The 1983 Compton Yearbook

A summary and interpretation of the events of 1982
to supplement Compton's Encyclopedia

F. E. Compton Company, a division of Encyclopædia Britannica, Inc.

CHICAGO
AUCKLAND · GENEVA · LONDON · MANILA · PARIS · ROME · SEOUL · SYDNEY · TOKYO · TORONTO

Library of Congress Catalog Card Number: 58-26525
International Standard Book Number: 0-85229-408-5
International Standard Serial Number: 0069-8091

The 1983 Compton Yearbook

Contents

compton's pictured highlights and chronology

2

1982

JANUARY

4 The foreign ministers of the European Community (EC), meeting in Brussels, denounce the imposition of martial law in Poland but do not endorse the economic sanctions imposed against both Poland and the U.S.S.R. by the U.S. The EC calls for an end to martial law and the resumption of dialogue with the Roman Catholic Church and Solidarity, the national federation of labour unions.

5 The government of South Korea declares an end to the four-hour nighttime curfew that has been in effect nationwide since the end of World War II.

6 Archbishop Jozef Glemp, the Roman Catholic primate of Poland, tells a congregation in Warsaw's St. John's Cathedral that those who signed oaths renouncing their membership in Solidarity, the national federation of trade unions, were coerced by the government. Such oaths, Glemp contends, have no validity.

7 Presidential counselor Edwin Meese III reads a statement by Pres. Ronald Reagan that reverses his pre-election stand against the registration of 18-year-old males for a possible future military draft.

8 Spokesmen for the American Telephone & Telegraph Co. (AT&T) and the U.S. Department of Justice announce that a seven-year-old antitrust case against AT&T has been tentatively settled.

11 The Reagan administration announces that the Chinese Nationalist government in Taiwan will not be given the advanced fighter aircraft it requested because "no military need for such aircraft exists." The U.S., however, says the Nationalists can continue to co-produce the U.S. aircraft that currently constitutes the mainstay of its air force.

13 Sir Ninian Martin Stephen is named next governor-general of Australia. He will replace Sir Zelman Cowen, who is scheduled to retire in July. The announcement ends speculation that Britain's Prince Charles might be given the post.

15 Spain announces successors to the top military commanders—the chiefs of staff of the Army, Navy, and Air Force and the chairman of the joint chiefs—retired summarily the day before. The Defense Ministry explains that it seemed appropriate to make the changes before Spain began negotiating its entry into NATO.

16 Great Britain and the Vatican establish full diplomatic relations after a period of four and a half centuries of estrangement. Relations between Britain and the Vatican were severed when King Henry VIII became head of the Church of England.

21 About 55% of Britain's nearly 250,000 coal miners reject the recommendation of their president-elect by voting to accept a 9.3% wage increase rather than strike. Outgoing president Joe Gormley had urged the miners to accept management's offer.

24 Egypt announces that it has invited 66 Soviet experts to assist on a number of industrial projects, reversing the policy of the late president Anwar as-Sadat, who in September 1981 ordered Soviet diplomats and technicians out. Pres. Hosni Mubarak explains that Egypt is now committed to a policy of nonalignment.

26 In his first state of the union message to the U.S. Congress, President Reagan reaffirms his support for supply-side economics and proposes a massive but gradual shift of federal social programs to the states. Reagan calls the bold concept "new federalism."

U.S. Secretary of State Alexander Haig and Soviet Foreign Minister Andrey Gromyko meet for eight hours in Geneva to review issues affecting relations between their two countries. The two leaders pointedly disagree on Poland. Gromyko insists that the imposition of martial law was an internal matter to be handled by Polish authorities; Haig declares that the military crackdown dealt a serious blow to U.S.-Soviet relations.

27 Salvadoran guerrillas stage a highly successful attack on the government's Ilopango air base outside San Salvador. According to reports, five or six fighter planes are destroyed as are also three C-47 transports, a trainer aircraft, and 5 of the 14 helicopters loaned to El Salvador by the U.S.

Honduras ends nine years of military rule with the installation of Roberto Suazo Córdova as president. During his inaugural address, Suazo pledges that officials of his administration will be "servants of the people and not beneficiaries of the state."

28 U.S. Brig. Gen. James L. Dozier is rescued from his Red Brigades kidnappers when Italian antiterrorist forces carry out a carefully planned raid on an apartment in Padua. Three men and two women are captured. Dozier is described as tired but otherwise in good health after his 42 days of captivity.

29 The U.S. government notifies nine of the nation's commercial banks that it will cover the $71 million in principal and interest that Poland was unable to pay on schedule. The Reagan administration chose to bypass the normal requirement that the banks first declare Poland in default on the loans, which had been guaranteed by the U.S. government.

30 According to a Warsaw radio report, more than 200 people are arrested in Gdansk after violent clashes with Polish police. The local military council responds by tightening curfew restrictions and suspending all sports activities and public entertainment. In other parts of the country, however, an easing of martial law is still expected to take effect on February 10.

31 The Israeli government signals its acceptance of France, Great Britain, Italy, and The Netherlands as part of a peace force that will patrol the Sinai after Israel's withdrawal in April.

(Above left) Salvage crews lift the tail of a jetliner that crashed into the Potomac River on January 13. (Above right) Pres. Ronald Reagan proposed a "new federalism" in his state of the union message on January 26. (Below) Brig. Gen. James L. Dozier was rescued by Italian police on January 28.

FEBRUARY

2 The Belgian Senate agrees to give the government of Prime Minister Wilfried Martens emergency powers until the end of the year so that it can initiate economic reforms without prior approval of the legislature. The Chamber of Representatives voted in favour of the same measures on January 18.

3 Egyptian Pres. Hosni Mubarak declares in Washington, D.C., that the "Palestinian problem" is the key to peace and stability in the Middle East. He also asserts that "both sides [Israelis and Palestinians] have an inherent right to exist and function as a national unity."

Soviet Pres. Leonid Brezhnev calls for a two-thirds reduction in medium-range nuclear weapons in Europe, but the U.S. rejects the proposal on the grounds that it would simply preserve the current imbalance in arms. The following day President Reagan counters by suggesting the elimination of all nuclear missiles in Europe.

7 Luis Alberto Monge is chosen president of Costa Rica in an election that also gives his National Liberation Party a substantial majority in the national assembly.

9 Philippine Pres. Ferdinand Marcos's son-in-law, Tommy Manotoc, is reported to have been rescued from leftist guerrillas the previous day. Manotoc, who mysteriously disappeared 41 days earlier, had angered the president and his wife by secretly marrying their daughter, Imee, on Dec. 4, 1981.

11 Eleven African leaders, members of the Organization of African Unity (OAU), end a special session in Kenya called to discuss the problems of peace in the Western Sahara and Chad. Morocco continues to refuse to negotiate directly with the Polisario Front, which is contesting Morocco's right to Western Sahara (former Spanish Sahara). The African leaders call on Chad's Pres. Goukouni Oueddei to accept a cease-fire with the rebel forces of Hissen Habré.

13 A civil court judge in El Salvador orders five former national guardsmen held for further investigation of the murders of three Roman Catholic nuns and a lay woman co-worker in December 1980. The news is gratifying to the U.S. On February 11 Pres. José Napoleón Duarte flatly declared, "These men are guilty."

17 Robert Mugabe, prime minister of Zimbabwe, relieves political rival Joshua Nkomo of his Cabinet post after accusing him of planning to take over the government. Mugabe claims that a sizable cache of arms was found on property owned by the Zimbabwe African People's Union (ZAPU), an organization founded and still headed by Nkomo.

18 The Iranian government announces that Ayatollah Ruhollah Khomeini will eventually be replaced by a four-, or five-man elected council. Concurrent reports that Khomeini is seriously ill are denied by the government as "imperialist and Zionist lies."

19 Pope John Paul II ends an eight-day pastoral visit to western Africa that included stops in Nigeria, Benin, Gabon, and Equatorial Guinea.

The De Lorean Motor Co. of Belfast, Northern Ireland, goes into receivership after the British government announces it can no longer provide money to the ailing manufacturer of the deluxe stainless steel sports cars.

21 Mexican Pres. José López Portillo, during a visit to Nicaragua, declares his willingness to act as a mediator to lessen tensions in Central America and the Carribean. On March 14 the U.S. responds by authorizing Mexico to sound out Cuba and Nicaragua on proposals that the U.S. believes could lead to a normalization of relations with Cuba and an end to alleged outside support for leftist rebels in El Salvador.

22 Kaytaro Sugahara, chairman of the Fairfield-Maxwell conglomerate, proposes a "foreign aid" program to alleviate unemployment in the U.S. Sugahara tells members of the National Governors Association during a meeting in Washington, D.C., that various Japanese industries could help create jobs for U.S. workers by providing $10 billion in low-interest loans.

23 The Japanese government announces that it will grant no new credits to Poland until it lifts martial law. Japan, however, promises to fulfill its earlier commitments of economic aid. The government also cancels some agreements with the Soviet Union.

24 President Reagan, in an address to the Organization of American States in Washington, D.C., warns that "new Cubas will arise from the ruins of today's conflicts" in Central America unless something is done to prevent it from happening. He proposes a "Caribbean Basin Initiative" to help Central American and Caribbean nations through trade, investments, technology, and military assistance.

25 The UN Security Council votes 13–0 to increase its 6,000-man peacekeeping force in southern Lebanon by an additional 1,000 troops. The vote is prompted by fears that continued Palestinian guerrilla attacks against Israel might provoke Israel to retaliate by sending troops across the border into Lebanon.

27 Wayne B. Williams, a 23-year-old black photographer and talent promoter, is convicted of murdering 2 of the 28 black children and young adults whose bodies were found in the Atlanta, Ga., area over a two-year period. Superior Court Judge Clarence Cooper immediately, in accordance with Georgia law, sentences Williams to two consecutive life terms in prison.

28 The Israeli Cabinet announces that if Egyptian Pres. Hosni Mubarak "refuses to visit Jerusalem during the course of his visit to Israel, we would have to do without this important visit. The Israeli demand effectively ends any hope that Mubarak will visit Israel in the foreseeable future.

(Top) The UN Security Council sent additional peacekeeping forces into Lebanon in hopes of forestalling open war between Israel and the PLO. (Left) Pope John Paul II made an eight-day visit to Africa. (Above) Wayne B. Williams was convicted on February 27 of murdering 2 of 28 young blacks who had disappeared in the Atlanta area.

MARCH

4 The American Petroleum Institute announces that U.S. refineries are operating at 63.9% of capacity because imports of crude oil have reached a seven-year low. The decline is attributed to conservation, the use of alternate fuels, and economic recession.

6 Arab members of the Organization of Petroleum Exporting Countries (OPEC) agree to cut their aggregate output of oil by more than one million barrels a day to shore up sagging oil prices.

8 The Standing Committee of China's National People's Congress approves sweeping changes in the structure of the government, including a reduction of vice-premierships from 13 to 2.

9 Ireland's Dail (parliament) elects Charles J. Haughey prime minister by a vote of 86–79.

10 The Reagan administration places an embargo on oil imported from Libya and on exports to Libya of certain high technology products. The decision, which affects only a small percentage of U.S. oil imports, means Libya will lose a market worth some $2 billion—about a quarter of its total annual oil revenues.

11 Sen. Harrison Williams, a Democrat from New Jersey, resigns from the U.S. Senate when it appears certain his colleagues are prepared to vote for his expulsion. Williams was convicted in 1981 of bribery and conspiracy in connection with the Abscam scandal.

12 Representatives of 35 nations adjourn their conference in Madrid as it becomes evident that discussion on East-West cooperation has reached an impasse. The U.S. and its allies use the occasion to denounce the Soviet Union for its role in imposing martial law in Poland. The Soviet bloc charges that Western nations are interfering in Poland's internal affairs.

The U.S. government is publicly embarrassed when a 19-year-old Nicaraguan tells reporters at a news conference arranged by the U.S. Department of State that he lied when he confessed to having been trained as a Marxist guerrilla in Cuba and Ethiopia and then sent to join leftist insurgents in El Salvador.

15 Daniel Ortega Saavedra, coordinator of Nicaragua's ruling junta, proclaims a month-long state of siege and suspends the nation's constitution one day after antigovernment rebels destroyed two important bridges near the Honduran border.

16 Commanders of an elite 45-man South African military unit claim they killed more than 200 members of the South West Africa People's Organization (SWAPO) while wiping out a guerrilla supply base in a desolate mountain area of southwestern Angola. Angola insists the raiders attacked a refugee camp.

17 Four members of a Dutch television crew, filming a report in an area of El Salvador controlled by leftist guerrillas, are killed by government troops during a 40-minute firefight.

21 French voters confirm a conservative trend set a week earlier in the first round of voting for departmental assemblies by giving the ruling coalition of Socialists and Communists control of only 37 of the country's 95 assemblies.

22 Iran launches a spring offensive to regain territory Iraq took from it more than a year earlier. After one week of fighting, Iran reports it has captured more than 13,000 Iraqi soldiers, while many more retreat in disarray.

The U.S. space shuttle "Columbia" is launched into orbit for the third time. An auxiliary power unit overheats in flight, two television cameras malfunction, and about 35 heat-shielding tiles are lost or damaged, but most of the planned experiments are successfully completed. Eight days later the "Columbia" lands at the White Sands Missile Range in New Mexico.

23 President Reagan sends Congress a plan to revitalize urban areas by offering businesses attractive incentives to invest in designated "enterprise zones." The inducements include tax breaks and a relaxation of government regulations.

Guatemalan army officers oust Pres. Fernando Romeo Lucas García from office and name a three-man military junta, headed by retired Gen. Efraín Ríos Montt. The rebel officers pledge to restore "authentic democracy." The following day the junta suspends the constitution and places a temporary ban on all political activities.

24 Lieut. Gen. Hussain Mohammed Ershad overthrows the government of Abdus Sattar, president of Bangladesh. Ershad says he seeks to end corruption in public life and to "reestablish democracy in accordance with the hopes and aspirations of the people."

25 Roy Jenkins, one of the founders of Britain's new Social Democratic Party (SDP), wins a seat in Parliament from the Hillhead district of Glasgow, a Conservative preserve for 60 years. Because preelection polls suggested the SDP had lost much of its initial momentum, the election assumes national significance.

A court in Verona, Italy, sentences 17 Red Brigades terrorists for their roles in the kidnapping of U.S. Brig. Gen. James Dozier on Dec. 17, 1981. The terrorists receive prison sentences ranging from 27 years to 2 years and 2 months.

28 Voters who turn out in surprisingly large numbers to elect members to El Salvador's Constituent Assembly give the Christian Democratic Party of junta president José Napoléon Duarte 24 of the 60 seats. Because of the combined strength of right-wing groups that oppose him, however, it is not certain that Duarte will continue to head the government.

(Top) French Pres. François Mitterrand addressed the Israeli Knesset on March 4. (Right) Space shuttle "Columbia" began its third trip into space on March 22. (Above) Voters in El Salvador elected a Constituent Assembly on March 28.

2 Several thousand Argentine soldiers seize control of the Falkland Islands off the southeastern coast of South America. On April 3 British Prime Minister Margaret Thatcher informs Parliament, convened in emergency session, that a large British naval task force is being dispatched immediately to retake the islands.

6 Egypt's UN Ambassador Ahmed Esmat Abdel Meguid outlines a peace plan for the Middle East during a meeting of nonaligned nations in Kuwait. It is the first high-level meeting of Arab states to which Egypt is invited since it signed a peace treaty with Israel in 1979. Meguid affirms that all countries in the Middle East have the right to security within borders mutually recognized by Israel and its neighbours.

8 President Reagan begins a five-day "working holiday" in the Caribbean during which he meets leaders of Jamaica, Barbados, St. Vincent and the Grenadines, Dominica, Antigua and Barbuda, and St. Kitts-Nevis.

U.S. Secretary of State Alexander Haig begins a series of intense diplomatic discussions with leaders in Britain and Argentina in an effort to resolve the growing crisis over Argentina's seizure of the Falkland Islands on April 2. Hopes for a peaceful settlement dim as Argentina refuses to meet British demands that it withdraw its troops as a precondition for negotiations.

10 The Iranian government confirms that Sadegh Ghotbzadeh, who became Iran's foreign minister shortly after the seizure of the U.S. embassy in November 1979, was arrested on April 7 for plotting to assassinate Ayatollah Ruhollah Khomeini.

11 Alan Harry Goodman, a 37-year-old U.S.-born Israeli soldier, runs amok in Jerusalem's Dome of the Rock, one of Islam's most sacred shrines. An unarmed mosque guard and an Arab youth are killed and a number of worshippers wounded before Goodman is subdued by Israeli policemen and border guards.

14 The U.S. and Nicaragua agree to try lessening tensions between their two countries, but no time or place for formal discussions is announced. On April 8, one day after Cuba offered Nicaragua $130 million in financial and technical assistance, the U.S. presented Nicaragua with an eight-point plan to improve relations between the two nations.

15 The two military men and three civilians convicted by a military court of assassinating former president Anwar as-Sadat are executed with the approval of Egyptian Pres. Hosni Mubarak, who rejects their final pleas for clemency.

17 Canada loses the last vestiges of legal dependence on Great Britain when Queen Elizabeth II proclaims the first formal Canadian constitution. Canada, which has been governed for more than a century by the British North America Act of 1867, retains the British monarch as its official head of state.

25 In a simple but significant ceremony, Egypt regains control over the eastern portion of the Sinai as stipulated in the peace treaty signed with Israel in 1979. Israel has occupied the territory since seizing it during the 1967 war.

26 The U.S. Immigration and Naturalization Service begins a week-long roundup of illegal aliens working in Chicago, Dallas, Denver, Detroit, Houston, Los Angeles, Newark, New York, and San Francisco. Of the 5,635 persons taken into custody, a few are able to produce proper documentation and return to work, but more than 4,000 agree to leave the country voluntarily.

28 Poland's Military Council of National Salvation announces that 800 detainees will be released outright and an additional 200 granted "conditional leave" as part of a program to relax martial law. Lech Walesa, the leader of Solidarity, is not among those freed.

The U.S. Central Intelligence Agency reveals that vital military secrets were given to a Polish spy by a defense industry radar engineer between 1979 and 1981. The information included details of the radar-evading Stealth bomber, various radar and missile systems, and a submarine sonar system.

29 El Salvador's 60-member Constituent Assembly elects Alvaro Alfredo Magaña Borjo provisional president of the country, thereby ending a month of partisan political strife that followed in the wake of elections for the assembly on March 28.

30 Canada's multibillion-dollar Alsands project to extract crude oil from the tar sands of Alberta is effectively killed when Shell Canada Ltd. and Gulf Canada Ltd., the last two private investors in the undertaking, announce an immediate end to their participation.

Corporate sponsors announce that they are delaying for two years construction of the U.S. segment of the 4,800-mi (7,689-km) Alaska Highway natural gas pipeline that would carry gas from Prudhoe Bay in Alaska into Canada and then into the lower 48 U.S. states. Canada has already completed part of its work on the pipeline, but it will have no access to Alaskan gas unless the U.S. company builds the northern section.

After eight years of complicated negotiations, delegates to the United Nations Law of the Sea Conference overwhelmingly adopt a final version of a comprehensive treaty governing the use of the seas and their natural resources. Though the U.S. votes against the treaty, it can still ratify the accord sometime in the future and become a signatory.

South African Prime Minister P. W. Botha and Zambian Pres. Kenneth Kaunda meet for several hours on the border separating South Africa and Botswana. It is Botha's first meeting with a black African leader. The two presumably discuss the issue of South West Africa/Namibia and the internal policies of South Africa.

(Top) Queen Elizabeth II proclaimed Canada's new constitution on April 17, ending the last trace of British rule in the one-time colony. (Centre) Argentine soldiers raised their flag over Port Stanley after seizing the Falkland Islands in a surprise invasion on April 2. (Bottom) A simple border marker remained after Israel returned the Sinai to Egypt on April 25.

2 Casualties in the war over the Falkland Islands dramatically increase when the Argentine cruiser "General Belgrano" is sunk by a British submarine with the loss of 321 lives. Two days later the British destroyer "HMS Sheffield" is hit by a plane-launched missile and sunk; 20 seamen lose their lives.

Exxon Corp. announces an end to its participation in the Colorado colony shale oil project in which it has a 60% interest. Exxon explains that the total cost of the operation could approach $6 billion by 1986–87, about twice the original 1980 estimate.

3 Israeli Prime Minister Menachem Begin, speaking to the Knesset, declares that Israel will assert sovereignty over the West Bank at the end of the five-year transitional period specified in the Camp David peace accords.

4 The federal trial of 26-year-old John Hinckley, Jr., for shooting President Reagan and three others gets under way in Washington, D.C.

5 The Canadian Wheat Board announces it has signed a contract to sell China between 3.5 million and 4.2 million metric tons of wheat each year for the next three years. It is the largest long-term grain deal between the two countries since they initiated such trade in 1961.

11 South Korea announces the arrests of Lee Chul Hi and his wife, Chang Yong Ja, for alleged fraudulent transactions on Seoul's unregulated curb (over-the-counter) market. Chang is related by marriage to the wife of Pres. Chun Doo Hwan. The fraud creates panic on the stock market and severely damages the financial structures of several corporations.

12 During a candlelight procession at the shrine of the Virgin Mary in Fatima, Port., a Spanish priest attempts to assault Pope John Paul II with a bayonet. The priest is identified as Juan Fernandez Krohn, an ultraconservative living in France. He reportedly opposes the reforms of Vatican Council II and calls the pope an "agent of Moscow."

13 Braniff International Corp. becomes the first major U.S. airline to file for reorganization under Chapter 11 of the federal Bankruptcy Act. Burdened with debts and mounting losses, the nation's eighth largest carrier cancels all its flights on May 12 and terminates about 8,000 employees.

14 Philippine Pres. Ferdinand E. Marcos swears in 15 members of the newly constituted Supreme Court four days after demanding and receiving the resignations of all 14 members of the former court. All but three of the new justices served on the former court.

16 Salvador Jorge Blanco, a member of the Dominican Revolutionary Party, is elected president of the Dominican Republic with something less than half of the popular vote. Pres. Antonio Guzmán Fernández did not run, but it is largely due to his efforts that the Army was depoliticized and played no significant role in the electoral process.

18 A crisis develops in the European Community when seven member nations vote to increase farm prices by 10.7% over Great Britain's forceful objections. Britain also resents the apparent disregard of a well-established tradition that requires unanimous approval of any measure that affects a "vital national interest" of any member nation. On May 25 a compromise is reached that at least temporarily settles the issue.

El Salvador's Constituent Assembly votes 37–18 to cancel for one crop year the right of tenant farmers and sharecroppers to apply for title to as much as 7 ha (17 ac) of land. The suspension is reportedly instigated by newly elected Pres. Alvara Magaña Borjo because he fears landowners would lack incentives to plant crops if they faced the prospect of losing their land.

21 British forces launch a major offensive against East Falkland Island and within a few days are in control of about 60 sq mi (155 sq km) along the west coast. Accurate casualty figures are unavailable, but material losses on both sides are heavy.

24 The Central Committee of the Soviet Union's Communist Party names 67-year-old Yury V. Andropov to the powerful ten-member Secretariat. He replaces Mikhail A. Suslov, who died in January. Andropov, a member of the Central Committee, was a career diplomat before being named head of Soviet security and intelligence in 1967.

Iran announces that it has recaptured its port city of Khorramshahr and with it about 30,000 Iraqi troops. Iraq won the fierce battle for control of Khorramshahr in late September 1980 but never succeeded in conquering nearby Abadan, especially important because of its huge oil refinery.

27 Japan announces the elimination of tariffs on 96 industrial goods, including machine tools and computers, and a reduction of import duties on 121 other items. The decision, which will be fully implemented within a year, is made public one week before the opening of an economic summit in Versailles, France.

30 Spain formally becomes a member of NATO following ratification by each of the other 15 member nations. Spain stipulated, as did Norway and Denmark before it, that no nuclear weapons would be based on its soil. Spain's contribution to the alliance will consist of 340,000 troops, nearly 200 planes, 29 warships, and 8 submarines.

31 Belisario Betancur Cuartas, a member of the Conservative Party, is elected to a four-year term as president of Colombia. On August 7 he will replace Pres. Julio César Turbay Ayala, who was not permitted to run for a second term.

(Top) Colourful but idle aircraft remained after the bankruptcy of Braniff International on May 13. (Left) The Knoxville World's Fair opened on May 1 for a six-month run. (Above) A dissident Spanish priest was taken into custody after attacking Pope John Paul II in Portugal on May 12.

JUNE

2 Pope John Paul II completes a historic visit to Great Britain that was highlighted by an ecumenical service in Canterbury Cathedral on May 29. On June 11 Pope John Paul arrives in Argentina, which is at war with Britain over control of the Falkland Islands and its dependencies.

3 The U.S. House of Representatives approves a bill forbidding the identification of current U.S. intelligence agents, informers, or sources of information, even if such information is available in public records.

A panel of 17 Spanish military judges hands down 30-year prison sentences to Lieut. Col. Antonio Tejero Molina and Lieut. Gen. Jaime Milans del Bosch for their roles in the abortive antigovernment coup of February 1981.

6 Israel carries out previous warnings by invading Lebanon by land, sea, and air. The announced objective is to destroy strongholds of the Palestine Liberation Organization (PLO). When a cease-fire is declared on June 11, Israeli forces control most of Lebanon south of Beirut. On June 19 Israel moves into the centre of Beirut.

The leaders of seven major industralized democracies conclude their eighth annual summit in Versailles, France. The official communiqué, signed by Canada, France, Great Britain, Italy, Japan, the U.S., and West Germany, declares that the participating nations have come closer together on such economic issues as currency exchange rates, aid to developing countries, and export credits to the U.S.S.R.

9 Brig. Gen. Efraín Ríos Montt dissolves Guatemala's three-man military junta. It is then announced that the Army has appointed Ríos Montt president of the country and commander in chief of the armed forces.

12 A massive parade and peace rally, organized by religious and secular groups, is held in New York City to coincide with a special UN session on disarmament. The crowd, including those who watched along the sidewalks, is estimated to be about 600,000.

13 King Khalid, who has ruled Saudi Arabia since 1975, dies of a heart attack. He is succeeded by 59-year-old Crown Prince Fahd, the country's foreign minister.

15 The Falklands war ends when the Argentine troops, surrounded in Stanley, the capital, surrender to the British. Britain later reports that 255 of its soldiers and civilians lost their lives in the fighting; Argentina's losses are believed to be three or four times heavier. On June 17 Lieut. Gen. Leopoldo Galtieri resigns as president of Argentina, as a member of the ruling junta, and as commander in chief of the Army.

The U.S. Supreme Court strikes down a Texas law that permitted local school districts to either bar children of illegal aliens from public schools or charge them tu-

ition. The ruling means that children of undocumented aliens must be granted free public education.

18 The U.S. Senate overwhelmingly approves renewal of the 1965 Voting Rights Act for an additional 25 years. Five days later the House of Representatives unanimously accepts the Senate version of the bill.

21 A federal jury finds John W. Hinckley, Jr., not guilty by reason of insanity of shooting President Reagan and three others on March 30, 1981. Hinckley is committed to a Washington, D.C., hospital for an indefinite period.

Buckingham Palace announces that a son has been born to Prince Charles and Lady Diana, the prince and princess of Wales. The child, named William Arthur Phillip Louis, is second in line to the British throne.

22 The U.S. Department of Justice charges 18 Japanese with conspiring to steal industrial secrets from IBM. Most of those charged are employees of Hitachi Ltd., which allegedly paid $622,000 for classified information about IBM technology. The defendants are accused of paying the money to an undercover FBI agent who posed as a "Silicon Valley" businessman.

The leaders of three Cambodian political factions form a coalition government-in-exile opposed to the Vietnam-controlled regime of Heng Samrin. The three leaders are Prince Norodom Sihanouk, former neutralist ruler; Khieu Samphan, head of the former Khmer Rouge regime; and Son Sann, a rightist.

Retired Army Maj. Gen. Reynaldo Benito Antonio Bignone is named president of Argentina over vigorous objections from the Air Force and Navy, which reportedly want a return to civilian rule.

24 The U.S. Supreme Court rules 5–4 that no president can be sued for damages connected with actions he took while serving as the nation's chief executive.

25 President Reagan announces the resignation of Alexander M. Haig, Jr., as U.S. secretary of state. George P. Shultz, who held a Cabinet post in the Nixon administration, is nominated as Haig's successor. The Senate confirms the appointment 97–0 on July 15.

29 A federal judge in Miami, Fla., rules that "it would not be just or equitable" to continue holding Haitian refugees in detention camps even though they entered the U.S. illegally. In ordering the parole of most of the 1,900 refugees, the judge stipulates that each Haitian have a written agreement from both a voluntary resettlement agency and an individual sponsor stating that they will abide by the terms of the release.

30 Efforts to pass the Equal Rights Amendment (ERA) to the U.S. Constitution end in failure when legislators in three additional states cannot be persuaded in sufficient numbers to vote approval of the measure before the midnight deadline.

(Above) British troops completed the recapture of the Falkland Islands. (Below left) Thousands of refugees fled as Israeli forces occupied southern Lebanon. (Below right) Leaders of the leading Western industrialized democracies met on June 4–6 at Versailles, France.

2 The U.S. Supreme Court overturns a Mississippi Supreme Court decision that held the National Association for the Advancement of Colored People (NAACP) liable for damages that resulted from a business boycott organized in Port Gibson.

4 Miguel de la Madrid Hurtado of the Institutional Revolutionary Party is elected president of Mexico with about 75% of the popular vote.

Pres. Antonio Guzmán Fernández of the Dominican Republic dies of a self-inflicted gunshot wound. He was reportedly depressed after discovering that some of his most trusted aides had been stealing government funds.

5 Federal regulators declare the Penn Square Bank of Oklahoma City, Okla., insolvent because of huge losses it has sustained on loans to small oil and gas companies whose collateral only partially covered the amounts they borrowed.

7 Private Western bankers try in vain to work out a settlement with Polish officials on that nation's multibillion-dollar debts. Poland wants new credits to cover its 1982 interest payments or deferment of both interest and principal payments until next year.

10 The UN special session on disarmament ends with all 157 members of the General Assembly acknowledging their inability to reach agreement on a comprehensive program of disarmament. Neither the U.S. nor the U.S.S.R. supports the progressive approach to disarmament put forth by nonaligned nations.

Ministers of the Organization of Petroleum Exporting Countries (OPEC) end an emergency two-day meeting in Vienna still divided over prices and production quotas. Iran, which along with Libya and Nigeria is accused of exceeding quotas agreed to in March, challenges Saudi Arabia's leadership.

12 Zail Singh, a close friend of Prime Minister Indira Gandhi, is elected president of India to replace N. Sanjiva Reddy, whose five-year term expires on July 25. Gandhi's nomination of a Sikh for the largely ceremonial post is seen by some as an attempt to pacify Sikhs in the state of Punjab who are clamouring for independence.

Peruvian Pres. Fernando Belaúnde Terry suspends constitutional rights in three of the country's southern provinces and orders 100 specially trained policemen into the area to quell violence instigated by a Maoist organization called Sendero Luminoso. All told, some 40 persons have been killed by the guerrillas since Belaunde assumed power in 1980.

13 Iranian troops cross the border into Iraq despite earlier protestations that the purpose of Iran's spring offensive is limited to recapturing the territory it lost in the early stages of the war.

16 A U.S. federal judge in New York City sentences the Rev. Sun Myung Moon, Korean founder of the Unification Church, to 18 months in prison for tax fraud and conspiracy to obstruct justice.

19 Bolivia announces that the resignations of Pres. Celso Torrelio Villa and his Cabinet have been accepted. A military junta composed of the chiefs of the Army, Navy, and Air Force take over the government. On July 21 Gen. Guido Vildoso Calderón, the army chief of staff, is installed as president by the junta.

Great Britain's House of Commons is told that the government plans to sell a majority share in British Telecom, the state-owned telephone company. The decision is in line with Prime Minister Margaret Thatcher's policy of selling off state-controlled operations to the private sector.

22 The French government announces that French companies have been told to honour contracts entered into for construction of the West European–Soviet natural gas pipeline. The policy defies a U.S. embargo on such cooperation by foreign companies operating under licenses from U.S. firms. West German Chancellor Helmut Schmidt's immediate support for France's decision is expected to be echoed by other members of the European Community.

Michele Sindona, already serving a 25-year prison sentence in the U.S. for banking fraud, is indicted in Milan, Italy, on charges of fraudulent bankruptcy, falsification of records, and violations of Italian finance laws. The charges are related to the 1974 bankruptcy of Banca Privata Italiana.

23 Japan's National Defense Council proposes a five-year military expansion program that will emphasize air and naval power to deter "limited and small-scale aggression." Implementation of the program will depend on annual appropriations voted by the Diet (parliament).

27 Indian Prime Minister Indira Gandhi arrives in the U.S. for her first visit in 11 years. During the visit Gandhi and President Reagan agree to a compromise solution over nuclear fuel for India's Tarapur power plant. The agreement prevents India from producing plutonium that could be used for nuclear weapons.

The Reagan administration sends a 48-page document to Congress certifying that El Salvador is making tangible progress on human rights and the implementation of economic and political reforms. Certification every six months is a condition for continued U.S. military aid to El Salvador.

29 A South African judge sentences 42 white mercenaries found guilty of air piracy after an unsuccessful coup in the Seychelles in November 1981. During the trial the government denied the leader's charge that it had backed the Seychelles coup attempt.

(Above left) Prime Minister Indira Gandhi of India addressed the National Press Club during her visit to the U.S. (Above right) A Pan American jetliner crashed into a New Orleans suburb on July 9, killing 154. (Below) George P. Shultz was sworn in as secretary of state on July 16.

AUGUST

1 Israeli planes bomb West Beirut for 14 hours in the most devastating attack against Palestinian guerrillas in Lebanon since June 6, when Israel sent its troops across the border. On August 12 Israeli planes again inflict severe damage on West Beirut in a sustained air attack that lasts 11 hours.

Army troops loyal to Kenyan Pres. Daniel arap Moi suppress an antigovernment revolt organized by members of the Air Force. About 3,000 persons are arrested, including all 2,100 members of the Air Force. On August 21 Moi dismisses the entire Air Force and directs a former army general to form a new one.

4 Panama's Supreme Court invalidates an order that closed down eight daily newspapers on July 30. Brig. Gen. Rubén Darío Paredes, commander of the National Guard, reportedly ordered the closedown to stifle criticism of government officials.

6 Lebanon announces that the Palestine Liberation Organization has agreed to terms for the peaceful withdrawal of its forces from the country. One of the few remaining problems is resolved the next day when Syria agrees to accept a large portion of the departing Palestinians.

Italian authorities order the liquidation of Milan's Banco Ambrosiano, Italy's largest privately owned bank. Roberto Calvi, head of operations at Banco Ambrosiano, was found dead in London in June, an apparent suicide. His bank had allegedly made unsecured loans amounting to $1.4 billion.

9 A White House spokesman confirms that the Reagan administration will not submit its new federalism plan to Congress until 1983. After six months of debate and negotiations, the governors of the states and federal representatives have been unable to reach agreement on several major issues.

12 The European Community (EC) rejects President Reagan's embargo on the use of U.S. technology for construction of the Soviet-Western Europe natural gas pipeline. The EC protests that the ban violates international law and that failure to participate in the construction would severely injure EC industries.

17 China and the U.S. announce an agreement whereby the U.S. will gradually decrease its arms sales to Taiwan. On August 19 President Reagan gives the required notification to Congress that he intends to sell Taiwan $60 million in spare parts for F-5E fighter jets.

The U.S. Senate approves a new immigration bill that would grant permanent resident status to illegal aliens who arrived in the U.S. before 1977. Those who arrived during 1977, 1978, and 1979 would be classified as temporary residents, but after three years they would qualify as permanent residents. Illegal aliens who had arrived in the U.S. after Dec. 31, 1979, would be subject to deportation.

Federal District Court Judge James C. Turk of Roanoke, Va., sentences 20-year-old Enten Eller to at least 250 hours of public service and places him on three years' probation for refusing to register for a possible future military draft. In addition, the judge orders Eller to comply with the law within 90 days or face a prison term of up to five years.

19 Both the U.S. House of Representatives and the Senate approve a $98.3 billion increase in tax revenues. President Reagan urged passage of the bill, saying it was "80% tax reform" and not, as some suggested, the largest tax increase in history. The bill's bipartisan support is unprecedented in an election year.

21 Mexican officials end a three-day emergency meeting in New York with bankers who are deeply worried about Mexico's ability to repay huge debts it has contracted. Mexico is given a 90-day moratorium on payment of $10 billion in principal but not on payment of interest due.

About 400 members of the Palestine Liberation Organization leave Lebanon by ship, the first step in what is planned to be the total evacuation of guerrillas from West Beirut within the next two weeks. Troops from France, Italy, and the U.S. are on hand to monitor the operation. Palestinian leader Yasir Arafat leaves for Greece on August 30. On September 1 the last of an estimated 15,000 Palestinians and Syrians leave the country.

23 Bashir Gemayel, a Maronite Christian, is elected president of Lebanon despite efforts by Muslims in the National Assembly to deprive the assembly of the quorum needed for such an election.

26 At the conclusion of their annual meeting in Halifax, Nova Scotia, Canada's ten provincial premiers call for a special conference with Prime Minister Pierre Trudeau to draft a comprehensive plan for the nation's economic recovery.

27 King Juan Carlos of Spain, acceding to the wishes of Prime Minister Leopoldo Calvo Sotelo, formally dissolves Parliament so that general elections can be held in late October.

28 U.S. Army Pfc. Joseph T. White of St. Louis, Mo., defects to North Korea while on duty at the Demilitarized Zone that separates North and South Korea. White is the first U.S. soldier to voluntarily flee to North Korea since 1965 and only the fifth to do so since the end of the Korean War in 1953.

31 Polish police use tear gas, water cannons, and noise grenades to control moderate-sized crowds of demonstrators who defy government warnings against holding rallies on the second anniversary of the founding of Solidarity, the outlawed federation of trade unions. It is later reported that at least five persons were killed during the turmoil and about 4,000 arrested.

(Above) The Palestine Liberation Organization guerrillas who had occupied west Beirut were evacuated under the eyes of an international force that included (below right) U.S. Marines. (Below left) The August 31 second anniversary of the Polish Solidarity union brought confrontation.

SEPTEMBER

1 Mexican Pres. José López Portillo closes all of the country's private banks so they can be "incorporated directly into the service of the nation." He also announces the imposition of a system of strict currency exchange controls.

Some 60% of all the farms in Australia are being harshly affected by one of the worst droughts in the nation's history. Government officials acknowledge that substantial government assistance will probably be needed to meet the emergency.

6 During a news conference organized by the Salvadoran Human Rights Commission, three women accuse government troops of indiscriminately killing 300 unarmed civilians during a seven-day antiguerrilla campaign in San Vicente Province.

9 The House of Representatives votes 301–117 to override President Reagan's veto of a $14.1 billion supplemental appropriations bill. The following day 21 Republican senators join 39 Democrats in voting 60–30 against the president. The override is the first legislative defeat that Reagan has suffered on a major issue since he assumed office.

Following a four-day conference in Fez, Morocco, the Arab League announces its unanimous approval of a peace plan for the Middle East. It calls for an independent Palestinian state and hints that such a move would bring about the formal recognition of Israel.

10 Argentina's navy and air force chiefs of staff decide to reconstitute the three-man military junta that was in effect dissolved when the two men announced in June that they would cooperate with the head of the Army only in matters of national defense.

11 The Chinese Communist Party adjourns its 12th National Congress after adopting a new party constitution. The document restructures the party organization in several ways to preclude the type of "personality cult" that prevailed under former chairman Mao Zedong (Mao Tse-tung).

14 Bashir Gemayel, president-elect of Lebanon since August 23, is assassinated when a bomb demolishes the headquarters of the Lebanese Christian Phalangist party in East Beirut. At least eight others are also killed. On September 21 Amin Gemayel, Bashir's elder brother, is elected president by Parliament.

15 Sadegh Ghotbzadeh, who became foreign minister of Iran shortly after U.S. hostages were seized in Teheran in November 1979, is executed by a firing squad. He was convicted of plotting to assassinate Ayatollah Khomeini and attempting to overthrow the government.

Philippine Pres. Ferdinand Marcos arrives in the U.S. for an official state visit, his first in 16 years. During an appearance before a group of congressmen, Marcos asserts that "there was no such thing as human rights" in the Philippines until he imposed martial law.

16 Christian militiamen begin a day-long slaughter of Palestinians in the Sabra and Shatila refugee camps in West Beirut. Worldwide condemnation of the atrocity is accompanied by anger directed against Israel for permitting the militiamen, whose hatred of the Palestinians is common knowledge, to enter the camps. On September 27 Lebanese officials report that more than 600 bodies have been removed from the two camps.

17 British Prime Minister Margaret Thatcher arrives in Japan on the first leg of her first official visit to Asia. After her arrival in China, Thatcher and Chinese officials discuss a wide range of topics, but none so pressing as the future of the British crown colony of Hong Kong. China seems certain to claim sovereignty over Hong Kong but appears willing to make certain concessions to ensure its continued prosperity.

19 Sweden's Social Democratic Party (SD) picks up 12 additional seats in elections for Parliament, enough to give it control of the government.

20 Indian Prime Minister Indira Gandhi begins a week-long visit to the Soviet Union. In Moscow, Gandhi thanks the Soviet Union for "standing by" India but also, according to reports, makes it clear that her country counts itself among the nonaligned nations.

21 Players in the professional National Football League (NFL) go on strike against all of the league's 28 teams. It is the first in-season strike in the 63-year history of the NFL.

22 Bolivian Finance Minister Alfonso Revollo reveals that his country is not able to pay $50 million in foreign debts that came due earlier in the month. The International Monetary Fund has refused to comply with Bolivia's request for help.

25 Twelve leftist guerrillas end their nine-day takeover of the Chamber of Commerce building in San Pedro Sula, Honduras. They had taken 107 hostages and demanded the release of captured Salvadoran guerrilla leader Alejandro Montenegro and others.

26 Japanese Prime Minister Zenko Suzuki arrives in Beijing (Peking) for a six-day series of meetings with top Chinese officials. Development of China's oil and coal reserves and continued aid to revitalize China's factories are among the topics discussed at length.

28 Israeli Prime Minister Menachem Begin reverses his earlier stand and agrees to have an independent three-man board of inquiry investigate the massacre of Palestinian civilians in Beirut on September 16–17. Two days earlier Israeli troops withdrew from West Beirut and were replaced by a peacekeeping force composed of French, Italian, and U.S. troops.

(Top) The Arab League meeting in Fez, Morocco, on September 6–9 produced a Middle East peace plan. (Left) Private banks in Mexico were closed by order of President López Portillo on September 1 and then nationalized. (Above) A massacre of Palestinians in Lebanese refugee camps on September 16 shocked the world.

OCTOBER

1 Helmut Kohl, leader of the Christian Democratic Union, replaces Helmut Schmidt as chancellor of West Germany. In a rarely used constructive motion of no confidence, the Bundestag (lower house of Parliament) votes 256–235 in favour of Kohl. Kohl and his Cabinet are sworn in on October 4.

A submarine is reported sighted in the restricted waters off Musko Island, the site of a Swedish naval base. The submarine is not identified, but the consensus is that it belongs to the Soviet Union or to a Soviet-bloc nation. After numerous depth charges fail to force the submarine to the surface, Swedish military officers conclude the submarine has either escaped or lies disabled on the bottom of the bay.

5 The Lebanese Army commences a sweep through West Beirut to begin reestablishing the government's authority over the capital. The goals of the search are to disarm combatants, ferret out caches of arms, and round up illegal aliens and criminals.

The Bolivian Congress votes 113–29 to elect Hernán Siles Zuazo president of the country. Three days later Siles Zuazo returns from exile in Peru and officially assumes office on October 10 as the first civilian president in 17 years.

7 Trading on the New York Stock Exchange sets a one-day record when 147,070,000 shares change hands. The rally continues through the following week, which registers the highest weekly total on record with 592,460,000 shares traded by Friday, October 15. The Dow Jones industrial average closes at 1012.79 on Monday, October 11, the first time the average has surpassed the 1,000 mark since April 1981.

8 The Polish Parliament overwhelmingly votes to outlaw Solidarity and all other existing labour unions. On October 11–12 thousands of workers at the Lenin shipyards in Gdansk go on strike to protest Parliament's action. Police use tear gas and concussion grenades to break up demonstrations. On October 13 all the shipyard workers are drafted into military service, which makes them subject to courts-martial for disobedience.

12 Japanese Prime Minister Zenko Suzuki, president of the ruling Liberal Democratic Party, stuns the nation by announcing that he will not run for reelection as party head in November.

King Hussein of Jordan and Yasir Arafat, head of the Palestine Liberation Organization, conclude four days of talks on the proposed establishment of a Palestinian state confederated with Jordan. No conclusions are made public but Arafat later declares there are "positive elements" in the plan suggested by President Reagan.

15 President Suharto of Indonesia ends a five-day visit to the U.S.

16 U.S. Secretary of State George P. Shultz announces that the U.S. is withholding an $8.5 million payment to the UN International Atomic Energy Agency because it canceled Israel's credentials. The action was instigated by Arab nations that wanted to exclude Israel from all UN bodies, including the General Assembly.

A Chinese Air Force pilot lands safely in South Korea in his MiG-19 fighter plane after successfully outrunning other Chinese jet fighters that pursued him. It is the third time since the Korean War that a Chinese pilot has fled to South Korea. The pilot obtains permission from Korean authorities to proceed to Taiwan, where the Nationalist government has a standing offer of $2 million for any pilot defecting from the mainland.

China announces that it has successfully fired a ballistic missile from a submarine. The event adds China's name to those of only four other countries that have developed such technology: France, Great Britain, the U.S., and the U.S.S.R.

19 John De Lorean, whose company has been producing luxury sports cars in Northern Ireland, is arrested in Los Angeles and charged with possession of 59 lb (27 kg) of cocaine and conspiracy to distribute it.

21 Hissen Habré is sworn in as president of Chad. The new government replaces the Council of State that has ruled since Habré's overthrow of Pres. Goukouni Oueddei in June.

26 About 50 unemployed Australian workers from Wollongong, New South Wales, fight their way into Parliament House in Canberra demanding to see Prime Minister Malcolm Fraser. The group represents some 800 laid-off miners and steelworkers who insist that the government take steps to put them back to work. When Fraser sends word that he will meet with union heads to see what can be done, the workers depart.

27 Trade talks between Japan and the U.S. are cut short in Honolulu when the U.S. delegation refuses to discuss any other topic except unrestricted Japanese importation of U.S. beef and citrus products.

President Reagan suspends Poland's most-favoured-nation trading status because it has outlawed Solidarity and other free labour unions. As a consequence, Polish goods entering the U.S. will have to be marketed at higher prices because of increased tariffs.

28 Felipe González leads the Spanish Socialist Workers' Party to resounding victories in elections for the lower house of Parliament and the Senate. The Socialists win 201 seats in the lower house, increasing their representation from 121 seats during the government of outgoing Premier Leopoldo Calvo Sotelo. Calvo Sotelo fails to win reelection to Parliament as his Union of the Democratic Centre Party suffers a devastating defeat. González will be Spain's first left-wing head of government in half a century.

(Above) The New York Stock Exchange enjoyed a record bull market. (Below left) Tylenol was removed from store shelves in the wake of seven poisonings. (Below centre) Automaker John De Lorean was arrested on October 19 on a drug charge. (Below right) Spain elected a Socialist prime minister on October 28.

NOVEMBER

2 U.S. voters go to the polls to elect 33 senators, 433 representatives, 36 governors, and hundreds of local officials. Republicans retain their 54–46 majority in the U.S. Senate but suffer a net loss of 26 seats in the Democrat-controlled House of Representatives.

4 Ruud Lubbers is sworn in as prime minister of The Netherlands, replacing Andreas van Agt. The new Parliament is expected to support NATO's decision to deploy medium-range nuclear weapons in Europe.

7 The Upper Volta government of Col. Saye Zerbo is overthrown by Jean-Baptiste Ouedraogo, an army commander and medical doctor.

9 Reports reach India that hundreds of Afghan civilians and Soviet soldiers were killed in a mountain tunnel disaster about one week earlier. It appears that a violent explosion occurred when the lead truck of a Soviet convoy collided with a fuel truck. Flames then engulfed other vehicles and toxic fumes swept through the tunnel.

Pope John Paul II concludes the first ever papal visit to Spain after making public appearances in 16 cities throughout the country.

10 The Mexican government announces that it has reached agreement with representatives of the International Monetary Fund (IMF) on terms for $3,840,000,000 in credits. Mexico agrees to cut spending, increase taxes, and curb imports to prevent badly needed capital from leaving the country.

Geoffrey A. Prime, a translator of Russian at Britain's Government Communications Headquarters in Cheltenham from 1976 to 1977, pleads guilty to having spied for the Soviet Union and is sentenced to 35 years in prison.

11 The Soviet people are officially informed that Leonid I. Brezhnev died the previous day of a heart attack. On November 12 the Communist Party Central Committee meets in emergency session and elects 68-year-old Yury V. Andropov head of the party, the most powerful position in the Soviet Union.

The U.S. space shuttle "Columbia" is successfully launched on its first commercial flight from the Kennedy Space Center in Florida. During the mission the flight crew places two communications satellites in orbit, but a planned space walk has to be canceled because the spacesuits malfunction.

13 President Reagan lifts his ban against the use of U.S. technology for the construction of a natural gas pipeline from Siberia to Western Europe.

14 Lech Walesa, released by Polish authorities after 11 months of detention, returns home to his family in Gdansk. The official Polish press agency refers to Walesa as "the former head of Solidarity."

16 Chinese Foreign Minister Huang Hua and his Soviet counterpart, Andrey Gromyko, meet for an hour and a half in Moscow following the funeral of Leonid I. Brezhnev. It is the first such high-level meeting between the world's two largest Communist countries since 1969.

The National Football League Players Association and the owners of the 28 teams reach a tentative agreement to end the strike that began on September 21. If the agreement is ratified by the players, each team will play only seven more regular season games. An expanded play-off series will involve 16 teams vying for a Super Bowl berth.

17 Edwin P. Wilson, a member of the U.S. Central Intelligence Agency from 1954 to 1970, is convicted by a federal jury on seven of eight counts of illegally transporting firearms to the Libyan government. The CIA denied his claim that he was part of a covert operation.

24 Representatives of the 88 nations that signed the General Agreement on Tariffs and Trade meet in Geneva for the first time since 1979. A major consideration in calling the meeting was President Reagan's concern that growing protectionist sentiment threatens world trade.

Irish voters go to the polls to decide, in effect, whether Prime Minister Charles Haughey, representing the Fianna Fail Party, will remain in power or be replaced by former prime minister Garret FitzGerald, the leader of the Fine Gael Party. Neither major party gains an absolute majority.

The Israeli commission investigating the slaughter of Palestinians in two Lebanese camps in mid-September notifies Prime Minister Menachem Begin and eight other top officials that they "may be harmed" by the findings and conclusions of the commission.

25 African leaders meeting in Tripoli, Libya, cancel a conference of the Organization of African Unity when it becomes evident that a dispute over Chad's representation cannot be amicably resolved.

26 The 60-member Central Council of the Palestine Liberation Organization issues a statement in Damascus, Syria, rejecting President Reagan's proposal that the Palestinians be given territory in the West Bank and Gaza Strip in association with Jordan. The terms of the rejection leave open hope for negotiation.

Yasuhiro Nakasone is, as expected, elected prime minister of Japan by the ruling Liberal Democratic Party. He had won the party presidency over three other contenders.

29 The UN General Assembly, for the fourth time in three years, condemns the presence of Soviet troops in Afghanistan. The vote, which calls for the "immediate withdrawal of foreign forces" from the country, is 114 to 21 with 13 abstentions.

(Above) The nation at last memorialized those who died in Vietnam with a controversial monument. (Below left) Leonid Brezhnev's death on November 10 forced the Soviet Union to find a new leader. (Below right) Polish Solidarity leader Lech Walesa was released on November 14 after 11 months in detention.

DECEMBER

2 Barney B. Clark, a 61-year-old retired dentist, receives the world's first permanent artificial heart during surgery at the University of Utah Medical Center in Salt Lake City. Clark was chosen because he was fast approaching death and had all the psychological attributes doctors desired in a patient undergoing such a critical operation. Doctors are cautiously optimistic that Clark could survive for a considerable period of time.

4 President Reagan concludes a visit to four Latin-American nations, undertaken to foster "democratic institutions in the hemisphere." The president was warmly welcomed in Brazil. In Colombia he was jeered in the streets and listened politely as Pres. Belisario Betancur Cuartas publicly criticized U.S. policies in Latin America. In Costa Rica Reagan signed an extradition treaty with Pres. Luis Alberto Monge and met briefly with Salvadoran Pres. Alvaro Alfredo Magaña. In Honduras Reagan conferred with Pres. Roberto Suazo Córdova and Guatemalan Pres. Efrain Ríos Montt.

The National People's Congress of China ratifies a new constitution, the fourth since the People's Republic was established in 1949. The document restores the post of president and in various ways institutionalizes China's program of modernization.

The trial of 280 Egyptians, all accused of conspiring to overthrow the government, gets under way in Cairo. Most of the defendants are members of Al Jihad, an Islamic fundamentalist group bent on turning Egypt into an Islamic state.

6 Pakistani Pres. Mohammad Zia-ul-Haq arrives in the U.S. for his first state visit. His request for economic and military aid is supported by President Reagan, but Congress is still debating the details of a proposed $3.2 billion aid package. On more than one occasion he tries to allay fears that Pakistan is seeking nuclear technology in order to develop nuclear weapons.

7 The U.S. House of Representatives rejects President Reagan's request for $988 million to build and deploy the first five of 100 MX missiles. The 245–176 vote is a major setback for the president, who has said the MX is vital to the nation's security and an essential bargaining chip in disarmament talks with the Soviet Union.

10 Peruvian Pres. Fernando Belaúnde Terry announces that he has accepted the resignation of Prime Minister Manuel Ulloa Elías. The president then announces that Fernando Schwalb López Aldana will replace Ulloa in January.

Representatives of 117 sovereign nations sign the United Nations Law of the Sea Treaty during a conference held in Montego Bay, Jamaica. Of the 23 countries that sent representatives to the meeting but do not sign, the U.S. is among the most outspoken in its opposition to that part of the pact calling for a global

authority that would determine who could mine metals under the high seas and how much they could remove. Other nonsignatories include Belgium, Ecuador, Great Britain, Italy, the Holy See, Japan, Spain, Venezuela, and West Germany.

12 Canadian auto workers overwhelmingly approve a new 13-month contract, thereby ending a 38-day strike against Chrysler Canada Ltd., a subsidiary of the U.S. company. Because the strike in Canada cut U.S. supplies and resulted in 4,600 layoffs in U.S. plants, U.S. workers decide to reopen their own contract negotiations, which had been postponed until January 1983.

15 The International Monetary Fund agrees to give Brazil $4.5 billion in credits so that it can service its huge foreign debt.

Roy L. Williams, president of the powerful Teamsters union, is convicted in Chicago along with four co-conspirators on 11 federal charges of plotting to bribe U.S. Sen. Howard W. Cannon and of defrauding the union's pension fund. Cannon, who was not indicted, denies having received a bribe offer.

19 Poland's Council of State announces that martial law will be suspended on December 31. The previous day Parliament authorized the government to suspend or reimpose martial law as it saw fit. Most political prisoners will be released, but certain ones will be charged with serious crimes and made to stand trial.

20 Italian Defense Minister Lelio Lagorio tells a special session of the Chamber of Deputies that the attempted assassination of Pope John Paul II in May 1981 by the Turkish terrorist Mehmet Ali Agca was "an act of war" perpetrated by Bulgaria. The Bulgarians, he indicates, acted as puppets of the Soviet Union, which wanted the pope killed because he had supported Solidarity, the Polish labour federation.

King Hussein of Jordan begins a series of talks in Washington, D.C., with top U.S. officials who are anxious to have Jordan join the peace negotiations between Israel and Egypt. The main sticking points are the establishment of a homeland for the Palestinians and Israel's withdrawal from occupied lands.

The Organization of Petroleum Exporting Countries (OPEC) ends its meeting in Vienna without reaching agreement on individual production quotas. Iran reportedly violated OPEC's earlier production quotas and price structures most flagrantly in order to finance its war with Iraq.

29 The Communist-dominated Finnish People's Democratic League (PDL) forces the resignation of Prime Minister Kalevi Sorsa, a Social Democrat, by opposing a parliamentary resolution to increase defense spending. Pres. Mauno Koivisto, however, refuses to accept Sorsa's resignation and appoints three Social Democrats to fill the Cabinet posts vacated by the PDL.

(Top left) One man's antinuclear protest at the Washington Monument ended in death. (Above) The MX missile was placed on hold until a place to put it could be agreed upon. (Below left) Surgeon William C. DeVries holds the Jarvik-7 artificial heart.

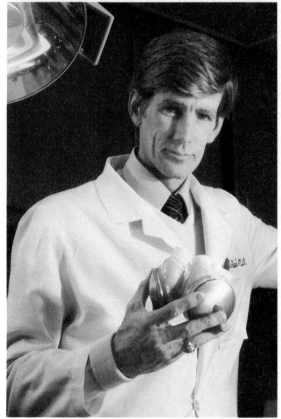

EVENTS OF THE YEAR

YEAR

1982

PRIGGEE/DAYTON JOURNAL HERALD

One of the year's most aggressive advertising campaigns was launched by Burger King, which took on rival fast-food chains McDonald's and Wendy's by name.

ADVERTISING

Advertisers on college football telecasts were affected by a federal district court ruling in September 1982 allowing individual schools, not the National Collegiate Athletic Association, to sell rights for their games. The ruling, if upheld, would create an open market in which each school would negotiate with networks and cable TV for the best deal. More immediately unsettling to advertisers was the strike of National Football League players in the fall that resulted in the cancellation of 112 games. Professional football had proved to be an unparalleled vehicle for advertising men's products. The networks substituted action movies and other sports events, principally boxing, but these did not have the same appeal.

The recession led many companies to offer more giveaways, sweepstakes, come-ons, and rebates to promote sales. Airlines, for example, offered free tickets and lower rates to frequent flyers. Manufacturers stressed quality, value, price reductions, and new uses of products in their advertising. General Electric, among others, used a technique called "flighting"—running a large number of high-visibility advertisements for fast-selling products over a short period.

Ted Bates Worldwide Inc. and William Esty Co. merged during the year, the largest merger in U.S. advertising agency history. Together, the agencies billed $2.4 billion in 1982. Bates paid $50 million for the Esty agency. The U.S. Supreme Court in 1982 rejected a Missouri state rule that barred lawyers from using direct-mail advertising and limited their advertising claims to specific, state-approved phrases. The decision could affect similar rules in 38 other states. As of March 1982, over 50% of U.S. households were "passed" by cable systems, and approximately half of them, 23 million, were subscribers. Fifty percent of cable households also subscribed to pay television. Advertisers were beginning to exploit this new medium, which allowed them to target particular consumer groups more selectively than with over-the-air television.

The $35 billion beef industry spent $7 million in advertising in 1982 in an effort to reverse declining beef sales. Beef thus joined such products as avocados, eggs, oranges, raisins, and potatoes in advertising directly to the public. The California Avocado Commission's campaign to change the perception that avocados are fattening had raised the percentage of U.S. households buying the fruit from 5 to 50.

In an effort to force Burger King, the U.S.'s second-largest fast-food chain, to withdraw a comparison advertising campaign, McDonald's (no. 1) and Wendy's (no. 3) filed suit in federal court, charging that the ads were false and misleading. The hard-hitting commercials, devised by the J. Walter Thompson agency, claimed that Burger King's hamburgers were broiled rather than fried, that they had been preferred in nationwide taste tests, and that Burger King's Whopper sandwich contained more meat before cooking than McDonald's Big Mac. An out-of-court settlement was reached in October under which Burger King agreed to phase out the ads.

Procter & Gamble also took to the courts, filing libel suits against individuals who allegedly had spread the rumour that the firm's man-in-the-moon trademark was a Satanist symbol. A publicity campaign had been launched to counter the persistent rumour, but an *Advertising Age* survey indicated that it had not reached the people most likely to believe the story and may actually have spread it. All advertising for Tylenol was withdrawn when seven people died after taking Extra-Strength Tylenol capsules contaminated with cyanide. In late fall Johnson & Johnson, makers of Tylenol, began a carefully calibrated campaign to restore confidence in the product.

Doylestown Township, Pa., lost a fight in the U.S. Supreme Court to curb unsolicited door-to-door distribution of "shoppers," free papers devoted to advertising. The trial court had upheld the township, which contended that the accumulation of unsolicited circulars at vacant homes identified targets for housebreakers. The appeals court had upheld the shopper, however, on First Amendment grounds, and the Pennsylvania Supreme Court had allowed the appeals court decision to stand.

Each year *Advertising Age* profiles the 100 top national advertisers in the previous year. In 1981 these advertisers spent an estimated $14.8 billion, a 14% increase over 1980. Procter & Gamble remained in the number one position, followed by Sears, General Foods, Philip Morris, and General Motors. Procter & Gamble had been the largest advertising spender in the U.S. since 1963, when it replaced General Motors. In 1981 it spent $671 million on advertising and promotion, 3.4% more than in 1980.

The four leading newspaper advertisers were R. J. Reynolds Industries, Philip Morris, General Motors, and Loews Corp. Procter & Gamble led in television advertising with an expenditure of almost $522 million. Next were General Foods, General Motors, American Home Products Corp., and the Ford Motor Co. The 100 leading national advertisers accounted for 36.5% of all newspaper advertising, 50% of all magazine advertising, 76% of network television advertising, and 61% of network radio advertising.

AEROSPACE

The sorry financial plight of the world's airlines took the edge off a major milestone in the aerospace industry—the entry into service of the Boeing 767 airliner, the intended replacement for a host of

mid-1950s, first- and second-generation transports such as the Boeing 707 and 737, Douglas DC-8, and Vickers VC-10. This all-new airplane first flew in September 1981, was certified in the extraordinarily short space of 11 months, and went into commercial operation on Sept. 8, 1982. It embodied the technical refinements developed since the days of the early jetliners: highly refined aerodynamic shape; new high-bypass, quiet, economical engines; computer-optimized structure; and digital, automatic, self-checking instruments and electronics.

A few months after the 767 came the same company's 757, for shorter ranges, and also Europe's Airbus Industrie A310, both of which made their first flights in 1982. The A310 and 767 were virtually identical to one another in performance, economics, and capacity. The European transport consolidated the reputation built by its predecessor, the A300 short-range airliner, the two designs putting Europe for the first time on equal footing with the U.S. in this class of aircraft.

Unfortunately, the airlines now lacked the capital to buy the new aircraft that were specifically designed to give them the profitability they so badly needed. Throughout the year airlines sought to delay, cancel, or transfer orders for the 767 and 757. United Airlines was discussing the possibility of canceling orders for 25 of the 767s, while American Airlines converted its order for 757s into 727s of similar capacity with a saving of about $8 million on

The newest product of the U.S. aircraft industry was Boeing's 757, which made its first flight during the year; it was intended to replace the aging 727 model.
WIDE WORLD

The European consortium Airbus Industrie introduced its new A310 wide-body aircraft to compete directly with Boeing's new 767, which entered service in 1982.

each aircraft. The latter airline was putting into practice the widely held conviction that expenditure on the new transports could be justified only at a time of steeply rising fuel prices, when the differences in operating costs between old and new aircraft would be greatest.

With the slump in orders, Lockheed in December 1981 announced the phasing out of production of the TriStar, perhaps the most advanced commercial transport in operation. Rumours that the almost identical rival, the McDonnell Douglas DC-10, might go the same way could have materialized had not the U.S. Air Force come to the rescue with orders for more of the KC-tankers, a military version of the DC-10. For the first time in its 50-year career, Lockheed was out of the commercial aircraft business and seemed likely to remain so for the foreseeable future.

With business so flat, little was heard of the 150-seat projects that in 1981 had looked so promising. Boeing still claimed that a viable aircraft could not be available before 1988 because the engine manufacturers would not be able to provide sufficiently advanced powerplants to justify the outlay before then. However, the Airbus A320 design might go ahead under the terms of the "order" announced by Air France at the 1981 Paris air show, thus getting the jump on Boeing (which was likely to be in cash-flow difficulties with the 767 and 757 for some time), Lockheed, and Douglas. The technically magnificent but economically disastrous supersonic Concorde, in the hands of its only two operators, British Airways and Air France, was gradually dying, with routes being closed down and aircraft being cannibalized for spare parts.

The year was also disastrous for the less-publicized but mammoth general aviation industry, cov-

ering everything from two-seater "fly-for-fun" aircraft to multimillion-dollar business and corporate jets. Sales in that sector were down by no less than 50%, with a mere 4,500 U.S. aircraft sold as compared with the previous figure of some 9,000 annually.

The principal military events were the air wars in the Falkland Islands and over Lebanon. The Falklands war was notable for being the first conflict to involve fixed-wing V/STOL (vertical/short take-off and landing) aircraft. The superiority of the British Aerospace Sea Harriers and their U.S.-supplied AIM-9L Sidewinder missiles was such that 31 Argentine aircraft—including 19 Mirages and 5 Skyhawks—were shot down in air combat with no losses to the British fighters. By a fluke of timing the Royal Air Force's Vulcan heavy bombers were used (to bomb the runway at Port Stanley airfield) within days of being retired after 25 years of service. It was their combat debut.

Israel's success in the air made one thing clear: the era of electronic battle management and automated combat was at hand. The Israeli Air Force in air combat and ground attack demonstrated a technical sophistication and integration of forces previously unequaled. Its E-2C Hawkeyes provided early warning of Syrian Air Force fighters taking off to intercept Israeli attackers, and its Boeing 707s then jammed the Syrians' radio communications. Meanwhile, Israeli fighter-bombers knocked out Palestine Liberation Organization and Syrian positions with great accuracy with laser-guided bombs, using ECM (electronic countermeasures) to protect themselves from antiaircraft missiles. To check on damage, Israel then sent in model-aircraft-sized RPV's (remote piloted vehicles) to monitor Syrian positions and radio and televise results.

AFGHANISTAN

Fighting in Afghanistan between the *mujaheddin* (Islamic guerrillas) and the Afghan Army backed by Soviet forces was less widespread during 1982 as the government appeared to be in better control of the insurgency problem in general. Pres. Babrak Karmal, whose position had been considered shaky, was also firmly in command as his Parcham faction of the ruling People's Democratic Party managed to eliminate most of the pro-Khalq elements from the government and the party.

Diego Cordovez, UN special representative for Afghanistan, visited the capitals of Afghanistan, Pakistan, and Iran to convince their leaders of the necessity to find a peaceful settlement. Afghan Foreign Minister Shah Mohammad Dost and his Pakistani counterpart, Sahabzada Yaqub Khan, met in Geneva in June, while Iran, after agreeing to attend, later backed out. Both sides, Cordovez maintained after the meeting, accepted the main agenda items: withdrawal of troops, resettlement of an estimated three million refugees, and international guarantees on noninterference in the internal affairs of Afghanistan.

President Karmal repeated in March that Afghanistan was ready to discuss proposals for a "flexible peace policy" with its neighbours but was thwarted by the hostile reaction of the U.S. and its allies. He also stressed his government's agreement with the U.S.S.R. on all policy matters.

The U.S., the U.K., and other Western countries again condemned the Soviet intervention in Afghanistan on March 21, the start of the Afghan new year, which was proclaimed Afghanistan Day by Western nations. On the same day, the U.S.S.R. declared its intention of staying in Afghanistan until the Kabul government was secure. The Soviet media criticized the proclamation of Afghanistan Day as part of a "slanderous campaign" against the Soviet presence in Afghanistan.

Clashes between insurgents and security forces were mainly centred on the Panjsher Valley, about 45 mi (70 km) northeast of Kabul. According to Western diplomatic sources, bitter fighting took place in this region during June–August. The Afghan Army and the Soviets committed a large number of ground troops supported by helicopter gunships and MiG jet fighters to dislodge rebels from the valley. Rebel sources in Pakistan admitted that the rebels had to take refuge in nearby mountains but insisted that they were preparing to fight back. As a result of large-scale operations by Soviet and Afghan forces, Kandahar City, in the south, also seemed more secure. Western news agency reports estimated casualties in fighting since the Soviet intervention at 20,000 Afghan and 10,000 Soviet troops. Little was known about rebel losses.

Early in November an explosion in a mountain tunnel north of Kabul was reported to have killed hundreds of Soviet soldiers and Afghan civilians. According to accounts that reached the West, the

KLINE–IMPACT

As fighting continued throughout the year, Soviet soldiers captured by rebels in Afghanistan were held in a rebel camp.

lead truck of a Soviet military convoy collided with an oncoming fuel truck. The resulting blast and burning gasoline ignited other vehicles, and most of the deaths were believed to have been caused by asphyxiation from the smoke and fumes that filled the tunnel.

In February Karmal signed a trade protocol with the Soviet Union that thrust Afghanistan further into the Soviet economic orbit. Most Afghan exports were going to the U.S.S.R., which allowed a credit of 10 million rubles to Afghanistan for essential imports. Agricultural production continued to suffer. The farm-labour force remained depleted, as able-bodied men, refusing to be forced into the Army, either fled the country or joined the rebels.

AFRICAN AFFAIRS

Africa's three major concerns during 1982 were the steadily worsening economic conditions throughout the continent, a serious crisis within the Organization of African Unity, and the failure to achieve an international settlement in regard to South West Africa/Namibia. These three elements contributed in varying degrees to political instability and to increasing military and political violence.

Libya's Col. Muammar al-Qaddafi was forced to adjourn a summit meeting of the Organization of African Unity in Tripoli when 19 African nations boycotted the meeting.

The Organization of African Unity

For the first time since its founding in 1963, the 50-nation Organization of African Unity (OAU) failed to muster a quorum for its annual summit meeting, which was scheduled for August in Tripoli, Libya. The two main reasons for the failure were, first, a decision to admit to membership in the OAU the Saharan Arab Democratic Republic (SADR), Western Sahara's government-in-exile led by the Popular Front for the Liberation of Saguia el Hamra and Río de Oro (Polisario Front), and, second, objections by a number of African leaders to the choice of Libya's capital as the site for the summit, since this automatically conferred the OAU chair for the ensuing year on Libyan head of state Col. Muammar al-Qaddafi.

Three months of intensive diplomacy produced a compromise formula that was acceptable to all the parties directly involved in the Western Sahara conflict. It required the Polisario Front to absent itself voluntarily from the summit but did not withdraw recognition of the SADR as a member, pending the holding of an internationally supervised referendum to test the wishes of the Saharans. Acceptance of this compromise appeared to allow the summit to be reconvened in Tripoli on November 23. However, a new dispute broke out concerning two rival delegations from Chad. Qaddafi wanted the one headed by former president Goukouni Oueddei to be seated. Oueddei had seized power with Libyan military backing in November 1981 but had been ousted in

1982 by forces led by Hissen Habré, head of the rival delegation. Several nations favoured Habré and walked out of the meeting. Again a quorum could not be obtained, and the summit was canceled.

Southern Africa

The level of military activity and political violence in southern Africa rose significantly during the year, with the South African Army making repeated military thrusts deep into Angola, and the guerrilla forces of the South West Africa People's Organization (SWAPO) and the African National Congress (ANC) intensifying their incursions into Namibia and South Africa, respectively. In addition to Angola, a number of other neighbours complained that the South African government was engaged in destabilizing their regimes; these included Zimbabwe, Mozambique, Lesotho, Zambia, and Botswana. Nevertheless, Zambia's Pres. Kenneth Kaunda agreed to meet with South Africa's Prime Minister P. W. Botha on neutral ground in Botswana to try to advance a negotiated settlement of the region's most pressing problems.

Substantial progress was made by the contact group of five Western countries (the U.S., the U.K., France, West Germany, and Canada) in persuading both South Africa and SWAPO to agree to terms for implementing the UN Security Council's resolution 435. The resolution called for an international settlement of the Namibian conflict and the introduction of a peacekeeping force to maintain a cease-fire during an 11-month transition period leading to free elections. By November most of the difficult problems relating to implementation had been resolved, and the only serious obstacle to agreement was the insistence by South Africa and the U.S. that Cuban troops should start to withdraw from Angola simultaneously with the confinement to barracks of South Africa's troops. Although the Angolan government remained publicly committed to the withdrawal of Cuban troops once agreement had been reached over Namibia, it firmly rejected the idea of linking the two issues. The U.S. sought to overcome this obstacle through separate talks with the Angolans.

Coups and Inter-African Affairs

Only one African government was changed by means of a military coup in 1982: in November the military regime of Upper Volta was overthrown by junior officers. An attempt by elements in the Kenya Air Force to oust Pres. Daniel arap Moi in August was quickly suppressed. The mercenaries who had attempted in November 1981 to overthrow the government of Seychelles were, after international pressure, brought to trial by the South African government and given stiff prison sentences.

The regime of Pres. Goukouni Oueddei of Chad was defeated in June by the military forces of Col. Hissen Habré, who was believed to have had the support of Sudan and Egypt. Libya, which had earlier withdrawn its army from Chad when an OAU peacekeeping force was introduced, was sharply critical of this new development in Chad. Sudan, which accused Qaddafi of wishing to intervene again

in Chad, remained on bad terms with the Libyan leader. The Ugandan government accused the Libyans of helping to arm the opponents of Pres. Milton Obote. However, Qaddafi's policies in Africa appeared to be less interventionist than in recent years, partly because of his wish to secure the chair of the OAU for 1982–83 and partly because of his involvement in the events in Lebanon.

The five-year conflict in the Western Sahara between Morocco and the Polisario forces, the latter strongly backed by Algeria, showed no sign of bringing military victory to either side. It continued to contribute to hostile relations between Morocco and Algeria. With 26 OAU members giving diplomatic recognition to the independence of the SADR and 14 giving their strong support to Morocco's claims on the territory, the conflict tended to polarize relations in Africa as few issues had done since the civil wars in Angola and Nigeria.

Political Systems

The decision of Senegal and The Gambia to establish the new Senegambia confederation—a decision prompted by an almost successful Gambian military coup in 1981—came into effect on Feb. 1, 1982. Sudan and Egypt also agreed in November to go ahead with their long-proposed plan for a union along confederal lines. In November Pres. Ahmadou Ahidjo of Cameroon decided to step down in favour of his prime minister.

The most sensational election held during the year was that in Mauritius when the ruling party of Prime Minister Sir Seewoosagur Ramgoolam failed to win

South African Prime Minister P. W. Botha (left) and Zambian Pres. Kenneth D. Kaunda (right) met in April. They discussed the role of black leadership in South Africa and the Namibia dispute.
UPI

a single seat in the new Parliament. Elections in Sierra Leone were characteristically violent and controversial. In Madagascar a hard-fought contest for the presidency was won by incumbent Pres. Didier Ratsiraka over the veteran nationalist Monja Joana.

External Relations

Although most African countries continued to pursue policies of nonalignment, their closest relations remained largely with the Western community, mainly owing to economic links. This relationship was considerably strengthened by the world economic crisis, which compelled African countries, more than ever before, to look for trade and aid from Western Europe, the U.S., and Japan. The two Marxist governments of Angola and Mozambique, which had previously indicated an intention to become associate members of the Soviet-led Council for Mutual Economic Assistance, signed the Lomé convention, a trade agreement between African, Caribbean, and Pacific countries and the European Communities.

The Soviet Union showed a renewed interest in Africa during the year, highlighted by a speech by Pres. Leonid I. Brezhnev in November in which he accused the U.S. of seeking to "encircle" Africa by acquiring bases and military allies around the continent's periphery. China's interest in the continent remained high, primarily because of its third world interest in strengthening the nonaligned alliance against the major powers, especially the U.S.S.R. But the Beijing (Peking) leadership told African visitors to China that, for the present, they were unable to give as much economic aid as in the past.

Israel's hopes of reestablishing relations with African countries, broken after the 1973 war, received a setback as a consequence of its military intervention in Lebanon. Only Zaire risked Arab League sanctions by restoring diplomatic ties with Jerusalem.

Social and Economic Conditions

For most of the continent, the only marginal exceptions being the larger oil producers, the state of the economy in 1982 was little short of disastrous. Every recognized indicator of economic and social development was markedly negative. The increase in the continent's real productive output averaged about 3.5%, just slightly above the average rise in its population; this meant that most countries were getting poorer. Export earnings continued to decline; they fell by $1 billion in 1981 to $28 billion and were expected to be still lower in 1982. Africa's aggregate trade deficit increased again, by $2 billion in 1981 to reach $13 billion. By early 1982 the continent's long-term external public debt stood at $38.5 billion, an increase of $4 billion over 1979. A World Bank forecast was that the annual income per head in the poorest of the African countries would fall by 10% during the 1980s to $235 by 1990.

The continuing failure of the continent to feed itself remained a critical factor in its economic development, both in terms of human suffering and because of the need to spend precious foreign exchange earnings on importing essential foodstuffs. Total food production increased by only 1.4% in 1979 and by 2.4% in 1980. Set against the average population growth of about 3%, these figures represented a growing gap between food needs and production. The UN-sponsored World Food Council (WFC) reported that food consumption was 10% per capita less than it had been ten years earlier, although grain imports had doubled in that period and were expected to triple by the mid-1980s. The WFC warned that hunger and malnutrition could be expected to become far more widespread in future years unless successful remedial action were taken. The WFC and the UN Economic Commission for Africa listed five major causes for Africa's serious economic condition: natural causes, the absence of adequate infrastructure, the failures of government policies, the adverse terms of international trade, and the severe impact of higher oil prices.

AGRICULTURE

Despite the leveling off of world agricultural production in 1982, the amount of output continued to support the buildup of stocks of a wide range of agricultural products, particularly in the major exporting countries. World prices of several agricultural farm commodities were depressed, and worldwide economic recession helped hold them down because of reduced demand by consumers. Those poor economic conditions also contributed to growing trade tensions throughout the world, particularly between the European Economic Community (EEC) and the United States over agricultural trade.

The agricultural sectors in both the U.S. and the EEC had faced serious difficulties in recent years, which intensified their trade differences. In the U.S. farm income was down because of the price-depressing effects of large agricultural supplies and also because operating costs had been driven up rapidly by inflationary forces. Thus, U.S. net farm income, which was $32.3 billion in 1979, fell to $20.1 billion in 1980, recovered to $25.1 billion in 1981, and slipped again to an estimated $19 billion in 1982. Under such conditions U.S. agriculture was particularly prone to look abroad for an outlet for its surpluses. During the last decade, when exports rose annually an average of 13%, U.S. agriculture had become much more dependent upon foreign sales for its income. About two acres out of every five on U.S. farms were used to produce for export.

The U.S., which had been concerned about its restricted access to the EEC's agricultural market, began in 1982 to press harder for the elimination of both import barriers and the subsidies on EEC exports that competed with U.S. products in third-country markets. The U.S. was already pursuing a number of complaints against the EEC under the General Agreement on Tariffs and Trade (GATT), including separate cases dealing with wheat flour,

ABOVE, STEVEN HUNTLEY/U.S. NEWS & WORLD REPORT; RIGHT, SARA KRULWICH/
THE NEW YORK TIMES

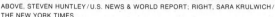

*A family farm in Minnesota (above) and an International Harvester
dealership in Marshalltown, Iowa (right), fell to the auctioneer's
hammer, illustrating the distress felt throughout agriculture as a
result of high interest rates and plummeting crop prices. Harvester
had been on the brink of bankruptcy for over two years.*

sugar, poultry, pasta, canned fruit, and citrus.

World agricultural and food production may have
declined somewhat less than 1% in 1982, according
to preliminary estimates (in December 1982) of the
U.S. Department of Agriculture's Economic Research Service. The heaviest losses in output were in
the Soviet Union, where the harvest was small again
for the fourth year in a row. Among the other centrally planned economies China registered gains in
production, and Eastern Europe matched its performance in 1981. Agricultural output fell slightly in
the developed countries as a group.

Agricultural output was unchanged in the less developed countries, as gains in West Asia and Africa
were offset by losses in Latin America and South
Asia. On a per capita basis world food production
may have fallen as much as 2% in 1982. The decline
was smallest in the developed countries and greatest
in the centrally planned economies.

Major Commodities

Another year of ample grain supplies (wheat,
coarse grains, and rice) was in prospect (in December) for 1982-83. The continuing increase in world
grain output was the result of an expected rise in
grain yields despite cutbacks in planted area. Most
of the estimated increases in 1982-83 grain production were in the EEC and in the centrally planned
economies, which should make possible a substantial recovery in world grain utilization.

World grain production was likely to exceed grain
consumption for the second year in a row. Thus,
world stocks of grain, which continued to grow in
1981-82, were forecast to become the largest (measured as a percentage of utilization) in a decade by
the end of 1982-83. Those stocks had become increasingly heavily concentrated in the developed exporting countries, and the U.S. share had increased
dramatically in recent years.

World wheat production was expected to reach a
record high in 1982-83 despite an estimated 1.4%
decline in harvested area. The largest increases in
output were in exporting countries other than the
United States—the EEC, Argentina, and Canada, all
of which had larger harvested areas—and in the centrally planned economies. Although Soviet wheat
output was estimated to be almost 8% above the 80
million-ton harvest in 1981-82, it was still one-third
lower than that of 1978-79. Severe drought cut Australian harvested wheat area and production by
nearly one-half, raising the possibility of a need to
import wheat in order to maintain that nation's export commitments. U.S. wheat production was little
changed from 1981-82; increased yields offset the
only partially successful influence of government
programs aimed at reducing wheat plantings in the
face of large domestic stocks. The U.S. captured
most of the rise in world wheat exports in 1981-82,
but it was also expected to face the largest cutback
in exports in adjustment to the rise in world wheat
output. The Soviet Union remained the single largest importer of wheat, almost 20 million tons in
1981-82, but China had been importing 13 million
to 14 million tons annually since 1980-81.

World rice production, which reached a record
high in 1981-82 based upon both expanded area and
rising yields, was forecast to decline in 1982-83. A
16% reduction in Indian rice output because of erratic rainfall was mainly responsible, although Thailand also experienced significant losses. The Chinese
harvest was estimated to rise about 3% above the 96
million tons of milled rice produced in 1981-82.
World rice consumption was expected to decline
slightly in 1982-83 after a strong rise in 1981-82. India, however, was expected to reduce its consumption of rice much less than its output by drawing
down rice stocks to their lowest level in eight years
and by sharply cutting its rice exports, 500,000 tons

A "vehicle operation simulator" was constructed at the John Deere Co.'s technical center to enable engineers to design safer and more comfortable farm equipment.

UPI

of which might otherwise have moved to the Soviet Union.

The strong expansion of world stocks of coarse grains that reached record levels by the end of 1981–82 was likely to continue unabated in 1982–83. For the second year in a row, stocks were expected to decline outside the U.S. while increasing there to about three-fourths of the world total. The vigorous expansion of North American coarse grain production in 1981–82, following the severe drought in 1980, pushed world output of coarse grains to a record high. An even larger crop was forecast for 1982–83 based mainly upon production increases in the centrally planned economies and Western Europe. Among the major exporters only the United States and South Africa were expected to register increases in output in 1982–83.

World production of cassava (also called manioc) rose only an estimated (in July) 1% in 1982, according to FAO, to the equivalent of about 50 million tons of grain. Output fell in Thailand because land previously devoted to cassava was being planted in corn, pulses, oilseeds, and rubber. Thailand accounted for about 90% of world cassava trade in 1981 with shipments of 6.3 million tons (processed product weight) and was estimated to export 6 million tons in 1982, almost all to the EEC.

Global output of oilseeds was forecast (in November) to increase about 8% in 1982–83 above the 161.4 million tons produced during the previous year. The increase reflected the expansion of the 1982 U.S. soybean harvest, the Soviet and Chinese oilseed harvests in 1982, and the predicted large

Southern Hemisphere soybean crops in early 1983. World production of protein meal and vegetable oil from oilseeds was expected to increase slightly faster than the output of oilseeds, but the production of fats and oils from other sources was not expected to change much in 1982–83.

World meat production in 1982 in the major producing countries was estimated (in November) to continue at about the same level as in 1981, with small increases in poultry output offset by declines in pork. Both cattle and hog numbers declined in some countries because of feed or forage shortages. Many producers also reduced herds or were reluctant to increase them because of expectations of continuing low revenues and dampened consumer demand.

The growth in world milk production accelerated in 1982, intensifying the problem of increasingly heavy surpluses of dairy products in several countries. With the exception of India the largest gains in productivity were in developed countries—particularly France, the United Kingdom, Italy, Ireland, and the United States—where daily output grew much faster than consumption. The world recession contributed to the problem by slowing the growth in demand for such dairy products as cheese and butter. Because consumption of fresh milk grew little or actually declined in many developed countries in 1982, most of the increased milk output was diverted to the manufacture of processed products, mainly nonfat dry milk (NFDM), butter, and cheese. Production of all those products exceeded their consumption in 1981, and the output of butter and NFDM was increasing more rapidly than consumption.

The world sugar surplus was expected (in November) to continue to expand in 1982–83, despite a likely decline in world sugar production. The sharp jump in world output of centrifugal sugar in 1981–82 led to a large buildup in sugar stocks until they represented nearly 40% of total world sugar production. The world price of sugar as measured under the International Sugar Agreement (ISA), which averaged nearly 29 cents a pound in 1980, had fallen to about 6.5 cents per pound in November 1982. Stocks could reach an unprecedented 45% of consumption by the end of 1982–83, even if low prices succeeded in stimulating a more rapid rise in the rate of world sugar consumption.

World production of cocoa was forecast (in November) to fall slightly in 1982–83, but stocks were expected to continue growing. Although Ivory Coast's output was expected to decline in 1982–83 because of weather problems and the tightening of the influx of contraband cocoa from Ghana, increases in its production were anticipated thereafter at least through 1985. One-fourth of the area planted to cocoa in the Ivory Coast had not yet matured. However, the Ivory Coast government reduced the rate of new cocoa plantings and eliminated planting subsidies because of low world cocoa prices.

Tons of surplus cheese were distributed from federal warehouse stockpiles to unemployed and needy recipients.
UPI

World cotton production was forecast (in November) to fall sharply in 1982–83, largely because of a nearly one-third reduction in planted cotton area in the U.S. Large U.S. stocks and sluggish demand favoured the adoption of a voluntary acreage reduction program there. China was expected to move ahead of the U.S.S.R. as the world's leading cotton producer, based on government incentives that had led to larger cotton plantings.

See also Fish and Fisheries; Food; Gardening.

ALBANIA

On Jan. 14, 1982, the Albanian People's Assembly approved Pres. Enver Hoxha's nomination of Adil Carcani as premier to succeed Mehmet Shehu, who allegedly had committed suicide in December 1981. Carcani, born in 1922 at Shkoder, had become first deputy premier in 1965 and a member of the Albanian Party of Labour's Politburo in 1974.

In his maiden speech Carcani did not refer to his predecessor; however, Mehmet Shehu's nephew, Fecor Shehu, formerly minister of the interior, was not included in the new government, and the late premier's widow, Ficreta Sandiaktari, was removed from her post of secretary in charge of ideology on the party's 81-member Central Committee. Haxhi Leshi, chairman of the Presidium of the People's Assembly (president), who had also been an associate of Shehu, was replaced in November by Ramiz Alia.

In his statement, Carcani reiterated Albania's resolve to persevere in seeking businesslike relations with all the countries of the world except the Soviet Union, the U.S., and Great Britain. Relations with Yugoslavia remained strained following further demonstrations in February by ethnic Albanians in the Yugoslavian province of Kosovo.

ALGERIA

The major issue for Algeria during 1982 was the prolonged struggle to gain a fair price for its major resource, natural gas. This was caused by Algeria's decision to index natural gas prices to crude oil prices. In February 1982 France agreed to buy Algerian gas at slightly more than the world price. Other agreements followed, including one with Italy for gas transported via the new Trans-Mediterranean pipeline, which was completed in 1981 but lay idle until September 1982 because of the dispute. These agreements meant that Algeria was able to counter the fall in crude oil sales, which dropped to 37.5 million metric tons for 1981.

A bilateral economic cooperation convention was signed between France and Algeria on June 21. Among other provisions, France was to supply 5,000 trucks, construct a subway system for Algiers, and build two gasification plants. The agreement was worth over $3 billion. This renewed cooperation between Algeria and France was crowned by the visit to Algiers of Pres. François Mitterrand on May 19. The Socialist government in France saw its for-

Pres. François
Mitterrand of France
(left) rode through
Algiers with Algerian
Pres. Chadli Bendjedid
(right) during his state
visit in May.
GAMMA/LIAISON

eign-policy objectives in the Mediterranean and Africa as complementary to those of Algeria.

Algeria also looked elsewhere for support. An economic agreement with Libya for cooperation over oil and gas exploration and production was signed in early April. However, despite Libyan requests, Algeria did not increase its support for the Popular Front for the Liberation of Saguia el Hamra and Río de Oro (Polisario Front) in the Western Sahara conflict.

Festivities planned for the 20th anniversary of Algeria's independence on July 5 were canceled because of the Israeli invasion of Lebanon. Internal unrest among industrial workers and young people occurred during the year. In April there were demonstrations in the Oran region protesting rumoured changes in the regulations governing entry into higher education.

National Assembly elections on March 5 underlined the domination of the National Liberation Front (FLN), the sole political party. Marxist tendencies within the FLN were purged in favour of Arabo-Islamic socialism. The government continued to emphasize Algeria's Arabo-Islamic heritage and commitment to Socialist development. When Foreign Minister Muhammad Seddik Benyahia died in May, his replacement was Ahmed Taleb Ibrahimi, a well-known Arabist.

The $16 billion budget for 1982 was directed toward infrastructure and communications. Industrial development continued to slow, and the private sector, responsible for one-third of industrial production, received modest encouragement. Algeria was considered sound by the international financial community, and this fact, together with its developing role as a mediator in international affairs, added to its growing international stature.

ANGOLA

Planning Minister Lopo do Nascimento announced early in January 1982 that Angola could not hope to avoid the food crisis that was affecting the whole of Africa, thus heralding another year of nationwide shortages. As a result of two years of drought and the continuing internal security problems, the amount of home-grown food sold in 1981 had declined by 26% from 1979; this could not be offset by purchasing food overseas because of the shortage of foreign exchange. The growing economic crisis prompted Pres. José dos Santos to assume emergency powers in December.

Angola's difficulties were aggravated by the fact that the government had to spend more than half of its revenue and foreign exchange earnings on financing military operations against Jonas Savimbi's National Union for the Total Independence of Angola (UNITA) guerrillas and in responding to South African armed incursions over the southern border. UNITA operations were undiminished along the Benguela Railway in the centre of the country as well as in the south, where there was more direct support from South Africa. Savimbi himself visited the U.S. and several African countries early in the year, raising money for his guerrilla campaign and collecting Soviet-made missiles. In January he claimed that he had been approached by the Angolan government with a view to negotiating a peace settlement. He had replied that UNITA was willing to negotiate but that a condition of any agreement must be the withdrawal of all Cubans from Angola.

This requirement was a clear reflection of the policy of UNITA's South African supporters, and it recurred throughout the year during the negotiations on the future of South West Africa/Namibia. In this way Angola was drawn still more deeply into discus-

Cuban troops remained in Angola during the year, and in July Cuban Pres. Fidel Castro declared they would not be removed until South Africa withdrew from Namibia.
WIDE WORLD

sions that involved the U.S. as well as a number of European countries. Pres. Fidel Castro of Cuba also intervened in July to confirm that Cuban troops would not pull out of Angola until South Africa withdrew from Namibia and ended its aggression toward Angolan territory. The Angolan government stressed that the two matters were in no way linked because the presence of Cubans in Angola was the result of a bilateral agreement between those two countries and was outside the jurisdiction of any other power. Nevertheless, it was widely believed that the U.S., in its anxiety to settle the Namibian problem, was bringing pressure on Angola to remove what appeared to be an important obstacle to South African participation in negotiations.

The Angolan government was itself anxious for a Namibian settlement, which, it was hoped, would remove the South African threat from the southern border and thereby weaken the challenge presented by UNITA. Angola could then concentrate on building up its economy with the assistance of the U.S. and Western Europe. Already Angola was trying to borrow $100 million from Western banks to help cover its balance of payments deficit.

South African troops continued to harass Angola's southern frontier. In March a member of Angola's defense staff stated that South Africa still occupied 50,000 sq mi (129,500 sq km) of Angolan territory. The South African government consistently denied all such claims but almost simultaneously announced that its forces operating in Angola had killed 201 guerrillas belonging to the South West Africa People's Organization (SWAPO) and had captured large quantities of ammunition. Again, in August, after repeated denials, South African defense headquarters admitted having pursued SWAPO guerrillas over the Angolan border, killing more than 300 of them. In May South African Air Force planes carried out a number of raids over the border, and in September South Africa claimed to have shot down a Soviet-made jet fighter over Angolan territory.

ANIMALS AND WILDLIFE

The Endangered Species Act was reauthorized in September, extending for three years a federal prohibition against buying, selling, possessing, importing, or exporting any products made from endangered or threatened species. Despite threats from conservative politicians after the 1980 elections, the nine-year-old conservation law was changed very little during the renewal process. In response to critics who claimed that the Reagan administration had been stalling decisions to add species to the endangered and threatened lists, the listing process was streamlined to allow faster action. The reauthorization also created exemptions in areas where industrial interests believed the law was too cumbersome.

The legislation continued the current funding level of $38.9 million per year, including $6 million in grants to state governments to assist them in creating and maintaining programs to protect endangered species. The maximum share of state costs that the federal government would pay was increased from 66.6 to 75% for single-state projects and from 75 to 90% for multistate projects.

The secretary of the interior would have one year to decide whether or not to declare a species endangered once the department received a petition to list that species. The time period was cut from two years after wildlife groups complained that up to 50 proposals had been repeatedly returned by the Interior Department's solicitor's office for "endless revisions." The actual decision to list or not list a species would now be based solely on the biological question of whether or not the species was threatened or endangered. Administration officials had been including the potential economic costs of listing a species in the decision. Economic factors could, however, be taken into account when designating critical habitat. Any decisions to reject a petition would be subject to judicial review.

Other provisions in the act would allow federal agencies or applicants for federal permits to seek,

Controversy continued to swirl around the use of poison against sheep-killing coyotes. A promising technique was the toxic rubber collar, such as the one worn by this lamb in a 1977 test.
UPI

much earlier in the application process than had previously been allowed, an informal consultation with the Interior Department over whether a project would jeopardize any endangered species. In order to encourage plans to introduce captive-bred members of endangered species to the wild, special provisions that would not trigger the full protective mechanisms of the law were established for "experimental populations."

Coyote Control

Western sheep ranchers won a partial victory in their struggle to be allowed to resume use of Compound 1080, a potent poison used to kill coyotes that was banned in 1972. In late October an administrative law judge recommended that the Environmental Protection Agency (EPA) permit ranchers to use 1080 in "toxic collars" attached to sheep's necks and to allow specially trained federal workers to scatter small amounts of meat laced with the poison over known coyote ranges. EPA Administrator Anne Gorsuch was expected to accept the judge's recommendations and lift the ten-year-old ban on 1080. Her decision, however, could be appealed in federal court, postponing a final settlement of the predator-control controversy.

Sodium fluoroacetate, or Compound 1080, was developed in Germany during World War II and was widely used in the U.S. as a predacide in the 1950s and '60s. At that time ranchers injected sheep or horse carcasses with large amounts of 1080, then dumped these "bait stations" where they would be eaten by coyotes. Wildlife groups demonstrated that this nonselective use of the poison was ecologically unsound, causing the deaths of other animals, including the endangered bald eagle and California

condor, who also ate the bait or who ate the bodies of poisoned coyotes. Other studies suggested that 1080 was so potent it posed a risk to humans who came in contact with it. Responding to this, the Nixon administration prohibited its use on federal lands in 1972, and shortly thereafter the EPA canceled the poison's registration.

Claiming a dramatic increase in stock losses, ranchers immediately began fighting the ban, even taking the issue to federal court, which upheld the EPA's action. But the Reagan administration proved more sympathetic to the ranchers' situation. In January President Reagan revoked the Executive Order that had prohibited the use of 1080; meanwhile, Gorsuch had reopened the case in December 1981, stating that new evidence suggested that "EPA overestimated the environmental hazard" of Compound 1080 in 1972.

According to some wildlife scientists, the bait station method is totally ineffective in controlling coyotes because studies have shown that a pack can quadruple its reproduction rate in order to counteract losses. Since a high percentage of the losses suffered by ranchers are the result of sheep-killing binges by specific members of a pack, the only effective way to cut down on stock losses, according to these scientists, is to kill specifically the individual coyotes who have developed a taste for sheep.

Spokesmen for the wool industry argue that through the use of the rubber "toxic collars," which release 1080 only when a predator bites through them in attempting to kill a sheep, only the harmful coyotes will be destroyed. No other wildlife will be endangered by the poison. Some environmentalists, however, fear that the repeal of the ban would make 1080 available to those willing to abuse it, including some ranchers who may not want to take on the expense of outfitting every sheep with collars.

Marine Mammals

The International Whaling Commission (IWC) voted July 23 to declare a worldwide moratorium on all commercial whaling starting in 1986. Brazil, Iceland, South Korea, Japan, Norway, Peru, and the Soviet Union voted against the measure, an attempt to halt the continuing slide toward extinction of many types of whales. Twenty-five other nations, including the United States, supported the ban, while five abstained and two were absent.

Some nations that opposed the measure threatened to file exceptions to the decision, which would permit them to continue to hunt whales under the commission's rules. Conservationists said that the U.S. attitude could be a major factor in determining the actions of the whaling nations, particularly Japan. The Pelly and the Packwood-Magnuson amendments to the Fishery Conservation and Management Act of 1976 permit the federal government to halt imports of fish and deny fishing rights within the U.S. 200-mi coastal zone to nations not complying with IWC rules. The Reagan administration strongly supported moves to end whaling, and U.S. delegates warned that the government "would take strong measures against countries defying commission decisions."

In order to ease the transition for whalers, the IWC moved to decrease the quota of whales that could be

Having failed to prevent a planned open hunt, volunteers moved into the Florida Everglades to rescue deer threatened by starvation.
UPI

caught each year until the total ban began in 1986. The member nations also agreed to review the moratorium in 1990 and to consider whether whaling might then resume. Under the terms of the ban, subsistence whaling by Eskimos and other native hunters would continue.

The populations of many kinds of whales have been declining sharply for years, with several species thought to be close to extinction. Over the past ten years the IWC has taken measures in an attempt to halt the decline, including prohibiting the use of "factory ships" in whaling, declaring the Indian Ocean a whale sanctuary, restricting the use of certain killing methods thought to be particularly cruel, and gradually decreasing quotas for especially endangered species.

Conservationists had unsuccessfully tried to establish a whaling moratorium since the idea was first proposed at the 1972 United Nations Conference on the Human Environment in Stockholm. Leading the opposition to the ban, Japan claimed that it would cause unemployment in that nation, where the world's biggest whaling industry employed 1,300 people, plus accounting for partial employment of another 50,000 in related processing and distribution trades. Conservationists argued that the strong measure was unavoidable in order to ensure the survival of the world's largest mammals.

Another marine mammal was the focus of an August controversy over a National Oceanic and Atmospheric Administration (NOAA) research project that called for killing 960 female and baby porpoises. The study was intended to investigate porpoise reproductive habits and thus determine the number of porpoises that Japanese fishermen would be allowed to take as "incidental catch." The Japanese had been salmon fishing in U.S. waters for three years under a National Marine Fisheries Service permit. The gill nets used by the Japanese also trapped porpoises swimming with the salmon, but the porpoises were usually discarded since they had no commercial value. The government had no scientific basis for restricting the number the fishermen should be allowed to take, so the permits placed no limit on the number of porpoises that could be caught. Senator Bob Packwood (Rep., Ore.) protested the planned study vigorously when he was informed of it by a constituent. Negotiations between Packwood's office and the Commerce Department, which oversees NOAA's work, resulted in a compromise under which the research was canceled in exchange for a three-year extension of the permit allowing foreigners to fish for salmon in the Bering Sea.

Hunting

A controversy arose in southern Florida in July when the state's Game and Fresh Water Fish Commission scheduled a two-day "mercy kill" of 1,500 starving deer in the Everglades. Heavy storms in June and drainage from upland sugarcane fields had flooded the marshlands in which the deer were liv-

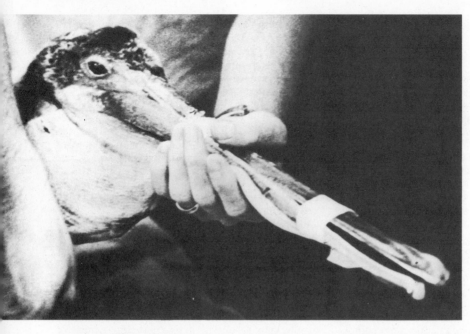

Pinocchio was one of several California brown pelicans to be fitted with prosthetic devices after unknown persons broke or sawed off the birds' beaks.
UPI

ing, and officials said many of the animals were dying of malnutrition and stress on tiny islands.

Animal protection groups tried to block the hunt in court, arguing that the deer ought to be caught and moved to safety; game officials responded that this would cause intolerable levels of shock in the animals. After a two-day delay, a federal judge dissolved the temporary restraining order, allowing the hunt to begin July 18. It lasted two days, during which 730 deer were killed; the hunt was ended two days earlier than planned when it was discovered that disease and starvation had taken a larger toll than anticipated. Only 19 animals were caught by animal welfare workers.

A similar protest in Washington, D.C., caused officials of the National Zoo to postpone plans for a deer hunt at the zoo's 3,300-ac (1,335-ha) exotic wildlife refuge in Virginia. An uncontrolled increase in the herd of whitetailed deer living in the refuge was posing a health threat to the exotic species as well as demolishing the alfalfa crop grown to feed zoo animals. Four previous efforts to drive the deer off the land had been unsuccessful.

Endangered Birds

The California condor rescue effort moved forward during the year, but not without suffering some discouraging setbacks as well. Observers from the U.S. Fish and Wildlife Service and the National Audubon Society, sponsors of the program, were delighted when a pair of condors produced an egg late in February. One biologist actually watched the female lay the egg from a blind about a half mile away from the cliffside nest in the coastal mountains north of Los Angeles. But several days later the parents began to quarrel over incubation rights to the egg. As the team watched in dismay, the squab-

ble escalated into a shoving match and then was carried into the air. When the birds returned to their nest after having left the egg untended for hours, they continued the brawl, and the egg was accidentally knocked out of the nest and over the edge of the cliff. It smashed on a ledge below, and its contents were eaten by a pair of ravens.

Happily, the condors mated again and produced a second egg in early April. But ravens had followed the condors to their new nest site and began harassing the huge birds there. The observers decided that the egg was in danger and obtained permission from Sacramento and Washington to shoot the ravens. The morning after the decision, before the condor team had time to take any action, one of the ravens invaded the nest. As the parent threw itself at the aggressor, the egg rolled to the edge of the cliff and over. The ravens then consumed its remains.

Later in the season the condor team discovered that two other chicks had been hatched in remote areas of the rugged range. On August 13 one of the chicks was removed and taken to the San Diego Zoo. There it was to form part of a captive breeding flock whose offspring would be released in the wild to replenish the critically endangered species.

Fifteen endangered brown pelicans were found in southern California during the year with their upper beaks sawed off, making it impossible for them to feed themselves. The California Fish and Game Department tried to capture as many as possible to keep the birds from starving. The unknown party mutilating the pelicans was thought to be a disgruntled fisherman, angry at the birds who sometimes steal fish from fishermen's lines. Veterinarians at the Crown Valley Animal Hospital in Laguna Niguel began a program to replace the pelicans' missing upper beaks with fiberglass ones.

Scientists from the University of California at Berkeley discovered in a remote Ethiopian desert bones believed to be remains of man's earliest known ancestor. Behind the four-million-year-old fragments are skulls of a modern human (left) and a chimpanzee.
UPI

ANTHROPOLOGY

Modern humans are characterized by specific physical and behavioural characteristics. The main physical features are a large brain, bipedal or two-footed walking, and certain features of the dentition such as small canine teeth and thick enamel covering the molars. Among the behavioural characteristics are the use of tools and fire, food sharing, and village or home-base sites. Although other species may be characterized by one or a few of these features, only humans possess the entire complex.

Since the early 1960s, a group of fossils known as *Ramapithecus* have been considered the first representatives of the human line because they possess relatively small canine teeth and have thick enamel on their molars. *Ramapithecus* is known from the middle of the Miocene period, approximately 16 million–10 million years ago, and has been found in East Africa, Europe, and Asia. However, over the past ten years the dental features common to hu-

mans and *Ramapithecus* have been recognized in other apelike fossils of the same age as *Ramapithecus*, known as *Sivapithecus*.

The major problem in interpreting the evolutionary significance of *Ramapithecus* and *Sivapithecus* has been the very fragmentary nature of their fossil remains. However, a relatively complete face of a large species of *Sivapithecus* (*Sivapithecus indicus*) was discovered in Pakistan in 1979–80. This skull shows clear affinities not only with the modern orangutan but also with *Ramapithecus*. The similarity between *Ramapithecus* and *Sivapithecus* is so great, in fact, that *Ramapithecus* was renamed *Sivapithecus punjabicus*. Because of the similarities between the orangutan and all of the *Sivapithecus* fossils, it was suggested that all of these fossils, including *Ramapithecus*, have only a remote relationship to the human line and are actually on that branch of the evolutionary tree leading to the orangutans.

A unique collection of prehistoric mud drawings—perfectly preserved by steady 55° F temperature and 100% humidity in a Tennessee cave—was disclosed by scientists in 1982. The exact location was not revealed in order to prevent vandalism or looting of the 13th-century artwork.
WIDE WORLD

The authors of this analysis point out that this interpretation is in line with the interpretation of the early course of human evolution drawn from the molecular evidence. Through the comparisons of proteins of living apes and humans, molecular biologists have claimed that the line leading to the modern orangutans could not have separated from that leading to humans and the African apes until the Middle Miocene, and the human line itself could not have separated from the line leading to the African apes prior to six million ± three million years ago. By removing *Ramapithecus* from the human line, the interpretation of the early course of human evolution based on the fossil material is brought more nearly into line with this alternative reasoning.

There are also no known fossils prior to those from Laetoli, Tanzania (3,750,000–3.6 million years old), and Hadar, Ethiopia (approximately 3.7 million–3.3 million years old), that are definitely on the human line (hominids). This more recent African material clearly shows the development of another hominid feature, bipedal locomotion. At the Laetoli site there is a trail of footprints showing that the gait of these hominids was virtually identical to that of modern humans except that the stride length appears to have been very short. Recent analyses of well-preserved skeletal fossils from Hadar support this conclusion. The muscle patterns on the bones indicate the possibility of a well-controlled bipedal gait, but the length of the hind limbs in relation to the inferred body size is very short compared with modern *Homo sapiens*. The author of this analysis concludes that bipedalism developed in an ancestral form with short hind limbs and, from the time of the Hadar and Laetoli material, the legs have lengthened in response to the need for greater efficiency associated with increased stride length.

The bipedal gait of these hominids has one important implication for the development of human culture. Bipedalism frees the forelimbs from their locomotor function. Ever since the time of Darwin, free forelimbs in hominids have been associated with the use and manufacture of tools. However, there is no evidence for the use of stone tools in sites of the same age as the early hominids from Hadar and Laetoli. Tools could have been made from perishable material, but there is no conclusive evidence that tool use was associated in a causal relationship with the evolution of bipedal locomotion.

It has been suggested that upright posture may have been associated with feeding on food that grew off the ground, at standing height. However, it has also been suggested that bipedalism may have been associated with another basic human feature, food sharing. If hominids collected food and brought it back to their home bases to share and consume, they would have had to carry it. Food sharing might also have developed from hunting and meat eating. Unfortunately, there is no convincing argument for the development of food sharing at this stage and nothing in the fossil record to support it.

There was also new evidence that fire may have been a relatively early occurrence. Until recently the earliest substantiated use of fire was from sites in northern latitudes dating around 500,000 years old, and it was associated with the spread of the hominids to more temperate environments. However, newly reported baked clay patches from Chesowanja, Kenya, have been interpreted as evidence of controlled hearths or "campfires" dating to 1.4 million years ago.

ARCHAEOLOGY

As often happens, what was probably the single most spectacular find of the year was not made by professional archaeologists. It was a magnificently decorated bronze Celtic helmet, discovered by speleologists in a cave near La Rochefoucauld (Charente), France. Covered with gold leaf, it was also ornamented with inlays of coral.

On October 10, the day before the U.S. national holiday celebrating Christopher Columbus's "discovery" of the New World, the *New York Times* reported that a "hunter of sunken treasure" had

Among the human remains discovered at Herculaneum was the skeleton of a Roman woman, perhaps a wealthy one. Her gold rings with gemstones were perfectly preserved.
WIDE WORLD

recovered specimens of Roman amphorae from a bay near Rio de Janeiro, Brazil. Encountered earlier by fishermen, the jars were said to be scattered over an area on the seabed comparable in size to three tennis courts. Both Plutarch and the elder Pliny remarked that the Romans knew the Atlantic as far as the Canary Islands. It is possible that a Roman vessel, caught in the trade winds, was blown across the ocean. Quite clearly, it never got back home again to announce its discovery.

The year had its usual archaeological whimsies. Mt. Ararat was again climbed in search of Noah's Ark. One of the climbers broke a leg, but no ark was found. Thanks, doubtless, to a current movie, another group sought and was even rumoured to have found a different ark, the "gold-plated Ark of the Covenant," on Mt. Pisgah in Jordan. The responsible authorities, both Jordanian and foreign, knew nothing of the matter.

The newly found fossil hominid bones from the Awash River valley, Ethiopia, at four million years old, predated the so-called Lucy fossils by about half a million years, but artifacts (hence, archaeology proper) discovered so far dated back to only about 2.5 million years. In 1982 a British-French-U.S. group, working in Kenya, pushed the use of fire back almost a million years to 1.4 million years ago. The firemakers were believed to have been of the *Homo erectus* taxonomic group.

In Israel a concentrated program of survey and excavation begun in the Sinai in 1970 was completed before the region was returned to Egypt. Ofar Bar-Yosef of the Hebrew University of Jerusalem reported on a variety of important prepottery Neolithic sites from the period in which agriculture was just beginning. In Jerusalem, despite the continued opposition of ultra-Orthodox zealots, Israeli archaeologists continued their work outside the old walled city. A French-Israeli excavation at Tell Yarmouth recovered new information from the 3rd-millennium BC levels at the base of the mound.

In Turkey, in a region where more new dams were being built on the Euphrates River, U.S., British, Dutch, French, West German, and Turkish salvage teams were at work. Much was being learned of the 4th- to 2nd-millennium BC developments in this previously unexamined region. It was becoming increasingly clear that the stretch of the Euphrates in upper Syria and southern Turkey, with its linkages to southern Mesopotamia, Anatolia, and Mediterranean coastal cities, is of critical importance for the understanding of ancient Near Eastern history.

The year's fresh news from Italy included word of further work at Pompeii and at Herculaneum, where the remains of more than 20 people who died in the fire and lava of Mt. Vesuvius's eruption were found. It now seemed likely, contrary to previous belief, that few of the people of Herculaneum had had time to escape the eruption by sea.

Farther east, in regions affected by Greco-Roman culture, a fine yield of gold jewelry was recovered in

THE MIAMI HERALD

Several amphorae discovered in a bay near Rio de Janeiro were of the type carried by Roman ships in the 2nd century BC.

a tomb in the Tadzhik S.S.R. The Jordanian government's Department of Antiquities organized a multinational team to investigate the great Greco-Roman site of Jerash.

In Western Europe the remains of nine Roman ships were recovered at Mainz, West Germany, on the Rhine, where foundations for a new hotel were being dug. They appear to have been in a shipyard abandoned by the Romans about AD 400, as the empire's garrison began to retreat. A large and well-planned Roman villa was being exposed at Echternach in Luxembourg. The fine bronze helmet from La Rochefoucauld, described above, has workmanship suggesting Greek or Italic models. In England there were also various finds of Roman date, the most important being the recovery in London of timbers believed to be from the Roman bridge and riverside wharves on the Thames. In January the old London market at Billingsgate was closed to permit excavations.

Despite fiscal and political limitations, 1982 was marked by several significant breakthroughs in applied technology that greatly expanded the ability of archaeologists to identify and define buried and vegetation-obscured archaeological sites. Radar equipment carried aboard the U.S. space shuttle demonstrated the capacity to see features below the surface of sand-covered desert regions in both Africa and the Americas. Scientists were able to identify the

PHOTOS, JET PROPULSION LABORATORY / NASA

Radar images from the space shuttle "Columbia" revealed that the Sahara Desert was once crisscrossed by a network of major waterways. The picture at left shows normal visual imaging; the one at right shows the same area in radar imaging.

presence of ancient rivers and landforms buried as much as 15 ft (4.5 m) below the desert sand. Because prehistoric peoples commonly worked or lived next to rivers, this new space-born radar technology held promise of helping to locate and identify deeply buried archaeological sites, which previously had been unrecognized and undetectable.

Between 1977 and 1982 airborne radar surveys provided scientists the first glimpses through this heavy overgrowth and, with them, some major new insights into the extent and economic foundations of ancient Maya culture. Using synthetic aperture radar (SAR), Walter E. Brown of the Jet Propulsion Laboratory, working with archaeologist Richard E. Adams of the University of Texas, identified an extensive system of between 500 and 1,000 sq mi (1,250 and 2,500 sq km) of prehistoric raised fields and canal networks in lowland swamp areas previously thought to have been uninhabited wastelands. The extent and magnitude of these previously unknown canal networks suggested how the Maya could have supported their large populations with an adequate agricultural food base.

In Mexico, despite the continuing economic crisis that curtailed or caused the cancellation of numerous ongoing and planned programs, work continued on the exposure of the Aztec Great Temple, which had been found by chance in 1978 during the installation of a power transformer by the Mexico City Light and Power Co. From 1978 Mexican archaeologists under the direction of Eduardo Matos Moctezuma continued to clear and stabilize the massive temple complex in what became one of the most energetic examples of New World urban rescue archaeology. This first look at the entire temple layout revealed seven major stages of construction and a

total area indicating that the previous hypothetical reconstructions were at least 30% larger than the actual structure.

In the southern Mayan area continuing work in Belize by Norman Hammond of Rutgers University revealed what could be the earliest lowland Maya stela yet discovered. The 32-in (80-cm)-long rectangular and undecorated stela was dated to the 1st century AD, contemporary with the earliest Mexican stone monuments found off the Pacific coast but several centuries earlier than the next most ancient stelae from the Maya lowlands.

In Cuzco, centre of the 15th-century Inca empire, a Peru National Institute team discovered an entire buried and previously unknown sector of the well-known Inca site Orllantaytambo in the Urubamba Valley to the east of Cuzco. This new sector consisted of a matrix of well-preserved buildings and courts with intricate fountains and baths buried below the fields. What appeared to be randomly deposited boulders protruding from the valley-bottom farmlands proved to be carefully engineered elements in a multilevel subterranean nonirrigation canal system for open-air baths and fountains.

Approximately 500 mi (800 km) to the north a second team of Peruvian archaeologists completed the excavation and stabilization of a large ceremonial complex at the 8th-century pre-Inca Huari capital. This find abruptly altered archaeologists' understanding of the development of pre-Inca architectural and cultural history. The shape and composition of this complex differed markedly from previously known Huari structures and helped link a continuum of development in Andean architecture from the 1000 BC Chavin civilization to the elaborate stone workmanship of the 15th-century Incas.

Special Report: The Raising of the "Mary Rose"

by Margaret Rule

At 9:03 AM on Oct. 11, 1982, the remains of the Tudor era warship "Mary Rose" were lifted through the surface of the Solent, one mile from the entrance to Portsmouth Harbour on the south coast of England. After being buried in the seabed for 437 years, less than half the hull survived, but the 200 metric tons of waterlogged oak recovered and brought ashore for conservation and display in the Royal Naval Base at Portsmouth will provide ship historians and naval architects with the only surviving example of a north European carrack fitted with a gun deck built for that purpose and equipped with a battery of guns capable of firing a broadside through lidded gun ports cut low in the side of the hull.

The Ship

The "Mary Rose" was built in Portsmouth by command of King Henry VIII in 1509-10, and a document dated July 29, 1511, refers to the payment of £120 by the king to Robert Brygandyne, the clerk of the king's ships, for the "conveyance of our two new ships from Portsmouth to the River Thames, the one being the 'Mary Rose' and the other the 'Peter Gernerde.' " By Christmas 1511 the ship lay in the Thames close to the royal palace at Greenwich, fully equipped, fitted out with banners and streamers and ready for war.

During the following spring the lord high admiral, Sir Edward Howard, chose the "Mary Rose" as his flagship for a short and successful campaign in the English Channel. Later that year the "Mary Rose" again served as his flagship during the English attack on the French fleet at Brest, which resulted in the destruction or capture of 32 French ships.

Undoubtedly the "Mary Rose" was a stable warship, and in 1513, after trials in the Channel, Sir Edward Howard reported to the king, "The 'Mary Rose,' Sir, she is the noblest ship of sail and a great ship at this hour that I trow to be in Christendom. A ship of 100 tons will not be sooner about than she." This ability to "go about" quickly and safely was essential in ships built like the "Mary Rose," with a high protruding summer castle at the bow and an even higher fighting castle at the stern causing it to be sluggish and unwieldy.

Although no drawings or plans survive to show how the "Mary Rose" was constructed in 1509, it seems possible that the hull lines remained unaltered after it was refitted and rebuilt in 1536. If so, it was a stable ship with a length-to-beam ratio of 3:1 and a keel length of 105 ft (32 m) from the skeg at the stern to the keel stem scarf. The only contemporary picture of the ship comes from an inventory of King Henry VIII's royal ships prepared by Anthony Anthony, an officer of the Board of Ordnance at the Tower of London in 1546, and it shows the ship after the rebuilding in 1536. At that time it was uprated from 600 to 700 tons and equipped with 91 guns, including 15 brass guns with iron shot, 76 iron guns with shot of stone or lead, and 50 hand guns.

The Sinking

Why an apparently stable ship should sink in calm weather within 1 mi (1.6 km) of its home port is a mystery, but the occasion was well documented, and both French and English eyewitness accounts of the tragedy survive. A fleet of 235 French ships under the command of Monsieur d'Annebault, admiral of France, lay in St. Helen's Roads off the northeast corner of the Isle of Wight on July 19, 1545. On board, 30,000 French soldiers waited the command to invade, but first Henry's small fleet of barely 60 ships had to be engaged and defeated. Henry had good intelligence reports of the proposed invasion, and on July 15 he had arrived in Portsmouth as commander in chief of his navy and his army.

The day was calm with only light winds, and the English carracks moved sluggishly through the water to meet the French fleet. Four French galleys, propelled by oarsmen, moved forward to challenge the English flagship the "Henry Grace à Dieu" and, as the "Mary Rose" moved forward to join its sister ship, it suddenly heeled on its starboard side and sank. English eyewitness accounts suggest that the disaster was caused by indiscipline among the crew, but the French admiral claimed that the "Mary Rose" was sunk by his ships.

The truth may lie somewhere between the two accounts. The ship's normal crew was 514 soldiers and mariners, but when it sank there were nearly 300 extra soldiers on board, many in armour and deployed high in the fighting castle. This extra weight may have made the ship dangerously unstable. The gun ports were open and secured against the sides of

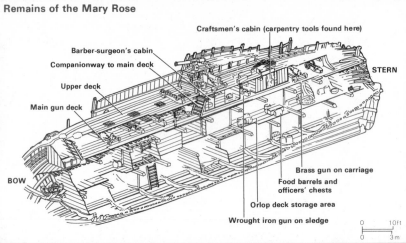

Remains of the Mary Rose

Craftsmen's cabin (carpentry tools found here)

Barber-surgeon's cabin

Companionway to main deck

Upper deck

Main gun deck

STERN

Brass gun on carriage

Food barrels and officers' chests

Orlop deck storage area

Wrought iron gun on sledge

BOW

the hull, and all the guns on the starboard side of the hull were loaded, primed, and run forward through the open ports. Under these conditions the normally stable ship would have been vulnerable, and any "undiscipline" or slow response to orders while hoisting sail would have been disastrous. As the ship heeled to go about, water poured in over the sills of the open gun ports, and some of the guns on the port side in the aftercastle broke loose and swept across the deck, carrying equipment and men with them. This additional weight and the extra weight of water pouring into the ship sealed its fate, and the "Mary Rose" sank rapidly to lie on its starboard side in the soft mud of the seabed 39 ft (12 m) below.

The Rising

There were immediate attempts to pull the ship upright and salvage it by securing it to two empty hulks and using the tide to lift it from the seabed, but eventually these attempts were abandoned. The ship lay forgotten until 1836, when John and Charles Deane, pioneer "hard-helmet" divers, recovered a bronze 32-pounder gun from the ship. During the following four years they recovered other guns, some longbows, pottery, and quantities of wood, but archaeological evidence reveals that they did not enter the surviving starboard section of the hull but simply "harvested" the material that lay among the collapsed timbers from the upper hull on the port side of the ship.

In 1965 a deliberate program of seabed search and documentary research was initiated to find the remains of the ship, but, although a buried mass was detected in the general wreck area in 1967, it was not until 1971 that the tops of eroded frames on the port quarter at the stern were seen for the first time. Between 1971 and 1979 an extensive series of excavations was conducted under the aegis of the Mary Rose (1967) Committee, and by 1979 enough evidence had been obtained to justify the formation of the Mary Rose Trust and the appointment of an archaeological team to excavate and survey the hull

and prepare it for recovery in 1982.

The program of underwater work was demanding, and between 1979 and 1982 almost 28,000 dives were made at the site by professional divers, archaeologists, and volunteers from aquatic clubs. Approximately 17,000 registered objects were removed from the wreck, and 3,000 timbers were surveyed and removed before the empty hull was strengthened and prepared for recovery. A steel cradle was built to conform with the hull lines deduced from the archaeological survey of the internal sections of the hull, and an underwater lifting frame was constructed of tubular steel to spread the load when the ship was lifted from the seabed and moved underwater to its final position in the cradle.

The underwater transfer was completed on Oct. 9, 1982, using acoustics (sonar) to locate the legs of the underwater lifting frame and fit them into the guides on the sides of the cradle. The total "package"— cradle, hull of the "Mary Rose," and underwater lifting frame—weighed 560 metric tons in the air. It was lifted and placed on a barge for transport ashore by the crane barge "Tog Mor," on loan from the Howard Doris Co. On October 11 the ship was towed through the harbour entrance, still looking much as it did when it sailed into battle 437 years earlier. Two months later, on December 8, the "Mary Rose" was "dry docked" at the Royal Naval Base alongside Lord Nelson's flagship HMS "Victory" and only a few hundred yards from where it was built 473 years earlier.

The current task is to restore the hull to the condition in which it was found underwater. The dismantled deck planks will be replaced on the deck beams, and the cabins, companionways, and bulkheads will be reconstructed. The objects of wood, leather, steel, and bronze will be prepared for display alongside the hull, and the public will then have a unique opportunity to study the material remains of a 16th-century community of seafaring men alongside a half section of the ship within which they worked, lived, and died.

John Outram's design for the McKay Trading Estate development in west London won a commendation from the Financial Times Industrial Architecture Award jury.

JOHN OUTRAM, LONDON

ARCHITECTURE

High interest rates and continuing recession throughout the Western world kept the construction outlook bleak in 1982, yet architects seemed full of ideas for new projects. Classicism was the dominant stylistic trend, much of it deriving from a renewed interest in architectural history and a renewed study of buildings of the past. Even where no distinct classical allusions appeared, there was often a discernible reliance on the straight line and the flat plane arranged geometrically, with colour and graphics as important accents.

The McKay Trading Estate in west London was strongly in the new classical idiom. Comprising a series of factory units, the estate was designed by architect John Outram. In an unprepossessing part of the city, between Kensal Road and the Grand Union Canal, Outram grouped together the factory elements to achieve a classical effect, complete with pediments, columns, recesses, and details, all somehow abstracted yet clearly derived from the temple model. Each individual element required by the function of the building was incorporated into a decorative and classical composition in an original and entertaining manner. The units had charm, something rare in industrial architecture, and were of human scale. The materials were simple. There was dark blue brick at the base, yellow London stock brick above, and a band of red brick for emphasis. This was as far removed from the "high tech" shed as imaginable.

Awards

Twelve projects received American Institute of Architects (AIA) Honor Awards, presented at the 1982 AIA national convention. Eight of the awards were for buildings designed and completed within the past seven years; the others were for older structures renovated or adapted to new uses. Included were the Illinois Regional Library for the Blind and Physically Handicapped, Chicago, by Joseph W. Casserly, city architect, and consulting architects Stanley Tigerman and Associates; a residence at East Hampton, N.Y., by Eisenman Robertson Architects; and an addition to the Schulman House, Princeton, N.J., by Michael Graves.

The AIA Gold Medal for 1982 went to Romaldo Giurgola of Mitchell/Giurgola Architects of New York City and Philadelphia. The firm's most recent competition success was for a new Parliament House for Canberra, Australia. The 1982 medal honouring artists whose work relates to architecture was given to Jean Dubuffet, a French sculptor who had made an important contribution to the harmony of sculpture and architecture.

Two widely contrasting buildings received Royal

A new west wing for Boston's Museum of Fine Art was designed by I. M. Pei to complement the original Beaux-Arts structure.
© STEVE ROSENTHAL

Institute of British Architects (RIBA) awards for architectural elegance. The Roman Catholic Church of St. John Ogilvie at Irvine in Ayrshire, Scotland, designed by Gerard Connolly and Douglas Niven, was a minutely detailed exercise in postmodernism. On a much larger scale, in high-tech style, was the radioisotope factory designed by the Percy Thomas Partnership for Amersham International Laboratories at Whitchurch, Cardiff, Wales.

The RIBA 1982 Royal Gold Medal was presented to Berthold Lubetkin, best known for his modern buildings of the 1930s, especially the Penguin Pool at London Zoo of 1938 and his High Point I and II apartment blocks in Highgate, London. Lubetkin was one of the leading proponents of the International Style in Britain.

Educational and Cultural Buildings

In 1982 museums seemed to be springing up everywhere and were often in the news for their architectural qualities. Indeed, the Whitney Museum of American Art in New York City devoted a summer exhibition to the wave of new U.S. art museums as well as museums that were planning large additions.

Architects Belzile Brassard Gallienne Lavoie; Sungur Incesulu; and Moshe Safdie and Desnoyers Mercure, Quebec, won a limited competition for a new National Museum of Civilization for Quebec City. The design was for a waterfront site with terraced steps and gardens integrating the building into the old street plan of the city. The galleries beneath

the terraces were skylit, and the design featured copper roofs with dormers punctuated by a tower.

A new west wing for the Boston Museum of Fine Art, opened in July 1981, was designed by I. M. Pei, architect of the East Wing of the National Gallery in Washington, D.C. The new air-conditioned galleries were not easily added to the 1909 Beaux-Arts building. The architect's instructions were to provide additional space for traveling exhibitions and contemporary art and also a new restaurant and other service functions. His design made a 250-ft (76-m)-long skylighted vault the heart of the wing. The new wing was clad in Maine granite to relate it visually to the old building.

Great public interest was generated in London by the competition for an extension to the National Gallery. The works of the seven finalists were put on public display in late summer and attracted such large crowds that the exhibition was extended. The addition was required to have some 30,000 sq ft (2,700 sq m) of toplit gallery space to house the Renaissance masterpieces of the collection. Underneath, the building had to provide 60,000 sq ft (5,400 sq m) of office space. Each architect teamed with a developer, who would gain an office building on a prime site in exchange for providing the galleries. The site would be leased for 125 years for a nominal rent but would then revert to the crown. Thus the government could gain its gallery space without having to foot the huge bill.

Of the seven plans chosen as finalists, by far the

most controversial was that by Richard Rogers & Partners. The Rogers design featured galleries raised on stilts above a metallic-looking office building with a curved face and a high tower at one side. The structure and metallic skeleton showed the technological bravura of the architect's Beaubourg Centre in Paris and was criticized by some as out of place on the sensitive site; others thought it the most exciting, romantic, and "architectural" entry. Although Skidmore, Owings & Merrill's entry was the one that came closest to satisfying the National Gallery's requirements, none of the competing designs was selected. Ahrends Burton and Koralek, however, were asked to submit an entirely new design.

Public, Commercial, and Industrial Buildings

The limited design competition for the Humana Headquarters for downtown Louisville, Ky., was won by Michael Graves & Associates of Princeton, N.J. The winning design was a formalist conception reminiscent of 19th-century buildings, featuring covered arcades, a tower, a loggia at the base, granite- and marble-clad façades red and bluish in colour, tripartite elevations, and a north-facing cantilevered porch. The mass of the 27-story-high building was broken into a number of disparate elements with classical overtones and was far removed from the traditional single-volume slab skyscraper. The building was to form the headquarters of an international hospital management committee and provide 450,000 sq ft (41,800 sq m) of space.

Two office buildings by Skidmore, Owings & Merrill were under construction and scheduled for completion in 1983. The Hartford Tower, CityPlace, Hartford, Conn., featured a cutaway corner design in which bay windows allowed a wide view from each office. The 38-story-high tower would be the tallest in Connecticut. In San Antonio, Texas, the First International Plaza, a $50 million project, would at 28 stories be the largest building in the downtown area. The arched façade with pointed detailing again showed the tendency to break up the slab.

Helmut Jahn, of the Chicago firm Murphy/Jahn,

won a design competition for an 82-story office building in Houston, Texas. The steel, granite, and glass design is reminiscent of the skyscrapers of the 1920s and 1930s. At 1,222 ft (373 m) the tower would be one of the tallest in the U.S.

In Los Angeles the Intercontinental Centre by Pereira Associates would replace the 1930s Streamlined Moderne Broadway Department Store (recently demolished) on Wilshire Boulevard. The project attempted to re-create some of the traditional Wilshire Boulevard motifs in the 30-story tower building with its stepped profile, monumental door, roof terraces, and motor court at the rear. The tower, which would have retail space at ground-floor level and ornate elevator lobbies in the traditional manner, would be the tallest in the immediate area.

Kohn, Pedersen, Fox Associates were architects for a new corporate headquarters for Procter & Gamble Co. in Cincinnati, Ohio. The building, which would provide 800,000 sq ft (74,300 sq m), featured squat twin octagonal towers rising from a downtown piazza to 17 stories from an L-shaped 6-story base. A gray granite colonnade at street level and open atria at fourth- and sixth-floor levels were features. A heat pump system was used to recover energy from lights, equipment, and people.

ARCTIC AND ANTARCTIC

Two British adventurers became the first to cross both the North and South poles in a single voyage when they planted the Union Jack at the North Pole on April 11, 1982. After covering 35,000 mi (56,300 km) of their planned 52,000-mi (84,000-km) trip, the attainment of the North Pole was the climax of a three-year voyage for Sir Ranulph Fiennes and Charles Burton.

In September the Associated Press reported that charter aircraft business to the North Pole was booming. The short mid-April to mid-May season is terminated when the ice breaks up, making landings dangerous. The visits to the area last no longer than 30 minutes because after that the planes' engines could freeze. After a year-long study by the U.S. National Petroleum Council, it was reported that unde-

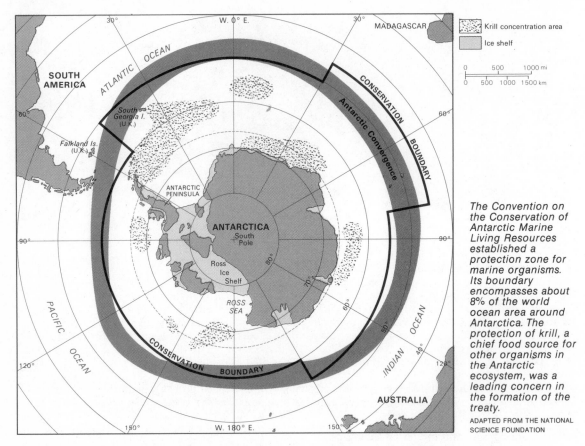

The Convention on the Conservation of Antarctic Marine Living Resources established a protection zone for marine organisms. Its boundary encompasses about 8% of the world ocean area around Antarctica. The protection of krill, a chief food source for other organisms in the Antarctic ecosystem, was a leading concern in the formation of the treaty.

ADAPTED FROM THE NATIONAL SCIENCE FOUNDATION

veloped Arctic regions in the United States contain enough oil and gas to make a significant contribution to the nation's energy supply. The report estimated that approximately 44,000,000,000 bbl of undiscovered recoverable oil and gas resources are expected to be found in those regions. In October, 23 firms made bids totaling $2.1 billion for the right to drill for oil in the Beaufort Sea off Alaska's North Slope.

In Canada planning for the Arctic Pilot Project (APP) continued during 1982. The joint undertaking by Petro-Canada, Nova Corp., Dome Petroleum Ltd., and Melville Shipping Ltd., if approved by the Canadian government, would eventually move natural gas from Melville Island through the Northwest Passage and Baffin Bay-Davis Strait to markets in eastern North America and Europe. Encouraging exploration results in the Beaufort Sea led the petroleum industry to begin designing systems to extract hydrocarbons and deliver them to market.

Some progress was made toward settling the many outstanding Indian land claims in Canada. In May the Dene Nation and Métis Association of the Northwest Territories announced that agreement had been reached upon the definition of "Dene" for the purposes of negotiating a land claims settlement in the western Canadian Arctic. "Dene" would include descendants of seven native groups including

the Métis, who traditionally used and occupied lands now in the Northwest Territories, Yukon, and northern British Columbia.

During the year the Northwest Territories and federal governments signed an agreement to create a 39,500-sq km national park on northern Ellesmere Island. Under the agreement the land would be withdrawn for two years from development for other purposes while public consultation and planning proceeded.

In July the Dene, Indians, Inuit, and Sami of the circumpolar countries participated in the first World Assembly of indigenous peoples held in Regina, Sask. The chairman of the conference stated that indigenous peoples did not intend to "ask for sovereignty, for they had never given it up" and that they wanted to coexist, as culturally and socially different nations, with those peoples who shared their lands. The Inuit (Eskimo) Circumpolar Conference, an organization that represents the Eskimo populations of Alaska, Canada, and Greenland, planned to ask for affiliation with the United Nations.

In May it was reported that Soviet scientists believed that relics ranging from 15,000 to 20,000 years old found in northeastern Siberia confirmed that the first inhabitants of America migrated from Asia. The relics indicated that the people hunted deer, mammoth, and bison and also tamed dogs.

Antarctica

The Antarctic Treaty nations began to formulate a regime for the exploitation of mineral resources during a consultative meeting in Wellington, N.Z. Major international research efforts occurred in the Weddell Sea, where a U.S.-U.S.S.R. expedition searched without success for the Weddell Polynya, an area of ice-free water; in North Victoria Land, where major geologic investigations were conducted by 60 scientists; and near the Antarctic Peninsula, where researchers in the BIOMASS (Biological Investigation of Marine Antarctic Systems and Stocks) program discovered a swarm of krill estimated at ten million metric tons. The Convention on the Conservation of Antarctic Living Marine Resources was ratified and went into effect. A permanent secretariat was organized in Hobart, Tasmania.

Disasters struck several expeditions. The West German expedition to North Victoria Land lost its ship "Gotland II" when it sank in heavy ice within 24 hours of being pinched by the pressure of the ice. The passengers and crew were rescued by the five helicopters on board, but all scientific equipment and supplies were lost. The British Antarctic Survey lost its two Twin Otter aircraft in a storm, eliminating much of the planned summer research program.

Australian glaciologists recovered an ice core to bedrock from fast-moving ice on the Law Dome at Cape Folger. The core was over 980 ft (300 m) in length and was returned to Australia for analysis.

Two active volcanoes were discovered by Chilean scientists working on the Weddell Sea side of the Antarctic Peninsula. Both volcanoes had erupted recently and covered parts of the Larsen Ice Shelf with debris. Tourist flights on Chilean aircraft between the mainland and Teniente Rodolfo Marsh base on King George Island were offered.

Some 160 scientists, including exchange scientists from four nations, participated in the New Zealand Antarctic Research Program. In addition to joining the North Victoria Land project, scientists worked on Mt. Erebus and at several locations between Cape Adare and the South Pole. The 25th anniversary of continuous New Zealand research in Antarctica was marked by a visit to Scott Base by Prime Minister Robert Muldoon and Sir Edmund Hillary, the conqueror of Mt. Everest. Hillary had been the first officer in charge of Scott Base.

The 27th Soviet Antarctic Expedition, which involved some 800 men and women during the summer, worked at seven permanent stations and established summer stations at the base of the Antarctic Peninsula and on the Ronne Ice Shelf. Soviet glaciologists discovered pollen, spores, and microorganisms at the 650-ft (200-m) depth of an ice core from Vostok Station and reported evidence of the occurrence of a major thaw of some kind about 15,000 years ago.

An important scientific discovery occurred on Seymour Island, where helicopter-supported U.S.

INSTITUTE OF POLAR STUDIES, OHIO STATE UNIVERSITY; ILLUSTRATION, R. W. TOPE

This inch-long jawbone was among the remains of a rat-sized marsupial that were the first fossils of land mammals ever found in Antarctica. The find helped confirm the theory that Australia, South America, and Antarctica were once joined.

geologists discovered the first fossil marsupial in Antarctica. The discovery supports the theory of marsupial migration from the Americas to Australia via Antarctica. Large-scale fieldwork was conducted in North Victoria Land. A 660-ft (203-m) ice core was drilled at the South Pole, and scientists estimated that it represents a 1,600-year climatic record. Laboratory analyses seemed to indicate that several meteorites discovered in Antarctica probably originated from Mars and not from the asteroid belt.

ARGENTINA

Lieut. Gen. Leopoldo Galtieri, who assumed the military presidency of Argentina on Dec. 22, 1981, faced increasing civilian opposition to military rule during the first months of 1982. The principal reason for this was the worsening economy. Gross domestic product fell by 6% in 1981; the foreign debt was $32 billion; and the annual rate of inflation, estimated at 138.1% at the end of 1981, was reported by the International Monetary Fund (IMF) to be the highest in the world in January 1982. The government introduced a program of austerity: cuts in public sector spending; denationalizations in the banking, energy, and military-industrial sectors; devaluation of the peso; and a wage freeze. Repeated outcries against these policies, rising unemployment, and falling wages led to a violent protest by the Peronist Confederación General de Trabajo on March 30, during which about 2,000 people were arrested.

The failure to resolve the dispute over sovereignty of the Falkland Islands/Islas Malvinas during 17 years of talks with the U.K. returned to the headlines in March. After reportedly cordial but unproductive talks in New York City on February 26–27, the Argentine Foreign Ministry stated that an alternative measure to negotiation would be taken if a solution were not found quickly.

Rumours of a possible Argentine invasion of the Falkland Islands met with no response from the U.K. until the arrival on March 19 of a group of Argentine scrap-metal contractors on South Georgia, a Falklands dependency, developed into a confrontation between Argentine warships and the British Antarctic patrol vessel HMS "Endurance." On April 2 Argentine troops landed on the Falkland Islands, easily overcoming the small garrison of U.K. Royal Marines stationed at Port Stanley.

The U.K.'s immediate reaction was to break off diplomatic relations and to dispatch a naval task force to the South Atlantic. On April 3 the UN Security Council supported the U.K.'s call for an Argentine withdrawal. During the three weeks that it took the British fleet to reach the vicinity of the Falklands, negotiations at the UN for a peaceful settlement and mediation attempts by U.S. Secretary of State Alexander Haig and by Pres. Fernando Belaúnde Terry of Peru proved unsuccessful.

Trade sanctions were imposed on Argentina by the European Communities (EC), and the U.K. received further support from many of its Commonwealth allies. Argentina, on the other hand, was backed by the majority of Latin-American countries, although many did not approve of the initial use of force as a means toward settlement. The U.S. delayed open support of the British until April 30.

On June 14 the Argentine military governor of the Falklands, Gen. Mario Benjamín Menéndez, surrendered. For Argentina the repercussions of defeat were serious. The Army's capitulation on the islands, the Navy's relative inactivity, and feelings that the U.S. could no longer be counted on as an ally brought a sense of pessimism.

Galtieri resigned as army commander and president on June 17. The former post was taken by Gen. Cristino Nicolaides; the presidency was temporarily given to Interior Minister Maj. Gen. Alfredo Oscar Saint Jean. After much debate within the armed forces, retired army general Reynaldo Bignone was named president until March 29, 1984. Since the plan for a speedy return to democracy seemed unlikely to be adopted, the Air Force and the Navy retired from the ruling junta in protest against Bignone's appointment. On September 10 the junta was restored in order to provide a stronger approach to the country's debt crisis. Opposition civilian parties were heartened by moves toward the signing of a statute on the organization and activity of political parties.

The politically sensitive issue of the *desaparecidos* ("disappeared persons") remained prominent in domestic affairs. Human-rights groups continued to press the government for a full investigation of the issue, especially after the claim that nearly 1,000 unidentified bodies found in six cemeteries during October and November were those of victims of the 1976–79 suppression of opposition. The government's proposed pact with civilian parties for a transition to democracy included an agreement not to investigate the armed forces' actions at that time or their handling of the Falklands campaign and the economy.

On the international front the war had forged some unexpected alliances, notably between Argen-

Argentine casualties were evacuated from the Falklands by helicopters and hospital ships to Río Gallegos.
SYGMA

tina and Cuba. Argentina's trading links with Latin America, socialist countries, and the Middle East were reinforced, but the end of hostilities brought a gradual reinstatement of trade ties with the U.S. and the EC. Argentina, however, retained some sanctions against selected EC countries. Argentine/British trade embargoes were not lifted, but in September financial sanctions were ended and in October agreement on Argentine debts to the U.K. was reached.

Since June 16 Argentina had been unable to make repayment on its external debts, which had risen to $37 billion. Economy Minister Jorge Wehbe succeeded in obtaining a delay in debt repayments to the country's major creditors. An IMF delegation arrived in September to study renegotiating the foreign debt, which by then stood at $40 billion.

ART AND ART EXHIBITIONS

There would be no more large loan exhibitions, or so the experts had been saying for some years. Certainly the lending policies of the major institutions, reflecting the increased costs of insurance and transport and the problems of conservation, militated against the major loan retrospectives that had been common 20 years earlier. Loans were approved only for works robust enough to travel and for shows of outstanding importance. Policy usually dictated that the same work was not lent frequently.

The rare large loan retrospectives were now greeted with more enthusiasm and excitement than ever. Such was the London Royal Academy's winter exhibition, "Painting in Naples from Caravaggio to Giordano," a loan exhibition devoted to Caravaggio and his followers which drew on many Italian private and public collections and churches. Not only were many of the paintings lent for the first time, but works often difficult to view properly in churches were displayed under gallery conditions. Of the more than 150 paintings comprising the show, the highlights were Caravaggio's "Seven Works of Mercy" and his "Flagellation." Jusepe de Ribera, Guido Reni, Francesco Solimena, and Giordano were other artists represented.

The largest exhibit of El Greco's paintings ever mounted opened at the Prado in Madrid in April before traveling to the National Gallery of Art, Washington, D.C., the Toledo (Ohio) Museum of Art, and the Dallas (Texas) Museum of Fine Arts. Titled "El Greco of Toledo," the show originated as part of the celebration of 50 years of "sisterhood" between Toledo, Ohio, and Toledo, Spain, where El Greco spent most of his career. Of the 66 paintings in the exhibit, 32 were from Spain and the remainder were on loan from museums and collections outside the country, several of them in the U.S.

If loan exhibitions in which works of art were borrowed from various owners were becoming less and less frequent, a new type of show was on the increase: the exhibition of a whole collection made by one man or family. Such exhibitions provided an insight into the history of private collecting, taste, and connoisseurship. The goals and achievements of private collectors differ from those of museums. A museum director, always under the watchful eye of the trustees, must bear in mind the suitability of a new acquisition for the whole collection. The great private collector can satisfy his own artistic taste. If he has a good eye, his collection will be coherent and unique.

The National Gallery of Art in Washington, D.C., mounted "Lessing J. Rosenwald: Tribute to a Collector" in the winter. Rosenwald was the foremost donor of prints and drawings to the gallery, and the Rosenwald collection contains works dating from medieval times to the present. It was described as the finest collection of its kind ever formed by a single individual in the U.S. Lessing Rosenwald was the son of the chairman of Sears, Roebuck & Co. and succeeded his father in that position, retiring in

"St. Martin and the Beggar" was among the 66 paintings by El Greco that were shown in Madrid, Spain; Toledo, Ohio; and elsewhere.
NATIONAL GALLERY OF ART, WASHINGTON, D.C.; PHOTO, AUTHENTICATED NEWS INTERNATIONAL

VICTORIA AND ALBERT MUSEUM, LONDON

"The Indian Heritage" exhibit at London's Victoria and Albert Museum featured many works of art from the Mughal period.

1939. Between 1926 and 1979 he collected about 22,000 Old Master and modern prints and drawings.

George Costakis, born in Moscow of Greek parents, formed a unique collection of modern Russian art between 1908 and 1932. A show based on his collection was organized by the Guggenheim Museum, New York City, in the winter of 1981–82 and later toured the U.S., Europe, and Asia, including the Museum of Fine Arts, Houston, Texas, and the Royal Academy, London. Titled "Art of the Avant-Garde in Russia: Selections from the George Costakis Collection," the show consisted of 275 works of art made in the first quarter of the 20th century by 40 artists, some little known in the West. There were important works of Futurism, Suprematism, and Constructivism and examples of works by the major artists of the period, including the sculptors Aleksandr Rodchenko and Vladimir Tatlin. Costakis, through his contacts in Moscow, was able to meet many of the artists personally and collect at a period when the works of this group lacked official recognition.

The families of artists sometimes have an unrivaled opportunity to collect. "Max Ernst—From the Collection of Mr. and Mrs. Jimmy Ernst" was organized by the Glenbow Museum, Calgary, Alta., and shown also at the Art Gallery of Hamilton, Ont. Jimmy Ernst was the son of the Surrealist artist Max

Ernst and was himself a leading American painter. The works forming the core of the show were from Max Ernst's personal collection. There were 16 paintings, 23 works of sculpture, 34 prints, and 15 pieces of primitive art from which the artist drew some inspiration. The exhibition included some of the concrete gargoyles made by Max Ernst to decorate his own home in Arizona.

"An American Perspective: Nineteenth Century Art from the Collection of JoAnn and Julian Ganz, Jr." was shown in the summer at the Los Angeles County Museum of Art. The Ganz collection, formed in the last 20 years, was considered one of the finest collections of 19th-century American art and included works by such major artists as Winslow Homer, Thomas Cole, and J. S. Sargent. An exhibition devoted to the works of the New York postwar Abstract Expressionist Adolph Gottlieb was shown in Los Angeles at the same time.

Shows with an American theme remained common, and one of the finest in 1982 was the definitive exhibition organized by the Philadelphia Museum of Art and devoted to the work of Thomas Eakins (1844–1916). The show was part of Philadelphia's celebrations of the city's 300th anniversary. Both the famous "clinical" scenes—"The Agnew Clinic" and "The Gross Clinic"—were on view. The show would travel to Boston later, but without a number of the paintings seen in Philadelphia.

"American Portraits in the Grand Manner, 1720–1920" was organized for the Los Angeles County Museum of Art and was also on view at the National Portrait Gallery, Washington, D.C. It was the first major loan exhibition to be devoted to formal portraiture in the U.S. as a distinct artistic genre. The works shown included notable examples by Frank Duveneck and Robert Henri as well as earlier works. The paintings were mostly full-length and many were life-size. Circus art was the subject of "Center Ring: The Artist," organized by the Milwaukee (Wis.) Art Center and also seen at the Corcoran Gallery of Art, Washington, D.C. Works on view included a nine-sheet poster for "Buffalo Bill's Wild West: Cody Shooting Glass Balls."

Many exhibitions in 1982 were again devoted to Far Eastern subjects. Indian art was shown at a number of places in London as part of the Festival of India. The British Museum's "From Village to City in Ancient India" focused on works dating from the neolithic period to the 10th century. "In the Image of Man" at the Hayward Gallery was devoted to 2,000 years of Indian painting and sculpture, with many works lent from India. The British Museum lent some examples of 3rd-century sculpture that were not normally on public view. At the Victoria and Albert Museum, "The Indian Heritage: Court Life and Arts Under Mughal Rule" included paintings and objects from private and public collections in Britain, India, France, and the U.S. Among the exhibits were a silver tiger's head from Tippu Sultan's throne, lent by the queen. Another exhibition at the Victoria and Albert, "India Observed," took as its theme British artists and photographers in India. It included 200 paintings, drawings, and prints. A number of commercial galleries also held shows with an Indian theme.

The Kimbell Art Museum, Fort Worth, Texas, celebrated its tenth anniversary with an exhibition of Japanese Buddhist sculpture from the 7th to the 13th centuries, the first show of its kind ever to travel from Japan to the West. Many of the fragile wooden pieces were lent by active Buddhist temples. Included were seven "national treasures" and over 30 "important cultural properties." The show was also seen at the Japan House Gallery in New York City. "Arts of the Islamic Book: The Collection of Prince Sanruddin Aga Khan" at the Asia Society Gallery, New York City, featured some of the finest examples of Islamic painting and calligraphy. It consisted of 90 paintings, drawings, manuscripts, and calligraphies collected by the prince over 30 years, most of which had never before been exhibited and many of which were unpublished. Said to be one of the most important collections of its kind in private hands, the show was slated to travel in 1983 to Fort Worth and Kansas City, Mo.

"Treasures of Asian Art from the Idemitsu Collection" was organized by the Seattle (Wash.) Art Museum and also seen in New York City at the Japan House Gallery and in Colorado at the Denver Art Museum. The Idemitsu Museum of Arts is a private Japanese museum, 15 years old, regarded as one of the finest in Japan. Its collection is particularly strong in Far Eastern ceramics and Japanese painting. Treasures of Chinese and Japanese art from the Kuboso Collection were shown at the To-

kyo National Museum and later at the Museum of Art, Osaka, Japan. Among the works on view were paintings and decorative art and a group of early Chinese bronze mirrors. The collection was formed by Sotaro Kubo and presented to the Imuzi municipality, where a new museum was built to house it.

Exhibitions held at the Israel Museum, Jerusalem, during 1982 included "Ethnic Arts" in March and April, a selection from the museum's own collection of African, Oceanic, and pre-Columbian objects. Also at the Israel Museum were an exhibition of photographs by Bill Brandt and "Royal Hunters and Divine Lovers," a display of 16th- to 19th-century Rajput miniatures.

An important Canaletto exhibition at the Fondazione Giorgio Cini in Venice, Italy, included many rarely seen privately owned paintings. Works from all phases of Canaletto's life were included, distinguishing this from the recent London exhibition devoted to his later works. Some of the paintings predated Canaletto's departure from Venice for England. Many of the later works had never before been exhibited in Italy. Three rooms were devoted to drawings and sketches, with many drawings lent by Queen Elizabeth. Works on show included the "View of the Piazza San Marco" from the Thyssen-Bornemisza Collection, Lugano, of about 1723, Canaletto's first painting of the Piazza and one that shows the influence of the theatre on his early works.

In the autumn the Museo Correr in Venice held a show called "Venezia: Piante e Vedute," which was made up of a series of plans and views of Venice, some taken from bound volumes. Works by Jacopo de'Barbari and the Combatti brothers and vistas by Dutch mapmakers were among the items shown.

"Card Players" by Theo van Doesburg was among examples of the Dutch avant-garde De Stijl movement shown in Minneapolis.
AUTHENTICATED NEWS INTERNATIONAL

NATIONAL GALLERY OF ART, WASHINGTON, D.C.; PHOTO, AUTHENTICATED NEWS INTERNATIONAL

Jan Steen's "Girl Eating Oysters" was among the 40 works of 17th-century Dutch painting shown at the National Gallery of Art in Washington, D.C.

"De Stijl—1917–1931: Visions of Utopia," organized by the Walker Art Center, Minneapolis, Minn., was also seen at the Hirshhorn Museum, Washington, D.C., and in The Netherlands at the Stedelijk Museum, Amsterdam, and at Otterlo. It included paintings by Mondrian and Theo van Doesburg and furniture by Gerrit Rietveld, the leading names in this Dutch modern movement.

London continued to attract important art exhibitions. The Arts Council staged the largest exhibition of new Italian art ever seen outside Italy at the Hayward Gallery from October 1981 to January 1982. The exhibition, called "Arte Italiana, 1960–1982," comprised a major roundup of what had happened in Italian art since 1960, from the abstract, the conceptual, and the minimal to the recent return to representation. The exhibition was organized by the city of Milan in exchange for the British exhibition "English Art Today," seen in that city in 1976.

The Mauritshuis in The Hague, Neth., held an exhibition devoted to the work of Jacob van Ruisdael which attracted an average 2,000 people daily. Forty paintings from the museum's permanent collection of Dutch masterpieces would travel to the U.S. and Canada as part of the bicentennial of diplomatic relations between The Netherlands and the U.S. The works, which would be seen in Washington, Boston, Chicago, Los Angeles, and Toronto,

included Vermeer's "Head of a Girl."

Two notable exhibitions were devoted to women. The Metropolitan Museum of Art, New York City, showed "The Eighteenth-Century Woman," an exhibition comprising costumes, clothing, furniture, desk sets, toilet articles, and other objects from the museum's collection. "The Substance or the Shadow: Images of Victorian Womanhood" was the first loan exhibition of Victorian painting to be organized by the Yale Center for British Art, New Haven, Conn. It included works by Millais, Frith, Rossetti, and others.

There were several important retrospectives devoted to modern artists. Among them was the first major show devoted to the Surrealist Giorgio de Chirico since his death in 1978. Organized by the Museum of Modern Art, New York City, it was seen in London at the Tate Gallery. The show emphasized the artist's early years, from 1911 to 1915, and included drawings and documents as well as 65 paintings. A large retrospective of the work of Fernand Léger was organized by the Albright-Knox Art Gallery, Buffalo, N.Y., in the winter. Most of the 65 paintings shown dated from 1905 to 1954 and were borrowed from European collections. Many were being shown in the U.S. for the first time. Included were "La Lecture" of 1924, lent by the Beaubourg Centre, Paris, and "Étude pour Adam et Eve" of 1939, from the Musée National Fernand Léger.

Works by the artist and sculptor Jean Tinguely were shown at the Tate Gallery. Many of his strange mobile constructions were made of scrap metal and found objects. The Swiss-born artist had worked in Paris from the mid-1950s and was influenced by the Dadaism of Marcel Duchamp. The Tate also held a comprehensive exhibition devoted to the work of English painter Graham Sutherland (1903–80), designed as a memorial to the artist. It included his 1977 self-portrait and a number of his menacing but characteristic thorn heads.

Chaim Soutine (1893–1943) was the subject of an exhibition at the Hayward Gallery, previously shown in West Germany. Soutine, a Russian-born artist who worked in Paris, produced works that are expressive in character, with strong colours, thick paint, and violent brush strokes. The exhibition comprised a number of works executed between 1919 and 1925 when the artist was living at Céret and at Cagnes in southern France. An exhibition at the Museum of Fine Arts, Ghent, Belgium, was devoted to the turn of the century work of Belgian sculptor Georg Minne (1866–1941). All of his works from the period 1886 to 1900 were shown.

An exhibition organized by the Tower of London Armouries, which has one of the finest collections of arms and armour in the world, was shown at the Sainsbury Centre for Visual Arts, University of East Anglia, Norwich, and later traveled to the U.S. and Canada. The arms and armour, displayed as works of art, included such historic and decorative items as the swords of Cromwell and Wellington.

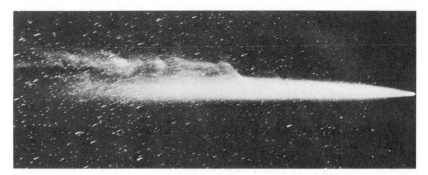

In October a team of astronomers at the Mt. Palomar Observatory in California photographed Halley's Comet, still more than a billion miles from its scheduled 1985 appearance.
LOWELL OBSERVATORY

ASTRONOMY

In 1979 a comet hit the Sun. But this remarkable event, the first evidence for the collision of an astronomical body with the Sun, only came to light in reports in late 1981 and 1982. The event was detected by an instrument aboard a U.S. Air Force research satellite, P78-1, launched in February 1979.

The SOLWIND orbiting coronagraph revealed the event in a series of photographs taken at ten-minute intervals. The Naval Research Laboratory group that built the coronagraph, headed by Donald J. Michels, reported that late on Aug. 30, 1979, the comet approached the Sun. The path of its head on the photo images was straight, and a typical cometary tail pointed away from the Sun. In succeeding photographs a brightly lit gassy region appeared around the Sun, but the comet did not reappear, suggesting that it either hit the Sun directly or totally evaporated because of the Sun's intense radiation. The calculated orbit suggested that it was a member of a previously known class of comets called sungrazers, comets whose highly eccentric orbits are opposite the orbital direction of the planets and bring them very close to the Sun.

Astonishingly, after their first announcements the same group reported that two more comets hit the Sun, on Jan. 27 and July 20, 1981, both with orbits similar to that of the first comet. Either cometary collisions with the Sun are quite common, possibly occurring as often as once a week, or the satellite was launched at a particularly auspicious time.

The year 1982 also marked the first sighting of Halley's Comet since it vanished from view in 1911. Using the 200-in Hale telescope on Mt. Palomar, David Jewitt and G. Edward Danielson spotted it early on October 16. At 24th magnitude it was still 100 million times too dim to be seen by the unaided eye. It was expected to pass the Earth in 1985, at which time a worldwide flurry of satellite- and ground-based observations would be made of the object. At its rediscovery the comet was within eight arc seconds of its predicted position in the sky.

In another story of belated discovery Edward F. Guinan, his student Craig C. Harris, and Frank P. Maloney of Villanova (Penn.) University announced in June 1982 the discovery of rings around the planet Neptune. In recent years all of the other giant gaseous planets of the solar system had been found to contain ring systems, though those of Uranus and Jupiter were far less easily seen from Earth than that of Saturn. The possible discovery (since it was unconfirmed, though not contradicted, by subsequent observations) was based on measurements made in 1968 to study Neptune's atmosphere. Guinan had been watching the occultation of a distant star by Neptune, looking for the diminution of the light as the star went behind the planet. The data, analyzed 13 years later, showed the partial drop in starlight characteristic of the presence of a ring system lying between 1.2 and 1.4 times the radius of the planet.

In May 1981, using the same stellar occultation technique, two independent groups at the University of Arizona had detected an eight-second period of total darkness as a dim star occulted by Neptune emerged from behind the giant planet. This was taken as an indication of the presence of a third moon of Neptune, approximately 100 mi (160 km) in diameter and orbiting roughly 30,000 mi (48,000 km) from the planet. If confirmed by future observations, this new satellite might prove to be the key for explaining the existence of the newly found ring system.

The one major planetary mission of 1982 was the soft landings by the twin Soviet probes Venera 13 and 14 on Earth's sister planet Venus on March 1 and 5. These two probes provided the sharpest images of the rock-strewn planetary surface to date. Though short-lived, the two craft managed to provide a wide array of information and insights, among them the findings that there are at least two major volcanic regions on Venus, Beta Regio and the "Scorpion Tail" of Aphrodite Terra; that Venus apparently has a thicker crust than that of Earth; and that the planet shows no evidence for the sort of plate tectonic activity that dominates Earth's surface features. Because of the thick crust most of the planet's internal heat vents itself through volcanically active regions. Not only are Venus's thick clouds the main absorber of sunlight for the planet; they appeared to be "upside down," with a thick smog layer on top. Finally, the probes found new evidence that the planet once had been covered with an ocean, which it lost early in its history.

Galaxies and Quasars

In recent years observations of spectacular outbursts or prodigious luminosities from quasars and active galaxies have tended to make our own Galaxy appear rather dull. The year, however, produced at least three independent lines of evidence that pointed to the presence of much greater activity within the nucleus of the Milky Way than had been suspected. Robert L. Brown of the National Radio Astronomy Observatory used the Very Large Array radio telescope in New Mexico to produce a radio "photograph" of the galactic centre. He found radio-emitting regions with an S-shaped symmetry around the galactic centre, suggesting the ejection of radiating material from some type of rapidly rotating central object.

A group using the Anglo-Australian Telescope managed to get a photograph of the same region in the near infrared, revealing what appeared to be a pair of objects at the position of the galactic centre. These could be simply two infrared stars, but the group interpreted them as a manifestation of nonthermal activity in the galactic centre. On the other hand, George Rieke of the University of Arizona's Steward Observatory reported on infrared observations of the galactic centre that he interpreted as evidence for a recent burst of star formation in the region. Complicating the interpretation further was the continuing gamma-ray observations of positron annihilation radiation from the galactic centre. Though no satisfactory explanation existed for the radiation, it was clearly tied to some sort of violently

In February astronomers at Kitt Peak National Observatory in Arizona photographed a spiral sunspot, a type never before observed.
KITT PEAK NATIONAL OBSERVATORY

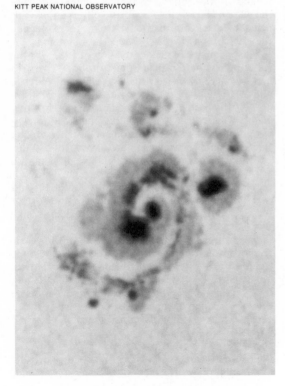

active object similar to the more luminous objects lying at the hearts of quasars.

The most distant known quasar, called OQ 172, had held that record for a decade—until a group of British and Australian optical and radio astronomers, headed by Bruce A. Peterson of Mount Stromlo and Siding Springs Observatories, bettered it in 1982. They found that the quasar called PKS 2000-330 has a red shift (shift of its spectral lines toward the red end of the spectrum due to its motion away from the Earth) indicating a distance of about 12,000,000,000 light-years.

Cosmology

Though the big-bang model of the universe enjoyed wide support based on its successful prediction of the microwave background radiation and helium abundance left over from the original cosmic fireball as well as its compatibility with observations of the overall expansion of the universe, a number of puzzles came to the forefront in 1982 to lead many astronomers to question the picture. In the usual scenario the universe formed in a vast explosion with all present-day matter and radiation ultimately emanating from an original singularity of space and time. But what caused the explosion? In recent years attempts to apply the so-called grand unified theories (GUTS) of the strong, weak, and electromagnetic interactions to the early universe led to a picture in which the universe forms spontaneously out of an original void. In 1982 A. D. Linde of the Lebedev Physical Institute in Moscow proposed a model in which the entire "universe" is essentially a bubble appearing in an even larger region of space and time in which other such "universes" form continuously, thus avoiding the problem of finding a unique origin of the universe.

Assuming that the expansion of the universe has continued at a constant rate, the ratio of the distance of a galaxy to its speed of recession from observers on the Earth is a measure of the time since the original explosion, or the age of the universe. T. Matilsky of Rutgers University, New Brunswick, N.J., and collaborators, reporting on X-ray observations of the quasar 1525-227, suggested this age to be about 9,000,000,000 years. Using observations of supernova explosions in distant galaxies, W. D. Arnett of the University of Chicago reported a value of about 13,000,000,000 years. Although these values lay between previously deduced ages for the universe, both were less than the ages determined for the oldest stars of about 15,000,000,000 years.

Probably the most intriguing (if true) cosmological report came from Paul Birch of the University of Manchester's Nuffield Radio Astronomy Laboratories at Jodrell Bank, England. Based on a study of 94 radio galaxies distributed over the sky, Birch concluded that the universe as a whole is rotating at a rate equivalent to one rotation every 6×10^{13} years. It was the first suggestion that the universe, like planets, stars, and galaxies, is rotating at all.

Antinuclear sentiment in Australia was highlighted by this march of thousands of demonstrators in downtown Melbourne.
MICHAEL COYNE—CAMERA PRESS/ PHOTO TRENDS

AUSTRALIA

The usual equilibrium of the Australian nation was disturbed during 1982 by a continual round of political crises. Prime Minister Malcolm Fraser and the leader of the opposition, William Hayden, faced challenges to their respective leaderships, and both the ruling coalition of Liberal Party and National Country Party (LCP) and the opposition Australian Labor Party (ALP) were shaken by unforeseen reverses.

Fraser tried to head off his problems by taking the battle to the enemy within his own Liberal Party. In April he seized the initiative and called a special party meeting to resolve the LCP leadership question "once and for all." At the meeting former Cabinet minister Andrew Peacock, who had resigned his office in 1981, challenged Fraser for the leadership. He was unsuccessful and later was treated without magnanimity by the prime minister, who excluded him from the fourth Fraser ministry when he announced a major Cabinet reshuffle on May 7.

The ALP had little time to capitalize on the disarray in the government camp. During the national conference of the ALP in July, tension surfaced between opposition leader Bill Hayden and the ALP's talented and temperamental industrial relations spokesman, Robert J. Hawke. A public opinion poll showed that the ALP would romp home in an election if Hawke were leader but might well lose under Hayden. When the vote was held, the result was 42 to 37 in favour of Hayden. There the similarity in the two unsuccessful challenges ended. While Peacock was temporarily exiled to the back bench, Hayden embraced Hawke, promoting him to the influential ALP Election Strategy Committee.

The leadership challenges were prompted by the result in Victoria's state election in April. The ALP was victorious in Victoria for the first time in 27 years. Peacock's supporters saw this as a portent for the LCP if Fraser's hard-line approach to economic management continued. The balance was maintained, however, when, in a similar upheaval in Tasmania in May, a long-term Labor administration was swept out by reformist Liberals.

The new ALP leader in Victoria was John Cain, a suburban lawyer who had led the state ALP for only seven months. Cain, however, embarrassed his leader, Hayden, with a serious miscalculation involving the sensitive issues of the Australian-U.S. alliance, nuclear weapons, and state rights. Cain announced in June that the Victorian government planned to introduce legislation that would make Victoria a nuclear-free state. Under the proposed new law, nuclear-powered and nuclear-armed vessels from the U.S. were not to be allowed to use the state's ports. Hayden supported Cain and precipitously announced that, if elected, a federal Labor government would follow the Cain approach and grant itself the right to ban visits to Australia by nuclear-armed ships.

Fraser was jubilant over this blunder. He pointed out that the states had no constitutional rights over what amounted to defense questions and that the ANZUS defense treaty, linking Australia, New Zealand, and the U.S., would be threatened by such a policy. Hayden changed his mind, and his vacillation helped draw supporters to the Hawke faction in the leadership conflict. Fraser sent the message home by sending federal police to oversee the visit of a U.S. warship to Melbourne.

On July 29 Sir Ninian Stephen succeeded Sir Zelman Cowen as governor-general.

The Economy

Tax avoiders and militant trade unions were the whipping boys chosen by the Fraser government to help explain the failure of Australia to live up to its economic promise in 1982. Billions of dollars were

Andrew Peacock, out of favour for challenging Prime Minister Malcolm Fraser's leadership of the Liberal Party, returned to the Cabinet in October as minister of industry and commerce.
THE CANBERRA TIMES, JOHN FAIRFAX & SONS, LTD.

said to have escaped the Taxation Department as a result of the promotion of such tax-avoidance measures as the notorious scheme involving "bottom of the harbour" companies—that is, companies that no longer existed.

By mid-1982 the Australian economy was in poor shape. The unemployment rate was then 6.6%, and in November, with 552,600 out of work, it reached 8%. Some of the unemployment was blamed on an estimated 50,000 illegal immigrants working in violation of their entry permits, and these illegal workers were threatened with deportation should they be caught.

High inflation joined unemployment as a major feature of the economy. During 1982 Australia's inflation rate reached its highest level in five years. The Australian Chamber of Commerce-National Bank survey revealed the worst trading situation since the survey was begun 14 years earlier and the worst profitability in 7 years. The Australian dollar also weakened in 1982, reaching its lowest value in history when measured against the U.S. dollar.

Things were scarcely any better on the farms than they were in the factories. The furor over the substitution of kangaroo, goat, and horse meat for beef being exported to the Japanese and U.S. markets had hardly died down when a royal commission reported in June that federal meat inspectors had been paid bribes of A$200 a week to turn a blind eye to the substitution of mutton for export lamb.

To make matters worse, the lack of rain in agricultural and pastoral areas led to widespread drought. By September it was so serious that massive government aid had to be granted to farmers.

Foreign Affairs

The Falklands crisis, the Australian-U.S. alliance, and instability resulting from the wars in the Middle East were the preoccupations of Australia's foreign-policymakers in 1982. Australia agreed to participate in the Sinai multinational peacekeeping force,

and Prime Minister Fraser called upon the U.S. to use its influence to restrain Israeli actions in Lebanon.

Australia's major diplomatic problem, however, was how to react to the conflict between Great Britain and Argentina in the Falkland Islands. Aware of its significant trading links with South America, Australia nevertheless threw its diplomatic weight behind the U.K. Australia did not follow New Zealand's lead in giving military assistance to the U.K. On the contrary, in the face of pro-British public opinion, Fraser detached Australian service personnel from British units due to be sent to the Falkland Islands. Fraser also used the Falklands crisis as the opportunity to withdraw from an agreement, widely criticized in Australia, to buy the British aircraft carrier HMS "Invincible." While the crisis gave the opportunity for a reappraisal of defense priorities, no immediate solutions presented themselves in regard to the problems of how to defend Australia's own huge coastline.

AUSTRIA

Under Austria's proportional representation system, results of the 1981 census necessitated a redistribution of provincial seats in the Nationalrat (National Council; the lower house of Parliament). Vienna's entitlement was reduced to four seats, while Upper Austria, Salzburg, Tirol, and Vorarlberg each gained one. The number of seats in the Bundesrat (Federal Council; the upper house) rose from 58 to 65.

After much political debate, construction began in July 1982 on a new conference centre that would greatly extend the facilities of Vienna's "UN City." Following an opinion poll in Vienna that indicated opposition to the new centre, the Austrian People's Party (ÖVP) had initiated a national referendum in which 1,360,000 (26% of those entitled to vote) rejected the project. A special parliamentary committee was named to consider the issue. The opposition

WIDE WORLD

Libya's Col. Muammar al-Qaddafi made his first state visit to a Western nation at the invitation of Austria's Chancellor Bruno Kreisky.

criticized the high cost of a "superfluous project," while the ruling Socialist Party (SPÖ) invoked undertakings given to the UN and the boost to employment that could be expected to result from construction of the centre.

Chancellor Bruno Kreisky continued to afford the Palestine Liberation Organization (PLO) diplomatic contact with the West. He was one of the sharpest critics of the Israeli government's intervention in Lebanon. The official visit to Austria in March, at Kreisky's invitation, of Libyan leader Col. Muammar al-Qaddafi brought a wave of protest from the opposition; it was also criticized by the U.S. and Western-oriented Arab states.

The arrest of Bahij Younis, believed to have organized the 1981 attack on a Viennese synagogue and the murder of Heinz Nittel, a Socialist city councillor, and the trial of two of the suspected assassins indicated that these acts of terrorism were instigated not by the PLO but by other Arab groups. Several bombings of Jewish homes and businesses in Vienna during 1982 were attributed to right-wing extremists and neo-Nazis.

Despite the unfavourable economic climate, Austria continued to admit refugees on a liberal scale. Some 35,000 were admitted in 1981, and a further 4,500 were granted, or applied for, asylum in the first eight months of 1982. The majority were Poles, whose care and administration caused considerable problems, since their onward movement to the traditional receiving countries was hindered by worldwide unemployment.

Austria's economic situation remained relatively favourable, with growth estimated at 1.5–2%, inflation at 5.5%, and unemployment at 3.6% for 1982. Nevertheless, insolvencies cost thousands of jobs; building and construction stagnated; and falling de-

mand and fluctuating raw-material prices necessitated massive financial support, especially for the nationalized industries. The important arms industry suffered a setback when the delivery of tanks to Argentina was suspended because of the Falklands conflict.

AUTOMOBILES

Chrysler Corp. seemed to be on the road to recovery in 1982, even though the automobile industry was still mired in a sales depression. After losing more than $1 billion in 1980, Chrysler trimmed its losses to $476 million in 1981 and expected to break even or perhaps earn slightly more than $100 million in 1982. Chrysler was able to retire all outstanding bank debt in 1982.

In contrast, De Lorean Motor Co. was placed in receivership by the British government, and production was halted after an estimated 7,000 to 10,000 of the $25,000 gull-wing sports cars had been built at the plant in Belfast, Northern Ireland. Ironically, the British government closed the plant only hours before founder and president John Z. De Lorean was arrested in Los Angeles for allegedly conspiring to sell cocaine for money to bail out his ailing firm.

Despite Chrysler's signs of recovery, the U.S. automobile industry was still struggling. In the 1982 model year, ended Sept. 30, 1982, sales totaled only 5.5 million units, down from the 6.5 million in the 1981 model year and the lowest total since 1961. General Motors sold 3,387,607 new cars, down from 4,032,727 in the '81 model year. Ford sold 1,289,987, down from 1,487,961; Chrysler sold 658,720, down from 764,535; Volkswagen sold 107,396 versus 159,588; and American Motors sold 99,300, down from 145,206.

Imports, which report sales on a calendar and not model-year basis, continued to hold around the 2.3 million-unit mark. Japanese automobiles were limited to sales of 1,680,000 units under voluntary agreements with the U.S. government to give U.S. manufacturers time to develop more fuel-efficient cars. Offsetting the effect of the limit, there was a marketing shift toward the luxury and sports models and away from the low-price, high-mileage economy cars. By midyear Detroit was complaining that the Japanese were selling fewer cars but making more money than ever before.

In an effort to spur car sales in 1982, U.S. automakers resorted to a variety of incentives. They used cash rebates, offers of free air travel, 24-month/24,000-mi or 36-month/36,000-mi free-service warranties that included oil and filter changes, and new car loans with interest rates below the national average of 15–16%. As a rule, sales picked up when the low interest rates were offered and then slid back when they were halted. Despite concern over reduced sales when the interest programs were off, GM and Ford gained a side benefit: both reported record earnings for their financing subsidiaries as a result of the increased loan business.

One other effort was made to bring buyers back into the showrooms. At the outset of the 1983 model year U.S. automakers limited price increases to less than 2% while either freezing the 1982 price or reducing it on selected small cars. In many cases, however, the price reductions were achieved by making previously standard equipment optional. GM raised the base price of its cars an average of $57 to $9,679; Ford by $515 to $8,819; Chrysler by $380 to $8,580; and AMC by $55 to $7,474. Industry-wide, the base price average was $9,157 for 1983.

Small-car demand cooled off during the year. One reason was that gas prices stabilized or declined, but also the industry's downsizing effort had resulted in mid- and full-size cars that could achieve 20 mi per gal (mpg). U.S. manufacturers also stalled demand for small cars in the 1982 model year by raising prices so that many subcompact models with typical options carried stickers of $10,000 and up and in some cases were priced at the same level or higher than full-size models.

There were only a few new models added for 1983. At GM the subcompact J-body Buick Skyhawk and Oldsmobile Firenza were added in the spring. Other midyear entries included the Buick Riviera convertible and a more powerful 1.8-l, Brazilian-built four-cylinder engine for use in the subcompact J-cars (Skyhawk, Firenza, Chevrolet Cavalier, Pontiac J2000, and Cadillac Cimarron). For 1983 an even more powerful 2-l, four-cylinder engine was added for use in all but the Pontiac car, which was waiting instead for a turbocharged 1.8-l engine in 1984.

GM's S-10 and GMC's S-15 new U.S.-built compact pickup trucks introduced late in '81 served as the basis for new small four-wheel-drive utility vehi-

Production of the luxury-priced De Lorean sports car ended after little more than a year in 1982; the firm left upwards of $180 million in debts.
BOWER—PICTURE GROUP

cles for 1983. These included the new "baby" Chevrolet Blazer and GMC Jimmy.

Changes at Ford were more numerous. The subcompact Escort and Lynx added larger engines for increased performance; the subcompact Mustang and Capri were restyled with Mustang adding convertible models and Capri glass-bubble hatchbacks; and the compact Granada and Cougar were discontinued, but their platform feature was retained to serve as the basis for new smaller LTD and Marquis models. The full-size LTD and Marquis remained but under the Crown Victoria and Grand Marquis names. The Thunderbird and Cougar XR7 were dramatically restyled, with the former sporting rounded lines and a laid-back aerodynamic grille while Cougar had a look similar to a Buick Riviera with a long hood, short deck, and notchback roofline. Thunderbird planned to add a five-speed transmission late in the model year.

The compact Fairmont and Zephyr were continued but only for a brief time, as the next line of front-wheel-drive models, a compact Ford Tempo and Mercury Topaz, were scheduled to replace them later in the 1983 model year. Tempo-Topaz were to be stretched versions of the Escort and Lynx with wheelbases expanded to 99 in from 94 in. Ford also planned a "baby" Bronco four-wheel-drive vehicle based on its new compact Ranger pickup.

At Chrysler a new series of front-wheel-drive offshoots from the compact K-body platform appeared, the Chrysler E-Class and Dodge 600. Both were offered in four-door models only and were built on stretched 103-in wheelbases versus 99 in on a compact Aries or 100 in on a mid-size LeBaron. Tagged for midyear entry were a front-wheel-drive New Yorker based on the E-body and a limousine based on the same but with the wheelbase stretched at least a foot. Early in 1982 Chrysler brought out the LeBaron and Dodge 400 convertibles.

At American Motors a subcompact, front-wheel-drive Fuego sports car from Renault was introduced in the spring of 1982, and later in the year came the new subcompact Alliance, the first joint venture car from the partnership between AMC and Renault. In the first month that it was offered, it accounted for 60% of AMC's sales and helped the firm report its highest one-month sales (12,722 in October 1982) in more than 14 months. To make room for the car, the subcompact Spirit sedan (at one time called the Gremlin) was discontinued.

Among the imports changes were few. Toyota restyled the subcompact front-wheel-drive Tercel and added a four-wheel-drive Tercel wagon. Datsun replaced the 210 rear-wheel-drive subcompact with a new front-wheel-drive Nissan Sentra and the 310 rear-drive model with the front-drive Nissan Pulsar. Mazda restyled its 626 and converted it to front-wheel drive.

Volkswagen, considered an import by the U.S. government and a U.S. producer by VW, added a sports GTI version of the Rabbit and a new engine for

One of the biggest attractions at the Automotive News World Expo held in Detroit in August was Ford Motor Co.'s high-styled "Flair."

UPI

a limited-edition Rabbit (only 3,000 were to be built) that automatically shuts off when the driver's foot is removed from the accelerator for more than 1.5 seconds. That engine, in a diesel-powered Rabbit, helped VW capture the top spot in the annual Environmental Protection Agency fuel economy rankings of 1983 cars. It was the sixth consecutive year in which a diesel Rabbit took the honours and the first year that any car reached the 50-mpg city mileage level. A diesel-engine Nissan Stanza and a Rabbit with nonshutdown engine tied for second with 48 mpg in the city. The lowest rated car was the Maserati Quattroporte at 8 mpg. The fleet average required of each automaker by federal law was set at 26 mpg for 1983.

In another ranking of some importance, the top ten sellers in the auto industry as the 1982 model year closed were the Ford Escort, Oldsmobile 88-98 duo, Chevrolet Chevette, Chevrolet Citation, Chevrolet Impala-Caprice duo, Honda Accord, Nissan Sentra, Toyota Corolla, Oldsmobile Cutlass Supreme, and the Buick LeSabre-Electra duo. Though the Toyota Corolla had previously finished in the top ten (highest was fifth in 1980), 1982 was the first year in which three imports (Corolla, Accord, and Sentra) were among the sales leaders.

In other developments Checker Motors Corp. stopped producing taxicabs and cars after 60 years in the business, and Avanti Motor Corp. of South Bend, Ind., was sold to S. Harvard Blake, a Washington, D.C., businessman. The Japanese industrial giant Mitsubishi began sales operations in the U.S. by marketing the Starion, Tredia, and Cordia cars on an exclusive basis without its normal ties with Chrysler dealers. Honda, on October 31, built the first Accord four-door model at its new Marysville, Ohio, assembly plant.

AUTO RACING

Indianapolis Motor Speedway paid out a record $2,067,475 in prize money in 1982, and that may be more important than the fact that veteran Gordon Johncock defeated Rick Mears to win the Indianapolis 500. Mears, driving a Penske PC-10, had blistered the course for a new pole record speed of 207.004 mph, and he nearly erased an 11-second deficit to pull even with one lap to go (1 mph = 1.61 km/h). But the veteran Johncock in a Wildcat-Cosworth held him off for his second 500 victory. Pancho Carter, a lap behind, was third, while Tom Sneva and Al Unser, Sr., were two laps farther to the rear in fourth and fifth.

Johncock earned $271,851 and Mears earned $205,151. This astonishing amount of money for averaging 162.029 mph for 500 mi (805 km) emphasized the continued importance of the United States Auto Club (USAC) as a prime factor in single-seater racing.

Johncock and most of the Indianapolis drivers competed during the year for the rival CART (Cham-

In the closest-ever finish in the Indianapolis 500, Gordon Johncock (car number 20) beat Rick Mears to the checkered flag by 1/1,600th of a second. It was his second win at Indy.
UPI

pionship Auto Racing Team) organization, which clearly established Champ Car primacy in the rest of the U.S. That group ran 11 races, including a new street race on the Cleveland lakefront, and also reclaimed the Pocono International Raceway in Pennsylvania. Following defending champion Mears in the drivers' standings were rookie of the year Bobby Rahal driving a March Ford, Mario Andretti in a Wildcat, Johncock, and Sneva in a March.

For NASCAR (the National Association for Stock Car Auto Racing) the highlight of the year was a points contest that was not settled until the final race at Riverside, Calif. There Darrell Waltrip, by virtue of taking third place, finally won the Winston Cup title over Bobby Allison, who failed to finish. Allison had won the classic Daytona 500 at an average speed of 153.991 mph in a Pontiac, only to switch brands to Chevrolet. Waltrip, the defending champion, stuck to a Junior Johnson-prepared Buick.

The most successful father-son combination in auto racing in 1982 was probably the Paul family. John Paul, Jr., won 9 of the 18 International Motor Sports Association's (IMSA's) Camel GT Series en route to the drivers' championship. John Paul, Sr., won a separate endurance race championship within the series. The Pauls won the two premier events of U.S. road racing, teaming with West Germany's Rolf Stommelin to take the 24 Hours of Daytona in Florida. Their Porsche Twin Turbo set a record average of 114.794 mph. At the 12 Hours of Sebring in Florida the Pauls won with an average of 105.401 mph. Mazda won the manufacturers' title for the third consecutive year. Jim Downing beat fellow Mazda RX-7 driver Roger Mandevelle in the November IMSA finale for the drivers' crown in the Champion Spark Plug Challenge Series.

In the Can-Am series of the Sports Car Club of America (SCCA), Al Unser, Jr., won the season crown driving a Chevrolet-powered GR-2 Frissbee and switching midseason to a GR-3. Unser edged Al Holbert in a VDS. In the other professional SCCA series, the Trans-Am, Elliott Forbes-Robinson won the top honours in a Pontiac Firebird.

Grand Prix Racing

Internal politics between the controlling body of the sport and the race-car constructors' "trade union" continued to cloud the running of a full season of racing, with the coveted drivers' world championship remaining open until the very last race, at Las Vegas, Nev., at which a young Finnish driver, Keke Rosberg, took the honours.

The first race, at Kyalami, South Africa, was delayed by a drivers' strike. It proved a runaway win for Renault, with Alain Prost (France) leading the Williams car of Carlos Reutemann (Arg.) home and René Arnoux (France) placing third in another turbocharged Renault. Prost set the fastest lap, at 216.386 km/h. At the Brazilian race in Rio de Janeiro, Nelson Piquet (Brazil) won in a Brabham after he had made the fastest lap at 187.525 km/h. In the U.S. Grand Prix West at Long Beach, Calif., Niki Lauda (Austria) won in a McLaren ahead of Keke Rosberg. Lauda set the fastest lap at 135.861 km/h. At Imola, Italy, the San Marino Grand Prix was a fierce battle between Renault and Ferrari, with victory for Pironi followed by Villeneuve; the two Ferraris crossed the finish line almost together. Third place went to Michele Alboreto of Italy in a Tyrrell. The Belgian Grand Prix at Zolder was won by John Watson (U.K.) in a McLaren from Rosberg (Williams) and Eddie Cheever of the U.S. (Talbot). Watson confirmed his expertise with quickest lap, at 191.278 km/h.

Riccardo Patrese (Italy) won the Monaco race in a Brabham, followed by Pironi and Andrea de Cesaris

(Italy) in an Alfa Romeo. Fastest lap was 138.073 km/h by Patrese. The inaugural Detroit Grand Prix on the new Downland circuit, run counterclockwise, was delayed by an accident and finished a lap short of the intended distance owing to a time-limit rule, with Watson first, Cheever second, and Pironi third. Prost (Renault) made best lap at 130.798 km/h. The Canadian Grand Prix at Montreal was won by Piquet for Brabham, with teammate Patrese second and Watson third; the winner recorded the fastest lap at 179.749 km/h.

In the Dutch Grand Prix Pironi's Ferrari won from Piquet and Rosberg, with best lap (191.867 km/h) by Britain's Derek Warwick (Toleman). The British Grand Prix at Brand's Hatch went to Lauda, with Pironi second and Patrick Tambay (France) third in the other Ferrari. In the French race at Le Castellet Renault took first and second places, Arnoux refusing to let Prost past to win. Pironi finished third, and Patrese had the fastest lap at 209.003 km/h. Tambay brought his Ferrari home first in the German Grand Prix, ahead of Arnoux and Rosberg; Piquet had the fastest lap at 214.576 km/h. In the Austrian Grand Prix Italy's Elio de Angelis (Lotus) won from Rosberg; Jacques Laffite (France) in a Talbot was third; and Piquet again lapped fastest at 228.315 km/h.

Rosberg won the Swiss Grand Prix (held at Dijon, France), ahead of Prost and Lauda, although Prost had the fastest lap (202.735 km/h). In the Italian race, at Monza, Arnoux's Renault finished before the Ferraris of Tambay and Mario Andretti (U.S.), the latter making a fine comeback. Arnoux's triumph was endorsed by fastest lap, at 223.031 km/h. The drivers' world championship remained in doubt until the Las Vegas Grand Prix, but Ferrari had already clinched the manufacturers' championship. The year ended with Alboreto winning for Tyrrell, in front of Watson and Cheever, and making best lap at 164.993 km/h; fifth place was sufficient to give Rosberg the championship.

BANGLADESH

The seizure of power and the proclamation of martial law on March 24, 1982, by Lieut. Gen. Hossain Mohammad Ershad came as no surprise, since the army chief of staff had often expressed dissatisfaction with the way the affairs of the country were being looked after by aging Pres. Abdus Sattar. Ever since his victory in the presidential election of November 1981, Sattar had steadfastly refused to yield to Ershad's demand that the armed forces be given a formal role in the administration. Appointing himself chief martial law administrator after a bloodless coup, Ershad attempted to justify his takeover, saying, "Bangladesh is facing a crisis on every front: economic, political, social, and law and order."

Ershad moved swiftly to keep control by arresting some government ministers suspected of corruption, banning political and trade union activities, and announcing stiff penalties, including the death sentence, for those found guilty of corruption or political agitation. Within days the military government was said to have arrested at least 200 persons, including six former ministers. Parliament was dissolved, and under a martial law order announced on April 12 Ershad was empowered to make laws that would have the same force as acts of Parliament.

To the people of Bangladesh, used to political upheavals, violence, and large-scale poverty, the peaceful changeover appeared to be welcome, at least on the surface. Ershad's choice of a new figurehead president fell on Justice Abul Fazal Mohammad Ahsanuddin Choudhury, a retired Supreme Court judge, who was sworn in on March 27. Soon after taking over, Ershad said that he would hand over power to a democratically elected government once stability was restored.

The economic situation in Bangladesh was extremely grave. Before the coup, the Bangladesh Bank reported that the balance of payments deficit had increased by more than 1 billion taka to 4,160,500,000 taka during 1981 (22.63 taka=U.S.

Keke Rosberg of Finland laid claim to the world driving championship with this win in the Swiss Formula One Grand Prix in Dijon, France, in August.
UPI

Military security was in evidence at Dacca airport following the Army's seizure of power in Bangladesh in March.
WIDE WORLD

$1). The International Monetary Fund continued to maintain that it would not release loans already sanctioned unless Bangladesh rectified its balance of payments position. Prime Minister Shah Azizur Rahman admitted before Parliament on March 2 that the food deficit was in the order of 2,265,000 metric tons; unofficial estimates had put it at approximately 2.8 million metric tons.

On June 1 Ershad denationalized almost all industries, 70% of which had been in the public sector. All public sector units operating at a loss were to be closed, and private participation in all existing industries was to be encouraged. Foreign investment was welcomed in the form of joint ventures.

Ershad tried to improve relations with India by inviting Indian Foreign Minister Narasimha Rao to visit Dacca in May. Relations had been strained for some time because of disagreement over the sharing of the Ganges River waters and the sovereignty of New Moore Island in the Bay of Bengal. Ershad himself visited India on October 6–7 in an attempt to find solutions to several bilateral issues.

BASEBALL

After the seven-week players' strike of 1981, baseball officials looked to the 1982 season with caution and some fear. Their apprehensions were unwarranted, however. The major leagues established an attendance record as the American League drew in excess of 23 million paid admissions and the National League topped 21.5 million. In November Bowie Kuhn was deposed as commissioner of baseball after 14 years when five National League team owners voted not to renew his contract.

World Series

The St. Louis Cardinals, who had finished fourth and were 14 games below .500 only two years earli-

er, captured the 1982 World Series by defeating the Milwaukee Brewers, four games to three. The Cardinals advanced to the World Series by sweeping the National League championship series from the Atlanta Braves three games to none. The Brewers had a more difficult time achieving the first pennant in their history. They lost the first two games of the American League series to the California Angels, but when they returned home they came to life and became the first team in play-off history to win despite losing the first two games.

The Brewers trounced the Cardinals 10–0 in the Series opener at St. Louis, Mo., on October 12. Mike Caldwell limited St. Louis to only 3 hits while Milwaukee pounded Cardinal pitchers for 17. In the second game the next evening the Brewers mounted an early 3–0 lead, but veteran right-hander Don Sutton was unable to hold it. A two-run double by St. Louis catcher Darrell Porter tied the game 4–4 in the sixth inning. In the eighth Milwaukee reliever Pete Ladd walked pinch hitter Steve Braun with the bases loaded to force home the winning run. The Cardinals prevailed 5–4.

The Series then moved to Milwaukee, Wis., where the Cardinals captured the third game 6–2 on October 15. Willie McGee, a 23-year-old rookie centre fielder, clubbed two homers and batted in four runs for St. Louis. In game four on October 16 the Cardinals were leading 5–1 when rookie pitcher Dave LaPoint dropped a throw while covering first base in the seventh inning. The Brewers seized the opportunity to score six runs. The Brewers triumphed 7–5 to even the Series at two games each. On October 17 Milwaukee shortstop Robin Yount registered his second four-hit game of the Series to pace the Brewers to a 6–4 conquest. Yount hit a home run before 56,562, the largest crowd in the history of Milwaukee's County Stadium.

At St. Louis on October 19 the Cardinals averted elimination by routing the Brewers 13–1 in a contest that was twice delayed by rain—once for 2 hours and 13 minutes. In the seventh game, on October 20, the Cardinals rallied for a 6–3 victory to win their first World Series championship in 15 years. The Cardinals garnered 15 hits (13 singles and 2 doubles) and won the game with a three-run outburst in the sixth inning to erase a 3–1 Milwaukee lead. Bruce Sutter used his split-fingered fastball to work two perfect innings and save the game.

Perhaps the happiest Cardinal was Porter, the bespectacled catcher who was voted most valuable player for the World Series. He batted a modest .286 for seven games but contributed several key hits and was a steadying influence for St. Louis pitchers.

Regular Season

Baseball was blessed with four uncommonly close division races during the season—a situation that no doubt contributed to the record attendances. Only one team, the Minnesota Twins, failed to draw one million fans; seven franchises cracked the two million barrier. The California Angels broke the American League season mark by attracting 2,807,360 customers. The Los Angeles Dodgers bettered their own major league record with 3,608,881 for 80 dates, an average of 45,111 fans per game.

The Brewers were an also-ran until Harvey Kuenn replaced Buck Rodgers as manager on June 2. Under Kuenn, the Brewers finished 72–43 and hit 216 home runs en route. But the Brewers had to win the last game of the season at Baltimore to take the American League East title.

The Angels finished three games in front of the Kansas City Royals in the American League West. The Angels were helped by off-season acquisitions such as Reggie Jackson, who hit 39 home runs, and Doug DeCinces.

LARRY DOWNING/NEWSWEEK

Catcher Darrell Porter indicated his satisfaction to pitcher Bruce Sutter as the St. Louis Cardinals won the World Series.

Rickey Henderson of the Oakland A's broke Lou Brock's eight-year-old record with this stolen base, his 119th of the year.
WIDE WORLD

The Cardinals, who hit fewer home runs than any team in the major leagues, employed speed and defense to win the National League East by three games over the Philadelphia Phillies. Their success was attributed mostly to their cagey manager, Whitey Herzog, who effected several trades in his role as general manager.

The Atlanta Braves probably had the most difficult time of any division champion. They began the season with a record 13 consecutive victories but then were inconsistent for much of the summer, at one point losing 19 of 21 games. With only 10 games left they were 3½ games behind the Los Angeles Dodgers. But the Dodgers then lost eight in a row.

Willie Wilson of the Kansas City Royals took the American League batting title with a .332 average. Hal McRae, also of the Royals, batted in the most runs (133), while Thomas of Milwaukee and Jackson of the Angels tied for home run leadership with 39. Rickey Henderson of the Oakland A's broke all base-stealing records with 130. Al Oliver batted .331 for the Montreal Expos to win the National League title. Dave Kingman of the New York Mets took the home run crown with 37, while Oliver and Atlanta's Dale Murphy shared the RBI leadership with 109.

Lamarr Hoyt of the Chicago White Sox recorded the most victories (19) among American League pitchers. Dan Quisenberry of the Kansas City Royals earned 35 saves. In the National League, Steve Carlton, the brilliant 37-year-old left-hander of the Philadelphia Phillies, was the only pitcher in the major leagues to win 20 or more games, with a record of 23–11. Sutter of the Cardinals was the front-runner in saves with 36.

Yount was named most valuable player in the American League and Dale Murphy of the Braves won in the National. The Cy Young awards for outstanding pitching went to Pete Vuckovich of the Brewers in the American League and the Phillies' Carlton (it was his fourth) in the National. Rookies of the year were Dodger second baseman Steve Sax in the National League and Baltimore shortstop Cal Ripken, Jr., in the American. Managers of the year were Joe Torre of the Braves for the National League and Kuenn for the American.

Little League

The five-year reign of Taiwan as Little League World Series champions ended when a team of 11- and 12-year-olds from Kirkland, Wash., blanked the youngsters from Pu-Tzu Town 6–0 in the championship at Williamsport, Pa. Cody Webster, Kirkland pitcher, struck out 12, gave up only 2 hits, and walked 3 during the 6-inning game. Webster also hit a 280-ft home run, longest in the 36-year history of the series.

There had been indications during the preliminary contests that this was not one of the powerhouse teams from Taiwan of other years, either at bat or in the field. But Taiwan beat Maracaibo, Venezuela, 8–2 and Rouyn, Que., 10–7 to reach the finals, while Kirkland was knocking out Sarasota, Fla., 5–3 and Wyoming, Mich., 3–2.

In the series for 13-year-olds, played at Taylor, Mich., Tampa, Fla., defeated Libertyville, Ill., 6–1. The Senior League play-off for ages 14–15 was won by Santa Barbara, Calif., over Orange Park, Fla., 11–4 at Gary, Ind. Victor in the Big League for ages 16–18 was San Juan, P.R., over Maracaibo, Venezuela, 2–0 at Fort Lauderdale, Fla.

There were three Little League Softball World Series. Glendale, Calif., became the 11- to 12-year-old champions by winning over Staten Island, N.Y., 2–1, and Naples, Fla., took the Senior League title, beating Rose City, Ore., 8–5. Both championships were played at Kalamazoo, Mich. In the first year of a Big League Softball series, Tampa, Fla., won 9–0 over Lyons McCook, Ill., at Mishawaka, Ind.

BASKETBALL

It was Earvin ("Magic") Johnson's turn to work wonders once more during the 1981–82 National Basketball Association (NBA) season. First, the charismatic superstar made Los Angeles Lakers' Coach Paul Westhead disappear merely by saying "I want to be traded." Then, with new coach Pat Riley permitting him to open his bag of tricks at will, the Magic Man conjured up another NBA championship.

It was the Lakers' second title in Johnson's three pro seasons, proving that the 6-ft 8-in guard was

Earvin ("Magic") Johnson of the Los Angeles Lakers was voted most valuable player of the NBA championship series.
WIDE WORLD

much more substance than shadow. Despite uproar about Johnson's 25-year, $25 million contract and the image-tarnishing Westhead incident, he regained the fans' favour.

When Westhead was fired, assistant coach Riley quickly ended grumbles about the Lakers' slow-down offense. Merely by letting Johnson and back-court running mate Norm Nixon trigger fast breaks at every opportunity, Riley unleashed a juggernaut on the NBA. And, even though he turned 35 on the eve of the play-offs, 7-ft 2-in centre Kareem Abdul-Jabbar was still at the top of his game, adding power to his teammates' speed.

That was fortunate, because the inspired Philadelphia 76ers staved off another collapse in the Eastern Conference finals to enter the championship round feeling like a team of destiny. They were not, despite Julius ("Dr. J.") Erving's valiant effort.

In a typical bitterly fought play-off with the Boston Celtics, the 76ers rolled to a 3-1 edge over the defending NBA champions in the best-of-seven series. Philadelphia had been in the same situation a year earlier and then had stunned their fans by dropping three straight games and the series to the Celtics. This time the 76ers again won three of the first four. They then lost the next two, forcing a showdown in Boston Garden, where the Celtics had humiliated them by 40 and 29 points earlier in the Eastern final. Even more ominous was the fact that in ten previous seventh-game play-off tests on their home court the Celtics had won nine times. But the magnificent Erving refused to let Celtic tradition prevail once more, sparking the 76ers to a convincing 120-106 triumph with 29-point artistry.

Meanwhile, Los Angeles had breezed through two Western Conference play-off rounds with 4-0 sweeps and then had to sit for a week while Philadelphia and Boston went the limit. Far from rusty, however, after their enforced idleness, the rested, relaxed Lakers landed the knockout punch against Philadelphia in the third quarter of the first game. They let the 76ers grab a big lead in Philadelphia and then shocked them with a 40-9 explosion in the third quarter to win going away. That made the outcome predictable, the new champions never losing control before they wrapped up the series with a 114-104 victory in the sixth game. Demonstrating his versatility, Johnson racked up 13 points, 13 rebounds, and 13 assists in the final game to earn the play-off's most valuable player award. Johnson was only the second man in NBA history to earn that award twice, the first being New York Knicks' centre Willis Reed, who did so in 1970 and 1973.

After the season the 76ers offered a $13.2 million, six-year contract to Moses Malone, all-professional centre of the Houston Rockets. The Rockets eventually traded Malone to Philadelphia for centre Caldwell Jones and a first-round draft choice.

The large amount of money for one superstar's services really reflected a league-wide struggle for survival. Caught in the squeeze between soaring sal-

James Worthy of the champion North Carolina Tar Heels was voted most valuable player of the NCAA tournament.

aries and sinking revenue, the NBA had a number of shaky franchises. The hope for salvation lay in the steadily increasing use of cable and home subscription television, but the players threatened to strike if they did not get a slice of that potential bonanza.

College

The jinx that had plagued North Carolina Coach Dean Smith finally was shattered in 1982. Seven proved to be Smith's lucky number when a pass stolen by All-America forward James Worthy in the closing seconds preserved North Carolina's first National Collegiate Athletic Association (NCAA) championship. The Tar Heels prevailed 63-62 over Georgetown in a splendid final played before a record crowd of 61,612 in the mammoth New Orleans Superdome.

One of America's most respected collegiate coaches, Smith had reached the final four in the NCAA tournament six times previously, only to be rebuffed. The spell was broken by his poised team's refusal to panic, despite a shaky start against Georgetown's shot-blocking 7-ft centre, Patrick Ewing.

Rallied by Worthy's clutch shooting, North Carolina gradually took control of the thrilling contest, getting the lead on a jump shot by freshman Michael Jordan with 16 seconds left. Coach John Thompson of Georgetown refused to call time out in order to set up a play, and that proved fatal to the Hoyas. Worthy capped a magnificent career at North Carolina with one more defensive gem, anticipating a midcourt pass by Georgetown's Fred Brown and stepping in for the interception.

That, plus a game-high 28 points, earned the tournament's most valuable player award for Worthy, soon to become the top choice in the NBA draft. Los Angeles made the 6-ft 8-in forward its number one pick, signing him to a lucrative contract.

But the exciting climax to another record-breaking season could not hide the fact that college basketball was in danger of being swallowed by its own success. With his coaching colleagues gathering in New Orleans for the NCAA finals, Notre Dame's Digger Phelps dropped a bombshell by disclosing that he knew of at least three schools illegally paying athletes up to $10,000 a year to play basketball. Phelps asserted that fewer than 10% of the top 100 universities were engaging in such practices, sticking to his guns despite criticism from coaches who felt he was tarring the profession with sweeping charges.

The pressure to make the NCAA tournament field provoked more controversy, even with 48 berths allotted. Coach Dick Versace of Bradley erupted when the Braves from Peoria, Ill., were not invited to the meet despite winning the Missouri Valley Conference title. He blasted the selection committee for alleged favouritism to Boston College and other Eastern schools.

Ironically, Boston College promptly recorded the tournament's most stunning upset by knocking out DePaul of Chicago. It was the third straight year the highly rated Blue Demons had been embarrassed in their NCAA opener. But Bradley had something to prove and did so convincingly, sweeping to its fourth National Invitation Tournament crown. Paced by

David Thirdkill's smothering defense, the Braves beat Purdue 67–58 for the title.

In women's basketball, Louisiana Tech took NCAA Division I honours, defeating Cheney (Pa.) 76–62. Rutgers beat Texas 83–77 to capture the Association of Intercollegiate Athletics for Women (AIAW) tournament. After losing a court challenge of the NCAA decision to stage women's championship events, the AIAW's major role in college athletics appeared over. Most nationally ranked teams switched to the NCAA.

BELGIUM

The new Social Christian-Liberal government led by Wilfried Martens, which took office in December 1981, immediately sought emergency powers to deal with Belgium's serious economic and financial crisis. Despite Socialist filibustering, the final vote in the Senate took place on Feb. 2, 1982, and the government at once published a first series of special decrees aimed at stimulating employment, in particular by a reduction of value-added tax on the construction of dwellings. The most surprising measure was an 8.5% devaluation of the Belgian franc, on February 21. This was accompanied by a prices and wages freeze to last until May 31, the previously sacrosanct automatic wage indexation system being replaced by a lump sum increase. On several occasions the Socialist Fédération Générale de Travailleurs Belges (FGTB) trade unions called a 24-hour general strike to protest the government's decisions. It failed to rouse the workers, however, except, to a limited extent, in French-speaking Wallonia.

The government, meanwhile, busied itself with the still pending 1982 budget, which had to be completely revised in order to bring down the expected deficit from BFr 322 billion to BFr 252 billion (48 BFr=U.S. $1). This was done in part by reducing child allowances and imposing wage reductions for childless couples and unmarried persons. The econ-

Distress in the Belgian steel industry led at one point to violence as steelworkers rioted in the streets of Brussels.
PHOTO NEWS–GAMMA/LIAISON

omies stirred up considerable discontent, and FGTB Secretary-General Georges Debunne, in an interview in early September, warned that he would initiate action to bring down the government. Martens stood his ground, proposing discussions over delicate questions such as the financial balance of the social security system, redistribution of the available amount of work, industrial policy, and the introduction of new technologies. Unemployment continued to climb but at a slower pace than in 1981. Most worrisome was the high proportion of unemployed under 25 (35% of the total).

The constitutional changes approved in 1980 were implemented with the designation of, on the one hand, a Flemish Executive (nine members) and, on the other, a French Community Executive (three members) and a Walloon Regional Executive (six members). The newly created bodies did not see eye to eye on several matters. Criticism was leveled repeatedly at the still incomplete state reform. While regional authorities wanted more power, other voices warned against growing separatist trends. Meanwhile, despite opposition by the Socialists, Parliament approved a bill transferring some powers to the German-language community. Early in September, antagonism between the two major language communities was rekindled when the European Economic Community included practically all of Wallonia in its list of economically distressed areas, while only two small districts in Flanders were recognized as such.

A long-awaited debate on Belgium's future energy policy was concluded with the carrying of nine resolutions, calling, among other things, for a new coal-powered, 600-Mw generating station near the Limburg coal mines that were still in operation, and the treatment by Eurochemic of no more than 90 tons of radioactive waste material annually.

BELIZE

During the year Belize celebrated the first anniversary of its independence and began to participate actively in regional and international affairs. Because the new nation is geographically bound to other Central American countries and is tied by political and cultural traditions to the English-speaking countries of the Caribbean, Belize's foreign policy was among its most important concerns. In March Belize became a full member of the African, Caribbean, and Pacific Group. The nation also opened its doors to 5,000 refugees from El Salvador, and a feasibility study got under way for the migration of some 600 Haitian families to Belize over a number of years.

Resolving the border dispute with neighbouring Guatemala remained a major priority for Belize. The possibility of violence crippled Belize's tourist industry despite the presence of a British security force. The British troops were to remain in Belize as a security guarantee until the agreement was terminated by both governments.

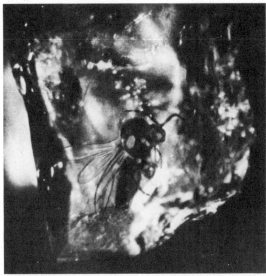

WIDE WORLD

This 40-million-year-old fly, found trapped in amber, was so perfectly preserved as to raise scientists' hopes that its genetic material was also intact.

BIOLOGY

Charles Darwin died in 1882, and hence the centenary year became a focal point for numerous conferences and symposia on evolutionary theory. The year's discussions and reviews could spawn new approaches, insights, and challenges to evolutionary theory, which stated that natural selection operates at the level of the individual organism and has been the primary force modifying species over time. Stephen Jay Gould of Harvard University concluded that the strictest interpretation of Darwin's basic premises eventually might be refuted. He based his opinion on recent scientific challenges to and extensions of Darwinism, such as the concept of punctuated evolution and hierarchical models in which natural selection operates on individual units at various levels of biological organization. Despite modern research tools, innovative interpretations, and new fields of science, such as molecular biology and biochemical genetics, most evolutionary biologists still considered Darwin's basic concepts to be solid. (*See* Special Report.)

The ongoing debates among evolutionary biologists did not at all question the fact that evolution took place but concerned the exact details of how it operated. The primary raw materials for resolving those details, *i.e.*, the fossilized remains of earlier life, continued to be unearthed and analyzed, and the results added to the emerging picture of life's pageant on Earth.

For example, new evidence documenting man's presumed transition from a tree-dwelling creature to an upright-walking, tool-using one was described during the year. Researchers in Antarctica offered their discovery of the first mammalian fossil ever found on that continent as support for a theory of early animal migration from South America to Australia.

E. M. Friis of the University of London and A. Skarby of the Geological Institute in Stockholm reported their find of whole, structurally preserved flowers in Sweden in clay beds dating from the Upper Cretaceous, about 80 million years ago. Only 2 mm (0.08 in) long, the rare fossils represented the oldest flowers known and came from an age in which it is believed that the flowering plants were diversifying and coming into dominance. Also reported in recent months was the discovery of the earliest known seeds, by William H. Gillespie of the U.S. Geological Survey and colleagues. About 5 to 6 mm (0.2 in) long and enclosed in seed-bearing cupules, the fossils lay in clays and shales associated with coal beds in West Virginia that were formed in the Late Devonian, about 350 million years ago.

A nearly complete skeleton of *Diacodexis*, the earliest known member of the order of mammals (Artiodactyla) that includes cattle, pigs, sheep, giraffes, hippos, camels, deer, and antelope, was described by Kenneth D. Rose of Johns Hopkins University, Baltimore, Md. Previous knowledge of this rabbit-sized species had been limited to a few bone fragments, from which it had been concluded that the animal had a short-limbed, generally unspecialized body and thus might well be the common ancestor of all present-day artiodactyls. The new skeleton, however, showed *Diacodexis* to have long, slender limb bones and other advanced features, suggesting a swift, graceful running and jumping animal much like today's mouse deer, or chevrotain,

Clay beds in Sweden yielded structurally whole fossil flowers, such as the one shown here in a scanning electron micrograph; at 80 million years old, they were the oldest known flowers.

COURTESY, E. M. FRIIS, BEDFORD COLLEGE, LONDON

and not the shrewlike creature first pictured.

George O. Poinar, Jr., and Roberta Hess of the University of California at Berkeley described one of the more spectacular paleontological events of the year: the discovery and microscopic examination of a fly whose abdominal soft tissues had undergone remarkable preservation in Baltic amber believed to be 40 million years old. Calling the find "an extreme case of mummification, involving the preservation of insect tissue by drying and natural embalming [with] plant sap," the researchers were able to observe cells, cell organelles such as mitochondria and ribosomes, nuclei, and clumps of genetic material called chromatin and to compare them with the structure of present-day insects. The level of preservation appeared to rival that previously seen in 3,000-year-old Egyptian mummies and mammoths exhumed from Siberian ice. Late in the year Poinar and colleagues were exploring the possibility that some of the fly's DNA had remained intact and might be cloned for further study.

Fossil finds resulted in advancements in understanding evolutionary relationships among vertebrates. In a development associated with human lineage, R. L. Susman and J. T. Stern of the State University of New York at Stony Brook reported on the earliest known human species (*Homo habilis*, 1,760,000 years ago from Tanzania). They presented evidence of a fossil specimen that shared both the primitive feature of being arboreal and the more advanced humanlike characteristics of walking upright and making tools, documenting the presumed transition from apes to humans. A significant discovery of lower mammals was made on a polar expedition led by William Zinsmeister of Ohio State University when Michael Woodburne of the University of California at Riverside found the jaw of a 40-million-year-old marsupial, the first mammal fossil ever found in Antarctica. The find supported the theory that early mammals migrated from the South American continent to Australia via the Antarctic continent, which at the time had a warmer climate.

Research findings associated with endangered species continued to occupy a significant portion of zoological news events. Removal of the Tecopa pupfish of Death Valley from the endangered species list was official recognition by the U.S. Fish and Wildlife Service that the species was presumed to be extinct. The fish was the first species to be removed from the list for this reason.

Donald Roberts and others from the University of Brazil and the U.S. Army Environmental Hygiene Agency, working on malaria control in the Amazon basin, investigated local stories of "DDT-eating bees" and found them to be males of a native bee, *Eufriesia purpurata*, that collect inside sprayed houses, noisily scraping DDT off walls and roofing with no apparent ill effects. The researchers postulated that DDT resembles some naturally occurring plant substance and is rapidly detoxified by the bees and used as a pheromone.

Special Report: Reevaluating Darwin

by Jeremy Cherfas

Charles Robert Darwin, who died quietly on April 19, 1882, at the age of 73, may safely be said to have changed the way we perceive the natural world of which we are a part. Although Darwin did not discover evolution, he documented the evidence that living things had undergone change and provided a mechanism to explain that change. Natural selection is the force that has shaped living things, and with it we can make sense of both the enormous variety of life and the seemingly exquisite perfection of design.

Darwin is believed to have become an evolutionist at some point on the voyage of the HMS "Beagle" around the world. In the Galápagos Islands he saw that each island had its own distinct giant tortoise. And the birds that he collected there turned out, despite their dissimilar appearance, to be closely related finches. Darwin could hardly suppose that a Creator had made each of the varieties independently. But then how had the varieties arisen?

When he returned to England he threw himself into the work of describing and cataloging the prodigious number of specimens—animal, vegetable, and mineral—that he had collected, giving the collections to the experts of the day. He began a notebook devoted specifically to "the species question" and filled it with observations, thoughts, and untried theories that might illuminate the transmutation of one type into another. The great insight came in 1838, when Darwin read again Thomas Malthus's *Essay on the Principle of Population.*

Theory of Natural Selection

Malthus explained how living things reproduce much more quickly than the resources they need and will very quickly outstrip those resources. This gave Darwin the selection he needed: potential growth coupled with constant resources means that there is an inevitable struggle for survival. This is the first part of Darwin's argument. He then documented the variability of living things. If any such variation gave its owner an advantage in the struggle for survival, so that it left more offspring, the variation would be favoured. The struggle for survival selects certain variants, and those variations come to dominate the population. That is the essence of natural selection, a phrase Darwin chose specifically to point up the analogy with artificial selection, in which man breeds specific varieties for his own purposes and in the process changes the plant or animal.

Natural selection, Darwin suggested, could account for all the diversity of life and for design. Anything that gave its possessor an advantage in the reproductive race would be favoured, and so organisms would come to exploit whatever niches they could. And because natural selection worked by accumulating modifications to a basic ground plan, it would produce the obvious similarities as well as the differences.

Darwin had worked out the theory by 1842, when he wrote the so-called "Sketch," later elaborated into the "Essay" of 1844, but only his closest colleagues were aware of his discovery. He knew that his ideas would create uproar, for the powerful doctrine of biblical creation still held sway, and so he settled down to gather the evidence and marshal the arguments that would make his case irrefutable. He was two-thirds of the way through this major work on natural selection when on June 18, 1858, a letter arrived from Alfred Russel Wallace, a young collector and naturalist in the Malay Archipelago. In a malarial fever Wallace had come up with exactly the same notion of natural selection to explain evolution. The timing of this coincidence was remarkable. Wallace had even been influenced by Malthus, but ever after Wallace regarded the theory as Darwin's and was unstinting in sharing the credit.

Darwin could delay no longer. His friends J. D. Hooker the botanist and Sir Charles Lyell the geologist arranged for a joint contribution from Darwin and Wallace to be presented to the members of the Linnean Society, of which Darwin was a member. This took place on July 1, and evolution by natural selection was made public. Darwin immediately set to and completed what he described as an "abstract" of the larger book. *On the Origin of Species by Means of Natural Selection* was published in November 1859 and sold out before noon on the day of publication. There was furious public debate of the subject, but most scientists of the day accepted the force of Darwin's argument and saw that natural selection could indeed operate like an intelligent designer. From the chaos of minute random variations, survival selected those best designed to do a particular job. The outcome looked as though an artificer had been at work, but in fact none was needed.

Creation Science

A century after his death, it may look as if Darwin's theory too is dead. Increasingly vociferous attacks, particularly by right-wing fundamentalist

Christians, culminated in the passage of legislation in several U.S. states demanding equal time within the educational system for an alternative doctrine, that of creation science. One such law in Arkansas was challenged by a group of religious leaders and teachers, coordinated by the American Civil Liberties Union, on the grounds that it infringed upon the constitutional separation between church and state. Judge William R. Overton, in his decision delivered on Jan. 5, 1982, agreed, saying that creation science "is not a science because it depends upon a supernatural intervention which is not guided by natural law." The Arkansas law was dismissed, as was another in Louisiana ten months later, but at the end of 1982 suits against similar legislation were still pending in other states, and anti-evolutionists continued to exercise considerable influence. In a counterblow the Board of Regents of New York State's Department of Education decided not to approve certain science textbooks because their treatment of evolution was not sufficiently thorough.

The fundamentalist attack on Darwin and evolution makes use of the considerable debate among biologists over the nature of the processes that underlie evolution, pointing to disagreements within biology as evidence that evolution is false. This is not the case. None of the biologists' disagreements involves doubts that evolution has taken place; they are arguing over the details of the mechanism.

Continuing Debate

One of the most prominent arguments is over the tempo of evolution and in particular the very question of the origin of species, which Darwin's great work does not really address. Darwin believed that evolution is slow and gradual, one species shading more or less imperceptibly into another with the passage of geological time. His friend and defender, Thomas Henry Huxley, found this the weakest part of his argument and warned Darwin that he had saddled himself with too great a burden in stating so forcibly that "*natura non facit saltum*" ("nature does not make jumps").

The fossil record does contain evidence of intermediate forms, like the famous *Archaeopteryx*, which is neither wholly bird nor wholly reptile, but there is little evidence of gradual change in the form of a given fossil species through the geological record. Rather, a species exists unchanged for some length of time and then is replaced by another species that is different and yet clearly related to the earlier form. Bearing this in mind, Stephen Jay Gould and Niles Eldredge, two U.S. paleontologists, put forward the theory of punctuated equilibrium in 1972. This stated that most change was concentrated into the event of speciation, and that speciation took place in a relatively brief period among a small subgroup of the original species. For these reasons, and the vagaries of fossilization, one would not expect to see intermediates or gradual change in the fossil record.

The theory received support in 1982 with the publication by Peter Williamson of Harvard University of his findings from the thick fossil beds around Lake Turkana in northern Kenya. Williamson was able to track certain fossil snails through the deposits, which are remarkably complete, and show that all change is indeed concentrated into the transition between species. The change could take place in as short a period as 5,000 years, with a million years or more of stasis thereafter. Other fossil series, however, are neither as detailed nor as complete as Williamson's, and arguments often can be made for either punctuated equilibrium or gradualism.

Other arguments concern such things as the level at which selection occurs and the role of nonselective forces in shaping evolution. Is it possible, for example, to account for certain trends in the fossil record, like the increasing size of ancestors of the horse, by saying that larger species were more successful and hence more likely to give rise to descendant species? And what part do random processes play in evolution? These are questions that cannot yet be answered, but they reveal that, even a century after his death, the legacy of Charles Darwin continues to provide considerable intellectual income.

An effigy of Charles Darwin presides over an exhibit on the theory of evolution entitled "The Hidden Link" at London's Natural History Museum.

THE TIMES, LONDON

BOATING

At the end of 1981 the Whitbread Round the World race had reached the halfway stage in New Zealand. Cornelis van Rietschoten's "Flyer" was leading with the shortest elapsed time, but with the handicap taken into consideration Andrew Viant's smaller Foers-design "Kriter III" was in first. The main interest in the race from the start of the second leg in Cape Town was whether or not the New Zealand entry "Ceramco" could catch "Flyer." "Ceramco" kept "Flyer" close company on that leg, and on the next legs from New Zealand to Australia, Australia to Argentina, and Argentina back to the U.K. This struggle continued until in the last 1,000 mi (1,600 km) to Portsmouth "Flyer" not only got away from "Ceramco" but also won first place on handicap as a huge high-pressure area left the smaller yachts struggling home in light fickle winds.

At the end of 1981 the Southern Cross series ended with the Sydney–Hobart race. Eleven teams, each consisting of three yachts, had entered the series, which was won by New South Wales.

During 1982 several syndicates were preparing for the 1983 America's Cup Challenge. From Britain Peter de Savery was challenging with his "Victory" syndicate. The Australians had three separate challenges with some five or six new 12-m yachts. The Canadians were awaiting completion of their new Bruce Kirby-designed boat. For the U.S. Dennis Connor and Tom Blackaller were the two best-known helmsmen involved. Connor's "Freedom" syndicate had two new boats, "Spirit" and "Magic," but neither seemed to be a match for "Freedom," the cup's successful defender in 1980.

In the Round Britain race the first leg of the course from Plymouth to Crosshaven was won by Robert and Naomi James in "Colt Cars GB," with Chay Blyth and Peter Bateman second in "Brittany Ferries GB." "Exmouth Challenge" won the second leg to Barra. "Britanny Ferries" won the third leg to Lerwick in record time and the fourth leg to Lowestoft with "Colt Cars" only 19 minutes behind. On the final leg to Plymouth the two large trimarans virtually match-raced all the way with "Exmouth Challenge" close behind. Robert and Naomi James were first home, closely followed by Blyth and Bateman and not long afterward by Mark Gatehouse and Peter Rowsell in "Exmouth Challenge." "Colt Cars" set a new Round Britain record of 8 days 15 hours and 3 minutes.

Motorboating

Lee ("Chip") Hanauer of Seattle, Wash., completed a storybook season in 1982 as he swept to his first American Power Boat Association (APBA) Gold Cup, APBA unlimited hydroplane national championship, and Union of International Motorboating (UIM) world championship aboard the new "Atlas Van Lines."

The 1982 hydroplane season opened with a victory in the Champion Spark Plug Regatta on June 6

WIDE WORLD

Bill Dunlop of Mechanic Falls, Maine, landed at Falmouth, England, after 78 days in the nine-foot one-inch "Wind's Will," the smallest boat to make a west–east Atlantic crossing.

in Miami, Fla., for defending champion Dean Chenoweth and "Miss Budweiser." Two weeks later John Walters made history, piloting the turbine-powered "Pay 'n Pack" to its first victory in the inaugural Seneca, N.Y., event.

The turning point of the season came two weeks later when the determined Hanauer staged a dramatic come-from-behind rally to pass Chenoweth and claim the Stroh's APBA Gold Cup in Detroit. Veteran driver Tom D'Eath, of Fair Haven, Mich., returning to unlimited competition after a six-year absence, claimed the Madison, Ind., event in "The Squire Shop" on July 4, but Hanauer returned to the winner's circle in Evansville, Ind., on July 11.

Tragedy struck in Pasco, Wash., on July 31, when Chenoweth was killed in a solo testing run. The four-time national champion (1970, 1971, 1980, 1981) and four-time APBA Gold Cup winner (1970, 1973, 1980, 1981) was the second most successful driver in the history of the sport.

The 1982 offshore racing season featured unprecedented competition. Defending national champion Betty Cook opened the season with a victory in the New Orleans/Michelob Light 200 but lost her APBA national title to 1981 world champion Jerry Jacoby of Old Westbury, N.Y. Jacoby piloted his "Cigarette Hawk" to victory in the Bacardi Trophy Race on May 8 in Miami, the only Class I win of the year for the traditional deep vee designs. Al Copeland of New Orleans, La., won the Stroh Light Challenge on June 22 in Detroit in his triple outboard-powered "Popeye's." Copeland also claimed the Harmsworth Trophy.

Rocky Aoki teamed with Howard Quam of Chicago to win the Benihana Grand Prix on July 14 at Point Pleasant, N.J. The boat was destroyed and Aoki injured two months later at St. Augustine, Fla. Ted Toleman of the U.K. posted a new world speed record for offshore boats with a 109.98-mph clocking at Lake Windermere in England.

BOLIVIA

Gen. Celso Torrelio Villa clung to power as Bolivia's president until July 1982 despite dissension among the armed forces, a burgeoning economic crisis, foreign debt difficulties, and the international isolation of his regime because of its alleged links with paramilitary groups and with the drug trade. As the crisis worsened, President Torrelio became desperate to reach agreement with civilian leaders so the Army could withdraw from the government. He decreed an amnesty to allow exiled political and trade union leaders to return and lifted the ban on the activities of political parties and unions. An army group, Nueva Razón de Patria, warned that it would start a "bloodbath" if the authorities carried through their plan for democracy by April 1983. Critics in the military stated that Nueva Razón's members were all officers linked to the drug trade who feared an investigation into their activities by an incoming civilian regime.

NICOLE BONNETT—GAMMA/LIAISON

Hernán Siles Zuazo became president of Bolivia in October, two years after his election. The junta that had prevented his taking office finally gave up trying to run the country.

On July 19 Torrelio announced his resignation from the presidency. Power was transferred to a junta composed of the commanders of the three armed services, and soon afterward they appointed Brig. Gen. Guido Vildoso Calderón, the army chief of staff, as head of state. The move was aimed at resolving a leadership crisis brought about by Col. Faustino Rico Toro, who had accused Torrelio of failing to halt deterioration in the economy and had named himself as the general's natural successor. On August 12 the new government announced that the forthcoming election would be contested under the electoral law of 1965 instead of that of 1980. Reaction by the political parties and unions was swift. Most of Bolivia was paralyzed by strikes, which hit all the main cities during August and September.

On September 17, after three days of inconclusive discussions, the senior military commanders decided to recall the Congress elected democratically in 1980. Under the plan the Congress was to reconvene at the beginning of October and confirm the results of the 1980 elections. These had been won by Hernán Siles Zuazo of the left-wing Unidad Democrática y Popular, but the Army had not allowed him to take power. The military junta's decision to resign came at a time when chaotic management of the nation's finances led Bolivia to default on interest payments on its renegotiated foreign debt. The generals had failed to reach agreement with the International Monetary Fund on austerity measures that might have helped to restart the flow of financial assistance to Bolivia.

On October 6 Congress elected Siles Zuazo president for a four-year term. Jaime Paz Zamora, a Socialist, was elected vice-president. The country's new president returned from exile in Peru and took office on October 10.

BOWLING

Pete Weber of St. Louis, Mo., the 19-year-old son of Bowling Hall of Fame member Dick Weber, emerged as one of the most formidable competitors in Professional Bowlers Association (PBA) tournaments in 1982. The young Weber, whose opponents on the national tour sometimes included his father, won the PBA meets in Hartford, Conn., and Portland, Ore., and his earnings of $75,935 placed him sixth in that category with several tournaments remaining on the schedule.

The dominant male professional was Earl Anthony of Dublin, Calif., voted bowler of the year in 1974–76 and 1981 and a likely choice for 1982. Anthony captured three PBA titles and was the money leader with $133,895.

Mike Durbin won the Firestone Tournament of Champions, the $200,000 event that concludes the PBA's nationally televised winter tour. Durbin, from Chagrin Falls, Ohio, rolled strikes in six of the first seven frames in the title match to defeat Steve Cook of Roseville, Calif., 233–203. Durbin received $40,000 for his victory.

In the Masters Tournament of the American Bowling Congress (ABC), the winner of the $40,600 first prize was Joe Berardi of New York City. He defeated Ted Hannahs of Zanesville, Ohio, 236–216, in the final game.

In the Regular Division team event of the ABC tournament, a club that competed on the final squad of the three-month-long meet, Carl's Bowlers Paddock, of Cincinnati, Ohio, rolled 3,268 to win. Rich Wonders of Racine, Wis., was the individual star of the tournament, as he won the Regular all-events title with a nine-game total of 2,076, shared the doubles honours with Darold Meisel of Milwaukee, Wis., with 1,364, and was a member of the Kendor Corp. unit from Racine that took the team all-events crown with 9,498. Bruce Bohm of Chicago bowled 748 to win the singles championship.

The largest prize in women's bowling again went to Japan's Katsuko Sugimoto, who triumphed in the Avon/Women's International Bowling Congress (WIBC) Queens tournament for the second successive year. Sugimoto won $20,525 by downing Nikki Gianulias of Vallejo, Calif., 160–137, in the final game. A week later in the women's U.S. Open, Shinobu Saitoh of Japan took the $9,000 first prize.

Open Division champions in the WIBC tournament were: team, Zavakos Realtors, Dayton, Ohio, 2,961; singles, Gracie Freeman, Alexandria, Va., 653; doubles, Shirley Hintz, Merritt Island, Fla., and Lisa Rathgeber, Palmetto, Fla., tied Pat Costello, Dublin, Calif., and Donna Adamek, Duarite, Calif., 1,264; all-events, Aleta Rzepecki, Detroit, Mich., 1,905.

European Tournaments

The fourth European Cup tournament for individuals was in May 1982 in Borås, Sweden. Each country in Europe was allowed to enter its national men's and women's champion of 1981. The cup was played in head-to-head round-robin matches. After the match games the four best women and men advanced to the finals. In the women's division Shelagh Leonard from Great Britain met Irene Groonert from The Netherlands in the final contest. Groonert won the first game 188–182, but in the second game Leonard closed with four strikes to score 242 and win the match and cup 424–381.

In the men's division the two finalists were Arne Svein Strøm of Norway, bowler of the year in 1981, and Olle Svensson of Sweden. Strøm showed again that world bowling writers had made the right selection when they voted him bowler of the year, winning the cup 374–357.

The European Youth Tenpin championships took place in Stuttgart, West Germany, in April. The nation that topped the tournament was Sweden, with five gold and five silver medals and one bronze. The host, West Germany, won the remaining three gold medals and also two bronze. The individual champions were Karin Glennert from Sweden for girls and Walter Meiburg of West Germany for boys.

The international bowling leaders approved membership applications from Bahrain and San Marino. This increased to 67 the number of national member federations in the Fédération Internationale des Quilleurs (FIQ), the world governing body for bowling sport.

Lawn Bowls

Open bowls and its relationship with the Commonwealth Games provided much of the news in 1982. The Games, held in September and October in Brisbane, Australia, greatly attracted amateur sports people, and in order to compete some decided not to accept money prizes in open tournaments. John Watson of Scotland won the Indoor Bowls World Championship, an amateur event, in February 1982 and was invited to the Target Bowls Championship, which carried the world's largest first prize, £5,050 ($8,707). He withdrew, however, in order to preserve his amateur status. Peter Bellis, winner of the New Zealand Open, refused the prize money and took the alternative award for an amateur. Outdoor world champion David Bryant had made his decision in 1980 when he accepted the £2,000 ($3,448) first prize at the first-ever open tournament. In 1982 he won the Kodak masters bowls tournament at Worthing, England, for the third time. Chris Ward won the English Bowling Association (EBA) singles championship.

The biggest surprise came from Australia when John Snell, a silver medalist at both previous world championships and Commonwealth Games, remained an amateur only to be omitted from the Australian team for the 1982 Games.

In the Games, W. Wood won the singles for Scotland, Zimbabwe won the triples, Australia the fours, and Scotland the pairs.

BOXING

World Boxing Council (WBC) champion Larry Holmes (U.S.) retained his heavyweight title by stopping Gerry Cooney (U.S.) in 13 rounds in June in the richest prizefight in history. Champion and challenger were reported to have grossed about $10 million each. The fight was witnessed by 32,000 in a stadium erected outside Caesar's Palace in Las Vegas, Nev., but millions watched it throughout the world on closed-circuit television. Holmes thus remained undefeated in 40 contests, while Cooney was defeated for the first time in 26 bouts. In November Holmes was again successful with a unanimous 15-round victory over Randall ("Tex") Cobb in Houston, Texas. Mike Weaver (U.S.), the World Boxing Association (WBA) champion, lost his title to Michael Dokes (U.S.) when he was stopped in the first round of a challenge late in the year.

In the cruiserweight division, with the weight limit raised to 195 lb, Carlos de León (P.R.) retained the title, stopping Marvin Camel (U.S.), the former champion, in seven rounds, but then lost it to S. T. Gordon (U.S.) in two rounds. The WBA, which had not previously competed in this division, recognized Ossie Ocasio (P.R.) as champion when he outpointed Robbie Williams (South Africa) in Johannesburg. He retained the title with a points victory over Young Joe Louis (U.S.) in December. Dwight Muhammad Qawi (U.S.), formerly Dwight Braxton, retained the WBC light-heavyweight title with wins over Jerry Martin (U.S.) and Matthew Saad Muhammad (U.S.), both in six. The WBA championship was retained by Michael Spinks (U.S.), who won his four defenses against Mustapha Wasajja (Uganda) in six rounds, Murray Sutherland (U.S.) in eight, Jerry Celestine (U.S.) also in eight, and Johnny Davis (U.S.) in nine.

Marvelous Marvin Hagler (U.S.) continued as undisputed middleweight champion recognized by the WBC and WBA, with knockouts against William ("Caveman") Lee (U.S.) in 67 seconds of the first round and Fulgencio Obelmejías (Venezuela) in five rounds. Wilfred Benítez (P.R.) surrendered the WBC junior middleweight crown to Thomas Hearns (U.S.) in a 15-round decision in December. Benítez held off a challenge to his junior middleweight title earlier in the year by outpointing Roberto Durán (Panama). Davey Moore (U.S.) became the new

WBA champion at that weight by stopping Tadashi Mihara (Japan) in six rounds in Tokyo. Moore then retained his title, stopping Charlie Weir (South Africa) in five rounds in Johannesburg and Ayub Kalue (Den.) in ten.

Sugar Ray Leonard (U.S.), the undisputed welterweight champion of the WBC and WBA and considered by many the outstanding boxer since Muhammad Ali, announced his retirement from the ring at the age of 26. This followed months of speculation after his eye operation for a detached retina.

Leroy Haley (U.S.) took the WBC junior welterweight crown from Saoul Mamby (U.S.) and defended it against Giovanni Giuseppe Giminez (Italy). Aaron Pryor (U.S.) kept the WBA junior welterweight title by stopping Miguel Montilla (Dominican Republic) in 12 rounds, Akio Kameda (Japan) in 6, and Alexis Argüello (Nicaragua) in 14.

Argüello kept his WBC lightweight title by stopping James Busceme (U.S.) in six rounds and Andy Ganigan (U.S.) in five. This was Argüello's 19th successive championship win in three divisions: featherweight, junior lightweight, and lightweight.

WORLD BOXING CHAMPIONS
As of Dec. 31, 1982

Division	Boxer
Heavyweight	Larry Holmes, U.S.*
	Michael Dokes†
Cruiserweight	S. T. Gordon, U.S.*
	Ossie Ocasio, Puerto Rico†
Light Heavyweight	Dwight Muhammad Qawi, U.S.*
	Mike Spinks, U.S.†
Middleweight	Marvelous Marvin Hagler, U.S.*†
Junior Middleweight	Thomas Hearns, U.S.*
	Davey Moore, U.S.†
Welterweight	vacant
Junior Welterweight	Leroy Haley, U.S.*
	Aaron Pryor, U.S.†
Lightweight	Alexis Argüello, Nicaragua*
	Ray Mancini, U.S.†
Junior Lightweight	Bobby Chacon, U.S.*
	Sammy Serrano, Puerto Rico†
Featherweight	Juan LaPorte, U.S.*
	Eusebio Pedroza, Panama†
Junior Featherweight	Wilfredo Gómez, Puerto Rico*
	Leonardo Cruz, Dominican Republic†
Bantamweight	Lupe Pintor, Mexico*
	Jeff Chandler, U.S.†
Super Flyweight	Rafael Orono, Venezuela*
	Jiro Watanabe, Japan†
Flyweight	Eloncio Mercedes, Dominican Republic*
	Santos Laciar, Argentina†
Junior Flyweight	Hilario Zapata, Panama*
	Katsuo Tokashiki, Japan†

*Recognized by the World Boxing Council.
†Recognized by the World Boxing Association.

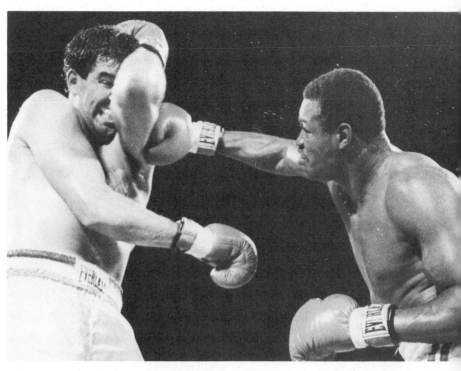

World Boxing Council heavyweight champion Larry Holmes (right) successfully defended his title against Gerry Cooney in June with a 13th-round TKO.

UPI

The WBA lightweight crown was taken over by Ray Mancini (U.S.) with a one-round win against Arturo Frias (U.S.). Frias earlier had retained the championship with a controversial points decision against Ernesto España (Venezuela). Mancini then knocked out Duk Koo Kim (South Korea) in the 14th round; the 23-year-old Korean never recovered consciousness and later died.

After Rolando Navarrete (Phil.) had retained the WBC junior lightweight championship, knocking out Chung Il-Choi (South Korea) in 11 rounds, Rafael Limón (Mexico), a former champion, regained the title by knocking out Navarrete in 12 rounds. Limón lost the crown on points to Bobby Chacon (U.S.). Sammy Serrano (P.R.) retained the WBA version of this division after a controversial finish against Benedicto Villablanca (Chile). The fight was stopped at the end of the tenth round after Serrano had sustained a badly cut eye, and the decision was given to Villablanca. But later the WBA changed the decision to a technical draw and, because Serrano had been ahead on points, he retained the title.

Salvador Sánchez (Mexico) was killed in an automobile accident a few weeks after retaining his WBC featherweight title with a victory over Azumah Nelson (Ghana) in 15 rounds. The vacant WBC crown was won by Juan LaPorte (U.S.), who beat Mario Miranda (Colombia) in ten rounds. Eusebio Pedroza (Panama) kept the WBA featherweight crown, outpointing LaPorte and drawing with Bernard Taylor (U.S.). Wilfredo Gómez (P.R.) remained WBC junior featherweight king with wins against Juan Meza (U.S.) in 6 rounds, Juan Antonio López (Mexico) in 10, Roberto Rubaldino (Mexico) in 7, and Lupe Pintor (Mexico) in 14. Sergio Palma (Arg.) won the WBA junior featherweight title from Jorge Luján (Panama) but lost it to Leonardo Cruz (Dominican Republic) on points.

Lupe Pintor (Mexico) continued as WBC bantamweight champion, stopping Seung-Hoon Lee (South Korea) in 11 rounds, and Jeff Chandler (U.S.) retained the WBA version and his unbeaten record by defeating Johnny Carter (U.S.) in 6 and Miguel Iriarte (Panama) in 9. Chul-Ho Kim (South Korea), the WBC super flyweight champion, won against Koki Ishii (Japan) and Raúl Valdez (Mexico) but in November was stopped in the sixth round by former champion Rafael Orono (Venezuela). The WBA gained a new champion when Jiro Watanabe (Japan) beat Rafael Pedroza (Panama) and retained the title against Gustavo Ballas (Arg.). Prudencio Cardona (Colombia) took the WBC flyweight title from Antonio Avelar (Mexico) with a one-round knockout but lost it to Freddie Castillo (Mexico). Later Castillo was outpointed by Eloncio Mercedes (Dominican Republic). The WBA flyweight crown was retaken by Santos Laciar (Arg.), who stopped Juan Herrera (Mexico) in 13 rounds and then beat Betulio Gonzáles (Venezuela) and Steve Muchoki (Kenya), both former champions. The WBC junior flyweight championship changed hands several times. Hilario Zapata (Panama) was knocked out in two rounds by Amado Ursua (Mexico). Then Tadashi Tomori (Japan) outpointed Ursua, but Zapata came back in a split decision against Tomori and then defeated Chang Jung-Koo (South Korea). WBA champion Katsuo Tokashiki (Japan) stopped Masaharu Inami (Japan) in the eighth round.

Supporters of Leonel Brizola, head of the Democratic Labour Party (PTD), rallied in Rio de Janeiro during the November election campaign. Brizola, who returned in 1982 from 18 years in exile, won the governorship of Rio de Janeiro State.

CAMERA PRESS/PHOTO TRENDS

BRAZIL

Political events in Brazil were dominated by the elections on Nov. 15, 1982, to the 479 seats in the Chamber of Deputies, one-third of the 69 seats in the Senate, the state governorships and assemblies, and the municipalities. These elections were in connection with the *abertura* policy of Pres. João Baptista de Oliveira Figueiredo's administration, aimed at gradually returning the country to civilian rule. The parties involved were the government-sponsored Partido Democrático Social (PDS) and four opposition groupings: the Partido Movimento Democrático Brasileiro (PMDB), by far the largest of the four; the Partido Trabalhista Democrático (PTD); the Partido Trabalhista Brasileiro (PTB); and the Partido dos Trabalhadores (PT). Preliminary results published at the end of November established that the PDS gained 234 seats in the Chamber of Deputies as against the four opposition parties' 245, of which 199 were won by the PMDB.

Nonetheless, the PDS gained an overall victory in the elections. Control of Congress was retained through its overall majority in the Senate, and it was expected to arrive at an accommodation with smaller opposition parties to ensure a majority in the Chamber of Deputies. The PDS also won 13 of the 23 state governorships and controlled most of the state assemblies and local councils.

The economic performance in 1982 was not good and was affected by the international recession. Growth in gross domestic product (GDP) was expected to be nil or slightly negative; a decline of 1.9% had been recorded in 1981. Overall industrial output fell by 0.6% in the period January–September 1982 and by 5.2% in the year ended in September. Agricultural production was expected to decline, owing to poor coffee and soybean crops and cuts in official

price and credit supports. On the other hand, industrial employment improved. The jobless rate in the six main industrial cities—São Paulo, Rio de Janeiro, Pôrto Alegre, Belo Horizonte, Salvador, and Recife—declined from 8% in December 1981 to 5.4% in September 1982.

The rate of inflation remained high, at 95.9%, in the 12 months ended in October 1982, and it was expected to be about 95% for the whole year. There was a trade surplus of $617 million in the period January–October, but the overall 1982 surplus was expected to be only $500 million, well short of the $3 billion target set in January. The current account deficit was estimated to have grown from $11 billion in 1981 to $14 billion because of interest payments on the external debt, which stood at $89 billion at the end of November. In December the International Monetary Fund tentatively agreed to extend to Brazil $4.9 billion in credit, and additional loans were also being sought from foreign banks to compensate for export revenue shortfalls resulting from low international commodity prices.

The Itaipú hydroelectric project on the Paraná River on the border with Paraguay was completed during the year, and it was inaugurated by President Figueiredo on November 5. It was reported to be the world's largest hydroelectric facility and was scheduled to reach full production in 1988.

During U.S. Pres. Ronald Reagan's visit to Brazil in late November and early December, agreement was reached on creating closer economic and military links between the two countries. President Figueiredo visited the U.S. on May 10–14, but his stay was cut short by one day in protest against U.S. support for the U.K. in its conflict with Argentina. He visited Canada in late July and signed agreements for transactions in excess of $1 billion.

BULGARIA

After a two-year trial period in selected state enterprises, Bulgaria launched a "new mechanism" to manage its national economy on Jan. 1, 1982. Its main aims were to make central planning less cumbersome and to improve industrial efficiency. One innovation was to link pay with productivity. General Secretary Todor Zhivkov and Premier Grisha Filipov initially positioned themselves between the Politburo members who supported the reform and those wishing to maintain traditional conservative ideology; they finally joined the reformers.

Filipov visited Moscow in June and signed two agreements: on joint production between appropriate industrial enterprises, and on cooperation in prospecting for oil and gas on the Bulgarian continental shelf. Gen. Kenan Evren, the Turkish head of state, and Greek Prime Minister Andreas Papandreou visited Bulgaria in February and June, respectively. Both discussed the idea of a nuclear-free zone in the Balkans, Papandreou supporting it and Evren rejecting it.

In March Peko Takov retired from the Politburo and was replaced by Milko Balev. On his appointment as premier in June 1981, Filipov had ceased to be a member of the Central Committee; he was replaced by Kiril Zarev. Zhivko Popov, a former deputy foreign minister, was deprived of party membership and sentenced to 20 years' imprisonment for offenses involving illegal hard-currency transactions. Joint maneuvers of land, sea, and air forces of the Warsaw Pact members took place in the Varna area from September 25 to October 1.

BURMA

After a lull lasting nearly two years, there were indications during 1982 that a new round of clashes had begun between Burma's government security forces and the pro-Chinese Burmese Communist Party (BCP) insurgents. First news of resumed fighting came when the government announced on June 15 that 67 Communists had surrendered with their weapons in April and May. Foreign Minister U Chit Hlaing visited Beijing (Peking) in July to persuade the Chinese government to stop giving moral and material support to the BCP. There was no official indication that he had succeeded in his effort, but unconfirmed reports circulating in Rangoon said the Chinese had indeed stopped giving aid to the BCP, which was left entirely dependent on the opium trade for funds.

On the surface, government-level relations between China and Burma appeared good as China continued to extend technical and financial assistance. The Thai and Burmese armies agreed to increase their cooperation in fighting the Communist, Karen, and other insurgents in border regions. In September a group of five Karens unsuccessfully attempted to take over the Burmese radio and television headquarters in Rangoon.

Relaxation of the rigid isolationist policy of for-mer chairman U Ne Win's government was benefiting the economy. Japan promised a $160 million loan for the fiscal year April 1982–March 1983, to develop liquefied petroleum gas and to modernize the railways. The Asian Development Bank sanctioned $18.5 million for upgrading half of the hospitals in the country and another $5 million for a crop intensification program.

BUSINESS AND INDUSTRY

In the midst of a major recession and the highest unemployment levels since 1940, American business witnessed in 1982 the bankruptcy of Braniff International Corp., the landmark divestiture of AT&T, one of the most acrimonious merger battles of recent times, and the tragedy of a former top official at General Motors arrested in a multimillion-dollar cocaine bust as his effort to found a new automobile company crumbled around him.

The work force took 10.8% unemployment on the chin, with the rate in older industries such as steel, autos, and mining running up to 25%, while the administration of Pres. Ronald Reagan obliged business to give back billions of dollars in tax breaks offered as a stimulus to new investment in the previous year's tax package. Meanwhile, the Federal Reserve Board's tight money policy, combined with the prolonged recession, seemed finally to bring inflation under control at the 5% level, about half the rate of the previous year.

In all, what was to have been a year of recovery was more of a patchwork year, perhaps a building year if the 300-point run-up in the Dow Jones industrial average in the late summer and fall was any indication of investors' faith in the near future. But with the recession in its 18th month in December, and with disappointed job seekers in such former employment havens as Texas living in Depression-style tent cities outside Houston, few economic seers were predicting great gains for 1983.

The pattern of growth in the Gross National Product (GNP) during the year was weak or falling for the four quarters reported in 1982, and the steel industry was unquestionably the hardest hit. Bethlehem Steel alone was projected to lose a total of $1 billion in 1982, following a cut in December of 8,000 jobs at its Lackawanna, N.Y., mills, once the world's fourth largest. That brought the total of unemployed steelworkers in the United States to 230,000. Lackawanna's declining output was tied directly to the low demand of its Detroit customers, who experienced the worst auto sales volume since 1961. But order cancellations by the hard-pressed airline industry also hurt steel, as did the depressed state of housing construction and purchases during most of the year, with their attendant demands for appliances. Foreign steel suppliers continued increasing their share of sales in the U.S. market, prompting suits by American steelmakers and diplomatic negotiations to curb import levels. The steel industry lost more than $100 million in the first quarter of the year, $20 million in the second quarter, and $650 million in the third quarter, when capacity utilization dipped to about 45%, a 44-year low.

Automakers, two years into a slump that had cost them billions of dollars in operating losses, did not experience the same accelerating skid as steel, even though auto imports grabbed a record 32% of the U.S. market during the fall of 1982. One reason was that Detroit had already taken its medicine, closing nonproductive plants and winning "givebacks" from its union work force in previous years. Though $128 million in the red for the first quarter, the four major American auto firms turned in a profit in the second quarter, then a $217 million loss in the third, mostly attributable to Ford Motor Co.'s loss of $325 million. Toward the end of the year, auto sales rebounded strongly to a level 37% greater than a year earlier on the strength of consumer interest in 1983 models and below-market loans offered by the auto companies to finance purchases of 1982 models. Closing inventories for the year were the lowest in 12 years, raising hopes that job callbacks and new steel orders would help spark a general economic recovery in 1983.

Chrysler's turnaround with a gain of $266.2 million for the first nine months of the year, although including extraordinary gains from the sale of some profitable operations, was a sign of austerity paying off and an ability to turn a profit even in a lower-volume environment. But it was also a signal to unions to drop the conciliatory attitude that had helped restore the industry's profitability. The United Auto Workers' future direction was not clear as its executive board picked the methodical Owen Bieber to succeed retiring president Douglas A. Fraser, but a strike by 10,000 Chrysler workers at Canadian plants late in the year gave some indication of a rank-and-file impatience to recover some lost ground.

There was also a change in union leadership in the coalfields, where 33-year-old Richard Trumka ousted incumbent Sam Church in a general election for the presidency of the United Mine Workers. Trumka took over a dwindling membership of less than 60% of all employees in an industry where one-quarter of the work force was on layoff in 1982. The steel industry's reduced output, combined with flat demand for electricity (electric utility companies consume 70% of U.S. coal production), caused the slack demand for coal. Many utility companies renegotiated contracts to defer shipments—a reneging that mine owners had to accept from their major customer. Moreover, the predicted export market for coal failed to materialize because of high European inventories and the falling price of the main competing fuel, oil.

Indeed, the worldwide recession seemed finally to

U.S. Steel demolished its blast furnace in Youngstown, Ohio, dramatizing the plight of many basic industries in the U.S.—technologically obsolete plants and production capacity far in excess of the demands of a recession-pinched economy.

PAUL R. SCHELL/THE YOUNGSTOWN VINDICATOR

have broken the back of the previous decade's oil price rises in late 1981 and 1982. Some OPEC (Organization of Petroleum Exporting Countries) members undersold the cartel's fixed price of $34 per barrel to make sales in the face of a worldwide petroleum glut. Steady and briefly dipping oil and gas prices were one bright spot for the U.S. economy and a key factor in the taming of inflation.

This proved slim compensation, however, to the airlines, for as fuel costs came under control, airline overcapacity sparked continued price wars. The industry lost $500 million in the first quarter of 1982 and seemed headed toward similar losses in the final quarter as $99 coast-to-coast and New York-to-Florida fares were heavily advertised. In promoting such potentially ruinous fares, airlines were floundering in a newly deregulated marketplace while attempting to fill flights, cover fixed costs, and win market shares. The collapse in May of Texas-based Braniff International, whose final tactic had largely consisted of a fare war, was apparently not warning enough to other carriers. It was also indicative of a competitive spiral they could not break in the deregulated marketplace. One stock market analyst, speaking to the *Wall Street Journal*, termed the airline fare wars a "bleeding contest" in which Braniff happened to bleed faster. Additional bankruptcies were anticipated, although some industry-wide restraint was apparent in the many cancellations of new aircraft orders in 1982. Ironically, cancellations on newer, more fuel-efficient and therefore economical aircraft were made easier by the softening of world oil prices.

Another contributing cause of those cancellations was government action—a reorientation in 1982 of administration policy toward capital investment that some termed a reversal of 1981. To stem federal budget deficits headed well over $100 billion in coming years, administration forces in Congress revoked such 1981 measures as superaccelerated depreciation and safe-harbour leasing and also reduced the investment tax credit from 10 to 8%. Sales of capital equipment had benefited from the 1981 changes in leasing because they enabled money-losing companies to sell to third parties the tax benefits they could not exercise, while the rapid depreciation and 10% investment tax credit made any investment, leased or bought, more attractive. The 1982 changes, due to go into effect in 1983 and accepted by many business leaders as the cost of keeping the federal deficit under control and avoiding reflation, were resisted by many supply-side Republicans who argued that the tax-cut philosophy of President Reagan's first year was more appropriate than additional taxes. But Reagan argued forcefully for the new approach, and the new taxes, projected to cost business $50 million over the next three years, narrowly passed Congress on the strength of Democratic Party votes and Republicans loyal to the president. The 10% individual income tax cut scheduled to go into effect in mid-1983 was left intact.

NEAL BOENZI / THE NEW YORK TIMES

Workers remove asbestos insulation from a classroom in New York City. Asbestos was implicated in a variety of health problems.

In other government action in 1982, the Justice Department brought to a close two mammoth antitrust suits, one by dropping a 13-year-old case against IBM Corp. and the other by accepting AT&T's proposed breakup. The charge that IBM had illegally dominated the computer industry fell before the evidence of rapid growth during the 1970s of minicomputer companies and IBM-compatible computer manufacturers. The AT&T case, on the other hand, was finally conceded in January by the nation's largest corporation, with $146 billion in assets and average quarterly earnings of $1.5 billion. The breakup plan would spin off the 22 Bell System operating companies as 7 regional telephone systems, while AT&T would retain its long-distance division, its Western Electric manufacturing division, and Bell Laboratories, its research arm. The divestiture, the largest in U.S. history, was to be set in motion in January 1983 but would not be completed until sometime in 1984.

While AT&T was divesting, Bendix Corp., the auto parts maker and 86th on the *Fortune* 500 list of American corporations, was dreaming of merging. But its bid to take over 130th-ranked Martin Marietta Corp. backfired when Martin Marietta began

"Hey, listen to this ... the president says the prime rate should drop this summer!"

ED GAMBLE © 1982 THE FLORIDA TIMES-UNION

buying Bendix stock in retaliation. The so-called "Pac Man" tactic of gobbling up its pursuers led Martin Marietta into a deal with United Technologies Corp., 20th on the *Fortune* list and a veteran of several successful takeover battles, to help with the Bendix purchases and to divide the company between them in the event they won. Bendix, effectively cornered, then arranged to be swallowed whole by 55th-place Allied Corp., and there the takeover visions of Bendix Chairman William Agee ended with his asking to have his company taken over. Other ironies involved Allied Chairman Edward L. Hennessy, Jr.'s victory over his former boss at United Technologies, Harry Gray, in a takeover battle, and the expenditure of millions of dollars in investment banking and legal fees, as well as future interest payments on loans taken to finance the stock tender offers, all of which added nothing to any company's productive capacity. Many in corporate circles viewed the spectacle as the sorry nadir of the merger mania of the past several years and a situation where ego outweighed economics. The participants replied that their goal had been to maximize shareholder value.

On August 26 the Manville Corp., a mining and manufacturing conglomerate that was 181st on the *Fortune* 500 list, filed a bankruptcy petition in federal court. The firm's financial condition was good, indeed enviable, with a net worth of $1.1 billion and 1981 after-tax earnings of $60.3 million. But the company was facing some 16,500 lawsuits, with 500 more being filed each month, stemming from the long-delayed health effects of asbestos on former miners and processors of the insulating material, a major Manville product. It was estimated that the company could eventually be liable for as much as $2 billion in legal costs and settlements. The claim of bankruptcy offered at least temporary protection from such suits, although it was unclear whether the courts would ultimately allow such a controversial maneuver, and it prompted Congress to begin con-

sidering some form of federally subsidized compensation program.

By far the most shocking event in American business in 1982 was the arrest of John Z. De Lorean for the possession of $24 million worth of cocaine. De Lorean had risen rapidly in a career at General Motors and at 47 had held the post of president of all North American auto and truck operations. He then left the $650,000-a-year post, grew his hair long, dyed it black, divorced his wife, and married a young New York model. He also began forming the De Lorean Motor Co. with investments by prospective

Atlantic Richfield Co. abandoned its credit card system in April and passed the savings along to its gasoline dealers and customers.

JOSEPH KUGLIESKY/THE NEW YORK TIMES

dealers of the stainless-steel sports car he envisioned and with loans from the British government in return for locating the first plant in Northern Ireland. The first plant was all there was to be, as the car was introduced to a strong novelty market that eventually faded while De Lorean boosted output in hopes of generating greater revenue. The company was declared bankrupt and its assets seized by British officials in October, just hours before De Lorean was arrested with the cocaine by undercover narcotics agents in a Los Angeles hotel room. One of the country's top business executives had been driven to extreme lengths in a chimerical attempt to save his automaking dream.

CANADA

Canada gained a new constitution in 1982. The document represented a striking personal achievement for Prime Minister Pierre Elliott Trudeau, who had made it a prized goal ever since his entrance into federal politics in 1965. Trudeau's popularity among Canadians slipped badly during the year, however, as his government failed to inspire confidence in its handling of the worst economic recession since the 1930s. Public opinion polls suggested that if an election were held, Trudeau's Liberals would be removed from office. But Trudeau, now 63 and enigmatic about his retirement, remained the dominant figure in Canadian political life.

Canada's new constitution was proclaimed by Elizabeth II, in her capacity as queen of Canada, in a dramatic ceremony on Parliament Hill in Ottawa on April 17. The document, called the Constitution Act 1982, contains the original statute that established the Canadian federation in 1867, the amendments made to it by the British Parliament over the years, and new material drawing on Trudeau's 1980 proposals and his later discussions with the provincial premiers. Of the ten premiers, all were present for the ceremony except René Lévesque, leader of the Parti Québécois (PQ) separatist government of Trudeau's own province. Lévesque's absence was unfortunate, for it had been Quebec's discontent with Canadian federalism during its "Quiet Revolution" in the 1960s that had launched the momentum for change. Quebec's demands for special status within the federal system had been rejected by Trudeau and the other provinces, as had its claim of an absolute veto over constitutional change.

The new constitution represented a compromise between Trudeau's vision of "one Canada with two official languages" and the particular concerns of the provinces. A novel part of the document was the Charter of Rights and Freedoms. This set down 34 rights to be observed across Canada, ranging from freedom of religion to language and educational rights based on the test of numbers. Many of the rights could be overridden by a "notwithstanding clause," which allowed both the federal Parliament and the provincial legislatures to set aside guarantees in the Charter. Designed to preserve parliamen-

tary supremacy, a basic political principle in Canada, "notwithstanding clauses" would have to be renewed every five years to remain in force. Thus the Charter of Rights was not fully entrenched in the Canadian constitution as the Bill of Rights was in that of the United States.

The Constitution Act also contained a formula for its amendment in Canada, a subject that had defeated attempts to gain agreement on a new constitution as far back as 1927. Under the formula, resolutions of the Canadian Parliament, accompanied by the concurrence of two-thirds of the provinces (7) representing at least 50% of the country's population, would be sufficient to approve a constitutional amendment. Other sections of the act recognized the aboriginal and treaty rights of native peoples, strengthened the provinces' jurisdiction over their natural resources, and committed the central government to provide public services of reasonable quality across Canada by ensuring revenue (equalization) payments to the provinces.

The constitutional changes having been extensively discussed in Canada since their presentation in 1980, and their mode of procedure having secured judicial endorsement in 1981, there was little opposition when they came before the British Parliament early in 1982. All major parties supported them, although some MP's felt that native rights were inadequately protected. The queen gave royal assent to the Constitution Act on March 29, 115 years to the day after Queen Victoria, her great-great-grandmother, had approved the federation act of 1867. Thus the last legal tie with Great Britain was severed, and Canada became a fully sovereign state.

Though the people of Quebec were deeply divided over the merits of the new constitution, Lévesque's government went ahead with its opposition to the changes. The PQ government took its case to the courts, but the Quebec Court of Appeal, on April 7, held that Quebec did not possess a veto over constitutional change, even if it affected provincial jurisdiction. Again, on September 8, the Superior Court of Quebec held that sections of Quebec's controversial language law, Bill 101, were unconstitutional because they conflicted with the new Charter of Rights. Bill 101 required English-speaking Canadian parents educated outside Quebec to send their children to French schools if they moved to Quebec. The Charter, on the other hand, guarantees minority language education in all provinces for children of Canadian citizens where numbers warrant the establishment of schools. Quebec's claim to a constitutional veto was decisively rejected by the Supreme Court of Canada, 9–0, on December 6.

The unpopularity of the Trudeau government derived from its inability to improve the country's weak economic condition. Finance Minister Allan MacEachen's budget of Nov. 12, 1981, had to be sharply modified in the face of widespread criticism. His second budget, proposed on June 28, 1982, was better received. Nevertheless, MacEachen left the

Finance Ministry on September 10, moving to External Affairs, a post he had held from 1974 to 1976. The new minister of finance was Marc Lalonde, who had promoted the Canadian national thrust in developing oil and gas resources while he was minister of energy, mines, and resources.

In August it was announced that public opinion polls showed the Liberal Party with a 28% popularity rating, its lowest in 40 years. Conservative support stood at 47%. Three federal by-elections on October 12 demonstrated the Liberals' unpopularity. The Conservatives won two seats, a gain of one, and the New Democratic Party (NDP) won the other. The results did not affect the Liberals' comfortable majority in the House of Commons, where the party occupied 146 of 282 seats. The Conservatives held 102 seats, the NDP 33, and there was one independent.

Five provinces went to the polls in 1982, and in four instances sitting governments were returned. The exception was Saskatchewan, where an 11-year-old NDP government under Allan Blakeney was soundly defeated on April 26. Led by Grant Devine, the Conservatives won 57 of the 64 seats in the legislature, the remainder going to the NDP. The party capitalized on popular discontent with the Blakeney government and offered tax cuts on gasoline and lower mortgage interest rates. Next door, in Alberta, another Conservative administration, under Edgar Peter Lougheed, won triumphant reelection on November 2. Having presided since 1971 over an oil boom that made Alberta the wealthiest province of Canada, Lougheed's Conservatives gained 75 of the 79 seats in the legislature. The once-powerful Social Credit Party, dominant in Alberta for 36 years before 1971, was eliminated in the legislature.

The other three elections were in Atlantic Canada. In Newfoundland Conservative Premier Brian Peckford won a resounding vote of confidence in his struggle with Ottawa over the control of offshore mineral resources. In an April 6 election the Conservatives captured 44 seats to the Liberals' 8 in the 52-seat House of Assembly. In a quiet contest in Prince Edward Island on September 27, Conservative Premier James Lee, sworn into office ten months earlier, led his party to a 22–10 victory over the Liberal opposition. Finally, in New Brunswick, Richard Hatfield, another Conservative who had been premier since 1970, won an unprecedented fourth term in office on October 12 when his party captured 39 seats in the 58-seat legislature. The Liberals won 17 seats, gaining another in a recount. For the first time in New Brunswick's history, an NDP member was elected. The elections left Conservative administrations in all four Atlantic provinces, in Ontario, and in Saskatchewan and Alberta. No Liberal government was in power in any province in 1982.

The Economy

Throughout 1982 Canada endured the longest and most severe economic slump since the great de-

THE CANADIAN CABINET

Members of the Canadian Cabinet in order of precedence:

Prime Minister . Right Hon. Pierre Elliott Trudeau
Deputy Prime Minister and Secretary
of State for External
Affairs . . . . Hon. Allan Joseph MacEachen
Minister of Transport . . . . Hon. Jean-Luc Pepin
Minister of Energy, Mines,
and Resources . . . . Hon. Jean Chrétien
Minister of Indian Affairs and
Northern Development . Hon. John Carr Munro
Leader of the Government
in the Senate . . . . . . Hon. Horace Andrew Olson
President of the Treasury
Board . . . . Hon. Herbert Eser Gray
Minister of
Agriculture . . . . . . Hon. Eugene Francis Whelan
Minister of Consumer and
Corporate Affairs . . . . Hon. André Ouellet
Minister of Finance . . . . Hon. Marc Lalonde
Minister of State
(Fitness and Amateur
Sport) . . . . Hon. Raymond Joseph Perrault
Minister of Public Works . . . Hon. Roméo LeBlanc
Minister of the Environment . . Hon. John Roberts
Minister of National Health
and Welfare . . . . Hon. Monique Bégin
Minister of Supply
and Services . . . . Hon. Jean-Jacques Blais
Minister of Communications . . . Hon. Francis Fox
Minister of Defence . . . . . Hon. Gilles Lamontagne
Minister of Fisheries
and Oceans . . . . Hon. Pierre DeBané
Minister of State (Canadian
Wheat Board) . . . . Hon. Hazen Robert Argue
Minister of State
(International Trade) . . . . Hon. Gerald Regan
Minister of Justice and
Attorney General
of Canada . . . . Hon. Mark MacGuigan
Solicitor General
of Canada . . . . Hon. Robert Phillip Kaplan
Minister of State
(Multiculturalism) . Hon. James Sydney Fleming
Minister of State (Small
Business and Tourism) . Hon. William Rompkey
Minister of National
Revenue . . . . Hon. Pierre Bussières
Minister of State
(External Relations) . . . . . Hon. Charles Lapointe
Minister of Industry, Trade,
and Commerce and Minister
of Regional Economic
Expansion . . . . Hon. Edward Lumley
President of the Queen's Privy
Council for Canada . . . . Hon. Yvon Pinard
Minister of State for Economic
Development and Minister
of State for Science and
Technology . . . . Hon. Donald Johnston
Minister of Employment and
Immigration . . . . Hon. Lloyd Axworthy
Minister of State (Finance) . . . Hon. Paul Cosgrove
Minister of State (Mines) . . . . Hon. Judy Erola
Minister of State
for Social Development . . . . . Hon. Jacob Austin
Minister of Labour . . . . . . Hon. Charles L. Caccia
Secretary of State of Canada . . . . Hon. Serge Joyal
Minister of
Veterans Affairs . . . . Hon. W. Bennett Campbell

Queen Elizabeth II, with
Canadian Prime Minister
Pierre Elliott Trudeau
looking on, signed the
proclamation of Canada's
new constitution on
April 17.
WIDE WORLD

pression of the 1930s. From mid-1981 to mid-1982 economic production slipped 6%. The gross national product, on a seasonally adjusted annual basis, was expected to total $349.9 billion, but this figure masked a real-term decline in output. The world recession, dampening mineral prices, severely affected the mining and energy sectors of the economy. Merchandise exports were surprisingly strong, and the cumulative surplus of exports over imports for the first nine months of the year amounted to a record $12.7 billion.

High interest rates, a serious problem in 1981, moderated as the Bank of Canada lending rate dropped steadily to 11.6% in mid-October. This brought down loan and mortgage rates, which in turn stimulated stock market gains. The Canadian dollar recovered somewhat from the shocks it had taken in 1981, moving from a low of 76 U.S. cents in June to 81–82 cents four months later. The rate of inflation also fell, although not as steeply as in the U.S. In October it stood at 10% over the previous 12 months, the lowest increase since the summer of 1980. The cost of checking inflation, the prime objective of the Trudeau government, was a disturbing increase in unemployment. The unemployment rate in November was 12.7% on a seasonally adjusted basis, a level unsurpassed since the '30s.

The dismal performance of the economy was symbolized by the collapse of several large projects in the energy field. The first to go was the $13.5 billion Alsands project to recover synthetic crude from the vast oil sands deposits of northern Alberta. It collapsed on April 30 when the last three of the eight companies in the consortium turned down an offer of tax and royalty concessions held out by the federal and Alberta governments. The high cost of construction, reduced cash flows for the oil companies, and uncertain world prices for oil killed the project. At the same time, the Alaska Highway gas pipeline suffered a blow when a further two-year delay in financing the project was announced in New York.

Since 1977, when Canada and the U.S. agreed to build the line, costs of construction had soared from about $10 billion to perhaps $35 billion. Completion was now scheduled for 1989, but there were doubts that the major part of the pipeline would ever be built. The southern portion of the line, the "prebuild" section, was completed on time within budget and began moving natural gas to U.S. markets on September 1. However, it represented only 520 mi (837 km) of the 4,800-mi (7,700-km) route.

The largest Canadian oil company, Dome Petroleum Ltd. of Calgary, Alta., required a massive injection of capital from the federal government and four chartered banks at the end of September. A total of $1 billion in new capital was put into Dome to help offset its $7.4 billion debt. Canada's hopes of achieving self-sufficiency in oil by 1990, a goal of the Trudeau government, now rested on the promising oil and gas exploration in the Beaufort Sea, a new oil field and pipeline at Norman Wells in the Northwest Territories, the Hibernia field off the coast of Newfoundland, and gas exploration activities around Sable Island off the Nova Scotia coast.

There was no agreement among the various levels of government in Canada on how to deal with the economy. This was demonstrated at a conference of first ministers in Ottawa, February 2–4, which broke up without reaching any consensus. In introducing his June 28 budget to the House of Commons, MacEachen admitted that the recession had undercut his efforts to reduce the federal government's deficit. The revised shortfall was placed at $19.6 billion, the largest in Canadian history. MacEachen's budget put limits on the indexing factor for personal income tax exemptions: 6% in 1983 and 5% in 1984. (Since 1973 indexing had been tied to the rate of inflation.) Wage controls at 6% for the current year and 5% for 1983 were imposed immediately on 500,000 federal public employees, ranging from civil servants to judges and members of Parliament. Old-age security payments and family allowances were also to be tied to the same 6 and 5% increases. MacEachen also gave a commitment to try to keep price increases down in all federally regulated industries.

Invited to endorse the federal government's restraint program at a special meeting held in Ottawa two days after the budget, the provinces balked. They insisted that they would control their spending in ways suited to their own circumstances and needs. Over the next few months all the provinces except Manitoba announced plans of restraint for public sector employees, and many of them imposed restraints on their municipalities as well. Lelonde, the new finance minister, issued an "economic statement" on October 27, when Parliament reconvened after the summer recess, explaining that the federal deficit had risen to $23.6 billion from MacEachen's June 28 forecast. The minister announced that $150 million would be redirected from government spending into job creation before April 1983.

Foreign Affairs

Trudeau's efforts to build a bridge between the industrialized North and the less developed South, a

Prime Minister Pierre Elliott Trudeau's problems with managing the Canadian economy caused his Liberal Party to suffer in popularity polls.

CANADIAN PRESS

strong thrust in his foreign policy since he returned to power in 1980, met failure in 1982. Global talks on restructuring the world economy did not get under way. The annual meeting of the International Monetary Fund in Toronto, September 6–9, largely failed to mention global negotiations for a new international economic order.

Trudeau made an 11-day trip to Europe to attend the Versailles economic summit (June 4–6), the results of which he described as "disappointing." Later, at the NATO meeting in Bonn, West Germany, on June 10, he was critical of the failure to discuss the deeper problems of the alliance. He said he did not agree with the Reagan administration's policy of linking disarmament talks to Soviet behaviour in other areas. On June 18, speaking before the UN special session on disarmament, he called on the two superpowers to give their undivided attention to arms reductions.

Canada imposed sanctions against Poland and the Soviet Union on February 23 in order to dramatize the government's unhappiness over the establishment of martial law in Poland. The sanctions, symbolic rather than substantial, resembled those laid down by other members of the Western alliance. Canada condemned Argentina's resort to force to settle the Falkland Islands dispute by banning imports and discouraging exports on April 12. Exports to Argentina amounted to only $150 million in 1981, much of it resulting from the sale of a Canadian-made CANDU nuclear reactor.

Canada was touched by international terrorism on August 27 when the military attaché at the Turkish embassy was murdered in Ottawa. The attack appeared to be the action of extremists seeking revenge for the Turkish massacre of Armenians during World War I. Another incident occurred on October 15 when a powerful blast damaged a Toronto plant making guidance systems for the U.S. nuclear cruise missile. Seven persons, including three policemen, were injured. The plant had been the focus of a number of antinuclear demonstrations since March 17, when the Trudeau Cabinet announced that approval in principle had been given to test unarmed cruise missiles in northern Canada.

A record grain sale worth $1.3 billion was made to the Soviet Union in October, the first signed with that country in the 1982–83 crop year. On June 10 Mexico announced the cancellation of its huge nuclear program, thus dashing Canada's hopes of selling it a CANDU reactor. This was a severe blow to the Canadian nuclear industry, which faced large layoffs unless new orders were found. Better news came on May 18 with the award of a contract to Bombardier Inc., a Quebec company, to build 825 subway cars for New York City. Valued at $1 billion, this was the largest export contract ever awarded a Canadian manufacturer. After strong representations by the Canadian government, Japan agreed to limit its car exports to Canada to 153,000 vehicles in 1982, down about 25% from the year before.

Canada

Special Report: Strains Along the Border

by Peter Ward

Hard economic times and conflicting political philosophies in 1982 created what some critics called the worst climate of the century between Canada and the U.S. U.S. policy in Central America came under fire from Canada; Canadian policies of economic nationalism annoyed Washington. Beset with rising unemployment, both countries competed for jobs in the staggering North American automotive industry. Neither capital thought its neighbour was taking the right approach to economic recovery.

Canadian politicians blamed the high-interest-rate policies of the Reagan administration for even higher Canadian interest rates; Americans were critical about the dismal Canadian performance in productivity, coupled with average wage increases greater than those in the U.S. In both nations businessmen went bankrupt by the thousands, while unemployment soared to post-Depression record levels. Paul Robinson, Jr., the U.S. ambassador to Canada, publicly criticized what he termed overly generous Canadian social policies, and Canada fought U.S. plans to cut back environmental protection budgets, even in the pages of U.S. newspapers.

Acid rain—the result of aerial pollution by industry in both countries—became an important political cause in Canada, and Canadians openly lobbied U.S. legislators to take action. As the year progressed, Americans grew angrier over Canada's Foreign Investment Review Agency, which monitors all foreign investment in Canada. Meanwhile, Canadians lashed out at the U.S. for flexing its economic muscle to stop other nations from cooperating with the Soviet plan to build a natural gas pipeline from Siberia to Western Europe.

Prime Minister Pierre Elliott Trudeau even backhanded Pres. Ronald Reagan in public with a verbal shot at the Bonn, West Germany, summer summit. While the leaders were lining up for photographs, a reporter yelled a question at the president. Trudeau loudly advised the reporter to "ask Al"—a clear indication that, in Trudeau's opinion, then U.S. secretary of state Al Haig was the one who should answer, not the president. Yet on several occasions Trudeau took pains to downplay the differences between Canada and the U.S. In September, during a lengthy radio interview, he said the Reagan administration, like previous U.S. governments, understood Canadian problems and the difficulties of solving them. Trudeau blamed the world economic recession for exaggerating the difficulties and politicians

on both sides of the border for trying to protect their constituencies, even at the expense of the other nation.

The Economic Disagreement

No matter what the economic times, it would be difficult not to notice the difference between the right-wing Reagan administration and Trudeau's Liberal government, which had become almost the North American equivalent of what the Europeans call social democratic.

Reagan's policy was to lessen government involvement with the economy and with business. Trudeau and his senior ministers believed in a partnership between business, government, and labour, with government exerting considerable influence over business and competing with the private sector through a myriad of government-owned enterprises. Canada's national energy policy of 1980, for example, was theoretically designed to increase Canadian ownership over the oil and gas industry, but in fact it increased government control over the industry much more rapidly. Canadian control over the private sector of the industry went from 22.3 to 24.9% during 1981, while government involvement rose from 3.8 to 7.9%. In addition, complex government regulations allowed Ottawa to keep a tight rein on privately owned oil and gas companies.

During 1981 the national energy policy was the pet peeve of the Reagan administration because, in the U.S. view, it allowed Canadians to take over U.S. assets in Canada at fire-sale prices. In 1982 the Foreign Investment Review Agency (FIRA) replaced the energy situation as the aspect of Canadian economic policy most disliked by U.S. critics. Trudeau added salt to the wounds when he switched Marc Lalonde, architect of the national energy policy, from the energy portfolio to the key task of finance minister. Both Trudeau and Lalonde defended FIRA as a mechanism that did for Canada what other governments do by more devious means. On the surface, FIRA appeared to be something of a paper tiger. The agency is empowered to allow or disallow takeovers of Canadian enterprises by foreign investors. It can also prevent a foreign firm from selling assets in Canada to another foreign company. In 1979–80 FIRA approved 92% of the cases it decided, and in 1980–81 it approved 88% of takeovers worth Can$5,350,000,000.

Thomas d'Aquino, president of Canada's presti-

TED SPIEGEL—BLACK STAR

Acid rain, one of the thorny issues dividing Canada and the U.S., was responsible for damage to the Parliament Building in Ottawa.

gious Business Council on National Interests, said the major areas of foreign investor concern over FIRA centred around the fact that the agency could block sales of assets by one foreign owner to another, thus diminishing the value of holdings. FIRA also sometimes required foreign investors to buy Canadian, and the agency could take months to make some decisions, then rule without offering explanations.

The reluctance of foreign investors to struggle through the FIRA process, coupled with the international recession, cut off much foreign capital that might have come to Canada. The result was downward pressure on the Canadian dollar, requiring higher Canadian interest rates as a counterbalance. The federal deficit, estimated by the government to be in excess of $23.6 billion for fiscal 1982–83, as well as deficits on other levels of government, placed a terrible strain on the nation's capital resources, again pressuring interest rates upward. Further pressure came from the estimated $20 billion that left the country during 1981 and '82 to buy out foreign ownership of various companies. Canadian government leaders blamed high interest rates in the U.S. for high rates in Canada. Americans argued that economic nationalism and the huge government deficit were the real villains.

Acid Rain

As predicted by economists on both sides of the border, the economic disagreements were spilling over into other areas. Acid rain was the issue that took the spotlight in 1982. Thousands of lakes in both Canada and the U.S. were dying and hundreds were dead because of increased acidic content in the rain and snow. Coal-burning electrical generating stations and smelters like the giant Inco mill at Sudbury, Ont., spew out toxic waste, particularly sulfur dioxide. This mixes with the moisture in the upper atmosphere and falls to Earth as a mild acid. The acid kills aquatic life in lakes and was already affecting the growth of timber. The $10 billion-a-year forestry industry of eastern Canada was in danger.

Canada's environment minister, John Roberts, called acid rain the greatest problem between the U.S. and Canada and probably the most serious long-term problem facing Canada. Opinion polls showed that most Canadians were aware of the threat of acid rain and were concerned about it, while a far lower percentage of Americans realized the dangers. Canada was particularly vulnerable because the lakes in the Precambrian Shield, which underlies much of Canada, are granite-based and have no natural protection against increased acid content. Lakes with limestone-base rock are better able to withstand the pollution onslaught because the limestone tends to neutralize the acid.

In the late summer a joint study by the C. D. Howe Institute in Montreal and the Washington-based National Planning Association warned that the acid rain situation was rapidly reaching crisis proportions. The study reported that 50% of the acid rain falling in Canada came from the U.S., primarily from utility generating sites in the Tennessee Valley, while only 15% of U.S. acid rain came from Canadian sources. However, the largest acid rain producer on the continent was the Inco smelter.

President Reagan was slashing environmental budgets and had rated industrial efficiency higher than fighting pollution. Environment Minister Roberts pledged to cut Canadian acid-rain-producing emissions 50% by 1990 if the U.S. would do the same, but installation of the necessary equipment to clean stack gases would add 10% or more to utility bills in the U.S.

Like many of the disagreements between the two close neighbours and best friends, acid rain and the economic issue were subtly related to a basic difference in national philosophies. The U.S. was founded on the ideals of life, liberty, and the pursuit of happiness, and the rights of the individual are considered to be paramount. It has been said that Canadians would rather have peace, order, and good government, even if that means more government involvement in society, more restrictions on freedoms of the individual, and a value system that places security for the poor ahead of creating a "good climate" for the business community.

Pres. Ronald Reagan reviews the troops on his arrival in Barbados in April for a meeting with Caribbean leaders on his proposed Caribbean Basin Initiative.
WIDE WORLD

CARIBBEAN STATES

Antigua and Barbuda

During its first year of independence Antigua and Barbuda set about forging a major regional role for itself in the eastern Caribbean. It was particularly active in the generation of the Organization of East Caribbean States and at the Caribbean Community summit at Ocho Rios, Jamaica, in November 1982. Despite this high regional profile, Antigua remained economically depressed, although tourism, the economic mainstay, continued buoyant in contrast to the downward regional trend. A dormant oil refinery was refurbished, and this generated additional employment. Aid came from South Korea, Venezuela, and Brazil in addition to that received from traditional sources in the U.S., Canada, and the U.K. The U.S. retained three military bases on the island for which Antigua received substantial rents.

During the year a left-leaning opposition party made allegations of corruption against the government, which were strenuously denied. Politically the opposition was weakened by factionalism. In contrast, the ruling Antigua Labour Party maintained its strong national support under the leadership of Prime Minister Vere Bird.

The Bahamas

In a general election on June 10, 1982, Prime Minister Lynden O. Pindling and his Progressive Liberal Party (PLP) were again returned to office. The PLP won 32 of the 43 seats in the House of Assembly, while the main opposition Free National Movement won the other 11 seats. The left-wing Vanguard Party won only a few votes.

During the year divisions between the Bahamian and U.S. governments became public. Pindling criticized the U.S. for not extending the same tax concessions granted to companies holding conventions in Jamaica to such companies wishing to hold such affairs in The Bahamas. Also criticized was the fact that to benefit from certain aspects of the Caribbean Basin Initiative, The Bahamas would have to provide tax information on nationals and nonnationals, thereby breaching its own banking secrecy laws. In May the Getty Oil Co. was awarded licenses to explore for oil at the northeastern end of the Bahama chain. Joint Bahamian-U.S. operations against the smuggling of narcotics through The Bahamas to the U.S. mainland were mounted.

Barbados

During 1982 Barbados began to experience problems similar to those of other less developed Caribbean nations. A reduction in tourism, a decline in sugar production, and increasing regional trade restrictions all served to depress the economy. In addition to putting forward a strongly deflationary budget, the government decided to seek special standby credits of $33.8 million over a 20-month period beginning in October 1982.

Relations with Grenada remained poor, but the personal acrimony between Prime Minister J. M. G. ("Tom") Adams and Prime Minister Maurice Bishop of Grenada evidenced in 1981 did not reemerge. Substantially closer relations with Trinidad and Jamaica developed in the period preceding the Caribbean Community (Caricom) summit meeting in Jamaica in November. In April U.S. Pres. Ronald Reagan visited Barbados in an effort to draw attention to the U.S. Caribbean Basin Initiative.

Barbados continued efforts toward establishing a

joint coast guard and fisheries protection service among eastern Caribbean governments. An agreement on cooperation in security matters was signed in November.

Dominica

A number of those arrested during the two attempted coups of 1981 were brought to trial in 1982. Among those accused was the former prime minister Patrick John, but in a court judgment, which the government decided to appeal, he and three others were acquitted. In September Alexander J. McQuirter, former "grand wizard" of the Canadian Ku Klux Klan, was sentenced in Ontario to two years in prison for plotting to break the laws of another country, namely Dominica. An aftermath of the coup attempts was that Dominica's complex opposition politics again became confused, with the leaders of three parties that had split from the Dominica Labour Party again joining together.

Despite these traumas Dominica began to show the first real signs of growth. After having forcefully presented a case for financial assistance to the U.S. government, substantial funding was made available

U.S. Coast Guards arrested 16 men in boats in the Florida Keys in March and confiscated a store of arms. The men were allegedly set to overthrow the Duvalier regime in Haiti.

for a number of capital projects, including much-needed road reconstruction. During the year Prime Minister Eugenia Charles was able to announce the creation of some 3,500 additional jobs; 28 new light industries were attracted by the Industrial Development Corporation. Most surprising, considering the political upheavals and previous natural disasters, was a 70% increase in tourism during the first eight months of the year.

Grenada

Throughout 1982 Grenada maintained an economic and political course unique in the eastern Caribbean. With aid from the European Communities, Eastern Europe, and the Middle East, the government concentrated on improving basic infrastructure. Work continued on construction of an international airport with Cuban assistance.

Prime Minister Maurice Bishop came away from a visit to Moscow with agreements for substantial aid from the U.S.S.R., a new source of assistance. Other new sources were Libya, East Germany, and Bulgaria. Grenada was excluded from the U.S. Caribbean Basin Initiative. During the conflict in the South Atlantic between the U.K. and Argentina, Grenada was the only English-speaking Caribbean government to support the latter.

At the Caribbean Community (Caricom) summit meeting in November, the government came under increased pressure, from Jamaica and Barbados in particular, to hold elections and to free political detainees. It was announced during the summit that 28 political prisoners had been released.

Haiti

Pres. Jean-Claude Duvalier ordered several Cabinet reshuffles during 1982. The most significant changes involved Marc Bazin, a former World Bank official, who was appointed minister of finance following pressure from the U.S. and international financial institutions to carry out a campaign against corruption and financial mismanagement. Bazin took up the post in February but was dismissed in July after losing a power struggle with Duvalier's wife, Michèle Bennett. In the main, the changes favoured the political hard-liners.

A retrial was ordered in the case of Sylvio Claude, leader of the suspended opposition Christian Democratic Party, whose 15-year prison sentence was thus reduced to 6. In September he was released from prison, but in December he was reincarcerated. In January and March there were reports of unsuccessful invasion attempts by small bands of Haitian exiles.

Haiti's real gross domestic product fell by 1% in 1982 and by 2.1% in 1981. The decline was attributed to bad weather, which affected agricultural production and bauxite output. The International Monetary Fund approved a standby credit of $37 million in August. Bilateral and multilateral aid in 1982 was estimated at $140 million.

Jamaica

Though the Jamaican economy under Prime Minister Edward Seaga had shown positive growth during 1981, it was clear toward the end of 1982 that some of the government's forecasts had been too optimistic. Low world prices for bauxite, sugar, and bananas meant that the planned growth rate of 4% had to be scaled down.

There was some concern among government supporters about the introduction of a structural adjustment program aimed at generating export industries and the government's decision to take over the Exxon petroleum refinery and a local port operation. The opposition People's National Party remained divided, though it became clear that former prime minister Michael Manley was determined to see the party chart a more moderate course.

The special relationship between Prime Minister Seaga and U.S. Pres. Ronald Reagan continued to develop. Jamaica was the main Caribbean beneficiary of the U.S. Caribbean Basin Initiative, receiving a $50 million share. In November the island was host to the Caribbean Community (Caricom) summit meeting.

Saint Lucia

After the resignation of the St. Lucia Labour Party government in January 1982, an interim government was appointed until elections took place on May 3. The opposition United Workers' Party led by former prime minister John Compton was returned to power.

The political unrest of the 12 months preceding the election had resulted in a decline in tourism and a general lessening of economic activity, so that 1981 figures showed a negative growth rate. Compton's right-of-centre approach to the problem placed heavy emphasis on construction, tourism, and agriculture. But in spite of generous assistance from the U.S., the U.K., Canada, and others, by late 1982 the prime minister was warning that economic recovery would be slow. In a speech at the UN he indicated that St. Lucia would follow a truly nonaligned path but would continue to look for help from traditional Western friends.

Saint Vincent and the Grenadines

St. Vincent continued its slow if unspectacular development during 1982. In common with other eastern Caribbean islands, the country suffered a decline in tourism caused by recession in North America. To this problem was added that of the low value of the pound sterling against the U.S. dollar, to which the currency was tied. Export earnings from bananas fell substantially, and the problems in the industry were compounded by disease and concern over the future of the protected U.K. market for Caribbean bananas.

The government introduced a 3% tax on the gross profits of businesses, and in response the business community organized a strike. However, support for the tax measure on the part of most Vincentians meant that the trades had little local sympathy.

Trinidad and Tobago

Though Trinidad and Tobago continued during 1982 to have the most buoyant economy in the Caribbean, doubts were beginning to be expressed toward the end of the year about the decline in revenue from taxes on the oil industry. Reduced local oil production, the slump in the world market price for crude oil, and new tax concessions to stimulate exploration were all expected to reduce government revenue by up to TT$500 million (TT$2.409 = U.S. $1). Concern grew despite a current account surplus forecast at TT$1,478,000,000 for 1982 and foreign exchange reserves of TT$7.8 billion. State corporations were instructed to reduce losses, and new credit restrictions were introduced.

Prime Minister George Chambers adopted the somewhat remote day-to-day approach of his predecessor, Eric Williams. However, he sought a leading role within the Caribbean Community (Caricom). Aid funds, concessionary loans, and joint ventures were agreed upon with most Caricom nations.

At the Caricom summit conference in Jamaica in November, Chambers emerged as the single most influential figure, taking a strong line on maintaining relations with Grenada. Unlike most other nations in the region, Trinidad maintained relations with the U.S. that were formal rather than close, with the government expressing reservations about the U.S.-inspired Caribbean Basin Initiative.

CHEMISTRY

The ever narrowing gaps between organic chemistry, biochemistry, and molecular biology were emphasized with the announcement in October of the 1982 Nobel Prize for Chemistry. The award went to Aaron Klug of the University of Cambridge in England for his fundamental work on the application of electron microscopy to solving the structure of nucleic acids and protein complexes. This achievement in turn led to a better understanding of the structure and development of viruses and the mechanisms of protein synthesis in animal cells. (*See* Nobel Prizes.)

Chemists continued to improve their skill at building bigger and bigger molecules, but because of the growing variety of synthetic methods and reagents available, they had to rely increasingly on computer assistance. New computing systems allowed chemists to draw the structure of the desired compound on a graphics tablet, to which the computer responded with possible routes of synthesis, starting materials, and reaction conditions using its built-in library. Computer graphics could also provide a colour picture of molecular shape in three dimensions.

Among the many compounds of biological importance synthesized during the year were human parathyroid hormone and the antibiotic milbemycin β_3, which also acts as a potent insecticide. Particularly exciting was the successful culmination of a 20-year research effort, involving more than 100 Chinese scientists and led by Wang Debao in Shanghai, to make biologically active transfer RNA (tRNA), a replica of a vital molecule found in living cells. Responding to the genetic code, tRNA brings the correct amino acids into alignment alongside the ribosomes for assembly into proteins. Also fascinating was the news of successful clinical trials in the U.S. of a perfluorocarbon emulsion used as a short-term substitute for human blood. Such blood substitutes bind oxygen reversibly like hemoglobin, last much longer than natural blood, and do not need matching for blood type.

Also newsworthy was the report that on August 29 scientists at the Heavy Ion Research Laboratory (GSI) in Darmstadt, West Germany, made element 109. Led by Gottfried Munzenberg and Peter Armbruster, the team bombarded a bismuth-209 target with iron-58 nuclei for a week. Even though only one atom was made by this fusion technique and decay began five-thousandths of a second later, researchers were confident of their identification. The work gave encouragement to the collaborative project with the Lawrence Berkeley Laboratory in California attempting to make element 116.

Zeolites held research attention as newly developed systems of this class of materials offered addi-

Bronze cancer, which affects ancient bronze works, was halted in this 5th century BC Greek piece by advanced chemical techniques.

Aaron Klug of the University of Cambridge was awarded the 1982 Nobel Prize for Chemistry for his electron microscope studies of the structure of nucleic acids.

tional possibilities for commercial application. These crystalline aluminosilicates have a sievelike structure that can sift molecules of different sizes; act as an absorbent or dessicant, trapping water from a solution; and offer a high surface area for catalysis. During the year increased volumes of zeolites replaced phosphates in detergents, regarded by environmentalists as major contributors to the biological degradation of lakes and streams. One new application for zeolites was for a simple synthesis of ammonia, an important raw material for fertilizers. Ammonia (NH_3) is normally produced by reacting hydrogen (H_2) and nitrogen (N_2) gases at high temperatures and pressures over an iron oxide catalyst. Researchers led by Po-Lock Yue at the University of Bath in England made their ammonia by shining light on water containing a titanium-based zeolite through which nitrogen was being bubbled.

Research funding for techniques to separate water photochemically into oxygen and hydrogen remained high during the year, and announcements of "breakthroughs" occurred regularly. By midyear the emphasis had turned to developing improved electron relays. In a typical water-splitting system, light energy is trapped by a semiconductor or an organic molecule called a sensitizer. This process frees an electron, which is passed on through an electron relay and which, with the aid of a platinum-based catalyst, reduces the hydrogen in water to elemental hydrogen. The main research teams were being led by Michael Grätzel of the École Polytechnique in Lausanne, Switz., Melvin Calvin at the University of California at Berkeley, and Sir George Porter at the Royal Institution in London. In October, however, lesser known researchers from Texas A & M University skipped formal publication of their work by excitedly (and exaggeratedly, according to some) disclosing their new process at a press conference. Marek Szklarczyk and A. Q. Contractor used a solar cell with cheap silicon electrodes coated with a very thin layer of platinum to convert solar energy to hydrogen with an efficiency of about 10%.

Of the many advances in spectroscopy recorded during the year, worth noting was the discovery by Canadian researchers of the largest molecule ever detected in space. With 13 atoms and molecular weight of 147 daltons, the molecule having the formula $HC_{11}N$ was detected in a shell of dust and gas surrounding the star CW Leonis in the constellation Leo.

Among the newsworthy analytical studies of the year were an elemental analysis of rocks on the surface of Venus by X-ray fluorescence equipment on the Soviet Venera 13 spacecraft and, back home, an investigation using scanning electron microscopy and X-ray microanalysis of the way in which interactions between aluminum wiring and iron screws in residential electrical outlets cause overheating and failure. Analytical chemists helped determine the exact metallic composition and thus prevented the corrosion of two rare 5th-century BC Greek bronze statues found in 1972. Other workers showed that Claudian quadrantes were the purest copper coins of any Roman coins found to date. These studies—and the confirmation that the pigment used to colour a beautiful limestone and plaster bust of Queen Nefertiti, who reigned in Egypt in the middle of the 14th century BC, was indeed the blue silicate of copper and calcium known as Egyptian blue—were able to shed light on the remarkable skills of these ancient civilizations.

CHESS

Anatoly Karpov's easy victory over Viktor Korchnoi in the world championship match at Merano, Italy, in October 1981 obscured the importance of the international tournament at Tilburg in The Netherlands during the same month. In that event, which attracted all the world's strongest players except for Karpov and Korchnoi, the Soviet grand master Aleksandr Beljavsky finished first, half a point ahead of former world champion Tigran Petrosian.

The 49th Soviet championship tournament, held at Frunze in November and December, ended in a tie between Lev Psakhis and Garry Kasparov. The Soviet women's championship at Ivano-Frankovsk ended in a tie between the former world champion Nona Gaprindashvili and Nana Joseliani. Soviet grand master Viktor Kupreichikwas won the annual Hastings International Tournament, finishing one point ahead of former world champion Vassily Smyslov and British grand master Jonathan Speelman. The European junior championship, held at Groningen in The Netherlands, was won by a 17-year-old Danish player, Curt Hansen.

In an official international rating list published on Jan. 1, 1982, Karpov was again ranked first with 2,720 points. He was followed by Jan Timman (The Netherlands) 2,655, Korchnoi (stateless) 2,645, and Kasparov 2,640. The highest placed British player, John Nunn, had a score of 2,590, and the highest placed U.S. competitor was grand master Larry Christiansen with 2,585.

Among the major events of the year were the interzonals, from each of which two players qualified for the candidates matches due to take place in 1983. These, in turn, would decide who should challenge Karpov for the world championship in 1984. The first interzonal was held at Las Palmas (Spain) in July, and the two qualifiers were Zoltan Ribli (Hungary) and the 61-year-old former world champion Vassily Smyslov. Among those who failed to qualify were Petrosian and Timman.

World chess champion Anatoly Karpov of the Soviet Union played 15 challengers simultaneously at UNESCO headquarters in Paris in February.
WIDE WORLD

The second interzonal took place in August at Toluca in Mexico, and the qualifiers were Hungarian grand master Lajos Portisch and the Philippine grand master Eugenio Torre. In the third interzonal, at Moscow in September, Kasparov won easily and Beljavsky was the second qualifier. Those six would be joined in the candidates matches by the two finalists from previous years, Korchnoi and Robert Hübner of West Germany.

Two women's interzonal tournaments took place during the year. In the first, at Bad Kissingen, West Germany, the three qualifiers were Gaprindashvili, Tatiana Lemachko (Bulgaria), and Semyonova (U.S.S.R.). It was later announced that Lemachko had defected to a Western country. The second interzonal, held in Tbilisi, was won by two Soviet players, Margareta Muresan and Irina Levitina.

At the world junior championship held near Copenhagen in August, the Soviet player, Andrey Sokolov, was the winner. During the same month, the world championship for players under 16 took place at Guayaquil, Ecuador; the winner was Yevgeny Bareyev of the U.S.S.R. The British championship, held at Torquay in August, was won by Tony Miles. At the Lucerne (Switz.) Olympiad, with a record entry of 91 countries, the Soviet team finished first with 42½ points. Second was Czechoslovakia with 36, and the U.S. was third with 35½. In the women's competition the Soviet team won with 33 points, ahead of Romania with 30 and Hungary with 26.

CHILE

The year 1982 proved to be one of the most difficult and testing of Pres. Augusto Pinochet Ugarte's term in office, as Chile faced a deepening economic crisis. The high level of growth, which averaged 6.8% per year during the period 1976–81, declined markedly.

Gen. Augusto Pinochet of Chile spoke at a ceremony marking the ninth anniversary of the military overthrow of Pres. Salvador Allende.
UPI

Contributing to this setback were the worldwide recession, low copper prices, and what many considered to be overvaluation of the peso in the first half of the year.

On economic policy, President Pinochet had to maneuver with increasing care between the Chicago-school proponents of the free-market economy (blandos, or "wets") and the military nationalists (duros, or "hardliners"), who believed in greater state intervention. The decision on June 14 to devalue the peso from 39 to 46 to the U.S. dollar, followed on August 6 by the floating of the peso, marked a dramatic end to Chile's three-year fixed exchange-rate policy and was a victory for those who had proposed that the government should take a more active role in economic management.

No fewer than three Cabinet reshuffles took place in quick succession. The annual change at the end of 1981 was followed by new appointments on April 23 and again on August 30. In the August reshuffle Rolf Lüders, a former executive of the Banco Hipotecario and like his predecessor a monetarist, was named to the joint post of minister of finance and economy; Samuel Lira became minister of mines; and Vice-Adm. Patricio Carvajal was named minister of defense, his appointment to take effect on December 15.

In foreign policy the Chilean government continued to strengthen its relations with the West and was one of the few Latin-American supporters of the U.K. during its conflict with Argentina over the Falkland Islands. The long-standing dispute with Argentina over the three islands of Picton, Lennox, and Nueva in the Beagle Channel and their territorial waters remained unresolved despite mediation by Pope John Paul II. Finally, in September, after much deliberation and on condition that Chile promise not to take the matter to the International Court of Justice, Argentina extended the 1972 agreement, thus allowing for a peaceful settlement.

Repression continued during 1982 with little sign of any political liberalization; books could not be published without the government's prior authorization, and the "state of emergency" that gave the president the power to carry out arrests, restrict labour union activity, and expel dissidents from the country was renewed again in 1982. The murder in February of the trade union leader Tucapel Jiménez Alfarao, following a speech made at a press conference in which he called for the formation of a "common front" to oppose the government's economic policy, aroused the suspicions of many; more than 50 people were arrested at the funeral. The International League for Human Rights claimed that a total of 837 political arrests occurred in the first six months of 1982, compared with 614 during the same period in 1981. Jaime Castillo, the president of Chile's human rights commission, who had been exiled in 1981, was again refused entry to the country.

Overall prospects for the Chilean economy were improved by the floating of the peso, but many economists considered that the measure had come too late to have a major effect. Gross domestic product plummeted in 1982 but was expected to pick up in 1983. Exports in the nontraditional sector, such as fruit, forestry, and fish, were likely to improve, but the outlook for copper remained bleak because of low world demand. International reserves, standing at $3.1 billion in July 1982, were depleted. It was predicted that inflation, reduced from an annual rate of 31.2% in 1980 to 9.5% in 1981 and to the remarkably low level of 2.4% during the first seven months of 1982, would rise to reach double digits by the end of 1982. Midyear figures showed that 21% of the work force was unemployed, and as the year progressed the situation showed no sign of improvement.

CHINA

During 1982 the new pragmatist leadership, effectively headed by Deng Xiaoping (Teng Hsiao-p'ing), carried out several political and economic reforms, most notably the streamlining of the administrative structure to weed out incompetent and undesirable officials and the punishing of economic criminals to eliminate corruption. A revised constitution was adopted by the fifth session of the fifth National People's Congress (the nominal legislature) in December.

The internal struggle for power between pragmatists and ideologues (or moderates and radicals) continued, with the former in the lead. In January the party newspaper called for a major ideological campaign to broaden and strengthen support for Deng's policies and to win the confidence of the people. A nationwide anticorruption campaign, which had begun in the summer of 1981, became a principal focus of political activity in February. In a detailed directive, the party's ruling Politburo cited 82 senior officials and their children in thefts of state property, bribe taking, and serious abuse of party and government positions. It directed all party organizations to undertake measures to expose corrupt officials and called on the people to rise up against them.

The campaign against corruption was related to the effort to reduce China's huge government and party bureaucracy, which was announced by Premier Zhao Ziyang (Chao Tzu-yang) at the fourth session of the fifth National People's Congress in December 1981. On March 2 Zhao presented to the Standing Committee of the National People's Congress his detailed proposals for reducing the 98 existing government ministries, commissions, and agencies to 52 and cutting their staffs by one-third, or about 200,000 people. The committee approved Zhao's plan but decided to carry out the streamlining of the State Council by stages. In April Zhao reported on a further trimming, which reduced the number of ministers and vice-ministers from 505 to 167. It was not until May that an official announcement was made on the abolition of 11 posts of vice-premier; only two vice-premiers were retained: Wan

Premier Deng Xiaoping addressed the opening session of the Communist Party's 12th party congress in Beijing in September.

Li and Yao Yilin (Yao I-lin), both veteran economic planners and close allies of Deng.

On November 19 the government announced that Foreign Minister Huang Hua and Defense Minister Geng Biao (Keng Piao) had been replaced, respectively, by Wu Xueqian (Wu Hsüe-ch'ien) and Zhang Aiping (Chang Ai-p'ing), both supporters of Deng. Huang had just returned from the funeral of Soviet Pres. Leonid I. Brezhnev in Moscow, and his sudden dismissal was unexpected.

Since the founding of the People's Republic in 1949, China had had three constitutions, promulgated in 1954, 1975, and 1978, each reflecting the internal power struggle at the time. The Committee for the Revision, established in 1980, prepared and circulated the draft of a revised constitution for public discussion. It proposed a number of changes, notably reinstatement of the post of president/chairman of the republic. As approved by the National People's Congress on December 4, the new constitution also extended the list of guaranteed civil rights, established family limitation as a national duty, and limited most top government officials to two five-year terms of office. A Central Military Council was created to replace the party's Military Commission. Provision was made for the creation of "special administrative regions," a category perhaps intended to encompass such areas as Taiwan, Hong Kong, and Macao.

The 12th Communist Party congress, with 1,545 delegates and 145 alternates in attendance, opened on September 1 with an address by Deng. He reiterated the basic tasks set out for China as follows: to strive for national reunification, including the return

Emphasis continued to be placed by Chinese officials on development of light industry and especially of new lines of consumer goods.

of Taiwan; to combat foreign hegemonism or expansionism; and to intensify efforts on the Four Modernizations (agriculture, industry, science and technology, and defense).

On September 6 the congress approved a new party constitution, superseding the constitution of 1978. It marked a complete break with the radicalism of the late Chairman Mao. The post of chairman was abolished to ensure that no one person would ever dominate the party as Mao had for over three decades. Advisory commissions were created in both Beijing (Peking) and the provinces to take over party posts from veteran leaders, who would retire to advisory roles. Lifelong tenure for leading party officials was eliminated.

In the last two days of the session (September 10–11), the congress elected 210 members and 138 alternates to the party's Central Committee and 172 members to the newly created Central Advisory Commission, to which elderly members of the leadership were encouraged to retire. Over 60% of the Central Committee's members were new, and two-thirds were under 60. About a dozen veterans over 70 remained on the new Central Committee, as did Hua Guofeng (Hua Kuo-feng), 61, who had been Mao's designated heir but was forced out as party chairman in 1981.

At the first plenary session of the 12th Central Committee, held on September 12–13, Hua was dropped from the Politburo, now composed of 25 full and 3 alternate members. Only 9 were new, and most of the elderly veterans remained in their posts.

The Economy

At the opening session of the party congress, party chairman Hu Yaobang (Hu Yao-pang) reaffirmed that the policy of economic reform included extensive reliance on market forces to spur economic development and growth, as well as expected foreign investment and trade. He stressed that improving conditions for the people would take precedence over new industrial projects. Nevertheless, it was hoped that the combined value of China's industrial and agricultural output would be quadrupled to over $1.7 trillion by the year 2000.

Since 1979 light industry had received priority in a number of fields, and production of major consumer goods had risen substantially. During 1978–81 the output of TV sets increased more than tenfold and that of radios and cameras more than threefold, while production of bicycles, sewing machines, wristwatches, and wine more than doubled. In the agricultural sector, acreage sown to grain crops was reduced and China continued to import 12 million to 16 million tons of grain.

Total foreign investment in China over the past three years was estimated at $2.9 billion, including $90 million in joint ventures. In March China invited foreign business to invest $900 million to help develop 30 new industrial projects. The foreign trade deficit for 1981 was $5.8 million, compared with $247 million in 1980. According to official figures, China registered a trade surplus of $2.4 billion in the first six months of 1982, achieved by a surge in exports coupled with severe import cutbacks. In February the newly established China National Offshore Oil Corporation took full charge of cooperation with foreign companies in exploiting oil reserves on China's continental shelf. On September 19 it signed an exploration agreement with the Atlantic Richfield Co., the first U.S. oil concern to win China's permission to start drilling for oil offshore.

Foreign Affairs

Since the normalization of Sino-U.S. relations in 1979, China had considered Soviet hegemonism rather than capitalist imperialism to be the major threat to world peace and security. During U.S. Secretary of State Alexander Haig's tenure, Washington's efforts to draw Beijing into strategic cooperation with the U.S. had met with some response. However, China differed sharply with the U.S. over such major issues as the Palestinian question, the Falkland Islands crisis, and the presence of U.S. troops in South Korea. Signaling a chill, Beijing reverted to its characterization of the U.S. as a hegemonistic superpower, like the Soviet Union. It revived Mao's three-world concept in international relations, criticizing both superpowers of the first world, soliciting the cooperation of the industrial nations of Europe and Japan (the second world), and championing the cause of the third world. By equating the two superpowers as hegemonists, China increased its flexibility in moving between them.

The status of Taiwan continued to complicate relations with the U.S. Under the Taiwan Relations Act of 1981, the U.S. was committed to supplying Taiwan with defensive arms, but a request by Taiwan for advanced fighter aircraft to deter Chinese aggression led to a threat by Beijing to downgrade its diplomatic relations with Washington. In January 1982 the Reagan administration rejected Taipei's request for advanced fighters, and it restricted arms sales to Taiwan to $60 million in spare parts. To demonstrate Pres. Ronald Reagan's interest in good relations with China, Vice-Pres. George Bush arrived in Beijing on May 7 to hold wide-ranging talks. Finally, after nearly a year's negotiation, Washington and Beijing reached a compromise agreement in late summer. In a joint communiqué issued on August 17, the Reagan administration acceded to the Chinese position that the People's Republic is the sole legal government of China. It also agreed that future arms sales to Taiwan would not exceed past sales but would be contingent upon peaceful relations between Taiwan and the mainland.

Early in 1982 both Moscow and Beijing appeared to be seeking common ground to improve trade and cultural contacts. Following the exchange of trade missions, Moscow offered to renew the suspended border talks and to revive scientific and technical consultations. A group of Chinese economists went to Moscow for a three-month study of Soviet management methods, and the two countries signed an agreement that allowed China to export goods to Eastern Europe via the Trans-Siberian railway. On September 27 it was announced that China and the Soviet Union would hold a new series of high-level talks. Soviet Deputy Foreign Minister Leonid F. Ilyichev arrived in Beijing on October 3 to open negotiations with Chinese Vice-Foreign Minister Qian Qichen (Ch'ien Ch'i-ch'en). After heading the Chinese delegation to the funeral of President Brezhnev in Moscow, Foreign Minister Huang Hua met on Nov. 16 with his Soviet counterpart, Andrey A.

TASS/SOVFOTO

Chinese Foreign Minister Huang Hua met with Soviet Foreign Minister Andrey Gromyko in a step to ease tensions between the two nations.

Gromyko, in the highest-level talks between the two countries in 13 years.

To celebrate the tenth anniversary of the normalization of relations with Japan, Zhao paid an official visit to Japan from May 31 to June 5. In talks with Zhao, Prime Minister Zenko Suzuki reaffirmed that Japan would continue to cooperate with China in its economic development and promised to pay a return visit to China in September. Sino-Japanese relations were strained in July, however, when Japan's Education Ministry disclosed a revision of school textbooks that mitigated accounts of Japanese aggression in Asia before and during World War II. (*See* Japan.) Beijing was particularly incensed by the suggestion that the "rape of Nanking," in which over 300,000 were massacred, was warranted by Chinese resistance to Japan. After two months of acrimony, China accepted Japan's pledge that the revision would be changed. On September 26 Suzuki arrived in Beijing for a six-day official visit.

Bilateral trade between China and Japan exceeded $10 billion in 1981. A new long-term Sino-Japanese

China vigorously protested new Japanese history textbooks that glossed over the brutality of Japanese aggression in China in the 1930s and in World War II.

UPI

A cloud of dust enveloped downtown Cleveland, Ohio, after the Cuyahoga and Williamson buildings were demolished to make way for a new headquarters for Sohio.
UPI

trade agreement signed a few days before Suzuki's arrival entitled Japan to 8.6 million tons of Chinese crude oil annually, as well as lesser amounts of Chinese coal. During his visit Suzuki signed an agreement giving China another $250 million in low-interest government loans, bringing total credit from Japan to over $1 billion in the past few years.

Accompanied by Sir Edward Youde, the governor of Hong Kong, British Prime Minister Margaret Thatcher arrived in Beijing on September 22 for a five-day official visit that included talks on Hong Kong's future. Hong Kong Island and the Kowloon Peninsula had been ceded to Britain in perpetuity, but the greater part of Kowloon and the New Territories, accounting for 90% of the colony's land, were under a 99-year lease, due to expire in 1997. Meanwhile, Hong Kong had become an economic gateway to China, which currently earned about 40% of its foreign exchange through the colony. On September 24 Thatcher and Deng issued a joint statement in which they agreed to enter negotiations through diplomatic channels "with the common aim of maintaining the stability and prosperity of Hong Kong" in working out a transition for the colony.

CITIES AND URBAN AFFAIRS

A recession that would not yield was the dominant fact of life for the nation's cities in 1982. Unemployment on a scale not known since the Great Depression gripped nearly all major cities, straining the capacity of local and state authorities to care for the destitute at a time when the administration of Pres. Ronald Reagan was arguing that the role of the national government should be reduced.

Even the fast-growing cities of the so-called Sunbelt found themselves deeply affected by the economic downturn. In Houston, the fastest-growing major city in the country over the previous decade, the slump in oil prices forced the layoff of tens of thousands of oil-company workers. By October unemployment in Texas had reached 7.6%, not quite as high as the national average but higher than at any time in living memory in a state once thought to be the state of perpetual boom. Ironically, joblessness in Texas was higher than in Massachusetts, which appeared to have found a new economic niche with high-technology industries. Still, it was the older cities, principally in the Midwest, dependent on declining heavy industry, that suffered the most, with the highest unemployment rates recorded, in October, for Flint, Mich. (20.6%), Rockford, Ill. (20.5%), and Youngstown, Ohio (19.7%).

Despite the recession, President Reagan pushed forward with his conservative economic remedies for urban ills, though not with complete success. A leaked draft of the administration's first urban policy statement argued that decades of federal aid had actually contributed to the decline of American cities by making them overly dependent on government programs. It contended that these programs, for street repairs, transportation, and other needs, had transformed local officials from "bold leaders of self-reliant cities to wily stalkers of federal funds" and had reduced the motivation of the poor to seek employment in areas of better opportunity. The draft, along with other statements, brought widespread complaints that the Reagan administration was callous toward the poor and unfortunate. It was roundly denounced as an "abdication" of responsibility by the United States Conference of Mayors at their meeting in Minneapolis, Minn., in June. And, indeed, the president disavowed the language of the report. Nevertheless, the final version still portrayed the central government's role in urban affairs as a limited one, saying, "It is the policy of this administration to return maximum authority and discretion over the use of resources to state and local governments."

The chief vehicle for this philosophy was the conversion of many federal programs into consolidated block grants administered by the states rather than the federal government. In all, 56 programs were thus reorganized, and the full effect began to be felt in 1982; there was no universal agreement that the results were entirely positive. A study by the Conference of Mayors found that 70% of 55 cities surveyed believed they were not fairly represented in the means by which the states distributed the federal monies. This had undermined the ability of cities to cope with the recession, the mayors claimed. "In cities across the country, there is emerging a group that may be termed the 'new poor'—people who are losing their jobs, exhausting their financial resources, exhausting their unemployment benefits, and losing their homes," the report stated. "These people are coming to human service agencies for the first time."

Indeed, across the country there were reports of growing numbers of homeless, many of them middle-class people who had never been without work or known hardship before. Columbus, Ohio, for example, had to open its first public shelter. So-called "tent cities," ad hoc communities created by families forced to move to find work, had sprung up in many places, and many other families were reported to be sleeping in their cars and vans. Texas cities found themselves unable to cope with the large number of Northerners who came seeking jobs that did not exist. In Houston the Travelers Aid Association reported 1,000 requests a month from desperate people, up 40% from a year earlier. Dozens of people set up a squalid tent city in a state park on the San Jacinto River north of Houston. In Los Angeles 30,000 homeless people were reported to be living on the streets.

President Reagan resisted suggestions that the federal government had an obligation to provide for these people. Rather, he said, the solution lay in general economic improvement in cities, and to that end he advanced the notion of urban "enterprise zones" as a means of "reindustrializing" American cities. The idea was founded on the premise that businesses would choose to relocate in depressed areas if given tax relief and other financial incentives to do so. The plan, as presented to Congress, would give the federal Department of Housing and Urban Development the authority to designate up to 25 such zones annually from among 2,000 officially designated depressed neighbourhoods. Businesses locating in these zones would receive a 50% tax credit on wages paid to disadvantaged employees for a three-year period and reduced credits over the next four years. In addition, some of the areas would be designated "free trade zones," in which businesses would get relief from import duties. President Reagan said the concept was "based on utilizing the market to solve urban problems, relying primarily on private sector institutions. The idea is to create a productive, free-market environment in economical-

UPI

Loretta Thompson Glickman of Pasadena, California, was believed to be the first black woman mayor of a U.S. city of 100,000 or more population.

ly depressed areas by reducing taxes, regulations, and other government burdens on economic activity." The proposal opened to mixed reviews from both Democratic and some Republican lawmakers, and its fate was uncertain. Many mayors argued that its potential benefits were speculative inasmuch as tax incentives are only one factor in corporate decisions. They also complained that the administration's cuts in the Summer Youth Employment Program would have immediate adverse effects.

The mayors' leadership, meeting in New York in November, proposed a multibillion-dollar public works program to be financed by a five-cent- to ten-cent-a-gallon gasoline tax. The president agreed to a version of this proposal, urging a five-cent tax to be used for repair of highways and bridges—the newly rediscovered "infrastructure" of the economy—and for mass transit. Though he insisted it was not a jobs bill, the president said the program would create 320,000 jobs. Congress passed the bill on December 23 after breaking a filibuster by two conservative senators that had threatened to block its consideration by the lame-duck session.

Later in November President Reagan personally met with urban officials at the meeting of the National League of Cities in Los Angeles. His message was not a welcome one: "It is time to give up temporary band-aids and placebos and get on to the business of a real cure. All the government boondoggles in the world won't fix what's ailing us. The only way to cure our problems is to get the economy moving again." However, he was applauded for hinting that he would not attempt to eliminate the general revenue-sharing program under which localities receive federal dollars for their own use.

New Colombian Pres. Belisario Betancur and his wife, Helena, greeted crowds gathered in Bogotá to witness his swearing in.

COLOMBIA

In the congressional elections of March 14, 1982, the Liberals led by ex-president Alfonso López Michelsen gained 54 of the 114 seats in the Senate and 96 of the 199 seats in the House of Representatives, respectively 3 and 12 more seats than the Conservatives of Belisario Betancur Cuartas. Luis Carlos Galán Sarmiento's New Liberals, whose only victory was in the capital district, took 8 of the Senate seats and 18 in the lower house.

Despite his disappointing results, Galán withstood pressure from López Michelsen to withdraw his presidential candidacy, thus splitting the Liberal vote in the presidential election on May 30 and preventing that party from repeating its congressional victory. Betancur gained the presidency by obtaining 47% of the vote (3.2 million), while López Michelsen won 41% (2.8 million) and Galán more than 11%. Voters' interest was spurred by Galán's challenges both to traditional Liberalism and to the long-established two-party system and by Betancur's pledges for job creation and low-cost housing. Betancur's first Cabinet maintained the practice of sharing posts between the Conservatives (six ministers) and the Liberals (also six); the Defense Ministry was a military appointment.

One of Betancur's initial tasks was to curb guerrilla activity. In the final months of his predecessor's term of office, military actions failed to diminish the operations of the various groups, including those of the right-wing death squad, MAS, formed in late 1981 to attack left-wing activists. An amnesty was proposed in February by the Peace Commission, led by ex-president Carlos Lleras Restrepo and set up to bring the guerrillas back into normal political life. Despite a number of surrenders, the leaders of M-19 (one of the most active movements) insisted that the state of siege, in force since 1976, be lifted before they would lay down arms.

The Peace Commission made direct contact with M-19 in March, but its proposals for negotiation were rejected by the government, causing Lleras and four commissioners to resign. After the commission's collapse, Pres. Julio César Turbay Ayala announced early in June that the state of siege would be lifted on June 20 because the congressional and presidential elections had taken place without the threatened disruptions. M-19 immediately called a cease-fire. On taking office, President Betancur initiated moves to hold direct talks with the guerrillas and recalled the Peace Commission. The guerrilla movements responded positively, and in September M-19 declared that it would cease all armed activity.

Although Betancur proposed that Colombia join the nonaligned movement, he stated that relations with Cuba would not be renewed. However, closer inter-American cooperation would be sought. During U.S. Pres. Ronald Reagan's December visit to Bogotá, Betancur was unusually blunt in his criticism of U.S. policies that "discriminated" among Latin-American nations.

The major economic tasks facing Betancur included reducing the government deficit and arresting the decline experienced by many sectors. Growth in the gross domestic product was not expected to be above the 2.5% rate of 1981 (4% in 1980). The balance of trade was again weakened by falling prices for the country's exports.

COMMUNICATIONS

Compared with the previous year, technological advances in the telecommunications industry slowed in 1982. But it was just as well that they did so, as legislative and regulatory agencies spent the year scrambling to come up with new rules that could cope with the flood of modern communications technology. The need for new regulations was equally evident in the home, office, and factory.

In the home and office there was great potential competition for the television viewer's eye from two new sources of information. The first of these, the direct broadcasting services, send their signals from an orbiting Earth satellite to an antenna at the viewer's site. The second comprises the suppliers of data base information for interactive television services such as teletex and videotext. These allow users to gain access to computer data bases at a place and time of their own choosing.

For direct broadcasting from an Earth satellite to the home to be successful, the home system must be small in size and low in cost. The most important component of the system for accomplishing this is the semiconductor gallium arsenide. Ideal for use at the microwave frequencies that a satellite uses to beam television signals down to the Earth, gallium arsenide also allows the making of inexpensive, mass-produced receivers of such great sensitivity that an acceptably small antenna—about 3 ft (1 m) in diameter—can provide high-quality reception.

France, West Germany, and the U.S. were all active in the development of direct broadcasting. But major regulatory questions remained to be answered. For example, it would have to be decided which microwave frequencies would be used and where in space the satellites would be placed.

While work on direct broadcasting was under way, the proponents of teletex and videotext made progress toward their goal of placing suitably modified television sets in living rooms and offices throughout the world. With teletex a viewer can watch a screen that provides him, by means of text and graphics, with various kinds of information, such as the times and places of airline flights to Chicago.

Mere transmission of the contents of a data base requires nothing from a viewer except a desire to watch. In contrast, videotext, while also transmitting data base contents, calls for interactivity. The viewer is expected to stop the transmission if he or she is not interested. Moreover, viewers can request different kinds of information or focus on those specific aspects of the data base in which they are interested. This interactivity is accomplished by means of a handheld keypad or a full keyboard to send requests—usually over telephone lines—back to the information provider.

As of 1982 teletex and videotext services were more popular in Europe than in the U.S. and, indeed, originated there. There were problems in marketing the services at both locations since they often

This collapsible eight-foot antenna could pick up all 105 U.S. television channels carried by satellite. The whole outfit could be carried in a station wagon.
UPI

duplicated what was otherwise available.

Another problem for the new technology to overcome involved the two conflicting standards for the technical details necessary for providing the service. Thus, several European nations had their own approach, while the U.S. and the Canadians had another. Fortunately, while the standards were different, in practice advanced versions of both teletex and videotext could be made to conform to either or both of them.

During the year the U.S. government dropped two long-standing lawsuits, against AT&T and IBM. One expected result of this action was increased competition between the two firms in areas where computer and communications technology overlap.

As part of settling its business with the U.S. Department of Justice, AT&T agreed to divest itself of its operating companies and make other adjustments in the way it does business. But, most important for AT&T, a new unregulated subsidiary, American Bell, Inc., was allowed to be established. This new firm was expected to compete directly with IBM and other computer firms. Its first offering was a computer-communications package known as the Advanced Information System. It was designed for customers with a need for extensive, nationwide, computer-based communication and data processing services.

COMPUTERS

The permeation of computers into people's daily lives became increasingly noticeable during 1982. Indications of this trend included the appearance of coin-operated microcomputers at some libraries, the proliferation of automated teller machines at banks, and home banking ventures that allowed selected customers to link their home computers to a bank's computer centre in order to perform transactions.

Increasing numbers of stores began stocking personal computers on their shelves. Personalities such as comedian Bill Cosby touted the utility of these systems on television, and magazines and newspapers carried extensive advertising about them. In fact, the competition among vendors to sell personal computers for home use resulted in a brief price war when Texas Instruments offered a $100 rebate on its 99-4A home computer.

"Computer literacy," knowledge about the operation of and language of computers, was at the root of this growing fascination with the microcomputer. As adults encountered computers more frequently at their places of work and as children used computers as learning tools at school, computer literacy was quickly spreading through society and paving the way for more extensive use of computer-based systems and acceptance of computer technology. Legislation was introduced into Congress during 1982 that would allow computer vendors to make tax-deductible gifts of computers to educational institutions.

Although microcomputers had recently begun to

capture the interest of the general public, particularly for use at home, the vast majority of computer systems were used for business or scientific purposes and were much larger than personal computers. These larger systems are known as mainframes and minicomputers.

Somewhere in between the personal computer and the larger systems was the domain of the desktop computers. Shipments of these powerful, economical devices, priced at below $5,000, were projected to increase annually by about 45% for the next five years. These computers, built around 16-bit or 32-bit processors, allow managers and professionals to access information. Their greatest potential is for distributed processing applications, in which data are downloaded from a company's mainframe to the desktop system, there to be used by managers and professionals for applications specific to their jobs. The communication of data to and among these devices is usually accomplished through a local area network. Many versions of these networks, such as Wangnet from Wang Laboratories, Inc., were introduced during 1982 by the makers of desktop systems.

Although there were no major technological breakthroughs during the year, new technologies

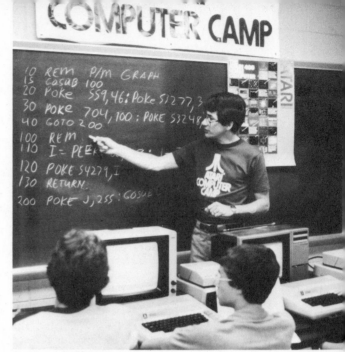

P.F. BENTLEY – PHOTOREPORTERS

Thousands of children attended summer computer camps to learn programming and problem-solving skills.

In Seattle, Washington, the Safeway supermarket chain experimented with selling low-priced personal computers from active displays.

GEOFF MANASSE / BUSINESS WEEK

such as artificial intelligence and a technique for "growing" computer circuitry in test tubes captured the imaginations of computer watchers. Artificial intelligence (AI) is a technique for programming computers to mimic human thought processes. Computers programmed in such a way are known as "expert" systems. They are designed to aid people in making judgments pertinent to their work specialties; an example is the diagnosis of diseases.

Scientists were also experimenting with growing biocircuits. Also called biochips, these were envisioned as a single layer of protein on top of glass and overlaid with metal tracks to form conventional two-dimensional chips. More complex versions consisted of enzymes used to organize a three-dimensional array of molecules that could fit into a human cell and direct pulses of current.

In September IBM introduced the 3084 computer. Almost twice as powerful as the firm's previous top-of-the-line model, it can process 26 million instructions per second. The 3084 consists of four smaller computers acting together as a single unit. A similar machine having almost as high a speed as the 3084 was unveiled earlier in the year by the Univac division of the Sperry Corp.

Electronic video games continued their rapid growth. Almost unknown five years earlier, they were plugged into television sets in approximately 15 million homes in the U.S. at the end of 1982. Revenues from these games, which operate with microprocessor chips, were estimated at $1.7 billion in 1982, and many industry observers believed that the figure would rise to $3 billion in 1983. In addition, electronic games in arcades enjoyed great popularity and profitability during the year.

Computers

Special Report: Logic Bombs and Other Crimes

by Donn B. Parker

Because of the speed and efficiency of computerized data processing, business and government have grown dependent on computer and data communication systems to carry on their activities. As the number of computers and the value of data stored and processed by them have increased, so too have reported cases of computers being involved in such crimes as fraud, theft, larceny, embezzlement, sabotage, espionage, extortion, and conspiracy. Therefore, computer crime and methods to prevent it have become important issues today.

Many definitions of computer crime are used for different purposes. One effective definition is any criminal activity in which a special knowledge of computer technology is essential for its perpetration, investigation, or prosecution. For example, a bank embezzlement accomplished by filling out standard forms for transferring funds among accounts could be a computer crime if the embezzler's knowledge of specific controls in the computer system was essential to avoid detection of the crime. Legal definitions of computer crime are being established in each jurisdiction that has a specific computer crime statute.

In computer crime, computers directly or indirectly play the role of objects, subjects, instruments, or symbols. A computer can be the object of an act when it or its content is attacked, damaged, or destroyed. For example, in five reported cases computers have been shot with guns. A computer can be the subject of a crime when it is the environment in which a criminal act occurs, such as the unauthorized change of personal credit data within a computer by altering a computer program, submitting false data or unauthorized instructions, or withholding authorized data. In addition, a computer can be a tool or an instrument in a computer crime when it is used to process data in an illegal act such as book-making, drug smuggling, or forging of investment statements. Finally, as a symbol in a crime, a fictitious computer could be claimed to be used in advertising of a fraudulent service. One or more of these four roles of computers have been found in all

of the more than 1,000 reported cases of computer abuse and crime.

Scope

Although many statistics have been reported on the extent of computer crime and its rate of increase, these statistics are not complete or representative of computer crime. As with other forms of business crime, acceptable mechanisms for collecting comprehensive or valid samples of incidence and loss data, even if a generally accepted definition of computer crime were in use, do not exist. The number and nature of cases that have been reported to criminal justice authorities, or prosecuted by them, has never been determined. Moreover, much suspected computer crime is thought not to be reported to the authorities.

Some analysts believe that the losses to business as a result of crime increase greatly when computers are used. In the Equity Funding insurance fraud in Los Angeles in 1973, for example, a computer was used to create 64,000 fake insurance policies and to disguise their false nature. A loss of $200 million was identified in the criminal trials, but it would be an estimated $2 billion if stockholders' losses were included. The largest recorded bank embezzlement, $21 million, occurred in Los Angeles in 1981. The embezzlers in the latter case had special knowledge about the controls in the targeted computer system. Crimes on this scale would be improbable without the concentration of assets and powerful processing capabilities within computer systems.

The Computer Criminal

For the most part, computer criminals exhibit the same characteristics as the traditional white-collar business criminal, although they more often are young people in the computer technology field. The challenge of winning the game plays a significant role during the perpetration of their crimes, but usually not as the initial motivating factor.

Known computer criminals have been mostly amateurs with no previous criminal history. In fact, they do not perceive themselves as criminals but only as problem solvers. They differentiate between doing harm to people, which they consider unacceptable and immoral, and doing harm to organizations or computers. These criminals are not necessarily exceptionally brilliant or even above average in intelligence, but they often have a capability for intense concentration on a narrow range of detailed activities.

The technical nature of computer crime limits its perpetration to those with sufficiently specialized skills, knowledge, access, and resources. This significantly reduces the number of people who are in a position to engage in business crime involving computers. Therefore, most known and reported computer crimes are perpetrated by trusted employees working in their authorized assignments. However, a growing number of mostly technically competent young people known as system hackers have been gaining access to computers through dial-up telephone connections from their own or their school's computer terminals. These are cases of technological trespassing into computers.

Few career criminals have been found among computer crime perpetrators. This situation is also changing, however, as an increasing number of prison inmates are taught electronic data processing. In addition, organized crime activities are often of such magnitude as to justify or require the use of computer technology for the same reasons that it is used in legitimate business activities.

Methods

The most common technical method in computer crime is false data entry, commonly referred to as data diddling. This technique of changing or withholding data intended for input to computers is least likely to be detected and can be performed by the largest number of people who might engage in business crime. Another basic method is called superzapping. It consists of using a computer program, usually referred to as a utility program, to change, copy, or destroy data and programs in a computer or on computer media. These utility programs do not come under the normal controls of the computer operating system and do not require the use of the more specialized and complex computer application programs that would normally be used to process the targeted data.

A third basic method used in computer crime is the Trojan horse technique of putting secret instructions into computer programs so that programs not only perform their normal functions but also execute the secret instructions so as to perpetrate an additional, unauthorized activity. For example, the program that debits and credits the accounts in a company's accounts payable and receivable system or in a bank's savings or checking system could be modified by inserting several computer instructions. Each time the program is run, these secret instructions would cause unauthorized transfers of credits and debits among the accounts being maintained by the computer program.

Using the Trojan horse method or a separate program, a computer criminal could transfer small amounts of money that might not be missed from each of a large number of accounts into one or more favoured accounts; from these the accumulated money could then be withdrawn by authorized methods. This is known as the salami technique—the taking of large numbers of small slices over a period of time to engage in a fraud not likely to be detected because few if any account holders would complain about small discrepancies. Another technique, known as the logic bomb, involves the use of control transfer and condition testing instructions in a program in order to cause fraudulent acts to be performed at a specific time when conditions are known to be opportune for the fraudulent purposes.

Safeguards

Because of the increasing number of powerful safeguards that can be built into and around computer systems, sophisticated computer crimes have become difficult to commit. Data stored in computer systems and computer media in a well-run computer centre are far safer than such data stored in human-readable form and used in noncomputerized business activities. Hundreds of highly cost-effective controls are routinely being used in computers to reduce the likelihood of business crime to a much greater extent than was ever possible in previous manual systems.

Technical controls are built into computers to create electronic "fences" that prevent or detect the attempts of people using computer programs from gaining access to the storage locations of other programs and data. Technical controls in the computer operating system also can limit the use of sensitive functions in the computer to only authorized persons or their computer programs. In addition, for computer systems accessed by many people from remote terminals, it is common to require knowledge of a secret password in order to gain access to the computer and subsequently to protected computer programs and data files.

At another level, business computer programs can be designed to prevent and detect any deviations from acceptable input data and activity within the computer system. For example, a wide range of controls that examine the reasonableness of data entering or leaving a computer system is available. These controls often trigger a special audit of any transaction that might exceed an acceptable or normal financial value.

One of the most powerful safeguards yet devised to protect data—cryptographic secret coding—is increasingly being used in computer systems and data communications. This technique scrambles or codes data and uses secret keys that must be employed for encoding and decoding the data.

CONGRESS, U.S.

The 97th Congress in 1982 continued the conservative approach to government mapped out by Pres. Ronald Reagan but took increasingly independent stands as the U.S. economy worsened and estimates of coming deficits mounted. Some additional cuts were made in welfare programs, but several administration initiatives for further cuts were rejected. Congress passed a $98.3 billion tax increase, and at the end of the session in December it also voted to increase the federal gasoline tax by five cents a gallon. Disputes over spending levels kept the legislators from adopting new appropriations bills for many government departments, and spending was continued in large part at current levels. The president's budget for the fiscal year 1983, ending in October 1983, was rejected, and a partial breakdown of the congressional budget process resulted. There was no action on several initiatives launched for conservative legislation on social issues and fiscal policy. An administration proposal for a balanced budget amendment to the Constitution was killed in the House. Measures to ban most abortions, virtually end court-ordered busing, and allow prayer in public schools also failed.

President Reagan proposed a budget of $757.6 billion, anticipated taxes of $666.1 billion, and projected a deficit of $91.5 billion. Both Republicans and Democrats assailed the deficit estimate as unrealistically low. In an effort to work out a modified budget, the president met with House Speaker Thomas O'Neill on Capitol Hill. The meeting failed to produce an agreement. Republican sources said the president offered reductions in defense spending, cancellation of $20 billion in requests for nondefense cuts, and $122 billion in taxes over three years. O'Neill charged that the only offer on taxes was to delay by three months the second 10% step in the scheduled three-year tax reduction, in return for which the president wanted $16.6 billion in Social Security reductions.

Speaker Thomas O'Neill (left) and Majority Leader Jim Wright led the fight to override Pres. Ronald Reagan's veto of a major funding bill.
UPI

At one point the House rejected all budget proposals before it. The budget that was finally adopted was evolved largely by the Senate Budget Committee. It envisioned outlays of $769.8 billion and revenues of $665.9 billion, for a deficit of $103.9 billion. Benefit programs such as Medicare, Medicaid, welfare, and nutrition were cut about $8 billion below what they would have been under existing law; discretionary programs such as education, housing, and health were cut by a roughly similar amount. Defense spending was cut $5.4 billion below the president's original request. The bill envisioned about $20 billion in new taxes.

Congress followed through with a so-called reconciliation bill to bring spending under the ceiling, as required by the budget procedure. The bill tightened spending for government pensions, veterans' benefits, food stamps, farm programs, and federal home loans. Savings were estimated at $3.3 billion for fiscal 1983, $13.3 billion over three years.

Soon afterward Congress passed a tax increase package that had the endorsement of the president. The bill, it was estimated, would raise $98.3 billion in three years, including $50 billion from business, $18 billion from individuals, and $21 billion from better compliance with tax laws. Businesses lost the right to sell deductible tax losses to other companies and to speed up recovery of assets through accelerated depreciation schedules. For individuals the tax on cigarettes was doubled to 16 cents effective Jan. 1, 1983. The tax on telephone service was raised from 1 to 3% in 1983 and would drop to zero after 1985. The tax on airplane tickets was increased from 5 to 8%, and an extra $3 fee was reimposed for overseas flights. Tax deductions for medical expenses and casualty losses were tightened. Restaurants with more than ten employees were required to report estimates of employee tips. Penalties for nonpayment of taxes were increased, and a 10% withholding tax on virtually all dividends and interest was imposed as of July 1, 1983.

Caps for Medicare payments to hospitals were extended and expanded, and premium rates were increased slightly. Health maintenance services and hospices for terminally ill patients were made eligible for Medicare payments. Some rules for Medicaid, Aid to Families with Dependent Children, and supplemental Social Security benefits were tightened. The Medicaid, Medicare, and welfare reductions totaled an estimated $17.5 billion.

Unemployment benefits were extended for up to ten weeks in states with the highest unemployment rates. Unemployment insurance taxes were raised, and the income level at which unemployment benefits become taxable was lowered. At the end of the session up to six weeks more of benefits were added, bringing the maximum up to 55 weeks for states with the highest unemployment.

The federal debt limit was increased from $1,080,000,000,000 to $1,143,000,000,000 and later to $1,290,000,000,000. The temporary increase in the debt limit is a formality needed to continue the government's borrowing authority.

Congress and the White House fought a continuing battle over extra appropriations in 1982. Early in the year the president vetoed two supplemental appropriations bills that he described as too high; he then signed a bill that contained $5.4 billion in new spending authority and canceled $5.8 billion in previous appropriations. Included were $2.4 billion for sewer construction, $1.3 billion for student loans, and $1 billion for food stamps. A $3 billion program to subsidize mortgage interest for new homes was deleted after the second veto.

Later in the year Congress overrode a veto of a second 1982 supplementary appropriations bill for $14.1 billion that the president described as a "budget buster"—a term the majority rejected because the total was $1.3 billion lower than the original presidential requests. Included were $211 million for community service jobs for the elderly, $217 million for aid to college students, and $148 million for education of handicapped children. In all, Congress cut $2.1 billion from the president's defense requests and added nearly $1 billion more than he wanted for social programs.

Meanwhile, work on appropriations for fiscal 1983 was hopelessly stalled. In September the president called on Congress to pass a stopgap money bill before it adjourned in October and to return after the November elections to complete work on the regular appropriations. A stopgap bill continuing spending at 1982 levels or lower levels recommended by congressional finance committees was passed on October 1 and signed October 2. This left the government technically without money for two days, but no important disruptions were reported. The bill provided money through December 17. In the postelection session Congress passed a catchall continuing resolution that Reagan said completed work on the 1983 budget in "favorable fashion" since it generally followed previous budget resolutions. The House had inserted a $5.4 billion public works jobs program in the money bill; the Senate had included a $1.2 billion jobs program. Under the threat of a presidential veto, both proposals were dropped from the bill.

An administration plan for a "dense pack" of 100 MX intercontinental missiles in Wyoming ran into heavy congressional opposition, and the continuing resolution denied a request for $988 million to produce the first five MX missiles. It allowed $1,734,000,000 for research and development of the MX, $215 million that could be used for basing projects without any strings, and an extra $560 million that could be used for engineering development of basing only after Congress had approved a basing system. Congress also denied $493.3 million for production of Pershing II missiles scheduled to be deployed in Europe in 1983. The conference committee said it would reconsider the request once the missile had been successfully flight tested.

In all, the continuing resolution allocated $232 billion for defense, in addition to funds for a military pay raise. This was $17.6 billion less than the president sought, but except for the two missile programs, major elements of his proposed weapons buildup survived almost intact. Included were funds for two nuclear-powered aircraft carriers, development of the B-1 bomber, a Trident submarine, two Los Angeles-class attack submarines, and reactivation of the battleship "Iowa." Earlier in the year the House defeated a resolution calling for negotiation of a U.S.-Soviet freeze on nuclear weapons. The vote was 204–202.

Another thorny issue in the bill was congressional pay. It was settled by allowing House members a 15% pay increase. Senators' salaries were kept at $60,662.50, but the senators were allowed to earn unlimited amounts from such things as legal fees, speeches, and writings. Raises of up to 15% also were allowed for about 32,000 high-ranking government officials; pay for members of the Cabinet went from $69,630 to $80,100.

The Clinch River breeder nuclear reactor project in Tennessee was allocated $181 million, less than the administration had sought but enough to continue engineering work and site preparation. Congress forbade major construction or contracts for major facilities during the fiscal year. In a separate bill Congress set a schedule for locating and building nuclear waste storage by the end of the century. Meanwhile, it ordered establishment of temporary storage of spent nuclear fuel from reactors that had exhausted their own storage capacity.

An omnibus anticrime bill was pocket-vetoed by President Reagan in December because it would have created a Cabinet-level "drug czar" post and a separate bureaucracy to conduct federal action against the illicit drug trade. No action was taken on administration proposals for stiffer laws on bail reforms, fines, prison terms, and parole.

After an angry battle to stop a conservative filibuster, the Senate passed a five-cent-a-gallon gasoline tax increase and adjourned on December 23. The House had passed the measure, designed to raise $71.3 billion for highway and transit systems over four years, and adjourned two days earlier. The tax on gasoline and diesel fuel was scheduled to increase from four cents to nine cents a gallon starting April 1, 1983. Gasohol was exempted from five cents of the tax. The bill also provided higher road-use fees for heavy trucks. The maximum was scheduled to go from $240 to $1,600 in 1984 and to $1,900 by 1988. Taxes on auto tires and other light-weight tires were repealed effective in 1984, but a graduated scale of taxes was imposed on heavy truck tires. Four cents of the new gasoline tax was earmarked for highways and one cent for mass transit—the first major allocation of Highway Trust Fund money for mass transit. While most of the money was designated for repair of existing highways and bridges, $4 billion a year was set aside for new construction on the

Interstate Highway System. Longer, heavier trucks—up from 73,280 to 80,000 lb—were allowed on Interstate and certain primary highways. Missouri, Arkansas, and Illinois had imposed lower limits. Operating subsidies for mass transit were limited to 80% of the 1982 level and guaranteed for four years. President Reagan had sought to have the subsidies cut one-third immediately and eliminated in 1985.

The House laid the groundwork for a constitutional confrontation with the president when it cited Anne Gorsuch, head of the Environmental Protection Agency (EPA), for contempt. At issue was Gorsuch's refusal to allow congressional access to certain documents relating to enforcement of hazardous waste laws. The EPA said Reagan had instructed her to refuse on grounds of executive privilege. That doctrine was most recently tested when the Supreme Court, in a somewhat different case, ordered Richard Nixon to turn over tapes of his Oval Office conversations to Congress. The Gorsuch case was complicated by a refusal of the Justice Department to prosecute the contempt citation.

The dairy price support program was tightened; tobacco growers were required to repay the government for any losses sustained in their price support program; and a sweeping ban was enacted against embargoes that interfered with existing contracts for grain exports, except in cases of war and national emergency. Rules enacted in 1902 limiting the amount of water available to Western farmers from federal reclamation projects were relaxed. The Endangered Species Act was renewed for three years after deletion of the administration's proposal that economic factors be considered in decisions on whether a species should be protected.

Congress allocated $350 million for emergency aid as part of President Reagan's Caribbean Basin Initiative. It failed to act on his proposal to ease trade barriers for Caribbean nations and never gave serious consideration to his request for tax benefits for U.S. companies investing in the region.

Enforcement sections of the 1965 Voting Rights

Act were renewed, for 25 years in the case of a number of requirements that had been scheduled to expire on Aug. 6, 1982. One section that was extended requires that 9 states and parts of 22 others get prior approval from the Justice Department for changes in election laws. However, beginning in 1984, government units would be allowed to escape this provision if they could prove to a three-judge panel in the District of Columbia that they had had a clean voting rights record for the previous ten years. Private parties were allowed to prove voting rights violations in lawsuits if they could show that a practice had resulted in discrimination. The administration had wanted the standard to be intent to discriminate, a much more difficult thing to prove. A requirement that some areas must provide bilingual election materials was extended to 1992. This provision had been scheduled to expire in 1985.

Sen. Harrison Williams, Jr., convicted of bribery in the Abscam scandals, resigned from the Senate on March 11, just before it was scheduled to vote on his expulsion for misconduct. He was the fifth person in the history of the Senate to resign after charges of misconduct and the first since 1922, when Sen. Truman Newberry (Rep., Mich.) quit while facing expulsion proceedings on charges of excessive campaign spending.

Manufacturers were given tax credits for development of so-called orphan drugs used to treat rare diseases and were given exclusive rights for seven years on marketing such drugs if they were not patentable. The bill was intended to make drugs available that otherwise would not be produced. Manufacturers estimated that sales of such drugs would amount to $3 million to $5 million a year; costs for tests needed for federal approval were estimated at $70 million.

In other congressional actions, banks and savings and loans associations were allowed to set up new kinds of federally insured accounts that would be competitive with money market funds. A ban on oil and gas leases in federal wilderness areas or areas being considered for wilderness status was extended to Sept. 30, 1983. Federal agencies were given the right to use private credit bureaus and bill collectors to collect from delinquent borrowers.

The assumption of existing home mortgages by new buyers was limited when Congress overrode state bans on due-on-sale clauses. These required home owners to pay off existing mortgages when they sold their property. Without the due-on-sale provisions, owners were able to transfer existing low-interest mortgages to buyers as part of sales agreements, depriving lenders of the opportunity to finance sales at current interest rates.

People whose Social Security disability benefits had been canceled were allowed to keep on collecting the benefits while they appealed cutoffs. A bill was passed to relax regulation of bus companies, making it easier for firms to start service, expand operations, or drop unprofitable routes.

BENSON © 1982 – THE ARIZONA REPUBLIC

Members of the Congress of the United States

1st Session, 98th Congress*

THE SENATE

President of the Senate: George Bush

State	Senator	Current Service Began	Current Term Expires	State	Senator	Current Service Began	Current Term Expires
Ala.	Howell Heflin (D)	1979	1985	Mont.	John Melcher (D)	1977	1989
	Jeremiah Denton (R)	1981	1987		Max Baucus (D)	1978	1985
Alaska	Ted Stevens (R)	1968	1985	Neb.	Edward Zorinsky (D)	1977	1989
	Frank H. Murkowski (R)	1981	1987		J. James Exon (D)	1979	1985
Ariz.	Barry Goldwater (R)	1969	1987	Nev.	Paul Laxalt (R)	1974	1987
	Dennis DeConcini (D)	1977	1989		Chic Hecht (R)	1983	1989
Ark.	Dale Bumpers (D)	1975	1987	N.H.	Gordon J. Humphrey (R)	1979	1985
	David Pryor (D)	1979	1985		Warren Rudman (R)	1980	1987
Calif.	Alan Cranston (D)	1969	1987	N.J.	Bill Bradley (D)	1979	1985
	Pete Wilson (R)	1983	1989		Frank R. Lautenberg (D)	1983	1989
Colo.	Gary W. Hart (D)	1975	1987	N.M.	Pete V. Domenici (R)	1973	1985
	William L. Armstrong (R)	1979	1985		Jeff Bingaman (D)	1983	1989
Conn.	Lowell P. Weicker, Jr. (R)	1971	1989	N.Y.	Daniel P. Moynihan (D)	1977	1989
	Christopher J. Dodd (D)	1981	1987		Alfonse M. D'Amato (R)	1981	1987
Del.	William V. Roth, Jr. (R)	1971	1989	N.C.	Jesse A. Helms (R)	1973	1985
	Joseph R. Biden, Jr. (D)	1973	1985		John P. East (R)	1981	1987
Fla.	Lawton Chiles (D)	1971	1989	N.D.	Quentin N. Burdick (D)	1960	1989
	Paula Hawkins (R)	1981	1987		Mark Andrews (R)	1981	1987
Ga.	Samuel A. Nunn (D)	1972	1985	Ohio	John H. Glenn, Jr. (D)	1974	1987
	Mack Mattingly (R)	1981	1987		Howard M. Metzenbaum (D)	1977	1989
Hawaii	Daniel K. Inouye (D)	1963	1987	Okla.	David L. Boren (D)	1979	1985
	Spark M. Matsunaga (D)	1977	1989		Don Nickles (R)	1981	1987
Idaho	James A. McClure (R)	1973	1985	Ore.	Mark O. Hatfield (R)	1967	1985
	Steven D. Symms (R)	1981	1987		Bob Packwood (R)	1969	1987
Ill.	Charles H. Percy (R)	1967	1985	Pa.	H. John Heinz, III (R)	1977	1989
	Alan J. Dixon (D)	1981	1987		Arlen Specter (R)	1981	1987
Ind.	Richard G. Lugar (R)	1977	1989	R.I.	Claiborne Pell (D)	1961	1985
	Dan Quayle (R)	1981	1987		John H. Chafee (R)	1977	1989
Iowa	Roger W. Jepsen (R)	1979	1985	S.C.	Strom Thurmond (R)	1956	1985
	Charles E. Grassley (R)	1981	1987		Ernest F. Hollings (D)	1966	1987
Kan.	Bob Dole (R)	1969	1987	S.D.	Larry Pressler (R)	1979	1985
	Nancy Landon Kassebaum (R)	1978	1985		James Abdnor (R)	1981	1987
Ky.	Walter (Dee) Huddleston (D)	1973	1985	Tenn.	Howard H. Baker, Jr. (R)	1967	1985
	Wendell H. Ford (D)	1974	1987		James R. Sasser (D)	1977	1989
La.	Russell B. Long (D)	1948	1987	Texas	John G. Tower (R)	1961	1985
	J. Bennett Johnston, Jr. (D)	1972	1985		Lloyd M. Bentsen (D)	1971	1989
Maine	William S. Cohen (R)	1979	1985	Utah	Jake Garn (R)	1974	1987
	George J. Mitchell (D)	1980	1989		Orrin G. Hatch (R)	1977	1989
Md.	Charles McC. Mathias, Jr. (R)	1969	1987	Vt.	Robert T. Stafford (R)	1971	1989
	Paul S. Sarbanes (D)	1977	1989		Patrick J. Leahy (D)	1975	1987
Mass.	Edward M. Kennedy (D)	1962	1989	Va.	John W. Warner (R)	1978	1985
	Paul E. Tsongas (D)	1979	1985		Paul S. Trible, Jr. (R)	1983	1989
Mich.	Donald W. Riegle, Jr. (D)	1977	1989	Wash.	Henry M. Jackson (D)	1953	1989
	Carl Levin (D)	1979	1985		Slade Gorton (R)	1981	1987
Minn.	David Durenberger (R)	1978	1989	W.Va.	Jennings Randolph (D)	1958	1985
	Rudy Boschwitz (R)	1979	1985		Robert C. Byrd (D)	1959	1989
Miss.	John C. Stennis (D)	1947	1989	Wis.	William Proxmire (D)	1957	1989
	Thad Cochran (R)	1978	1985		Robert W. Kasten, Jr. (R)	1981	1987
Mo.	Thomas F. Eagleton (D)	1968	1987	Wyo.	Malcolm Wallop (R)	1977	1989
	John C. Danforth (R)	1977	1989		Alan K. Simpson (R)	1979	1985

* Convened January 1983.

THE HOUSE OF REPRESENTATIVES*

Speaker of the House: Thomas P. O'Neill, Jr.

Alabama
Jack Edwards, 1 (R)
William L. Dickinson, 2 (R)
Bill Nichols, 3 (D)
Tom Bevill, 4 (D)
Ronnie G. Flippo, 5 (D)
Ben Erdreich, 6 (D)
Richard C. Shelby, 7 (D)

Alaska
Donald E. Young (R)

American Samoa
Fofo I. F. Sunia (D)†

Arizona
John McCain, 1 (R)
Morris K. Udall, 2 (D)
Bob Stump, 3 (D)
Eldon D. Rudd, 4 (R)
James F. McNulty, Jr., 5 (D)

Arkansas
Bill Alexander, 1 (D)
Ed Bethune, 2 (R)
John P. Hammerschmidt, 3 (R)
Beryl F. Anthony, 4 (D)

California
Douglas H. Bosco, 1 (D)
Eugene Chappie, 2 (R)
Robert T. Matsui, 3 (D)
Vic Fazio, 4 (D)
Phillip Burton, 5 (D)
Barbara Boxer, 6 (D)
George Miller, 7 (D)
Ronald V. Dellums, 8 (D)
Fortney H. (Pete) Stark, 9 (D)
Don Edwards, 10 (D)
Tom Lantos, 11 (D)
Ed Zschau, 12 (R)
Norman Y. Mineta, 13 (D)
Norman D. Shumway, 14 (R)
Tony Coelho, 15 (D)
Leon E. Panetta, 16 (D)
Charles (Chip) Pashayan, Jr., 17 (R)
Richard H. Lehman, 18 (D)
Robert J. Lagomarsino, 19 (R)
William M. Thomas, 20 (R)
Bobbi Fiedler, 21 (R)
Carlos J. Moorhead, 22 (R)
Anthony C. Beilenson, 23 (D)
Henry A. Waxman, 24 (D)
Edward R. Roybal, 25 (D)
Howard L. Berman, 26 (D)
Mel Levine, 27 (D)
Julian C. Dixon, 28 (D)
Augustus F. Hawkins, 29 (D)
Matthew G. Martinez, 30 (D)
Mervyn M. Dymally, 31 (D)
Glenn M. Anderson, 32 (D)
David Dreier, 33 (R)
Esteban Edward Torres, 34 (D)
Jerry Lewis, 35 (R)
George E. Brown, Jr., 36 (D)
Alfred A. McCandless, 37 (R)
Jerry M. Patterson, 38 (D)
William E. Dannemeyer, 39 (R)

Robert E. Badham, 40 (R)
Bill Lowery, 41 (R)
Dan Lungren, 42 (R)
Ronald C. Packard, 43 (R)
Jim Bates, 44 (D)
Duncan Hunter, 45 (R)

Colorado
Patricia Schroeder, 1 (D)
Timothy E. Wirth, 2 (D)
Ray Kogovsek, 3 (D)
Hank Brown, 4 (R)
Ken Kramer, 5 (R)
vacancy, 6

Connecticut
Barbara B. Kennelly, 1 (D)
Samuel Gejdenson, 2 (D)
Bruce A. Morrison, 3 (D)
Stewart B. McKinney, 4 (R)
William R. Ratchford, 5 (D)
Nancy L. Johnson, 6 (R)

Delaware
Thomas R. Carper (D)

District of Columbia
Walter E. Fauntroy (D)†

Florida
Earl D. Hutto, 1 (D)
Don Fuqua, 2 (D)
Charles E. Bennett, 3 (D)
Bill Chappell, Jr., 4 (D)
Bill McCollum, 5 (R)
Buddy MacKay, 6 (D)
Sam M. Gibbons, 7 (D)
C. W. (Bill) Young, 8 (R)
Michael Bilirakis, 9 (R)
Andy Ireland, 10 (D)
Bill Nelson, 11 (D)
Tom Lewis, 12 (R)
Connie Mack, 13 (R)
Dan Mica, 14 (D)
E. Clay Shaw, Jr., 15 (R)
Lawrence J. Smith, 16 (D)
William Lehman, 17 (D)
Claude Pepper, 18 (D)
Dante B. Fascell, 19 (D)

Georgia
Robert Lindsay Thomas, 1 (D)
Charles F. Hatcher, 2 (D)
Richard Ray, 3 (D)
Elliott H. Levitas, 4 (D)
Wyche Fowler, Jr., 5 (D)
Newt Gingrich, 6 (R)
Lawrence P. McDonald, 7 (D)
J. Roy Rowland, 8 (D)
Ed Jenkins, 9 (D)
Doug Barnard, 10 (D)

Guam
Antonio Borja Won Pat (D)†

Hawaii
Cecil Heftel, 1 (D)
Daniel Akaka, 2 (D)

Idaho
Larry Craig, 1 (R)
George V. Hansen, 2 (R)

Illinois
Harold Washington, 1 (D)

Gus Savage, 2 (D)
Martin A. Russo, 3 (D)
George M. O'Brien, 4 (R)
William O. Lipinski, 5 (D)
Henry J. Hyde, 6 (R)
Cardiss Collins, 7 (D)
Dan Rostenkowski, 8 (D)
Sidney R. Yates, 9 (D)
John E. Porter, 10 (R)
Frank Annunzio, 11 (D)
Philip M. Crane, 12 (R)
John N. Erlenborn, 13 (R)
Tom Corcoran, 14 (R)
Edward R. Madigan, 15 (R)
Lynn M. Martin, 16 (R)
Lane Evans, 17 (D)
Robert H. Michel, 18 (R)
Daniel B. Crane, 19 (R)
Richard J. Durbin, 20 (D)
Melvin Price, 21 (D)
Paul Simon, 22 (D)

Indiana
Katie Hall, 1 (D)
Philip R. Sharp, 2 (D)
John P. Hiler, 3 (R)
Daniel R. Coats, 4 (R)
Elwood Hillis, 5 (R)
Dan Burton, 6 (R)
John T. Myers, 7 (R)
Frank McCloskey, 8 (D)
Lee H. Hamilton, 9 (D)
Andrew Jacobs, Jr., 10 (D)

Iowa
James A. S. Leach, 1 (R)
Tom Tauke, 2 (R)
Cooper Evans, 3 (R)
Neal Smith, 4 (D)
Tom Harkin, 5 (D)
Berkley Bedell, 6 (D)

Kansas
Pat Roberts, 1 (R)
Jim Slattery, 2 (D)
Larry Winn, Jr., 3 (R)
Dan Glickman, 4 (D)
Robert Whittaker, 5 (R)

Kentucky
Carroll Hubbard, Jr., 1 (D)
William H. Natcher, 2 (D)
Romano L. Mazzoli, 3 (D)
M. G. (Gene) Snyder, 4 (R)
Harold Rogers, 5 (R)
Larry J. Hopkins, 6 (R)
Carl D. Perkins, 7 (D)

Louisiana
Bob Livingston, 1 (R)
Lindy Boggs, 2 (D)
W. J. (Billy) Tauzin, 3 (D)
Buddy Roemer, 4 (D)
Jerry Huckaby, 5 (D)
W. Henson Moore III, 6 (R)
John B. Breaux, 7 (D)
Gillis W. Long, 8 (D)

Maine
John R. McKernan, Jr., 1 (R)
Olympia J. Snowe, 2 (R)

Maryland
Roy Dyson, 1 (D)

Clarence D. Long, 2 (D)
Barbara A. Mikulski, 3 (D)
Marjorie S. Holt, 4 (R)
Steny H. Hoyer, 5 (D)
Beverly Byron, 6 (D)
Parren J. Mitchell, 7 (D)
Michael D. Barnes, 8 (D)

Massachusetts
Silvio O. Conte, 1 (R)
Edward P. Boland, 2 (D)
Joseph D. Early, 3 (D)
Barney Frank, 4 (D)
James M. Shannon, 5 (D)
Nicholas Mavroules, 6 (D)
Edward J. Markey, 7 (D)
Thomas P. O'Neill, Jr., 8 (D)
John Joseph Moakley, 9 (D)
Gerry E. Studds, 10 (D)
Brian J. Donnelly, 11 (D)

Michigan
John Conyers, Jr., 1 (D)
Carl D. Pursell, 2 (R)
Howard Wolpe, 3 (D)
Mark D. Siljander, 4 (R)
Harold S. Sawyer, 5 (R)
Bob Carr, 6 (D)
Dale E. Kildee, 7 (D)
Bob Traxler, 8 (D)
Guy Vander Jagt, 9 (R)
Donald J. Albosta, 10 (D)
Robert W. Davis, 11 (R)
David E. Bonior, 12 (D)
George W. Crockett, 13 (D)
Dennis M. Hertel, 14 (D)
William D. Ford, 15 (D)
John D. Dingell, 16 (D)
Sander M. Levin, 17 (D)
William S. Broomfield, 18 (R)

Minnesota
Timothy J. Penny, 1 (D)
Vin Weber, 2 (R)
Bill Frenzel, 3 (R)
Bruce F. Vento, 4 (D)
Martin Olav Sabo, 5 (D)
Gerry Sikorski, 6 (D)
Arlan Stangeland, 7 (R)
James L. Oberstar, 8 (D)

Mississippi
Jamie L. Whitten, 1 (D)
Webb Franklin, 2 (R)
G. V. (Sonny) Montgomery, 3 (D)
Wayne Dowdy, 4 (D)
Trent Lott, 5 (R)

Missouri
William (Bill) Clay, 1 (D)
Robert A. Young, 2 (D)
Richard A. Gephardt, 3 (D)
Ike Skelton, 4 (D)
Alan Wheat, 5 (D)
E. Thomas Coleman, 6 (R)
Gene Taylor, 7 (R)
Bill Emerson, 8 (R)
Harold L. Volkmer, 9 (D)

Montana
Pat Williams, 1 (D)
Ron Marlenee, 2 (R)

Nebraska
Douglas K. Bereuter, 1 (R)
Hal Daub, 2 (R)
Virginia Smith, 3 (R)

Nevada
Harry M. Reid, 1 (D)
Barbara F. Vucanovich, 2 (R)

New Hampshire
Norman E. D'Amours, 1 (D)
Judd Gregg, 2 (R)

New Jersey
James J. Florio, 1 (D)
William J. Hughes, 2 (D)
James J. Howard, 3 (D)
Christopher H. Smith, 4 (R)
Marge Roukema, 5 (R)
Bernard J. Dwyer, 6 (D)
Matthew J. Rinaldo, 7 (R)
Robert A. Roe, 8 (D)
Robert G. Torricelli, 9 (D)
Peter W. Rodino, Jr., 10 (D)
Joseph G. Minish, 11 (D)
James A. Courter, 12 (R)
Edwin B. Forsythe, 13 (R)
Frank J. Guarini, 14 (D)

New Mexico
Manuel Lujan, Jr., 1 (R)
Joe Skeen, 2 (R)
Bill Richardson, 3 (D)

New York
William Carney, 1 (C-R)
Thomas J. Downey, 2 (D)
Robert J. Mrazek, 3 (D)
Norman F. Lent, 4 (R)
Raymond J. McGrath, 5 (R)
Joseph P. Addabbo, 6 (D)
Gary L. Ackerman, 7 (D)
James H. Scheuer, 8 (D)
Geraldine Ferraro, 9 (D)
Charles E. Schumer, 10 (D)
Edolphus Towns, 11 (D)
Major R. Owens, 12 (D)
Stephen J. Solarz, 13 (D)
Guy V. Molinari, 14 (R)
Bill Green, 15 (R)
Charles B. Rangel, 16 (D)
Ted Weiss, 17 (D)
Robert Garcia, 18 (D)
Mario Biaggi, 19 (D)
Richard L. Ottinger, 20 (D)
Hamilton Fish, Jr. 21 (R)
Benjamin A. Gilman, 22 (R)
Samuel S. Stratton, 23 (D)
Gerald B. H. Solomon, 24 (R)
Sherwood L. Boehlert, 25 (R)
David O'B. Martin, 26 (R)
George C. Wortley, 27 (R)
Matthew F. McHugh, 28 (D)
Frank Horton, 29 (R)

Barber B. Conable, Jr., 30 (R)
Jack F. Kemp, 31 (R)
John J. LaFalce, 32 (D)
Henry J. Nowak, 33 (D)
Stan Lundine, 34 (D)

North Carolina
Walter B. Jones, 1 (D)
Tim Valentine, 2 (D)
Charles Whitley, 3 (D)
Ike F. Andrews, 4 (D)
Stephen L. Neal, 5 (D)
C. Robin Britt, 6 (D)
Charles Rose III, 7 (D)
W. G. (Bill) Hefner, 8 (D)
James G. Martin, 9 (R)
James T. Broyhill, 10 (R)
James McClure Clarke,
 11 (D)

North Dakota
Byron Dorgan (D)

Ohio
Thomas A. Luken, 1 (D)
Willis D. Gradison, Jr., 2 (R)
Tony P. Hall, 3 (D)
Michael G. Oxley, 4 (R)
Delbert L. Latta, 5 (R)
Bob McEwen, 6 (R)
Michael DeWine, 7 (R)
Thomas N. Kindness, 8 (R)
Marcy Kaptur, 9 (D)
Clarence E. Miller, 10 (R)
Dennis E. Eckart, 11 (D)
John R. Kasich, 12 (R)
Donald J. Pease, 13 (D)
John F. Seiberling, 14 (D)
Chalmers P. Wylie, 15 (R)
Ralph S. Regula, 16 (R)
Lyle Williams, 17 (R)
Douglas Applegate, 18 (D)
Edward F. Feighan, 19 (D)
Mary Rose Oakar, 20 (D)
Louis Stokes, 21 (D)

Oklahoma
James Rogers Jones, 1 (D)
Mike Synar, 2 (D)
Wes Watkins, 3 (D)
Dave McCurdy, 4 (D)
Mickey Edwards, 5 (R)
Glenn English, 6 (D)

Oregon
Les AuCoin, 1 (D)
Robert F. Smith, 2 (R)
Ron Wyden, 3 (D)
James Weaver, 4 (D)
Denny Smith, 5 (R)

Pennsylvania
Thomas M. Foglietta, 1 (D)
William H. Gray III, 2 (D)
Robert A. Borski, 3 (D)

Joe Kolter, 4 (D)
Richard T. Schulze, 5 (R)
Gus Yatron, 6 (D)
Robert W. Edgar, 7 (D)
Peter H. Kostmayer, 8 (D)
E. G. (Bud) Shuster, 9 (R)
Joseph M. McDade, 10 (R)
Frank Harrison, 11 (D)
John P. Murtha, 12 (D)
R. Lawrence Coughlin, 13 (R)
William J. Coyne, 14 (D)
Donald L. Ritter, 15 (R)
Robert S. Walker, 16 (R)
George W. Gekas, 17 (R)
Doug Walgren, 18 (D)
William F. Goodling, 19 (R)
Joseph M. Gaydos, 20 (D)
Thomas J. Ridge, 21 (R)
Austin J. Murphy, 22 (D)
William F. Clinger, Jr., 23 (R)

Puerto Rico
Baltasar Corrada (D)‡

Rhode Island
Fernand J. St. Germain, 1 (D)
Claudine Schneider, 2 (R)

South Carolina
Thomas F. Hartnett, 1 (R)
Floyd Spence, 2 (R)
Butler C. Derrick, Jr., 3 (D)
Carroll A. Campbell, Jr., 4 (R)
John M. Spratt, Jr., 5 (D)
Robin Tallon, 6 (D)

South Dakota
Tom Daschle (D)

Tennessee
James H. Quillen, 1 (R)
John J. Duncan, 2 (R)
Marilyn Lloyd Bouquard,
 3 (D)
Jim Cooper, 4 (D)
Bill Boner, 5 (D)
Albert Gore, Jr., 6 (D)
Don Sundquist, 7 (R)
Ed Jones, 8 (D)
Harold E. Ford, 9 (D)

Texas
Sam B. Hall, Jr., 1 (D)
Charles Wilson, 2 (D)
Steve Bartlett, 3 (R)
Ralph M. Hall, 4 (D)
John Bryant, 5 (D)
Phil Gramm, 6 (R)
Bill Archer, 7 (R)
Jack Fields, 8 (R)
Jack Brooks, 9 (D)
J. J. (Jake) Pickle, 10 (D)
J. Marvin Leath, 11 (D)
James C. Wright, Jr., 12 (D)
John Hightower, 13 (D)

William N. Patman, 14 (D)
E. (Kika) de la Garza, 15 (D)
Ronald D. Coleman, 16 (D)
Charles W. Stenholm, 17 (D)
Mickey Leland, 18 (D)
Kent Hance, 19 (D)
Henry B. Gonzalez, 20 (D)
Tom Loeffler, 21 (R)
Ron Paul, 22 (R)
Abraham Kazen, Jr., 23 (D)
Martin Frost, 24 (D)
Michael A. Andrews, 25 (D)
Tom Vandergriff, 26 (D)
Solomon P. Ortiz, 27, (D)

Utah
James V. Hansen, 1 (R)
Dan Marriott, 2 (R)
Howard C. Nielson, 3 (R)

Vermont
James M. Jeffords (R)

Virginia
Herbert H. Bateman, 1 (R)
G. William Whitehurst, 2 (R)
Thomas J. Bliley, 3 (R)
Norman Sisisky, 4 (D)
W. C. (Dan) Daniel, 5 (D)
James R. Olin, 6 (D)
J. Kenneth Robinson, 7 (R)
Stan Parris, 8 (R)
Frederick C. Boucher, 9 (D)
Frank R. Wolf, 10 (R)

Virgin Islands
Ron de Lugo (D)†

Washington
Joel Pritchard, 1 (R)
Allen Swift, 2 (D)
Don Bonker, 3 (D)
Sid Morrison, 4 (R)
Thomas S. Foley, 5 (D)
Norman D. Dicks, 6 (D)
Mike Lowry, 7 (D)
Rod Chandler, 8 (R)

West Virginia
Alan B. Mollohan, 1 (D)
Harley O. Staggers, Jr., 2 (D)
Robert E. Wise, Jr., 3 (D)
Nick Joe Rahall, 4 (D)

Wisconsin
Les Aspin, 1 (D)
Robert W. Kastenmeier, 2 (D)
Steven Gunderson, 3 (R)
Clement J. Zablocki, 4 (D)
Jim Moody, 5 (D)
Thomas E. Petri, 6 (R)
David R. Obey, 7 (D)
Tobias A. Roth, 8 (R)
F. J. Sensenbrenner, 9 (R)

Wyoming
Richard Cheney (R)

* Numbers after names indicate congressional districts; where no number is given, the representative is elected at large.
† Nonvoting elected delegate.
‡ Nonvoting elected commissioner.

CONSUMER AFFAIRS

March 15, 1982, was the 20th anniversary of the "consumer bill of rights." In a speech to the U.S. Congress on that date in 1962, Pres. John F. Kennedy announced four basic rights of consumers: the right to safety; the right to be informed; the right to choose; and the right to be heard. The rights to redress, to consumer education, and to a healthy environment were subsequently added. The president of the International Organization of Consumers Unions (IOCU) proposed that March 15 be marked as "Consumer Rights Day" throughout the world.

In 1982 IOCU's membership stood at 118 organizations in 50 countries. In recent years IOCU had played an increasing role as an "international consumer advocate," particularly through a number of groups that it was instrumental in forming: the International Baby Food Action Network (IBFAN, formed in 1979), Health Action International (HAI, 1981), and the Pesticide Action Network (PAN, 1982). A major IOCU project for the 1980s, Consumer Interpol, was launched in 1982 to provide a worldwide warning and information exchange system on newly discovered hazardous products, wastes, and technologies.

A coalition of nongovernmental organizations based in 16 countries, PAN was formed during a meeting in Penang, Malaysia, organized by IOCU and Friends of the Earth in May 1982. With the objective of stopping the indiscriminate sale and misuse of hazardous chemical pesticides, PAN members called for, among other measures, the expansion of traditional, biological, and integrated pest management and an end to the unnecessary sale and use of chemical pesticides. It urged that nine Green Revolution research centres, including the International Rice Research Institute based in the Philippines, reverse their practice of developing and distributing seed varieties that are heavily dependent on chemical pesticides and fertilizers.

Mounting evidence of the dumping of hazardous or potentially hazardous products pointed to the need for an independent worldwide alert system. Consumer Interpol, inaugurated for this purpose in 1982, consisted of a network of correspondents representing consumer groups within the IOCU, as well as IBFAN, HAI, and PAN. The correspondents were to notify the Consumer Interpol coordinator when they received information on any newly discovered or recently regulated hazard. The coordinator, in turn, would inform other correspondents. In recognition of the inception of this system, IOCU president Anwar Fazal was awarded the 1982 Alternative Nobel Prize.

The Bureau Éuropéen des Unions de Consommateurs (BEUC), the lobby organization of consumer

A proposal by the Department of Agriculture to revise the system of grading beef by lowering the standards for the prime and choice grades to include leaner, lower-priced meat was strongly opposed by consumers at both retail and wholesale levels.

PATRICK D. PAGNANO/NEWSWEEK

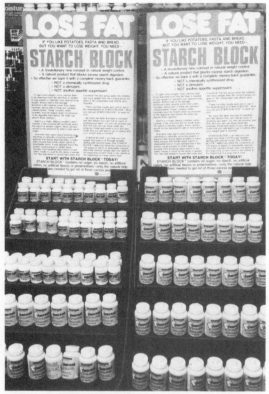

JACQUES M. CHENET/NEWSWEEK

So-called starch blockers became the latest diet fad with the promise of easy weight loss, but the FDA moved to remove them from the market until proved safe and effective.

groups in the European Community (EC) countries, identified two areas related to the current economic recession as cornerstones of its programs for 1982. First, it felt that consumers should be more alert with regard to price-fixing mechanisms, competition problems, and price and quality comparisons. Second, safety and consumer protection should not be foregone because they placed a financial burden on industry. As a direct result of the second consideration, BEUC set up an alert system on hazardous products that would be linked to Consumer Interpol.

U.S. Actions

In the U.S. a study released by the Insurance Institute for Highway Safety in 1982 found that U.S.-made automobiles were safer than Japanese-made automobiles of comparable size. The study used government records on fatal automobile crashes that occurred from 1978 through 1980. A rule reinstated by the Civil Aeronautics Board (CAB) on Oct. 1, 1982, allowed passengers of commercial airlines to collect double the face value of a one-way ticket, up to $400, if they were bumped from an airline flight and were unable to arrive at their destinations within two hours of their original scheduled flight.

The CAB also changed a rule to allow passengers to obtain $1,000 rather than $750 if their luggage was lost or damaged.

The Federal Trade Commission (FTC) completed its work in 1982 on proposed regulations requiring funeral homes to provide price lists to consumers. The rule was subject to congressional veto. In 1982 Congress vetoed a proposed FTC regulation that would have required used-car dealers to tell customers about known mechanical defects.

In September the Food and Drug Administration (FDA) proposed labeling aspirin containers with a warning that aspirin had been linked to Reye's syndrome, a rare and sometimes fatal childhood disease. A House of Representatives subcommittee approved three tough warning labels to be put on cigarette packages. The subcommittee's recommendations would be reviewed by Congress in 1983.

Consumer groups and restaurateurs were opposing revisions of beef grading standards proposed by the U.S. Department of Agriculture that would allow leaner and lower-priced beef to qualify for higher grades and higher prices. USDA officials contended that the current grading system put a price premium on fat content, which may cause health problems. A U.S. district court upheld the FDA's decision to give industry more time to complete safety reviews of 23 colour additives used in foods, drugs, and cosmetics. The colours were on the agency's provisional list, permitting their use until safety tests determined whether they were to be "permanently" approved or withdrawn from the market. In July the FDA issued an ultimatum to 125 marketers and distributors of "starch blocker" diet aids to halt distribution of the products until they were proved safe and effective. Starch blockers were said to assist weight control by impeding the digestion of starch.

Federal restrictions on offering discounts to customers who pay cash were removed, but the ban on surcharges for credit-card purchases was extended to 1984. Several oil companies discontinued or discouraged the use of credit cards at their gasoline stations. In some cases consumers were offered discounts if they paid in cash.

COSTA RICA

General elections held in Costa Rica on Feb. 7, 1982, resulted in a clear victory for Luis Alberto Monge Alvarez and his social democratic Partido de Liberación Nacional, which gained an absolute majority in the Legislative Assembly. The new president took office on May 8.

Costa Rica was allocated $70 million, more than any other country apart from El Salvador, under the U.S. Caribbean Basin Initiative, and further promises to bolster the country against Communism were forthcoming. Israel granted aid, and the International Monetary Fund provided a standby agreement for $105 million scheduled for November. In January Costa Rica established the Central American Democratic Community (CDC) with El Salvador and

Luis Alberto Monge Alvarez, shown casting his ballot in Costa Rica's February general election, took office as president in May.
RANDY TAYLOR—SYGMA

Honduras (Guatemala joined later in the year), and in September it organized a forum of nine Caribbean Basin countries to seek peace in the region. U.S. Pres. Ronald Reagan visited San José in December.

The economic chaos inherited from the previous administration was partially resolved by austerity measures. Chief among the remaining problems were a foreign debt of $4.4 billion, an inflation rate of 100%, and a three-tier exchange rate (official rate 20 colones to the U.S. dollar, commercial 40, and free-market 69).

CRIME AND LAW ENFORCEMENT

The hatred and bitterness flowing from long-festering political conflicts, many of them centred in the Middle East, sparked a rash of terrorist incidents in 1982. Western Europeans, especially the French, bore the brunt of much of this violence. During August and September more than 20 bombings and shootings were reported in Paris alone, including an August 9 machine gun and grenade attack on customers lunching at a famous Jewish restaurant in the French capital. The attack, believed to have been committed by the Black June terrorist group, left 6 people dead and 22 wounded.

Led by Abu Nidal, a renegade Palestinian leader, Black June was known to have waged a six-year campaign of terror against a wide range of targets, including rival Palestine Liberation Organization leaders and Israeli diplomats. It claimed responsibility for the attempted assassination in London on June 3 of Shlomo Argov, Israel's ambassador to Britain, an incident used by Israel as the immediate pretext for its June 6 invasion of Lebanon. Black June was also thought to be responsible for a bloody attack in Rome on October 9, when terrorists wielding machine guns and lobbing grenades cut down worshipers leaving a synagogue. The incident resulted in the death of a two-year-old boy and the wounding of 34 people, many of them children.

In March Italian authorities in Verona put on trial 17 (8 in absentia) Red Brigades terrorists accused of the December 1981 kidnapping of U.S. Brig. Gen. James L. Dozier. After 42 days in captivity, Dozier was rescued on January 28 in a dramatic raid on an apartment in Padua by Italy's elite antiterrorist commando unit, the Leatherheads. The massive manhunt for Dozier resulted in the penetration of the Red Brigades' elaborate underground network as captured terrorists traded information for shorter sentences. In April one of these terrorists, Antonio Savasta, 27, who received a prison term of 16 years for his leading role in the Dozier kidnapping, became a key prosecution witness in the Rome trial of more than 50 Red Brigades members. The defendants faced charges arising out of 19 murders and many gun attacks between 1977 and 1981, including the 1978 kidnapping and murder of former Italian premier Aldo Moro. Italian authorities achieved another success in October with the capture in Bolivia of Pierluigi Pagliai, 28, wanted in connection with the 1980 bombing of the Bologna railway station in which 85 people were killed. In this case, neo-Fascists had committed the outrage.

An international assassination campaign by Armenian nationalists directed against Turkish diplomats claimed several victims during the year, including Kemal Arikan, Turkey's consul general in Los Angeles, and Orhan Gunduz, the honorary Turkish consul general for New England. Gunduz was the 22nd Turkish diplomat or member of a diplomat's family or staff slain by Armenian terrorist

A terrorist attack on Goldenberg's, a well-known Jewish restaurant in Paris, left 6 dead and 22 hurt. Itself the worst single anti-Semitic episode in France since World War II, the attack was only part of a wave of terrorism that swept France in 1982.

PATRICE HABANS—SYGMA

groups since the launching of their assassination campaign in 1973. On August 7 one of these groups, the Armenian Secret Army for the Liberation of Armenia, made a major assault on Turkish soil for the first time. Three men armed with machine guns and bombs killed at least 9 people and wounded 72 at Ankara's Esenboga Airport.

Pope John Paul II, who survived an assassination attempt in St. Peter's Square on May 13, 1981, was attacked again almost exactly one year later while visiting the shrine of Fatima in Portugal to thank the Virgin Mary for sparing his life. Juan Fernandez Krohn, a rebel Spanish priest, was apprehended at the scene after lunging at the pope with a bayonet. Controversy continued to surround the earlier assassination attempt by Turkish right-wing terrorist Mehmet Ali Agca. There was speculation that Agca may have had links to the Bulgarian secret service and that the Bulgarians, in turn, acted as agents for the Soviets, who desired the death of the Polish-born pontiff because of his support for the Solidarity movement in Poland.

In June John W. Hinckley, Jr., who narrowly missed killing U.S. Pres. Ronald Reagan on March 30, 1981, was found not guilty by reason of insanity on each of 13 counts arising from the assassination attempt. The verdict provoked a storm of protest across the U.S. and led to a wave of legislative attempts to tighten or abolish the insanity defense. Hinckley was hospitalized for psychiatric treatment.

A man identified as Norman Mayer, 66, was shot and killed by police on December 8 after he had threatened for ten hours to blow up the Washington Monument. He had demanded a nationwide debate on the use of nuclear weapons.

On July 9 Michael Fagan, 31, an unemployed labourer, was arrested in Buckingham Palace after gaining access to the royal bedchamber and talking to Queen Elizabeth II. Fagan, it was discovered, had also sneaked into the palace on June 7 and drunk some wine belonging to Prince Charles. On July 9 Fagan had merely trespassed, a civil rather than a criminal offense, so he was charged only in connection with the June 7 incident. In September a jury acquitted him, but in October, after he had pleaded

guilty to a charge of car theft, a judge ordered him detained indefinitely in a mental hospital.

The British public's confidence in its security forces was further weakened by the explosion on July 20 of two bombs planted by the Irish Republican Army (IRA) in the heart of London. The first blast, in Hyde Park, killed three members of the Queen's Household Cavalry as they rode to a changing of the guard ceremony at Whitehall. Twenty-three persons were injured in the explosion, which also killed or wounded a number of horses. Two hours later 6 army musicians were blown apart and 28 people were injured when a second bomb exploded under a Regent's Park bandstand during a lunchtime concert by the Royal Greenjackets Band. An IRA splinter group claimed responsibility for an explosion that collapsed the roof of a popular bar in Ballykelly, Northern Ireland, on December 6, killing 11 British soldiers and 5 civilians and injuring an estimated 66 others.

Murder and Other Violence

In a sharp departure from the soaring crime rates reported to the police in recent years in the U.S., the FBI's *Uniform Crime Reports* showed that the overall rate of crime in 1981 remained about the same as that of 1980, while violent crimes as a group rose only 1%. Despite these slightly encouraging trends, there were still almost 25,000 murders committed in the U.S., or roughly 500 per week.

Proponents of gun control pointed out that handguns were used to kill about 10,000 Americans each year and to commit another 500,000 violent crimes. Opinion polls continued to show that a large majority of Americans favoured stricter handgun controls, and a few municipalities adopted local ordinances barring possession or sale of handguns by almost all citizens. In California, however, Proposition 15, which would have mandated regulation of handguns, was rejected in the November election.

A nationwide consumer alert was triggered early in October by the sudden deaths of seven Chicago-area residents who had taken capsules of Extra-Strength Tylenol, a popular over-the-counter pain-relieving drug, that were found to contain cya-

IRA terrorists claimed responsibility for two bomb blasts in London on July 20. The first bomb killed 3 and injured 23 members of the Queen's Household Cavalry in Hyde Park; a number of horses were also killed or wounded.
WIDE WORLD

nide. Authorities determined that the capsules had been tampered with after they left the factory and probably after they had been placed on store shelves. The police began a massive hunt for the person or persons responsible for these terrifying acts of random, impersonal mass murder, but they had few clues to go on. Attempts at extortion aimed at the manufacturer were thought to have been made by persons other than the murderer. Meanwhile, there were reports across the country of "copycat" incidents of product tampering.

Nonviolent Crime

U.S. Sen. Harrison A. Williams, Jr., of New Jersey was sentenced in February to three years in jail and fined $50,000 by a federal court in Uniondale, N.Y. He had been convicted in 1981 on charges of bribery and conspiracy arising from the FBI's Abscam investigation of political corruption. Williams resigned his seat rather than face almost certain expulsion from the Senate, but he continued to claim he had been victimized by the FBI and appealed both the conviction and sentence. In December Roy L. Williams, president of the teamsters' union, and four others were convicted of attempting to bribe Sen. Howard J. Cannon (Dem., Nev.) to oppose a bill deregulating the trucking industry.

A much publicized investigation by a special federal prosecutor, Leon Silverman, into the conduct of U.S. Secretary of Labor Raymond J. Donovan came to a close in September when the prosecutor said he was unable to find "sufficient credible evidence" to corroborate allegations that Donovan had consorted with known Mafia figures and committed various illegal acts. During the course of the Donovan probe, two government witnesses, both connected with organized crime, were murdered.

A complex scandal that shook the international banking system and reached into the secret financial apparatus of the Vatican began to take shape after the collapse of the Banco Ambrosiano, Italy's largest private bank, and the apparent suicide of its president, Roberto Calvi. According to investigators, some $1.2 billion in bank funds had been used to provide unsecured loans to "shadowy" Latin-Amer-

ican companies, in association with letters of patronage (financial guarantees) issued by the Institute for Religious Works, or Vatican bank. (*See* RELIGION.) As the inquiries continued, Licio Gelli, an Italo-Argentine financier associated with Calvi and the alleged recruiter of the mysterious Masonic lodge known as P2, was arrested by Swiss police in Geneva. Gelli's arrest came as he sought to withdraw up to $60 million, believed to have come from the Banco Ambrosiano, from numbered accounts in a

Flamboyant automaker John Z. De Lorean was arrested for his part in an alleged $6.5 million cocaine deal.
WIDE WORLD

Swiss bank. Gelli faced possible charges of fraud, political and military espionage, and illegal possession of state secrets in Italy and was thought to be implicated in the Bologna railroad station bombing. The exposure of P2, which allegedly included many prominent Italian politicians, military men, and police, had brought down the Italian government in 1981.

In another case involving a prominent figure, automaker John Z. DeLorean was arrested by federal agents in California in October on charges of dealing in drugs. After a meteoric career at General Motors, DeLorean, with British government participation, had begun manufacturing expensive sports cars in Northern Ireland. Officials alleged that he became involved in a scheme to sell cocaine in an effort to obtain funds to shore up his failing company.

In Canada's Arctic territories, the Royal Canadian Mounted Police (RCMP) launched a campaign to crack down on the smuggling of rare falcon eggs and live birds to Saudi Arabia and other Middle Eastern countries where falconry remained a popular royal sport. Smuggled eggs were said to fetch as much as $8,000 in Saudi Arabia, while a fully grown falcon brought $60,000. The first conviction resulting from the crackdown was of a West German citizen, arrested in possession of five falcon eggs in a special incubator as he was about to fly out of northern Quebec.

In the U.S. the FBI reported a 4% decline in car and truck thefts in 1981. Even so, about 1.1 million such thefts occurred during the year, and only 55% of the stolen vehicles were returned to their owners. Police officials stated that the proportion of vehicles recovered had continued to drop over the last 25 years, reflecting increased professionalism among car thieves. In many cases vehicles were worth more as parts than as a whole, and "chop shops" had sprung up which could reduce a stolen vehicle to pieces within a very short time.

A new U.S. record for a cash robbery was set on December 12. Robbers sawed through the roof of an armoured car service depot in the Bronx, New York City, backed a truck up to the loading dock, and filled it with bales of cash. They made off with an estimated $10.4 million.

Law Enforcement

President Reagan announced in October that a major offensive would be launched by federal law enforcement agencies to "cripple the power of the mob in America." The president, who pointed to the enormous profits gained by crime syndicates from illicit drug operations around the nation, said 12 new task forces of federal prosecutors and investigators would be established to focus on drug trafficking. Earlier in the year the FBI had been given an expanded role in domestic drug trafficking investigations.

In a September press interview, FBI Director William Webster said that almost 20% of his agency's resources now went into fighting organized crime. In the first nine months of 1982, the FBI obtained 587 convictions in organized crime cases. Among a further 245 cases in the process of prosecution was one involving a dramatic FBI undercover operation that infiltrated fencing operations in New York City. In August five alleged members of New York's Bonanno crime syndicate went on trial on racketeering charges stemming from the operation, which included three murders, gambling, hijacking, drug conspiracy, and armed robbery. The main witness against the Bonanno group was an FBI agent, Joseph D. Pistone, who was sent undercover in 1976 and posed as a thief named Don Brasco for more than six years.

Italy's top Mafia fighter, Gen. Carlo Alberto Dalla Chiesa, and his wife died in a hail of bullets as they drove through the streets of Palermo, Sicily, on September 3. Following his considerable success in leading the battle against political terrorism, Dalla Chiesa had been sent to Sicily in May by Premier Giovanni Spadolini's government on a special mission to combat the Mafia. In the wake of the assassination, the government created a new and powerful post of high commissioner against organized crime, and a bill was pushed through Parliament giving investigators unprecedented powers to look into Mafia sources of wealth and influence. The bill made it an offense, for the first time, to be a member of a Mafia clan.

Technicians tested millions of capsules of Extra-Strength Tylenol in the wake of seven deaths in the Chicago area from cyanide-contaminated Tylenol.
WIDE WORLD

Special Report: The New Prohibition

by Richard Whittingham

Deep in the night a large fishing boat plows through the ocean under a star-studded sky. A little more than 12 mi off the Florida coast, the engines are cut, and the ship's anchor splashes into the water. A short while later the silence is broken by the harsh rasp of a speedboat's motor, then another, and another. . . . The sleek boats close on the mother ship like metal shavings drawn to a magnet. As they tie up alongside, the deck above is suddenly awash with activity as men rush to pass the cargo down to those in the speedboats. Satchels of cash are thrown up to eager hands on the fishing boat. Minutes later the small boats are racing back toward shore, every cubic inch filled with contraband. At a remote docking place trucks wait to take the illicit cargo on the next leg of its journey, one that will eventually end with the surreptitious sale of the goods to a variety of consumers.

Scenes like this were played out countless times in the 1920s and early '30s, and they are occurring in almost the same fashion in the 1980s; only the commodities have changed. Marijuana, cocaine, heroin, and Quaaludes have replaced the beer and bootleg whiskey of Prohibition. The smugglers, once called "rum runners," are now known as "reefer runners."

The illegal manufacture of the substance, the methods of smuggling, and the channels of distribution are astonishingly similar. For example, raw alcohol was manufactured in one place, distilled in another, watered down in still another; pure cocaine or heroin goes through a similar process of reduction before it hits the street. In both cases huge profits were—or are—made at each stage. From the astronomical amount of cash involved to the killings and the political and police corruption, the parallels cut deeply into the moral and economic heart of the United States.

The Noble Experiment

The Prohibition era began one minute after midnight on Jan. 16, 1920. The 18th Amendment to the U.S. Constitution had rendered the nation dry, and the Volstead Act was passed to enforce the ban on the manufacture, importation, and sale of alcoholic beverages. But the nation was hardly ready for that kind of reform. On the contrary, the "flappers and philosophers" of the 1920s, as F. Scott Fitzgerald

called them, were about to launch what he termed "the greatest gaudiest spree in American history."

To supply the wants of the wets, a vast illicit trade arose, manipulated by organized crime. In the lucrative but bloody business, names like Al Capone, Johnny Torrio, Dion O'Banion, Hymie Weiss, Bugs Moran, Machine Gun Jack McGurn, Legs Diamond, Dutch Schultz, Frank Costello, and Detroit's Purple Gang soon became infamous.

Throughout the U.S., secret stills and breweries were set in operation. (Some distilleries controlled by crime bosses turned out as much as 2,000 gal of whiskey a day.) Their crude output was bottled and trucked to the speakeasies and roadhouses that catered to a legion of thirsty consumers.

On the coasts the rum runners (who ran everything from whiskey and beer to raw alcohol) flourished. Whiskey that was "right off the boat" was known to be far superior to that manufactured in the clandestine stills. The smugglers loaded up in the West Indies, the Bahamas, Cuba, and other south-of-the-border ports and moved their cargo into the U.S. through Florida, the Louisiana bayous, and the Virginia capes. Farther north other boats set out from Canada and delivered their illegal freight along the shores of Long Island, New Jersey, and the Great Lakes. Even the fragile airplanes of the '20s were pressed into service to ferry loads of booze on short hops from Canada to U.S. soil.

Competition was fierce. There were "rum wars" waged between rival importers on the high seas and in the ports, and there were "beer wars" in the cities between factions of the crime syndicate that sold and distributed the "hootch." Blood flowed freely. The "St. Valentine's Day Massacre" of 1929, when seven men were machine-gunned to death in a Chicago garage, was a notorious but relatively minor incident, measured against the 300 to 400 bootleg-booze-related murders that took place in Chicago each year during those times.

The government tried to combat the rampant disregard for the new law, but it was a hopeless task. The Coast Guard captured thousands of boats used to smuggle alcohol into the U.S., but they were only a drop in the proverbial bucket. In the cities practically everyone was on the take. In New York City alone there were an estimated 32,000 speakeasies by

1929 (and 219,000 nationwide). As Mayor Fiorello La Guardia said: "To enforce the Volstead Act in New York you would need 250,000 policemen and another 200,000 to keep the police within the law."

A Case of Déja Vu

It all ended when Prohibition was repealed in 1933 by the 21st Amendment. The stills disappeared; the smugglers went back to fishing; and the gangsters channeled their energies into prostitution, gambling, and other sordid endeavours.

Some 50 years after repeal of the 18th Amendment, however, there has been a reprise of Prohibition-type activities. Instead of stills and breweries turning out illicit beverages, there are fields and gardens sown with marijuana and clandestine chemical laboratories for refining and cutting narcotics and manufacturing other drugs. As in the '20s, the best quality goods are imported (now from places like Colombia and Bolivia). And the smugglers use the same methods, although today's reefer runners may have $250,000 speedboats capable of reaching 70 mph (113 km/h) and equipped with radar scanners, infrared night-vision scopes, and even satellite navigational gear.

There is the same intramural warfare, though leisure suits and gold chains have replaced the shoulder-padded suitcoats and flip-brim hats of the hoodlums who once killed each other over territories and profits, and today's feuding parties often speak Spanish. (One thing remains the same as in the Prohibition days: among the preferred weapons for drug-related executions is the machine gun.) Like Chicago in the '20s, Miami, as the capital city of the illicit drug business, has the worst crime rate in the nation. Of the 250 to 300 murders committed in Miami each year in the 1980s, approximately one-third are believed to be drug-related.

Big Business

In an inflationary era the drug trade involves sums of money that dwarf the crime syndicate operations of the '20s. Whereas Al Capone allegedly grossed between $100 million and $200 million a year from his Chicago bootlegging operation, the drug industry's figures are calculated in the multibillions. One federal bust alone (a government operation called "Grouper") resulted in the confiscation of $1 billion worth of drugs and the indictment of 155 people. It is estimated that cocaine with a street value of $28 billion is smuggled into the U.S. each year. The drug-smuggling traffic in south Florida is estimated at between $7 billion and $12 billion annually. In California the largest agricultural cash crop in that fertile land of fruits and vegetables is thought to be marijuana.

Offenders commonly come up with $1 million in bail—in cash—within hours of being arrested. Smugglers abandon $200,000 yachts and $500,000 airplanes after a single run; when the cargo is worth perhaps $10 million, such losses are a small proportion of sales.

Putting the financial aspect of today's drug trade in startling perspective, *Time* magazine reported the story of a young drug dealer in Florida, one Donald Steinberg. At 28 he owned an estate in Fort Lauderdale, a townhouse in Manhattan worth $2 million, a fleet of cars that included a Rolls-Royce and a Ferrari. At his peak earnings (1978) Steinberg, according to estimates by the U.S. Drug Enforcement Administration, had an annual revenue of $100 million from the sale of 500,000 lb (227,000 kg) of marijuana. In one 90-day period he reaped a $12 million profit.

Steinberg was caught, convicted, and sent to prison, but others have taken up where he left off. The Coast Guard and Customs Service are continually fighting the smuggling of narcotics and marijuana, and federal agents and local authorities are combating the dissemination and use of the drugs inside the country. Their job is no less difficult than it was in the 1920s.

Drugs constitute a criminal and economic problem of international proportions. The United Nations Commission on Narcotic Drugs has established a major five-year program (1982–86) aimed at developing a strategy to mobilize international efforts to check both drug abuse and the proliferating international traffic in drugs. Among its stated objectives are the improvement of drug-control systems, eradication of illicit sources of supply, prevention of the inappropriate use of narcotic drugs, and reduction of the demand for them.

It will not be as easy to achieve these aims as it was to curb the abuses of the old Prohibition era. There is no simple solution like Repeal.

Narcotics agents in Miami seize a shipment of cocaine worth millions of dollars; while not as picturesque, perhaps, as emptying barrels of illicit beer into a sewer, their work is more than a little reminiscent of that of Prohibition agents of the 1920s.
MAURICE COHN – MIAMI HERALD/BLACK STAR

Pres. Fidel Castro of Cuba talked with Argentine Foreign Minister Nicanor Costa Mendez before calling on a meeting of ministers of nonaligned nations to condemn Great Britain for "colonialist aggression" in the Falkland Islands.
WIDE WORLD

CUBA

Political stability was maintained in Cuba during 1982, but little economic progress was made apart from modest improvements in productivity. The National Assembly of People's Power was inaugurated for its second five-year term in December 1981. Fidel Castro, head of state and first secretary of the Cuban Communist Party, was reelected by the Assembly to the post of president of the Council of State, and Gen. Raúl Castro was reelected as first vice-president.

In January 1982 it was revealed that two months earlier U.S. Secretary of State Alexander Haig had met in secret with Carlos Rafael Rodríguez, a vice-president of the Cuban Council of State, in Mexico. In a bid to begin negotiations that might resolve the differences between the two countries—and perhaps also bring an end to economic sanctions—Cuba had offered to halt military aid to revolutionary forces in Central America if the U.S. would make a similar pledge not to intervene militarily in the area. Cuba had also offered to withdraw troops from Angola as soon as South African troops began to leave South West Africa/Namibia.

During the remainder of 1982, however, Cuba's relations with the U.S. wavered. U.S. Pres. Ronald Reagan clearly indicated his administration's attitude to Cuba when he launched the Caribbean Basin Initiative in February. His projected program of economic and development assistance to Caribbean nations was strongly underscored by the political objective of strengthening the region against "the expansion of Soviet-backed Cuban-managed support for violent revolution in Central America." The U.S. planned to set up a Spanish-language radio station—to be named Radio Marti, after Cuban national hero José Marti—to broadcast to Cuba from Florida. In April new limitations were imposed on U.S. citizens traveling to Cuba, further straining relations between the two countries. In August, apparently in response to the Radio Marti proposal, Cuba disrupted U.S. radio programming for one night.

Castro announced that he regarded as a "real threat" the U.S. military maneuvers that took place in the Caribbean in March; these followed major exercises earlier in the month by NATO forces, the aim of which was to practice the protection of merchant shipping in the Florida Strait. Any attempts to normalize relations with Washington were further jeopardized in July when President Castro, during his speech at the annual ceremony to celebrate the start of the Cuban revolution, resorted to a hard-line attitude over Cuban troops in Angola. In August Wayne Smith, who had served the U.S. government's interests section in Havana since being appointed by Pres. Jimmy Carter in 1977 and was regarded as a moderate, resigned in protest over U.S. policy toward Cuba, particularly what he saw as missed opportunities for serious negotiations.

Cuba's position in Latin America and the Caribbean was strengthened during the year, mainly as a result of its stance during the Falkland Islands conflict between the U.K. and Argentina. In its capacity as chairholder of the nonaligned movement, Cuba called on the members of the group to condemn the "colonialist aggression of Great Britain against Argentina." Although the movement did not adopt the resolution in its entirety, in general Cuba gained credibility among the members by its solid support for Argentina.

In September the Cuban government sought to reschedule $1.2 billion of its debt to Western banks, delaying repayment of the principal until 1986. Cuba's debts to the West totaled about $3.5 billion, and falling sugar prices, rising interest rates, and the drying up of credit from Western banks had led to severe difficulties with debt repayment. It was estimated that the Soviet Union was subsidizing up to 20% of Cuba's national income, though much aid was in the form of subsidized trading agreements between the two countries.

Real economic growth in 1981 was abnormally high at 12%, compared with the 1980 growth rate of 3%, chiefly as a result of recovery within the agricul-

Cyprus was a staging point for many of the Palestinian guerrillas evacuated from Beirut, such as this group on its way to Jordan.
WIDE WORLD

tural sector from diseases that affected tobacco and sugar crops in 1980. The forecast for 1982 was much lower, in spite of a good harvest, because world prices for sugar were depressed. Sugarcane still dominated the economy, providing about 80% of export earnings. The 1981–82 sugar crop was officially put at 8.2 million metric tons, just short of the record 1969–70 crop of 8.6 million metric tons. Cuba exported 7.1 million metric tons of sugar during 1981, as against 6.2 million metric tons a year earlier. To achieve improved levels of agricultural output and stem migration to the cities, the government allowed the establishment of limited free markets, where farm produce in excess of state quotas could be sold at freely negotiated prices.

Diversification of the economy away from sugar had been the prime economic policy aim since 1971. There had been some broadening of the manufacturing base, an expansion of fishing, and a development of nonsugar agriculture. The 1982 economic plan aimed at 2.5% growth, offsetting the still low world sugar prices with reduced demand for imports. A new law published in February 1982 encouraged direct foreign investment, particularly in the tourist sector, where the number of visitors had risen from 3,000 in 1968 to about 200,000 in 1981.

In October the poet Armando Valladares, imprisoned for 22 years after he broke with Castro over Cuba's ties to Moscow, was released following the personal intervention of French Pres. François Mitterrand. He left Cuba for Paris.

CYPRUS

The major political development of 1982 in Cyprus was the announcement of an alliance between Pres. Spyros Kyprianou's ruling Democratic Party and the Communist party, AKEL. Its objective was to secure victory for President Kyprianou in the presidential election scheduled for February 1983. Kyprianou announced his candidacy for a second term after reaching agreement on a minimum program of cooperation with AKEL.

The new political alliance brought strong reactions from the main opposition parties, the right-wing Democratic Rally Party of former president Glafcos Clerides and the Socialist EDEK party of Vassos Lyssarides. Both these opposition leaders intended to stand for election but realized that they had little chance of matching the 54% electoral support that President Kyprianou and AKEL proved they could muster in an August by-election.

A more serious result of Kyprianou's alliance with the Communists was a sharp deterioration in relations between Cyprus and Greece after Greek Prime Minister Andreas Papandreou indicated his displeasure with the pact. The Cyprus Communists sharply rebuked Papandreou for "interference," to the great embarrassment of the government, which had accorded the Greek leader a hero's welcome when he visited the island in February–March.

Greek-Cypriot disappointment over the progress of talks with Turkish Cypriots led the government to seek more international action on the Cyprus problem, a move that angered Turkish Cypriots who saw the problem as an internal one. The Turkish-Cypriot administration in the north showed signs of internal instability and, with both sides having internal divisions, problems between the Greek and Turkish communities tended to be exploited. The result was a number of sharp exchanges between Greek and Turkish leaders, each accusing the other of stockpiling arms. The new tensions reached a dangerous level in September when a Greek-Cypriot national guardsman was shot dead by a Turkish-Cypriot sentry on the Nicosia "green line." Both sides were shocked by the incident and afterward were careful to keep the confrontation at the propaganda level.

All major industries in Cyprus, apart from tourism, appeared to be in decline, a result of the island's reduced competitiveness in traditionally labour-intensive enterprises such as clothing manufacture and citrus farming. Inflation had been cut back from 13.5% in 1980 to 10.8% in 1981 and an estimated 7% in 1982, and the total unemployment rate during

1982 was about 3%. However, Cyprus began during the year to experience its first labour problems ever. Trade unions began to show a militancy previously unknown as fears for the future of jobs grew. The government gave assurances that its pact with AKEL would not in any way affect the island's free-enterprise economy.

CZECHOSLOVAKIA

The problem of the economy, which had dominated Czechoslovakia's affairs for several years, continued to overshadow virtually all other considerations in 1982. If anything, the situation grew more alarming and the leadership's inability to apply remedies more obvious. The figures for 1981 were the second worst since the Communist Party of Czechoslovakia (CPC) took over in 1948. The increase in national income was 0.2% over 1980. In 1981 industrial output went up by 2%, while agricultural output fell by 3.4%. These and other statistics made it clear that Czechoslovakia had exhausted its reserves and was paying for the policies of the 1970s by low output. In effect, the failure to improve investment structure, the continued preponderance of heavy industry, and the reliance on inflexible command planning had resulted in stagnation. Responsibility lay with the CPC leadership, which had rejected economic reform projects on political grounds and remained wedded to rigid central control.

In the first place, the leadership stressed austerity. There were to be serious cutbacks in consumption, both individual and social. Affecting the former were the steep increases in meat, drink, and tobacco prices announced in January; energy prices were also raised. Collective consumption, which as a proportion of the budget had risen steadily in the 1970s, would be cut back, with unavoidable deterioration in the provision of health, education, culture, rented accommodation, and transportation. The second goal of the leadership's strategy was autarchy. This had inherent difficulties for a relatively small, industrial country short of many raw materials. Czechoslovakia relied on imports for 40% of its energy needs, 69% of nonferrous and 93% of ferrous metals, and 34.3% of its feed grains.

The raising of productivity, the most pressing requirement according to outside observers, ran into obstacles of inflexibility deriving from politically determined centralization. The scale of inefficiency in Czechoslovak industry was alarming. The rate of consumption of materials was 30–40% higher in Czechoslovakia than in the West. In engineering, waste amounted to one-quarter of the total output of steel.

Despite countless official exhortations to the population to improve their working habits and to "face up to the challenge of the economic situation," there was no evidence of any improvement in the figures for the first half of 1982. Although at first the press attempted to present these figures in an optimistic light, by October the newspapers were openly refer-ring to "an emergency situation" in the economy. The January–June increase in industrial output over the same period of 1981 was on the order of 0.4%.

In the midst of this economic gloom, political developments were of secondary significance. The Czechoslovak leadership was evidently relieved at the suppression of Poland's reform process before it might spread. The popular mood was one of skepticism and apathy. Shortages of consumer goods, services, and foodstuffs were reported, but the response did not go beyond grumbling and deeper involvement in the secondary economy.

While the official hard-line attitude to religion was sustained, making Czechoslovakia the most repressive country in Eastern Europe (Albania excepted) in its policy toward the churches, the Charter 77 opposition movement appeared to have found a new lease on life. After the inactivity of 1981, the Charter issued a large number of documents in 1982. They dealt with a variety of subjects, ranging from the situation in Poland to religious freedom, price increases, education, miscarriages of justice, the situation in prisons, and discrimination against certain writers. Nonetheless, the political isolation of the Charter from the population as a whole continued, and apathy characterized the mood of the bulk of the population.

DANCE

The year 1982 was a disquieting one for dance in the U.S. Major ballet companies were beset with labour disputes, financial crises, and injuries to dancers and choreographers. Large and small troupes struggled to hold ground in a shrinking economy with reduced government support for touring.

American Ballet Theatre (ABT) completed its second season under the artistic helm of Mikhail Baryshnikov, whose contract was renewed through the 1985–86 season. Baryshnikov promoted many young dancers from the ranks but was criticized for his revisions of 19th-century ballets and unfruitful commissions. ABT staged new ballets by Kenneth MacMillan (*The Wild Boy*, music by Gordon Crosse, sets by Oliver Smith, costumes by Willa Kim), Choo San Goh (*Configurations*), Lynne Taylor-Corbett (*Great Galloping Gottschalk*), and Peter Anastos (*Clair de Lune*). The company also acquired its first Merce Cunningham ballet, *Duets*. Other ABT premieres included George Balanchine's *Bourrée Fantasque*, Eliot Feld's *Variations on 'America,'* and Roland Petit's *Carmen*.

Injuries plagued many ABT dancers, including Baryshnikov, who underwent knee surgery and was out most of the season. At the expiration of their contracts on August 31 ABT dancers were locked out by management, and engagements in Paris, Boston, and Washington, D.C., were canceled. A two-month layoff ended in November with a four-year contract (a first for ABT). Dancers won major salary gains, an increased number of performance weeks, and improved fringe benefits. The company resumed

Eliot Feld's Over the Pavement, *to music by Charles Ives, was premiered by the Feld Ballet at the Joyce Theater, New York City, in July.*

LOIS GREENFIELD

rehearsals for a delayed season to begin January 1983 in Washington, D.C. Aleksandr Godunov, who defected from the Soviet Union in 1979, left ABT; soloist Gelsey Kirkland was rehired.

New York City Ballet (NYCB) mounted an ambitious Stravinsky Centennial Celebration in June at the New York State Theater, despite the infirmity of the artistic director, George Balanchine, who first underwent cataract surgery and later suffered a fall that necessitated lengthy hospitalization. Compared with the NYCB's landmark 1972 Stravinsky Festival, the 1982 celebration was disappointing. Eleven of the 28 Stravinsky works were newly choreographed. Balanchine mounted new productions of *Persephone* (with Vera Zorina) and *Noah and the Flood* (designed by Rouben Ter-Arutunian) and three short works, *Tango*, *Elegie*, and *Variations*. There were new ballets by Jerome Robbins (*Four Chamber Works*), John Taras (*Concerto for Piano and Wind Instruments*), Jacques d'Amboise (*Serenade en La* and *Pastorale*), and Peter Martins (*Concerto for Two Solo Pianos* and *Piano-Rag-Music*). Lew Christensen's *Norwegian Moods* had its NYCB premiere; Robbins's *Circus Polka* and Balanchine's *Scherzo à la Russe* were revived.

With Balanchine ill there was considerable speculation as to his possible successor, with Martins the most frequently mentioned prospect. The regular season featured Martins's *The Magic Flute* (Riccardo Drigo), staged first in 1981 for the School of American Ballet, Robbins's *The Gershwin Concerto*, and Joseph Duell's *La Création du Monde*. Mel Tomlinson of Dance Theatre of Harlem and David MacNaughton of San Francisco Ballet joined NYCB.

The Dai Rakuda Kan company of Japan performed Sea-Dappled Horse, *one of their* buto *("dark soul") pieces, at the American Dance Festival in Durham, North Carolina, in July.*

WALLY McNAMEE/NEWSWEEK

Joffrey Ballet, strapped financially, announced that it would acquire a second home in Los Angeles in 1984 as resident dance company of the Los Angeles Music Center. It thus became the first major company with a home on both coasts of the U.S. The Joffrey celebrated its 25th season with performances of a new work by Gerald Arpino (*Light Rain*), the first U.S. productions of John Cranko's *The Taming of the Shrew* and Jiri Kylian's *Transfigured Night*, revivals of Kurt Jooss's *The Green Table*, Twyla Tharp's *Deuce Coupe II*, the pas de six from Arthur Saint-Léon's *La Vivandière*, Robbins's *Moves*, and Arpino's *Trinity* and *Secret Places*.

Pennsylvania Ballet survived the disclosure of an accumulated debt of close to $2 million; the resignation of founder Barbara Weisberger, a protégé of George Balanchine; and Balanchine's withdrawal of his ballets. Under Benjamin Harkarvy's direction the dancers toured nationally before a layoff. Harkarvy, who joined the company in 1972, resigned when he was unable to regain the Balanchine repertory. Robert Weiss, principal dancer with NYCB, replaced him as artistic director on a one-year contract, with Martins as artistic adviser.

San Francisco Ballet produced a Stravinsky celebration with in-house choreographers Michael Smuin, Val Caniparoli, John McFall, Robert Gladstein, and Tomm Ruud. The season also included *Vilzak Variations*, staged by ballet master Anatole Vilzak, and a newly designed production of Lew Christensen's *Beauty and the Beast* by José Varona.

The Metropolitan Opera's Stravinsky tribute was designed by painter David Hockney. It comprised *Le Sacre du Printemps* (Jean-Pierre Bonnefous), *Le Rossignol* (Frederick Ashton for Natalia Makarova and Anthony Dowell), and *Oedipus Rex* (narrated by Dowell).

Dance Theatre of Harlem toured widely during 1982, staging company premieres of Valerie Bettis's *A Streetcar Named Desire*, Geoffrey Holder's *Songs of the Auvergne* and *Banda*, Domy Reiter-Soffer's *Equus*, and Ruth Page and Bentley Stone's *Frankie and Johnny*. There was also a world premiere of John Taras's *Firebird*, with sets and costumes by Geoffrey Holder.

Ballet West presented *Swan Lake*, newly staged by Denise Schultze and Louis Godfrey (formerly from South Africa), and there were premieres by Helen Douglas and company director Bruce Marks. The Feld Ballet, directed by Eliot Feld, inaugurated its home in New York City, the Joyce Theater, a 500-seat converted movie house designed for Feld and other small companies. Feld's new ballets included *Play Bach* and *Over the Pavement*.

The Boston Ballet mounted Rudolf Nureyev's *Don Quixote*, with sets and costumes by Nicholas Georgiadis, and took it on the road with Nureyev. In Miami, Fla., Norbert Vesak's New World Ballet Company made its debut in the New World Festival of the Arts with premieres by Vesak, Vicente Nebrada, Lynn Seymour, and Oscar Araiz. Patricia

MARTHA SWOPE

Nina Fedorova and Adam Lüders starred in Noah and the Flood, *one of the principal productions in the New York City Ballet's Stravinsky Centennial Celebration.*

Wilde, former director of the ABT School, which closed in 1982, replaced Patrick Franz as artistic director of Pittsburgh Ballet. Flemming Flindt and Ted Kivitt completed their first seasons directing the Dallas and Milwaukee ballets, respectively. Indianapolis Ballet Theatre staged the first Western production of Marius Petipa's one-act *Cavalry Hall*. Following its production of Bronislava Nijinska's *Les Noces*, the first by a U.S. company, the Oakland Ballet staged Nijinska's *Les Biches*.

Martha Graham, 88 and in ill health, presented two new works in her City Center season, *Dances of the Golden Hall* (Andrzej Panufnik) and *Andromache's Lament* (Samuel Barber), and revived *Dark Meadow*, *Primitive Mysteries*, and *Herodiade*. The José Limón Dance Company celebrated its 35th anniversary and tenth year since Limón's death with a tribute at the Joyce Theater. The Alvin Ailey troupe celebrated its 25th anniversary season with new works by Rodney Griffin (*Sonnets*) and Elisa Monte (*Pigs and Fishes*). In City Center seasons Merce Cunningham presented *Trails* and *Gallopade* and his latest film/dance collaboration with Charles Atlas,

Channels/Inserts; Paul Taylor created *Lost, Found and Lost* and *Mercuric Tidings* and revived *Orbs.* Twyla Tharp presented two new works in Vancouver, B.C. (*Bad Smells* and *Nine Sinatra Songs*). David Gordon's *T.V. Reel* and *Trying Times*, Meredith Monk's *Specimen Days*, and Bill T. Jones's *Social Intercourse* were among notable new works that mixed media, movement, and language.

Foreign companies visiting the U.S. for the first time included Ballet Rambert from Great Britain, the Norwegian National Ballet, and the Cullberg Ballet from Sweden. The Royal Danish Ballet played two-week seasons at the Kennedy Center in Washington, D.C., and New York City's Metropolitan Opera House, with a rich selection of August Bournonville ballets, including the first U.S. showing of *Kermesse in Bruges.* Other major imports included the Grand Kabuki from Japan, Netherlands Dance Theatre, and Dutch National Ballet. Les Grands Ballet Canadiens made its first U.S. appearance in ten years at New York City Center. There were tributes to Igor Youskevitch in Austin, Texas, and to Katherine Dunham in Chicago.

DEFENSE AND ARMS CONTROL

Continuing Palestine Liberation Organization (PLO) attacks on Israeli territory from Syrian-occupied Lebanon led Israel to invade Lebanon on June 6, 1982, in an effort to neutralize Palestinian and Syrian troops based there. After several weeks of fighting, the Palestinians evacuated the Lebanese capital of Beirut during August 21–September 1, under the supervision of an international U.S., French, and Italian force. (*See* MIDDLE EASTERN AFFAIRS.)

Chief among the basic causes of conflict in the area was the Arab-Israeli dispute. After more than 30 years, the Arab countries (other than Egypt) still refused to accept the existence of Israel. At the same time, their insistence on the creation of a state for the displaced Palestinians was unacceptable to Israel, in large measure because of the dominance within the Palestinian nationalist movement of violent extremists. Adding to unrest in the region were the emergence of Islamic fundamentalism as a major ideological and political force, epitomized by the Ayatollah Ruhollah Khomeini's theocratic regime in Iran; the centuries-old division between the Sunni and Shi'ah branches of Islam; and border disputes such as that leading to the stalemated Iran-Iraq war. Against this background, Israel's reliance on military means to provide for its security was unavoidable. The U.S. had little choice but to support Israel with massive military aid—since Israel could not afford to defend itself—but could influence Israel's military actions only marginally. The U.S. also had to try to protect its interests and those of its allies, including NATO-Europe and Japan's continued access to Persian Gulf oil at stable prices.

In the Lebanese fighting the latest U.S. equipment operated by the Israelis proved far superior to older Soviet equipment manned by the Syrians. Syrian losses were estimated at 70–80 interceptors (out of 244), as against Israeli losses of 2–3 fighter-bombers. The Israeli Air Force (IAF) also destroyed Syria's Soviet-built SA-6 mobile surface-to-air missiles (SAM's) and radar deployed in the Bekaa Valley. Israel's success was attributed to, first, superior electronic countermeasures (ECM/ECCM), including anti-SAM weapons; second, the use of EC-2 Hawkeye airborne warning and control systems (AWACS) aircraft; and, third, superior pilots and equipment.

It would be incorrect to conclude, however, that the results proved the overwhelming supremacy of U.S. military technology, although it performed much better than its critics had predicted. The IAF had not had to fight the latest generation of Soviet fighters and air defense systems, manned by Soviet personnel. Similarly, the supremacy of Israeli ground forces, especially armour and artillery, could not be extrapolated to the East-West land balance.

United States

Contrary to the widespread impression that Pres. Ronald Reagan was undertaking a massive defense buildup, U.S. defense spending as a proportion of gross national product (GNP) increased only slightly, from 5.5 to 6.1%. Because of inflation, the monetary amount seemed large—some $215.9 billion for 1982–83—but U.S. gross domestic product (GDP) had risen to some $3 trillion. The administration's projection for 1984–85 was for a defense budget of about 7% of GNP, compared with average defense spending of 10% of GNP from 1950 to 1965. The impact of this increase was generally overestimated, however. The proportion of GNP spent by the federal government had increased sharply in recent years, and the proportion of government spending allocated to defense had dropped from 41.7% in 1964 to 25.2% in fiscal year 1982.

U.S. strategic nuclear forces (SNF) remained inferior to those of the Soviets. The main changes in U.S. SNF and intermediate nuclear forces (INF) involved the retirement of obsolete systems, including the last of 10 Washington/Allen-class nuclear ballistic missile submarines (SSBN), each carrying 16 Polaris A-3 ballistic missiles (SLBM); 52 Titan II liquid-fueled intercontinental ballistic missiles (ICBM); and 75 B-52D bombers. The only new system deployed was one Ohio-class SSBN with 24 Trident C-4 SLBM's; one more was on trials and seven were building. The first B-52G/H squadron equipped with long-range air-launched cruise missiles (ALCM) became operational. Production of the B-52's replacement, the B-1B, was under way, but the first squadron would not become operational before 1986. The 1,000 aging Minuteman II/III ICBM's were being upgraded; some 300 of the 550 Minuteman III's were being retrofitted with the improved Mk 12A multiple independently targetable reentry vehicle (MIRV).

Controversy continued to surround the basing mode for Minuteman's successor, the MX ICBM, scheduled to become operational in 1986. The pro-

While its political fate was undecided, work proceeded on this prototype MX missile. The black cones are dummy warheads used to align elements of the nose assembly.
MARTY KATZ

posal advocated by President Reagan was to space MX very close together in a "dense pack" system. Attacking Soviet reentry vehicles would, it was hoped, destroy each other with their own blasts—the fratricide phenomenon—enabling a large proportion of the 100 MX in each dense pack field to survive. The defeat of the dense pack proposal and the delay of MX production funding by Congress in December left the entire system in doubt. (Future funding was made contingent on congressional approval of a basing mode.) Loss of the MX, according to the administration, would leave the U.S. without a survivable ICBM force by the late 1980s.

Nonetheless, the administration began to announce a new strategy of prevailing in any major conflict with the Soviets; that is, that the U.S. and its allies would win. This was linked to a strategy of horizontal escalation. A direct, or proxy, Soviet attack on one area of vital U.S. interests (*e.g.*, the Persian Gulf) would be met by U.S. retaliation against one of the Soviets' direct or indirect assets (*e.g.*, Cuba). Hence the administration's emphasis on rebuilding U.S. power-projection forces, notably the Navy, Air Force, and Marine Corps.

The 553,000-strong Navy's 600-ship goal was ambitious, given its current force of 201 major surface combat ships and 90 attack submarines (85 nuclear-powered [SSN]). The core of the fleet remained the attack carrier battle group, built around four nuclear carriers and seven conventional carriers. Each normally carried one air wing of 70–95 aircraft. There were also three older carriers, as well as the "Intrepid," used for training. Major surface combatants included 9 nuclear-powered guided weapons (GW) cruisers and 20 conventionally powered GW cruisers, plus the first of the new Aegis-class fleet air-defense cruisers, the USS "Ticonderoga" (8,000 tons). There were also 41 GW and 43 gun/antisubmarine warfare (ASW) destroyers and 24 GW and 55 gun frigates. Major Navy aircraft included some 400 F-14A/RF-14A Tomcats, 116 A-6E Intruders, 164 A-7E's, and 110 S-3A Viking ASW aircraft.

The U.S. Marine Corps had 192,000 men and 576 M-60A1 tanks, divided into three heavy divisions,

103

In its first test at Cape Canaveral, on July 22, the Army's new Pershing II missile malfunctioned and was destroyed by flight controllers.

each with its own air wing. Aircraft totaled 440, including the first 28 F-18 Hornet fighters. Deployment afloat was in marine amphibious units, each comprising a composite Marine battalion group (1,800 men). One was deployed with the international force in Lebanon.

The 581,000-strong Air Force had some 3,650 combat aircraft. Major aircraft types, excluding the Strategic Air Command, included 624 F-4 Phantoms, 312 F-16 Falcons, 376 F-15 Eagle interceptors, 252 F-111A/D/E/F medium bombers, 288 A-10A Thunderbolt ground-support fighters, and 126 RF-4C reconnaissance Phantoms. Conversion to modern aircraft types (F-15, F-16, and A-10) was nearly complete.

The Army, with 790,800 personnel, provided four armoured, six mechanized, four infantry, one airmobile, and one airborne division. These contained more men but fewer tanks than a Soviet division. U.S. tank holdings totaled 12,130, including 300 new Abrams M-1s.

The central U.S. commitment remained the defense of NATO-Europe, where some 348,600 personnel, including 221,300 troops, were deployed. Other

major commitments were in defense of South Korea (28,500 U.S. troops) and Japan (2,500), plus the Persian Gulf. Overall, U.S. military forces had improved, especially in quality, although not enough to counter the Soviets' formidable qualitative and quantitative advantages.

U.S.S.R.

The growth of Soviet military expenditure and power continued in 1982. Estimates of Soviet defense expenditure as a percentage of GNP remained at the high end of the 9–15% range, with an annual real growth rate of 4–10%. Soviet S/INF reflected this. Modern Soviet SSBN included 1 Typhoon class (20 SS-NX-20 SLBM's; larger than the "Ohio") and 13 D-III class (16 SS-N-18 SLBM's; more of both classes building), as well as 4 D-II's, 18 D-I's, 1 Y-II, and 25 Y-I's. Five Y-I's had been converted to attack submarines. ICBM launch silos totaled some 1,398, but this was not an accurate indication of Soviet ICBM numbers since an estimated 2,000–3,000 reserve ICBM's were available. A new strategic bomber, the Ram-K (NATO code name Blackjack), comparable to the B-1, was deployed, while the number of Backfire long-range (8,000 km; *c.* 5,000 mi) bombers rose to 180.

Deployment of modern INF continued rapidly despite Pres. Leonid Brezhnev's claim of a moratorium. By September there were 333 SS-20 intermediate-range ballistic missile (IRBM) launchers deployed in 37 complexes. Each launcher had one or more reload missiles, each with three warheads, for a total of 666 SS-20 IRBM's with $1,998 \times 150$-kiloton warheads. The Soviets retained 16 SS-5 and 275 SS-4 intermediate/medium-range ballistic missiles (I/MRBM). They also led in the development of space weapons, including antisatellite weapons.

Soviet conventional forces were still the most powerful in the world. Personnel totaled 1,825,000 (1.4 million conscripts), and the quality of their equipment was now comparable to that of the West. This included 50,000 tanks (12,000 new T-72 and older T-62 and 38,000 T-54/55 main battle tanks); 62,000 armoured fighting vehicles (AFV), including the new BTR-70 armoured personnel carrier (APC) and BMP mechanized infantry combat vehicle (MICV); and some 20,000 artillery pieces. These were organized into 46 tank (armoured), 126 motor rifle (mechanized), and 8 airborne divisions, each with more striking power than the Soviet division of a decade earlier.

The Soviet Navy had grown to 450,000 personnel, with 290 major surface combat vessels, 273 cruise-missile and attack submarines (105 nuclear, 168 diesel), 755 combat aircraft in the Naval Air Force, and 300 helicopters. Newer Soviet vessels were designed to project Soviet power as well as to defend Soviet SSBN, attack Western SSBN's, and deny the West use of the sea lines of communication. Construction of a Soviet nuclear-powered attack carrier continued, and a third Kiev-class carrier/cruiser (37,000 tons) was deployed, armed with 14 Yak-36 Forger vertical/short take-off and landing (v/STOL) aircraft, similar to the British Harrier. The new Sovremenny-type GW destroyers and Udaloy-type ASW GW destroyers were joining the 39 existing GW destroyers and 77 GW frigates.

The Soviet Tactical Air Force of 475,000 personnel continued to expand its deep-interdiction capability. Older strike aircraft (100 MiG-21s, 150 Su-7s, and 650 Su-17s) were being phased out and replaced by the MiG-27 Flogger D/J and Su-24 Fencer (current deployment 550 each). A new ground-attack aircraft, the Su-25 Frogfoot (formerly Ram-J), comparable to the U.S. A-10 Thunderbolt, was being deployed in Afghanistan. A new fighter, the MiG-29 Fulcrum (Ram-L), was reported.

NATO

The divisions within NATO, symbolized by the controversy over implementation of the 1979 INF modernization program, remained serious. In the view of the U.S. and the U.K., there was a real Soviet politico-military threat that should be contained by rebuilding NATO military capabilities for deterrence and defense. To the NATO-Europeans and Canada, this view exaggerated the threat while understating the importance of détente and arms control. These legitimate differences of interest had been exacerbated by the reemergence of antinuclear, neutralist, nationalistic, and anti-American sentiment in Britain, Belgium, The Netherlands, and West Germany, fanned by a Soviet propaganda campaign.

NATO's chief military problem remained the weakness of its conventional forces on the crucial Central Front from Norway to southern Germany. NATO could offer an effective conventional defense of only ten days or less before resorting to nuclear weapons. But the Soviets seemed likely to win a theatre nuclear exchange, forcing the U.S. to use its SNF and thus bring on a Soviet strategic counterstrike. Static force comparisons underestimated NATO's weakness because the Soviet forces could mobilize more quickly and concentrate superior forces at chosen points for a breakthrough. But the crude figures themselves pointed up NATO's inferiority on the Central Front, even if the French forces were counted: 10,356 tanks to some 17,000 Soviet tanks, plus reserves; the equivalent of some 66 divisions to 119 for the U.S.S.R./Warsaw Pact.

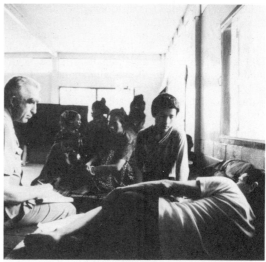

BOWIE/DISCOVER

Evidence continued to accumulate of the use of outlawed chemical weapons by Vietnamese forces in Laos, this victim's home, and Cambodia.

Arms Control and Disarmament

Further evidence emerged, confirmed by an independent Canadian investigation, of massive Soviet violations of the 1925 Geneva Protocol banning the first use of chemical weapons and the 1972 Biological Warfare Convention banning the manufacture, stockpiling, and use of biological weapons. The evidence showed that the Soviets (and their Vietnamese allies) had used CBW in Southeast Asia since 1976–78 and in Afghanistan from the start of the occupation in 1979. This called into question Soviet reliability in observing the terms of any arms control agreement and indicated that U.S. requirements for verification would have to be more rigorous, as would requirements for enforcing compliance by a credible U.S. threat to abrogate any agreement the Soviets violated. The Soviets had also exceeded the limits on strategic delivery vehicles contained in the 1972 SALT I and 1979 SALT II agreements (although the latter remained unratified). They were in violation of the 1972 ABM treaty, which was undergoing its second five-yearly review in 1982, and of the unratified 1974 Threshold Test Ban Treaty, which banned underground tests of more than 150 kilotons.

The French Exocet missile gave Argentina its chief success in the Falklands war, the sinking of the HMS Sheffield.
WIDE WORLD

Despite this pattern, the Reagan administration was still pursuing arms control in the strategic arms reduction talks (START) and the intermediate nuclear force (INF) talks. President Reagan had set out the U.S. START objectives as elimination of the Soviet land-based ICBM first-strike capability and reduction of U.S. and U.S.S.R. strategic forces. He proposed a mutual reduction of warheads to 5,000 on ICBM's and SLBM's (not more than 2,500 on ICBM's), with a ceiling of 850 on ICBM and SLBM launchers. The Soviets replied by proposing a 25% reduction in their ICBM/SLBM launchers in exchange for a 10% reduction in U.S. forces, limiting U.S. SLBM's and banning U.S. cruise missiles. These positions were unreconcilable. It was ironic that a movement supporting a bilateral nuclear freeze should emerge in the U.S. at this juncture, but the movement—however impractical—reflected a growing realization that traditional approaches to arms control had failed.

DENMARK

The major economic problems facing Denmark in 1982 were the rising foreign debt, accumulated over several years, and a growing budget deficit. The balance of payments deficit was estimated at 20 billion kroner (8.73 kroner=U.S. $1), bringing the foreign debt up to a little more than 25% of Denmark's gross national product (GNP).

The Social Democratic minority government on February 21 announced a 3% devaluation of the krone, and in May it set forth plans to raise an extra 6 billion kroner in taxes. About one-third of the total was to be raised from taxing the previously tax-free pension fund and other similar funds. The remainder was to come from increasing the traditional indirect taxes—on wine, beer, liquor, tobacco, gasoline, and heating oil—and from new taxes on coal for heating, videotapes, and bus trips by tourists. Not all the proposals were accepted; the new pension tax in particular was resisted violently.

In February the people of Greenland voted to leave the European Communities (EC). Greenland—like Denmark itself—was involved in the continuing struggle over fishing rights within the EC.

The grim realities of Denmark's economic situation were spelled out by the finance minister on August 16 when he presented his 1983 budget. It showed national expenditures of 191 billion kroner against income of 117 billion kroner, producing a deficit of 74 billion kroner. This deficit was later revised upward to a little over 80 billion kroner, some 14–16% of the estimated GNP.

Prime Minister Anker Jørgensen tried to find parliamentary support for a way to reduce the deficit by 10 billion kroner. However, there was opposition from right-wing parties to the taxing of pension funds, while the Progress Party claimed that the government should be cutting spending by 60 billion–70 billion kroner. On the left wing, the Socialist People's Party wanted nothing to do with tax increases and was even less in favour of spending cuts.

FRANCIS DEAN—SYGMA

Anker Jørgensen (right) was succeeded as prime minister of Denmark by Poul Schlüter (with flowers) at the head of a conservative coalition.

All this dissent resulted in the resignation of Prime Minister Jørgensen on September 3. Six days later Denmark had its first Conservative prime minister in more than 80 years, Poul Schlüter, at the head of a minority coalition government comprising the Conservative, Liberal Democratic (Venstre), Centre Democratic, and Christian People's parties.

On October 5 Prime Minister Schlüter presented his government's program to the Folketing. It was an austerity program similar to (though more severe than) that which Jørgensen had proposed. Among many other features, it planned to cancel automatic wage indexation for two years, to freeze unemployment benefits (according to analysts this represented a real decrease in purchasing power over two years of 15–20%), to introduce the much-debated tax on pension funds for an interim period of two years, to reduce the state old-age pension for those with earned incomes, and to freeze wages from October 5 until March 1983. This package was approved by 90 votes to 85 on October 17.

DENTISTRY

In a sweeping report on the future of dentistry the American Dental Association (ADA) during 1982 projected that, although new methods of financing and delivering dental care were gaining popularity, the mainstream of services would continue to take place in the offices of the private practitioner. As an example of alternate care the ADA noted the slowly growing number of dental centres in department and drug stores, which increased from one such clinic in

California in 1977 to 91 retail-store dentistry centres in 17 states and in the District of Columbia in 1982.

A specific strain of bacterium that inhibits the function of certain white blood cells offered a new clue to researchers at the State University of New York at Buffalo who were studying ways of fighting periodontal, or gum, disease. Gum disease, the major cause of tooth loss in adults, causes the underlying bone to resorb into the jaw, thus allowing the teeth to loosen. T. E. Van Dyke reported that cells of the immune system called neutrophils guard the gum crevices against bacterial attacks. His research suggested that the bacterium specifically inhibits binding of stimulatory molecules to the neutrophil surface, indicating that periodontal disease may be of local rather than of systemic nature.

One successful attempt at a less expensive substitute for increasingly costly silver-based dental alloys came from L. B. Johnson of the University of Virginia. A conventional alloy contains mainly tin, silver, and copper, which generally are melted together and then powdered. This powder is then mixed with mercury at the time of treatment. The outside of each alloy particle reacts with the mercury to form a matrix in which the unreacted portions of each particle set, resembling pebbles in cement. These particles, however, still contain about 60% silver. Johnson replaced the powdered alloy with copper granules to which enough silver and tin had been plated to allow the matrix to form as usual. The difference is that the particles set in the matrix are mostly copper and thus much less expensive than granules of silver alloy.

In recent years one approach to the prevention of cavities has been to replace sucrose with nonsucrose sweeteners. According to Larry Breeding of the University of Kentucky College of Dentistry, two such sweeteners, saccharin and Acesulfame-K, may curb dental caries (decay) by means other than simple substitution. Breeding found that these synthetic sweeteners actively inhibit the growth of the tooth-decay bacterium, *Streptococcus mutans*, and also restrict its ability to use such dietary carbohydrates as sucrose in the development of caries.

DISASTERS OF 1982

The loss of life and property from disasters in 1982 included the following:

Aviation

January 13, Potomac River, Washington, D.C. An Air Florida Boeing 737 jetliner crashed into a crowded bridge, broke into pieces, and sank into the river moments after takeoff from National Airport during a snowstorm; the crash claimed the lives of 74 of the 79 persons on the plane and 4 others in vehicles on the bridge.

February 5, Cheju, South Korea. A C-123 military transport plane carrying 53 persons crashed into Mt. Halla, the country's highest mountain, when strong winds jerked the aircraft as it approached a landing strip; there were no survivors.

February 9, Tokyo Bay. A DC-8 jetliner dived into Tokyo Bay some 900 ft (275 m) short of the runway at Tokyo International Airport when its captain, who had been experiencing mental difficulties, pushed the control stick forward moments before the crash; 24 persons were killed and some 150 others were injured.

April 13, Near Erzincan, Turkey. A U.S. C-130 cargo plane crashed into a mountain and burst into flames; all 28 military personnel aboard were killed.

April 26, Near Guilin (Kuei-lin), China. A Chinese jetliner carrying 112 persons from Guangzhou (Canton) to the scenic city of Guilin crashed some 28 mi (45 km) short of its destination; all aboard were killed.

June 8, Near Fortaleza, Brazil. A Boeing 727 Brazilian airliner crashed in the Pocatuba Mountains during heavy rains; all 137 persons aboard were killed.

July 6, Near Moscow, U.S.S.R. An Ilyushin-62 jetliner crashed moments after takeoff in the area of Sheremetyevo Airport; all 90 persons aboard reportedly were killed.

July 9, Kenner, La. A Pan American World Airways Boeing 727 jet carrying 145 persons crashed shortly after taking off from New Orleans, exploded, and plowed through four residential streets; the

Twenty-four passengers died when their Japan Air Lines DC-8 plunged into Tokyo Bay 1,000 feet short of the runway at Haneda International Airport.
UPI

accident, which killed 153 persons including 8 on the ground, was the second worst air disaster in U.S. history involving a single plane.

September 11, Mannheim, West Germany. A U.S. Army helicopter carrying an international parachuting team crashed minutes after taking off from Neuostheim airfield, the site of an air show; all 44 persons aboard the copter were killed.

October 17, Near Taft, Calif. A C-45H Beechcraft airplane, carrying 12 skydivers, a jumpmaster, and a pilot, crashed and exploded into flames moments after takeoff; all aboard were killed.

December 9, Near San Andres de Bocay, Nicaragua. An air force helicopter carrying Indian children crashed and burst into flames; 75 children and 9 women were killed in the crash.

Fires and Explosions

February 8, Tokyo, Japan. An early morning fire ripped through the top two floors of a ten-story luxury hotel; 32 persons were killed and more than 60 others were injured.

March 6, Houston, Texas. A fire in one room of a new 165-room high-rise hotel was confined to that room, but 12 persons died of suffocation when thick billowing smoke infiltrated their rooms. The tragedy was complicated by a hotel employee who unwittingly and repeatedly turned off the fire alarm.

April 30, Hoboken, N.J. A predawn fire in a four-story hotel claimed the lives of 12 residents; police confirmed that arson was the cause of the blaze.

May 15, Baltimore, Md. A residential home caught fire after a candle affixed to a wall tipped over and ignited a sofa; four persons escaped with minor injuries but ten others were killed.

May 25, Aire, France. A fire in a privately run home for mentally handicapped teenagers resulted in the deaths of 18 persons, including 2 staff members.

July 5, Waterbury, Conn. A fire set by an arsonist ripped through two brick tenement buildings; 11 persons were killed.

August 17, Luanco, Spain. A block of three-story apartment buildings was reduced to rubble after some propane gas containers exploded in a ground-floor restaurant; 10 persons were killed in the blast and 11 others were injured.

September 4, Los Angeles, Calif. A fast-burning fire swept through a four-story tenement house and claimed the lives of 18 persons including 5 children and 4 infants.

November 8, Biloxi, Miss. A fire believed to have been started by an inmate at the county jail claimed the lives of 27 prisoners, many of whom succumbed after inhaling toxic fumes from burning polyurethane padding in the jail cells.

November 11, Tyre, Lebanon. An explosion rocked an Israeli military headquarters building and claimed the lives of 47 persons; an investigation was being made into the cause of the blast.

December 19, Near Caracas, Venezuela. A fire erupted at a power plant when a storage tank containing 80,000 bbl of fuel oil ignited while it was being discharged; the tank exploded, ignited two other tanks, and blazed for three days before firemen could control the fire; at least 129 persons were killed and 500 others injured in one of the country's worst disasters.

Marine

January 6, Aleutian Islands. The ship "Akebono Maru" capsized while being boarded by fishermen in the Aleutian Islands; 27 fishermen were missing and presumed dead.

February 16, Off the coast of Canada. A Soviet freighter, the "Mekhanik Tarasov," carrying some 35 to 40 crewmen, sank in heavy North Atlantic seas; 7 men were rescued by a Danish trawler, but all other lives were lost because the remaining men insisted on waiting for a Soviet rescue vessel.

March 28, Boca Raton, Fla. A wooden Haitian freighter called "The Esperancia" broke up and sank in 15-ft (4.5-m) seas; at least 20 persons drowned, many of them believed to be Haitian refugees who were smuggled aboard by crewmen.

March 28, Near Rangoon, Burma. A passenger ferry capsized in a canal and claimed the lives of nearly 130 passengers.

April 11, Near Henzada, Burma. A double-decker ferry carrying more than 300 persons sank after slamming into a sandbar; at least 160 persons were missing and presumed drowned.

April 17, Near Cairo, Egypt. A 36-ft (11-m) ferryboat sank in the Ismailia Canal after overzealous factory workers forced their way onto the small craft in order to attend a soccer match; as many as 100 persons were feared dead.

October 17, Java Sea. The "Karya Tambangan" cargo ship sank off the coast of central Indonesia; 89 of the 120 persons aboard were missing and presumed drowned.

Mining

May 12, Zenica, Yugos. Two methane gas explosions in a coal mine claimed the lives of 39 miners; the cause of the blast was unknown.

October 6, Northwestern Liberia. After three days of torrential rain, an avalanche of iron-ore waste descended on sleeping workers at a mining camp on the Mano River; 45 miners were known dead, 150 others were missing and presumed dead, and 29 workers were injured.

Miscellaneous

January 17, Near Guaíra, Brazil. A footbridge suspended over a waterfall on the Paraná River collapsed and dropped tourists into the waterfall or the river; at least 30 persons were feared dead at Guaíra Falls, which is on the Brazil–Paraguay border.

February 15, Off the coast of Newfoundland, Canada. The "Ocean Ranger," the world's largest submersible oil rig, listed and sank in 50-ft (15-m)

Pres. François Mitterrand, Prime Minister Pierre Mauroy, and other dignitaries attended the funeral of 44 schoolchildren who died in a fiery bus crash, France's worst highway disaster in history.
ROBERT COHEN – AGIP / PICTORIAL PARADE

seas; all 84 men aboard the rig, including those who tried to escape from the structure in lifeboats, were presumed drowned.

February 17, Moscow, U.S.S.R. When the moving surface of an escalator broke during rush hour at the Aviamotornaya subway station, at least 15 persons were killed when they were pitched into the mechanism or thrown down a 150-ft (46-m) shaft beneath the escalator.

April 15, East Chicago, Ind. Two sections of an unfinished bridge collapsed and hurled 12 construction workers to their death; 17 others were hospitalized with serious crushing injuries.

July 10, Mwinilunga, Zambia. A measles epidemic claimed the lives of 51 children.

Early September, Kerala, India. Poisoned homemade liquor that was sold to revelers at a festival killed 54 persons and left more than 600 others hospitalized.

November 29, Igapo, Brazil. A power line fell on a crowd of people who were watching rescuers remove victims from a wrecked van that had crashed into a power post; of the 29 persons killed, some were electrocuted and others died after being hurled into a barbed wire fence.

December 3, Cairo, Egypt. A five-story house collapsed and 55 persons were killed; 15 persons were injured and 32 others escaped unharmed.

Natural

January–March, Madagascar. Five tropical cyclones, named Benedict, Frida, Electra, Gabriel, and Justine, ravaged various regions of Madagascar; more than 100 persons were killed, 117,000 others were left homeless, and over 98,800 ac (40,000 ha) of crops were destroyed.

January 3–5. San Francisco Bay area, Calif. A devastating rainstorm that lashed the area with more than 12 in (30 cm) of precipitation triggered flooding and mudslides that killed at least 37 persons in the counties of Santa Cruz, San Mateo, Contra Costa, Marin, and Sonoma.

January 9–12, Europe. Frigid cold and wind-whipped snowdrifts battered Europe and claimed the lives of at least 23 persons; hardest hit was Wales, which was cut off from the rest of Britain by 12-ft (3.7-m)-high snowdrifts, making travel impossible.

January 9–17, United States. An onslaught of record-breaking arctic-cold temperatures, combined with fierce, icy winds and, in some cities, heavy snow, was blamed for the deaths of more than 230 persons nationwide.

January 23–24, Western Peru. The swollen Chuntayaco River burst its banks after several days of rain and swept away 17 villages along a 60-mi (97-km) stretch of the river; at least 600 persons were killed and some 2,000 others were missing.

January 31, Near Salzburg, Austria. An avalanche on the Elmau-Alm slope in the Tennen Mountain range killed 13 members of a West German student group, including their teacher.

March 14, France. A spate of avalanches in the French Alps claimed the lives of at least 11 skiers; a late winter thaw triggered the massive slides of snow, rock, and dirt.

Late March, Philippines. Typhoons Mamie and Nelson rampaged across the central and southern islands of the country, leaving some 17,000 people homeless and claiming the lives of at least 90 others.

March 29, Near Pichucalco, Mexico. El Chichón, a 7,300-ft (2,200-m) volcano that had been dormant for centuries, erupted, spewed nearly a billion tons of hot ash and rock, and killed as many as 100 persons living in villages on its slopes.

April 2–3, Midwestern and southern U.S. A series

Twelve workers died when several spans of a bridge under construction in East Chicago, Indiana, collapsed in a mass of wreckage.

of deadly tornadoes swirled through Ohio, Texas, Arkansas, Mississippi, and Missouri and left 31 persons dead; hardest hit were Paris, Texas, where 10 persons died, and Arkansas, where 14 were killed.

April 6, United States. An unseasonable blizzard moving from the Rocky Mountains to the northeastern states inflicted severe damage to crops and property, forced some airports and schools to close, and killed 33 persons.

May 11–12, Kansas, Oklahoma, Texas. A cavalcade of tornadoes rampaged through Oklahoma, Texas, and Kansas and killed at least seven persons.

Mid-May, Guangdong (Kwangtung) Province, China. Torrential rains precipitated the worst flooding in 30 years; at least 430 persons were killed, 450,000 others were marooned, and some 46,000 homes collapsed.

Late May, Honduras and Nicaragua. The worst flooding in 50 years killed 75 persons in Nicaragua and 125 others in Honduras; the damage to homes, roads, bridges, and crops was estimated at $200 million.

May 29, Marion, Ill. A deadly tornado left a 15-mi (24-km) swath of destruction and killed at least ten persons.

Late July, Southern Japan. Monsoon rains touched off landslides and the worst flooding in 25 years. The death toll stood at 245 persons; 117 others were missing.

August 12–13, South Korea. A raging typhoon battered the country's southwestern coast; 38 persons were known dead, 26 others were missing, 6,000 were left homeless, and 100 persons were injured in flash floods and landslides.

Mid-August, South Korea. Typhoon Cecil blasted the country, claimed the lives of at least 35 persons, left 28 missing, injured 42 others, and caused more than $30 million in damage.

Early September, Orissa, India. The worst monsoon flooding in memory displaced nearly 8 million people and swept away more than 2,000 head of cattle; at least 1,000 persons were feared dead in the coastal districts and 5 million others were receiving aid from air force planes dropping food and supplies to those marooned on rooftops and islands.

September 11–12, Japan. Typhoon Judy battered the country with 110 mph (175 km/h) winds and caused hundreds of millions of dollars in damage; 26 persons were killed, 94 were injured, and 8 others were missing.

September 17–21, El Salvador. Five days of relentless torrential rain triggered floods and huge mudslides that buried hundreds of people. The El Salvador government reported that 700 persons were known dead, 18,000 were injured, and 55,000 others were made homeless. Neighbouring Guatemala reported 615 deaths related to the storm and hundreds of others missing.

November 8, Gujarat, India. A devastating hurricane struck the western coast of the country with gusting winds of 125 mph (200 km/h); the storm leveled 30,000 homes, destroyed crops, cut power and communication lines, and claimed the lives of at least 275 persons.

Early December, Arkansas, Illinois, Missouri. Torrential rains precipitated heavy flooding that caused at least $500 million in damage in three states; 20 persons lost their lives and 4 others were missing.

Early December, Western U.S. Blizzards, rainstorms, and tornadoes swept across the western states; heavy rains and high winds in California burgeoned into a blizzard that dumped 6 ft (1.8 m) of snow in the Sierra Nevada and 4 ft (1.2 m) over the Rocky Mountains. At least 34 persons were killed in the storms.

December 13, Dhamar Province, Yemen Arab Republic. A deadly earthquake measuring 6.0 on the Richter scale struck the province, killing more than 2,800 persons and injuring some 1,500 others; nearly 300 villages were either damaged or destroyed.

December 16, Baghlan, Afghanistan. A powerful earthquake measuring 6.0 on the Richter scale killed more than 500 persons, injured 3,000 others, and destroyed thousands of homes.

Railroads

January 27, Near Beni Helouane, Alg. A passenger train carrying 450 persons broke free from its locomotive, sped backward down an incline, and struck a stopped cargo train at Beni Helouane station; 130 persons were killed and at least 140 others were injured.

July 11, Tepic, Mexico. A passenger train carrying 1,560 persons to Guadalajara plunged into a mountain gorge when an eroded roadbed caused the tracks to collapse beneath the coaches; 120 persons were killed.

September 12, Near Zürich, Switz. A locomotive slammed into a tourist bus carrying West German soccer fans after the signalwoman failed to lower the railroad barriers at the crossing. Thirty-nine of the 41 passengers aboard the bus were killed and at least 10 others were injured, including the signalwoman, who was severely burned.

Traffic

January 27, Near Baguio, Phil. A bus carrying a group of Canadian tourists to the resort city of Baguio was struck by a larger tourist bus traveling in the opposite direction; the smaller bus's fuel tank was smashed and the bus exploded, killing 12 persons.

July 31, Near Beaune, France. A ten-vehicle pile-up resulted in the deaths of 44 children and 9 adults; the worst road disaster in France's history occurred when a bus stopped, two cars smashed into the bus, and then a second bus slammed into the wreckage and exploded in flames. A third bus and five other cars were also involved in the accident.

Early November, Northern Afghanistan. A Soviet fuel truck collided with another vehicle in the Salang Tunnel and exploded, sending noxious fumes throughout the 1.7-mi (2.7-km)-long tunnel. Eyewitnesses reported that hundreds of Soviet soldiers and Afghan civilians were asphyxiated by the fumes or burned to death when the Soviets sealed off the tunnel in fear that they were being attacked by Afghans.

December 26, Brahmanbari, Bangladesh. An overcrowded passenger bus plunged into a riverbed when the bridge it was traveling over collapsed; of the more than 100 persons aboard, 45 were killed and 80 others were seriously injured.

DOMINICAN REPUBLIC

Presidential and congressional elections held on May 16, 1982, showed a shift to the left with 56-year-old lawyer Salvador Jorge Blanco, a moderate leftist within the ruling Partido Revolucionario Dominicano (PRD), being elected president with 48% of the votes cast. Former president Joaquín Balaguer of the Partido Reformista received 35% of the votes. The PRD achieved a majority in both houses of Congress for the first time.

On taking office, President Jorge Blanco stated that he would seek closer links with the U.S. and would hesitate over establishing ties with Cuba. The period leading up to the transfer of power was marred by the suicide of Pres. Antonio Guzmán Fernández. Vice-Pres. Jacobo Majluta Azar completed the last six weeks of President Guzmán's term of office.

The country faced an economic crisis in 1982, with the main export crop, sugar, selling at less than half the cost of production, no foreign reserves, 28% unemployment, and a budget deficit of more than $450 million. President Jorge Blanco announced an austerity program that included a wage freeze, price controls, higher taxes, and an import ban on such farm products as poultry, pork, rice, and beans.

DRUGS

Far overshadowing any other news about drugs during 1982 were the deaths of seven persons in the Chicago area from poisoned Tylenol capsules. While this tragic episode certainly conveyed the message that drugs are not risk-free, it remained the case that the risk of injury from nonprescription medicines is almost infinitesimal. Federally mandated tamper-resistant packaging standards for nonprescription medicines were the direct result of the Tylenol episode. (*See* Safety.) An advisory by the surgeon general of the U.S. Public Health Service cautioned against the use of salicylates (aspirin) and salicylate-containing medications by children with influenza or chicken pox because of the possible link between salicylates and Reye's syndrome, a rare and often fatal childhood disease.

Prescribing instructions for the "morning sickness" drug Bendictin were altered to include information about the relationship between high doses of the drug and birth deformities in some rats and monkeys. Nonprescription drug labels were changed to include a warning that pregnant women and nursing mothers should "seek professional advice" before taking any drug product. Stocks were recalled and sales suspended of a new and widely hailed antiarthritis drug, Oraflex, after reports of deaths associated with its use.

A controversy about the risks of vaccination against pertussis (whooping cough) grew out of a television documentary emphasizing the risks of encephalopathy—brain disease—among children taking the pertussis vaccine. The program apparently caused many parents to decide against having their children vaccinated. While a risk was associated with pertussis vaccine, there was a much greater risk in not being vaccinated. According to Kenneth J. Bart of the Centers for Disease Control, one in

100,000 children who contracted whooping cough suffered some form of permanent brain damage. The American Academy of Pediatrics pointed out that the number of cases of permanent brain damage associated with the vaccine was one in 310,000 injections. Before introduction of the vaccine 40 years ago, whooping cough killed some 7,000 children per year; currently 5 to 20 die.

Counterbalancing this increased concern over the risks associated with medicines was the unusually

Doctors in 250 U.S. hospitals were shown this televised demonstration of the action of the newly approved antibiotic piperacillin sodium. In this sequence the drug causes bacilli to elongate while preventing them from multiplying; finally the cell wall ruptures.

COURTESY OF LEDERLE LABORATORIES, DIVISION OF AMERICAN CYANAMID CO.

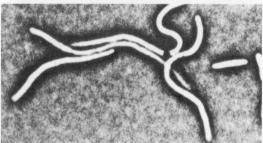
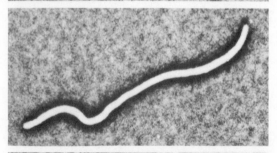
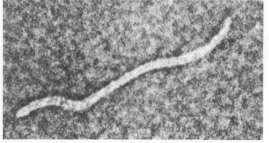

large number of beneficial new drugs approved by the FDA during the year:

Procardia (nifedipine) was approved as a potentially important alternative treatment for patients with angina—the vise-like chest pain that ensues when narrowed or contracting arteries starve the heart muscle of oxygen-bearing blood. The drug was the first oral form of an important new group of drugs called calcium blockers.

Accutane was approved for treating the most severe and disfiguring form of acne, cystic acne. The drug, 13-cis-retinoic acid, also known chemically as isotretinoin, is a derivative of vitamin A. It was not intended for common uncomplicated cases of acne but for the chronic disorder that usually causes deep pitting and scarring. This form of acne affected about 350,000 Americans. (*See* Medicine.)

Zovirax (acyclovir sodium) was the first drug available to help manage genital herpes. Used as an ointment or in intravenous infusion, it could shorten episodes of the disease but not cure it. Genital herpes affected between 5 million and 20 million Americans. Carafate (sucralfate), a basic aluminum salt of polysulfated sucrose, was approved for short-term (up to eight weeks) treatment of duodenal ulcer. Niclocide (niclosamide) was designed for treating tapeworm infestations. It acts on contact with the parasite by killing the scolex, or head. For control of severe, recalcitrant psoriasis, Puva, a treatment using the drug methoxsalen (8-methoxypsoralen) in conjunction with ultraviolet A light, was approved.

Prostin VR Pediatric (alprostadil or synthetic prostaglandin) was designed to treat those children born with heart defects that do not permit adequate flow of oxygen through the body—the so-called blue babies. Since the drug had limited commercial appeal (there were only about 1,500 children each year with this heart defect) it had been classified as an "orphan drug," one not developed because it was for a rare disease or otherwise lacked commercial interest. The FDA began making special efforts to find sponsors (manufacturers) for orphan drugs.

Humulin, the first health care product manufactured by recombinant DNA technology, or genesplicing, is synthetic human insulin. While not offering significant therapeutic advantage over the most highly purified insulin of swine origin, Humulin was important because the development of drugs and biologics by means of DNA technology would ensure a virtually limitless supply of products.

Visken (pindolol), the first of a new class of betablockers, differed from other beta-blockers in maintaining the resting heart rate closer to normal. This avoided a potential complication in treatment of hypertension that was a troublesome side effect of earlier beta-blockers. Chymodiactin (chymopapain), an injectable drug derived from the papaya, could be used as an alternative to surgery in treating such back problems as herniated lower back disks ("slipped disks") when more conservative measures, such as bed rest and traction, failed.

EARTH SCIENCES

Seismically 1982 was comparatively quiet, experiencing no great earthquakes (Richter magnitude 8.0 or greater). Among several shocks that reached magnitude 7.0 or greater, the largest occurred on June 19 in El Salvador. At magnitude 7.4 it caused 16 deaths and many injuries. Extensive damage due to seismic vibration and landslides left thousands homeless in El Salvador and southeastern Guatemala. The shock was also felt in Costa Rica, Honduras, and Nicaragua. On December 13 a series of shocks of magnitude 5.4–6.0 shook North Yemen, killing over 2,000 and leaving hundreds of thousands homeless. Two shocks of special interest occurred on January 9 in New Brunswick. Although they were not damaging, they had magnitudes of 5.7 and 5.4 and were the largest in the region since 1855.

Volcanic activity was less destructive than usual. In the state of Washington, Mt. St. Helens, which continued to be studied intensively, exhibited moderate and varied activity until March 19, when it produced the most significant eruption in 17 months. A cloud of tephra (solid particles) rose to an altitude of more than 13.5 km (1 km = 0.62 mi), and a directed blast caused an avalanche down the north slope into Spirit Lake and a mud flow down the North Fork of the Toutle River, where it did minor damage. The volcano remained rather active during succeeding months.

A phenomenon that evoked considerable interest among meteorologists and geophysicists was a stratospheric aerosol cloud first detected by lidar (laser radar) at Fukuoka, Japan, on January 23. On January 28 it was detected at Mauna Loa, Hawaii, and four days later it was reported at Garmisch-Partenkirchen, West Germany. On February 13 a lidar-equipped plane flew from Wallops Island, Va., 3,000 km to Costa Rica, encountering an unbroken cloud along the entire path at altitudes of 16.5 to 19.5 km. Subsequent analysis of cloud samples showed that it contained none of the debris that would have resulted from either a nuclear explosion or a meteorite; instead it had a high sulfuric acid content indicative of a volcanic origin. After considering several previous eruptions, experts decided that the eruptions of Mt. Nyamulagira in Zaire in late December 1981 were the probable source. Some uncertainty remained because the cloud was detected as far north as West Germany, whereas the volcano is located at latitude 1° S.

While these investigations were in progress, El Chichón in Mexico became active for the first time in modern history. Eruptions began on March 26 and continued through mid-May. A particularly violent blast on March 29 killed as many as 100 persons living in nearby villages. On April 4 an explosive eruption produced a cloud that by May 1 had circled the Earth. The cloud reached an altitude of more than 32 km in late June with the densest portions detected at 28 km altitude. On the slopes of El Chichón pyroclastic deposits trapped subsequent rains and formed several lakes. One of these natural dams failed on May 27, releasing the waters of a lake 5 km in length into a nearby river and inundating a hydroelectric plant 35 km downstream.

After a series of four earthquakes ranging in magnitude from 5.5 to 6.1 occurred in Long Valley Caldera in California during May 1980, the U.S. Geological Survey (USGS) began monitoring the area very closely. An earthquake hazard watch was issued in May 1980 and remained in effect at the end of 1982. By May 1982, when seismic activity decreased, 22 earthquake swarms had been recorded in a limited area about 3.5 km from the town of Mammoth Lakes, Calif. The first occurred at a depth of nine kilometres, but as time went on the swarms

Yemeni villagers looked on as a Swiss search party sought survivors in their devastated village following a December earthquake that killed over 2,000.
KEYSTONE

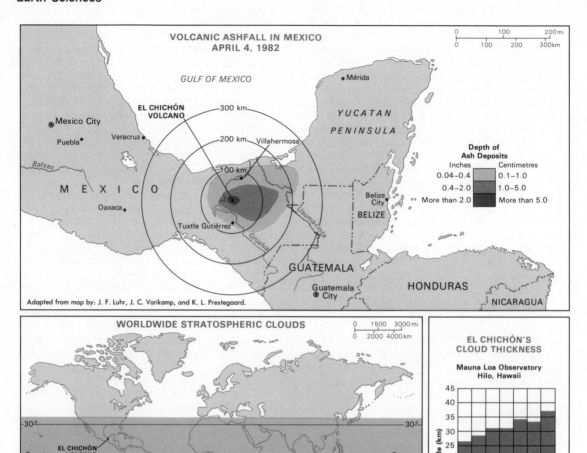

VOLCANIC ASHFALL IN MEXICO
APRIL 4, 1982

GULF OF MEXICO

Mérida

EL CHICHÓN VOLCANO

300 km.
200 km. · Villahermosa
100 km.

Mexico City

Puebla · · Veracruz

Balsas

M E X I C O

Oaxaca ·

Tuxtla Gutiérrez

YUCATAN PENINSULA

Depth of Ash Deposits

Inches	Centimetres
0.04–0.4	0.1–1.0
0.4–2.0	1.0–5.0
More than 2.0	More than 5.0

Belize City

BELIZE

Usumacinta

Grijalva

GUATEMALA

Guatemala City

HONDURAS

NICARAGUA

Adapted from map by: J. F. Luhr, J. C. Varikamp, and K. L. Prestegaard.

WORLDWIDE STRATOSPHERIC CLOUDS

EL CHICHÓN VOLCANO

Equator   Equator

El Chichón's volcanic cloud dispersion three months after eruption, July 1982.

"Mystery Cloud's" latitudinal distribution three months after detection, March 1982.

Source: NASA Solar Mesosphere Explorer operated by the Laboratory for Atmospheric and Space Physics, U. of Colorado.

EL CHICHÓN'S CLOUD THICKNESS

**Mauna Loa Observatory
Hilo, Hawaii**

Altitude (km)

APRIL 10 · MAY 5 · MAY 14 · JUNE 3 · JUNE 22 · JULY 2 · JULY 30

Source: NOAA

became progressively shallower until the final hypocentres were only three kilometres deep. In addition to the seismic activity the central dome in the caldera deformed progressively. Because of this combined continuing activity, the USGS issued a volcano notice. A notice is much less definite than a watch and, in this instance, indicated that a volcanic eruption was a possibility but was not nearly as likely as a moderate-size earthquake. The Long Valley Caldera was formed by the Bishop eruption more than 700,000 years ago. That catastrophic event deposited 580 cu km (140 cu mi) of ash over western North America, more than 500 times the amount from Mt. St. Helens. The current deformation of the dome and the upward migration of hypocentres were believed to result from a tongue of lava pushing up from a magma chamber situated eight kilometres below the surface.

Hydrology

In contrast to the prolonged droughts and water shortages of 1981, streamflow was at or above the normal range in most of the U.S. during 1982. The combined flow of that nation's "big five" rivers—the Mississippi, St. Lawrence, Ohio, Columbia, and Missouri—was 12% above normal in 1982. Several regions, including the Pacific and Gulf coasts, the Midwest, and southern New England, experienced severe flooding. More than 150 lives were lost, and monetary damages were in the billions of dollars. The Federal Emergency Management Agency reported that 80% of presidential disaster declarations were related to floods. In the Maumee River basin in Indiana and Ohio severe flooding occurred during March, and many streams were at or close to the highest discharge of record. As a result 9,000 residents of Fort Wayne, Ind., had to evacuate their homes. Torrential rains in June and July caused flooding on several streams in Connecticut, Iowa, Illinois, Indiana, and Pennsylvania. In early December a week of rainstorms flooded extensive regions of Illinois, Missouri, Arkansas, and other states from the Great Lakes to the Gulf of Mexico, forcing tens of thousands from their homes.

Spirit Lake, a large body of water on the northeast flank of Mt. St. Helens, had presented a potential for catastrophic flooding along the Toutle and Cowlitz rivers since the eruption of the volcano on May 18, 1980. During the summer of 1982 the lake reached a dangerous level because of damming by volcanic debris. On August 19 Pres. Ronald Reagan issued a Declaration of Emergency and ordered action by federal agencies. As a result geologic and hydrologic data were being collected and analyzed to determine the best method to stabilize the dam and to prevent additional rises of water levels. The U.S. Army Corps of Engineers was pumping water from the lake to ease pressure on the dam.

Acid precipitation, thought to be responsible for deterioration of lakes, crops, and buildings since about 1950 in the northeastern U.S. and the Maritime Provinces of Canada, was the subject of much discussion in the news media in 1982. Many federal and state agencies in the U.S. conducted coordinated, nationwide programs to monitor the chemical composition of streams and lakes that were or could be affected by acid rain or snow. An interagency task force on acid precipitation, consisting of 12 federal agencies, received $18 million in funding in 1982, which would increase to $22 million in 1983. Research also was conducted by state and federal agencies on natural and man-made sources of acidic substances in precipitation. The studies were intended to provide the scientific basis for a national policy on the control of damage due to acid rain. The USGS reported that the acidity of lakes and rivers in New York State had showed little change since the late 1960s. Hydrologic data from 1965 to 1978 indicated that acidity had increased slightly in eastern New York but declined slightly in western New York.

The mining or withdrawal of groundwater in the High Plains area in excess of what was returned received attention during the year. The High Plains Aquifer underlies 451,000 sq km (174,000 sq mi) extending from Texas to South Dakota. The region has abundant sunshine and moderate precipitation (400–460 mm, or 16–18 in, annually). These advantages along with a plentiful supply of groundwater to support irrigation have permitted development of the region into one of the major agricultural areas of the U.S. The increase in groundwater withdrawal since 1949, however, has resulted in extensive declines in water level in the High Plains Aquifer. Since irrigation began, water levels have declined more than 3 m (10 ft) in 130,000 sq km (50,000 sq mi) of the aquifer and more than 15 m (50 ft) in 31,000 sq km (12,000 sq mi) of the aquifer. Declines of as much as 61 m (200 ft) have been measured in Texas, where most of the depletion has occurred.

The aquifer underlying Cape Cod, Mass., was designated by the U.S. Environmental Protection Agency (EPA) as a sole-source aquifer. This designation requires that all federally funded projects be evaluated to determine their possible effect on the aquifer. The Cape Cod aquifer supplies drinking water to more than 100 municipal wells and 15,000 private wells. The EPA indicated that localized contamination from chemical spills, leaking fuel tanks, waste-water treatment systems, and individual disposal systems had occurred in the past.

Accumulating dust and ash created both physical obstructions and health hazards in towns and villages surrounding El Chichón volcano.
R. TAYLOR–SYGMA

ECUADOR

The already shaky coalition governing Ecuador came under increasing strain in 1982. Several Cabinet changes were made, reflecting the fluctuations in power within the coalition. In September Energy Minister Eduardo Ortega resigned both that post and the presidency of the Organization of Petroleum Exporting Countries (OPEC) as a result of a congressional vote of censure over his handling of energy policy. Jaime Morillo also resigned as minister of finance rather than face a similar vote. Pres. Osvaldo Hurtado Larrea replaced those ministers with independents so that only four Cabinet posts were affiliated with political parties.

The economy deteriorated rapidly at the beginning of the year as oil revenues declined and international interest rates remained high. In May the official exchange rate for the sucre was devalued, for the first time in over a decade, from 25 to 33 sucres to the U.S. dollar. In spite of this move, the free-market rate continued to depreciate to over 70 sucres to the dollar in July before making a slight recovery later in the year. Foreign borrowing was still necessary to support the balance of payments, and a debt crisis was seen to be imminent as international reserves declined; negotiations were started to reschedule part of the $5.2 billion foreign public debt. It was hoped that new legislation would attract foreign investment and thus increase oil exports, as rising domestic consumption threatened to make Ecuador the first net oil importer within OPEC.

The government faced severe criticism from organized labour. A general strike protesting austerity measures took place October 21, despite the government's declaration of a state of emergency. The private sector was also disaffected with the government's economic management, as companies suffered from slack demand coupled with rising costs and falling exports.

EDUCATION

Judging from UNESCO's statistics, the world illiteracy rate continued its decline in 1982. UNESCO's projections showed that it would fall to 25.7% by 1990 (from a figure of 44.3% in 1950). However, because of the increase in population the actual number of illiterates continued to rise. What caused particular concern in 1982 was evidence of illiteracy in some of the advanced countries. A report drawn up for the European Parliament by Phili Viehoff, on behalf of the Committee on Youth, Culture, Education, Information, and Sport, said that there were some 10 million to 15 million illiterates in the countries of the European Community (not including Greece). Based on an earlier survey, some two million of these were in the United Kingdom. France, West Germany, and Luxembourg denied the existence of illiteracy within their borders, but the evidence suggested that this was untrue. In Greece it was estimated that 14% of the adult population was illiterate and in Portugal 23%.

As the 1982–83 school year opened, some 57,320,000 elementary, secondary, and college students were enrolled in the United States. That was a decrease of 522,000 students from the previous year. Elementary and secondary students numbered 44.8 million, continuing the steady decline since 1970, when there were 51.3 million. College students increased by 100,000 to a record enrollment of 12.5 million. The U.S. Census Bureau reported that private school enrollments, especially those of Roman Catholic systems, had declined markedly.

Primary and Secondary Education

A nearly 6% cut in federal elementary-secondary school support followed the previous year's 8% reduction in the U.S. The federal dollars dropped from $5,610,000,000 in 1981–82 to $5.3 billion in the 1982–83 school year. In keeping with Pres. Ronald

Soldiers and police patrolled the streets of Quito, Ecuador, in the wake of an October strike that turned violent.
WIDE WORLD

Reagan's "new federalism," there was a shift in federal funding away from categorical grants for specific programs to block grants for use in broadly defined areas. However, for the 30 educational programs that were combined into block grants, total federal funding declined from $535 million to $484 million. Hardest hit by the cutbacks would be those districts that had large numbers of students targeted by the federal programs—the economically disadvantaged, handicapped, and non-English speaking. It was estimated that by the time President Reagan's policies were fully implemented, the federal contribution to education would have been halved. Federal officials pointed out, however, that the federal component of local school budgets was relatively small and that, overall, the proportion of local school budgets funded by the federal government only fell from 8.7% in 1981 to 8.2% in 1982.

The Reagan administration concluded that forced busing was ineffective. It explored the idea of assisting school districts that sought to modify busing plans that were not working. At the same time, the administration said that it was not reversing basic policy and was only seeking better, voluntary means of encouraging desegregation.

The Northeast trailed in promoting school integration, according to a report to the House of Representatives. The Joint Center for Political Studies told a House committee that between 1968 and 1980 the Southern and border states made great progress in achieving integration in the classroom. By 1970 the South was the least segregated region for U.S. blacks. The Northeast had become the most segregated area. The Center reported that segregation of Hispanics had increased in each region.

In its first opinion of the law that provided "free and appropriate" education to handicapped children and youth, the U.S. Supreme Court said that provisions for the handicapped could be limited. In their opinion on the Education for All Handicapped Children Act of 1975, the justices concluded that the Congress intended that education be accessible to the handicapped but did not intend a specific type of education—nor that it necessarily be equal to that provided other children.

A Texas law prohibiting the free education of children of illegal aliens was overturned by the U.S. Supreme Court. State officials estimated that 5% of the Texas population was there illegally. Texas had the only law in the U.S. limiting the free education of the children of illegal aliens. The law required exclusion of the children or the payment of tuition for them. A court majority held that without education the children would suffer a lifetime of hardship and the stigma of illiteracy.

The Reagan administration changed the role of the Internal Revenue Service in denying tax exemptions to private schools that practice racial discrimination. The Department of Justice said that the IRS simply does not have the legal right to deny exemptions. The department denied that its action signaled

a retreat on the enforcement of civil rights.

The U.S. Supreme Court decided that when a school district bans certain books and thus deprives students' access to ideas, those students have the right to take their case to federal courts. The Nassau County, N.Y., school board had removed some books from library shelves, an act that could be challenged on First Amendment grounds, said the court. The justices did not provide specific guidelines for the trial, which was to be heard in the U.S. Second Circuit Court of Appeals.

Few teachers' strikes marked the opening of school in the U.S. Teachers in Detroit staged the largest, with 9,880 teachers out of classes and 200,000 students at home. In Teaneck, N.J., striking teachers were "jailed" in a school for two days for defying a judge's order to return to their jobs. Scattered strikes took place in other Michigan communities and in Illinois, Pennsylvania, Ohio, and Montana. The number of teachers affected in those states was about the same as in Detroit. In some cases teachers worked without contracts. Key issues in negotiations were economic—pay freezes or reductions, layoffs, and job security.

Teacher layoffs increased. The teachers' unions estimated that 40,000–55,000 teachers were laid off for the 1982–83 school year, more than 20% percent higher than in 1981–82. The American Federation of Teachers said it was the worst year ever for firings.

Teacher of the Year for 1982 was Bruce Brombacher, an eighth-grade teacher at Jones Junior High School, Upper Arlington, Ohio.
WIDE WORLD

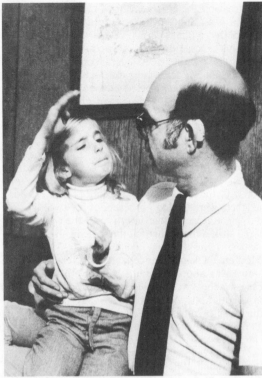

JAMES NACHTWEY/THE NEW YORK TIMES

The Supreme Court ruled in June that deaf student Amy Rowley's Westchester Co., N.Y., school district was not required to provide a sign-language interpreter in her classroom.

After a long decline and a leveling off in 1981 of Scholastic Aptitude Test scores, there was a 3% improvement in 1982. Approximately one million high-school seniors take the test each year to help colleges determine who will be admitted. The producers of the test claim that it predicts academic success in college. Educators believed that the rise in SAT scores indicated that the general quality of the schools had improved.

There was a report in August of differences of opinion between West German and U.S. historians about the postwar images of their respective countries presented in textbooks. The evidence came from the Georg Eckert Institute, which since 1979 had coordinated annual meetings of historians from West Germany and the U.S. The complaint on the West German side was that U.S. schoolchildren were presented with an image of Germany as it was during the era of Adolf Hitler and that little was written about Germany after the Hitler era. U.S. historians complained that German history books concentrated on the Vietnam war and on Watergate and other scandals.

Higher Education

Federal funding for colleges and universities in the United States was cut by 17%, from $5,540,000,000

to $4,570,000,000. The aid provided for loans to students, for construction, and for a variety of other kinds of support. Overriding a presidential veto, the U.S. Congress provided $169 million more for financial aid for college students. The additional money would ensure full funding for student loan programs.

Students in the U.S. found on the average that going to college in 1982–83 cost 11% more than in 1981–82, according to the College Board. The average per-year cost of attending a public four-year college was estimated at $4,388, while expenses for those in private four-year colleges averaged $7,475.

College enrollments in the U.S. could drop by 15% by the mid-1990s, according to a study by the Brookings Institution. The decline would result from the fall in births and the subsequent decrease in high-school graduates. For three decades colleges in the U.S. had experienced uninterrupted growth.

U.S. colleges raised tuition and other direct costs for students. The situation for students worsened as women found it more difficult to find jobs to help pay for their children's educational expenses. A study by the Education Commission of the states found that most education and state officials expected state appropriations to trail inflation. This would require higher tuitions, which were already rising about 15% per year, according to the National Association of Student Financial Aid Administrators. State-supported schools provided education for some 78% of U.S. college students.

The college graduating class in the U.S. in 1983 would be the largest ever. It would also be the most diverse in regard to student backgrounds, would be divided almost equally between men and women, and would have more older students. The number of persons planning to enter graduate schools was expected to decline.

In what two dissenting judges branded "benign neglect" of earlier government pressures to desegregate state education systems, a U.S. Court of Appeals upheld a North Carolina–U.S. Department of Education settlement. The decade-long case was settled when the state agreed to provide new programs at historically black colleges. In a change of policy the state was permitted to leave duplicate programs intact in nearby white institutions.

The traditional open-door admissions policies of U.S. junior and community colleges began to change. The schools began to establish entrance requirements and to drop students who did not maintain acceptable academic standards.

In Canada the number of students in Quebec was allowed to go on rising. Although the Quebec government cut funds to universities, student enrollments continued to increase. The government took the view that the universities must become more productive. In practice this led to a dispute over the allocation of funds between the newer universities, attracting a new class of French-speaking students, and some of the older universities.

Computer literacy was the newest addition to many schools' curricula. This classroom in Roseville, Minnesota, benefited from a state program encouraging the use of computers.
GEORGE HEINRICH/BUSINESS WEEK

In Europe it was only in France that there was conspicuous growth. In 1982 the higher education budget was up 15% from the previous year. In March the Claude Jeanette Commission was established by the minister of education, Alain Savary, to draw up a framework for a new higher education law. Savary also spelled out the expectations of the French government for higher education. First was a contribution to combat the recession through teaching and research; the second expectation comprised ways of developing those industrial sectors that would be important in the future, such as biotechnology and computers; the third was collaboration between universities and research bodies; and the fourth was increased effectiveness in spreading new knowledge to the population as a whole.

Several governments declared a need to create more productive institutions. There was much argument in the U.K. about the need to reduce the security of tenure held by university teachers. In France, Savary announced something of a crackdown on absentee university teachers. The university academic year was to be lengthened from 25 to 32 weeks (like the institutes of technology in France), and professors were required to increase the number of lectures they gave per annum from 75 to 96.

There was, unhappily, ample evidence of interference with freedom of inquiry in many parts of the world. In Israel there was serious trouble in the three West Bank universities—Al-Najah, BirZeit, and Bethlehem—over the official demand that teachers refrain from any kind of support for the Palestine Liberation Organization. One hundred foreign teachers in the universities, including 30 from the U.S. and 10 from Great Britain, objected to the "loose and ambiguous wording" of the demand and complained of interference with the rights of free expression. Politics actually closed down the University of Nairobi in Kenya in September because during August a number of university students had taken part in an abortive coup against Pres. Daniel arap Moi.

In Seattle, Washington, students protested the reduction in federal funds supporting educational programs for the handicapped.
WIDE WORLD

Special Report: The Promise of Early Learning

by James M. Wolf

Interest and support for early learning have been expressed by philosophers and scholars throughout history. Comenius, in the 17th century, espoused the teaching of all knowledge to the child and advocated the "School of the Mother's Knee." John Locke, whose thinking dominated the 18th century, wrote, "I have always had a fancy that learning might be made play and recreation for young children." Lord Henry Brougham in 1828 argued that the child can and does learn more before the age of six than during any other period in his life. It was not until the late 1950s and 1960s, however, that evidence was accumulated to support Lord Brougham's notion.

Two books are frequently cited as catalysts for the revolution in early learning that began at that time. Joseph McVicker Hunt's *Intelligence and Experience* (1961) documented the importance of adequate environmental stimulation for a child's optimal development. Benjamin Bloom's classic *Stability and Change in Human Characteristics* (1964) demonstrated that there is a growth curve for each human characteristic. For example, half of a child's future height is reached by age two and a half. By the time a child enters school at age six, he has developed as much as two-thirds of the intelligence he will have at maturity.

As a result of these findings, a wide variety of experimental early childhood programs emerged to challenge the older concepts of child development. The idea of fixed intelligence was no longer a tenable theory. Bloom found that extreme environments— either very favourable or underprivileged—could affect the development of intelligence during the first four years of life. According to Hunt, the preschool years, especially the first four, appear to be highly important for the achievement of initiative, trust, compassion, curiosity, and intelligence.

The Pathfinders

In 1967 Maya Pines published her epochal book *Revolution in Learning*. It is historically significant because it was written for parents and summarized the work of many of the pathfinders in early learning. Pines discussed such projects as the talking typewriter experiment, in which Omar Moore taught some 60 children as young as three and four to read, write, and compose poetry. The americanization of Montessori methods was also described, particularly the work of Nancy Rambusch at the Whitby School in Connecticut, where she demonstrated the learning potential of three- and four-year-olds from advantaged homes. Bettye Caldwell's work in children's centres where six-month-old babies received cognitive training demonstrated that culturally determined mental retardation in young babies was reversible. Two of the more controversial pathfinders were Carl Bereiter and Siegfried Engelmann, who developed a special preschool program for disadvantaged children that enabled them to start first grade on an equal footing with more privileged children.

Efforts to aid children and adults with deviant conditions frequently provide insights and approaches that can be used for enrichment of the so-called normal child. Glenn Doman and his colleagues, pioneers in the treatment of brain-injured children, have applied their concept and findings about neurological dysorganization in brain-impaired children to the enhancement of neurological organization in the average and superior child. The mastery of reading skills is one of the intervention strategies Doman uses in the treatment of very young brain-injured children. His book *How to Teach Your Baby to Read* has been used successfully by mothers of nonimpaired children throughout the world and is now published in 15 languages. Sylvia Ashton-Warner in New Zealand is another pathfinder in early reading.

Teaching young children to read is a controversial topic among U.S. educators. Some still oppose the practice of having a parent engage in systematized reading instruction with preschool children. Skepticism is also expressed by some teachers, who surmise that learning to read at home interferes with the method used in school and that most children are not ready for reading before the age of six. Too often, it is said, early reading efforts are the result of parental anxieties and pressure and serve primarily to satisfy the parent's ego. In addition, teaching preschoolers to read is an infringement on their precious childhood. However, these statements are more myth than fact.

The Confirmers

Beginning in the mid-'60s, early learning and early childhood enrichment became acceptable to greater numbers of parents and educators. However, there was a need for research to corroborate the pathfinders' results.

Federal programs provided the major source for confirmation of early learning among children from low-income families. In 1965 Pres. Lyndon Johnson hailed Head Start, an early education program, as the principal weapon in his administration's attempt to achieve a Great Society. The results of a national evaluation released by the Westinghouse Learning Corp. and Ohio University in 1969 came close to destroying Head Start and discrediting the concept of early learning and intervention. However, *The Carnegie Quarterly* notes, in an article entitled "New Optimism About Preschool Education," that ". . . recent studies based on new data or reanalysis of the old suggest that the Westinghouse conclusions were premature. . . . Preschool education [early learning] apparently gives youngsters a lasting effect over their peers who get no special help. . . ."

Other research findings have supported this statement. In 1977 Irving Lazar of Cornell University completed his compilation of data from 14 longitudinal studies of children from low-income families who participated in Head Start programs. The findings indicate that, as compared with control groups, children who participated in early childhood and family development programs were placed in remedial special education classes less often, were held back in a grade less often, scored higher on intelligence tests, and were superior in social, emotional, cognitive, and language development after entering school. In a chapter on "Enrichment of Early Childhood Experiences," Caldwell and her associates describe projects that started intervention before age three and that also provide evidence of the effectiveness of these programs in modifying intellectual development.

The Advocates and Resource Materials

Joan Beck was among the first journalists to make a case for early learning. In her book *How to Raise a Brighter Child*, she wrote about the pathfinders in early learning and detailed how all parents can raise their child's useful level of intelligence significantly. Siegfried Engelmann and his wife, Therese, drawing on their extensive experience with preschool children, developed a programmed step-by-step guide for parents called *Give Your Child a Superior Mind*.

In a 1982 issue of the *Elementary School Journal*, Richard Norton and Doman wrote: "The potential of the young human brain, whether injured or intact, is virtually unlimited and varies inversely with age. Given proper informational, social, nutritional, and emotional nourishment (*e.g.*, speaking, understanding, reading, writing), most children are capable of functioning at the level which is called gifted." The authors propose that an ". . . entire new generation of 'gifted' children is possible." Doman has developed a program on *How to Multiply Your Baby's Intelligence* in which parents are taught how to teach their infants to read, do math, do gymnastics, play the violin, and speak a foreign language.

A group of child development specialists at the Princeton Center for Infancy have condensed the viewpoints of leading experts from over 800 books on child-rearing practices in a complete and easy-to-use guide entitled *The Parenting Advisor*. There are also a number of newsletters that deal with early learning. One of the most interesting, produced monthly by Dennis Dunn and Edwin Hargitt, is called *Growing Child*, with a supplement issue called *Growing Parent*. It should be noted that there is no one method of achieving the goals of early learning, but these materials contain many useful and practical ideas.

The Future

Early learning is an idea whose time has come. Methods now exist to increase the intelligence, creativity, and sociability of all children. However, like most new knowledge, it has the potential for misuse and abuse, and it must be applied with loving care and joyfulness. Early learning, to be successful, must be made "play and recreation" for babies and young children.

Research on early learning during the past two decades has produced exciting findings on how to teach very young children. The next two decades will produce refinements and a new set of challenges. New knowledge gained from brain research will provide more definition for the frequency, duration, and intensity of appropriate early learning activities. This new knowledge will also provide more specific information on the relationship between nutrition and brain chemistry. Although the "School of the Mother's Knee" will never be completely replaced, advancements in technology will affect early learning techniques. The transformation of the ordinary television set into a home-entertainment and educational centre and the proliferation of home computers will offer new opportunities for research and innovative home programs in early learning. Most important, early learning will become more accepted and will be demanded by parents and professionals as a common practice to ensure that all children come closer to reaching and expanding their potential.

EGYPT

During 1982 Pres. Hosni Mubarak's strong personality enabled him to steer Egypt back toward the Arab fold while retaining the confidence of Western leaders, particularly U.S. Pres. Ronald Reagan. At home his grim economic inheritance proved a heavy burden. Although much emphasis had been put on economic reform since the assassination on Oct. 6, 1981, of Pres. Anwar as-Sadat, little had materialized by the end of 1982. The trade gap widened during the year, and remittances from Egyptians working in other nations fell. On January 2 President Mubarak appointed Ahmad Fuad Mohieddin to the post of prime minister; Mubarak himself had held the office since he assumed the presidency in October 1981. The day after his appointment the new prime minister announced a reshuffled and enlarged Cabinet, in which the most important reorganizations involved the economic portfolios.

Relations with Israel remained a thorny question for President Mubarak in his dealings with the other Arab nations. In a low-key ceremony on April 25, Israel handed back to Egypt the last remnants of the occupied Sinai Peninsula as part of the agreement reached at Camp David. Egypt's ambassador to Israel was recalled in September, however, in response to the massacre by Lebanese Christians of Palestin-

In a simple flag-lowering and flag-raising ceremony, Egypt regained control of the entire Sinai Peninsula from Israel on April 25.

BARRY IVERSON—GAMMA/LIAISON

ians in Beirut. Nevertheless, Israel remained Egypt's main oil customer, taking 40,000 bbl a day.

In welcoming the unified Arab position on the Middle East reached at the Arab summit meeting in Fez, Morocco, in September, Foreign Affairs Minister Kamal Hassan Ali suggested Egypt's ambivalence. Hailing Fez as "an important landmark and turning point in the Arab countries' position, directed toward achieving peace and recognizing the existence of Israel," Ali added that the proposals that emerged were "goals and principles" that still needed to be discussed further by the Arab countries and the U.S. government. Although the Fez declaration was closer to Egypt's position than the solution proposed by President Reagan, Egypt nevertheless supported the Reagan plan. This was because President Mubarak took the view that the U.S. held the key cards in any comprehensive Middle East peace plan. (*See* Middle Eastern Affairs.)

Egypt's drift back toward Arab orthodoxy was emphasized by the president's enthusiastic espousal of a union with Sudan. On October 23 at El Arish, where six months earlier the Sinai had been formally handed back, a ceremony took place at which Mubarak and Pres. Gaafar Nimeiry of Sudan formally declared the "integration" of Egypt and Sudan. It was the third time since the overthrow of King Farouk in 1952 that Egypt had attempted a confederation with another Arab nation. The other two attempts, with Syria and with Libya, both broke down. This time, under President Mubarak, the union was to be more gradual, with a ten-year trial period. At the same time, Foreign Minister Ali was at pains to stress in September that while Egypt welcomed resumed relations with the Arab world, it was in no hurry and would not put pressure on any Arab country over the issue of Egypt's exclusion from the Arab League.

Five men convicted of killing Sadat were executed in Cairo on April 15, two by firing squad and three by hanging. Prison sentences on 17 other conspirators were upheld. A crackdown on Muslim fundamentalists announced on September 16 resulted in 58 arrests. The government was forced to ask the People's Assembly for a renewal of the emergency powers granted for one year after Sadat's death. The Coptic patriarch, Shenuda III, having been stripped of his official status in 1981 for allegedly contributing to tension between Copts and Muslims, remained incommunicado.

Egypt's economic problems included a trade gap that had deteriorated in 1981 to $4.8 billion; declining remittances, down 19%; lower income from tourism, down 24%; and reduced income from Suez Canal tolls. Tourism, particularly from the U.S., was affected by the aftermath of Sadat's assassination. On September 24 a young Muslim extremist attacked a tourist bus near the pyramids at Giza, slightly injuring two Soviet visitors. In addition, Egypt had become the world's tenth largest debtor nation, with foreign debts estimated at $16 billion.

Three hundred Muslim fundamentalists went on trial in Cairo in December on charges of conspiring to overthrow the government.
WIDE WORLD

Although inflation was officially estimated at 9.6%, a more realistic figure was thought to be 20–30%. Maintenance of subsidies—currently budgeted at $2.4 billion a year—was becoming increasingly burdensome. Some $975 million, equivalent to more than the entire annual income from the Suez Canal, was being used to subsidize bread sales alone. With a population increasing by 1.2 million a year, Egypt had become partly dependent on imported food. Where once it had been an exporter of more than 640,000 metric tons of rice a year, the nation had exported no rice since 1980.

Crude oil production was expected to rise to 740,000 bbl a day in the financial year ending July 1, 1983, compared with 660,000 bbl a day in the financial year 1981–82. Gas output in the same period was expected to rise to 2.8 million metric tons, compared with 2.5 million metric tons in the previous year.

An aid agreement worth $284 million was signed in Brussels on May 25 by Minister of State for Foreign Affairs Boutros Boutros-Ghali and Léo Tindemans, chairman of the Council of Ministers of the European Communities. U.S. aid to Egypt remained the largest single commitment of any Western nation; on May 26 contracts were signed with the U.S. for the enrichment of uranium for four proposed nuclear power plants. On March 26 the World Bank announced a $90 million loan to finance development of the Abu Qir offshore gas field.

Energy remained the brightest element in the economy. Substantial oil finds, particularly one discovered in the Gulf of Suez in November 1981 by the Suez Oil Co., were expected to yield between 50,000 and 100,000 bbl a day. On the basis of the find, British Petroleum, a partner in the Suez Oil Co. along with Royal Dutch Shell, Deminex of West Germany, and the Egyptian General Petroleum Corp., proposed to make Egypt, over the next five- or six-year period, second only to the North Sea in

its development budget. The output of the Morgan Field, Egypt's largest in production in 1982, was 150,000 bbl a day. The Suez find was, therefore, a substantial addition to known reserves. Royal Dutch Shell also announced that it had struck oil in the Western Desert.

ELECTIONS

Democrats made major gains in the House of Representatives, in state governorships, and in control of state legislatures in 1982 elections. The Republican Party maintained its previous 54–46 control of the Senate and took over the governorship of the nation's largest state. Voter turnout in November was 64,172,541 on the basis of complete but unofficial returns for 47 states and the District of Columbia. (Louisiana had voted earlier.) It was expected that final, official returns would show a turnout of about 41% of eligible voters. This reversed a downward trend in midterm congressional elections that had been under way ever since 1962.

House of Representatives

In the House, Democrats made a net gain of 26 seats. Before the election there were 241 Democrats, 192 Republicans, and 2 vacancies in districts that had been held by Democrats. After the election was completed with a November 30 vote in two Georgia districts where redistricting disputes caused delays, the members elected to the House included 269 Democrats and 166 Republicans. It was the most severe midterm loss for a party that had just gained the presidency since 1922, when Republicans lost 75 seats in the middle of Warren Harding's term.

The change in the House weakened the coalition of Republicans and conservative Democrats that had given Pres. Ronald Reagan a number of major victories in 1981. Most of the so-called Boll Weevil Democratic conservatives won reelection. There was a net gain of nine Democratic congressmen in the

New senators elected in November included Frank Lautenberg of New Jersey (left) and Jeff Bingaman of New Mexico.

South, but few of the newcomers were expected to join the conservatives.

Twenty-one women were elected to the House, a net gain of one. Three incumbent women did not seek reelection to the House, and one other congresswoman, Rep. Margaret Heckler (Rep., Mass.) was defeated in a campaign in which her opposition to abortion aroused some women's groups. Twelve of the women elected to the House were Democrats; nine were Republicans. New woman U.S. representatives were Barbara Boxer (Dem., Calif.), Nancy

Among Democrats elected to the House were Barney Frank of Massachusetts (left) and newcomer Marcy Kaptur of Ohio.

Johnson (Rep., Conn.), Katie Hall (Dem., Ind.), Barbara Vucanovich (Rep., Nev.), and Marcy Kaptur (Dem., Ohio).

Sixteen black incumbents were reelected to Congress, as was Delegate Walter Fauntroy of the District of Columbia. The 17th black incumbent, Shirley Chisholm (Dem., N.Y.), did not seek reelection. Four other victories brought the number of black representatives up to 21, all Democrats. The new black congressmen were Alan Wheat (Mo.), Edolphus Towns and Major Owens (N.Y.), and Katie Hall (Ind.). All eight Hispanic congressmen were reelected, and three more Hispanics won seats in the House. They were Esteban Torres (Dem., Calif.), Bill Richardson (Dem., N.M.), and Solomon Ortiz (Dem., Tex.).

Senate

In the Senate, where there were 19 Democratic and 13 Republican seats at stake, the election was a standoff. The lineup remained at 46 Democrats, 54 Republicans. Only two incumbent senators were defeated, one from each party. Three other new senators came from states in which the incumbents were not running.

Frank Lautenberg (Dem.), 58, spent $1.3 million of his own money to defeat well-known Rep. Millicent Fenwick (Rep.), 72, in New Jersey after trailing by 18 percentage points in early polls. It was Lautenberg's first elective office. Paul Trible (Rep.), 35, a lawyer and three-term congressman, defeated Lieut. Gov. Richard Davis (Dem.) for the Virginia Senate seat vacated by Sen. Harry F. Byrd, Jr., an independent who had voted with the Democrats on organizational matters.

Pete Wilson (Rep.), 49, three-term mayor of San Diego, Calif., defeated Gov. Edmund Brown to win the seat vacated by Sen. S. I. Hayakawa (Rep., Calif.). Wilson had a reputation as a low-key conservative and a competent administrator as mayor. Chick Hecht (Rep.), 53, a former minority leader in the Nevada state Senate, defeated Howard Cannon, a veteran of 23 years in the U.S. Senate. Although not charged with any crime, Cannon appeared to be hurt to some degree by the trial of Teamsters Union president Roy Williams and others on charges that they tried to bribe the senator. Attorney General Jeff Bingaman, 39, defeated Sen. Harrison Schmitt in New Mexico. Bingaman described himself as a mainstream Democrat and had union backing.

Governorships

The Democrats took nine governorships from the Republicans. These included Nebraska, Minnesota, Wisconsin, Michigan, and Ohio in the Midwest; Arkansas and Texas in the South; and Nevada and Alaska in the West. The Republicans took New Hampshire and California from the Democrats. The net Democratic gain of seven gave the Democrats 34 statehouses, the Republicans 16.

The closest major contest in the nation was in

Illinois, where Gov. James Thompson (Rep.) defeated former senator Adlai Stevenson III (Dem.) by 1,816,101 to 1,811,027, a mere 5,074 votes, according to the official canvass. In Texas, Attorney General Mark White (Dem.) succeeded in a populist-style campaign against the well-financed Gov. William Clements. While White was generally regarded as a conservative, the economy appeared to be a major factor in deciding the election. In Alabama, former Gov. George Wallace (Dem.), once a symbol of segregationism, won the governorship. He had strong support from blacks, who preferred him to flamboyant Emory Folmar, Republican mayor of Montgomery. In New York, Lieut. Gov. Mario Cuomo (Dem., Liberal) defeated Lewis Lehrman (Rep., Conservative) in an unexpectedly close contest. Lehrman spent heavily from his private fortune and countered Cuomo's generally liberal campaign with strong emphasis on crime issues.

Mayor Thomas Bradley (Dem.) lost in his campaign for governor in California by less than 1% of the popular vote. Three percent of voters surveyed in exit polls indicated they voted against Bradley because of his race. However, Bradley also campaigned for gun control, which lost by a wide margin in a statewide referendum. The California winner for governor, Attorney General George Deukmejian, had a reputation as a stern advocate of law and order and stressed crime issues in his campaign.

In the Midwest, the Democrats elected Anthony S. Earl, a former state Cabinet member, in Wisconsin, former governor Rudy Perpich in Minnesota, former lieutenant governor Richard Celeste in Ohio, and Rep. James Blanchard in Michigan to succeed four of the Republican governors. Democrat Bob Kerrey, a restaurant owner who won the Medal of Honor in Vietnam, defeated Nebraska's Republican Gov. Charles Thone. In Iowa, Lieut. Gov. Terry Branstad defeated Roxanne Conlin to hold the statehouse for the Republicans. At 35, Branstad be-

came the nation's youngest governor.

In addition to Wallace and Perpich, former governors Bill Clinton (Dem., Ark.) and Michael S. Dukakis (Dem., Mass.) regained governorships. Clinton defeated Republican Gov. Frank White, who had ousted him in 1980; Dukakis won easily after winning the Democratic primary on September 14 from Gov. Edward King, who had defeated him in the 1978 primary. Hotel owner Bill Sheffield (Dem.) was elected governor of Alaska at the same time voters were giving the Republicans control of the legislature. In Nevada, state Attorney General Richard Bryan (Dem.) defeated Gov. Robert List (Rep.). List was hurt by charges of indecisiveness and by problems with a program to reduce real estate taxes and increase sales taxes. In New Hampshire, former state representative John Sununu (Rep.) defeated Gov. Hugh Gallen (Dem.) largely on the basis of Gallen's refusal to promise that he would veto any bill for an income tax or sales tax.

In a rare foreign policy referendum, nine states, the District of Columbia, and 29 cities and counties voted on asking the administration to negotiate a bilateral U.S.-Soviet freeze on production of nuclear weapons. The proposals won in most local elections and in statewide elections in California, Massachusetts, Michigan, Montana, New Jersey, North Dakota, Oregon, and Rhode Island. It lost in Arizona and in counties in Arkansas and Colorado.

Maine's voters rejected a proposal to phase out the state's only nuclear power plant, Maine Yankee. A bid for a shutdown had failed in the 1980 election. In Massachusetts a proposal was passed to require voter approval of any new nuclear plants or nuclear waste facility. Proposals to require deposits on beverage bottles were defeated in Arizona, California, Colorado, and Washington, but Massachusetts voted to keep its bottle-deposit law. Californians rejected a plan to freeze the number of handguns in the state and require gun registration.

George Deukmejian (right) won a narrow victory over Los Angeles mayor Tom Bradley in the race for governor of California. In New York, Lieut. Gov. Mario Cuomo (far right) defeated a heavily financed rival for the state house.

Special Report: PAC's—The New Force in Politics

by David C. Beckwith

Early in 1982, the U.S. Congress overwhelmingly vetoed a Federal Trade Commission (FTC) regulation that would have required used car dealers to inform buyers of any hidden defects they knew about in the autos they were selling. "There was no public interest reason on earth to oppose that rule," Sen. William Proxmire (Dem., Wis.) complained. "The vote can be explained only by campaign contributions." Proxmire's analysis was illuminated later in the year, when campaign finance reports were made public. The National Automobile Dealers Association had donated $950,680 to congressional candidates, the vast bulk of it to incumbents who helped defeat the defect-disclosure rule. The money was channeled through NADA's political action committee, one of the most generous association donors of campaign contributions and clearly one of the most successful.

A Matter of Money

The history of the used car rule illustrates a phenomenon in recent U.S. politics: the rapidly growing influence of the political action committee. PAC's were authorized to gather and spend money freely only ten years ago, and the 113 in existence then accounted for less than $10 million in congressional campaign contributions in 1974. By 1982, however, 3,479 PAC's raised over $200 million, fed about $90 million into congressional campaign coffers, and threatened to overwhelm both individuals and political parties as the dominant source of "the mother's milk of politics." In other words, lobbyists for special interests were fast becoming the dominant financiers of the U.S. electoral process.

The rise of PAC influence paralleled—and encouraged—a dramatic increase in the cost of running for office. The average U.S. House campaign, for example, cost a mere $50,000 in 1974, but that had grown to $150,000 by 1980 and $200,000 in 1982. In some hotly contested races, expenditures of $500,000 or more were not uncommon. The costs of other major campaigns soared proportionately. More than $18

million was spent in the 1982 Texas gubernatorial and Senate races alone, and $2 million was raised and expended on a single race for a seat in the California state legislature (won by former radical Tom Hayden).

Part of the reason was inflation and the expense of reaching a larger population, but most of the increase reflected an indulgence made possible by ever more efficient fund raising. Instead of volunteers, campaign workers now were often paid staffers who were provided with meals and expenses out of campaign funds. Most important, expensive image-building television advertisements were soaking up more and more campaign cash.

Birth of a "Reform"

PAC's began taking on major importance in 1974 when, in the wake of the Watergate scandal, Congress approved an election law reform designed to end under-the-table payments by corporations and unions and to put a lid on the influence of wealthy individual contributors. At that time PAC's were viewed as part of the solution, a well-regulated way for individuals to pool their resources in support of candidates. That much had worked. Reports of secretive, bribe-like payments to candidates had almost vanished, and the identity of most contributors was now a matter of public record. Many small donors to PAC's thought they could have a significant effect on elections, and the power of the smoke-filled room had diminished.

But like many other well-intentioned laws, the "reform" bred new problems. The law attempted to curb spending by limiting the amount any single entity could donate. An individual could give only $1,000 to both a congressional candidate's primary and general election campaigns, for example, while a PAC was restricted to $5,000 gifts in both races. But the U.S. Supreme Court subsequently threw out a provision limiting the amount a wealthy person could donate to his own campaign, giving an inordinate advantage to millionaire politicians. Also, the law failed to control the proliferation of separate PAC's. The result: more money was pouring into elections every year; the price of running a competitive race was escalating steadily; and the value of an individual citizen's contribution was dwindling apace.

More ominously, the role of major political parties, the great broadening influence in U.S. public life, was being diminished as well. Even with abnormally heavy spending by the Republican Party in 1982, the average congressional candidate got three times as much money from PAC's as from his party. That alarmed PAC critics such as former House legislative counsel Jerome Ziefman. "A whole raft of bills to weaken the antitrust laws is now in danger of passage," he noted. "The principles of both parties support vigorous antitrust enforcement, so you have to conclude that PAC's are driving the process." Added former presidential counsel Stuart Eizenstat: "The PAC's are balkanizing the process, shifting attention away from broad national concerns and towards single-issue, special interest topics." That, in turn, often led to costly special-interest legislation. According to PAC critic James Leach (Rep., Iowa), one of only a dozen congressmen who refused to take PAC money in 1982: "It's not surprising there are no balanced budgets."

Paying the Piper

Four categories of PAC's dominated in national and state elections. In 1982, 613 trade associations such as the National Association of Realtors and the American Medical Association contributed $22 million to congressional campaign war chests. Some 1,500 individual corporation committees, technically funded by employee contributions, gave $30 million more; 350 labour union PAC's, also aggregating individual contributions, added $20 million; and 644 ideological or nonconnected PAC's, of which the National Conservative Political Action Committee (NCPAC) was the most publicized, provided candidates with $6 million and spent at least $25 million on their own advertising and administration.

Whether this money promotes good government and participation in the political process or whether it amounts to an organized payoff system was at the heart of the debate over PAC growth. PAC defenders, such as Rep. Bill Frenzel (Rep., Minn.), asserted that the PAC vehicle allows like-minded individuals to aggregate their contributions and have a legal, wholesome effect on an election. He noted that while $5,000 is a significant contribution, it is not sufficiently overwhelming to cause the abandonment of principles. Other backers of the system suggested that PAC contributions do not buy votes but merely reward those who, by the contributor's lights, voted correctly in the past. Another contention was that a PAC contribution merely ensures access to a congressman and exposure for one's point of view. "Talking to congressmen is fine," said California businessman Justin Dart, "but with a little money, they hear you better."

Critics emphatically rejected that argument as disingenuous. "There's no reason to give money except in the expectation of votes," said Rep. William Brodhead (Dem., Mich.), who retired in 1982, partly because he tired of constant fund raising and subsequent pressures for voting allegiance. "Money doesn't always win—just 95 to 98 percent of the time." The relative ease of securing big four-figure checks from lobbyists rather than laboriously scraping up individual $25 contributions also distorts the democratic process. Concluded Common Cause president Fred Wertheimer: "Dependency on PAC's has grown so much that PAC's, not constituents, are now the focus of a congressman's attention."

Certainly, virtually every PAC contribution had some legislative interest behind it. The American Medical and American Dental associations, which had given $2.3 million to House members since 1979, were struggling to exempt doctors and dentists from FTC price-fixing regulation. The beer lobby's PAC, appropriately named SixPAC, was similarly rewarding House members who supported their bill to allow monopoly territory for beer distributors. A half-dozen PAC's led by the American Bankers Association passed out $704,297 to 255 congressmen cosponsoring a bill that would require individuals to repay debts after they declared bankruptcy.

Looming over the fray was the dark spectre of the independent, ideological PAC's, groups that enjoyed constitutional free speech protection. They would doubtless benefit if other PAC activities were somehow curbed. These committees were unaffiliated with any candidate, and they often produced their own advertising—much of it scathing personal assaults on candidates with whom they disagreed. NCPAC, for example, claimed credit for the defeat of four liberal U.S. senators in 1980 via expensive negative television advertising. Two years later, however, the targets were better prepared. Seventeen of 18 NCPAC targets won their races in 1982, but the independent PAC's remained a potent, unguided political force.

There were plenty of ideas for new and improved reforms. One congressman proposed a constitutional amendment to place a ceiling on campaign spending. Another bill would limit a candidate's total PAC take to $75,000 per election. Others would attempt to reduce PAC influence by increasing the limits on an individual citizen's contributions to candidates and political parties. Among academic thinkers, a growing consensus called for public financing of all elections, similar to the system used for presidential campaigns. The prospects for immediate action by Congress were dim, however, and many critics thought a national embarrassment would have to precede any serious effort at reform. Concluded Rep. James Shannon (Dem., Mass.): "Eventually this scandal—and it is a scandal—will attract so much attention that public financing of elections will be seriously considered."

EL SALVADOR

The elections to El Salvador's Constituent Assembly held on March 28, 1982, failed to provide, as the U.S. and many others had hoped, a clear majority for the Partido Demócrata Cristiano (PDC) and Pres. José Napoleón Duarte. Instead, they resulted in an unstable and unruly coalition of five parties: the PDC; Alianza Republicana Nacionalista (Arena); Partido de Conciliación Nacional (PCN); Acción Democrática (AD); and Partido Popular Salvadoreño (PPS). All parties were to the right of the political spectrum because the left-wing umbrella organization, the Frente Democrático Revolucionario (FDR), did not participate in the elections. Duarte was forced to resign from the presidency and was replaced on May 2 by Alvaro Magaña Borjo, a man previously involved not in mainstream politics but in banking and economics. The leader of the far-right party Arena, Maj. Roberto d'Aubuisson, was elected president of the assembly and planned to campaign in national presidential elections scheduled to take place in the spring of 1984.

U.S. policymakers regarded the elections, in the words of one official, as a "unique experiment in democracy." In the U.K. they were also seen as a legitimate process, and the two official observers sent to cover the elections were reasonably satisfied with their fairness. However, all other nations of the European Community remained skeptical. In March the European Parliament passed a resolution declaring that the elections "cannot be regarded as free elections as no political liberties have been guaranteed and opposition politicians have to face the possibility of assassination." Within El Salvador itself allegations were made about intimidation and bribery, and a report produced by the Jesuit-run University of Central America suggested that the number of votes had been inflated to represent an unusually high level of participation.

In July U.S. Pres. Ronald Reagan certified that the Salvadoran government had made a "concerted and significant effort" to comply with international human rights standards. However, the U.S. Congress was not convinced, rejecting a proposed increase in military aid from $66 million to $166 million and securing a reduction in the proportion allocated to El Salvador from the much-publicized U.S.-funded Caribbean Basin Initiative; El Salvador's share was reduced from $128 million to a maximum of $75 million. The International Monetary Fund also laid down conditions to be met before it released the remainder of the 75 million Special Drawing Rights promised for balance of payments assistance in 1983.

Polarization between the left and right continued, leading to increased guerrilla and counterinsurgency activity. According to the majority of sources, the number of civilian deaths amounted to approximately 13,000 during 1981, with a somewhat lower total for the first eight months of 1982.

All attempts at reconciliation, even within the government, failed. The Pact of Apaneca, signed in August by Arena, the PCN, and the PDC, which proposed three commissions to discuss municipal elections, human rights, and peace, was termed a panacea. No agreement was reached upon the dates for municipal elections, nor indeed their procedure, since the far-right parties feared that the PDC would win a majority if there was no prior distribution of seats. Relations with neighbouring countries deteriorated despite the formation of the Central American Democratic Community in January by El Salvador, Honduras, and Costa Rica, later joined by Guatemala.

The widespread political unrest resulted in severe disruption of the economy. Some 45 bridges, 20 railway lines, and 650 electricity generators were attacked over the period of 18 months up to mid-1982, and guerrilla kidnappings continued. Gross domestic product fell by 9.6% in 1981 and was expected to decline still further in 1982. The trade deficit for 1981 showed a marked deterioration. Exports fell by 18% to $792 million, while imports increased by 1.5% to $986 million. In September the government introduced a parallel exchange rate of 3.50 colones to the U.S. dollar beside the official rate in an attempt to prevent a further decline in the level of international reserves.

Despite threats from antigovernment terrorists, voters in El Salvador turned out in large numbers to elect a Constituent Assembly on March 28.
UPI

The Jesse H. Jones Memorial Bridge over the Houston Ship Channel in Texas, with its 750-ft main span, was built with advanced techniques for casting concrete forms in place.

ENGINEERING PROJECTS

In the U.S. the battle of concrete versus steel for long-span bridges followed the pattern already set in Europe, with concrete being used where, a few years earlier, steel would have been the automatic choice. A showdown developed between concrete and steel interests over the replacement for the Sunshine Skyway Bridge across Tampa Bay, Florida, a structure requiring a 1,200-ft cable-stayed main span and 7,600 ft of high-level approach spans. The final decision was that concrete would be used throughout. However, the encroachment by the concrete contractors into bridge work formerly the preserve of the U.S. steel firms did not go technically unchallenged. For the 418-m-long (1 m = 3.3 ft) four-lane Bonners Ferry Bridge across Idaho's Kootenai River, the contractors all chose a cable-stressed steel bridge rather than the alternative of cast-in-place, post-tensioned concrete design. By using cables to stress the top flange, the designers reduced by 10% the steel required for a conventional plate-girder structure; in so doing they exploited the principles developed by the concrete engineer.

North America also followed Europe with the construction of large concrete cast-in-place cantilevered bridges. Several such projects were under way in the U.S., including the Houston Ship Canal Bridge with a main span of 750 ft (228 m). Not only was it the longest span of its kind in North America; the largest traveling forms ever made were used for pours of 60 to 84 cu m. This method of bridge construction, described as an "on-site assembly-line factory," reduced costly labour to a minimum.

The French and British governments appeared finally to have abandoned the Channel Tunnel project, which could handle only rail traffic, and were moving in favour of a bridge crossing that could cope with the ever increasing demands of road traffic. A principal objection to such a bridge had been the possible damage if it were hit by a ship. To forestall this, engineers proposed an ingenious protection of the piers utilizing a large "hydraulic cushion." Each pier would be built at the centre of a water-filled flexible structure resembling a large inverted umbrella. If struck by a ship, the "umbrella" would distort inward, raising the level of the contained water and generating a hydraulic head that would resist the continued movement of the ship toward the pier. Model tests indicated that this protection would be effective and relatively cheap.

Buildings

The U.S. engineer Fazlur Khan pioneered the use of the "tube within a tube" principle of resisting lateral loads on tall buildings. In Khan's concept advantage was taken of the external mullions and spandrel beams to provide an external pierced tube that would share the load with an internal core, thereby saving construction material. The recently completed 49-story First City Tower in Houston, Texas, used this principle. The building also made extensive use of composite steel and reinforced concrete construction in the floors, columns, and the elevator and service core. It was believed to be the first time that these two concepts had been used in one high-rise structure.

Another recently constructed building of note in the U.S. was the 84-m-clear-span Moscone Convention Center in San Francisco. A requirement was that the main exhibition hall roof was to be at

TURNER CONSTRUCTION COMPANY

The Moscone Convention Center in San Francisco used novel engineering techniques to achieve the longest-span underground space in the world.

ground level and designed to support a public park, amusement area, or low-rise shop and theatre buildings. In order to provide maximum headroom without having to excavate deeply into the ground and incur excessive groundwater problems, a shallow arch solution was chosen. Because the arch was shallow, the side thrusts were large, and the ground could not carry the loads without excessive movement. The floor was therefore prestressed to fulfill a threefold function: to tie the arch, to enable an initial prestress to be put into the arch, and, by appropriately profiling the tendons, to resist the water pressures in the ground under the floor.

In Europe much use was made of the external structural frame with the roof suspended underneath. Notable examples of this concept were the factory of the Fleetguard International Corp. in northwestern France and the Inmos factory in south Wales. The object in France was to allow the perceived height of the building to be kept to a minimum and to leave the interior roof zone free for services and unhampered by internal structure. The suspension principle was continued throughout the building with the cooling towers, air handling units, and ducting all being supported in this way. The Inmos factory took a different form, having a relatively heavy spine structure housing the main services plant above the roof and using its height to support sloping tendons that provided intermediate support to long-span (36-m) steel trusses. In this way

large areas uninterrupted by internal columns were provided.

A recently completed institutional building of note was the European Investment Bank in Luxembourg. The site chosen for the bank was the Kirchberg Plateau, a broad ridge separated from the old city of Luxembourg by a gorge. The architect developed a double-L plan with four fingerlike wings and chose a stratified appearance having a horizontal emphasis. The narrow wings allowed natural light and ventilation, and this showed considerable economy in energy costs over a deep plan building. The structure of the building was in concrete, partly poured at the site and partly precast.

Dams

Dam building continued throughout the world in 1982, although activity was more pronounced in less developed countries where the demand for water for irrigation and energy was greater. Brazil had the greatest number of large dams actively under way. The main dam of the $14 billion Itaipú project was completed in October, and initial power delivery from the 12,600-Mw plant was scheduled to begin in April 1983. When the plant began full operation, Brazil expected to save an equivalent of 300,000 bbl of oil per day. The dam was designed as a hollow gravity type, in which large segments are made to form a hollow chamber with the upstream face supported by two buttress sections and with a downstream face slab. This feature saved about 25% of concrete and about $130 million in cost as compared with other gravity dams. While not the first of this type, Itaipú was the highest and largest.

In Europe Sweden planned to construct 1,300 mini-hydroelectric plants in the next five years in order to conserve oil use. The U.S.S.R. announced plans for large-scale diversion of several Siberian rivers, the Ob, Irtysh, and Yenesey, which flow into the Arctic Ocean, to supply water to the arid lands in the Kazakh, Kirghiz, and Uzbek regions in the south. The Soviets also planned to divert the Pechora and Kolva rivers to the Volga. While these projects might take many years to complete, environmentalists were alarmed that they could have a worldwide impact.

In the U.S. work was under way on the first roller-compacted concrete dam, Willow Creek in Oregon. Its dimensions included a volume content of 300,000 cu m, a height of 52 m, and a crest length of 518 m. It represented a major change in the method of construction of a concrete gravity-type dam. The principal difference was that damp gravel is blended with cement and spread and compacted by large, efficient earth-moving equipment, eliminating the labour-intensive, bucket-by-bucket placing procedures used in the past.

In Thailand and Laos the proposed Mekong River project would include a dam 100 m (330 ft) high and require $2 billion to construct. Thailand had under way the 100-m-high Khao Laem dam, scheduled for completion in 1984. China announced plans for ten hydroelectric dams at a cost of $6.7 billion to supply 10,000 Mw of power. During 1982 China constructed more than 1,000 small hydroelectric dams. Even so the nation had developed only 3% of its hydroelectric potential.

Roads

In many of the industrialized nations, revenues from vehicle and fuel taxes were no longer sufficient to meet current and projected highway financing needs. Inflation was raising costs at a faster rate than revenues, while the increased fuel efficiency of vehicles was reducing income from gasoline taxes. This situation, coupled with the deterioration of many major highways constructed after World War II, resulted in exploration of new methods of financing highway construction and maintenance.

In the U.S. federal tax receipts fell below outlays by $5.6 billion in 1980 and $5.2 billion in 1981. Legislation to add 5 cents in taxes to the cost of each gallon of gasoline was approved by the U.S. Congress in December, with four cents dedicated to rehabilitation of roads and one cent dedicated to financing of urban transit projects. In the United Kingdom representatives of the Department of Transport proposed a road financing system under which highway contractors would arrange financing and pay for new road projects and then would be repaid by the government over a period of 15 years.

Despite a variety of economic problems major highway programs were initiated or completed in all continents. Approximately 95% of the 68,260-km (1 km = 0.62 mi) Interstate System in the U.S. was in service, while extensive reconstruction and rehabilitation programs were under way on some segments of the system that had been in heavier than antici-pated service for more than a quarter of a century.

The Inter-American Development Bank was helping finance construction of 61,587 km of roads in eight countries in Latin America and the Caribbean, with a combined value of $7,329,000,000. The last link in the section of the Pan-American Highway between Buenos Aires, Arg., and Santiago, Chile, was opened to traffic in 1982 at Punta de Vacas, Arg., in the Andes Mountains.

Thirty-nine African countries submitted plans for highway projects worth $26 billion as part of the second phase of the UN Transport and Communications Decade in Africa. Included were the 1,200-km highway connecting Annaba, Constantine, Algiers, and Oran in Algeria and the 1,085-km Aaium–Akjoujt road in Morocco.

More than 1,800 km were completed on the Trans-European North-South Motorway, which was to pass through Austria, Bulgaria, Czechoslovakia, Greece, Hungary, Italy, Poland, Romania, Turkey, and Yugoslavia. Italy's government lifted a six-year ban on the building of new expressways and was expected to implement a new $5 billion program that included a bypass around Rome.

Tunnels

Hard rock tunnel boring machines (TBM's) continued to improve their performance and reliability when used under suitable conditions. Norwegian engineers claimed a world record for an advance of 240.5 m in one week achieved by a Robbins 3.5-m-diameter TBM in a rock tunnel for a hydroelectric project. A TBM achieved an impressive performance at the Hausling pumped storage project in Austria, where in eight months it bored a 950-m-long, 4.2-m-diameter pressure shaft inclined at 42° through a hard grained gneiss. In the U.K. the machine-driven

The Itaipú Dam on the Paraná River, largest hydroelectric dam in the world, was dedicated by the presidents of Brazil and Paraguay on October 5.
UPI

Kielder water tunnel through hard rock between the Rivers Tyne and Tees was finally completed in 1982. The 29-km-long, 3.5-m-diameter tunnel was Britain's longest.

The need to ensure that ground conditions were suitable for the employment of TBM's was demonstrated at the Talave irrigation tunnel in Spain; during construction of the 31.6-km-long rock tunnel, the longest in Spain, a roof fall buried a 4.2-m-diameter TBM, which was eventually recovered two years later. Altogether the Talave tunnel penetrated 300 faults during its construction.

Despite the increasing use of TBM's, they were unlikely to supersede drill and blast methods in the foreseeable future. In Finland the Pajainne 18-sq-m-section tunnel providing water to Helsinki was completed by drill and blast methods. This 120-km-long unlined tunnel was claimed to be the longest in the world.

At Frankfurt am Main, West Germany, one of Europe's largest tunnel shields began to be used in 1982 on the new extensions to the city's subway. Weighing 450 metric tons, the 10.56-m-diameter shield was equipped with three excavators. The equipment could be rebuilt to excavate the 8.7-m-diameter tunnels in the same project.

In the U.S. bids were asked for in the construction of the largest soft ground tunnel in the country, at Seattle, Wash.; estimated to cost up to $100 million, it would be 19 m in diameter and 457 m long. The interesting feature of this huge tunnel was the proposed method of construction, using a minimum of 24 drifts located around the circumference of the tunnel.

ENVIRONMENT

Congressional leaders postponed final decisions on controversial rewrites of the Clean Air and Clean Water acts after budget debates and the worsening economic situation monopolized national attention in 1982. Since the original deadlines of the air pollution law were not extended, 144 counties across the nation faced cutoffs of federal aid because they had not met clean air standards in time.

Auto industry and electric power lobbyists had fought hard for a thorough rewrite of the Clean Air Act, but the five-year extension of the law proposed by the Senate Environment and Public Works Committee in August merely relaxed a few provisions of the air pollution control law. Amendments designed to combat acid rain—a product of airborne pollutants combined with water vapour in the atmosphere that has been blamed for millions of dollars of damage to fish, water, and timber resources in the northeastern U.S. and Canada—were added to the measure. The legislation would also require the Environmental Protection Agency (EPA) to decide within three years if 40 substances, most already designated as "potentially harmful" by the agency, should be subject to special regulation. Other provisions would support an August 23 EPA decision ordering the reduction of lead emissions in car exhausts, require the EPA to research the harmfulness of indoor air pollution, and assist the domestic copper industry by relaxing deadlines requiring the installation of antipollution equipment in nonferrous smelters. A different bill in the House would have made a number of industry-backed changes in the act, weakening existing auto emissions standards and loosening deadlines requiring certain types of auto air pollution control equipment.

The Reagan administration announced its proposals for a rewrite of the Clean Water Act on May 26, but Congress was unable to act on them before the end of the year. The administration asked Congress to extend deadlines requiring industries that dump wastes directly into rivers and streams to install advanced water pollution control equipment as well as to move back deadlines for municipal sewage treatment plants whose construction depends on federal funding. Other proposals would loosen a requirement that the EPA set industry-by-industry standards for treating toxic waste before it is discharged into municipal sewage systems, authorize the EPA to charge fees to process applications for exemptions from some of the Clean Water Act's more stringent requirements, exclude dams from discharge permit rules, and extend from five to ten years the period of industrial and municipal discharge permits in order to reduce the EPA's workload.

Pollution and Toxic Waste

Hundreds of protesters were arrested at a North Carolina landfill in September while demonstrating against the disposal there of dirt contaminated with polychlorinated biphenyls (PCB's), which are suspected carcinogens. The dirt was contaminated in 1978 when three New York men and a Raleigh, N.C., businessman illegally spread oil containing the PCB's along highways in the state in order to avoid the costs of proper disposal. Local residents charged that racism had motivated the choice of the landfill as a disposal site for the soil in a county where 64% of the population was black.

The toxic waste issue was again a focus of attention in the House of Representatives in 1982. On September 8 it passed, by a vote of 317 to 32, legislation strengthening the federal law governing the management and disposal of hazardous wastes. In reauthorizing the 1976 Resource Conservation and Recovery Act (RCRA), the House closed several loopholes in the law. Companies that generate less than 1,000 kg (2,200 lb) of hazardous waste per month had been exempt from federal regulation and were allowed to dispose of their wastes in ordinary landfills or sewer systems; the House bill lowered this to no more than 100 kg (220 lb) per month. The EPA would have to report to Congress within one year on the type and amount of hazardous wastes that were being dumped into municipal sewage treatment plants. These wastes were supposed to be covered by the Clean Water Act, but the EPA had not

This 1,250-foot smokestack in Sudbury, Ontario, was believed to be the largest single source of the pollution that mixes high in the air with water vapour to form acid rain.

yet finished the regulations that would govern them under that law, and some legislators were concerned about the delay. The reauthorization bill would ban the disposal of toxic wastes directly into or above underground drinking water supplies. It would also establish a National Groundwater Commission to study and report on the problems of groundwater contamination.

In other congressional action, the House passed a bill on August 11 reauthorizing the Federal Insecticide, Fungicide, and Rodenticide Act (FIFRA) for two years. A coalition of environmental and health groups, state governors, and agriculture officials persuaded the representatives to kill two major revisions to the federal pesticide law that had been backed by the chemical industry. States' rights advocates joined with environmentalists to defeat one provision that would have limited state authority to regulate pesticides more strictly than the federal government did. The other scrapped provision would have kept information about pesticides from public view for five years after the information was given to the EPA, preventing independent scientists from reviewing key health and safety research data. The final bill did honour some industry goals, such as extending by five years a company's period of "exclusive use" of data it submits to the EPA to support its application for registration of a pesticide. Another provision in the bill would give individuals the right to sue companies for violations of FIFRA, but they would be allowed to seek only an injunction requiring the company to stop violating the law; they would have no claim to either damage payments or attorney's fees. After the reauthorization bill went to the Senate, it was halted by debate over reinstituting the industry-backed amendments.

On July 13 the EPA issued new rules governing the design and construction of toxic waste disposal sites. Also outlining how the EPA would monitor disposal operations and correct problems, the more than 500-page document stated that new facilities had to have an impermeable liner preventing the seepage of pollutants from the site, but this regulation would not apply to already-existing facilities. All operations had to control runoff from their sites and were required to carry liability insurance. Closed facilities had to be capped, and their owners would have to monitor their safety for up to 30 years after closure.

One of the largest inland oil spills ever reported in the U.S. occurred on August 1, when a pipeline near Byron, Wyo., broke, spilling an estimated 6,000 bbl of crude oil into Whistle Creek, the Shoshone River, and the Big Horn Reservoir.

On December 20 the EPA released a list of the 418 hazardous waste dumps "most dangerous to public health." The sites would become the top priorities for the $1.6 billion Superfund, a program financing the cleanup of hazardous waste dumps. The announcement was unrelated to the December 16 vote by the House of Representatives to hold EPA Administrator Anne Gorsuch in contempt of Congress for refusing, on President Reagan's order, to turn over to Congress legal documents related to the EPA's management of the Superfund program.

Land Use Policy

The Interior Department published plans to drop 805,000 ac of land from consideration for designation as wilderness late in December. The action, coming only days after Congress adjourned, was denounced by conservationists. A few days later, on December 30, Interior Secretary James Watt announced that he would ban all oil and gas leasing in wilderness areas, ending one of the most controver-

As debate continued over oil and gas drilling in wilderness areas, this oil pumping station, one of several in the Los Padres National Forest in California, continued to operate at the edge of a sanctuary for the endangered California condor.

DAVID STRICK/THE NEW YORK TIMES

sial issues of his tenure. Shortly after taking office, Watt began to accelerate the process under which oil and gas leases in wilderness areas were granted. Congress moved several times to halt the secretary's actions, and under an amendment to the Interior appropriations bill, passed December 19, leasing was banned until Sept. 30, 1983. Since the Federal Wilderness Act forbids oil and gas leasing in wilderness areas after 1983, the congressional move left only a three-month period when wilderness leasing would have been legal.

The Reagan administration also faced opposition to its plan to expand offshore oil and gas drilling by offering up to one billion acres, nearly the entire outer continental shelf, for leasing over the following five years. The plan, devised to raise revenue for the deficit-ridden federal government as well as to increase domestic energy production, came under fire from critics who pointed out that in the midst of a worldwide oil glut, the oil industry had neither the interest nor the ability to explore one billion acres over the next five years. With oil more plentiful than it had been for years, the administration plan would put up for lease almost 40 times as much offshore acreage over the following five years as had been offered in the previous 28 years. Some critics believed that the very loose system of tract evaluation in the administration plan, combined with oil supply conditions, would lead to the tracts' being let for less than fair market value, cheating the public of billions of dollars. The General Accounting Office, in a report requested by 17 members of Congress, questioned the ability of the Interior Department to handle an expanded leasing program with a reduced budget and staff.

Similar criticism was aimed at an administration plan, unveiled when the fiscal 1983 budget was announced in February, to raise $17 billion over the following five years by selling federal lands. According to Secretary Watt, the government planned to sell up to 5% of all U.S.-owned land, more than 35 million ac, an area about the size of Florida. Critics

said that the current depressed real estate market could not possibly absorb such an area at fair market value and that dumping so much federal land on the market would only further depress prices, injuring private land sellers.

Barrier islands are unstable as a result of flooding, erosion, and other natural forces. Structures built on them are likely to wash away, and the government had to pay in the past both to subsidize development and to bail out property owners struck by disaster. In addition, human activities on barrier islands can damage fragile dunes and complex wetland ecologies. A bill banning federal subsidies for development of coastal barrier islands cleared Congress on October 1. The bill mapped out undeveloped areas to be called the "Coastal Barrier Resource System" and prohibited use of federal funds for sewers, bridges, highways, boat landings, airports, housing loans, and some erosion control in these areas. It also renewed a prohibition on the sale of new federal flood insurance. The measure would allow continued federal funding for fish and wildlife projects, maintenance of essential roads and existing channels and structures, coastal energy development, military activities, navigation aids, and research, as well as for programs unrelated to development.

Water Resources Policy

Legislation revising the Reclamation Act of 1902 was passed in 1982, ending a long-running battle between western businessmen who want cheap irrigation water and small farmers who want to limit the growth of corporate farms. Under the old law, federally subsidized water had been provided to farms of 160 ac or less in 17 western states. Large growers had found ways to circumvent the acreage limits in the reclamation law and receive full subsidies for all their farmland. In 1976 a federal court ruled that the law had been administered illegally in favor of large growers and said that, unless Congress revised the act, the Interior Department would have to enforce the 160-ac limitation. During the battle over the rewrite of the law, environmentalists came out in favour of the small farmers, arguing that limiting cheap irrigation water would foster water conservation on western farms. The revision passed by Congress raised the limit to 960 ac for individuals or small corporations. Farmers could also lease an unlimited number of additional irrigated acres but would have to pay substantially more for water to the extra land. It also canceled a requirement that farmers live on or near their farmland in order to qualify for the subsidized water.

Parks and Recreation

A bill designating three new national scenic trails passed the House on May 11. The 704-mi (1,133-km)-long Potomac Heritage Trail in Maryland and Virginia and the 1,300-mi (2,092-km)-long Florida Trail were to be carved from existing federal lands. A $500,000 land acquisition fund was authorized for the Natchez Trace Trail, stretching 694 mi (1,117 km) from Nashville, Tenn., to Natchez, Miss. Studies were authorized for six additional trails. The trails bill was approved by the Senate Energy and Natural Resources Committee on September 15. A similar bill stalled short of enactment in 1980.

On August 26 the president signed a bill creating the Mt. St. Helens National Volcanic Monument. The bill set aside about 110,000 ac of land devastated by the May 18, 1980, eruption for the purposes of scientific research and resource preservation. The new monument included about 30,000 ac of land owned by Weyerhaeuser and Burlington Northern timber companies and by Washington State that will be exchanged for other federal forest land.

Five bills adding more than 120,000 ac to the federal wilderness system were passed in the final days of the lame-duck session in December. New wilderness areas were created in Florida, Missouri, West Virginia, Alabama, and Indiana.

Judicial Action

One of the nation's longest running environmental lawsuits ended in 1982 when the Reserve Mining Co. of Silver Bay, Minn., agreed to pay the city of Duluth and three other communities $1,840,000 to cover the costs of filtering drinking water polluted by the company's mining wastes. Between 1955 and 1980 Reserve dumped some 67,000 tons of asbestos-laden taconite tailings into Lake Superior, creating a potential public health hazard to people who drink the lake's water unfiltered, since microscopic asbestos fibres are known to cause gastrointestinal cancer and other ailments when ingested. Environmentalists first filed suit to stop the dumping in 1969.

In other court action, on March 22 the U.S. Supreme Court let stand a lower court ruling upholding the power of the EPA to set air-quality standards. The oil industry and the city of Houston, Tex., had challenged the agency's 1979 adoption of standards limiting the level of ozone—a major component of smog—on the grounds that the EPA had failed to subject those regulations to cost-benefit analysis, which would have taken into account the cost of installing and maintaining antiozone equipment. The high court agreed with the Court of Appeals in rejecting that argument.

On April 27 the Supreme Court held that the Clean Water Act did not require the Navy to stop using an uninhabited island off Puerto Rico for target practice while it applied for a required federal permit to discharge ordnance into coastal waters. The 8–1 ruling said that the law allows lower courts discretion in determining remedies for violations.

ETHIOPIA

The keynotes of Ethiopian domestic policy in 1982 were the fight against corruption, the consolidation of worker-peasant alliances, and the launching in January of the "Red Star Campaign" in the northern region of Eritrea. The campaign combined intensified military activity against the secessionists with the diversion of funds to the region from other parts of the country for the reconstruction and development of basic facilities, industry, and social services. Government sources claimed successes against rebel guerrillas, and there was much evidence of the revi-

Dangerously radioactive nuclear waste stored in canisters under water awaited a solution to a growing problem: how to dispose of it safely.
THE NEW YORK TIMES

Despite some economic progress, Ethiopia remained one of Africa's ten poorest nations.
KEYSTONE

talization of the Eritrean economy. The government's hand was strengthened by the growing accord with Sudan on border control. Since 1979, the government claimed, more than 8,000 Ethiopians had returned from Sudan or voluntarily abandoned their association with rebel groups.

A concerted program for the elimination of corruption began during the year. People's and workers' control committees were established in neighbourhood associations (Kebeles), peasant associations, industry, and government organizations. A special hierarchy of courts was set up to deal with offenders. The objective was to underline the fact that the means of production and the wealth of the country were no longer to be regarded as the monopoly of an elite and that this transfer of real power brought with it new responsibilities. This action was closely linked with the reorganization of the All-Ethiopia Trades Union and the All-Ethiopia Peasants Association, which was carried out in 1982.

In October it was announced that the second national congress of the Commission to Organize the Party of the Working People of Ethiopia (COPWE) would be held in the near future. An accompanying commentary explained: "Although COPWE is not a party, it is a political organization which functions as a party in its day-to-day operations, guided by the decisions of its periodic Central Committee plenums to intensify the class struggle and provide leadership in the political, ideological, organizational, economic, military, and social fields."

In September 716 detainees imprisoned in 1974–75 were released. These included senior officials of the previous regime and a number of former ministers, several of whom were recruited into the government.

The ten-year (1983–93) social and economic development plan was in preparation. There was expected to be a heavy emphasis on the development of agriculture and an underlying general requirement for self-reliance and the mobilization of national resources. However, projected economic growth rates depended upon a continuing high level of external assistance.

Nevertheless, significant progress was made in the economic sector. The road between Mizan Teferri and Tepi was completed. The construction industry was reorganized and supported by measures taken to increase cement production. In general the industrial sector, hampered by lack of capital input over the previous two decades, found it difficult to meet production targets. However, new industry was progressing. A car and truck assembly plant in Addis Ababa produced more than 24,000 vehicles over a six-year period; the printing industry provided over 42 million books between 1979 and 1982; and the tourist industry expected to benefit from the construction of new hotels.

The government commitment to action against "ignorance, ill health, and want," announced in the early years of the revolution, was producing a noteworthy effect. In the three years since the national literacy campaign was launched in mid-1979, more than six million certificates had been issued to new literates. The health sector also made great strides forward in primary health care and immunization. The national population and housing census, to be implemented with support from the UN Development Program in 1983, was to be the country's first complete census.

A visit by the head of state, Mengistu Haile Mariam, to Moscow in October resulted in an agreement to broaden cooperation between Ethiopia and the U.S.S.R. In January the fifth session of the Ethiopian-East German Cooperation Commission was conducted in Addis Ababa. In July an agreement pledging Ethiopian-Italian cooperation was signed in Addis Ababa.

In October Addis Ababa was the site of a meeting of the Organization of African Unity Contact Committee, established after the failure of the OAU summit meeting in Tripoli, Libya. Its objective was to define the conditions under which a full meeting of the OAU could take place in the near future.

EUROPEAN AFFAIRS

Throughout 1982 the European Communities (EC; the European Economic Community [EEC], the European Coal and Steel Community [ECSC], and Euratom) faced both unresolved internal problems and increasingly difficult relations with the U.S., their major political, defense, and commercial partner. The internal problems had their origins in the stresses induced by the EC's enlargement to include three new member states—above all, Britain—in 1973 and Greece in 1981. The external problems with the U.S. owed much to the failure of the Western economies as a whole to find a way out of the protracted recession that had really begun with the 1973 oil

price rise. Another year of recession and high unemployment brought to the surface of Community relations with the U.S. and other partners a potentially serious number of trade conflicts.

Economic Affairs

The danger of a trade war with the U.S. was sparked in January when U.S. steel producers sought to impose higher import duties on the exports of European steel firms, which, they claimed, were unfairly benefiting from governmental financial aid. This was followed during the summer by U.S. Pres. Ronald Reagan's decision, announced just after the Western economic summit that had been held at Versailles, France, to impose sanctions on European firms supplying equipment for the planned Soviet gas pipeline from Siberia to Western Europe. The pipeline issue, unlike the dispute over steel and—later in the year—agricultural trade, was by no means a purely commercial question. It went to the heart of differences that had developed between the Reagan administration and most EC governments in regard to relations with the Soviet Union. The closing months of 1982 were largely preoccupied with urgent diplomatic moves aimed at defusing what had become known as the "transatlantic trade war" and ensuring that it did not under-

The leaders of the industrialized democracies met in Versailles, France, in June to discuss trade, East-West relations, and other vital issues.
SIPA PRESS/BLACK STAR

mine the wider Western alliance in NATO.

The tensions between the EC and the U.S. first attracted wide attention on January 4 when the EC refused to join the wholesale economic sanctions that the U.S. proposed should be established against the Soviet Union for its moral involvement in the Polish government's suppression of the Solidarity free trade union movement. Although subsequently the Community countries—other than Greece—did agree to make some minor adjustments in trade with the Soviet Union, the U.S. administration was clearly disappointed by the reaction of its European allies. There were hopes that the Versailles summit, which was held June 4–6, would find a formula designed to express the West's criticism of Soviet policy toward Poland, and it was agreed there that the Soviet Union should have to pay more for export credits provided by the West and that the seven leading economic powers would exercise more caution in increasing trade with the Soviet Union in the future.

Shortly after the Versailles summit it became clear that the EC countries did not intend to cut back heavily on trade with the Soviet Union, and most European governments made it clear that they would not be parties to a Western campaign of trade sanctions that might threaten détente between Eastern and Western Europe. At this point President Reagan announced the pipeline sanctions and provoked a storm of condemnation in EC capitals—including London, where the Conservative government of Margaret Thatcher, as a firm advocate of "Reaganite" policies, felt betrayed by Washington's action.

Throughout the spring and summer months efforts were made by both the European Commission and the U.S. administration to head off the imposition of higher import duties on U.S. steel producers. At the same time, other trade frictions surfaced, and there were fears that, unless answers were found, the autumn ministerial meeting of the signatory countries of the General Agreement on Tariffs and Trade might be wrecked. In the event, the GATT ministers, after considerable wrangling, agreed to "resist protectionist pressures." There were widespread warnings on both sides of the Atlantic that trade war and spreading protectionism would make a concerted international recovery from the recession even more difficult to achieve. In October agreement was finally reached, less than two hours before U.S. import duties were to have been introduced, on limitation of European steel imports.

Friction between Europe and the U.S. over trade was matched by continuing difficulties between the EC and Japan over Japan's mounting trade surplus with the Community. Visits by Japanese ministers to Brussels and other EC capitals in March and June resulted in some action in Tokyo to liberalize import restrictions, but the yen's declining value tended to exacerbate the trade imbalance.

European Community summit meetings in Brussels in March and June and in Copenhagen in December were largely preoccupied with the continuing recession and the seemingly relentless rise in unemployment within the EC. The numbers out of work rose to more than 11 million during the year, with industries such as steel, textiles, and automobiles particularly hard hit by plant closings and production cutbacks. However, the consensus among EC leaders was that priority should be given to reducing government budget deficits and public spending rather than to expanding output and reducing unemployment. The political swing to the right in Belgium, Denmark, and The Netherlands and financial and currency pressures brought to bear on France, whose Socialist government had until August given priority to growth, ensured that conservative financial orthodoxy prevailed.

The severe budget pressures on member nations ensured that the negotiations about the future of the EC's own budget and finances would be particularly difficult. This problem involved a wholesale review of the Community's spending policies—above all on agriculture—and the distribution of the burden of financing the budget among member governments. Between January and May, under the chairmanship of Belgium, which currently held the presidency of the Council of Ministers, efforts were made to secure an agreement. Britain insisted on major reforms of the common agricultural policy, curbs on higher farm prices, and a long-term arrangement limiting its own net contributions to the EC budget.

The negotiations eventually overlapped with the annual fixing of farm prices by the EEC. On May 18 a majority within the EEC Council of Agriculture Ministers pushed through a decision increasing prices by an average of more than 10%, despite British protests and an attempt by the U.K. government to use its veto powers. The disregard of the veto triggered a major political row in Britain, where it had been thought that the national veto (known as the Luxembourg compromise) was sacrosanct.

At the end of May it was agreed in principle to extend the ceiling on Britain's budget payments for 1982 and to consider a longer term arrangement later in the year. Although this gave Britain a smaller rebate on its budget payments than the nation's ministers had wanted, it was accepted, and Britain withdrew its opposition to the farm price decision. The conclusion of the Community policy reform was widely seen in Britain as a disappointment, and in the closing months of 1982 there were warnings that, with agricultural spending rising once again and with the strains likely to result from the planned admission of Portugal and Spain, the EC could face its most serious ever budgetary crisis in 1983 or 1984. The establishment of a common fisheries policy by the end of 1982 was blocked by Denmark.

Political Relations

Statements by French Pres. François Mitterrand during an official visit to Spain in June appeared to

The foreign ministers of the European Community nations refused to go along with a U.S. call for sanctions against the Soviet Union. Among those meeting in Brussels in January were, from left, Max van der Stoel (Netherlands), Claude Cheysson (France), Hans-Dietrich Genscher (West Germany), and Léo Tindemans (Belgium).
WIDE WORLD

throw doubt on the possibility of completing the negotiations about Spain's accession to the EC in time to permit it to join in January 1984. However, the electoral successes of the Spanish Socialists in the general election, combined with fears about the political consequences of the EC's shutting the door on Spain, put pressure on the negotiators to break the deadlock. It became clear by the middle of September that the negotiations with Portugal were proceeding much more rapidly than those with Spain, and there was even speculation that the two nations might join the Community on different dates. Although the joining of NATO by Spain (May 30) was widely welcomed in the EC, the continuing problems with Britain, even after the border with Gibraltar was opened in December, cast a further shadow over Community-Spanish relations.

In a referendum held on February 23, Greenland became the first territory in the EC to vote for withdrawal from the Community. Negotiations were due to begin at the end of 1982 on Greenland's future relations with the EC, a subject in which Denmark took a very close interest, both as Greenland's sovereign power and as holder, for the half year from July 1, of the presidency of the Council of Ministers. In Denmark itself the anniversary of the October 1972 referendum that preceded the country's entry into the EC the following year was marked by widespread demonstrations by anti-EC groups.

Despite the difficulties experienced by the EC in resolving its internal problems, European political cooperation—the coordination of a common Community foreign policy—also assumed great significance in 1982. The ten member states met frequently during the year to draw up their own policies on issues such as the Middle East, Poland, and the war between Britain and Argentina.

Relations between EC governments and Israel reached a new low when the former denounced the massacre of Palestinian refugees by Israel's Lebanese Phalangist allies in September. France and Italy joined the U.S. in providing troops for the international peacekeeping force in Beirut, and EC foreign ministers were active in the autumn seeking common ground between the ideas of the U.S., the EC, and the Arab League countries for a political settlement of the Palestine problem.

The same unity that the Community displayed over the Middle East and Poland was not quite so evident in the discussions on the Falkland Islands war. Although the EC countries condemned Argentina's invasion and initially backed Britain with trade sanctions against Argentina, Italy and Ireland subsequently withdrew their support for the sanctions.

The European Parliament (of which a new president, Pieter Dankert of The Netherlands, was elected on January 19 to succeed Simone Veil of France) made it clear during the year that it expected to play a more influential role in the formulation of Community policy. The European Court was very active throughout the year, particularly in giving judgments affecting interpretations of EC rules. At the end of October the court gave a provisional judgment that obliged the Ford Motor Co. of Britain not to restrict the import of right-hand-drive cars from the continent to Britain—a move seen as threatening the British motor industry's desire to keep out inexpensive automobiles.

FASHION

During the winter of 1981–82 women's fashion focused on ponchos and knickers. The latter, carried through into spring, culminated in the rhinestone-trimmed black satin pair worn by Nancy Reagan at a reception given on the occasion of the Versailles summit meeting in June 1982. Ponchos, glorifying in their seamless cut, gave a pleasing alertness to the winter street scene. Adding to their whirl and swirl, stunning giant shawls were tossed over one shoulder and left to flow freely. They came in muted plaids or bold florals, fringed, and often with metallic threads running through the soft wool material like streaks

UPI

Calvin Klein designed this ensemble, featuring revivals from an earlier age, the spencer jacket and the hat.

topped with a mannish slouch hat, this was the typical hard chic look worn by the young executive. Suit materials were borrowed from men's wardrobes, mainly small or large checks and preferably black and white. But a blue cornflower or a red poppy slipped through the buttonhole, a brooch at the throat, dangling earrings, and high-heeled sandals or the newest bicolour pumps revived from the 1930s in black and white relieved the stark look and reminded one that the young executive was also feminine.

Though at first quite a few were taken with the bright red of the Socialist rose that crowded the early displays of spring clothes in Paris shop windows, very soon all that remained of the vivid red was on the plain low-heeled pumps worn with the all-white summer look. All white were the two- or three-flounced petticoat skirts worn with a fitted corselet top with wide straps, dairy-maid style, or with a high-necked frilly blouse in the "square dance" manner, with a wide belt with metal disks adding a Western touch. The above-knee hemline, however, had made its point and shared honours with a low and droopy waistline. In this case there was very little skirt left. Short, soft, and wavy, it was reduced to a high flounce below a high-necked, bloused top with full sleeves and was christened the "Charleston" dress.

For dressy occasions, wedding receptions, or gar-

Patterned sweaters and wing collars played major roles in the 1920s look popularized by nostalgic television and movie dramas.
S.H. COSTIN, LONDON

of lightning. Shawls were an essential part of dressing during the winter and early spring.

Knickers served their purpose in getting the eye accustomed to more leg and were instrumental in the rapid acceptance of the above-knee hemline. The same applied to Bermudas and sturdy, cuffed shorts in the spring, followed by the miniskirt for full summer. The cuffed bubble dress, which hung down straight from the shoulders, came closest to knickers, with one knee-level cuff instead of two. In view of its tightness at the knees, this type of dress was reserved for fancy occasions; quick movement was limited and measured steps were advisable. Pert little hats, feather-trimmed, veiled, and tipped forward, signaled that this manner of dressing was part of a game and not to be taken seriously.

Hemlines were very much in the news. Snappy, knee-level skirts accompanied the new spencer suit jacket as well as the more traditional one over the hipline, fitted at the waist with darts and seaming and squared off at the shoulders. Completed by a silk blouse with a ruffle-trimmed high neckline and

den parties the "Charleston" dress hovered around knee level and the top had a boat neckline edged with wide triple or quadruple ruffles—all very gentle and feminine and emphasized by wide-brimmed floppy capeline hats in fine straw, usually untrimmed. The accompanying high-heeled sandals were made of narrow strips of leather, multicolloured and metal-hued. A "gondolier bag," shoulder-slung and reduced to the needed size for indispensables, was worn hanging in front to discourage purse snatchers.

After dark there was a lot of glitter and shimmer, in checked silk gauze for shawls and in shot taffeta for blouses featuring "fin de siècle" shades such as puce, bronze, and ruby. Knits sparkled with metallic threads, a persistence of the Midas touch. In the fall the new short suit jacket was puffed out at the shoulders and fitted at the waist, sometimes trimmed with velvet at the collar, lapels, and cuffs. Great, gyrating skirts in full flare balanced the short jacket.

The black and white of spring pumps was replaced by russet or claret red, with black arrow-shaped insets front and back. Low boots with high cuffs continued the summer trend in all colours. Worn with trousers or with a slim skirt, the spencer jacket surfaced again in subdued autumn shades such as Burgundy red or black. In some cases the points were omitted, the fit was looser, and black braid trimming was added. In contrast with the fully flared skirt and big-sleeved top for short evening wear, the "smoking" or black dinner jacket with a white blouse frilled at the neck, a narrow ribbon tie, and a slim knee-length skirt also had its supporters.

Autumn colours ranging from black currant and puce to misty mauves, heather, and deep purple were worn in graduated effects, typically a dark heather for the poncho, a light misty mauve for the full skirt, and both colours combined in the bulky knitted sweater. A bright fuchsia pink was the winner for light wool sweaters trimmed with a little frill at neck and cuff, like the blouses. Ponchos took on a new lease. The finest were in soft plain cashmere in natural shade, black, or red; the others were in more rustic and weatherproof woollen materials.

Men's Fashions

The year 1982 was one of pure nostalgia. What the film version of *The Great Gatsby* did for men's fashions in the mid-1970s, the television series "Brideshead Revisited," shown originally in Great Britain and subsequently in Europe, the U.S., and Australia, achieved even more dramatically in 1982. This adaptation of Evelyn Waugh's novel of the 1920s and 1930s, and to a lesser extent the film *Chariots of Fire*, helped to revive at least some of the fashions of that period, while the British Menswear Guild's promotion of the "Duke of Windsor" look for 1983 also drew its inspiration from the flamboyance of those halcyon days for men's fashions.

Wing- and pin-collar shirts and the cutaway-style collar for accommodating the Windsor knot of the tie were part of this nostalgic fashion image; so too were scarlet cloth braces, metal armbands, and Fair Isle, argyle, and cable-patterned knitwear, the last in white wool and worn with white flannel trousers and a club or regimental striped blazer. Gloves, too, were worn on many more occasions; panamas and boaters, striped scarves, tweed hats, and caps all enjoyed a resurgence; and one did not have to be either a Liberal politician or a family doctor to carry the Gladstone bag. It was hardly surprising, then, that Anthony Andrews, one of the stars of "Brideshead Revisited," was designated the "Best Dressed Man of 1982" by the Menswear Association of Britain.

The business suit itself changed little in style. It was still elegant but less formal, and the interest was centred in the cloths, both lighter in weight and colour and with a greater diversity of designs. The country suit was again influenced by the fashions of the '20s and '30s, with full and semi-hacking jackets in colourful tweeds in big and bold designs. Another touch of nostalgia was the attempt to revive the spencer, a truncated and tailless version of the tailcoat worn with a black tie for either day or evening wear.

FINANCIAL INSTITUTIONS

For the nation's banking industry 1982 was a year marked by some costly mistakes at home and trouble with borrowers abroad. It also saw the start of a long-overdue effort to strike back at alternative financial services that had snapped up tens of billions of dollars in consumer deposits over the previous five years.

The mistakes brought heavy losses and executive shakeouts to two of the nation's top bank holding companies when a small, high-flying Oklahoma bank that had sold more than $2 billion in energy industry loans to its larger colleagues went under in July. The failure of the Penn Square Bank in Okla-

Most individual depositors were covered by federal insurance, but some banks lost millions in the failure of Penn Square Bank.

DAVID LONGSTREATH–AP

The new money market accounts, introduced by banks in December, offered high interest rates and the security of federal insurance. They proved even more popular than had been anticipated.
KEN FIRESTONE

homa City was an exception to federal regulators' practice in recent years of negotiating the purchase of small, ailing banks by larger institutions. Penn Square's books were so riddled with poor record keeping and doubtful loans to the oil and gas business that no larger bank would consider a buy-out without considerable guarantees of the bank's credits, and the government declined to offer those sweeteners. When sixth-ranked Continental Illinois National Bank and Trust Co. took a close look at more than $1 billion in loans generated by Penn Square and sold to Continental for fees of ½ to 1% of the interest, the Chicago bank wrote off over $200 million of the credits, reported a $61 million second-quarter loss, and accepted the resignations of several top lending officers. Chase Manhattan, the nation's third-largest bank, reported a $16 million loss that quarter owing to its Penn Square loans and to an additional $117 million in guarantees called when the small Drysdale Government Securities Inc. defaulted on loans from other government securities dealers. The governments's refusal to work for a Penn Square solution was viewed as a warning to bankers now commonly buying loans packaged and syndicated by other banks that federal help would not be forthcoming when the bankers neglected their own homework.

The U.S. government and other nations did step in, however, in the cases of several foreign countries facing default on interest payments to private banks in 1982. Argentina's defeat in the Falkland Islands war, Mexico's declining oil revenues in the face of slack world demand, and overexpansion of foreign debt in Brazil caused these countries to run short of cash needed to make payments on multibillion-dollar loans even as their problems caused their currencies to tumble in value, requiring still more funds to make the dollar-denominated payments. A crisis was averted by a combination of direct low-interest loans from Washington and from the International Monetary Fund.

In consumer banking there were few bright developments in the gloomy picture of the past few years. Competition for funds remained fierce as withdrawals from savings banks exceeded new deposits at a rate similar to that of 1981, about $1 billion each month. Money market mutual funds continued to be the clear beneficiaries of this trend, running up a total of nearly $250 billion under management in 1982 from virtually nothing five years before. Their growth rate seemed to have slowed somewhat toward the year's end, however, when the Federal Reserve Bank began a sharp drop in the discount rate on loans charged to member banks, from 12% in July to 8½% in December. Where federal observers had predicted up to 200 insolvencies for the coming year requiring "fold-ins" to larger banks and, in many cases, government guarantees, the number of problem cases seemed likely to decline with interest rates.

The plight of bank deposit-taking was also mitigated somewhat by what became a bewildering variety of new financial instruments. Aside from the tax-exempt All-Saver certificates authorized in 1981 and due to expire at the end of 1982, there were new 91-day floating rate certificates and the bank-sponsored money market funds, newly authorized in December 1982. A typical bank advertisement might promote nearly a dozen investment options with different interest rates, including one rate that was not printed since it fluctuated daily with the securities markets.

Meanwhile, banks were testing the limits of the 1933 Glass-Steagall Act that had separated commercial banking from stock and bond dealing. After the spectacle of 1981, when bankers watched as powerful "financial supermarkets" were created in the mergers of Prudential Insurance with the Bache Group and of American Express Co. with Shearson Loeb Rhoades, bringing insurance, brokerage, and credit services under one umbrella, the banks answered back in 1982. Several commercial banks and thrift institutions started their own brokerage firms, arranged to act as agents for stockbrokers, or bought out brokers, the largest such purchase being BankAmerica's $53 million deal for Charles Schwab Co., the discount broker. It was clear that federal regulators were softening on the distinction between banks and securities dealers while Congress continued to debate changes in Glass-Steagall without a satisfactory bill emerging. Brokers were concerned that U.S. banking industry assets—many times the value of the securities industry's assets—and the banking network's far more numerous retail outlets posed a clear and present danger if entry by banks into brokerage went unfettered.

FINLAND

Mauno Koivisto was sworn in as Finland's ninth president on Jan. 27, 1982, ending almost 26 years of unbroken rule by Urho Kekkonen, who had resigned in October 1981 because of illness. In the popular vote for an electoral college, the Social Democratic and independent candidates backing Koivisto secured 43.4%, against 18.7% for Conservative nominee Harri Holkeri, best placed of the other seven contenders. Koivisto then secured 167 of the 301 votes in the electoral college, thus gaining a decisive majority in the first round of voting.

Koivisto, the first Finnish head of state to emerge from the left, vowed to continue the external policy pursued by his post-World War II predecessors, based on good-neighbourly relations with the U.S.S.R. During a visit to the U.S.S.R. in March he was amiably received by Soviet Pres. Leonid Brezhnev. Koivisto also traveled to Sweden, Norway, Iceland, and Hungary.

As a result of Koivisto's elevation from prime minister to president, his centre-left government resigned. A new coalition drawn from the same four parties—Social Democratic, Centre, Swedish People's, and Communist—took office on February 25. Again, a Social Democrat became prime minister: Kalevi Sorsa, who had occupied the post twice before (1972–75 and 1977–79).

Domestic politics were overshadowed by the approach of a general election due in March 1983. Opinion polls showed the Social Democrats and Conservatives poised to pick up votes, the Centre holding its own, and the Communists clear losers. The most heat was generated at an extraordinary Communist Party congress in mid-May, when retiring chairman Aarne Saarinen, a reformist, made a sensational attack on Moscow for siding with the Finnish hard-line minority and implicitly charging the party with harbouring "anti-Soviet elements." In December the Communists left the government to go into opposition, preparatory to the upcoming election. Sorsa's resignation was refused by Koivisto, and on December 30 the prime minister reconstituted his Cabinet with Social Democrats replacing the three Communist ministers.

Attempts to balance bilateral trade between Finland and the U.S.S.R. over a five-year period posed problems. By the fall the Finns had built up a 5 billion markkaa surplus. To restore equilibrium, they needed to reduce eastward-bound deliveries. This factor, coupled with the continued recession in Western markets and a loss of competitive edge, served to dull economic prospects. Unemployment rose toward 6% as growth rates, forecast at 1% or lower, were insufficient to sustain jobs. Inflation, though waning, was not brought significantly below the average within the Organization for Economic Cooperation and Development. In October the government finally followed the example of the other Nordic countries and devalued the markka—twice in a single week.

In some respects the economy remained well balanced, however, with a reasonably healthy current account, a respectable foreign debt profile, and no need to apply sharp monetary adjustments. In the budget only 12.4% of expenditure had to be financed by borrowing, a low percentage by Scandinavian standards.

Mauno Koivisto became president of Finland in January, succeeding Urho Kekkonen, who resigned after 25 years in office.
ALAIN NOGUES—SYGMA

FISH AND FISHERIES

The UN Food and Agriculture Organization announced a 2% rise in the world fish catch during 1982, but this was by no means a sign that the industry's problems were coming to an end. High operating costs continued to threaten some fisheries with extinction.

The year's most notable casualty was undoubtedly the U.S. Pacific tuna industry, which experienced an unprecedented slump in demand that tumbling prices did little to check. The blame was placed on the recession, which swung consumer buying to cheaper chicken and cheese products. By August half the Inter-American Pacific tuna fleet was idle, and both Bumble Bee and Van Camp Seafoods had closed big canneries in California. Sales of canned salmon declined when a perforated can caused a death from botulism in Belgium, requiring the recall of enormous quantities of U.S. salmon in cans produced by a certain type of can-forming machine. Untold damage was done to the salmon canning industry, leading to a massive lawsuit by the industry against the machinery manufacturers.

The U.S. total catch had risen by 27% since the advent of the 200-mi fishing limit, and in 1982 it was nearing four million tons, valued at $2.4 billion at dockside. The potential value was estimated at $8 billion–$10 billion, and it was believed that continued growth would lead to the possible creation of 300,000 new jobs. Much of this potential lay in the estimated 20 million tons of Alaskan pollack that were within reach of U.S. vessels.

Canada had been suffering from an oversupply of canned mackerel, and the government had to support the market by buying stocks for distribution to third world countries. Measures were introduced to cut the fleet by 25%; these included a subsidy for scrapping old vessels and restrictions on the introduction of newer and more efficient ones.

Europe was trying desperately to adjust to a situation of overcapacity. While vessels were becoming ever more efficient, their number had not decreased accordingly, and the EEC nations were finding it difficult to divide a "mutually owned" resource in a way that was satisfactory to all concerned. Quota allocations were bitterly argued, as was the total allowable catch (TAC) for popular species such as herring, mackerel, and haddock. Denmark was accused of taking ten times its permitted share of the herring TAC and of ignoring requests to stop fishing. Faced with falling prices and costs that were 33% higher than in 1981, EEC nations were tempted to save the industry at the expense of the fish stock.

In Britain demands by the industry for financial aid were loud and desperate, particularly in Scotland, but were frustrated by the economic climate and by the inability of the EEC to agree on a common fisheries policy. Under the Treaty of Rome the rich and carefully husbanded fish stocks around Britain's coasts could be opened to an "up to the beaches" free-for-all in 1983, failing a new agreement.

With so much uncertainty in the marine fisheries, it was not surprising that greater attention was being given to the more stable aquaculture industry. This was one of Western Europe's fastest growing industries, worth approximately $400 million a year. China's aquaculture production had risen 30% since 1978 to 370,000 tons a year, and Chinese researchers were claiming a breakthrough in the induced spawning of freshwater prawns. Prawn ponds in Central America continued to develop their enormous potential, and Panama received a $13 million loan from the Inter-American Development Bank for prawn farm development.

What was seen by the International Whaling Commission (IWC) as a major step toward a total ban on whaling was regarded by others as a shift of emphasis from one species to another. Whaling nations such as the U.S.S.R., Japan, and Iceland joined in condemning a total ban, claiming that it would cause additional unemployment and a reduction of food supply. (*See* Environment.)

Ralph Maggioni, president of L.P. Maggioni & Co., the last remaining oyster cannery on the Atlantic coast of the U.S., surveys his empire from atop a mountain of oyster shells. Fifty other oyster canneries had succumbed to pollution, coastline development, and hard times.

UPI

JACQUES M. CHENET/NEWSWEEK

Community gardening plots such as this one in New York City turned unpromising urban wasteland into sources of produce, pride, and even profit for growing numbers of city dwellers.

FLOWERS AND GARDENS

The number of U.S. households engaged in gardening has generally paralleled changes in the Consumer Price Index for food, with a one- to two-year lag. According to surveys by Gardens for All, a national nonprofit gardening association, 47% of the nation's households, or 38 million, grew some or all of their own vegetables. This represented a gain of one million households a year. Of these gardeners, 51% were between the ages of 18 and 29, and more than half lived in the Midwest and South, although the West was the fastest growing area. About 15 million households indicated they would like to garden if they had land, and 52% of them would support community gardening programs.

Outdoor bedding plants continued to win favour with home gardeners, who found that these seedlings were good shortcuts to instant garden displays. Geraniums, grown primarily from seed by commercial growers, showed a 14% rise in sales. Tissue culture or test-tube production of perennials increased the availability of these relatively permanent summer flowers. Garden centres and mail-order catalogs had stimulated interest in these plants, as well as renewed interest in home fruit orchards and berry patches. Most mail-order sources reported sales increases of up to 33%. With the housing market depressed, many homeowners were revamping their old houses, a process that often included the redesigning of old landscapes with renovation plantings. The most important plants for this purpose were

dwarf or low-growing evergreens, longer-lasting lawn-grass mixtures, and the smaller flowering trees.

In the continuing battle against the gypsy moth, which destroyed more than 12 million ac (4.8 million ha) of forest and residential trees and shrubs in 21 states and Canada during the year, progress was reported in the use of biological controls. Several parasitic wasps were proving effective in attacking the moth larvae; one species imported from the Kulu Valley in India had excellent prospects since it multiplies rapidly and is harmless to humans. The synthetic sex attractant or pheromone Disparlure was also being integrated successfully into pest management.

A herbicide for the control of a pernicious perennial weed, couch grass (*Agropyron repens*), was introduced in the U.K. in small packs for amateur gardeners. The active ingredient, alloxydim-sodium, acts systemically and will control the weed without damaging most ornamental plants.

In the annual all-Europe seed trials (Fleuroselect), the 1983 award and bronze medal went to the F_1 hybrid grandiflora petunia Red Picotee, which was raised in Japan (T. Sakata & Son of Yokohama). The flower is dark red with a white margin and measures about three inches across when wide open. (It also won a 1983 bronze medal in the All-America seed trials.) At the Royal National Rose Society's trials in the U.K., the President's International Trophy for the best new rose and a gold medal went to a blood red, cluster-flowered seedling (tentatively called Korpeana), raised in West Germany by W. Kordes and Son.

The use of micropropagation techniques (increasing plants vegetatively from very small parts, such as buds) for roses received considerable publicity in 1982. One firm in the U.K. multiplied a miniature rose by micropropagation to produce a large quantity of plants for marketing. Another firm was using the technique for several varieties, although it was known that not every variety would grow satisfactorily on its own roots. Some 20 varieties of large flowered and cluster-flowered roses could be grown from bud to salable plant in 21 months. The main advantage for the gardener was that roses propagated by this method produced no unwanted suckers from the roots.

FOOD

The continuing recession, escalating legislative controls, health controversies, and the costly complexities of safety assurance absorbed an undue proportion of manufacturers' resources in 1982. They contributed to the liquidation of many food processors and the absorption of others by multinational corporations.

A wild fruit extremely rich in vitamin C, yielding 2.3 to 3.1 g per 100 g, was discovered in Northern Australia. The fruit, *Terminalia ferdinandiana*, was eaten by the aboriginal people and especially by children. Spanish technologists made a significant development in paprika processing by replacing the

Paper Bottle containers utilized newly approved aseptic packaging technology that yields a six-month shelf life without refrigeration.
GENE MAGGIO/THE NEW YORK TIMES

traditional sun-drying with a continuous process involving washing, dicing, seed separation, liquidizing, low-temperature concentration, pasteurization, and, finally, aseptic packaging. New potato strains were developed in The Netherlands for chip manufacture in less developed countries; when dried, they did not require refrigeration or special storage. The discovery that the local potatoes of Taiwan were particularly suitable for french fries led to a fast-food development there.

The proportion of brown to white bread consumed in Britain increased substantially. A gastroenterologist told the Royal Society that consumption of brown bread could eliminate the National Health Service's £20 million-a-year expenditure on laxatives. In the U.S. pasta became a fashionable food, and stores specializing in different varieties of pasta opened in a number of cities. China launched a campaign to encourage bread consumption, assisted by a Japanese company that installed a large plant for bread and doughnut manufacture.

World stocks of dairy products continued to rise. At the International Dairy Federation conference in Moscow there was discussion of how to reconcile overproduction in developed countries with undernutrition in the third world. One proposal was to blend milk fat and protein with vegetable oils and proteins to make cheaper products. However, the growing market for such cheaper products in the U.S., Britain, and other Western countries had already increased the surpluses. Imitation cheese had captured 7% of the U.S. market, and imitation mozzarella was used in 35% of the pizzas sold there.

The concentration of milk by ultrafiltration (UF) on the farm was studied in the U.S. as a means of reducing transportation costs. The concentrate could be stored for four days without deterioration, and it improved the yields of cheese and cultured products. Canadian workers used milk powder made from UF-concentrated milk in cheese manufacture, making it possible for dairies to cope with the summer surge and to keep operating throughout the year.

British scientists demonstrated that the storage of refrigerated milk could be improved by the use of carbon dioxide, which prevented the growth of cold-tolerant bacteria. French scientists made the interesting discovery that the adverse effect of refrigerated milk in cheesemaking could be overcome by the use of certain proteolytic enzymes that also improved cheese quality.

Serological tests developed in Austria and West Germany made it possible to differentiate between different kinds of meat in manufactured products. A similar test developed in Britain detected 3% kangaroo meat in beef products. A British company developed a fluorimetric method for determining "lean meat" content, and the Danish Meat Research Institute (DMRI) developed a rapid method for determining the collagen content of meat.

A great many of the new products that appeared during the year were specially formulated preparations with reduced fat and/or energy content, variously combined with nonnutrient fillers and sometimes aerated or with increased water content. Such products satisfied the desire for variety and customary levels of food consumption without exceeding calorie requirements; they also helped to maintain manufacturing and sales turnover. Other growth areas included new low-salt and low-cholesterol products and sugarless foods. The growth of new products high in polyunsaturated fats was affected by medical statements that they increased the risk of cancer, although other medical spokesmen expressed the opinion that high intake of saturated fats was actually the culprit.

The transition of Japan toward a Western lifestyle resulted in a spate of new products that were compromises between traditional and Western-style foods. Among them were a soy protein-derived blue cheese resembling Roquefort, soymilk yogurt, snacks made from meat and algae (*Chlorella*), and food preparations made from gelatinized seaweed combined with fruit juices, fish eggs, meat products, or noodles. Kangaroo meat was reported to have become popular in Japan, where it was known as "jumping steak."

Similar new product adaptations were made in many other countries to meet tourist and ethnic demands. A line of cheese spreads made from soy flour was developed in Yugoslavia, and a custard-like product was made in the U.S. from *villia* (a Scandinavian cultured milk), soy milk, and honey. The Chinese developed a cola drink prepared from haws and another soft drink from soy flavoured with hibiscus. A line of ethnic Mexican-style products was developed in Britain, including tacos, tostados, and taco casserole. Mexican foods, often adapted to American tastes, were also gaining in popularity in the U.S.

(*See also* Agriculture; Fish and Fisheries.)

FOOTBALL

The Washington Redskins emerged from the abbreviated 1982 National Football League (NFL) season as the undisputed champions. While critics could object that they had arrived at the play-offs in part by having some of their toughest games canceled, there could be no doubt of their skill and determination. And no one disputed the choice for most valuable player in the championship game: running back John Riggins, who set Super Bowl records for rushes (38) and yards gained rushing (166) and who electrified fans by taking a fourth-and-one off left tackle for a 43-yd touchdown that put Washington ahead to stay. The final score at the Rose Bowl in Pasadena, Calif., on January 30, 1983, was 27–17 over a Miami Dolphins team whose defense had been tops in the league. Redskin coach Joe Gibbs was NFL coach of the year in his second season.

Washington reached the Super Bowl with playoff wins over Detroit (31–7), Minnesota (21–7), and Dallas (31–17) for the National Football Conference title. Miami beat New England (28–13), San Diego (34–13), and the New York Jets (14–0) for the American Conference crown.

The season was most memorable for its 57-day players' strike, which reduced the schedule from 16 games to 9. The strike ended November 16, when player unrest coaxed Players Association executive director Ed Garvey to withdraw his demand for a fixed pay scale distributed from a league fund drawn from television revenue. Before the season the NFL had signed a five-year contract worth $2.1 billion with three television networks, attesting to its economic stability but also igniting a share-the-wealth uprising that contributed to the lengthy strike.

After the strike the league temporarily abandoned its six-division structure and expanded its postseason play-offs from 10 teams to 16. Even so, four 1981 play-off teams failed to return to the tourna-

John Riggins got 43 of his record 166 yards rushing in the Super Bowl on this fourth-and-one play that produced the game-winning touchdown for the Washington Redskins.
WIDE WORLD

Football

DRAWING BY BARSOTTI © 1982 THE NEW YORKER MAGAZINE, INC.

"Go, go, go, Winnipeg or Saskatchewan or whoever the hell you are!"

ment: Buffalo, the New York Giants, Philadelphia, and San Francisco, the defending Super Bowl champion, which fell from a 13–3 record to 3–6.

The most improved team was New England, which climbed from 2–14 to 5–4 under new coach Ron Meyer. The Raiders, who moved from Oakland after years of legal battles that still were being appealed at the year's end, had been 7–9 the previous season. Their star rookie halfback, Marcus Allen, led the league in touchdowns with 14, and their defense led the league with 38 quarterback sacks.

Washington improved its record from 8–8 to 8–1, largely because kicker Mark Moseley set two league records with 23 consecutive field goals (20 of them in 1982) and with a .952 field-goal percentage (20 for 21). The Redskins also allowed the fewest points in the league, and their quarterback, NFC passing leader Joe Theismann, threw to unheralded first-year wide receiver Charlie Brown, the league leader with 21.6 yd per catch.

San Diego's average of 324.7 passing yards per game set an NFL record, and its average of 450.8 total yards per game was the highest since 1951. Quarterback Dan Fouts became the first quarterback to pass for 400 yd in consecutive games and tied Terry Bradshaw of Pittsburgh with a league-high 17 touchdown passes. Wide receiver Wes Chandler led the league with 1,032 yd on pass receptions and nine touchdown catches. San Diego's Kellen Winslow led the AFC with 54 receptions, and the Chargers also led the league in points, first downs, and yards per play.

Cincinnati quarterback Ken Anderson won his fourth NFL passing championship, broke a 37-year-old record by completing 70.6% of his passes, and completed a record 20 consecutive passes on January 2. When San Diego defeated Cincinnati 50–34 on December 20, the teams combined for 66 completions and 883 passing yards, both NFL records.

San Francisco led the NFC in total yards and passing yards as quarterback Joe Montana passed for at least 300 yd in five consecutive games, another record. Also for San Francisco, Dwight Clark led the league with 60 receptions and the conference with 913 yd on receptions.

On the ground Tony Dorsett of Dallas set a record with a 99-yd run, but with the shortened season he was unable to extend his own record of five 1,000-yd seasons in five years. Dorsett's 745 yd rushing led the NFC, trailing only Freeman McNeil of the New York Jets, who led the NFL with 786.

Defensively, Miami led the NFL by allowing 256.8 yd and 114.1 passing yards per game. Tampa Bay led the NFC in those categories. Pittsburgh led the league in rushing defense, yielding 84.1 yd per game.

As the year ended, the NFL's first U.S. competition in nearly eight years was preparing to begin its first season in March 1983 with network television backing. The United States Football League had 12 franchises: in Birmingham, Ala.; Boston; Chicago; Denver, Colo.; Los Angeles; Philadelphia; Tampa, Fla.; Washington, D.C.; Oakland, Calif.; suburban Phoenix, Ariz.; Detroit; and New York–New Jersey.

Collegiate Football

Pennsylvania State University won the national collegiate football championship on Jan. 1, 1983, by defeating the University of Georgia 27–23 in the Sugar Bowl game at New Orleans. Georgia, the Southeastern Conference champion, had been the only major college team with a perfect record before the bowl games. Its star junior halfback, Herschel Walker, won the Heisman Trophy, honouring the best college player. Walker finished his third season just 824 yd short of the four-year career rushing record. Penn State's national championship with a record of 11 victories and 1 defeat was the first for Joe Paterno, named college football's coach of the year in his 17th season at Penn State.

Southern Methodist University, the Southwest Conference champion with a 11–0–1 record and a 7–3 Cotton Bowl win over Pittsburgh, ranked second. Penn State had beaten both Pittsburgh and third-ranked Nebraska, which finished 12–1 with a 21–20 Orange Bowl victory against Louisiana State. Georgia (11–1) ranked fourth.

The other top ten teams in the Associated Press writers' poll were, in order: UCLA (10–1–1), Arizona State (10–2), Washington (10–2), Clemson (9–1–1), Arkansas (9–2–1), and Pittsburgh (9–3). The coaches voting in the United Press International poll omitted Clemson, the Atlantic Coast Conference champion and defending national champion, because the NCAA had put it on probation for more than 100 rules violations. UPI otherwise ranked its top ten teams the same as did the AP and made Florida State (9–3) number ten.

Alabama coach Paul ("Bear") Bryant retired after 38 seasons and the most victories in college football history. Bryant's record was 323–85–17, including 232–46–9 in 25 years at Alabama. But Alabama, the only team to beat Penn State, lost three games in a row before defeating Illinois 21–15 in the Liberty Bowl. Ray Perkins, who resigned as coach of the NFL New York Giants, was named Bryant's successor.

Pacific Ten Conference champion UCLA defeated

Curt Warner (25) scored Penn State's first touchdown in a 27–23 victory over Georgia in the Sugar Bowl.
WIDE WORLD

Big Ten champion Michigan 24–14 in the Rose Bowl. Other conference champions were: Montana in the Big Sky; Fresno State in the Pacific Coast Athletic; Brigham Young in the Western Athletic; Tulsa in the Missouri Valley; Bowling Green State in the Mid-American; Furman in the Southern; Louisiana Tech in the Southland; Jackson State in the Southwestern; and Harvard, Dartmouth, and Penn sharing the Ivy League crown.

Nebraska was the national leader in total offense (518 yd per game), rushing offense (394 yd per game), and scoring (41 points per game). Its centre, Dave Rimington, became the first player ever to win a second Outland Trophy, honouring the best collegiate lineman. Long Beach State led the country in passing offense with 327 yd per game, and its quarterback, Todd Dillon, was the individual leader with 3,587 yd of total offense.

Stanford had a more prominent passing attack as John Elway's 24 touchdown passes and Vincent White's 68 pass receptions in ten games were individual highs, but Stanford lost the season's wildest finishing game against California November 20. Stanford took a 20–19 lead with four seconds to play, but then California players exchanged the ball five times on a kickoff return and ran through the Stanford band for the winning touchdown. Northwestern ended its losing streak at 34, a record for major colleges.

Canadian Football

The Edmonton Eskimos extended their record of Canadian Football League (CFL) championships to five when they defeated the Toronto Argonauts 32–16 for the Grey Cup on November 28 at Toronto. The Eskimos won ten straight after lounging in last place of the Western Division with a midseason record of 3–5. The Argonauts improved from 2–14 the previous season to win the Eastern Division with a regular-season record of 9–6–1 behind rookie coach Bob O'Billovich and quarterback Conredge Holloway, named the league's outstanding player.

Edmonton quarterback Warren Moon set a CFL record with 5,000 yd passing, led the league with 36 touchdown passes, and won his second award in three years as the outstanding offensive player in the Grey Cup game. Edmonton linebacker James Parker led the league with 17½ quarterback sacks and was named its outstanding defensive player, and Dave Cutler led the league with 170 points.

Joey Walters of Saskatchewan set a CFL record with 101 pass receptions and led the league with 1,670 yd on receptions. Ottawa had three award winners: Rudy Phillips was outstanding offensive lineman; quarterback Chris Isaacs was rookie of the year; and Alvin Walker led the league with 1,141 yd rushing and 18 touchdowns.

Association Football (Soccer)

Italy's captain and goalkeeper Dino Zoff led his men up the steps of the Santiago Bernabeu stadium in Madrid on July 11, 1982, to receive the golden World Cup and medals from King Juan Carlos after Italy's victory in the final of that tournament. Italy decisively defeated West Germany 3–1 in a match estimated to have been watched on television by 1,000,000,000 people. The Italians equaled Brazil's record of three victories in the World Cup, the finals of which had been enlarged to accommodate the teams of 24 nations playing in 17 centres in Spain during June and July.

The Italians started the final without one of their key midfielders, Giancarlo Antognoni, injured in the semifinals against Poland, and Francesco Graziani limped out of the game after ten minutes with further damage to a shoulder hurt also against the Poles. Italy also withstood the disappointment of Antonio Cabrini's driving a penalty kick wide of Harald Schumacher's goal in the first half, the first time a penalty had not been converted in a World Cup final. But Paolo Rossi, Marco Tardelli, and Bruno Conti hit peak form and made the West Germans' attacks look stereotyped and robotish.

There was no fluke about the triumph of the Italians. They had already eliminated the favoured Brazil and defending champion Argentina. France lost one semifinal (3–3) to West Germany on penalty kicks and then went down 3–2 to a spirited Polish team in Alicante, Spain, in the play-off for third place.

West Germany was involved in a boring clash against Austria with the worst aspects of possession play being paraded in an exploitation of the "league" points system to enable both teams to qualify for the second phase. The tournament did produce some surprises. The unheralded Cameroon team tied its three games against Poland, Italy, and Peru; Kuwait showed remarkable resilience, and

Antonio Cabrini (left) and Claudio Gentile were on top of the celebration after their Italian team won the World Cup final in Madrid.
UPI

Honduras rocked Spain by holding the tournament hosts to a draw.

North American Soccer League

The New York Cosmos regained their champions' tag when they beat the Seattle Sounders in the Soccer Bowl in San Diego, Calif., on Sept. 18, 1982, with a single goal after 30 minutes by Italian-born striker Giorgio Chinaglia, again the league's leading scorer with 20 goals and 15 assists in 32 games. It was the Cosmos' fourth title in six years.

The small crowd of 22,634—some 14,000 fewer than the previous year—demonstrated the trend of declining attendance in the NASL. Even the Cosmos dropped to below an average of 30,000 for the first time since the arrival of Pelé in 1975; six teams attracted average attendances of less than 10,000, and three put their franchises up for sale at the end of the season. High ticket prices, unexciting play, and general economic depression contributed to the decline.

FRANCE

The "honeymoon" period that marked the start of Pres. François Mitterrand's term of office was followed in 1982 by a deterioration in the political and economic situation. This led to a notable success for the conservative opposition in the spring cantonal elections and a second devaluation of the franc, resulting in the adoption of austerity policies by the Socialist government.

The government's success in carrying its nationalization bill was the major event of the start of Mitterrand's seven-year term. In February the Constitutional Council declared that the bill was consistent with the constitution; it was published two days later in the *Journal Officiel*, thus becoming law. Accordingly, the state found itself in control of a public sector the extent of which was unequaled in the West. It managed 75% of credits and deposits in the banking system, held 29% of industrial turnover, exerted its influence in 3,500 firms or industrial concerns, and employed 23% of industrial wage-earners. In mid-February the Cabinet appointed "general administrators" (in effect, managing directors) of the 5 nationalized industrial groups, the 2 financial companies, and the 18 banks.

Soyouz Gas Export and Gaz de France signed an agreement in Paris for the annual delivery to France of 8 billion cu m (282.5 billion cu ft) of gas over a period of 25 years, beginning in 1984. This would make France dependent on the U.S.S.R. for some 35% of its gas. A third Franco-Algerian agreement on gas was signed in early February, under which France was to receive from 1983 on 9,150,000,000 cu m of Algerian gas annually at a price slightly above that on the world market.

Despite the enactment of a statute reducing the workweek from 40 to 39 hours and introducing a standard five weeks' paid vacation, there were tensions in the government's relations with the trade unions, and the number of strikes increased. The

Hundreds of sympathizers attended the funeral of PLO deputy director Fadel el-Dani, who was killed by a bomb in Paris in July.
LAURENT MAOUS—GAMMA/LIAISON

government was confronted with discontented white-collar workers, angry farmers, impatient trade unionists, and restless Socialists. Farmers protested over the level of subsidy being offered by the Ministry of Agriculture, headed by Edith Cresson. The situation on the industrial front deteriorated, with factory occupations and sometimes violent clashes. The confrontation between the two main trade union confederations, the Confédération Général du Travail (CGT) and the Confédération Française Démocratique du Travail (CFDT), intensified.

In this hostile climate, the Socialist government suffered some stunning political defeats. In January four by-elections were all won by the opposition. The cantonal elections on March 14 and 21 to fill half the seats on the *conseils généraux* appeared to be an undeniable defeat for Mitterrand and the government. Final results for the 2,014 seats contested showed that—except for the far left, which took five seats for a gain of one—all the parties in the government coalition lost. The Communist Party (PC) took 198 seats, a loss of 44; the Socialist Party (PS) took 509 seats, a loss of 5; the Left Radicals (MRG) took 61 seats, a loss of 27; and the remaining left-wing parties took 54 seats, a loss of 24. The opposition parties, on the other hand, all improved their positions. The Rassemblement pour la République (RPR) took 336 seats, a gain of 146; the Union pour la Démocratie Française (UDF) took 470 seats, a gain of 69; and the various right-wing parties took 380 seats, a gain of 51. The far right retained its one seat. Of the *conseils généraux* in metropolitan France, the left now controlled 35 as against the opposition's 58.

On June 12 in Brussels, the finance ministers of the European Communities (EC) decided to adjust parity of four out of seven currencies in the European Monetary System. The West German mark and the Dutch guilder were revalued by 4.25% each, while the French franc and the Italian lira were devalued, the first by 5.75% and the second by 2.75%. Thus the franc was effectively devalued by some 10% against the West German currency. This adjustment was accompanied by a number of other measures, including a freeze on all wages and prices until October 31 except for producer agricultural prices, fresh food prices, and fuel prices.

A major problem facing the government was the renewed wave of terrorist attacks in various parts of the country, especially Paris. In the Rue Marbeuf, near the Champs-Elysées, a car bomb killed or injured some 60 people and caused extensive damage, and in the Rue des Rosiers a terrorist gang opened fire in a Jewish restaurant, leaving 6 dead and many wounded. In August, after several other outrages in the capital, the government set up an antiterrorist plan involving the dissolution of the *Action directe* group and surveillance of foreign diplomats suspected of illegal activities.

Among the measures approved by the National Assembly were the government's economic and financial program; an amended bill on security and freedom; an electoral reform bill; and a bill on transport, which for the first time set out to reorganize transport within France on a national basis. Also passed was a social security bill that represented a turning point in social and political policy because it aimed to balance the social security budget. Most French people would have to make sacrifices in order to achieve this goal.

The debate on the 1983 finance bill in the National Assembly confirmed the government's wish to pursue a policy of austerity. The proposed budget was marked by considerable restraint in public expenditure, the curbing of taxes, and limiting of the deficit.

ARAL–SIPA PRESS / BLACK STAR

Protesters carrying red flags and banners demonstrated in Paris when U.S. Pres. Ronald Reagan arrived in June to take part in the Versailles conference.

The government laid down strict guidelines for the relaxation of the freeze on prices and incomes after November 1. The resulting dissatisfaction was manifested in an unprecedented wave of strikes—especially in the automobile and steel industries and in transport—as well as protest demonstrations.

Unlike domestic policy, French foreign policy under the PS government was not subject to any major change. The Falkland Islands conflict between the U.K. and Argentina generally strengthened the solidarity of the ten members of the EC behind the U.K. However, the fact that France had supplied the Argentine Air Force with its Super-Étendard fighter planes, equipped with the Exocet missiles that caused so much damage to Royal Navy ships during the hostilities, resulted in strained relations between France and the U.K. Nevertheless, the seventh Franco-British summit took place in Paris early in November in a cordial atmosphere, and relations improved overnight after France decided to abstain in the UN vote on a Latin-American motion calling for a resumption of negotiations on the sovereignty of the Falklands.

Following several meetings between West German Chancellor Helmut Schmidt and President Mitterrand, the 40th Franco-German summit in October brought together, for the second time, the French president and the new West German chancellor, Helmut Kohl. It confirmed that cooperation remained a constant factor in the diplomacy of both countries, despite any changes in the political complexion of the governments of France and West Germany.

Mitterrand also went to Washington, where he met Pres. Ronald Reagan; to Tokyo on the first official visit of a French president to Japan; to Denmark; to Hungary, where no French head of state had been for eight centuries; and to India. In August, when the U.S. imposed sanctions on companies supplying hardware to the U.S.S.R. for the Soviet-European gas pipeline, the government ordered French companies to defy the ban. Sanctions were lifted in November as part of a wider agreement between the U.S. and Western Europe on the nature of East-West trade, but France immediately declared that it was not a party to the agreement.

FUEL AND ENERGY

The slack demand for petroleum as a result of the continuing worldwide recession kept oil prices soft throughout the year and created severe strains within the Organization of Petroleum Exporting Countries (OPEC). During the first quarter of 1982 there were many price cuts by both OPEC members and other exporting countries. Iran, desperate for income to support its war with Iraq, cut its price three times within two weeks in February. An emergency OPEC meeting in July broke up in disagreement as members quarreled over production allocations and the price differentials that reflect the quality of the crude oil. For the remainder of the year official posted prices were maintained, but all countries engaged in discounting. Saudi Arabia, with mounting dissatisfaction, countered other members' above-quota production by cutting its own output. This brought the Saudi production level down to 5.5 million bbl a day, less than one-half capacity. The action was prompted by the fear that, without it, the relatively small discounting would degenerate into an all-out price war, possibly leading to a collapse of the international market.

As it was, the persistent slack oil demand and weak prices had many unpleasant consequences. The unexpected decline in oil revenues brought Mexico to the brink of formal default on its international loans, from which it was rescued by emergency arrangements with international financial institutions and by the advance payment of $1 billion by the United States for additional oil to be delivered to the U.S. Strategic Petroleum Reserve. (A $12 billion loan offer from Saudi Arabia was not accepted, reportedly because it was conditional on either Mexican membership in or formal cooperation with OPEC.) The number of laid-up oil tankers reached a record high. Utilization of U.S. refining capacity declined to 61.5% in February, the lowest level since the 1930s. The permanent closing of some entire refineries and obsolescent facilities at others occurred in the U.S., Canada, and Europe. (U.S. refining capacity dropped by more than 10% in the first nine months of the year.) The slump in oil drilling in the U.S. led to many bankruptcies in the drilling and supply industry and to the failure of one bank that had specialized in oil industry loans.

In the oil industry there were also noteworthy events not associated with markets and prices. After several years of planning and success in obtaining all other government permits and approval, a project to transport Alaskan oil by pipeline from Puget Sound to Minnesota met with rejection from the governor of the state of Washington, who refused on environmental grounds to issue the necessary final permit. In February the world's largest semisubmersible drilling rig sank in a storm off Newfoundland with the loss of all 84 aboard. Also in February China announced that its offshore waters were open for exploration and production by foreigners and sent letters of notification to 46 companies in a dozen countries, inviting bids. In June the first oil production from the Dutch sector of the North Sea was delivered ashore. This sector had previously produced only natural gas.

Oil companies drilling offshore from Point Conception, Calif., revealed the largest discovery in the U.S. since the gigantic Prudhoe Bay field was found on the north coast of Alaska in 1968. The new discovery was estimated to have reserves of 500 million to 1,000,000,000 bbl. In October deliveries through the Trans-Panama Pipeline System began. The pipeline was built to bypass the Panama Canal in delivering crude oil from Prudhoe Bay to refineries on the Gulf and East coasts of the U.S. The pipeline reduced transportation time by four days and enabled the use of larger tankers on the eastern leg of the route.

News of natural gas was dominated by a dispute

At the "Solar One" power plant near Barstow, California, a computer-guided array of 1,800 movable mirrors focuses sunlight on a boiler atop a 300-foot (90-metre) tower to produce 10,000 kilowatts of electricity.

UPI

JOHN BARR/GAMMA—LIAISON

The "Zapata Concord" was one of many offshore platforms set up to exploit huge new oil deposits discovered off Santa Barbara, California.

between the U.S. and its European allies over a project to deliver gas from the Soviet Union to Austria, Belgium, France, Italy, The Netherlands, Switzerland, and West Germany. Delivery was scheduled to begin in 1984 through a 2,800-mi (4,500-km) pipeline from western Siberia at an eventual rate of 1.4 trillion cu ft (39,620,000,000 cu m) per year. The project was to be financed by loans from the buying countries and would involve the purchase of equipment and the use of technology from those countries.

Contracts for the equipment had been signed in 1981, and during 1982 several Western European countries signed gas purchase contracts with the Soviet Union. The U.S. government attempted to discourage the Europeans from proceeding with the project on the grounds that it would make them energy hostages to the Soviets and constitute acquiescence, in trade policy, to Soviet actions in Afghanistan and to the Polish military dictatorship. In June U.S. Pres. Ronald Reagan brought the dispute to a head by prohibiting U.S. firms and their European subsidiaries from supplying the Soviet Union with pipeline equipment that was based on U.S. technology. Viewing this as an unwarranted infringement on their sovereignty, France, Italy, West Germany, and the United Kingdom promptly ordered the local firms to honour their contracts, which they did. The U.S. retaliated by invoking sanctions against the firms involved, prohibiting them from receiving U.S. oil and gas equipment. The end result was that the equipment was delivered to the U.S.S.R., some firms were placed at a competitive disadvantage, and work proceeded on construction of the pipeline. In November the sanctions were quietly lifted.

An equally large pipeline project in North America ran into difficulties of its own. The Alaska Highway gas pipeline would bring gas through Canada from the giant Prudhoe Bay field on the Beaufort Sea to the lower 48 states. After several years of struggle to raise the necessary capital in the face of rising costs, backers of the project decided in May to postpone for two years the construction of the Alaskan portion of the line. In the meantime a portion

from Montana to Iowa was completed. In the absence of Alaskan gas it was to be used to bring gas from Alberta to the midwestern states.

In June it was announced that exploration in the Atlantic Ocean off Sable Island, near Nova Scotia, had found sufficient gas to justify commercial development. Construction of the offshore structures and the pipeline facilities necessary to bring the gas to the Canadian Maritime Provinces and New England was scheduled to begin in 1984, with deliveries in 1987 or 1988.

The coal industry, like the oil industry, faced slack demand as a result of the recession. Coal stockpiles mounted in consuming countries, and the anticipated boom in coal exports from the U.S., Australia, Canada, and South Africa failed to materialize. Polish coal miners confounded the expectations of Western observers by responding to government inducements such as extra food rations, and Polish coal exports in 1982 began to increase from the near total halt that had resulted from the imposition of martial law at the end of 1981. In May the first commercial use of a coal-oil mixture began at a power plant near Tampa, Fla. The mixture of one-half finely ground coal and one-half heavy fuel oil is burned in a conventional boiler designed to burn straight oil. The result is a considerable cost saving.

One of the richest uranium deposits ever found in the U.S. was discovered during the year in Pittsylvania County, Va. If developed, it would provide the first commercial production of uranium east of the Mississippi. In March Brazil's first nuclear power reactor went critical, the first of an eventual eight plants to be operating or under construction by the year 2000. The Canadian National Energy Board in April authorized the first export of nuclear-generated electricity, from a plant at Point Lepreau, N.B., to consumers in Maine and Massachusetts.

The November election in the U.S. included several referenda on nuclear power. In Maine a proposal to force the closing by 1987 of the state's only nuclear power plant was defeated. Nuclear power also received support from Idaho voters, who prohibited the state legislature from blocking, without voter approval, construction of any new nuclear plant. In Massachusetts, on the other hand, voters approved a proposition requiring a referendum on the construction of any nuclear plant or nuclear waste facility.

There were several noteworthy events in unconventional energy. The most dramatic was the sudden and wholly unexpected cancellation, in May, of the most ambitious oil shale project in the United States, an undertaking that would have produced more than 50,000 bbl a day of synthetic crude oil by 1987. Exxon Corp., the project's sponsor, cited the combination of continuing cost increases and lower oil prices as the reason for the cancellation. An almost simultaneous announcement by other oil companies signaled the end of a similarly ambitious project to produce synthetic oil from the huge deposit of tar sands in the Athabasca region of Alberta, Canada, for the same reason.

Progress continued, however, in the harnessing of solar energy for commercial use. In April a solar thermal power facility began operation in the Mojave Desert near Barstow, Calif. Known as "Solar One," the plant uses an array of mirrors to track the Sun and reflect its light onto a boiler mounted on a central tower. The steam thus generated drives a conventional turbine with a capacity of ten megawatts. Two other solar installations to supply utilities with power also began operation during the year. A plant using Sun-tracking photovoltaic cells to produce one megawatt of electricity started up at Phoenix, Ariz., in July, and in December a one-megawatt photovoltaic plant went on-line in San Bernardino County, Calif.

Other new projects began supplying energy directly to industrial plants. In May a 400-kw facility began supplying electricity and steam for heating, cooling, and process use to a knitwear plant at Shenandoah, Ga., and in the same month another installation began supplying steam to a chemical plant at Haverhill, Ohio. In February construction began on a "solar breeder" factory at Frederick, Md., for the manufacture of photovoltaic cells with 600 kw of electricity supplied by cells on its roofs.

In still another unconventional energy application, construction began in March on a compressed-air power plant near Springfield, Ill. When completed in 1986 the plant would use electricity generated by conventional power plants during the offpeak period at night to store compressed air in caverns 1,800 ft (545 m) below ground at a pressure of 800 psi. This would provide enough energy to generate 220 Mw for 11 hours during daytime periods of peak electricity demand.

In December 1981 President Reagan announced his plan to abolish the Department of Energy and shift about 70% of its functions to the Department of Commerce, with the remainder to be scattered among other departments. (The Department of Energy had been created in 1977.) This proposal fulfilled one of Reagan's pledges made during his 1980 election campaign. Congressional reaction to the proposal was so lukewarm, however, that it was never formally submitted, and the administration contented itself with continuing the reduction in the department's work force and programs that it had begun on taking office. In March the U.S. Senate sustained the presidential veto of a bill that would have given him the power to allocate oil and control its price during a future emergency. Reagan said that he was declining the authority because he believed the free market would work better during a crisis than would any system of government controls. In September the U.S. Congress continued the funding for the controversial Clinch River (Tenn.) demonstration breeder reactor project. Work on the project had been halted while opponents of the project sought to kill it on environmental grounds through court action. Almost simultaneously with the congressional action a federal appeals court overturned a lower court order that had blocked site-clearing work. Bulldozing began the day after the court decision. In another court action, in January, the U.S. Supreme Court upheld the right of Indian tribes to impose severance taxes on mineral resources produced on their lands.

GERMANY

West Germany

The year 1982 proved to be one of change in West Germany. A steady deterioration of relations between the government coalition partners, the Social Democratic Party (SPD) and the liberal Free Democratic Party (FDP), reached a dramatic climax on September 17. In a statement to the Bundestag the federal chancellor, Helmut Schmidt, made it clear that he could no longer cooperate with the Free Democrats, whom he accused of plotting to switch support to the Christian Democratic Union (CDU) and its Bavarian wing, the Christian Social Union (CSU). The Free Democrats thereupon resigned from Schmidt's government and joined forces with the CDU–CSU. On October 1 Schmidt was replaced as chancellor by the CDU chairman, Helmut Kohl.

The SPD–FDP alliance had endured since 1969, with Schmidt succeeding Willy Brandt as head of the alli-

Despite U.S. attempts to embargo advanced technology, construction of the Soviet pipeline from Siberian gasfields to Europe continued through the year.
SYGMA

ance and chancellor in 1974. At the 1980 federal election it was returned with an increased majority of 45 seats, compared with only 10 in the previous Bundestag. All seemed set for another stable four-year term in office. But decay set in rapidly. The Social Democrats, divided over defense policy and bearing the brunt of the blame for the country's economic malaise, suffered an alarming loss of public support. The Free Democrats, who had always lived in fear of their parliamentary lives, were confronted with the prospect of going down with a sinking ship. Moreover, genuine political differences between the two parties became increasingly evident as the government got down to the task of balancing the federal budget in a period of economic recession.

By mid-1981 the chairman of the FDP, Hans-Dietrich Genscher, had begun to talk of an approaching "turning point" in German politics, and thereafter there was constant speculation as to whether the coalition would stay the course. Matters came to a head quickly after the summer recess. A memorandum presented in early September by the Free Democrat minister of economics, Count Otto Graf Lambsdorff, was widely interpreted as a statement of grounds for divorce. The minister's strategy for restoring economic growth and combating unemployment contained proposals for severe cuts in social welfare and was unacceptable to the SPD.

In his statement to the Bundestag on September 17, Schmidt said that the Lambsdorff memorandum had indeed marked a turning point—from the concept of a socially caring state to that of an "elbowing society." The chancellor repeated an earlier demand for new elections, although he admitted that his party was in poor shape to contest them. The Free Democrats left the coalition, and Schmidt carried on as head of a minority government.

To secure election as federal chancellor, Helmut Kohl needed at least 249 votes, 23 more than the total parliamentary strength of the CDU-CSU. In the event, in a secret ballot on October 1, he polled 256, indicating that 30 of the 53 Free Democrat members had voted for him. Kohl, who was sworn in as chancellor on the evening of the same day, announced his intention to hold a federal election on March 6, 1983.

The new Cabinet included four Free Democrat ministers, one fewer than before. Genscher remained as foreign minister, Lambsdorff as economics minister, and Josef Ertl as minister of agriculture. But the leftish liberal Gerhart Baum of the FDP was replaced as minister of the interior by a right-wing conservative, Friedrich Zimmermann of the CSU.

Four weeks after losing office, Helmut Schmidt announced that he would not stand again for the chancellorship. This robbed the Social Democrats of their biggest electoral asset and opened up the prospect of a move to the left. The leader of the opposition in the West Berlin assembly, Hans-Jochen Vogel, a 56-year-old lawyer with a distinguished career as mayor of Munich and later as federal minister of justice, was nominated to succeed Schmidt as the SPD's candidate for the chancellorship.

The policy statement by Chancellor Kohl to the Bundestag on October 13 should have caused no unease, at home or abroad. He described his government as a coalition of the centre, dedicated to giving society a human face, and there was nothing in his rather vaguely phrased program to suggest that the label was false.

The year was one of economic disappointments, and 1983 seemed unlikely to prove better. Almost everyone's projections turned out to be too optimistic—those of government, banks, and economic research institutes. An export boom came and went without proving to be the forerunner of an economic

Helmut Kohl (centre, with glasses) succeeded Helmut Schmidt as chancellor of West Germany in October.
BOCCON-GIBOD—SIPA PRESS/ BLACK STAR

upswing at home. Kohl was planning a federal election campaign as the unemployment figures rose to around two million. Soon after taking office the new administration announced measures to stimulate the crisis-ridden building industry and to encourage those planning to found businesses of their own.

Kohl's government stressed continuity in foreign and security policies. In his first few weeks of office Kohl visited Paris and London, and soon afterward he received Pres. François Mitterrand of France and U.K. Prime Minister Margaret Thatcher in Bonn. In mid-November Kohl went to Washington for talks with Pres. Ronald Reagan. In his policy statement on October 13, he declared that West Germany's foreign and security policies were founded on NATO and friendship with the U.S. The federal government, the chancellor went on, was wholly committed to the NATO dual-track decision of 1979, which proposed negotiations on the reduction and limitation of Soviet and U.S. intermediate-range nuclear systems. It would stand by the two parts of the decision, both the part relating to negotiations and, if necessary, the part on arms modernization.

The NATO summit meeting in Bonn in June reiterated the Western alliance's determination to seek détente from a position of military balance. As the NATO leaders met, some 300,000 people gathered on the other side of the Rhine to demonstrate for peace. When the summit meeting was over, President Reagan spent a few hours, closely guarded, in West Berlin. Relations with the U.S. were strained by the Reagan administration's attempts to obstruct the Soviet-European gas pipeline project.

West Germany's initial support for the U.K. in its reaction to Argentina's aggression against the Falkland Islands gave way to strong misgivings once the military campaign began. In the interests of Western solidarity the West German government voted for the indefinite extension of trade sanctions imposed against Argentina by the European Communities, but this action belied Bonn's true feelings. Schmidt's government believed that the British response to the seizure of the islands was inappropriate and anachronistic. But the Falklands conflict did not seem to impair relations between West Germany and the U.K. Thatcher visited West Berlin in October and was widely applauded for her powerful speech in defense of freedom.

East Germany

The East German people increasingly felt the pinch of the world economic recession during 1982. There were severe shortages of food items, including meat, butter, and cheese. Reports of a drop in morale and falling production came from various parts of the country. Lack of foreign currency caused a sharp cutback in imports of vital components for industry, and in some sectors short-time working had to be introduced.

In March the East German Parliament adopted a law regulating the use of firearms by East German

JEAN GUICHARD—SYGMA

The growing European antinuclear movement was particularly strong in West Germany, where new Pershing missiles were to be deployed.

border guards. It did not, however, make them less trigger-happy. The ink was hardly dry on the statute book when an East German farmer, trying to escape across the demarcation line into the West German state of Hesse, was shot and killed. Since 1961 at least 180 East Germans had died attempting to reach West Germany. The motive in passing the legislation was not clear, but it was assumed that East Germany wished to demonstrate that it was a *Rechtsstaat*, a state based on the rule of law.

The people's Parliament also passed a law obliging schools, universities, factories, and all state organizations to ensure that the "citizen is prepared for defensive service." One of the reasons the law was needed, according to Gen. Heinz Hoffmann, the defense minister, was that in a crisis the strength of U.S. forces in West Germany, at the time numbering 230,000, could be increased to 480,000.

Contrary to expectations, the East German government decided not to extend the period of conscription beyond 18 months. Instead, reservists were to fill the gaps in the ranks caused by an approaching shortage of recruits, a consequence of the introduction of the contraceptive pill. Should mobilization be necessary, the law provided for the call-up of women between the ages of 18 and 50. Otherwise, the new legislation was not expected to

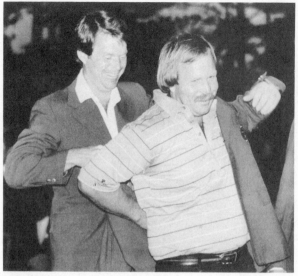

WIDE WORLD   UPI

In April Craig Stadler was helped into the winner's green coat by Tom Watson, the previous year's winner, after taking the Masters title. In August JoAnne Carner secured a place in the LPGA Hall of Fame by winning the World Championship of Women's Golf tournament.

cause much change in East German life, already firmly militarized. One of the purposes of the legislation was to counter the propaganda of the burgeoning peace movement.

In a leading article headed "No to Nuclear Madness," the Communist Party newspaper, *Neues Deutschland*, expressed sympathy for the hundreds of thousands of people in Western Europe who were standing up for the elementary right to life and peace. A demonstration of 50,000 people in Potsdam in October protested against NATO nuclear rearmament. But the authorities said nothing about the peace movement, centred in the church, which was campaigning against the nuclear buildup in both East and West.

The West German government had no success in persuading East Germany to reduce the compulsory currency-exchange fee imposed on Westerners entering East Germany. This had been tripled in October 1980, with the effect that the East German authorities managed to achieve a 40% drop in the number of Westerners visiting relatives and friends while maintaining the amount of hard currency derived from the border traffic.

GOLF

Although Craig Stadler, winner of the Masters and the World Series of Golf, was the leading money winner in the United States during 1982, Tom Watson's victories in the U.S. and British Open championships made him the outstanding golfer of the year. This feat had been achieved only five times previously, by Bobby Jones (1926, 1930), Gene Sarazen (1932), Ben Hogan (1953), and Lee Trevino (1971). It stamped Watson as one of the great players of the generation.

Prior to his triumph in the U.S. Open at Pebble Beach, Calif., there had been reservations as to Watson's overall quality. He had never won a U.S. Open, and that tournament seemed always to be a stumbling block in his career. In 1982, however, he survived a tremendous contest with Jack Nicklaus and deprived Nicklaus of a record fifth victory. No recent Open had produced a more fitting climax than that between the two foremost competitors of the time, and the way it was contested was magnificent.

Watson began the last round tied for first with Bill Rogers, runner-up in 1981 and reigning British champion, and three strokes ahead of Nicklaus. The latter, however, quickly charged for the lead with five successive birdies beginning with the third hole. A long putt on the 14th green put Watson two ahead, but Nicklaus birdied the 15th and when Watson bogeyed the 16th the match was even. The 17th is a menacing short hole, and Watson's no. 2 iron shot drifted into thick rough just off the green and about 40 ft (12 m) from the pin. Nicklaus, watching on television in the scorer's tent, then felt certain that Watson would need a birdie on the 18th to win, but Watson thought differently. The lie was better than he expected, and he told his caddie that he was going to hole the delicate little chip shot. To everyone's astonishment and Watson's boundless delight he did just that. It would be remembered as one of the great winning shots. That Watson's lay-up putt for a winning par on the last green went in for a birdie and victory by two strokes was purely academic.

Watson was no stranger to harsh disappointment and could sympathize with Nicky Price of South Africa, who had the British Open lead during the last round but could not take the pressure. If Price could have played the last four holes at Troon in one over par, he would have won. By then Watson had finished in 284, four under par, having just missed his putt for a birdie on the 18th hole. The 15th had proved the most difficult hole in relation to par throughout the Open, and on it Price shot a double bogey six; he then underclubbed to the short 17th green, and when his putt of 30 ft missed, Watson won by one stroke his fourth British Open in eight years, all of them in Scotland.

An opening 77 proved too great a burden for Nicklaus, but the British made a good showing. Peter Oosterhuis, not for the first time, was runner-up, sharing second place with Price; and Nick Faldo (286) and Sandy Lyle (287) were each a stroke farther behind. Watson had now won seven major championships and by the end of the season lacked only a victory in the Professional Golfers' Association (PGA) championship to share the rare distinction with Sarazen, Hogan, Gary Player, and Nicklaus of having won all four major titles—the U.S. and British Opens, the U.S. Masters, and PGA.

One of the worst experiences that can befall any golfer is to suffer the erosion of a commanding lead. When Stadler was six ahead at the last turn in the final round of the U.S. Masters, many thought that he was assured of the victory. But while Stadler was bogeying the 12th, 14th, and 16th, Dan Pohl was posting a second successive 67 after starting with a pair of 75s. Jerry Pate and Severiano Ballesteros were also making moves, and eventually Stadler came to the 18th needing a par to win. An awful first putt finished six feet short, and one could imagine the agony he felt when he missed the second one and had to go into a sudden-death play-off with Pohl. That Stadler played the 10th, the first extra hole, in a solid par, while Pohl went one over spoke highly of his composure and proved that he could control the lively temperament that on occasion in the past had betrayed him. For once at Augusta the air was alive with complaint at the pin positions and pace of the greens on the second day. The committee admitted that some of the contours were wrong and said that 12 greens would be reshaped for 1983. The greens for the second round proved so troublesome that the cut score of 154 was the highest ever.

Stadler made almost certain of leading the money list by beating Ray Floyd and winning $100,000 on the fourth sudden-death hole of the World Series of Golf at Akron, Ohio. Had the result been reversed, Floyd would probably have retained the honour. He had won the PGA championship in commanding style with a score of 272, shooting a 63 in the first round at the Southern Hills course in Tulsa, Okla., and he won by three strokes.

Discounting the major championships, the golfer of the year was Calvin Peete. His four victories, two by seven shots, and total winnings of well over $300,000 far surpassed the achievements of any other black golfer in the history of the game. The PGA statistics also proved that he was the most accurate golfer in terms of hitting fairways and greens in regulation figures. In 1981 and 1982 he was first in both categories.

For the second time Greg Norman, the most powerful of Australian golfers, headed the European money list with £66,405 ($114,491), and Lyle, leader in 1979–80, was second. Lyle lost a memorable final to Ballesteros in the Suntory match play championship at Wentworth, England. Otherwise Ballesteros had, for him, a moderate season.

The victory of Jay Sigel in the U.S. amateur championship was a triumph for a generation of amateurs who had gradually been thrust aside by the uprush of young golfers from colleges and universities. Sigel, whose attractive style and easy rhythm had impressed everyone when he won the British title in 1979, had every right to be counted the premier amateur (in the true sense of the term) in the world. He led the U.S. to victory in the World Team championships in Lausanne, Switz. In this he was assisted by Jim Holtgrieve, Robert Lewis, and Nathaniel Crosby, whose 68 on the final day steadied the U.S. performance when Japan and Sweden were mounting a serious threat. Considering the attention al-

Jan Stephenson sank a long putt on the 15th green on her way to winning the LPGA championship in June.
WIDE WORLD

ways upon him as Bing Crosby's son, Nathaniel Crosby, who had won the U.S. amateur championship in 1981 and was leading amateur in the U.S. Open, showed remarkable golfing character.

In women's golf the U.S. professional scene was dominated by JoAnne Carner with five victories and record winnings of $308,759, a total surpassed by only a few on the men's tour. No woman had ever approached this total before, and one of the greatest natural talents the game had known showed no sign of waning at 43. Sandra Haynie, who turned professional in 1961 but lost some years through injury, returned to peak form and was Carner's closest challenger, together with Sally Little, Patty Sheehan, and Beth Daniel. In view of the supremacy of these women, one of the most remarkable achievements was that of Janet Alex, wife of a professional, who joined the small and distinguished group whose first victory as a professional was in the most important event of all. Her final round of 68 swept her clear of the field, and she won the U.S. Women's Open by six shots from Carner, Daniel, Haynie, and Donna White.

The outstanding woman amateur of the season was Juli Inkster, who won the U.S. championship for the third successive year, a feat that had not been accomplished since Virginia Van Wie did so in 1932–34. Inkster also played a leading part in overwhelming U.S. victories over Britain and Ireland in the Curtis Cup match in Denver, Colo., and over New Zealand in the World Team championship in Geneva, Switz.

GREAT BRITAIN

Nobody could have dreamed that 1982 would be a year in which Britain went to war. But that was what happened on April 2, when Argentine forces invaded and quickly captured the Falkland Islands (Islas Malvinas), a tiny British possession 8,000 mi (12,800 km) distant from the U.K. in the South Atlantic. The war for the recovery of the Falklands lasted until June 15, when the British flag flew once again over Government House in Port Stanley. This wholly unexpected incident totally commanded the nation's attention while it lasted—theatre and motion picture attendances fell sharply—and continued to colour its political life for the remainder of the year.

The U.K. had been engaged for some years in desultory talks with Argentina concerning the future of the Falkland Islands. In December 1980 the Conservative Party government, led by Prime Minister Margaret Thatcher, had gone so far as to suggest a leaseback arrangement whereby sovereignty would pass to Argentina in exchange for continuing British administration over the islands for a substantial period of time. This arrangement was not acceptable to the islanders. A proposal that the sovereignty question be "frozen" for 25 years was unacceptable to the Argentines.

Not much attention was paid when on March 19 a group of Argentine scrap-metal merchants disman-

SUTTON–GAMMA/LIAISON

The war in the Falklands dominated the British press, which helped feed a national outpouring of patriotism.

tling a disused whaling station raised the Argentine flag on South Georgia, a dependency of the Falkland Islands. The incident had too much of low comedy about it. Even in the hours preceding the invasion there was no sense in London of impending crisis. On the evening of March 31 Thatcher was informed for the first time that an invasion was imminent or in progress.

The prime minister was determined from the outset to recapture the islands. The news of what was happening did not break until the night of April 1–2, and throughout the following day the Foreign Office, fueling the accusations of incompetence that were to follow, was unable to confirm to Parliament that an invasion had taken place. The magnitude of the crisis did not begin to become apparent to the public until the morning of Saturday, April 3, when for the first time since the Suez crisis of 1956 Parliament met in an emergency session that was broadcast live to the public. At the close of the debate it was announced that a naval task force would be immediately dispatched to the South Atlantic.

The first contingent sailed out of Portsmouth on April 5 to the playing of bands and the waving of flags. Lord Carrington resigned as foreign secretary, stung by criticism leveled at him from some sections of his party and in some right-wing newspapers. The excited, patriotic tone of the Saturday debate had encouraged the public to regard the loss of the Falklands as some kind of major national disaster. Thatcher quickly made plain her own war aims, which were, first, to show to the world that aggression did not pay and, second, to secure for the Falkland islanders the right to self-determination. The collapse of the peace initiative by U.S. Secretary of State Alexander Haig led to a declaration of unequivocal support for the U.K. from the U.S. on April 30. The intransigence of the Argentine military junta convinced senior ministers around the prime minister that further dealings with Gen. Leopoldo Galtieri, the president of Argentina, were likely to be useless.

On April 25–26 the Argentine garrison on South Georgia Island was captured, along with the submarine "Santa Fe." As the task force took up positions around the Falklands, a British submarine sank the Argentine cruiser "General Belgrano" on May 2. Despite good account given by the Sea Harrier aircraft from the carriers "Hermes" and "Invincible," the task force was ill equipped for air defense, however, and was subjected to heavy attacks by Skyhawk, Mirage III, Dagger, and Super Étendard fighter-bombers from the mainland. One of the last, armed with an Exocet air-to-surface missile fired from long range, sank the destroyer "Sheffield" on May 4. The amphibious landing of British troops at Port San Carlos on May 21 was particularly vulnerable to air attack, and over the next several days two frigates, a destroyer, two landing ships, and a container ship were sunk. Progress overland was rapid, however, as Argentine defenses proved poorly organized and the troops poorly trained. With British forces occupying the high ground all around Port Stanley, the Argentine garrison of some 5,000 troops surrendered on June 14.

When the war broke out, the state of British politics was that the three parties were running approximately neck and neck in voter popularity. This indicated that some recovery had already taken place in the fortunes of the Conservative Party during the winter and some decline—in fact about 10%—in the standing of the Social Democratic Party (SDP)-Liberal Party Alliance, which had peaked in November 1981 at an astounding 50% according to a Gallup Poll. The local elections on May 6 showed the Conservatives with 40% support against the Labour Party's 32% and the Alliance's 26%. By June the government had notched up a remarkable 20-percentage-point lead. Most of this Conservative gain—the so-called Falklands factor—was at the expense of the Alliance.

When the political season resumed in late September with the annual party conferences, it began to look as if factors other than the Falklands might be responsible for the high standing of the government in spite of the fact that unemployment was well in excess of three million. With the most probable date for a general election being the autumn of 1983,

party politics began to revolve around the distinct possibility that Thatcher might win a second majority.

During the Falklands crisis the reputation of Labour Party leader Michael Foot reached an unprecedented low in the opinion polls. In by-elections in the Glasgow Hillhead constituency in March and in the Merton, Mitcham, and Morden constituency in June, Labour finished in third place amid the by now familiar canvass reports that the activities of Tony Benn and the left wing were causing disaffection and desertion among the party's traditional supporters. In September and again in November, Foot was obliged to deal with speculation that his leadership of the party was under threat. By the end of the year there were signs of a modest Labour revival, but few of the party's own leaders could find much hope or confidence of victory at a general election.

Meanwhile, the Alliance was having troubles of its own. The war in the South Atlantic had deprived it of the limelight in which it had thrived since the launching of the SDP in March 1981 and the formation of an alliance with the Liberal Party in September of that year. Roy Jenkins, the former Labour Party chancellor of the Exchequer and home secretary, was returned triumphantly to Parliament at the Glasgow Hillhead by-election and later was elected leader of the SDP in a contest with David Owen, the former Labour Party foreign secretary.

The state of the economy was overshadowed by

Pope John Paul II and Archbishop of Canterbury Robert Runcie prayed together in Canterbury Cathedral in May.
UPI

the Falklands war. By the autumn, with interest rates having fallen sharply and the rate of inflation down into single figures, it had become popular to suppose that the government might be able to win the coming election even with some 3,250,000 unemployed, a total scarcely thinkable a few years earlier. One explanation could be what had happened to actual living standards. In the years 1977–80 real disposable income had risen on average by 5% a year, and during that time there had been a sharp increase in savings. In 1981 and again in 1982 real living standards fell by about 2% each year, but consumption held up for the most part as people drew upon their savings or borrowed. Moreover, falling interest rates, combined with a faster than expected decline in the rate of inflation, to around an annual 6% by the end of the year from 12% at the beginning, gave the government some claims to success for its economic policies.

The fall in production flattened out, but none of the forecasters saw better than a sluggish growth prospect for the economy. Competitiveness improved somewhat, owing to a depreciation of the pound sterling and a slower increase in labour costs. Britain's share in international trade continued to decline during the international trade recession and, in spite of hopes that improvements in productivity might prove lasting, there was little sign in 1982 that the fundamental weaknesses of the British economy were responding to disciplinary treatment.

In three showdowns with trade unions the government came out on top. The most important and the most politically charged of these involved the coal miners. As the agents of the destruction of former prime minister Edward Heath's Conservative government in February 1974, the miners had a special place in British political mythology. Their newly elected national president, the ultraleftist and mili-

Roy Jenkins won a striking victory for himself and for his Social Democratic Party in capturing a parliamentary seat.
THE TIMES, LONDON

tant Yorkshireman Arthur Scargill, invited his members in the autumn to authorize a national strike on the twin issues of pay and pit closings. The National Coal Board stood firm with the government behind it, and the miners roundly rejected Scargill's strike call. Earlier in the year the British Railways Board had succeeded in facing down the railway unions, although not until Board Chairman Peter Parker threatened to close down the entire system.

The third dispute of the year was a more protracted and a murkier affair, involving nurses and ancillary workers employed by the National Health Service. There was a good deal more public sympathy for their cause than there was for the well-paid miners or the railwaymen; nevertheless, after a day of action in sympathy for the poorly paid health workers, which was organized by the Trades Union Congress in September, the dispute slowly petered out in the face of the government's firmness. By the end of the year such fears as there had been that Thatcher might be plagued by a "winter of discontent" of the kind that had destroyed the Labour Party government of former prime minister James Callaghan in 1978–79 had disappeared.

A happier event was the birth of a son, and eventual heir to the throne, to the prince and princess of Wales on June 21. The child was named William Arthur Philip Louis. The princess was soon back in action, and scarcely a day passed in which the popular newspapers did not carry gossip, malicious rumour, or fetching photographs of her. What with an intruder at Buckingham Palace who sat on Queen Elizabeth II's bed and chatted to her, and spies galore, Britain was not without diversion in 1982.

Foreign Affairs

As with everything else, foreign affairs were overshadowed by the preoccupation with the Falkland Islands. The war broke out just as Britain's annual wrangle with the European Economic Community (EC) over the costs of the common agricultural policy and the scale of Britain's contributions to the EC budget was coming to its climax. Needing EC support for economic sanctions against Argentina, the government was obliged to abandon hope of achieving any lasting solution and to settle, once more, for a temporary rebate. The continental members of the EC took the opportunity of Britain's distraction to, in effect, override a British veto (in breach of the previous convention) and increase farm prices by more than the British had been willing to agree to.

Northern Ireland

In the face of considerable opposition from his own Conservative Party, James Prior, the new secretary of state for Northern Ireland, persisted in his plan to revive somewhat the politics of the province by the restoration of an elected, although only consultative, assembly. In spite of the declaration by the Roman Catholic parties that they would boycott the assembly by refusing to take their seats, the elections

Yasir Arafat, chairman of the Palestine Liberation Organization, was welcomed by Greek Prime Minister Andreas Papandreou and a naval guard of honour upon his arrival in Greece in September.

JEAN-CLAUDE FRANCOLON—GAMMA/LIAISON

took place in late October. The Protestant parties, predictably, won a substantial majority, but the chief significance of the event was the success of the Sinn Fein, the political wing of the Provisional Irish Republican Army (IRA). Competing for the first time across a broad electoral front, it won 10% of the vote and five seats, puncturing the British claim that the IRA terrorists lacked political support. The more moderate, pro-Irish Social Democratic and Labour Party was outflanked in the process, and politics in Northern Ireland became more polarized than ever before along sectarian and nationalist lines. Accompanying this endeavour to restore civilized political life to the province was a rash of incidents of sectarian violence involving further loss of life.

GREECE

During 1982, the first full year of Socialist change in Greece, Prime Minister Andreas Papandreou and his government tackled the country's problems with a vigorous realism that spared them untimely confrontations but was not without political cost. In foreign affairs the government sought to reassert the independence of its opinions at international meetings on such topics as the Middle East, Poland, and détente. However, on the issues that were truly vital for Greece, it showed a moderation that was, in practice, a renunciation of its election slogans about leaving NATO and the European Communities (EC) and dismissing the U.S. bases. Faced with a rapidly deteriorating economy, the government refrained from introducing its more radical reforms.

The effect of these contradictions was reflected in the results of municipal elections held in October. Although the ruling Panhellenic Socialist Movement (Pasok) gained control of three-fifths of Greece's towns and villages, it did so only with the help of the pro-Moscow Greek Communist Party (KKE), which had deplored the government's failure to fulfill its campaign promises.

The Socialist government was forced to agree to the resumption of diplomatic dialogue after Turkish

aircraft systematically challenged Greek sovereignty and jurisdiction in the Aegean. Preliminary Greek-Turkish talks were resumed at the foreign minister level in October, but only after Turkey had promised to discontinue its Aegean sorties. Pasok's plan to alienate Greece from NATO was shelved in the hope of extending the protection guaranteed by the alliance to Greece's frontiers with Turkey.

Negotiations with the U.S. to determine the status of U.S. military bases in Greece were begun in October, in exchange for the supply of sophisticated U.S. weapons that would help Greece preserve the balance of power with Turkey. A plan to get rid of Western nuclear warheads stockpiled in Greece, as a first step toward the creation of a nuclear-free zone in the Balkans, was put on ice, partly because of reservations expressed by Yugoslavia but also because Papandreou had become more sensitive to the exigencies of maintaining the East-West equilibrium.

Cyprus was declared a top priority, and Papandreou made a triumphant visit to the island on February 28. However, his opposition to continuing the intercommunal dialogue between Greek and Turkish Cypriots under UN auspices brought him into direct conflict with Pres. Spyros Kyprianou of Cyprus; to ensure his reelection in February 1983, Kyprianou made an alliance with the island's powerful Communist party, AKEL, which, like Moscow, wanted the dialogue to continue.

The most flamboyant aspect of Papandreou's foreign policy was his unstinted support of the Arabs and of the Palestine Liberation Organization cause. Greece became the only EC country to grant the PLO diplomatic recognition. This policy sprang naturally from Pasok's ideological affinity with several Arab states. It was also designed to distract Pasok's supporters from foreign-policy reversals. But if the government hoped that it would trigger an avalanche of Arab petro-investments, it was disappointed.

With Greece still financially dependent on the West, the government drastically revised its attitude toward the EC. Before coming to power, the Socialists had promised to call a nationwide referendum to decide whether or not Greece should stay in the EC. One year later, faced with a foreign payments deficit of over $2 billion, the government no longer talked about a referendum. Instead it applied to the EC for help in solving its economic problems.

Perhaps the government's most disappointing performance was in its handling of the economy. Pasok let 1982 go by without introducing a program that could have stimulated enough confidence to curb the recession. A change of guard in the economic ministries in July reversed whatever trust the previous ministers had managed to inspire. By the end of the year, the only hope for the economy was the promise of a 1983–87 five-year plan that would allow businesses to plot their course.

The government systematically purged the public administration. All directors general and their deputies were retired, and civil servants loyal to Pasok were appointed to key positions. Through some legalistic devices the court deposed several antigovernment trade union executives and appointed temporary councils consisting of Pasok trade-unionists. Most of the militant unions, however, remained under KKE control, and they tended to cause trouble whenever Pasok's relations with KKE soured.

The municipal elections in October allowed the government to go ahead with its plan for drastic administrative decentralization. Other reforms included a new law giving university students a say in the advancement of their professors, the abolition of illiberal labour legislation, the lowering of the voting age to 18, the introduction of civil marriage, and the recognition of wartime left-wing resistance organizations as patriotic. Minister of Culture Melina Mercouri campaigned for the return of the Elgin Marbles from the British Museum.

GUATEMALA

Presidential elections held in Guatemala on March 7, 1982, were won by Gen. Angel Aníbal Guevara, the candidate chosen by the outgoing regime. On March 23, however, a coup brought Gen. Efraín Ríos Montt and two other officers to power, and the election results were declared void. General Ríos Montt dissolved the junta and declared himself sole leader and head of the armed forces on June 9.

Violence escalated in the countryside, and only a temporary lull was experienced in urban areas. An Amnesty International report estimated that over 2,600 Indians and peasant farmers had been killed in the period March–July. Political parties boycotted the Council of State, which was established on September 15 in an attempt to provide a forum for discussion between politicians and members of the university, judiciary, and private banks.

Relations with the U.S. administration were strengthened following the admission of Guatemala to the Central American Democratic Community on July 7. However, as a result of the deterioration in human rights, full resumption of U.S. military aid was no longer assured, and Guatemala received only $10 million of the total $350 million in direct aid granted under the U.S. Caribbean Basin Initiative. Relations with the U.K. remained uneasy, since the president refused to recognize the independence of Belize. The economy was adversely affected by the decline in Central American trade and a marked fall in investment. The trade deficit widened to $409 million in 1981, compared with $63 million in 1980.

GYMNASTICS

In the World Cup championships held in Zagreb, Yugos., from October 22 to 24 Soviet athletes captured both team titles. The U.S.S.R. women also took home the lion's share of the individual medals. In the men's team competition, China finished second and East Germany third. The Soviet women's team finished far ahead of the teams from East Germany, China, Romania, and the U.S.

In the men's all-around, Li Ning and Tong Fei (China) outperformed Yury Korolev (U.S.S.R.), the 1981 world champion, who had to be content with third place. In the head-to-head competition for

The military junta that took control of Guatemala in March included (left) Gen. Horacio Maldonado, (right) Col. Francisco Gordillo, and (centre) Gen. Efrain Ríos Montt, who in June dissolved the junta and proclaimed himself sole leader.

UPI

UPI

Bart Conner was the men's champion, and Julianne McNamara and Bulgaria's Zoya Grantcharova shared the women's title in the American Cup gymnastics competition.

medals in individual events, Li was superb. He won the floor exercise, the pommel horse, and the long horse vault. In addition, he tied for the gold medal in both the horizontal bar and rings competitions and placed third in parallel bars. The top U.S. competitor was Jim Hartung in tenth place.

In the women's all-around, Olga Bicherova (U.S.S.R.), the 1981 world champion, shared first place with newcomer Natalia Yurchenko (U.S.S.R.). In the individual events, Bicherova won a gold medal for the floor exercise and shared the vaulting title with Yurchenko; the latter captured a second gold medal for her balance beam routine. Maxi Gnauck (East Germany) was crowned champion in the uneven parallel bars competition. Julianne McNamara of the U.S. placed eighth overall.

At the International Invitational held in Fort Worth, Texas, the U.S. won both team titles, defeating both China and the Soviet Union. Though Li Ning won the all-around title, Hartung was second, Mitch Gaylord fourth, and Scott Johnson sixth. Li again displayed his remarkable talents by winning the floor exercise, the pommel horse, and the rings. None of the U.S. gymnasts won a gold medal in the individual events. Kathy Johnson captured the women's all-around title, finishing just ahead of her teammates Diane Durham and Amy Koopman. Johnson and Michelle Goodwin shared first-place honours on the balance beam, and Durham was tops in the vault.

In the U.S. national championships for men held

in early June in Syracuse, N.Y., Peter Vidmar succeeded Hartung as all-around champion. Gaylord was second, Hartung third, Tim Daggett fourth, Scott Johnson fifth, and Phil Cahoy sixth. Hartung, however, won four of the six individual events: the floor exercise, pommel horse, rings, and long horse vault. Vidmar won the parallel bars and Gaylord the horizontal bar. During the women's U.S. nationals held in Salt Lake City, Utah, in May, Tracee Talavera retained her crown as national all-around champion by defeating Julianne McNamara 75.95 to 75.75. The next four top places were taken by Koopman, Gina Stallone, Goodwin, and Lynne Lederer. First-place honours in the individual events went to Koopman in the floor exercise, McNamara on the balance beam, Marie Roethlisberger on the uneven parallel bars, and Yumi Mordre in the vault.

HONDURAS

The election of a civilian president, Roberto Suazo Córdova, in November 1981 ended nearly nine years of military rule in Honduras and raised hopes for peace. But these were shattered in 1982. On the one hand, Gen. Gustavo Alvarez Martínez, commander-in-chief of the Army, consolidated his position and strengthened the Army to 20,000; on the other, leftist guerrilla activity increased, culminating in an eight-day siege in San Pedro Sula in September when about 80 people, including the finance minister, the economy minister, and the president of the central bank, were held hostage. In December President Suazo's daughter was held captive for several days by leftists in Guatemala.

Turmoil in neighbouring countries spread into Honduras. Refugees from El Salvador entered the country, and supporters of the late president Anastasio Somoza of Nicaragua continued to use Honduras as a base from which to conduct raids. In an attempt to maintain Honduras as a buffer state, the U.S. sent additional military advisers there. U.S. President Ronald Reagan visited Honduras in December.

Because of its vulnerability to fluctuating commodity prices and severe lack of working capital, Honduras seemed likely to remain one of the poorest countries in the region. On September 1 trade was resumed between Honduras and El Salvador, following a 13-year break after the 1969 war.

HORSE RACING

Conquistador Cielo was voted horse of the year for 1982 in the closest result since the Eclipse Award balloting was inaugurated in 1971. The three-year-old colt narrowly defeated the four-year-old colt Lemhi Gold and the two-year-old filly Landaluce, both of which were awarded titles in their divisions, as was Conquistador Cielo in his.

Conquistador Cielo (Mr. Prospector-K D Princess, by Bold Commander), owned by Henryk de Kwiatkowski and trained by Woodford C. ("Woody") Stevens, defeated older rivals in the

Conquistador Cielo, ridden by Laffit Pincay, breezed to a 14-length victory in the Belmont Stakes on June 5.
UPI

Metropolitan Handicap with a track record of 1 min 33 sec for the mile in late May and six days later won the Belmont Stakes by 14½ lengths. A recurring leg problem ended his career after he finished third to Runaway Groom and Aloma's Ruler in the Travers Stakes in August. He was syndicated for $36.4 million and retired to stud. Winners of the other Triple Crown events (with the Belmont Stakes) for three-year-olds were Gato del Sol, owned by Arthur Hancock III and Leone J. Peters, in the Kentucky Derby

Gato del Sol, with Eddie Delahoussaye aboard, moved up from last place to lead the field of 19 across the finish line in the Kentucky Derby on May 1.
UPI

Speed Bowl won a close victory in the Hambletonian on August 7. At 25 Tommy Haughton became the youngest driver ever to win the 57-year-old event.

UPI

and Aloma's Ruler, owned by Nathan Scherr, in the Preakness.

Misfortune struck many other promising three-year-olds but none as severely as Timely Writer, which suffered a broken left front cannon bone during the running of the Jockey Club Gold Cup and had to be destroyed. Landaluce, the unbeaten two-year-old daughter of Seattle Slew-Strip Poker, by Bold Bidder, succumbed to a bacterial infection. Racing exclusively in California for owners L. R. French and Barry Beal, Landaluce had made a spectacular turf debut in early July at Hollywood Park by winning a six-furlong race by seven lengths in 1 min 8.2 sec. Her second start was a still more dramatic 21-length decision in the Hollywood Lassie in 1 min 8 sec.

Aaron U. Jones's Lemhi Gold accumulated $1,066,375 while winning stakes over both turf and dirt. His most important victories were in the Marlboro Cup and the Jockey Club Gold Cup. Other Eclipse Award winners included: two-year-old colt, Roving Boy; three-year-old filly, Christmas Past; older filly or mare, Track Robbery; male turf horse, Perrault; female turf horse, April Run; sprinter, Gold Beauty; steeplechase, Zaccio, for the third consecutive year.

Jockey Angel Cordero, Jr., apprentice jockey Alberto Delgado, owner Viola Sommer, breeder Fred W. Hooper, Jr., and trainer Charles Whittingham also won Eclipse honours, Whittingham for the second time. Cordero's mounts earned more than $9.7 million in purses to establish a one-year record for a jockey. Whittingham's horses earned $4,588,897 to break his own record. Sommer's stable was the top money winner with earnings in excess of $2 million.

Robert E. Hibbert's Roving Boy captured his title in head-to-head competition with Eastern champion Copelan in the Hollywood Futurity. Cynthia Phipps's Christmas Past won five stakes, including the Coaching Club American Oaks, Monmouth Oaks, and the Ruffian Handicap to defeat several other aspirants to the crown. Competition for the older filly and mare award was close, but Summa Stable's Track Robbery gained the honours with triumphs in four stakes.

Perrault, a five-year-old English-bred, earned $1,197,400 for owners Serge Fradkoff and Baron Thierry van Zuylen after winning four stakes, including the Budweiser Million. A versatile campaigner, he triumphed in the Hollywood Gold Cup on dirt in the excellent time of 1 min 59.2 sec. for 1¼ mi.

Harness Racing

World race records were broken frequently in the U.S. in 1982. In races on mile tracks they included: fastest two-year-old pacer, Trim The Tree 1 min 53⅗ sec; fastest three-year-old, Trenton 1 min 51⅗ sec; fastest older horse, Genghis Khan 1 min 51⅘ sec. Among the trotters, more than one-third of the age, gait, and sex records were broken, notably by New Zealand's Arndon, which took the mile race record of 1 min 57⅖ sec on ⅝-mi tracks and then trotted an incredible 1 min 54 sec at Lexington, Ky., which made him the fastest trotter in standardbred history. Fan Hanover paced a one-mile time trial in 1 min 50⅘ sec to become the fastest mare ever.

The final of the International World Cup at the Meadowlands in New Jersey went to Genghis Khan. The Hambletonian for three-year-old trotters was won by Speed Bowl; Idéal du Gazeau of France won the Roosevelt International Trot; Jazz Cosmos took the Kentucky Futurity; Merger won the Little Brown Jug; and Hilarion won the Million Dollar Meadowlands pace.

Two of Michigan's most depressed industries joined forces in a novel promotion in a subdivision of Farmington Hills.
ERIC SMITH—GAMMA/LIAISON

HOUSING

The long-awaited housing rebound seemed to take shape toward the end of 1982 following a devastating spring and a full three years after the homebuilding industry began its slide toward record low rates of new home sales and housing starts. But observers predicted a long, slow recovery in the industry that normally provided 10% of the gross national product.

The trough in housing was reached in March, with new home sales down to an annual rate of 334,000 houses versus the 874,000 annual rate of October 1978, before rising prices and rising interest rates began their heavy downward pressure. Sales reached a 465,000 annual rate in September, 24% above that of the previous month and the largest increase since the deceptively temporary recovery of May 1980.

"The cork is coming out of the bottle," remarked Paul Schosberg, executive director of the Savings Association League of New York State, in early November. Schosberg spoke from a vantage point of 14% fixed-rate mortgages, down from the 17% rates typical of the previous year and most of 1982 at his member institutions, the thrift banks that provide the bulk of the nation's mortgage money. The rate decline had tracked the falling prime rate, which was down to 11½% in November, its lowest level in two years. In December the Federal Reserve Board's cut from 9 to 8½% in the discount rate charged on loans to banks and thrifts signaled a further drop in the prime.

But the housing recovery promised to be slow and fitful, in part owing to the 10.8% unemployment rate that prevailed at year-end. If mortgage rates bottomed out at 13%, as many predicted they would, that would still be higher than rates had been at the low end of any previous business cycle. An effort by Congress at midyear to ease the burden of

the mortgage rate by enacting a five-year subsidy program at a cost of $3 billion failed when backers could not secure the votes to override Pres. Ronald Reagan's veto. "We will not promote a housing recovery by going even deeper in debt," the president said.

An existing subsidy program at the Department of Housing and Urban Development (HUD) was largely credited for a late summer leap in housing starts to an annual rate of 1.2 million units, with the bulk of the increase occurring in multifamily housing fueled by $900 million in HUD financing released in the spring. (Housing starts are normally higher than new home sales because builders construct for anticipated demand and the starts figure includes multifamily dwelling such as apartment buildings.)

The pressure on affordable housing during the year left only one strong sector in the homebuilding industry—mobile, or "manufactured," homes. Sales of this least expensive of housing options stood 15% over 1980 levels and 5% above 1981, with 250,000 units sold. Another business that did well was home auctioning, which enabled builders in some overbuilt or overpriced areas like California and the Mountain West to work down inventories through the tried-and-true method of encouraging impulsive, competitive bidding. Most auction sales netted a loss against the construction price of the house, but with houses remaining on the market for more than a year, some builders were eager to be rid of the carrying costs and collect the cash.

With the mortgage rates and home prices still high, it was an open question in November whether homebuilding would ever regain its traditional role of leading the economy out of recession. "We're in a new ball game," chief economist Michael Sumichrast of the National Association of Homebuilders warned his members. But, he added, "Things are most certainly looking up."

HUNGARY

The two major events of 1982 were Hungary's admission to the International Monetary Fund (IMF) and the official visit of Pres. François Mitterrand of France. On May 5 the executive board of the IMF approved Hungary's application for membership, and the following day Jozsef Marjai, a deputy prime minister, signed a certificate of membership by which his country became the 146th member of that institution. Hungary's quota was set at $415 million, giving it access to up to $2 billion of credit. Automatically, Hungary also became a member of the World Bank. A $580 million IMF credit was agreed to on November 11.

Seven months earlier, on Oct. 1, 1981, the National Bank of Hungary had taken the unprecedented step—for a member country of the Soviet-dominated Council for Mutual Economic Assistance (Comecon)—of introducing a single official rate for the Hungarian forint in relation to each of the convertible Western currencies. This decision, however, did not mean a change in the rates of the forint against the "transferable" ruble and other Comecon currencies. It seemed certain that Hungary had not taken such an initiative without clearing it in advance with the U.S.S.R.

A $260 million loan to the National Bank of Hungary was signed on August 9 in London. At the end of 1982 the total Hungarian debt in hard currencies was estimated at $7.2 billion, representing about $770 per head of population, not an enormous burden for a country with a gross national product estimated at $2,000 per head by IMF officials and as high as $3,850 per head according to the World Bank.

In order to reduce state subsidies and ensure economic equilibrium, the government introduced a series of considerable price increases. They included 100% on the price of rail travel, 14–25% on fuel, and 20–25% on bread, flour, and rice.

President Mitterrand's visit on July 7–9 was formally a reciprocation of the official visit to France undertaken by First Secretary Janos Kadar in November 1978, but in reality it became something more. In his public statements the president described his trip to Budapest as "the shortest road toward the East-West dialogue," and he duly acknowledged Hungary's unique position within the Socialist camp. He brought with him five ministers, including Foreign Relations Minister Claude Cheysson and Foreign Trade Minister Michel Jobert, and promised to expand Franco-Hungarian economic and cultural relations.

Kadar replied that though Hungary and France belonged to different political regimes and were members of opposite alliances, President Mitterrand's visit was of particular importance because it went beyond the normal framework of bilateral relations. Kadar also alluded to the fact that the part played by France in Hungary's foreign exchanges was too modest and expressed a hope that it would increase as a result of talks between the French min-

isters and their Hungarian counterparts. At the time France was occupying 59th place in the list of countries supplying goods to Hungary.

In 1981 Hungarian foreign trade amounted to $9.2 billion in imports and $8.7 billion in exports. Although in 1975 about two-thirds of Hungary's total trade was with other Comecon countries, that share was reduced in 1982 to slightly more than one-half of the total.

In June Gyorgy Aczel was replaced as deputy premier by Istvan Sarlos. Aczel then succeeded the retiring Andras Gyenyes as secretary of the Central Committee, a post he had held in 1967–74.

ICE HOCKEY

The New York Islanders capped a brilliant season-long effort by winning their third consecutive Stanley Cup, defeating the Vancouver Canucks in four straight games. The greatest peril to their success came in the five-game opening round of the play-offs when the Pittsburgh Penguins led by two goals late in the last game before the Islanders rallied to win that series in overtime.

The Islanders went on to a rousing series against the New York Rangers, rejuvenated by U.S. Olympic coach Herb Brooks, and then eliminated the

Mike Bossy of the New York Islanders happily hoisted the Stanley Cup after his team won the championship in Vancouver in May.
UPI

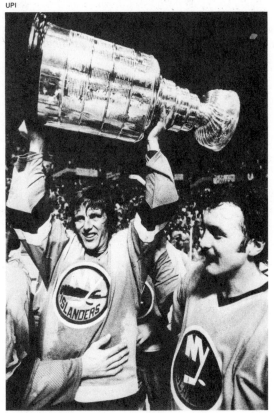

Quebec Nordiques in the Wales Conference championship before defeating the Canucks. It was the first year of the divisional play-off format in which most of the National Hockey League's strongest teams were in the Islanders' conference.

During the season the Islanders set a league record for consecutive wins of 15. The ascendancy of their dynasty was paralleled by the decline of another: the Montreal Canadiens were ousted in the opening round of the play-offs by the Quebec Nordiques.

The 1981–82 season also was notable for the greatest individual performance by a player in NHL history. Twenty-one-year-old Wayne Gretzky, in his third season with Edmonton, swept through the record book again, setting marks for most goals in one season (92), most assists (120), and most points (212). His point total broke his own record of the previous year and gained him the Art Ross Trophy. For the third year in a row Gretzky was also awarded the Hart Trophy as the most valuable player during the regular season.

Gretzky's performance overshadowed another great year for the New York Islanders' 25-year-old right wing, Mike Bossy, who scored 147 points, the fourth highest in league history. Bossy also won the Conn Smythe Trophy for most valuable competitor in the play-offs.

During the summer there were some ownership changes, including the transfer of the Colorado Rockies to the New Jersey Meadowlands Arena, where the team was to be known as the New Jersey Devils. The Devils would take their place in the heated Patrick Division with the New York Rangers, New York Islanders, and Philadelphia Flyers, creating a tight geographical rivalry.

Another ownership change was the sale of the Detroit Red Wings by Bruce Norris, whose family had owned the team for 50 years. The new owner was Mike Ilitch, who promptly induced a management defection from the championship Islanders, hiring their assistant general manager and chief scout, Jimmy Devellano, to be Detroit's general manager. Herb Brooks, who sharpened the Rangers considerably in his first year as coach, signed a new contract with the team for $200,000 annually. This made him the highest paid coach ever in the league.

The league, still unable to woo national television revenues because of ice hockey's regionalism, turned to the new technology of cable television and signed a contract with the USA network for exclusive national cable TV rights over the next two years. Individual teams increasingly were turning to this medium in their local areas. For example, the New York Islanders signed a groundbreaking 30-year agreement with the SportsChannel network.

The year was not without the usual controversy over violence on the ice, but this time there was a new twist. A federal jury in Detroit awarded $850,000 in damages to Dennis Polonich, who had brought a personal injury suit against Wilf Paiement, then with the Colorado Rockies. Polonich had sued Paiement for hitting him with a stick during a game, breaking his nose and giving him a concussion and numerous cuts. It was the first suit of its kind in NHL history.

Among end-of-year honours, the Vezina Trophy for the single top goalkeeper was awarded to the Islanders' Bill Smith. The Jennings Trophy for goalies with the best goals-against average went to Denis Herron and Rick Wamsley of Montreal, who posted a 2.79 average. The rookie-of-the-year award was won by Dale Hawerchuk, a forward with Winnipeg.

Wayne Gretzky of Edmonton scored his record-breaking 77th goal of the season against goalie Don Edwards of the Buffalo Sabres. He scored twice more in the next six minutes.
UPI

Rick Middleton of Boston received the Lady Byng Trophy for sportsmanship and standard of play. The Masterton Trophy for perseverance went to the Colorado Rockies' embattled goalie, Glenn ("Chico") Resch. The Norris Trophy for best defenseman was won by Doug Wilson of Chicago. The best defensive forward was Steve Kasper of Boston, who wrested the Selke Trophy from Montreal's Bob Gainey, the recipient for each of the four previous years it had been awarded.

The Adams Trophy for coach of the year was won by Tom Watt of Winnipeg. His team showed the greatest one-year improvement, 48 points, in NHL history.

The American Hockey League champions were the New Brunswick Hawks. In the Central Hockey League the winners were the Indianapolis Racers, a team affiliated with the New York Islanders.

ICELAND

The Icelandic economy gradually entered into recession in the course of 1982. Real gross national product (GNP) was estimated to have declined by some 3.5%, and the current account deficit for the year as a whole was expected to amount to 10–11% of GNP. This followed several years during which production had grown slowly but steadily and the balance of payments had been close to achieving equilibrium. Inflation rose from a 40–45% annual rate at the beginning of the year to some 55–60% at the end. The main cause was the fall in the fish catch, the result of declining fish resources off Iceland's coast. Sales of fish were also suffering because of difficulties in certain export markets, especially Nigeria, where there was an important market for Icelandic stockfish.

The economic downturn led to considerable strain within the three-party government coalition, composed of members of the left-wing People's Alliance, the Progressive Party, and a splinter group from the Independence (Conservative) Party. With some difficulty, the government agreed in August to economic measures that consisted mainly of an attempt to break the inflationary spiral by cutting wage increases that were due in compensation for price rises. At the same time, the currency was devalued by 13%, in addition to a 12% devaluation at the beginning of 1982 and gradual devaluation during the course of the year.

During the summer, when Parliament was not in session, one member who had previously supported the government in the upper house switched his allegiance to the opposition, with the result that the government lost its majority in that house. However, it still commanded a majority of one vote in the lower house and a similar majority in a joint legislative session. This situation created a stalemate in Parliament, since the government was unable to pass any legislation other than the fiscal budget, which was dealt with in joint session.

It was the intention of all the political parties to pass a constitutional amendment redrawing electoral districts to reflect population movements in the previous two decades. Since the last such amendment was passed in 1959, large population shifts had taken place toward urban areas, which as a result were underrepresented in the legislature.

On May 22 local elections were held throughout most of the country. The results showed considerable gains for the Independence Party, the main opposition party, while the chief losers were the People's Alliance and the Social Democrats. The election outcome indicated a substantial swing to the right, reflecting dissatisfaction with the government.

Iceland's Pres. Vigdís Finnbogadóttir paid state visits to the U.K. in February and to the U.S. in September. In the U.S. she also represented all the heads of state of the Nordic countries at the opening of the exhibition "Scandinavia Today."

ICE SKATING

Keener interest in nonchampionship figure-skating competitions and increased participation in indoor short-track racing were notable trends during 1982.

Judy Blumberg and Michael Seibert successfully defended their dance pairs title at the U.S. figure-skating championships in January.
WIDE WORLD

WIDE WORLD

Peter and Caitlin Carruthers won their second straight U.S. pairs title in the figure-skating championships in Indianapolis, Indiana.

The International Skating Union had 32 member nations.

Figure Skating

The first world figure championships to be held in Denmark drew 132 skaters from 25 countries to Copenhagen on March 9–13. The four events produced two victories for the U.S., one each for Great Britain and East Germany, and, for the first time in 18 years, none for the Soviet Union.

Scott Hamilton retained the men's title for the U.S. with apparent ease. His almost flawless long free skating included six triple jumps in a widely varied program entertainingly presented. Norbert Schramm, the season's new European champion from West Germany, finished second ahead of a Canadian, Brian Pockar, whose third place was commendably achieved after he missed much training because of appendicitis complications. Another Canadian, fourth-place Brian Orser, completed a perfect triple axel—3½ midair rotations—which only he and his compatriot Vern Taylor had previously accomplished in a world championship. After leading in the compulsory figures, Jean-Christophe Simond of France could only finish fifth.

Elaine Zayak, 16, became the sixth U.S. skater to gain the women's crown, remarkably pulling up from seventh place in the long free skating after an otherwise undistinguished season. Katarina Witt from East Germany was runner-up despite three faulty landings, and Claudia Kristofics-Binder, the outstanding woman figure tracer from Austria, took the bronze medal in a contest marred by erratic judging. Rosalynn Sumners and Vikki de Vries, sixth and seventh for the U.S., each demonstrated considerable potential.

Tassilo Thierbach and Sabine Baess became the first East Germans to take the pairs title, with a sound display of powerful overhead lifts, deft throws, and well-controlled death spirals. Neither the winners nor the Soviet runners-up, Stanislav Leonovich and Marina Pestova, appeared to be in the same league as other champions of recent years. An upsurge of North American strength was evident in this division when a U.S. brother and sister team, Peter and Caitlin Carruthers, narrowly defeated Canadians Paul Martini and Barbara Underhill in a close duel for third place. Igor Lisovsky and Irina Vorobieva, the Soviet defending champions, were humbled in fifth position, Vorobieva skating with suspected injured cartilage and looking clearly under stress.

Christopher Dean and Jayne Torvill, widely considered to be the best performers ever in their branch of skating, retained the ice dance title for Britain with bewildering technical brilliance. They secured the highest marks ever for a compulsory dance, five of the seven judges awarding 5.9; no one had yet received a six in this section of the event. For their free dance five judges gave them maximum sixes for presentation. Andrey Bukin and Natalia Bestemianova gained a hard-fought silver medal from their Soviet compatriots Andrey Minenkov and Irina Moiseyeva.

During the European championships a month earlier in Lyons, France, Dean and Torvill had received the highest score from a single set of marks in any figure-skating competition when awarded sixes for presentation from eight of the nine judges. They received three additional sixes for technical merit, making 11 sixes, a record for any ice dance event.

Speed Skating

Hilbert van der Duim won the men's world championship for the host country at Assen, Neth., on February 20–21. Dmitry Bochkarev of the U.S.S.R. was runner-up, and Rolf Falk-Larssen of Norway came in third. In the individual events Gaetan Boucher of Canada won the 500 m, van der Duim the 1,500 m, and Bochkarev the 5,000 m and 10,000 m.

An East German, Karin Busch, became the new women's world champion at Inzell, West Germany, on February 13–14. Second place went to Andrea Schöne, also of East Germany, and third to the Soviet title defender, Natalia Petruseva. Busch finished first in the 500 m, 1,000 m, and 1,500 m, while Schöne won the 3,000 m.

In the separate world sprint championships, decided at Alkmaar, Neth., on February 6–7, Sergey Khlebnikov of the U.S.S.R. gained the men's title, ahead of Boucher and Frode Rønning of Norway.

The women's championship was won by Petruseva, followed by Busch and a West German, Monika Holzner.

Two new men's world records were set. Aleksandr Baranov of the U.S.S.R. skated the 5,000 m in 6 min 54.66 sec at Medeo, U.S.S.R., and a Swede, Tomas Gustafson, covered the 10,000 m in 14 min 23.59 sec in Oslo. In the second world short-track (indoor) championships, at Moncton, N.B., on April 2–4, the men's and women's titles were gained, respectively, by Guy Daigneault and Maryse Perneault of Canada.

INDIA

During 1982 India made several moves to improve its relations with other countries. Agitation for an autonomous state for Sikhs by the Akali Dal in Punjab caused anxiety, and the three-year-old Assam issue remained unresolved. The republic acquired its seventh elected president in Zail Singh, who succeeded N. Sanjiva Reddy on July 25.

The year started with the rejection by the Akali Dal of Prime Minister Indira Gandhi's award on the sharing of the waters of the Ravi and Beas rivers among Punjab, Haryana, and Rajasthan. The demands of the party included the declaration of Amritsar as a holy city, an all-India act for *gurudwaras* (Sikh temples), the right to carry *kirpans* (daggers) on aircraft, the transfer of the territory of Chandigarh to Punjab, and the acceptance of the party's 1973 Anandpur Sahib resolution, which declared Sikhs to be a separate nation and demanded greater powers for Punjab, including a separate constitution. Having obtained no satisfaction during talks with the union government in April, the Akali Dal asked its members to defy laws and court arrest. Some 25,000 were arrested but later released.

Several rounds of talks were held during the year regarding the demand of Assam students that "foreigners" who had come to that state from Bangladesh be detected, deleted from the electoral rolls, and deported. Some opposition parties joined the discussions, but no breakthrough was achieved. In January K. C. Gogoi of the Congress (I) formed a government in Assam, but he resigned in March, and president's rule was reimposed.

Elections were held in May to legislative assemblies in West Bengal, Haryana, and Himachal Pradesh, where the five-year legislative terms had been completed, and in Kerala because the government led by K. Karunakaran of Congress (I) had fallen in March after being in office for less than three months. In West Bengal the Left Front, led by the Communist Party of India (Marxist) or CPI(M), retained power, capturing 238 out of 294 seats; Jyoti Basu continued as chief minister. In Kerala an alliance led by Congress (I) won 77 seats as against the Left Front's 63 in a house of 140. Karunakaran was sworn in as chief minister. In Himachal Pradesh, Ram Lal of Congress (I) formed a government again with the support of independents. In Haryana no party secured a majority. The governor called Bhajan Lal of Congress (I) to form the government, and several members elected on other tickets crossed over. Elections were held in Nagaland in November, resulting in a Congress (I) ministry under S. C. Jamir.

There were governmental changes in four other states. In January A. R. Antulay, chief minister of Maharashtra, was adjudged by the Bombay High Court to be guilty of misuse of office. Following his resignation Congress (I) chose Babasaheb Bhosale to succeed him. T. Anjiah resigned as chief minister of Andhra Pradesh in February and was succeeded

Responding to a call by the Akali Dal party, Sikhs mounted several demonstrations in New Delhi that quickly turned violent.

CAMERA PRESS, LONDON

BALDEV—SYGMA

Zail Singh was installed as India's seventh president in July. It was hoped that Singh, a Sikh, could pacify the turbulent Punjab.

by B. V. Reddy, who made way for Vijaya Bhaskar Reddy in September. In Uttar Pradesh, Vishwanath Pratap Singh resigned in June, and Sripat Mishra was sworn in as chief minister. The chief minister of Jammu and Kashmir, Sheikh Muhammad Abdullah, died in September, and his son, Farooq Abdullah, was appointed in his place.

The presidential election held in July evoked considerable excitement, although the victory of the Congress (I) nominee, Home Minister Zail Singh, was a foregone conclusion. He secured 754,113 electoral votes against 282,685 for the candidate of the combined opposition, H. R. Khanna, a former Supreme Court judge. In elections for one-quarter of the seats in the Rajya Sabha (upper house of Parliament) in March, the Congress (I) improved its strength to 125 seats out of 244. Of the eight by-elections to the Lok Sabha (lower house) during the year, the Congress (I) won three, BJP two, and the Democratic Socialist Party, the CPI(M), and the All-India Anna Dravida Munnetra Kazhagam one each. The opposition, although unable to unite, was heartened by the decision of Maneka Gandhi, widow of Sanjay Gandhi, to defy Prime Minister Gandhi. After being ordered from her mother-in-law's residence in March, Maneka Gandhi formed a

group to promote the ideas of her late husband and vowed to turn it into a political party.

The Economy

Grain production in the agricultural year ended June 1982 was placed at 133,060,000 metric tons, compared with 129,590,000 metric tons the previous year. But the June–September monsoon was erratic, subjecting vast areas to drought and others to floods. Orissa, Andhra Pradesh, Maharashtra, and Gujarat were hit by cyclones. Sugar production reached a record 8,430,000 metric tons. The wholesale price index on Oct. 9, 1982, was 0.6% above the level of Oct. 10, 1981.

In February railway fares and freight rates were increased to bring in additional income of Rs 2,-614,000,000 (Rs 9.62 = U.S. $1). The union government's budget for 1982–83 provided some relief in direct taxes, but overall revenue was increased by Rs 5,330,000,000. With revenue and capital receipts of Rs 278,540,000,000 and disbursements of Rs

Thousands of housewives marched in New Delhi in August to protest the dowry system and its attendant bride burnings.
UPI

292,190,000,000, the uncovered deficit amounted to Rs 13,650,000,000.

In June the Aid-India Consortium undertook to give development assistance of $3,660,000,000 for 1982–83. Among the major projects completed during the year were the thermal powerhouses of Korba, Ramagundam, and Singrauli, a hydroelectric station of Srisailam, and a bridge across the Ganges River in Bihar. A strike by 160,000 textile workers in Bombay that began in January remained unresolved throughout the year.

Foreign Affairs

Prime Minister Gandhi visited the U.S. and the Soviet Union in quick succession. After her talks with U.S. Pres. Ronald Reagan in Washington, D.C., it was announced that the two countries would work more closely in scientific research and that the U.S. obligation to supply nuclear fuel to the Tarapur power station would be taken over by France. In Moscow arrangements for increased trade and economic cooperation were agreed on. Gandhi returned to Moscow in November to attend the funeral of Soviet Pres. Leonid Brezhnev and to have talks with his successor, Yury Andropov. There were major developments in relations with Pakistan, culminating in a brief visit to New Delhi by Pres. Mohammad Zia-ul-Haq on November 1, when a decision to establish a joint commission was announced. Senior officials of the two countries were to meet to examine proposals for a no-war pact put forward by Pakistan and a treaty of peace, friendship, and cooperation suggested by India.

In March Prime Minister Gandhi went to the U.K. to launch a six-month-long "Festival of India." While there, she had discussions with Prime Minister Margaret Thatcher, which were continued when Thatcher stopped in New Delhi in September. India undertook to play host in March 1983 in New Delhi to the seventh summit conference of the non-aligned movement. The conference, scheduled for Baghdad in September 1982, had been postponed because of the Iran-Iraq war.

INDONESIA

On May 4, 1982, Indonesia's 82 million registered voters went to the polls to elect a new (lower) House of People's Representatives (DPR) to a five-year term, amid sporadic acts of violence that claimed 81 lives. Two thousand candidates contested for 364 seats. (The remaining 100 seats were appointed by the president, largely from the military, who were barred from the general election.) The outcome was no surprise. The government-sponsored Golkar (Functional Groups) won 246 seats, 14 more than in 1977, to retain control of the DPR. The Islamic-oriented United Development Party (PPP) garnered 94 seats for a loss of 5, and the largely secularist Indonesian Democratic Party (PDI) won 24 seats, also for a loss of 5. The parties were essentially strained coalitions of the many traditional parties, which Presi-

UPI

President Suharto cast his ballot in the Indonesian general election after a six-week campaign punctuated by violence.

dent Suharto had compelled to merge in an effort to simplify the country's fractious party system. The opposition charged irregularities at the polls.

The election was only a step toward the selection of a president in 1983 by the People's Consultative Assembly (MPR). The MPR consisted of 924 members, including the DPR, 140 regional delegates, 113 additional party representatives, and 207 appointed members. Suharto was expected to win a fourth five-year term. In 1981 he had announced that his fourth term would be his last. In another internal development, the DPR adopted a defense act in September that bolstered the concept of *Hankam Rata* ("people's defense") and the "dual function" of the Army in Indonesia's sociopolitical and military life.

Indonesia denounced the continuing Soviet occupation of Afghanistan and the Vietnamese occupation of Kampuchea. Many Indonesians considered Vietnam a Soviet client state. Relations with Moscow worsened in February when the Indonesians broke up a major Soviet spy ring in Jakarta. Radio Moscow was assailed on the floor of the DPR for broadcasts defending the abortive Partei Kommunist Indonesia (PKI) coup of 1965.

While relations with Moscow cooled, Jakarta was dismayed by Washington's policy of weapons sales to China and its promotion of Japanese rearmament. Indonesia viewed both China and Japan as potential threats to Southeast Asia. In July Defense Minister Mohammed Jusuf flew to Washington to confer with Pres. Ronald Reagan. Suharto followed this up in October with a state visit to the U.S., during which he elicited a pledge from President Reagan that the U.S. would not let its China and Japan policies undermine Indonesian security. During Suharto's visit 102 members of Congress called on the U.S. to investigate allegations of starvation and violations of human rights in East Timor, which had been integrated into Indonesia. In 1975, after the end of Portuguese colonial rule, the Indonesians had moved into East Timor to prevent a takeover by Fretilin, a left-wing independence faction supported by Moscow and the Portuguese Communists. The U.S. State Department strongly refuted the allegations. During the year independent visitors to East Timor reported a relatively quiet situation with about 100 to 200 armed Fretilin guerrillas holed up in the mountains.

Despite the world recession, Indonesia's economy maintained one of the world's highest growth rates at 7.6% annually. During the year Indonesia entered the ranks of the middle-income nations when its per capita gross national product rose to $520. (The World Bank defined a middle-income nation as one with a per capita GNP of at least $410.) Inflation eased to 7%, compared with 16% the year before, and rice output, a barometer of political stability, rose by 10% to 22.2 million tons.

INSURANCE

Record losses in widespread winter storms and the growing disparity between premium income and claims payouts troubled the nation's insurance industry during the first half of 1982. First-quarter profits fell 46% from earnings a year earlier, and confidence in the three largest publicly traded companies was reflected in their stock prices' tumbling 20% or more between April and June.

Although the easing of inflation had been expected to curb the rising cost of damage claims, this had not occurred by the third quarter. Added to that was the fear that the investment income that had seen the industry through four years of low rates would also fall off with inflation, even as price cutting seemed likely to continue as firms sought to secure market shares in anticipation of an economic recovery. By one estimate, negotiated rates for some commercial lines of insurance had fallen 60% during the past four years in a recession-generated climate of fierce rate competition.

The persistent problem for the big multiline insurance companies was that so-called cash-flow underwriting in property-casualty policies had become standard practice by 1982. Where firms had formerly devised premium schedules to return a profit over expected claims and expenses, they now typically aimed premiums at underselling the competition in order to get cash to invest. Claims and expense exceeded premiums by 6% in 1981, but the industry earned $13.4 billion in investment income against only $6 billion in pretax underwriting losses. Net earnings in the property-casualty industry were $6 billion for the year. By the second half of 1982, however, the industry had booked pretax underwriting losses of $5.5 billion, nearly equaling the figure for all of 1981, and projections were that the loss would total $10 billion for the full year, with the gap between losses and premiums reaching 9%.

Selling at a loss inevitably eroded the amount of investible cash over the long run, by the margin of claims and expenses over premiums. Also, investments toward the end of 1982 yielded nothing like the 20% returns available for short-term lending during parts of 1981. The increase of 16% in investment income for the first half of 1982 was well below the 21% increase in the first half of 1981.

Moreover, unprecedented claims were paid in 1982 for numerous minor storms and other natural disasters—a record $400 million in the first quarter and topping $1 billion by July, more than in all of 1981. Major losses were predicted in airline underwriting following three disasters early in the year: an Air Florida flight slammed into Washington, D.C.'s, 14th Street bridge on takeoff from National Airport in January, killing 78 people; 154 people died in July when a Pan Am 727 crashed shortly after takeoff from New Orleans; and in January two persons were killed when a World Airways DC-10 skidded off a runway at Logan Airport into Boston Harbor. A conservative estimate placed damages at $165 million against $100 million in premiums for aircraft insurers in 1982, although the payment of claims was expected to stretch out over several years.

Business failures also cost the industry in 1982 as Braniff International airline went bankrupt in May and the Manville Corp., the giant asbestos maker, took the unusual step in August of seeking protection from lawsuits claiming billions of dollars in damages for diseases linked to the product (*see* Business and Industry). Life insurance companies were among the firm's largest creditors, with Prudential Corp. alone holding some $68 million in debt from Manville, and property-casualty companies were next in the line of attack for the plaintiffs in the cases.

Corporate activities on the insurance side saw several mergers during the year, the one between Connecticut General Corp. and INA Corp. creating the nation's second-largest publicly held insurance company, with $30 billion in assets. The new firm, renamed CIGNA Corp., was designed to capitalize on Connecticut General's strength in employee benefit insurance in combination with INA's strength in marketing commercial casualty products. In a less friendly takeover, in July American General Corp. finally won control of NLT Corp., a Nashville-based insurance holding company, creating the fourth-largest insurance company, with $13 billion in assets. For about $1.6 billion Xerox Corp. entered the insurance business in September with its purchase of Crum & Forster, another large insurer in the commercial casualty field.

John Saladino's "post and beam" sofa with an ash frame won the best of show prize in the second annual judging for the Daphne Awards for hardwood furniture design.
DUNBAR

INTERIOR DESIGN

The year 1982 could be described as one of ambivalence and ambiguity as three growing movements converged: a fondness for things foreign, a yearning for the quality and romance of yore, and a need for streamlined designs to suit today's tighter-than-ever living quarters. An exhibition of Scandinavian furniture at the Cooper-Hewitt Museum in New York City and the enthusiasm for Italian designs at the Milan furniture show underscored an affection for a new "international style" that went far beyond eclecticism. At the annual spring Southern Furniture Market in North Carolina, Ethan Allen showcased a living room filled with imports, and, as part of its expanded "Four Corners" import program, Thomasville began reproducing such designs as a Queen Anne lacquered bureau.

American consumers saw much more attention being paid to such classic cabinetmaking techniques as dowel and tongue-and-groove joinery in response to a renewed interest in "craftsmanship,"albeit contrary to an equally avid cost consciousness. An award-winning sofa designed by John Saladino with a solid bleached ash frame, upholstered back and sides, a single seat cushion, and two back cushions exemplified an inclination toward the decidedly pragmatic. Judges cited its "good value and multi-purpose flexibility." The Saladino sofa's 22-in depth took into account tightening living spaces.

A more formal and generally stiffer look in seating eclipsed slouchy designs as sofas and chairs tended toward firmer and higher postures. The rather formal camelback sofa style of the 18th century appeared regularly. Lane Co.'s American Folk Museum collection included a camelback sofa in a quiltlike fabric, and Heritage offered a triple camelback in a flowered cotton. Several new reproductions were revealed during the year, including a 1785 Pembroke mahogany and kingwood table by Henredon, a Hepplewhite sideboard and Duncan Phyfe breakfast table from Kaylyn, and leather-trimmed Jacobean designs from Sutton.

A group of 18th-century American reproductions from the Winterthur, New York's Metropolitan, the Museum of Early Southern Decorative Arts, and Boston's Museum of Fine Arts was launched under the name "Sutton Reproductions." Yale and Frances Forman Designs introduced "An American Legacy," a collection of furniture, wallcoverings, rugs, bedding, accessories, and fabrics based on late 18th- and early 19th-century Federal designs.

To punctuate the soft colours and soft lines that dominated so many of the year's interiors, bright and glistening metals were introduced on sofa bases, table frames, and wall systems. Brass was the big favourite, but Selig offered "almost neutral" nickel frames on a line of glass-topped occasional tables. In fabrics, flowered chintzes blossomed as part of the sentimental mood, along with balloon shades, multilayered window treatments, fringed lampshades, and tassled chair skirts.

Some of the industrial materials that were part of the "high-tech" movement—rubber flooring, brushed steel, rugged hardware—were still holding their own. Ceramic tiles for both floors and walls in living areas reappeared in one-inch squares and in dull clay colours. Reminiscent of commercial installations of the 1950s, the tiles' renaissance was all part of the nod to that era, as was a fondness for old bamboo furniture, once relegated to back porches but now welcomed as the "Florida look," sometimes retrofitted with polished cotton pillows in the newly popular deep pastels. But more often than not, the familiar old sofas and chairs were seen with cushions covered in reproductions of the garish florals they originally wore. An interest in fauna grew, too. Herons and cranes in all manner of finishes, ranging from brasses and bronzes to pale woods and ceramics, moved into dining rooms, entry halls, atriums, and spa-proportioned bathrooms.

Several manufacturers introduced special cabinets designed to house expensive entertainment equipment, large-screen televisions in particular. "Electroniture," created by Phil Noelke for the Bench Collection of Santa Rosa, Calif., included an oak cabinet-desk to hold a video display terminal, a shelf

Reminiscent of the 1950's, this room design by Peter Culhane featured pastel shades and a pair of decorative herons.
SELIG

for a keyboard, a document holder and work surface, plus an optional printer stand and paper bale.

Teal was but one of the new deep pastels to appear in everything from dishes to fabrics and wall coverings. Other grayed pastels, grayed reds, and gray itself turned up as pet colours, and they were so often shown set off by black accessories, walls, fabrics, lamps, and furniture that a Macy's representative called black "important."

INTERNATIONAL FINANCE

Several economic and political events combined to generate major disruptions in international financial markets in 1982. A global recession continued throughout the year, significantly reducing demand for imported goods and severely constricting export markets. World trade was further hampered as sagging domestic economic conditions increased internal pressures in a number of countries to restrict imports from abroad. Multilateral negotiations under the auspices of the General Agreement on Tariffs and Trade (GATT) in November succeeded only partly in avoiding protectionist measures that would limit mutually advantageous trade between nations and slow the expected recovery of the world economy. In October the European Community Commission estimated that the volume of aggregate world imports would decline by 1% for 1982 as a whole, reversing the net gain of the previous two years.

The predicament of recession and declining world trade had its roots in the economic policies of the 1970s. Faced with declining growth due to escalating burdens of taxation and disruptions resulting from unexpected shocks such as oil price changes, most governments chose the panacea of monetary stimulus. Higher money growth rates resulted in temporary spurts of economic growth but also led to an inflationary spiral. From 1979 the industrial countries, led by the United States, pursued restrictive monetary policies. Inflation abated slightly in 1981 and fell substantially in 1982 in response to this policy shift. For instance, consumer price inflation declined in each of the "big seven" industrial countries for the 12 months ending in November 1982, compared with the 1981 average. Inflation fell from 10.3 to 4.6% in the U.S., from 12.5 to 9.8% in Canada, from 4.9 to 2.3% in Japan, from 5.9 to 4.7% in West Germany, from 13.3 to 6.3% in the U.K., from 13.3 to 9.4% in France, and from 18.7 to 16.7% in Italy.

Although the success in lowering inflation improved the outlook for future economic development, the cost was high. In addition to recession and declining international trade, the anti-inflationary policies raised interest rates well above underlying inflation levels, in turn contributing to substantial exchange rate volatility.

The average value of the U.S. dollar reached its highest level in 12 years in June 1982. The dollar, weighted by the size of foreign trade flows against the currencies of 15 major countries as reported by the Morgan Guaranty Trust Co., equaled the value last achieved in June 1970, the end of the fixed exchange rate era. The trade-weighted dollar rose nearly 4% more by the end of October, then declined to close the year at the June level. In addition, the dollar touched all-time record levels during the second half of 1982 against the French franc, Canadian dollar, Italian lira, and a number of lesser currencies.

The value of the dollar had declined steadily between 1970 and 1973 as the U.S. progressed from the end of the Bretton Woods pegged exchange rate regime and an overvalued dollar to a system of freely floating rates. By 1973 the dollar had fallen 16%

from the 1970 parity, but economic fundamentals suggested that some of the lost ground could be regained. In 1973 the U.S. inflation rate was 2.5% lower than the international average, and interest rates were higher than the international average by 2.2% after adjusting for inflation (international inflation and interest rates are a weighted average for Canada, France, West Germany, Japan, Italy, and the U.K.). The higher real interest rate increased worldwide demand for the dollar as international investors sought the highest possible return, and this gradually led to dollar appreciation. At the same time, the lower U.S. inflation rate resulted in smaller price increases for U.S. goods. As world traders shifted to U.S. markets to buy these cheaper goods, the demand for dollars increased until the dollar's appreciation just offset the benefits of lower inflation. As a consequence of these combined actions, the dollar rose from 16% below the 1970 benchmark in 1973 to a shortfall of only 11% in 1977.

Economic fundamentals supporting the dollar deteriorated sharply from 1977 to 1980. Stimulative monetary policies and deteriorating productivity growth increased U.S. inflation, and a 2.5 to 4% inflation differential in favour of the dollar in 1973–77 became a 2.5% differential against the dollar in 1979–80. The unfavourable inflation experience was reinforced by falling real rates of return as stimulative monetary policies held nominal U.S. interest rates below accelerating inflation. Consequently, a positive real interest rate differential of 1.2 to 2.5% in 1973–77 had become a 1.5% disadvantage by 1980. As a result of these inflation and interest rate developments, the trade-weighted dollar fell from an annual average of 11% below the 1970 parity in 1977 to annual averages near 17% below the 1970 parity in 1978, 1979, and 1980. Moreover, the dollar

hit monthly lows of 20% below parity during 1978 and 1980.

The year 1980 marked the turning point for fundamental strength behind the dollar. The international inflation differential improved significantly as the U.S. was more successful than its trading partners in curbing inflation. By 1982 U.S. inflation averaged 3% lower than in the major industrial countries, the first positive differential since 1977. At the same time, sharply higher real U.S. interest rates boosted the real interest rate differential to 1.5% in favour of the dollar in 1982. In response to these favourable developments, as well as to gains due to political turmoil in the Middle East, the South Atlantic, and Eastern Europe, the dollar rose sharply to a 12-year high and averaged only 1% below the 1970 parity for 1982 as a whole, a 14% gain from the 1980 value and a 10% gain from 1981.

In addition to increasing on a trade-weighted basis, the dollar appreciated against every freely traded currency in 1982. From January to December the value of the dollar in terms of foreign currency increased 4.4% against the Canadian dollar, 19% against the British pound, 18.2% against the French franc, 5.6% against the West German mark, 13.9% against the Italian lira, 9.5% against the Swiss franc, and 7.3% against the Japanese yen. The greatest gains—from 88% upwards—occurred against the Mexican peso (562%), the Argentine peso (443%), the Israeli shekel, the Brazilian cruzeiro, the Peruvian sol, and the Chilean peso. The massive devaluations for each of the latter currencies resulted from a history of high domestic inflation rates, the failure of long-standing efforts to peg exchange rates in spite of large inflation differentials, or both.

The major exchange rate adjustment involving currencies other than the dollar during 1982 was the

"The peso must be down again . . . it's another batch of Mexican bankers."

PETERS/©1982 DAYTON DAILY NEWS

Roberto Calvi, president of Milan's Banco Ambrosiano, was found dead in London soon after fleeing a major bank scandal.

June 12 realignment of currencies within the European Monetary System (EMS). In the EMS the currencies of West Germany, The Netherlands, Belgium, Denmark, France, Italy, Luxembourg, and Ireland are pegged to each other and must be maintained within certain ranges of central intervention rates, but the currencies of the EMS as a unit are free to float up or down against the U.S. dollar. Because divergent national economic policies maintained significantly different inflation rates among European countries, the central intervention rates came under increasing speculative attack until changes in these rates were made in order to reflect changes in purchasing power. As a result, at midyear the French franc was devalued 5.75% and the Italian lira was devalued 2.75% against the EMS central rates, while the West German mark and the Dutch guilder were each increased in value by 4.25% against the central rates.

The most exotic international development in 1982, and the most serious, was a liquidity crisis in less developed countries that interrupted normal debt payment patterns. Estimates indicated that the foreign debts of less developed countries that were not members of the Organization of Petroleum Exporting Countries (OPEC) doubled between 1978 and 1982, to reach $700 billion. While this borrowing was occasionally used to subsidize nonproductive activities in the less developed countries, the majority of the borrowing was invested productively and was thought capable of producing adequate income to service the growing indebtedness. However, the economic disruptions of 1982 severely limited the ability of less developed countries to earn income and service their debts in the short run and reduced banks' willingness to refinance debts or to lend further capital, consequently endangering the international lending institutions involved and ultimately the international financial system itself.

Less developed nations experienced a variety of external shocks during 1982 that were perhaps worse than the first oil price increases in 1974. The world recession significantly lowered the prices of many primary commodities that were important exports of these countries, and the decline in world trade exacerbated the shortfall in expected export revenue. At the same time, persistently high levels of real interest rates and an appreciating dollar greatly increased the costs of debt payments already contracted. The squeeze of falling export earnings and rising debt servicing costs forced as many as 40 countries to delay external payments during 1982. Moreover, the problem for a growing number became so serious that creditors were forced to agree to extended schedules for debt repayment.

Economic difficulties generated a record number of reschedulings in 1982; 20 countries were estimated to have rescheduled $28 billion. Countries rescheduling debt in 1982 included Argentina, Bolivia, the Central African Republic, Costa Rica, Guyana, Honduras, Liberia, Madagascar, Malawi, Pakistan, Peru, Poland, Romania, Senegal, Sierra Leone, The Sudan, Togo, Uganda, Vietnam, and Zaire. Moreover, Mexico and Brazil between them requested $24 billion in debt relief in 1983. Because of the number and size of debt problems in 1982, Western leaders began taking steps to restore economic growth at a faster pace. In addition, negotiations were begun at the meeting of the International Monetary Fund in September to increase the amount of emergency funds available for lending to countries with balance of payments problems.

IRAN

The tide of the Gulf war turned strongly in Iran's favour during 1982. The main breakthrough began on March 22, when Iraqi forces in Khuzestan were driven back across a broad front. In a further offensive launched at the end of April, an Iranian bridgehead was established west of the Karun River. At the end of May the final withdrawal from Khuzestan was effected when Iraqi troops left Khorramshahr. The Iranian leadership could claim with some truth that the Islamic Republican Army had swept all before it in the liberation of Iranian territory. Iraq announced that it would unilaterally withdraw from all remaining Iranian lands captured earlier and seek a peace agreement through the Islamic Conference.

Encouraged by its military successes, the Iranian regime hardened its stance on peace conditions. It demanded that Iraqi Pres. Saddam Hussein at-Takriti be removed from office, that an independent commission be established to allocate blame for the war, and that reparations be paid to Iran. In addition to these publicly stated aims, there appeared to be consensus in Teheran that the war should continue until the regime in Baghdad was changed, that the

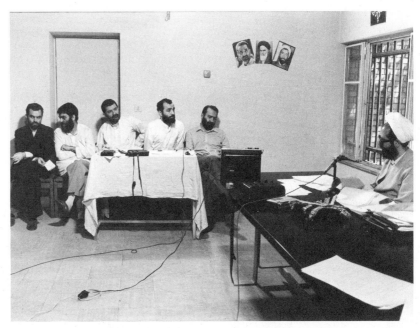

Sadegh Ghotbzadeh (fourth from left), familiar to U.S. audiences as the suave spokesman of the Iranian government during the hostage crisis, was executed in September.

ALFRED ZADEH—GAMMA/LIAISON

Shi'ah Muslims of Iraq should be liberated by force if necessary, and that all Iranian territorial claims should be met.

A first step toward implementing these expanded goals came with the invasion of Iraq that began on July 14. The offensive was directed toward Basra in southern Iraq. Although some early gains were made, Iranian troops were ultimately expelled with heavy losses. On October 1 a major Iranian assault on the border town of Mandali was followed by a drive westward from Dezful on November 1, when a number of roads and oil installations were captured. A thrust into Iraqi territory in the region of Amarah opened up the road to Baghdad.

The war had an appreciable impact on Iran's foreign relations. Both the U.S. and the U.S.S.R. re-

Several thousand Iraqi troops were captured by Iranian forces during a major counteroffensive launched on March 22 in Khuzestan.

SYGMA

mained officially neutral and refused arms supplies to both sides, though materials slipped through these embargoes with comparative ease. Iranian relations with the Arab world deteriorated sharply when Iranian troops invaded Arab soil; only Syria and Libya remained aligned with Iran.

Domestic political events were largely controlled by the ruling Islamic Republican Party, which became increasingly associated with policies of an Islamic and conservative nature. Left-wing influences were attacked and removed wherever possible. The threat from the Mujaheddin-i Khalq opposition was largely negated during the year, though occasional violence erupted. The Tudeh (Communist) Party was no longer tolerated. While the aging Ayatollah Ruhollah Khomeini showed increasing signs of frailty, he remained the final point of reference for all political forces. In September Sadegh Ghotbzadeh was executed for plotting to overthrow the government.

Iran's economic plight worsened in 1982. Poor demand for Iranian oil, Iraqi air attacks on the Kharg Island oil terminal, and prohibitive insurance rates for vessels visiting Iranian ports exacerbated existing problems. Oil output, averaging 1,519,000 bbl a day in the first half of 1982, rose to 1.7 million bbl a day in November. However, the recovery was bought with large discounts on oil prices; revenue flows, though improving, were barely adequate to buy imports.

Economic development activity came to a virtual halt. Changes were effected in the organization of foreign trade, much of which was nationalized. Otherwise, unemployment persisted and economic activity diminished. Industry suffered shortages of electricity and raw materials, while agriculture, an officially favoured area, showed a further decline in output. Imports of agricultural products rose dra-

matically to an estimated $4.5 billion. By November Iranian holdings of foreign exchange were thought to be worth $3 billion, compared with $500 million four months earlier.

IRAQ

Iraq suffered severe military setbacks in the war with Iran during 1982, and this, coupled with lower oil production and the need for austerity at home, gave Pres. Saddam Hussein at-Takriti a difficult year. The military pressure began in September 1981 when the Iraqi Army was pushed back across the Karun River. This phase culminated on May 24, 1982, with a humiliating capitulation at the Iranian port of Khorramshahr. The Iraqis appeared to hold the line with a successful defensive action in the Basra sector in July, and an Iranian offensive at Mandali in October was also contained. Casualty estimates stood at 40,000 dead, 70,000 wounded, and some 40,000 Iraqis held as prisoners of war.

President Hussein survived a difficult political period in May and June but emerged with a stronger hand. On June 27 a shake-up in the ruling Revolutionary Command Council was announced. The average age of the new ministers was 46; most had university degrees; and two had military backgrounds. Ten new ministers were appointed, and a new Ministry for Light Industries was created. Prominent among the new appointees was Oil Minister Qassem Ahmad Taki, a former deputy industry minister.

Hussein's position was secure enough for him to ride out the cancellation of the nonaligned movement summit, scheduled to take place in Baghdad in September 1982. The president suggested that the eighth summit be held in Baghdad in 1985, when he could assume the chair of the movement. There was some evidence that Iranian-inspired terrorism in

*"Operation Ramadan,"
an Iranian invasion
aimed at Basra, was
finally thrown back with
considerable losses by
Iraq.*

MANOOCHER—SIPA PRESS/BLACK
STAR

Iraq was responsible for the cancellation.

Arab aid to Iraq, estimates of which varied from $16 billion to $30 billion since the start of the war with Iran, were vital to Iraq's survival. By October 1982 oil exports had fallen to 600,000 bbl a day, and only the pipeline to Turkey was in use. Annual revenue from the sale of this oil in depressed world market conditions was estimated at some $6 billion–$10 billion. Foreign currency reserves held by Iraq were down to about $8 billion. The war effort was estimated to be costing Iraq $1 billion a month, while development spending for 1982 was put at about $12 billion.

Against this background of austerity, it seemed likely that the ambitious $130 billion, five-year (1981–85) development plan would be shelved. Instead, new projects would be amended annually within the guidelines of the plan and annual budget allocations. A further worry was that Iraq might have to pay war reparations to Iran for a guarantee of peace. It was thought likely, however, that in such an event Arab Gulf neighbours would step into the breach. Hussein made it clear that the war would take priority as long as he governed. He was quoted as saying, "If we are required to stop any of our development projects to meet battlefield requirements, we will do so."

Within the nonaligned movement, Iraq had a powerful friend in Yugoslavia, with which it had strong business relations. There were similar ties with India and certain other third world countries, which had been helped in the past by the Iraqi Fund for External Development. The president retained a pragmatic view of relations with the Soviet Union and the U.S. but had no diplomatic relations with the latter. Within the Gulf, Hussein was still regarded with suspicion as a past supporter of elements hostile to the sheikhly system. Iraq was pointedly not invited to join the Gulf Cooperation Council grouping of conservative Arab Gulf states formed in 1981.

IRELAND

Political instability cast a shadow over events in Ireland again in 1982. The recession deepened, and unemployment rose. John Bruton, minister for finance in the Fine Gael-Irish Labour Party coalition government, brought in a particularly harsh budget in January in an effort to reduce the massive borrowings abroad. As a result of the vote on this budget, the government of Prime Minister Garret FitzGerald was defeated. In the general election on February 18, the second within nine months, neither of the two main parties, Fine Gael and Fianna Fail, gained a majority in the Dail (parliament).

Until the Dail reconvened on March 9, there was uncertainty about who would form a government. In the event, the 81 Fianna Fail deputies, supported by 3 left-wing Sinn Fein Workers' Party deputies and 2 independents, elected Charles J. Haughey as prime minister. Losses of Fianna Fail members by death

PETER JORDAN–GAMMA/LIAISON

Charles J. Haughey (left) and Garret FitzGerald continued to succeed one another as prime minister in Ireland.

and illness, however, placed the administration in an almost untenable position when the Dail resumed in October after the summer recess.

Haughey faced further embarrassment in August when a murder suspect was found in the apartment of the attorney general, Patrick Connolly. As details emerged, it became clear that Haughey had permitted the attorney general to leave the country for a holiday in the U.S. the day after the suspect was arrested. Recalled to Dublin, Connolly resigned the next day.

In spite of the unstable situation, the government adopted stringent measures to deal with the economy. Nevertheless, the current budget deficit soared, and unemployment rose to a record 160,000. There was some reduction in inflation from 20 to 14%, but it was still the second highest among the country's main trading partners. The popularity of the Haughey administration sank to an all-time low.

This grave situation was seriously aggravated by discord within the Fianna Fail party. A motion of no confidence in Haughey's leadership was moved in October, and in an open roll-call vote an unprecedented 22 deputies supported it. Two Cabinet ministers resigned, and the open wrangle did major damage to the administration. Finally, a motion of no confidence moved on November 4 was passed, resulting in the downfall of the government. Elections were called for November 24. The outcome was once again indecisive, but after nearly three weeks the Fine Gael-Irish Labour coalition was reforged with a combined 86 seats in the Dail. On December 14 FitzGerald was returned to office.

Ireland's relations with the U.K. deteriorated considerably during the year. Ireland withdrew from the economic sanctions imposed by the European Communities against Argentina during the Falklands hostilities. The rift was widened in the autumn when Haughey withheld approval from the October 20 elections to set up a consultative assembly in Northern Ireland. Haughey claimed that this initiative toward devolution had been carried out by the U.K. government without consulting the republic.

Abortion continued to be a widely debated issue. This was the result of efforts by a pro-life group to have a referendum on the proposal that the country's antiabortion laws be incorporated into the constitution. Although abortion was already illegal (it was estimated that 7,000 Irishwomen annually traveled to the U.K. to attend abortion clinics), the pro-life group feared that a test case might be taken to the Supreme Court and that abortion might be made legal as a result. Political leaders had agreed to the referendum without considering the implications, and it seemed likely that they might be faced with a dilemma as the issue gained momentum.

ISRAEL

For the first four months of 1982, Israel's attention was focused on one date, April 25, when Israel was to complete its withdrawal from the Sinai Peninsula as agreed under the Camp David accords. While it waited for this military process to be completed, Egypt, in its relations with Israel, had been correct and friendly if not fulsome. Pres. Hosni Mubarak of Egypt had assured the Israeli government that there would be no change and that Egypt would stand by its peace treaty with Israel. Nevertheless, in Israeli eyes the move was the one big gamble in the Camp David agreement. There was no lack of voices abroad suggesting that, once Israel had withdrawn,

Egypt would proceed to mend its fences with the rest of the Arab world.

In the event, the military withdrawal presented the least difficulty, despite the costly dismantling of the two largest and most sophisticated military airfields in the Middle East and other sensitive Israel Defense Forces (IDF) installations. Far more serious for the government of Prime Minister Menachem Begin was the opposition of the civilian settlers—religious and nationalist—who refused to abandon and dismantle their homes. They had built up a flourishing community—in places literally making the desert bloom—and they resented the government's agreeing to Egypt's demand that no Israeli be permitted to remain in Sinai once it was returned to Egyptian sovereignty. The Begin government called in troops specially selected for the difficult and unpopular task of forcing the settlers to leave.

A small multinational peacekeeping force supervised the demilitarization of the Sinai region, with only nominal Egyptian forces on the Sinai banks of the Suez Canal. Egypt belied the many Western and Arab forecasters who had predicted the abandonment of the Camp David undertakings once Egypt regained possession of Sinai. President Mubarak and his government maintained their strict adherence to the treaty with Israel, and neither then nor later in the year, when other crises intervened, did Egypt take any action that might undermine the peace.

Possibly the most important consequence of the withdrawal went largely unnoticed, even in Israel. In a remarkable interview on Israeli television on April 27, Israel's chief of staff, Lieut. Gen. Raphael Eitan, spoke frankly about the new character of the IDF in

Israel's invasion of Lebanon provoked an unprecedented level of domestic opposition. In July thousands of demonstrators chanted "No more war!" in Tel Aviv.

UPI

Defense Minister Ariel Sharon (centre foreground) testified for several hours before the Israeli commission investigating the massacre of Palestinians in Lebanon.
MILNER–SYGMA

the post-Sinai era. He emphasized that Israel's armed forces needed virtually no more quantitative growth. Their efforts would be concentrated on improving the quality of their equipment and the training of their troops.

But even while attention was centred on Sinai, there were ominous rumblings on Israel's northern border with Lebanon and Syria. The Palestine Liberation Organization (PLO) in Lebanon had not been quiescent during Israel's preoccupation with the south. Both Israeli and U.S. intelligence sought to establish an accurate profile of the PLO presence and strength in southern Lebanon. The Israelis concluded that a formidable PLO arms buildup was under way and that this presented a real threat to Israel's security. The U.S. did not agree. However, when U.S. Secretary of State Alexander Haig appeared before the U.S. House Foreign Affairs Committee on March 2, he appeared to share the Israeli rather than the U.S. assessment. This discussion about the status of the PLO was refueled by media reports and claims by PLO leadership that Israel was about to launch a major attack on the PLO in Lebanon.

Meanwhile, Israel was receiving decisive support from the U.S. in blocking punitive proposals in the UN directed at Israel because of the application in December 1981 of Israeli law to the Golan Heights, occupied by Israel in 1967. The UN described the move as tantamount to annexation. There was clear recognition in Israel that U.S. support was all that stood between Israel and much greater condemnation by the UN, including the possible suspension of Israel's membership as proposed by Syria on January 29.

On January 19 Prime Minister Begin assured U.S. Pres. Ronald Reagan that Israel would not attack Lebanon without unquestionable provocation from either the Palestinian or the Syrian forces there. Thereafter the Israeli government repeatedly assured President Reagan that no action against Leba-

non had been ordered, especially after terrorist attacks inside Israel and attacks on Jewish or Israeli targets elsewhere.

In March a third element was added to Israel's preoccupations in the form of widespread unrest among elements of the Arab population of the West Bank, stemming from the dismissal by the Israeli authorities of elected Palestinian councils and mayors in several West Bank districts. A number of people died when Palestinian demonstrators clashed with Israeli troops. Menachem Milson, civil administrator of the West Bank, accused some Arab mayors of being PLO agents and questioned the fairness of the elections that had brought them to power in 1976. Further Arab protests followed the shooting of two Muslims by a deranged Jewish immigrant in Jerusalem on April 11.

Despite the repeated limited assurances given to the U.S., and also to France's Pres. François Mitterrand during his state visit to Israel on March 3–5, it was evident in Jerusalem that an Israeli strike against the PLO would not be delayed much longer. Negotiations between the Israeli authorities and the leaders of Lebanon's Maronite Christian community—especially with the commanders of its military forces, led by Bashir Gemayel—had been under way for years rather than months. The Lebanese Christian leaders were becoming impatient for action against the PLO. According to the information relayed to the Israelis by Gemayel and his associates, the PLO was preparing to block Gemayel's intended candidacy in the Lebanese presidential election due in September. But the PLO could do this effectively only if it first neutralized Israeli assistance to the Maronites. In order to do this, PLO forces began to deploy guns and rockets directed at northern Israel. Convinced by Gemayel's arguments, the Israelis agreed that the operation against the PLO, if it was to be of lasting effect, would have to aim at Beirut and the PLO heartland position.

MILNER–SYGMA

Hundreds of Israeli squatters had to be removed by force from illegal settlements in the Sinai before the April transfer to Egypt.

On June 3 Israel's ambassador to the U.K., Shlomo Argov, was shot and gravely wounded in London. Two days later Israeli jets bombed PLO targets in Beirut. By the early hours of June 6, the operation against Lebanon was under way: Tyre was occupied on June 7; Sidon on June 8; Damur on June 9. The encirclement of Beirut was complete by June 14. At this point the Israeli government came under heavy pressure from the U.S. not to let its troops enter Beirut. Prime Minister Begin and a majority of Cabinet ministers agreed, and Defense Minister Ariel Sharon had to accept the majority opinion. The advance was halted and replaced by indirect negotiations with the PLO through U.S. special envoy Philip Habib and the Lebanese government. These proceeded inconclusively while the military situation remained suspended.

By July 4 Habib had informed the Israeli negotiators that the PLO was ready to sign an undertaking to evacuate Beirut. This was followed by a long process of equivocation and delay while the PLO leaders sought political reassurances from the U.S. In the event, it was only after massive Israeli bombardments of West Beirut, which resumed toward the end of July and reached their fiercest pitch on August 12, that the PLO accepted the evacuation terms.

The PLO evacuation on August 21, supervised by a multinational force of U.S., French, and Italian troops, was followed by the election of Bashir Gemayel as president of Lebanon. On September 14, however, Gemayel was assassinated, and Israeli plans were hastily revised. Reversing previous policies and undertakings, Defense Minister Sharon ordered the IDF into West Beirut in order, he claimed, to make certain that there would be no large-scale massacre of Palestinians and Muslims in the wake of Gemayel's death. Nevertheless, Lebanese Christian forces entered the Sabra and Shatila refugee camps in West Beirut on September 16, and hundreds of Palestinian men, women, and children were massacred. Israel received widespread condemnation for its alleged complicity in the tragedy. Yielding to internal and external pressure, the Cabinet finally voted on September 28 to set up a state commission inquiry under Chief Justice Yitzhak Kahan to ascertain Israel's responsibility. The inquiry was still under way at year's end.

While virtually all the Israeli media were hostile to the government's position and particularly toward Sharon, the government's popularity among the voters remained high. It far surpassed that of the opposition Labour Alignment parties who, in varying degrees, had criticized the inception and conduct of the war in Lebanon.

The validity of the government's justification for launching the attack on the PLO would depend on the extent to which it could uphold its indictment of the PLO as a "form of gangster state within the state of Lebanon." The display of equipment captured in southern Lebanon lent credence to the claim that the PLO was preparing a major assault on northern Israel. The IDF took intact some 500 pieces of artillery from PLO positions in southern Lebanon. On the other hand, the IDF was singularly unwilling to produce its estimates of civilian casualties. At the end of December, Israeli and Lebanese delegations, with a U.S. delegation headed by special envoy Morris Draper in attendance, began talks on relations between the two countries. The initial meetings, held at Khaldah in Lebanon and Qiryat Shemona in Israel, produced no substantive results.

Other events during the year were no less traumatic for Israelis. They included the dismantling of much of the Israel built by the founding fathers and dramatic changes in the economic basis of the state. A number of enterprises were returned to the private sector, not least among them the national airline, El Al, which went into liquidation after a long series of punishing labour conflicts. The Begin regime was replacing Labour stalwarts with its own people in the administrative and diplomatic fields.

(*See also* Middle Eastern Affairs.)

ITALY

The release on Jan. 28, 1982, in Padua by a special police commando unit of Brig. Gen. James Dozier, a senior U.S. NATO officer taken hostage by Red Brigades terrorists from his Verona home in December 1981, marked a turning point in the Italian authorities' fight against terrorist crime. Dozier's five captors, including two women, were arrested inside the apartment where they had held him captive. They were sentenced to long terms in prison.

Information gathered by police from the Padua operation and from captured terrorists who decided to turn state's evidence in exchange for promises of leniency in sentencing led to the arrest and prosecution of hundreds of terrorist suspects during the year. The most important and longest terrorist trial ever held in Italy began in Rome on April 14, when 63 alleged members of the Red Brigades appeared in a heavily guarded courtroom to face charges of kidnapping and murdering former premier Aldo Moro in 1978. The accused were also charged with a total of 16 murders and 11 attempted murders during a four-year period from 1976. A verdict was expected in the spring of 1983.

Another terrorist trial, of members of the Front Line Urban Guerrilla Organization, ended in Bergamo in August after eight months of hearings. The jury took a record 16 days to reach its verdict. Sentences totaling more than 450 years in prison were handed down to 87 of the accused.

Middle East violence spilled over into Italy in two incidents in Rome. In June Kamal Hussein, second in command of the Palestine Liberation Organization's office in Italy, was murdered by a bomb placed under his car. In October unidentified gunmen opened fire on a group of worshippers coming out of Rome's main synagogue, killing a two-year-old boy and injuring 35 Jews in Italy's worst anti-Semitic incident in years.

Italy's most serious single act of terrorism in 1982 was, however, carried out as a warning by the Sicilian Mafia. Gen. Carlo Alberto Dalla Chiesa and his wife were assassinated in Palermo, Sicily, on September 3. Dalla Chiesa, the antiterrorist chief credited with a major role in previous battles against the Red Brigades, had been sent to Sicily in May as the civilian prefect of Palermo with a mandate to chal-

lenge and beat the power of the Mafia, which was based on the lucrative heroin trade with the U.S.

The Rome government responded to the assassination by pushing through Parliament a new anti-Mafia law that gave the police wider powers to tackle Mafia crime. Pope John Paul II visited Palermo in November to add his voice to the general denunciation of the Mafia and to confirm the decision of his bishops in Sicily to excommunicate those committing Mafia crimes of violence.

The arrest of a Bulgarian airline official, Sergey Antonov, in Rome on November 25 was the first official confirmation of the Italian government's allegations that there had been a plot hatched in Eastern Europe to kill Pope John Paul II in May 1981. An Italian investigating magistrate, Ilario Martella, acting mainly on evidence from Mehmet Ali Agca, the Turkish terrorist who actually shot the pope and was sentenced to life imprisonment for his crime, also accused two Bulgarian diplomats formerly accredited to Rome of complicity in the shooting. But the prospects of the Italian judiciary's finding out the truth about a Bulgarian connection with the plot to kill the pope appeared dim.

In May Italy's ruling Christian Democrat Party elected a new party secretary, Ciriaco De Mita. The Christian Democrats, despite a series of government crises during the year, showed no signs of loosening their hold on power. They regained the premiership after a hiatus of almost 18 months when in November the veteran Christian Democrat politician Amintore Fanfani, 74, took over from Giovanni Spadolini, leader of the small Republican Party, who had headed the two previous coalitions.

Foreign Affairs

Italy and the Vatican exchanged diplomatic notes over the involvement of the Vatican bank, the Institute for Religious Works (IOR), in a major Italian

An October 9 attack by terrorists on the main synagogue in Rome left one child dead and 35 persons injured and caused extensive damage.
FABIAN—SYGMA

banking scandal. The Banco Ambrosiano of Milan, formerly Italy's biggest private banking group, in which the Vatican bank was a shareholder, went into forced liquidation after the death in London in mysterious circumstances of its chairman, Roberto Calvi. A joint commission was set up by Italy and the Vatican to sort out the losses involved in a series of complex financial deals concluded between Calvi and Archbishop Paul C. Marcinkus, president of the Vatican bank.

The Italian government rejected U.S. Pres. Ronald Reagan's ban on U.S. technology for turbines manufactured in Italy for the Siberian gas pipeline, due to bring Soviet natural gas to Western Europe by the mid-1980s. The government signed a long-term agreement with Algeria for the supply of natural gas through a newly completed undersea pipeline between North Africa and Sicily.

The Economy

In June Italy's employers' federation, Confindustria, announced that it was pulling out of a wage-indexing agreement because of its inflationary effect. Protracted negotiations between labour unions and employers to find a substitute basis for wage indexing failed to produce any agreement. The economy stagnated, while inflation stood at 16% at year's end, one of the highest rates in Western Europe.

A $1 billion joint venture between the Italian state oil company, ENI, and Occidental Petroleum Corp. of the U.S. aimed at helping Italy's ailing chemical industry was abandoned shortly after it came into force when the U.S. parent company objected to plans to take over an unprofitable factory.

JAPAN

In November 1981 Prime Minister Zenko Suzuki had reshuffled his Cabinet with an eye on factional strength within the ruling Liberal-Democratic Party (LDP) and a view toward the next election for LDP president, scheduled for late fall of 1982. He named Susumu Nikaido to be secretary-general of the par-

ty. Nikaido had been nominal head of the powerful 106-member faction actually led by former prime minister Kakuei Tanaka. A veteran politician, Yoshio Sakarauchi, was selected as foreign minister, and Kiichi Miyazawa was retained as chief Cabinet secretary. Among established faction leaders, Yasuhiro Nakasone remained director general of the Administrative Management Agency, charged with the sensitive issue of administrative reform, and Toshio Komoto was retained as head of the Economic Planning Agency (EPA).

On Jan. 18, 1982, the 96th regular session of the Diet (parliament) was reconvened in the presence of the emperor. In his policy speech, Prime Minister Suzuki promised to restructure the government in order to rehabilitate the national finances, burdened with a cumulative debt of 82 trillion yen. On February 3 Suzuki declared that he would assume "political responsibility" if his fiscal program failed to achieve the goal of eliminating deficit bond issues by the end of fiscal year 1984. The press interpreted the statement as a de facto declaration that he intended to remain in office at least two more years.

Nevertheless, according to a *Yomiuri* newspaper opinion poll taken February 20–21, support for the Suzuki administration had dropped by 6.2 points in the space of a month, to 31.7% of those polled. It was the lowest level since the regime was inaugurated in July 1980.

Yet another factor affecting the fate of the Suzuki government—and, indeed, of the LDP majority leadership—was the long-awaited outcome of the Lockheed affair, which had first surfaced in February 1976. The scandal, directly involving former prime minister Tanaka, had to do with procurement of aircraft for All Nippon Airways (ANA). On January 25 Tokuji Wakasa, board chairman of ANA, was given a suspended three-year prison sentence. On June 8 former transport minister Tomisaburo Hashimoto and his ex-vice-minister were also found guilty, of "accepting bribes upon entreaties." A ruling on Tanaka was expected within a year.

Prime Minister Zenko Suzuki (right) toasted Chinese Premier Zhao Ziyang during Zhao's visit to Japan in May.
WIDE WORLD

On October 12 Suzuki suddenly announced that he would not stand in the forthcoming party primary and, therefore, would also relinquish the prime ministership. Although LDP leaders tried desperately to settle the succession issue behind the scenes, four faction leaders entered the preliminary party primary on November 23. In the poll Nakasone received 58% of the nearly one million votes cast by eligible members of the LDP. On November 25 the 421 LDP members of the Diet selected Nakasone to be president of the party, and the next day he was elected Japan's 17th postwar prime minister.

Final figures for the fiscal year April 1980–March 1981 showed Japan's gross national product (GNP) at 239,155,000,000,000 yen (264 yen=U.S. $1) in nominal terms; in real terms (1975 prices) the growth rate was 3.7% over fiscal 1979. In December 1981 the EPA estimated nominal GNP at 250,658,300,000,000 yen ($1.2 trillion), with an adjusted annual growth rate of between 4 and 5% for fiscal 1981.

Late in December 1981 the Cabinet had approved a 1982 budget incorporating expenditures of 49,680,800,000,000 yen, a 6.2% increase over the previous year (the lowest rate of expansion in 26 years). Defense appropriations accounted for a 7.8% increase (to a total representing 0.9% of GNP), the first time in several decades that defense expenditures had outpaced the increase in general accounts. The press interpreted the defense buildup as a response to U.S. pressure. On July 9 the Cabinet apreduced budgetary requests for fiscal 1983 by 5% across the board; however, defense, foreign aid, and pensions were exempt from cuts.

During the year the Japanese staggered under a series of blows dealt by man-made and natural disasters. On February 8, in the worst hotel fire since World War II, 32 guests were killed and 30 injured in a predawn blaze that swept through the Hotel New Japan in Tokyo. The next day a Japan Air Lines DC-8 crashed in shallow waters off Tokyo's Haneda Airport, killing 24 and injuring 150. On March 14 a violent earthquake (force 6 on the Japanese scale of 7) shook Hokkaido and northern Honshu, injuring 99 persons and causing extensive damage. In August in Nagasaki a public funeral service was held for 275 victims who died in the July 23–25 flood that wreaked havoc throughout Kyushu. On August 1 Typhoon No. 10 cut a swath of destruction across central Honshu, leaving 59 persons dead and 24 missing.

Foreign Affairs

During June Japan, represented abroad by Prime Minister Suzuki, played out the role of an advanced industrial power. At the eighth summit meeting of industrialized Western democracies, held at Versailles, France, June 4–6, Suzuki emphasized the importance of "assurance of employment through promotion of science and technology" in order to overcome world economic problems.

UPI

Yasuhiro Nakasone was elected prime minister in November by the Liberal Democratic Party, which had ruled Japan for 27 years.

After the summit, on June 9, Suzuki flew to New York to attend the UN special session on disarmament. As the first speaker, he spelled out a three-point proposal calling for disarmament, the transfer of resources to promote economic development, and reinforcement of UN peacekeeping functions.

At Versailles Suzuki found himself under considerable pressure because of trade surpluses with the U.S. and with the European Community (EC). Customs clearance statistics for 1981 revealed that Japan had chalked up its biggest ever surplus with the U.S., a total of $13.4 billion. With the EC, a record surplus of $10.3 billion was recorded.

With the U.S., Japan's closest ally, Tokyo faced a number of critical issues, including the trade surplus, the sanctions proposed against the Soviet Union for its actions in Poland, and the question of the level of Japan's defense effort. In March, in Washington, U.S. Secretary of State Alexander Haig, in talks with Foreign Minister Sakarauchi, openly criticized congressional moves toward protectionist legislation directed at Japan. The two failed, however, to agree on the U.S. request that Tokyo delay fulfillment of a contract between Komatsu, the nation's largest earth-moving-equipment firm, and the Soviet Union. On June 4 in Paris, Suzuki asked U.S. Pres. Ronald Reagan to exempt the Japan-Soviet Sakhalin oil-development project, which had been agreed

After the arrest of six Hitachi and Mitsubishi employees by the FBI, a Hitachi executive explained that his people had been caught in an elaborate "sting" operation.
WIDE WORLD

upon before sanctions were suggested.

In the area of trade, Washington was calling on Tokyo to abolish some 22 import quotas on fishery and agricultural products, specifically on beef and on citrus fruits. On April 16 in Tokyo, the president of a national federation of agricultural cooperatives, Shizuma Iwamochi, told about 8,000 demonstrating farmers that his organization would defend the nation's agriculture "to the death."

In spite of the increase in defense expenditures in the current budget, Washington was not satisfied. U.S. Defense Secretary Caspar Weinberger, visiting Tokyo in March, proposed that expansion of Japan's defense capability be designed to protect sea lanes up to 1,000 nautical miles from its coasts.

In what was called in Tokyo a "sting" operation, the FBI on June 22 arrested five employees of the Hitachi and Mitsubishi electronics firms in the San Francisco area on charges that they had paid $648,000 to an undercover agent to steal computer data from IBM. Warrants were also issued for 12 employees in Japan. By July 21 the men had been indicted by a federal grand jury in San Jose, Calif. Hitachi claimed that its employees had "bought" computer technology from "a consulting firm," while Mitsubishi flatly denied the FBI allegations. Meanwhile, on July 20 in San Francisco, a federal grand jury indicted Mitsui & Co. (U.S.A.) for allegedly conspiring to sell steel in the U.S. below market prices. Mitsui, claiming that the case involved a misunderstanding of import procedures, agreed to seek an out-of-court settlement.

Japanese-Soviet relations during the year were dominated by developments in Poland. In December 1981, Zdzizlaw Rurarz, Poland's ambassador to Japan, was protected until he left Tokyo for the U.S., after Washington had granted him political asylum. He was the first ambassador in Japan ever to defect. On February 23 Japan joined the U.S.,

Britain, and West Germany in imposing limited sanctions on Poland's military regime and its Soviet supporters. The government announced that it would honour pledges for "humanitarian aid" to the Polish people.

Japan's relations with its nearer neighbours were mixed. In July Foreign Minister Lee Bum-suk of South Korea, in consultation with Foreign Minister Sakarauchi in Tokyo, agreed to accept Japan's offer of $4 billion in aid to help Seoul's five-year plan (1982–86). At a joint ministerial meeting in Tokyo in December 1981, Japan pledged to provide $1.4 billion in aid to China to help revive China's stalled industrial projects. Chinese Premier Zhao Ziyang (Chao Tzu-yang) visited Tokyo in May–June.

Ties with both China and Korea were severely strained, however, by the so-called Japanese textbook issue. Late in July it was revealed that Japan's Education Ministry had approved alterations in schoolbooks so that, for example, the nation's aggression in China prior to 1945 was described as an "advance." Similarly, pre-World War II opposition to Japanese colonial rule in Korea was called a "riot" against authority. The Chinese reacted angrily, and in Seoul sentiment built steadily as the August 15 anniversary of Korea's national liberation from 35 years of Japanese rule approached. On August 4 Prime Minister Suzuki stated that there was no change in his government's policy, first articulated in the 1972 Sino-Japanese joint communiqué, that Japan "repents its faults in the past." On August 20 Tokyo offered reassurances to Seoul that the issue would be settled in good faith, and on August 26 it was announced that Japan intended "to do its best to make textbook descriptions in question more appropriate." Despite expectations that his return visit would be postponed, Suzuki arrived in Beijing (Peking) on September 26 to commemorate a decade of normalized Sino-Japanese relations.

Special Report:
Japan's Economic Secret

by Frank Gibney

The rest of the world's business leaders—not to mention the economists and the politicians—continue to be alternately impressed, puzzled, or angered by the extraordinary success of Japan's "economic miracle" and the alert, toughly competitive business society that made it. During the past two decades Japan's economy has weathered oil shortages, foreign export restrictions, and domestic recessions; and its statistics are business history. In 1960 Japan's $39.1 billion gross national product (GNP) was not quite 8% of that of the U.S. Japan's $1 trillion GNP in 1980 was almost 40% of the U.S. total. In per capita GNP Japan will probably pass the U.S. before 1990. Exports worth $12 billion in 1968 had become $140 billion by 1980.

Nowhere has the rate of productivity risen so fast or so steadily. If the 1960 level of Japanese productivity in manufacturing is set at 100, the 1980 level is more than 450. Japanese steel, Japanese cars, Japanese television sets, ships, cameras, and chemicals—and now Japan's semiconductor chips, computers, and overseas factories—have made consumers throughout the world satisfied and dependent. No other nation's private entrepreneurs have carried off such brilliant marketing strategies.

Although the Japanese over the past two years have experienced something of a recession in the domestic economy, their productivity and GNP figures continue to rise—if at a reduced rate—and the flood of high-quality exports continues to pose problems for home-grown industry in the U.S., Europe, and some of the other East Asian countries. Despite their economic successes the Japanese have not been good international politicians. Their attitude remains determinedly insular. Continuing trade restrictions on some imports into Japan—especially on such highly visible products as tobacco and citrus fruits—have brought angry threats of retaliation from U.S. producers. Suffering unemployment and the worst business depression of recent history, U.S. automakers and labour union officials alike are demanding protectionist legislation; and congressmen are listening to them.

People-Centred Capitalism

There is some truth to their charges of "unfair" competition in certain areas. But instead of simply dismissing Japan's success as "unfair competition," it would be more useful to see how this success was achieved—and what lessons can be learned from it.

One can neither understand the nature of Japan's economic success nor learn from it unless it is seen in its social as well as economic context. Much of Japan's business society is strange to those in the West. Everyday words such as law, contract, board of directors, labour union, manager, and stockholder—even such basic terms as company and employee—hold different meanings for the Japanese and for those in the Western world. Whereas business society in the West is based on the Christian ethic of individuals, that in Japan grew from the Confucian ethic of relationships. The Japanese have different priorities—different views of wealth, of sufficiency, and of satisfaction. Yet the philosophy of their business as well as its techniques—indeed their modern version of free enterprise democracy—resembles that of the U.S. more than it does anyone else's, and owes much to it.

To begin with, the Japanese are for our time the original practitioners of supply-side economics. They accumulated capital and used it in the classic way—for plant modernization and technology development. They saved prodigiously to provide ever more investment funds. But then they took the standard idea of capital one step further. Western economists tended to think of capital in terms of money, plant, material, and technology. To this, however, the Japanese capitalist adds people. The most conspicuous characteristic of Japanese capitalism is its belief that long-term investment in people—which includes training them, partly educating them, and developing them within a company—is fully as important as long-term investment in plant.

Those in the West have worried about the individual worker's self-fulfillment or alienation. They have shaken their heads at "soulless" corporations that treat workers as virtually interchangeable parts—by definition separated from the management and ownership of their companies. The Japanese, partly from old tradition and partly from modern necessity, simply infused human values into the corporation. They made the company a village. And in so doing not only have they given the worker a sense of belonging; they have also given the company a constituency that speaks up for it: its own workers. A variety of practices—the system of lifetime employment used by Japan's major corporations, the seniority system, the companywide bonuses or "base-ups" founded on profits and paid out to blue-collar and white-collar workers alike—all add up to a unique

MIYAZAWA–BLACK STAR

Two employees of Matsushita Electric are married in the company club, epitomizing the family atmosphere in many Japanese firms.

kind of "people-centred" capitalism.

Once in charge of a corporation, the average U.S. businessman will want to make the major decisions himself and lead his people after him. By contrast, the Japanese leader's ideal is to encourage those under him to formulate decisions. Although there are "dynamic leader" types in Japan and "consensus" types in the U.S., the ideals of the two capitalisms differ. A Japanese economist contrasted them this way: "Our system is rather like an electric train, with each car having its own motor, whereas your system is more like a long train drawn by two or three strong locomotives, with no motors in the other cars. You tell your workers to follow. We like people to have their own motivation—and move together."

Japan's top executives continue to be distinguished also by their relatively low rates of compensation, at least compared to the galloping expansion of corporate salaries in the U.S. The gap between the president's salary and stock option package and the wages of the average worker is nowhere so vast in Japan as it is in the U.S. Prestige and power the Japanese president seeks. But money does not seem to be a primary motivation.

Role of the U.S.

Yet despite their strong work ethic—and the advantages of a well-educated, homogeneous society—the Japanese could not have got where they are today without U.S. aid and example. In the first years after World War II the U.S. occupation first fed the Japanese and then supplied enough technical skill, money, and direction to start the wheels of Japan's industry slowly turning again. And without the sweeping "rationalization" of Japanese business and industry under the 1949 Dodge Plan, the economy could not have gone ahead. The Korean War also provided Japan with an unexpected windfall, in the form of $3 billion worth of arms, military equipment, and supplies purchased there for the U.S. and UN war effort.

Through the 1950s and 1960s there was a rush to acquire U.S. technology. This the Japanese imported wholesale, through a variety of licensing arrangements used and adapted to great advantage. Although the Japanese have had since 1973 a favourable trade balance in technology licensing revenues, the opposite was once true. The Japanese drive to a greater productivity was inspired by the U.S. as part of the effort during the postwar occupation to make Japan more self-sufficient. The Japan Productivity Center, a pioneer in this work, was originally set up with U.S. government funds. In the 1960s, as postwar Japanese business came of age, a procession of pilgrims crossed the Pacific to worship at the shrines of U.S. management efficiency techniques, as taught by various U.S. business schools. These lessons were duly brought back to Japan, digested—and modified.

Besides these tangible contributions there has been the effect, less measurable but immense, of U.S. democracy, innovation, and optimism on the thinking of the Japanese. The attempted U.S. "democratization" of Japan served to ventilate the closed world of Japanese capitalism and semidemocratic practice. It imposed on the Japanese—some would say restored—a feeling for wider freedoms and broader horizons.

Nihachiro Hanamura, vice-chairman of the powerful Keidanren (Federation of Economic Organizations), has labeled this U.S. influence, along with Japan's political stability, one of the major factors underlying Japan's high-growth economy. He said: First, there was a thorough democratization by the Occupation forces in the early postwar years of all old systems—political, economic, social, cultural, and educational. The breaking up of the zaibatsu—giant financial, industrial, and business groups—and agricultural land reform was at the core of the policy of economic democratization. As a result every Japanese stood at the same starting point, and an environment was provided in which everyone was rewarded according to the effort that was exerted. This generated in every Japanese a willingness to study and work hard, just as in the frontier days of the U.S.

One should not underrate the importance of this U.S. inspiration, however much it may have been modified. The so-called 21st-century capitalists of Japan owe much to the 20th-century capitalism of the United States.

DAVID KENNERLY—GAMMA/LIAISON

While discussing advanced military hardware in Jordan in February, U.S. Secretary of Defense Caspar Weinberger (left) toured an army base with King Hussein.

JORDAN

Jordan was assured a central role in talks on a Middle East peace settlement when, on Sept. 1, 1982, U.S. Pres. Ronald Reagan revived what had come to be termed the "Jordanian option." This option ruled out the Palestinians' principal demand for total independence, substituting instead proposals for "self-government by the Palestinians of the West Bank and Gaza in association with Jordan." The proposal implicitly revived U.S. plans for the Middle East that originally had circulated in 1978 at the time of the Camp David agreement.

There was no immediate reaction from Jordan, but only days earlier, after greeting a contingent of Palestine Liberation Organization (PLO) guerrillas who had been evacuated from Lebanon, King Hussein reiterated his support for the efforts of the PLO to recover the West Bank and Gaza and declared that the PLO was not finished as a force in the Middle East. In mid-September Hussein described the U.S. peace plan as "a very constructive and a very positive move." Following two days of talks in mid-December, the Jordanian government and the PLO agreed that Jordan should have a "special and distinctive relationship" with any future Palestinian entity. During a visit to Washington later in the month, however, Hussein indicated that conditions were not yet ripe for Jordan to enter the negotiations for Palestinian autonomy.

Israel's outraged reaction to a visit by U.S. Secretary of Defense Caspar Weinberger to Jordan in February elicited a denial by President Reagan that his administration was planning to sell advanced military hardware to Jordan. Nevertheless, reports in the *New York Times* in September suggested that the U.S. was indeed prepared to sell Jordan a package that was thought to include mobile Hawk anti-aircraft missiles, F-5 interceptors, and possibly F-16 fighter-bombers. Jordan advanced as the reason for the request the threat to its air space from Syria.

Jordan's support for Iraq in the latter's war against Iran continued. In January King Hussein announced that a contingent of Jordanian volunteers, to be named the "Yarmouk Brigade," was to be formed to fight alongside Iraqi forces. He called for an "arabization" of the war against Iran.

Another type of assistance granted to Iraq put considerable pressure on the southern Jordanian port of Aqaba, where in 1981 some 62% of incoming shipments were in transit and in the main destined for Iraq. Jordan offered to help in the building of a terminal for Iraq's proposed trans-Arabian oil pipeline, while, if Iraq's finances improved, it was to pay for three new berths south of Aqaba's container terminal. Even if the Iran-Iraq war were to end quickly, it was predicted that it would take years to clear the Shatt al-Arab waterway of bombs and wreckage.

The Arab Potash Co.'s ambitious Dead Sea extraction plant was opened on March 18 by the king. Commercial production started late in 1982, with a planned rate of 240,000 metric tons a year to be achieved by 1986. Overall the economy was guided by the five-year (1981–85) social and economic development plan. Revisions to the plan in 1982 raised projected spending to $9,970,000,000. As in the previous plan, a heavy commitment from the private sector was envisioned as well as a continuing reliance on foreign aid. Remittances from Jordanians in other countries were also forecast to grow, despite a decline in the number of Jordanians going to work in the Persian Gulf nations. Income from this source had grown from the equivalent of $100 million in 1974 to more than $2 billion in 1980. In an interview in June, Crown Prince Hassan said that Jordan's manpower pyramid was "upside down"; technical skills acquired by Jordanians working abroad had not been exploited at home because of the failure to build a technical base there.

Prince Norodom Sihanouk (left) and former premier Son Sann formed a Kampuchean coalition government-in-exile with Khieu Samphan of the Communist Khmer Rouge in June.
UPI

KAMPUCHEA

Kampuchea reemerged into the international limelight in 1982 as the three principal anti-Vietnamese Khmer forces formed a coalition to combat Vietnam's continued military occupation of their homeland. At the same time, there were continued efforts by the Vietnam-backed government of Pres. Heng Samrin to consolidate its position and restore normal life to the war- and famine-ravaged country.

Not long after agreeing in principle in September 1981 to form a "loose coalition," the Communist Khmer Rouge, former premier Son Sann of the anti-Communist Khmer People's National Liberation Front, and Prince Norodom Sihanouk of the neutralist National Liberation Movement of Kampuchea (Moulinaka) were publicly at odds over power distribution and administrative arrangements. In February 1982 the trio's principal backer, the Association of Southeast Asian Nations (ASEAN), voiced impatience over the lack of progress. Apparently fearful that ASEAN might drop its support for the Chinese-aided Khmer Rouge as the legitimate occupant of the Democratic Kampuchea seat at the UN, China agreed to act as host to a meeting of the Khmer resistance leaders. In late February Sihanouk parleyed with the Khmer Rouge's Khieu Samphan in the Chinese capital and, after making certain compromises, announced he had reached "initial agreement" with his former enemies.

It took a few more months before the firm-principled Son Sann was brought around to joining forces with the Khmer Rouge, under whose regime in 1975–79 more than a million Kampucheans were reportedly killed. Prodded by ASEAN and China, however, Sihanouk, Son Sann, and Khieu Samphan met in Kuala Lumpur, Malaysia, and on June 22 signed a declaration that they would form a coalition government of Democratic Kampuchea. Sihanouk, once his country's head of state, became president, while the post of premier went to Son Sann. Khieu Samphan was made vice-president.

Though Vietnam publicly scorned the coalition, privately it was clearly worried, particularly about

the political respectability Sihanouk and Son Sann lent Democratic Kampuchea. It tried to gain ASEAN's goodwill by withdrawing some 8,000 of its estimated 180,000 troops in Kampuchea, but the move was widely decried as a "meaningless" rotation of soldiers. Vietnam's fears became reality when the UN General Assembly voted that Democratic Kampuchea should retain its seat.

Kampuchea's once-critical food situation improved. Increased agricultural yields, together with international assistance, made starvation largely a thing of the past. Further increases in food production, however, were slowed by increased collectivization of agriculture. Attempts to raise a national army met with limited success; problems included desertion, draft evasion, low-quality training, and lack of enthusiasm in fighting resistance forces. Though most Kampucheans continued to fear the return of the Khmer Rouge, there was also growing resentment of the Vietnamese presence.

KENYA

A bitter and wholly unexpected attack on Asian businessmen by Kenya's president, Daniel arap Moi, was made during a speech in February 1982. Asians, the president said, were guilty of hoarding essential goods and selling them on the black market and were ruining the economy by smuggling currency out of the country; any Asians, even citizens of Kenya, found guilty of these charges would be deported.

Kenya suffered from serious shortages throughout 1982, and the economy faced considerable problems. This may have been one reason for the reshuffling of the Cabinet in February; although no minister was dropped, only 9 out of the 26 retained their original portfolios. Most surprising was the transfer of Vice-Pres. Mwai Kibaki from the Ministry of Finance to the Home Affairs Ministry and his replacement by Arthur Magugu, who was not known to have had any experience of financial issues.

Vigorous criticism of the government's economic

policies was voiced by former vice-president Oginga Odinga in February. He claimed that Kenya's resources had been subjected to systematic plunder, leading to mass unemployment, and that this situation could not be explained away by reference to high oil prices and international inflation. Odinga was not the only critic of the government; a play by the novelist and playwright Ngugi wa Thiong'o was banned without explanation in May. It was known that the play pursued the theme of some of Ngugi's novels, which had drawn parallels between the condition of Kenyan Africans under the colonial regime and that of peasants under the independent government.

Army troops in Kenya celebrated after successfully crushing an attempted coup by members of the Air Force and university students.
DUNCAN WILLETTS—CAMERAPIX/KEYSTONE

The government reacted severely to Odinga's speech. In May he was expelled from the ruling Kenya African National Union (KANU) by the president, in July his passport was withdrawn, and in November he was placed under house arrest. Meanwhile, in June three other persons were detained under the Preservation of Public Security Act. One, Mwangi Stephen Muriithi, had been deputy director of intelligence until relieved of his post in 1981. The second, George Anyona, had been expelled from KANU along with Odinga after advocating the formation of another political party. (Kenya became officially a one-party state in June 1982 when Parliament amended the constitution.) The third, John Khaminwa, was a lawyer who had acted on behalf of the other two. In July George Githii, editor of Kenya's *The Standard* newspaper, was dismissed after writing an article critical of the detention of the three.

Whether the government's fear of its critics was justified or whether its severe action against alleged subversives actually provoked resistance was difficult to determine, but on August 1 a number of air force personnel, enlisting the support of several hundred university students, tried to overthrow the government. The government reacted swiftly, and the uprising was soon put down by the Army and police. There was a brief wave of opportunist looting, mainly of Asian shops and houses because of the feeling that had been generated against the Asian community, but there was little overt support for the attempted coup.

The organizers of the uprising were difficult to locate. Although an air force private and sergeant who had fled to Tanzania claimed to have been its leaders, there was some doubt about their ability to plan such an operation. In any case the Tanzanian government refused to repatriate the two refugees as requested by Kenya. As a precaution against further troubles the president disbanded the Air Force, and heavy sentences were passed by courts-martial on a number of persons accused of some responsibility for the coup attempt. Some civilians, members of the Luo tribe, were also arrested, including the son of Oginga Odinga.

KOREA

Just over a year after North Korean leader Kim Il Sung announced his plan for reunification of the country, South Korean Pres. Chun Doo Hwan responded with the most detailed blueprint ever to emerge from Seoul. The proposal called for the convening of a bilateral, Cabinet-level conference to set up a summit meeting between the two heads of state; they would then negotiate a provisional agreement that would ultimately lead to a new and mutually acceptable constitution and also to free elections for a unified government on the peninsula. The proposal would leave intact South Korea's mutual defense treaty with the U.S. as well as the North's alliances with China and the U.S.S.R.

Chun's plan was quickly rejected by North Korean Vice-Pres. Kim Il, who merely repeated Kim Il Sung's proposal for a Korean confederation and such demands as the withdrawal of the 40,000 U.S. troops in the South, President Chun's resignation, abrogation of internal security laws, and the release of political prisoners. Analysts believed that, in the absence of drastic changes, neither side was likely to alter its position on reunification.

Pres. Chun announced in January 1982 that the country's 36-year-old midnight-to-4 AM curfew was to be scrapped and that Prime Minister Nam Duck Woo was to be replaced by Yoo Chang Soon, an economics expert. The lifting of the curfew, widely welcomed, was seen as a sign of confidence in increased social stability since Chun's seizure of power during the turbulent period following the assassination of former president Park Chung Hee in 1979.

Chun proclaimed a general amnesty on March 3, the first anniversary of his inauguration as president. Religious groups and human-rights activists complained, however, that only one-tenth of the 2,863 people pardoned were political offenders. The country's best known opposition leader, Kim Dae Jung, had his life sentence reduced to 20 years. In December, in a surprise move, Kim was freed. He immediately left for the U.S., and there were questions as to whether he was in fact exiled.

On April 26 a young policeman shocked the nation by going on a murderous rampage in rural Uiryong, killing 56 innocent people before blowing himself up. Questions were raised as to why security personnel had been unable to stop the killer and whether there had been a serious neglect of duty on the part of those who, among other things, were supposed to protect the country from North Korean infiltration and sabotage.

A much bigger scandal erupted in May. Socialite Chang Yong Ja and her husband, Lee Chul Hi, were charged with defrauding six companies of $250 million by manipulating South Korea's vast underground "curb" money market, in which private loans were transacted. Chang, whose brother-in-law was an uncle of President Chun's wife, and Lee were also accused of using connections in high places to extract large sums of money from government-controlled banks.

The political repercussions were drastic. Chun, whose presidency had been marked by a strong stress on integrity and moral purity, found himself obliged to replace half of his 22-member Cabinet. Chun again revamped his Cabinet in June. Yoo Chang Soon was replaced as prime minister by educationist Kim Sang Hyup.

After two decades of remarkably rapid growth, the economy since 1980 had been buffeted by rising oil prices, the global recession, soaring interest rates, and increasing foreign restrictions on Korean exports. The government announced a series of dramatic steps to lift the country's debt-ridden big business out of recession. Bank interest rates were immediately cut by four percentage points, while corporate taxes were to be trimmed by up to 18 percentage points by 1983.

South Korea's efforts to negotiate a massive development loan from Japan were suddenly disrupted in July by a fierce controversy over the latter's attempt to revise its history textbooks in order to downplay Japanese atrocities during the occupation of Korea in World War II. The storm abated in September, however, and the two governments settled on a Japanese aid package worth $4 billion.

Democratic People's Republic of Korea (North Korea)

Events in North Korea centred on the continuing efforts of Pres. Kim Il Sung to pass power on to his son, Kim Chong Il. Over the past few years Kim Chong Il had been in charge of most day-to-day affairs of the Workers' Party of Korea, and he was expected to be named a vice-president in 1982. But he failed to gain any top government post when a

Chang Yong Ja, socialite wife of Lee Chul Hi, former deputy director of the Korean CIA, was taken to court in July.
WIDE WORLD

new Cabinet was selected in April, after general elections in February. Analysts attributed this to resistance to the younger Kim by veteran military officers, who believed that he was too young and inexperienced to inherit his father's mantle.

Even so, the apparent setback was likely to be only temporary, for Kim Chong Il continued to appear by his father's side. The prospect of Kim Chong Il's eventual rise to supreme power worried South Korea, which viewed him as being even more dogmatic and martial-minded than his father.

With North Korea currently spending a quarter of its $16.2 billion gross national product on defense (against South Korea's 6% of $58 billion), South Korean and U.S. intelligence analysts feared that the North might be tempted to strike at the South while it enjoyed a distinct military advantage. Reliable economic indicators for North Korea were difficult to obtain, but economists believed that the country's performance had been generally indifferent. It continued to have problems repaying its $2 billion foreign debt. It was largely to boost North Korea's limited overseas trade that Premier Li Jong Ok undertook a 12-day tour of non-Communist Southeast Asia in February. A more important trip was that of Kim Il Sung to China in September. China was North Korea's chief trading partner and political ally, and it was reported that the Chinese, anxious to ensure that Kim was friendlier to them than to the Soviets, gave him 20 MiG-21 jet fighters.

KUWAIT

In 1982 Kuwait experienced a year of introspection brought about by the continuing Iran-Iraq war, lower prices for crude oil, and a liquidity crisis on the unofficial Kuwaiti stock exchange or curb market. A U.S. survey ranked Kuwait as the 17th most prosperous country in the world. Yet Finance Minister Abdel Latif al-Hamad warned in April that Kuwait faced bankruptcy within four years if the increase in government spending was not checked.

Early in 1982 oil production dropped as low as 600,000 bbl a day, about half the ceiling introduced in 1981. Part of the fall was cushioned by government investment income, estimated at $9 billion a year. Foreign currency reserves were reported to be in excess of $60 billion.

The greatest challenge to Kuwait's free economy and system of government was posed by the Gulf war. An Iraqi defeat or a change of government in

Baghdad would be deeply embarrassing to Kuwait, which had supported Iraq with grant aid of more than $6 billion since the beginning of hostilities.

The stock market crisis, brought about by uncontrolled forward trading using postdated checks, some of which were not honoured, brought the government into direct conflict with elements of the merchant community. Some estimates put the value of the outstanding checks at more than $60 billion. In late December the government began paying off some of the investors.

LABOUR AND EMPLOYMENT

For organized labour in the United States, 1982 was a year of challenges, changes, and contrasts in collective bargaining; of growing problems for unions in an economy shifting from industrial, blue-collar jobs—the hard-core of labour's past strength—to service-oriented jobs; and of waning union influence in politics and legislative halls. And it was a year in which swelling imports of steel, automobiles, shoes, and other manufactured products took a further toll of U.S. jobs. Organized labour increased its demands for stronger protection through fair-trade treaties or government curbs on imports. For many unions saving jobs became more important than increasing wages.

The American Federation of Labor-Congress of Industrial Organizations (AFL-CIO) and unions generally showed signs of responding to hard times and deepening problems in 1982 by a "back to basics" strategy designed to recruit younger workers with no background in trade unionism and to extend labour union membership and influence into new fields offering growth opportunities.

Labour Unions

Unions in the United States continued to suffer from the weakened national economy, the erosion of the country's industrial base, and occupational, geographic, and demographic shifts in the labour force. The AFL-CIO reported 15 million members in its affiliates in late 1981. The U.S. Labor Department about the same time reported that labour organizations (unions and employee associations that bargain for members) had 22,223,000 members in the U.S., with an additional 1,546,000 in Canada. Totals to be reported in 1983 were expected to show substantial losses in industrial unions hardest hit by layoffs and plant shutdowns and cutbacks. Unions in the ser-

The United Auto Workers union made significant concessions in a contract with Ford Motor Co. signed in March by (left to right) Donald Ephlin, UAW vice-president; Douglas Fraser, UAW president; Philip Caldwell, Ford chairman; and Donald Petersen, Ford president.

UPI

vices and those representing public employees could show small offsetting gains—the Food and Commercial Workers, for example, reported gains through "an absolutely monumental organizing effort."

Among industrial unions, the United Auto Workers reported in June 1982 that its membership had dropped to 1,225,000. In 1959 it was 1,124,362; in 1969, 1,530,870; and in 1979, 1,527,858. In steel, membership in the United Steelworkers dropped from 1.3 million in early 1981 to less than a milllion in June 1982. The International Brotherhood of Teamsters, the largest union in the U.S., also saw its membership shrink by hundreds of thousands in 1981 and 1982.

Relatively little organizing was under way. A year-long AFL-CIO campaign in Houston, Texas, netted a reported 5,000 new members. Efforts to recruit new members were too expensive for many unions. Hard times led to mergers, reducing the number of AFL-CIO affiliates to 99.

Important leadership changes occurred in 1982. Owen Bieber was named to succeed the retiring Douglas A. Fraser as president of the United Auto Workers in 1983. Gerald W. McEnlee moved to the top in the American Federation of State, County and Municipal Employees, a union with more than a million members and one of the AFL-CIO's largest. He succeeded Jerry Wurf, who died in 1982.

Marvin J. Boede succeeded Martin J. Ward as president of the Plumbers and Pipefitters; Ward, one of the country's most respected construction union leaders, died during the year. Patrick J. Campbell succeeded William Konyha as head of another major building trades union, the Carpenters. William H. Bywater moved into the presidency of the International Union of Electrical Workers on the death of David J. Fitzmaurice. Ellen Burstyn, the actress, became the first woman to head the AFL-CIO's 30,000-member Actors' Equity, and Doris Turner was elected president of unionized hospital and nursing care workers. Outside the AFL-CIO, Richard L. Trumka, 33, an attorney, defeated the United Mine Workers' president, Sam L. Church, Jr.

Government investigations of corruption in organized labour continued to focus in 1982 on the International Brotherhood of Teamsters. Several lower level officers were convicted and, in December, the union's president, Roy L. Williams, was found guilty after a complex seven-week trial with four co-defendants on charges of conspiring to bribe Sen. Howard Cannon (Dem., Nev.) to help defeat a congressional bill to deregulate the trucking industry. Senator Cannon, defeated for reelection in 1982, was not indicted.

Bargaining and Strikes

Organized labour was facing a heavy bargaining agenda in 1983 after a year of stunning concessions by unions produced some of the cheapest contracts in decades. In the meatpacking, trucking, auto, rubber, and airline industries, unions agreed either to forgo wage increases or to sign for modest gains. Job and income security were more important than larger pay increases at bargaining tables.

Major collective bargaining settlements in the first nine months of 1982 averaged in wage increases 3.8% in the first contract year and 3.5% annually

Militant members of the United Steelworkers union rejected concessions and twice blocked industry efforts to negotiate early contract agreements.

KEITH SRAKOCIC–PICTURE GROUP

over the terms of the contract. The averages were the lowest since the Labor Department's Bureau of Labor Statistics began keeping such records in 1968. When the same parties negotiated in the previous bargaining round, most in 1979 or 1980, first-year raises averaged 8.3%, and increases averaged 6.4% over contract terms. Nearly half, or 45%, of 2.7 million workers covered by settlements through September received no wage increase, although some got cost-of-living adjustments (COLA). Workers who got first-year raises averaged 7.1%.

In a key settlement in 1982, the trucking industry and the International Brotherhood of Teamsters froze basic wages for at least two years and limited COLA increases but added 25 cents and hour to employer contributions to welfare funds. Meatpackers and the Food and Commercial Workers negotiated a 44-month freeze on wage increases. The United Rubber Workers agreed to forgo wage increases in contracts with major employers, but a continuing COLA clause could boost pay as much as $2.44 an hour. Breaking with the concession trend, the Oil, Chemical and Atomic Workers won what the union called "justifiable" hourly raises of 9% in 1982, then 90 cents an hour in 1983, in oil industry bargaining.

The United Auto Workers (UAW), worried about future prospects of the U.S. auto industry, made substantial concessions in contract negotiations with Ford and General Motors, agreeing to forgo 3% annual pay raises, defer COLA payments, and give up paid holidays, in return for more job security and guarantees against plant closings. Savings for Ford alone were estimated as high as $1 billion over 30 months. The UAW reached an innovative contract with American Motors under which COLA and annual wage increases would be retained by the company as employee investments, to be repaid at 10% interest beginning in 1985. The pact was expected to yield $115 million or more for new product development. However, the UAW refused to make concessions to the Chrysler Corp., which had won substantial concessions from the UAW when the company was on the brink of bankruptcy in 1980 and 1981. Chrysler workers, receiving about $2.60 an hour less than General Motors and Ford workers, demanded immediate raises and won 75 cents an hour in added pay and COLA after Canadian UAW workers struck the company in November and December. In the farm equipment industry, the UAW settled in May with International Harvester, giving up raises for a profit-sharing plan, but its Caterpillar Tractor locals struck on October 1, rejecting concessions.

Efforts by the basic steel industry and the United Steelworkers (USW) to negotiate an early contract with union concessions to cut mill labour costs failed twice as USW's rank and file militantly demanded contract gains. In other negotiations, General Electric and Westinghouse signed new contracts with wage increases of 7% or more in 1982 and 3% in 1983 and 1984. AFL-CIO men's clothing workers signed for $1.05 an hour over 38 months and ladies'

WIDE WORLD

UAW members employed by Chrysler Corp. in Canada refused to join their U.S. counterparts in a no-strike agreement and won significant raises for workers in both countries.

garment workers for 19% through June 1984.

Generally, strikes continued to be few and minor in 1982 after dropping to a 15-year low in 1981, when only 0.11% of total work time (24.6 million days) was lost by strikes. A major railroad tieup was averted when Pres. Ronald Reagan and Congress stepped in to bar a serious disruption of service and produce a settlement at about 11% more pay over 39 months, plus cost-of-living adjustments.

Teacher and public employee strikes declined in 1982, but stoppages increased in the arts and sports. A number of major symphonies were struck, and the American Ballet Theatre was forced to cancel performances in Paris, Boston, and Washington, D.C., before settling with a dancers' union. More Americans were affected by a profesisonal football players' strike than by any other in 1982. Games were canceled during an eight-week labour dispute, leaving millions of fans without hours of Sunday and Monday televised football.

Labour and Government

Labour's relations with the Reagan administration, and with President Reagan himself, deteriorated even more in 1982. The AFL-CIO and unions

Michigan's staggering 14.5% unemployment rate, one of the nation's highest, was centred in Detroit, which, like other old industrial cities of the Northeast and upper Midwest, felt the brunt of recession.
ANDREW SACKS

generally severely criticized administration policies as responsible for high unemployment. Labour also criticized Congress for its part in budget, tight money, tax, and other policies that labour said were unfair. The AFL-CIO and its unions increased political action in the congressional and state elections in 1982 and claimed to have had an important part in electing more Democrats to the House of Representatives and to governorships and state legislatures.

Employment

Unemployment in the United States climbed to 10.8% in November, with nearly 12 million out of work by the government's count and at least a million more as estimated by organized labour. Of a labour force of 111 million, more than 99,032,000 were working in the week of November 15, when the government took its count. An increase of 436,000 in the number of jobless was mainly a product of a loss of 165,000 jobs and the entry into the labour force of 375,000 who were unable to find work. Married men were 7.7% jobless. A 20.2% rate among blacks and a 24% rate for teenagers were unchanged.

In addition to the unemployed, about 1.6 million were listed by the Bureau of Labor Statistics as "discouraged workers" who had given up looking for jobs, and more than 6.5 million were listed as underemployed—working less than full time. The rates in all categories were the highest since 1947.

The government also reported that fewer than half of those without jobs were collecting unemployment benefits, varying from $84 a week for a single person in Indiana to $234 a week for a worker with dependents in Massachusetts. The national average was $116 for a jobless worker with no dependents.

The normal duration of benefits was 26 weeks, with workers in states with high, long-term joblessness eligible for an additional 13 weeks of aid. Supplemental payments for 10 additional weeks were being paid at year's end.

Interpretations of year-end economic figures differed, with few economists showing optimism. The housing industry was making a recovery, rebounding by 31% from a low level in October 1981, but heavier construction remained sluggish. Construction unemployment in some areas was 75% or higher. Factory orders, the basis of industrial production and jobs, remained weak in October, with a discouraging 3.9% drop. However, auto production showed new but weak signs of improvement.

Total U.S. personal income rose $19.1 billion in October, but private wages and salaries declined by $1.8 billion owing to layoffs and shorter working hours. Most of the overall income gain resulted from Social Security benefits, jobless compensation, and other federal or state money. The personal income total represented an annual $9,553 for every man, woman, and child in the United States, based on 1982 population estimates of 232,700,000. The Consumer Price Index rose month by month, and the level in October was 294.1% of the base prices in 1967. Real earnings—workers' buying power—fell 1.3% in the first ten months of the year, largely as a result of fewer hours worked and higher prices.

Industrial production fell eight-tenths of 1% in October as factories operated at just 68.4% of capacity, the lowest rate in 35 years. Production had fallen 11.4% since the recession began in July 1981. Interest rates dropped a little but, still on a seesaw, remained historically high.

LANDMARKS AND MONUMENTS

As of August 1982, 67 states had deposited an instrument of ratification or acceptance of the International Convention Concerning the Protection of the World Cultural and Natural Heritage; the "World Heritage Convention," as it was usually called, was adopted by the General Conference of the United Nations Educational, Scientific, and Cultural Organization (UNESCO) in 1972 and came into effect in 1975 after the requisite 20 UNESCO member states had adhered to it.

By the end of 1981, 112 sites had been inscribed on the World Heritage List. Among the most recent were the Roman and romanesque monuments of Arles, the Roman theatre and triumphal arch of Orange, and the Chateau of Chambord (all in France); the archaeological park and Maya ruins of Quirigua (Guatemala); and the Olympic National Park (Washington State). *A Legacy for All: The World's Major Natural, Cultural and Historic Sites*, published by UNESCO, presented 57 sites on the World Heritage List that were inscribed in 1978 and 1979. Essentially a photographic essay with descriptive text, this publication was the first in a series that would be updated approximately every two years.

Monumentum, the international architectural conservation journal of the International Council of Monuments and Sites (ICOMOS), had a new format and now appeared as a quarterly. It continued to have a leading role in the international dissemination of general and technical knowledge in the field of historic preservation. A third exchange of East-West specialists in the "Field of Preservation and Rehabilitation of Historic Quarters in the European Region," co-sponsored by ICOMOS and UNESCO, took place in October–November 1982, pursuant to the recommendations of the Conference on Security and Cooperation in Europe held in Helsinki, Fin., in 1975. There was a growing recognition of the importance of this program among those concerned with European and North American cooperation for the safeguarding, restoration, and presentation of historic monuments and sites.

Two of UNESCO's 27 campaigns to preserve monuments and sites of international significance had ended successfully. The Nubian campaign had been completed in 1980, and work on the 9th-century Buddhist monument of Borobudur on the island of Java was finished in 1981. A grand ceremony at Borobudur paid tribute to this immense undertaking and to the remarkable demonstration of international support it elicited. The government of Indonesia contributed approximately $14 million, and over $6 million was donated by 25 member states of UNESCO.

Another of UNESCO's international campaigns, launched in 1974, was to save the archaeological site of Mohenjo-daro in Pakistan, one of the main urban centres of a civilization that flourished in the Indus Valley about 5,000 years ago. Since the initial excavations over 50 years ago, Mohenjo-daro had been threatened by rising groundwater caused by the development of irrigation in this arid area of Sind and by the wanderings of the Indus River. A system of pumping stations, drainage canals, and protective embankments was almost complete, but work had yet to begin on the essential deflector spurs at the river's edge. In 1981 the U.S. government contributed almost $1 million to support the project.

At the invitation of the Mexican government, the World Conference on Cultural Policies (Mondiacult) took place in Mexico City during July 26–Aug. 6, 1982. Convened by UNESCO, its purpose was to review the experience acquired since the Intergovernmental Conference on Institutional, Administrative and Financial Aspects of Cultural Policies in 1970; to consider fundamental problems regarding culture in the contemporary world; and to formulate new guidelines. Over 200 resolutions were adopted, the significance of which—particularly in relation to historic preservation—had yet to be assessed. Nevertheless, in Mondiacult's "Mexico Declaration," the international community affirmed its belief in the importance of culture (defined as the identity of a people) as an essential element for "development." This came at the time when the preservation and, indeed, the very existence of such monuments as Angkor Wat (Kampuchea) and Tyre (Lebanon) were in

Restoration of the Borobudur temple on the island of Java, a job involving the reassembly of some 750,000 pieces, was completed.
WIDE WORLD

A scaffold erected about the Erechtheum temple on the Acropolis in Athens enabled workers to replace corroding iron brackets installed over 80 years earlier.

question, and when the survival of many national preservation programs was being threatened by severe budgetary cuts.

The return or restitution of cultural property also figured prominently in the Mondiacult discussions. In recent years support had grown for the principle that art treasures whose absence "causes the greatest anguish" should be returned to their countries of origin. The process of restitution was not seen in isolation but as accompanied by the strengthening of museums and the training of personnel.

LAOS

The highlight of 1982 for Laos was the convening in late April of the third national congress of the ruling Lao People's Revolutionary (Communist) Party (LPRP). It had been a decade since the last congress was held, and the 1982 meeting took up the tasks of assessing and defining the country's leadership structure, economic and political development, and foreign policy.

The third congress unequivocally confirmed the leading position of Kaysone Phomvihan, secretary-general of the LPRP and premier. There had been rumours that Kaysone, who had headed the party since its founding in 1955, would relinquish the premiership, but he emerged apparently all the stronger as several of his closest allies, as well as his wife, were elevated to the important LPRP central secretariat. Though he shed his finance portfolio in Sep-

tember, Deputy Premier Nouhak Phoumsavan seemed secure in his standing as the regime's second most powerful figure. The composition of the seven-member Politburo remained unchanged, but 30 new faces, including representatives of ethnic minorities and women, graced the 49-member LPRP Central Committee.

The congress struck a decidedly reformist note as it drafted the country's first five-year (1981–85) development plan. Of the rigidly Marxist line pursued by the LPRP since its accession to power in 1975, Kaysone said candidly: "We . . . indulged in subjectivism, failed to grasp economic laws and strongly promote the people's mastery as a motive force." Remedies prescribed included a slowdown in the drive toward full-scale socialism, the lifting of restrictions on private trade, wage increases, and the training of technocrats and efficient economic managers.

The third congress also scrapped the earlier target of eliminating Laos's huge trade deficit by 1985, and it halved the projected increase in internal revenue to about 90%. A bright spot was rice production, which had risen from 700,000 metric tons in 1976 to over 1 million metric tons in 1981, when the country became self-sufficient in the food grain for the first time. Laos was also increasingly able to obtain finance for its projects from non-Communist countries and international institutions.

Vientiane remained a loyal ally of Vietnam in Vietnamese-dominated Indochina. At the third party congress, Kaysone hailed his country's "special relationship" with Vietnam and identified Hanoi's archfoe China as "the most dangerous enemy" of Laos. Vientiane's ties with neighbouring Thailand continued to be strained by what the Laotians saw as Bangkok's sanction of Lao rebel activity on Thai soil. Late in the year, former Lao deputy premier Phoumi Nosavan, who had lived in exile in Thailand since 1965, announced his intention to form an anti-Communist "United Front of Lao People for the Liberation of Laos." He claimed to have some 40,000 supporters inside the country.

LATIN-AMERICAN AFFAIRS
During 1982 Latin-American affairs were dominated by the crisis that resulted in armed conflict between Argentina and the U.K. in the South Atlantic. On March 19 a group of scrap merchants who had been contracted to dismantle a disused whaling station raised the Argentine flag on South Georgia, a dependency of the British colony of the Falkland Islands/Islas Malvinas. The crisis escalated quickly. On April 2 Argentine forces occupied the Falkland Islands, and the U.K. broke off diplomatic relations with Argentina. The U.K. called an emergency session of the UN Security Council, which on April 3 passed Resolution 502 condemning the Argentine actions; on the same day, the British government announced the dispatch of a naval task force to the South Atlantic area.

On April 17 the European Communities (EC) imposed trade sanctions on Argentina for 30 days, and in May some member countries renewed their support for the U.K. in this way. On April 7 Britain imposed a 200-nautical mile (370-km) exclusion zone in waters around the islands. U.S. Secretary of State Alexander Haig shuttled between London, Washington, D.C., and Buenos Aires from April 8 to 19 in an endeavour to find a peaceful solution to the dispute. British forces retook South Georgia on April 25, and soon afterward the U.S. formally declared its support for the U.K. Extended negotiations on peace formulas sponsored by Peru and the UN broke down on May 6 and May 20, respectively.

The main military action between Argentina and the U.K. took place between May 1 and June 14, the date on which the Argentine commander on the Falklands surrendered to the British. (*See* Argentina; Great Britain.)

Latin-American countries supported Argentina throughout the crisis in varying degrees. Their attitude was expressed in the resolution passed by the Organization of American States meeting in Washington, D.C., in late April. The resolution supported Argentina's claim to the Falklands but called for a truce; it was passed by 17 votes to 0 with 5 abstentions. Peru and Bolivia offered limited military assistance to Argentina, which was not taken up. Chile followed a policy of strict neutrality, as it was already in dispute with Argentina over the islands of Picton, Lennox, and Nueva in the Beagle Channel at the southern tip of South America. Brazil adopted an evenhanded stance and made available reexport facilities for Argentine goods from its southern ports and some aircraft for submarine-tracking purposes.

At the April meeting of the Organization of American States in Washington, D.C., Argentine Foreign Minister Nicanor Costa Méndez unsuccessfully called on the OAS to demand that Great Britain withdraw its fleet from the South Atlantic.

CONSOLIDATED NEWS PICTURES/
KEYSTONE

Early in November the UN voted for a Latin-American draft resolution calling for renewed negotiations between Argentina and the U.K. over the sovereignty of the islands. The fact that the U.S. voted in favour of the resolution was interpreted as a gesture toward repairing relations with Latin America that had been damaged when the U.S. declared its formal support for the U.K. during the hostilities. U.S. Pres. Ronald Reagan visited Brazil, Costa Rica, Honduras, and Colombia in late November and early December as part of the process of restoring links. British efforts to ameliorate relations with the region in the wake of the crisis centred on a visit by Peter Rees, British trade minister, to Chile, Paraguay, and Ecuador in September.

At a meeting of the board of governors of the Inter-American Development Bank (IDB), held in Rio de Janeiro, Brazil, in late October, the U.S. was in dispute with Brazil, Mexico, Venezuela, and Argentina over access to multilateral finance. The U.S. delegation insisted that those four countries were to limit credits from the IDB in the period 1982–86 to a maximum of $3 billion; Latin-American countries requested an 18% annual growth in bank lending, as opposed to a U.S. proposal of 12%, and a large volume of concessionary lending, totaling at least $2,750,000,000.

The Latin American Integration Association (LAIA), set up by the August 1980 Montevideo Treaty to replace the 20-year-old Latin American Free Trade Association (LAFTA), was fully ratified in March by the signatories (Argentina, Bolivia, Brazil, Chile, Colombia, Ecuador, Mexico, Paraguay,

Peru, Uruguay, and Venezuela). The Montevideo Treaty provided for regional preferential tariff arrangements, to be applied by all members on their internal trade within the grouping; regional agreements on trade, industrial and agricultural cooperation, science and technology, tourism, financial flows, and environmental protection, which also extended to member countries; and partial agreements between some members, which were eventually to be extended to other members through negotiation.

At a meeting in Jamaica in August, central bank representatives of LAIA member countries and the Dominican Republic agreed to bring under the aegis of LAIA a multilateral reciprocal payments and credits system that had been operated by central banks in the region since 1965. The system provided for clearing bank services for payments of intraregional trade transactions. About 85% of all intraregional trade, valued at $9.3 billion, was channeled through the system in 1981. Under the arrangement the Peruvian central bank settled balances stemming from 63 credit lines every four months, eliminating the need for member countries to make available foreign exchange for individual transactions. A further strengthening of LAIA took place when private-sector representatives from Argentina, Brazil, Mexico, and Uruguay met in Montevideo, Uruguay, in July to discuss mutual tariff reductions for imports of office machinery under its auspices.

In August a ministerial meeting of the Latin American Economic System (SELA) was held in Caracas, Venezuela, to outline a new strategy for Latin-American economic relations. This body,

On the first stop of his Latin-American tour in November, U.S. Pres. Ronald Reagan exchanged toasts with Brazil's Pres. João Figueiredo.
WIDE WORLD

established in October 1975 by 25 Latin-American and Caribbean nations, including Cuba, was designed to complement rather than rival or replace the existing regional organizations.

The Andean Group was in the doldrums during the year. The one event of significance was an agreement on new rules for multinational Andean corporations. By Group Decision 169 of March, these corporations were required to have at least 80% Andean ownership, with foreign, non-Pact, holdings limited to 20%. In the case of concerns to be established in Bolivia and Ecuador, the decision allowed for a gradual transition from a maximum of 40% foreign capital down to a maximum of 20%.

In Central America events were dominated by political violence and social disturbances, especially in El Salvador and Guatemala, and by economic difficulties, in Costa Rica in particular. The Central American Common Market was largely in a state of suspension, but there were some encouraging developments. At a meeting of the Central American Monetary Union in April, the central bank presidents of the five member countries (Costa Rica, El Salvador, Guatemala, Honduras, and Nicaragua) authorized credits of $80.4 million to finance intraregional trade. In February Honduras and El Salvador ratified a bilateral free-trade treaty, which ended an 11-year gap in trade between the two countries. The European Parliament in October discussed the granting of an aid package worth approximately $30 million to Central America and the Caribbean. The Central American Democratic Community, a regional body established to promote cooperation in political and security matters, was formed in January by El Salvador, Costa Rica, and Honduras, which were joined in July by Guatemala.

On February 24 U.S. Pres. Ronald Reagan announced a program of aid and of trade and investment incentives designed to develop the economies of countries of the Caribbean Basin, excluding Mexico, Cuba, Grenada, and Nicaragua; it was known as the Caribbean Basin Initiative (CBI). The CBI sought to achieve economic benefits through a reduction in state controls, liberalization of trade, and encouragement of foreign investment. Its centrepiece was the proposed free entry of Caribbean products into the U.S. market for 12 years. (Exceptions included textiles, clothing, and sugar, which were subject to quotas.) The U.S. Congress passed the aid component of the program, and a total of $350 million was made available in 1982 for short-term balance of payments support, including $75 million for El Salvador, $50 million for Jamaica, $70 million for Costa Rica, and $40 million for the Dominican Republic. Also envisioned was longer-term development aid, which would total $675 million by 1984. The trade and investment sections of the CBI proposal failed to gain congressional approval during the year. Concomitantly with the program the U.S. was negotiating bilateral treaties for investment, and the first of these was signed with Panama in October.

Latin America's economic performance in 1981 was its worst in 35 years. Overall growth in the region was only 1.2%, a large drop from the 5.8% of 1980 and well below the population increase. The average rate of inflation in Latin-American countries during the year was 60%, the worst figure ever recorded except for 1976. The overall balance of payments registered a deficit for the second successive year. Although the volume of exports rose by 11%, there was a record current account deficit of $33.7 billion in 1981; this was an increase of nearly $6 billion over 1980. The region's disbursed foreign debt was estimated to have grown by 15% to $240 billion by the end of 1981. During 1982 Mexico, Bolivia, Brazil, Costa Rica, Honduras, Ecuador, and Argentina were at various stages of discussion with their creditors about debt renegotiation and with the International Monetary Fund (IMF) about stabilization programs. Cuba also sought the rescheduling of some of its $3 billion debt to non-Communist countries in August. (*See also* articles on the various countries.)

LAW

Acquittal of the man who tried to assassinate Pres. Ronald Reagan focused new attention in 1982 on insanity defenses in criminal trials. A federal jury in Washington, D.C., found 27-year-old John W. Hinckley, Jr., innocent by reason of insanity of all charges relating to his shooting of the president, White House Press Secretary James Brady, police officer Thomas Delahanty, and Secret Service agent Timothy McCarthy on March 30, 1981.

Hinckley's defense maintained successfully that

Mayor Dianne Feinstein of San Francisco turned in her .38-calibre handgun to dramatize the city's controversial ban on such weapons.
UPI

he was schizophrenic and compelled by his delusions to commit the assault. He lacked remorse, the defense continued, because he could not understand that his deed was wrong.

Hinckley was committed to St. Elizabeths Hospital in Washington. In committing him, U.S. District Judge Barrington D. Parker found he was both mentally ill and dangerous. Hinckley waived his right to a hearing on release within 50 days, required by District of Columbia law in such cases.

After the surprise verdict, U.S. Attorney General William French Smith and others called for new laws to prevent innocent verdicts in such cases. President Reagan, without mentioning the Hinckley case, later submitted legislation to Congress that would restrict the insanity defense by focusing on whether a suspect knew what he was doing and intended to commit a crime, rather than on whether the suspect knew right from wrong or acted on an impulse that could not be resisted. There were parallel moves in some legislatures to change state laws on criminal insanity.

In a complex settlement of an antitrust lawsuit that began in 1974, American Telephone & Telegraph (AT&T) agreed to sever its ties with its 22 local operating companies. The settlement allowed AT&T to keep its other subsidiaries, such as Bell Laboratories and Western Electric. The company was barred from entering the field of electronic publishing for seven years. The action ended one of the most complicated antitrust cases in U.S. history.

A federal appeals court decided that the word Monopoly, as applied to the board game, had become part of the language and could no longer be used as an exclusive trademark. The court decided that a competitor was within his rights in calling a game Anti-Monopoly as long as he informed buyers that the game was not made by Parker Brothers, the makers of Monopoly.

The Justice Department dropped a 13-year-old antitrust suit against International Business Machines (IBM). IBM's counsel noted that since the suit was filed, there had been tremendous gains by IBM's competitors in the field of electronic computers.

The Rev. Sun Myung Moon, founder of the controversial Unification Church, was convicted of conspiracy to evade personal income taxes and filing false tax returns from 1973 to 1975. The federal court jury decided that $162,000 in bank accounts and stock held by Moon were his personal property, not the property of the church, and thus should have been reported as taxable income. Despite his attorney's contention that a jail sentence would amount to religious persecution, Moon was sentenced to 18 months in prison and fined $25,000.

Wayne Williams, 23, a free-lance photographer, was convicted of murdering 2 of 28 young blacks who disappeared in the Atlanta area over two years. The prosecution relied heavily on expert testimony that matched strands of fabric found on the victims' bodies with fabric from Williams's car and from a rug in the home Williams shared with his elderly parents. Williams was sentenced to two life terms.

In a highly publicized Rhode Island case, financial

The settlement of the biggest antitrust suit in U.S. history was announced, eight years after it was instituted, by U.S. Assistant Attorney General William Baxter (left) and Chairman Charles Brown and Vice-Pres. and General Counsel Howard Trienes of AT&T.
WIDE WORLD

Twenty-year-old Enten Eller, a member of the pacifist Church of the Brethren, became the first American since the Vietnam war to be convicted of refusal to register for the draft.
WIDE WORLD

consultant Claus von Bulow was convicted of twice trying to murder his wealthy wife by injections of insulin. After the second injection Mrs. von Bulow went into an irreversible coma. Von Bulow was sentenced to 30 years in prison.

Joseph Paul Franklin, an admitted racist, was acquitted of shooting Vernon Jordan, president of the National Urban League, in Fort Wayne, Ind., in 1980. Franklin earlier had been convicted of killing two joggers in Utah. Joseph Christopher, an army private, was convicted of three racially motivated killings of blacks in Buffalo, N.Y., and sentenced to 60 years to life in prison.

A California parole board revoked a scheduled 1984 hearing on the release of Sirhan Sirhan, the convicted killer of Robert Kennedy. The board found that Sirhan had threatened several persons and that an earlier parole board had not known of the threats when it set the 1984 date. The request of James Earl Ray, convicted of the murder of the Rev. Dr. Martin Luther King, for a Tennessee parole hearing was deferred until at least May 1985.

An appeals court upheld the murder conviction of Jeffrey MacDonald, former army Green Beret doctor charged with killing his wife and two daughters in 1970. He was convicted in 1979, but an appeals court voided the conviction because he had not been brought to trial promptly. The U.S. Supreme Court had restored the conviction but opened the possibility of appeals on other grounds.

San Francisco adopted a far-reaching ban on ownership and sale of handguns. However, a state court of appeals later ruled that the city had no authority to impose the rule. At the other extreme, Kennesaw, Ga., adopted a rule that every head of household must own a firearm. The ordinance, which imposed no penalties, was challenged in federal court.

Enten Eller, 20, a student at Bridgewater College in Harrisonburg, Va., and a conscientious objector, became the first American since the Vietnam war to be convicted of refusal to register for military draft. He was placed on probation, ordered to do community service work, and also ordered to register within 90 days or face a prison term. Later Benjamin Sasway, 21, the first man indicted for failure to register, also was convicted in San Diego, Calif.

In August, New Jersey became the 37th state to adopt a death penalty law. Frank Coppola, 38, was executed in Virginia for beating a woman to death in a 1978 robbery. In December Charlie Brooks, Jr., became the first person in the U.S. to be executed by lethal injection; the controversial "humane" execution took place in a Texas state prison.

LEBANON

The Israeli invasion, which began on June 6, 1982, and the assassination of President-elect Bashir Gemayel on September 14 were the key events in a year that saw Lebanon occupied by foreign troops. The Israeli invasion rapidly escalated into a full-scale pursuit of the Palestine Liberation Organization (PLO) guerrillas by the Israeli Army. By mid-June Beirut was effectively surrounded, and a long siege began. Thousands were reported to have died during the bombardment of the city. The Israelis' second objective—to drive the Syrians from their military positions in Lebanon—was also being achieved. Israeli military successes against Syria were largely attributable to superior military hardware supplied by the U.S.

The PLO fighters and their leader, Yasir Arafat, finally agreed to leave Beirut, and on August 21 the evacuation began under French, U.S., and Italian military supervision. The plans for their departure to other Arab countries were negotiated by U.S. special envoy to the Middle East Philip Habib.

Worse was to come for Lebanon, however. An election brought about by the retirement of Pres. Elias Sarkis was won by Christian (Phalangist) militia leader Bashir Gemayel on August 23. His election was not popular with some Lebanese leaders because of his association with sectarian violence, but he himself was to die violently, when a bomb planted in the Phalangist headquarters in East Beirut exploded on September 14. The assassination triggered an immediate advance by the Israeli forces into Beirut on September 15. Various theories were put forward about the responsibility for the assassination, among them one that suggested the Israelis were to blame.

On September 16 a massacre of hundreds of Palestinian men, women, and children began at the Sabra and Shatila refugee camps in West Beirut. The final toll was placed at 328 dead and 991 missing. Reports suggested that those responsible for the killings were Christian militia forces loyal either to the late Bashir Gemayel or to Maj. Saad Haddad. Allegations were subsequently made about Israeli complicity in the killings. The Israeli government claimed it was not aware of the massacre until September 18, but an Israeli inquiry later in the year cast some doubt on this assertion.

The election of Pres. Amin Gemayel at the end of September brought hopes of a new start. Bashir Gemayel had been hailed as a "messiah" by some Christian groups in Lebanon, and it was feared that his presidency would be divisive. Amin Gemayel, on the other hand, was a more moderate figure than his brother. It was thought that the new government would take a strong line with Israel and refuse to agree to a peace treaty except within the context of an overall Arab-Israeli settlement.

Amin Gemayel immediately sought to achieve three objectives: the withdrawal of all foreign troops from Lebanon, the restoration of security, and the reconstruction of a country devastated by war and sectarian strife. In October he visited the U.S., France, and Italy. In an address to the UN, Gemayel pleaded for the withdrawal of Israeli, Syrian, and Palestinian forces from Lebanon. He also requested that the 7,000-strong UN Interim Force in Lebanon remain for a further three-month period until Jan. 19, 1983; this request was granted.

Prime Minister Shafiq al-Wazzan named an entirely new Cabinet on Oct. 8, 1982. The Lebanese press heralded the administration as a technocratic rather than a political group. Wazzan had the respect of Muslims and Christians and the backing of the PLO. Beirut airport was reopened on September 30 after the last Israeli soldiers had left it. This event appeared to mark the return of normality to the city. Late in the year, however, factional fighting was reported between Christian and Druze militiamen in the mountains east and southeast of Beirut and between pro- and anti-Syrian Muslims in Tripoli. On December 28, largely as the result of intense U.S. pressure, negotiations began between Lebanese and Israeli delegations.

(*See also* Israel; Middle Eastern Affairs.)

Palestinian civilians in Beirut chanted patriotic slogans as contingents of Palestinian Liberation Organization gunmen were evacuated under Lebanese and French supervision.
PIERRE PERRIN—GAMMA/LIAISON

LIBRARIES

The Index of American Public Library Circulation, released in July 1982 by the University of Illinois, showed that U.S. circulation figures for 1981 had passed the 1,000,000,000 mark for an all-time high. U.S. public libraries spent some $2 billion in 1981, but with barely a one-point increase in purchasing power. Although state aid to libraries was up 9% overall, federal funding was flat, and many urban communities cut library services severely.

District-level allocation of federal funds for schools, along with school-based management trends, resulted in increased spending for microcomputers and software, and school media centres were eager to ride the wave. In October the second national conference of the American Association of School Librarians in Houston devoted some 20 sessions to microcomputers. An American Library Association (ALA) survey showed that most libraries were charging fees to help support on-line reference searching, one of the proliferating nonbasic library services.

In April, Dallas, Texas, opened its new state-of-the-art Central Library, with on-line computer catalogs for patrons, a cable television studio, and a full range of community services. The Newberry Library

The new logo adopted by the American Library Association, a stylized blue and white figure of a person reading a book, was to be used on T-shirts, tote bags, and other items.

of Chicago completed a ten-story, free-standing facility with 77,000 sq ft (7,150 sq m) for storage of rare materials. The Library of Congress began a deacidification program to prolong the life of some 50,000 items that were self-destructing because of chemicals used in the paper.

The ALA and other library groups waged a yearlong battle against qualification standards for federal library posts proposed by the U.S. Office of Personnel Management. Librarians charged the standards would diminish the importance of the master of library science degree and raise the status of managerial posts above that of service posts.

The worldwide drift into recession created problems for library and information services in other nations as well in 1982. Budgets for the purchase of books and periodicals were reduced, while prices continued to rise. Reactions varied from country to country. In the U.K. economies in the operation of public library services that had begun in 1973–74 reached a stage where further reductions would make it difficult to provide the comprehensive library service required by statute.

But if most other countries in Europe suffered badly, the standards of library and information services in the less developed countries faced greater threats. Not only was the purchase of books and periodicals made difficult by increased costs and transport charges; problems were exacerbated by the inability to purchase new technology and to provide the necessary skilled manpower to use it.

Indeed, the increasing confluence of computers and telecommunications, the development of cable networks for television and radio, the evolution of videotext systems and of relatively inexpensive microcomputers, and the introduction of microcomputers into educational institutions were changing the environment in which library and information services were provided. The coincidence of technological developments and reductions in expenditure forced the library and information science professions to consider ways to best exploit the resources already allocated to them. Many countries in Europe continued to examine the machinery—and in some cases the legislation—required to improve resource allocation to library and information services. Library and information science education programs were also being reexamined.

The U.S. Postal Service issued a 20-cent "America's Libraries" commemorative stamp in Philadelphia on July 13.

Special Report: The "New" Censors

by John N. Berry III

When officials of the Mark Twain Intermediate School in Fairfax, Va., decided to restrict the use of the novel *The Adventures of Huckleberry Finn* in that school, the incident became the most widely reported censorship story of 1982. No reporter could resist the delicious irony of a case where school officials banned a book by the namesake of the school in which they served. In the eyes of U.S. intellectual freedom fighters, the incident proved what they had been anxiously asserting for nearly two years: Censorship is on the rise, and the freedoms guaranteed in the First Amendment to the U.S. Constitution, particularly those of speech and the press, are in danger.

In June Judith F. Krug, director of the American Library Association's Office for Intellectual Freedom, which monitors censorship activity in the U.S., told reporters that the number of censorship complaints reported to her office had tripled in the last three years. According to Krug, at the beginning of the 1970s the ALA received about 100 complaints of attempted library censorship a year, but this number grew to 300 in the later years of the decade, "and since mid-1980 we get nearly 1,000 a year."

Recent Attempts at Censorship

A sampling of the censorship challenges of 1982 provides some insight into the motivation and beliefs of those who would "protect" others from words and pictures on paper, on the screen, or in live public utterances. Commissioners in Coral Gables, Fla., voted to ask the Miami-Dade Public Library System to ban the showing of several "racy" films (*Airplane, The Wiz, Ordinary People, Urban Cowboy, The Shining, Stripes, The Blue Lagoon*) in branch libraries. The complaint was brought by two Protestant ministers on the grounds that the films presented premarital sex, foul language, and the occult in a favourable light. In Orlando, Fla., a group called the Movement for Moral Decency objected to having works by author Judy Blume (*Deenie; Forever; Are You There God? It's Me, Margaret;* and *Then Again, Maybe I Won't*) in Orange County schools.

In Coleman, Wis., the school board voted to restrict access to *A Handbook for Conscientious Objectors* and *Words of Conscience: Religious Statements of Conscientious Objectors*. The books were requested by a mother who wanted her two teenage sons to have access to their point of view, as well as to the views of military recruiters who were allowed to work in the schools. In Renton, Wash., a group of parents formally complained against the use of Peter Stillman's *Introduction to Myth* in the schools, because by including it in the book Stillman implied that Christianity was a myth.

During the past year Chicago author Studs Terkel traveled to Girard, Pa., to defend his book *Working*. Students and parents in Girard objected to the use of profanity in the interviews of workers describing their work that make up the book. *Huckleberry Finn* was also the target of complaints by parents in Houston, Texas; Warrington, Pa.; and a host of other cities.

Challenged books came from nearly every era (*Huckleberry Finn*, 1884; *Gone with the Wind*, 1936; *The Grapes of Wrath*, 1939; *The Stupids Die*, 1981) and ranged across subjects from science fiction to psychology. Under fire since its publication in 1951, J. D. Salinger's *The Catcher in the Rye* returned to the fray in 1982, along with two Kurt Vonnegut novels of the 1960s, *Slaughterhouse-Five* and *Cat's Cradle*.

Magazines caught in the attack included *Ms., National Lampoon, Penthouse, Playboy, The Humanist*, and even such apparently "safe" titles as *McCall's, Ladies' Home Journal*, and *Newsweek*. The censors' lists also included games (Dungeons and Dragons), television programs ("Lou Grant"), and a number of newspapers.

New Sources of Censorship

Censorship challenges have always been a part of life in the U.S. They have come from every place on the political, social, racial, and religious spectra of American society. In 1982, however, observers claimed that attempts at censorship had increased dramatically, and most agreed that conservative political and religious individuals and groups were responsible for the increase over what used to be a "normal" amount of censorship activity. The "new" censors, then, are apt to be politically conservative and believers in what are usually labeled "fundamentalist" Christian religious principles.

It was an organization called the Christian Research Center that wanted to ban Isaac Asimov's *In the Beginning* from high-school libraries in San Diego, Calif. The campaign to remove several psychology and sociology textbooks from schools in Escambia County, Fla., was led by members of the Crossroads Baptist Church. In Shreveport, La., the charges against two Guidance Associates films were brought by a group called the Pro-Family Forum. Other censors have called themselves "creationists" (opposed to scientific theories of evolution) or "pro-life" (opposed to abortion).

The objections that arise from such would-be censors centre on three areas: sex, religion, and politics. The use of dialogue that is perceived to be obscene or profane is the fastest way to get a book challenged by the new censors. Books or movies that appear to condone activities that are threatening to what are called "traditional" values are always in danger of being challenged. Materials that portray premarital sex or any of a number of other varieties of sexual activity are regularly challenged, even in works recommended as purely educational. Any public or published views that oppose defense spending, draft registration, or favour sex education in public schools will draw opposition. The broadest brush with which the new censor paints his or her target, however, is the label "secular humanism." By that the censor means any work or works that either convey doubts about or disbelief in a more or less literal interpretation of the King James Version of the Christian Bible.

Not all censorship efforts originate from these "new" censors, however. There are still substantial attempts at censorship emanating from other segments of the political and religious spectra. It was black parents who objected to Twain's use of the word "nigger" in *Huckleberry Finn*, and it was feminists who campaigned under the banner of Women Against Pornography. Still, it is apparent that the increase in current attempts to censor is coming from the political and religious right.

First Amendment Rights

It is also important to note that, of the "nearly 1,000" complaints that ALA's Judith Krug reports, most (about 750) are aimed at books and other materials in institutions serving children. One of the most perplexing questions that this raises, and that the courts have been unable to resolve, concerns the nature of the First Amendment rights of children and of the librarians and teachers who serve them. One side takes the view that only parents can decide what these rights are and that tax money should not be spent on the purchase of books or other materials for use in schools and libraries serving children if taxpayers and parents disapprove of those materials. The other side asserts that such materials are protected by the First Amendment, as are the teachers, librarians, and children. Court decisions in such cases have been less than definitive.

To complicate the situation, many observers seriously doubt that the incidence of censorship is as great as the reports would suggest. Even if the reported increase in censorship activity is real, there is evidence that the censors are defeated more often than they succeed. Lillian Gerhardt, the editor of *School Library Journal*, points out that U.S. libraries number more than 83,000, "So, we have less than 0.01% of the libraries serving the young encountering some parent or patron disapproval." Gerhardt goes on to assert, "In a citizen-run democracy, a rate of one percent or less . . . of complaints, or even demands of any public institution probably represents democratic good health."

This society has never experienced a time with fewer constraints on freedom of expression. It is inevitable that attempts at censorship will increase as freedom of expression is enhanced. As Ervin Gaines, director of the Cleveland Public Library, pointed out in the *Cleveland Press*, would-be censors are "more of a nuisance than a threat." He cited the series of censorship decisions of the U.S. Supreme Court in the 1960s as dramatically reducing constraints on freedom of expression.

The censors are seldom victorious. In August a school board that removed nine books (including *Slaughterhouse-Five*, *The Fixer*, *Black Boy*, and *Soul on Ice*) from the school library ordered them returned to the shelves. *The Adventures of Huckleberry Finn* is back in use in the Mark Twain Intermediate School. A federal court ordered *365 Days* returned to the school library in Baileyville, Maine. Studs Terkel convinced the authorities and students in Girard, Pa., to keep and read his book *Working*. Throughout the U.S. school boards, library trustees, judges, and librarians have turned away the censors, "new" and old. Thus, in 1982 the freedoms guaranteed by the First Amendment held their own.

Book burning—long the symbol of the censor's zeal—has become an increasingly frequent phenomenon in America. Books are often accompanied into the flames by magazines and records similarly judged offensive.

CLIFF SCHIAPPA, ©1982 THE KANSAS CITY STAR

LIBYA

For the first time in more than two decades, Libya in 1982 entered a protracted period of reduced oil revenues, with important consequences for both consumption and economic development. The scale of the reduction in revenues could not be determined exactly because a significant proportion of oil was moved through barter arrangements with Eastern-bloc trading partners, and oil was also offered under a barter agreement to Ireland and Cyprus, among many others. Revenues fell from over $20 billion in 1980 to only $10 billion in 1982.

The shortages reported in Libyan shops could be attributed only partly to a shortage of the means to pay suppliers. The Libyan marketing system continued to adjust to the nationalization of all wholesaling and retailing initiated in 1980. State supermarkets dominated the urban retail trade, and smaller versions were set up throughout the country. These adjustments were more significant than any dislocations in imports.

At a special emergency session of the General People's Congress on March 3, a number of changes were made in the composition of the General People's Committee (GPC). Jadallah Azzuz at-Talhi retained the post of secretary-general of the GPC (premier). At a regular session of the Congress in January, it was decided to draft a bill that would bring into force the plan to replace the Army with a national militia composed of all Libyan citizens. It was also determined that the necessary measures for the merger with Syria that were proposed in September 1980 should be undertaken immediately.

During Col. Muammar al-Qaddafi's visit to Algeria in January, a merger between Libya, Algeria, and Syria was discussed. Relations with Egypt were resumed, and some border movements took place for the first time since 1977. Colonel Qaddafi maintained a statesmanlike demeanour prior to the August summit meeting of the Organization of African Unity in Tripoli. Nevertheless, 19 countries boycotted the meeting, with the result that the necessary two-thirds quorum was not attained, and no formal sessions could take place. A second effort to convene the summit in November failed because of a dispute over the seating of Chad.

Libya blamed the U.S. for influencing members to stay away, and relations with the U.S. remained poor; no oil was exported there, and U.S. nationals were impeded by their own government from going to Libya. In late summer, when the U.S. fleet once again exercised in the southern Mediterranean Sea, the anniversary of the 1981 clash between U.S. and Libyan forces passed without incident.

Qaddafi continued to cultivate relations with Eastern-bloc countries and visited Poland September 8–10. In his first official visit to a Western state, Qaddafi spent four days in Austria in March. On November 3 some 100 armed forces officers were arrested for planning a coup to coincide with Qaddafi's return from a visit to China and North Korea.

LITERATURE

The 1982 Nobel Prize for Literature was awarded to Gabriel García Márquez (*see* Nobel Prizes). A Colombian exiled in Mexico, he was one of the Spanish-American writers who had contributed to what was known as "el boom" in Western publishing circles. His most celebrated novel, *One Hundred Years of Solitude*, was often described as a classic. In 1975 he declared that he would not publish any fiction until the president of Chile was deposed; nevertheless, his new novel, *Chronicle of a Death Foretold*, appeared in English in 1982.

United States

Fiction. The threat of nuclear war was the subject of a large number of the year's books, both fiction and nonfiction. Bernard Malamud's *God's Grace* was an odd, muddled fable, both sardonic and silly, that began with a nuclear holocaust and a second Flood and ended with the destruction of an Eden peopled by the last man and his primate companions, including a gifted chimpanzee with an artificial larynx that allows him to speak. Another version of (among other things) *Robinson Crusoe* was Paul Theroux's *The Mosquito Coast*, a brilliantly executed story of the rise and fall of Allie Fox, self-taught polymath and freethinking dropout, who decides to abandon a corrupt, doomed America with his wife and children and create a utopia in a backcountry village in Honduras. Kurt Vonnegut's *Deadeye Dick*, the usual catalog of grotesque disasters climaxing this time in the depopulation of a Midwestern town in the explosion of a neutron bomb, was a mechanical, uncertain work.

Although it did provide some of the pleasures for which his work has been celebrated, *The Dean's December*, Saul Bellow's first novel since winning the Nobel Prize in 1976, was a disappointment. Chicago journalist-turned-academic Albert Corde, Bellow's thinnest and most complacent fictional disguise to date, is stranded in Bucharest one Christmas. While

Bernard Malamud
IRA WYMAN/NEWSWEEK

his Romanian wife, a distinguished emigré scientist, is baffled by malicious bureaucrats in her attempts to visit her dying mother, he kills the time thinking chiefly about a murder trial back in Chicago, contrasting the "hard nihilism" of the Communist countries and the "soft nihilism" of the West. Another disappointing work was John Barth's *Sabbatical: A Romance*. Like Bellow, Barth seemed unjustifiably enamoured of his central characters, a pair of married academics who confront a number of "life-choices" and nautical perils while on a cruise in their sailboat; the book founders in self-satisfied liberal priggishness and Barthian scholarly apparatus.

John Cheever, who died in June at the age of 70, published his last novel, the elegiac *Oh What a Paradise It Seems*, a brief, beautiful story that included a wealth of narrative invention within its small, elegant compass. At its centre is elderly, affluent Lemuel Sears, a typical Cheever suburbanite, made melancholy by the fragile fading beauty around him. He asserts his hold over life by taking a mistress and battling an attempt to turn a pond he had loved as a child into a garbage dump. A less satisfactory last novel was *Mickelsson's Ghosts* by John Gardner, who was killed in a motorcycle accident in September at the age of 49. It was a vast, loosely organized, and ponderously speculative work about a philosophy professor who attempts to flee from a variety of personal and professional problems by holing up in an old farmhouse on the edge of a decaying town in eastern Pennsylvania.

Louis Auchincloss's *Watchfires*, based on an incident from the diary of George Templeton Strong, "the Pepys of nineteenth-century New York," was another of his accomplished studies of manners, full of the "enthusiasm for personalities" with which he credits Strong in a note to the book. Less conventional in their approach to historical subject matter were Stanley Elkin's *George Mills* and Joyce Carol Oates's *A Bloodsmoor Romance*. Elkin's book was a rambling, thousand-year chronicle of the ancestral line of his working-class hero. Moving back and forth from the life of the present George Mills to those who drudged in the past, the novel is enlivened by a colloquial, blackly comic lyricism. *A Bloodsmoor Romance* was a massive, mock-gothic tale of five independent-minded sisters in late-19th-century U.S., an irreverent blending of fact and fiction in the manner of Oates's recent *Bellefleur*.

The pseudonymous William Wharton published a powerful antiwar novel, *A Midnight Clear*, about a small group of bright, teenaged GI's trying to survive Christmas 1944 in a snowbound no-man's-land. Like Wharton's highly original earlier novels, *Birdy* and *Dad*, *A Midnight Clear* powerfully integrated fantasy into a realistic narrative. Another strongly didactic work was Marge Piercy's typically blunt and energetic seventh novel, *Braided Lives*. Largely autobiographical, it was a middle-aged writer's frequently powerful account of the painful process of growing up female in the 1950s. Gail Godwin's qui-

THOMAS VICTOR ©1982

Marge Piercy

etly affirmative and carefully detailed *A Mother and Two Daughters* told of three women coping with change today and triumphing in an idyllic epilogue set in 1984.

Poppa John by Larry Woiwode was largely the events of a single day in the life of an elderly actor who had been idled several months previously by the television "death" of the famous soap-opera character he had long played. An untypically brief and spare narrative for Woiwode, *Poppa John* was also unlike his earlier work in being somewhat implausible and unrewardingly awkward in style. Anne Tyler's ninth novel, *Dinner at the Homesick Restaurant*, a witty and compassionate study of an unhappy family, demonstrated a new mastery of both character and form. Glimpsed through the eyes of their dying mother and at their brief, calamitous family reunions, two brothers and a sister reveal their bondage to a childhood diminished by a father's truancy. Alice Walker's *The Color Purple* was a brilliant and affecting novel covering 30 years in the lives of two Southern black women, sisters separated as adolescents.

A number of impressive first novels were published during the year. Ivan Doig's *The Sea Runners*, an account of four men's flight from indentured labour in Russian Alaska in the 1850s, had the convincing matter-of-factness and understated violence of an Icelandic saga. Another powerfully realistic novel was John M. Del Vecchio's *The 13th Valley*, a massive, vivid documentation of the day-to-day horrors of the Vietnam war that is only occasionally flawed by improbable philosophizing by his characters. Two interesting debuts were comic novels about publishing. Alice McDermott's *A Bigamist's Daughter* was a lively, cynical story about a young woman working for a sleazy vanity press who drifts into a love affair with one of her hapless authors. *A Novel Called Heritage* by Margaret Mitchell Dukore consists of the correspondence between an 18-

year-old precociously determined to write the Great American Novel and her somewhat bewildered editor, alternating with chapters of her odd, incipient masterpiece. *Sassafrass, Cypress & Indigo* by black playwright Ntozake Shange was a strange, poetic story of three sisters that was realistic and fantastic by turns.

Among the year's popular fiction were books by publishing phenomena Robert Ludlum and Stephen King. Ludlum's new thriller, *The Parsifal Mosaic*, longer than any of his previous books and at least as opaquely byzantine, led the *New York Times* bestseller list a week before publication. King's latest book, *Different Seasons*, was a quartet of short novels. Although the stories were uneven in execution (and only the last contained any element of supernatural horror), *Different Seasons* had a sufficiently Grand Guignol character to recommend it to King's legions of fans. In his latest research project, *Space*, James Michener presented the entire history of the space program (along with a half dozen major plots). The first novel in ten years by otherwise prolific Isaac Asimov, *Foundation's Edge*, was the well-executed sequel to his 30-year-old science-fiction classic, the Foundation trilogy.

Among the year's notable short fiction was a new, expanded edition of *Progress of Stories* by poet, critic, and controversialist Laura (Riding) Jackson. Praised by critics when it first appeared in 1935, *Progress of Stories* was challenging, rewarding reading from a major, if neglected, 20th-century writer. In the seven stories of *Bech Is Back*, John Updike brilliantly reintroduced Henry Bech, Jewish academic and reluctant novelist, who first appeared a dozen years ago in *Bech: A Book*. Ursula LeGuin, one of the few writers of science fiction and fantasy who had become known to a wider audience, gave further evidence of her depth, versatility, and growing virtuosity in *The Compass Rose*. Other fine col-

lections of short fiction included Alice Adams's *To See You Again*, Cynthia Ozick's *Levitation: Five Fictions*, Ann Beattie's *The Burning House*, and poet Maxine Kumin's *Why Can't We Live Together like Civilized Human Beings?*

History, Biography, and Belles Lettres. The year's nonfiction also showed the effects of a rapidly worsening arms race. Among the dozens of books on the subject of nuclear war, the most discussed was Jonathan Schell's *The Fate of the Earth*, first published in installments in *The New Yorker* magazine. In the first of the book's three essays Schell presented technical information about nuclear weapons and the possible effects of their use; in the second he offered moral reflections about human extinction; and in the third he discussed political responses to the problem of the arms race.

A number of the year's books dealt with the U.S. presidency. In *The Kennedy Imprisonment: A Meditation on Power*, columnist and academic Garry Wills produced a vigorous if somewhat simplistic piece of debunking in which he traced an almost unremittingly hostile history of the family, leading to an Edward Kennedy both created and crippled by a self-serving, self-defeating dynastic myth. Robert Caro's *The Years of Lyndon Johnson: The Path to Power* was an illuminating account of Johnson's youth and his political apprenticeship in Franklin Roosevelt's New Deal. *Tumultuous Years: The Presidency of Harry Truman, 1949–1953*, by Robert J. Donovan, was an ably done reappraisal of Truman's second term. For all its 1,300-page bulk, Henry Kissinger's second volume of memoirs, *Years of Upheaval*, dealt only with the 19 months from his first visit to Hanoi in February 1973 to Richard Nixon's resignation as president in August 1974.

Louise Brooks, ex-Ziegfeld showgirl and impassively beautiful femme fatale in a number of silent films, recalled her brief movie career in *Lulu in Hol-*

John Updike
WIDE WORLD

Richard Reeves
SIGRID ESTRADA/TIME MAGAZINE

(Left) Carolyn Forché; (right) Thomas Keneally
(Left) THOMAS VICTOR ©1982; (right) CAMERA PRESS, LONDON

lywood, an elegant, perceptive memoir. Another book on Hollywood was David McClintick's *Indecent Exposure*. Journalism given a novelistic treatment, McClintick's book was an account of the scandal and corporate power struggle that resulted when, early in 1977, it was accidently discovered that David Begelman, then president of Columbia Pictures, was guilty of forgery and theft.

Pursuing an intriguing journalistic experiment, columnist Richard Reeves described in *American Journey* his retracing of the route traveled in 1831 by the young French aristocrat Alexis de Tocqueville, whose nine-month tour of the U.S. produced the classic *Democracy in America*. The hindsight of 150 years only confirmed Tocqueville's brilliant insight.

Poetry. Many major poets published books during the year. *This Journey* was a ninth, posthumous collection of the work of James Wright, who died in 1980 at the age of 52. *Our Ground Time Here Will Be Brief* by Maxine Kumin included selections from her six earlier books as well as a number of new poems, some of her best work to date. Mona Van Duyn published the elegiac *Letters from a Father and Other Poems*, her first substantial collection since *To See, to Take*, which won the National Book Award in 1971. Among the other new volumes were Denise Levertov's *Candles in Babylon*, Adrienne Rich's *A Wild Patience Has Taken Me This Far*, A. R. Ammons's *Worldly Hopes*, Robert Bly's *The Man in the Black Coat Turns*, and Carolyn Forché's *The Country Between Us*, winner of the 1982 Academy of American Poets Lamont Award.

United Kingdom

Readers of fiction looked back a century to 1882, the year when Anthony Trollope died and James Joyce was born. It was noted that the Victorian conservative was still popular and the experimental Irishman was still obscure, needing interpreters.

Trollope's novels were dramatized and entertainingly broadcast on radio and television. Joyce was discussed and read aloud on BBC's Radio Three, for a smaller audience. Shirley Robin Letwin published *The Gentleman in Trollope*, a provocative account of Trollope's conservative values. There were also several new books about Joyce—*The Joycean Way, A Starchamber Quiry*, and *James Joyce's Odyssey: A Guide to the Dublin of Ulysses* among them—but none of the large scholarly enterprises engaged in Joyce research were ready for the centenary.

Anthony Burgess continued to celebrate and, to some degree, emulate Joyce. A composer as well as a novelist, Burgess brought Joyce to the fore in his set of essays about the relationship of music to literature, *This Man and Music*, and in his charming disquisition *On Going to Bed*. Burgess's third book of 1982 was a playfully experimental novel, *The End of the World News*, in which he mingled the lives of Freud and Trotsky with a science-fiction yarn with Joycean musicality and wordplay.

Fiction. The prestigious Booker Prize attracted strong interest in the mass media, and the prizewinning ceremony was televised. The winner was an Australian, Thomas Keneally, with *Schindler's Ark*. This choice caused argument. Keneally's book seemed more like a factual report than an example of fiction. Apparently a true story about a German who protected Jews during World War II while pretending to collaborate with the Nazis, *Schindler's Ark* offered encouragement to well-meaning, unheroic spirits.

It was contrasted with Lawrence Durrell's fictional treatment of wartime life, *Constance: Or Solitary Practices*, fanciful, gamy, and surrealistic. Another unsuccessful competitor was Alice Thomas Ellis with *The 27th Kingdom*, a Roman Catholic fantasy about a flying nun. Also on the list for the Booker were two more down-to-earth novels. William

Boyd's *An Ice-Cream War*, a historical novel about the clash between British and German troops in East Africa during World War I, was a worthy successor to his *A Good Man in Africa* of the previous year (which received a 1982 Somerset Maugham Award). *Sour Sweet* by Timothy Mo was an intriguing novel about a Chinese family in the catering trade. The sixth competitor was John Arden, the left-wing historical playwright; his first novel, *Silence Among the Weapons*, was a historical romance, set in the world of the theatre in ancient Rome and imaginatively expressing his concern for subject races and classes. John Wain and Alan Sillitoe, who made their names in the 1950s—that decade of youthful, antisnobbish radicalism—both returned with the quieter work of their maturity. Wain's novel (which won the Whitbread Prize) was *Young Shoulders* and movingly described the bereavement of a young boy after the death of his sister. Sillitoe's *Her Victory* came to terms with feminism, persuasively representing the struggle of a downtrodden middle-aged housewife while retaining a gruff masculine courtesy.

Graham Greene, the senior British novelist, offered a light, humorous variation on his old theme—dialogue between Catholics and Communists. *Monsignor Quixote* was set in Spain and told of the travels of an innocent priest (a descendant of Cervantes's hero) in the company of his friend, a Communist ex-mayor, who acts as his Sancho Panza. This pleasing morality, with its odd thoughts about faith, dogma, and permissiveness, won immediate popularity. Doris Lessing, who continued her science-fiction series *Canopus in Argos—Archives* with *The Making of the Representative for Planet 8*, received the Shakespeare Prize awarded annually by the West German FVS Foundation.

Lives and Letters. The most admired biography of the year was George Spater's new account of William Cobbett, the great 19th-century journalist and political reformer, appraising his soldierly combination of conservatism and radicalism. The Falklands crisis stimulated many books but, so far, little "literature"—apart from one collection of angry letters, *A Message from the Falklands*, written by a young naval officer, David Tinker, who was killed during the fighting.

Several British prime ministers were commemorated in biographies and collections of letters, with interesting new material about Benjamin Disraeli, William Gladstone, H. H. Asquith, and Clement Attlee. The cuckoo in this nest of politicians was the British Fascist Sir Oswald Mosley, whose talents were wasted by selfish arrogance and inconsideration. His son, Nicholas Mosley, attempted the difficult task of appraisal in *Rules of the Game: Sir Oswald and Lady Cynthia Mosley 1896–1933*.

Admirable biographies of poets, including Roy Campbell and Robert Graves, were appreciated. Among the theatrical lives, Sir Laurence Olivier's *Confessions of an Actor* attracted particular attention; usually unwilling to be interviewed, Olivier ap-

BERNARD GOTFRYD/NEWSWEEK

Robertson Davies

peared in two television programs that offered a physical, visual illustration of his contentious, well-written book. The thoughtful novelist C. P. Snow was currently out of fashion and favour; a biographical essay by his brother, Philip Snow, *Stranger and Brother*, offered his detractors an opportunity of which they took advantage.

Poetry. The most severe critic of English verse, Geoffrey Grigson, now 77, brought out his own *Collected Poems, 1963–1980*. No one dared to flatter him. At the same time, he published *The Private Eye: A Poetry Notebook*, with valuable reflections on good poets of the past, and a collection of his reviews, *Blessings, Kicks and Curses*, offering an opportunity for readers to complain of his severity.

Grigson responded by writing fairly gently about his juniors' new anthology, *The Penguin Book of Contemporary Verse*. He highly praised James Fenton, whose collection, *The Memory of War*, was the most acclaimed of 1982, and he was not unsympathetic to Fenton's 32-year-old contemporary, Christopher Reid, whose new book, *Pea Soup*, was described elsewhere as "the acceptable face of Martianism." The Scottish poet Douglas Dunn won the 1982 Hawthornden Prize.

Canada

The exuberance of Canadian poetry continued unabated during 1982. Among the more experimental offerings were *Sa N His Crystal Ball* by Bill Bissett, in which Sa enters the occult and encounters weird beings described in a language of cracked, distracted, haunting beauty. Another enchanter from the West Coast with her first major collection was Maxine Gadd with *Lost Language*, while b. p. Nichol was up to tricks new and old in *Zygal*.

Among other notable volumes of selected poems were *Earthlight: Selected Poetry of Gwendolyn MacEwan*, with poems from 1963 to 1982 marking the development of this magical voice; *Into a Blue Morning: Poems Selected and New* by C. H. Gervais, edited by Al Purdy; *The Land They Gave Away: Selected and New Poems* by Andrew Suknaski, edited by Stephen Scobie; *The Beauty of the Weapons: Selected Poems 1972–1982* by Robert Bringhurst; and a definitive selection of Irving Layton's best and best known works, *A Wild Peculiar Joy, 1945–1982*.

The long poem was also well represented, including a sonnet sequence by Milton Acorn, *Captain MacDougal and the Naked Goddess*, and *Kissing the Body of My Lord: The Marie Poems*, in which Douglas Beardsley uses the life and times of Marie de l'Incarnation to explore the conflicts between the Old World and New.

Other collections of new works by well-known authors included Patrick Lane's *Old Mother; The Presence of Fire* by George Amabile, dealing with such themes as love and friendship, the family and the self; *The Phases of Love*, in which Dorothy Livesay explores her theme over a span of 60 years; and *I Might Not Tell Everyone This* by Alden Nowlan, a bold look at some very private mysteries.

The fiction lists were fat and sassy. They included Katherine Govier's *Going Through the Motions*, the story of a stripper's struggle for justice and survival; Elizabeth Brewster's *Junction*, a time-travel novel in which a woman finds the fantastic and romantic inextricably entangled in the realistic; Graeme Gibson's *Perpetual Motion*, in which an obsession for the impossible culminates in a lunatic but moving tragedy; *The Ruined Season* by M. T. Kelly, a bleak, brawling story in an imaginary northern Ontario setting; the fourth in David Helwig's Kingston tetralogy, *It Is Always Summer; Cutting Through*, Keith Maillard's sequel to *The Knife in My Hands;* and *A Fairly Conventional Woman*, the other side of the coin from Carol Shields's previous *Happenstance*.

First novels included *The Ivory Swing* by Janette Turner Hospital, the $50,000 Seal First Novel Award winner of 1981; Aviva Layton's *Nobody's Daughter*, in which a poet's ex-wife finally finds her own voice; and Gail Scott's *Spare Parts*, a comic-tragic treatment of a woman's confrontations with crisis from puberty to womanhood.

The short story also continued to flourish, as exemplified by Guy Vanderhaeghe's *Man Descending;* Robertson Davies's *High Spirits*, which having once enlivened the annual Gaudy Nights at Massey College are now free to entertain us all; and Alice Munro's *The Moons of Jupiter*.

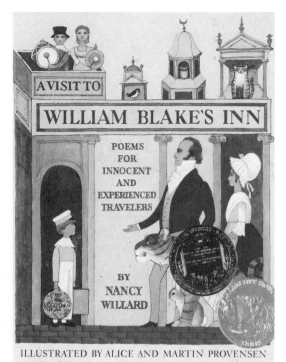

©1981 BY NANCY WILLARD. USED BY PERMISSION OF HARCOURT BRACE JOVANOVICH

Nancy Willard won the Newbery Medal for A Visit to William Blake's Inn, *which was also given a Caldecott Honor award.*

LITERATURE FOR CHILDREN

Books published in 1982 for children and young people reflected, as they always do, the trends, mores, and interests of our society as a whole. There were many books about the elderly and the handicapped, many that portrayed nontraditional sex roles, and many that dealt with such subjects of current interest as computer programming and the threat of nuclear war. There were also, among the almost 3,000 new titles published, hundreds that followed traditional patterns of folk literatures, fairy tales, poems, family and school stories, and picture books.

For Younger Readers

Several books were notable for the beauty of their illustrations. One such was Barbara Cooney's *Miss Rumphius*, the story of an elderly woman who believes that one should leave a gift of beauty to the world; the pictures are filled with light and sun and with the soft colours of flowers. Another was *Shadow*, a poem by Blaise Cendrars translated from the French and illustrated by Marcia Brown; based on African folklore, the poem is strikingly complemented by collage pictures that combine strong, vivid colours and bold silhouettes.

There were several books designed for very young children. Helen Oxenbury's *Shopping Trip* was one of a series of such books, printed on board pages and geared to the toddler's interests and experiences.

The Caldecott Medal went to artist Chris Van Allsburg for Jumanji.
©1981 BY CHRIS VAN ALLSBURG. USED BY PERMISSION OF THE HOUGHTON MIFFLIN CO.

Here the round-faced baby's investigations leave Mama limp by the end of a shopping expedition. Another set of concept books, also small and with baby-resistant pages, was done by Colin McNaughton to illustrate opposites. In *At Home*, for example, "wet" shows a happy bath-splasher, while "dry" has an equally happy baby wrapped in a towel. Another wordless picture book is Jan Ormerod's *Moonlight*, which depicts with humour and beauty the stages of a child's bedtime.

Some of the year's books for younger children focused on relationships with others. In Miriam Cohen's *So What?* a first grade nonachiever gets perspective from a classmate's "So what?" and gains enough self-confidence to adjust to being himself. In Judith Vigna's *Daddy's New Baby* a small girl describes her victory over jealousy when her father and his second wife have a baby. Also jealous is Alex in Mary Dickinson's *Alex and the Baby;* here it's a visiting infant over whom his mother coos; to Alex's delight, the baby proves to be noisy and messy. There's a strong mother-child relationship in Russell Hoban's *The Flight of Bembel Rudzuk*, a very funny story of children's imaginative play amusingly illustrated by Colin McNaughton.

Dramatic linoleum-cut pictures by Marcia Horvath illustrate Betty Baker's *And Me, Coyote!*, based on the creation myths of the California Indians. An Oriental tale is romantically illustrated by Michael Hague for Nancy Luenn's *The Dragon Kite*, in which the magical kite comes to the aid of an apprentice kitemaker. The storytelling tradition is strong in Leonard Kessler's *Old Turtle's Baseball Stories*, a simply written book for beginning readers in which a group of animals sit around a potbellied stove and reminisce about old baseball stars like Melvin Moose and Carla Kangaroo.

Of nonfiction books for younger children, one of the most innovative was the wordless *Anno's Counting Book*, by the Japanese artist Mitsumasa Anno. In Hans-Heinrich Isenbart's *A Duckling Is Born*, fine colour photographs by Othmar Baumli are smoothly integrated with a text gracefully translated by Catherine Sadler. In Jeannie Baker's *One Hungry Spider* the striking mixed-media collage complements a text that provides information about spiders, teaches the numbers 1–10, and tells a story.

For the 8–to–11 Group

It is for this group that some of the best realistic fiction is written. Constance Greene's warm and funny *Al(exandra) the Great*, one of a series about two lively girls in New York City, has a serious core. In Betsy Byars's *The Animal, the Vegetable, and John D Jones*, John D goes with his mother to the vacation cottage where two girls are staying with their father; he is accepted only when a near drowning makes the girls see how petty they've been.

In *Story for a Black Night*, by Clayton Bess, a Liberian father talks about his childhood, when an abandoned infant with smallpox brought tragedy to his family. A poignant quality is also found in Tormod Haugen's *The Night Birds*, translated from the Norwegian by Sheila LaFarge, in which a child's fears fluctuate with the condition of his emotionally unstable father. *Happily Ever After . . . Almost*, by Judie Wolkoff, is the story of a second marriage in which the children of both parents like each other. In Elaine Konigsburg's *Journey to an 800 Number*, a snobbish boy spends a summer with his father, who travels with a camel to fairs and conventions.

Jane Cardam's *The Hollow Land* is a series of closely linked stories about a lifelong friendship in rural England. Another fine story from England is Nina Bawden's *Kept in the Dark*, in which three children who are staying with their grandparents are terrorized by an older cousin. Rosemary Minard's *Long Meg* is the true tale of a young girl who, posing as a man, fought in France with the troops of Henry VIII. Lloyd Alexander's *The Kestrel*, an adventure story with depth and wit, describes a hero known as the Kestrel and his successful war against the invaders of his country.

One of the most imaginative stories of the year was *Witch Week*, by Diana Jones; a teacher in an English school is upset by an anonymous note that says someone in the class is a witch. In *The Haunting* noted New Zealand author Margaret Mahy wrote a cleverly crafted tale of a family in which there are hereditary psychic powers. Another excellent fantasy is set in Australia; Ruth Park's *Playing Beatie Bow* knits past and present together in a time-shift story in which the fanciful and the realistic are merged. *Pigs Might Fly*, by Dick King-Smith, is a witty tale about a runt pig who becomes a hero.

Notable among informational books was Piero Ventura's profusely illustrated *Man and the Horse*, describing the ways in which human beings have used horses from prehistoric times to today. Carol Lerner's handsome botanical drawings illustrate biblical quotations in *A Biblical Garden*, which also gives facts about each plant mentioned.

Many of the best books of nonfiction dealt with scientific subjects. Franklyn Branley's *Dinosaurs, Asteroids, and Superstars: Why the Dinosaurs Disappeared* discusses the many theories that attempt to explain the extinction of the dinosaurs. Shelley Lipson and Janice Stapleton's *It's Basic: The ABC's of Computer Programming* uses technical terms only when necessary in giving easy-to-follow instructions for creating computer programs. In *Messing Around with Water Pumps and Siphons*, Bernie Zubrowski holds a lively discussion of, and suggests home experiments to illustrate, various devices that move water for different purposes. *Journey to the Planets*, by Patricia Lauber, incorporates findings from recent space probes.

Several fine books of poetry for older readers can be enjoyed by younger children as well. Myra Cohen Livingston's *A Circle of Seasons* is an oversize book with seasonal poems that are paired with Leonard Everett Fisher's bold, stylized paintings. In an anthology by Helen Plotz, *Saturday's Children: Poems of Work*, a broad range of poems has been chosen with discrimination; all of the poems in William Jay Smith's anthology *A Green Place: Modern Poems* are by 20th-century poets, chiefly U.S. or British.

For Older Adolescents

A subtle shifting between past and present is a feature of *The Visit*, by T. Degens, a story in which a German girl gets a new perspective on her aunt when she reads a diary written in a World War II political camp for girls. Another fine historical novel is *Whistle down a Dark Lane*, by Adrienne Jones, set in the South just after World War I and featuring a trenchant handling of the protagonist's encounter with the Ku Klux Klan.

In Robert Lehrman's *Juggling* Howie plays on an all-Jewish soccer team and cannot understand why his father does not want him to go to a college that stresses soccer. A choice of school is an issue also in Mildred Walter's *The Girl on the Outside*, a story of the discrimination against black students who try to integrate a Southern high school.

Among the best fantasy of 1982 was Virginia Hamilton's *Sweet Whispers, Brother Rush*, in which occult elements broaden a story about a black family faced with a hereditary disease. Robin McKinley's adventure novel *The Blue Sword* also blends fantasy and realism adroitly in the story of a young woman who becomes a warrior-hero. In a vastly different type of fantasy, Delia Huddy's *The Humboldt Effect*, a submarine-based group of scientists uses a time-travel machine.

Like many of the best informational books for older adolescents, Robert Goldston's *Sinister Touches: The War Against Hitler* is equally appropriate for an adult audience. World War II is also the setting for *Behind Barbed Wire*, by Daniel Davis, a sympathetic description of the treatment of Japanese-Americans in the United States. Mitsumasa Anno's *Anno's Britain* is a beautifully illustrated depiction of a trip through the British Isles.

Awards

The Newbery and Caldecott Medals, selected by a committee of the American Library Association, went respectively to Nancy Willard for her poems in *A Visit to William Blake's Inn: Poems for Innocent and Experienced Travelers* and to artist Chris Van Allsburg for *Jumanji*. The winner of the National Council of Teachers of English Award for Poetry, given for the body of a poet's writing for children, was John Ciardi, and the Regina Medal of the Catholic Library Association, also given for the body of an author's work, went to Theodore Geisel, better known as Dr. Seuss. Winner of the award given to a new author by the International Reading Association was British writer Michelle Magorian, for *Good Night, Mr. Tom*. The Library Association of Great Britain gave its major award for a children's book, the Carnegie Medal, to Robert Westall for *The Scarecrows* and its artistic prize, the Kate Greenaway Medal, to Charles Keeping for his illustrations for *The Highwayman*, by Alfred Noyes. The Canadian Library Association's Book of the Year for Children was *The Root Cellar*, by Janet Lunn, and the Howard-Gibbon Medal for the best illustrated Canadian book went to Heather Woodall for her pictures in Garnet Hewitt's *Ytek and the Arctic Orchid: An Inuit Legend*.

MAGAZINES

Just as the effects of recession really began to affect the mainstream of magazine publishing, the titles actually doing well were those like *Vogue*, whose cover price and ethos were increasingly beyond the reach of the vast majority. In fashionable London it seemed at times that everyone's enterprising son or daughter was involved in planning a new title to be laden with high-gloss photography and aimed at café society, the traditionally rich, or Arabs.

The conventional wisdom that controversy is a sure method of building magazine circulation proved correct in 1982 for *The Atlantic*. After running a controversial interview with U.S. Pres. Ronald Reagan's budget director, David Stockman (December 1981), the monthly magazine experienced a threefold increase in readership, as well as gaining wide publicity in other media. Perhaps illustrating Stockman's doubts about the economy, the 58-year-old *Saturday Review* suspended publication after losing $3 million in a two-year effort to remake itself into a monthly cultural journal.

According to a 1982 study, the number of successful commercial periodicals had increased from 500 in 1964 to 1,200 in 1982. The primary reasons were a high literacy rate, higher incomes, and interest in specialized fields. The most popular growth areas were art and antiques; business and finance; crafts, hobbies, and models; dressmaking; cooking; and fishing and hunting. In decline were magazines about babies, campers, and youth.

The usual 100 to 200 new magazines appeared in 1982. Most of the titles were self-explanatory. *Better Times* offered articles on stretching the dollar; *Fit* aimed to help women design their own physical fitness programs; *New Body* offered hope for both men and women; *Performance Horseman* was in step with renewed interest in horse care; *Collectibles Illustrated* came from the publishers of *Yankee;* and *Popular Computing* was directed to microcomputer fans. The most promising new title, to be published early in 1983, was Time Inc.'s challenge to *TV Guide*. Called *TV-Cable Week*, the *Time*-sized magazine would offer news and program listings. The record start-up expense, expected to last five years before profit, was an estimated $100 million.

Still another way of viewing magazines was offered in 1982 when BRS (Bibliographic Retrieval Service) put the prestigious *Harvard Business Review* on line. Readers could sit at a computer terminal and call up articles or parts of articles on a display screen. Full text computer availability of numerous other periodicals seemed inevitable in the years to come. The problem with on-line computer searching of magazines, however, was cost. The *Review* royalty was $40 per connect hour, contrasted with an annual subscription for the printed version of $24. At the same time, magazine readers were faced with ever increasing prices. The cost of periodicals rose 14.5% in 1982, bringing the average annual subscription price of a periodical to $44.80. Labour and printing costs continued to rise, while advertising revenues in the first half of 1982 were only even with the same period in 1981.

Alongside the demise of older general-interest magazines came continued growth in magazines aimed at special interests and services, among them personal computers and cable TV.
(LEFT) ROBERT R. McELROY/NEWSWEEK; (RIGHT) TIME, INC.

MALAYSIA

Elections to the federal Parliament and all 11 state assemblies in peninsular Malaysia were held on April 22, 1982, while the two east Malaysian states voted only for federal seats on April 22–26. With the slogan "clean, effective, and trustworthy government," the ruling National Front (Barisan Nasional) coalition achieved an electoral triumph, securing 132 parliamentary seats out of 154 and retaining control of all the peninsular state assemblies.

A notable feature of the parliamentary results was the loss of seven seats by the Chinese-based opposition Democratic Action Party, which won only nine seats. The dominant Malay party, the United Malays National Organization (UMNO), consolidated its strong position within the ruling coalition through the efforts of Prime Minister Datuk Seri Mahathir bin Mohamad and also by attracting as a parliamentary candidate the charismatic figure of Anwar Ibrahim, who resigned as head of the Malaysian Islamic Youth Movement in order to run for office.

An election for one state seat in Negri Sembilan was postponed until May because of the murder on April 14 of UMNO candidate Datuk Mohamad Taha Abdul Talib, speaker of the outgoing state assembly. In July federal Minister for Culture, Youth, and Sports Datuk Mokhtar bin Haji Hashim and four others were arrested and charged with the murder.

Malaysia's economic circumstances declined. In March Deputy Prime Minister Datuk Musa bin Hitam announced an early review of the country's fourth economic plan. During the same month, the prime minister assured senior executives of 45 multinational firms from the U.S., Europe, Japan, and Australia that Malaysia would continue to offer stability and a good investment climate. With a serious drought affecting the rice harvest, in April the National Padi and Rice Board announced its intention to import approximately 400,000 metric tons of rice.

In August, alongside an independence-day amnesty for 47 people detained under the Internal Security Act, Datuk Harun Idris, the former chief minister of Selangor imprisoned for six years in 1978 on charges of fraud and corruption, was granted a full pardon. He had already been released from prison by remission of sentence in August 1981, but the pardon permitted him to hold political office.

In June Kuala Lumpur served as the site for a meeting between leaders of Khmer Communist and non-Communist Kampuchean factions, who agreed to form a coalition government to challenge the Vietnamese-backed administration in their country. Australian Prime Minister Malcolm Fraser visited Malaysia in August in an attempt to improve relations, which had deteriorated since Mahathir came to office in 1981. A more fruitful visit was made by Singapore's prime minister, Lee Kuan Yew, also in August; agreements were reached on the purchase by Singapore of Malaysian liquefied natural gas and also on the operation of an air shuttle service between Kuala Lumpur and Singapore.

MICHAEL GRECCO–PICTURE GROUP

Winners of the 1982 Nobel Prize for Physiology or Medicine were (left to right) John Vane, Sune Bergström, and Bengt Samuelsson.

MEDICINE

Much of the medical news during 1982 reflected the increasingly complex relationship between the providers of health care and the rest of society and pointed up a growing awareness of the effect of life-style on health and longevity.

The Institute of Medicine, part of the U.S. National Academy of Sciences (NAS), issued a report that claimed that as much as 50% of the mortality from the ten leading causes of death in the U.S. could be traced to life-style, adding that three of four Americans die from heart disease, stroke, cancer, accidents, or violence, in all of which behaviour plays a part. The report quoted the surgeon-general's estimate that 320,000 deaths a year in the U.S. are related to smoking and stated that more than 200,000 deaths a year are due to alcohol-related causes, including accidents and violence.

The World Bank and the UN Food and Agriculture Organization announced their intention to reduce support for tobacco cultivation in the less developed nations but showed reluctance to condemn the trade altogether because of short-term profitability. Stronger action would have been welcomed by the World Health Organization (WHO), which stated that controlling cigarette smoking in the less developed countries "could do more to improve health and prolong life than any other single action in the whole field of preventive medicine."

In another report from the Institute of Medicine, chronic, heavy marijuana smoking was blamed for inflammation and precancerous changes in the bronchial airways similar to those produced by tobacco smoking. The report stated that although marijuana may be less toxic in the short term than cigarettes, in combination the two are more dangerous than either alone. Total opposition to any attempts to legalize cannabis was pledged by ministers from 12 Council of Europe countries at the end of a two-day conference on drug abuse and illicit trafficking.

During the summer the NAS advised the American public that it could reduce its risk for cancer by following a diet that emphasizes fruit, vegetables, and whole-grain cereals and that is low in fat, alcohol, and cured or smoked foods. The anticancer diet was similar to the prudent diet recommended in 1977 by the American Heart Association to prevent heart disease, although it seemed to partially contradict an NAS report that was released in 1980, which had found no reason for healthy Americans to reduce fat intake.

The NAS committee that made this latest recommendation had worked for two years, studying worldwide epidemiological evidence that what people eat affects their likelihood of getting cancer. Although it admitted that the cancer-diet hypothesis was only about as firm as the link between cancer and smoking had been in the late 1950s, the committee ventured that diet is responsible for 30–40% of cancer in men and 60% of cancer in women.

The American Cancer Society announced in September that it was beginning the largest cancer study in U.S. history. The study would be similar to one conducted between 1959 and 1972, which helped demonstrate that smoking causes cancer, and would involve more than a million Americans aged 30 and older, who would be followed for six years. At the end of that time cancer researchers expected to learn a great deal about the relationships between environment, life-style, and cancer.

In 1982 a mysterious disease that killed 40% of its victims came under medical scrutiny. Called acquired immunodeficiency syndrome (AIDS), the disease results in failure of the body's immune system, which normally wards off cancer and infection. AIDS victims are ravaged by disease, including rare cancers and stubborn fungal infections. In some cases doctors were able to control patients' cancers and infections with drug treatments, but no AIDS victim regained normal health.

At first it was thought that AIDS was a new disease of homosexual men. Continued investigation, however, identified other groups of people with the disease; of the approximately 500 AIDS victims identified by late 1982, 27 were women and more than 60 were men who said they were not homosexual. Nevertheless, the epidemiological pattern strongly suggested that whatever triggers the disease can be sexually transmitted. Some medical researchers thought the cause to be a virus harboured in

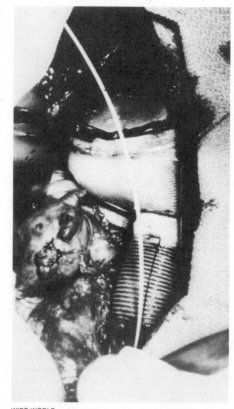

WIDE WORLD

The Jarvik-7 artificial heart replaced Barney Clark's worn out original in a historic medical development.

blood, semen, and other body fluids. They feared that, like hepatitis, the virus may be spread to the general population through blood transfusions and noted that several nonhomosexual AIDS victims were hemophiliacs who required frequent transfusions. The alarming spread of AIDS was arousing immense concern among public health specialists.

In May the 35th World Health Assembly in Geneva endorsed WHO's recommended list of 240 essential drugs that could serve virtually all the needs of the less developed nations and that would reduce their dependence upon imported and expensive pharmaceuticals, many of which were of doubtful use. The following month Bangladesh became the first country to adopt the WHO guidelines and announced legislation establishing a list of 250 essential medicines, banning 237 as dangerous, and directing that supplies of 1,500 others should not be renewed. The pharmaceutical industry worldwide expressed concern at the WHO policy, which threatened a large and expanding export trade to the third world.

Iatrogenic disease—disease resulting from the effects of treatment—claimed attention, most notably in the case of benoxaprofen, marketed under the trade name Opren in the U.K. and Oraflex in the U.S. Benoxaprofen is one of a group of nonsteroidal, anti-inflammatory agents widely used for the treatment of rheumatoid arthritis and osteoarthritis. It was approved for use in the U.K. in 1980 but was given clearance in the U.S. by the Food and Drug Administration (FDA) only in April 1982. Its manufacturer, Eli Lilly and Co., vigorously promoted benoxaprofen as being different from similar drugs already on the market.

Concern over the drug began in May with publication in the *British Medical Journal* of two papers recording an unacceptably high incidence of side effects, notably death from liver poisoning. These papers stimulated a rash of reports from other sources, and by the beginning of August 3,500 reports of adverse reactions, including 61 fatal cases, prompted prohibition of further sales of benoxaprofen in the U.K. with immediate effect and for an initial period of three months. Almost immediately Eli Lilly suspended sales worldwide. In Washington a congressional hearing was told that Eli Lilly had made unsubstantiated claims for benoxaprofen when it was launched in a blaze of publicity, but the manufacturers made it clear that they still thought it to be safe when properly used. Benoxaprofen might yet return to the market, depending on the results of further studies, but not likely as the best-seller it was in the summer of 1982.

A major study of heart disease in the U.S. was concluded in 1982 with a surprising result: widely prescribed diuretics used to treat high blood pressure could be dangerous to some patients. The study, called the Multiple Risk Factor Intervention Trial (MRFIT), was conducted by the National Heart, Lung and Blood Institute at a cost of $115 million over ten years. Its aim was to determine whether men who reduced their blood cholesterol, blood pressure, and cigarette smoking—three major risk factors for heart disease—would live longer. The 12,866 MRFIT participants were divided into two groups. One group, the experimental group, was given intensive counseling and assistance in reducing its risk factors, whereas the other group, a control group, was referred to its members' doctors for medical treatment.

Both groups of men reduced their risk factors, but the experimental group reduced them more. So the MRFIT analysts predicted that this group would have a lower mortality rate. But the two groups had the same mortality rate. On the face of it, risk factor reduction was not beneficial. The MRFIT investigators, however, suspected that something unforeseen had influenced the results. They proposed that most of the subjects who reduced their risk factors indeed had been helped but that these positive results were canceled by negative ones in certain men who appeared to have been harmed by reducing their risk factors. In particular, those participants who had high blood pressure and abnormal electrocardiograms and who were given diuretics to control their blood pressure had a 66% higher death rate than expected. It was felt that most men in the control group who had high blood pressure were given lower doses of diuretics or none at all.

The MRFIT researchers speculated that diuretics, particularly in high doses, may be depleting the body of potassium. For people whose hearts are already damaged, as evidenced by their electrocardiograms, this depletion may encourage rhythm disturbances leading to sudden death. The MRFIT study was the first in which it was ever suspected that diuretics may be toxic to some patients. The implications were far-reaching because diuretics were among the most commonly prescribed medicines.

In August Great Britain's Association of Anaesthetists produced a report suggesting that about 300 people in the U.K. die from surgical anesthesia every year and that in a further 1,800 postoperative deaths the anesthetic was a significant factor. The report stated that doctors were still making the same mistakes with anesthetics that they did 30 years earlier,

Nan Davis, paralyzed by a spinal cord injury, was able to ride a tricycle and later to walk by means of a computerized system of electronic muscle stimulation developed at Wright State University, Dayton, Ohio.

COURTESY, WRIGHT STATE UNIVERSITY

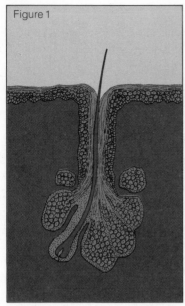  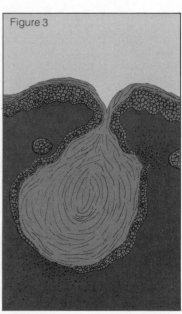

Sufferers from acne were given hope by a new drug, Accutane. Acne develops in hair follicles when surrounding sebaceous glands (Fig. 1) oversecrete oily sebum; pressure grows within the follicle (Fig. 2); the wall of the follicle then ruptures, forming a deep lesion filled with sebum, bacteria, and pus (Fig. 3).

despite improved knowledge, equipment, and drugs. Too many patients were given anesthetics without having been previously examined by the anesthetist for the presence of heart or lung disease or other relevant disabilities, and too many were anesthetised by insufficiently supervised trainees.

Doctors at the Karolinska Institute in Stockholm transplanted tissue into the living human brain for the first time in May. They injected cells taken from an adrenal gland of a patient with Parkinson's disease into a part of his brain known as the caudate nucleus in the hope that the cells would continue to secrete a key chemical, dopamine, that is deficient in the brains of Parkinson's disease victims. After several months the patient was showing slight improvement, but whether the effect was due to the transplant was not certain.

In early December medical history was made again when a surgical team led by William C. DeVries of the University of Utah Medical Center implanted a permanent artificial heart into a human for the first time. The aluminum-and-plastic device, called the Jarvik-7 after its inventor, bioengineer Robert Jarvik, replaced the two lower chambers (ventricles) of the natural heart; its two rubber diaphragms, designed to mimic the pumping action of the natural heart, were kept beating by an external compressor connected to the implant by hoses. At year's end recipient Barney Clark, a 61-year-old retired dentist, was making remarkable progress despite setbacks that included a bout of brain seizures and further operations to close air leaks in his lungs and to replace one of the artificial ventricles, which had developed a crack.

More than $1,200 in medical costs were spent on

the average American in 1981, compared with $350 in 1970. According to a report from the U.S. Department of Health and Human Services (HHS) issued in July, national health care expenditures reached $287 billion in 1981, which represented a record 9.8% of the gross national product and a 15% increase over 1980. While inflation accounted for 70% of the increase, 10% was attributed to population growth and 20% to the growing proportion of elderly in the population. Medicare costs totaled nearly $45 billion for 1981—up 21.5% over 1980—and averaged $2,400 per beneficiary. The report noted that in 1981 the average person paid only one-third of personal health care expenses directly, compared with slightly more than half in 1965; two-thirds were covered by governments, private insurers, and other "third party" agencies.

Regulation and Legal Matters

HHS announced in June that it would seek a warning label on aspirin sold in the U.S. The popular drug was suspected of being linked to Reye's syndrome, a serious and often fatal disease that strikes children recovering from flu or chicken pox. Reye's syndrome starts with vomiting and progresses to coma and brain swelling; patients who survive often suffer brain damage. But the link between aspirin use and Reye's syndrome was not well established, and some medical researchers felt that a warning label was unwarranted. Nonetheless, HHS Secretary Richard Schweiker announced that the agency would run a public awareness campaign to publicize the putative link between aspirin and Reye's syndrome as well as press for warning labels on the drug. (*See also* Safety.)

In April the British government took the unprecedented step of rejecting the advice of its official Committee on Safety of Medicines (CSM) by refusing to approve the use of the injectable contraceptive Depo-Provera for long-term use. Over the past decade the drug had been given to some ten million women, amassing a safety record better than that of oral contraceptives, with no deaths attributed to its use. A single injection is effective for three months, and the agent had been approved for short-term use in the U.K. under special circumstances; for example, to provide protection against pregnancy for the limited period after a male sexual partner has been vasectomized but is still capable of delivering sperm.

The CSM decided that the drug was safe for long-term use, and the government's refusal to grant a license for such use was based on political rather than scientific considerations. Objectors had claimed that the injectable contraceptive might be used, for example, to produce functional sterility in the mentally disabled without their informed consent, an injection every three months being far more readily administered without protest from the recipient than, say, the fitting of an intrauterine contraceptive. This appeared to be the first time that any drug apart from drugs of addiction had its use limited on social rather than clinical grounds. The decision produced strong protests from doctors and the manufacturer, Upjohn.

The FDA began deliberations in September on whether Depo-Provera should be approved for use in the U.S. More than 80 countries had approved the drug in the 15 years since Upjohn first applied to market it, but the FDA was hesitating because of hints from animal studies that the drug might cause cancer.

During the year a new prescription drug to help acne sufferers was approved by the FDA. Accutane, a synthetic derivative of vitamin A, had been shown effective in clinical trials against cystic acne, a disfiguring disorder that afflicts 360,000 Americans. Although neither the FDA nor Hoffman-La Roche, the manufacturing company, knew how Accutane works, both believed it to be a major medical breakthrough.

In November 1981 a major medical cause célèbre came to an end when respected British pediatrician Leonard Arthur was acquitted of the attempted murder of a three-day-old victim of Down's syndrome (mongolism). The infant had been rejected by his parents, and the doctor had written on the case notes "Parents do not wish baby to survive" and the instructions "Nursing care only." He was further alleged to have prescribed a morphinelike drug at a dosage that could have favoured the development of the pneumonia from which the child died. The jury decided that Leonard had committed no crime or, in the words of the judge, "strayed beyond the bounds of proper medical ethics." Although the verdict was greeted with great relief by the medical profession and made similar prosecutions unlikely for some time to come, it did nothing to clarify the law concerning the legal position of doctors who must handle grossly disabled newborns.

U.S. courts saw an increase in a novel variety of lawsuits during the year. With the legalization of abortion more and more couples were suing doctors for "wrongful birth" or (on behalf of a child) "wrongful life" following unsuccessful sterilization or the birth of a diseased or deformed infant after doctors had assured the parents of a normal birth. South Dakota and Minnesota had laws banning suits on such grounds, and at the instance of antiabortion groups similar legislation was pending in Illinois, Michigan, and Missouri.

In September abortion foes were blocked in the U.S. Senate after 18 months of efforts to pass some sort of federal antiabortion legislation. The bill that was defeated was sponsored by Sen. Jesse Helms (Rep., N.C.), who had tried to attach it to a debt-ceiling bill that had to be passed by October 1 to keep the government operating. Before its defeat, Sen. Orrin G. Hatch (Rep., Utah) withdrew a companion bill he had sponsored for a constitutional amendment that would have permitted Congress and each state to restrict abortion. Hatch later said his bill would be brought to the Senate floor in the spring of 1983 for a full debate.

Starch blockers, one of the hot diet fads of 1982, came under attack by the FDA. Marketed as tablets in pharmacies, health food stores, and supermarkets under many different brand names, the products contain a protein obtained from beans that reportedly prevents the body from digesting starch, thus allowing consumption of starchy foods like breads and pasta without weight gain. The FDA contended that starch blockers are not a food, as their manufacturers claimed, but unapproved drugs that should be removed from the market. The agency was concerned that the drugs may be ineffective in promoting weight loss, may interact with prescription drugs, may harm diabetics and pregnant women, and may have serious long-term effects. In addition, some users reported nausea, flatulence, diarrhea, vomiting, and stomach pains. Following orders in July that manufacturers discontinue marketing starch blockers, the FDA began seizure of the tablets in several states in September. The following month a federal district judge legally classified starch blockers as drugs and issued a ban on further manufacture and sale until experts could evaluate their safety.

MENTAL HEALTH

The use of electroconvulsive therapy (ECT) in the treatment of mental illness remained a matter for dispute. At the end of 1981 Great Britain's Royal College of Psychiatrists published a major report based on more than 3,000 questionnaires that had been sent to every doctor in the U.K. known to be using ECT. The investigators also visited many of the 400 hospitals and clinics where the treatment was

WILLIAM THOMAS

Demonstrators in Berkeley, California, campaigned to ban the use of electroconvulsive therapy (ECT) through a voter initiative.

employed. More than 80% of the psychiatrists interviewed agreed that the technique was of greatest value in treating severe depression that had proved resistant to drug therapy, but there was great divergence of opinion concerning its value in such other conditions as acute schizophrenia, for which half thought it occasionally appropriate and a quarter said it was "probably not appropriate." Only 1% thought that ECT should never be used, which

Supporters of ECT maintained that it was still a viable therapy in many cases of depression and schizophrenia.

PHYLLIS CROWLEY

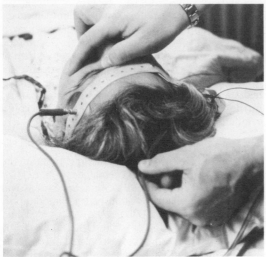

seemed surprising in view of the controversy that had surrounded this treatment in recent years.

A disturbing aspect of the report revealed that administration of ECT usually was left to junior members of the medical staff who had received little training or guidance in the use of the technique and who had to be told what to do by attendant nurses or anesthetists familiar with the routine. Very few of the clinics displayed diagrams showing the correct positioning of ECT electrodes. ECT machines are so made that the strength and duration of the current pulse can be varied to suit the needs of individual patients, but in 72% of the clinics visited the settings on the machines were never altered. In more than a quarter of the clinics the machines were obsolete and did not conform to hospital safety standards. Many of the older machines had no automatic timer, so that the duration of the delivered shock depended entirely upon the manipulations of the operator, a particularly serious fault because overdoses can lead to prolonged memory impairment. Although research had shown that ECT is beneficial only if a convulsion is induced, many patients do not convulse, but this fact was unrecognized by some doctors, who mistook a tonic jerking of muscles for the desired effect.

As a result of the report the college set up a working party to prepare improved guidelines on the use of ECT for members, and the secretary of state for social services set up another working group to investigate the adequacy of apparatuses available in National Health Service hospitals.

A worrisome tendency among old people toward violence was noted during the year by Bernard Knight of the University of Wales, Cardiff, and William Petrie of Vanderbilt University, Nashville, Tenn. In a survey of patients in the geriatric unit of a state psychiatric hospital in Nashville, Petrie discovered that 139 had committed or had threatened acts of violence. The weapon of choice was a gun or a knife. He classified 18 of the 139 as "violent." The patients had an average age of 74. Knight told a British Medical Association symposium that he had dealt with three cases of extreme violence among elderly people within as many weeks. He said that in such cases years of pent-up frustrations seemed to be released in one great outpouring and suggested that brain degeneration of the elderly might release inhibitions in much the same way as alcohol.

A panel convened by the National Institutes of Health in the U.S. concluded that there was insufficient evidence to support claims for the efficacy of the Feingold diet first proposed by California allergist Ben Feingold in 1973. He advocated the exclusion of all artificial food additives and natural salicylates as an effective treatment for hyperactivity in children. Children diagnosed as hyperactive had been subjected to various forms of treatment in recent years, including administration of amphetamines and even brain surgery. In the early 1980s the condition was still poorly understood, too loosely defined, and sometimes confused with behaviour resulting from other, better understood disorders such as lead poisoning and perhaps in some cases with the natural ebullience of youth.

Guy Chouinard, director of clinical psychopharmacology at the Royal Victoria Hospital in Montreal, reported that one-third of all patients taking major tranquilizers, or antipsychotic drugs (*e.g.*, Thorazine, Stelazine), are likely to suffer from tardive dyskinesia as a side effect. This condition involves distressing involuntary muscular movements, particularly of the face, lips, and tongue. His findings supported earlier recommendations that these drugs should be used only for the short-term treatment of patients with acute schizophrenia, who can benefit greatly from such medication.

MEXICO

The year 1982 in Mexico was dominated by a financial crisis engendered by the lack of early adjustments in economic policy as oil prices continued to decline. In February Minister of Finance David Ibarra Muñoz introduced a stabilization program under which the peso was devalued by 40%, but the crisis was not averted. Ibarra and Gustavo Romero Kolbeck, director of the central bank, resigned in March. They were replaced by Jesús Silva Herzog and Miguel Mancera, both close associates of the presidential candidate of the ruling Partido Revolucionario Institucional (PRI), Miguel de la Madrid Hurtado, and both known for economic caution.

Miguel de la Madrid was elected president on July 4 with 74.4% of the vote. Pablo Emilio Madero of the Partido de Acción Nacional (PAN), the main opposition party, polled 16.4%, while Arnaldo Martínez Verdugo, leader of the Partido Socialista Unido de México (PSUM), obtained 3.7%. In concurrent congressional elections the PRI won all 64 seats in the Senate and 299 of the seats in the Chamber of Deputies, with the remaining one going to the PAN. Of the 100 seats allocated by proportional representation to parties outside the PRI, 54 were gained by the PAN and 17 by the PSUM; three centre and left-wing parties shared the remaining 29.

The new president, who assumed office on December 1, inherited the economic problems caused by the sudden drop in international oil prices in 1981 at a time of rapid domestic expansion. Massive outflows of capital drained the country's foreign exchange reserves between January and August 1982, particularly as inflation began to gain momentum after the first devaluation. Wage increases of 10–30% were granted to compensate for the rise in prices. In spite of strong denials prior to a further devaluation, partial exchange controls were introduced in August, and the International Monetary Fund (IMF) was called in to discuss a $4.5 billion standby credit. At the beginning of September a stringent two-tier exchange rate was finally established, involving a preferential rate of 50 pesos to the U.S. dollar for foreign-debt interest payments and essential imports and an ordinary rate of 70 pesos to the dollar for all other purposes, including conversion of dollar deposits. In December the preferential rate was changed to 95 pesos to the dollar, and a free rate for other transactions was introduced.

Outgoing president José López Portillo announced that all Mexican private banks were being nationalized in order to reestablish financial stability. Following this move, Mancera resigned as head of the central bank and was replaced by Carlos Tello Macias, a former planning minister who advocated greater public-sector involvement in the economy. The government later said that compensation to shareholders in the banks of at least 144 billion pesos would be paid over ten years. At the end of

Miguel de la Madrid Hurtado was elected president of Mexico on July 4 and inaugurated on December 1, continuing the 53-year reign of the Institutional Revolutionary Party.
RANDY TAYLOR–SYGMA

UPI

The bank holiday declared by Pres. José López Portillo in September caught many unawares, including these Canadian tourists.

September, however, bank owners and major shareholders filed a lawsuit against the government, stating that the takeover was unconstitutional. In mid-November the government announced that it would close 106 of its 743 state companies and agencies to help reduce the public-sector deficit.

At the end of October there were demonstrations in Mexico City calling for an emergency wage increase of at least 50%. The minimum wage was subsequently raised by 30%; the average increase in private-sector salaries was 12%. Also in October, 17 officials of the Communications and Transport Ministry were charged with misappropriating funds to the value of some $1 million. Two senior officials of Petróleos Mexicanos (Pemex), the state oil company, were charged in November with receiving almost $12 million in bribes from a U.S. oil equipment company.

Two natural disasters affected Mexico in 1982. In March the El Chichón volcano near Pichucalco, southeastern Mexico, became active and showered ash, killing over 100 people. At least 200 people were injured and thousands were made homeless in

October by a hurricane that battered the coast of Baja California, northwestern Mexico.

Relations with the U.S. were mixed in 1982. The two countries failed to agree on a bilateral trade arrangement under which proof of damage to U.S. economic interests would be required before countervailing duties could be imposed on heavily subsidized Mexican exports. Following the August devaluation, Mexico banned exports of foodstuffs across the U.S. borders in order to safeguard supplies to its own residents. In mid-1982 Mexican politicians were angered by a U.S. television program in which the U.S. ambassador to Mexico, John Gavin, stated that Central American turmoil could spread into Mexico. Relations worsened in August when it was alleged that two U.S. State Department documents predicted that Mexico would adopt a lower profile in international affairs and become a more willing partner at the economic level. In October U.S. Pres. Ronald Reagan met President-elect de la Madrid at Tijuana. Both men pledged to cooperate while respecting each other's independence.

Within Central America, relations were affected by incursions from Guatemala into Mexican territory. At the end of September Mexico protested against counterinsurgency troops operating inside its borders. Guillermo Ungo, leader of the Frente Democrático Revolucionario in El Salvador, met Mexican political leaders in October in an attempt to gain support for ending the civil war in his country.

MIDDLE EASTERN AFFAIRS

The Arab-Israeli dispute entered a new dimension in 1982 when the Israeli Army invaded Lebanon on June 6. Israel had two objectives: the first was to destroy Palestine Liberation Organization (PLO) bases in Lebanon, and the second was to drive the Syrians out of the Chouf Mountains of central and southern Lebanon back toward the Bekaa Valley. While these military aims could in no sense be described as a "sixth Middle East war," their consequence was to harden Arab resolve and to rally international opinion behind the anti-Zionist cause.

Elsewhere in the Middle East Iran made considerable gains in the conflict with Iraq that had erupted in September 1980. With the incursion into Arab territory represented by Iran's invasion of Iraq in July 1982, there followed a considerable hardening of attitudes among other Arab nations, though most maintained their officially neutral stance.

Arab-Israeli Relations

Two important political initiatives toward a settlement of the Middle East's problems were launched during 1982. On September 1 U.S. Pres. Ronald Reagan revived the so-called Jordanian option for the future of the Palestinians and their occupied territories on the West Bank and Gaza Strip. Reagan recommended the establishment of an autonomous entity for the Palestinians that was to be linked with Jordan, thus reviving the 1978 proposals originally circulated at the time of the Camp David accords. Arab nations considered this the most evenhanded approach yet by a U.S. president. On September 2 the Israeli Cabinet rejected the proposals. Deputy Prime Minister David Levi declared, "They will lead to the establishment of a Palestinian state, even if this is not intended."

The Reagan declaration mentioned the PLO only in passing and gave little indication as to how the U.S. believed the question of the 2.5 million Palestinian refugees should be settled. Nor did it mention the issue of the Golan Heights, which Israel effectively annexed in December 1981 after having captured the area from Syria in 1967. It was believed that the hand of U.S. Secretary of State George Shultz, who replaced Alexander Haig on June 25, could be seen in the proposals; Shultz was considered to be an Arab sympathizer, close to the Saudi Arabians in particular.

The Arab League Summit

At a resumed Arab League summit in Fez, Morocco, in September, an eight-point peace plan was adopted as a response to the Reagan proposals. Under this plan: (1) Israel would withdraw from all Arab territories occupied in 1967, including Al Qods (Arab East Jerusalem); (2) Israeli settlements established in Arab land after 1967 would be dismantled; (3) all religions would be guaranteed freedom of worship in holy places; (4) the rights of the Palestinian people to self-determination, the exercise of their rights under the leadership of the PLO (their sole and legitimate representative), and the compensation of those Palestinians who did not wish to return would be reaffirmed; (5) the West Bank and the Gaza Strip would be placed under UN supervision for a transitional period not exceeding a few months; (6) an independent Palestinian state would be set up with East Jerusalem as its capital; (7) the UN Security Council would guarantee peace among all nations of the region, including the independent Palestinian state; and (8) the UN Security Council would guarantee the respect of these principles.

Thus, for the first time, the Arab nations made positive and collective proposals for peace. With the exception of Libya, all the members of the hardline Arab Steadfastness Front agreed to the plan. It had been the absence of those—Syria, Algeria, and Yemen (Aden), together with Libya and the PLO—that had effectively wrecked the first meeting of the Fez summit in November 1981. That meeting floundered over a peace plan put forward by King Fahd of Saudi Arabia, at the time crown prince. In particular the radical states could not bring themselves to recognize implicitly the right of Israel to live within secure boundaries.

The new plan was virtually identical to the Fahd scheme with two important exceptions. First, it explicitly recognized the PLO as the sole legitimate representative of the Palestinian people in their progress toward achieving statehood within the Arab nation. Second, the plan specifically called upon the UN Security Council to guarantee the security of all nations in the region. This latter alteration was seen as

U.S. Marines joined the international peacekeeping force sent to oversee the evacuation of Palestine Liberation Organization guerrillas from Beirut, Lebanon.
CHIP HIRCO—GAMMA/LIAISON

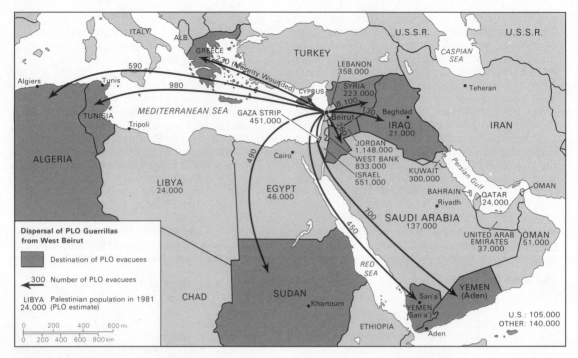

Dispersal of PLO Guerrillas
from West Beirut

Destination of PLO evacuees

300 Number of PLO evacuees

LIBYA Palestinian population in 1981
24,000 (PLO estimate)

a means of bringing the Soviet Union back into the Middle East peace process and thereby helping to quell Syrian objections. In early December a committee of seven Arab League members visited the U.S.S.R. in an attempt to rally support for the plan.

Israel reacted by rejecting the summit proposals out of hand. A Cabinet representative in Jerusalem described the plan as "a declaration of war." The U.S. welcomed the implicit recognition of Israel that was retained from the August 1981 Fahd proposals but reiterated objections to the establishment of a Palestinian state. Shultz told Congress that the U.S. opposed the dismantling of existing Israeli settlements in occupied Arab territories, a condition that formed a linchpin of the Arab plan. PLO chairman Yasir Arafat accepted all eight clauses of the peace plan, although it was thought likely that Palestinian fringe groups would reject the terms because their attitude to Israel was not sufficiently hard-line.

The Fez summit was considered a triumph for King Hassan II of Morocco, although beyond the main issue of agreement on a peace plan diplomatic progress was slow. Pres. Gaafar Nimeiry of Sudan was voted down when he proposed the readmission of Egypt, expelled in 1979 for signing an agreement with Israel. Egypt seemed likely to remain out in the cold at least until the 1983 summit in Saudi Arabia. Hassan failed to bring about a reconciliation between Syria and Iraq. A clear diplomatic winner from the summit was Arafat, who was received as a head of state by the other Arab leaders. Later in September Arafat continued his diplomatic rehabilitation in Italy, where he had a 20-minute audience with Pope John Paul II, talked with Italy's Pres. Alessandro Pertini, and gave an address to the Inter-

Parliamentary Union in Rome.

Following the summit President Reagan gave Arab leaders the option of allowing King Hussein of Jordan to represent the Palestinians in new talks with Israel and the U.S. over the future of the occupied territories. He warned an Arab delegation to Washington led by King Hassan that unless talks got under way, the Israeli government of Prime Minister Menachem Begin was likely to proceed with a mass escalation of its policy of settling the occupied territories. The Reagan suggestion put King Hussein in a quandary. Accepting that the king should act as a spokesman for the Palestinians would imply rejection of a principle adopted in 1974 and reaffirmed in 1982, that the PLO was the sole and legitimate representative of the Palestinian people.

The Crisis in Lebanon

The Israeli invasion of Lebanon was triggered by the shooting in London on June 3 of the Israeli ambassador to the U.K., although a full week earlier Israeli Foreign Minister Itzhak Shamir had publicly stated that Israel perceived the need to destroy the PLO as a fighting force. At first Israel stated that its aims were the same as those pursued in March 1978: to push the Palestinians back from the border with Israel in order to create a buffer zone. It became clear within 24 hours of the start of the invasion, however, that the Israelis aimed to clear the PLO from the whole of southern Lebanon, cutting off the 4,000 Syrian troops in Beirut from reinforcements in the Bekaa Valley. Later this objective led to a siege of the PLO strongholds in Beirut itself.

On June 9 Israeli jets attacked Syrian missile positions in the Bekaa. Syrian Pres. Hafez al-Assad's

government was quick to agree to a cease-fire on June 12. Skirmishing continued to take place after that, but on June 22 the Israelis declared a unilateral truce with the Syrians. With Beirut under siege from mid-June onward, law and order in the city broke down. Israeli forces kept a stranglehold on the city to starve out the PLO. On June 28 Israeli planes dropped leaflets making it clear that their bombardment of Beirut would not cease until the PLO's 6,000 fighters left the city. After intensive negotiations by U.S. special envoy Philip Habib, this was accomplished with the signing of a document providing for the withdrawal of the Palestinians under French, Italian, and U.S. military supervision; the evacuation began on August 21.

On September 20 President Reagan announced that U.S. troops would go back into Lebanon as part of a peacekeeping force to supervise the withdrawal of Israeli troops from Lebanon. The decision was prompted by the fact that the Israelis had pushed back into West Beirut in the aftermath of the assassination on September 14 of Lebanese President-elect Bashir Gemayel. It was on September 18 that the world learned the first details of massacres at the Palestinian refugee camps of Sabra and Shatila. Israeli soldiers were alleged to have stood by while Lebanese right-wing militiamen killed hundreds of men, women, and children in scenes of savagery unprecedented even for Lebanon. In the aftermath of the tragedy the Israeli government set up a commission of inquiry at which Defense Minister Ariel Sharon and Prime Minister Begin, among others, testified.

U.S. Marines returned to Lebanon on September 25 to join a reconstituted peacekeeping force. Disagreements arose almost immediately about how long the foreign troops should remain. Israel maintained that its conditions for withdrawal were the expulsion of the remaining PLO fighters, mainly in the north and the Bekaa plain; a simultaneous withdrawal of Syrian troops and Israeli forces; and a special status for the Israeli-backed Christian militia followers of Lebanese Army rebel Maj. Saad Haddad. Arafat said that the PLO would not leave before the Israelis. Syria agreed to withdraw its forces if the Lebanese government asked them to go and if Israeli troops also left. The U.S. expressed the hope that the evacuations could be achieved by the end of 1982, but Israeli-Lebanese talks did not get underway until December 28.

Gulf Cooperation Council

The GCC, which grouped Saudi Arabia, Kuwait, Qatar, Bahrain, Oman, and the United Arab Emirates (U.A.E.), held its third heads of state meeting on November 9–10 in Bahrain. The summit concentrated on the objectives of strengthening regional security and improving economic integration. The main topics for discussion were reported to have been agreement on a security pact, closer military cooperation, and the establishment of a $2 billion Gulf investment fund. The latter was to include private-sector participation. In addition, the leaders of the Arab world's wealthiest nations reviewed the results of numerous ministerial and technical committees that had met earlier. The proposed abolition

Arab heads of state gathered to celebrate the success of their summit meeting at Fez, Morocco, at which they agreed upon a unified peace proposal for the Middle East. The group included PLO chief Yasir Arafat (giving the victory sign).
ALAIN NOGUES/SYGMA

of customs tariffs and trade and travel restrictions among member countries—the first major implementation of the June 1981 economic agreement—was to be delayed until March 1983.

Kuwait gave notice of its reluctance to sign a mutual security pact at a meeting of interior ministers held before the summit. Kuwait was the only GCC member state to have refused to sign a bilateral security agreement with Saudi Arabia. The provisions that the agreement contained concerning the cross-border pursuit of criminals aroused fears in Kuwait that its democratic traditions were being threatened.

Shortly before the GCC summit Kuwait's foreign minister called for the GCC to work for a negotiated settlement between Iran and Iraq. This continued to be official policy. With the war costing Iraq about $1 billion a month, the GCC had already lent Baghdad some $30 billion. The GCC states apparently believed that it was in their interests to fund the Iraqi war effort rather than to meet claims for reparations from a victorious Iran.

(*See also* Defense; Fuel and Energy; articles on the various political units.)

Heavy casualties were the price of Iran's invasion of southern Iraq in July as early success gave way to retreat.

SIPA PRESS / BLACK STAR

MINES AND MINING

Production cutbacks and mine closings dominated the news about mining in 1982. Responding to a recession in heavy industry among the industrialized nations, demand for most metals and minerals declined and prices fell. Mining companies reported financial losses and furloughed thousands of employees. In the iron mines of Minnesota and Michigan 70% of the workers were idle during the summer of 1982, and in the fall in Arizona, after some callbacks, over 40% of the copper workers employed a year earlier were still idle. In the less developed countries the mines continued producing, but those nations' foreign exchange earnings suffered because the mine products brought low prices.

In 1981 there were six oil shale projects in the U.S., but by mid-1982 that number had dwindled. The shutdown by Exxon Corp. of the Colony oil shale project in Colorado came as a surprise because in the spring Exxon and its partner Tosco had reaffirmed that they were proceeding with the 50,000-bbl-per-day facility. Exxon cited escalated costs as the reason for the closing. In the aftermath Exxon purchased Tosco's 40% interest, which was in accord with their agreement. Surviving the debacle was Union Oil Co. of California, moving ahead at Parachute, Colo., with its 10,000-bbl-per-day facility. When the plant became operational in 1983, it would be the first commercial shale oil producer; the cost was estimated at $600 million.

Existing overcapacity in minerals was discouraging new developments. The oil companies that had diversified into minerals were taking a second look. Phillips Petroleum Co. and Conoco Inc. wiped out their minerals departments. Occidental Petroleum Corp. and Cities Service Co. were attempting to sell their mineral units.

Whereas minerals acquisitions had been frequent in 1981, that scene was comparatively quiet in 1982. Even so, mining men noted actions by big corporations in which Occidental acquired Cities Service and U.S. Steel Corp. took over Marathon Oil Co.

Molybdenum miners watched with interest as U.S. Borax, a division of Rio Tinto Zinc of the U.K., pressed ahead with the large Quartz Hill molybdenum project in Alaska. This development continued in the face of a depressed molybdenum market, existing mines operating at reduced capacity, and rich undeveloped deposits in Colorado and Nevada.

Quartz Hill was typical of the mining conundrum: whether to build during the market troughs and hope to come into production during the market highs, or build when cash flow and courage are better. Anaconda Minerals Co. did the latter when it announced its Nevada molybdenum project in December 1979 and reached design capacity of 12 million to 15 million lb of molybdenum annually early in 1982.

Kennecott Minerals Co., a subsidiary of Sohio, announced plans with Mitsubishi Corp. to modernize the Hurley, N.M., smelter. When completed in

The sudden closing of the Colony Shale Oil Project by Exxon in May caught the project's 2,100 workers by surprise and threatened to leave ghost towns in its wake.

1985, the facility would comply with environmental regulations and have 66% greater capacity, at 450,000 tons per year of copper metal. In December 1981, Asarco Inc. started up a new mine and concentrator at Troy, Mont. At capacity the facility would produce 130 tons of silver and 18,000 tons of copper annually and would employ 300 people.

A one million-ton-per-year soda ash mining and milling facility was started up by Tenneco Minerals Co. near Green River, Wyo. The plant began operating at a time when the market was depressed and plans for the expansion of other soda ash mines had been set back.

The most northerly metal mine in the world, on Little Cornwallis Island at latitude 77° N in Canada, was put into operation by Cominco Ltd. of Canada. The facility produced lead and zinc concentrates and employed about 240 persons. Construction methods were noteworthy for the high degree of prefabrication, the centrepiece being a barge-mounted concentrator that was towed to the site where the barge was settled on a pad as the foundation for the mill.

In New Brunswick, Canada, the Mt. Pleasant tungsten mine was scheduled to come into production at a cost of Can$120 million. In June the Real de Angeles silver mine in the state of Zacatecas, Mexico, started production. When it reached full capacity, producing 220 tons of silver annually, it would be the world's largest silver mine.

The first production of aluminum was achieved by Valesul Aluminio early in 1982 at its new smelter

southwest of Rio de Janeiro, Brazil. For the state-owned company Cia Vale do Rio Doce, Valesul was one unit of a much larger enterprise, including the Alunorte 800,000-ton-per-year alumina refinery and the Albras 320,000-ton-per-year aluminum smelter at Bacarena southwest of Belem. These last two projects, costing an estimated $2.5 billion, were to be commissioned in 1985.

Brazil set its sights on even higher goals in its projected development of the Carajás mineral province in the Amazon River area. Since the discovery of iron ore in 1967, a remarkable assemblage of mineral deposits containing 18,000,000,000 tons of iron ore, 60 million tons of manganese ore, 1,200,000,000 tons of copper ore, 50 million tons of nickel ore, 4,600,000,000 tons of bauxite, 37 million tons of cassiterite, and significant deposits of gold had all been located in a 36-mi (58-km) radius centred in the Carajás Range. Development of iron ore for export was launched by 1982 with construction of a mine, railroad, and port well advanced.

The Olympic Dam project, near Roxby Downs, South Australia, with a metal content worth $140 billion, held the potential of being one of the largest mining operations in Australia. Owned 51% by Western Mining Corp. and 49% by BP Australia, the deposit was expected to yield an annual 150,000 tons of copper, 3,000 tons of uranium, and 120,000 oz of gold.

A complete mining system for the new phosphate mine of the Agrico/Williams group in North Caroli-

The Polaris mine on Little Cornwallis Island—the world's most northerly at 77° N latitude—began producing lead and zinc concentrates in March for the Canadian mining concern Cominco Ltd.

ANDREW H. MALCOLM/THE NEW YORK TIMES

na was purchased from PHB Weserhutte AG of West Germany. The system utilized four bucket-wheel excavators and materials-handling equipment to remove overburden and phosphate from the pit area in a continuous mining system. It was the first packaged mining system operated in a mine of this type in the U.S.

Continuous mining of coal, first introduced in the early 1950s, continued to grow, and *Mining Journal* in 1982 estimated that more than 2,000 fixed-head continuous miners were in operation throughout the world. The machines cut the coal away from the face, load it, and deliver it to a transportation system in a virtually continuous system. In June and July the world record was broken three times by a 120-H2 Heliminer manufactured by Jeffrey Mining Machinery Division of Dresser Industries. The records were for eight-hour shifts producing 3,148 tons, 3,513 tons, and 3,668 tons. The records were set at the Sigma coal mine in South Africa.

MINORITIES, AMERICAN

American minorities continued in 1982 to defend rights and opportunities achieved in earlier and more favourable years. At the same time, they struggled to adapt to profound alterations in the nation's economic and political climate. More minority organizations began to stress self-help efforts combined with greater pressure on American corporations to expand opportunities for minority enterprise. The recession's shrinkage of economic opportunity hit American minorities with particular severity and also played a role in stimulating review of the nation's immigration laws. Underlying the year-long debate over immigration policy was one fundamental issue. How was America to apportion its opportunities between the disadvantaged at home and the dislocated from abroad?

Civil Rights

In the early months of the year, interest focused on the extension of the Voting Rights Act of 1965 and the strength of Pres. Ronald Reagan's support for the extension. Both the Senate and the House of Representatives approved the extension bill by substantial margins in June, and President Reagan praised the bill as a "statesmanlike measure" when he signed it. In September, however, the chairmen of 33 state civil rights commissions held President Reagan responsible for "dangerous deterioration" in civil rights enforcement and, a few days later, the Washington Council of Lawyers released a study of the Department of Justice that alleged a clear lack of vigorous civil rights enforcement.

Decisions of the Supreme Court during the year included several victories for minorities. The court affirmed the right of illegal aliens' children to a free public education, ruled that the mentally retarded in state institutions are entitled to training as well as basic care, and exempted the National Association for the Advancement of Colored People (NAACP) from liability for losses in a Mississippi boycott.

In October Vietnam began permitting "Amerasian" children of U.S. servicemen to leave the country and resettle in the U.S. Among the second group of such children to arrive were the 10-year-old son and 12-year-old adopted daughter of Frederick Eilerman of Manchester, Connecticut.

WIDE WORLD

Immigration

For the first time in decades, significant reform of the nation's immigration policies appeared on the political agenda. President Reagan opened the year with a set of proposals for extensive changes in immigration policy. The Senate in August passed a reform bill by a vote of 81–18; the bill clarified the status of illegal aliens, imposed penalties on employers who knowingly hire illegal aliens, and created a new category of labourer called "guest worker." Its provisions engendered considerable controversy, particularly among Hispanic groups, and the House took no final action on its bill.

Throughout the year the status and future of refugees from Cuba and Haiti occupied federal and state officials, particularly in Florida and New York. The Krome Detention Center in Miami kept over 600 Haitians in custody for over ten months. A federal appeals court ruled in May that the Immigration and Naturalization Service (INS) had violated the due process rights of 4,000 Haitians for whom the INS had held mass deportation hearings. Under court pressure the INS began during the summer to release Haitians from Florida and Puerto Rico detention camps. Florida officials battled for several months with the U.S. government over the issue of federal financial assistance for refugees; the federal government in June finally agreed to extend more than $30 million for resettlement costs.

Blacks

The early months of 1982 witnessed a number of heated exchanges between black leaders and spokesmen for the Reagan administration on the question of the president's sensitivity to black and other minority concerns. The president's nominee for a post on the U.S. Commission on Civil Rights, the Rev. B. Sam Hart, proved to be damagingly controversial, and in February his name was withdrawn.

The NAACP's annual convention in July reflected a growing trend among minorities toward self-help programs. A July gathering in Gary, Ind., of some 700 black leaders focused largely on strategies for using black economic power as leverage to expand economic opportunities.

The fall elections brought generally encouraging results for black candidates. Tom Bradley, the former mayor of Los Angeles and the Democratic candidate for the California governorship, came within 50,000 votes of victory. In Illinois, Roland Burris led the Democratic ticket in winning reelection as the state comptroller. In the Alabama gubernatorial race, former governor George Wallace, who had built an earlier career on segregationist politics, won with a substantial number of black votes.

235

Hispanics

The November elections afforded evidence of growing political power among Hispanics. Toney Anaya, candidate for governor in New Mexico, won office with 53% of the vote and became the highest ranking Hispanic elected official in the U.S. Hispanic candidates won three new congressional seats in Texas, New Mexico, and California.

Throughout the year immigration and the status of illegal aliens—many of whom are Mexican—were issues that aroused Hispanic leaders. The immigration reform passed by the Senate created a new category called "guest worker" that was, in Hispanic eyes, simply the old bracero program under a new name. Operation Jobs, launched in April by the Immigration and Naturalization Service, tracked down and in many cases deported illegal aliens employed in the U.S.; by May INS agents had taken into custody some 5,500 illegal aliens, amid strongly critical reactions from religious leaders, politicians, and civil rights spokesmen, as well as from Hispanic leaders.

Asian-Americans

In the centennial year of the Chinese Exclusion Act of 1882, census figures revealed that Asian-Americans were the fastest growing nationality in the U.S. In the period 1970–80 the Asian-American population increased by 125% to a total of 3.5 million. While the educational and income indexes for Asian Americans were among the highest in the country, the most recent arrivals—sometimes called the "second wave"—included many unskilled and uneducated immigrants who experienced considerable difficulty in establishing footholds in American life. In a pattern consistent with earlier waves of immigration, Asians tended to cluster in certain geographic areas; 10% of all Asian immigrants since 1965 settled in Orange County, Calif., and clusters also existed in a number of cities like Chicago, Dallas, and New York.

Native Americans

Land and tribal rights issues continued to dominate the news among native Americans. In Utah the Paiute tribe battled the U.S. government over its plan to take over portions of two national forests under the provisions of a 1980 law establishing the tribe's reservation and tribal rights. The U.S. Department of the Interior in May issued a finding that supported allegations from several Wyoming tribes that oil companies drilling on the Wind River Reservation had violated record-keeping procedures and paid the tribes inadequate royalties. The Penobscot and Passamaquoddy tribes in Maine, having finally settled their massive land claim in 1981, struggled throughout the year to convert their victory into concrete economic gains. Under the 1981 settlement the tribes were given a $27 million trust fund and additional money to buy 300,000 ac of land. By September the tribes had purchased close to 150,000 ac, but only a handful of members had begun successfully to make a living on the newly acquired land.

In a decision handed down in June, the Supreme Court sustained the right of Indian tribes to levy severance taxes on minerals extracted from their

Looting and heavy property damage marked a four-day riot in the Overtown section of Miami, Florida, in December, sparked by the shooting of a young black man by a Hispanic policeman.
UPI

HORAN–PICTURE GROUP

Supporters of the Equal Rights Amendment chained themselves to a brass railing outside the Illinois Senate in June to "dramatize the economic slavery we are in."

land; the case originated in a suit brought by a Jicarilla Apache tribe. Alaskan natives won a victory in November when the state's voters defeated a referendum that would have repealed a 1979 law granting natives special hunting and fishing rights for subsistence purposes.

Women

For women's groups the first half of 1982 was largely occupied by the struggle to secure passage of the Equal Rights Amendment (ERA), while the second half centred around organizing and fund raising for the November elections. ERA bills failed in key states, notably Illinois and Florida, and the midyear deadline passed with the amendment still three states short of ratification. The results of the November elections constituted clear evidence that the "gender gap" had become a reality that would weigh heavily in future elections. Postelection analysis confirmed that women had distributed their votes among candidates in a pattern significantly different from that of male voters.

Research studies released during the year further documented evidence of the barriers faced by women in the work force. A U.S. Department of Labor survey of earnings revealed that women performing the same work as men consistently earned lower wages. The National Research Council submitted an employment study to the Equal Opportunities Employment Commission that confirmed a 40% disparity between the sexes in average earnings.

The Handicapped

The U.S. Congress extended the 1981 International Year of Disabled Persons for an additional year in the U.S. But while Congress thus symbolically af-

firmed its commitment to strengthening the rights and opportunities of the disabled—who numbered some 35 million Americans—the Reagan administration sought regulatory changes affecting the disabled in the areas of education, employment, and physical access and encountered formidable resistance throughout the country. Proposed changes in the Right to Education of All Handicapped Children Act drew particularly strong criticism, and the administration finally withdrew a number of the most controversial changes. In May the Architectural and Transportation Barriers Compliance Board, ordered by Congress in 1978 to create guidelines governing access of the disabled to federal buildings, issued its regulations amid continuing uncertainty about the future of the board.

Homosexuals

In a year of some breakthroughs in legal status and political acceptance, homosexual rights groups had also to cope with an unexpected and sometimes fatal health threat—the acquired immune deficiency syndrome (AIDS). Although by the end of the year AIDS had begun to appear in other groups, its initial manifestations occurred predominantly among homosexual males. (*See* Medicine.)

An August decision handed down by the U.S. District Court in Texas invalidated a state law prohibiting homosexuality, thus making Texas the 26th state to decriminalize homosexuality. During the fall election period, several national political leaders appeared at homosexual-rights fund-raising events and elicited strong praise from rights leaders for their willingness to do so. In San Francisco a federal district court judge invalidated an INS rule barring foreign homosexuals from entering the U.S.

Special Report: The Latinization of the U.S.

by John T. Kenna

They are known as Hispanics, Latinos, Spanish-surname, Spanish-speaking, or Hispanos. They themselves usually prefer to be identified by their national heritage. Thus, they are Mexican-Americans (or Chicanos), Puerto Ricans, Cuban-Americans, or people from any of 16 Spanish-speaking Central or South American countries.

Unlike European Spaniards, Hispanics in the United States are not sociologically classified as whites. In popular terminology, they are often referred to as "browns." When the Spaniards colonized areas with indigenous populations of Native Americans, they intermarried and produced a mixed race (mestizos). These groups also mixed with Africans brought to the Americas as slaves, producing a new breed of people that mingles three races.

Similarities and Differences

The Spanish language is the unifying factor among the Hispanics in the U.S., as it is for the more than 250 million persons who make up Hispanidad throughout the world. Another source of common identity is religion. At least 85% of Hispanics are Roman Catholic.

There are also certain social, economic, and cultural characteristics that most Hispanics share. Eighty-four percent are congregated in large metropolitan areas, compared with 66% of the general population. They are, with some exceptions, poor, having lower incomes per family and higher levels of unemployment than the average American family. Hispanics also have a high degree of family stability and a larger than average number of children per family. With increasing acculturation, however, there is a consistent decline in these factors.

Politically, Hispanics are the most underrepresented ethnic group in the nation. They have only nine members in the U.S. House of Representatives, no U.S. senators, one state governor, mayors of only two major cities (San Antonio, Texas, and Miami, Fla.), and, except for New Mexico, disproportionately low representation in state legislatures.

Descriptions of common characteristics should not obscure the vast differences that exist. Within the Hispanic community, there is a rich variety of histories and traditions. Even the way Spanish is spoken differs among the various groups. Some observers believe these differences impede the unity that is necessary for the political success of the Hispanic community as a whole.

A Growing Population

The 1980 U.S. census recorded 14.6 million Hispanics in a total national population of 226.5 million. This made them the nation's second largest minority, after the blacks, who numbered 26.5 million. It also gave the U.S. the distinction of having the sixth largest Hispanic population in the world.

During the 1970s the national growth rate was a low 11.4%, reflecting the decline that began after the baby boom of the 1950s. In sharp contrast, the growth rate for Hispanics during the 1970s was 61%, and even faster growth was likely in the 1980s and 1990s. As of 1980 the median age for Hispanics was 23 years, compared with 30 for non-Hispanics. If the Cubans, who have a surprisingly high median age of 38, were excluded, the median age for Hispanics would be 19 or 20. Hispanic women have a higher fertility rate than that of any other group in the country. Based on these data, together with projected immigration figures, many population authorities believe that by the early 1990s Hispanics could be the largest single ethnic group in the U.S.

Minorities Within a Minority

Mexicans account for 60.6% of the U.S. Hispanic population. They are heavily concentrated in the Southwest and West, areas that were claimed by Spanish explorers and evangelized by Spanish missionaries. Almost all the Hispanics in the Southwest chose to become U.S. citizens in 1848, following the Mexican War.

Until the 1930s it was common for people to come and go at will across the relatively unguarded 1,900-mi (3,060-km) Mexican-U.S. border. The Mexican Revolution that began in 1910 caused thousands of political refugees to seek asylum in the U.S. Thousands more came later in search of better economic opportunities. Beginning in the early 1940s temporary seasonal farm workers (braceros) were allowed to come into the U.S. from Mexico in large numbers. A decade later "illegal alien" or undocumented workers began to pour into the U.S., driven by economic and population pressures and attracted by the

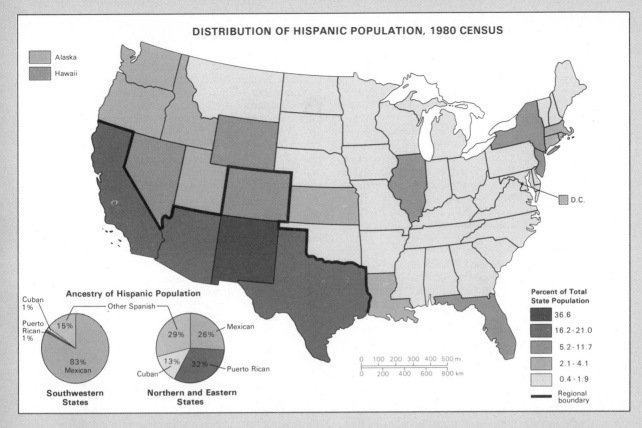

DISTRIBUTION OF HISPANIC POPULATION, 1980 CENSUS

Alaska
Hawaii

Ancestry of Hispanic Population

Southwestern States

Cuban 1%
Puerto Rican 1%
Other Spanish
15%
83% Mexican

Northern and Eastern States

Mexican 26%
Other Spanish 29%
Puerto Rican 32%
Cuban 13%

D.C.

0 100 200 300 400 500 mi
0 200 400 600 800 km

Percent of Total State Population
36.6
16.2 - 21.0
5.2 - 11.7
2.1 - 4.1
0.4 - 1.9
Regional boundary

need of U.S. industry for low-paid, unskilled labour.

Puerto Ricans, who constitute 14.5% of the country's Hispanic population, are U.S. citizens because Spain ceded the island to the U.S. in 1898 after the Spanish-American War. Internal migration by air between the island and the mainland became heavy in the 1950s and 1960s. Most of the Puerto Ricans settled in the Northeastern states, especially in New York City, but there are also fairly large clusters in the big cities of western Pennsylvania and some Midwestern states. Among Hispanics, Puerto Ricans are at the low end of the economic scale.

The most successful economically are the Cubans, who make up 6.6% of U.S. Hispanics. They did not migrate to the U.S. in substantial numbers until 1959, when Fidel Castro came to power. Since then, successive waves of political refugees have flocked to Miami from Communist Cuba, led by the skilled, entrepreneurial classes, then followed by lower-middle-class workers. Their number exceeds 500,000. Most have remained in the Miami area, where they have become a major success story.

About 125,000 more arrived in 1980, when Castro first eased restrictions on emigration, then emptied Cuban jails and mental institutions and forced the inmates into small boats waiting in Mariel Harbour to take the refugees to the U.S. These less desirable newcomers, many of whom were incarcerated upon arrival, caused serious disruptions among the Cuban-Americans already established in Miami.

Immigrants from Central and South American countries, who account for 7% of the U.S. Hispanic

population, have come to the U.S. both as political refugees (the most recent being Guatemalans and Salvadorans) and as seekers after economic opportunity. They are a diverse group, ranging from uneducated and unskilled labourers to highly trained professionals. Many of them, especially the affluent and well educated, tend to remain aloof from the other groups of Hispanics. Their aim is to be assimilated into the larger U.S. society.

Issues for the Future

Several broad issues face Hispanics and the rest of the nation in the years ahead. Should the U.S. try to reduce immigration across the Mexican-U.S. border—at a huge cost—because, as some claim, the immigrants take jobs Americans need? Or should the U.S. relax border surveillance and/or grant amnesty to undocumented workers and their families who have established themselves in the U.S.?

Should Spanish truly become a second language in the U.S., especially in public schools? Can Hispanics, who have tended to be inactive politically, secure proper representation in federal, state, and city governments? To what degree will Hispanics compete or cooperate with other organized groups, such as blacks and women? Finally, are Hispanics going through the same phase of balancing cultural integrity and acculturation that other ethnic groups have experienced?

Their numbers, their youth, and the goal of attaining full entry into the mainstream of U.S. life could make the 1980s the decade of the Hispanics.

239

MOROCCO

During 1982 the continuing war in the Western Sahara against the Popular Front for the Liberation of Saguia el Hamra and Río de Oro (Polisario Front) again dominated events in Morocco. The Moroccan Army completed a defensive wall from southern Morocco through the Western Sahara down to Cape Bujdur, thus preventing Polisario attacks and allowing the Bou Craa phosphate mines to reopen in July. However, Morocco suffered diplomatic reverses. In February Polisario representatives were admitted to the Organization of African Unity (OAU) meeting at Addis Ababa, Eth. In protest, Morocco and 18 other nations walked out, thus halting OAU activities.

Morocco reaffirmed its pro-U.S. stance when King Hassan II visited the United States in May. Although the U.S. Congress refused Pres. Ronald Reagan's request for a $70 million increase in military aid to Morocco, raising it instead by $50 million, Morocco nevertheless granted the U.S. Air Force landing and refueling facilities.

Morocco also reinforced its position in the Middle East when King Hassan in September was host to the Arab heads of state summit at Fez. There the position of the Palestine Liberation Organization was reaffirmed despite the Israeli occupation of Beirut, Lebanon, and a new plan to resolve the Arab-Israeli dispute was adopted. France moved away from traditionally close relations with Morocco, mainly over the Saharan issue, but a visit to Rabat by Pres. François Mitterrand in October helped to improve the situation.

Political wounds after the Casablanca riots in June 1981 were partly healed when the major opposition party, the Socialist Union of Popular Forces, and its associated trade union were allowed to operate again in April, 1982. A new loyalist party, the National Democratic Party, replaced the old Independents Group. Nonetheless, social and political tensions persisted, marked by violent Muslim fundamentalist demonstrations in several cities. There were widespread student protests over arrests of student union officials in February.

Morocco continued to suffer from the adverse effects of the 1980–81 drought. The trade balance by mid-1982 had worsened by 18%; the inflation rate had risen to 15%; and phosphate sales were down. Foreign debt had increased to $7 billion. Discriminatory trade practices by European nations forced Morocco to seek markets in the third world, Eastern Europe, and the U.S.S.R. Attempts were made to attract foreign investment; a new law no longer demanded majority Moroccan shareholding in any foreign company based in Morocco. Nevertheless, in April the International Monetary Fund had to grant Morocco a $579 million loan, with a special facility to pay for cereal imports necessitated by the drought.

MOTION PICTURES

By 1982 in almost all of the technologically developed countries of the West, the videocassette recorder had firmly established its place alongside the television set and record player in the standard equipment of the average home. For film industries everywhere this presented a whole new series of problems. With the possibility of renting the cassette of a recent box-office success for less than the cost of a single theatre ticket, the decline in audience numbers could only accelerate. Also, the potentially profitable market for the distribution of feature films in cassette form could be critically eroded by massive, easy piracy—a problem that increasingly

E.T. phones home.
SYLVIA NORRIS–PHOTO TRENDS

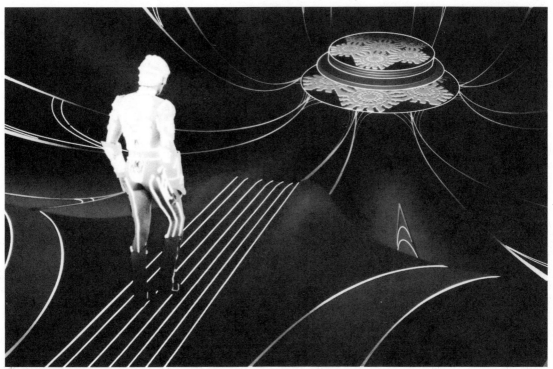

SYLVIA NORRIS—PHOTO TRENDS

Tron

was exercising the wisest heads of the film industry in many countries.

In a search for certainties in an essentially unpredictable industry, Hollywood increasingly tended toward a policy of making sequels to past successes. As *Variety* explained, "With the general decline of the traditional star vehicle, [exhibitors] have latched onto series films as an easily definable, steady source of product." Thus the year saw a *Rocky III*, a *Friday the 13th Part III*, a *Grease 2*, an *Amityville II: The Possession*, a *Star Trek II: The Wrath of Khan*, and other successors, whether signified in Roman or Arabic numerals.

Clearly responding to the tastes of an audience largely made up of late adolescents, two themes predominated in the year's studio production: horror and visions of future worlds. With titles like *Madman*, *The Beast Within*, *Bloodsucking Freaks*, and *Basket Case*, the horrors were mostly cheap and very deliberately nasty; but some (John Carpenter's *The Thing*, Paul Schrader's *Cat People*—both new versions of classic horror subjects) were more ambitious, and others (Tobe Hooper's *Poltergeist*, Amy Jones's *The Slumber Party Massacre*) more imaginative than the general run.

The films that speculated on future worlds and technology were generally costly productions. Among them Steven Spielberg's *E.T. The Extra-Terrestrial* was the major box-office success of the year and one of the most profitable films in motion-picture history. Much of its success seemed due to the innocent charm of its story about a stranded creature from outer space befriended by Earth children. Ridley Scott's *Blade Runner* projected a detective story into a gloomy future of urban decay and general pollution. Steven Lisberger's *Tron* was a more cheerful fantasy, a kind of electronic *Alice in Won-*

Annie

JOHN BRYSON—SYGMA

An Officer and a Gentleman
PHOTO TRENDS

derland whose characters enter into a video game to become luminous participants in combat.

Other favoured popular entertainment formulas were the high-school film, in which the excitement of adolescent sexual discovery was an important element (Robert Freedman's *Goin' All the Way;* Amy Heckering's *Fast Times at Ridgemont High*), martial-arts fantasies (*The Bushido Blade*), and the "sword and sorcery" picture. The principal representatives of this last genre, John Milius's *Conan the Barbarian* and Albert Puyn's *The Sword and the Sorcerer*, both sacrificed great cost and effort to scripts whose tedium and childishness could not entirely be attributed to the intention of parody. The year's leading animated features included Don Bluth's *The Secret of N.I.M.H.*, made by former employees of Walt Disney Productions, and Jim Henson's $25 million fantasy *The Dark Crystal*.

Among Hollywood's old traditional genres the Western remained in eclipse, the only notable representative during the year being the Australian Fred Schepisi's *Barbarosa*. Two costly though lively and successful musicals were adaptations from Broadway successes—John Huston's *Annie* and Colin Higgins's *The Best Little Whorehouse in Texas*. In contrast, an original musical by Francis Ford Coppola, *One from the Heart*, set in the gambling city of Las Vegas, Nev., achieved no distribution success.

The year's most successful love story was Taylor Hackford's *An Officer and a Gentleman*, about a young man's coming of age during naval officer training, while George Roy Hill made a successful film from John Irving's picaresque novel *The World*

According to Garp. Sidney Lumet's *The Verdict* dealt with the struggle of a down-and-out lawyer to regain his earlier idealism. Walter Hill's *48 Hours* was a thriller teaming a white policeman with a hip young black convict.

The year brought several notable comedies. Woody Allen's *A Midsummer Night's Sex Comedy* appeared as a farcical pastiche of Ingmar Bergman's *Smiles of a Summer's Night*, with a Shakespearean plot line about three ill-assorted couples in a rustic romp. Other comedies had a darker hue: Paul Bartel's low-budget *Eating Raoul* showed a middle-class suburban couple finding fun and profit in murder and cannibalism; Ron Howard's *Night Shift* was set in a morgue whose employees were using it as a call-girl centre; Carl Reiner's *Dead Men Don't Wear Plaid* was a witty spoof of the 1940s private-eye film, using extracts of period films as direct quotation. Richard Pryor made a second solo concert film, *Richard Pryor Live on the Sunset Strip*, and appeared in Richard Donner's disappointing *The Toy*.

Another highly successful comedy, *My Favorite Year*, which starred Peter O'Toole as an aging, alcoholic, swashbuckling movie star in the Errol Flynn mold, marked the directorial debut of the actor Richard Benjamin. Other distinguished debuts in the course of 1982 were Barry Levinson, with *Diner*, a study of a group of disenchanted young people, habitués of a Baltimore, Md., eating place in the late 1950s; Wayne Wang, with *Chan Is Missing*, a low-budget independent production that used the device of two Chinatown taxi drivers in pursuit of a defaulting debtor to illuminate much about the situation of the U.S. Chinese community; and Jonathan Kaufer with *Soup for One*, a bright and funny portrait of a young Jew encountering the everyday problems of life and sexuality.

Unanimous critical acclaim greeted Sydney Pollack's *Tootsie*, starring Dustin Hoffman in a bravura performance that required him to play an actor, the actor masquerading as an actress in order to win a job, and the actress acting in a soap opera. *Tootsie* also featured notable performances by Teri Garr, Jessica Lange, Bill Murray, and Pollack himself. Another year-end candidate for best film was Alan J. Pakula's *Sophie's Choice*, based on the William Styron novel and starring Meryl Streep. Jason Miller directed a film version of his own Pulitzer prize-winning *That Championship Season*.

At the annual awards ceremony of the Academy of Motion Picture Arts and Sciences in Hollywood, a British production, Hugh Hudson's *Chariots of Fire*, took Oscars for best film of 1981, best original screenplay (Colin Welland), best musical score (Vangelis), and best costume design (Milena Canonero). The best foreign-language film was the Hungarian *Mephisto*, directed by Istvan Szabo. The winning director was Warren Beatty, whose film biography of John Reed, *Reds*, also received awards for the best supporting actress (Maureen Stapleton) and best cinematography (Vittorio Storaro). Henry Fonda, who died shortly afterward, and Katharine Hepburn were adjudged best actor and actress for

Tootsie
WIDE WORLD

their work in *On Golden Pond*, which also took the Oscar for best screenplay adaptation (Ernest Thompson). The film *Raiders of the Lost Ark* was recognized for the best film editing (Michael Kahn), best art direction, best sound, and best visual effects. The best supporting actor was Sir John Gielgud, for his role as the butler in *Arthur*.

Some Notable Foreign Films

With the world's highest per capita average of videocassette recorders in use in the U.K., British distributors and exhibitors felt their position more insecure than ever. This was, however, something of a wonder-year for British film production. The success of *Chariots of Fire* in the Oscar awards had given the industry new confidence, and the launching of the fourth television channel provided new stimulus and finance for production. Channel 4 commissioned or financed a considerable group of films, on modest but sufficient budgets, providing overdue opportunities for new directors.

Co-produced by Channel 4 and the British Film Institute, Peter Greenaway's *The Draughtsman's Contract* was one of the most individual and inventive films made in England for many years: an ironic little anecdote set in the end of the 17th century and treated in a highly formalistic manner. Greenaway's style, already illustrated in his earlier short films, was a game with words, images, and music, enlivened by a rich and quirky sense of humour. Another distinguished Channel 4 production, Colin Gregg's *Remembrance*, was a sad, sympathetic portrayal of young peacetime sailors in port.

Moonlighting, Jerzy Skolimowski's fine comedy and a metaphorical reflection on the tragic events of December 1981 in his native Poland, was jointly financed by Channel 4, the producer Michael White, and the National Film Finance Corporation. Opening late in the year was Richard Attenborough's $22 million success *Gandhi*, a more than three-hour biography of the Indian leader. Lindsay Anderson's *Britannia Hospital*, though arguably the most important film of its era, was greeted with hostility from the British critics and indifference from the public; the foreign press (it was shown at the Cannes Film Festival) was more ready to acknowledge the Swiftian energy of this comic metaphor for a society in which institutions had become the masters of the people for whose service they were created. Among more conventional commercial productions, *Victor/Victoria*, a reworking of a German musical of the early 1930s, directed by the American Blake Edwards and starring his wife, Julie Andrews, as a woman who poses as a male transvestite artiste, enjoyed considerable international box-office success.

While government investment in films in Australia dropped during the year, a generous tax-shelter scheme encouraged sizable new private investment. The results were more than a score of films, the majority with the combination of technical assurance and indigenous character that could assure

SYGMA

Parsifal

international acceptance. Among these the outstanding box-office success of the year was George Miller's *The Man from Snowy River*, adapted from a favourite Australian novel by "Banjo" Peterson. Another early-century book, *We of the Never Never*, Mrs. Aeneas Gunn's memories of the dramatic change in her life when she left a comfortable existence as a Melbourne teacher to join her husband on a remote cattle station, was sensitively and spectacularly brought to the screen by Igor Auzins. Other notable productions of the year were David Atkins's *Squizzy Taylor*, a stylish re-creation of the career of a small-time gangster of the 1920s; Paul Cox's *Lonely Hearts*, about an unlikely romance between two quirky, middle-aged people; and Michael Caulfield's *Fighting Back*, about a young teacher's efforts to reclaim a delinquent child.

Tax-shelter schemes and other government measures to help promote quality film production in Canada had as yet had little time to show results. The outstanding French-speaking production of the year was Jean-Pierre Lefebvre's *Les Fleurs Sauvages*, a gentle and humorous account of family relationships, focused on the annual ritual of a mother's visit to her children. The most notable English-speaking films of the year were Rex Bromfield's *Melanie*, a touching story of a backwoods woman who comes to the city to reclaim her child, abducted by its father on his return from the Army; and Phillip Borsos's *The Gray Fox*, a period piece about a turn-of-the-century bank robber endowed with Robin Hood instincts.

In a year of generally undistinguished French production two major box-office successes were scored by Francis Veber's detective comedy *Le Chèvre* and Alexandre Arcady's *Le Grand Pardon*, a kind of French *Godfather*, in which Algerian Jews fill the role in organized crime played in the U.S. by Italian immigrants. More distinguished was Eric Rohmer's *Le Beau Mariage*. A fine comedy of manners, it was the intimate observation of a young girl determined on marriage but with not much success in choosing a quarry among the men of her acquaintance.

The death of Rainer Werner Fassbinder confirmed that for most of the past decade he had been the dominant figure in West German filmmaking. He left two new films, by far the better of which was *Die Sehnsucht der Veronika Voss*, a scenario based on the life and death of a well-loved star, Sibylla Schmidt, which won the main prize at the Berlin Festival in February. Of Fassbinder's contemporaries, Werner Herzog completed a much-fraught epic shot in the Amazonian jungles, *Fitzcarraldo*, recalling the crazy undertaking of a turn-of-the century Irish adventurer who set out to build an opera house in the jungle and to carry a steamship over a mountain range. Hans-Jürgen Syberberg directed a mammoth, five-hour screen version of *Parsifal*, and Hans Geissendorffer produced a faithful adaptation of Thomas Mann's *The Magic Mountain*.

MOZAMBIQUE

Instead of reducing their activities in 1982, the guerrillas of the Mozambican National Resistance (MNR) began to operate on a much broader front. In May the Army launched a strong attack in an attempt to clear the road and rail links with Zimbabwe, which had been sabotaged. The following month Pres. Samora Machel announced that arms would be distributed to civilians, but guerrilla activities increased, supported by arms supplies from South Africa and sometimes, it was believed, by South African troops.

Apart from severing communications with the inland countries of Zimbabwe and Zambia to make them more dependent on South Africa for supplies, the guerrillas seemed intent on discouraging foreign technicians from working in Mozambique. In May 40 Swedish workers sought refuge in Zimbabwe after two men were killed. A Portuguese technician working at a sawmill was shot by guerrillas. Six Bulgarian engineers were held hostage in the north of the country, and in October, in Manica Province, three Portuguese working on the oil pipeline to Zimbabwe were seized, together with their families. This latter action was accompanied by sabotage of the pipeline itself. Particular horror was felt in August when Ruth First, an exile from South Africa, was killed by a letter-bomb explosion in Maputo. First, a member of the South African-banned African National Congress, was at the time of her death a lecturer at Eduardo Mondlane University.

These guerrilla activities placed a heavy strain on an economy that showed only limited signs of recovery, and the failure to restore Mozambique's role as a transit state for goods traveling to countries in the interior seriously weakened an important source of income. Agricultural production, the country's main source of wealth, was threatened by the drift of people from rural areas to the towns. In June it was decided to issue identity cards to all city dwellers in an effort to stop this movement.

The need for foreign aid presented a challenge to a government committed to a socialist ideology. In June a Portuguese delegation headed by the premier visited Maputo for discussions that led to the signing of economic cooperation agreements between the two countries. Four months later the government asked to take part in negotiations for the next Lomé Convention, whereby African countries shared in the European Economic Community's common market.

The minister of defense visited the U.K. in November to discuss the purchase of communications systems that would facilitate joint action with Zimbabwe against the MNR. President Machel visited Zimbabwe in November with a further appeal for assistance. This followed a secret meeting between Machel and Pres. Julius Nyerere of Tanzania in October, when it was believed that Machel had asked that the 2,000 Tanzanian troops already assisting his forces be reinforced.

MUSEUMS

An exhibition at the Whitney Museum of American Art in New York City, "New American Art Museums," with its focus on eight diverse building projects across the U.S., highlighted the oddity of continuing construction of visual art institutions amid economic recession. Some included in that exhibition, such as the $11.8 million Hood Museum of Art at Dartmouth College in Hanover, N.H., and the Dallas (Texas) Museum of Fine Arts, were already under construction; others, including the Museum of Contemporary Art in Los Angeles and the Virginia Museum of Fine Arts in Richmond, were in advanced planning stages. Among other major museums that announced the construction of large additions were the Cleveland (Ohio) Museum of Art, the Whitney Museum of American Art, and the Des Moines (Iowa) Art Center.

In Baltimore, Md., the Museum of Art completed its three-year renovation with the opening of a new wing, while in St. Petersburg, Fla., the world's largest Dali collection, the Morse from Cleveland, was placed in the permanent Salvador Dali Museum, a $2 million renovated structure. The Asiatic wing of the Boston Museum of Fine Arts reopened in November after a four-year, $6 million renovation.

The J. Paul Getty Museum of Art, in Malibu, Calif., became the richest museum in the world

Elaborately carved memorial poles from the Pacific line one wall of the Metropolitan Museum of Art's new Rockefeller Wing in New York City.
JACK MANNING/THE NEW YORK TIMES

RICARDO FERRO / THE NEW YORK TIMES

The Salvador Dali Museum opened in March in St. Petersburg, Florida, to house the world's largest collection of works by the controversial artist.

when it received $1 billion from the estate of its founder, with another $100 million expected. The National Gallery of Art, Washington, D.C., inaugurated a $50 million endowment fund and was granted $5 million by Paul Mellon. In Pittsburgh, Pa., the Museum of Art at the Carnegie Institute received a grant of $2 million from the Mellon Trust that enabled the museum to resume its international survey of art begun in 1896 and discontinued in 1970.

A new gallery at the Victoria and Albert Museum, London, known as the Boilerhouse Project, opened in January. Established by Terence Conran, founder of Habitat Designs Ltd., it was to provide underground exhibition space dedicated to "encouraging professional and popular interest in the practice, history, and theory of design." The Conran Foundation would own and run the gallery independently of the museum for five years, after which it would move to permanent premises of its own, but the Boilerhouse space would remain a part of the museum as a gift.

In March a new art museum opened in Silkeborg, Den., as a permanent exhibition centre for the large collection of contemporary art formed by the Danish painter Asger Jorn, amassed from 1953 until his death in 1973. The Museo Civico of Pistoia, Italy, which had been closed for many years for restoration, reopened to the public in February. The Mauritshuis in The Hague, Neth., was closed temporarily for restoration in March. Many of its treasures were on view elsewhere in The Hague; some were part of an important traveling exhibition. (*See* Art and Art Exhibitions.)

The new Australian National Gallery in Canberra was opened by Queen Elizabeth II. It housed the Australian national collection of art and provided more than 75,600 sq ft (7,000 sq m) of exhibition space in 11 main galleries on three levels. The building was designed by Australian architect Colin Madigan and was described by one critic as combining the "munificence of a cathedral with the austerity of Fort Knox."

A new private museum devoted to the cat opened at Reihen, Switz. The "Katzen Museum," with some 10,000 items collected over 20 years, would hold small exhibitions on such subjects as "The Cat in Antiquity" and "Famous Cat-lovers."

New Acquisitions

Museums continued their recent practice of sharing works of art. Rather than compete with one another, the Minneapolis (Minn.) Institute of Arts and the Des Moines (Iowa) Art Center jointly acquired the Grant Wood painting "The Birthplace of Herbert Hoover." Each museum will display the work in alternate years. The Guggenheim Museum in New York City began a collection decentralization program. Ten museums in other parts of the U.S. would be allowed to borrow art works on a long-term basis from the Guggenheim's permanent collections.

The Metropolitan Museum of Art in New York received two extraordinary gifts from private collections: the Linsky Collection of small-scale three-dimensional works from the Renaissance and Baroque periods included 500 objects valued at $60 million; and 60 examples of Chinese painting and calligraphy, from the John M. Crawford, Jr., collection, were appraised at $18 million. The Art Insti-

The Australian National Gallery in Canberra was opened in October by Queen Elizabeth II. The $40 million worth of art already installed included works by Australia's own Sidney Nolan.

tute of Chicago incorporated the extensive collections of the long-closed Chicago Harding Museum to give it a comprehensive medieval and Renaissance arms and armour collection. Also in Chicago the Museum of Science and Industry showed the Morse Foundation collection of glassware by Louis Tiffany.

"Gimcrack, with John Pratt up on Newmarket Heath" by George Stubbs was acquired after a successful appeal by the Fitzwilliam Museum, Cambridge, England. The picture had been "sold" to a U.S. buyer, though prior to the sale it had been on loan to the museum for a long period. In order to prevent the picture's export the museum required over £600,000 ($1,034,483), nearly half of which it had to raise itself in only 12 weeks.

New acquisitions at the Tate Gallery included Max Beckmann's "Carnival," painted in 1920 in Frankfurt am Main and the first treatment of his later favourite theme, the costume procession. It was the last in a series of important modern German pictures acquired in recent years. Stanley Spencer's last "Self-Portrait," painted in 1959, was presented to the gallery by the Friends of the Tate. The Friends had given Spencer's first "Self-Portrait" of 1914 to the Tate nearly 30 years earlier.

The Scottish National Portrait Gallery acquired the first portrait from life of Mary, Queen of Scots, a small bronze bust modeled in 1559–60 when she was in her teens in France. Four Hogarth drawings related to the series of engravings "Industry and Idleness" of 1747 were acquired by the British Museum. The drawings represent different stages in the development of the series.

MUSIC

Classical

Symphonic Music. "Safe box office is best" was clearly the watchword among the world's leading orchestras in 1982. Except for a few sparsely scattered, generally undistinguished, and, as always, poorly attended premieres, the symphonic scene in the U.S. reflected the economic climate in its slimmed-down productions and blandly safe programming. The fact that, on the basis of just one album, the Minnesota Orchestra under conductor-in-chief Neville Marriner failed to achieve the expected long-term recording contract with the giant Phonogram empire probably had as much to do with economics as with any short-term weaknesses in the orchestra.

Elsewhere, the Pittsburgh Symphony continued to improve steadily under principal conductor André Previn (himself a steadily improving practitioner), and Italian-born Riccardo Muti, now fully in charge of the "fabulous Philadelphians" (as their brochure not unreasonably had it), at last got around to promoting at least one piece by a U.S. composer: the late Samuel Barber's second orchestral *Essay.* Under the circumstances it was a shame that the orchestra's previously rich, well-oiled style of playing (qualities well to the fore during a widely applauded European tour) sometimes seemed to be taking on a more hectoring, rasping edge; a Muti/Philadelphia *Petrushka* (Stravinsky) proved an especially ear-lacerating experience. In the same way, a Sir Georg Solti/Chicago Symphony Haydn *Creation* (subsequently recorded at Orchestra Hall for

London-Decca as part of Solti's 70th birthday celebrations) showed plenty of fire but little humour or stylistic adroitness. Cleveland Orchestra music director Lorin Maazel (still saddled with a fearsome reputation as a martinet) renewed and strengthened an uncommonly rewarding relationship with the Vienna Philharmonic, which lent a particularly bright sparkle to the annual Strauss family jamboree held each New Year's morning in the Austrian capital's historic *Musikverein*.

Despite sundry financial problems it was, however, London that once again provided the richest pickings during the year under review. If quantity decreased, quality was undoubtedly on the advance. Bernard Haitink's Royal Festival Hall (London) performance with the Philharmonia of Sir William Walton's firebrand First Symphony (subsequently recorded for Angel EMI) caused a considerable stir. News that additional classics by British masters (among them the two symphonies by Sir Edward Elgar and Gustav Holst's *The Planets* suite) were scheduled for performance and recording by so winning a combination was welcome indeed.

Opera. So far as the world's opera houses were concerned, old standards with established stars were the most frequent offerings in 1982. New York City's Metropolitan Opera enjoyed a particularly jaded season; the fiasco during an October staging of Amilcare Ponchielli's tuneful but glutinous *La Gioconda* (when an indisposed Placido Domingo's understudy was half-booed, half-tittered off the stage

and the conductor, Giuseppe Patane, suffered something approaching a nervous breakdown during the third act) provided light relief to audiences increasingly restless at having to pay $50 and more to hear sometimes inferior productions of box-office regulars. In two of its most successful productions the Metropolitan featured Luciano Pavarotti in Mozart's *Idomeneo* and Joan Sutherland in Donizetti's *Lucia di Lammermoor*.

If opera blossomed anywhere during 1982, it was undoubtedly in France, where (however recklessly) the ruling Socialist regime poured money into the arts in an attempt to ginger up French interest in something other than food, drink, and sports and to improve the nation's standards of music making and music teaching. Apart from English-born Baroque specialist John Eliot Gardiner's unearthing, as part of the 1982 Aix-en-Provence Festival, of yet another lost opera by the 18th-century French master Jean-Philippe Rameau, *Les Boréades*, Paris (courtesy the Opéra) witnessed a new production of Tchaikovsky's *Eugene Onegin*, directed by Gian-Carlo Menotti and conducted by Mstislav Rostropovich, and an enjoyable revival of Gounod's faded but tuneful and ever engaging *Roméo et Juliette;* l'Opéra de Lyon (a centre for excellence for some seasons now) announced a Mozart *Le Nozze di Figaro* starring France's leading dramatic soprano, Colette Alliot-Lugaz, that hailed initially from Italy's Teatro Comunale, Bologna; and the Théâtre de la Ville de Rennes staged a wide range of events from Bizet's

The New York Philharmonic, the oldest symphony orchestra in the U.S. (founded in 1842), gave its 10,000th performance on March 7 under the baton of Zubin Mehta.
UPI

Carmen (Antoine Bourseiller producing) and Pergolesi's *La Serva Padrona* to a visit by the Pansori "traditional opera" from Korea.

Sir Peter Hall (artistic director at the U.K.'s still unsteady-at-the-knees National Theatre) displaced Patrice Chéreau as producer in chief at West Germany's Wagner shrine, the Bayreuth Festspielhaus; the prime attention there focused on a new *Ring* cycle under the musical supervision of Sir George Solti, at threescore years and ten still the most dynamic Wagnerite around. In London mezzo-soprano Dame Janet Baker announced her retirement from the operatic stage, giving a farewell performance at a Henry Wood Promenade concert at the Royal Albert Hall singing Gluck's *Orfeo ed Eurydice*.

La Scala in Milan went through a difficult period in 1982, with the resignation reported in April of artistic consultant Giorgio Strehler because of his "profound suspicion" of the principles governing the theatre's management. The impending departure of La Scala's artistic director, Claudio Abbado, was also announced. The year marked the demise of the D'Oyly Carte Opera Company, formed in 1876 to perform the operas of Gilbert and Sullivan.

Albums and Cassettes. If 1981 had been a difficult year for the recording and hi-fi industries, 1982 was even more so. News that the European launch of the revolutionary Polydor/Sony-developed compact laser disc system had been postponed (though not in Japan) until spring 1983 was hardly surprising; with

the death knell of the 30-year-old long-playing disc now officially sounded (most authorities gave it at most a further decade's life), consumer resistance in certain markets was running high.

On the whole, the small companies with the lowest overheads generally fared best. Numerous interesting (and often trailblazing) releases hailed from apparently homespun but in truth highly professional operations. These included an album coupling U.S. composer Roger Sessions's Pulitzer Prize-winning *Concerto for Orchestra* with Polish-born, U.K.-domiciled Andrzej Panufnik's Eighth Symphony, the *Sinfonia Votiva* (Hyperion); Elizabeth Maconchy's Symphony for double string orchestra and *Serenata Concertante* (Lyrita); Alexander Goehr's *Metamorphosis/Dance* and cello *Romanza* (Unicorn Kanchana); William Wordsworth's fifth and sixth string quartets (CRD); and Robin Holloway's *Sea-Surface Full of Clouds* (Chandos).

Best news from the big names tended to centre less on star-filled new releases (a Herbert von Karajan Wagner *Lohengrin* on Angel EMI and Puccini *Turandot* on DGG notwithstanding) than on an active reissues policy. These included the late Italian maestro Tulio Serafin's masterly late-1950s Verdi *Missa de Requiem* (Angel EMI), pianist Julius Katchen's long-absent issue of George Gershwin's Concerto in F Major and *Rhapsody in Blue* (French Decca), Poulenc's *Les Mamelles de Tirésias* and *Dialogue des Carmélites* (both French EMI), and a considerable quantity of material conducted by Sir Thomas Bee-

The Silva Concert Hall of the Hult Performing Arts Center opened in Eugene, Oregon, in September. The hall features an advanced system of "acoustic resonance" to adapt it to both operatic and symphonic performance.

MARY KATZ

SIMON FOWLER – RETNA

The Human League, from Great Britain, made purely synthetic pop music with the latest in electronic gadgetry.

cham (Columbia CBS). Columbia CBS also scored with a lavish "Stravinsky conducts Stravinsky" reissue, in which 31 of the master's albums (many of them long unobtainable) were sumptuously repackaged as a limited edition.

Top choice among new issues (in a year in which pressing quality, even in The Netherlands, slipped generally) included *The Cunning Little Vixen*, a further installment in Sir Charles Mackerras's outstanding peregrination around the operas of Leos Janacek (London Decca); Eliot Carter's Symphony for Three Orchestras and *A Mirror on Which to Dwell* (Columbia CBS); Alexander von Zemlinsky's *Lyric Symphony* (DGG); a sequence of middle-period Beethoven piano sonatas played by Charles Rosen (Nonesuch); and a four-disc album of Mozart's complete sacred music conducted by Herbert Kegel (Philips).

Jazz

Little of lasting significance took place during the year. Connoisseurs of the best in jazz saxophone playing were saddened during 1982 by the deaths of two of the most accomplished apostles of that art. Arthur Edward ("Art") Pepper was among the earliest white players to understand and echo effectively the ideas of Charlie Parker, and after some years of ill health he had returned in recent years to give further evidence of the incisiveness of his technique. An even more gifted player was Edward ("Sonny") Stitt, a contemporary of Parker's who remained true to the teachings of the master through the decades. A player of brilliant facility, ferocious passion, and a truly wonderful melodiousness, Stitt was also one of the few considerable soloists in the history of the

saxophone to show equal mastery of the alto, tenor, and baritone instruments. As an alto player he was the wittiest of all of Charlie Parker's shadows, while as a tenor saxophonist he showed some allegiance to the works of Lester Young.

Another modern lion who died in 1982 was that most enigmatic of pianists and composers, Thelonious Monk. In conventional terms Monk's piano playing was hamstrung by severe limitations of technique, but a quirky harmonic originality allied to a sly sense of musical humour enabled him to overcome the handicaps of his own style. Monk achieved much as a composer of jazz themes and, whatever the fate of his idiosyncratic and occasionally willfully eccentric solos, there was no question that such themes as "Round Midnight," "Blue Monk," "Straight No Chaser," "Off Minor," and "Epistrophy" would continue to engage the attentions of sophisticated instrumentalists.

Popular

There was no orderly development of pop music in 1982. It was a year of rapid change, of styles coming and going, when for economic reasons there was a greater emphasis on single records than on albums and on the happenings in small clubs rather than in big stadiums. The major concert events seemed like relics from the past and exercises in nostalgia rather than pointers to the future, and the most successful bands of the year—in purely economic terms—were the two most famous survivors from the British pop golden years of the 1960s, the Rolling Stones and The Who.

The Rolling Stones followed their 1981 U.S. tour, which had earned them an estimated £60 million, with their first European and British tours in six years. Through the summer of 1982 they gave 40 shows in ten countries, playing to audiences numbering over two million people. Later in the year The Who gave a lengthy tour of North America, announcing that it would be their last on that continent. Thus an economically depressed record industry was able to thank a bunch of veteran rock stars for bringing young audiences swarming back to the vast sports stadiums that rock bands had found so easy to fill in the 1970s.

In both Britain and the U.S. the reaction against big-stadium rock led to a flourishing of new styles. As in the 1930s, a period of austerity led to flamboyance in the dress of those with any money to spend, and this apparently escapist trend was reflected in pop music. Much of the new music was based on electronic technology, utilizing synthesizers and computers that could allow one or two performers to sound like a full band, drums and all. The Human League were the most successful exponents of this new "electro-pop" dance music, and they exported the style to the U.S., where they had a massive hit with "Don't You Want Me." Like several other bands they made use of female singers to add glamour to the electronics. Two- or three-piece synthesizer-based bands such as Dépêche Mode, Soft Cell, Yazoo, and Blancmange also made an impact. In keeping with the high-tech mood of the times, some of these bands preferred to make video discs rather than appear live.

The new British fascination with dance music, style, and exotic foreign sounds was best summed up by the massive success in Britain of a New York artist, August Darnell, with his band Kid Creole and the Coconuts. Using a big band with a horn section, a comic percussionist (Coati Mundi), and three deadpan, slick dancing girls and singers, Darnell mixed black rhythm-and-blues and disco styles from the U.S. with a variety of Latin influences.

The U.S., with its enormous size, differences in regional tastes, and musically conservative radio stations, was slower to change to the whims of pop fashion. The very popular John Cougar was a beat balladeer in the tradition of Bob Seger, while such best-selling bands as REO Speedwagon were in the slick, easy-listening tradition, and even the energetic all-girl group the Go-Gos presented a spirited rerun of old styles.

Changes and innovation were taking place, however, and black American styles were leading the way. "Rap" was the skill of snappily, wittily, and rhythmically talking over a piece of music, and the rap artists of New York, such as Grandmaster Flash and the Furious Five, developed the style to a fine art. Their rap was fast, exhilarating, and funny, but it could also express the hopes and fears of the black community in a poignant and even startling way. "The Message," a rap single that was also a big hit in Britain, was a brilliant description of the sights, smells, and fears of the New York City ghettos, as expressed by a nervous, battered figure who admitted he was "close to the edge."

Elsewhere in the U.S. there was a surprising growth in the new wave or punk scene. Such bands as the blues-based Gun Club or X showed that not everyone in California was "laid-back." Once again the greatest U.S. performer of the year was the balladeer Bruce Springsteen, and again he surprised his followers by going against all the trends. *Nebraska*, recorded at home with his own guitar and harmonica backing, was his most bleak, chilling vision yet of the U.S. and blue-collar working life.

THE NETHERLANDS

On April 27, 1982, Willem Duisenberg, president of The Netherlands Bank, presented his 1981 annual report. While pointing out the possibility of recovery in the world economy and the opportunities this would present for Dutch industry, he was more concerned about the immediate situation. The number of unemployed had doubled in two years; in real terms the income of the average worker had declined by 4%; and the profits of trade and industry had been seriously undermined.

On May 12 the Socialist Party (PVDA) Cabinet ministers submitted their resignations to Queen Bea-

WIDE WORLD

Crosses bearing the names of four Dutch journalists killed in El Salvador were planted in front of the U.S. consulate in Amsterdam in March.

trix. The differences of opinion among the coalition partners—the Christian Democratic Appeal (CDA), the Democratic Party (D'66), and the PVDA—had become too great. The immediate cause of the split was the social-economic and financial policy of the government. The CDA and D'66 wanted to give highest priority to measures intended to reduce the government's financial deficit and thus stimulate economic activity. The PVDA, while acknowledging the desirability of such measures, wanted a policy directed toward the creation of employment. Personal animosity among the leading politicians added to the tensions.

On May 29 Prime Minister Andreas van Agt presented a new Cabinet that excluded the PVDA. The main task of this Cabinet was to prepare for elections to the lower house of Parliament on September 6. One thing was evident from the election results: D'66 had lost its political influence. As a result, Jan Terlouw, the D'66 leader, quit the national political arena. The Liberal Party (VVD) under its new leader, Ed Nijpels, greatly increased its representation, but the PVDA became the largest single party. The CDA lost three seats, and van Agt declared that he was no longer available for the position of candidate-prime minister.

By convention the biggest single party, in this case the PVDA, was given first chance to form a Cabinet. From the beginning the attempt was doomed to fail. Both the CDA and the VVD let it be known that their differences with the PVDA could not be bridged. After renewed consultations, Queen Beatrix appointed Willem Scholten, vice-president of the State Council and member of the CDA, to form a Cabinet. On November 4 the new Cabinet, headed by Ruud Lubbers as prime minister and supported by the CDA and the VVD, was sworn in. The Cabinet was at once confronted with a five-day strike by teachers. On November 22 the government announced tough new austerity measures, including a public-sector wage freeze that prompted a strike threat by government workers' unions.

On March 18 the Ministry of Foreign Affairs announced that four members of a Dutch television team had been killed in a gun battle between guerrillas and the Army in El Salvador. Some days before the shooting, Koos Koster, one of the four journalists, had been interrogated by the El Salvador police because a message with his name on it had been found on the body of a guerrilla. The results of an inquiry did not exclude the possibility that the attack was intentional but provided no conclusive evidence.

On March 1 Queen Beatrix and Prince Claus were welcomed to West Germany by Pres. Karl Carstens. During April 19–25 the royal couple visited the U.S., where the queen addressed both houses of Congress, and during November 16–19 they visited the U.K.

NEWSPAPERS

During 1982 newspaper publishers, faced with mounting costs and, more often than not, falling circulations, fought to keep mastheads afloat. There were some successes: The *New York Daily News*, in dire straits at the end of 1981, faced a brighter future a year later after reaching agreement with unions on manning reductions and an innovative profit-sharing scheme.

Total daily circulation declined 1.2% to 61,430,745 from the previous year's 62,201,840, according to the 1982 *Editor & Publisher International Year Book*. The total number of daily newspapers published in the U.S. dropped by 15, from 1,745 to 1,730. However, these figures did not tell the entire story. The U.S. was becoming a nation of two newspaper industries: a dwindling core of ailing afternoon papers, most of them published in big cities; and a prosperous group of morning papers in cities large and small. Total afternoon circulation declined 5.8% to 30,878,429, the lowest point in more than two decades, and the number of afternoon papers dropped to 1,352, 36 fewer than the year before. At the same time, morning circulation hit an all-time high of 30,552,316, up 3.9% from the previous year, and the number of morning papers rose to 408, a

gain of 21. (The number of dailies publishing editions throughout the day remained constant at 30, and their circulation is divided evenly between the morning and evening categories in the above figures.) It appeared certain that in 1983, for the first time, more Americans would read morning than evening papers.

Two of the nation's oldest dailies were among the large number of U.S. newspapers that folded in 1982: the Philadelphia Bulletin, *founded in 1847, and the* Buffalo (New York) Courier-Express, *founded in 1834.*
(TOP) UPI; (BOTTOM) WIDE WORLD

USA Today, *intended as a national newspaper by its publisher, the Gannett chain, made its debut on September 15.*

WIDE WORLD

One of the nation's oldest afternoon dailies, the *Philadephia Bulletin*, founded in 1847, folded after years of slow decline. A new owner had managed to raise circulation to 405,000 in 1982 from a 64-year low of 397,000, but the paper's share of the city's advertising market had dropped to 24%. The next major afternoon paper to die was the *Minneapolis Star*, which was folded into the city's morning *Tribune* by the firm that owned them both, Cowles Media Co. Though the *Star* was turning a profit at the end, circulation had slipped from 300,000 to 170,000 since the 1950s. The *Star* had attracted attention in recent years for its attempts to introduce a measure of democracy into the newsroom, in the manner of some European newspapers. Shortly after the *Star*'s fall, the afternoon *Cleveland Press* also folded. Circulation had risen from 304,000 to 316,000 under a new owner, Joseph E. Cole, but with stiff competition from the morning *Plain Dealer*, the *Press* continued to lose $500,000 a month.

A few big-city morning papers were in trouble as well. The morning *Seattle Post-Intelligencer* was saved from extinction when the U.S. Justice Department approved a joint operating agreement with a more prosperous all-day rival, the *Times*. The *Boston Herald American* got a last-minute reprieve when Rupert Murdoch bought it from the Hearst Corp. The nation's largest general-interest daily newspaper, the morning *New York Daily News* (circulation 1.5 million) came close to folding. Circulation had fallen by nearly 500,000 over the past decade, and the paper lost $12 million in 1981. The parent Tribune Co. of Chicago offered it for sale, but there were no buyers. As Tribune Co. executives were deciding whether to close it, 11 of its key production unions agreed to the elimination of the equivalent of 1,340 jobs, saving the company $50 million per year. The company then promised to invest $44 million in new equipment and declared that the paper was saved.

Another major U.S. journalistic institution was rescued from the edge of oblivion. United Press International, which had lost $32 million since 1975, was sold by the E. W. Scripps Co. to a group of young entrepreneurs. Despite UPI's reputation for quality and its heavy investment in new technology, the news service had been unable to gain ground on the Associated Press, and the problem became acute as newspapers that subscribed to both services were forced by rising costs to choose one.

Unlike many countries, the U.S. for years had had no general-interest national newspaper, but that picture began to change in 1982. The *New York Times* started printing a version of the paper, minus local news, on a limited basis in Florida and the western U.S. The *Washington Post* announced plans for a tabloid-size national weekly that would be basically a compilation of the daily *Post*'s major nonlocal articles. In the most important development of all, the Gannett Co., which published 88 dailies around the country, launched a true national daily. *USA Today*, with a start-up press run of 200,000, was initially available in four U.S. metropolitan areas and was scheduled to appear in ten more in 1983. By year's end Gannett was able to announce that circulation was running ahead of projections.

Five of the 12 major Pulitzer Prizes went to Western papers. The *Kansas City Star* and *Times* were both cited for reporting construction flaws in a walkway that collapsed at a local hotel, killing 113 people. *Seattle Times* reporter Paul Henderson received an award for proving that a man had been wrongly convicted of rape, and the *Detroit News* won a prize for its investigations into the deaths of two U.S. Navy personnel. *Los Angeles Times* music critic Martin Bernheimer received the award for criticism, and syndicated humorist Art Buchwald received the award for commentary. The only two prizes won by papers in the northeast went to the *New York Times*, for editorials by Jack Rosenthal and dispatches from Poland by John Darnton.

Across the Atlantic, *The Times* of London, Rupert Murdoch's prestigious but unprofitable flagship, drifted close to crisis yet again at the end of 1982 when a union dispute over new technology halted production. At *The Times* the year had begun with a double crisis. It took Murdoch's threat of closure to enforce a major reduction in staffing. Then an unseemly public slanging match ended with the resignation of Harold Evans, whom Murdoch had appointed editor only the previous year. The affair raised doubts about the efficacy of the national directors appointed when Murdoch took over the papers, supposedly to protect editorial independence. The proprietor was evidently in command, and he appointed Charles Douglas-Home to replace Evans.

During the Falkland Islands war, New Zealand offered the HMNZS "Canterbury," its most modern frigate, to the British Navy to replace ships committed to the South Atlantic action.

NEW ZEALAND

After providing a speaker in the New Zealand Parliament, which reconvened in April 1982, the National Party (Conservative) administration of Prime Minister Robert Muldoon had a margin of one over the combined opposition of Labour and Social Credit. But Social Credit had agreed not to block government funding measures if it held the balance of power, and in the key political crisis it voted with the government to overturn a planning tribunal's denial of water rights for a major hydroelectric project. The government was committed to a number of major projects to make the country less dependent on imported fuels and to developing large-scale industry to provide jobs. These policies had a rocky first year in North Auckland, where continuing disagreement with boilermakers threatened a refinery extension.

Tight voting lines did not deter the prime minister from introducing a 12-month wage and price freeze in June, after labour unions had declined an income tax trade-off in place of a wage increase. (The Institute of Economic Research in early October forecast that the 15% inflation would fall to single figures by mid-1983.) The budget, presented in August, increased diesel-oil prices, and inevitably higher transportation costs would be reflected in retail prices. Thaws in the price freeze increased pressure on the government to make exceptions with wages. The budget eased the tax burden on middle-income earners, with less relief for lower earners. It also increased duties on fuels, liquor, and cigarettes; abolished allowances on regional investments, export investment, and fishing investment; and increased an international departure tax from NZ$35 to NZ$40 ($55).

In June the prime minister called for the resignation of one of his most outspoken colleagues, Derek Quigley, from his post as minister of housing, works, and development. Quigley had publicly questioned the direction of free-enterprise policies and the extent of government intervention. Muldoon's elderly and most trusted lieutenant, Deputy Prime Minister Duncan MacIntyre, underwent heart surgery during the year, and the National Party elected its first woman president, Sue Wood. In a February reshuffle, Associate Minister of Finance John Falloon relinquished his post office portfolio to Minister of Tourism Rob Talbot. There was some pressure on Labour opposition leader Wallace ("Bill") Rowling, a three-time general election loser, to step down, but he appeared determined to retain his position.

Muldoon moved to the forefront of the Commonwealth finance ministers' conference when he called for the convening of a conference to reform the collapsing international monetary system. He carried the campaign to the International Monetary Fund and World Bank meetings in Toronto. For once he had third world powers behind him. In the Falkland Islands conflict, New Zealand took the lead in supporting the U.K.

Parliamentarians were surprisingly in accord in their response to a Privy Council (U.K.) ruling on an appeal by a Western Samoan woman who had allegedly overstayed a visitor permit. The council ruled that she—along with thousands of other Western

Samoans—could regard herself as a New Zealand citizen because of a succession of acts in connection with a trusteeship phase of Western Samoa's development. Western Samoans protested when the New Zealand government offered a deal by which 40,000 Samoans in New Zealand, some of them "overstayers," could regard themselves as legally resident there in return for the cancellation of automatic New Zealand citizenship rights for the Samoans at home. One count estimated that 60,000 people in Western Samoa might be penalized by the decision.

NICARAGUA

The Sandinista National Liberation Front government faced serious political problems in 1982. On the international front Thomas Enders, U.S. assistant secretary of state for inter-American affairs, promised that the U.S. administration would not help the opponents of the Sandinistas if Nicaragua stopped sending arms from Cuba to El Salvador. The Sandinistas replied that negotiations must be linked to a change in the U.S. policy of aiding the military buildup in Honduras. A new military base was established in that country only 12 mi (19 km) from the Nicaraguan border.

Daniel Ortega Saavedra, coordinator of the Sandinista junta, expressed the opinion that a war between Nicaragua and Honduras appeared to be inevitable if the U.S. continued to contribute assistance to the former Nicaraguan national guardsmen, followers of the late president Anastasio Somoza (Somocistas), who still operated from bases within Honduras. An incident between a Honduran naval ship and a Nicaraguan coast guard vessel was reported on September 18.

In October the Sandinista government received assurances of international backing when Nicaragua was chosen to fill the UN Security Council's Latin-American seat beginning in January 1983.

A serious confrontation was developing between the government and a sector of the Miskito Indian communities on the Atlantic coast. Following heavy fighting in northern Zelaya Province, about 10,000 Indians living along the Coco River were transferred early in 1982 to a new settlement farther from the Honduran border. The Sandinistas justified the transfer on the grounds that it was necessary in order to defend the border more effectively against incursions from Honduras. The Miskito communities opposed to the government were divided; some formed a guerrilla force that supported the Somocistas, while others joined former Sandinista leader Edén Pastora and opposition leader Alfonso Robelo in a new, non-Somocista united front of opposition, the Alianza Revolucionaria Democrática.

Nicaragua's gross domestic product grew by 7% in 1981, as compared with 10.7% in 1980. A similar performance was expected for 1982.

More than 10,000 Miskito Indians in Nicaragua were uprooted from their villages on the Atlantic coast and along the Honduran border and forced into refugee camps in Honduras.
RANDY TAYLOR—SYGMA

NIGERIA

During 1982 Nigeria suffered from its almost total dependence on income from petroleum in the face of world recession, falling demand, and price restrictions imposed by the Organization of Petroleum Exporting Countries (OPEC). Crude-oil exports fell by 41% in 1981, while the cost of living rose by 21%.

In June the National Party of Nigeria (NPN) chose Pres. Alhaji Shehu Shagari as its candidate in the 1983 presidential election. Meanwhile, four opposition parties combined to form the Progressive Parties' Alliance, and a new party, the Nigerian Advance Party, was registered in May. Odumegwu Ojukwu, who had led Biafra during the civil war in the late 1960s, was granted a presidential pardon and returned to Nigeria in June, ending a 12-year exile in the Ivory Coast; later he joined the NPN.

The 1983 elections would be the first test of democracy since the 1979 return to civilian rule. In September the registration of electors was officially completed amid complaints of inefficiency and corruption. Nigeria, which had not had a reliable census for 30 years, was estimated to have 66 million voters. However, there were fears that the new method of establishing voters' lists—registration was carried out at booths rather than door-to-door—could result in fewer Muslim women registering.

Nigeria mended fences with its neighbours in West Africa. A visit from a Ghanaian delegation in March was designed to quash rumours that Nigeria supported the deposed Ghanaian president, Hilla Limann, while a state visit by Pres. Ahmadou Ahidjo of Cameroon wrote finis to the May 1981 border incident in which five Nigerian soldiers were killed. Pope John Paul II's successful visit in February pointed up the tolerance of Shagari, himself a Muslim in a country with a sizable Muslim population. Nigeria played a neutral role at the abortive summit meeting of the Organization of African Unity (OAU) in Tripoli, Libya, in August.

Attempts to increase agricultural production and to stem the population drift away from the countryside continued to fail in the face of corruption and lack of technical skills. Once the leading African exporter of peanuts (groundnuts) and palm oil, Nigeria was paying more than 1 billion naira a year for food imports by the 1980s. Shagari's 1982 budget, announced in December 1981, showed a 1981 balance of payments deficit of more than 1 billion naira. Estimates for 1982 stood at 7.4 billion naira (1.47 naira=U.S. $1) for capital expenditure, 3.5 billion naira for recurrent expenditure, and revenues of 11.6 billion naira. Despite austerity measures in the budget, President Shagari was obliged to pass an Economic Stabilization Act in April to meet an increasing economic crisis, indicating that the budget had been based on overoptimistic estimates of oil production. New measures included import cuts, closing of private jetties, salary cuts for government workers, strict control over external borrowing, and a clampdown on smuggling.

Nigeria's 22nd independence celebrations, held for the first time at the future capital, Abuja, took place on October 1. President Shagari's speech, covering economic planning, education, and the new "ethical revolution," struck a note of cautious optimism. In late October there were violent clashes between Muslim fundamentalists and police in Kano, Kaduna, and Maiduguri. It was reported that more than 450 people died during the riots. An extremist Muslim sect blamed for the violence was banned in November.

Pope John Paul II ordained a large number of priests in an outdoor mass during his visit to Kaduna, Nigeria.
FRANCOIS LOCHON–GAMMA/LIAISON

The Nobel Prize for Peace was won by Alfonso García Robles of Mexico and Alva Myrdal of Sweden, here being congratulated by King Olav V of Norway. Standing behind Mrs. Myrdal is her husband, Gunnar, a Nobel laureate in economics.
WIDE WORLD

NOBEL PRIZES

Prize for Peace

Two senior ambassadors of disarmament who shared the 1982 Nobel Prize for Peace, Alva Myrdal of Sweden and Alfonso García Robles of Mexico, were honoured for "patient and meticulous" work spanning several decades. The twin choice seemed to reflect the times because many Western countries have been experiencing antinuclear protests. The Nobel Committee, appointed by the Norwegian Parliament, expressed the hope that this year's award might be "a stimulus to the climate of peace that has emerged in recent years." Alva Myrdal and Alfonso García Robles have both served at the UN and worked for the UN Disarmament Commission in Geneva. In addition, both have sharply criticized the Soviet Union and United States alike for carrying the world to the brink of thermonuclear disaster.

While serving as ambassador to Brazil, García Robles first encountered the proposition of making Latin America a nuclear-free zone, an idea he pursued so successfully that it was deemed worthy of a Nobel Prize for Peace. Following the Cuban missile crisis of 1962, he persuaded the Mexican government to pursue the cause of a nonnuclear Latin America. His efforts led to the 1967 Treaty of Tlatelolco, a pact that committed 22 nations to bar nuclear weapons from their territories. A year later he helped write the Nuclear Non-proliferation Treaty.

When the Swedish foreign minister asked Myrdal to become his special disarmament adviser in 1961, she set out to become an expert on the subject. A year later she was elected to Parliament as a Social Democrat and was named head of the Swedish delegation to the Geneva Disarmament Conference. In 1966 she became minister with portfolio covering disarmament and church affairs and held that post and the one in Geneva until 1973. Since that time she has written and spoken frequently on behalf of disarmament.

Prize for Economics

George J. Stigler, winner of the 1982 Nobel Memorial Prize in Economic Science, wears the "conservative" label and teaches at the University of Chicago, where he has been Charles R. Walgreen Distinguished Professor of American Institutions since 1958. He often collaborates with Milton Friedman, who is also associated with the university and was awarded the Nobel Prize in 1976. Stigler is an advocate of free market economics and a particular proponent of reduced government intervention in marketplaces.

Stigler confesses that he is more interested in why things happen than in how to change them. This inclination has led him to study the history of economics as well as contemporary phenomena. Along the way he has scrutinized numerous regulating agencies, ranging from those overseeing local public utilities to the Securities and Exchange Commission. His overall conclusion is that government regulators have, at best, no effect.

Prize for Literature

When the Swedish Academy announced that Gabriel García Márquez had been awarded the Nobel Prize for Literature, it noted he was not "an unknown writer." Indeed, the committee's choice recognized a novelist whose works have been translated into at least 32 languages. Ten million copies of *Cien años de soledad* (1967; *One Hundred Years of Solitude*, 1970) have been printed. Pablo Neruda, the Chilean poet who won a Nobel Prize for Literature in 1971, described the book as "perhaps the greatest revelation in the Spanish language since the *Don Quixote* of Cervantes." García Márquez has frequently been compared with Balzac and sometimes also with William Faulkner because both rooted their stories in fictionalized versions of the places of their origin.

In 1948 García Márquez became so intrigued with the political turmoil that surrounded him, he aban-

The Nobel Prize for Literature was won by Gabriel García Márquez (left). George J. Stigler of the University of Chicago was the winner in economics.

(RIGHT) WIDE WORLD; (LEFT) UPI

doned law for journalism. A naturally gifted reporter, he worked first in Bogotá, then Geneva, Rome, Paris, and New York. He soon became a noted advocate of leftist causes but never joined the Communist Party. Finding conditions in Colombia too inimical, he entered a semi-self-imposed exile in Mexico after severing his relationship with Fidel Castro's propagandists. During the past two decades he has lived mostly in Mexico City.

Prize for Physiology or Medicine

An Englishman and two Swedes shared equally in the Nobel Prize for Physiology or Medicine for 1982. The Englishman is John R. Vane, a pharmacologist who is research director of the Wellcome Research Laboratories, a pharmaceutical manufacturing firm in Beckenham, Kent. The Swedish laureates are biochemists at the Karolinska Institute at Stockholm: Sune K. Bergström, who retired as rector in 1977 but continues to do research, and Bengt I. Samuelsson, who succeeded Bergström as dean of the medical faculty in 1967. The three have isolated and identified numerous prostaglandins, a family of natural compounds widely distributed (although in minute amounts) in the bodies of mammals, and they have systematically clarified their biological effects.

Bergström undertook the isolation and identification of prostaglandin in 1947. By 1962 he and Samuelsson had determined the molecular structure of a prostaglandin, and in 1964 they announced their finding that the substances are produced in the body from arachidonic acid, a constituent of polyunsaturated oils present in certain meats and vegetables.

In 1969 Vane found that, in allergic shock, the lungs of rabbits release a substance that causes the aorta to contract. He demonstrated that the same substance also causes blood platelets to clump together. Samuelsson found a prostaglandin in this substance, then went on to prove that another component was present. This newcomer proved to be a thromboxane, the first member of a class of compounds similar to the prostaglandins but differing somewhat in molecular structure. In 1976 Vane, in turn, noted that the prostaglandin found by Samuelsson is convertible to a compound of still another class, the prostacyclins; this compound proved to be the most powerful agent yet found to dilate blood vessels and prevent the clumping of platelets. The confusion was finally resolved when it was found that the prostaglandin released by the lung tissue is transformed to a thromboxane by the platelets but to prostacyclin by the walls of the blood vessels.

Prize for Chemistry

The Nobel Prize for Chemistry was conferred upon Aaron Klug, a South African expatriate who is joint head of the division of structural studies of the Medical Research Council at Cambridge, England. Klug was cited for his investigations of the three-dimensional structure of the combinations of nucleic acids and proteins, the forms in which the genetic material is present in living cells and viruses; his work on the tobacco mosaic virus, in particular, has resulted in a highly detailed understanding of the arrangement of its components and of the selective process by which the single-stranded molecule of ribonucleic acid and more than 2,000 identical molecules of its protective protein assemble to form the rodlike virus particle.

Klug has made his discoveries in biology in conjunction with an outstanding achievement in physics, namely, the development of a versatile technique for studying crystalline materials by taking advantage of the way they diffract electron beams. By use of this innovative technique, which established the new science of crystallographic electron microscopy, Klug unified the concepts of image formation and the diffraction of beams of X-rays, light, or electrons. Klug has shown how series of electron micrographs, taken from different angles, can be combined to produce three-dimensional images of particles. His method has been widely used to study proteins and viruses.

Prize for Physics

The Nobel Prize for Physics was awarded to Kenneth G. Wilson of Cornell University, Ithaca, N.Y., who has developed a general procedure for constructing improved theories concerning transformations of matter called continuous or second-order phase transitions. Exact understanding of these changes had been unattainable, partly because of the mathematical difficulties of accounting for effects that involve neighbouring atoms or molecules as well as those that influence the whole of a specimen of material large enough to be observed.

In 1971 Wilson published a demonstration that these effects could be quantitatively framed by applying the mathematical strategy of the renormalization group. This approach had been developed during the 1950s to unite quantum mechanics and the theory of relativity in explaining the interactions of elementary particles with electromagnetic fields.

NORWAY

Norway entered 1982 with a recently elected Conservative government at the helm. Prime Minister Kåre Willoch's minority administration had pledged to cut corporate and personal taxes, reduce public spending, curb inflation, abolish unnecessary bureaucratic controls, and scale down selective subsidies to industries.

Several factors hampered the achievement of these goals. One was the government's dependence on support from the small Christian People's and Centre parties in order to achieve an overall majority in the Storting (parliament). The two parties were only lukewarm about some of the Conservative proposals, particularly spending cuts that threatened welfare or regional development. The main problem, however, was the continuing world recession. World demand and prices slumped for traditional exports such as paper and pulp, ferroalloys, aluminum, and shipping services. The only important industrial sector still working at capacity, and earning good profits, was offshore oil and gas production.

Industrial employment, on the decline since 1974, dropped to 360,000 in 1982 and was expected to fall still further in 1983. The number of registered unemployed climbed steadily throughout the first half of 1982, hitting a postwar record of 43,900, representing 2.7% of the labour force, in August.

The first test of the new government's policies came in the spring, when the unions traditionally bargain with employers over pay and conditions for the coming year. The Conservative government promised to leave bargaining entirely to the unions

The "Hjemkomst" ("homecoming"), a 76-foot (23-metre) replica of a Viking ship, was begun in 1971 by Bob Asp, a Minnesotan of Norwegian descent. Asp died in 1980, but his family continued the project. "Hjemkomst" set sail from Duluth on May 6 and arrived in Bergen, Norway, on July 19.
WIDE WORLD

and employers, although it pointed out that a moderate settlement of around 6.5% would help hold down inflation and stop the decline in Norwegian industry's competitiveness. In the event, settlements averaged 10–11%, slightly less than the rate of inflation, and there were few strikes. A nationwide transport strike was stopped when the government ordered a compulsory settlement.

Offshore production workers, however, failed to reach agreement with their employers during the spring wage bargaining. The union was reluctant to order a strike because it feared the government would enforce a settlement, as the previous Labour government had done in 1980 and 1981. Only in mid-October, when members had voted to reject a final compromise proposal, did the union send out strike notices. The government immediately announced that it would ask the Storting to approve a compulsory settlement order. The dispute cost the state an estimated 145 million kroner a day in lost revenues. Because of the strike, moreover, 1982 oil and gas output was expected to be only slightly higher than in 1981. A new field, Valhall A, came on stream in October.

The government's budget for 1983, introduced in October, proposed real reductions in direct company and personal taxation, partly offset by increased indirect taxes and charges for public services. At the same time, spending was to be curbed, in real terms, in virtually every sector except defense and law and order. The result would have been a tightening of fiscal policy. The very week that the draft budget was published, however, the new Swedish government of Prime Minister Olof Palme announced a 16% devaluation of the Swedish krona. This immediately undermined many of the assumptions on which the government's economic strategy had been based.

Despite the Conservatives' opposition, in princi-ple, to selective industrial subsidies, the government announced a package of measures to assist the Norwegian industries hardest hit by the move. Sweden's sudden, steep devaluation was condemned by Norwegian government ministers, who accused the Swedes of "exporting their problems" and undermining "Nordic solidarity." This overlooked the fact that Norway itself had already devalued its currency twice in 1982, in August and September, by 3% each time.

OCEANOGRAPHY

In more than a century of measuring temperature and salinity in the oceans, oceanographers had never detected any changes of either property in the deep waters of the ocean. Then in recent months it was discovered that water in the North Atlantic many thousands of metres below the surface had cooled by about 0.1° C (0.18° F) and freshened by about 0.02 g of salt per kilogram of seawater between 1972 (when a survey of water properties was made as part of the Geochemical Ocean Sections program) and 1981 (when participants in the Transient Tracers in the Ocean program returned to some of the 1972 stations). These changes occurred in a region of the Atlantic occupied at great depths by water that was once at the surface in the Norwegian and Greenland seas; subsequently this water sank below the surface there and flowed southward into the Atlantic along the Mid-Atlantic Ridge. Examination of still earlier data showed no evidence for similar changes in the decade or so prior to 1972 for which data existed in this region.

The importance of these observations is that they provided the first direct evidence of how much the heat stored in the deep oceans may vary with time, a critical question in understanding global climate fluctuations. It is possible that these changes oc-

Scientists in the research submarine "Alvin" discovered colonies of giant clams living near hot volcanic springs in the Pacific Ocean floor south of Baja California.
SCRIPPS INSTITUTION OF OCEANOGRAPHY

curred in response to changes in atmospheric behaviour over the Norwegian and Greenland seas. If this could be demonstrated, these observations would reveal a great deal about the way in which the deep circulation of the ocean is driven.

Success in applying an entirely new observational technique, called acoustic tomography, for mapping ocean currents over many hundreds or even thousands of kilometres was reported in 1982. A number of buoys containing acoustic transmitters and receivers are placed around the perimeter of the region within which currents are to be mapped. As the study progresses, the travel time of sound from each buoy to every other buoy is measured repeatedly with high accuracy. Since the travel time of sound from one buoy to another depends on the velocity of water between the buoys as well as on the sound speed of the intervening water, all of the travel times measured at any instant may be combined to produce maps of water velocity and sound speed in the region enclosed by the buoys.

Sound speed in seawater depends on the temperature and salinity of the water. Because these are closely correlated with the flow, the sound speed map itself furnishes a great deal of flow information. Sound traveling from one buoy to another does so along a number of paths, all centred on a region of minimum sound speed usually about a kilometre or so (about 0.62 mi) beneath the surface but departing vertically from this region by varying amounts. As a result, different paths give information about the flow at different depths throughout the measurement region. Resolution of detail depends on the number of buoys available. With about a dozen buoys, flow features with a size on the order of 100 km may be resolved in a study region many hundreds of kilometres on a side.

Although this technique was demonstrated by resolving such flow features in a region in the Atlantic, its greatest potential appeared to lie in monitoring flow variations over very large regions such as an entire ocean current gyre. As of 1982 no other technique was able to average small features out of a measurement of the large-scale flow without a prohibitive number of instruments in the water. Since large-scale changes in ocean flow are accompanied by similarly large-scale changes in ocean heat transport and storage, monitoring them is of great importance for climate studies.

In recent years a number of seafloor vents emitting water at temperatures of more than 100° C (212° F) had been discovered along the East Pacific Rise, a mid-ocean ridge running from near Antarctica toward the Pacific coast of Mexico. In 1982 clear evidence of similar vents in an entirely different tectonic setting was found in the form of high methane concentrations in the deep water of the Mariana Trough in the western Pacific (not to be confused with the much deeper Mariana Trench to the east). Such vents are important because they are major sources of metals both in seawater and in ores.

BALDEV–SYGMA

Pakistan's Pres. Mohammad Zia-ul-Haq met with India's Prime Minister Indira Gandhi in New Delhi, India, in November.

PAKISTAN

To consolidate his martial law regime, Pres. Mohammad Zia-ul-Haq in December 1981 set up a handpicked 350-member Federal Advisory Council, which, he said, would act as a bridge between the martial law administration and a future Islamic democratic government. The council, of which all federal ministers and ministers of state were ex-officio members, had no decision-making powers. After the general elections for a National Assembly of Pakistan, the council would cease to exist. President Zia told the council when it began its first session in Islamabad on Jan. 11, 1982, that general elections could not be held under current circumstances without endangering the country's security and integrity.

On Pakistan's national day, March 23, President Zia described Pakistan's armed forces as the only sector in the country that was organized, disciplined, and united. In May President Zia suggested the formation of a Higher Command Council, to consist of the president, the prime minister, the defense minister, and the chiefs of the Army, Navy, and Air Force.

The government denied allegations by Amnesty International in January 1982 that an estimated 6,000 political prisoners had been under arrest at one time in the past and that 193 of them had undergone torture. Refuting the charges, federal Minister of the Interior Mahmood Abdullah Haroon reported that only 62 political prisoners were under detention.

Universities in Karachi, Lahore, and other cities were closed from March to June when teachers went on strike demanding higher salaries and students demonstrated against right-wing political elements in academic life. Lawyers and barristers in Karachi and elsewhere boycotted courts in July to protest President Zia's order banning legal practitioners from political activity. From mid-1981 to mid-1982 a number of violent incidents between Shi'ah and Sunni Muslims rocked Pakistan. Terrorists linked to Al Zulfikar, an organization headed by Murtaza Ali Bhutto, son of executed former prime minister Zulfikar Ali Bhutto, also carried out several hit-and-run attacks against police guards and pro-Zia politicians in June and September.

The Islamic Shari'ah law reforms and their application in public life came under criticism. After the Women's Action Forum publicly demonstrated against them in Karachi in April, President Zia gave an assurance that the policy of islamization would not involve women being "shunted back into the home." However, Pakistan's women's field hockey teams were banned from playing overseas or in front of men; their national championships were canceled; and the women's athletic events in the national games were also scrapped.

After his successful state visit to China in October, President Zia met Indian Prime Minister Indira Gandhi in New Delhi on November 1 en route to Singapore, Malaysia, and Indonesia. Despite continuing suspicions about each other's motives, India and Pakistan continued attempts to narrow their differences. A U.S. economic aid and military assistance package for Pakistan, spread over a six-year period and estimated to be worth approximately $3 billion, was made final at the end of 1981. Agreements were signed for the delivery to Pakistan of the first part of a consignment of 40 U.S.-built F-16 fighter aircraft. In December 1982 President Zia visited Washington for talks with Pres. Ronald Reagan.

Pakistan's budget for the 1982–83 fiscal year envisioned an overall economic growth rate of 6.2%. There was to be a 16% increase in government spending for development and a 12% increase in defense spending.

PANAMA

The arrangement dividing governmental authority between the National Guard and the president worked badly in 1982. Col. Florençio Flórez (the successor of military strong man Brig. Gen. Omar Torrijos) found the friction so uncomfortable early in the year that he retired. Late in July Pres. Aristides Royo yielded to pressure and resigned. Their successors, Col. Rubén Darío Paredes del Río and Ricardo de la Espriella, were no more successful. Royo, charged with corruption and blamed for economic troubles, was swept out with hundreds of his government officials. Paredes displayed his dominance by suspending operation of the nation's press.

Many Panamanians had been disturbed by leftist indications in Royo's foreign policy. In the press and at the United Nations he frequently denounced Great Britain during the Falkland Islands conflict. The Panamanian Air Force rescued a number of guerrillas from Honduras and brought them to a sanctuary on the isthmus. A Soviet trade delegation, interested in a west coast port as a fishing base, was welcomed.

Much attention centred on the economy. The annual rate of inflation reached 15%, and unemployment rose to an estimated 130,000 persons. Panama's financial obligations raised its foreign debt to more than $3 billion. Compared with this figure,

WIDE WORLD

Pres. Aristides Royo (left) resigned under pressure in July and was succeeded by his vice-president, Ricardo de la Espriella.

the new source of revenue from the canal treaties, $70 million annually, seemed small and of no benefit. Depression and disenchantment prompted marches, demonstrations, and strikes.

On the other hand, the transition from U.S. to Panamanian operation of the canal on April 1 went smoothly. Passage of ships and cargo reached record levels. The prospect of a new oil pipeline across Panama aroused attention. In October the Morrison Knudsen Co. completed the 80-mi (130-km) line not far from the Costa Rican border. It was expected to carry some 800 bbl a day.

PARAGUAY

Uncertainty as to whether Gen. Alfredo Stroessner would run in the presidential elections, scheduled for February 1983, strengthened rumours circulating in 1982 that the president was suffering from ill health. Stroessner had remained in power for 28 years by balancing his two main power bases, the military and the Partido Colorado, and no one had emerged who appeared able to continue the act. The four permitted extraparliamentary parties, which together formed a loose grouping known as the Acuerdo Nacional, seemed likely to run independently in the election. Despite the lack of an organized opposition, the government was anxious to prevent any focus of dissent from appearing in Paraguay. The authorities kept human rights advocate Adolfo Pérez Esquivel of Argentina, as well as a group of exiled Paraguayan politicians, from entering the country.

The economic slowdown continued throughout 1982. International reserves and exports fell, capital inflows slowed, and the balance of payments surplus evaporated. The start of the Yacyreta hydroelectric project, to be built jointly with Argentina, was delayed by that country's financial crisis, and expected revenues from the Itaipú reservoir were postponed by the lack of a high-tension line linking the project to São Paulo, Brazil.

PEOPLE

Among the milestones in the lives of people making news in 1982 were the following:

Births

To former senator **Birch Bayh** and his wife, Katherine, on July 24, a son.

To **King Carl Gustaf** of Sweden and Queen Silvia, on June 10, a daughter, Princess Madeleine.

To actress **Jill Clayburgh** and her husband, playwright **David Rabe,** on June 29, a daughter.

To **Diana, Princess of Wales,** and **Prince Charles,** on June 21 in London, a son, Prince William.

To television personality **David Hartman** and his wife, Maureen, on Nov. 23, a son.

To boxer **Larry Holmes** and his wife, Diane, a son.

To actor **Tommy Lee Jones** (*Coal Miner's Daughter*, *The Executioner's Song*) and his wife, Kimberlea, in November, a son.

To playwright **David Mamet** and his wife, actress **Lindsay Crouse,** on June 28, a daughter.

To singer and actress **Michelle Phillips** and her husband, Grainger Hines, in March, a son.

To rock singer **Suzi Quatro** and her husband, guitarist Len Tuckey, on Sept. 26, a daughter.

To TV actor **John Ritter** ("Three's Company") and his wife, Nancy, in March, a daughter.

To novelist and playwright **Budd Schulberg** and his wife, Betsy, on Aug. 14, a daughter.

To **Margaret Seddon** and her husband, **Robert Gibson,** on July 26, a son, the first child of astronaut parents.

To actress **Jane Seymour** and her husband, David Flynn, on Jan. 7, a daughter.

Princess Madeleine joined the Swedish royal family on June 10, to the delight of King Carl XVI Gustaf, Queen Silvia, Prince Carl Philip, and Princess Victoria.

WIDE WORLD

UPI
On June 21 Prince William Arthur Philip Louis of Wales became second in line for the British throne.

To actress **Jaclyn Smith** and her husband, Tony Richmond, on March 19, a son.

To actress **Sissy Spacek** (*Coal Miner's Daughter*) and her husband, **Jack Fisk,** in July, a daughter.

To actor **McLean Stevenson** and his wife, Ginny, on Jan. 22, a daughter.

To singer **Donna Summer** and her husband, songwriter Bruce Sudano, on Aug. 11, a daughter.

To actor **Donald Sutherland** and his wife, actress Francine Racette, on Sept. 10, a son.

To pitcher **Fernando Valenzuela** and his wife, Linda Valenzuela-Burgos, on Sept. 30, a son.

To actress **Lindsay Wagner** and her husband, stunt driver Henry Kingi, on Sept. 25, a son.

To Polish Solidarity leader **Lech Walesa** and his wife, Danuta, on Jan. 27, a daughter.

Marriages

Grammy-winning rock singer ("Hit Me with Your Best Shot") **Pat Benatar,** 29, to guitarist Neil Geraldo, 30; Feb. 20, Maui, Hawaii.

Author and columnist **Jimmy Breslin,** 51, to Ronnie Eldridge, 51.

Business executive **Mary Cunningham,** 30, to Bendix Corp. chairman **William M. Agee,** 44; June 5, San Francisco.

Singer **Karla DeVito,** to actor **Robby Benson;** July 11, Mokena, Ill.

Singer and songwriter **Jose Feliciano,** to Susan Omillian; Aug. 2, Villa Park, Calif.

Actress **Zsa Zsa Gabor,** 54 or more, to lawyer Felipe de Alba, count of Pardela, 52; April 13, Puerto Vallarta, Mexico.

Olympic ice-skating medalist **Dorothy Hamill,** 25, to actor **Dean Paul Martin,** 30; Jan. 8, Beverly Hills, Calif.

Actor **James Earl Jones** (*Othello*), 51, to actress Cecilia Hart, 31; March 15, New York City.

Entertainer **Carol Lawrence,** 49, to businessman Greg Guydus, 46; in March, Los Angeles.

Broadway producer **David Merrick,** to dancer Karen Prunczik; July 19, at an undisclosed location.

Composer and conductor **André Previn,** 52, to

UPI

The Rev. Sun Myung Moon of the Unification Church officiated at the mass marriage of 2,075 young couples at Madison Square Garden, New York City, on July 1.

Heather Hales, 33; Jan. 6, in Pittsburgh, Pa.

Actress **Diana Rigg,** 43, to producer Archibald Stirling, 40; March 25, New York City.

Songwriter ("They're Playing Our Song") **Carole Bayer Sager,** 36, to songwriter ("Raindrops Keep Falling on My Head") **Burt Bacharach,** 52; April 3, Santa Monica, Calif.

2,075 young men to 2,075 young women, many of whom had only recently met, at a mass ceremony at Madison Square Garden conducted by the Rev. Sun Myung Moon of the Unification Church; July 1, New York City.

Mary E. Cunningham, vice-president of Joseph E. Seagram & Son, Inc., was married to Bendix Corp. Chairman William Agee on June 5.

WIDE WORLD

Singer-actress Marie Osmond married Stephen Craig at the Mormon Temple in Salt Lake City, Utah, on June 26.

WIDE WORLD

Obituaries

Goodman Ace, U.S. humorist who wrote for radio and TV comedians including Milton Berle, Sid Caesar, Danny Kaye, Perry Como, and Bob Newhart; with his wife, Jane, he wrote and starred in "Easy Aces" on radio in the 1930s and '40s; later he wrote a column for the *Saturday Review;* March 25, New York City, age 83.

Harriet Stratemeyer Adams, U.S. writer of nearly 200 children's books under the pseudonyms Carolyn Keene ("Nancy Drew" series), Franklin W. Dixon ("Hardy Boys"), Victor W. Appleton 2d ("Tom Swift, Jr."), and Laura Lee Hope ("Bobbsey Twins"); March 27, Pottersville, N.J., age 89.

Louis Aragon, French poet and novelist who abandoned the Dada and Surrealist movements in the arts to become an ardent Marxist and one of the intellectual and literary leaders of the French Communist Party; he was best known in English for novels as *The Bells of Basel, Residential Quarters, Holy Week,* and *To Be Killed;* Dec. 24, Paris, age 85.

Sir Douglas Bader, British flier who lost both legs in a plane crash in 1931 and went on to become an ace in World War II, shooting down at least 24 German planes; later captured, he made four escape attempts before German authorities took away his artificial legs; Sept. 5, London, age 72.

Pierre Balmain, French couturier who helped revive the custom-made dress business in France after World War II and became known especially for his elegant gowns favoured by royalty and film stars; June 29, Paris, age 68.

Djuna Barnes, U.S. poet and novelist who was a member of the expatriate avant-garde literary set of Gertrude Stein in Paris in the 1920s and '30s but who spent the last 41 years of her life a virtual recluse in a Greenwich Village apartment; her most famous book was *Nightwood* in 1941; June 18, New York City, age 90.

Stringfellow Barr, U.S. educator who as president (1937–46) of St. John's College in Annapolis, Md., introduced a curriculum based on the study of 100 great books of the past; Feb. 2, Alexandria, Va., age 84.

Hugh Beaumont, U.S. actor best known for his role as Ward Cleaver, the ever patient father in the TV series "Leave It to Beaver" in the 1950s and early '60s; May 14, Munich, West Germany, age 72.

John Belushi, U.S. comedian whose manic presence and outrageous antics helped make a hit of the TV series "Saturday Night Live" from 1975 to 1979 and who appeared in the movies *Animal House, 1941, The Blues Brothers,* and *Continental Divide;* he also recorded an album of blues songs with comedy partner Dan Aykroyd; March 5, Hollywood, Calif., age 33.

Ingrid Bergman, Swedish-born actress who won three Academy Awards and countless admirers in such films as *Intermezzo, Gaslight, Spellbound, The Bells of St. Mary's, Notorious, Casablanca, Anastasia, Murder on the Orient Express, Autumn Sonata;* her last role was a portrayal of Golda Meir for television; Aug. 29, London, age 67.

William Bernbach, U.S. advertising executive who in 1949 was a founder of the Doyle Dane Bernbach agency and its president and later its chairman; he was a noted advocate of the "soft sell" approach in advertising; Oct. 2, New York City, age 71.

Vinoba Bhave, known as Acharya ("teacher") Vinoba, Indian reformer who joined Mohandas K. Gandhi's movement in 1916 and was widely regarded as Gandhi's spiritual heir after his assassination in 1948; in the 1950s he led an agrarian reform movement that distributed over 1.5 million ac of tillable land to the poor; Nov. 15, Maharashtra, India, age 87.

Alfred Bloomingdale, U.S. businessman who from 1955 developed the Diners' Club as a pioneer in the field of credit card retailing; Aug. 20, Santa Monica, Calif., age 66.

Ken Boyer, U.S. baseball player who starred for the St. Louis Cardinals from 1955 to 1965, was chosen to the National League's All-Star team seven times, and was the league's Most Valuable Player in 1964, the year he hit a grand-slam home run in the fourth game of the World Series against the New York Yankees; he managed the Cardinals from 1978 to 1980; Sept. 7, St. Louis, Mo., age 51.

UPI
HARRIET S. ADAMS

NBC PHOTO
JOHN BELUSHI

UPI
INGRID BERGMAN

SVEN SIMON—KATHERINE YOUNG
LEONID BREZHNEV

UPI
VICTOR BUONO

UPI
JOHN CHEEVER

Leonid I. Brezhnev, Soviet leader who ruled for 18 years as general secretary of the Communist Party of the Soviet Union and from 1977 combined that post with the less powerful but symbolic one of president; he was the chief Soviet architect of the policy of détente, intended to improve relations with the West in the aftermath of the invasion of Czechoslovakia in 1968; the policy foundered largely as a result of the invasion of Afghanistan in 1979; Nov. 10, Moscow, age 75.

Arthur Bryant, U.S. restaurateur whose "House of Good Eats" in Kansas City, Mo., was a mecca for lovers of barbecued ribs; he entered the business in 1931 and in 1946 took over the restaurant from his brother; over the next few years he perfected a secret sauce that coated some 2,000 lb of ribs daily and that some aficionados hoarded like vintage wines; Dec. 28, Kansas City, Mo., age 80.

Victor Buono, U.S. actor whose corpulent figure and courtly manner made him a popular film and TV villain (*The Strangler, Hush, Hush, Sweet Charlotte,* the "Batman" series); he was known also as a raconteur and writer of whimsical verse; Jan. 1, Apple Valley, Calif., age 43.

Ernie Bushmiller, U.S. cartoonist who took over the comic strip "Fritzi Ritz" in 1925 and developed it into "Nancy," which he continued to draw with gentle humour and an inexhaustible store of sight gags almost until his death; Aug. 15, Stamford, Conn., age 76.

Clifford P. Case, U.S. politician who was representative (1944–54) and senator (1954–78) from New Jersey, a liberal Republican who helped draft Dwight D. Eisenhower for the presidency in 1952, and who supported many social and civil-rights reforms; March 5, Washington, D.C., age 77.

Colin Chapman, British designer and builder of racing cars, who founded Lotus Engineering Co. in 1952 and produced a long line of innovative racers that won seven world championships with such drivers as Jim Clark, Graham Hill, and Mario Andretti; he was considered one of the greatest of automotive engineers; Dec. 16, Norfolk, England, age 54.

John Cheever, U.S. writer who explored the material satisfactions and spiritual frustrations of modern upper-middle-class life in over a hundred stories, including "The Enormous Radio" and "The Swimmer," and four novels, *The Wapshot Chronicle, The Wapshot Scandal, Bullet Park,* and *Falconer;* June 18, Ossining, N.Y., age 70.

John Cardinal Cody, U.S. prelate who devoted 50 years to the Roman Catholic priesthood and served dioceses in Missouri and Louisiana before becoming archbishop of Chicago in 1965; he was made cardinal by Pope Paul VI in 1967; April 25, Chicago, age 74.

Hans Conried, U.S. actor whose versatility enabled him to play elegant villains, supercilious dandies, and a variety of crackpots and zanies on Broadway and in films; on television he was a popular panelist; Jan. 5, Burbank Calif., age 66.

Herbert O. ("Fritz") Crisler, U.S. football coach who developed the two-platoon system of offensive and defensive teams while coaching at the University of Michigan (1938–47); he remained at Michigan as athletic director until 1968; Aug. 19, Ann Arbor, Mich., age 83.

Criswell (originally Charles Jared Criswell King), U.S. prognosticator whose "Criswell Predicts" newspaper column and radio and television shows were popular in the 1950s and '60s; he also appeared in a few movies, including the classic *Plan 9 from Outer Space;* Oct. 4, Burbank, Calif., age about 75.

Sir Clifford Curzon, British pianist who was considered the premier British keyboard virtuoso of his day; he was noted especially as an interpreter of Schubert, Schumann, and Mozart; Sept. 1, London, age 75.

Frederic Dannay, U.S. writer who with the late Manfred Lee produced over 35 novels, dozens of story anthologies, movie and radio scripts, and a magazine, all featuring the detective Ellery Queen; Sept. 3, White Plains, N.Y., age 76.

Mario del Monaco, Italian operatic tenor who was celebrated for the stentorian power of his voice; he enjoyed a successful career at New York City's Metropolitan Opera in 1951–59 and was a highly popular recording artist; Oct. 16, Venice, Italy, age 67.

Babette Deutsch, U.S. novelist and poet who was best known as a critic and as a translator; with her husband, the late Avrahm Yarmolinsky, she published anthologies of Russian verse; the ten volumes of her own verse culminated in her *Collected Poems* in 1962, and her critical works included *Poetry in Our Time* (1952) and *Poetry Handbook* (1957); Nov. 13, New York City, age 87.

David Dubinsky, U.S. labour leader who emigrated from Russian Poland in 1911 and became one of the most effective and respected unionists of his day as president (1932–66) of the International Ladies Garment Workers Union; he was a noted foe of Communist and racketeer influence in labour; Sept. 17, New York City, age 90.

Rene Dubos, French-born bacteriologist who taught at the Rockefeller Institute (later University) from 1944 and who became a leading critic of environmental pollution; among his 20 books were the Pulitzer Prize-winning *So Human an Animal* (1969), *Only One Earth* with Barbara Ward (1972), and *A God Within* (1972); Feb. 20, New York City, age 81.

Marty Feldman, pop-eyed British comedian who gained a devoted following for his own brand of zaniness in the Mel Brooks farces *Young Frankenstein* and *Silent Movie* and who wrote, directed, and starred in *The Last Remake of Beau Geste;* Dec. 2, Mexico City, age 48.

Henry Fonda, U.S. actor who in more than 100 roles over 48 years became a quintessential American hero; his natural acting style enabled him to portray a succession of modest but morally strong characters in such films as *Young Mr. Loncoln, The Grapes of Wrath, The Ox-Bow Incident, My Darling Clementine, 12 Angry Men, Mister Roberts, The Best Man,* and *Fail Safe;* he won an Academy Award for *On Golden Pond* in 1982; Aug. 12, Los Angeles, age 77.

Abe Fortas, U.S. lawyer and jurist who was named an associate justice of the U.S. Supreme Court by Pres. Lyndon Johnson in 1965 and four years later became the first justice ever to resign under pressure following disclosure of his financial involvement with a controversial financier; April 5, Washington, D.C., age 71.

Harold Foster, U.S. cartoonist who drew the "Tarzan" comic strip from 1931 to 1937 and then created his own strip, the popular "Prince Valiant," which he continued until retiring in 1979; July 25, Spring Hill, Fla., age 89.

Brenda Frazier, U.S. socialite who for newspaper and magazine readers became the epitome of glamorous cafe society in the 1930s and '40s; she later wrote of the meaninglessness of debutante life; May 3, Boston, age 60.

Anna Freud, Austrian-born psychoanalyst and daughter of Sigmund Freud who became a noted psychoanalyst of children and a principal defender of her father's theories; she was long the director of the Hampstead Child Therapy Clinic in London; Oct. 9, London, age 86.

Karl von Frisch, Austrian zoologist who won a share of the 1973 Nobel Prize for Physiology or Medicine for his pioneering studies of animal behaviour and sense perception; he demonstrated that fish have colour vision and acute hearing and, in his best known work, that bees communicate the location of pollen-bearing flowers to one another by means of "dance" movements; June 12, Munich, West Germany, age 96.

Dave Garroway, U.S. television personality who was the first host of NBC's "Today" program (1952–61) and made the experimental morning news and features show a tremendous success; July 21, Swarthmore, Pa., age 69.

John Gardner, U.S. writer who attracted critical notice with *Grendel* (1971), written from the viewpoint of the monster of the *Beowulf* saga; later works included *The Sunlight Dialogues, October Light,* the polemic *On Moral Fiction,* verse, children's stories, and criticism; Sept. 14, Susquehanna, Pa., age 49.

Sadegh Ghotbzadeh, Iranian politician who became familiar to Americans as the suave spokesman for the Iranian government of the Ayatollah Khomeini during the American hostage crisis of 1979–80; he was accused of plotting against the government and was executed; Sept. 15, Teheran, Iran, age 46.

William F. Giauque, U.S. chemist who won the 1949 Nobel Prize for Chemistry for his studies of the properties of substances at temperatures near absolute zero; March 28, Oakland, Calif., age 86.

Nahum Goldmann, Lithuanian-born Zionist leader who in 1936 founded and for many years headed the World Jewish

UPI
JOHN CARDINAL CODY

UPI
HANS CONRIED

CAMERA PRESS, LONDON
SIR CLIFFORD CURZON

DAVID DUBINSKY

HENRY FONDA

ABE FORTAS

Congress; in 1951 he began negotiations that secured West German commitment to pay reparations to Jewish victims of Nazism; Aug. 29, Bad Reichenhall, West Germany, age 87.

Wladyslaw Gomulka, Polish Communist who survived imprisonment during the Stalin years and became party leader in the wake of a wave of domestic unrest in 1956; his "Polish road to socialism" frequently angered Soviet leaders and failed to solve the economic problems that led to his downfall in 1970; Sept. 1, Warsaw, age 77.

Freeman F. Gosden, U.S. comedian who with his partner, Charles Correll (1890–1972), created and played the title characters in "Amos 'n Andy," one of the most popular radio shows of all time; the program aired from 1929 to 1960, when protests against its supposed stereotypes of blacks and black life caused its cancellation; Dec. 10, Los Angeles, age 83.

Glenn Gould, Canadian pianist who was almost as well known for his personal eccentricities as for his highly individual approach to performance and interpretation of classic works, especially those of J. S. Bach; he gave up concert appearances in 1964 to devote himself to perfecting the art of recording music; Oct. 4, Toronto, age 50.

Princess Grace of Monaco, the former Grace Kelly, who gave up a career in the movies to marry Prince Ranier in 1956; she had starred in such films as *High Noon, Dial M for Murder, Rear Window, The Country Girl,* for which she won an Academy Award, and *High Society,* and her poise and patrician beauty translated effortlessly into the royal role that seemed to her admirers a fairy tale come true; Sept. 14, Monte Carlo, Monaco, age 52.

Melville Bell Grosvenor, U.S. editor and traveler who followed his family's tradition of service to the National Geographic Society, founded by his great-grandfather Gardiner G. Hubbard and later presided over by his maternal grandfather, Alexander Graham Bell; he was president of the Society and editor of the *National Geographic Magazine* from 1957 to 1967; April 22, Miami, Fla., age 80.

Joyce Hall, U.S. businessman who as a teenager sold postcards and then founded Hallmark, which grew to dominate the greeting card business in the U.S.; he served as president of Hallmark from 1910 to 1966 and was responsible for the firm's sponsorship of the acclaimed "Hallmark Hall of Fame" television programs; he also personally selected the firm's slogan, "When you care enough to send the very best"; Oct. 29, Leawood, Kan., age 91.

Granville Hicks, U.S. novelist and literary critic who was a leading figure in the "proletarian" literary movement of the 1930s and wrote controversial Marxist analyses of American literature; he later publicly resigned from the Communist Party; June 18, Franklin Park, N.J., age 80.

Stanley Holloway, British actor who was best known to American audiences for his portrayal of Eliza Doolittle's father in the original Broadway production of *My Fair Lady* in 1956; he also played Shakespearian roles and appeared in such films as *The Lavender Hill Mob* and *The Titfield Thunderbolt*; Jan. 30, Littlehampton, Sussex, England, age 91.

Sam ("Lightnin' ") Hopkins, U.S. musician who was one of the greatest and most influential of his generation of blues singers and guitarists; Jan. 30, Houston, Texas, age 69.

Jiro Horikoshi, Japanese engineer who designed the Zero fighter plane, noted for its agility and firepower; more than 10,000 of them were produced during World War II; Jan. 11, Tokyo, age 78.

Edward S. ("Ned") Irish, U.S. sportsman who began promoting college basketball games at New York's Madison Square Garden in 1934 and in 1946 helped found the Basketball Association of America, which three years later merged with a rival to become the National Basketball Association; he was the founder, and from 1946 to 1974 president, of the New York Knickerbocker team; Jan. 21, Venice, Fla., age 76.

Leon Jaworski, U.S. lawyer who was best known for his work as special prosecutor in the Watergate case in 1973–74; his argument before the Supreme Court in July 1974 led to the court-ordered release of White House tape recordings that implicated Pres. Richard Nixon in the coverup of misdeeds by his subordinates and led, in turn, to Nixon's resignation; Dec. 9, near Wimberley, Texas, age 77.

Maria Jeritza, Austrian-born opera singer who was one of the great sopranos and perhaps the greatest of the prima donnas of opera's golden age; she enjoyed and encouraged popular and critical adulation during her career at New York's Metropolitan Opera (1921–32); her best known role was Tosca; July 10, Orange, N.J., age 94.

Dame Celia Johnson, British actress who was best known for her role in the 1946 film *Brief Encounter;* she also appeared in *In Which We Serve, This Happy Breed,* and *Captain's Paradise;* for more than 50 years she was a mainstay of the British stage; April 26, Nettlebed, Oxfordshire, England, age 73.

Murray Kaufman, better known as "Murray the K," U.S. disk jockey who first gained attention by his hysterical broadcasting style on various New York City stations and became a major promoter of rock concerts and performers, especially the Beatles; Feb. 21, Los Angeles, age 60.

King Khalid, ruler of Saudi Arabia who came to the throne on the death of his half brother Faisal in 1975 and continued his family's program of national development financed by petroleum; he was noted for his love of hunting and falconry; June 13, Taif, Saudi Arabia, age 69.

George Kistiakowsky, Russian-born chemist who fled Russia after serving in the anti-Communist White Army; he taught at Harvard from 1930 to 1971, and in 1944–46 he headed the explosives division of the Los Alamos, N.M., laboratory where the first atomic bomb was built; later he became a leading advocate of the banning of nuclear weapons; Dec. 7, Cambridge, Mass., age 82.

Fernando Lamas, Argentine-born actor who starred as a dashing Latin lover in dozens of movies; a champion swimmer, he married aquaqueen Esther Williams in 1963; Oct. 8, Los Angeles, age 67.

Will Lee, U.S. actor whose more than 50-year career included work in the Group Theater of the 1930s, on Broadway, off Broadway, in films and television, and a period on a 1950s blacklist; he was best known for his 13 years as Mr. Hooper, the kindly storekeeper of television's "Sesame Street"; Dec. 7, New York City, age 74.

Sybil Leek, British writer and lecturer on occult subjects who claimed to be a witch, a calling she said her family had followed since the year 1134; among her books was *Diary of a Witch* (1968); Oct. 26, Melbourne, Fla., age 65.

Richard Lockridge, U.S. writer who created the fictional detective team of Pam and Jerry North and with his wife, Frances Lockridge, published 49 books of their adventures; "Mr. and Mrs. North" were featured in a movie and on radio and television; June 19, Tryon, N.C., age 83.

Helen M. Lynd, U.S. sociologist who, with her husband, the late Robert S. Lynd, wrote *Middletown in Transition* (1937), classic studies of a small American city (Muncie, Ind.); she taught at Sarah Lawrence College from 1928 to 1964; Jan. 30, Warren, Ohio, age 85.

Paul Lynde, U.S. actor and comedian who gained attention in the Broadway musical *Bye Bye Birdie* in 1960 and appeared in numerous movies but was probably best known as a regular on the television game show "Hollywood Squares"; Jan. 9, Los Angeles, age 55.

Dwight Macdonald, U.S. author and critic who for decades played the role of gadfly in discussions of contemporary letters and politics; his wry and acerbic wit and combative nature kept him out of parties and movements but won him wide respect; Dec. 19, New York City, age 76.

Archibald MacLeish, U.S. poet and playwright who won three Pulitzer Prizes—for the long poem *Conquistador* (1932), for his *Collected Poems* (1952), and for the verse play *J.B.* (1958)—and found time to serve as librarian of Congress in 1939–44, as assistant secretary of state for cultural affairs in 1944–45, and as professor at Harvard in 1949–62; he was also a founder of UNESCO in 1946; April 20, Boston, age 89.

Dame Ngaio Marsh, New Zealand writer whose more than 30 novels featuring Chief Inspector Roderick Alleyn earned her recognition as one of the very best creators of detective fiction; Feb. 18, Christchurch, N.Z., age 82.

Pierre Mendès-France, French politician who was a Socialist member of the National Assembly from 1932 and who served as prime minister for seven months in 1954–55, during which

UPI
DAVE GARROWAY

SVEN SIMON—KATHERINE YOUNG
SADEGH GHOTBZADEH

UPI
PRINCESS GRACE

SVEN SIMON—KATHERINE YOUNG
KING KHALID

WIDE WORLD
WILL LEE

UPI
ARCHIBALD MacLEISH

time he negotiated an end to France's war in Indochina; Oct. 18, Paris, age 75.

Harry Mills, U.S. singer who, as one of the popular Mills Brothers, entertained professionally for more than 50 years and made over 2,200 records, including such hits as "Tiger Rag," "Sweet Sue," "Paper Doll," "Lazy River," and "Glow Worm"; the brothers, a quartet until 1968, imitated musical instruments on their early records but later sang in easy, close harmony to band arrangements; June 28, Los Angeles, age 68.

Thelonius Sphere Monk, U.S. jazz musician whose highly individual rhythmic and harmonic devices marked him as one of the most original and influential pianists of his time; his compositions included "Round Midnight" and "Straight No Chaser"; Feb. 17, Englewood, N.J., age 64.

Stanford Moore, U.S. biochemist who shared the 1972 Nobel Prize for Chemistry for his studies of enzymes and particularly for his success in discovering the exact chemical structure of a human enzyme, pancreatic nuclease; from 1939 he was associated with the Rockefeller Institute (later University) in New York City; Aug. 23, New York City, age 68.

Thruston B. Morton, U.S. politician who represented Kentucky in the House of Representatives from 1947 to 1953 and in the Senate from 1957 to 1969; during 1959–61 he served as chairman of the Republican National Committee; Aug. 14, Louisville, Ky., age 74.

Cathleen Nesbitt, British actress who played some 300 character roles in her 70 years on the stage and was best known for portrayals of grand dames and elegant mothers in such plays as *The Cocktail Party, Gigi,* and *My Fair Lady;* Aug. 2, London, age 93.

Ben Nicholson, British artist whose strongly geometric paintings and drawings made him the outstanding British abstract artist of his time; his best known works were a series of all-white reliefs carved from wood and synthetic board in the 1930s; Feb. 6, London, age 87.

Lord Philip Noel-Baker, British internationalist who won the 1959 Nobel Prize for Peace for his activities in support of the League of Nations and for disarmament; he was a member of the British Olympic teams of 1920, 1924, and 1928, served in Parliament as a Labour member from 1929 to 1970, and was created Baron Noel-Baker by Queen Elizabeth II in 1977; Oct. 8, London, age 92.

Juan O'Gorman, Mexican painter and architect whose works included the library of the National University of Mexico with its stone and glass mosaics and murals and frescoes for the National Museum of Anthropology and for the Museum of National History; Jan. 18, Mexico City, age 76.

Carl Orff, German composer and teacher who was best known for *Carmina Burana* (1937), a setting of a 13th-century collection of Latin, Old French, and Middle High German song texts; his system of musical education for children was widely translated and adopted; March 29, Munich, West Germany, age 86.

Leroy ("Satchel") Paige, U.S. baseball player who was perhaps the greatest pitcher of the old Negro leagues and who, after the major league colour bar was finally broken, pitched briefly for the Cleveland Indians and the St. Louis Browns; at the age of 45 he was named to the American League's 1952 All-Star team, and in 1965 he pitched three innings against the Boston Red Sox; June 8, Kansas City, Mo., age 75.

Jack Pearl, U.S. comedian whose career spanned vaudeville, radio, Broadway, and films; his radio sketches as Baron Münchhausen, employing a burlesque German dialect, made "Vas you dere, Sharlie?" a national catchphrase; Dec. 25, New York City, age 88.

Eleanor Powell, U.S. actress who tap danced through dozens of movie musicals such as *Broadway Melody of 1936, Born to Dance, Rosalie,* and *Lady Be Good;* after a long retirement she returned successfully to the Broadway stage in a 1961 revue; Feb. 11, Beverly Hills, Calif., age 69.

William Primrose, Scottish-born musician who was considered to be the greatest violist of his time; he was known especially as an exponent of chamber music and introduced many important works by such contemporary composers as Bartok, Hindemith, Milhaud, and Walton; he was also a noted teacher; May 1, Provo, Utah, age 77.

Dame Marie Rambert, Polish-born ballet director who worked with Diaghilev and Nijinsky from 1912 to 1917 and in 1920 settled in London, where she founded in 1931 the company that became Ballet Rambert, one of the most influential dance groups in the world; June 12, London, age 94.

Ayn Rand, Russian-born writer and philosopher who developed and expounded a doctrine of "rational selfishness" and promoted unfettered capitalism in books, essays, her own *Objectivist* journal, and especially in the widely read novels *The Fountainhead* (1943) and *Atlas Shrugged* (1957); March 6, New York City, age 77.

Kenneth Rexroth, U.S. writer who influenced several American literary movements, especially the Beat Generation of the 1950s; he was noted as a poet, essayist, novelist, translator, and critic and won particular acclaim for his *Autobiographical Novel* (1966); June 6, Montecito, Calif., age 76.

Marty Robbins, U.S. singer whose country and western hits included "El Paso," which won the first Grammy award for best country and western song in 1960, "A White Sport Coat and a Pink Carnation," "Devil Woman," and "My Woman, My Woman, My Wife," which also won a Grammy; Dec. 8, Nashville, Tenn., age 57.

Arthur Rubinstein, Polish-born pianist who made his concert debut in Berlin in 1898 and over the next 80-odd years gained recognition as one of the very greatest pianists of the century and probably the most popular concert musician in the world; his musicianship, technique, vitality, appetite for life, and longevity were equally celebrated; he became a U.S. citizen in 1946 and toured tirelessly until the late 1970s; he was also a highly successful recording artist with a huge repertory; Dec. 20, Geneva, age 95.

T(ubal) Claude Ryan, U.S. aircraft builder who opened a flying service in San Diego in 1922, opened the first year-round regular passenger service in the U.S. in 1925, and in 1927 built the "Spirit of St. Louis" for Charles Lindbergh; from 1933 to 1969 he ran Ryan Aeronautical Co.; Sept. 11, San Diego, Calif., age 84.

Walter W. ("Red") Smith, U.S. journalist who was the most widely read and respected sportswriter of his day; his column appeared in the *New York Herald Tribune* from 1945 to 1966 and in the *New York Times* from 1971, and in 1976 he became only the second sportswriter to win a Pulitzer Prize; several collections of his columns were published; Jan. 15, Stamford, Conn., age 76.

King Sobhuza II, ruler of Swaziland who was the world's longest reigning monarch, having succeeded his father, Ngwane V, as king in 1900; he reigned under British protection until Swaziland became independent in 1969, and in 1973 he assumed absolute power; he left scores of wives and, at least in popular belief, some 600 children; Aug. 21, Mbabane, Swaziland, age 83.

Charlie Spivak, U.S. musician who played trumpet in bands led by the Dorsey brothers, Ray Noble, Ben Pollack, Bob Crosby, and others and later led a series of successful bands and orchestras of his own; March 1, Greenville, S.C., age 77.

Edward ("Sonny") Stitt, U.S. musician who was widely considered the heir and successor of Charlie Parker as a jazz stylist and innovator; he played alto saxophone with various groups in the 1940s and '50s and later worked as a single, developing gradually an individual style that was admired for its speed, polish, and consistency; July 22, Washington, D.C., age 58.

Lee Strasberg, Polish-born acting teacher who was active in New York City's Theatre Guild from 1925, helped found the experimental Group Theater in 1931, and as guiding force in the Actors Studio from 1948 introduced Method acting to the U.S. and trained such stars as Marlon Brando, James Dean, Rod Steiger, Anne Jackson, Shelley Winters, Paul Newman, and Robert DeNiro; Feb. 17, New York City, age 80.

Monty Stratton, U.S. baseball player who pitched for the Chicago White Sox from 1934 and whose courageous attempt at a comeback after a hunting accident that resulted in the loss of a leg in 1938 inspired a Hollywood motion picture; Sept. 29, Greenville, Texas, age 70.

Mikhail A. Suslov, Soviet politician who was the Kremlin's chief Marxist ideologist and a powerful conservative force in the government; he was believed to be mainly responsible for

UPI
THELONIOUS MONK

UPI
LEROY ("SATCHEL") PAIGE

UPI
ELEANOR POWELL

UPI
WALTER ("RED") SMITH

UPI
EDWARD ("SONNY") STITT

WIDE WORLD
BESS TRUMAN

the decisions to crush liberal tendencies in Hungary, Poland, Czechoslovakia, and other satellites; Jan. 25, Moscow, age 79.

Jack Swigert, U.S. astronaut who was one of three crewmen who narrowly averted disaster on the Apollo 13 moon mission in 1970; in November 1982 he was elected to the U.S. House of Representatives from Colorado despite the discovery that he was suffering from cancer; Dec. 27, Washington, D.C., age 51.

Jacques Tati, French actor, writer, and director who created the role of Mr. Hulot and won worldwide acclaim by bumbling amiably through the films *Mr. Hulot's Holiday* (1954), *Mon Oncle,* for which he won an Academy Award (1958), *Playtime* (1967), and *Traffic* (1971); Nov. 5, Paris, age 75.

Hugo Theorell, Swedish biochemist who won the 1955 Nobel Prize for Physiology or Medicine for his pioneering studies of enzymes in the process of cell respiration; Aug. 15, Sweden, age 79.

Bess Truman, former First Lady who earned universal admiration for her unassuming manner and refusal to seek the limelight and who was credited by her husband, the late Pres. Harry S. Truman, with having been a full partner in all his undertakings; Oct. 18, Independence, Mo., age 97.

Merle Tuve, U.S. physicist whose experiments with short-pulse radio waves in the 1930s helped lay the groundwork for the development of the proximity fuze and of radar during World War II; May 20, Bethesda, Md., age 80.

Gen. Nathan F. Twining, U.S. Air Force officer who commanded the 13th Air Force in the Pacific during World War II and served as chief of staff of the Air Force from 1953 to 1957; from 1957 until his retirement in 1960 he was the first chairman of the Joint Chiefs of Staff selected from the Air Force; March 29, Lackland Air Force Base, Texas, age 84.

King Vidor, U.S. film director whose more than 50 feature films included such silent classics as *The Big Parade* (1925) and *The Crowd* (1928), the pioneering *Hallelujah* with an all-black cast (1929), *The Champ* (1931), *Our Daily Bread* (1934), *The Citadel* (1938), *Northwest Passage* (1940), *Duel in the Sun* (1947), *The Fountainhead* (1949), and *Ruby Gentry* (1952); Nov. 1, Paso Robles, Calif., age 88.

Lloyd Waner, U.S. baseball player who, as "Little Poison" to his elder brother Paul's "Big Poison," starred in the Pittsburgh Pirates outfield from 1927 through 1941; he was elected to the Baseball Hall of Fame in 1967, 15 years after Paul; July 22, Oklahoma City, age 76.

Jack Webb, U.S. actor who was best known—and widely imitated—for his portrayal of the stone-faced, laconic Sgt. Joe Friday on the "Dragnet" radio and television shows; he also appeared in several films and produced other television programs including "Adam-12," "Emergency," and "Escape"; Dec. 23, Los Angeles, age 62.

Peter Weiss, German-born playwright who lived in Stockholm from 1942 and achieved worldwide fame in 1964 with his startling and disturbing *The Persecution and Assassination of Marat as Performed by the Inmates of the Asylum of Charenton Under the Direction of the Marquis de Sade,* known as *Marat/Sade;* May 10, Stockholm, age 65.

Gluyas Williams, U.S. cartoonist who contributed his wry, lucid drawings to many publications, most notably *The New Yorker* magazine; he also illustrated many of the humorous books of his Harvard classmate Robert Benchley; Feb. 13, Boston, age 93.

Don Wilson, U.S. radio and television personality who was Jack Benny's announcer and foil for more than 40 years; April 25, Palm Springs, Calif., age 81.

Korczak Ziolkowski, U.S. sculptor who devoted his last 35 years to carving a gigantic monument to Chief Crazy Horse out of a granite mountain in the Black Hills of South Dakota; he financed the work out of private donations and achieved a rough outline of the work before his death; Oct. 20, Sturgis, S.D., age 74.

Vladimir Zworykin, Russian-born electrical engineer who patented the iconoscope and the kinescope—the basic devices of electronic television—in 1923 and 1924 and a system of colour television in 1929; as a researcher and later director of the RCA Laboratories in Princeton from 1929 to 1954, he also contributed to the development of the electron microscope; July 29, Princeton, N.J., age 92.

WILLIAM CAMPBELL/TIME MAGAZINE

A British officer (left) directs Baluchi troops on the Oman side of the troubled border between Oman and South Yemen.

PERSIAN GULF STATES

Bahrain

The first half of 1982 was dominated by the aftermath of an attempted coup planned for Dec. 16, 1981. The plot was foiled as a result of information supplied to the security police by Saudi Arabia and the United Arab Emirates. The plotters belonged to an Iranian-backed underground movement, the Islamic Front for the Liberation of Bahrain.

The trial of 73 accused, most of whom were Shi'ah Muslims, ended late in May. All were found guilty, and three were sentenced to life imprisonment. Prior to the coup attempt, it had been thought that the rift between Sunni and Shi'ah Muslims in Bahrain was healing. Prime Minister Khalifah ibn Sulman al-Khalifah accused Iran of involvement in the plot and said that training camps existed in that country for revolutionaries bent on creating unrest in all the Arab Gulf states.

The attempted coup had little effect on development plans for the island or the growth of its banking, insurance, refining, and aluminum industries. Bahraini politicians continued to have faith in the Gulf Cooperation Council as a sign of stronger relations with their Arab neighbours. Contracting work on the $600 million causeway link to Saudi Arabia was begun; an important new project agreed on in 1982 was a $1 billion heavy-oil conversion plant, a joint venture with Saudi Arabia and Kuwait.

Oman

During 1982 Oman was affected by reduced oil revenue resulting from weak world demand. The five-year plan launched in early 1981 depended on a crude-oil production ceiling of 320,000 bbl a day, but by late 1982 the Cabinet was considering raising production to 350,000 bbl a day to make up for the revenue shortfall. Sultan Qabus ibn Sa'id continued to pursue a policy of friendship with Western countries and hostility toward the U.S.S.R.

Security remained a high priority in view of the support given by neighbouring Yemen (Aden; South Yemen) to guerrillas hostile to Qabus. About 30 guerrillas were believed to be at large in the mountains above the southern city of Salalah. Oman professed its readiness to cooperate with mediation efforts by Kuwait and the Arab League. On October 27 it was announced that Oman and South Yemen had agreed to a cessation of hostilities.

Qatar

Falling oil revenue and setbacks over a major planned gas field development provided a gloomy outlook for the Arab world's smallest state in 1982. Oil revenue for the year, from production levels of 300,000 bbl a day, was expected to gross $3 billion, significantly less than the $5 billion a year earned in 1980 and 1981. Oil production was reduced by 25% in April 1982 as part of the Organization of Petroleum Exporting Countries (OPEC) strategy aimed at eliminating the world oil glut.

Qatar's biggest projects, for the recovery of gas at the offshore North Field, advanced more slowly than anticipated. Potential joint venture partners were reluctant to commit new funds for investment in the Gulf because of the Iran-Iraq war, and slackness in the world markets for liquefied gas was another inhibiting factor. The government decided, nevertheless, to go ahead with an interim scheme to harness gas for power generation and desalination.

A number of development projects were completed in 1982 for Emir Sheikh Khalifah ibn Hamad ath-Thani's tenth anniversary as ruler. They included the Hamad Hospital, to service the health needs of Qatar well into the 21st century, and the Sheraton West Bay government hotel and conference centre.

United Arab Emirates

The resignation of Brig. Sheikh Sultan ibn-Zaid as commander of the defense forces of the United Arab Emirates on February 22 was the major political event of 1982. The appointment of Sheikh Sultan, second son of Sheikh Zaid of Abu Dhabi, had caused strained relations with the Dubai ruling family; his resignation followed an incident in which soldiers under his command assaulted a group of Bahraini women.

Sheikh Sultan of Sharjah, considered the most radical of the rulers of the seven emirates, opened the Sajaa oil and gas field on June 20. This was expected to boost the emirate's revenues, although by mid-1982 Sharjah was in default on a $200 million loan.

Among the important economic developments were a tightening of laws requiring foreign companies to use local agents and the opening on March 10 of Abu Dhabi's Ruwais industrial zone. Cuts in crude oil production to about one million barrels a day had little effect on government spending, which continued to be high.

PERU

Terrorist activity in Peru, which began in 1980 when democracy was restored under Pres. Fernando Belaúnde Terry, reached new heights in 1982. Most of the attacks were attributed to the Maoist group Sendero Luminoso. In March an attack by 150 guerrillas on a prison in Ayacucho led to the breakout of some 250 prisoners. Subsequent guerrilla violence included dynamite and firebomb attacks in many parts of the country. In several provinces a state of emergency was imposed, lifted, and then reimposed in accordance with the fluctuating levels of violence. There was a lull in June, although bands of escaped prisoners carried out sporadic attacks on isolated villages and summarily executed several suspected police informers. An intensification of terrorism followed in July and August. There was a spate of assassinations of local politicians and community leaders in the Ayacucho region, and in a night of violence in Lima and its port of Callao, electricity py-

A group of "Sinchis," members of a special police force trained for antiterrorist work, search for guerrillas in the Ayacucho region of Peru.
ALAIN KELER—SYGMA

lons were sabotaged, shops vandalized, and public buildings attacked.

The guerrilla organization proved difficult for the police to infiltrate. It had close links with the peasant community, but claims of foreign involvement remained unproved. Public disquiet led the government to introduce a bill that would bring back the recently abolished death penalty for political killings and premeditated murder.

The economy remained depressed. Low prices for exports coupled with high international interest rates were detrimental to the balance of payments. A trade deficit of up to $700 million and a current account deficit of at least $1.7 billion were anticipated. In July, after months of negotiations, the government signed a loan agreement with the International Monetary Fund (IMF) for $960 million over three years on condition that immediate steps be taken to introduce stringent austerity in public finance. Initially it was believed that the public sector deficit could be reduced to 4% of gross domestic product (GDP), compared with 8.3% in 1981, but by August Prime Minister Manuel Ulloa Elías was admitting that it was likely to be around 9%.

Steps were taken to meet the conditions of the IMF loan. Cuts in spending on investment projects were difficult to implement, as many had been contracted one or two years previously, but the government aimed to save 270 billion soles by this means. Plans to reduce subsidies were also difficult because fuel and food price rises had already exacerbated social tensions and led to many strikes and wage claims. Nevertheless, the Cabinet announced further monthly increases of 10–12% in gasoline prices from August, saving 30 billion soles. The wheat subsidy was cut by lifting the control on the price of bread, and other food subsidies were reduced to save 40 billion soles. The government hoped to bring the deficit down to a more acceptable 6% of GDP. However, the spending cuts were expected to provoke a downturn in economic activity. An inflation rate of 65% was predicted, only marginally lower than the 1981 rate of 73%. Faced with increasing economic difficulties, Prime Minister Ulloa resigned on December 9 and was replaced by Fernando Schwalb, formerly ambassador to Washington.

One of Peru's leading diplomats, Javier Pérez de Cuéllar, was appointed secretary-general of the UN in December 1981. President Belaúnde gained a reputation as an international mediator during the Falkland Islands dispute when he proposed a peace plan that was debated, but later rejected, by the U.K. and Argentina.

PETS

The role of pets in child development and human care came under greater scrutiny in 1982 than ever before. Scientists grew more certain that the interaction of human and animal had a great deal to do with the physical and mental well-being of both. Institutes established by the Humane Society of the

MODELL © 1982 THE NEW YORKER MAGAZINE, INC.

"All right, come out and we'll talk about it."

United States in Washington, D.C., and by the schools of veterinary medicine at the University of Pennsylvania in Philadelphia and Washington State University in Pullman joined other groups in examining the human–pet bond.

One of the most inflammatory issues in the humane movement was "pound seizure." Biomedical researchers require animals for experimental surgery and for testing new drugs, for veterinary as well as human medical use. Very often the dogs and cats they use come from pounds and shelters. Humane groups were fighting pound seizure bitterly, claiming that the laboratory was not a proper reward for an animal that had served as a faithful pet.

Six states had outlawed the use of shelter animals by laboratories. Seven states required pounds and shelters to surrender animals requested by laboratories. The other states had let the matter be settled on the local level. The city of Los Angeles, for example, had an ordinance against pound seizure, while Los Angeles County did not. An effort in California to adopt the Los Angeles policy statewide failed in 1982 but was to be an issue again in 1983.

Opponents of pound seizure, many claiming not to be antivivisectionists, said the animals should come from colonies where they were bred for that purpose. Researchers pointed out that shelter animals were generally destroyed anyway. It seemed unlikely that the issue would be resolved easily or soon.

The exotic pet trade continued to flourish in 1982, with reptiles suffering terribly from poor shipping conditions and from ill-equipped owners with little or no experience in handling them. Hundreds of thousands of reptiles, often of questionable species and some of endangered species, continued to flow through dealerships across the country. The traffic included venomous snakes, leading inevitably to numerous accidents over the course of the year.

Although there were slightly fewer dogs registered with the American Kennel Club than there had been a few years earlier, the dog fancy continued to broaden its base. Dog showing, once a hobby of the very wealthy, continued to attract enthusiasts from every social level. The appreciation of purebred dogs had universal appeal. The larger dogs continued to lead in popularity. While the poodles (all three sizes—standard, miniature, and toy combined) still led the parade and the cocker spaniel was in second place, the Doberman pinscher was third in popularity and the German shepherd was fourth.

Cats continued to increase in popularity; at least 40% of the homes in the United States had at least one cat. At least 52% of American homes had dogs. With the trend toward multiple pets, the likelihood of there being two cats or a cat and a dog continued upward.

The latest fad seemed to be miniature horses. These are not ponies but true horses that have been bred down until they are not much taller at the shoulder than a terrier. They are generally ill-tempered, impossible to housebreak, and extremely expensive. The appeal of the creatures was strongest in the South and Southwest. Undeniably a self-limiting enthusiasm, the fad seemed likely to pass soon.

Despite restrictions because of the threat of Newcastle disease to domestic fowl, birds continued to be popular with pet fanciers. Birds were imported by the hundreds of thousands, and many of them, cockatoos and macaws particularly, sold for thousands of dollars each.

PHILIPPINES

The National Assembly passed, and Pres. Ferdinand E. Marcos signed into law on Sept. 11, 1982, a bill providing for the succession in case of the president's "permanent disability, death, removal from office or resignation." It gave succession powers to a 15-member Executive Committee, headed by Prime Minister Cesar Virata.

Marcos named his wife, Imelda, and his eldest daughter, Imee, to the committee. Mrs. Marcos was already minister for human developments and the governor of greater Manila, where a fifth of the nation's people lived. Imee headed the National Youth Movement. The appointments strengthened speculation that Marcos intended his wife to succeed him. He said, however, that "she is not going to be my successor" but that she would be needed to help a successor.

Marcos, president since 1966, said that he intended to ask the New Society Movement, the nation's dominant political party, to find another candidate for president when his term ended in 1987. He added that an emergency or party pressure could make him decide to seek reelection.

Nationwide elections were held May 17 for

SHOOTERS/TIME MAGAZINE

Imelda Marcos was sworn in as a member of the new Executive Committee of the Philippines by her husband, Pres. Ferdinand E. Marcos.

280,000 members of 40,000 barangay (village council) units. After more than eight years of martial law, this was a step back toward elective government, to be followed by National Assembly elections in 1984 and the 1987 presidential election. Legislative assemblies were elected June 7 for autonomous regions created for Muslims in the south. Voter turnout was poor, and the government party candidates prevailed.

Political opponents of Marcos united in February as the United Nationalist Democratic Organization. It called for restoring political freedom, which it accused Marcos of suppressing; justice for the oppressed and exploited; and economic development.

Marcos said on August 8 that his opponents were conspiring to stage nationwide bombings, assassinations, and strikes in September while he visited the United States. Labour leaders were particular targets of a crackdown. By early September, 39 had been arrested and 42 others accused of plots.

From September 15 to 27 Marcos made his first state visit to the U.S. since 1966. He was accorded a cordial reception by Pres. Ronald Reagan, but some Filipinos in the U.S. demonstrated against him.

The government searched for ways to get the country out of its worst economic situation in more than a decade. The 1983 budget was austere, offering little hope of breaking out of deficits or improving living standards unless worldwide demand for the Philippines' primary products (coconut oil, metal ores, fruit and vegetables) increased significantly.

Economic problems contributed to continued growth of the New People's Army, a Communist guerrilla force. The president of the National Defense College estimated that 20% of the nation's villages were under NPA control or soon would be. One government tactic for combating guerrillas, a program of village relocation under which some 100,000 persons had been gathered into 35 strategic settlements on Mindanao Island, was abandoned because of human rights complaints.

Sporadic insurgency operations by Muslim separatists in the southern islands continued to cause bloodshed in armed clashes with the Army. The separatists' Moro National Liberation Front intensified efforts to win political backing from Muslim countries but had little success.

PHOTOGRAPHY

By far the outstanding event in photography for mass consumers in 1982 was Kodak's introduction in February of its ultraminiature-format Disc system, the result of a long and intense research-and-development effort. Heart of the system was a wafer-thin disk containing 15 tiny (8 × 10-mm; 0.3 × 0.4-in) radially arranged frames of a new high-resolution ISO (ASA) 200 Kodacolor HR Disc film. Three models of Disc cameras, the 4000, 6000, and 8000, were all small and flat enough to slip into a shirt pocket and incorporated a sophisticated 12.5-mm $f/2.8$ four-element glass lens, a built-in flash with a recycling time of about one second, lithium batteries with a claimed life expectancy under normal amateur use of five years, and automatic film advance. As a further attempt to supply what Kodak termed "decision-free" photography, the Disc cameras provided a bright-light exposure of 1/200 sec at $f/6$ but automatically switched to the flash mode, with an exposure of 1/100 sec at $f/2.8$, when the light level dropped sufficiently. In addition, the 6000 and 8000 models included a built-in close-up lens that provided a minimum shooting distance of 18 in (46 cm). The top-of-the-line 8000 also had a self-timer, rapid-sequence film advance, and digital alarm clock.

By year's end other models of the Disc camera had been introduced by manufacturers in Europe and the Far East under Kodak license arrangements, many of which omitted some of the high-technology convenience features of the Kodak models. Kodak hoped that the Disc system would reinvigorate the mass market of snapshooters as the introduction of its 126 and 110 cameras had done before. The initial response was hopeful; late in the year Kodak announced that it had sold more than eight million Disc cameras and that sales were exceeding those of the 110 for the same period following the latter's introduction.

Sales of 35-mm single-lens-reflex cameras (SLR's) declined as a result of overproduction, saturated markets, recession, and shifts in the international monetary exchange rates, but important developments continued. Nikon introduced its FM2 SLR with a titanium focal-plane shutter providing speeds to 1/4,000 sec and electronic flash synchronization at an unusually fast 1/200 sec.

Continued attempts were made to provide sensitive, fast-responding autofocusing and autofocus aids for interchangeable-lens 35-mm cameras. Canon incorporated its own CCD (charge-coupled device) technology in the Canon AL-1, an aperture-priority 35-mm SLR that provided three focus indicators visible in the viewfinder: a green dot that lit when the focus was correct and two red arrows to indicate which way to turn the lens if the subject was out of focus. Nikon introduced a modified Nikon F3 autofocusing camera and two specially designed lenses, an 80-mm $f/2.8$ and a 200-mm $f/3.5$. When the new lenses were used with the F3 AF, full autofocusing was provided. With conventional Nikon lenses, autofocus aid was supplied.

Olympus was the last of the major Japanese 35-mm SLR makers to bring forth an autofocus model, the OM-30 (OM-F in the U.S.). This camera used the Honeywell TCL (through-camera-lens) focus-detecting module to provide full autofocus with a new 35–70-mm $f/4$ autofocusing zoom lens and autofocus aid with conventional Olympus lenses.

Anxious to keep their highly automated factories busy, major Japanese camera manufacturers intro-

Eastman Kodak's new pocket-sized Disc camera replaced the usual film roll with a wafer-thin disk containing 15 radially arranged film frames.

PHOTOGRAPHS, JACK MANNING/THE NEW YORK TIMES

duced dozens of new compact, fixed-lens, leaf-shutter 35-mm cameras with numerous convenience features including built-in flash, power film advance and rewind, automatic exposure, and autofocus. Canon dramatically led the way with its line of Snappy compacts available in several colours and set to challenge Kodak's Disc system by offering nearly equivalent decision-free photography plus the advantage of 35-mm format at a competitive price.

The year's unusually large number of innovations and technical developments in silver-image sensitized materials was led by Kodak's remarkable ISO 1000 Kodacolor negative film, which provided unprecedented speed with moderate grain. The key to this accomplishment was a new type of light-sensitive silver halide grain that was wafer-flat rather than chunky. Called T-grain (T for "tablet"), the new emulsion was expected to lead to other high-speed films and printing papers.

Polaroid demonstrated a unique rapid-process 35-mm colour transparency film, Polachrome, plus high-contrast and continuous-tone black-and-white instant emulsions. These were used like conventional film in any 35-mm camera, but they could be developed and ready for mounting and projection about 1½ minutes after exposure with provided chemicals and a crank-operated processing unit.

Kodak augmented its Ektaflex colour printing system with a new material, Ektaflex PCT Reversal Film, designed for the rapid production of colour prints from positive transparencies. Agfa announced a rival, even simpler system based on Agfaspeed, a positive-to-positive printing material that developed within 1½ minutes in any tray or processing tube and required only a single-bath activator solution plus a water rinse.

During the year Sony gave public demonstrations of a Mavigraph system for producing colour prints from its prototype all-electronic Mavica camera. Innovative as the Sony concept was, the Mavica was still far from being a practical, available item. At the Photokina trade fair held in Cologne, West Germany, in October, Kodak demonstrated its potential for creating interfaces between conventional and electronic photography with a device that converted Kodak Disc photographs into images on a colour television screen. The unit allowed one to zoom in on the image and reframe it by shifting to the left or right. The data could then be encoded on the film disk's magnetic core to automatically guide a photofinishing machine in making a print according to the customer's directions.

Cultural Trends

The market for photographic prints, which had begun to soften in the previous year, was severely affected in 1982. A number of galleries found themselves in serious financial difficulties, while others, including New York City's Light Gallery and Photograph Gallery, were forced to close their doors. Print prices at major auctions were erratic. Although the work of 19th-century masters and some contemporary photographers continued to fetch high prices, other work dropped. The volume generally was down, and a number of photographs were withdrawn because they did not meet the minimum bid.

Among the year's more ambitious photographic exhibitions was "Color as Form," a major attempt to trace the medium's evolution and define its function, mounted by the International Museum of Photography at George Eastman House in Rochester, N.Y. The work of contemporary Chinese photographers was seen in the U.S. for the first time in "China from Within," which opened at the National Academy of Sciences in Washington, and in "The Face of China" in connection with the first U.S. visit by a cultural delegation from the Chinese Photographers Association. An unusual photojournalistic project, organized by American Rick Smolan and Australian Andy Park, brought 100 photographers from all over the world to photograph "A Day in the Life of Australia" and resulted in an impressive picture book and a major exhibition at the International Center of Photography.

The 1982 Pulitzer Prize for spot news photography went to Ron Edmonds of the Associated Press for his coverage of the assassination attempt against U.S. Pres. Ronald Reagan and for feature photography to John H. White of the *Chicago Sun Times*. Among top winners of the 1982 Pictures of the Year awards, co-sponsored by the University of Missouri School of Journalism and the National Press Photographers Association, were Dan Dry of the *Louisville* (Ky.) *Courier-Journal* and *Louisville Times* as Newspaper Photographer of the Year and Harry Benson of *Life* magazine as Magazine Photographer of the Year; winner of the World Understanding Award was Cincinnati free-lancer Gordon Baer for his photographic report on "Vietnam: The Battle Comes Home." The Hasselblad Foundation Award for photography went to Frenchman Henri Cartier-Bresson.

PHYSICS

For some years it has been known that appropriate laser design allows the production of laser light in the form of pulses rather than as a continuous wave. These pulses are normally much shorter than a second in duration and can have considerably higher peak power than continuous-wave emission. In the early 1980s standard techniques were available to decrease this time to a few picoseconds (a millionth of a millionth of a second).

These very intense, very short pulses of light have many possible applications, ranging from the cutting and welding of metals to the study of the kinetics of chemical reactions. For some studies in chemical kinetics the shorter the light pulse, the more precisely controlled is the experiment and the less ambiguous are the results. In 1982 brevity achieved a new meaning at Bell Laboratories, where C. V. Shank and co-workers generated the shortest ever flash of

Kenneth G. Wilson of Cornell University won the Nobel Prize for Physics for his theory of "critical phenomena in connection with phase transitions."

UPI

laser light and therefore the "fastest act of man." Their laser pulse lasted for 30 femtoseconds, or 0.03 picoseconds. The experimenters put such a small period of time into perspective in the following way: in one second a light beam can travel from the Earth to the Moon and back; in 30 femtoseconds light travels about ten micrometres, or one-tenth the thickness of a human hair.

With light pulses this short it might be possible to study in far more detail not only the result of a chemical reaction but also the reaction itself while it is in progress. Applications for picosecond-pulse lasers had grown rapidly in recent years, and it was expected that the femtosecond laser soon would become yet another useful tool for the spectroscopist, the reaction chemist, the medical physicist, the metallurgist, and many other specialists.

Magnetic Monopole

Schoolchildren study the permanent magnet with its one north pole and one south pole and are taught that like poles repel whereas unlike poles attract. The origin of these magnetic effects, in the electric charge of the electron, is well understood. The orbiting electron carries its charge around the nucleus of the atom and, as such, is equivalent to a current loop. It will appear as a very weak, permanent magnet. Since an orbiting electron is the fundamental origin of magnetism and since it produces a small magnet with north and south poles, the two poles seem to be parts of an indivisible whole.

In 1931 British physicist P. A. M. Dirac was studying the theoretical aspects of electromagnetism, and he found it necessary to propose a particle with a single quantum of magnetic charge, which became known as the magnetic monopole. Dirac was able to deduce its strength, and much more recently its mass was estimated to be about 10^{16} times the mass of the proton. Nevertheless, despite considerable experimental effort direct observation of this particle remained elusive. Because of its heavy mass, searches for the magnetic monopole had been carried out, for example, in the depths of the deepest underwater gorges and in the middle of some of the oldest and densest rocks on Earth—all unsuccessfully until a report in April 1982 by Blas Cabrera of Stanford University that a single monopole appeared to have been detected.

The experiment performed by Cabrera was centred around a monopole detector consisting of a

Charles V. Shank and co-workers at Bell Laboratories produced the smallest slice of measurable time ever created—a burst of laser light 30 femtoseconds long, or 30 millionths of a billionth of a second.

AUTHENTICATED NEWS INTERNATIONAL

superconducting ring of four turns of niobium wire. When cooled to a few degrees above absolute zero by liquid helium the wire loses all electrical resistance, allowing a current to flow indefinitely in the coil. This current will not decay even though no external power is supplied.

Quantum theory holds that the current in the ring can only have "allowed" quantized values that are separated by a forbidden gap. Another way of stating this is that the magnetic flux produced by the current in the ring is quantized and increases in quantum jumps. If a monopole were to pass through the detector's four-turn coil, it should produce a change equivalent to eight flux quanta. Cabrera monitored his detector for more than 200 days and during that time observed one change in current that corresponded to the passage of a single monopole to an accuracy of $\pm 5\%$.

There are many other possible causes of such jumps in current, and Cabrera took great care to eliminate all of them. He argued that effects due to voltage fluctuations, radio-frequency interference, external magnetic fields, ferromagnetic contamination, mechanical effects, earthquakes, and cosmic rays could all be discounted. Nevertheless, he pointed out that a possible effect due to the release of internal stresses in the coils could not be ruled out.

Given the diameter of the detector loop (five centimetres) and making certain assumptions, one can calculate the maximum expected number of monopoles passing through the loop in a particular period of time. Carrying through this analysis yields a maximum of three monopoles passing through a five-centimetre coil every two years. One would surmise that Cabrera was rather fortunate to have made an observation in only 200 days. The statistics would soon be put to the test since the experiment was to be repeated with a ring having a much larger detection area, which should be penetrated by a monopole every 15 days. Since the analysis includes some highly conservative assumptions, one should expect the average interval between observations to be more than 15 days.

Physicists working in magnetism, however, remained unruffled by all of this excitement. Confirmation of the existence of the monopole would hardly solve their problems. In 1982 details of the origins of magnetism in two of the most fundamental magnetic materials, the elements iron and nickel, were still not understood. Indeed they were the basis of an enthralling controversy. Is the magnetism produced by electrons that are mainly localized around their parent atom? Or, on the other hand, is it the electrons that are free to wander through the metal, the conduction electrons, that are responsible? What actually happens to iron and nickel when they are heated to a temperature at which the overall magnetism is destroyed? Do the atoms still have magnetic moments that interact with their neighbours or not? These and other questions would continue to be studied in years to come.

POLAND

At the end of another eventful year for Poland, on Dec. 12, 1982, Gen. Wojciech Jaruzelski "suspended" martial law, which had been in force since Dec. 13, 1981, promising to remove all its restrictions as soon as he was able to judge that the "enemy" was totally crushed. A month before the suspension Lech Walesa, leader of the independent trade union Solidarnosc (Solidarity), had been released from his almost year-long detention; and at the same time, there were indications that the Polish Roman Catholic hierarchy, in the interest of preserving public order, might be prepared to modify its support for Solidarity in favour of some 2,000 new labour unions that the government intended should become operational on Jan. 1, 1983, and to which Solidarity's assets were to be transferred.

According to Jaruzelski, who besides being first secretary of the Polish United Workers' (Communist) Party (PUWP) was also head of the Military Council of National Salvation and premier, the "enemy" included the people who had organized a "counterrevolution" directed against the Polish "socialist statehood" and the Polish-Soviet alliance. In his speeches and press interviews during 1982 General Jaruzelski constantly reiterated the importance of the Polish-Soviet alliance, describing it as "the cornerstone of Poland's security."

Not only Polish Communists—a minority of the

Lech Walesa, head of the outlawed Solidarity union, was released in November after 11 months of detention.
C.A.F. / WIDE WORLD

UPI

Demonstrators who gathered in Gdansk in August to mark the second anniversary of Solidarity were met by police firing tear gas.

Polish nation—recognized the soundness of this statement. Poles dwelling in the basins of the Vistula and Oder rivers understood that the existing resolution of Poland's long-standing conflict with Germany was a matter of common interest to both Poland and the U.S.S.R. That major consideration explained why Soviet rulers of the post-Stalin era, starting with Nikita Khrushchev, reconciled themselves with the existence of two anomalies differentiating Poland from other members of the Soviet bloc: first, that 70% of Poland's agricultural land was still privately owned by 2.9 million farmers who were responsible for 80% of the nation's total agricultural production; second, that the spiritual influence of the Roman Catholic Church remained strong in the minds and hearts of the Polish people. Instead of drawing the present Soviet rulers' attention to the importance of accepting a third anomaly—making "socialist statehood" popular among the ten million Polish workers who had joined Solidarity—Jaruzelski had accepted Leonid Brezhnev's advice that the movement must be crushed.

Despite the proclamation of martial law, strikes and violent confrontations continued during 1982. During clashes in Gdansk at the end of January, 205 demonstrators were arrested; two weeks later 194 were arrested in Poznan, including many students, after the reopening of the universities on February 8.

By mid-February some 4,000 faced charges for breaches of martial law. Meanwhile, social and economic conditions worsened; there were severe food shortages and price increases of up to 400%.

Solidarity leaders who had escaped the December 1981 roundup formed an underground Coordination Commission, which started organizing demonstrations against martial law. These continued throughout the summer and included a mass gathering in Poznan to mark the anniversary of the 1956 riots that had preceded the advent to power as PUWP secretary-general of Wladyslaw Gomulka. The demonstrations culminated in a series of violent confrontations with security forces in Warsaw and other towns at the end of August, marking the second anniversary of Solidarity's birth as a union. During the summer four workers were killed. On October 5 the authorities announced the arrest of Wladyslaw Frasyniuk, one of the leading Solidarity underground organizers. Then on October 8 the Sejm (parliament) passed an act dissolving all registered trade unions including Solidarity; out of 460 deputies, 10 voted against and 9 abstained.

Underground Solidarity's response to the ban was to call for an eight-hour general strike and public protest meetings on November 10. However, on November 8 Archbishop Jozef Glemp, Roman Catholic primate of Poland, had talks with Jaruzelski,

JEFF MACNELLY—CHICAGO TRIBUNE

after which it was announced that Pope John Paul II was to be invited to pay a second official visit to Poland in June 1983. The talks were said to have centred on the "common concern" of the church and the government over the trend of events. Before the talks Archbishop Glemp had made it clear that the church would not support street demonstrations. With the government having taken massive security precautions, the November 10 protest strike was a failure. The following day it was announced that Lech Walesa was being released from his internment as a "private person."

In an interview that Polish state television had taped just before his release, Walesa stated that he wanted a "fair, proper agreement" with the government. On December 18 the Sejm voted unanimously for the suspension of martial law already announced by Jaruzelski six days earlier. But there were nine abstentions when it approved measures maintaining a tight grip on vital sectors of the economy. Archbishop Glemp sent to the Council of State a letter complaining, in the name of the Roman Catholic hierarchy, of the "repressive" nature of the measures. On December 23 all the remaining 250 or so of those detained when martial law was promulgated were released, with the exception of seven Solidarity leaders who remained under formal arrest and would be charged with unspecified contraventions of martial law.

On November 4 the representatives of 500 Western banks and heads of the Polish state Bank Handlowy signed in Vienna an agreement on the new spread of Poland's financial commitments for 1982, amounting to $3.4 billion.

POLITICAL PARTIES

Preparations for the 1984 presidential campaign were to be the major concern of both major political parties in the United States in 1983. For the Republicans the question as 1982 ended was whether Pres. Ronald Reagan would seek reelection. The indications—far from decisive—were that he would.

The president himself hinted in July 1982 that he was thinking about reelection. At a press conference he said he had told his aides, "It would be unlike me, I think, to walk away from an unfinished job. And I've suggested to them that they shouldn't waste their time reading the help wanted ads." Former president Richard Nixon predicted that Reagan would run again and would win.

In October Richard Richards announced he would quit as chairman of the Republican Party and return to private ventures when his term expired in January. He denied there had been pressure from the White House for his resignation but added, "Every clerk in the White House thinks he can do my job better than I do. If I had my choice, I would not have a political shop in the White House."

On November 6 President Reagan appointed Sen. Paul Laxalt (Nev.), a close personal friend and chairman of his 1980 election campaign, as general chairman of the Republican National Committee. Party rules required that the chairman be a full-time, paid employee; special action to exempt Laxalt from the rule was expected at a meeting of the Republican National Committee in January. Besides supervising the national committee, he was expected to coordinate the activities of the Republican House and Senate campaign committees. Laxalt indicated

Sen. Paul Laxalt (right) of Nevada, long a close friend and adviser of Pres. Ronald Reagan, succeeded Richard Richards (far right) as chairman of the Republican Party in November.

PHOTOS, WIDE WORLD

he expected Reagan to run for reelection. "If I didn't think he was running for president, I wouldn't be taking this position," he said.

The Republican National Committee on June 18 unanimously approved Dallas as the site for the Aug. 20–23, 1984, party convention. The site had been recommended by the president. At the meeting of the Republican National Committee June 18, Finance Chairman Richard DeVos said in a speech, "This recession has been a beneficial thing and a cleansing thing for this society." This remark and, it was reported, complaints of high-pressure tactics in fund raising, led then-chairman Richards to replace him in August. Richards named Lieut. Gov. Mike Curb of California as the new finance chairman.

The Democratic Party began to inch backward from a decade of reform that had been intended to give more power to grass-roots voters and less to party leaders. Rules adopted in 1982 provided that about 550 delegates to the 1984 convention would be party and government officials not committed to any candidate. These delegates could include up to three-fifths of the Democrats in the House and Senate. The rest would be named by state parties, with priority given to governors and big-city mayors. Since the party and government officials would be the only uncommitted delegates at the 1984 convention, they could be decisive in a close contest for the presidential nomination.

Under its previous reform rules, the party had apportioned delegates from each congressional district among top candidates for the presidential nomination. Rules adopted in 1982 would allow the top candidate to win all the delegates in a district. Delegates pledged to a specific candidate no longer would be bound to support that candidate on the first convention ballot. The new rules merely required that delegates "in all good conscience reflect the sentiments of those who elected them."

The rules called for presidential primaries or caucuses to be held between the second Tuesday in March and the second Tuesday in June. Exceptions were granted for Iowa, which could hold its caucus 15 days early, and New Hampshire, which could hold its primary 8 days early; both states thus retained their traditional lead on the primary season.

The shape of the Democratic campaign for the presidential nomination changed radically in December when Sen. Edward Kennedy (Mass.) announced he would not be a candidate. Kennedy was at the time leading in presidential preference polls among Democrats. But he said he did not want to subject his three children—Kara, 22, Ted, Jr., 21, and Patrick, 15—to another campaign at a time when he and his wife, Joan, were involved in "painful" divorce proceedings. Kennedy said he would not accept a draft nomination in 1984, but he left open the possibility of a 1988 campaign.

The surprise announcement sent potential Democratic presidential candidates and their aides rushing to telephones to enlist known Kennedy supporters. It also appeared to strengthen labour's influence in the Democratic nomination process. The AFL-CIO Executive Council set up procedures in March for early endorsement of a presidential candidate. Previously, the 15 million-member federation had endorsed candidates only after party nominations were made. The Executive Council called for a meeting of the federation's general board in December 1983. A two-thirds vote for a single candidate would be needed to make an endorsement.

It had been assumed that Kennedy and former vice-president Walter Mondale would each have enough labour support to prevent endorsement of the other, thus deadlocking the process. With Kennedy out of the campaign, the chance of Mondale's winning the endorsement seemed improved. To gain enough union support to block an endorsement, any other candidate would have to take significant pro-union stands. Besides Mondale, Democrats who

SACK—MINNEAPOLIS STAR AND TRIBUNE

"On your mark, get set—go: The longest, most expensive race ever"

were actively considering presidential bids were former governor Reubin Askew, Fla.; Sen. Alan Cranston, Calif.; Sen. John Glenn, Ohio; Sen. Gary Hart, Colo.; and Sen. Ernest Hollings, S.C.

The Democrats' midterm convention in 1982 was about half the size of the similar 1978 convention, and party regulars were heavily represented—all 374 Democratic National Committee members were among the 897 participants. The convention adopted a broad series of stands critical of the Reagan administration but avoided most issues that might have divided their own ranks. All of the potential candidates except Askew, who chose not to attend, addressed the convention.

In June the Democratic National Committee finally liquidated a long-standing debt that had ranged up to $10 million. Efforts were made in 1981 and 1982 to bolster the party's direct-mail fund raising and thus reduce heavy dependence on large contributions. Contribution figures indicated that the Republicans were far ahead in direct-mail activities and, consequently, in total receipts from small donations.

POPULATION

World population, increasing at a rate of almost 2% per year, was estimated at 4,600,000,000 at mid-1982. New UN projections to the year 2000 ranged from 5,800,000,000 to 6,300,000,000. An analysis by the Population Reference Bureau emphasized the continuing disparity in the growth of the more developed countries (Europe, North America, Australia, Japan, New Zealand, and the U.S.S.R.) and the less

developed countries. The latter contained twice as many persons as the more developed countries in 1940 and three times as many in 1982; by the year 2000, they would have four times as many. At current growth rates, time required to double the population in the more developed countries averaged 116 years (Sweden 999 years), while in the less developed countries the average was 33 years (Kenya 18 years).

In the U.S. immigration added over one million persons to the population in 1980 and 1981, reminiscent of the numbers that entered the country in the early 20th century. According to the Population Reference Bureau, 808,000 persons were legally admitted as immigrants or refugees in 1980, while an estimated 400,000 were illegal migrants.

Birth Statistics

For the sixth consecutive year, the number of births in the U.S. increased; an estimated 3,646,000 live births occurred in 1981, compared with 3,598,000 in 1980. The birthrate was 15.9 live births per 1,000 population, somewhat lower than for 1980. The fertility rate was 67.6 live births per 1,000 women aged 15–44, about the same as in 1980. These trends continued into 1982. For the 12-month period ended in June, there were 3,662,000 births, a 1% increase over the previous 12 months, while the rate continued at the 1981 level.

An analysis by the National Center for Health Statistics of the phenomenon of delayed childbearing in the 1970s revealed that not since the 1930s had such large numbers of women postponed marriage and motherhood. The proportion of women aged

Chinese census takers interview residents of the Hongqi commune in Lhasa, Tibet, as part of the largest population count ever undertaken.

25–29 who were still childless in 1979 was almost twice that in 1970.

Reflecting the increased significance of the Hispanic population in the U.S., 19 states now included an item on ethnic or Hispanic origin of the parents on birth certificates. In the nine states where data were available in 1979, the Hispanic birthrate was 25.5 births per 1,000 population, compared with the non-Hispanic rate of 14.7. The Hispanic fertility rate was 100.5 births per 1,000 women aged 15–44, while that for non-Hispanic women was 63.2.

As their total fertility rates continued to drop, developed industrialized countries became increasingly aware of the problem of population replacement. A total fertility rate of 2.1 to 2.5 children per woman in her childbearing lifetime indicates replacement level fertility, below which a population will eventually decline. Two-thirds of all European countries, Australia, Cuba, Canada, Japan, and the U.S. had rates below replacement level. In contrast, the total fertility rates of most less developed countries were well over replacement levels. Many less developed countries had policies directed toward reducing population growth. China had the most drastic policy, with a national goal of a one-child family.

Expectation of Life

The provisional life tables prepared by the National Center for Health Statistics indicated a life expectancy at birth of 74.1 years for the total U.S. population in 1981, a new record. The average length of life for males was 70.3 years and for females, 77.9 years. Nonwhites had made greater gains than whites; since 1970 total white life expectancy had increased by 4% and nonwhite by 8%. White females had the highest life expectancy in 1981, 78.5 years; nonwhite females were next at 74.5 years. Life expectancy for white males was 71 years and for nonwhite males, 66.1 years.

Death Statistics

The number of deaths in the U.S. in 1981 was estimated at 1,987,000. The provisional death rate per 100,000 population (866.4) was somewhat lower than in 1980 (874.2). The decrease resulted from declines in deaths for infants under one year of age and for persons 55 and over. The rate continued to fall in 1982; for the 12-month period ended in June it was 8.5 deaths per 1,000 population, as against 8.8 for the corresponding period ended June 1981.

In 1981 there were decreases in deaths from diseases of the heart (2%), cerebrovascular disease (5%), motor vehicle accidents (4%), all other accidents (6%), chronic liver disease and cirrhosis (7%), and leukemia (9%). Increases were noted for malignant neoplasms of respiratory and intrathoracic organs (3%) and of the breast (5%), chronic obstructive pulmonary diseases (7%), and ulcer of the stomach and duodenum (20%). Two-thirds of all deaths were attributed to heart disease (38%), cancer (21%), and stroke (8%). Accidents, suicide, and homicide accounted for 8%.

The leading causes of death in the U.S. in 1981 were:

Cause of death	Estimated rate per 100,000 population
1. Diseases of the heart	330.6
2. Malignant neoplasms	184.3
3. Cerebrovascular diseases	71.7
4. Accidents	44.5
5. Chronic obstructive pulmonary diseases	26.1
6. Pneumonia and influenza	23.7
7. Diabetes mellitus	15.2
8. Chronic liver disease and cirrhosis	12.9
9. Atherosclerosis	12.5
10. Suicide	12.3
11. Homicide and legal intervention	10.7
12. Conditions of the perinatal period	9.2
13. Nephritis, nephrotic syndrome, and nephrosis	7.6
14. Congenital anomalies	5.8
15. Septicemia	4.4

Infant Mortality

There were 42,000 deaths of infants under one year of age in the U.S. in 1981, compared with 45,000 in 1980, and the infant mortality rate fell from 12.5 deaths per 1,000 live births to 11.7, the lowest on record for the U.S. Both neonatal mortality (deaths to infants under 28 days) and postneonatal mortality (deaths to infants aged 28 days to 11 months) decreased by 7%. The declining trend continued into 1982. The rate for January–June 1982 was 11.7, compared with 12.4 for the corresponding period in 1981, and the rate for the 12-month period ended June 1982 was 11.4, a new record low. At the same time, differences in rates continued to exist among various segments of the population. In 1979 the black infant mortality rate was about twice the white (21.8 black infant deaths per 1,000 live births, compared with 11.4 for white infants).

Infant mortality continued to be high in certain African countries, with estimates of about 200 infant deaths per 1,000 live births in The Gambia, Sierra Leone, and Upper Volta. Northern and Western Europe continued to report extremely low rates (Iceland 5.4; Sweden 7; Finland 7.7).

Marriage and Divorce Statistics

Marriages in the U.S. increased for the sixth consecutive year, to an estimated 2,438,000 in 1981, a new national record. The marriage rate was 10.6 per 1,000 population. The trends continued into 1982. For the 12 months ended in June there were 2,444,000 marriages, 13,000 more than in the previous corresponding period.

People married later in life than they had a decade earlier. The Census Bureau reported that the median age at first marriage in 1981 was 24.8 years for men and 22.3 years for women, about 1.5 years higher than in 1970. The proportion of never married persons rose significantly for young men and women in the age groups from 20–24 through 30–34.

Divorces also reached a record high in 1981, with 1,219,000 being granted, 3% more than in 1980 and 72% more than in 1970. The divorce rate was 5.3 per 1,000 population, compared with 5.2 in 1980. During the first six months of 1982 there were 582,000 divorces, with a rate of 5.1 per 1,000 population, 4% below the rate for the corresponding period in 1981.

According to the Census Bureau, the number of families headed by one parent had doubled in a decade, from 3.3 million in 1970 to 6.6 million in 1981. In the same period, the number of one-parent families headed by divorced women rose 182%, from 956,000 to 2.7 million. Reflecting both increased divorces and births to unmarried mothers, 54% more children under 18 lived in a one-parent family in 1981 than in 1970.

Censuses and Surveys

The field enumeration of the long-awaited census of China began July 1, 1982. About five million enumerators, one million supervisors, and one million or more additional workers, including advisers, took part. Through the UN Fund for Population Activities, the UN provided 21 computers for data processing, as well as consultation. Simple statistical summaries, available on October 1, showed a total population of 1,008,175,288 persons. Complete results of the census would be available to the government of China at the end of 1985.

PORTUGAL

The governing Democratic Alliance (AD) coalition's plan to revise Portugal's 1976 constitution, purging it of its references to the achievement of socialism, the People and the Armed Forces Movement, and the irreversibility of nationalizations, led the Communist Party into overt extraparliamentary opposition. As a result, the Communists fully backed the country's first general strike in 40 years on Feb. 12, 1982. Public transport was the principal service disrupted. Without the official support of the Socialist Party-led General Union of Workers (UGT), the striking CGTP-Intersindical trade-union federation represented just slightly more than one-third of the work force.

After the strike was over, the government alleged that a violent coup had been planned to take place at the same time as the union action. The Socialist Party (PSP) introduced a motion of no confidence in the government in March, but it was defeated by 130 votes to 116. Shortly afterward the Communist Party introduced its own motion, which was withdrawn after Premier Francisco Pinto Balsemão declined to appear for the debate. On May 1 two men were shot dead and 80 people were injured in Oporto when riot police opened fire to quell violence between rival UGT and CGTP May Day demonstrations. The Com-

Juan Fernández Krohn, a Spanish fundamentalist priest, attempted to stab Pope John Paul II in Fatima, Portugal, in May.
JEAN CLAUDE FRANCOLON/
EDORADO FORNACIARI—GAMMA/
LIAISON

munist union then called a second general strike, but again support was patchy.

Amid accusations of drift in economic policymaking and rumours of renewed disagreements within the premier's own Social Democratic Party (PSD) over his capacity for leadership, four ministers and six secretaries of state were affected in an unexpected Cabinet reshuffle in June. The education, foreign affairs, and labour ministers were dropped, and a new minister for parliamentary relations was drafted into the government to speed up the constitutional revision, which had stalled in the Assembly. Amid general surprise from the politicians, Pres. António Ramalho Eanes expressed strong disapproval of the reshuffle since he had not been informed of the changes in advance, as required by the constitution. Meanwhile, however, moves were taking place to reduce the president's powers substantially as part of the constitutional amendments. After a week of haggling in early June, the Assembly agreed to devote 100 hours to debate of the new constitution, and the legislature's two-month summer recess was postponed.

In July the Assembly, as part of the constitutional revision process, voted to abolish the military Council of the Revolution—the body, headed by President Eanes, that was charged with vetting legislation for conformity with the requirements of the constitution. The outgoing military council reacted loudly, and the left-wing majority pushed through a resolution calling the vote "unjust and disgraceful." The Council of the Revolution was to be replaced by a civilian Council of the Republic with representatives from the political parties, a supreme military defense board, and a constitutional tribunal.

A month later, on August 12, the Assembly completed its debate and approved the revised text of the constitution by 197 votes to 40. The Communist Party and its sympathizers were opposed. Under the new rules the president was deprived of the right to nominate the military chiefs of staff, though he re-mained supreme commander. Although shorn of their left-wing wording, clauses in the old 1976 constitution governing nationalization and agrarian reform were largely unamended; this was insisted upon by the PSP, which agreed to vote in favour of the new constitution.

President Eanes's dissatisfaction with the drift of political events was manifest in the fact that his promulgation of the new constitution, which was required by law, was delayed until the end of September. He also threatened to veto the law governing local government elections and did in fact veto the decree ordering the closure of ANOP. In the event, a compromise on the date for local elections was reached, and the president insisted that all new laws be delayed until the new constitution came into effect, 30 days after its promulgation.

PRISONS

How the courts and the penal system should deal with mentally abnormal offenders was a question that came to the fore during 1982. It arose in the U.S. as a result of the trial of John Hinckley, Jr., who, the year before, had attempted to assassinate Pres. Ronald Reagan. After eight weeks Hinckley was found not guilty by reason of insanity. The verdict aroused much controversy. In many other countries such a decision could not have been made by the courts. In the U.K. a verdict of guilty but insane would have been possible. The courts of most European countries could also have passed verdicts involving the concept of diminished responsibility. This might have permitted a reduction in the charge but would still have been likely to lead to long confinement in a secure psychiatric hospital for the criminally insane or one for those with major mental or behavioural abnormalities.

Ordinary prisons nevertheless had to house a great many mentally abnormal prisoners. This occurred despite efforts to establish more secure psychiatric units, and it placed additional burdens on

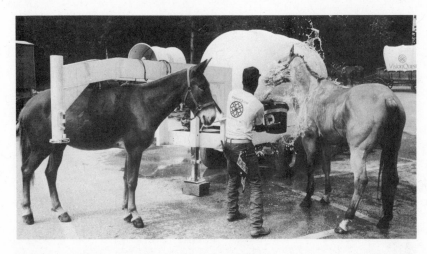

In a Vision Quest rehabilitation program in Arizona, young offenders were challenged to develop self-reliance and self-respect in a trek across the desert.
DIEGO GOLBERG—SYGMA

already overstrained penal facilities. Prison nursing staffs were usually briefly and poorly trained. It was this situation that led to a major scandal in the U.K. Barry Prosser, a prisoner, had died a year earlier in the hospital wing of Birmingham prison of injuries that could not have been self-inflicted. An inquest jury decided that Prosser was "unlawfully killed." But at two different trials it proved impossible to obtain a conviction against the accused prison staff members.

An official report on this same prison later recommended that there should be more training for prison hospital officers, more assignments to outside psychiatric hospitals, and more exact record-keeping of incidents and action taken. Ordinary psychiatric hospitals were generally unsuitable for the containment of mentally disturbed criminals. Nor did nurses and physicians not specialized in forensic psychiatry necessarily have sufficient experience in the management of these often extremely difficult patients to deal with them appropriately. With not enough secure hospitals they had somehow to be coped with in jails.

Overcrowding was a serious problem in many countries. So many prisoners, cooped up in inadequate and out-of-date buildings in so many countries, could not fail to produce riots and disturbances. At the Archambault Institute, a jail near Montreal, three guards were killed and seven injured and two prisoners committed suicide in July, and at Brushy Mountain State Penitentiary in Tennessee in February seven white prisoners took four guards hostage and shot four black inmates, killing two of them. Perhaps not surprisingly, uniformed staff sometimes began to take matters into their own hands. An official report on a particularly bad incident of staff overreaction that had occurred the previous year at London's Wormwood Scrubs prison criticized prison management for letting the staff run the place according to their own rules instead of those laid down by the Prison Department.

Fresh means were being sought to devise alternatives to imprisonment. These were not always probation or community service but sometimes imaginative projects run by voluntary agencies. Some of the best schemes were those of the U.S. Vision Quest organization. Vision Quest had pioneered some programs for apparently hopeless young offenders, who were often from chaotic homes and usually had prolonged experience of detention in a penal or mental institution. The programs were action-oriented, posing a physical and mental challenge to these alienated boys and girls, who found that they could overcome considerable hardship and dangers and learn to trust others and themselves. The effort required gave them pride, resourcefulness, self-respect, and a new sense of responsibility. They were confronted instantly with the consequences of their own actions and, whenever possible, were helped to rebuild relationships with their parents. So far these schemes had had an approximately 80% success rate. Although not cheap, they were less expensive than juvenile detention.

However, it was early prevention that continued to get the attention of most researchers. Even in Japan, with much the lowest crime rate in any industrialized society, juvenile crime and vandalism continued to rise. The massive work by the Center for Urban Affairs and Policy Research at Northwestern University in Evanston, Ill., suggested broad general factors associated with crime, such as increased affluence; the availability of more and sometimes unguarded goods; and the existence of a large pool of potential offenders, for reasons that were not well understood. Narrower but more specific studies suggested possible practical action. For example, there was proof of a link between television violence and aggressive behaviour in susceptible youngsters, obtained from careful research in the U.S., the U.K., and other countries. Truancy was also connected with juvenile crime. In 1982 in London alone, every day about 20,000 children missed school and roamed the streets, often committing offenses while doing so. Unemployment, too, was a factor, producing a sense of purposelessness, of not being a part of productive society.

REFUGEES AND MIGRANTS

Although the status of refugees in 1982 improved in some areas, the worldwide situation was a cause for deep concern by the office of the UN High Commissioner for Refugees (UNHCR). In November there was a sudden influx of some 40,000 refugees from Uganda into Rwanda, a small country extremely ill-equipped to care for an additional population. The massive relief operation continued in Pakistan, where the number of Afghan refugees passed the 2.5 million mark. More than 200,000 Indochinese refugees still awaited resettlement in camps throughout Southeast Asia at the end of the year, while many resettlement countries began to show signs of reluctance toward maintaining high resettlement quotas.

In Africa, home of about one-half of the world's refugees, it became possible to shift the emphasis of several major UNHCR programs—notably in the Horn of Africa and the Sudan—from care and maintenance exclusively to self-reliance projects and income-generating activities. A major voluntary repatriation program was successfully concluded in Chad, where UNHCR assisted a total of 200,000 people by repatriating them and/or providing emergency food, tools, and other items needed to repair their damaged homes. The special program for returnees in Ethiopia was expanded in an effort to encourage continued voluntary repatriation.

During the year UNHCR participated in the overall UN relief effort to aid victims of the conflict in Lebanon. The high commissioner authorized allocations of $5.5 million from the UNHCR emergency fund to assist displaced persons in Lebanon as well as Lebanese citizens in a refugee-like situation in Syria.

The number of arrivals of Indochinese refugees continued to decrease throughout the world, and the number of refugees resettled also declined. A total of 47,115 Indochinese refugees arrived by boat or overland in countries of temporary asylum in the region between January 1 and November 30, 1982, while 71,641 were selected for resettlement. By the end of 1982 more than 800,000 Indochinese had been resettled with the assistance of UNHCR.

The work of UNHCR in Central America had to focus on emergency relief for Salvadoran, Nicaraguan, and Guatemalan refugees. Camps had to be enlarged and facilities improved to accommodate continuous arrivals throughout the year. Several hundred refugees were able to be integrated into small agricultural developments in Belize, Costa Rica, Nicaragua, and Panama.

Migration

The patterns of international migration from the poor countries to the richer continued during 1982. At the same time, rising levels of unemployment in the latter—over 11 million in the European Community countries and 10 million in the U.S.—reinforced the tendencies toward greater restrictions on immigration, rising levels of racism and violence directed against migrants, and increasing pressures—both official and unofficial—to "encourage" migrants to return home.

The political controversies surrounding immigration to the U.S., particularly from Latin America and the Caribbean, continued. In mid-1981 Pres. Ronald Reagan had proposed new legislation that would create a category of "temporary residents," admitted on renewable (subject to acceptability) three-year visas, who would pay full taxes but would be ineligible for welfare, food stamps, and other benefits. "Permanent resident alien" status would be granted only after ten years' continuous residence, and only those with such status would be allowed to bring in families. "Amnesty" would be offered to undocumented workers who could show five years' continuous residence—a requirement that limited its applicability. Fines would be levied on firms employing four or more undocumented workers.

In March and July 1982 federal courts ruled that the 1,800 Haitians being held in camps throughout the U.S. had to be released subject to later court appearances to determine their status. In 1981 only five Haitians were granted political asylum, and the administration continued to restrict political refugee status to those coming from Communist countries.

Abel Dorvilier (foreground), here congratulated by a resettlement official, was one of the last Haitian refugees released in October under a federal court order.
WIDE WORLD

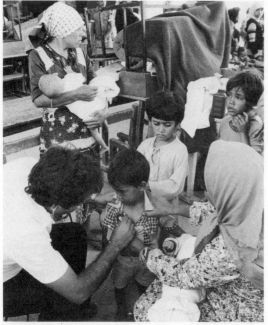

UNRWA/KEYSTONE

A physician from the UN's Relief and Works Agency examines Palestinian refugees in a temporary camp in southern Lebanon.

The Population Reference Bureau projected immigration into the U.S. of up to one million people a year during the 1980s. The bureau estimated that half would enter illegally and would come primarily from Latin America. Changes in agriculture throughout the hemisphere and the shortage of permanent urban employment, combined with demand for migrant labour—particularly in low-paid, undesirable jobs in the U.S.—ensured that such migration would continue.

In 1981 Canada admitted 128,000 immigrants, down from 142,439 in 1980. The two largest sources were Asia, 48,000, and Europe, 46,000 (21,000 from Britain). The effect of rising levels of unemployment on immigration policy could be seen in new regulations laid down in May 1982. All future potential in-

dependent immigrants would have to have a prearranged job, cleared through a government employment centre on the basis that there were no qualified Canadian residents available to fill it. In September Australia introduced measures to reduce the number of illegal immigrants, estimated at 50,000. Responding to trade union demands, the federal government also agreed to restrict legal immigration in 1983.

RELIGION

"Religion and Power" was the theme when the Society for the Scientific Study of Religion gathered for its annual October convention in Providence, R.I. Conference organizers noted the "unusually large number" of scholarly papers submitted that dealt with "religion and politics" in all parts of the world. It was a timely theme. News of religion in 1982 was dominated by the relationship between religion and power. Next in importance were stories about major developments in the ecumenical movement.

Worldwide, religious leaders increased the momentum of their efforts to ward off the threat of nuclear war. The religious peace movement crossed the dividing lines among denominations and normal differences between "conservatives" and "liberals." At a Boston rally in April, evangelist Billy Graham began what aides described as the most ambitious crusade of his career—to alert the nations to the peril of nuclear war.

A month later, Graham and 587 other religious leaders of all "living faiths" met in Moscow at the World Conference of Religious Workers for Saving the Sacred Gift of Life from Nuclear Catastrophe. Called by the Russian Orthodox Church, the session prompted the U.S. State Department to warn 28 American participants about the dangers of being used as pawns of Soviet propaganda. Although some acrimonious statements were made, the conference ended with the delegates in basic accord on the need for an end to "hostile rhetoric" and for a freeze on the development, deployment, and testing of nuclear weapons.

In May the World Council of Churches (WCC), representing 300 churches in more than 100 nations,

Hierarchies and laities of several churches engaged the issue of nuclear arms and warfare during 1982.
WALLY MCNAMEE/NEWSWEEK

Evangelist Billy Graham (at right) attended an ecumenical service at Yelokhovsky Cathedral in Moscow during a week-long conference on religion and peace.
UPI

contributed to the peace debate by issuing a document, "Before It's Too Late." The declaration stated that "the time has come when the churches must unequivocally declare that the production and deployment, as well as the use, of nuclear weapons are a crime against humanity." Especially noteworthy was the participation in the antinuclear movement by the American hierarchy of the Catholic Church. The religious peace movement was not without its backlash, however. Typical of the critics was "neoconservative" Catholic commentator Michael Novak, who charged that the peace bishops were guilty of promoting a "Catholicism of very simple judgments that are deeply felt. The liberal Catholic has become mush-headed."

Caught in the clash between religion and power—or, more accurately, between the power of religion and the power of secular states—was Pope John Paul II, whose planned visit to his troubled Polish homeland was postponed until 1983. The pope also faced problems at home when the Vatican was rocked by a scandal centring around its Institute for Religious Works, popularly called the Vatican bank. The Vatican bank and its president, U.S.-born Archbishop Paul C. Marcinkus, gained unwanted world publicity after auditors uncovered $1.4 billion in questionable loans made by Italy's largest private bank, the Banco Ambrosiano. Convicted the year before on charges of violating Italian laws by exporting $26.4 million to Switzerland, Roberto Calvi, Ambrosiano's president, fled to England. A short time later, his body was found hanging from the Blackfriars Bridge in London. The day before, his secretary had fallen to her death from a fourth-floor window in Milan.

Faced with heavy losses and damage to the church's credibility, John Paul took the unprecedented step of appointing four international financiers to examine the relationship between the Vatican Bank and the Banco Ambrosiana. At a special meeting of the College of Cardinals, the pope pledged that the Vatican would cooperate with Italian authorities to see that the whole truth came to light.

In the U.S. piety and politics were interwoven throughout 1982. Elected in 1980 with help from the well-organized "New Christian Right," Pres. Ronald Reagan disappointed his most conservative backers at the beginning of his term by putting on the "back burner" some of the issues most important to his right-wing constituents. As the 1982 congressional elections neared, however, Reagan began to push for legislation that would solidify his support in conservative constituencies. In particular, he urged adoption of tuition tax credits for parents of children attending nonpublic schools and passage of two constitutional amendments, one sanctioning prayers in public schools, the other aimed at circumventing the Supreme Court decision legalizing abortion. The amendments were defeated by liberal filibusters just before Congress's pre-election recess, but their supporters vowed to continue the fight.

All these issues sharply divided the nation's religious communities. Civil libertarians joined numerous mainline church leaders in opposing the "prayer amendment." Reflecting this viewpoint, Dean M. Kelley of the National Council of Churches charged that the amendment "makes the rights of members of the religious minorities dependent upon the self-restraint of religious majorities." Countering this point of view, E. E. McAteer of the Religious Roundtable called upon Congress to undo court decisions that declare "God unwelcome in our classrooms." After the votes were counted in the November election, it became obvious that the political power of the New Christian Right had waned significantly since 1980.

The power of religion and the power of secular government also met head-on in the nation's courts. In Little Rock, Ark., a federal judge struck down a state law passed in 1981 that required the teaching of "scientific creationism" in the public schools. Judge William R. Overton ruled that the legislation violated constitutional separation of church and state by introducing "the biblical version of creation into the public school curricula." In November a federal judge handed down a similar ruling in Louisiana, arguing that the state legislature had exceeded the limits of its power by enacting legislation that dictated to public schools "not only that a subject must be taught, but also how it should be taught."

In New York City the Rev. Sun Myung Moon, Korean-born evangelist and founder of the controversial Unification Church, was sentenced to an 18-month prison term after being found guilty of tax fraud and conspiracy to obstruct justice. The prosecution accused him of using his organization to avoid personal income taxes, but his followers contended that the verdict was an act of "religious persecution." Moon had incurred widespread hostility from parents of his youthful followers, who believed their children had been brainwashed by cultic indoctrination techniques.

The ecumenical movement began to move again after more than a decade of near stagnation. In January the Faith and Order Commission of the WCC unanimously approved a resolution that, in the words of one ecumenist, provided a "framework for church union" by reaching general consensus on such issues as baptism, the Eucharist, and the nature of ministry.

The Anglican-Roman Catholic study commission completed 12 years of work on an ecumenical document stating that there was no reason in principle why Anglicans could not unite with Catholics under the primacy of the bishop of Rome. Old wounds were healed within Presbyterianism and Lutheranism as well. The general assemblies of the United Presbyterian Church and the Presbyterian Church in the United States approved resolutions that soon could rejoin those two bodies, separated since the Civil War. Three branches of Lutheranism in the U.S. approved steps leading to a merger that would bring a 5.4 million-member denomination into being

The Dalai Lama (right), exiled leader of Tibet, was greeted by followers in Rome in September before meeting with Pope John Paul II.
WIDE WORLD

by Jan. 1, 1988. Meanwhile, these same three branches of Lutheranism and the Episcopal Church reached a historic accord allowing "common joint celebrations" of communion led by clergy of both traditions.

Although ecumenical relations flowered, interfaith relations withered under the pressures of war. Jewish-Christian relationships deteriorated sharply after the Israeli invasion of Lebanon. Numerous mainline church leaders denounced Israel for attacking civilian populations in and around Beirut and for failing to prevent the massacre of Palestinians by Lebanese Christians in two West Beirut refugee camps. Tensions were further exacerbated in September when Pope John Paul agreed to meet in Rome with Yasir Arafat, the leader of the Palestine Liberation Organization (PLO). A senior Israeli official charged: "The same church that did not say a word about the massacre of Jews for six years in Europe [during World War II] and did not say much about the killing of Christians in Lebanon for seven years is ready to meet the man who perpetrated the crime in Lebanon and is bent on the destruction of Israel, which is the completion of the work done by the Nazis in Germany." In an unusually angry response, the Vatican described that statement as an "outrage to the truth."

Although the ecumenical outlook was much brighter than it had been, it was not completely rosy. Some Anglicans and Roman Catholics were both mystified and angry when a former Episcopal priest, married and the father of two daughters, was accepted into the priesthood of the Roman Catholic Church. At a rite on June 29 in Springfield, Mo., the Rev. James Parker was reordained and two days later celebrated his first mass, serving communion to his wife. The angriest outcries came from Roman Catholics who for years had called for an end to mandatory clerical celibacy and recognition of priests who were ordained in the Catholic Church and later married.

A federal grand jury investigation into charges that John Cardinal Cody, Roman Catholic archbishop of Chicago, had diverted tax-exempt church funds to a lifelong friend ended when Cody, the chief target of the probe, died in April. He was succeeded by Archbishop Joseph L. Bernardin of Cincinnati, Ohio, a major figure in world Catholicism, who was received with joy by Chicago Catholics.

Although moderates made a strong showing, biblical literalists continued to dominate the Southern Baptist Convention, the largest Protestant denomination in the U.S. with 13.6 million members. Conservative dominance was reaffirmed when James T. Draper was elected president, defeating his more moderate rival, theologian Duke McCall.

Leaders of the Baha'i faith continued to report that their co-religionists in Iran were being systematically persecuted and put to death by the radical Shi'ah Muslim regime of Ayatollah Ruhollah Khomeini.

Religion

Special Report: New Roles for Women

by Martin E. Marty

The defeat of the Equal Rights Amendment to the U.S. Constitution in 1982 led to much stocktaking on the part of American women. Behind the political activities that brought about the defeat were cultural attitudes. Those who make profound studies of culture are agreed that religious symbols, fears, and hopes animate troubling issues such as those having to do with feminism. Proponents of the ERA had long recognized that opponents like Phyllis Schlafly appealed to conservative religious forces. The New Christian Right also spoke of the biblical commands for women to be "submissive," to know that their place was in the home and not in the arena where they had to be guaranteed full rights.

The Ordination Issue

The stocktaking has uncovered many positive changes in the way women and religion meet. Some of these can be chronicled with hard data. An important symbolic issue is the ordination of women to the Jewish and Christian clergy. The elites in religion have enormous power in determining what is taught, who has authority to bring about change, and even how God is to be thought of and addressed. Whether or not women are admitted to the ordained and professional ministry tells much about the deepest religious beliefs of a faith-system.

The hard data on progress come from the Association of Theological Schools in the United States and Canada. The authors of its annual *Fact Book* recognize that far more than half of practicing religionists in America are women and that far fewer than half of the seminarians and even fewer of the active clergy are women. In the decade since the ATS started keeping track, the percent increase of women in theological schools was 241.4%, while the number of men rose only 35.3%. Even so, these 12,473 future religious professionals still make up only 23.7% of the seminary population.

What is more, many of the women are in two-year programs that prepare them for traditional roles in nonordained religious education positions. What counts for symbolic change is the number in pre-ministerial courses. There they make up only 16% of the total. The figure varies greatly by denomination. The United Church of Christ and the United Church of Canada are highest, with 49.5 and 41.1%, respectively. About one-third of the United Presbyterian, United Methodist, and Lutheran Church in America seminarians are women.

Roman Catholicism forbids the ordination of women, so only 6.5% of the Catholic theological students are women—yet they make up much higher percentages in select schools. The Southern Baptist Convention, the largest Protestant body, allows for women's ordination but discourages it, and only 9.7% of the students in its huge seminaries are women. More and more women are completing doctorates and going on into teaching in colleges and universities, a fact that portends more change in the future.

The bad news for women accompanying the good news of high enrollments is the existence of a low ceiling in their profession. Few Conservative or Reform Jewish women ordained to the rabbinates have congregations of their own. After a decade of women's ordination in the Episcopal Church, some bishops still refuse to do the ordaining and few parishes have a woman as head rector. Even in the mainline Protestant and Lutheran churches, where the ministry of women is very widely accepted, most women remain assistant pastors, educators, or in other posts outside the highest congregational ministry.

Many denominations have had women as presidents, moderators, and high executives and have seen to it that they are in important policymaking roles. Thus when three Lutheran bodies voted in September 1982 to form a single Lutheran church, they stipulated that a large percentage of the 70-member commission that would effect the new church policies would be women.

A Matter of Language

Controversies have raged in recent years over the language denominations use in their constitutions, liturgies, and sacred texts. Even the more conservative church bodies have had no difficulty removing sexist language from their constitutional vocabularies and procedural documents. Only the moderate-to-liberal groups, however, have changed the language of their hymns and orders of public worship. Some opposition to the changes has come from people of aesthetic sensitivity who believe that words about "men" should not be changed to language about "persons," since this is taking license with others' art. Others have opposed it because they see feminist ideology as subverting the religious message.

The most heated debate has come about in the aftermath of efforts by some to produce what the public press seized upon as a "Non-Sexist Bible" translation. In this case, the translators would take liberties with the text. God would no longer be God the Father, a male patriarchal figure. While the work in progress was more tempered and moderate than some of the rumours and releases first suggested, there is no question but that such Bible translations will continue to meet opposition, not only from those who oppose feminism, but also from language purists and those who fear violation of the integrity of sacred texts.

Jewish and Christian feminist thinkers recognize that while women may have had honoured and dignified roles in biblical literature, the texts of these scriptures reflected and reinforced a culture in which women were secondary human beings, subject to men. These theologians, therefore, lift out and accent the biblical passages that *do* point to female roles for the deity: God is pictured in the prophets as giving birth to Israel and nurturing it. The word for the divine presence, the *shekinah*, is feminine. There were women prophets, judges, and visionaries in Israel and women deacons and preachers in early Christianity. Over against the biblical texts that preach female submission there are others that envision the breaking down of barriers as a result of Jesus' work: in Christ there is to be "neither male nor female," for "all are one in Christ" (Gal. 3:28).

Old and New Roles

Battles of this sort are most intense in evangelicalism, the moderately conservative Protestant form of church life that is less rigid than fundamentalism. Many of the best-selling books in this camp have appealed to what Marabel Morgan called *The Total Woman*. The writers are expressive, fulfilled women in the bounds of marriage, devoted chiefly to pleasing their husbands and bringing up their children.

In the opposite camp is the Evangelical Women's Caucus, led by theologians like Virginia Ramey Mollenkott of William Paterson College. She argues that the biblical message of liberation shatters even the cultural limits of women in the biblical world. The Evangelical Women's Caucus takes pains not to be seen as a mere religious branch of secular feminism. Instead, it argues that women have always had a higher potential in the context of biblical faith than the church has permitted until now.

A small but articulate group of women has not only given up on the Judeo-Christian tradition but has openly rejected it. Charlene Spretnak, in her introduction to the essays in *The Politics of Women's Spirituality* (1982), blasted "patriarchal religion" of biblical descent. At the same time, she and her co-authors do advocate a "spirituality" that draws on other sources. Violently rejecting "God the Father," they appeal to goddesses, mythic Heras and Amazons, and witchcraft lore. Some of this spirituality is both lesbian and antimale. Others simply argue that male imagery has reinforced men's hold on power.

As important as radical feminist spirituality may be in the culture at large, the decisive battles in cultures influenced by Jewish and Christian faith and institutions will take more moderate and persistent forms. Pope John Paul II will not authorize the ordination of women, but Catholic women will still prepare and press for extensions of their ministry. The evangelical patriarchs and their female allies will still preach submission, but every year more women become ministers, more people see their consciousness changed, more women find new roles, more men "see the light."

Only the most sanguine Jewish and Christian women would say that all this amounts to "the end of patriarchy," but it does contribute greatly to the spiritual realization of women's being and power. The issue of "women and religion" is not yet settled in the synagogues, churches, or culture at large. It promises drama long after Equal Rights Amendment battles have been quieted.

Sandra Antoinette Wilson, here with the Rev. James Parks Morton, dean of the Cathedral of St. John the Divine, was ordained in the Episcopal Church in January. She became the first black female Episcopal priest in the New York diocese and the fourth in the nation.
SARA KRULWICH/THE NEW YORK TIMES

Pres. Nicolae Ceausescu
(right) of Romania met
with U.S. Secretary of
State Alexander Haig in
Bucharest in February.
WIDE WORLD

ROMANIA

The year 1982 was critical for Romania both economically and politically. The standard of living, always among the lowest in Europe, had deteriorated markedly during the previous five years. In February food prices were increased by an average of 35%, while salaries went up 16%. There were shortages of meat, while quality wines and *tsuica* (the national plum brandy) were added to the list of goods for export only. The *Lumea* political weekly announced on October 15 that the 1982 harvest of grain, including corn (maize), was expected to reach 22 million metric tons—almost one ton per person.

Speaking on October 7 at a session of the RCP Central Committee, Pres. Nicolae Ceausescu proclaimed that Romania had modern, competitive industry and that by 1985 the country would be self-sufficient in energy. That goal was to be reached by building new hydroelectric and nuclear power stations and by increasing the output of coal. There was some evidence to suggest, however, that these objectives were unrealistic. In 1981 Romania extracted 11.6 million metric tons of crude, compared with the planned 12.5 million tons, and imported 13.1 million tons; for the first time the quantity imported was higher than that produced at home.

Ceausescu's reaction to policy setbacks was to conclude that members of the Council of Ministers (Cabinet) were to blame. A few were replaced in 1981, but the announcement of May 21, 1982, was more like a mass purge, as about one-third of the 50-odd portfolios changed hands. Ilie Verdet was replaced as premier by Constantin Dascalescu, but the former was compensated by his appointment as a vice-president of the Council of State. In November Chairman of the State Planning Committee Emilian Dobrescu was replaced by Stefan Birlea.

On July 29 Pres. François Mitterrand of France canceled his planned visit to Romania, apparently because Virgil Tanase, a Romanian dissident writer, had reportedly been killed on the order of the Romanian security services. A few days later, however, the French newspaper *Le Monde* revealed that the kidnapping of Tanase from the Place de la Bastille, Paris, on May 20 had been staged by the French counterespionage service to foil an assassination attempt, and that Tanase was alive and well. It was also claimed that Mitterrand had known all along of the subterfuge. The affair soured relations between France and Romania.

On December 7 an agreement signed with 14 of Romania's biggest Western bank creditors rescheduled over 6½ years 80% of the country's 1981–82 outstanding debt of almost $2 billion. The remaining 20% of the debt to Western commercial banks was due to be paid by the end of March 1983. Romanian hard-currency debts were estimated in December 1982 at $10 billion–$14 billion.

SAFETY

In 1981 an estimated 99,000 Americans died as a result of accidents, according to *Accident Facts*, an analysis of accident statistics published annually by the National Safety Council. This was a 6% decline from 1980 and was the first time since 1962 that the total had been less than 100,000. The death rate per 100,000 persons was 43.2, the lowest on record. Another 9.4 million persons suffered disabling injuries as a result of accidents, down from 10 million the previous year. (A "disabling" injury is one that incapacitates the victim beyond the day of the accident.)

Declines were reported in all four classes of accidents used by the council. Deaths in motor-vehicle accidents were estimated at 50,800, a decline of 3% from the previous year. The motor-vehicle mileage death rate was 3.29, down 5% from 1980 and the lowest on record. Accidents in the workplace resulted in an estimated 12,300 deaths, a decline of 5%. Accidental deaths in the home were estimated at 21,000, a decline of 9%. The large decline in this class of accident was certainly partly due to the great increase in home deaths during 1980, owing mainly to severe, prolonged hot spells in the South and Southwest that produced large numbers of deaths attributed to excessive heat. Public accidents during 1981 resulted in an estimated 19,500 deaths, a decline of 7%. ("Public" accidents include those taking place in transportation other than motor vehicles, in public buildings, and during recreation such as swimming and hunting.)

There were indications, however, that economic hard times were adversely affecting health and safety. In July researchers from the University of California at Irvine reported the results of extensive interviews conducted with 6,130 Los Angeles County residents between 1978 and 1980 to determine the economy's impact on their lives and health. According to urban planner Ray Catalano, "What we found was that people who experienced undesirable job and financial events have about twice the risk of being ill or injured as people who don't experience those events. And they have 2½ times the risk of some psychological disorder." The adverse impact of the economy on health and safety is particularly likely to affect middle-class people, he said, since the economic conditions of both the poor and the rich change relatively little during hard times.

Another factor likely to be adversely affected by economic hard times is the condition of the country's infrastructure—the vital network of roads, bridges, sewers, rails, and mass transit systems. According to a nationwide study by the Department of Transpor-

tation reported in June, nearly half of all the bridges in the U.S. were deficient or obsolete, and the number was rising. A *Newsweek* article in August reported that "one-quarter of the interstate-highway system is worn out and needs resurfacing. One-half of Conrail's rails and roadbeds are seriously decayed. Half of all American communities cannot expand because their water-treatment systems are at or near capacity. . . . All told, the cost of needed repairs around the country could run as high as $3 trillion. But the bills are coming due at a time when there is little money to spare."

The safety of nonprescription, over-the-counter drugs, however, was unquestionably the major concern of the American public in 1982, following the deaths in late September of seven Chicago-area residents resulting from using Tylenol capsules contaminated with cyanide. In Chicago a federal, state, and local law-enforcement team conducted a massive search for a suspect who the authorities say took Extra-Strength Tylenol capsules from the shelves of area stores, replaced the powder they contained with cyanide crystals, and returned them to the shelves. The unsuspecting victims included two men, four women, and a 12-year-old girl. Early in October, after a similar but apparently unrelated incident in California in which a man was stricken after taking Tylenol capsules laced with strychnine, the McNeil Consumer Products Co., makers of Tylenol, announced a nationwide recall of all Tylenol capsules,

Bernard Neff of Kessler Memorial Hospital in Hammonton, New Jersey, was one of several volunteers who X-rayed Halloween treats for hazardous material.
WIDE WORLD

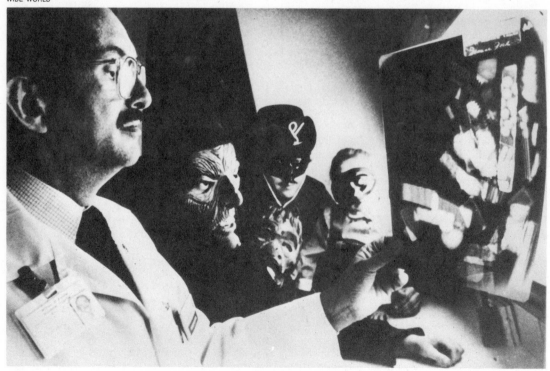

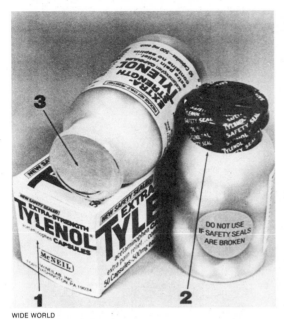

WIDE WORLD

Safety precautions introduced after the Tylenol tragedy included (1) glued box flaps, (2) plastic neck seal, and (3) foil seal.

both Regular and Extra-Strength, and said it was halting production. (Tylenol tablets, which are more difficult to tamper with than the capsules, were not considered suspect.) In mid-October the Proprietary Association, a trade group representing the nation's major pharmaceutical manufacturers, asked the Food and Drug Administration to enact regulations that would require sealed packaging of nonprescription drugs to prevent tampering. Early in November Richard S. Schweiker, secretary of health and human services, approved regulations that would require tamper-resistant packaging on almost all nonprescription drugs on store shelves in the U.S. within 15 months. The most vulnerable products, capsules and liquids, had to meet the new safety standards within 90 days.

Another safety issue that was given increased attention was that of contaminated Halloween candy. Each year more and more incidents of tampering—sweets containing such items as pins, razor blades, sleeping pills, and insecticide—had been reported, prompting many communities across the country to bar trick-or-treating altogether. In a number of places hospitals offered to X-ray suspicious items.

In late October in a report titled "Poisons on the Job," the Sierra Club, the Natural Resources Defense Council, and the Urban Environment Conference accused the Reagan administration of weakening critical health standards in the workplace and refusing to issue new standards for toxic substances. The groups charged that an estimated 100,000 Americans die of job-related diseases each year while the administration neglects to enforce the Occupational Safety and Health Act.

SAUDI ARABIA

Khalid ibn 'Abdal-'Aziz, king and prime minister of Saudi Arabia, died of a heart attack on June 13, 1982. He was immediately succeeded in both these capacities by his half brother Fahd, who had been crown prince and first deputy prime minister. Fahd's half brother Prince Abdullah, previously second deputy prime minister and commander of the National Guard, was named crown prince.

While pledging himself to continue the work of the late King Khalid, Fahd showed every sign of continuing the modernizing stand that he had espoused as crown prince. The smoothness of the transition was not surprising to most observers because of the perceived need of the royal house of Saud to stand together. As crown prince Fahd took the brunt of responsibility for government from his saintly brother Khalid, who had been regarded as a caretaker monarch. Even the most important foreign-policy effort during Khalid's reign was associated with Fahd: the Fahd plan, an eight-point plan proposed by Saudi Arabia in August 1981, that aimed to bring about a Middle East peace settlement based on recognition of Israel's right to exist within secure boundaries as well as the establishment of an independent state for the Palestinians.

On July 23 Fahd renewed Khalid's promises to introduce the country's first democratic institution—the *majlis al-shura*, a consultative assembly of commoners—into the political administration. He pledged himself to continue Khalid's work and said that the next five-year (1985–90) development plan would ensure a "wide distribution of the national income." Fahd could be expected to fulfill this pledge, since he himself had largely inspired the last two Saudi Arabian development plans.

In his address to mark the Hajj (pilgrimage to Mecca) on September 27, Fahd attacked Israel for its intervention in Lebanon. He also condemned the Soviet Union for its actions in Afghanistan. In calling for an end to the Gulf war between Iran and Iraq, King Fahd was identifying strongly with his partners in the Gulf Cooperation Council (GCC): Kuwait, the United Arab Emirates, Qatar, Bahrain, and Oman. The Hajj was disrupted by demonstrations mounted in the holy cities of Mecca and Medina by Iranian pilgrims. With the memory of the 1979 siege of Mecca fresh in the minds of Fahd and his associates, subversion and incitement in the holy cities by foreign pilgrims was clearly a matter of intense concern.

Although the official attitude of the GCC toward the Gulf war was one of neutrality, these internal disruptions and other, earlier incidents served to bring Saudi Arabia, as well as other members of the council, into closer alignment with Iraq. Saudi Arabia signed a frontier treaty with Iraq at the end of 1981, after which Interior Minister Prince Nayef called on all Arab countries to abandon their neutrality in favour of Arab solidarity with Iraq in its fight to defend the entire Arab nation.

Led by the new king, Fahd, mourners carried the shroud-wrapped body of King Khalid through the streets of Riyadh following his death in June.

Saudi Arabia and Libya restored diplomatic relations on Dec. 31, 1981, after a break of 14 months. However, this move did not result in a significant improvement in relations between the two countries during 1982. In March Libya's Col. Muammar al-Qaddafi accused Saudi Arabia of acting in league with the U.S. by "drowning the world market with crude oil at the cheapest price." Saudi Arabia, in turn, called for the expulsion of Libya from the Arab League and the Organization of African Unity, in condemnation of Qaddafi's foreign policies.

At the Arab summit meeting in Fez, Morocco, in September, consensus on a Middle East peace plan was achieved among the Arab nations. The set of proposals was a slightly modified version of the Fahd plan, which the same summit had rejected a year earlier. The revised version put greater emphasis on the role of the UN Security Council in guaranteeing "peace among all states of the region including the independent Palestinian state."

Within the Organization of Petroleum Exporting Countries (OPEC), Saudi Arabia absorbed much of the slump in demand for crude oil in 1982. Output in late 1982 was running at less than 6 million bbl a day, compared with the all-time high of 10.5 million bbl a day achieved at one point in 1981. In the same period, combined OPEC production fell by not more than 3 million bbl a day. The loss of about one-half of the kingdom's export revenue appeared to have little immediate effect on the development plan. The 1982–83 budget called for spending the equivalent of $91 billion, but most analysts agreed that the king-

dom needed no more than 7 million bbl a day to finance that sum. Unofficial reports in early November suggested that the Saudi Arabian government might consider drawing down its official reserves, possibly by as much as $25 billion, in order to avoid incurring a budget deficit. In oil policy, Saudi Arabia was committed to maintaining the $34-a-barrel price for Arabian light crude oil with no discounts.

With imports estimated at $9.8 billion in the first quarter of 1982, Saudi Arabia maintained its attraction for Western business as a buoyant market for capital goods and consumer products. The Saudi Arabian economy had grown used to massive injections of public funds in the 1979–82 period. The squeeze on oil revenue in 1982 dictated that the private sector and the commercial banks would have to play a bigger role in financing projects.

SHIPPING

In 1982 the international shipping industry was faced with the worst shipping recession since the early 1930s, and as a result the level of idle tonnage reached a new all-time high. Slightly over 10% of world merchant ship tonnage, representing 1,098 ships of nearly 69 million tons deadweight (dw), was laid up for lack of cargo by the end of the summer, compared with about 17 million tons dw in August 1981. By far the largest portion (57 million tons dw) of the laid-up total was tankers, representing 16% of the world's tanker tonnage.

The merchant fleets of many of the traditional

IRA WYMAN / THE NEW YORK TIMES

In contrast to economic woes in the rest of the industry, the Bath Iron Works in Maine undertook a $46.7 million expansion on the strength of a nearly $1 billion backlog in ship orders.

maritime nations suffered severe reductions because of idled vessels. Denmark led with 33% of Danish-flag vessels laid up; it was followed by Norway with 32%, Greece 20%, The Netherlands 12%, Liberia 11%, and Panama 8%. The volume of tonnage being sent to scrapyards increased as many owners gave up hope of finding employment for older vessels; this fact, coupled with only a modest influx of new tonnage, kept the tonnage total of world shipping almost the same as a year earlier. At the end of 1982 the total was 75,151 ships of 424.7 million gross registered tons (grt) or 702 million tons dw. For the first time since such tables were kept, Greece with 42 million grt moved into second place in the overall table of national tonnages, well behind Liberia with 74 million grt and just ahead of Japan with 40 million grt.

The war between the U.K. and Argentina over possession of the Falkland Islands had little effect on world freight markets with the exception of grain, which suffered from a reduction in movements from Argentina to the U.S.S.R. A world surplus of steel resulted in cutbacks in production by all the major steel-producing countries, and this in turn led to less demand for ore. Part of the loss in ore cargoes was recovered by an increase in the movement of steaming coal for use in power stations that were converted from oil to coal-firing and in certain industrial processes. It was expected that the long-term future for coal would be good enough to justify the expansion of coal-handling facilities at the major coal ports. At Los Angeles work neared completion on a

new $40 million coal terminal, and facilities were improved at New York City and Mobile, Ala. The Sri Lanka government approved a plan to develop the Port of Colombo, and in Taiwan a $35 million coal-discharging terminal was to be built offshore from Hsinta to serve the Taiwan Power Corporation's electricity generating station.

Despite predictions to the contrary, world shipbuilding did not continue the slow recovery that had appeared to be under way in 1981, and by the end of 1982 the amount of tonnage on order showed a reduction from 1981 of more than 13 million tons deadweight (dw) to 61 million tons dw. New construction of bulk carriers and oil–bulk–ore carriers declined sharply as owners finally acknowledged that an over-tonnage situation existed. The situation was worse in the tanker sector as a result of reduced oil production, and even a fairly high scrapping rate did little to help. The ship category having the largest drop in orders during the year was tankers, where orders fell from over 20 million tons dw to just under 15 million tons. Orders for bulk carriers decreased from 41.5 million tons dw to 33.3 million tons. Dry cargo ship orders recorded only a modest fall from 9.3 million tons dw to just under 9 million tons. The only sectors to show increased orders were cruise ships and certain types of specialized tonnage such as a new generation of containerships and ships serving the offshore oil and gas fields.

Japan stayed at the top of the world shipbuilding table with 27.2 million tons dw on order, followed at some distance by South Korea with 6 million tons,

Spain with 3.8 million tons, and Brazil with 3.2 million tons. A newcomer to the upper part of the table was Taiwan with 3,140,000 tons, just ahead of Poland with 2,830,000 tons.

For most of the shipyards in Europe and the U.S., the situation remained very bad in terms of new orders. The worst hit yards were those in the U.S., where no orders were placed for new merchant ships above 5,000 tons dw. It was significant, however, that even the Japanese shipbuilding industry, which had been drastically streamlined, was facing an acute shortage of new orders and had turned its attention to more specialized ships, such as the 100,000-ton-dw coal carrier with an ultrashallow draft, a very wide beam, and a "split" stern with a propeller at the after end of each skeg. This remarkable vessel, which was offered as a standard design, had the same draft as the popular Panamax-class bulk carrier of 60,000 tons dw; the large beam provided the greatly increased cargo capacity.

It became generally accepted that without some form of state financial aid many European shipyards could not survive the current crisis. In Belgium the important Cockerill shipyard virtually shut down with four bulk carriers still to be completed, and in France negotiations started for the merging of the three shipyards at Dunkirk, La Seyne, and La Ciotat as well as of the shipyard of Dubigeon Normandie with the St.-Nazaire yard of Alsthom Atlantique. The major reason for the desperate plight of the U.S. shipbuilding industry was the virtual ending of the construction differential subsidy, which had been a valuable cushion for the yards against the realities of the commercial market.

SKIING

Extensive additions in various methods of mechanical ascent, ranging from spectacular aerial cabin-car cableways to chair lifts and T-bar tows, generally lengthened the season, particularly for holiday skiers, by opening up more high-altitude terrain. Thus, skiing became a more familiar activity in countries associated with warm climates.

Alpine Racing

The 16th annual Alpine World Cup series covered 28 men's and 27 women's events spanning four months at 34 sites in nine countries. Retaining the men's trophy, Phil Mahre of the U.S. headed both the slalom and giant slalom standings. Ingemar Stenmark of Sweden was the overall runner-up; Steve Mahre, Phil's twin brother, finished third. The best downhill skier was Steve Podborski of Canada.

Erika Hess of Switzerland won the women's trophy. Irene Epple of West Germany and Christin Cooper of the U.S. finished second and third, respectively. Hess topped the slalom and giant slalom ratings; the leading downhiller was Marie-Cecile Gros-Gaudenier of France. Austria regained the concurrently decided Nations Cup. Switzerland was runner-up and the U.S. finished third.

The 27th biennial world Alpine championships were held at Schladming, Austria, during January 17–February 7. Stenmark won the slalom, the first man to do so in three successive world championships. Bojan Krizaj of Yugoslavia was second and another Swede, Bengt Fjällberg, took the bronze medal. Steve Mahre gained the first American giant slalom win in international competition, with Sten-

The "Hitachi Venture" was launched in January for a Hong Kong shipping concern. The bulk carrier, largest in the world, featured the latest in electronics and the world's biggest hatch cover.
UPI

Steve Mahre of the U.S. (right) beams with pleasure after edging defending champion Ingemar Stenmark of Sweden (left) in the world championship giant slalom race in Schladming, Austria, in February.
UPI

mark second and Boris Strel third for Yugoslavia. Harti Weirather of Austria won the downhill; his fellow Austrian Erwin Resch finished third behind Conradin Cathomen of Switzerland. The combination event went to Michel Vion of France in front of Peter Lüscher of Switzerland and Anton Steiner from Austria.

Hess dominated the women's events, taking three of the four gold medals. Cooper was her runner-up in both the slalom and giant slalom, the respective bronze medals going to Daniela Zini of Italy and Ursula Konzett of Liechtenstein. Cooper finished third in the combination, behind Perrine Pelen of France. In the downhill Gerry Sorensen and Laurie Graham won gold and bronze medals for Canada, split by Cindy Nelson of the U.S.

Nordic Events

At the 34th biennial world Nordic championships at Holmenkollen, Oslo, February 15–28, North Europeans took all the cross-country medals except one. In the 15 km Oddvar Braa of Norway outpaced Aleksandr Zaviolov of the U.S.S.R. and Harri Kirvesniemi from Finland. The 30 km went to Thomas Eriksson of Sweden, with Norway's Lars Erik Eriksen runner-up and Bill Koch of the U.S. third—the first American to win a Nordic world championship medal. Thomas Wassberg of Sweden won the 50 km from Yury Burlakov of the U.S.S.R., with Eriksen third. Braa and Zaviolov, anchoring their Norwegian and Soviet 4 x 10-km relay teams, crossed the finish line in a dead heat, with Finland third.

The Nordic combination (jumping and cross-country) was won by Tom Sandberg of Norway with two East Germans, Konrad Winkler and Uwe Dotzauer, second and third. A team competition (jumping and relay race) was won by the Soviet Union. The silver medal was shared by Finland and Norway. An Austrian, Armin Kogler, took the 70-m event, with Jari Puikkonen of Finland and Ole Bremseth of Norway placing second and third. In the 90-m jumping finals, Finland's Matti Nykaenen beat Olav Hansson of Norway; Kogler finished third. The team jumping was won by Norway, followed by Austria and Finland.

Berit Aunli became the first Norwegian woman to win a world skiing championship gold medal when she took the 10 km. She subsequently won the 5 km and achieved a third gold medal as a member of the winning Norwegian 4 x 5-km relay team, which finished ahead of the U.S.S.R. and East Germany. Aunli placed second in the 20 km behind the Soviet veteran Raisa Smetanina, with Hilkka Riihivuori of Finland third. Riihivuori was runner-up in both the 5 km and 10 km, the bronze medals going to Brit Pettersen of Norway and Kvetoslava Jeriova of Czechoslovakia.

The third Nordic World Cup series saw the first U.S. victory, as Koch won the men's cross-country events, and a women's triumph for Aunli. The men's silver and bronze medals were gained by Wassberg and Kirvesniemi. The women's runner-up was Pettersen, followed by Jeriova. The Nordic World Cup jump title was retained by Kogler, followed by his compatriot Hubert Neuper and Horst Bulau of Canada. The Nordic Nations Cup was retained by Austria, with Norway second and Finland third.

Maria Epple of West Germany won the women's giant slalom in the World Cup competition in Aspen, Colorado, in February.
WIDE WORLD

East Germans and Norwegians dominated the world biathlon championships at Raubichi, U.S.S.R., February 12–17. Frank Ulrich won the 20-km title for East Germany, ahead of two Norwegians, Erik Kvalfoff and Terje Krokstad. Kvalfoff won the 10 km, with Ulrich second and Vladimir Alikin of the U.S.S.R. third. East Germany retained the 4 x 10 km-relay title, with Norway second and the U.S.S.R. third.

Other Events

In international speed-skiing championships at Silverton, Colo., on April 19–25, a world record men's time of 126.24 mph (203.16 km/h) was set by Frans Weber of Austria. A new women's record of 111.29 mph (179.10 km/h) was achieved by Marty Martin-Kuntz of the U.S.

The men's world cup for freestyle skiing was won by Frank Beddor of the U.S. The women's overall title went to Marie-Claude Asselin of Canada.

SOCIAL SERVICES

The revolution in social welfare policy, promised and begun by Ronald Reagan in the first year of his presidency, expanded in 1982. The number of persons receiving welfare and food stamps stopped growing, and spending was cut for subsidized housing, public services, employment and job training, and other programs. One notable exception to this trend was Social Security, the largest social program of all. It continued to grow, as did concern about its future.

The new direction for social welfare programs had been set by the budget passed in 1981, which cut family support spending by $25 billion. However, the effect was not fully felt until the cuts took effect in the fiscal year running from Oct. 1, 1981, to Sept. 30, 1982. Another $8.5 billion was trimmed from these programs for fiscal 1983, bringing the human resources share of the federal budget to about 50.8%, compared with 53.8% in the peak year of 1976.

The number of people receiving Aid to Families with Dependent Children (AFDC) fell from 11.1 million in 1981 to 10.4 million in 1982, and the federal outlay dropped from $7.9 billion to $7.6 billion. A major change in the structure of the AFDC program took effect in 1982, as benefits to the working poor were eliminated or cut back sharply. In addition, inflation continued to take its toll. The Department of Health and Human Services reported that welfare benefits had fallen by an average of 29% in real terms over the past decade.

Although food costs rose, the federal outlay for food stamps declined from $11.4 billion in 1981 to $11.3 billion in 1982, and the number of recipients dropped from 22.4 million to 22.2 million. Food stamp recipients received their first cost-of-living increase in almost two years on October 1—an 8% boost that raised the maximum allotment for a family of four from $233 a month to $253. The number of children participating in the school lunch program fell from 26.8 million in the 1980–81 school year to 23.6 million in 1981–82, and more than 2,700 schools dropped out of the program.

State Medicaid officials used new authority to restrict eligibility and reduce benefits. Medicaid provided $32.4 billion in 1982 to help pay the medical bills for 22.9 million Americans, about one in every ten. The Comprehensive Employment and Training Act (CETA) expired on Sept. 30, 1982, but Congress approved new legislation that could provide job training for as many as one million disadvantaged workers and youths. Unlike CETA, it would not subsidize public service jobs but would concentrate on skills instruction and other employment-related assistance for low-income workers.

In his state of the union address in January, President Reagan introduced his "New Federalism" proposal to transfer at least 30 federal programs to state and local control, including AFDC, energy assistance, legal services for the poor, and child nutrition. In return, the federal government would assume full responsibility for Medicaid. No action was taken on this plan during the year.

The Urban Institute, a nonprofit, nonpartisan research organization, reported that President Reagan's domestic policies had brought about the most dramatic shift in economic and social policy since Franklin D. Roosevelt's New Deal. The report said the full impact of the Reagan "revolution" was yet to come and would continue long after Reagan left office. The Census Bureau reported that 2.2 million additional Americans had joined the ranks of the poor in 1981, for a total of 31.8 million or 14% of the population. The poverty line was defined as $9,287 for a family of four in 1981.

With unemployment at its highest level since the depression of the 1930s, the Reagan administration estimated that 10.9 million people received a total of $21.1 billion in unemployment benefits during the year. The average payment was $115 a week (in July). Even so, a study by the Center on Budget and Policy Priorities found that 59%, or 6.2 million, of those out of work in September received no unemployment benefits. One reason was that the "extended" benefits program, which had increased the basic 26 weeks of insurance to 39 weeks in hard-hit states, had been cut back by a 1981 law. Another factor was the length of the recession, which resulted in workers using up their benefits before they could find new jobs. Congress passed a temporary $2.1 billion supplemental benefits program in 1982, providing six to ten additional weeks of coverage.

Meanwhile, there was only debate over Social Security, which paid about $156 billion to 36.2 million persons in 1982. After decades of unchecked expansion, Social Security was running out of cash. The largest of the system's three trust funds, Old-Age and Survivors Insurance, was borrowing from the

A Roman Catholic nun brings food to a family in New York City's East Harlem district. Voluntary welfare agencies were hard pressed to keep up with demand.

others (Medicare and disability), but these, too, would be without money in 1984. In the long term, the system faced a major crisis when the huge baby-boom generation reached retirement age in about 30 years. A 15-member National Commission on Social Security Reform, appointed by President Reagan and headed by economist Alan Greenspan, was to have reported at the end of the year, but the members failed to agree and it was given an extension. Some of the possibilities included increased payroll taxes; extension of coverage to federal, state, and local employees; a delay or reduction in cost-of-living increases; taxes on all or part of retirement benefits; and borrowing from general federal revenues.

Critics feared that returning welfare responsibilities to states and local communities might lead to their abandonment.

SOMALIA

In 1982 Pres. Muhammad Siyad Barrah of Somalia continued to demonstrate his staying power in spite of considerable pressures. In February and again in April disturbances in the northern city of Hargeisa resulted in several deaths. This apparently reflected feelings among the population of the north of the country that they were being neglected by the Mogadishu government, which drew most of its strength from the south.

Despite the troubles in Hargeisa, President Barrah felt sufficiently secure in March to end the national state of emergency that he had declared more than 16 months earlier. He disbanded the Supreme Revolutionary Council, through which he had ruled during this period, and reinstated the People's National Assembly and also the state party, the Somali Revolutionary Socialist Party (SRSP). He went on to make a tour of Western countries, including the U.S., which had become Somalia's principal ally since its break with the U.S.S.R. after the latter supported Ethiopia in the 1978 Ogaden war.

In July fighting began near the Ethiopian border, where Somali Army units were attacked. Responsibility was claimed by the Somali Democratic Salvation Front (SDSF), a Somali group opposed to Barrah's regime. However, there were also reports, strongly denied by the Ethiopian government, that most of the invaders were Soviet-armed Ethiopian troops backing an SDSF initiative. In response to this allegation the U.S. finally delivered the $40 million package of defensive armaments that had been promised to Somalia since 1980 in exchange for the use of the port of Berbera as a naval and air base; an additional $40 million worth was promised by the U.S. for future delivery.

After August, however, the fighting appeared to die down. The antigovernment forces held territory about 20 mi (32 km) inside Somalia. In October the SDSF announced that it had formed a joint military committee with the northern-based Somali National Movement, another major opposition group.

The situation of the refugees who had fled from the war in the Ethiopian-ruled province of Ogaden had apparently become stabilized, in that the people still living in camps—who according to the official estimate of the UN High Commissioner for Refugees numbered 700,000—were said to be receiving adequate food and health care. There remained the problem of what was to become of them and also of the unknown but perhaps equally large number of refugees scattered among the general population of Somalia.

In the middle of the year the government ordered several measures aimed at financial stabilization, including devaluation of the Somali shilling, easing of import restrictions, and firmer control of government expenditure. This was the second phase of a program begun in 1981 and backed by the International Monetary Fund.

Some 700,000 Ethiopian refugees were reported living in camps in Somalia.
Y. MILLER – UNHCR

Thousands of striking black mine workers were rounded up by police after they violently protested meagre wage settlements offered by South Africa's Chamber of Mines.

SOUTH AFRICA

The year 1982 was marked by significant political developments. An open split in the ruling National Party (NP) was the culmination of a period of internal strife that was primarily focused on the issue of nonwhite participation in government. The central figure in the rift was Andries Treuernicht, minister of state administration and of statistics and Transvaal leader of the NP. He and his supporters, including Minister of (Black) Education and Training Ferdinand Hartzenberg, accused Prime Minister P. W. Botha of deviating from the traditional policies of the NP by proposing to extend political rights to the Coloured and Asian populations.

In March Treuernicht and Hartzenberg, with a group of some 20 members of Parliament and provincial councillors, chiefly in Transvaal, seceded from the NP. They formed the Conservative Party of South Africa (CP), with a parliamentary representation of 18, and were joined by other dissidents outside Parliament. While opposing any form of political sharing in decision making in South Africa, they were prepared to concede limited rights of self-determination and some participation, with advisory powers, to Coloureds and Asians in their own areas. But they were not willing to extend these rights to urban blacks who, they contended, could exercise political rights in their respective homelands.

The right-wing opposition Herstigte Nasionale Party (HNP) under Jaap Marais turned down Treuernicht's offer of an alliance but later agreed to a future election pact. In the first test of strength for the new arrangement, a provincial by-election in the Germiston district, the two groups fought the NP

separately. The NP retained the seat with a slender majority over the CP and a substantial minority against the combined opposition. In a later series of by-elections in the Cape and the Orange Free State, the NP retained all its seats.

In May the President's Council submitted a draft constitution designed, it was declared, to break with the "Westminster" system of parliamentary democracy. The draft embodied a far-reaching range of proposals. Among them were the appointment by an electoral college, for a seven-year term, of an executive president who would have a white, Coloured (mixed black and white), and Asian Cabinet not chosen on party lines and with authority to choose a prime minister; the setting up of separate parliaments for each group; representation for blacks not at the government level but in their own local authorities; multiracial representation on metropolitan councils and on Group Areas Act committees; replacement of provincial councils by eight regional councils with white, Coloured, and Asian representation; and residential separation on ethnic lines but with no enforced segregation or integration. The principle of "one man: one vote" was ruled out. The Council later supplemented and to some extent modified the proposals in a second report.

The government, on the whole, accepted the Council's original draft. The main alteration it proposed was to replace the suggested three parliaments by three chambers in one parliament, each to manage its own affairs but with an elaborate system of consultation and consensus subject to a final decision by the President's Council. There would also be an overall Cabinet to deal with matters of common

305

South African Prime Minister Pieter W. Botha met with Zambian Pres. Kenneth Kaunda on the South Africa-Botswana border in April.

interest. The general effect was to give the executive president and the President's Council, with its white majority, the dominant voice.

The draft had a mixed reception, largely critical, from other quarters. The official opposition, the Progressive Federal Party, while prepared to discuss the plan, objected to the omission of blacks from virtually all participation and argued that in fact it entrenched apartheid (racial separation) and white supremacy. Coloured and Asian opinion was strongly critical of the exclusion of blacks. Black leaders, with KwaZulu's Chief Gatsha Buthelezi in the forefront, rejected proposals that left their people in the cold. Right-wing Nationalists were firmly opposed to the draft.

Security legislation as a whole had come under review by a judicial commission. Its recommendations, broadly accepted by the government, included provisions for tighter safeguards against terrorism and subversion, the protection of secret information, and the power to intercept mail and telephone calls. It endorsed the principle of detention without trial but proposed some changes in prison procedure affecting detainees and special ministerial approval for detentions exceeding 30 days. An official code on the treatment of detainees, though welcomed, was regarded as not going far enough.

Foreign Relations

The search for a peaceful independence settlement in South West Africa/Namibia remained a central factor in South Africa's foreign relations. Headed by the U.S. representatives on the five-nation Western contact group (the U.S., the U.K., France, West Germany, and Canada) that was acting on behalf of the UN, discussions with the southern African frontline states, South Africa, and the South West Africa People's Organization (SWAPO) produced a broad agreement in principle on a cease-fire and the holding of a free and fair UN-supervised election as required by UN Resolution 435.

However, fresh issues were raised even before the first phase of actual implementation was reached. Above all, the problem of the presence of Cuban forces in Angola emerged as the most formidable stumbling block. South Africa called for the withdrawal of the Cubans as a precondition to Namibian independence. The argument was that, in the event that SWAPO achieved victory in the envisioned election, it would have Cuban backing for the establishment of a pro-Communist regime that might become a threat to South Africa itself. The U.S., for other reasons, also pressed for a Cuban withdrawal, while the Angolan government maintained that the presence of the Cubans was its own affair and had nothing to do with Namibia.

In the meantime, sporadic military activity continued on the Namibian border. South Africa launched periodic raids into Angola with the declared object of preempting a buildup of SWAPO forces or countering the less and less frequent SWAPO incursions into Namibia. A ministerial-level meeting between Angola and South Africa in early December discussed terms for a cease-fire. In December South African troops carried out a raid on African National Congress (ANC) bases in Maseru, Lesotho; 42 people were reported to have been killed. The ANC claimed responsibility for the bombing of the Koeberg nuclear power plant, still under construction, on the day some of the dead were being buried.

Efforts at the UN to secure international approval for mandatory economic and general sanctions against South Africa failed in the face of U.S. and other mainly Western opposition. UN investigators found no conclusive evidence of alleged official South African complicity in an unsuccessful bid by a group of mercenaries to overthrow the Seychelles government in November 1981. The allegations were denied by South Africa. At their trial in a South African court on a hijacking charge, they were sentenced to terms in prison.

The Economy

Introducing his budget in March, Minister of Finance Owen Horwood stressed that it was being presented against a background of serious and long-term world recession. He pointed out that while South Africa had in real economic terms outperformed most other countries up to then, it had become more and more evident that the decline in the gold price and the worldwide recessionary situation were adversely affecting the balance of payments in particular. The situation, Horwood said, called for firm control of state spending, the cash and liquidity base of the banking system, and the money supply.

As the year proceeded, a series of measures to that end were taken in conjunction with the Reserve Bank. They took the form of fluctuating interest rates and bank credit adjustments. An imports surcharge and a de facto depreciation of the rand in dollar terms (to R 1.15 = U.S. $1) cut down a balance of payments shortfall of approximately R 3 billion. Further relief for the balance of payments situation came in the form of a loan of R 1,240,000,000 granted by the International Monetary Fund against strong UN and third world opposition.

Amid growing concern, shared by the government and the general public, at the continued depopulation and underdevelopment of rural areas and small towns, first steps were taken to implement a policy of economic decentralization. The scheme was a comprehensive attempt to arrest the drift of both black and white people to a few highly developed metropolitan areas by creating favourable conditions for the development of the economically backward regions. The country was divided into eight regions, each with a central growth point and each incorporating one or more of the existing and former homelands. Industrialization was to be the main target of the plan, but the development of mineral, agricultural, and commercial potentials was also an essential part of the program.

SOUTHEAST ASIAN AFFAIRS

In 1982, for the fourth consecutive year, Kampuchea (Cambodia) was the issue upon which the political and strategic interests of both Southeast Asian countries and global powers converged. Though the divergences of those interests continued to produce much tension, the Kampuchean imbroglio seemed to be edging more distinctly toward a resolution than at any time since Vietnamese troops toppled the Khmer Rouge regime of Pol Pot in 1979 and replaced it with one headed by their ally, Heng Samrin. At the same time, the five members (Indonesia, Singapore, Malaysia, Thailand, the Philippines) of the Association of Southeast Asian Nations (ASEAN) felt sufficient pressure from big-power rivalry in the region to address again the controversial subject of closer military cooperation.

Kampuchea was undoubtedly the question that consumed the most energy among diplomats of both ASEAN and the Communist Indochinese nations in the opposite camp. Through patient, deft, behind-the-scenes maneuvering, ASEAN was able to pull off a major political coup by persuading leaders of the three principal anti-Vietnamese Khmer groups to form a coalition to combat Hanoi's occupation of their troubled homeland. (*See* KAMPUCHEA.) Reconstituted with former head of state Prince Norodom Sihanouk as president, former Cambodian premier Son Sann as prime minister, and Khieu Samphan of the Khmer Rouge as vice-president, the tripartite alliance of Democratic Kampuchea and its backers, ASEAN and China, scored a major diplomatic victory against the Phnom Penh regime and its Vietnamese and Soviet supporters when the UN General Assembly voted in October 90–29 to recognize the alliance as the sole legitimate government of Kampuchea.

Vietnam spared little effort trying to prevent formation of the alliance and to weaken the unity and resolve of ASEAN members. In chorus with its clients in Phnom Penh, Hanoi continued to remind the world of the atrocities that took place under Khmer Rouge rule and to paint a picture of a Kampuchea gradually returning to normal under Heng Samrin's administration. In July, shortly after the tripartite coalition was born, Vietnam offered ASEAN an ostensible olive branch by withdrawing some 8,000 of its 180,000 troops from Kampuchea. ASEAN, however, spurned the overture, judging it a mere rotation of soldiers. The association made it plain to visiting Vietnamese Foreign Minister Nguyen Co Thach that it would not be satisfied with anything less than full compliance with a UN resolution calling for a complete withdrawal of foreign forces from Kampuchea, followed by free elections. After a stiff confrontation in Singapore, Thach dropped hints that if ASEAN continued to maintain its tough stance, Vietnam might consider supporting long-festering Communist insurgencies within the association's member countries and also might grant the Soviet Union freer access to military facilities in Vietnam.

Yet toward the year's end it seemed that developments were becoming increasingly unfavourable to continued Vietnamese occupation of Kampuchea. With an accelerating thaw in Sino-Soviet relations, many analysts thought it increasingly likely that the Soviets might, in great-power terms, concede that Kampuchea was within the Chinese "sphere of influence" in return for improved ties with China. In such circumstances Moscow would scale down its support for Vietnam, China's archenemy. Indeed, Vietnam had since mid-1982 given subtle hints that it might be prepared to compromise.

The continued interest of the great powers in the Kampuchean question and the resulting competition was unsettling for the smaller countries of Southeast Asia. At a meeting of ASEAN foreign ministers in June, conference host and Singapore Prime Minister Lee Kuan Yew noted that "over Indochina, China and the Soviet Union are engaged in a sustained contest of will and power for preeminent influence. Until one side finds it burdensome and not worth the cost, there is little hope for peace [in the region]." Lee, one of Southeast Asia's most astute strategic thinkers, added that "we were premature in assuming that the congruence of American and Chinese interests in containing Soviet expansionism will make them de facto allies." He concluded that "the present balance of relationships among the U.S., the U.S.S.R., and China is more fluid and uncertain than a year ago."

It was amid such uncertainty that Lee raised in September the delicate issue of a possible military role for ASEAN, which since its formation in 1967 had concerned itself largely with economic and social matters. While on a visit to Indonesia, Lee suggested multilateral military exercises involving all five ASEAN member countries. Though observers noted that this was the closest thing ASEAN had heard to a call to arms, the extremely cautious response seemed to indicate that the association's other members were not quite ready to put Lee's suggestion into practice.

In the absence of a fully developed defense capability of its own, ASEAN was generally reassured by renewed U.S. pledges to protect non-Communist Southeast Asia. U.S. Defense Secretary Caspar Weinberger made two separate visits to the region, during which he reaffirmed his country's "unshakable" commitment to its Southeast Asian allies. In his first trip to the White House in 16 years, Philippine Pres. Ferdinand Marcos was pleased to hear U.S. Pres. Ronald Reagan declare that the security relationship between the two countries, founded on the U.S.'s giant Clark and Subic military bases in the Philippines, "is an essential element in maintaining peace in the region and is so recognized." Reagan's assertion also cheered other Southeast Asian leaders, who had good cause to doubt the resolve of the U.S. to stand up to Communist expansionism after the trauma of the war in Vietnam. Specific acts by the U.S. included an agreement to renegotiate the lease on its Philippine bases a year early in 1983 and its provision to Thailand of an additional $12 million in military assistance.

Australia, under the conservative government of Prime Minister Malcolm Fraser, also decided to contribute more actively to the security of the Asian and Pacific region. Over several months Fraser traveled to Malaysia, the Philippines, China, New Zealand, and Fiji, offering aid packages to some countries and discussing defense strategies with others to keep "enemy" (*i.e.*, Soviet) influence at bay. Australia planned to double its assistance (to $1.8

million) to Thailand in 1982–83 and was considering prolonging its small but significant military presence in Malaysia, Singapore, and Thailand. Practical defense cooperation was the leading discussion topic when Australian Defense Minister Ian Sinclair toured Southeast Asia in the fall.

One capitalist power that ASEAN was reluctant to see assume a higher military profile was Japan. Though the U.S. had been consistently urging Japan to assume a share of responsibility for regional security more in keeping with its economic strength, memories of Japanese aggression in World War II continued to haunt Southeast Asia. Such unpleasant recollections were sharpened when a region-wide furor erupted at midyear over Japan's efforts to tone down descriptions in secondary-school history textbooks of Japanese Imperial Army atrocities during the war. Despite Tokyo's protests that it would continue to adhere to its no-war constitution, Ferdinand Marcos proclaimed himself "wary, very wary" of Japan's U.S.-encouraged defense buildup and warned the U.S. against "strengthening Japan so it becomes a threat to us small nations in Southeast Asia."

The Soviet Union also did not contribute to ASEAN's sense of security. The region's misgivings about Moscow's sustained military expansion in the Pacific were exacerbated by two of the most sensational spy scandals to come to light in Southeast Asia for some time, both involving Soviet agents. In early February Indonesia expelled two Soviet officials for illegal espionage activities and closed the Jakarta office of Aeroflot, the Soviet airline. Though the Indonesian government tried to play down the affair, there were angry demonstrations outside the

Prince Norodom Sihanouk (left) visited and spoke at a refugee camp at Kao-I-Dan in Thailand, where some 45,000 refugees from Kampuchea were living.
YVES-GUY BERGES–SYGMA

The Canadian Anik 3-C communications satellite was deployed into orbit from the U.S. space shuttle "Columbia" in November.
NASA

Soviet embassy. Barely two weeks later the Singapore government announced that it had caught two Soviet spies trying to gain access to sensitive military information. The pair were quickly deported.

China, however, another traditional bugbear of Southeast Asia, offered some reassurance. After finding some common ground with ASEAN on the Kampuchean issue, Chinese leaders publicly hinted that Beijing (Peking) would restrict its support for "fraternal" Communist parties in Southeast Asia to purely the moral kind.

In trade the main challenges that faced the open economies of Southeast Asia in 1982 were the global recession and one of its most insidious by-products, protectionism. When ASEAN's economic ministers met in Manila in May, the battle against mounting international trade barriers was at the top of the agenda. The commodity-rich association concluded that a key weapon would be for member nations to increase trade with one another.

(*See also* articles on the various countries.)

SPACE EXPLORATION

Throughout 1982 the U.S. space shuttle continued to record progressively greater achievements, justifying the nation's faith in it as the space transportation system of the future. The space shuttle orbiter "Columbia" lifted off for its third mission from the Kennedy Space Center at Cape Canaveral, Fla., on March 22 with astronauts Jack R. Lousma and C. Gordon Fullerton. The mission lasted more than eight days and ended at White Sands Missile Range in New Mexico on March 30. There were few problems, and the crew performed a variety of experiments, including further operation of the manipulator arm to lift an experiment package from the cargo bay, extend it into space, and return it to the bay. Other experiments included materials processing in near-zero gravity and an insect study developed by Todd E. Nelson, a student at Southland High School in Adams, Minn. The astronauts also checked out a payload canister for future "getaway specials," experiments to be flown by individuals, schools, industry, and other organizations as space aboard the orbiter permitted.

"Columbia's" fourth launch was on June 27, with astronauts Thomas K. Mattingly and Henry W. Hartsfield, Jr. Fittingly enough it landed on July 4 at Edwards Air Force Base (AFB) in California, greeted by Pres. Ronald Reagan and an estimated 500,000 fellow citizens. During the mission a major problem occurred when the two booster rockets plunged into the Atlantic and were not recovered, apparently because of parachute failures. Experiments included the first one to be developed by a private company. It was designed to produce certain pharmaceuticals continuously with high purity. The astronauts also helped save the first "getaway special" when a defec-

WIDE WORLD

The "Conestoga 1" rocket, launched on September 9 from Matagorda Island, Texas, was a first step toward a private space program.

tive circuit prevented power from reaching the canister.

The shuttle's fifth flight, November 11–16, was described by NASA as its first "operational" mission. Two commercial communications satellites, the American SBS-3 and the Canadian Anik 3-C, were carried aloft in the cargo bay and deployed directly into orbit. To handle the deployment "Columbia" carried two mission specialists, Joseph P. Allen and William B. Lenoir, in addition to pilots Vance D. Brand and Col. Robert F. Overmyer; it was the first shuttle flight to carry a crew of four. The mission was marred only by failures in two newly designed spacesuits that forced cancellation of a planned "space walk" by Allen and Lenoir. At the end of the mission "Columbia" was grounded for extensive refitting; shuttle missions in 1983 were to be flown by the more powerful sister ship "Challenger."

On July 29 the Soviet Salyut 6 space station reentered the atmosphere and burned after four years and ten months in orbit. But the Salyut 7 had been successfully launched on April 19 and its primary crew on May 13. Cosmonauts Anatoly N. Berezovoy and Valentin V. Lebedev, in Soyuz T-5, docked with Salyut 7 on May 14. Their mission was a mixture of scientific experiments and military observations. After a record 211 days in space, they returned to Earth on December 10.

On May 24 the unmanned supply satellite Progress 13 docked with Salyut 7. It brought mail, fuel, water, oxygen, and other supplies. Having been resupplied, the space station was in shape to receive its first visiting cosmonauts. Soyuz T-6 was launched on June 24. Its crew consisted of Vladimir Dzhanibekov, Aleksandr Ivanchenkov, and Jean-Loup Chrétien of France, the first astronaut from the West to be orbited by the U.S.S.R. The international crew returned to the Earth on July 2.

The next visitors to Salyut 7 arrived aboard Soyuz T-7 on August 20. They were Leonid I. Popov, Aleksandr A. Serebrov, and the second woman in space, Svetlana Y. Savitskaya. (Valentina Tereshkova, also of the U.S.S.R., orbited the Earth in 1963.) This crew continued the experiments of previous visitors with special attention to the effects of weightlessness upon female physiology. The T-7 crew returned to the Earth on August 27.

Launch Vehicles

As 1982 progressed, so did development of a lightweight external propellant tank for the space shuttle. By September the manufacturers of the huge tank had succeeded in reducing its weight by more than 10,000 lb (4,545 kg). Approximately 600 lb (273 kg) were saved simply by not painting the tank.

The European Space Agency's (ESA's) Ariane made its final developmental flight on Dec. 20, 1981, orbiting two satellites. However, on its first operational mission, on Sept. 10, 1982, from Kourou, French Guiana, a failure in its third-stage propulsion system sent the launch vehicle crashing into the Atlantic Ocean. Two satellites were lost. Despite the failure ESA made the decision to develop the much more powerful Ariane L4, capable of payloads up to 9,460 lb (4,300 kg).

The Soviet Union during 1982 continued development of its heavy booster vehicle, which had a larger payload capability than NASA's former Saturn V. Western experts believed that the booster, variously known as the Lenin and G-1 vehicle, had a payload capability of 484,000 lb (220,000 kg). First launch was expected in 1984. It was expected that the new booster would be used primarily for the orbiting of large space stations with crews of 12 and, later, 20.

Joining the primary crew of the Soviet space station Salyut 7 in June were (left) Aleksandr Ivanchenkov, (right) Vladimir Dzhanibekov, and (centre) Jean-Loup Chrétien of France, the first Western astronaut to be orbited by the U.S.S.R.

UPI

Looking forward to the need for a vehicle to ferry such crews to such space stations and back to Earth, the Soviet Union for several years had been developing a mini-shuttle. An unmanned version of it, weighing approximately 2,000 lb (900 kg), was launched on June 3 and designated Cosmos 1374. It traveled for a little more than one orbit and was recovered after impact in the Indian Ocean.

Ventures concerning privately developed launch vehicles during the year experienced both bad and good fortune. The bad news came from West Germany's Otrag Corp., which had to close down its launching site in Libya to avoid political problems with several North African nations. The good news was from Space Services, Inc., of Houston, Texas. On September 9 its Conestoga 1 lifted off from a small island off the coast of Texas and successfully performed a suborbital flight.

Unmanned Satellites

As 1981 ended, the Solar Maximum Mission Satellite, launched on Feb. 14, 1980, detected several important new kinds of emissions from solar flares. It also observed gamma rays with energies never recorded before. On Nov. 11, 1981, the Orbital Test Satellite, launched in 1978 by ESA, was successfully pressed into service as a telephone and telegraph exchange when a terrestrial exchange at Lyons, France, was destroyed by fire.

Designed for a lifetime of only three years, Applications Technology Satellite (ATS) 1 marked its 15th year of continuous operation in space on Dec. 6, 1981. Shortly after its birthday, the satellite helped save the eyesight of a crewman on a research vessel in the Pacific. Radio communications with his ship were interrupted while a doctor was giving instructions on treatment of the man's infected eye. The ship's radio operator switched to ATS 1, and the instructions continued.

On April 4 the GOES 5 environmental satellite spotted the eruption of the Mexican volcano El Chichón and tracked its dust cloud. Similar observations were made by the NOAA 7 weather satellite. Measurements made by both satellites assisted scientists in evaluating the effects of the dust on the Earth's weather.

On May 17 the crew of Salyut 7 placed Iskara 2, an amateur radio satellite, into orbit from an air lock in the space station. On September 10 a Soviet satellite, Cosmos 1383, was instrumental in saving the lives of three men whose plane had crashed in northern British Columbia. The satellite had on board a developmental search-and-rescue transponder that detected signals from the plane and provided positional data to Canadian rescue aircraft.

Probes

Soviet Venus probe Venera 13, launched on Oct. 30, 1981, landed March 1, 1982, on a plain to the east of the Phoebe region of the Beta area. The lander took 62 minutes to traverse the thick atmosphere, and it transmitted data from the surface for 127 minutes. The lander reported that the ground temperature was 855° F (457° C) and the atmospheric pressure was 89 times that of Earth at its surface. Elements found in the soil included magnesium, silicon, aluminum, sodium, potassium, titanium, manganese, and iron. Photographs showed rust-coloured rocks and an orange or reddish-brown sky.

Venera 14, launched Nov. 4, 1981, landed on March 5, 1982, some 600 mi (965 km) to the southeast of Venera 13 after a 63-minute descent. However, it transmitted data for only 57 minutes. The lander reported a temperature of 869° F (465° C) and an atmospheric pressure 94 times that of Earth.

Information on Saturn continued to accumulate as data from the U.S. Voyager probes were analyzed. There was evidence that at least two of Saturn's rings might be composed of ice rather than the remains of a shattered moon of the planet. Early in 1982 Voyager 2, on its way to an encounter with Uranus in 1986, began to experience failures after a 2,000,000,000-mi (3,200,000,000-km) flight that began in 1977.

In March Pioneer 10, the first successful probe to Jupiter, completed ten years in space and was continuing to function. It was halfway between the orbits of Uranus and Neptune, 2,500,000,000 mi (4,000,000,000 km) from the Sun.

SPAIN

Defections from the ruling Unión Centro Democrático (UCD), which had begun in November 1981, intensified in 1982 when Francisco Fernández Ordóñez formally established the Democratic Action Party (PAD) in March and when the right-wing Popular Democratic Party and the Liberal Democratic Party were both set up in July. During the following month former premier Adolfo Suárez González registered the Democratic and Social Centre. To halt the disintegration of the UCD in the face of these defections and to attain some degree of unity in preparation for general elections, Premier Leopoldo Calvo Sotelo y Bustelo held several meetings in early July with the president of the Congress of Deputies, Landelino Lavilla Alsina.

After a meeting on July 6 Calvo Sotelo told the press that Suárez represented the main obstacle to resolving the crisis in the UCD and accused him of trying to regain his powers through control of the party apparatus. Accordingly, Sotelo offered his res-

ignation as UCD president and proposed Lavilla Alsina as his successor; the latter was elected on July 13. Before consenting to run for the UCD presidency, Lavilla Alsina obtained broad new powers from the national political council. These included the rights to nominate the party secretary-general, to reorganize the national executive, and to nominate the majority of the electoral committee.

The controversial Organic Law on the Harmonization of the Autonomy Process (LOAPA) was approved in the Congress of Deputies on June 30. Supporting it were the UCD and the Partido Socialista Obrero Español (PSOE), while the regional parties, the Partido Communista Español (PCE), and independents opposed it. Opponents of the law, most notably the Basques and Catalans, maintained that the LOAPA represented a disfigurement of the spirit of the constitution and of the autonomy statutes since it reinforced central government controls; its proponents argued that the law filled the gap between the more general demands of the constitution and the specific requirements of differing autonomous regions.

The statutes for the uniprovincial regions of Cantabria (Santander) and that of the principality of Asturias entered into force on February 1. Autonomy statutes for Valencia, Murcia, and La Rioja came into effect on July 10, and those for Aragón, Castille-La Mancha, the Canary Islands, and Navarra on August 16. In elections held on May 23 for a regional parliament in Andalusia, the PSOE won 66 seats in the 109-member assembly, while the right-wing Alianza Popular (AP) won 17 and the UCD 15.

Defections from the UCD from March onward meant that the government lost its majority in the Cortes, and by late August its strength was reduced to 149 deputies. The PSOE had 117, the Communists 23, and the Coalición Democrática 9. Final blows to

Felipe González takes the oath of office before King Juan Carlos (right) and other Spanish dignitaries. González became Europe's youngest prime minister.
UPI

Alonso Alvarez de Toledo (left), Spain's chargé d'affaires, shakes hands with U.S. Deputy Secretary of State Walter Stoessel, Jr., after depositing the instrument of NATO ratification at the State Department on May 30.
UPI

UCD hopes for reelection were their poor showing in the Andalusian elections and the tensions that were generated in June when light sentences were passed on 32 members of the armed forces and one civilian accused of trying to overthrow the Spanish government in February 1981.

King Juan Carlos I signed a decree on August 27 dissolving the Cortes in preparation for an early election on October 28. During preparation for the election the national executive of the UCD rejected a proposal to form an electoral alliance with the AP. Lavilla Alsina had threatened to resign as UCD president if the proposal were accepted. His principal complaint concerned the AP's plans to reform the constitution should it gain power in the elections. The PSOE, meanwhile, made a preelectoral alliance with the PAD and proposed in a manifesto that a referendum be held on Spanish membership in NATO, which had become effective on May 30, and that no postelectoral alliance would be formed with the Communists.

The PSOE swept to a landslide victory in the general elections. In a 75% turnout they gained 202 seats in the lower chamber and 134 senators. The AP placed second with 106 deputies and 54 senate seats. The UCD representation was reduced to 12 deputies; the premier and 11 Cabinet ministers were among those who lost their seats. On November 18 the Cortes convened and took the oath to the constitution. Gregorio Peces Barba and José Federico de Caravajal, both Socialists, were elected speakers of the Congress and the Senate, respectively. Following the election results the UCD executive committee resigned; Santiago Carrillo was replaced as PCE secretary-general by Gerardo Iglesias; and Blás Piñar's Fuerza Nueva, the extreme right-wing Fascist organization, decided to cease operating as a political party because it failed to return a single member to the new Cortes.

King Juan Carlos formally opened the new session of the Cortes on November 25. During his discourse the king lent crucial support to the normalization process of Spain's young democracy by condemning terrorism and any future attempt to overthrow the system by military or civilian elements. The following day Premier-elect Felipe González Marquez announced a 14-member Cabinet. Among the first measures taken by the new government were the devaluation of the peseta by 8% and the opening of Spain's frontier with Gibraltar.

SRI LANKA

The government of Pres. Junius Jayawardene announced in August 1982 that Sri Lanka's presidential election would be held on October 20, more than a year ahead of schedule, giving a splintered opposition little time to select a common candidate. The main opposition to President Jayawardene, candidate of the ruling United National Party (UNP), was provided by Hector Kobbekaduwa, nominee of former prime minister Sirimavo Bandaranaike's Sri Lanka Freedom Party (SLFP). Bandaranaike herself was barred from contesting the election because of the 1980 court order stripping her of civil rights for seven years for alleged abuses of power. Four other candidates, representing the Trotskyist groups and the Tamil Congress, commanded only limited support. In the election Jayawardene was returned with almost 53% of the vote.

Jayawardene declared a state of emergency on July 30 after Sinhalese and Muslims clashed in the southern part of the island, leaving three dead and more than 100 injured. There was another state of emergency on election night as UNP and SLFP supporters clashed. After the election Jayawardene claimed that a faction of the SLFP had planned to assassinate him if their candidate had won. He announced that, rather than wait for elections due in 1983, a referendum would be held to decide whether the current Parliament should be extended to August 1989. The referendum was held on December 22, and a 55% majority approved the measure.

STAMPS AND COINS

During an unsettled year, an important development concerned arrangements for the future of Stanley Gibbons International. The Swedish conglomerate Esselte disposed of the purely philatelic stock to a consortium of Gibbons directors headed by David Stokes, the managing director, who remained when Letraset (the owners since 1978) sold out to Esselte in 1981.

Values continued to slump for stamps in general but held up well for really rare stamps and excep-

The highest price ever paid for an ancient coin—$120,000—was fetched by a Roman coin struck about 300 AD. It had been in the collection of a Chicago brewer who died in 1926.
UPI

tional pieces of postal history. As expected, the collapse was most marked in the 1977 and 1978 "omnibus" issues for the British Silver Jubilee and 25th anniversary of the coronation of Queen Elizabeth II.

A three-day Robson Lowe-Christies sale in Zürich, Switz., in May realized SFr 1,500,665 ($701,245); Swiss stamps accounted for SFr 119,278, with an 1849 Vaud 4-centime cantonal on cover selling at SFr 40,500 ($18,925). In London, Sotheby's philatelic department enjoyed outstanding progress handling, among other specialized properties, the remarkable collection of Cape of Good Hope stamps formed by Sir Maxwell Joseph.

The U.S. and Sweden approved a common design for a stamp to be issued in 1983 commemorating the 1783 treaty between the two nations.
WIDE WORLD

Sotheby's also sold a copy of the rare *Official History of Postage Stamps of Japan* (published by the Japanese Post Office in 1896) for a remarkable £1,700 ($2,931), a new record for a philatelic publication. A world record for a Chinese stamp, $44,000, was realized in May for the 1897 one-dollar (Chinese) postal surcharge on a three-cent revenue stamp at a George Alevizos sale held in Santa Monica, Calif.

The first International Philatelic Federation-sponsored international exhibitions to be held in India and Japan took place in New Delhi and Tokyo, respectively, at the end of 1981. The main awards at Tokyo were: Grand Prix d'Honneur, E. M. Bustamente (Spain) for Peru; Grand Prix International, G. Barcella (Italy) for Papal States; and Grand Prix National, Y. Watanabe (Japan) for Japan 1871–79. The major international exhibition, PHILEXFRANCE, was held in Paris in June 1982. The main awards were: Grand Prix d'Honneur, E. Antonini (Switz.) for specialized Egypt; Grand Prix International, "Vreneli" (Switz.) for Switzerland 1843–82; and Grand Prix National, F. Pineau (France) for French postal reform of 1848. At the British Philatelic Federation congress held in July at Southampton, two new signatories to the Roll of Distinguished Philatelists were Herman Branz (West Germany) and Bernard A. Henning (U.S.). The Philatelic Congress medal was awarded to Bernard Lucas of Leeds, England, and the Lichtenstein Medal of the Collectors Club of New York to Robert G. Stone of Blue Ridge Summit, Pa.

Coins

The U.S. was one of several countries making major coinage changes in 1982 to reduce the cost of manufacturing money. In January U.S. Federal Reserve banks released into circulation the first Lincoln cents minted out of zinc plated with copper. By year's end government bureaucrats had discontinued production of the "traditional Lincolns," comprised mostly of copper, despite warnings of some experts that the new zinc coins would not wear well. Except for the wartime "steel pennies" of 1943, copper had been the primary metal used in all U.S. one-cent pieces since the federal government began issuing coins in 1793. Treasury Department executives estimated that the new metal composition would save taxpayers at least $25 million annually starting in 1983.

The government also abandoned production of the Susan B. Anthony dollar coin following a three-year experiment that failed. The coins were supposed to reduce the demand for $1 bills, thus lowering government printing costs. However, most merchants and consumers refused to use the metal dollars, complaining that people mistook Anthonys for Washington quarters.

In another cost-cutting move, Canada introduced a 12-sided one-cent coin dated 1982 that contained about 10% less copper than the country's traditional round cent. Officials also replaced much of the nickel in Canada's five-cent piece with copper, making the 1982-dated coins cheaper to produce than the pure-nickel specimens minted from 1955 until 1981.

Artists in Great Britain prepared designs for a one-pound coin scheduled for introduction in April 1983. Undaunted by the failure of the Anthony dollar in the U.S., the British believed the coin would lessen demand for one-pound notes.

Besides cutting costs with zinc cents, the U.S. Mint generated more than $45 million in revenue during 1982 by selling millions of commemorative half-dollars to collectors. The 1982-dated coins, the country's first commemorative halves since 1954, marked George Washington's 250th birthday by depicting a middle-aged Washington astride a horse. They were identical in size and metal composition to half-dollars made for circulation before 1965, the so-called 90% silver specimens. Each contained more than a third of an ounce of silver mixed with a much smaller amount of copper.

The U.S. Congress passed a bill authorizing three new coins to mark the 1984 Summer Olympics in Los Angeles. During 1983 and 1984 the Mint would produce and sell two types of silver dollars and a $10 gold piece, in part to raise money for the Olympics. The country had last struck a gold coin in 1933.

For persons owning rare coins as an investment, 1982 was a disappointment as prices plummeted. By year's end several numismatic collectibles were worth only half their value at the peak of the market boom in 1979 and early 1980. Still, over the past ten years, the annual return on the typical rare coin collection had been a robust 22.5%, according to a midsummer survey by a Wall street securities firm.

STATE GOVERNMENTS, U.S.

Democrats made major gains in 1982 state elections, adding a net seven governorships and extending their domination of state legislatures. After picking up 200 seats in the November balloting, Democrats controlled both chambers in 34 state legislatures, while Republicans had a two-house majority in only 11. All states were solidly Democratic except Alaska, Arizona, Colorado, Idaho, Indiana, Kansas, New Hampshire, South Dakota, Utah, Vermont, and Wyoming (where Republicans had control in both houses); Montana, New York, North Dakota, and Pennsylvania (where Republicans controlled the upper house and Democrats the lower); and Nebraska (a nonpartisan, one-house legislature). Republicans captured the governorship from Democratic control in California and New Hampshire, but Democrats regained the gubernatorial office from the GOP in Alaska, Arkansas, Michigan, Minnesota, Nebraska, Nevada, Ohio, Texas, and Wisconsin.

Government Structures and Powers

Economic hard times and single-issue enthusiasm led to a 50-year high in voter ballot initiatives during 1982. The National Conference of State Legislatures counted nearly 300 measures on the ballot in 42 states, the highest total since the depression of the 1930s. Some observers feared that the development represented a lack of confidence in elected officials and a weakening of representative democracy.

It was not a boom year for state government. Financial pressures, including declining federal aid, caused employment in state and local public jobs to decline for the first time since World War II. Numerous bond issues were defeated. Georgia voters approved a new state constitution, but proposals to liberalize gubernatorial term length or succession restrictions in Georgia, New Hampshire, North Dakota, and Rhode Island were rejected. New Hampshire voters called for a state constitutional convention. Alaska voters refused to fund, and thus apparently killed, a $2.8 billion project to move the state capital from Juneau to the village of Willow. Voters in the District of Columbia narrowly approved a constitution for a new state of New Columbia. The controversial document guarantees a job or adequate income for all, but observers doubted that even a model draft would prompt Congress to establish a 51st state in the foreseeable future.

Government Relations

For the second consecutive year Pres. Ronald Reagan's "new federalism" program bogged down in controversy over funding. Reagan made an attempt to revitalize the concept in his January 1982 state of the union address, calling for "a single bold stroke" that would have the states take over responsibility for basic welfare and food stamp programs while the federal government assumed all costs of Medicaid. He also offered to turn back to the states up to 40 federal programs, from child nutrition to sewerage aid, along with some revenue to fund them.

But critics charged that the presidential initiative was merely a thinly disguised effort to divert attention from shortcomings in the administration's federal budgetary proposals. A Congressional Budget Office study faulted early administration estimates that the Reagan program would be a no-cost "wash," calculating instead that the swap would cost hard-pressed states about $15 billion in the first year and more after that.

Alaska became the 31st state to demand a constitutional convention that would consider a balanced federal budget; 34 states are required in order to convene such a body. Under that pressure the U.S. Congress hastened to consider a balanced budget amendment, but the House of Representatives defeated it in September. Amendment advocates promised a renewed drive in state legislatures during 1983. Alaska joined the "Sagebrush Rebellion" as voters laid formal claim to most federal lands within the state. Backers of a worldwide nuclear weapons freeze were successful in persuading 11 states to register advisory opinions on the question during 1982. Legislators in Connecticut and Vermont and voters in California, Massachusetts, Michigan, Montana, New Jersey, North Dakota, Oregon, and Rhode Island approved the freeze recommendation, while Arizona voters rejected it.

States engaged in a significant number of squabbles among themselves, some of them serious. A "Great New England trucking fee war" escalated after Vermont began charging entering truckers a toll of $15, but the warfare wound down after six states agreed to a compact banning all such fees. Another short-lived flare-up started late in the year when New York City authorities discovered that 17-cent Connecticut highway tokens fit into 75-cent city subway turnstiles.

Finances and Taxes

Buffeted by a prolonged recession, cuts in federal aid, high unemployment, and reduced tax revenue, state treasury officials faced unprecedented problems in attempting to balance their budgets during 1982. By midyear 17 states had taken the unpopular election-year step of raising taxes, but many of those same states were forced to cut budgets and boost tax rates again later in the year. Even so, seven states ended their fiscal years with an illegal deficit, and a record six states had their bond ratings lowered by a major market service.

A survey by the Tax Foundation reported that 22 states enacted well over $3 billion in tax increases during the year, with four-fifths of the additional revenue being derived from broadly based general sales and personal income taxes that are especially unpopular with voters. Michigan, Minnesota, New Jersey, Ohio, and Oregon raised their personal income taxes, usually by adding a surcharge to existing rates. Florida, Minnesota, Missouri, Nebraska, New Jersey, Washington, and Wisconsin boosted sales taxes, Missouri doing so in exchange for property tax reductions. Nebraska, Rhode Island, and Vermont increased their personal income tax rates to offset decreases in federal taxes to which the state levies are tied.

The fiscal situation forced many states into dramatic belt-tightening measures. The U.S. Bureau of the Census reported that the number of state and local government workers declined in fiscal 1982 from 13.3 million to 13.1 million as 43 states reported laying off workers during the year. Indiana, Kentucky, Missouri, New York, Nebraska, and Michigan admitted that they were slowing down payment of income tax refunds in order to harbour cash.

Figures accumulated in 1982 showed that state revenue from all sources totaled $310.8 billion during the 1981 fiscal year, an increase of 12.2% over the preceding 12 months. General revenue (excluding state liquor and state insurance trust revenue) was $258.2 billion, up 10.5%. Total state expenditures rose 13.1% to $291.5 billion, creating a surplus of $19.3 billion for the year. General expenditures,

A nationwide crackdown on drunken drivers was fueled by scenes such as this one in Washington, D.C. Some 25,000 persons die yearly as a result of drunken driving.
© MARK REINSTEIN—
PHOTOREPORTERS

GOOD LUCK!

AUTH

CALIF

OHIO

PENNA

States found themselves left more and more to their own resources and ingenuity as continuing economic distress eroded the federal government's ability to assist them.

©1982 PHILADELPHIA INQUIRER

not including outlays of the liquor stores and insurance trust systems, amounted to $253.7 billion, up 11.1% for the year.

While most states grappled with drastic funding problems, oil-rich Alaska arranged to give $1,000 in excess tax receipts to each person residing in the state for at least six months. An earlier plan to give citizens $50 for each year of state residence was struck down by the U.S. Supreme Court as discriminatory. The giveaway quickly hit a snag, however: although latest census data listed Alaska's population at 400,418, more than 475,000 "residents" signed up for the $1,000 payment.

Ethics

For the first time in a decade present and past state governors avoided involvement in major misconduct charges, a development partially attributable to a national shift in FBI priorities away from white-collar crime and toward combating drug trafficking and organized crime. Charles Roemer, former Louisiana administration commissioner, was sentenced to three years in prison in January after his conviction for conspiring to receive kickbacks from state insurance contracts. New Jersey state senator William V. Musto was convicted in March and sentenced to seven years for arranging kickbacks on school renovation projects. Rep. Tommy Burnett, majority leader of the Tennessee House of Representatives, pleaded guilty in June to three misdemeanour charges; he was accused of failing to report $768,088 in income over three years. Richard Wertz pleaded guilty in October to theft of $18,685 from the Arizona Justice Planning Agency, which he formerly had headed; Wertz was fined $21,800 and sentenced to five years in prison. Nevada state senator Eugene Echols was indicted on bribery charges in December after allegedly accepting $6,000 from an FBI undercover agent.

Oklahoma legislators revamped county commissioner financial laws in the aftermath of a statewide bid-rigging scandal over paving contracts. Alaska

also tightened state contracting safeguards. Louisiana mandated financial disclosure for state political candidates. Virginia strengthened legislative ethics rules but weakened its freedom of information act by allowing more meetings and records to be closed. Arizona opened additional meetings to the public while reducing some penalties for violation of disclosure laws. Ohio and Michigan voters decisively rejected proposals for public financing of utility commissioner election campaigns.

Education

Southern states were stunned by a U.S. Supreme Court decision requiring that a free public education be provided for children of illegal aliens. Federal courts struck down Louisiana and Arkansas laws requiring the teaching of "scientific creationism," the biblical version of creation, alongside scientific evolutionism in public schools. Joining ten other states with existing programs, California, New Mexico, Oklahoma, South Carolina, and Texas provided for mandatory testing of public-school teachers.

West Virginia and Vermont moved to equalize spending between wealthy and poor school districts, but a Colorado appellate court overturned a 1979 lower court decision requiring similar action. Iowa and Massachusetts began selling tax-exempt bonds to replace dwindling federal student loan funds.

Drugs

A nationwide lobbying effort by traffic victim groups such as Mothers Against Drunk Driving (MADD) and Remove Intoxicated Drivers (RID) resulted in a marked stiffening by 27 states of their driving-while-intoxicated laws during 1982. Some states mandated minimum jail terms even for first offenders under aggravated circumstances. Iowa provided for automatic revocation of license for some first offenders. Maryland, Minnesota, Utah, and Idaho slashed the blood alcohol content level required for a drunk-driving conviction, and Arizona, Kansas, and Wyoming eliminated plea bargain-

Among the 45 delegates to the District of Columbia's constitutional convention were (left to right) Talmadge Moore, Hilda Mason, Harry Thomas, and Franklin Kameny. Their final proposal was narrowly approved by voters.

GEORGE TAMES / THE NEW YORK TIMES

ing to ensure integrity of records for repeat offenders.

Connecticut, Maryland, New Jersey, New York, and Ohio raised the minimum drinking age during the year. Of the 29 states that lowered the drinking age during the mid-1970s, 20 had reversed themselves by the end of 1982; only 5 still allowed 18-year-olds to drink liquor. Many states claimed markedly improved traffic death figures following the law changes.

Law and Justice

Reacting to perceived abuses, several states moved to curtail the use of the insanity defense in criminal trials. The acquittal of would-be presidential assassin John W. Hinckley, Jr., by reason of insanity added momentum to a growing protest over alleged misuse of the plea. The most radical reform was taken by Idaho and Montana, which abolished the defense altogether. Alaska, Delaware, Georgia, and Kentucky joined four other states in establishing a new verdict—guilty but mentally ill—that provides treatment for a convict but requires a set period of incarceration in the event he or she is cured.

New laws protecting children were enacted by several states. California, Colorado, and Washington toughened laws against child molesting, with California voters abolishing a special diversion program for disordered offenders. Iowa, Vermont, and Washington strengthened laws against child abuse. The U.S. Supreme Court approved a New York law banning the depiction of children in sexually suggestive poses even if the scene is not legally obscene.

Massachusetts joined nine states that had recently expanded the right to use deadly force against intruders in one's home. California, Maryland, and Virginia toughened legal penalties for the use of firearms in commission of a crime, but California voters rejected a major handgun-control initiative. Alabama and Alaska prohibited localities from regulating gun possession, and New Hampshire and Nevada voters expressly reaffirmed their right "to keep and bear arms." New Jersey and Massachusetts during the year became the 36th and 37th states

to enact capital punishment provisions for first-degree murderers.

Environment

An environmentalist-backed drive to require deposits on beverage containers enjoyed mixed success during the year. New York became the ninth state to require a five-cent deposit on plastic, glass, and aluminum containers of beer and soft drinks, and Massachusetts voters rejected a move to repeal that state's similar law. But well-publicized initiatives to extend the idea were rejected overwhelmingly by voters in Arizona, California, Colorado, and Washington, dampening hopes for a national deposit law.

Massachusetts, New Hampshire, New York, and Rhode Island, suspecting adverse impacts on their citizens, sued over plans to build extra-tall smokestacks at several Midwestern pollution centres. And three downstream states, Iowa, Missouri, and Nebraska, filed a legal challenge against South Dakota's 50-year, $1.4 billion contract to provide Missouri River water for a coal slurry pipeline.

Controversy over nuclear energy continued to bubble. Idaho and Massachusetts voters ordered a statewide referendum before any new nuclear plant construction could begin, but a federal judge voided a similar Washington law as an undue impairment of existing contracts. For the second time in three years, Maine voters rejected a move to shut down the state's mammoth Maine Yankee nuclear plant.

Equal Rights

A proposed U.S. constitutional amendment to ban sex discrimination finally died during 1982. The measure received 35 of 38 necessary state ratifications in four years following its approval by Congress, but no state ratified it after 1977 despite congressional extension of the deadline to June 1982.

The U.S. Supreme Court threw out a Washington State initiative to curb school busing because it was "effectively drawn for racial purposes." The high court let stand a similar 1979 California initiative, however, noting the absence of civil rights violations in the state's history.

GOVERNORS OF THE STATES
(With Party Affiliations and Current Terms)

Ala. .... George C. Wallace (D), 1983–87
Alaska .... Bill Sheffield (D), 1982–86
Ariz. .... Bruce Babbitt (D), 1983–87
Ark. .... Bill Clinton (D), 1983–85
Calif. .... George Deukmejian (R), 1983–87
Colo. .... Richard D. Lamm (D), 1983–87
Conn. .... William A. O'Neill (D), 1983–87
Del. .... Pierre S. (Pete) du Pont IV (R), 1981–85
Fla. .... Robert Graham (D), 1983–87
Ga. .... Joe Frank Harris (D), 1983–87
Hawaii .... George Ariyoshi (D), 1982–86
Idaho .... John V. Evans (D), 1983–87
Ill. .... James R. Thompson (R), 1983–87
Ind. .... Robert D. Orr (R), 1981–85
Iowa .... Terry Branstad (R), 1983–87
Kan. .... John Carlin (D), 1983–87
Ky. .... John Y. Brown (D), 1979–83
La. .... David C. Treen (R), 1980–84
Maine .... Joseph E. Brennan (D), 1983–87
Md. .... Harry R. Hughes (D), 1983–87
Mass. .... Michael S. Dukakis (D), 1983–87
Mich. .... James J. Blanchard (D), 1983–87
Minn. .... Rudy Perpich (D), 1983–87
Miss. .... William Winter (D), 1980–84
Mo. ..... Christopher S. (Kit) Bond (R), 1981–85
Mont. .... Ted Schwinden (D), 1981–85
Neb. .... Bob Kerrey (D), 1983–87
Nev. .... Richard H. Bryan (D), 1983–87
N.H. .... John H. Sununu (R), 1983–85
N.J. .... Thomas H. Kean (R), 1982–86
N.M. .... Toney Anaya (D), 1983–87
N.Y. .... Mario M. Cuomo (D), 1983–87
N.C. .... James B. Hunt, Jr. (D), 1981–85
N.D. .... Allen I. Olson (R), 1981–85
Ohio .... Richard F. Celeste (D), 1983–87
Okla. .... George Nigh (D), 1983–87
Ore. .... Victor G. Atiyeh (R), 1983–87
Pa. .... Richard L. Thornburgh (R), 1983–87
R.I. .... J. Joseph Garrahy (D), 1983–85
S.C. .... Richard W. Riley (D), 1983–87
S.D. .... William J. Janklow (R), 1983–87
Tenn. .... Lamar Alexander (R), 1983–87
Texas .... Mark White (D), 1983–87
Utah .... Scott M. Matheson (D), 1981–85
Vt. .... Richard A. Snelling (R), 1983–85
Va. .... Charles S. Robb (D), 1982–86
Wash. .... John Spellman (R), 1981–85
W.Va. .John D. (Jay) Rockefeller IV (D), 1981–85
Wis. .... Anthony S. Earl (D), 1983–87
Wyo. .... Ed Herschler (D), 1983–87

STOCKS AND BONDS

The stock market turned in one of its best postwar performances in 1982, with record highs achieved by the leading indexes and very heavy turnover as a result of major institutional participation. On August 18 volume on the New York Stock Exchange (NYSE) reached 132.7 million shares, the first time in the history of the exchange that trading during one day had exceeded 100 million shares.

On August 17 Henry Kaufman, a leading stock market economist, predicted that interest rates would decline in 1983. This set off a major rally that lasted until November 3. The Dow Jones Industrial Average advanced 37% from 777 to 1,065 in the period. It ended the year at 1,046.54, a 19.6% gain for the year. The Standard & Poor's 500 at 140.64 was up 14.8% for the year, and the Nasdaq composite index of over-the-counter issues gained 18.7% to 232.41. The American Stock Exchange (Amex) market value index, however, gained only 6.2% for the year to end at 340.60.

The fundamental explanation for the market's sharp advance and its volatility lay in the sharp decline in interest rates, expectations of a lower rate of inflation, and optimistic projections for economic recovery. The markets were increasingly dominated by institutional investors making trades of large blocks of shares. Erosion in the size of stock commissions, largely owing to the work of discount brokers, improvements in communications, and the development of options and stock futures all contributed to the boom in the last half of 1982.

The Dow Jones Industrial Average rose by 171.54 points over the year as a whole. From its starting point at 875, the average trailed irregularly through March, when the lowest level in 23 months was achieved at 795.47. In mid-August the bull market took off, and records began to be established on a daily basis as volume and price levels climbed. On December 27 the Dow Jones reached 1,070.55, an all-time high.

Interest rates remained at 1981 levels during the first half of 1982, with the prime rate beginning the year at 15.75%, rising to 17% in February, and remaining in the 16.5% range until July. At that time interest rates began one of their sharpest plunges in postwar history, to end the year at 11.5%. Thirty-year U.S. Treasury bonds, which started 1982 at 14% and peaked at 14.1% in June, dropped to 10.4% by the year's end. The discount rate, which is the rate charged by the Federal Reserve on loans to banks and savings institutions, was 12% in mid-July but only 8.5% at the end of the year.

Volume on the NYSE established many records in 1982. Stock sales were 16,458,036,768, up 39% from 1981. The largest daily volume was set on November 4, when 149,385,480 shares were traded; the largest number of blocks (10,000 shares or more) traded was 2,530, set on October 7; and the largest single block, 6,290,700 shares of Federal National Mortgage Corp., was traded on September 10. Av-

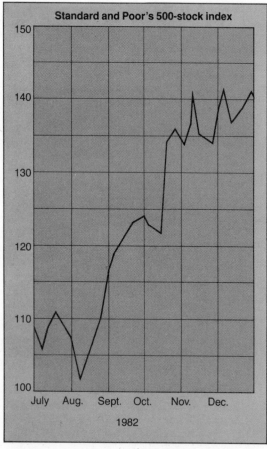

Standard and Poor's 500-stock index

150
140
130
120
110
100

July Aug. Sept. Oct. Nov. Dec.

1982

erage daily turnover was 65 million shares, well above the 1981 level of 46.8 million per day.

Spurred by institutional investors, the well-known stocks led the turnover race. The most active stocks on the NYSE were IBM Corp. with 216,642,200 shares traded, Exxon Corp. 213,104,000, AT&T 181,655,700, Sony Corp. 137,316,600, and Sears, Roebuck and Co. 129,202,300. The leading gainers in 1982 were the automobile companies, the average prices of which rose 81.62%; they were led by Chrysler Corp., which increased 419% for the year. The worst performing groups were offshore drilling, coal, and oil-well equipment. Bond sales on the NYSE were $7,155,443,000 (at par value), up 41% from the 1981 level of $5,059,309,000.

While all of the major exchanges topped their 1981 volume totals, the gains were less impressive than those posted by the NYSE. On the Amex turnover was 1,337,820,000 shares, a slight decline from the 1981 figure. Bond sales on the Amex rose $325,240,000 in 1982, up only 8% from 1981 and below the level achieved in 1980. The regional markets enjoyed a banner year in regard to their turnover in NYSE-listed issues. The Midwest Stock Exchange recorded a volume of 983,988,000 shares for the first 11 months, a gain of 283,158,000 shares over the 1981 total. The Pacific Stock Exchange traded

593,559,000 during the first 11 months, up 141,968,000 over all of 1981. The National Association of Securities dealers reported 484,651,000 NYSE stocks traded over-the-counter through November 1982, up 165,570,000 over the full year of 1981. Over-the-counter activity expanded by 7.7% as volume on Nasdaq reached 8,432,274,885 shares.

Mutual funds of all types enjoyed record sales growth in 1982, with total industry assets of $300 billion and 21 million shareholder accounts by the year's end. Mutual funds other than short-term funds registered sales of $14.9 billion in 1982, a 50% gain over the record set in 1980. Short-term funds set sales records of their own. Assets of short maturity tax-exempt bond funds rose to $14 billion in 1982, three times their size in 1981. Money market funds, which fell sharply in the last half of December, had assets of about $215 billion, up nearly 20% in 1982. Common stock funds also posted record sales. Equity mutual funds gained an average of 25.03%. Money market fund assets began dropping in December as new deposit accounts offered by banks and thrift institutions drained off funds.

The Standard & Poor's Composite Index of 500 stocks, which had drifted downward listlessly in 1981 and early 1982, made a turnaround in August. The 400 stocks represented in the Industrial Average paralleled the composite, surpassing the monthly figure for 1981 in September.

Yields on U.S. government long-term bonds began 1982 at 13.73, well above the corresponding January 1981 figure of 11.65, but they then dipped progressively through May. After a short pickup in June to 13.32, the average dropped steadily through the remainder of the year. Although the rally cooled off in the final two months of 1982, prices of long-term Treasury issues at the year's end were up more than 30% from June levels and about 25% from the end of 1981. High-grade U.S. corporate bond prices were well below 1981 levels in the early months of 1982 but rose from 30.9 in January to 34 in May. After an interruption in June and July, prices rose throughout the last half of the year.

Options trading rose sharply in 1982 as the bull market took hold and new products, new markets, and the internationalization of financial futures became more widespread. Volume on the Chicago Board of Trade Options Exchange (CBOE) rose nearly one-third in 1982 to 75.7 million contracts. Options trading on the Amex increased 11% to 38.7 million contracts.

During 1982 U.S. Treasury bond futures became the most widely traded futures in the world, ahead of wheat, soybeans, and pork bellies. Market participants used financial futures to reduce interest-rate risk. Daily dollar volume of trading in Treasury bill futures ranged between $25 billion and $30 billion. While Treasury bonds and bills were the most actively traded contracts, Certificates of Deposit, Eurodollars, Treasury notes, and stock indexes were also listed for trading.

The Supreme Court struck down a Texas statute that had effectively barred children of illegal aliens from free public education.

SKELTON/DALLAS TIMES HERALD

SUPREME COURT, U.S.

A president of the United States cannot be sued for his official actions even if they are illegal, the Supreme Court ruled in 1982. In other decisions the court strengthened the powers of law enforcement officials, put a new restriction on the death penalty, gave schools responsibility for teaching children of illegal aliens, eased rules for education of the deaf, and strengthened the rights of natural parents to custody of their children.

The ruling on the presidency came in a suit against former president Richard M. Nixon. Former Pentagon budget analyst A. Ernest Fitzgerald charged he had been fired in 1969 because of a White House conspiracy after he exposed an embarrassing cost overrun in the construction of the C-5A transport plane. Nixon already had paid Fitzgerald $142,000 to settle the case without a trial on its merits and had agreed to pay an extra $28,000 if the court turned down his claim of immunity.

In a bitterly contested 5–4 decision, the justices ruled no president may be sued for his official actions in office. This absolute immunity is necessary, the court said, because the president's energies must not be diverted by concern over possible private lawsuits. The immunity does not apply to criminal cases; the court specifically reaffirmed its 1974 ruling that Nixon had to deliver tapes related to the Watergate trials. Further, Justice Lewis F. Powell, Jr., noted in the majority opinion, "There remains the constitutional remedy of impeachment," as well as congressional and press scrutiny.

Nevertheless, the minority opinion by Justice Byron White insisted the ruling "places the president above the law. It is a reversion to the old notion that the king can do no wrong." White called the ruling "tragic."

Presidential assistants are entitled only to qualified immunity, the court ruled in a related 8–1 decision. The conditions for this immunity, previously extended to Cabinet officers, governors, and other high officials, were eased. Immunity formerly depended on an official's proving that he acted without malice and that he could not have been expected to know that his action was illegal. The new decision dropped the need to prove absence of malice, in effect making it easier for officials to defend themselves in court. Fitzgerald's suit against Nixon assistants Bryce Harlow and Alexander Butterfield then was sent back to lower federal courts for further action under the new rules.

Death sentences for people who participate in a crime that results in murder, but who did not intend to kill anyone, were barred as cruel and unusual punishment. Justice White noted that state laws and recent jury verdicts had overwhelmingly rejected death sentences for so-called nontriggermen.

A death sentence for an Oklahoma man who was 16 when he murdered a state trooper was overturned. However, the court based its decision only on the trial judge's failure to consider all mitigating factors. Thus, the ruling did not indicate whether there were any circumstances under which the death penalty could be ordered for crimes committed by a juvenile.

The court in effect overturned a 1981 ruling that police need a warrant to search sealed containers in a suspect's car. The new ruling held that when police lawfully stop a car, they can search anything in it that they believe contains incriminating evidence. Auto searches had been a difficult issue for the court ever since 1925, always involving interpretations of the constitutional guarantee against unreasonable searches and seizures. Another decision held that when police accompany an arrested person into his home, they do not need a search warrant to seize evidence that is in plain view. The case involved a student who went to his dormitory room with police to pick up identification papers. While there, the police seized marijuana that was on a desk.

The Illinois village of Hoffman Estates, a Chicago suburb, was allowed to enforce its ordinance regu-

The Supreme Court decided that the president is immune from private lawsuits arising from his official acts. The case involved former air force budget analyst A. Ernest Fitzgerald (right) and former president Richard M. Nixon (left).

LEFT, AGIP/PICTORIAL PARADE; RIGHT, RICARDO WATSON—PICTORIAL PARADE

lating shops that sell drug-related paraphernalia such as rolling papers and water pipes. The village requires such shops to bar minors, to keep a list of customers, and to pay a license fee. Justice Thurgood Marshall, who wrote the majority opinion, noted that 21 states and many localities have laws about so-called head shops. He warned that these might be unconstitutional if they were overly broad or enforced unfairly. This was not the case in Hoffman Estates.

The court acted to curb repeated appeals by state prisoners to the federal courts. An opinion by Justice Sandra Day O'Connor ordered federal courts not to hear petitions charging violations of constitutional rights unless all aspects of the petitions had been heard in state courts. She warned that if a prisoner goes ahead with an appeal of one part of a so-called mixed petition—containing some issues not previously raised in state courts—he risks having federal courts turn down appeals on other parts after the state courts decide on them. This warning, however, did not have the force of an actual decision, since it was not backed by a majority of the court.

Prosecutors were given the right to seek new trials for prisoners whose cases were dismissed because of prosecution misconduct. The court ruled that this did not amount to double jeopardy unless the prisoner could show that the prosecutor intended to cause a mistrial.

In the field of labour law, agreements that require building contractors to do business only with union-labour subcontractors were upheld. State-operated railroads, it was decided, are governed by the national Railway Labor Act, and thus their employees are entitled to strike under certain circumstances.

The legal status of strikes and boycotts for political purposes was left unclear. The court ruled that a boycott of stores in Port Gibson, Miss., by the Na-

tional Association for the Advancement of Colored People was a legitimate use of free speech unless merchants there could prove they were damaged by violence. The boycott was called to force the merchants to expand opportunities for black residents. The court also ruled that a strike by longshoremen who refused to load Soviet-bound cargo because of the Soviet invasion of Afghanistan was a labour dispute covered by a law against court-issued antistrike injunctions. But earlier in 1982 the court allowed companies affected by a similar longshoremen's action to sue for damages caused by an illegal secondary boycott. Chief Justice Warren Burger, in a dissent, complained that there is "no rational way" to reconcile the two rulings on the longshoremen.

So-called testers working for fair-housing groups were allowed to sue landlords who showed bias in leasing practices, even though the testers never actually intended to rent from the landlords they asked about vacancies. Rules for proving that local election laws are racially biased were eased. The court ruled that complainants need not have direct evidence of intentional bias if they can show that a "totality of circumstances" reveals bias. The decision found that an at-large system of electing commissioners in Burke County, Ga., was illegal.

The court let stand a provision in the Copyright Act under which a retail chain was required to pay royalties to the American Society of Composers, Authors and Publishers for broadcasting radio music through loudspeakers in its store. A bankruptcy reform law passed by Congress in 1978 was declared unconstitutional because it vested special bankruptcy judges with broad powers that should belong only to regular federal judges. Under the Constitution, regular judges hold tenure for life and are guaranteed against salary cuts; special judges do not. Congress was given a deadline of October 4—later extended to December 24—to repair the bankruptcy law.

Cities and counties were denied access to raw census records in order to protect the public's confidence in the privacy of the records. The local governments seeking the information wanted to prove that their populations had been undercounted, thus cutting their share of federal aid.

States were forbidden to prevent utilities from exporting electric power to other states. Similarly, a Nebraska rule barring landowners from shipping groundwater to states without reciprocal water agreements was struck down. Cities that regulate private businesses were put on notice that they are governed by antitrust laws unless they are granted exemptions under state law.

An effort by the Oglala Sioux Indian tribe to regain possession of the Black Hills of South Dakota was rejected because the tribe had not made the request to the Indian Claims Commission. In 1980 the court awarded the Sioux Nation $122.5 million for land seized from it. The Oglala tribe, however, was not party to the case but pushed a separate suit for $11 billion in compensation and for the land itself. The tribe also lodged a complaint with the United Nations.

The Jicarilla Apache tribe's right to impose severance taxes on oil and gas taken from its reservation was upheld. The right to tax, the court said, is an essential element of Indian self-government. About 30 tribes had imposed or were considering such taxes.

States were given broad powers to forbid taking or showing sexually explicit photos of children. The ruling included not only legally obscene photos but all others that show sexual conduct by children. State rules against sexual exploitation of children were described as of "surpassing importance." The ruling created a new exception to the constitutional guarantee of freedom of expression.

States were forbidden to take children away from their natural parents without clear proof of neglect or abuse. The question of school library censorship moved a step closer to a decision. The court ruled that students can sue a school board for banning certain books and that the boards cannot suppress ideas simply because they disagree with them.

"Free appropriate education" for all public school children, required under a 1975 law, does not necessarily involve a free sign-language interpreter for a deaf student, the court decided. All the act requires is that handicapped children be provided with enough special services to give them "meaningful access" to education. Federal courts were warned to beware of imposing their own teaching theories on school systems.

The Mississippi University for Women was ordered to admit a male nursing student. This effectively left Texas Women's University as the nation's only all-women state-supported university.

A Maryland law permitting the charging of higher college tuition to foreigners who live in the state but pay little or no state income tax was struck down. A Texas law barring children of illegal aliens from free public schooling was voided as a denial of equal protection under the law. A California law requiring that peace officers be citizens of the United States was upheld.

SWEDEN

Sweden ended a six-year flirtation with non-Socialist rule when, in a general election on Sept. 19, 1982, the Social Democratic Party led by Olof Palme swept back to power, gaining 166 seats in the 349-seat Riksdag (parliament). With the Communists retaining 20 seats, the left-wing parties had an overall majority of 23 over the non-Socialist parties. The latter had governed since 1976, when the Social Democrats were defeated after an unprecedented 44 years in office. The result reflected dissatisfaction with a succession of weak coalition governments and one minority Liberal government. The prime minis-

Former prime minister Olof Palme was returned to power when his Social Democratic Party won Sweden's general election in September.
WIDE WORLD

Supporters of Sweden's extreme right-wing Nordic National Party (NRP) were responsible for defacing this hamburger stand owned by a Turkish immigrant.
WIDE WORLD

ter for most of this time had been Thorbjörn Fälldin, a sheep farmer from the far north and leader of the agrarian-based Centre Party.

The Social Democratic election manifesto contained a pledge to introduce so-called wage-earner funds, under which elected committees of trade unionists would buy shares in private industry. This proposal became the central issue in the election, opposed by the three non-Socialist parties and the subject of a massive advertising campaign by Swedish industry.

After his return to power, however, Palme offered "an outstretched hand" to industry in future negotiations on the funds issue, choosing instead to devalue the krona by a massive 16% and to impose an indefinite price freeze. Palme said the devaluation was intended to restore confidence in the krona and improve conditions for Swedish industry on the international and home markets.

Another of Palme's first actions on assuming office was to announce that in the future foreign submarines caught inside Swedish waters ran the risk of being sunk on direct orders from the government. His tough statement came after the Swedish Navy claimed to have trapped a foreign submarine off its top-secret naval base on the Baltic island of Muskö, 20 mi (32 km) south of Stockholm. Journalists from all over the world had flocked to the site, expecting a rerun of the 1981 incident in which a Soviet Whisky-class submarine ran aground on rocks near the southern naval base of Karlskrona, but they were disappointed. The submarine was generally thought to have smashed its way through an underwater barrier six days after the hunt started on October 1 and to have escaped back into international waters.

The incident raised grave questions concerning Sweden's traditional policy of armed neutrality and the Navy's ability to defend its coastline, and the government announced a commission of inquiry into the affair. This followed a summer during which more than 50 sightings of unidentified submarines in Swedish waters were reported. A further reminder of Sweden's proximity to the Eastern bloc was the

steady stream of refugees from Poland following the imposition of martial law on Dec. 13, 1981. More than 3,000 Poles were granted political asylum in Sweden. The most spectacular escape was the flight of 20 refugees in an old-fashioned crop-spraying biplane across the Baltic Sea to Malmö in October.

There was also a reminder of Sweden's vulnerability to the phenomenon known as acid rain when a four-day ecological symposium took place in Stockholm in June to mark the tenth anniversary of the Stockholm UN Conference on the Human Environment. The symposium called for urgent action to cut sulfur emissions from heavy industry. Scientists claimed that the acid was responsible for killing plant and animal life in about 20,000 Swedish lakes. Sweden was particularly sensitive because its topsoil lacked significant quantities of chalk, which might have had a neutralizing effect on the acid.

SWIMMING

The IV World Aquatics Championships, from July 30 to Aug. 7, 1982, at Guayaquil, Ecuador, were expected to produce the best swimming since the 1976 Olympic Games. Fifty-six nations entered the competition, which consisted of swimming, diving, water polo, and synchronized swimming (synchro).

The medal count proved the U.S. was the top nation overall with 13 gold, 10 silver, and 11 bronze in swimming, diving, and synchro. For the first time points were scored, and the combined total from swimming, diving, water polo, and synchro determined the overall champion. The U.S. scored 840, followed by the Soviet Union with 587.5 and East Germany with 583.5. But in swimming, at the new multimillion-dollar Alberto Vallarino pool, the U.S. team won 8 of 29 events. The East Germans won 12 gold medals, 8 silver, and 5 bronze. Ten of the gold were won by women. The U.S. won 8 gold (6 by men), 8 silver, and 9 bronze. The Soviet Union was third, with 4 gold, 7 silver, and 3 bronze.

The ten-day tournament produced seven world swimming records. The outstanding swimmer of the meet was East Germany's Petra Schneider, who set a world record of 4 min 36.10 sec in the 400-m individual medley. Her old mark was 4 min 36.29 sec. Schneider also won the 200-m individual medley, placed second in the 400-m freestyle, and placed fourth in the 800-m freestyle. Another outstanding East German was Cornelia Sirch, who swam the 200-m backstroke in 2 min 9.91 sec, lowering the previous world mark by almost two seconds. An East German team of Kristin Otto, Ute Geweniger, Ines Geissler, and Birgit Meineke set a new 4 x 100-m medley relay world record of 4 min 5.88 sec. Annemarie Verstappen of The Netherlands became the first Dutch woman to win a major swimming title since the 1968 Olympics, taking the gold in the 200-m freestyle and a silver in the 100-m freestyle. The U.S. women gold medalists were Kim Linehan in the 800-m freestyle and Mary T. Meagher in the 100-m butterfly.

In men's competition Canada's Victor Davis was timed in 2 min 14.77 sec in the 200-m breaststroke to erase the six-year-old mark of 2 min 15.11 sec by David Wilkie of the U.K. at the 1976 Olympics. Steve Lundquist, the U.S. world record holder in the 100-m breaststroke, held off Davis by 0.07 sec to win his specialty. On July 19 at the U.S. team trials Lundquist had lowered his world record with a 1 min 2.62 clocking, and then on August 21 at the U.S. championships in Indianapolis, Ind., he set another new record of 1 min 2.53 sec. Ricardo Prado of Brazil set a world record and won the first world title by a South American by taking the 400-m individual medley in 4 min 19.78 sec, faster by 0.27 sec than the old mark established by Jesse Vassallo of the U.S. in the 1978 world meet. U.S. relay teams set two world records; the 4 x 100-m freestyle mark was lowered to 3 min 19.26 sec and that of the 4 x 100-m medley relay to 3 min 40.84 sec.

Rowdy Gaines, the U.S. world record holder in the 100-m and 200-m freestyle, could do no better than second in those events, losing to East Germany's Jorg Woithe in the 100 m and West Germany's Michael Gross in the 200 m. Gaines did win three gold medals, but he did so as a member of three winning relays. In July Gaines had set a world mark of 1 min 48.93 sec for the 200-m freestyle at the U.S. team trials.

Earlier in the year Soviet Olympic champion Vladimir Salnikov set new world records in the 400-m, 800-m, and 1,500-m freestyle events with times of 3 min 49.57 sec, 7 min 52.83 sec, and 14 min 56.35 sec, respectively. Salnikov and teammate Sviatoslav Semenov finished 1-2 in both the 400-m and 1,500-m freestyle in the world championships.

For the first time since the event was included in the world championships the U.S. failed to win the synchronized swimming team title. Nor did it win the duet crown. The Canadians won two gold medals and one silver, led by Kelly Kryczka and Sharon Hambrook, victors in the duet. Tracie Ruiz won the solo for the only U.S. gold medal.

At the XII Commonwealth Games, September 30–October 9 at Brisbane, Australia, the outstanding swimmer was Alex Baumann of Canada, who on October 4 lowered his world record in the 200-m individual medley from 2 min 2.78 sec to 2 min 2.25 sec. He also won the 400-m individual medley crown. Lisa Curry of Australia was the outstanding woman swimmer, winning titles in the 100-m butterfly and 200-m and 400-m individual medley. Commonwealth records were set in five men's events and five women's. Canada won six gold medals in men's races, followed by Australia with five and the U.K. with four. In women's competition Australia won eight gold medals, with Canada and the U.K. winning three each.

Diving

At the world championships in Guayaquil the U.S., led by Greg Louganis, made diving history. Louganis completed an almost faultless dive by scoring four 10s out of a possible seven for a forward 3½ somersault. His winning springboard aggregate of 752.67 was an amazing 116.52 points over silver medalist Sergey Kuzmin of the Soviet Union. In the platform competition, for the first time in modern international diving, Louganis obtained a clean sweep of seven 10s for his inward 1½ somersault. This perfect dive enabled him to outpoint Vladimir Aleinik of the Soviet Union 634.26 to 629.85. In the women's springboard U.S. divers finished first and second, the first time a nation had ever achieved this in world championship diving. Megan Neyer out-

Tracy Caulkins (right) won her 37th U.S. swimming title in April, bettering Johnny Weismuller's 54-year-old record. Ricardo Prado (far right) of Brazil set a world record in the 400-metre individual medley in August.

PHOTOS. UPI

World Swimming Records Set in 1982			
Event	Name	Country	Time
MEN			
200-m freestyle	Rowdy Gaines	U.S.	1 min 48.93 sec
400-m freestyle	Vladimir Salnikov	U.S.S.R.	3 min 49.57 sec
800-m freestyle	Vladimir Salnikov	U.S.S.R.	7 min 52.83 sec
1,500-m freestyle	Vladimir Salnikov	U.S.S.R.	14 min 56.35 sec
100-m breaststroke	Steve Lundquist	U.S.	1 min 2.62 sec
100-m breaststroke	Steve Lundquist	U.S.	1 min 2.53 sec
200-m breaststroke	Victor Davis	Canada	2 min 14.77 sec
200-m individual medley	Alex Baumann	Canada	2 min 2.25 sec
400-m individual medley	Ricardo Prado	Brazil	4 min 19.78 sec
4 × 100-m freestyle relay	U.S. national team (Chris Cavanaugh, Robin Leamy, David McCagg, Rowdy Gaines)	U.S.	3 min. 19.26 sec
4 × 100-m medley relay	U.S. national team (Rick Carey, Steve Lundquist, Matt Gribble, Rowdy Gaines)	U.S.	3 min 40.84 sec
WOMEN			
200-m backstroke	Cornelia Sirch	E. Ger.	2 min 9.91 sec
400-m individual medley	Petra Schneider	E. Ger.	4 min 36.10 sec
4 × 100-m medley relay	East German national team (Kristin Otto, Ute Geweniger, Ines Geissler, Birgit Meineke)	E. Ger.	4 min 5.88 sec

pointed teammate Chris Seufert by 11.01 points, 501.03 to 490.02. In the platform event Wendy Wyland moved up on the leaders from China, and after her seventh dive she had clinched the gold medal with a score of 438.78. Ramona Wenzel of East Germany slipped by the favoured Chinese for second place.

At the Commonwealth Games Chris Snode of the U.K. repeated his 1978 performances, winning both the springboard and platform titles. In women's competition Australia's Jenny Donnet and Valerie Beddoe won the springboard and platform, respectively.

SWITZERLAND

The year's most dramatic event was the federal plebiscite of Nov. 28, 1982, in which a majority of voters unexpectedly approved introduction of a constitutional amendment calling for a system of permanent price control. The amendment was proposed in a popular initiative launched by consumer organizations. In a rather normal 32% turnout, 57.9% voted in favour and 42.1% against. As in the case of other popular initiatives, the federal government submitted its own counterproposal, which called for control of prices only in emergencies and for a limited period. This counterproject was defeated by a vote of 75% against. The simultaneous submission of a popular initiative and a government counterproposal, with the proviso that the citizens could vote "no" for both but "yes" for only one, was in itself a topic of controversy, involving as it did the increasingly complex procedures of "direct" democracy.

Against a general background of prosperity, apprehension about the future of the economy spread toward year's end in the wake of successive statistical reports on the "partial" unemployment introduced in the machine and watchmaking industries, in particular. While the proportions involved were modest compared with those experienced in other industrialized nations, one high official noted that "we are approaching dimensions to which our country is unaccustomed." It was feared that outright dismissals might follow the partial layoffs and reductions in working hours.

The inflationary economic trend continued, though the rate remained much lower than in other industrialized countries. In October the cost of living was reported to have risen by 6.2% during the previous year. The rise of public indebtedness was a cause for concern; the deficit of the federal budget was expected to approach the SFr 3 billion mark (SFr 2.14 = U.S. $1).

Social security and national defense continued to

In a precision 12-minute operation, Swiss police stormed the Polish embassy in Bern and released hostages who had been held for three days by a band of Polish dissidents.
UPI

Members of the fundamentalist Muslim Brotherhood, shown here plotting strategy, staged a fierce three-week-long rebellion that left much of Hamah, Syria, in ruins.
SPENGLER–SYGMA

be the two main priorities of the budget, receiving SFr 4,227,000 and SFr 3,995,000, respectively. While the federal government pleaded for a reduction in military expenditure, the head of the military department called for spending SFr 6 billion on new armaments and installations during 1984–87. At the same time, he appealed for a vote in favour of final and total adhesion to the UN. (The referendum on the issue was unlikely to take place before 1984.) Meanwhile, a committee of centre and right-wing parliamentarians was founded to combat adherence to the UN.

Assistance to less developed countries followed the "Swiss pattern," giving preference to selected bilateral arrangements. Total governmental aid still failed to reach the level stipulated by international authorities. The occupation of the Polish embassy in Bern by a group of Polish dissidents in September was quickly and efficiently ended by the Swiss police, the federal government having declined an offer of assistance from Warsaw.

SYRIA

Pres. Hafez al-Assad of Syria survived a difficult year in 1982, with military setbacks in Lebanon and an uprising by the banned Muslim Brotherhood in the city of Hamah. The balance of payments deficit reached crisis proportions. The Soviet Union was approached for aid on a number of development projects. Crude-oil supplies were being purchased from Iran, underlining a radical alliance between Assad's government and the regime of Ayatollah Ruhollah Khomeini.

The Israeli invasion of Lebanon, which began on June 6, met no significant resistance from the 26,000 troops of the all-Syrian Arab Deterrent Force in Lebanon. They had been deployed in a wide arc curving from Tripoli in the north through the town of Shtawrah in the centre to Sidon in the south. The Syrian Air Force challenged the Israelis as they fired on Syrian missile sites in the Bekaa Valley, but to no avail. Israel claimed to have shot down 86 Syrian aircraft and reported no losses, although in October

Syria claimed that it had shot down 26 Israeli aircraft. The Bekaa sites were destroyed. A further blow to Syrian prestige was its agreement to withdraw its forces from Beirut after August 20. On November 20 President Assad said that Syria would impose no conditions for the withdrawal of all its troops from Lebanon "after a total evacuation of Israeli troops."

The Hamah uprising dramatized the continuing internal opposition to Assad. On February 11 government forces started a drive against antigovernment Muslim Brotherhood militants in the city. Heavy fighting ensued, resulting in the destruction of the city centre and a death toll estimated by Western sources at 3,000–10,000. On February 24 Assad claimed the fighting was over. Government spokesmen alleged that Iraq had supplied weapons to the dissidents.

Syria's antagonism toward Iraq was evident in a decision in April to close its border with Iraq and also the trans-Syrian pipeline. This corresponded with a move to buy 8.7 million metric tons of crude oil a year from Iran starting on April 1. Teheran subsequently announced its willingness to supply Syria with phosphate. This was a far cry from the mood of 1979, when Syria had ambitions for a political union with Iraq. The plans had foundered after the discovery of a coup attempt in which Iraqis were said to be implicated.

The economic picture was bleak. Although oil exports brought in more than $1 billion in 1981, the economic trends bore almost no relation to the optimistic forecasts contained in the five-year (1980–85) plan. The plan targeted an average annual increase in imports of 3.4%, but in 1981—the first full year of the plan—imports rose by 22%. Exports, which had been scheduled to grow by 6.5%, remained almost static. Several European countries complained that they had not been paid for goods or services supplied, while letters of credit were experiencing delays of six to eight months. The only bright spot in the economic outlook was the announcement in August by Marathon Petroleum of a significant gas find at the western edge of its Homs block concession.

In January it was reported that the Soviet Union had agreed to supply additional arms to Syria, while Soviet technical help was expected to increase significantly as the result of an economic cooperation agreement signed on October 31. A specific agreement was initialed on a Soviet study for converting the Damascus-Dara railway to standard gauge. Land improvement, dam building, oil drilling, and expansion at Latakia port were covered in the protocol. It was reported on October 27 that agreement had been reached on the supply of nuclear expertise by the Soviets in exchange for power generation.

At home a rigorous crackdown against corruption was mounted by the government. On September 4 in Hamah, security forces arrested 29 government employees accused of offenses against the state. The manager of a bank in Dara was hanged on August 23 after being convicted of embezzling public funds.

TAIWAN

The future security and status of Taiwan continued in 1982 to cause serious concern to the government and the people of the islands. In 1981 the Chinese Communists laid down a nine-point "peace proposal" for reunification with the mainland. The Communists also pressured the United States to discontinue arms sales to the Nationalists and demanded that countries that had recognized mainland China not have representative agencies on Taiwan. In the midst of those actions and in spite of the strong protests and boycott by China, the fifth World Women's Softball Championship was held in Taipei July 2–12, 1982, with two dozen countries participating.

Because of the development of new weapons by the Communists in recent years, the Nationalists sought to maintain air superiority over the Taiwan Straits by purchasing FX aircraft from the U.S. The administration of U.S. Pres. Ronald Reagan rejected Taiwan's request for the purchase of such advanced aircraft because of China's threat to curtail diplomatic relations with the U.S. if it did so. Instead, the U.S. decided to limit arms sales to Taiwan to spare parts and to extend the F-5E co-production line in Taiwan to strengthen its defensive capability.

The four-day visit to China in May by U.S. Vice-Pres. George Bush demonstrated the interest of the U.S. in maintaining good relations with the Communist regime. From his arrival to his departure Bush reaffirmed that the Reagan administration unequivocally accepted that the Communist regime was the sole legal government of China and that Taiwan was a part of China. While Bush was in Beijing (Peking), President Reagan's letters to the three top Chinese leaders were released; in them Reagan restated the "one China policy" of the U.S. and linked the reduction and termination of U.S. arms sales to Taiwan with the peaceful resolution of the Taiwan question. The Nationalist government and the general public on Taiwan viewed the pronouncements of Reagan and Bush as a setback in relations between the U.S. and Taiwan.

On August 17 the U.S. and China issued a new communiqué on arms sales to Taiwan. In it the U.S. government "recognized the government of the PRC [Communist China] as the sole legal government of China" and stated that it had no intention of "infringing on Chinese sovereignty and territorial integrity'. . . or pursuing a policy of 'two Chinas' or 'one China, one Taiwan.' " Acceding partly to China's demand that arms sales to Taiwan be terminated, the U.S. pledged, for the first time, to reduce, limit, and eventually end such sales. President Reagan stated that the pledge was made on the basis of the Chinese promise to seek reunification with Taiwan

The U.S. told the Chinese Nationalists on Taiwan that they could not purchase advanced FX jet fighters but could continue co-producing the F-5E jets that were the mainstay of its Air Force.

by peaceful means only. On August 21 the New China News Agency on the mainland denied any commitment by China to the U.S. to pursue only a peaceful solution of the Taiwan question. In Taipei the Nationalist government expressed profound regret over the U.S. statement that "it does not seek to carry out a long-term policy of arms sales to Taiwan."

The official Nationalist response to Communist overtures and pressure for unification negotiations, as stated repeatedly by Pres. Chiang Ching-kuo, remained "no contacts, no talks, no compromise" with the Communists. It was feared that under the present circumstances negotiations would only lead to Taiwan's surrender.

The economy of Taiwan, primarily under the system of free enterprise, was approaching the status of a developed country; per capita income rose from $2,378 in 1980 to $2,570 in 1981, ten times that of the Chinese mainland.

The economic growth rate declined from 6.7% in 1980 to 5.5% in 1981. The slowdown was caused by a number of factors, including stagnation in the international economy and a wall of protectionism in world markets.

TANZANIA

To mark the 20th anniversary of Tanzania's independence on Dec. 9, 1981, Pres. Julius Nyerere released 2,749 prisoners and commuted 48 death sentences. The released prisoners did not include persons charged with economic sabotage, and the government's campaign against those believed to have damaged the country's economy continued into 1982.

The prospect of the country's starting the year with a desperate food shortage because of severe drought in 1981 was averted when a number of nations volunteered assistance. Nevertheless, Tanzania's economic position continued to be grave, and President Nyerere announced on March 25 that in its next budget the government would be concentrating upon improving existing industries and services.

The annual congress of the ruling Revolutionary Party (Chama Cha Mapinduzi, or CCM) in October put into effect some of the constitutional changes recommended by an extraordinary session in January. The proposals were aimed at increasing the power of the party and reducing the power of the state, which, in the president's view, had grown disproportionately.

In the 1982 election President Nyerere, chairman of the CCM for 20 years, and Vice-Pres. Aboud Jumbe, vice-chairman since 1972, were elected for additional terms of five years. The president took the opportunity offered by his reelection to reaffirm his commitment to a policy of socialism whatever the difficulties ahead.

At a meeting between President Nyerere and Zambian Pres. Kenneth Kaunda in Lusaka, Zambia, in March an agreement was signed establishing a joint commission of cooperation between their two countries. The presidents also agreed on measures to improve the operation of the Tanzam Railway, which had been working at only a fraction of its capacity because of frequent breakdowns and congestion in the port of Dar es Salaam. Relations with Kenya were further strained when, in October, Tanzania granted political asylum to two men believed to have led the attempted coup against the Kenyan government in August.

TELEVISION AND RADIO

In some form television and radio service was available in all major countries in 1982. Approximately 850 million radio sets were in use, of which about 470 million, or 55%, were in the United States. Television sets numbered about 430 million, of which 171 million, or 40%, were in the U.S.

The Soviet Union ranked next to the U.S. in number of television sets; its total was about 65 million, and Japan was third with 28.8 million, according to estimates prepared for the 1982 *Broadcasting and Cable Yearbook*. Other *Broadcasting* estimates for television sets included West Germany, 21 million; United Kingdom, 18.3 million; France, 17.6 million; Brazil, 15 million; Italy, 13.2 million; Canada, 11.3 million; Spain, 9.4 million; Mexico, 7.5 million; Poland, 7.2 million; Australia, 5.5 million; East Germany, 5.2 million; Argentina, 5.1 million; and The Netherlands, 4 million.

Approximately 7,850 television stations were in operation or under construction throughout the world. Some 2,200 were in the Far East, 2,110 in Western Europe, 1,240 in the U.S., 920 in Eastern Europe, 180 in South America, 105 in Mexico, 100 in Canada, and 45 in Africa. There were about 16,400 radio stations, most of which were amplitude modulation (AM) stations, though the proportion of frequency modulation (FM) outlets was growing. In the U.S. there were 9,698 radio stations, of which 4,892 were FM.

Organization of Services

Broadcasting organizations throughout the world used communications satellites almost routinely to exchange coverage of important news events. Among the most widely distributed in 1982 were the U.S. elections, events surrounding the death of Soviet president Leonid Brezhnev, the war between Great Britain and Argentina over the Falkland Islands, the visit of Pope John Paul II to Spain, the fifth launch and landing of the U.S. space shuttle "Columbia," and such sports events as the baseball World Series and the Wimbledon tennis matches.

In the United States Pres. Ronald Reagan's policy of deregulation continued to free both broadcasters and cable television operators from some of the restrictions that had limited them. The Federal Communications Commission (FCC) formally opened a proceeding aimed at allowing TV networks to again own cable TV systems, a move it had signaled in

Among NBC's brighter new
shows in 1982 was
"Cheers," featuring Ted
Danson and Shelley Long.
NBC PHOTO

1981 when it granted CBS an exception to its network/cable cross-ownership ban. In another, more controversial, proceeding the FCC was considering whether to repeal its prohibition against the ownership by networks of financial interests in programs produced by others and against their engaging in domestic syndication of any programs.

Along with deregulation there was during the year official authorization of several new services, including FCC grants for low-power television stations capable of serving relatively small communities; for direct broadcast satellite distribution of TV programming, which had the potential of rendering local television stations obsolete except for purely local news and programming; and for experiments in teletext, which offered a virtually limitless variety of information on home screens. In radio the FCC authorized the start of AM stereo broadcasting on a free-market basis, allowing stations—and listeners—to decide which of several FCC-approved systems they preferred.

The U.S. Corporation for Public Broadcasting (CPB), dependent on both federal and private financing, found itself in difficulties under the administration's reductions in federal spending. CPB officials told a congressional hearing in February that cuts contemplated for fiscal year 1984 and 1985 could threaten public television's existence, requiring curtailment of program production, hampering stations' ability to attract funds from private sources, and forcing some stations to close. Over a presidential veto Congress restored the 1984 budget to $130 million from the $105.6 million recommended by the administration, but it deferred action on 1985.

Programming

For the first time in three years the opening of the new prime-time season in the U.S. was not delayed by a strike of actors or writers. The season opened

"officially" the week of September 27, although for tactical reasons the networks introduced a few series intermittently before that date and held a few others until later. To make room for the new entries some 18 shows were dropped, including such hits of earlier seasons as "Mork & Mindy," "Barney Miller," and "Taxi" on ABC; "Lou Grant" and "WKRP in Cincinnati" on CBS; and "Harper Valley PTA" on NBC. The new shows replacing them continued, as a group, to reflect a diminishing emphasis on sex and a somewhat more cautious approach to violence. The law-and-order theme evident in 1981–82 lost some of its foremost vehicles with the cancellation of "Today's FBI," "Code Red," and "Strike Force," but adventure shows, often containing violent action, remained numerous.

CBS, first in the prime-time ratings again in the 1981–82 season, prepared a new schedule aimed especially at young adults. Its new series included four half-hour situation comedies and three one-hour dramas. Among the comedies were "Square Pegs," about two high-school girls; "Newhart," starring Bob Newhart as the owner of a Vermont inn; and "Gloria," a spin-off from the original "All in the Family" hit series. The new dramas were "Bring 'em Back Alive," based on the exploits of Frank Buck, the big-game hunter; "Seven Brides for Seven Brothers," based loosely on an earlier hit movie of the same name; and "Tucker's Witch," about a private detective whose wife and partner possesses psychic powers.

ABC, second in the 1981–82 prime-time ratings, brought in three new half-hour comedies and four new one-hour shows. The comedies included "Star of the Family," about a fireman whose daughter is a pop singer; "It Takes Two," about the conflicts of a physician husband and his attorney wife; and "The New Odd Couple," a black-cast version of the former hit. ABC's new one-hour entries were "Tales of the Gold Monkey," an adventure set in the South Pacific; "The Quest," a madcap adventure set in a mythical Mediterranean kingdom; "Matt Houston," a detective story; and a drama based on "Ripley's Believe It or Not."

NBC offered 11 new series. These included the comedies "Family Ties," about liberal parents bringing up conservative children; "Cheers," set in a Boston bar; and "Silver Spoons," about a young boy adapting to a rich father. The dramas were "Gavilan," the adventures of a former CIA agent; "St. Elsewhere," set in a hospital; "The Devlin Connection," an adventure story with Rock Hudson as star; "Knight Rider," about a former policeman and an "indestructible" car; "Remington Steele," about a female detective; and "Voyagers," a time-travel adventure drama.

The early weeks of the new season produced a somewhat mystifying decline in network prime-time audience ratings. Together, the three networks normally achieved a national Nielsen rating of about 54 at that time of year (each rating point representing 1% of all U.S. TV homes, which in late 1982 numbered about 83.3 million). In October and November 1982, however, their combined ratings were ranging between 49 and 52 each week, and their combined shares of audience—the percentage of sets actually in use that were tuned to one of the networks—had slipped from about 86 to 82. Researchers were unable to agree on where the missing viewers had gone. There were strong suspicions that many had switched to independent stations, cable TV, or public television.

Program executives at the networks were concerned about the ratings trends but were nevertheless slower than usual to make major changes in their schedules, in part because of the suspicion that perhaps in past years they had been too quick to cancel low-rated programs; some series, they noted, had become big hits only after enduring months of low ratings—"All in the Family" was one of the earliest and most notable examples, and "Hill Street Blues," initially low rated but retained because of the critical acclaim it received, was one of the most recent. In the opening months the programmers did

more tinkering than canceling. CBS withdrew "Alice," "Filthy Rich," and "Tucker's Witch," replacing them with a weekly movie, but said that the programs would return to the schedule, probably in midseason. Similarly, ABC announced that it would put "The Greatest American Hero" and "The Quest" on the shelf for an indefinite period and fill their time period with a movie.

For the period from September 27 through November 21 only three new series were in the top 20: "Newhart" was tied (with "Three's Company") for 6th place; "9 to 5," a comedy that had been given a test run before the season opened, was 9th; and "Gloria" was 17th. The top of the list was dominated by established programs, led by the "60 Minutes" newsmagazine, the comedy "M*A*S*H," and the nighttime soap opera "Dallas."

News was in the forefront of television programming in 1982. Unable to convince their affiliated stations that the early-evening network newscasts should be expanded from the current half hour to an hour, ABC, CBS, and NBC expanded the number of newscasts they offered. ABC, which had introduced a late-night half-hour newscast during the hostage crisis in Iran, added a one-hour weeknight report and also launched a new early-morning half-hour newscast. CBS added an early-morning half hour of news and also a four-hour report running from 2 AM to 6 AM (Eastern time). NBC added both a late-night hour and an early-morning half hour to its news schedule.

In the 34th annual Emmy awards the Academy of Television Arts and Sciences named "A Woman Called Golda," based on the life of the late Israeli Prime Minister Golda Meir, as the year's outstanding drama special. Ingrid Bergman, who starred in it, was named outstanding lead actress in a limited series or special. "Hill Street Blues," a police drama whose audience ratings were beginning to live up to its critical acclaim, was chosen as the outstanding drama series for the second straight year, and "Barney Miller" was voted the outstanding comedy series. "Night of 100 Stars," a one-night extravaganza that featured more than 100 television, motion-picture, and Broadway stars, was named the outstanding variety, music, or comedy program, and "Marco

Banking on an audience of night owls, insomniacs, and newsaholics, CBS launched its all-night "Nightwatch" program in October.
MARIO RUIZ

NBC PHOTO

"The Smurfs Christmas Special" on NBC was a pleasant holiday feature for children.

to Michael Conrad of "Hill Street Blues" and Nancy Marchand of "Lou Grant" in the drama category; Laurence Olivier of "Brideshead Revisited" and Penny Fuller of "The Elephant Man" for limited series or specials; and Christopher Lloyd of "Taxi" and Loretta Swit of "M*A*S*H" for comedy, variety, or music series.

Sports continued to be one of the most popular—and most expensive—forms of programming, with professional and college football and major league baseball the most consistent drawing cards. The popularity of professional football was demonstrated during the eight-week early-season strike by National Football League players. The networks substituted other sports on Sunday afternoons and movies on Monday nights, but the audience ratings plunged, in some cases to less than half of what they were when NFL games were shown. The appeal of sports was also reflected in ratings for the 1982 NFL Super Bowl football game; it was seen in 49.1% of all U.S. television homes, commanded a 73% share of audience, and became the highest rated live television program of all time.

Public television's audiences continued to grow, though its producers, faced with budget cutbacks, had to watch their dollars more closely. In January a special ratings study showed that the Public Broadcasting Service's audiences—which in 1981 reached an average of some 75 million persons a week—had increased 17% in prime time, compared with the previous January, while its full-day audiences had grown by 9.6%. PBS's presentation of "The Sharks," also in January, was hailed as "the all-time most-watched public television program," and its "Life on Earth" as the highest rated weekly series in PBS history.

Polo," a ten-hour, $25 million production shown on four nights in May, was chosen the outstanding limited series.

Emmys for lead actor and actress in a dramatic series went to Daniel J. Travanti of "Hill Street Blues" and Michael Learned of "Nurse," and for lead actor and actress in a comedy series to Alan Alda of "M*A*S*H" and Carol Kane of "Taxi." Mickey Rooney, for his work in "Bill," was voted outstanding lead actor in a limited series or special. Supporting actor and actress Emmys were presented

The ten-hour-long "Marco Polo," which cost $25 million to produce, won the Emmy for outstanding limited series.
NBC PHOTO

Special Report: Revolution in the Soaps

by Robert Feder

On a Friday night in November 1980, an estimated 89.9 million people in the United States gathered in front of television sets to watch the climactic "Who Shot J.R.?" episode of the top-rated CBS prime-time soap opera "Dallas." Besides registering the highest Nielsen audience rating ever achieved for a TV series, that program represented a turning point in television history. After 30 years as the most durable and most maligned staple on TV, the soap opera finally had come of age.

Now in full cry, the soap opera revolution has taken television—and mass culture—by storm. Twelve daytime serials air five days a week on the three commercial networks; four soaps air weekly during evening hours; and several more have been created specifically for the burgeoning cable and pay-television markets. Major motion picture stars who used to regard soap operas with disdain now make cameo appearances on them with increasing frequency.

A multimillion-dollar industry has sprung up to merchandise soap-related paraphernalia and exploit the public's fascination with the phenomenon. And, largely based on the success of their nighttime offspring, the daytime soap operas are attracting more men and more young viewers among their 30 million daily devotees than ever before. In short, Americans' attitudes toward the soaps have changed dramatically in the 1980s, prompting more serious attention from the press, greater consideration by scholars and academics as a legitimate social force, and staggering financial returns to the networks and companies that produce them.

Radio to Television

Soap operas made the transition smoothly from radio to television in the 1950s. So named because the first radio serials were sponsored largely by soap companies, they changed little through the 1970s. Housewives comprised the bulk of the audience, and the soaps spoke to them mainly about matters that the networks and sponsors believed would appeal to them most: old-fashioned morality, small-town family virtues, and contrived romantic entanglements. By and large, the dialogue was unrealistic; the acting and technical quality were uninspired; and the story lines were conceived so as to advance almost imperceptibly from day to day, save for the obligatory cliff-hanger at the end of each episode.

Although some shows tried to break from the hopelessly corny mold of their radio ancestors, few people bothered to notice the exceptions. Agnes Nixon, the most gifted and prolific creator and writer of soap operas (and a housewife herself), summed up the prevailing belief that "soap opera is a Never-Never Land where hack writers and inferior producers, directors, and actors serve melodramatic pap to a lunatic fringe of female children who grow older but never grow up."

True or not, that unfortunate stereotype persisted for decades until the term soap opera itself became, in Nixon's words, "the classic cliché of derogation." Anyone who had anything to do with soaps, including the millions who watched them faithfully each day, was looked upon with censure or pity by society, the media, and even the networks that profited from them.

New Viewers, New Respectability

Several factors have combined in recent years to change that perception dramatically, most notably the emergence and popularity of evening soap operas, including "Dallas," "Dynasty," "Falcon Crest," and "Knots Landing." Thanks to their acceptance, viewers could follow the week-to-week tribulations of the characters in these high-budget, lavishly produced programs (and discuss them in public) without feeling guilty or fearing the stigma attached to fanatics of the drearier daytime dramas. And, as a result of these converts' becoming "hooked" on nighttime serials, the whole soap opera genre suddenly gained new respectability.

A few years earlier another trend had begun to sweep the daytime soaps, fueled by the fact that more and more housewives—the shows' traditional audience—were getting jobs and leaving the home during the day. In an effort to expand their audiences, programmers at ABC deliberately decided to tap into the youth market by centring much of their action on younger characters, thereby attracting more young women and drawing in high-school and college viewers for the first time. Once the mainstay of the soaps, stories about older, long-established characters were shunted aside to make room for sexier, faster-paced plots about younger people. The strategy worked for ABC, and soon shows on all three networks were courting youth with a vengeance.

The fierce competition for ratings reflected the networks' realization that soap operas make money. While the cost of producing one episode of a weekly one-hour series on prime-time television often exceeds $600,000, daytime soaps cost far less than that for a full week of five hour-long installments. Altogether, in 1981 daytime television accounted for $1.4 billion of the three networks' $5.6 billion in advertising revenue; a few top-rated soap operas each generated as much as $150 million per year in net profits. With stakes that high, the networks frequently resorted to various new devices to improve their ratings, including the use of celebrities for brief appearances and the export of cast and crew to exotic places around the world for taping on location.

New Story Lines

Although none of the soap operas strays far from its mandate to provide entertainment and try to draw the largest share of viewers, several have been noted for their efforts at educating and enlightening their audiences as well. Because they air 260 original episodes a year with no reruns, the daytime soaps have the opportunity to infuse their story lines with thinly disguised messages of public service and social conscience.

Over the years the best of the soaps have explored everything from drug abuse and wife beating to the war in Vietnam and unemployment. Viewers see these issues from various characters' standpoints, and in this way some may come to understand the

Rod Arrants and Sherry Mathis were flown to a remote Caribbean island to film this scene for NBC's "Search for Tomorrow."
NBC PHOTO

problems and how to deal with them. For this reason, psychologists and other professionals have begun to pay increased attention to the soap operas as therapeutic devices and as mirrors of society. One university dean observed: "With their realistic characters, daytime serials provide a more accurate representation of the real world than prime-time shows. Prime time is a world of action, power and danger. Daytime is a world of interior turbulence that hits much closer to home."

On ABC's "All My Children," creator and head writer Agnes Nixon, who pioneered the injection of serious social issues on soap operas, conceived two story lines about rape that ran concurrently in 1982. One concerned the effect of rape on the families of both the victim and the rapist, while the other explored the consequences of a situation in which a young white woman falsely accuses a young black man of raping her.

Just before NBC announced the cancellation of "The Doctors" in late 1982, the show launched a major story line involving the dangers of cigarette smoking. Viewers who followed the plight of a physician who tried to kick the habit were invited to send for a free brochure prepared by NBC and the American Cancer Society on how to stop smoking. More than 100,000 of the pamphlets were distributed.

Spin-offs

The television networks are not alone in profiting from the viewers' increased appetite for soap operas. A sizable industry has been spawned to capitalize on the popularity of the genre. Soaps now can be seen on cable and pay-TV systems across the country, and since they are not bound by rigid network censorship, they tend to be more sexually explicit and enjoy greater freedom to employ graphic language. Other new shows to cash in on the soap craze include several nonnetwork programs devoted to following developments on the soaps and the private lives of the shows' stars.

Soap-opera fan magazines, once relegated to lowly places on supermarket checkout racks, have become more critical and incisive while attracting significantly wealthier and better educated readers. They also are making more money than ever before, with the three largest periodicals in the field boasting a combined monthly circulation of almost two million. Add to that the money made by promoters of soap opera "festivals" held throughout the year; the merchandisers of various books, games, calendars, clothing, mugs, tote bags, and other soap-inspired items; and the syndicators of "Dallas" throughout the world, and the total value of the new soap craze is beyond estimate.

But the soap opera revolution relies most, not on audience ratings or money, but on the insatiable curiosity of the public to find out what will happen next. For that, the only answer is: Tune in tomorrow.

TENNIS

The organization of the leading events in men's tennis lost its cohesion in 1982. World Championship Tennis (WCT), controlled by Lamar Hunt of Dallas, Texas, withdrew from the Grand Prix series and revived its independent circuit with a sequence of 22 tournaments in the U.S. and Europe. The Grand Prix series, controlled by the Men's International Tennis Professional Council (MITPC), comprised 85 tournaments played on five continents.

The relationship between the Women's Tennis Association and the Women's Professional Council functioned more smoothly. The women's game was organized in two distinct circuits, the Avon Series played early in the year in the U.S. and a wider ranging International Series under the sponsorship of Toyota. For 1983 one circuit, comprising fewer tournaments in all, was arranged under a revised sponsorship by Virginia Slims cigarettes.

There was controversy early in the year about the decision of Björn Borg (Sweden) not to fulfill the requirements of the Grand Prix rules by undertaking to compete in at least ten tournaments. It meant automatic relegation to the qualifying rounds of all Grand Prix events. Borg did in fact challenge in the Monte Carlo tournament in April after qualifying, but without notable success. He competed in no major event during 1982.

Men's Competition

The Australian championship, the last event of the 1981 Grand Prix, was won in Melbourne by Johan Kriek (South Africa). The Volvo Masters' Tournament, the climax event of the series, was again staged in Madison Square Garden, New York City, in January 1982. It was won by Ivan Lendl (Czech.), who dominated the early part of the season. Lendl beat John McEnroe (U.S.) in the semifinal 6–4, 6–2. In the final he beat Vitas Gerulaitis (U.S.) 6–7, 2–6, 7–6, 6–2, 6–4. Lendl also won the principal WCT tournament, the Dallas Finals in April, by beating McEnroe 6–2, 3–6, 6–3, 6–3.

The Italian championship was won in Rome by Andres Gomez (Ecuador). He beat Eliot Teltscher (U.S.) 6–2, 6–3, 6–2 in the final. The French championship had a precocious singles winner, Mats Wilander (Sweden), victor in the junior event the year before. Wilander, unseeded, beat Lendl 4–6, 7–5, 3–6, 6–4, 6–2 in the fourth round; subsequently he beat Gerulaitis, José-Luis Clerc (Arg.), and, in the final, Guillermo Vilas (Arg.) by 1–6, 7–6, 6–0, 6–4. Wilander's age when he won was 17 years 288 days, making him the youngest man ever to win a major singles title.

The Wimbledon championships, extended for the first time to 13 playing days, suffered from wet weather, with only one day free from rain. McEnroe, seeded first, was successful in defense of his 1981 title only as far as the final. In the final Jimmy Connors (U.S.) rose to the occasion and won 3–6, 6–3, 6–7, 7–6, 6–4 after a contest more notable for its tension than for the quality of play. It was the fifth final and second championship for Connors in nine years, his first victory occurring in 1974.

Connors established himself as the player of the year when he won the U.S. Open championship at Flushing Meadow in New York City. Lendl beat Wilander in the fourth round and in the semifinal defeated McEnroe, the defending champion, 6–4, 6–4, 7–6. Connors won a semifinal against Vilas 6–1, 3–6, 6–2, 6–3 and then triumphed in the final against Lendl 6–3, 6–2, 4–6, 6–4. It was the fourth U.S. singles championship for Connors since 1974.

In men's doubles Peter Fleming and McEnroe won the Master's title in New York City. The runners-up there, Kevin Curren (South Africa) and Steve Denton (U.S.), took the U.S. Open title later in the year. Peter McNamara and Paul McNamee (both Australia) won the Wimbledon title, where the bad weather caused a reduction to the best of three sets for the first time. The World Team Cup, formerly the Nations Cup, was again staged in Düsseldorf, West Germany, on clay courts in May. The U.S. (Gene Mayer, Teltscher, and Sherwood Stewart) beat Australia (Kim Warwick, McNamara, and Mark Edmondson) 2–1 in the final.

In Davis Cup play Ireland, Denmark, Paraguay, and Indonesia were zone winners and qualified for the main competition of 1983. Mexico, India, Spain, and West Germany dropped out of the championship group for 1983 when they lost in both the first round and play-off matches. The U.S. beat India 4–

Jimmy Connors defeated fellow American John McEnroe in five sets in July to win his second Wimbledon championship.
UPI

SYNDICATION INTERNATIONAL/PHOTO TRENDS

Martina Navratilova won her third Wimbledon women's title by defeating defending champion Chris Evert Lloyd.

1, Sweden 3–2, and Australia 5–0 to reach the final. The contest with Sweden, held in St. Louis, Mo., was narrowly won in the fifth match when McEnroe beat Wilander 9–7, 6–2, 15–17, 3–6, 8–6 after 6 hours 32 minutes. France beat Argentina 3–2, Czechoslovakia 3–1 (one match unplayed), and New Zealand 3–2 to reach the final. Yannick Noah, from Cameroon, was France's number one competitor in that nation's most distinguished progress since its tenure as champion from 1927 to 1932.

The final round, U.S. versus France in Grenoble, was the first between those nations since France won in Paris in 1932. Led by McEnroe, who won two singles matches and teamed with Fleming to win the doubles, the U.S. triumphed 4–1 and thus won the cup for the 28th time. McEnroe defeated Noah 12–10, 1–6, 3–6, 6–3, 6–2 and Henri Leconte 6–2, 6–3 and then, with Fleming, beat Noah and Leconte 6–3, 6–4, 9–7. Gene Mayer triumphed over Leconte 6–2, 6–2, 7–9, 6–4, and Noah gained France's only victory by defeating Mayer 6–1, 6–0.

Women's Competition

The Australian championship, staged in Melbourne in December 1981, was won by Martina Navratilova (U.S.). From a strong field she won the final against Chris Evert Lloyd (U.S.) 6–7, 6–4, 7–5. Later in the month the Toyota championships, the climax of the International Series, was held at the Meadowlands Arena in New Jersey. Tracy Austin (U.S.) beat Evert Lloyd 6–1, 6–2 in the semifinal and Navratilova 2–6, 6–4, 6–2 in the final. On the Avon circuit Navratilova won 5 of the 11 tournaments. In the Avon championship at Madison Square Garden in March, Sylvia Hanika (West Germany) surpris-

ingly beat Navratilova 1–6, 6–3, 6–4 in the final.

Evert Lloyd won the Italian championship, played in Perugia separately from the men, beating Hana Mandlikova (Czech.) 6–0, 6–3 in the final. In Paris Navratilova won the French championship for the first time. Andrea Jaeger (U.S.) beat Evert Lloyd 6–3, 6–1 in the semifinals. Mandlikova, the defending champion, beat Austin 7–6, 6–7, 6–2 in the quarterfinals, but Navratilova defeated her 6–0, 6–2 in the other semifinal. In the final Navratilova triumphed over Jaeger 7–6, 6–1.

The Wimbledon championship brought notable success to Billie Jean King (U.S.), 38 and competing there for the 21st time. She defeated Austin 3–6, 6–4, 6–2 in the quarterfinals to record her record 90th singles victory at the tournament. Evert Lloyd then beat King 7–6, 2–6, 6–3 in the semifinals. This was King's 104th Wimbledon singles match, and her overall Wimbledon tally was 252 matches played, 214 won, unique on both counts. Navratilova reached the final without losing a set and beat Evert Lloyd 6–1, 3–6, 6–2.

Navratilova's victory gave her three legs on the "Grand Slam," holding the Australian, French, Wimbledon, and U.S. titles at the same time, achieved by only two women, Maureen Connolly (U.S.) in 1953 and Margaret Court (Australia) in 1970. However, Navratilova was disappointed in the U.S. championship at Flushing Meadow. Pam Shriver (U.S.), her doubles partner, beat her 1–6, 7–6, 6–2 in the quarterfinals. Also in a quarterfinal match Mandlikova defeated the defending champion, Austin, 4–6, 6–4, 6–4, and then reached the final by beating Shriver 6–4, 2–6, 6–2. Evert Lloyd beat Jaeger 6–1, 6–2 in the other semifinal and in the final defeated Mandlikova 6–3, 6–1 to win the championship for the sixth time.

In women's doubles Navratilova rivaled her singles achievements. With Shriver she won both the Toyota and Avon championships. She paired with Anne Smith (U.S.) to win the French title and with Shriver again to triumph at Wimbledon. The U.S. title went to Rosemary Casals (U.S.) and Wendy Turnbull (Australia). The Federation Cup tournament was staged in July at Santa Clara, Calif., and was won by the U.S. (Evert Lloyd, Navratilova, and Andrea Leand) for the seventh consecutive year and the 11th time in all. Navratilova played number one for the U.S. Navratilova's status as the outstanding player of 1982 was clear-cut.

The Wightman Cup was won for the 44th time by the U.S. (Evert Lloyd, Barbara Potter, Anne Smith, Casals, and Sharon Walsh). At the Royal Albert Hall, London, they beat Great Britain (Sue Barker, Jo Durie, Virginia Wade, and Anne Hobbs) by six matches to one. For the British, Wade played for the 18th successive year and extended her total of matches to a record 52. On the U.S. side, Evert Lloyd increased her total to 32, a record for a U.S. player, and, unique for either side, won her 22nd singles match out of 22 played.

TEXTILES

There was growing polarization in 1982 between the textile industries of the developed countries (mainly Western Europe, North America, and Japan) and those of the less developed countries. In the future the labour-intensive industries of the latter would have to fight against the products of highly automated manufacturing in those countries that could afford new technology.

An example was the almost completely automatic, open-end spinning machine. This produced yarn that, though about 10% weaker than conventionally made yarns, was of much greater regularity and thus highly suitable for weaving on air-jet looms (in which a jet of air—or water, if man-made fibres are being processed—replaces the shuttle). Also reliant on very regular yarn was the multiphase loom currently being developed, which would be able to produce cloths at more than double the speed of conventional weaving.

World production of wool in the 1981–82 season (ended June 1982) was 1,644,000 metric tons clean, 1½% higher than in the 1980–81 season and the highest recorded since the mid-1960s. Only a nominal increase was expected in the 1982–83 season as drought in Australia, the largest producer, reduced sheep numbers. Preliminary estimates of virgin wool consumption showed a slightly declining trend overall in 1981, amounting to 4% in 11 leading reporting countries. The fall was most substantial in Western Europe; there was a rise of 11% in the U.S., but manufacturing activity there declined toward the close of the year. Early statistics suggested that the overall downtrend in consumption was not halted in 1982.

After hovering around the 22 million-bale mark for some time, world stocks of raw cotton suddenly advanced sharply in the 1981–82 season. At more than 27 million bales, carry-over supplies were the highest in seven years, covering requirements for almost five months. The basic reason was a major gain in production. Global output was a record 17.4 million bales, an improvement of 5.8 million bales over the previous season. Better yields accounted for about 75% of the increase, while the acreage planted was around 2.4% higher. The gain centred on the U.S., China, India, and Sudan. There was a fallback in the Soviet Union, Mexico, Egypt, and Zimbabwe, largely caused by bad weather.

Developments in 1982 confirmed that China, now the world's premier producer of silk, was fostering the export of finished goods with the aim of increasing the industry's capacity as a foreign currency earner. For some years China had been providing funds for the promotion of silk in Europe. Other Asian silk-producing countries—such as India, Thailand, and to some extent the U.S.S.R.—had traditionally confined their exports of fabric to silk that was surplus to domestic requirements. However, China, since the demise of Japan as an exporter in 1967, had set itself up as a consistent supplier of raw silk to the West, fulfilling that role with much discretion.

Japan, meanwhile, faced the problem of unwieldy stocks. Even with stricter import controls, a lighter crop of cocoons, and domestic promotion, the volume of stocks was reduced by no more than 10%. Worldwide demand for silk was healthy throughout the year, but Japan's contrived price plateau debarred exports except at a considerable loss. Hopes of restoring the kimono to its ancient status did not seem promising.

The continuing decline of the textile industries in the richer countries resulted in the closing of a number of man-made fibre production facilities. This affected not only polyester and polyamide (nylon) but also the cellulosics such as viscose rayon. Since they are based on raw materials other than petroleum, the cellulosics had seemed to have a secure future.

THAILAND

For the people of Thailand, 1982 above all marked the 200th anniversary of the establishment of the kingdom's ruling Chakri dynasty. Three months after the nationwide celebrations, King Bhumibol Adulyadej fell ill, but he recovered some six weeks later.

The administration of Prime Minister Prem Tinsulanond faced numerous challenges as the nation geared up for general elections in 1983. The tone was set in December 1981, when Prem brought back into his Cabinet members of the country's largest political grouping, the Social Action Party (SAP), which had left the coalition government nine months earlier. Though it promised a measure of political stability, the move nonetheless brought to the surface the SAP's own severe internal divisions. The factionalism came to a head in March when the long-time SAP leader, former prime minister Kukrit Pramoj, announced that, at 71, he would not run in the 1983 election. Front-runner in the party succession stakes was economics expert Boonchu Rojanastien, former deputy prime minister and head of the Bangkok Bank.

Pressure on the prime minister mounted in June when the parliamentary opposition introduced a no-confidence motion against the government, alleging ineptitude in the conduct of economic and foreign affairs. The motion was defeated.

In an unconfirmed incident on July 16, one or more assailants ostensibly fired an antitank rocket at the prime minister's motorcade as it was traveling in one of Thailand's northern provinces. The attack was unsuccessful. Despite tightened security, a grenade was lobbed into Prem's residential compound on August 15. Prem again escaped unscathed, but so did his assailant. Some insiders said the attacks were the work of elements within the Army disgruntled by the swift rise of Gen. Arthit Kamlang-ek, a Prem protégé who had played a leading role in crushing a coup attempt in April 1981. The controversial

Arthit was named commander in chief of the Thai Army in the annual military reshuffles in September, making him effectively the second most powerful man in Thailand.

Prem, himself a former commander in chief, displayed the Thai military's traditional reluctance to participate in democratic politics when he announced in October that he would not join a political party and stand in the upcoming election. However, analysts said that Prem's support within the armed forces virtually guaranteed him another term as prime minister, since no party was expected to win an outright parliamentary majority.

The Thai Army launched three major assaults against the 5,000-strong Shan United Army of the notorious "Golden Triangle" narcotics leader, Khun Sa. An offensive in January succeeded in driving the drug runner's troops from their base in northernmost Thailand into Burma. Follow-up operations in May and October were deemed necessary when it became clear that Khun Sa was determined to reestablish a foothold on Thai soil. Bangkok also reaped results from its judicious carrot-and-stick policy against the Communist Party of Thailand. Promised lenient treatment, thousands of Communists came out of the jungle to surrender to the authorities.

Though affected by the worldwide recession, Thailand's economy performed creditably in 1982. Gross national product was expected to grow at about 5%, and improvements were recorded in several key areas. The current-account deficit was estimated at $1,220,000,000, just half the 1981 figure.

After two devaluations the previous year, the baht recovered in 1982 and gained ground against the Japanese yen and most major Western European currencies. However, the government was obliged to introduce sweeping tax changes toward year's end to raise an additional $440 million in revenue.

THEATRE

Although professional theatres throughout the U.S. and Canada continued to be active in 1982, most attention during the year was focused on Broadway. A drab and depressing economy was surely the reason. Audiences seem to have an interest in serious drama when they can enjoy leisure time, but if it becomes escapist time they prefer glamour and tinsel. For that reason primarily the Broadway commercial theatre dominated the U.S. drama in 1982.

During the year the cost of producing a Broadway show hit a new high of $5 million. The show was *Cats*, a musical extravaganza based on T. S. Eliot's collection *Old Possum's Book of Practical Cats*, set to music by Andrew Lloyd Webber, who also wrote the music for *Evita* and *Jesus Christ Superstar*. This import was a rare example of the British succeeding in an area that Americans had long considered their exclusive domain: the musical theatre. The show became so popular that the record $50 price tag for a ticket did not deter audiences.

Cats was the biggest hit to arrive on Broadway during the year, although *Nine* ran it a close second. *Nine* was also a musical, this time based on a film—Federico Fellini's *8½*. For legal reasons that source could not be credited in the program. *Nine* won

King Bhumibol Adulyadej and Queen Sirikit of Thailand, with other family members, celebrated the bicentennials of the city of Bangkok and of the monarchy.
UPI

©1982 MARTHA SWOPE

The biggest and most expensive hit on Broadway in 1982 was the musical Cats, *a British import based on a book by the poet T. S. Eliot.*

Broadway's Tony award for the season's best musical, *Cats* not being eligible at the time.

These productions dominated an otherwise thin season during which most of Broadway's theatres were empty and two were even demolished. The biggest noise along Broadway was in fact not the cheering for *Cats* or *Nine* but the explosion of dynamite and the crash of the wrecker's ball as the Helen Hayes and Morosco theatres were razed so that a new hotel could be built.

It seemed as if there were no inclination to put dramas or comedies on any stages or to maintain theatres suitable for them. Zakes Mokae won a Tony award for best featured actor in *Master Harold . . . and the Boys* by the South African Athol Fugard. It was a well-conceived drama but small in scale and without the muscle usually found in prize-winning plays.

Other Broadway dramas produced during the year included *Hothouse*, an early play that Harold Pinter had relegated to his trunk. William Alfred, a Harvard professor, achieved his second New York production in 20 years, but *The Curse of an Aching Heart* was not the success that his *Hogan's Goat* had been. Another futile follow-up was *The Wake of*

Jamey Foster, written by Beth Henley, whose *Crimes of the Heart* had won a Pulitzer Prize.

The only play to originate on Broadway and succeed at all was an uncertainly written religious mystery called *Agnes of God*. Its popularity stemmed from fine performances by Geraldine Page, Elizabeth Ashley, and Amanda Plummer. Broadway audiences do not usually seek out Shakespeare or Euripides, but a star can attract them. In 1982 the stars were Christopher Plummer and James Earl Jones in *Othello* and Zoe Caldwell and Dame Judith Anderson in *Medea*.

Nonprofit and regional theatres had emerged precisely to do such plays. However, New York's institutional theatres had been floundering in recent years, and in 1982 they continued to do so. The theatre at Lincoln Center remained shut for still another season, presumably for renovations. Hopes for its eventual reopening grew dimmer with every work delay and cutback of funds. New York's other major theatrical institution, the New York Shakespeare Festival, continued to operate at a reduced pace. The Circle in the Square produced a popular revival of Noël Coward's *Present Laughter* with George C. Scott and then canceled the rest of its

SECOND CITY PRODUCTIONS, CHICAGO; PHOTOGRAPH, CAROL ROSEGG—MARTHA SWOPE

*The Great Lakes Shakespeare Festival mounted a highly successful touring production of the 8½-hour
The Life and Adventures of Nicholas Nickleby.*

schedule in order to capitalize on the hit.

Stars do not always attract audiences. Television's Donny Osmond notwithstanding, a revival of the George M. Cohan musical *Little Johnny Jones* lasted only a single performance. Movie director Robert Altman turned to the stage with a play called *Come Back to the Five and Dime Jimmy Dean, Jimmy Dean* featuring another television star, Cher. The play closed after running little more than a month.

Yet all was not gloomy. Off-Broadway theatre continued to flourish. Despite ticket prices as high as $20, it attracted audiences who were still faithful to serious drama. The year's best plays in fact came from off-Broadway. They were Lanford Wilson's *Angels Fall*, a study of the crisis of faith in a nuclear age, and Harvey Fierstein's *Torch Song Trilogy*, three related one-act plays about a middle-class transvestite. Both were naturalistic works dealing with personal problems.

Throughout the rest of the U.S., theatres presented many costume classics, whether Greek, Elizabethan, Restoration, or Chekhovian. It seemed as if the concert-hall mentality of familiar programming had overtaken these theatres. Audiences, however, were hungering for something more recognizable and sympathetic than costume drama. The Actors Theatre of Louisville, Ky., met this need during its popular annual festival of new plays. The Mark Taper Forum in Los Angeles also seemed conscious in its programming of a thirst for relevance, staging Charles Fuller's prizewinning *A Soldier's Play* and Jules Feiffer's *Grown Ups*.

Although there is a commercial theatre in Canada, that nation's stage life has always centred on the established and prestigious Stratford Festival. With John Hirsch finishing his second year as artistic director, this theatre's days of uncertain leadership seemed over. Playing a 22-week season to an audience that averaged 75% of capacity, the Festival presented *Julius Caesar, The Merry Wives of Windsor, The Tempest,* and Shaw's *Arms and the Man* in the main theatre and *Blithe Spirit* and *The Mikado* in the smaller house.

Arms and the Man was a surprising discourtesy to the nearby Shaw Festival, which is much smaller than Stratford and poses no great competitive threat. The Shaw Theatre in its own summer season presented popular favourites, obviously seeking broad appeal: Shaw's *Too True to Be Good* and *Pygmalion* and Edmond Rostand's *Cyrano de Bergerac*. These were not daring choices but rather the selections of a theatre trying to survive difficult economic times. In that respect it was representative of many U.S. and Canadian theatres in 1982.

Great Britain and Ireland

The world recession, rising ticket prices, lower attendances, and soaring production costs placed the theatre in Great Britain in increasing jeopardy. Several theatres remained "dark" or closed permanently, though the Old Vic was saved by Ed Mirvish of Canada, who paid £550,000 for it and was spending £1 million on refurbishment. The National Youth Theatre was rescued by a grant from Texaco Inc. and the takeover of its home (the Shaw Theatre) by Camden Council.

Among the annual Arts Council prizes were six playwrights' bursaries, the John Whiting Prize (David Pownall), and the George Devine Prize (shared by Louise Paget and Andrea Dunbar). A record number of Plays and Players (PP) and Society of West End Theatre (SWET) awards went to the NT, whose spectacular production of the U.S. musical *Guys and Dolls* rated seven: two each to Richard Eyre, director, and John Gunter, designer, the SWET award for best actress in a musical to Julia Mackenzie, for best actor in a supporting role to David Healy, and the outstanding achievement in musicals award to the play. Bill Paterson won the PP best actor award for the title role in *Schweik in the Second World War*, in which Julia Mackenzie also was impressive as Anna Kopecka. In the NT's *The Importance of Being Earnest* the SWET supporting actress award went to Anna Massey and the PP best actress to Judi Dench (as Lady Bracknell and as the lead in Harold Pinter's one-act *A Kind of Alaska*, about a sleeping-sickness patient). This play also shared the PP best new play award with Tom Stoppard's *The Real Thing*, a brilliant Pirandellian comedy of love and marriage among theatricals, which Peter Wood directed in the West End.

Other fine productions at the NT were Edward Bond's *Summer* with Anna Massey, *The Beggar's Opera* with the exciting Imelda Staunton as Lucy, *The Prince of Homburg* with Patrick Drury, a Victorian *A Midsummer Night's Dream* with Paul Scofield as Oberon (also memorable as Don Quixote in Keith Dewhurst's adaptation at the Olivier), and Samuel Beckett's *Rockaby* directed by Alan Schneider, all at the Cottesloe; *Major Barbara* with Penelope Wilton, Alan Ayckbourn's cynical *Way Upstream*, and Chekhov's *Uncle Vanya*, newly translated by Pam Gems, at the Lyttelton; and, at the Olivier, *Danton's Death* (adapted by Howard Brenton) and a revival of the Peter Hall *Oresteia*.

Following the move of the Royal Shakespeare Company (RSC) to the Barbican Centre in the City of London, the company earned four SWET awards: the best musical for Peter Nichols's *Poppy*, a Christmas pantomime type of show with Monty Norman's music, about Britain's opium trade in China in Victorian times; the best comedy actor for Geoffrey Hutchings's pantomime-dame in *Poppy;* and two for best performances in a revival, for Cheryl Campbell's Nora and Stephen Moore's Helmer in *A Doll's House* on the RSC's small stage, The Pit. Before the move to the Barbican the RSC was seen in Schnitzler's *La Ronde* and Ostrovsky's *The Forest* at the Aldwych. Thereafter came charming productions, at the Barbican, of the two parts of *Henry IV* (with Gerard Murphy as a plebeian Prince Hal), *A Midsummer Night's Dream* and *All's Well That Ends Well* (with Peggy Ashcroft), *A Winter's Tale*, and a new version of *Peter Pan*, staged by Trevor Nunn and John Caird, using a male actor for the first time in the title role. At The Pit the RSC staged classics (Bulwer-Lytton's *Money*, *The Twin Rivals*, and *The Witch of Edmonton*) and first-rate plays by Peter

South African playwright Athol Fugard directed his new play, Master Harold . . . and the Boys, at the Lyceum Theatre, New York City. The production featured (left to right) Lonny Price, Zakes Mokae, and Danny Glover.

MARTHA SWOPE

Flannery (*Our Friends in the North*, about corruption in modern society) and Peter Whelan (*Clay*, about growing old in a nuclear society).

SWET awards in the private sector went to Rosemary Leach in *84 Charing Cross Road* (best actress in a new play), Roy Hudd in *Underneath the Arches* (best actor in a musical), and Julian Mitchell's *Another Country* (transferred from Greenwich, where it was seen in 1981) as the year's best play; in it Kenneth Branagh won the most promising newcomer awards, given by PP and by SWET and Benson and Hedges jointly. *Andy Capp*, transferred from the Manchester Royal Exchange Theatre, won the PP best musical, and the philosophical comedy *Insignificance*, by Terry Johnson, gained the most promising new play award. Ian McDiarmid won the SWET best actor in a new play award in *Insignificance*, while the comedy of the year award went to Michael Frayn's backstage *Noises Off*, earlier seen at the Lyric Theatre in Hammersmith. Of interest at the Royal Court were Louise Page's drama of old age, *Salonika; Top Girls* by Caryl Churchill; G. F. Newman's drama of police corruption, *Operation Bad Apple;* and the John Byrne working-class trilogy *The Slab Boys*, from Glasgow. The Lyric Theatre, Hammersmith, presented Claire Luckham's *Trafford Tanzi* en route from Liverpool to London's Mer-

Harvey Fierstein starred as a transvestite entertainer in his own Torch Song Trilogy, *an off-Broadway hit.*
KEN HOWARD

maid, William Gaskill's production of *She Stoops to Conquer*, and Shared Experience's stage version of Evelyn Waugh's *A Handful of Dust*.

Other novelties in the subsidized sector included a new version of Ayckbourn's *Season's Greetings* and Noël Coward's *Design for Living*, at the Greenwich, both later seen in the West End; *Skirmishes* by Catherine Hayes and *Dreyfus* (Tom Kempinski's version of a J. C. Grumberg play), at Hampstead; *The Lucky Ones* by Tony Marchant and *A Star Is Torn*, starring Robyn Archer, who took it to the West End, at the Theatre Royal, Stratford East; Foco Novo's *Edward II* by Brecht at the Round House and *Woza Albert!* from South Africa at the Riverside Studios; and Robert Walker's rock-and-roll musical, *Yakety Yak*, at the New Half Moon.

The Theatre Royal, Haymarket, launched a repertory season that included Ronald Millar's version of C. P. Snow's *A Coat of Varnish*, starring Peter Barkworth. Among other highlights were Penelope Keith and Trevor Peacock in *Hobson's Choice*, Donald Sinden in *Uncle Vanya*, Peter O'Toole in *Man and Superman*, and Leonard Rossiter in *The Rules of the Game*. Comedies ranged from the farcical *Key for Two* starring Moira Lister to Eric Idle's absurdist *Pass the Butler*, while more serious fare included *The Little Foxes* with Elizabeth Taylor, Susannah York in *Hedda Gabler*, Glenda Jackson (as Hitler's mistress) in *Summit Conference*, *Nuts* by Tom Topor, and, more renowned for its authorship than its dramatic skill, *The Jeweller's Shop* by Karol Wojtyla, alias Pope John Paul II.

Helped by the Irish Arts Council grant of £1.9 million, the Abbey Theatre, Dublin, though facing future cuts, staged Fr. Desmond Forrestal's *Kolbe*, a tribute to the canonized anti-Nazi wartime martyr, at the Dublin Festival. Other new works there included Hugh Leonard's *Kill*, Mary Halpin's *Irish Times*, the prizewinning *Semi-Private*, Jim Sheridan's *The Immigrant* (first seen in Canada), and Fergus and Rosaleen Linehan's *Mary Make-Believe*, a musical based on James Stephens's *The Charwoman's Daughter*. Harveys' of Bristol Theatre Awards went to Frank Conway (*She Stoops to Conquer* at the Abbey, shifted to an Irish setting), Neil Donnelly's *The Silver Dollar Boys* at the Peacock, Alan Standford (for the role of Antonio Salieri in *Amadeus*), Maureen Toal (in *All My Sons*), and Patrick Mason's production of *The Pirates of Penzance*.

TOURISM

International tourism continued to weather the recession in 1982, though a slight decrease in overall arrivals marked a year in which stagnation of arrivals was frequent and declines were not uncommon. World Tourism Organization (WTO) preliminary estimates revealed a 1.3% drop in international arrivals to 279,900,000, while dollar receipts edged forward by 4% to about $110 billion.

As demand for energy continued to decline, concern for supplies ceased to be a problem, though the

EASTMAN KODAK CO.

A futuristic monorail and the pyramids of Kodak's "Journey into Imagination" exhibit were features of Epcot Center, opened in Florida in October by Walt Disney Productions.

relatively high cost of energy, especially for transport, consolidated the trend for travelers to stay closer to home. While the stronger U.S. dollar stimulated outbound U.S. travel, it made North American destinations relatively expensive, leading to a sharp decline in travel to the U.S. Likewise, recovery of Caribbean tourism was delayed because of the high prices of these destinations, the currencies of most of which were linked to the U.S. dollar.

Countries faring well in 1982 included Spain, where 37.7 million visitors were received in the first ten months of the year, a 5% increase over 1981. Receipts for the first nine months of 1982 reached $5.6 billion, almost 10% more than in 1981. Despite the considerable publicity that attended the World Cup football (soccer) championships held in Spain in June and July 1982, the success of the season seemed to have been attributable mainly to poor summer weather in northern Europe and a weak peseta (devalued in December 1982 by 8%). In the United Kingdom, where arrivals rose by 4% to 9.5 million during the first nine months of the year, the North American segment of the market was the most buoyant, with a 7% increase attributable to the use

of marketing skills to halt an incipient decline in the "stately home" industry. In comparison, arrivals from European Economic Community countries rose less than 1%, those from all of Western Europe by 3%, and the small "rest of the world" segment by 9%. Receipts expressed in pounds sterling grew by 13% in 1982 over the first nine months and, though expenditures grew by only 9% over the same period, the travel account deficit that had marred 1981 persisted as U.K. tourists spent £265 million ($425 million) more on foreign travel than international tourists spent in the U.K.

Other countries reporting favourable trends in 1982 included Japan with a 20% increase, while Finland, Yugoslavia, Austria, Portugal, France, and Greece all showed positive growth rates of up to 10% in the early months of the year. The tiny Indian Ocean nation of the Maldives reported a half-year increase of 28%, bringing arrivals to 38,000.

In North America there were declines of 11% in arrivals in Canada, though hopes were that the weakness of the Canadian dollar in comparison with the U.S. dollar would shift the balance in Canada's favour as the year progressed. Arrivals in the U.S.

were reported down by more than 7%, and a mid-summer survey of U.S. travel intentions foreshadowed a 14% decline in person-trips (covering both domestic and international travel). However, the number of U.S. tourists intending to travel by air continued above 1981 levels, while business and convention travel intentions were strong, implying that the U.S. economy was beginning to climb out of its recession. The 1982 declines should be compared with the 12% increase in total travel volume in the U.S. in 1981 according to final figures published by the U.S. Travel Data Center.

In the Caribbean, tourism demand continued to be mixed. Jamaica showed a 26% increase at mid-year with 271,000 visitors. This success was attributed to a return of customer confidence and a strong marketing effort. Antigua registered a 5.5% increase over eight months, aided by a considerable increase in hotel capacity. But Barbados declined 12% over the first eight months, possibly owing to dependence on Canadian visitors and the collapse of some leading Canadian tour operators. Aruba, the Cayman Islands, and The Bahamas also declined from their 1981 visitor levels. Currency movements were seen as undermining the competitive position of some Caribbean destinations, notable exceptions being the French overseas territories of Guadeloupe and Martinique, where the weakness of the French franc led to higher visitor levels. Mexico's successive peso devaluations made that country an especially good value for money, leading to strong off-season demand from U.S. travelers.

TOYS AND GAMES

The major growth segment of the toy market in 1982 was electronics, and during the year there was a significant trend in the U.S. toward video games. The coin-operated electronic arcade games, which throughout the U.S. had been satisfying youngsters' need for a place to congregate, paved the way for the rapid development of home games of the same kind. But the video games market was very different from the battery-operated, hand-held games market because, unlike the latter, it was not predominantly concerned with products designed to amuse children. As a result, in the U.S. the growth of video games brought the greatest sales benefits not to the specialty toy shops but to the electronic stores, and the same pattern was developing in the U.K. and other European countries. Understandably, there was some reluctance on the part of toy stores to deal in the hardware of electronic games, mainly because of the lower than usual profit margins. Furthermore, since adults were the main purchasers of these items, manufacturers were distributing their products to retail outlets that could provide good demonstration facilities and electronics know-how.

The importance of the growth of video games was emphasized during the year when two major U.S. manufacturers entered the field for the first time. CBS Inc. unveiled plans to market, through its subsidiary

As the market for home video games continued in grow, retail displays such as this one at Macy's in New York City became common sights.
THOM O'CONNOR/BUSINESS WEEK

Gabriel Industries, Inc., home versions of Bally Manufacturing Corp. arcade games. CBS then followed this by purchasing Ideal Toy Corp., which had outlets for video games in the U.K., France, and West Germany, and merged Ideal with Gabriel. In another development Quaker Oats Co., the parent company of Fisher-Price Toys, acquired the home video games assets of the U.S. Games Corp.

Solar power came to the toy field in 1982 through the enterprise of the Bandai group of Japan. The company evolved a line of hand-held electronic games that operated when exposed to the Sun or to any normal electric light. In the U.K. the Mettoy Company Ltd., the manufacturers of Corgi diecast toys, launched a family computer in midyear. This surprising move by a leading British toy company was further evidence that the toy industry was coming to grips with the needs of the modern market. Traditional toys were ceasing to be of interest to children at a much earlier age. In elementary school they were using computers, and Mettoy decided that a home computer, when added to its traditional toy products, spanned the age spectrum of consumers and would be a family purchase with year-round sales potential.

In June Lesney Products & Co. Ltd., the British-owned Matchbox toys group, went into receivership. The company owed £25 million ($43 million) to the British banks and a further £10 million ($17 million) to trade creditors. In addition, its overseas marketing subsidiaries had £10 million in bank loans. Many companies were involved in the possible purchase of the Matchbox firm, whose brand name was a world leader in the field of diecast toys. Eventually the company was acquired by Universal International (Holdings) Ltd. of Hong Kong. The new owners quickly announced the closing of one of the two Matchbox factories. Universal International also acquired subsidiary companies of the former Lesney group operating in France, West Germany, and Australia.

Much of the financial difficulty experienced in recent years by the toy industry had been due to the uneven pattern of business, which in the majority of countries continued to be heavily concentrated in the Christmas gift-buying season. In an effort to alter this pattern, trade associations representing toy manufacturers, wholesalers, retailers, and importers in the U.K. carried out an experiment in 1982. They launched a pilot scheme in northern England under the title "Give a toy at Easter." The promotion was widely advertised in the chosen area and achieved sufficient success to warrant the holding of a fully national promotion in the U.K. in 1983.

Rubik's Cube, the best-selling toy of 1981, declined in popularity in 1982. Taking its place along with video games were dolls and toys based on the successful motion picture *E.T. The Extra-Terrestrial*.

In September the European Parliament called on European Community governments to ban war toys. The European MP's voted 82 to 45 in favour of a resolution recommending a progressive reduction in the manufacture and sale of such toys and their replacement by toys that were "constructive and develop creativity." The governments of the member countries of the Community planned to consider the resolution. The International Committee of Toy Industries (ICTI), meeting in Montreal in April, agreed to set up a committee to examine all current advertising standards in its 11 member countries. Canada had proposed that ICTI members should adopt a voluntary international standard for advertising directed at children. The ICTI had already achieved a measure of success in harmonizing safety standards for toys throughout the world.

The venerable game of Monopoly, which had sold some 80 million sets since 1934, entered the electronic age in 1982 with the new "Playmaster" version, which rolls the dice, keeps track of property ownership, and plays "Taps" when a player is bankrupted.

COURTESY, PARKER BROTHERS, INC.

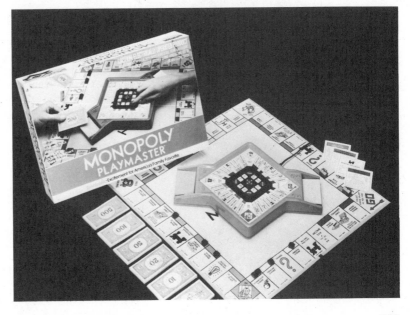

TRACK AND FIELD

Competition was keen throughout the year, but 1982 failed to produce the excitement of either the Olympic Games year of 1980 or of 1981, the "year of the mile." This was especially true of the men's competition, in which world records were set in only four events, but both sexes seemed to be holding something back for the sport's first world championships, scheduled for Helsinki, Fin., Aug. 7–14, 1983.

Four of the world's top performers of 1981 missed all or most of the year. Sebastian Coe and Steve Ovett of the U.K., each of whom set three new world standards in mile and 1,500-m runs in the two previous years, were injured for most of the season and did not approach their form of 1980–81. Also missing were Renaldo Nehemiah and Edwin Moses, the fastest hurdlers in history. Nehemiah retired from hurdling to play professional football in the U.S., and Moses was injured.

Steve Scott of the United States nearly made up for the loss of Coe. He twice broke the U.S. mile record, running 3 min 48.53 sec at Oslo on June 26 and coming back to record 3 min 47.69 sec on July 7. The latter was the second fastest mile ever run, only 0.36 sec off Coe's mark.

Carl Lewis of the U.S. fell just short of Bob Beamon's wind- and altitude-assisted long jump record in August.
WIDE WORLD

Of the six new men's world marks in 1982, three were made in the decathlon. Two of them went to Daley Thompson of the U.K., who had stayed away from major competition in 1981. Rested and eager, Thompson returned in May to Gotzis, Austria, scene of his non-Olympic 1980 record. There he again set a new mark with a total of 8,704 points. But Thompson's record did not stand for long, falling on August 15 at Ulm, West Germany, to Jurgen Hingsen. Competing in his national championships, Hingsen bettered Thompson's record with a score of 8,723. The two met again in the European Championships, and Thompson won, this time with a best ever 8,743 points. Torsten Voss of East Germany set a new world junior mark of 8,387 points.

First of the other three records set in 1982 was made by Sergey Litvinov of the U.S.S.R. He threw the hammer 83.98 m (275 ft 6 in) at Moscow on June 4. It was an unusually large improvement (2.18 m; 7 ft 2 in) on the record of his countryman Yury Sedykh. The biggest surprise among the record breakers was Dave Moorcroft of the U.K., who lowered the 5,000-m mark by 5.8 sec to 13 min 0.42 sec at Oslo on July 7. Moorcroft finished third in the European title meet but won the Commonwealth race. Sixth of the records to fall was in the 4 x 800-m relay, a non-Olympic event. The U.K. team of Peter Elliott, Garry Cook, Steve Cram, and Coe ran the event in 7 min 3.89 sec at London on August 30.

Indoors, U.S. athletes accounted for nine world bests—indoor records are not approved officially—with Billy Olson responsible for four of them. The Abilene Christian University pole vaulter raised the vault record a centimetre at a time, beginning with 5.71 m (18 ft 8¾ in) at Toronto. In quick succession he vaulted 5.72 m (18 ft 9¼ in) at Louisville, Ky., and 5.73 m (18 ft 9½ in) at San Diego, Calif., concluding his spectacular series at Kansas City, Mo., on February 27, when he cleared 5.74 m (18 ft 10 in).

Two other jumping records were set, Carl Lewis long jumping 8.56 m (28 ft 1 in) at East Rutherford, N.J., and Willie Banks triple jumping 17.41 m (57 ft 1½ in) at San Diego. Lewis just missed the outdoor long jump record in August with a leap of 28 ft 9 in. On the track Nehemiah ran the 60-yd hurdles in 6.82 sec at Dallas, Texas, and Don Paige lowered his own world indoor best at 1,000 yd with a 2 min 4.7 sec clocking at Inglewood, Calif.

Women's International Competition

In 1982 the women rebounded from a poor year in 1981, when only two new world marks had been produced. They established 13 records in 11 events, with East Germany leading the way.

The East Germans accounted for four of the records, and Marita Koch, already holder of the international best at both 200 m and 400 m, had a hand in two of them. She dashed 400 m in a rapid 48.16 sec at the European Championships and followed by anchoring the record-breaking 4 x 400-m relay team. Koch's 47.9-sec leg was the second fastest ever, as

Kirsten Siemon, Sabine Busch, Dagmar Rubsam, and Koch ran the distance in 3 min 19.04 sec. Ramona Neubert bettered her own heptathlon figure with 6,772 points at Halle.

A third record was set at the European Championships when Ulrike Meyfarth of West Germany leaped 2.02 m (6 ft 7½ in) in the high jump. Finland's Tiina Lillak hurled the javelin 72.40 m (237 ft 6 in) at Helsinki, and Sofia Sakorafa of Greece later produced a throw of 74.20 m (243 ft 5 in) at Canea, Greece. Two Romanians bettered the long jump standard on the same day in Bucharest. Anisoara Cusmir leaped 7.15 m (23 ft 5½ in) but soon had her mark eclipsed by Vali Ionescu, who reached 7.20 m (23 ft 7½ in).

Most of the action on the track came in the longer runs, and Mary Decker Tabb of the United States was the leading lady. She established new records for the 5,000-m, 10,000-m, and mile runs. Anne Audain of New Zealand ran a record 15 min 13.3 sec for 5,000 m before it was Tabb's turn. The latter reduced the mark to 15 min 8.3 sec at Eugene, Ore. Her home city also was the site of the 10,000-m record six weeks later, when she ran that distance in 31 min 35.3 sec. In between the Eugene performances she cut the mile best to 4 min 18.08 sec at Paris. But the season ended with the mile mark in the possession of Maricica Puica of Romania, who ran a race in 4 min 17.44 sec at Rieti, Italy. The final record went to Svyetlana Ulmasova of the U.S.S.R., who covered 3,000 m in 8 min 26.78 sec at Kiev.

Indoors, U.S. women were as prominent as the U.S. men. Tabb started her big year with three new mile marks, running 4 min 24.6 sec, 4 min 21.5 sec, and, finally, 4 min 20.5 sec. At 60 yd, a distance not run in Europe, first Jeanette Bolden (6.60 sec) and then Evelyn Ashford (6.54 sec) lowered the world record. At the same distance, but over hurdles, Stephanie Hightower and Candy Young had the unique experience of tying with a best ever 7.47 sec and then repeated two weeks later when they were each timed in 7.37 sec.

The high-jump record was raised twice, Debbie Brill of Canada clearing 1.98 m (6 ft 6¼ in) before Coleen Sommer of the U.S. jumped 2.00 m (6 ft 6¾ in). In the long jump two Soviet Union women matched or increased the standard three times. Margarita Butkiene equaled the record of 6.77 m (22 ft 2½ in) before Svyetlana Vanyushina first jumped 6.82 m (22 ft 4½ in) and then 6.83 m (22 ft 5 in). The only European track record was a 49.59-sec 400-m run by Jarmila Kratochvilova of Czechoslovakia.

U.S. Competition

U.S. men failed to produce a world record for the third year in a row. And for the first time since 1946 no men's world record was established in the United States. But 18 national records were produced.

Scott, who set two U.S. mile marks in Europe, also broke the U.S. 2,000-m figure twice, clocking 4 min 58.8 sec and 4 min 54.8 sec. Multiple records

WIDE WORLD

Mary Decker Tabb of the U.S. set a new women's world record for the mile in Paris in July with a time of 4 minutes 18.08 seconds.

also were set by Alberto Salazar, the marathon record holder. After Matt Centrowitz ran a record 13 min 13.0 sec for 5,000 m, Salazar lowered the U.S. mark to 13 min 12.0 sec. Two weeks earlier Salazar had run 10,000 m in 27 min 25.7 sec, a U.S. best.

National standards were established in five of the eight field events with the vaulters most active. Olson opened with 5.71 m (18 ft 8¾ in) and in the national championships tied with Dan Ripley at 5.72 m (18 ft 9¼ in). Dave Volz soon moved the record to 5.73 m (18 ft 9½ in) and then to 5.75 m (18 ft 10¼ in), best in the world for 1982. The high-jump best of 2.32 m (7 ft 7¼ in) was equaled by Del Davis.

Dave Laut set a shot put record; Dave McKenzie improved the hammer throw mark twice; and Bob Roggy broke the javelin standard three times. Laut's 22.02-m (72-ft 3-in) heave equaled Brian Oldfield's 1981 mark, while McKenzie improved on his own record. He threw 73.56 m (241 ft 4 in) and 74.34 m (243 ft 11 in). Close to the world best was Roggy,

Billy Olson of Abilene (Texas) Christian University set a series of new U.S. records in the indoor pole vault during the year.
UPI

who made 93.72 m (307 ft 6 in) and 94.46 m (309 ft 11 in) and then became the second best thrower ever with 95.80 m (314 ft 4 in).

Tabb earned a U.S. record when she ran the 3,000 m in 8 min 29.8 sec. Hightower and Sommer set U.S. marks, too. The former equaled the 100-m hurdle standard of 12.86 sec and then lowered it to 12.79 sec, while Sommer again high jumped 1.98 m (6 ft 6 in). Veteran Jane Frederick was a two-time record breaker, scoring 6,423 and 6,458 in the heptathlon. And the U.S. national 4 x 100-m relay team ran 42.47 sec with Alice Brown, Florence Griffith, Randy Givens, and Diane Williams carrying the baton.

In team competition the United States men beat East Germany 120½–102½, lost to the Soviet Union 118–100, and defeated West Germany 123–99 and Africa 136–69. U.S. women lost to the East Germans 105–52 and to the Soviets 89–67 but defeated the West Germans 90–56. In team competition within the U.S. the University of Texas at El Paso won the National Collegiate Athletic Association (NCAA) title for the third consecutive time indoors and the fourth straight time outdoors. Nebraska won the Association of Intercollegiate Athletics for Women indoor tournament, while in outdoor competition UCLA captured the first women's NCAA tournament, held in conjunction with the men. The Athletic Congress national championships went to Athletic Attic

Tiina Lillak of Finland set a new women's world record in the javelin throw at the World Games in Helsinki in July.
UPI

for the men both indoors and outdoors and for the women to Tennessee State and Wilt's Athletic Club indoors and Los Angeles Naturite outdoors.

Marathon Running

Alberto Salazar continued his domination of the marathon, but his margins of victory were thin. He won at Boston on April 19 with a race record time of 2 hr 8 min 51 sec, just two seconds ahead of Dick Beardsley. Six months later Salazar won his third consecutive New York City Marathon, running just four seconds faster than Rodolfo Gómez of Mexico, with a winning mark of 2 hr 9 min 29 sec. Salazar was unbeaten in four marathons and was the only man to have broken 2 hr 9 min twice. Charlotte Teske of West Germany led the women at Boston in 2 hr 29 min 33 sec, while Grete Waitz of Norway returned to her winning ways in New York, timed in 2 hr 27 min 14 sec. It was her fourth win in five starts there, after being forced out in 1981.

TRANSPORTATION

Aviation

The air transport industry's problems continued unabated in 1982, highlighted dramatically by the collapses of Laker Airways in February and of Braniff, the eighth largest airline in the U.S., in May. The director general of the International Air Transport Association (IATA), the organization representing most international scheduled carriers, described the

problems in his annual report as "staggering." He added that the industry was on a financial tightrope with "the abyss of bankruptcy on the one hand and the slippery slope of subsidization or permanent bondage to the loan market on the other." The IATA airlines were expected to suffer a collective operating loss on scheduled services of $260 million in 1982, a figure slightly worse than that for 1981. The association anticipated further deterioration to a $370 million operating loss in 1983 but after that expected a return to profitability.

The full picture, however, was worse. After allowing for interest payments of $1,610,000,000 in 1982, the IATA members' net result for the year was put at a loss of $1,870,000,000. A loss of more than $2 billion was anticipated in 1983, and only a modest improvement was expected in the following year.

The bleak situation was blamed on such factors as stagnant markets, uneconomic fares combined with illegal discounting, rising costs, overcapacity on many routes, and, in the case of 30–40 airlines, the blocking of some $600 million of their earnings in about 30 countries, mostly in Africa.

In the U.S. the 11 major airlines reported an operating loss of $118.1 million for the first nine months of 1982, compared with a loss of $18 million for the comparable period of 1981. Although 9 of the 11 airlines improved their operating results in the third quarter of 1982 compared to those of a year earlier, and although the group as a whole managed a net profit in that quarter, it was considered too early to

Laker Airways, created by Britain's Sir Freddie Laker in 1977 to pioneer in low-cost transatlantic flights, was forced to cease operations in February.
LONDON EXPRESS/PICTORIAL PARADE

September's strike by members of the Brotherhood of Locomotive Engineers idled trains across the nation for four days.

declare these the first signs of an improving trend.

A review by the U.S. Civil Aeronautics Board considered the effects of deregulation on the U.S. transport industry. It showed that, with the freeing of competition over the years 1978–82, the trunk carriers consistently lost market share to local service carriers and new entrants. In that period the trunks' share fell from 87.2 to 78.9%. The study detected a shift in service patterns, with the trunks pulling out of smaller markets and the locals expanding into longer-haul markets. Fuel and labour costs more than doubled in the period, yet average fares increased by 65%. Certificated airline service to 74 communities was discontinued, but in general the public's travel convenience improved in large markets and declined only slightly in small ones.

Final figures for world scheduled air traffic in 1981, issued by the International Civil Aviation Organization, showed that the number of passengers, 743 million, represented a decline of 0.8% from 1980. The volume of freight rose 2.8% to 11 million metric tons. Thanks to an increase in the average distance flow, total traffic increased 2.5% to 133,940,000,000,000 metric ton-km, but this was the lowest percentage increase recorded in ten years.

U.S. Railroads

The beleaguered national economy severely affected freight railroads in 1982 and tempered the industry's optimism for a postderegulation renaissance. On the bright side, however, the nation's railroads endured the lingering economic downturn without suffering the bankruptcies that had marked previous recessions. In 1982, operating classically as a "demand-derived" industry, commodities carried by rail declined precipitously. Grain loadings were down 6.3%; lumber and wood products were down 22.8%; and motor vehicles and equipment dropped 11.9% from already depressed 1981 levels.

Coal, the railroads' largest single commodity, experienced a 1.8% decline—contrary to predictions that coal traffic would increase. Piggyback, the movement of containers and trailers on flatcars, was the notable bright spot with a 9.9% increase in loadings. Many experts believed this increase reflected a continuing shift in high-rated consumer goods from trucks to more fuel-efficient rails.

As a result of the overall drop in traffic, however, the freight railroads often had more than 12% of their freight cars and more than 20% of the locomotive fleet standing idle. The depressed traffic levels also were reflected in the industry's disappointing financial performance. Net revenue for the first three quarters of the year was off by almost 50% from the comparable 1981 period, and the industry's rate of return for the 12 months ending September 30 was 2.16%, compared with 5.17% a year earlier.

While weathering the immediate impact of the recession, the rails looked to the future and continued to move toward a basic restructuring. On March 25 the Interstate Commerce Commission (ICC) approved the merger of the Norfolk & Western and the Southern Railway. The new system—the Norfolk Southern—had nearly 18,000 mi of road in 21 states. The ICC also approved the consolidation of the Union Pacific, Western Pacific, and Missouri Pacific railroads to form Pacific Rail System Inc., a 22,740-mi system spanning 21 states.

The year also saw significant developments in rail labour relations. The National Railroad Passenger Corporation (Amtrak) signed a historic agreement with the Brotherhood of Locomotive Engineers (BLE) to change the basis of pay from the traditional combination of hours worked and miles traveled to one of hours worked only. The precedent-setting contract at last removed the concept of the "100-mi day" that had originated in the days of steam.

The Amtrak-BLE agreement came shortly after the nation endured a four-day strike by the engineers against most freight railroads. The strike—the first nationwide action by a rail union since 1971—ended when Pres. Ronald Reagan signed a quickly passed congressional resolution mandating an end to the action, which threatened to cripple the country's already weakened economy. The BLE then accepted basically the same agreement that the 12 other rail unions already had signed.

Finally, with budget cuts promising to close the federal Transportation Test Center in Pueblo, Colo., the Association of American Railroads took over management of the facility, where state-of-the-art freight, passenger, and transit equipment is tested.

Pipelines

While pipelines had occasionally led to some regional controversy, they rarely formed a focus of international dispute. A major exception to this general rule was the Siberian-Western European gas pipeline. The scheme involved pumping between 21 billion and 30 billion cu ft per annum of natural gas 2,200 mi (3,550 km) from the Urengoi field in the U.S.S.R. (the largest in the world) to the Czechoslovak border and then on into Western Europe. The contracts, signed in October 1981, would bring relatively cheap gas to energy-poor Western Europe and also would result in substantial orders for pipes, generators, and other engineering equipment. Meanwhile, in response to the continuation of martial law in Poland, the Reagan administration embargoed the use of equipment made by U.S. manufacturers and their European subsidiaries. Understandably,

this led to tension between the U.S. and Western Europe, while the U.S.S.R. maintained that the pipeline could be built without U.S. technology (notably 25-MW compressors). Spiced with rumours of the use of forced labour on the pipeline, the controversy ended when Reagan lifted the embargo in the fall of 1982.

Roads and Traffic

The number of automobiles on the world's highways rose to 330 million in 1982. The maintenance of existing roads was a major issue in both developed and less developed countries. In order to keep down construction and maintenance costs, greater emphasis was placed on the use of local materials. In the U.K. the first stage of the widening of one of the world's most densely traveled interurban expressways (the M1) was opened; apart from the problems of designing, constructing, and managing the remodeling of a busy operational motorway, the project provided lessons for long-term highway planning.

Whereas in the past the most spectacular highway projects were to be found in the Western world, the balance was changing. The $460 million Aberdeen Tunnel and East Kowloon Way in Hong Kong and the $175 million Olympic Expressway between Taegu and Kwangju in South Korea were examples of this. The latter project was initiated to mark the holding of the 1988 Summer Olympic Games in Seoul. Traffic congestion was becoming a major problem in some Asian cities, and Hong Kong introduced stiff vehicle taxes to help moderate the growth of car ownership there.

Intercity Rail

The most remarkable event of the year was the near completion of the fourth Shinkansen line between Tokyo and Niigata, Japan. This 170-mi (270-km) line had taken 11 years to build through some of Honshu's most difficult terrain. The link through to the Tokyo suburbs was made by the opening of the Di-Shimiyu tunnel, which, at 13.8 mi (22.3 km), was the longest mainline rail tunnel in the world. The opening of this line, which was to extend to central Tokyo in 1986, brought the length of the "bullet train" network to 1,118 mi (1,800 km). In California a "bullet-type" railway service between San Diego and San Francisco was being planned.

Expansion of national railway networks continued in other countries, especially those earning oil revenues. In Iraq, despite the war with Iran, work was under way on rail links between Baghdad and Basra (565 mi, 910 km) and Baghdad and Husaiba (250 mi, 404 km). In Venezuela the capital, Caracas, was to be connected to La Guaira on the coast, and in Libya work began on the 120-mi (194-km) Tripoli-Misratah line.

In the U.K. the high-technology Advanced Passenger Train had to be withdrawn from passenger service because of difficulties with its braking system. In West Germany the Lufthansa airline intro-

Souvenir collectors placed coins on the tracks as the last car headed into the barn before a 20-month shutdown of San Francisco's famed cable-car system began.
WIDE WORLD

duced express service between Düsseldorf, Cologne, and Bonn and the Frankfurt airport.

Urban Mass Transit

During the year the most advanced urban mass transit system came into revenue service in Lille, France, and one of the oldest mechanized systems, the San Francisco, Calif., cable cars, shut down temporarily for rehabilitation. In the U.S. progress was made on rapid transit rail projects in Portland, Ore., and Buffalo, N.Y., and the line from Cleveland, Ohio, to the suburb of Shaker Heights was renovated. In Canada Light Rail Transit (LRT) projects were under way in Vancouver, B.C., and Pickering, Ont. A light rail scheme was approved for London's Docklands, and in The Netherlands the Coalhaven-to-Copelsburg line in Rotterdam was to be extended as a streetcar line to Binnerhof. This form of technology, able to operate as both railway and streetcar, appeared to be increasingly popular where full subways were not merited but good quality of service was required.

Work on subways proceeded in Paris; in West Germany at Bochum, Dortmund, Duisburg, and Essen; and in Berlin, Rome, Stockholm, Hong Kong, Seoul, Tokyo, Boston, New York, and Mexico City. Openings during the year included Helsinki and the Tsuen Wan line in Hong Kong. By the end of 1982 the system in Mexico City was 53 mi (85 km) long, and the planners were aiming at a 272-mi (438-km) system by the year 2000. Authority to proceed was given to new subways in Singapore and Riga (U.S.S.R.) as well as to extensions of several existing systems, including the connection to the new terminal at Heathrow Airport (London).

Noteworthy developments in urban buses included the successful guided bus in Stuttgart, West Germany, which was to be introduced in Adelaide, Australia. Work also continued on new drive systems including battery diesel hybrids. The number of exclusive urban busways was growing steadily, and there were now at least ten such systems. One of the highest bus flows in any city was in São Paulo, Brazil, where platooning of up to six buses in convoys was used to increase busway capacity by 100%.

In London transit fares were first cut by one-third and then doubled. In 1981 many transit fares had been more than doubled on some lines in Chicago. This reflected pressures to keep down revenue support for transit on the part of public agencies. In the U.K. new legislation was proposed that sought to restrict external support from either local or central sources. In the U.S. reduction of federal funding led to the crisis in Chicago. In southern California a decision to "go it alone" led to a reduction in transit fares, and in New York and other cities freedom from federal "buy American" policies allowed a wide choice of equipment procurement. This especially benefited Japanese and Canadian train builders and West German bus builders.

TUNISIA

On the domestic scene the main events of 1982 in Tunisia were a series of strikes in February that led to a general increase in wages and violent confrontations between university students and police in March. There also were a number of anti-Jewish incidents at Zarzis, Ben Gardane, and Djerba in October.

The main thrust of Tunisian foreign policy was toward a rapprochement with Libya. At Pres. Habib Bourguiba's invitation, Libyan chief of state Col. Muammar al-Qaddafi paid a five-day official visit to Tunisia in February; this followed a brief unofficial visit by Qaddafi on January 24, when he met Tunisia's Prime Minister Mohammed Mzali. A cooperation agreement was signed during the February visit, but although Qaddafi reportedly again brought up the question of a union between Libya and Tunisia (first proposed by him in 1974), no mention was made of this in the joint communiqué.

Despite the improved relations with Libya, Tunisia was among those member nations that boycotted the August summit in Tripoli of the Organization of African Unity, being opposed to the admission of the self-proclaimed (West) Saharan Arab Democratic Republic. Meanwhile, the dispute between Tunisia and Libya over their respective rights to the oil-rich continental shelf in the Gulf of Gabès was before the International Court of Justice in The Hague.

Following a private visit to the U.S. in January by President Bourguiba, Mzali in April went to Washington, D.C., for talks with Secretary of Defense Caspar Weinberger. An agreement was signed for the sale to Tunisia of military equipment that included 12 F-5 fighter aircraft and 54 M-60 tanks; to help pay for this, U.S. aid for 1983 was to be almost doubled from the 1982 figure of $82 million to $140 million.

Following Israel's intervention in Lebanon and the escalation of the civil war there, Tunisia's ruling Parti Socialiste Destourien and the Union Générale des Travailleurs de Tunisie proclaimed their solidarity with the Arab people in Lebanon and Palestine. In August, at President Bourguiba's invitation, Palestine Liberation Organization (PLO) leader Yasir Arafat set up his new headquarters in Tunis, and more than 1,000 Palestinian guerrillas evacuated from Lebanon were housed in the Beja region west of Tunis.

Franco-Tunisian relations were reinforced. Bourguiba visited France for medical treatment in January and September, and members of the French government visited Tunis on several occasions during the year. In March Tunisia became a member of the Organization of Petroleum Exporting Countries, Libya having withdrawn its opposition. In November serious flooding caused a number of deaths and much damage.

Guerrillas of the Palestine Liberation Organization cheered as they left Bizerte, Tunisia, for their camp in the remote Beja region.
WIDE WORLD

TURKEY

The armed forces commanders who formed the National Security Council (NSC) and took over the government of Turkey in the bloodless coup of Sept. 12, 1980, continued during 1982 to follow their plan for the reform of institutions with a view to the reestablishment of parliamentary rule. A new constitution, drafted by a nominated Consultative Assembly and amended by the NSC, was submitted to a referendum on November 7 and approved by 91% of the votes in a voter turnout also of 91%. Criticism of individual constitutional provisions was allowed before the final text was established. Thereafter the campaign was one-sided, as no one was allowed to urge its rejection.

Under provisional articles, acceptance of the constitution carried with it the election of Gen. Kenan Evren, chairman of the NSC, to the presidency of the republic for a seven-year term, and a ban varying from five to ten years on leading members of the old political parties. The constitution provided for a single-chamber Parliament, elected every five years; for an executive headed by a president who was to be elected by Parliament (after the end of General Evren's term) and given enhanced powers; for a Cabinet responsible to Parliament; and for an independent judiciary. Political activity by trade unions and professional associations was banned, as were totalitarian, Marxist, and religious fundamentalist politics. After the constitution was approved, the Consultative Assembly began drafting a law on political parties and an electoral law in preparation for elections scheduled for late 1983.

Bulent Ecevit, leader of the dissolved left-of-centre Republican People's Party, was the only politician to challenge the ruling generals. He served two short prison sentences for giving interviews to foreign publications. On September 1 there were some 18,000 persons under arrest and facing charges for politically motivated offenses, while another 6,500 had received sentences of imprisonment. The military authorities examined 540 complaints of torture and maltreatment and concluded that in four cases death had been caused by torture.

While Turkish political terrorism was largely suppressed, attacks by Armenian terrorists continued. The number of Turkish diplomats and their dependents killed outside the country by Armenian terrorists rose to 24, and on August 7 nine people were killed and 72 injured in an Armenian attack on the Ankara airport.

General Evren in 1982 visited Kuwait, Pakistan, Romania, and Bulgaria, while Prime Minister Bulent Ulusu took part in the Islamic mediation mission in the Iran-Iraq war. Relations with Greece were strained by repeated Greek accusations of Turkish violations of Greek territorial waters and airspace in the Aegean Sea, by Turkish accusations of Greek maltreatment of the Turkish minority in western Thrace, and by the Greek campaign against the presence of Turkish troops in Cyprus, where Turkey continued to support intercommunal talks as the only means to a solution. The situation was temporarily eased, however, when the two governments decided on June 22 to refrain from further polemics.

Relations with Europe were soured by frequent European criticism of the military regime; the European Communities continued to block aid to Turkey. Close relations with the U.S. were promoted by the visit to Ankara in May of U.S. Secretary of State Alexander Haig. The killing of two Turkish soldiers by Soviet border guards on August 10 emphasized the basically antagonistic nature of the outwardly correct relationship between Turkey and the U.S.S.R.

Former Turkish premier Bulent Ecevit was escorted from a military courthouse in April after being convicted of violating the government's gag order.
WIDE WORLD

Inflation fell below 30%, and exports increased significantly. However, the tightly controlled monetary policies caused difficulties. The largest private finance house in Turkey, Banker Kastelli, was unable to meet payments and had to be taken over by the government on June 22. This was followed by the resignations of Turgut Ozal, deputy prime minister in charge of the economy, and of the ministers of finance and of housing.

UGANDA

Early in 1982 Pres. Milton Obote of Uganda released nearly 200 detainees, including four opposition members of Parliament. His action was dismissed as an empty gesture by a group of his critics meeting in London on January 7 to form a popular front to overthrow the government. The prime mover of the group was former president Godfrey Binaisa; another former president, Yusufu Lule, chairman of the National Resistance Movement, was also present, together with the chairman of the Uganda Freedom Movement. Both Binaisa and Lule insisted, however, that they had had no contact with former president Idi Amin, whom they grouped with Obote as an oppressor of Uganda and its people.

In February Obote appealed to Ugandan exiles to return to their homes, assuring them that they need not fear attack from other tribes. However, acts of violence by guerrillas, particularly in the neighbour-hood of Kampala, continued throughout the year, followed by vigorous reprisals from the Army. In February a large group of guerrillas carried out a heavy but ultimately unsuccessful attack on the Malire barracks in Kampala. Both sides claimed to have inflicted serious casualties, and it was reported that 2,000 civilians were subsequently arrested and interrogated. The rough handling meted out by the Army on such occasions aroused further resentment against the government. A small force of Commonwealth soldiers arrived during the year to train and discipline the Ugandan troops.

In areas at a distance from Kampala, security and stability were more in evidence, and a recovery program, backed by the World Bank and the International Monetary Fund, was beginning to take effect. In the drought-threatened northeastern district of Karamoja, however, there were fears that food shortages would again be acute.

A further measure aimed at restoring confidence in Uganda's economy was taken in September; a law was enacted by Parliament guaranteeing the return of their property to Asians who had been forced to surrender it by the order of Idi Amin in 1972. It was a condition of the bill that Asians must return to Uganda to register their claim within three months of its becoming law and that they could not resell their property for a period of five years. The law was strongly criticized by many Ugandans who thought it unfair that Africans who had acquired property in

Kitchen utensils and agricultural tools were part of the self-help assistance provided by the United Nations to these Ugandan refugees in The Sudan.
UNHCR/KEYSTONE

good faith and had made good use of it should now have to surrender it.

In August a further 1,160 detainees were released, many of them former soldiers under Amin. Almost immediately it was announced that a plot engineered by Binaisa to overthrow the government with the aid of white mercenaries had been postponed owing to lack of money to fund the enterprise. The government was challenged from another quarter, however, when Amnesty International published a report charging Obote and his ministers with responsibility for the torture and group killings of civilians by the Army. The government replied in September that ever since taking office it had been subjected to a hostile campaign of criticism from inside and outside the country and had been given no opportunity to comment on charges before they were published.

In the southwest a new problem arose in October. In the absence of the president, who was receiving medical attention in Europe, officials in Ankole ordered thousands of Rwandan refugees who had been given asylum in Uganda during Obote's first presidency to leave their settlements and enter refugee camps. Finally, the government decided to permit the refugees to live in certain fixed zones. It was announced shortly afterward that thousands of Ugandans living in Kenya who had previously been exempt from the normal immigration laws would have to leave the country because the exemption no longer applied to them.

UNION OF SOVIET SOCIALIST REPUBLICS

An era came to an end on Nov. 10, 1982, with the death of Leonid Ilich Brezhnev. The news of his demise was kept from the Soviet and international public until the following day. Then it was announced that Yury Vladimirovich Andropov had been made chairman of the funeral commission, clear evidence that he was the front-runner in the struggle to become the new general secretary of the Communist Party of the Soviet Union (CPSU). An extraordinary plenum of the Central Committee duly elected him party leader on November 12. Shortly afterward, the Supreme Soviet convened and elected Andropov to its Presidium but did not make him president. Vasily Kuznetsov, the deputy president, was to continue to act as president.

Andropov's hopes of succeeding Brezhnev had improved in January when Mikhail Suslov died. Rumoured to have turned down the post of party leader in 1964, he was the keeper of the CPSU's ideological conscience. Had he lived he would have played a key role in deciding the next party leader. Andropov, head of the KGB security force since 1967, moved back into the Central Committee Secretariat in May, a position he had to hold in order to make an effective bid for the succession. At the same time, Vladimir Dolgikh, Central Committee secretary for heavy industry, was made a candidate (nonvoting) member of the Politburo.

Andropov's main competitors were Konstantin Chernenko and Andrey Kirilenko, but it soon became apparent that the latter was slipping from prominence. Andropov struck a tactical alliance with Defense Minister Dmitry Ustinov and the military. Andropov could also rely for support on the KGB under Col. Gen. Vitaly Fedorchuk. The security policy-military complex, Andropov's tactical alliance, proved too powerful for Chernenko and his supporters. At 68, Andropov, a Russian, was the oldest man ever to become party leader, ten years older than Brezhnev when he took over in 1964.

The Soviet Union needed incisive leadership after the drift of the late Brezhnev era, and Andropov appeared capable of providing it. Since his power base was the party apparatus, he would need to ease out all those closely associated with Brezhnev. The first demotion was that of Kirilenko, who was dropped from both the Politburo and the Secretariat.

Geidar Aliev, first secretary of the Communist Party of Azerbaijan, was the first man to advance under Andropov. He was promoted from candidate to full member of the Politburo and was also made first deputy premier in preparation, it seemed likely, for the post of premier. Before becoming party leader in Azerbaijan in 1969, he was a professional KGB officer and headed the organization in that republic in the years 1967–69. The new administration's KGB connection was further emphasized on December 17 when Andropov made Fedorchuk minister of the interior, replacing Nikolay Shchelokov, a close Brezhnev associate. The new KGB head was Viktor Chebrikov. Andropov soon set in motion other changes, promoting younger, more capable officials. This contrasted with the remarkable stability of cadres under Brezhnev, which had led to complacency and inefficiency.

The military lobby strongly argued its case for higher defense spending and eventually won the day. Chief of Staff Marshal Nikolay Ogarkov, however, was unhappy about the attitude of many Soviet citizens toward the West. Some thought that any peace was good, any war was bad. He advocated an increase in political and educational work in order to inculcate a "class point of view" in foreign affairs. At the parade in Red Square on November 7—Brezhnev's last public appearance—Ustinov stated that the armed forces were ready to do their "patriotic and internationalist duty" if called upon. The tone of military self-confidence continued after Andropov became party leader.

A tougher line toward dissent, opposition, corruption, and other social misdemeanours was taken throughout the year. The Helsinki monitoring group, formed six years earlier to check Soviet observance of the 1975 Helsinki accords, was dissolved. Direct dialing between Western Europe and the Soviet Union ceased in July, clearly a move to restrict unofficial contacts, but it was partially restored in September. Soviet citizens were warned

The pomp and ceremony of Leonid Brezhnev's funeral in Moscow on November 15 were the most elaborate seen in the Soviet Union since the death of Stalin 29 years before.

against unofficial contacts with Westerners in the Soviet Union. The dissident scientist Andrey Sakharov accused the KGB in October of drugging him and stealing several hundred pages of personal manuscripts and documents.

An unofficial peace committee was set up on June 4 with the aim of establishing trust between the U.S.S.R. and the U.S. It put forward a list of "confidence-building measures," including the suggestion that the Moscow region be twinned with the District of Columbia as a nuclear-free zone. It also wanted war games banned in both states and the introduction of a course on the "propagation of peace" in the schools. It was claimed that some 170 people signed the proposals. The authorities quickly made arrests and threatened signatories with loss of career prospects. Sergey Batovrin, a founding member, was confined in a psychiatric hospital in August but was released after strong protests by Western scientists and nuclear disarmers.

The battle against corruption was given prominence in the press. The most senior official executed was Vladimir Rytov, a former deputy minister of fisheries, for his part in a caviar-smuggling scandal. Parnaoz Ananiashvili, former minister of finance in Georgia, was sentenced for embezzlement, and it was said that his ministry had been riddled with bribery over the last ten years. Thousands of officials, managers, and sales personnel were dismissed, fined, or sentenced for corruption during the year.

Alcoholism continued to be the main social problem. According to a survey, 62% of women filing for divorce cited the "husband's drinking or alcoholism" as the main reason for the breakup of the marriage.

Among those granted exit visas were Igor, son of chess grand master Viktor Korchnoi, his mother, and his stepmother. Korchnoi, who defected in 1976, had campaigned ceaselessly on their behalf. New defectors included the violinist Nelli Zhkolnikova. It became much more difficult for Jews to emigrate. In 1982 only about 3,000 received exit visas, compared with over 51,000 in 1979. Most of those allowed to leave in 1982 were elderly people with relatives in the U.S. or other Western countries. Soviet officials told Western politicians that all those wanting to leave were being allowed to do so but that the number of requests was decreasing. However, Jewish sources put the number wishing to leave at 380,000.

The Economy

Industry and agriculture failed to achieve their planned targets. Instead of 3.4% industrial growth, only 2.8% was claimed. The harvest was disappointing for the fourth successive year and was unlikely to exceed 185 million metric tons, far short of the planned 239 million metric tons. Labour productivity again failed to meet planned targets, and a whole range of industries turned in disappointing performances.

In the opinion of Western experts, the level of investment scheduled for the five-year (1981–85) plan was not sufficient to achieve the planned industrial targets. Investment in the fuel and energy complex had increased sharply, while investment in the industries that provided the support base (*e.g.*, the machine-building industry) had slowed. The goal of the plan was to raise the share of consumption in total national income, and social goals were accorded priority, but at the same time, investment in housing, health, and services had dropped. The performance of the economy in 1982 was the poorest since World War II, with growth in gross domestic product, in real terms, probably zero.

The food situation was serious. Reports circulated that even bread was rationed in certain areas—a psychological blow, since the regime had always been capable of ensuring that enough bread was produced. One of the reasons for the shortage was excessive demand. Prices of all staple foods, including meat, had been frozen for 20 years, while incomes had doubled over the same period. During the agricultural year July 1981–June 1982, the Soviet Union imported an estimated 45 million metric tons of grain at a cost of about $8 billion. In 1982 the state subsidy to agriculture—the difference between what the state paid the farms for their produce and what it got back from retail sales—topped 27 billion rubles.

The dismal performance of agriculture galvanized the Brezhnev leadership into action, and a massive agricultural program, covering the years 1982–90, was announced in May. One of the reasons was the grain embargo imposed by the U.S. Moscow did not wish to find itself in a position where the U.S. could offer grain for Soviet concessions. Because of the high cost of Soviet food production, it might be cheaper to import grain, meat, and other products. However, the leadership rejected this solution because it would make the Soviet Union dangerously dependent.

The agricultural program introduced a new hierarchy of coordinators headed by a deputy premier in Moscow. All the agencies serving agriculture, especially those involved in processing, packing, and transporting produce to the consumer, were to be brought together. Another large increase—totaling 16 billion rubles—in the prices paid by the state for farm produce was to take effect from January 1983, and many farm debts to the state bank were to be written off. Over the next eight years, 160 billion rubles were to be spent on improving rural roads and homes, building new farms, and providing amenities in the villages so as to stem the flow of young people from the countryside. An effort was to be made to improve the quality of machinery and fertilizer delivered to the farms; currently, about 20% of all fertilizer was lost in transit.

Foreign trade turnover rose by only 5% in 1982, despite considerable sales of gold, diamonds, and precious metals on the world market. One of the reasons for the modest growth was the drop in oil sales on the spot market. However, U.K. trade with the Soviet Union showed a healthy increase, one of the reasons being the purchase of Soviet oil offered at very advantageous prices. The Soviet Union was obliged to run down its hard-currency holdings in Western banks in order to cover its imports of grain and industrial goods. Moscow was slow in reacting to the U.S. offer of an additional 15 million metric tons of grain after the grain embargo was lifted.

Foreign Affairs

Relations with the outside world were unsatisfactory throughout the year. The U.S. administration took a noticeably harder line toward the Soviet Union and set in train heavy increases in defense spending. Although the grain embargo and sanctions against firms participating in the construction of the Urengoi natural-gas pipeline to Western Europe were lifted by Washington, Soviet-U.S. relations deteriorated during the last period of Brezhnev's rule. On November 7 Brezhnev warned "potential aggressors" that the Soviet Union would deal them a crushing retaliatory blow. On the other

Yury Andropov delivered Brezhnev's eulogy at Lenin's tomb, flanked by (left to right) Politburo members Kunayev, Shcherbitsky, Ustinov, Tikhonov, Chernenko, Gromyko, Grishin, and Gorbachov.
UPI

"Freeze!"
OLIPHANT ©1982, WASHINGTON
STAR / UNIVERSAL PRESS
SYNDICATE

hand, he stated that the U.S.S.R. would fight consistently for détente. In late October he accused the U.S. government of launching a political, ideological, and economic offensive against Moscow.

Considerable prominence was accorded Sino-Soviet relations throughout the year. Leonid Ilichev, a deputy foreign minister, journeyed to Beijing (Peking) in October for talks. On the day that Brezhnev died, however, the party newspaper *Pravda* attacked China for "linking up with imperialist reaction" on the Kampuchean question. Evidently there had been little progress on the three main Chinese demands: that the Soviet Union stop aiding Vietnam in Indochina; that Soviet forces withdraw from Afghanistan; and that Soviet troops along the Sino-Soviet border be thinned out. *Pravda* attacked Chinese support for the Khmer Rouge regime, which occupied the Kampuchean seat at the UN, and accused Beijing of distorting the situation inside Kampuchea and the Soviet Union's support of Vietnam.

At Brezhnev's funeral, Huang Hua, the Chinese foreign minister, was warmly welcomed by Andropov. He reciprocated by referring to Brezhnev as an "outstanding statesman" and proposing a "genuine improvement" in relations between the two countries. He also wished the Soviet Union well under its new leadership.

In Afghanistan the war against the Islamic guerrillas continued, with no end in sight. Over 100,000 Soviet soldiers dominated the towns, but the countryside remained in rebel hands. Soviet losses continued to mount, as did those of the guerrillas and the civilian population. The latter were particularly hard hit by the bombing raids carried out by Soviet helicopter gunships. Capture usually meant death for Soviet troops, but two soldiers were handed over to the International Red Cross for internment for two years in Switzerland. Several hundred Soviet personnel were reportedly asphyxiated in the Salang tunnel en route to Kabul in November. According to some reports, the Soviet commander, fearing a guerrilla attack, had closed both ends of

the tunnel after a vehicle pileup and explosion. At the UN the Soviet Union failed for the third successive year to convince the third world majority that its troops were in Afghanistan at the request of the Afghan government. In November a resolution calling for the immediate withdrawal of Soviet troops was carried by 114 votes to 21 (13 abstentions).

The situation in Poland stabilized, thus allowing martial law to be suspended after a year. Nevertheless, Poland became a greater burden to the Soviet Union, especially economically. Elsewhere in Eastern Europe, most leaders were in their 70s and well entrenched. Their room for maneuver in relations with the Soviet Union had expanded during the late Brezhnev era, and Andropov was expected to meet resistance if he tried to impose stricter Soviet control. The whole region was in need of economic reform to head off stagnation and decline.

In Western Europe the Soviet Union was encouraged by the strength of the peace movement, which was especially strong in the U.K., The Netherlands, and West Germany. However, Moscow did not welcome the change of government in Bonn when Helmut Kohl replaced Helmut Schmidt as federal chancellor. Moscow continued its polemics against the Eurocommunists, hitting out especially against the Italians. The latter called into question the historical value of the Soviet experience and the contribution of Lenin to Marxism, as well as criticizing Soviet behaviour in Poland and Afghanistan. The French Communists remained loyal to Moscow and defended Soviet policy in Afghanistan and Poland, but this made them unpopular with French voters.

The Soviet naval attaché, Capt. Anatoly Zotov, was expelled from the U.K. in December for allegedly trying to set up a spy ring. Since U.K. government policy was not to permit replacement of those expelled, the Soviet diplomatic community was reduced from 46 to 45.

Soviet commitments around the world became more onerous. The subsidy extended to Eastern Europe amounted to about $20 billion. The Afghan

Some 300 Western advocates of nuclear disarmament, most of them Swedish, were allowed to march in Moscow and other cities in the Soviet Union in July although participation and even watching by Soviet citizens was closely controlled.
UPI

conflict was costing an estimated $7 million a day and Cuba $10 million a day, while Vietnam was also receiving considerable financial support. In total, the burden of empire may have cost the Soviet exchequer about $30 billion in 1982.

UNITED NATIONS

On September 7 UN Secretary-General Javier Pérez de Cuéllar warned the world that it was "perilously near to a new international anarchy." He asked nations to reverse their "exceedingly dangerous course" and urged them "to render the UN more capable of carrying out its primary function" of preserving international peace and security.

Instead of surveying UN activities broadly, as secretaries-general have usually done, Pérez de Cuéllar focused, in his first report on the work of the organization since he assumed office on January 1, on the "central problem" of the UN: its "capacity to keep the peace and to serve as a forum for negotiations." Often during 1982, he said, the UN had been set aside or rebuffed. Frequently, the Security Council could not act decisively to remove international conflicts, but even its unanimous resolutions were "increasingly defied or ignored by those . . . strong enough to do so."

Middle East

Throughout the year, charges and countercharges by disputants in the Middle East came before the Council and the Assembly, with just such results. On March 24 Arab nations asked the Council to consid-

er "deliberate provocations, assaults, abductions and murder, perpetrated by heavily armed Israeli troops and intruding settlers" in occupied Arab territories. Israel replied that Jordan and the Palestine Liberation Organization (PLO) were conspiring "to eliminate any emerging and promising alternative to the PLO method of violence and terror," were intimidating Arab leaders who favoured peace, and were stirring up violence against Israeli troops.

The Assembly met on April 28 in a resumed emergency session and condemned Israel (86–20–36) for not being a peace-loving state, for not carrying out its Charter obligations, for not complying with resolutions on Jerusalem and not dismantling settlements in occupied territories, for not applying the Geneva Conventions that protect civilians in wartime, and for frustrating the exercise of Palestinian rights. It called on the Security Council to recognize the Palestinians' rights to independent statehood and urged the secretary-general to consult with all parties, including the PLO, to find ways to achieve a comprehensive, just, and lasting peace. Israeli delegate Yehuda Blum denounced the resolution as a "miserable concoction" that "regurgitates" the main components of other anti-Israeli resolutions "steamrollered" through the Assembly by parties seeking to destroy Israel.

The resolution certainly did not alleviate tensions in Lebanon. The Council had on April 22, after three Israeli air strikes against Lebanon, authorized its president to demand an end to all armed attacks and cease-fire violations. On May 9 Israel launched "retaliatory" raids against Lebanon to put an end to the "terrorist PLO operating from Lebanese territory."

After Israel's ambassador to Great Britain was critically wounded by Arab assailants in London on June 3, Israel bombed PLO sites in Lebanon again for two days. Then, on June 6, calling Lebanon "the centre of world terrorism," Israel launched an attack that overran positions of the UN Interim Force in Lebanon (UNIFIL) and did not end until nearly all of Beirut was under Israeli control. UN reactions included calls on June 4 by the secretary-general for both sides to "desist from hostile acts" and from the Security Council to "adhere strictly" to the cease-fire. On June 5 and 6 other Council resolutions followed calling for an end to military action, but the Israeli representative asked, "How many Israelis have to be killed by terrorists for this Council to be persuaded that the limits of our endurance have been reached?" On June 26 the U.S. vetoed a resolution calling for all forces to pull back from Beirut because of its "fatal flaw" in not requiring "the elimination from Beirut and elsewhere of the presence of armed Palestinian elements, who neither submit to nor respect" Lebanese sovereignty.

On September 17 the world learned that a massacre of Palestinian and other civilians had occurred in Beirut refugee camps. The Council on September 18–19 unanimously condemned the slaughter and authorized the secretary-general to increase the number of UN observers in the area from 10 to 50.

Senji Yamaguchi held a picture of himself taken after the 1945 atomic bombing of Nagasaki as he addressed the UN disarmament session in June.
UPI

On September 24 the Assembly also condemned (147–2) the Beirut massacre. The U.S. and Israel, which voted no, argued that the resolution would only prolong and embitter conflict.

UN officials continued their efforts to end the fighting between Iran and Iraq, which had begun in 1980, but neither the secretary-general himself nor his special representative, Olof Palme of Sweden, succeeded in bridging the gaps between the parties. Security Council resolutions (July 12 and October 4) were likewise unavailing. On October 22 the Assembly affirmed (119–1–15) the Council's calls for a cease-fire, but Iran, which cast the sole negative vote, objected that the Assembly had ignored the fact that Iraq started the war and occupied a portion of Iranian territory for more than two years.

Falkland Islands

On April 1 the U.K. warned the Security Council that Argentina was preparing to move militarily against British dependencies in the South Atlantic; at the same time, Argentina complained of "continuous acts of aggression" by Britain over 150 years. The Council and the secretary-general both urged restraint, but on April 2 Argentina invaded and seized the Falklands (which it calls the Malvinas). The Council demanded (10–1–4) that Argentina withdraw and that hostilities cease immediately, but Argentina went on to take South Georgia Island on April 3. Britain sent a naval task force to the area, and on April 12 Argentina announced that it would comply with the Council resolution if the British would. The U.K. pointed out, however, that Argentina had already violated the resolution by invading South Georgia and increasing its forces on the Falklands and asserted that Britain would do whatever was necessary "in exercise of its inherent right of self-defense" under Article 51 of the Charter.

British military action proceeded while the secretary-general and Council tried without success to resolve the dispute peacefully, and on June 14 Argentina surrendered. It reported its surrender to the Council on June 18, announced a "de facto" end to hostilities, and asked for negotiations within a UN framework to settle the dispute finally. Britain responded on June 23 by saying that its forces would remain to defend the islands against further Argentine attacks.

On November 4 the Assembly called (90–12–52) for Britain and Argentina to settle their "sovereignty dispute." Britain opposed the resolution as coming too soon after military conflict and insisted that the islanders themselves must choose who should govern them. Argentina insisted, however, that the issue was not self-determination but the right of states to maintain their territorial integrity.

Other Political Questions

In Afghanistan the secretary-general and his personal representative, Undersecretary-General Diego Cordovez, could report only "tentative progress" in continuing efforts to arrange for 100,000 Soviet troops to withdraw, to allow the voluntary return of an estimated 3.5 million refugees, and to establish in the dispute the principle of noninterference in the internal affairs of nations. On November 29 the General Assembly renewed its demand (114–21) that the U.S.S.R. withdraw from Afghanistan.

The Assembly on October 28 reiterated (105–23–20) its call for all foreign troops to withdraw from Kampuchea in order to give back the independence and territorial integrity that the people of that nation needed to determine their own destiny and that was lost when 150,000 Vietnamese troops invaded in 1978. The Assembly continued to seat the Pol Pot government, deposed at that time.

On December 15 the Security Council unanimously voted to condemn "strongly" a raid on Lesotho on December 9 that resulted in some 30 deaths. South Africa described the dead as guerrillas belonging to the outlawed African National Congress, but Lesotho called them refugees from South Africa. On December 20 the secretary-general announced that a UN team would go to Lesotho to ensure the safety of refugees there.

International Law

The concluding session of the third UN Conference on the Law of the Sea met in Jamaica from December 6 to 10 to sign the treaty and open it for ratification by governments. Nine years in the making, the treaty was completed during two final sessions at UN headquarters (March 8–April 30; September 22–24) despite strong U.S. pressure to change it substantially. Called "possibly . . . the most significant international legal instrument [formulated] in this century," the treaty was signed on December 10 by 117 nations, with the U.S., the U.K., and several other industrialized nations among the 45 declining.

UNITED STATES

In national elections held in November 1982 the Democratic Party scored a gain of 26 seats in the U.S. House of Representatives as voters expressed dissatisfaction with the economic program of Pres. Ronald Reagan but stopped short of repudiating it altogether. The outcome indicated a considerable amount of voter frustration with a party only two years into national power. The Democrats won 269 seats to 166 seats for the Republicans, giving the Democrats a 103-seat advantage in the House. The total included two districts in Georgia where redistricting problems forced postponement of the general election until November 30.

In sharp contrast to the House, the only remarkable thing about the 1982 Senate results was the lack of change. Not only did the party ratio remain the same—54 Republicans and 46 Democrats—but 95 of the 100 senators in the 97th Congress were assured of seats in the 98th. The class of five newcomers was the smallest such group in the history of popular Senate elections.

The outcome was different at the state level, where the Republicans suffered a net loss of seven governorships, leaving them with a total of 16. Of the Republican governors' seats that switched to the Democrats, five were in the Midwest, where the recession was most acute. Michigan, Minnesota, Nebraska, Ohio, and Wisconsin elected Democratic governors. Republican incumbents had decided to retire in all those states except Nebraska, where Gov. Charles Thone was turned out by a margin of about 10,000 votes for Bob Kerrey.

In a surprise announcement on December 1, Sen. Edward Kennedy of Massachusetts said that he would not run for the Democratic presidential nomination in 1984 because he did not want to expose his children to the rigours of another national campaign. Kennedy also said that he would not accept a

Amin Gemayel, newly elected president of Lebanon, appealed to the UN for aid in rebuilding his country in an address to the General Assembly in October.
UPI

"Last week, interest rates went down again, the Dow-Jones went up, inflation dropped, unemployment dropped, tension between the United States and the Soviet Union eased, our balance of payments stabilized, the gross national product grew very nicely, but still everything seemed to get worse."
DRAWING BY FRADON ©1982 THE NEW YORKER MAGAZINE

draft for his party's nomination in 1984, but he did not rule out a presidential candidacy in 1988 or later. The senator's withdrawal appeared to leave Walter Mondale, vice-president in the administration of Pres. Jimmy Carter, as the early favourite to become the Democrats' 1984 presidential candidate.

Domestic Affairs

Economic developments dominated national news in 1982 as the U.S. continued to suffer through its deepest recession since World War II. Unemployment climbed steadily during the year, reaching a rate of 10.8% of the work force in December. This was the highest level of joblessness since 1940. The rising number of unemployed workers severely strained the ability of state and local governments to provide benefits to the jobless.

Also of concern were the more than 30 bank failures, the largest number since 1940. Two events in particular shook the financial community's confidence. The first came in May, when Drysdale Government Securities Inc., a small New York City firm that had been in business only four months, defaulted on $160 million owed to other dealers. Chase Manhattan Bank and Manufacturers Hanover Trust Co., which had acted as Drysdale's intermediaries in the government securities market, were obliged to absorb the firm's losses, at an after-tax cost of $117 million and $8.8 million, respectively.

Then, in July, federal regulators forced the closing of Penn Square Bank, of Oklahoma City, which had managed to make more than $2 billion in loans although it had only about $500 million in deposits. The Continental Illinois National Bank, the nation's sixth largest, was left holding $1 billion in Penn Square credits. Chase Manhattan and Seattle First National Bank also were major partners in Penn Square loan syndications.

Of the many business bankruptcies in 1982, that of Braniff International Corp., the nation's eighth largest airline, was among the most notable. The carrier filed for reorganization under Chapter 11 of the federal Bankruptcy Act on May 13, becoming the first major U.S. airline to do so. Struggling under heavy losses and laden with debt, Braniff the day before had suspended all its flights. The announcement of the suspension came as a surprise to the company's 9,500 employees, most of whom were told not to come to work the next day.

Manville Corp. filed a bankruptcy petition in August in an effort to gain relief from thousands of asbestos-related health lawsuits filed against the company. The company was "completely overwhelmed" by the cost of the lawsuits, according to John McKinney, Manville's chief executive officer and president. The firm faced approximately 16,500 lawsuits at the time, and more were being added at the rate of 500 a month.

Not all the economic news was bad. Inflation eased during the year, triggering a gradual decline in interest rates. The interest rate on government-insured home mortgages issued by both the Veterans Administration and the Federal Housing Administration, which had risen as high as 17.5% in 1981, declined in stages to 12%. Conventional mortgage rates fell also, and housing industry spokesmen expressed cautious optimism that the long-awaited revival of the residential construction industry might be at hand. In November home building starts rose 27% above October and were 64% higher than in November 1981.

There was no question about the stock market's revival. Several New York Stock Exchange records were set in frenzied trading during the last two weeks of August. In the week ended August 20, the closely watched Dow Jones industrial average climbed

81.24 points to finish at 869.29 and surpass the record of 73.61 points gained in the week ended Oct. 11, 1974. Volume for the week ended August 27 was 549,830,000 shares, also a record. The Dow Jones eventually reached a record closing high of 1070.55 in trading on December 27.

While some businesses were failing, others were merging. Marathon Oil Co. shareholders on March 11 approved a $6 billion merger with U.S. Steel Corp., the second-largest merger in history. The Interstate Commerce Commission on March 25 approved the merger of the Norfolk and Western Railway and the Southern Railway. Directors of Cities Service Co. in August accepted a merger proposal by Occidental Petroleum Co. valued at $4 billion. And on October 26 the California Federal Savings & Loan Association and the American Savings and Loan Association, respectively the third- and fourth-largest savings and loans in the nation, announced an agreement in principle for a merger. The combination would result in the country's biggest savings and loan institution.

But the merger that attracted the most attention in 1982 was the four-way battle involving the Bendix, Martin Marietta, United Technologies, and Al-

Protesters with a variety of grievances turned out during Pres. Ronald Reagan's visit to Philadelphia in May.

UPI

lied corporations. Bendix initiated the takeover fight in August by announcing an unsolicited tender offer for 45% of Martin Marietta stock; it already controlled 4.5% of Martin Marietta. In retaliation Martin Marietta made a tender offer for 50.3% of Bendix's outstanding stock. United Technologies entered the fray on September 7, allying itself with Martin Marietta by making a similar bid for Bendix.

For a time it appeared that Bendix and Martin Marietta were headed for a bizarre situation in which each company would own a controlling interest in the other. Then, on September 22, Allied and Bendix reached a tentative agreement calling for Allied to purchase 55% of Bendix's outstanding shares. In a separate deal with Martin Marietta, Allied agreed to allow that company to remain an independent concern.

Perhaps the most significant business story of the year was the settlement of the U.S. Department of Justice's eight-year-old antitrust suit against American Telephone & Telegraph Co. Among other things AT&T agreed to divest itself of its 22 Bell System companies in return for the department's promise to drop the case. U.S. District Court Judge Harold H. Greene, who had jurisdiction of the case, withheld his approval of the agreement until major modifications were made in it. The changes ordered by Greene would (1) prohibit AT&T from entering the field of electronic information services for a minimum of seven years; (2) allow the divested Bell System companies to publish their own Yellow Pages advertising directories; (3) allow the divested companies to market, but not manufacture, telephones and switchboards. Greene gave his final consent to the amended pact on August 24.

In another antitrust case the Department of Justice dropped its suit against IBM Corp., an action that it had begun in 1969. The suit had charged IBM with monopolizing the general-purpose computer market, but the government finally decided that it was "without merit."

President Reagan scored a major victory in Congress on August 19, when the House and the Senate approved a $98.3 billion tax-increase bill. Reagan, who had committed the prestige of his presidency to passage of the legislation, praised Congress's action as an important part of "our crusade to get this country's economy moving again." Also pressing for the bill's approval was Democratic House Speaker Thomas P. ("Tip") O'Neill, normally an opponent of the president.

Reagan's biggest legislative setback of the year occurred on December 7, when the House voted to delete initial production funds for the controversial $26 billion MX missile program. It was the first time since World War II that either house of Congress had voted to deny a major weapons system to a president. Reagan reacted angrily, saying: "I had hoped that most of the members in the House had awakened to the threat facing the United States."

One day later the House voted to keep the MX

missile alive but only in the development stage, and in a compromise hammered out with the Senate it was agreed that the matter would be reviewed in 1983. Part of the opposition to the MX had concerned the so-called dense pack basing mode recommended by Reagan. However, the controversy over the weapon was viewed as a sign that some members of Congress believed that the administration's military buildup had gone too far.

The proposed Equal Rights Amendment to the U.S. Constitution, banning discrimination on the basis of sex, failed to gain ratification by three-fourths of the state legislatures before the deadline of June 30. Supporters of the amendment vowed to continue their efforts to gain equality for women.

In a widely publicized trial, a U.S. District Court jury in Washington, D.C., on June 21 found John W. Hinckley, Jr., not guilty by reason of insanity on all charges of shooting President Reagan and three others in the nation's capital in March 1981. The verdict, reached after four days of deliberation, surprised and shocked many observers, in and out of government. There were calls, including one from Attorney General William French Smith, for a change in the law permitting acquittal in such cases.

Hinckley was committed to a hospital in the District of Columbia. Under the District's law he was entitled to a hearing within 50 days on whether he was capable of being released from custody. After that hearing, in August, U.S. District Court Judge Barrington D. Parker ordered Hinckley confined to a mental hospital for an indefinite period.

After a strike lasting 57 days, negotiators for National Football League players and owners agreed on November 16 to a five-year, $1.6 billion settlement. Two regular-season games had been played before the players struck, and eight were lost during the walkout. It was agreed to play out the remainder of the regular season as originally scheduled and to play one additional game, for a total of nine, prior to the play-offs. A new, one-time play-off format was instituted with a total of 16 teams, 8 from each conference, qualifying for the postseason tournament.

Foreign Affairs

As usual, U.S. foreign policymakers were preoccupied in 1982 with relations with the Soviet Union and the continuing search for a lasting peace in the Middle East. Their task was complicated somewhat by a midyear change of secretaries of state. Alexander Haig, Jr., who had held the post from the beginning of the Reagan administration, resigned in June and was replaced by George Shultz, who had served previous presidents as secretary of labour, director of the Office of Management and Budget, and secretary of the treasury. The nomination of Shultz was unanimously approved by the Senate on July 15.

Another complicating factor was the death on November 10 of Leonid I. Brezhnev, head of the Soviet Communist Party since 1964 and president of the U.S.S.R. President Reagan sent a letter to the

JEAN-LOUIS ATLAN–SYGMA

A black granite memorial inscribed with the names of 57,939 Americans killed or missing in Vietnam was dedicated in Washington, D.C.

Soviet leadership the following day expressing regret for Brezhnev's death and willingness to work for improved relations with his successor. Brezhnev was "one of the world's most important figures for nearly two decades," Reagan wrote to Vasily V. Kuznetsov, first vice-president of the Presidium of the Supreme Soviet. "I look forward to conducting relations with the new leadership in the Soviet Union, with the aim of expanding the areas where our two nations can cooperate to mutual advantage."

In what may have been meant as a conciliatory gesture to the new Soviet leadership, Reagan announced on November 13 the lifting of sanctions against U.S. and foreign companies selling U.S.-developed technology for use in the Soviet-Western European natural gas pipeline. "We've achieved an agreement with our allies that provides for stronger and more effective measures," Reagan declared in a nationwide radio broadcast. By lifting the sanctions Reagan removed a persistent irritant in relations

"The public has got the idea that Dense Pack is a Rube Goldberg." — Sen. Henry Jackson.

with Western European allies. Most of them had announced that they would defy the sanctions because they constituted an unacceptable intrusion on their national sovereignty.

According to Reagan, the U.S. and its allies had agreed to the following provisions: (1) "not to engage in trade arrangements which contribute to the military or strategic advantage of the U.S.S.R.," with particular attention to trade in high technology, including that used in gas and oil production; (2) not to sign any new natural gas contracts with the Soviet Union, pending the results of "an urgent study of Western energy alternatives"; (3) a strengthening of "existing controls on the transfer of strategic items to the Soviet Union"; (4) establishment of "procedures for monitoring financial relations with the Soviet Union," with the goal of developing a coordinated policy on export credits.

Reagan decided in July to authorize U.S. officials to seek a one-year extension of the U.S.-Soviet grain agreement. He called for preserving the terms of the current accord, due to expire on October 1. By the provisions of the agreement the Soviet Union had to purchase a minimum of six million metric tons of grain and was entitled to buy up to eight million metric tons, with larger amounts subject to negotiation.

Early in August Reagan told U.S. farmers that they would be able to sell a "record volume" of grain to the Soviet Union in 1982. "The granary door is open and the exchange will be cash on the barrelhead," the president promised in a speech to the National Corn Growers Association in Des Moines, Iowa. In a radio talk broadcast to U.S. farm states in October, Reagan said that the United States would soon offer to sell 23 million metric tons of grain to the Soviet Union. He conceded that the

Soviets might not buy the full amount offered. "But we know they are shopping," he said, "and they still have large needs." Reagan's announcement followed reports of a large Canadian grain sale to the Soviet Union.

The United States and the Soviet Union continued to discuss nuclear arms limitation, although no formal agreements were reached. In a commencement address May 9 at his alma mater, Eureka College in Illinois, Reagan called for "significant reductions" in U.S. and Soviet nuclear arsenals. He proposed a one-third reduction by both countries of ballistic missile nuclear warheads. In a second stage of his plan an "equal ceiling" would be set on other components of each country's strategic nuclear forces, including "throw weight," or the total payload of destructive power. The president said he had proposed to the Soviet Union that strategic arms reduction talks, known by the acronym START, get under way by the end of June.

Soviet leaders responded favourably to Reagan's initiative, with the result that the START talks opened June 29 in Geneva. The chief Soviet negotiator was Viktor P. Karpov, and his U.S. counterpart was Edward L. Rowny, a retired army lieutenant general. The talks recessed on August 12 and reopened October 6. Rowny expressed optimism early in October: "With good will on both sides, we can make progress toward an equitable and verifiable agreement." But Karpov urged the U.S. to abandon its "one-sided" proposal and "open up the road toward a mutually acceptable agreement."

In the meantime, also in Geneva, negotiations continued between the U.S. and the Soviet Union on limiting intermediate-range missiles stationed in Europe. Negotiators for both sides publicly differed in September on ways to resolve the differences that

THE 13 EXECUTIVE DEPARTMENTS
as of December 1982

Secretary of State	George P. Shultz
Secretary of the Treasury	Donald T. Regan
Secretary of Defense	Caspar W. Weinberger
Attorney General	William French Smith
Secretary of the Interior	James G. Watt
Secretary of Agriculture	John R. Block
Secretary of Commerce	Malcolm Baldrige
Secretary of Labor	Raymond J. Donovan
Secretary of Health and Human Services	Richard S. Schweiker
Secretary of Housing and Urban Development . . .	Samuel R. Pierce, Jr.
Secretary of Transportation . . . . :. . .	Andrew L. Lewis, Jr.
Secretary of Energy	Donald Hodel (acting)
Secretary of Education	Terrel H. Bell

had emerged during the talks, begun in November 1981. The U.S. offer to cancel its scheduled deployment of 572 new missiles in Europe, starting in 1983, if the Soviet Union dismantled its nuclear arsenal aimed at Western Europe was still "the best prospect for an enduring and verifiable agreement," said Paul H. Nitze, head of the U.S. delegation. Some progress had been made, Nitze maintained.

The U.S. response to Israel's invasion of southern Lebanon on June 6 was restrained at first. In a formal statement issued on June 7 the Department of State did not directly condemn the Israeli assault. "A divided Lebanon must not be the outcome of this violence," the statement said. "Israel will have to withdraw its forces from Lebanon, and the Palestinians will have to stop using Lebanon as a launching pad for attacks on Israel." President Reagan, who

was attending economic and military summit meetings in Europe, dispatched special envoy Philip C. Habib to the Middle East to try to arrange a new cease-fire in Lebanon, as he had done in 1981.

Two weeks later, on June 21, Reagan met for three hours at the White House with Israeli Prime Minister Menachem Begin. In remarks that emphasized their general accord on long-term objectives, the leaders agreed that all foreign troops should be withdrawn from Lebanon as soon as Israeli territory could be made permanently secure from Palestinian attacks.

U.S. involvement in the Lebanon crisis deepened in July, when Reagan confirmed that he had agreed to the use of U.S. Marines in the country to guard a withdrawal of Palestinian forces from West Beirut. The plan called for 800–1,000 U.S. Marines to form the core of an international evacuation and peacekeeping force in Lebanon.

But the Israeli siege of Beirut continued, culminating in an 11-hour bombardment of the city on August 12 by Israeli aircraft. The bombardment was finally ordered halted by the Israeli Cabinet after an angry confrontation involving Defense Minister Ariel Sharon, who had ordered the raid on his own authority. While the Israeli Cabinet was in session, U.S. Ambassador Samuel Lewis delivered a message from President Reagan sharply condemning the bombardments. Reagan followed with a personal call to Begin in which, as the White House described it, the president "expressed his outrage over this latest round of massive military action."

Taking a broader view of the Middle East situation, Reagan on September 1 called for a "fresh start" in the effort to achieve peace in the region. The president advanced new proposals urging "self-government by the Palestinians of the West Bank

Vice-Pres. George Bush (centre) and Secretary of State George Shultz (right) met with Communist Party Chairman Yury Andropov at the Kremlin following the funeral of Leonid Brezhnev in November.
TASS/SOVFOTO

and Gaza in association with Jordan." To this end he called for the "immediate adoption of a settlement freeze by Israel"; that is, an end to the establishment of additional Jewish settlements in the occupied territories.

The U.S. also became embroiled in the short war that broke out unexpectedly in April between Great Britain and Argentina over ownership of the Falkland Islands in the South Atlantic, a dependency of Britain long claimed by both countries. The conflict was precipitated by Argentina's military occupation of the Falklands and South Georgia island and Britain's decision to send a naval task force to the South Atlantic to retake them.

The U.S., which counted both combatant countries as allies, at first tried to act as mediator, with Secretary of State Haig conducting shuttle diplomacy. Starting April 8, Haig flew back and forth between London and Buenos Aires in an unsuccessful effort to reach a diplomatic solution to the crisis. The U.S. abandoned this role on April 30, declaring that Argentina was not willing to negotiate. At the same time, the U.S. offered to provide military supplies to Britain and invoked limited sanctions against Argentina, including a suspension of all military exports and certain types of aid.

The U.S. decision to side with Britain in the Falklands conflict caused deep bitterness in Argentina and indeed in much of Latin America. Some Latin-American officials asserted that it would take years to undo the diplomatic damage. As a first step in that direction, Reagan flew to Brazil on November 30 on the first leg of a five-day trip to Latin America that also took him to Colombia, Costa Rica, and Honduras. On December 1 he announced in Brasília that the U.S. had agreed to extend to Brazil $1,230,000,000 in short-term credit until the government of Pres. João Baptista Figueiredo had finished negotiating with the International Monetary Fund for a possible long-term credit.

Reagan's other major initiative in hemispheric affairs was his program for improving economic conditions and ensuring military security in the Caribbean basin and Central America. Outlined on February 24 in an address to the Organization of American States, the president's plan included $350 million in additional economic aid for the region in fiscal year 1982 and $60 million more in military assistance. The program's other points included special duty-free status for imported products from the Caribbean, tax incentives to encourage U.S. business investment in the region, technical assistance, and efforts to increase international aid programs.

URUGUAY

The Council of State approved a law on political parties on June 3, 1982. Although the legislation introduced a limited form of democracy in preparation for presidential elections due in November 1984, the final text was much more restrictive than had been predicted. Only the Partido Colorado, the Blancos (Nationalists), and the tiny Unión Cívica (a splinter group from the Christian Democrats) were allowed to organize. The Christian Democrats and the left remained excluded. On November 28 the approved parties held internal elections, which also acted as presidential primaries.

There was an increase in the repression of dissent. Magazines opposed to the junta's policy were closed down, and the military threatened that continued criticism of its actions could lead to a slowdown in the program of political liberalization. Discussion of the bleak economic situation was forbidden. The already faltering economy was adversely affected by the Falkland Islands conflict since Uruguay's economy was heavily influenced by that of Argentina. The country obtained a standby loan from the International Monetary Fund to compensate for a fall in export earnings and held talks with the IMF on wider-ranging support in November.

A number of Argentine soldiers captured in the British retaking of the Falkland Islands were sent home via Uruguay.
WIDE WORLD

VENEZUELA

The economy of Venezuela suffered from a severe cash crisis in 1982, resulting from falling oil revenues, a sharp decline in international reserves, and a lack of confidence by investors. Devaluation of the bolívar and exchange controls were not considered necessary, but by September the government was forced to take action to stem the capital flight, which was reaching alarming proportions, similar to the peak recorded in March when fears about oil income were rife. Dollar sales by commercial banks reached the level of $80 million a day, and private capital flight caused a $3.5 billion drop in international reserves to $5 billion by mid-September. Oil revenues were expected to be 20% below the $16.5 billion earned from this source in 1981, and the money supply was falling despite an increase in oil output to over 2 million bbl a day in September, more than 500,000 bbl a day above the production limit agreed on by the Organization of Petroleum Exporting Countries (OPEC) in March.

In order to improve the country's financial image abroad, the government then resorted to certain accounting methods to boost reserves. These included revaluing its 11.5 million oz (326 million g) of gold holdings from the official price of $42.22 per oz to nearer the market value at $300 an ounce, recalling about $1.5 billion deposited in Venezuelan banks in which the state had a shareholding and $850 million from the central bank's stock-market support fund, and placing the foreign reserves of all state agencies (most importantly the state oil company, PDVSA, with reserves worth $5 billion) under central bank jurisdiction. This last step was important because it ended PDVSA's financial independence, which had been maintained since the oil industry was nationalized in 1976.

By these means the government was able to raise international reserves to $15 billion against a total public foreign debt of $18.5 billion. Attempts were also made to reorganize the debt profile and obtain loans on a longer term; the government negotiated with international banks to convert some $2.5 billion–$3 billion of the total $8.8 billion short-term debt into medium-term obligations.

The domestic political scene was dominated by the launching by the political parties of their campaigns for the December 1983 presidential elections. The ruling Social Christian party, COPEI, chose former president Rafael Caldera as its candidate, while the main opposition party, the social democratic Acción Democrática, nominated Jaime Lusinchi to stand for election.

Guerrilla activity reemerged in 1982 in the eastern part of the country, causing a series of confrontations between police patrols and bands of armed left-wing terrorists. One of the worst incidents, a shoot-out between army and guerrilla forces in October, left at least 25 people dead.

The dispute with Guyana over the border region of Essequibo reached a critical stage when the treaty

UPI

A policeman carries an infant to safety as smoke billows from a Caracas power plant; at least 129 were killed in the December fire.

granting a 12-year moratorium on the issue expired on June 18 and was not renewed. Tension had been heightened by news of the discovery of oil by a Canadian firm in the disputed region, and there were frequent Guyanese protests about alleged military incursions across the border by Venezuela. Under the 1966 Geneva agreement signed by Venezuela, Guyana, and the U.K., the two countries in dispute had three months after the expiration of the 1970 treaty to agree to a means of settlement. Venezuela rejected Guyana's proposal to submit the dispute to the International Court of Justice, and in September Venezuela's president, Luis Herrera Campins, asked the UN to intervene after direct negotiations had failed. In the event that the UN was unable to bring the dispute to a satisfactory conclusion, UN Secretary-General Javier Pérez de Cuéllar was to decide the issue.

VIETNAM

For Vietnam, 1982 brought important developments on both the domestic and international fronts. The convening in March of the fifth congress of the Vietnamese Communist Party (the last congress had been held in 1976) signified a determined attempt by Hanoi to come to grips with the country's two most pressing problems—putting the tottering economy back on track and infusing the leadership with younger and more capable cadres. Internationally, the formation in late June of a coalition by three leading

Deputy Assistant Secretary of Defense Richard Armitage (left) headed a U.S. delegation to Hanoi in February to discuss the issue of 2,553 U.S. servicemen still listed as missing in Vietnam.
UPI

anti-Vietnamese Khmer resistance forces provided Vietnam with its toughest political challenge over Kampuchea since its troops rolled into Phnom Penh in January 1979 and toppled Pol Pot's Khmer Rouge regime.

Despite widespread rumours that he might resign, 75-year-old Le Duan retained the party secretary-generalship that he had held since 1959. Duan struck a keynote of the fifth party congress when he told delegates that "the party's Central Committee wishes sternly to criticize itself." "Objective conditions," he said, had contributed to the country's many difficulties, but so had the "shortcomings and errors committed by our party and state organs."

The dismissal of inefficient and elderly cadres announced at the party congress continued throughout the year, most notably during the major reshuffles of the Council of Ministers (Cabinet) and National Assembly in April and July, respectively. The most notable promotions were those of Politburo member Vo Van Kiet, 59, to vice-premier and head of the State Planning Commission (Vietnam's top economic post) and Foreign Minister Nguyen Co Thach, 62, to alternate membership in the Politburo. The most surprising demotion was the dropping of Dien Bien Phu war hero Vo Nguyen Giap from the Politburo. However, the refusal—or inability—of the most senior men in the hierarchy to step aside triggered doubts about the rejuvenation campaign. Despite their obviously failing health—all three visited the U.S.S.R. for medical treatment during 1982—veterans Le Duan, Pres. Truong Chinh, 75, and Premier Pham Van Dong, 76, retained their positions.

The economy was Vietnam's prime concern throughout the year. Among the nation's "acute problems," Premier Dong told the fifth party congress, were shortages of clothing, medicines, paper, housing, and materials and transport for production; a yawning trade deficit; and fluctuating markets and prices.

The unmitigated failure of the 1976–80 five-year development plan led Hanoi's leaders to approve one for 1981–85 that displayed marked departures. While the earlier scheme was rigidly Marxist, the new one incorporated such "capitalistic" features as individual enterprise, incentives for workers and peasants, unrestricted movement of goods, and special attention to the production of consumer items. Nonetheless, a flourishing black market remained, and the underground exchange rate for the dong passed 60 to the U.S. dollar (more than six times the official rate of 9.60:1) despite a 400% devaluation.

Vietnam continued to depend heavily on subsidies and aid from the Soviet Union—the reason good relations with Moscow remained the cornerstone of Vietnamese foreign policy. Yet strains in the alliance became conspicuous. Insiders reported that the Soviets encountered stiff resistance from Hanoi on such sensitive issues as greater Soviet control of Vietnamese economic management and increased access to military facilities. For its part, Moscow came under growing pressure from its Eastern European allies to reduce its massive aid to Vietnam, estimated at some U.S. $3 million a day.

More important to Moscow—and thus disquieting to Hanoi—were the moves, largely on the U.S.S.R.'s initiative, toward improving ties with China, Vietnam's archenemy. Shortly after Soviet Pres. Leonid Brezhnev made his country's most serious "peace overture" in years to China in March, observers wondered how the Kremlin's apparently sincere desire to normalize relations with China would affect Soviet-Vietnamese ties. Hanoi's announcement in July of a withdrawal of some of its occupation troops from Kampuchea was seen in many quarters as the result of Soviet pressure aimed at conciliating China.

The pullout offer came on the heels of the formal announcement of a coalition government-in-exile formed by the three major Khmer groups resisting Vietnamese occupation of their country. (*See* Kampuchea.) Proclamation of the coalition, after almost a year of difficult negotiations among its mutually suspicious partners, posed the biggest obstacle yet to Vietnam's campaign to gain diplomatic recognition for its client regime in Phnom Penh under Heng Samrin.

In the event, Vietnam's offer of a partial troop withdrawal met widespread skepticism in non-Communist Southeast Asia, as Foreign Minister Thach discovered when he toured key capitals of the Association of Southeast Asian Nations (ASEAN) in July. He was bluntly told that ASEAN still abided by the UN resolution calling for a complete withdrawal of foreign armed forces from Kampuchea. Although Hanoi pulled back thousands of its estimated 180,000 troops in Kampuchea, intelligence sources confirmed that at least as many fresh replacements were being sent in. By early October a conspicuous military buildup by Hanoi near Kampuchea's border with Thailand had led to new fears of a major Vietnamese offensive against Khmer resistance forces based in the vicinity.

A group of U.S. Vietnam war veterans visited Vietnam during May 29–June 3, 1982; discussions with Vietnamese officials centred on missing U.S. servicemen and the effects of chemical defoliants used by the U.S. In what some interpreted as another gesture of goodwill, the Vietnamese government permitted the largest number of Amerasian children in some years to be reunited with their American fathers.

WEATHER

Record severe weather events in 1982 left indelible scars across the nation in lost lives and property damage from January into December. Preliminary figures collected by the National Oceanic and Atmospheric Administration (NOAA) revealed that more than 600 Americans died in the blizzards, subzero temperatures, avalanches, floods, tornadoes, hurricanes, and high winds that struck the United States during the year. Total damage was estimated conservatively at $10 billion.

January proved to be the worst opening month for any year in the century, with five major storms that swept across large regions of the U.S. less than a week apart. Their cumulative weather tax on the nation amounted to 300 lives lost and more than $6 billion in direct losses.

Thousands of students pitched in to build and patrol sandbag dikes in Fort Wayne, Indiana, during a March flood.
UPI

UPI

Iwa, Hawaii's first hurricane in 23 years, battered the islands of Kauai, Oahu, and Niihau, leaving $230 million in damage behind.

More than 100 temperature and numerous snow-fall records were broken during the month. Sioux City, Iowa, Minneapolis, Minn., and Muskegon, Mich., all broke long-standing snowfall records, with Muskegon recording a monthly accumulation of nine feet (three metres). In Chicago temperatures dipped to -26° F (-32° C), the lowest there since 1872. Augusta, Ga.'s, temperature of 1° F (-17° C) broke a 100-year record there. Citrus crops froze solid on the trees when temperatures for much of Florida plummeted to the low 20s.

NOAA weather satellites, used by the agency's National Weather Service, revealed that 75% of the nation was covered with snow at one time during January. This was a record for the 17 years of weather satellite operation.

The transition to spring was a violent one, marked by flooding and a monstrous storm that struck the West Coast and swept across the country. Before the unusual spring storm was finished, it had taken more than 80 lives and caused millions of dollars in damage. The storm started with avalanches in the Sierra Nevadas, 100-mph (161 km/h) winds in Wyoming and Colorado, blizzards in the upper Midwest, and tornadoes in Texas, Oklahoma, and Arkansas. It ended with blizzards in New England that equaled the worst of the winter past with 80-mph (129 km/h) winds and 2-ft (61-cm) snowfalls.

Flooding and flash floods during 1982 reached major proportions in many parts of the United States owing to snowmelt and unusual storms. At least 150 lost their lives in the year's flooding. Damage exceeded $2 billion. Record rains of 10 to 15 in (25 to 38 cm) in 24 hours deluged San Francisco in early January, causing flash floods and mudslides. Property damage exceeded $300 million and the death toll reached 39, despite storm and flash flood warnings issued nine hours before the storm hit.

The winter's record snowfall in the Midwest set the stage for severe spring flooding in Ohio and Indiana. Fort Wayne, Indiana's second largest city, was hardest hit by the mid-March floods. Rivers bloated by melting snow surged nine feet (three metres) over flood stage, drowning nine people and destroying $150 million in property. Thousands of residents fled the area's worst flood in 69 years.

Heavy rains fell on southern New England in June, producing the worst floods there since 1955. The combined toll of dead and missing persons reached 22. Connecticut was hardest hit when rainfall amounts over 10 in (25 cm) created record flooding along parts of the Yantic River at Norwich. The rupture of numerous small dams in the state added to the complexity of the flooding.

The central Mississippi Valley suffered record-breaking flooding as a result of an unusual December storm that drew massive amounts of moisture from the warm and humid Gulf of Mexico, dumping it as rain on Arkansas, Missouri, and Illinois. At least 20 people were killed, and damage reached at least $600 million. The slow-moving storm dropped from 10 to 12 in (25 to 30 cm) of rain on Arkansas, causing the Buffalo River in the north central area of the state to rise from 4 to 52 ft (1 to 16 m) in one day. The Meramec River in east central Missouri exceeded flood stage by 23 ft (7 m).

Over 900 tornadoes killed at least 63 people and caused millions of dollars in damage in 1982. On the average, there are 673 tornadoes causing 111 deaths each year. At least one-third of the year's fatalities resulted from tornadoes spawned in severe April thunderstorms that swept across northern Texas, southeast Oklahoma, Arkansas, and points east. In all, 16 states recorded tornadoes. May was the most active month with 326 tornadoes, the highest number for any month since reliable records were first kept in 1913. At least ten people were killed by tornadoes in Marion, Ill., on May 29.

The 1982 Atlantic hurricane season—June through November—was the most tranquil in half a century. The Atlantic, Caribbean, and Gulf of Mexico waters bred five tropical storms. Only two of these reached hurricane strength, but neither storm made landfall. By contrast, the central and eastern Pacific Ocean was active this year with 23 tropical storms, 12 of which became hurricanes. The most noteworthy of these storms was Iwa, the first hurricane to strike Hawaii in 23 years. It pounded the islands on November 23 and 24. Advance storm warnings helped keep the death toll to one, but damage to the islands of Kauai, Oahu, and Niihau was

extensive, amounting to some \$230 million.

The day after Iwa struck Hawaii, NOAA's GOES West weather satellite failed. Positioned in a stationary orbit 23,000 mi (37,000 km) above the Equator southeast of Hawaii, this satellite had provided vital day-night coverage of the weather from Australia to the central U.S. To help fill the gap until the planned April 1983 launch of a replacement satellite, NOAA reactivated GOES 1, previously used to monitor weather in the Pacific and the U.S. This satellite, however, was limited to daylight coverage.

During the year atmospheric scientists from the U.S. and 12 other nations completed a major experiment in the Alps of Central Europe. Called the Alpine Experiment, it was conducted to develop a better understanding of how mountains affect weather and climate. This experiment was the final field project of the World Meteorological Organization's Global Atmospheric Research Project (GARP).

The U.S. scientists were primarily interested in learning how best to represent mountains in computer models used for weather forecasting. They also were studying the physical processes that cause winter storms downwind of mountain barriers. NOAA and National Science Foundation scientists expected to learn more about meteorological dynamics in the Rocky Mountains from this experiment.

The greatest warming episode in the equatorial waters of the central and eastern Pacific since the

Blizzards, seasonal and unseasonal, such as this one in St. Paul, Minnesota, wreaked havoc with traffic while producing record snowfall totals for much of the nation.
WIDE WORLD

1940s was observed by NOAA researchers during the last half of 1982. Sea-surface waters there increased five degrees Fahrenheit above normal temperatures, based on measurements by NOAA research ships and deep-ocean buoys moored along the Equator due south of the Gulf of California. This information provided new understanding of the apparent linkage between sea-surface temperatures and variations in the climate, a primary goal of NOAA's Equatorial Pacific Ocean Climate (EPOCS) program. Initiated in 1980, EPOCS was slated to continue through 1993.

WORLD TRADE

The dramatic trade story of 1982 was the U.S. government's struggle and ultimate failure to induce its European allies to curb trade with the Soviet Union in retaliation for Soviet political and military policies abroad. The backdrop was a sluggish world economy where double-digit unemployment in some of the major industrialized nations, and triple-digit inflation in some less developed countries, created fertile ground for protectionism. Instances of subsidized exports and barriers to imports to prop up domestic industries became increasingly common, even as the focus of economic summitry during the year was to reaffirm the West's commitment to a semblance of open trading policies.

Certainly the world recession was one factor in the Reagan administration's failure to build a united economic front against the Soviet Union's behind-the-scenes role in Poland's crackdown on the trade union Solidarity. The chip Pres. Ronald Reagan wanted Europe to play was a halt to the Soviet gas pipeline project linking Siberian wells to Western Europe. At stake, beyond the energy supply, were $11 billion in equipment and construction contracts

for more than a dozen European firms—deals so eagerly sought that some countries, France in particular, made or guaranteed loans at well below market rates to finance the contracts.

President Reagan's first step covered U.S. companies with roughly $2 billion in additional contracts for the pipeline, barring them from following through on the work. When allied countries failed to follow suit, the administration attempted unilaterally to extend the sanctions in June to equipment made in Europe with U.S. parts or U.S.-licensed technology. France was the first to defy this action when it allowed engineering firms, only recently nationalized by the Socialist government of Pres. François Mitterrand, to deliver to the Soviets turbines that used General Electric Co. technology. West Germany, Britain, and Italy endorsed the French stand, with Britain terming the Reagan sanctions "unacceptable interference." The Europeans were especially rankled by ongoing U.S. grain sales to the Soviet Union that jumped to some 15 million tons, with a value far exceeding the American stake in the pipeline.

Under pressure from farmers to increase these grain sales, the administration finally backed off the pipeline issue in November, when Reagan announced the end of the sanctions on U.S. companies as well as on U.S.-licensed know-how. But the acrimony remained as France disclaimed any part in an agreement the U.S. said had been worked out with its allies to apply other strategies in the context of East-West trade to punish the Soviets for Poland.

It was not, then, a wholly agreeable spirit that marked the two high-level economic conferences in 1982, the Geneva session of the General Agreement on Tariffs and Trade (GATT) talks in late November, directly following Reagan's capitulation on the pipe-

The seemingly inexorable flood of Japanese exports produced a rising tide of protectionist sentiment in the U.S. and Europe.
J. P. LAFFONT—SYGMA

The UN's Law of the Sea Treaty was adopted in April by a vote of 130 to 4, with 17 abstentions. The United States and some other industrial nations voted against and later declined to ratify the treaty.
MILTON GRANT—UNITED NATIONS

line issue, and the earlier meeting of seven heads of state at Versailles, France.

The Versailles summit of industrialized nations (the U.S., West Germany, France, Italy, Britain, Japan, and Canada) aimed at restoring order to the system of export credits nations offer to their trading partners in the form of subsidized loans or loan guarantees to foreign buyers. There were concerns that some countries had undercut others on these loans, making their exports more attractive, and hopes that a general hike in the rates would save money for the treasuries of all conferees. The latter aim was accomplished in an agreement in late June that retained 10% as the loan rate for poor countries but raised rates to "middle-income" and "rich" countries, also upgrading such rapidly developing nations as Brazil and Taiwan to middle-income. But the friction over the pipeline issue, a symbol of the

degree to which the Western nations are economic rivals as well as trading partners, was not resolved at Versailles and broke out later in the French resistance to Reagan's expanded sanctions. And protectionism to shelter domestic industries and domestic markets continued. A notable example was a French decree that all imported videotape recorders must pass through an undermanned customs post at Poitiers, which slowed the stream of these imports and was a clear effort to protect the French videotape recorder industry at the expense of Japan's exports of that new technology. A flap also developed over low financing provided by Canada to New York City's Metropolitan Transit Authority to help a Montreal manufacturer win a bid over French and American companies to supply 825 subway cars.

In the United States continued protectionist pressure by a steel industry running at less than 50% ca-

The GATT talks in Geneva in November brought together trade ministers and some 900 delegates from 88 nations to attempt to head off threats to free trade.
UPI

pacity with 25% unemployment led trade regulators there to hammer out a "voluntary" quota agreement with European steel producers limiting them to 5% of the U.S. market. The steel industry then turned on Japanese imports late in the year, suing to curtail Japan's 7% share of the U.S. market on claims that collusion between Japan and the Europeans had diverted pressure by Japanese steelmakers from European markets to the U.S. This matter was unresolved at year's end. The U.S. also retained formal and informal quotas on imports of automobiles, colour television sets, shoes, and textiles.

Designed to go beyond export credit issues and address the broader issues of protectionism, the GATT talks in Geneva brought together 88 trade ministers from developed and less developed countries. It also was host to a group of U.S. legislators, the most vocal of whom, Sen. Jesse Helms (Rep., N.C.),

treated the ministers to a threat of "fighting fire with fire" in the world market for agricultural exports, which he claimed were heavily subsidized by European producers at the expense of U.S. exporters. The United States accounted for more than 50% of the world's grain exports, yet 1982 saw a surplus of over 30 million tons in the U.S. and depressed prices that pushed farm incomes to their lowest levels since the Great Depression.

The GATT conferees did agree to take a close look at agricultural trading and to produce recommendations within two years and also planned a study of trade in services such as banking and insurance—never covered by GATT but now accounting for $600 billion of the estimated $2 trillion world trade in goods and services annually, versus only $100 billion in 1970. The ministers also reaffirmed a commitment to open trade and opposition to trade sanctions as a political weapon—an implied criticism of the U.S.

Pres. Ronald Reagan's imposition of sanctions against European firms involved in the Siberian pipeline project angered U.S. allies and was later reversed.
ED GAMBLE ©1982 THE FLORIDA TIMES-UNION

pipeline stand. These actions did not impress most observers as particularly dramatic, but they were perhaps the best that could be expected amid the trade tensions of a world recession.

One agreement not reached in 1982 involved the long-drawn-out Law of the Sea Treaty. Launched by the United Nations a decade earlier to assure freedom of the sealanes and regulation of ocean mining, the treaty was negotiated by a succession of governments in the 140 nations involved. The final document, presented for signature at Montego Bay, Jamaica, in December, was ratified by 117 nations but ignored by the United States and most industrialized nations owing to provisions obliging them to share ocean-mining technology with third world countries. Mining of manganese, cobalt, nickel, and other minerals from the ocean floor was potentially worth billions of dollars but was also a long way from being realized. World leaders came no closer to finding a way to share these common resources when that day arrived.

YOUTH ORGANIZATIONS

Big Brothers/Big Sisters

The Big Brothers/Big Sisters of America program continued to expand in 1982, with affiliated agencies numbering more than 420. Through its 100,000 matches between adult volunteers and children, it provided the opportunity for concerned, civic-minded adults to offer their friendships to community youth. School-age children, many from single-parent homes, were given the chance to develop a special relationship with a volunteer who served as both adult role model and friend. The need for more volunteers remained a priority in 1982, with the number of youngsters waiting to be matched with a Big Brother or Sister paralleling the soaring increase of single-parent families.

The Service to Girls Task Force was formed to provide a deeper understanding of youth service by examining the side of the program that benefits young girls. A nationwide survey of Big Brothers/Big Sisters affiliates was conducted, and its findings were to be incorporated in the organization's course in fulfilling the needs of today's children.

Boys Clubs of America

Boys Clubs of America (BCA) launched a new health initiative, SuperFit All-Stars, in 1982. Funded by PepsiCo, the program was designed to promote health-related fitness evaluations and exercise prescriptions. More than 200 Boys Clubs around the country were expected to be trained to conduct the program in 1983.

More than 700 teen leaders from around the country gathered in Orlando, Fla., to attend BCA's 15th annual National Keystone Conference. Internationally known grooming and health care specialist Vidal Sassoon, actress Cathy Lee Crosby, and Chicago Bears tight end Bob Fisher spoke on the importance of proper self-image and of keeping in good physical and mental condition. More than 1,000 Boys Clubs career professionals and directors gathered in Washington, D.C., for BCA's 76th annual National Conference. Edward Alameda, 16-year-old member of the Boys Club of Tucson, Ariz., was named 1982–83 National "Boy of the Year."

Boy Scouts of America

In 1982, with its new theme "Catch the Scouting Spirit," the Boy Scouts of America (BSA) invited rededication to and revitalization of its 73-year-old tradition of service to the youth of America. The ingredients for this revitalization were identified in a research study and were embodied in such programs as Tiger Cubs, which opens up Scouting to seven-year-old boys, and Prepared for Today, which

For some 60,000 handicapped boys, such as these in Milwaukee, Wisconsin, Boy Scouts activities supplemented other educational and physical therapy resources.

BOY SCOUTS OF AMERICA

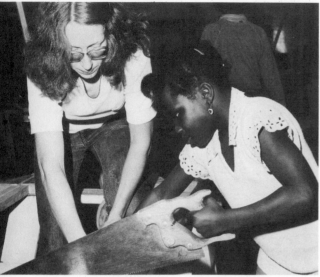

A member of the Girls Club of Omaha, Nebraska, learns to handle a saw in the "Tools Aren't Tricky" program.

teaches self-reliance and independence to "latch-key" boys and girls, who go from school to homes from which adults are away at work.

Members of Exploring/BSA had eight scientific experiments accepted for a January 1984 space shuttle flight. The experiments were placed through the National Aeronautics and Space Administration's "get-away specials" program.

Camp Fire

In 1982 Camp Fire comprised more than 300 local councils nationwide, with a total membership of 500,000 boys and girls. Development began on a new program about personal safety, designed specifically for kindergarten and first grade members. Work also began on updated programs for fourth, fifth, and sixth grade Adventure members that would emphasize the importance of working with and giving service to others. Revision was completed on programs for junior high Discovery members and high school Horizon members to reflect the inclusion of both girls and boys in Camp Fire and the agency's commitment to nonsexist programming for all youth.

To advance Camp Fire's efforts in helping young people grow into caring, responsible individuals, the board of directors voted to make sexuality education a part of its programming services and advocacy efforts.

Camp Fire members across the country participated in a significant conservation effort by building nesting boxes for the endangered North American bluebird. Project Save the Bluebirds had been a joint effort of Camp Fire and the U.S. Air Force for many years. On March 27, 115 nesting boxes were placed on the grounds of the U.S. Air Force Academy in Colorado. The Denver Museum of Natural History was to study the impact of this project on the bluebird population.

4-H

An important milestone for 4-H in 1982 was the introduction of a new 4-H history, *4-H: An American Idea—1900–1980*, in special ceremonies at the U.S. Department of Agriculture on June 24. Simultaneously, delegations of 4-H'ers across the nation presented copies of the book to the governors of more than 30 states. A "Salute to Excellence" program for volunteer leaders was launched in which an outstanding volunteer leader from each state was to participate in a week's training at the National 4-H Center near Washington, D.C. Nearly five million youth took part in 4-H in 1982 through organized 4-H clubs, 4-H special interest groups, 4-H expanded food-nutrition education programs, 4-H school enrichment programs, and 4-H instructional TV.

More than 6,000 4-H youth participated in the 1982 Citizenship-Washington Focus summer training program at the National 4-H Center. A National 4-H Youth Employment Career Education pilot program was completed in early 1982, carried out in cooperation with the National Collaboration for Youth and the U.S. Department of Labor, to help economically disadvantaged and other youth learn about jobs and careers and develop work skills.

Future Homemakers of America

Future Homemakers of America is a national vocational student organization of 400,000 junior and senior high school home economics students. It is dedicated to helping youth assume their roles in society through home economics education in the areas of personal growth, family life, vocational preparation, and community involvement.

Major areas of activity in 1982 included a building campaign for the organization's new National Headquarters and Leadership Center in Reston, Va., with chapter members raising over $300,000 in the campaign's first year. Other highlights were expansion of peer education projects on teen nutrition and sexuality, formation of a Future Homemakers of America Foundation, and the student-developed 1982 National Leadership Meeting in Atlanta, Ga., with the theme "Operation Outreach: Move to Improve."

Girls Clubs of America

In 1982 Girls Clubs of America (GCA) marked its 37th year as a national voice for girls and girls' issues. In its first year of operation, the GCA's new National Resource Center sponsored several seminars and workshops on issues related to girls' needs. The Center housed the nation's most comprehensive collection of data on girls and young women.

The GCA National Youth Employment and Children's Creative Theatre projects involved more than 4,000 girls in special training. GCA received funding from the U.S. Department of Health and Human

Services for a Family Life Education for Adolescents project. Other activities that spotlighted GCA's leadership as an advocate for the special needs of girls were the continuation of the Today's Girls: Tomorrow's Women project, co-sponsorship of three seminars on New Directions for Young Women, and lobbying efforts at the federal level on issues of youth employment, juvenile justice, teenage pregnancy, and charitable contributions.

Girl Scouts of the U.S.A.

In March 1982 Girl Scouts of the U.S.A. began its 70th anniversary with a commitment to carry out a wide variety of community services related to the protection and conservation of the world's water resources. The yearlong effort, called the Gift of Water, supported the United Nations' declaration naming the 1980s as the Water Decade.

The project was launched at the United Nations with a symbolic pouring ceremony of water samples gathered by Girl Scouts from 50 states and Puerto Rico. The samples, gathered from rivers, lakes, snowmelt, and glacier ice, were mingled to represent the waters of America. The crowning contribution was water from the tidal basin in the nation's capital, sent by Pres. Ronald Reagan.

A milestone in Girl Scout history was achieved in May with the opening of the Edith Macy Conference Center in Briarcliff Manor, N.Y. In June Girl Scouts from the United States and Girl Guides from Canada were the first girls to benefit from the modern learning and living facilities at the new conference centre. They were participants in a Girl Scout wider opportunity program called You Can Shape the Future. In October the conference centre was the site of a women's history conference sponsored by Girl Scouts and the Wonder Woman Foundation.

YMCA

The Young Men's Christian Association (YMCA) operated more than 2,200 branches, units, centres, and camps in the United States in 1982. More than 11 million persons were members of those YMCA's or registrants in YMCA programs.

Egie Huff of Rome, Ga., became the first woman president of the National Council of YMCA's. Three major national YMCA task forces met to recommend new programs for older youth, for wellness, and for child care. A major new after-school child care program, based on YMCA experience, was drawn up and offered to YMCA's in the fall.

The annual YMCA Swimming and Diving Championships, which had grown into the largest event of its kind in the world, attracted 1,800 young people, aged 12 to 19 and from 250 YMCA's in 37 states, to Fort Lauderdale, Fla. The team from Sarasota, Fla., won the overall title.

YWCA

The Young Women's Christian Association of the U.S.A. (YWCA), with a membership of approximately 2.5 million, observed in 1982 its 124th year of providing services to women and girls, involving them in activities, programs, and policymaking. Made up of some 450 community and student associations in 49 states, the YWCA operated in nearly 5,000 locations.

At its 29th National Convention in June the YWCA, in its continuing public affairs program, selected seven issues on which to focus the work of the 1982–85 cycle: ratification of the Equal Rights Amendment and support of legislation ending sex-based discrimination against women; promotion of a national policy of full employment, mandating affirmative action and equal pay for work of comparable value; prevention of teenage pregnancy; protection against violence for every individual, particularly for those most vulnerable; child care services; peace and disarmament; and human rights.

YUGOSLAVIA

Elections were held in Yugoslavia for local, republican, and federal assemblies in March and April 1982. In May the Federal Assembly in Belgrade appointed a new Federal Executive Council with Milka Planinc as premier. Lazar Mojsov became foreign minister, and Stane Dolanc was appointed interior minister. Gen. Nikola Ljubicic, defense minister during the years 1967–82, was replaced by Adm. Branko Mamula. In May the Collective Presidency elected Petar Stambolic president for one year, with Vladimir Bakaric as vice-president.

The congress of the League of Communists in June reaffirmed the main principles of Titoism: self-management, economic decentralization, and nonalignment. It elected a 163-member Central Committee, which in turn elected a 23-member Presidium with Mitja Ribicic as president and Nikola Stojanovic as executive secretary.

Political tension in Kosovo, the scene of nationalist riots in 1981, continued throughout 1982. In November it was officially stated that in the period March–September 1982 some 700 Kosovo Albanians had been arrested for political offenses and that more than 300 had been sent to trial. Three bombs exploded in Pristina, the province's capital, in November. A large-scale purge of Kosovo's state and party administrations, police, and university was carried out. The continuing emigration of Serbs and Montenegrins from Kosovo caused tension in Serbia. Yugoslavia reacted sharply to a speech in November by Albanian leader Enver Hoxha expressing support for the struggle of the Kosovo Albanians. Nevertheless, work was resumed on the joint project for a railway linking Albania with Yugoslavia.

Throughout 1982 Yugoslavia continued to be active in the nonaligned movement, seeking to counter attempts by Cuba and other pro-Soviet members to steer the group toward the Soviet bloc. During the year Yugoslavia was visited by senior representatives of the Sudan, Malaysia, and Cuba as well as Egypt's Pres. Hosni Mubarak, Malta's Prime Minis-

UPI

Milka Planinc became the first woman premier of Yugoslavia; she was named in May to head the new Federal Executive Council.

ter Dom Mintoff, and Libya's leader Col. Muammar al-Qaddafi. Lazar Mojsov traveled to Tunisia and Cyprus in September and to Iran in November. Radovan Vlajkovic, a member of the Collective Presidency, visited India. Petar Stambolic visited Ethiopia in October.

Yugoslav leaders criticized the military takeover in Poland in December 1981, one party official describing it as "a trampling on democracy." Although Soviet Foreign Minister Andrey Gromyko visited Yugoslavia in April, relations between the two countries remained cool.

Yugoslavia encountered severe financial problems in 1982. In order to pay its hard-currency debt, the government in May ordered businesses to sell to the state a percentage of the foreign currency they had previously been allowed to hold for their own purposes and also to repatriate foreign-currency earnings from abroad within 60 rather than 90 days as before. This measure caused much opposition and controversy, particularly in Croatia and Slovenia, which had large tourist earnings and close trade connections with nearby Western countries. In October the dinar was devalued by 20%, and an austerity package was introduced that included gasoline rationing, restrictions on heating and lighting, a prohibitive tax on private journeys abroad, a ban on personal imports above the value of 1,500 dinars, and incentives for exporters to hard-currency areas.

Yugoslavia's request for credit from the Bank for International Settlements in Basel, Switz., in September was turned down. However, in November a

consortium of banks granted a $200 million, 18-month credit. Industrial output increased by 0.6% in the first ten months of 1982, the lowest figure since the end of World War II. Inflation remained at about 30% instead of dropping to 15% as planned. Exports to non-Communist countries fell by 3% during the first nine months of 1982.

ZAIRE

With receipts from Zaire's main exports—cobalt, coffee, copper, and industrial diamonds—falling well below their anticipated levels and inflation soaring, any prospect of adequately servicing the foreign debt was shattered. The International Monetary Fund (IMF) consequently withdrew permission for Zaire to make use of the loan in the form of Special Drawing Rights agreed upon in 1981. A delegation from the IMF paid a 15-day visit in June 1982, and the government agreed to proposals for reorganizing the mining industry.

This serious economic situation was further undermined by a dispute with the U.S. in May. Following allegations by members of the U.S. Congress that aid given to Zaire had been embezzled, it was proposed that the grant for 1983 should be severely cut. Pres. Mobutu Sese Seko, however, preempted Congress's decision by renouncing all aid from the U.S. because of the "insulting" statements directed against his government.

Internal opposition to the government was taking an increasingly political form. Thirteen people's commissioners (members of the Legislative Council) who in December 1980 had accused the government of irregular financial dealings were sentenced along with 25 others on July 1, 1982, to 15 years in prison on the charge of having founded a new political party, the Union pour la Démocratie et le Progrès Social (UDPS). They had held political rallies calling for an end to Mobutu's government and, according to the president, had stirred unrest among the supporters of the ruling Mouvement Populaire de la Révolution. Their actions, he said, were in direct conflict with the 1978 constitution, which stated that Zaire should be a one-party nation.

The most immediate result of the sentences was an increase in tension in the government's relations with Belgium, which had already been under strain because of the activities of Zairian exiles in that country. Mobutu planned a visit to Brussels in July, expecting that this would be treated as a state occasion. However, criticism of his action by some of his opponents in exile was so vigorous that the Belgian authorities, fearing demonstrations, preferred to regard the proposed trip as merely a working visit. Such an interpretation would, in Mobutu's view, have constituted a rebuff. He therefore canceled the visit, ostensibly on account of the declaration of state mourning after the death of Gen. Bobozo Adurama, a former army chief of staff. Zairian exiles nevertheless continued their campaign against the government, and in October a number of them formed a popular front aimed at restoring democracy in Zaire.

In May the president himself reformed his government. The membership of the National Executive Council was reduced from 27 to 19, and ten state commissioners lost their ministries. Economies were achieved in the main by assigning the portfolios of those who had been dismissed to those who had been retained.

It was alleged by Zambia that in February Zairian troops had seized a bus and a truck carrying cornmeal inside Zambian territory. This had led to an exchange of shots between Zairian and Zambian soldiers, and thousands of Zambian villagers had fled the area. On March 2 Zaire closed its border with Zambia, and tension continued in the border region in spite of a meeting between President Mobutu and Zambian Pres. Kenneth Kaunda in August. Two meetings of a joint commission were held in September, and both sides agreed to seek a solution to their border problems.

The government restored diplomatic relations with Israel on May 16. The president had earlier announced his intention to take this step because Egypt had already restored diplomatic relations with Israel and the last of the occupied Egyptian territory would be vacated by the Israelis in April. In response, Saudi Arabia, Qatar, Libya, Kuwait, Bangladesh, and the United Arab Emirates broke off diplomatic relations with Zaire, while Algeria and Tunisia recalled their ambassadors.

Zaire did not send a representative to the abortive Organization of African Unity summit meeting in Tripoli, Libya, in August. President Mobutu had been inclined to respond to the appeal by the Libyan foreign minister who had urged him to rally to the support of the meeting. However, it was thought that he changed his mind as a result of pressure brought to bear by Israel. In December it was reported that Israel was to sell arms worth $18 million to Zaire.

In June President Mobutu visited China. Before he did so, an accord was signed between the two countries that granted Zaire military sales credits worth $3.5 million. But the visit brought no significant improvement in relations between the two countries.

ZAMBIA

Economic problems continued to loom large in Zambia during 1982. In presenting his budget the minister of finance stated that foreign exchange earnings from the mining industry, the country's main source of wealth, were more than 20% below forecast. Subsidies were reduced by one-third, and taxes on fuel, sugar, cigarettes, alcohol, and soft drinks were increased. Subsequently the mining industry was declared exempt from taxes for the current year. The International Monetary Fund refused to allow the government, because of its poor economic performance, to draw further on the loan that had been negotiated in May 1981. Aid from Japan, the U.S., West and East Germany, and the Arab Bank for Economic Development partly ameliorated the situation; however, the corn (maize) crop produced only one-half of the 1981 yield, thus necessitating large-scale imports.

A meeting between Pres. Kenneth Kaunda and Prime Minister P. W. Botha of South Africa in April was strongly criticized by other southern African nations, but the president maintained that the discussions on the future of Namibia/South West Africa and on racial policies in South Africa had been of value. Border incidents strained relations with Zaire, but links with both Tanzania and Zimbabwe were strengthened.

As a prolonged drought threatened the harvest in Zambia, one farmer near Lusaka dejectedly examined his scorched corn crop.
ALAN COWELL/THE NEW YORK TIMES

ZIMBABWE

The relative tranquillity that had followed the independence struggle in Zimbabwe was disturbed in 1982 by conflicts between the ruling Patriotic Front party, the Zimbabwe African National Union (ZANU [PF]), and Joshua Nkomo's Patriotic Front party, known as the Zimbabwe African People's Union (ZAPU [PF]). In a New Year's message Prime Minister Robert Mugabe forecast an increasingly Socialist program with the state playing an important role in farming, mining, and all other aspects of the economy. He also stated that in the future only policies approved by ZANU (PF) would be adopted by the government. This was denounced by Nkomo, who claimed that it ran counter to the idea of the supremacy of Parliament contained in the 1979 Lancaster House agreement signed by Mugabe and himself. Ignoring this remark, Mugabe insisted that he was seeking support for a one-party state and that it was only a matter of time before this would be achieved.

In February Nkomo rejected a plan to merge the two Patriotic Front parties. Relations between the two leaders then took a turn for the worse with the discovery of large quantities of armaments on farms belonging to Nkomo's supporters. This led on February 17 to the dismissal of Nkomo from the government, along with three others belonging to his party, on the grounds that they allegedly plotted to overthrow the ruling party. Fears that these events would result in violence among Nkomo's angry supporters were not immediately realized, and U.K. Foreign Secretary Lord Carrington, who visited Zimbabwe in February, congratulated the government on the country's stability. Moreover, the three remaining ZAPU (PF) members of the government

Joshua Nkomo, head of the Zimbabwe African People's Union, was removed from the Cabinet by his old rival, Prime Minister Robert Mugabe.

PETER JORDAN—GAMMA/LIAISON

decided that they would not resign in protest.

Links between Nkomo's supporters and the Republican Front (RF; previously the Rhodesia Front) were given an ominous twist after four white men were found guilty of plotting to overthrow the government and force the secession of Matabeleland, Nkomo's home province. Nine RF members of Parliament resigned from their party after disagreement over some of its policies. One of the defectors stated that senior members of the RF had known and approved of a proposed armed coup in which Nkomo's supporters would be involved.

In June the government was forced to launch a large-scale campaign against the dissidents in Matabeleland, and Nkomo denounced those who were resorting to violence and called for an all-party inquiry into their activities. Only days later armed men attacked the home of the prime minister and another of his ministers, Enos Nkala, in Harare (the name given in April to Salisbury). Nkomo unreservedly condemned the attacks and called for peace and stability, but nonetheless Mugabe accused Nkomo of being linked with the Harare attacks.

Worse was to follow. Toward the end of July a night raid on the air base near Gweru resulted in the destruction of 12 fighter planes. A number of both white and black members and former members of the Air Force were arrested by security police. On August 2 Mugabe and Nkomo met, on Nkomo's initiative, and there appeared to be some prospect of discussions between their two parties. On September 14 Nkomo again called for a political solution to the violence in the west of the country, but at the same time he accused security forces of mistreating civilians. These forces belonged to the 5th Army Brigade, which had been recruited from Mugabe's supporters and trained by North Korea.

On September 30 two condemned murderers became the first people to be executed since independence. They were not political dissidents, but observers believed that their execution was meant to be a warning to dissidents engaged in similar violence for professed political ends. On December 24, 3 people were killed and 21 wounded when a band of supposed ZAPU (PF) supporters attacked cars, buses, and a train in western Matabeleland.

In early December it was reported that Ian Smith, former Rhodesian prime minister and leader of the RF, had had his home searched and several papers removed by security forces. The search was believed to be in response to controversial statements made by Smith during a trip to the U.S. and the U.K.

These political activities overshadowed serious economic problems. In March the preferential trade agreement with South Africa, which was due to expire in the same month, was renewed. Not to have done so, an advisory report maintained, would have cost Zimbabwe $50 million in exports and would have put 6,500 jobs at risk. Such a result could not be contemplated after the nation had experienced in 1981 its first visible balance of trade deficit since

1968. One of the main problems was the lack of foreign investment, which the prime minister was inclined to blame on adverse foreign press reports. In fact, world recession and government policy were more important factors. The announcement in March that the constitution was to be rewritten caused consternation among potential investors in spite of an assurance that any change would be introduced by constitutional means and that the property rights of foreign investors would be secure.

In May the economy suffered a further setback when the oil pipeline from Mozambique was sabotaged. The prime minister himself paid a visit to seven European countries in late May and early June in an attempt to reassure would-be investors that Zimbabwe offered secure opportunities for their activities. More important was the government's announcement in October, after prolonged external pressure, of a code to protect foreign investment. The government also reduced subsidies on some basic foods, and the minister of finance cut the allocation of foreign currency to industry and for travel.

These changes took effect against a background of concern as the country prepared to negotiate a loan with the International Monetary Fund (IMF) to offset the balance of payments deficit. The government announced a 20% devaluation of its currency on December 8, a move that was interpreted as necessary in order to secure IMF credits. Meanwhile, the long-awaited three-year economic development program was published in late November.

ZOOS AND BOTANICAL GARDENS

Worldwide recession, with rapidly rising costs, increasing wages, and declining numbers of visitors caused financial problems for many zoos, especially those in Europe and North America. For totally self-supporting zoos the position in some cases became critical. In Britain, where admissions to the London Zoo had fallen by more than 20% in 1981, a symposium was held in October 1982 at which the reasons for the situation were discussed and a number of possible remedies put forward. It was agreed that to increase attendance it might be necessary to emphasize the entertainment aspect of zoos, although this should not detract from or diminish their essential functions in the areas of conservation, education, and science.

During 1981–82 the American Association of Zoological Parks and Aquariums committed itself to developing a species survival plan to coordinate the captive breeding of endangered animal species. Thirty species were designated, and detailed plans were drawn up for nearly half that number. A coordinated scientific and practical breeding program was a necessary step forward. There were now fewer sources of wild animals, and high purchasing and shipping costs further reduced the supply. In addition, international and national laws on endangered species, and stricter quarantine regulations, limited animal import and export.

UPI

What was believed to be the first albino wallaby born in captivity in the U.S. arrived at the Jackson (Mississippi) Zoo in the spring.

The desire to preserve species for future generations and to maintain a rich genetic pool that might some day be returned to the wild had radically changed the policies of many zoos, replacing competition with cooperation. Modern technology, particularly the use of computer records, was being used more and more. On an international scale, the Captive Breeding Specialist Group, an important committee of the Species Survival Commission of the International Union for Conservation of Nature, advised and helped to coordinate management and breeding programs. At its meeting in August in London, the committee made a number of important decisions, particularly in relation to the international management of the Asian wild horse (Przewalski horse) in captivity and its release into reserves in the wild. This meeting followed a well-attended symposium on the status and management of African and Asian rhinoceroses in the wild and in captivity, organized by the International Union of Directors of Zoological Gardens.

In September pandas again stole the headlines when the female Shao Shao in Madrid gave birth to twins after artificial insemination with semen from the London Zoo's male, Chia Chia. This was the second successful artificial insemination but the first outside China. There were no birth complications, but the mother rejected the smaller offspring and, although it was placed in an incubator, it died after a few days. The other cub was being looked after by the mother and was progressing well.

Massa, the world's oldest gorilla in captivity, celebrated his 52nd birthday at the Philadelphia Zoo with cake and fruit.

More refined techniques of artificial insemination led to successful births or hatchings in other species. Two particularly important examples in 1982 were the first whooping crane (*Grus americana*) at the International Crane Foundation in Wisconsin and the first parrot, a cockatiel (*Nymphicus hollandicus*), in Florida.

Successful first-time breedings of special note in 1982 included Mexican wolves (*Canis lupus baileyi*) in St. Louis, Mo. (only about 30 left in the world; only one female in captivity); a killer whale (*Orcinus orca*) in Marineland of the Pacific, near Los Angeles; a Lear's macaw (*Andorhynchus leari*) in Tampa, Fla.; and Houston toads (*Bufo houstonensis*) in Houston, Texas.

Botanical Gardens

The economic recession seriously affected botanical gardens as well as zoos, and plans for new establishments and the extension and modernization of existing ones were severely curtailed in many cases. Cuts in personnel had a particularly bad effect on the care and maintenance of large collections. In the U.S. the national parks, invaluable reservoirs of naturally occurring species, were threatened by proposed changes in their status.

This state of affairs, combined with the current trend of environmentalist thought, focused interest on "wilderness gardens." The theory was that areas given over to natural growth (as, for example, disused railroad station sites in West Berlin) would be richly colonized by flora and fauna, providing valu-

able material for study without the need for attention. Experience suggested, however, that it was fallacious to assume that no human intervention would be required.

An outstanding development during the year was the provision of extensive new hothouses for the 50-year-old Zürich, Switz., succulent collection. This secured the continuance of one of the most comprehensive protective collections of cacti and other succulents for development and scientific research.

At the Royal Botanic Gardens, Kew, England, the extensively restored temperate house was opened by Queen Elizabeth II in May 1982. The queen planted a young Chilean wine palm (*Jubaea chilensis*) that would eventually replace the one grown from seed in 1846 and transplanted to the temperate house at the original opening in 1860, and which now reached the roof.

Among the year's negative aspects, certain environmental factors predominated. "Acid rain," the precipitation of emissions in the form of various acids, increasingly threatened forests and hothouse cultivation as well as lakes with their plant and animal life. In Hamburg, West Germany, substantial deposits of zinc, lead, and cadmium were recorded in the leaves, roots, and stamens of orchids and bromeliads; protective measures against this threat would be difficult and costly.

Shao-Shao, the Madrid Zoo's giant panda, gave birth to twins in September; although one soon died, the other flourished.

82

FOCUS

THE GREAT DISARMAMENT DEBATE

by Lawrence Freedman

"Great armaments lead inevitably to war. The increase of armaments . . . produces a consciousness of the strength of other nations and a sense of fear." This comment of British foreign secretary Sir Edward Grey on the Anglo-German naval arms race gained immense authority with the subsequent onset of World War I. He appeared to have identified a virtual Law of International Relations. According to this law, those who wished to prevent further war must prevent further arms races. The key to this was disarmament: fixing the armed forces of all countries at the lowest possible level.

Seventy years later voices are warning once again that an arms race must inevitably end in catastrophe. The warnings are given even greater urgency by the fact that the weapons involved are nuclear and the consequences of their use would move beyond mass slaughter to the destruction of whole civilizations. In these circumstances, the cause of disarmament is understandably popular. However, the relationship between arms races and war is not a simple one of cause and effect. Wars are not just the product of the accumulation of armaments but reflect real conflicts over such things as territory and ideology. To address the arms race without considering the political differences between nations is often to address the symptoms rather than the cause. Furthermore, as is evident from a survey of postwar efforts at disarmament and the current debate, unless the underlying political differences can be moderated, the "arms race" symptoms are extremely resistant to treatment.

After Hiroshima

The pro-disarmament sentiment of 1918 was not evident in the international community in 1945. Explanations of the origins of World War II looked more to a failure to react to the German military challenge of the 1930s than to an arms race. There had been no equivalent to the Anglo-German naval competition, nor was it possible to point to military machines impressing their own timetables on a crisis and forcing the hand of the diplomats. Memories of interwar efforts to promote disarmament were of cynical wrangling and deadlocks. Those treaties that had been adopted failed to affect the course of the war, with the possible exception of the 1925 Geneva Protocol outlawing the use of poison gas. No disarmament treaty could have prevented Belsen and Auschwitz.

In plans for a postwar world, centred on the new United Nations, the prevention of further conflicts was seen to lie in the political rather than the military sphere. The victorious powers expected to maintain military capabilities that would enable them to act swiftly and decisively against any renewed outbreaks of aggression. Otherwise, as in 1918, after years of full mobilization and having imposed total disarmament on their defeated enemies, the Allies were only too happy to run down their own armed forces as quickly as possible.

Nevertheless, disarmament was still high on the international agenda. The reason was the impression of awesome power and destructiveness created by the atomic bomb, whose use against the Japanese cities of Hiroshima and Nagasaki was the war's dramatic finale. Whatever might be done about the generality of weapons, urgent action was needed in this special case. Even in the United States, with its monopoly of atomic weapons, there was a disposition to nip this dangerous new development in the bud. Accordingly, in 1946 the U.S. put forward a plan to internationalize atomic technology and prevent its full exploitation for military purposes.

Unfortunately, the U.S. plan was framed in such a manner as to excite Soviet suspicions, and it soon got bogged down with the onset of the cold war. The political conditions became unfavourable, and the relevant UN committees began to devote themselves to scoring propaganda points rather than to serious negotiating. The warning signs were the tendencies toward utopian and all-embracing plans. Argument could not be limited to the area of atomic weapons, where for much of the 1950s the U.S. had a clear lead, but inevitably began to include all other weapons as well. Why, it was asked, should the West forgo its nuclear superiority if the East would not relinquish its conventional superiority? So the discussion got tangled up in military and political complexities. Agreement depended on an understanding between the superpowers, but their antagonism prevented any agreement. American suspicions of Soviet secrecy meant that the U.S. put an enormous premium on methods to verify compliance with the provisions of any treaty by making the closed Soviet society as transparent as possible. Still, neither side wished to appear responsible for dashing international disarmament hopes, so Washington and Moscow engaged in a sort of competitive bidding, putting forward ever more elaborate and fanciful schemes to ensure General and Complete Disarmament.

Arms Control

Long before this futile process reached its peak at the start of the 1960s, moves had begun on a more fruitful approach to the regulation of armaments. This approach came to be known as arms control. It accepted that nuclear weapons and East-West antagonism would be features of international life for many years. The challenge was to find ways to reduce the consequent dangers. If the nuclear threat could not be eliminated, it could at least be contained. If a military paralysis based on a balance of terror was developing, then perhaps this could be fortified to remove temptations to settle differences once and for all in some decisive battle, or to rush from crisis to war in a preemptive strike through fear of being caught napping.

Superpower political relations had to ease to give even this modest approach an opportunity to show its potential. The opportunity came after the October 1962 Cuban missile crisis when, having gone so close to the brink, the leaders of the U.S. and the

Although no atomic weapon has been used in anger since Aug. 9, 1945, at Nagasaki, Japan, there is a growing anxiety that the failure of disarmament could lead to disaster.
YOSUKE YAMAHATA–G. T. SUN CO., TOKYO

GENE BASSET / UNITED FEATURE SYNDICATE

U.S.S.R. resolved to develop a less stressful relationship. Additional help was provided by advances in satellite reconnaissance that began to open up Soviet and U.S. territories to each other's penetrating gaze. As there was little that could be done about this, it became recognized as a reliable means of verification. In the ensuing decade, arms control chalked up some impressive achievements: the 1963 Nuclear Test-Ban Treaty, which, while failing to be comprehensive, banned atmospheric explosions and so eased public anxieties over the harmful effects of radioactive fallout; the 1966 Outer Space Treaty, which kept nuclear weapons out of space; the 1968 Non-proliferation Treaty, which constrained the spread of military nuclear technology; the 1970 Seabed Treaty; and, as the first substantive result of the strategic arms limitation talks (SALT) begun by the superpowers in 1969, the 1972 treaty limiting anti-ballistic missiles. This last pact, combined with a short-term agreement putting a ceiling on the numbers of offensive nuclear weapons, became known as SALT I.

By 1972, with détente in full swing, there seemed every reason to believe that the pattern of regular agreements would continue. The next stage was to be a more comprehensive treaty on offensive nuclear arms, and at Vladivostok, U.S.S.R., in December 1974, Leonid Brezhnev, general secretary of the Communist Party of the Soviet Union, and U.S. Pres. Gerald Ford announced the framework for an agreement. Meanwhile, in 1973, NATO and the Warsaw Pact had begun to discuss ways of reducing the burden of conventional forces in central Europe in the Vienna talks on mutual and balanced force reductions.

Loss of Momentum

This promise was not fulfilled. After acrimonious and difficult negotiations, a SALT II treaty was agreed on in June 1979, but it was not ratified by the U.S. Senate. The Vienna talks failed to overcome fundamental disagreements over data. A set of arms control initiatives undertaken in 1977 to breathe life into the enterprise—concerning a variety of issues ranging from a comprehensive test ban to limits on anti-satellite and chemical weapons and reform of the arms trade—all faltered. One reason was the loss of momentum in détente, largely as a result of superpower rivalries and interventions in the third world (particularly by the Soviet Union). Under these conditions, negotiations became tougher, with greater domestic suspicion of the motives of the other side.

Another problem was uncertainty over objectives, at least in the West. This was part of a general uncertainty about strategic doctrine, revolving around arguments over whether all that was necessary for deterrence and stability was for both sides to be able to assure destruction of the other. Even if a balance of terror was firmly in place, were there other forms of superiority that might be translated into a decisive political advantage? The promoters of arms control were generally doubtful. In 1974, in a moment of frustration, U.S. Secretary of State Henry Kissinger exclaimed: "We have to ask ourselves . . . what in the name of God is strategic superiority? What is the significance of it, politically, militarily, operationally, at these levels of numbers? What do you do with it?"

There was no agreed answer to this general question, or to the specific question: if "superiority" was believed to be significant, exactly what type and degree of superiority made the difference? For negotiating purposes it seemed sensible to concentrate on simple numbers and rectify any imbalances with common ceilings. East and West could then claim to be "second to none." However, such visible parity seemed artificial to the technically minded, who were more interested in what each side could do in actual warfare than in comparing static inventories. U.S. technicians noted asymmetries in force structure that escaped treaty language, particularly the growing Soviet lead in warheads on intercontinental ballistic missiles (ICBM's). They began to worry that under cover of SALT and an irrelevant numerical parity, the U.S.S.R. was being allowed to attain a potentially decisive strategic advantage.

Even those unimpressed by such fears found the calculation of parity difficult. The negotiations were becoming less manageable as attention moved from the first stage—setting limits to military activity by marking boundaries that few had shown an inclination to cross—to making substantial adjustments to existing capabilities and plans. There was no self-evident formula for "parity," for the two force structures were quite different in composition. Did one count launchers or warheads? How should targeting accuracy be ascertained and balanced against warhead yield? Should an ICBM count the same as a bomber? Should one make allowances for the British, French, and Chinese forces facing the U.S.S.R.? In each country programs with strong political support had to be protected from arms control. To the other country, these were precisely the programs to which a stop had to be put if the exercise was to be worthwhile. Under adverse political conditions, this mix created a barely tractable set of problems.

In retrospect, many of the early successes seemed easy. Underground testing of nuclear weapons was a ready substitute for atmospheric testing; there was no great military interest in putting nuclear weapons in space or in Antarctica or on the seabed; the technology of antiballistic missiles was not showing great promise. Once negotiators began to address the more dynamic offensive weapons, they found themselves barely able to cope, bypassed by new developments and outpaced by production programs.

The eventual SALT II treaty of June 1979 was hardly satisfactory. It was enormously complex yet imposed only marginal changes on the nuclear arsenals. If anything, it required most of the U.S.S.R., but that did not prevent a powerful opposition, largely mounted on the right, from developing in the U.S. Critics charged that the treaty threatened valuable U.S. military options, failed to constrain the most dangerous aspects of the Soviet military buildup, and perpetuated an illusion of détente. Although U.S. Pres. Jimmy Carter had answers to all these points, after the Soviet invasion of Afghanistan in December 1979 he no longer felt disposed to make an effort on SALT II's behalf. The treaty languished, unratified, in the Senate.

Pres. Ronald Reagan, entering office in January 1981, described SALT II as "fatally flawed" and argued for a major program of rearmament to regain ground lost in the 1970s. According to his officials, the U.S. had been so preoccupied with arms control that it had neglected to take full note of the Soviet buildup.

Some 30,000 antinuclear protesters linked arms to form a human chain around a U.S. Air Force base at Greenham Common, England, where U.S. cruise missiles were to be based.

U.S. Pres. Jimmy Carter
and Soviet Pres. Leonid
Brezhnev exchange
copies of the SALT II
agreement after signing
them in June 1979.
SVEN SIMON/KATHERINE YOUNG

The Nuclear Debate

Distrust of all forms of diplomatic contact with the Soviet Union, interest in the possibility of conducting nuclear wars to produce results approximating "victory," and a readiness to increase purchases of all types of military hardware generated some consternation among the U.S.'s allies. The fear in Western Europe was that a breakdown in U.S.-Soviet relations would unravel all the local benefits of détente, from the settlement of the territorial status quo to East-West trade. In addition, a renewed arms race would aggravate the general sense of tension, raise the terrible spectre of nuclear war, and, if the U.S. was deemed responsible, put an added strain on the NATO alliance.

In the early 1980s there was widespread protest in Western Europe against the nuclear policies of NATO. In the latter part of 1981 many of the continent's capitals were filled with demonstrations, sometimes involving up to 250,000 people. The origins of this renewal of the antinuclear movement, which had last peaked in the late 1950s and 1960s, go back to 1977, when the "neutron bomb" gained notoriety. To NATO officials this was an "enhanced-radiation weapon" designed to disable tank crews; to its opponents it would "kill people but leave buildings intact"—the ultimate "capitalist weapon." Revulsion against the neutron bomb led to a massive public outcry. In The Netherlands, with the encouragement of religious leaders, some one million signatures were collected in opposition.

The outcry led President Carter in April 1978 to defer production of the neutron bomb. The protest groups calmed down but then re-formed in 1979 to oppose plans by NATO to base 464 Tomahawk cruise missiles in Belgium, Britain, The Netherlands, Italy, and West Germany, along with 108 Pershing ballistic missiles in West Germany. This deployment was designed to modernize a well-established capability. U.S. nuclear weapons had been based in Europe

since the early 1950s, partly to offset Soviet superiority in conventional forces but increasingly to couple the defense of Western Europe with the U.S. nuclear arsenal. The theory was that the Kremlin was deterred from any aggression by the risk that war would "go nuclear" but that the risk would be insufficient if U.S. weapons were stored out of harm's way in North America. In the mid-1970s concern grew in defense circles, at first mainly in Europe, that gradual obsolescence of the long-range aircraft on the NATO side was being exploited by determined improvements in equivalent Soviet capabilities, most notably the Backfire bomber and the SS-20 triple-headed missile. From this perspective, NATO's decision on Dec. 12, 1979, to deploy the cruise and Pershing missiles was seen as merely a prudent measure to fill a gap.

In an attempt to ward off the expected protest, NATO added to the armament program a second track of arms control, offering to limit the number of new NATO missiles in return for severe restrictions on comparable Soviet missiles. Unfortunately, the credibility of this diplomatic alternative was shattered within weeks. The Soviet invasion of Afghanistan undermined all East-West diplomacy and made early ratification of SALT II impossible.

New Fears

The Carter administration then announced, in June 1980, a new doctrine for targeting nuclear weapons that emphasized selectivity, flexibility, and command and control, thus implying an expectation that nuclear exchanges could turn into old-fashioned battles rather than orgies of mutual destruction. No such confidence was actually claimed, only a worry that the U.S.S.R. might try to fight in such a manner, but the critics feared that the U.S. government was now harbouring dangerous notions concerning the military utility of nuclear weapons.

In Europe opponents linked this new doctrine (known officially as Presidential Directive 59) with the highly accurate weapons coming into Europe and the low state of East-West relations. From this, they concluded that the U.S. was shaping up for some confrontation with the Soviet Union which it intended to fight with nuclear weapons all over Europe. This fear grew after the U.S. presidential election in November 1980. Ronald Reagan was known to be distrustful of arms control, a believer in energetic schemes for rearmament, and interested in active nuclear strategies.

Vigorous and determined protest movements gathered strength in Europe. Some, like the "Greens" in West Germany, reflected an environmentalist bias and a history of campaigning against nuclear energy facilities. The British-based campaign for European Nuclear Disarmament, inspired by the social historian E. P. Thompson, linked opposition to cruise missiles with an aspiration to dissolve the two alliances—NATO and the Warsaw Pact—dividing Europe. These movements soon influenced political parties. In Britain the Labour Party resolved to have nothing whatever to do with nuclear weapons. In West Germany immense strains were put on the Social Democratic Party; even the Christian Democrats, whose leader, Helmut Kohl, replaced Helmut Schmidt as federal chancellor in October 1982, were not immune to antinuclear influences. In The Netherlands all but the centre Liberal Party reflected the same trend. The trend, in fact, could be detected throughout northern Europe, though it was much less evident in the south. Pres. François Mitterrand of France, despite his Socialism, upheld the established French faith in nuclear deterrence, while in Italy protest against cruise missiles was rather late in starting.

It came to be assumed that, whereas opinion in the U.S. was robustly anti-Communist and ready for high levels of defense spending, opinion in Europe was drifting in exactly the opposite direction. This picture was always somewhat misleading. Polls in both the U.S. and Western Europe demonstrated strong support for established policies as well as increasing nervousness over the risk of nuclear war. Toward the end of 1981 the U.S. was beginning to develop its own protest movement, organized around the call for a "nuclear freeze"—that is, cessation of all new work on weapons development, production, and deployment. The idea was to halt the arms race before it was beyond control. The Freeze Resolution was put to both the Senate and the House of Representatives (where it just failed) and to a number of state referenda (where it passed in most cases). Although bipartisan in leadership—Democrat Edward Kennedy and Republican Mark Hatfield sponsored the resolution in the Senate—the movement was animated by opposition to the policies of the Reagan administration.

The Reagan administration's image was not helped by regular Soviet disarmament initiatives. In October 1979 President Brezhnev promised unspecified concessions if NATO would abandon its plans for new missiles in Europe. Then he offered a moratorium: no new missiles on either side. Later Brezhnev even claimed to have ordered a unilateral freeze on the Soviet side. The impact was not enormous. There was nothing particularly magnanimous about offering to freeze deployments of weapons in an area of substantial Soviet superiority. Nevertheless, the rhetoric and regular initiatives from the Warsaw Pact helped to put the Reagan administration on the defensive.

Reagan's Response

President Reagan insisted that he was not opposed to the principle of arms control negotiations but was only reluctant to sit at the same table with

U.S. negotiator Lieut. Gen. Edward L. Rowny (left) greeted his Soviet counterpart, Viktor Karpov, at the opening of the Strategic Arms Reduction Talks (START) in Geneva in June 1982.
UPI

the U.S.S.R. while it was still indulging in unacceptable behaviour in such places as Afghanistan. When, in response to domestic and international pressure, he did eventually put forward initiatives of his own in late 1981, he was anxious to avoid repeating what he saw as the deficiencies of SALT: its failure to deal adequately with the most menacing aspects of the Soviet buildup and its imposition of permissive ceilings, rather than substantial reductions, in armaments.

In the second of these complaints against SALT, President Reagan was quite close to the critique made by the antinuclear movements. They also castigated previous arms control efforts for not achieving disarmament. In fact, Reagan's first major proposal was surprisingly close to an antinuclear slogan. In November 1981 U.S.-Soviet discussions began in Geneva on intermediate nuclear forces—a new name for the longer-range nuclear weapons based in and around Europe. At a speech to the National Press Club, President Reagan proposed the "zero option," offering to abandon plans for cruise and Pershing missiles in return for the dismantling of all Soviet SS-20s, along with the older generation SS-4s and SS-5s.

In the West this was politically effective, but it was certain to be unacceptable to the U.S.S.R. because it required the Soviets to give up something for nothing. Soviet proposals emphasized the need to bring in the British and French nuclear forces and U.S. aircraft in Europe. The asymmetry of the two force structures and the technical problems of deciding on what to count (location or type of weapon; launchers or warheads) make it hard to envision a satisfactory conclusion to the talks. The first anniversary passed without any breakthroughs.

In principle, strategic arms talks appeared to be a better prospect. Many of the technical details and problems of definition had been ironed out in a decade of discussions. The forces were sufficiently comparable to permit some agreement based on parity. However, the political context was less favourable, with every move surrounded by controversy. President Reagan's approach was again calculated to disarm his critics as much as the U.S.S.R. He proposed radical cuts in strategic arms on the eve of the resumption of talks—after a gap of three years—in June 1982. He renamed the negotiations Strategic Arms Reduction Talks (START) and proposed common ceilings of 5,000 missile warheads, half of which could be on ICBM's, and 850 deployed missiles—only 50% of current levels. Skeptics noted that this posed maximum inconvenience to the U.S.S.R., with its heavy dependence on multiple-warhead ICBM's, and minimum disruption to U.S. plans. Nevertheless, the philosophy of cuts was compelling, and the Soviet proposal of ceilings of 1,800 for all missiles and bombers reflected this mood. The two positions were not hopelessly apart, but neither appeared flexible and there were many negotiating pitfalls in the incidental details.

The Future

Arms control was hardly bursting with promise in 1982, but at least serious discussions were beginning once more. Those anxious for more urgent and fundamental action had little cause for comfort. Despite a number of years of sustained pressure by the antinuclear movement, no major NATO country had opted for unilateral disarmament of any sort. Those who dreamed of parallel movements in Eastern and Western Europe, working together to expel nuclear weapons from the continent, saw their hopes dashed with the imposition of martial law in Poland and the crushing of the small independent "peace" groups in East Germany and the Soviet Union. The vision of a "nuclear-free zone"—always unlikely because of France's attachment to its *force de frappe* and the fact that some 40% of all Soviet nuclear forces are based in the European part of the country—seemed even more impractical. The more modest proposal of a nuclear freeze was critically dependent on a change in U.S. administration, impossible before January 1985.

Meanwhile, there was no progress in attempts to organize old-fashioned disarmament through the UN. In 1978 a special session of the UN achieved a common agenda for disarmament. At a second special session in the summer of 1982, the attempt to move beyond that agenda failed, a victim of the prevailing state of international distrust. A group of senior statesmen and others from all sections of the international community, including the U.S. (former secretary of state Cyrus Vance) and the U.S.S.R. and chaired by Sweden's Olof Palme (the Independent Commission on Disarmament and Security Issues), produced a report for the session that gained credibility only by the moderation of its objectives; these were mainly to urge expeditious completion of all the various negotiations begun in the 1970s.

Thoroughgoing schemes for disarmament require a degree of international accord that is not likely to exist for some time to come. The most optimistic construction on the current situation is that some sort of marriage is taking place between the arms controllers' preoccupation with stability and the disarmers' desire for tangible reductions in armaments. But there is no prospect of reductions to a point where war is anything less than catastrophic—to reduce "overkill" still leaves "kill"—and even progress in this direction is highly dependent on improvements in superpower relations. Ultimately, it is in the political sphere that answers to the problems of war and the peacetime burden of armaments must be found.

Lawrence Freedman is professor of war studies at King's College, University of London. He is the author of The Evolution of Nuclear Strategy *and* Britain and Nuclear Weapons.

PHOTO. DEPARTMENT OF ENERGY

THE RUSSIAN GIANT: 60 YEARS AFTER FORMATION OF THE SOVIET UNION

by Zhores A. and Roy A. Medvedev

The Union of Soviet Socialist Republics was declared a multinational federative state at the very end of 1922, the draft of the new constitution having been written by Lenin. There was no unanimous agreement about this draft among Lenin's Bolshevik colleagues. Lenin wanted a federation of "equal" republics, with the right of each to independence. Joseph Stalin and Leon Trotsky wanted more formal Russian domination, with strict subordination of the other national republics. Lenin won the constitutional battle, but when he died in January 1924, he left the power over the country and the Communist Party to the newly emerged Communist bureaucracy, which had no intention of respecting the constitutional rights either of citizens or of the nations that formed the Soviet Union. The constitution acknowledged the importance of democratic rights, but it included no formula to guarantee them at all levels of social life. Furthermore, it did not solve the problem of leadership succession; the possibility of a power struggle made the choice of leader by democratic process difficult even within the party system.

The year 1982 was declared an official Jubilee year. The Soviet population was reminded of this by countless posters, slogans, and news headlines. While the country had changed enormously in many ways during the intervening 60 years, the lack of consistency and the contradictions between real and constitutional rights were by now even more visible than they were in 1922.

Growth of the U.S.S.R. and World Communism

In 1922 there were only four constituent republics of the U.S.S.R.: the Russian Federal Republic, the Ukraine, Belorussia, and the Transcaucasian Republic. Lenin insisted on a federation of independent republics because he believed that the Union would grow in the future, both through internal development and by the voluntary accession of other countries that would become socialist. The Union did indeed grow; the Uzbek and Turkmen republics, formed in 1924, became constituent members in 1925, and the Tadzhik Republic joined in 1929. By 1936, when the new Stalin Constitution was adopted, the number of republics was already 11. A few more were incorporated in 1939 and 1940—the Karelo-Finnish Republic, Moldavia, Estonia, Latvia, and Lithuania; however, they joined not voluntarily but under coercion. The war against Nazi Germany in 1941–45 and against Japan in 1945 brought several Eastern European states and North Korea under Soviet domination, though these did not become republics in the Union.

But it was not only Soviet military power that was responsible for the spread of Communism. The defeat of Fascism in Europe and militarism in Asia increased the worldwide influence of Communist movements. The new Communist regimes in Albania, Yugoslavia, and China emerged essentially as a result of national revolutions and civil wars within those countries. Although the Soviet Union supported their revolutions, it was unable to transform them into satellite states. Greece came very close to Communism in the years from 1944 to 1946. The Communist Party of Italy might also have come to power if the country had not been under Anglo-American occupation during the last stage of World War II. Even France was not immune from the possibility of a Communist takeover during this period because the traditional ruling groups in that nation had collaborated with Germany. When Stalin died in 1953, about one-third of the world's population lived under the banner of Marxism-Leninism. But the structural unity of the world Communist system proved unable to survive nationalistic and ideological disputes. Nevertheless, the Communist move-

ment has continued to attract new adherents, although at a much slower pace. Cuba, Vietnam, Laos, Kampuchea, Angola, Mozambique, South Yemen, Ethiopia, Zimbabwe, and several other smaller nations can now be considered to have Marxist-Leninist regimes.

When the capitalist economic system takes the form of Nazism, feudal monarchy, or military dictatorship, and when this is aggravated by poverty and social polarization, the confrontation between right and left often develops into a revolutionary struggle. Thus new Marxist regimes will continue to appear, particularly in Africa, Latin America, and Asia. In the modern world of superpowers the final outcome of a revolutionary struggle often does not depend upon internal factors alone—the examples of Chile,

In April 1982 Yury Andropov addressed a Lenin's birthday celebration in the Kremlin's Palace of Congresses. He was then head of the KGB intelligence and security agency; seven months later he would succeed to the highest post in the Soviet Union.

UPI

Vietnam, and Angola show this clearly. External aid in the form of arms, training, financial grants, and direct military assistance may be decisive. Who helps whom often (but not always) depends upon ideological considerations.

The survival of the Communist system in the Soviet Union, in China, and even in Eastern Europe is not in serious doubt. It is unrealistic to expect the imminent collapse of the world Communist system, even if some observers see signs of this in Poland. The question of "Whither Communism?" is relevant not to the survival of already well-established Communist states but rather to their ability to generate and support Communist ideology in the rest of the world, to be an attractive model for others. Active assistance to radical Marxist regimes and revolutionary movements in the third world is of huge economic and political cost. Will the Soviet Union be able to continue carrying this burden? This question can be answered only by analyzing the economic and political situation within the Soviet bloc. Since the changes in the Soviet leadership following the death of Leonid Brezhnev, the probable priorities of his successor, Yury Andropov, and the latter's new team are equally important aspects of the question.

Successes and Failures

The Soviet Union has an impressive list of achievements to show for its 60 years of existence:

the rapid industrial reconstruction of agrarian and undeveloped Russia; the difficult victory in World War II against Nazi Germany and its allies; the educational revolution; the building of a modern and powerful army.

But 60 years of Soviet history have also recorded some events that are hardly mentioned in relation to the jubilee. The forced and brutal collectivization of agriculture (1930–33) cost the lives of millions of people; it did not solve the food problem but instead retarded the production of grain, meat, and dairy products for years to come. Stalin's rule of terror and repeated purges from 1928 to 1953 took almost the same toll of human lives—about 20 million—as did the war against Germany. Although the situation began to change during Nikita Khrushchev's era, the image of the Soviet Union as the most repressive postwar regime remained for years. It damaged the structure of the "just society" that the first Communist thinkers had expected would be built upon the foundations of the proletarian revolution.

The plight of the Soviet population under Stalin's regime shows that the current economic and political crisis is certainly not the most serious in Soviet history. The current crisis does not threaten the Communist system, because it has not developed as an isolated problem unique to the Soviet bloc. It appeared simultaneously with the deep postwar recession in Western Europe and the U.S. and the

Lenin (centre), seen here strolling in Moscow's Red Square with several of his military commanders, ruled the Soviet Union as leader of the Communist Party.

CAMERA PRESS, LONDON

desperate economic plight of many major countries of Latin America and Africa. It can also be seen in relation to China's apparent failure to modernize rapidly and the economic difficulties of the unique Yugoslav model of socialist self-management. However, if the crisis in the West can be explained in economic terms, the problems of the U.S.S.R. are essentially related to an accumulation of errors and the political and economic mismanagement of an inept leadership.

The most serious economic crisis of Lenin's government in 1921 was the result of the arbitrary and repressive system of War Communism. Lenin was the only leader in Soviet history who was bold enough to acknowledge a failure. He replaced War Communism with the successful New Economic Policy, with its mixed socialist and capitalist sectors that competed with and complemented each other. When Stalin became leader, this balanced development quickly became distorted. Stalin's model of rapid industrialization was based mainly upon the forced extraction of human and economic resources from the rural agricultural sector and from the private trade and light industrial sectors. The historical necessity for these methods was far from certain. The losses in light industry, trade, and food production during the 1930s and the horrendous purges did little to help prepare the country for the inevitable war against Germany. The most important factors for the outcome of the war were the enormous size of the country and the significant reserves of the population.

After the war, during the last years of Stalin's life, the economic crisis manifested itself primarily in the form of acute shortages of food and consumer goods and the extreme poverty of the collective farm peasants. Soviet agriculture was now dependent upon a semifeudal system that attached peasants to the collective farms and made them work under the threat of prison camps. During the period 1950–53 the total production of food reached only the level of 1913, and the urban population had significantly increased. Stalin's death in 1953 saved the country from the gloomy prospect of rural starvation and a new series of purges.

After Stalin

Khrushchev's reforms quickly improved the economic and political situation. From 1954 to 1958 the growth of all sectors of the economy was about 11–12% per annum. The most visible growth was in agriculture. The annual production of grain rose from an average of 80 million metric tons (1950–53) to 130 million–140 million metric tons. However, Khrushchev's subsequent reorganizations were carried out hastily. Attempts to produce an artificially accelerated growth rate miscarried and had the reverse effect—the production of food declined again. The bitter quarrel with China split the Communist system into two hostile camps and made it necessary to increase the Soviet defense budget. Khrushchev's

errors and blunders continued to mount until they reached a critical level in 1964, when his Politburo colleagues voted him into retirement.

The new leadership of Leonid Brezhnev managed to restore a more balanced economy and began to transform the country into a modern consumer society. However, the leadership was already too old and inflexible to introduce the necessary political and economic reforms when new serious problems started to emerge at the end of the 1970s.

As the history of the U.S.S.R. clearly shows, then, the performance of the system is closely linked to the performance of the men at the top. What is more, their style, their knowledge, their character, and even their tastes are reflected not only in the methods of rule but in almost everything, ranging from literature and the arts to industry, agriculture, and international policy. The dependence of the fate of a country on individual leaders is not, of course, restricted to the Communist system. But in the West this dependence is often temporary, and it is less comprehensive than in the Soviet Union. Western leaders are less involved in day-to-day economic and industrial decision-making processes. The Soviet economy is much more centralized, and it is entirely dependent upon government decisions. Because the Soviet Union is now the centre of a large group of countries linked in the Council for Mutual Economic Assistance (CMEA or Comecon), which is responsible for about 30% of the world industrial output, possible changes of economic policy related to leadership transition attract intense attention.

The Leadership Problem

In no Communist country does the constitution make provision for an orderly succession, nor are the criteria for changing the leader made explicit. In fact, the durability of individual rule has become an integral part of the legitimacy of most such regimes. Aging and ill health are still the main indicators of possible changes at the top, which, when they happen in large powers like the U.S.S.R. or China, can alter the course of world politics.

In the Soviet Union Khrushchev's dismissal prompted the Politburo to set a compulsory retirement age of 70 for its leaders. However, when Brezhnev was approaching 70, the compulsory retirement age was canceled "for outstanding figures of the party and state." The venerable age of the current leaders relates them to the revolutionary period and is a part of their claim to legitimacy. That is why the deaths of Brezhnev, Premier Aleksey Kosygin, and chief party ideologue Mikhail Suslov, together with the retirement of Andrey Kirilenko, mean for the Soviet Union much more than the change of a few leaders—they mean the end of a whole political era. At 68, Andropov is older than any of his predecessors were when they assumed power, but for replacements in many important positions he is selecting much younger men who will probably remain in office for at least a decade. They belong to a generation that not only does not remember the Revolution and Civil War but often took only a minor part in World War II. This will make it difficult for them to build up the kind of "personality cult" that proved to be so important for their predecessors. Moreover, they will face difficult decisions. The economy of the U.S.S.R. is in poor shape, and Soviet-style Communism is in a critical condition in such neighbouring countries as Poland and Afghanistan.

Power Base of the Soviet Leadership

Lenin's main power base was the October Revolution itself and all its institutions and reforms. The party had not yet developed a bureaucratic apparatus, and Lenin ruled the country as the chairman of the first revolutionary government, the Council of People's Commissars. When Stalin was appointed general secretary of the Communist Party Central Committee in 1922, he was not a popular figure and was not considered a possible successor to Lenin. But he skillfully began to form an influential party apparatus, which he used as his power base in the struggle with the left and right opposition in the 1920s. When he started to become de facto dictator rather than party leader, he made the state security system the powerful instrument of his personal rule, able to carry out comprehensive purges of all ranks of the party, military, and state systems. The party apparatus was not abolished, but its influence declined. From 1934 to 1953 the Soviet Union was, in all practical senses, a police state. Before World War II Stalin abolished the post of general secretary of the Central Committee and assumed the post of chairman of the government, one more convenient for direct rule.

Khrushchev is best remembered in Soviet political history for his elimination in 1953 of Lavrenty Beria and his top security henchmen and for his "secret speech" in 1956, which exposed and condemned many of Stalin's crimes. The exceptional position of the security system was abolished, and the party system and party bureaucracy regained priority. Khrushchev himself was not a typical party bureaucrat—his style of rule was more open, though still far from being democratic. Party power had been restored, but the party only made directives. Final decisions had to be made and implemented by the government. It was, therefore, to Khrushchev's advantage to assume the post of premier in addition to his position as leader of the party in 1958. This step, however, restored the possibilities for personal dictatorship, and Khrushchev was not immune from the misuse of power and the creation of a personality cult. Khrushchev was a de facto dictator, but the party apparatus remained his power base. When he introduced an unpopular reorganization of the party apparatus that reduced the influence of local bosses, his relations with the party bureaucracy were seriously damaged. His seven-year plan for economic development failed, and he had no powerful security

system to protect him from his angry colleagues. His removal was a comparatively painless leadership change. Only one man—Khrushchev himself—lost his post. As a precaution against repetition of personal rule, the Central Committee decreed that the positions of party leader and head of government should be separated forever.

The Brezhnev Era

Brezhnev's power was, therefore, much more limited. Leadership was effectively collective, based on Politburo consensus, even after the restoration of the position of general secretary in 1966. Kosygin had independent views about the economy, and both Suslov and Nikolay Podgorny had independent sources of influence. But like previous Soviet leaders, Brezhnev began to consolidate his power. In 1977 he assumed Podgorny's post of chairman of the Presidium of the Supreme Soviet and managed to remove him from the Politburo. This made Brezhnev titular head of state. When Kosygin became ill in 1980, Brezhnev succeeded in replacing him with Nikolay Tikhonov, a rather weak premier but an old friend and protégé. Brezhnev's personality cult grew. But by the time he achieved this concentration of power, he was already too old and too ill to use it or to lead the country efficiently. When his old friends and relatives started to assume important state and party positions, the more technocratic members of the Politburo and Central Committee objected. Brezhnev failed to secure Suslov's position for Konstantin Chernenko, his aide and confidant since the 1950s. Instead, Andropov, then head of the security force (KGB), was appointed to this post, the second most important in the party hierarchy. Until 1967 Andropov was the secretary of the party Central Committee responsible for Soviet relations with other socialist countries. He had his own political objectives, and his rise, supported by the more technocratic group in the Politburo (Dmitry Ustinov, Andrey Gromyko, Mikhail Gorbachev, and Vladimir Shcherbitsky), secured his election as general secretary after Brezhnev's death.

Few new bold initiatives were adopted during Brezhnev's era. Most of the reforms—a limited attempt to introduce market forces into the economy; an increase in the procurement prices paid to farmers; increasing investment in agriculture; the encouragement of more effective use of private plots of land—were Kosygin's ideas. Many of these reforms were half measures, and they generated very modest incentives. But the absence of reorganization and the lack of coercion were welcomed by the managerial groups, and economic growth was persistent, although slower than before. However, the absence of strong leadership also encouraged official corruption.

The policy of détente with the West improved the international position of the U.S.S.R. The decline of U.S. influence in the world was not directly related to Soviet actions. It was more the result of errors

Stalin's death in 1953 set off a five-year power struggle; the losers included Malenkov and Bulganin (flanking the bier), the winner was Khrushchev (second to right).

and miscalculations by the administrations of U.S. Presidents Richard Nixon, Gerald Ford, and Jimmy Carter. Just when Soviet international policy was predictable and consistent, U.S. policy was unstable. The peak of Brezhnev's success at home was reached in 1978, when the U.S.S.R. reaped a record harvest of 230 million metric tons of grain. The peak of his détente policy was in June 1979, when the new SALT II (Strategic Arms Limitation Treaty II) was signed in Vienna. However, there were new challenges at home and abroad at the start of the 1980s, and the aging Soviet bureaucracy responded inadequately. The situation was complicated by four poor harvests in a row; 180 million metric tons of grain per annum and a decrease in the production of meat and dairy products created food shortages and the need for massive purchases of food abroad. The popularity of the leadership declined sharply, and the closed, secretive style of Brezhnev's rule increased the gap between the Soviet people and their leaders.

However, discontent did not develop into real opposition, as happened in Poland, where the crisis was much more serious. In the Soviet Union there was a visible slowing down of the growth rate but no actual decline in the gross national product (GNP) or in living standards. The Soviet political system was also much more stable than that of Poland. The alternative extraparty opposition was represented by small and weak groups of dissidents who had no links with workers or peasants. The influence of the Orthodox Church and other religions had been weak ever since religious institutions were repressed under Lenin, Stalin, and Khrushchev. Soviet people tend to wait for change to occur at the top.

From Bureaucracy to Technocracy

The most likely outcome of the Andropov ascendancy is an increase in the influence of the technocratic elements in the Soviet leadership. The emergence of a younger, more pragmatic, and more flexible generation of state and party leaders is inevitable within two to three years, if not sooner. Any significant reduction in the dominant role of the Communist Party is unlikely—it is still the most efficient apparatus of power. But the essence of the Communist doctrine concerning economic and political processes will probably change. Some modest experiments with a mixed economy in agriculture and in the service sectors are likely. The new leadership may also try to reduce the international commitments of the Soviet Union. They may decide that there is no point in giving generous economic assistance to countries that, like Egypt and Somalia, easily change sides after a change of leadership or for other reasons.

The new generation of Soviet politicians lived through the exposure of Stalin's crimes and of Khrushchev's errors and mismanagement. They will, therefore, realize that public support for party objectives cannot be taken for granted. They will probably be more ready to accept criticism and to introduce the political and economic reforms that are badly needed. The generation born between 1923 and 1935 is much better educated, and its representatives have occupied professional positions for much longer. They should, therefore, know that a Communist economy as such does not guarantee rapid economic progress and that the capitalist system can achieve rapid technological innovation and high productivity, even if it is cyclical. This generation will not be inclined to dogmatism or fanaticism, qualities usually born of revolution. Because they did not occupy high positions before 1980, they often have no basis for claiming past great successes and for building personality cults. They will try much harder to be successful after promotion. In general they will be technocrats rather than bureaucrats. The government may develop more decision-making power, independent of the party, than it has at present. If the new leaders want to be popular, they will have to introduce some liberal reforms. Repression does not win popular support, and probably no one understands this better than Andropov, former head of the KGB.

Economic Problems

This section is purposely headed "economic problems" rather than "the economic crisis." While the economic situation in Poland is critical, and in Romania near critical, it has not reached crisis level in the U.S.S.R. During the last few years the Soviet economy has experienced a decline in the growth rate, but there has been no reduction in total output. Although living standards have not risen, neither have they fallen. The price of food and other essentials has not risen; there has been no budget deficit and no unemployment; and the inflation rate has remained very low. There has been no serious foreign debt problem. Consumers complain about the quality of goods and the lack of diversity but not about empty shelves. There are shortages of meat and some dairy products but not of bread and other staple foods. The problems are those of rising expectations and of the disproportion between consumer demands and available stocks. However, the disappointment of consumers and especially their complaints about the quality of their diet indicates that they are disillusioned with the official promises and programs reiterated at party congresses and in official plans. The older generation remembers the deprivation and rationing of food and consumer goods during Stalin's time and is less disturbed about the current problems. But the younger generation, more consumer oriented and Westernized, clearly sees the system as being responsible for the country's poor economic performance.

The promises of economic growth made in the 1950s and 1960s and included in the official party program were very inflated. They seemed to ignore the fact that the Soviet Union has natural limits of economic growth. The targets for the 1958–65 seven-year plan and for the subsequent five-year plans were unreasonably high, and the plans were not fulfilled. Nevertheless, the growth of industrial output was substantial, increasing by 270% in the period 1965–80. But agricultural production grew only 35% during those 15 years, and it did not increase at all from 1980 to 1982. Because the urban population grew by 30–32%, there was no improvement in the food situation throughout this period. Nonetheless, the situation in rural areas improved substantially. Rural incomes increased because higher procurement prices were paid for state purchases and because the prices paid for food on the private and collective farm markets in towns were very high. The gap between the incomes of urban workers and peasants was markedly reduced.

The centralized Soviet economy still gives priority to defense and heavy industry. In the production of some military hardware (*e.g.*, tanks) and in the total output of steel, iron, some metals, and some kinds of machine tools and heavy equipment (locomotives, electric trains, tractors, steel pipes), the Soviet Union has already surpassed the U.S. The U.S.S.R. produces more oil and gas than does the U.S., and more gold and diamonds. However, the U.S. has the ascendancy in the production of such high-technology equipment as computers and in the production of consumer goods per capita. The construction of housing in "modernized" Soviet villages and in cities has been impressive. After food, housing is the second most important indicator of living standards. Between 1965 and 1982 about 1.8 million square metres (19 million square feet) of apartment space was built in the Soviet Union, more than for the whole preceding period from the Revolution to 1964. But the annual growth of GNP declined from an average of 10% in the 1960s to 3.5% at the end of the 1970s and 2.8% in 1982.

In the 1970s, however, the Soviet Union improved its internal domestic situation by radically increasing foreign trade. The deficiencies of agricultural production were partly compensated for by large purchases of food abroad. This turn of events became possible because of the dramatic increase in the world prices for oil and gas. The U.S.S.R. is the world's largest producer of these commodities. In Stalin's time the Soviet Union, with even worse food problems, had to export grain to obtain hard currency. In the 1970s oil sales became the main source of export revenue. The world prices for other traditional Soviet exports, such as timber, fur, gold, and diamonds, also increased, and the new revenue was used to import significant quantities of food, machinery, and high-technology equipment. Between 1970 and 1980 Soviet foreign trade rose from 22 billion to 109 billion rubles a year, and there were no signs that this trend would be changed by U.S. attempts to restrict further increases in the export of Soviet energy.

The overall picture of Soviet industrial development reveals some problems, disproportions, and errors of planning but no signs of real crisis. The Soviet bureaucracy has been conservative in using foreign credits. Soviet foreign debts are mostly related not to cash payments but to payments in kind by goods and commodities. Other Eastern European countries were much more liberal in their foreign borrowing, and this has put them in a difficult position. It has also created a great deal of financial difficulty for their Western creditors. While a significant number of economic problems have certainly accumulated in the final stages of Brezhnev's era, they are of a very different kind from those that occurred at the end of Lenin's, Stalin's, or Khrushchev's tenure. The new leadership will not need to make an economic U-turn but will no doubt make some adjustments and modifications. If Andropov's attempts to be more pragmatic and more efficient

Khrushchev's victory, bolstered by much-needed reforms, was nonetheless incomplete. In 1964 he was shunted into retirement.

and less tolerant of the widespread official corruption are reflected in reforms that will give more encouragement to local initiative in the industrial and agricultural sectors, that in itself would be enough to stimulate the economy.

The Future: An Optimistic View

The most urgent priority for the future will remain food. The recently introduced ten-year "food program" has been received by Soviet public opinion, with justified skepticism, as yet another empty long-term promise. Something must be done and can be done more quickly. If the new government were to open up a free discussion of the problem, this could help to solve it more quickly; an effective food program should be open for democratic discussion, not simply introduced by the Politburo. Although

Brezhnev tried hard to improve agricultural performance, having no wish to leave the political arena as a possible future scapegoat for food shortages, he did not introduce basic changes, such as price reforms. Increases in food prices are certainly not popular. But when food is too cheap, when prices have not changed for decades, much agricultural produce goes to waste. About 20% of cereals are lost in the Soviet Union because of waste, poor storage, and inadequate transport; the proportion of vegetables lost is even higher. Moreover, all the available resources are not being used for food production. Although hydroelectric projects, nuclear power stations, and other industrial projects have absorbed land, there are still large resources available for individual agricultural exploitation, for small, privately cultivated farms. In the early 1960s, when the government gave permission to workers and other urban dwellers to grow fruit and vegetables on small allotments on unused land outside towns, there was no problem in finding land. There are now some four million allotments, and they are extremely popular. This is primitive private agriculture, and it is tax-free. Many thousands of small, productive private farms would cause no harm to the socialist sector of agriculture. Leasing land for private farms and offering credits is a project that can be effective immediately. Gigantic schemes, like using the waters of northern and Siberian rivers to irrigate the drought-prone south, may be technically feasible but would take many years and hundreds of billions of rubles to realize.

The socialist idea that essential services must be free has brought benefits in the form of free health services and free education to many countries. In the U.S.S.R. this idea has led to cheap public transport and cheap rent. These services are state controlled and not easy to misuse. But much public housing is poorly built and inadequately maintained because of lack of funds normally provided by rate (local property tax) or rent payments. Without some such provision a deterioration of living conditions in the near future is inevitable. The provision of free gas for cooking and heating water is not really justified and leads to the misuse of this important energy source. There is nothing wrong with making people pay for some services. The old Communist dream, reiterated by Khrushchev, that "mature Communism" will mean that everything is free, is utopian. The slogan "to each according to his needs" probably seemed reasonable 100 years ago, but it is naive when material needs constantly expand. Moreover, people's needs include not only food and consumer goods but also cultural and intellectual values and freedoms. As soon as food and minimal consumer requirements are met, demands for democratic freedoms are inevitable. What the Soviet public values most about the countries of the West is not the quality of consumer goods but civil liberties and democratic traditions. The propaganda image of an eternally prosperous West is now very tarnished—recession, unemployment, inflation, and other problems are too visible. But trade with the West helps to satisfy demands for consumer goods and makes it more likely that in the course of time the Soviet people will come to demand civil liberties.

Soviet Foreign Policy

Contrary to many Western predictions, the new Soviet international policy will almost certainly be more restrained. There have already been some signs of restraint in the last two years. The Soviet Union has not been actively involved in the major conflicts of 1981–82, the Iraq-Iran war, Poland, the Argentine-British conflict, the Israeli-Palestinian war. Soviet support for radical revolutionary regimes has become a costly economic and political burden and

Brezhnev, seen here visiting West Germany in November 1981, seemed to personify an aging and enfeebled leadership.

SVEN SIMON/KATHERINE YOUNG

will probably be reduced in the future, although the Soviet Union will continue to exploit the situation in the third world indirectly by capitalizing on economic and political difficulties. But the U.S.S.R. needs partners, not dependents, and the technocrats understand this much better than the bureaucrats and revolutionaries.

The entry of new countries into Comecon will certainly be restricted. Cuba and Vietnam have been admitted but have not become active participants. Experience has shown that real integration is possible only among equally developed countries. The failure of Poland and Romania to westernize their economies through credits and to increase their independent cooperation with the West has helped the long-term Soviet aim of completely integrating the Eastern European economies. Although this project is unpopular in Poland, Hungary, and Romania, these countries have little choice since they are unlikely to receive further economic assistance from the West. Within a few years they will have to redirect their industries and standardize their equipment, technological processes, research and development programs, and distribution of manufactured goods. This will almost certainly mean a parallel increase in political integration.

For centuries traditional Russian foreign policy was centred on relations with immediate neighbours. The Soviet Union has the longest border in the world, more neighbours than any other country, and an economy relatively independent of overseas resources. Thus the improvement of relations with close neighbours will be the most urgent foreign policy priority for the future. China, Iran, and Turkey will mean more to the U.S.S.R. than Mozambique or Nicaragua. The failure of Soviet-U.S. détente may become less important as the chance of Sino-Soviet détente increases—neither country has anything to gain from the continuing conflict.

A return to a more rational, traditional foreign policy is, certainly, an optimistic prediction for the future. Many chances of better relations with neighbours have been lost by Soviet leaders in the past because of ideological disputes. One can only hope that the new leadership will not repeat the errors and miscalculations of its predecessors.

Zhores and Roy Medvedev are co-authors of Khrushchev—The Years in Power *and* A Question of Madness. *Zhores Medvedev, a biologist who until leaving the U.S.S.R. held important posts in Soviet research institutes, has worked at the National Institute for Medical Research, London, since 1973; besides numerous scientific publications, his books include* The Rise and Fall of T. D. Lysenko, The Medvedev Papers, *and* The Nuclear Disaster in the Urals. *Zhores's twin brother, Roy, a historian and sociologist still resident in the U.S.S.R., is the author of* Let History Judge, The October Revolution, Khrushchev, On Soviet Dissent, Leninism and Western Socialism, *and other books.*

"YOU CAN'T FORECLOSE A COUNTRY" DEBTOR NATIONS WORRY BANKERS

by F. John Mathis

During 1982 major commercial banks in the United States, Canada, Europe, and Japan were confronted with a number of very large borrowers who could not make interest and principal payments on their loans. Mexico, Argentina, Venezuela, and a host of other smaller Latin-American and African countries faced a liquidity shortfall and were forced to reschedule their foreign indebtedness to governments and banks.

Mexico and Argentina are among the largest borrowers from commercial banks. During the year they ran out of funds to service their bank debt of $78 billion, almost $40 billion of which matured before the end of 1982. Venezuela, also a major borrower, initiated renegotiation talks with its banks to lengthen the maturity of its debt. Worldwide, 40 countries were in arrears in their foreign debt-service payments, including Poland, which, together with Romania, had rescheduled its debt in 1981. Even countries that were not facing severe economic difficulties or liquidity problems, such as Brazil and South Korea, suffered adverse side effects and found it troublesome to obtain the funds that they needed to maintain their debt payments.

Rescheduling debt is not a new phenomenon for commercial banks—they have done it often for their domestic loans—but the magnitude of the international debt being rescheduled in 1982 was tremendous. For some banks it represented a significant percentage of their capital and reserves. This was particularly true of U.S. banks, which had the largest loans to Latin-American countries. In the case of Mexico, for instance, loans of the ten largest U.S. banks averaged almost 55% of their shareholders' equity, including common and preferred stock. Even so, Mexican exposure accounted for only 3% of total loans for those same banks and, unlike companies that can declare bankruptcy, countries seldom go out of existence.

Since 1975 principal payments have been renegotiated for payback over a longer period for 22 countries, including Poland. However, most of this rescheduled debt has been owed to governments in industrial countries rather than to banks. Between 1975 and 1981 commercial banks participated in only eight renegotiations—with Peru, Yugoslavia, Zaire, Nicaragua, Sudan, Jamaica, Turkey, and Bolivia—involving about $5.5 billion. Actual bank losses on those loans were negligible in most cases, and in general bank losses on international loans are about half the loss rate on domestic loans.

Beginning in 1982, however, reschedulings with commercial banks began to increase. These financial difficulties have been made more serious because of

severe problems in domestic lending by banks as bankruptcies rose sharply after 1979, reflecting persistent worldwide recession. As large corporations in many industrial countries neared collapse and oil prices weakened, the Penn Square became the largest bank to fail in the U.S. In Italy Banco Ambrosiano collapsed, in part because of fraud but also owing in part to depressed economic conditions.

These developments made it more difficult for even the largest banks to raise funds in international financial markets. Therefore, banks were unable to continue to extend their loan portfolios. This, in turn, led to a major slowdown in the amount of net new international lending during 1982, resulting in

further strains on the international financial system. During the first half of 1982 net new lending of $50 billion was well below the $65 billion increase recorded in the first half of 1981. It seems likely that because of the external financing difficulties of some major borrowing countries in Latin America, net new lending slowed further in the second half of 1982. Thus, total lending for the year will be well below the $165 billion increase recorded in 1981.

Growth of International Bank Lending

Following the quadrupling of oil prices in 1973, major banks participated aggressively in the recycling of funds from the oil-exporting countries to the oil importers. Between 1974 and 1982 international lending by commercial banks grew by an average annual rate of 26%, significantly higher than before 1974. This growth was concentrated in a relatively small number of large banks, with the world's 50 largest banks accounting for nearly two-thirds of total international lending and the top 200 banks representing almost 80%.

Total international loans outstanding rose to $1,550,000,000,000 at the end of 1981. If interbank transactions and redepositing among banks are excluded, the net amount was $945 billion, compared with $155 billion in 1973. European banks accounted for almost two-thirds of total international loans; the share of U.S. banks and their offshore branches was almost 30%; while Japanese banks represented 5% and Canadian banks 2%. Almost three-quarters of international loans were to industrial countries and offshore money centres. The remaining 26%, or $415 billion, was loaned to less developed countries, including $61 billion to Eastern Europe, $51 billion to southern Europe, and $72 billion to nations in the Organization of Petroleum Exporting Countries (OPEC). More than 60% of the total amount of loans to the less developed countries was concentrated in 12 countries, as shown in the table.

Offshore loans by U.S. banks and their foreign branches rose to $286 billion at the end of 1981, up from $65 billion in 1973. The 12 largest less-developed-country borrowers from U.S. banks represented 34% of total offshore borrowing and 70% of all U.S. bank loans to less developed countries. Most international lending by U.S. banks is concentrated in a few of the largest banks. For example, in the case of Mexico the ten largest U.S. banks account for 70% of the loans to that country.

Commercial bank loans are only part of the total debt owed by less developed countries. These nations also receive funds from governments and international institutions, such as the World Bank, the International Monetary Fund (IMF), and corporations in the form of suppliers' credits. Altogether the total debt of less developed countries rose to $530 billion at the end of 1981 and is estimated to have increased to $630 billion during 1982. About 80% of those funds were received by foreign governments or guaranteed by them. The remainder went to businesses in the private sector and was not guaranteed by the governments. Countries with the largest total foreign debt are ranked in the table.

Debt owed by less developed countries to private creditors rose from 23% of total debt in 1970 to 55% in 1982. In contrast, the share of debt accounted for by official (public-sector) sources dropped from 57% in 1970 to below 40% in 1982. Consequently, the proportion of debt contracted on concessional terms (loans with at least a 25% grant element) declined from 41 to 25% over the past decade. Moreover, almost 70% of the public-sector debt and almost all of the private-sector debt owed to private creditors carries variable interest rates. The trend of

rising interest rates over the past decade, combined with heavy reliance on private credit markets, has fundamentally increased the cost of borrowing. This has reduced the amount of funds left to invest in economic development.

Foreign Debt Structure

In evaluating the seriousness of present debt problems, a number of indicators show that there has been a significant change in the structural aspects of foreign debt. For example, during the past five years the ratio of foreign debt to gross national product (GNP) for less developed countries increased little, from 22% in 1977 to 24% in 1981. However, in 1973 foreign debt as a percentage of GNP was below 14%, and in 1982 it was estimated at 28%. Similarly, foreign debt service payments as a percentage of export earnings changed little between 1977 and 1981, remaining about 16%, but in 1973 it was only 11% and it may reach 25% in 1982. These ratios refer primarily to public or publicly guaranteed debt because similar information on private debt is not readily available. The World Bank estimated that the amount of foreign debt held by the private sector in less developed countries and not guaranteed rose to $94 billion in 1981 from about $25 billion in 1973.

Evaluating the maturity structure of less developed countries' foreign debt indicates that the debt servicing problem may continue for several years because debt service payments will be bunched until the mid-1980s. This bunching of service payments is the result of the sharp increase in lending that began in 1974 immediately after the first oil price increase. Also, lending continued to be strong after the second oil price increase in 1979 and 1980. Commercial bank loans averaging eight years in maturity began to come due in 1982 and will continue to do so until 1984. However, for a less developed country an eight-year loan usually does not allow enough time to finance the establishment of sufficient productive capacity to service the debt.

Deteriorating Economic Conditions

The sharp increase in external borrowing by less developed countries and the resulting debt burden were caused by a number of factors, but particularly important were the two oil price rises of 1973 and 1979. Less developed countries have been especially hard hit by the oil price increases, and their deteriorating economic conditions forced significant policy changes. The less developed nations initially suffered a sharp deterioration in their balances of payments. Subsequent stimulative policies of industrial countries boosted world trade growth temporarily, and commodity export earnings rose sharply with world inflation, causing the less developed countries to stimulate their economies.

The second oil price increase further worsened the current account deficits of the less developed countries, but this time there were no stimulative policies by industrial nations. Consequently, real world trade growth stopped, interest rates on foreign borrowings rose to record levels, and the foreign currency reserves of the less developed countries were drawn down to finance their balance of payments deficits. Less developed countries were then forced virtually to abandon economic development goals in order to meet the more pressing need for balance of payments adjustment. This process was uneven, and some countries such as Brazil began to adjust sooner than others such as Mexico.

The restrictive economic policies of industrial countries were designed to reduce inflation, but they also caused growth in the volume of world trade to decline from about a 10% average annual rate of increase prior to 1973 to an average of 3 to 4% since, with almost no growth occurring since 1979. Slower world trade growth will continue to hinder the recovery of export earnings for less developed countries and to slow the successful completion of their economic development programs. Also, it will be increasingly difficult for them to earn foreign exchange to meet scheduled debt service payments.

Those less developed countries whose exports are dominated by basic raw material or agricultural products have been hit particularly hard. Not only did the volume of their exports slip but commodity export prices (for both agricultural and industrial materials) also fell, resulting in a deterioration in terms of trade, particularly with respect to oil imports. Thus, the growth in the purchasing power of export earnings was severely eroded, and with oil import costs sharply rising, non-oil imports were reduced adversely, affecting general economic growth. Even the relatively prosperous exporters of manufactured goods experienced only a 1% annual rise in the purchasing power of exports during 1980 and 1981, compared with a 5% yearly increase in 1978 and 1979 and 10% growth in both 1976 and 1977. The less developed countries reacted by depreciating their currencies more often and by larger amounts.

However, this aggravated their liquidity problem by raising the cost of imports, which drained scarce foreign exchange reserves.

Another factor adversely affecting the less developed countries is the growing interest rate burden, which since 1973 has led to a hardening of borrowing terms. Increasingly, foreign borrowing by less developed countries has been at variable interest rates based on the London interbank offered rate (LIBOR), adjusted every three or six months, plus a fixed spread. The general trend of rising interest rates over the past ten years was accelerated by the jump in U.S. interest rates beginning in 1979.

Eurodollar rates parallel interest rate movements in the United States and have risen sharply from an average of 6% in 1977 to 12% in 1979, 14% in 1980, almost 17% in 1981, and 14.5% for 1982. The yearly increase in debt service due solely to the increase in interest rates totaled at least $16 billion between 1978 and 1981. Interest payments by less developed countries now take about 10% of export earnings, up from just 3% in 1973. Consequently, the net inflow of funds (taking into account debt-service outflows) to less developed countries has declined since 1978 and in 1982 was smaller than it was in 1975. This decline was entirely accounted for by private lenders, whose share of the net inflow of new funds fell from 70% in 1978 to about 20% in 1981.

Mixed Prospects for Commercial Banks

Each country will react differently to changes in its external or internal economic environment depending on such factors as social pressures, international reserve levels, and resource endowment. Countries in the newly industrialized category will react differently from oil exporters or the centrally planned economies of Eastern Europe. Consequently, each country's situation and adjustment options must be reviewed independently. In international lending most U.S. and other industrial-country com-

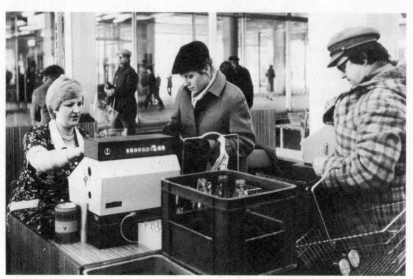

Poland's massive international debts meant fewer foreign goods on store shelves and a lower standard of living for its people.
DANIEL SIMON—GAMMA/LIAISON

Eldon Beller, president of the failed Penn Square Bank in Oklahoma City, Oklahoma, testified in August before a special congressional hearing on the bank's failure.

mercial bank loans are concentrated either in the high-income less developed countries or in those that have shown the most potential for strong economic development. Most of those countries are exporters of manufactured goods and should best be able to adjust to economic problems and service their foreign debt.

Significantly, since World War II only Cuba has defaulted on its foreign debts, and even in that case efforts are under way by the country to reschedule its loans. Unless a nation is prepared to leave the free world economy—either because it does not need to sell its exports and import products from abroad or because it is no longer in need of substantial funds from private banks, governments, or international institutions—it must continue to service its foreign borrowings. Not only is it in the country's self-interest to service its foreign debt but it also has little choice, since it needs access to world products and capital markets to raise its standard of living. As illustrated by the reschedulings of debts of Poland and Romania, even members of the Soviet bloc want to maintain access to the free world markets.

Western governments generally have encouraged private banks to take an active part in the transfer of resources to the less developed countries. This is based on the belief that free market forces will yield the most efficient distribution of resources. A conflict in government policy has developed as increased commercial bank lending has prompted attempts to monitor and regulate the growth of this lending. Governments have denied responsibility for bailing individual banks out of any rescheduling

problems but, at the same time, they have reacted quickly when the problem was perceived to be a political issue, as in the case of Mexico and Yugoslavia. In the case of Eastern European debt problems, particularly with Poland and Romania, the issue of forced default to embarrass the Soviet Union politically was openly discussed. Such government involvement, as in the case of Eastern Europe, shifts international lending from the realm of economics into that of politics. It undermines the role market forces can play in inducing the required economic adjustment.

Some analysts accuse commercial banks of overaggressive lending and maintain that it is the source of current debt problems. However, governments and international agencies worry that banks now may withdraw from offshore lending, causing major hardship to the vast majority of the world's population. Furthermore, the lender-of-last-resort responsibility of central banks comes into play when a major liquidity shortfall threatens to jeopardize the confidence of the international financial community. In this respect governments and international organizations moved quickly in the cases of Mexico, Brazil, and Argentina to provide substantial amounts of funds. These funds have been made available until the liquidity shortfall can be resolved through domestic policy adjustment under IMF guidelines.

Thus, during December 1982 solutions to the liquidity problems of the large less developed countries began to be worked out. Mexico agreed to implement the necessary economic-adjustment measures to improve its international financial position.

In return it received access to $4.5 billion over three years from the IMF, $1 billion in U.S. Commodity Credit Corporation guarantees, $700 million from the U.S. Federal Reserve, and $1,850,000,000 from industrial countries acting through the Bank for International Settlements. Net new funds needed for Mexico from commercial banks were estimated at $1.5 billion in 1982 and $5 billion in 1983. Similarly, Argentina obtained commitments for $1.8 billion from the IMF and in 1982 was attempting to obtain $2.6 billion from commercial banks in short-term loans in order to refinance $4.8 billion of unpaid 1982 debt. Brazil received access to $4.5 billion over three years from the IMF and may obtain an additional $1.5 billion from that agency; Brazil also gained several short-term loans totaling $1,230,000,000 from the U.S. government and a $1.5 billion loan from the United States and three European governments. It also was attempting to arrange a $2.4 billion short-term loan from commercial banks. Finally, Venezuela is in the process of arranging a $3 billion short-term refinancing loan from commercial banks.

Additional Funds Needed

These developments, plus smaller debtor requests, have exhausted a substantial amount of the IMF's loanable resources. If the IMF is to continue to be effective in guiding countries' economic and balance of payments adjustment process, it will require additional funds to lend. The growth in the IMF's resources has lagged far behind the expansion in world trade and inflation and thus diminished its ability to cope with rising imbalances. The U.S. originally objected to a large increase in IMF resources, but more recently it has agreed with other major industrial countries to expand the IMF's resources by 50% and to make those funds available as early as 1983 instead of in 1985, as had originally been scheduled.

Despite these additional funds from official sources, there is still a strong need for new funds from commercial banks. These banks will be in-

volved in rescheduling or rolling over outstanding loans, which in the case of Mexico may approximate a $16 billion public-sector debt and as much as $9 billion in the private sector falling due by the end of 1983.

Although the vast majority of offshore lending is done by the 200 largest banks in the world, many of the remaining smaller institutions that comprise the 1,000 to 1,500 banks involved in international lending are likely to reduce their overseas exposure. Since smaller banks tend to emphasize short-term loans, often in the form of trade finance, they are able to reduce their foreign exposure rather quickly. However, both large and small banks have discovered that when a country is experiencing a liquidity shortfall, there may be little difference between short- and long-term debt. The Mexican rescheduling also made clear the distinction between lending to the public versus the private sector as public loans received priority access to available dollars to make service payments. Even so, in some cases the Mexican government has assumed responsibility for private debt and is eventually expected to make dollars available to facilitate the servicing of almost all foreign debt.

The withdrawal of smaller banks from offshore lending may adversely affect creditworthy borrowers and reinforce the slowdown in international lending. The impact of this slowdown, even with increased official lending, will deter world economic growth. The extent of this adverse effect may be softened somewhat by slower world inflation, so that the actual purchasing power of international lending may be maintained.

Rescheduling has certain costs for commercial banks, although it has some benefits. The costs relate to depressed stock prices and management time. So far, actual outright loan losses have remained small. The benefits of a rescheduling are associated with an increase in the average interest rate spread on outstanding debt. In addition, the country concerned may receive special economic management assistance from the IMF. Nevertheless, it may take some time before full confidence is restored in the commercial banking system. In an effort to improve the flow of information on countries' financial situations, commercial banks in major countries are attempting to establish a new institution. This institution, first discussed at Ditchley, England, in early 1982, would attempt to make member banks aware of payment problems in countries and would serve as a forum for banks to communicate their concerns to foreign governments. The objective is to resolve balance of payments difficulties in a more orderly manner so as to avoid repetition of the liquidity problems confronting a number of major countries.

John Mathis is vice-president of the Continental Illinois National Bank and Trust Company of Chicago.

STRESSES IN THE WESTERN ALLIANCE

by Edward Heath

Ever since the creation of the Atlantic Alliance more than 30 years ago, there has never been a shortage of those who have concentrated on the strains and tensions to which it has been subjected. Moreover, the issues of policy that have divided it have been a constantly recurring feature of its existence. Differences of opinion over nuclear strategy, over the Arab-Israeli conflict, over the disputes between Greece and Turkey, and, more indirectly, over trading activities between East and West, industrial protectionism, and differing agricultural systems are nothing new.

Ascendancy of Unilateralism

That the Alliance has survived these seemingly endless disagreements and conflicts of national interest should have caused observers, until recently, to regard the prophets of doom with more than a little skepticism. However, there is today a new, and what can only be described as pernicious, tendency within the Alliance that compels one to view its prospects with greater foreboding. This new tendency is the deliberate downgrading, by the present United States administration in particular, of the concept of joint management of the international economy and global security. Inflation is to be solved by each country on its own. Security outside the North Atlantic Treaty Organization (NATO) is to be assured by an unwarranted reliance on the unilateral deployment of military might. Diplomacy is to be downgraded; and partnership with the overwhelming majority of less developed countries is shelved, thus excluding two-thirds of the world's population as far as possible from the governance of the international system.

It is not merely frustration or exhaustion or even plain selfishness that motivates this abdication from international cooperation. Nor is it growing public indifference toward the Alliance that is enabling political leaders increasingly to pursue unilateral policies. It is rather the ascendancy of an ideology in which cooperation is denigrated as a sellout to foreign interests, in which the utility of military power is asserted to be almost absolute, and in which the pursuit of moderation and consensus is dismissed as the negation of strength and fortitude. Under these circumstances consultation between allies, when it is allowed to take place at all, is inevitably in real danger of becoming a ritual, emptied of all substance and direction.

After the disarray among the Allies following the Soviet invasion of Afghanistan and the U.S. unilateral decision to produce the neutron bomb, this alarming conclusion is borne out by at least two further transatlantic disagreements: the first over how to react to the imposition of martial law in Poland and the second over the pipeline to transport natural gas from the Soviet Union to Western Europe.

Concerning Poland, discussions within the Alliance had been going on for one and a half years before the imposition of martial law in that country. Yet it still failed to produce a united reaction or even an agreement on how to gear the extension of credit to Eastern Europe more closely to Western political priorities. As far as the pipeline is concerned, the U.S. administration unilaterally imposed sanctions against European companies that had signed contracts for the export of components made under license to the Soviet Union—a policy that was inconsistent with international law and with all the accepted limitations governing the sovereignty of nations. Subsequently, the U.S. administration uni-

At one end of the political spectrum, differences between the U.S. and its European allies were expressed violently, as in this demonstration against Pres. Ronald Reagan's visit to West Berlin.

laterally lifted the sanctions. As a result, the strain imposed on the Alliance has been substantial; and the West has conveyed a signal of disunity and inconsistency to the new Soviet leadership.

Disruptive Forces

The real question that now must be asked, and to which this article is addressed, is whether this new autarchy in political and economic affairs is merely a temporary phenomenon, brought about by the strains of a world recession and by the group of political leaders who happen to be in office at the present time, or whether forces are at work that will make this a far longer and deeper crisis in the Alliance—forces that challenge the whole of the set of assumptions that have governed Western policy-making for more than three decades. It is impossible to disguise the fact that strong forces of this kind do indeed exist.

First, the pursuit of unilateral policies is in danger of becoming a self-sustaining process, not only in the realm of economics but also in matters of security. This is because the inevitable failure of such policies, and the consequent worsening of the problems they are designed to solve, serves to enhance rather than reduce the inclination of governments to be introspective and to pursue national rather than international solutions to their problems. This was seen only too clearly in the 1930s, and with catastrophic results.

The monetary policy of the U.S. provides an example of this process. The unilateral imposition of high interest rates by the U.S. authorities was originally conceived to be a temporary measure to reduce the rate of inflation, after which business confidence, investment, and output would rapidly be revitalized. Nothing of the kind happened. On the contrary, high interest rates increased the cost of borrowing for governments and private investors alike so enormously that investment by both virtually ceased and long-term business planning became all but impossible. At the same time, spiraling public and private debt increased the competition for available funds, which in turn was used by the authorities concerned as a justification for continued upward pressure on interest rates—pressure that resulted not only in thousands of bankruptcies but also in a continuing decline in investment. Yet the deeper the economic quagmire in which the Reagan administration found itself, the more resolutely it seemed to believe in the pursuit of national autarchy in its economic policies.

The second force that is perpetuating the crisis in the Alliance is the continuing shift of the political centre of gravity in the U.S. away from the East Coast. The growing intellectual and political assertiveness of other parts of the U.S., which do not have the tradition of internationalism or the network of contacts in Europe so characteristic of the Eastern Seaboard, appears now to be an irreversible process. As a result, it is increasingly improbable that a president from this old political group will be elected; or, if he is, he will need to be far more closely attuned to the ascendant political views of the rest of the country than was ever necessary in the past.

The third disruptive force stems from the threats to the security of the Alliance and the interests of its members, which have become so much more numerous and complex in recent years that unity has become far more difficult to maintain and far more costly for political leaders to insist upon. This is an inevitable result of the new challenge to Western policy created by the global reach of Soviet power, the growing inhibitions on the full use of Western power—whether military or economic—to deter aggression in the modern world, and the increasing economic strength of countries outside NATO, particularly in East Asia, the Arabian peninsula, and Latin America. Although the Alliance does not formally act as one in economic affairs or in upholding international security outside its own perimeter, it is condemned to seek unity on these matters because the failure to do so would seriously damage both its interests in those areas and its cohesiveness in the face of the Soviet threat to Western Europe.

The crisis precipitated by the Argentine invasion of the Falkland Islands provided a vivid illustration of these realities. It showed how difficult unity is to achieve given the increasingly complex interests of the major countries in the Alliance—for example, in their respective relations with Latin America. At the same time, it demonstrated the overriding and inescapable need for the Alliance to remain united, even on an issue that was clearly outside the scope of its formal purpose—to defend itself from a direct Soviet military threat.

Fourth, there is a danger that the growing cost of defense will heighten tensions between Europe and the U.S. over military strategy. The recession in the West and the rapidly rising cost of conventional forces are exacerbating the old dilemma between placing greater reliance on nuclear weapons for the defense of NATO, so as to minimize costs, and diverting public expenditure from social or economic purposes to conventional defense in order to reduce the need for the use of such weapons. Today, both courses of action are extremely difficult for politicians to undertake, the first because of the unprecedented strength of the antinuclear lobby and the second because the recession is making every additional cut in other spheres of public expenditure to make way for that on conventional arms the object of increasingly strong public opposition.

The absence of any easy solution to this dilemma is undermining the attempt by some European members of NATO to achieve a durable domestic consensus on the priorities for their own defense. This has been reflected in the changes in attitude within some European countries toward the neutron bomb, from being in support of it to opposing it; and it has been seen in the vacillation of some who had previously given full support to the modernization of NATO's

long-range theatre nuclear forces, to name but two major issues of defense policy.

These changes in attitude are wrongly interpreted by many in the U.S. administration and Congress as symptomatic of a tendency on the part of governments in Western Europe to appease the Soviet Union rather than to stand up to its growing military strength. One of the dangers of this misconception about European behaviour is that in the minds of many Americans it may justify the current tendency of their administration to pursue unilateral policies. To these people the European allies will no longer seem to be worthy of the sacrifices and the compromises that are constantly required to maintain unity within the Alliance.

Opportunities for Renewal

What do these various threats to the cohesion of the Alliance portend for the future? Are there any developments within the Alliance that may counterbalance these disruptive forces and thereby give it fresh vigour in the years ahead? There are, in my view, three opportunities for the Alliance to inject itself with renewed vitality and purpose.

The first is the increasingly close cooperation between Spain and the rest of the Western world. Even if Spain decides not to join the integrated military command of NATO, its desire to cooperate with the Alliance reflects the confidence and hopes that the Spanish people have placed in it and the remarkable reintegration of that nation into the family of Western democracies. If Spain does decide to remain in NATO, this will provide an opportunity both to strengthen the Alliance and to rekindle popular support in all its countries for its basic aims of preserving democracy and freedom in the West.

Second, it is a sign of vitality in NATO, and not of decay, that some of its members are now seriously beginning to question doctrines of nuclear warfare that are no longer credible in an age of nuclear parity between the superpowers. In particular, more and more senior generals and politicians on both sides of the Atlantic openly doubt whether a U.S. president would really authorize the first use of nuclear weapons, and thereby the potential destruction of the U.S., in response to a successful conventional assault on Western Europe by the Warsaw Pact forces. That these doubts are now openly voiced has added considerably to the need to find an answer to this question: What happens if deterrence breaks down?

The answer to the question is *not* that more complicated means of fighting "limited" nuclear wars must be elaborated. For one thing, nobody has yet shown that a nuclear war could be kept limited, nor that the military has mechanisms for command and control to keep it as such, nor that the Soviets would believe that it would remain so. For another, the attempt to make nuclear "war-fighting" seem more credible will have the effect of making NATO's overall military posture less credible because it will powerfully inflame the anxieties of those in Europe who fear that it will increase the probability of a nuclear exchange between the superpowers that is confined to the European battlefield. This argument will therefore play directly into the hands of the growing army of "pacifists" who favour the unilateral disarmament of Western Europe.

Strategic logic dictates one overriding answer to the question of how to address the crisis of NATO's nuclear doctrine. It demands an improvement of NATO's conventional forces to such a degree that the Alliance is relieved of the political and psychological burden of appearing to have to rely on the threat to use nuclear weapons in a first strike. This will be expensive, but so great is the fear of nuclear weapons in Europe—and in much of the U.S.—that it would be presumptuous to regard the political obstacles to a major improvement in conventional defense as insurmountable.

Such a strengthening of NATO's conventional defenses would be the single most effective way of diminishing the strength of the pacifist movement. At present, reliance is being placed on arms reduction talks to achieve this objective. Yet the process of arms reduction is likely to be too slow to mollify the fears of Europeans about nuclear war or to prevent fresh calls for unilateral disarmament. And as the technological sophistication of armaments relentlessly increases, so it will become even more difficult to find ways of limiting not only the numbers of weapons but also improvements in their quality.

However, arms reduction talks are, and must remain, a top priority for the Alliance. In particular they can help to make clearer and more visible the capabilities and the military options available to both East and West in conventional as well as nuclear warfare. President Reagan's proposals leading to the strategic arms reduction talks (START), now under way in Geneva, on the limitation of intermediate-range nuclear warfare could make a major contribution to building greater stability into the East-West relationship. Indeed, the growing political consensus in the U.S. on the need for arms control provides a fresh opportunity for a major step forward toward the limitation of nuclear weapons.

What Europe Should Contribute

The third long-term opportunity for the Alliance is the increasing balance in power between the U.S. and Western Europe. Today Western Europe has a gross national product larger than that of the U.S., and it has the potential, through the European Community, to play a major diplomatic role in international affairs. Militarily, the gap between European and U.S. capabilities continues to be reduced. Indeed, if tomorrow NATO had to counter a conventional attack by the Warsaw Pact, 90% of its ground forces and 75% of the sea and air forces available from the outset would be Western European troops.

The existence of a more equal relationship between Western Europe and the U.S. may well make the achievement of consensus more difficult, but it provides a major opportunity to revitalize the Alliance and give added effectiveness to its policies. In particular, it enables Europe to make a far greater contribution to a genuine division of labour in the Alliance. For example, in the diplomatic sphere European governments are sometimes allowed considerably more flexibility by their electorates than is the U.S. administration. This is true of the Cyprus problem and the lingering dispute in the Aegean, where Europe has uniquely close contacts with all the parties involved. And it is true of the Arab-Israeli dispute, where Europe often has better and more trusted relations with key Arab countries than the U.S. One of the advantages of working through the institutions of the European Community in these tasks is that they are untainted by the legacy of mistrust—justified or unjustified—that the superpowers have acquired for themselves.

In the economic sphere Europe has technological and financial resources with which it can help countries whose security is threatened by their economic weakness—Turkey, Yugoslavia, and Pakistan, particularly after the Soviet invasion of Afghanistan.

In the military sphere Europe can also make a substantial contribution without deploying large numbers of troops outside the NATO area. It can do this by providing military equipment and training to countries threatened by external aggression. It can also provide logistical and financial support for U.S. military deployments around the world. And it can strengthen the defense of the European theatre itself.

In all these spheres it is essential that Europe should be seen to make an effective and willing contribution to the solution of the problems with which the Alliance is faced. Unless the Europeans do this, the people of the U.S. will inevitably become disillusioned with their allies, and the effectiveness of the Alliance will be further undermined.

At this point, however, a nagging question arises, which refers back to the starting point of this article: What if the U.S. is unwilling to pursue a partnership of equals with Western Europe in the nonmilitary tasks that currently face the Alliance? What if it refuses to cooperate with Europe in the development of the underprivileged regions of the third world or if it designs its economic policies without regard to the interests of Europe or the stability of the international economy?

It is obviously desirable for Europe to resist as far as it possibly can the temptation to go it alone. Indeed, in the areas of military security and relations with the Soviet Union it remains of overriding importance to maintain compatibility between European and U.S. policies. Moreover, there is still much that can be done to improve mechanisms of consultation within the Alliance. The democracies still have no institutional machinery for addressing economic issues or those relating to the third world. The summit meetings of Western and Japanese leaders are an attempt to fulfill this need, but they are too infrequent and unsystematic in the way they relate to decision-making procedures at lower levels to solve the many substantive problems on the agenda of the Alliance.

Thus, where consultation between Europe and the U.S. can be improved, where the possibility of a convergence of their views and policies remains, and where time permits, every effort must be made to preserve unity of action within the Alliance. However, the new reality of our times is that we must be prepared to face the fact that in some areas of policy this may not be possible, and that Europe will need to take its destiny more into its own hands. It is in the area of economic affairs that this is perhaps most urgent and most immediately feasible.

The Monetary Factor

The constant threat of conflict across the Atlantic over trade and monetary policy can be averted by Europe only if the Community makes a determined effort to insulate its monetary policies and interest rates from those of the U.S. I have proposed that this should be done by devising a "ring fence" of ex-

change controls around the Community that can be imposed as and when necessary in order to preserve monetary stability in Europe. I have never pretended that this would be easy, either politically or technically. In particular, it would be difficult to attempt without harmonizing taxation on portfolio investments in the different member nations. It would also require that greater control be achieved over the Eurocurrency markets, whose unchecked expansion in any case threatens the attainment by each member state of its own monetary objectives.

Some will say that exchange controls cannot work and that the proposal for a ring fence is therefore doomed to failure. History shows otherwise. For example, the British operations over 50 years, including the experience with the old investment dollar premium, which was often around 20–30% for long periods of time, are evidence that they can work. Others will say that the ring fence is no more than a protectionist device that militates against free trade and all the principles of an open international economy on which the post-World War II prosperi-

Sections of gas pipeline destined for the Soviet Union are readied at a factory in West Germany in defiance of the U.S. embargo.

"Well. . . . it looks like I'm going to have to explain the trickle down theory again."

ED GAMBLE / THE FLORIDA TIMES-UNION

ty of the West has been based. Such a view is founded on little more than ideological prejudice, for exactly the reverse would occur. Such a ring fence would enable Europe to pursue lower interest rates and therefore higher growth and expanded trade. It would help to reduce the instability of exchange rates, which is a potent cause of protectionist pressures. And, as a result, it would enable the less developed countries to increase their trade with Europe and to reduce their crippling payments of interest. This in turn would help those countries to escape from the appalling quagmire of spiraling debt in which they now find themselves and that seriously threatens the integrity of the international private banking system. The result would be to underpin the international system of payments and trade rather than to endanger it.

It is the alternative course along which Europe is now being dragged that is more likely to lead to the breakup of the international systems of trade and private lending. It is the relentless multiplication of restrictive trading practices, the futile attempt to defend currencies by constant changes in interest rates, and the irresponsible financing of the internal projects of countries like Poland that most gravely threaten the international economy.

It is now vital to bring into being a system of international monetary affairs of which the U.S. need no longer be the ultimate guarantor. In this system a central role for Europe can be neither escaped nor postponed, even if the U.S. once again becomes more cooperative in international monetary affairs. Indeed, what is needed is the development of a regional approach to the management of global economic and monetary affairs, for no one country is any longer powerful enough to underwrite the system, however benign or altruistic its policies. Under this approach only those responsibilities that cannot be dealt with effectively by cooperation between the major economic zones of the world would be handled by the International Monetary Fund or other

such bodies with global constituencies.

The responsibility of Europe in giving renewed strength and purpose to the Alliance is today greater than ever before. This responsibility can be exercised only by a united Europe. This is true whatever the climate of relations with the U.S. happens to be. It will require the European Community to devise a far wider range of policies than those that are currently its mainstay, namely the common policies that exist in the spheres of agriculture, foreign affairs, and the customs union. This would in turn enable the development of a broader constituency with a conscious stake in the growing unity of Europe.

With over nine million people unemployed in the Community, with billions of dollars worth of idle industrial plant, and with Europe's currencies adversely affected by wildly gyrating foreign exchange markets, the ability of the Community to take bold common action to develop the new high-technology industries on which its international competitiveness depends, to create a forward-looking energy policy, to coordinate further monetary and exchange rate policies, and to remove the plethora of nontariff barriers that frustrate millions of businessmen in Europe will be the prime determinant of its ability to rekindle the confidence of the public in its direction and purpose. And the ability of Europe to grow in unity and strength will in turn determine whether the Atlantic Alliance possesses the resilience to withstand the many disruptive forces and conflicting national interests to which it is being increasingly subjected.

The Rt. Hon. Edward Heath, MBE, MP, was Conservative prime minister of the United Kingdom from 1970 to 1974, having held office in previous Conservative governments from 1952 onward. He is a member of the Brandt Commission (Independent Commission on International Development Issues) and a firm supporter of European unity, and his publications include Old World, New Horizons.

CHINA'S UNCERTAIN FUTURE

by Richard H. Solomon

China and Japan began their struggles to transform agrarian, feudal societies into industrial nation-states at about the same time in the late 19th century. But while Japan, since the Meiji Restoration of 1868, has single-mindedly grown to become the world's third largest industrial power, China, from the time of Li Hung-chang's self-strengthening movement in the 1870s and '80s, has repeatedly floundered in its search for a path to national political and economic restoration.

Sun Yat-sen's 1911 revolution against the Manchu dynasty, the intellectual ferment of the May Fourth (1919) era, the decade of the Nationalist government at Nanking after 1928, and the 1949 Communist victory in the civil war now seem notable as false starts or periods in which high hopes for national rebirth were dashed by domestic political turmoil, foreign intervention, and the burdens of bringing a vast, decentralized peasant society into the mainstream of 20th-century industrial civilization. In contrast, the Japanese—despite the destructiveness of World War II—have hardly missed a step on the difficult road to social and economic modernization.

The past three decades of Communist Party rule of China—the era of Mao Zedong's (Mao Tse-tung's) leadership—have been no less a time of shifting experiments and disappointed hopes that a way could be found to modernize China rapidly. During the early 1950s the Chinese Communists adopted the Soviet model of development, only to reject it after 1958 in favour of a Great Leap Forward in economic construction. This experiment in the mass mobilization of peasant labour had failed by 1961, and it was followed by a decade of uncertainty in economic policies as the country succumbed to leadership feuds and the political chaos of the Cultural Revolution.

The decade of the 1970s was one of continuing leadership conflict and policy alterations as the Communists who established the People's Republic of China (PRC) continued to search for a path to China's modernization. Three developments give special meaning to the past decade:

- Communist Party Chairman Mao Zedong and many of the other senior revolutionary figures who led the People's Liberation Army to victory in the civil war, and who subsequently shaped policy during three decades of national reconstruction, died in the 1970s.
- China's foreign relations, which in the first two decades of Communist rule shifted from alliance with the Soviet Union to self-isolation during the years of Cultural Revolution turmoil, took a major turn toward an opening to the non-Communist world—to Western Europe, the United States, and Japan.
- Efforts of China's revolutionary leaders to bring about economic development through political mobilization of the country's 800 million peasants gave way to the building of socialism through the training of a technically competent party cadre, material incentives for the workers and peasants, and the bureaucratic management of China's huge agricultural economy.

Mao and the Succession

Mao Zedong—Chairman Mao—emerged as a leading figure in the Chinese Communist movement after the 1935 emergency leadership conference held at Zunyi (Tsun-yi) during the Long March. From that time until his death he played the primary role in developing the military and political strategies

and the organizational forms that led the Communists to victory in the civil war and, after the founding of the People's Republic in 1949, that built a socialist economy. A major issue in China's leadership politics from the early 1960s was Mao's effort to ensure that his policies would survive his death and that leaders who he believed would sustain his revolutionary legacy would remain in control of the Communist Party. In both respects Mao's final years of rule were a failure.

The Cultural Revolution that began in the spring of 1966 was, in part, an effort by Mao to remove from positions of leadership men such as State Chairman Liu Shaoqi (Liu Shao-ch'i) and Party General Secretary Deng Xiaoping (Teng Hsiao-p'ing), who—according to the chairman and his supporters—wanted to take China down the "capitalist road" of national development. While such leaders were purged in 1967, by the end of the 1960s the chaos and violence of what the Chinese now term the "ten wasted years" of political terror had generated a strong reaction against Mao's more radical policies and serious leadership factionalism.

At the second plenum of the 9th Central Committee in August 1970, Mao's long-time associate Chen Boda (Ch'en Po-ta), the theoretician of the Great Leap Forward and the Cultural Revolution, was purged on grounds of having incited Red Guard violence and factional intrigue within the party. Just over a year later, in September 1971, the man named in the ninth party constitution as Mao's heir to party leadership, Defense Minister Lin Biao (Lin Piao), mysteriously died in a plane crash while fleeing to the Soviet Union. It was later said that Lin had organized an assassination plot against the strong-willed and unpredictable chairman.

During the next three years it appeared that under the pragmatic direction of Premier Zhou Enlai (Chou En-lai), China was finally emerging from its nightmare of political violence. Zhou even succeeded in bringing Deng Xiaoping back to national leadership to assist him in his efforts. But Zhou's attempt to reestablish regularized bureaucratic administration of China's huge state system and economic planning mechanism was criticized by radicals within the party leadership centred on Mao's wife, Jiang Qing (Chiang Ch'ing). As Mao's health deteriorated after 1974 because of a series of debilitating strokes, Zhou and his plan to bring the Four Modernizations to China (the modernization of agriculture, industry, science and technology, and national defense) were attacked as being contrary to the chairman's legacy. The popular Zhou succumbed to cancer in January 1976, and not long thereafter the radicals engineered

the second purge of Zhou's choice for the succession, Deng Xiaoping.

Thus, on the eve of Mao's death on Sept. 9, 1976, China's leadership seemed firmly in the hands of his wife and the radicals. Indeed, less than a month after Mao's passing, party leadership was placed in the hands of a provincial official from Mao's home province of Hunan, Hua Guofeng (Hua Kuo-feng). It was said that Mao's deathbed testament was that with Hua in charge of his revolution, he—the chairman since 1935—was "at ease" as he passed on to a Marxist heaven.

However, the deep hatred within China for Mao's wife and the radicals who had led the country into the decade of Cultural Revolution turmoil erupted within only weeks of Mao's death. Jiang Qing and her close supporters were arrested and accused of being a "gang of four" who acted against the will of the party and the chairman. Deng Xiaoping was rehabilitated for the second time nine months later, and by 1978 he had begun restoring to leadership many of the senior figures of China's Communist movement who had been purged by Mao during the Cultural Revolution. Liu Shaoqi was exonerated posthumously, and Mao's chosen successor, Hua Guofeng, was demoted from the posts of party chairman and premier in 1981 and replaced by associates of Deng Xiaoping. Hu Yaobang (Hu Yao-pang), a former Communist Youth League official, assumed the post of Communist Party general secretary, and the Sichuan (Szechwan) provincial official Zhao Ziyang (Chao Tzu-yang) became premier of the State Council.

Pragmatic Bureaucratism

More significant to the ending of Chairman Mao's revolution than the intrigues within the party leadership that followed his death has been the almost complete abandonment of Mao's policies for build-

PHOTOS. (LEFT) FRANCOIS LOCHON—GAMMA/LIAISON; (RIGHT) EASTFOTO/SOVFOTO

China's largest single resource—population—has had to make up for lack of capital and advanced technology. The organization of peasants into military-style work brigades, however, was not always successful.

The excesses of the infamous Cultural Revolution bred a profound hatred of the "gang of four" who were its leaders.

HENRI BUREAU—SYGMA

ing China into a socialist state. A party leadership plenum in the summer of 1981 paid lip service to the chairman's role in bringing the Communist Party to power in China, but it also attacked him for his "cult of personality," for serious policy misjudgments dating back to the time of the Great Leap Forward, and for his "gross mistakes" made during the Cultural Revolution. And while Mao's contributions to the revolution were said to outweigh his errors, in fact, China's contemporary leaders have all but eliminated the style of leadership and the policies for economic development that were the distinguishing characteristics of his three decades of rule.

From the mid-1960s until Mao's death the Communist Party had become little more than an instrument for the chairman's personal rule. During those years the party's propaganda machinery preached "the thought of Mao Zedong" as the only vision of China's future. Mao's successors, at the 12th party congress in September 1982, abolished the post of party chairman and asserted their intention to "break the fetters of dogmatism and the personality cult" by rebuilding a party that would "seek truth from facts" and perfect a socialist legal system to guard against abuses of power. In the Maoist era the party cadre had asserted its authority by means of "redness" or political loyalty. The new party leadership proclaimed its intention to train a younger generation of leaders that instead had both technical competence and organizational ability.

To give force to these intentions party General Secretary Hu Yaobang asserted that all of the Communist Party's membership of 38 million would have to turn in their party cards and be examined for reregistration based on these new criteria for leadership. But future political battles can be expected as Deng Xiaoping and his associates seek to purge the party of the aged and incompetent as well as those members who still support the now discredited "ultraleft" policies.

Under Chairman Mao the Communist Party, or its Cultural Revolution incarnation of "revolution-

ary committees," had virtually run China—formulating policies, assigning personnel, and administering the economy, the Army, and the state bureaucracy. In the era of Deng Xiaoping the party's role, it is asserted, will be restricted to that of a policy-formulating institution. The power to make laws and administer a society of more than 1,000,000,000 people will be returned to the National People's Congress, the State Council, and its various administrative organizations. Whereas in Mao's time "class struggle" and the promotion of policies through military-style mass campaigns were the hallmarks of economic and political life, the Deng Xiaoping leadership now seeks to stabilize administrative power in the various bureaucracies of the State Council.

Intellectual Liberalization

Deng Xiaoping's modernization program, by its very definition, will transfer power in China from the rural "masses" to the urban intellectuals and bureaucrats. This shift in emphasis became evident in the summer of 1978 as Deng began to assert his alternative to Mao's policies. Invoking the slogan of past periods of intellectual liberalization, "Let a hundred flowers bloom," Deng and his colleagues encouraged China's intellectuals to vent their bitterness against the turmoil and persecution suffered during the Cultural Revolution. "Big character posters" were displayed on what was known as Democracy Wall in Beijing (Peking) and in other cities; on them personal tales of mistreatment during Jiang Qing's reign of terror were recounted for China, and the world, to see. Writers and artists purged during the 1960s by the gang of four were rehabilitated and their works published. Even Western literature, music, and films were widely circulated.

To compensate for the destruction of China's educational system during the Cultural Revolution, Deng ordered in 1978 that more than 10,000 students be sent abroad—largely to the United States—to gain the scientific, technical, and managerial skills that they needed to become leaders in a more pragmatic Communist Party. Also, such institutions as the Chinese Academy of Sciences and the newly created Academy of Social Sciences were given the resources to help formulate policies for China's modernization.

The intellectual ferment unleashed by Deng, however, was not long in generating a political reaction from more conservative elements in the party and the People's Liberation Army. By late 1979 criticism of the Communist Party and socialism by the intellectuals had reached sufficient proportions that fears were raised of a loss of all party authority. Counter-criticism of the danger of "bourgeois liberalism" began to appear in official publications. Democracy Wall was closed down. And the party asserted its authority once again by proclaiming that intellectual life had to remain within the bounds of the Four Fundamental Principles: Communist Party leadership, the working class dictatorship, a commitment to Marxism-Leninism, and the building of socialism.

Economic Development

For Mao Zedong and the other Communist revolutionaries who struggled for more than three decades to gain political power in China, the establishment of the People's Republic in 1949 presented a profound personal challenge to their leadership skills. Could they be as successful as economic developers as they had been as political revolutionaries? From the perspective of 1982 it is clear that Mao, in particular, tried to adapt the style of leadership that had succeeded in the years of revolutionary warfare to the tasks of economic construction—but with catastrophic results.

In the early 1950s the Chinese Communists adopted the Stalinist approach to economic construction, with its stress on the development of heavy industry through a centralized bureaucratic planning system that set production targets and allocated key resources. It did not take long for Mao, a man of rural background, to see that such an approach would not work in a technologically backward and undercapitalized country like China, in which more than 80% of the population were unlettered peasants. Some of the first strains in Sino-Soviet relations appeared in the mid-1950s as Mao rejected the Stalinist approach and began to formulate his own solution to China's economic development dilemmas.

The Great Leap Forward of 1958 represented Mao's answer to China's modernization needs: to substitute for capital the country's great surplus resource, its labour power, and to mobilize the peasants for agricultural and industrial production by organizing them into military-style units as had been done during the years of revolutionary warfare—into production "brigades" and agricultural communes. Mao went so far as to encourage population growth because, he said, it would enlarge the country's labour force.

The Great Leap Forward was a drastic failure. Between 1959 and 1962 China's national income dropped by 35%, a greater decline than occurred in the United States during the Great Depression of the 1930s. While some economic recovery was achieved during the years 1962–65, the onset of the Cultural Revolution in 1966 destroyed China's economic management system and central planning bureaucracy as party members were attacked by student Red Guards for practicing "revisionism." Labour productivity similarly dropped as peasants and workers devoted considerable time to studying Mao Zedong's "little red book" of quotations and attending political rallies. In 1978 China's leaders had to face the stark fact that over the 20-year period 1957–77 per capita income in the nation had actually declined somewhat as unabated population growth outpaced the increases in agricultural and industrial output attained during two decades of economic experimentation and political turmoil.

Mao devoted scant attention to economic matters in his last decade of rule, instead concentrating his failing energies on the political succession struggle and on China's growing national security problems with the Soviet Union. It was only in 1975 that the ever pragmatic Zhou Enlai—only a year from death—raised again the need for China to pursue the Four Modernizations, a theme he had first expressed in 1964 just before the country was engulfed in the Cultural Revolution. Zhou's call for a return to economic construction was delayed for several

In one of many attempts to stimulate trade in consumer goods, China held its first international Auto Salon in January 1981.
JONQUESTION–GAMMA/LIAISON

For a brief period after the fall of the gang of four, the Democracy Wall in Beijing (Peking) flourished as a public medium for the expression of bitterness and dissent.

GAMMA/LIAISON

years, however, first by the struggle against the gang of four, and then by two years of renewed Soviet-style planning in 1977–78 under the leadership of Hua Guofeng. In an effort to restart the engine of economic development rapidly, Hua stressed the development of heavy industry through high levels of capital accumulation (at the expense of popular consumption) and unrealistically high production targets. His policy, however, did not survive Deng Xiaoping's reassertion of power in the summer and fall of 1978.

China's current policy lines for pursuing the Four Modernizations were basically set at the third plenum of the 11th Central Committee in December 1978—the leadership convocation at which Deng Xiaoping reaffirmed the Zhou Enlai approach to economic development. Deng stressed that in pursuit of the goal of quadrupling national income by the year 2000, China would abandon Mao's mass campaign style of economic construction and return to a pattern of planned, centralized management of the economy by technically proficient bureaucrats. Deng sustained Mao's legacy to the extent that he stressed the primacy of agricultural output and encouraged a significant decentralization of decision making in the rural economy to the production teams and individual peasant households. But material incentives rather than political appeals were to be used to motivate the labour force, including allowing the peasants to earn extra income by selling the produce of their private plots at free markets.

By the end of 1982 Deng Xiaoping's policies had begun to improve China's economic performance, particularly in the rural areas. Yet even if the Communist Party is able to sustain these policies until the end of the century, it faces major barriers to sustained economic growth. Among these the most significant are the difficulty of increasing agricultural productivity given China's fixed quantity of arable land and the great effort needed to modernize rapidly the nation's agricultural technology, serious bottlenecks in the production of energy and in

transportation, and the country's limited number of well-trained scientists, engineers, and managers.

Although the Western world has been prepared to help facilitate China's economic modernization program through sales of advanced production technologies, the Chinese discovered in the late 1970s that they lack the economic and managerial capacity to absorb large quantities of foreign technology, even if they can find ways of financing such imports. And although the Chinese economy, in aggregate terms, is likely to rank among the world's largest by the end of the century, unless the country is able to stabilize its population growth quickly, further gains in agricultural and industrial production will do little to raise per capita income—estimated in 1982 to be less than $320 (compared with $9,780 in Japan and $2,460 in Taiwan).

Foreign Relations

China's foreign relations since 1949 fall into three distinct, decade-long periods of shifting alignments, each of which was influenced in a major way by Mao Zedong. In the summer of 1949 Mao proclaimed that the soon-to-be-established People's Republic of China would "lean to one side"—to an alliance with the Soviet Union and the socialist world. By 1960, however, after a decade of experimenting with the Stalinist model of development, leadership and policy differences in the Sino-Soviet relationship had grown so serious that China's "unbreakable" friendship with the U.S.S.R. had dissipated in public feuding. During the 1960s China withdrew from active involvement with the world—despite Mao's calls for revolution in the third world—as the leadership preoccupied itself with the domestic chaos of the Cultural Revolution. All but one of China's ambassadors were recalled home during the latter half of the decade. In 1969, however, serious military clashes along the Sino-Soviet frontier forced the Chinese to confront a major and growing Soviet military buildup. This development led Mao to initiate the third major phase in China's foreign relations—

an opening to the United States and other non-Communist countries of the West.

In early 1970 China and the United States privately informed each other, after 134 unproductive ambassadorial talks at Warsaw, that they wished to normalize relations. This set the stage for what was probably the most dramatic development in international relations since the end of World War II, the journey to Beijing of U.S. Pres. Richard Nixon. Concurrently, Premier Zhou Enlai initiated efforts to establish diplomatic relations between China and the countries of Western Europe and the third world. During the 1970s 70 governments broke ties with the Republic of China on Taiwan and established diplomatic relations with Beijing.

Intrigue and political pageantry marked the opening of the high-level Sino-U.S. dialogue in the summer of 1971 as President Nixon's national security adviser, Henry Kissinger, traveled secretly to Beijing to pave the way for Nixon's visit to the Chinese capital in February of the following year. The Kissinger trip probably accelerated China's long-resisted admission to the United Nations, which finally occurred in October 1971—along with Taiwan's expulsion from the world organization.

The Nixon visit to China in early 1972—projected worldwide by satellite television—concluded with publication of the Shanghai Communiqué, a political document in which China and the United States agreed to seek the full normalization of their bilateral relations while expressing a common opposition to Soviet "hegemony." Trade and cultural exchanges between the two countries were initiated, and the leaderships continued to discuss ways of reconciling their differences over Taiwan—with which the U.S. continued to maintain formal diplomatic relations.

Normalization did not come quickly, however. President Nixon's resignation over the Watergate scandal in August 1974, conservative Republican resistance to breaking U.S. ties with Taiwan, and political uncertainties in China associated with the deaths of Zhou Enlai and Mao in 1976 slowed down the process of Sino-U.S. accommodation until 1978. In December of that year the administration of U.S. Pres. Jimmy Carter and Deng Xiaoping finally reached agreement on establishing diplomatic relations, which was accomplished on Jan. 1, 1979. The U.S. severed formal ties to the government of the Republic of China on Taiwan and agreed to maintain only unofficial relations with the island even as it asserted its intention to sustain the island's defenses through continuing sales of American arms.

For both China and the United States the process of normalizing relations, from its beginning in 1970, was given political impetus by a common concern with the worldwide growth of Soviet military power. Indeed, the timing of the establishment of diplomatic relations in early 1979 was influenced, in part, by Moscow's support for Vietnam in its invasion of Kampuchea—a development highly threatening to

China's security. By the late 1970s, however, China's post-Mao leadership had begun to place its highest priority on economic development, and it was in this context that Deng Xiaoping in the summer of 1978 ordered the training abroad of a new generation of scientists, engineers, and managers. At the same time, China began to import sizable amounts of foreign technology in order to speed up the process of economic development. Nonetheless, Soviet military pressures continued to impart a national security rationale to the Sino-U.S. relationship. After Moscow invaded Afghanistan in December 1979, the U.S. and China exchanged visits of senior defense officials in order to explore ways of cooperating in response to the seemingly implacable military threat from Moscow.

This decade of positive developments in U.S.-China relations slowed abruptly after 1980, however, as the Chinese began placing greater emphasis on reunification with Taiwan and the administration of U.S. Pres. Ronald Reagan asserted its intention to sustain U.S. arms sales to the island. During the 1980 presidential campaign in the U.S., Reagan had stressed his desire to strengthen ties with Taiwan. In this context the Chinese curtailed defense-oriented contacts between the two countries and threatened to downgrade relations with the U.S. if arms sales to Taiwan were not terminated. This impasse led to more than a year of negotiations, which culminated on Aug. 17, 1982, with the publication of a joint Sino-U.S. communiqué. In this document the U.S. pledged to gradually reduce its sales of defense weaponry to Taiwan in view of Beijing's "fundamen-

Pressed by a huge population and a lagging standard of living, China's moderate leadership has sought openings to the West.

FRANCOIS LOCHON—GAMMA/LIAISON

"China's economic progress and political stability will be hostage to the effectiveness with which

tal policy of striving for peaceful reunification" with the island.

Not long after publication of this understanding, the Chinese initiated what may turn out to be a major new phase in their foreign relations by opening talks with the U.S.S.R. designed to explore the possibility of normalizing Sino-Soviet relations. In the era of Chairman Mao unremitting hostility to the Soviets had been almost a touchstone of political virtue, but under Deng Xiaoping's more pragmatic leadership diplomatic efforts to defuse the growing Soviet military threat to China are seen as holding the promise of allowing China to concentrate its scarce resources on economic development. However, China's intention is not to reestablish the Sino-Soviet alliance of the 1950s but to create for itself an independent foreign policy of balance between the two "superpowers." Thus, Hu Yaobang, in his political report to the 12th party congress in September 1982, stressed that "China never attaches itself to any big power or groups of powers." At the same time, PRC propaganda began to criticize *both* the United States and the Soviet Union as "hegemonic" states and stressed China's alignment with the third world of less developed countries.

Whether China, in fact, can pursue a more independent foreign policy will be shaped primarily by actions of the Soviet Union. If the new leadership in Moscow significantly reduces the Soviet military threat to China, the latter can conduct a more balanced foreign policy between the U.S. and the Soviet Union. Conversely, unremitting Soviet pressures on China will sustain Beijing's resistance to Moscow's "hegemonic" actions. Also of importance for the evolution of China's foreign relations will be the future China policy of the U.S., which in 1982 was still being pulled between a strategic interest in good relations with the PRC and long-standing ties of friendship, cooperation, and trade with Taiwan.

The Uncertain Future

The death of Mao Zedong marked the onset of a new phase in China's struggle for economic and social development. Given Mao's profound influence over the Chinese people for more than a quarter of a century, it is remarkable that his policies dissipated so rapidly after his death. Deng Xiaoping and China's other contemporary leaders have all but abandoned the chairman's legacy in favour of policies of bureaucratic pragmatism, and these must now be tested against several intractable realities.

Four problem areas will have particular influence on this new phase in China's struggle for modernization. First, Deng Xiaoping's efforts to rejuvenate the

population growth can be restrained while . . . technical modernization . . . is promoted."

Communist Party with a technically competent younger generation will face resistance from the aged, the radical, and the reactionary among the party membership. Further leadership feuding could seriously disrupt the country's development efforts, as it has so often in the past.

Second, current attempts to reestablish centralized planning and the bureaucratic management of the Chinese economy will once again expose the country to the stifling weight of the state bureaucracy, something that Mao fought against during much of his life. As is attested to by the Soviet economy, the bureaucratic control of an economic system of continental size can be as stultifying as political turmoil can be disruptive. Only the future will tell if the Chinese can find an effective balance between centralized planning and managerial initiative given to industrial enterprises and farm families.

The third problem area involves the new generation of scientific and managerial talent that has been trained abroad since Mao's death. This is a valuable human resource that compensates only in part for the destruction of China's educational system during the Cultural Revolution. Many times in China's past, however, a xenophobic reaction to foreign ways has led to the rejection of those trained abroad. If the Chinese fail to use effectively their newly trained talent, they are likely to pay a great cost in terms of the pace of modernization.

Finally, and most profoundly, China's economic progress and political stability will be hostage to the effectiveness with which population growth can be restrained while the technical modernization of agriculture and industry is promoted. The Chinese people today seem cynical of ideology and distrustful of Communist Party rule after so many years of political turmoil, and they are likely to measure their contemporary leaders according to how rapidly their living standard improves rather than in terms of the promotion of "class struggle," as characterized the era of Mao Zedong.

Richard H. Solomon is director of International Security Policy research at the Rand Corporation and head of Rand's Political Science Department. A professor of Political Science at the University of Michigan from 1966 to 1971, he subsequently served on the National Security Council staff with particular responsibility for Chinese affairs (1971–76). His books include Mao's Revolution and the Chinese Political Culture *(1971),* A Revolution Is Not a Dinner Party *(1976),* Asian Security in the 1980s *(1979), and* The China Factor: Sino-American Relations and the Global Scene *(1980).*

Asides

Not all the news events of 1982 made prominent headlines. Among items reported less breathlessly in the worldwide press were the following:

Dorsey Connors of the *Chicago Sun-Times* supplies her readers with a wide variety of practical household hints. During the summer she gave space to Helen Kiska, who said she saved a great deal of sorting time by marking plastic containers and their corresponding lids with identical numbers. She then went on to say, "If you run out of numbers, use the alphabet." No follow-up story appeared on the number of mathematicians who suffered cardiac arrest at the thought of running out of numbers.

Most who listened to 66-year-old Yvonne Mary Henderson's ramblings presumed she was merely exhibiting signs of incipient senility. After all, other bag ladies were known to talk in much the same way. For several years Henderson was able to survive on food given to her by a community centre in Miami Beach, Fla., but no one really believed she had been born in China and was the daughter of Sir Herbert Phillips, who once headed the Far East Department of the British Foreign Office. Then an English newspaper published a story about the curious bag lady in Florida who said she had lived in luxury before divorcing her fifth husband and moving to the U.S. Anthony Phillips read the account with great attention. In June he flew to the U.S., identified Henderson as his sister, and made preparations to take the bag lady aristocrat home.

Adrian Pugh, an 18-year-old Londoner, was not much of an art critic, but he knew what he liked in the way of picture frames. In fact, he liked one small frame so much he stole it. When Pugh was brought before an Old Bailey judge in March and charged with theft, he told the court he liked the picture frame but not the etching it enclosed, so he tossed the picture into a Piccadilly Circus sewer. The unrecovered etching was a Rembrandt.

City marathons have become major sports events in recent years, but the annual Bay to Breakers Race in free-spirited San Francisco was in several ways more memorable. Among the 50,000 people who ran across the city on May 16 were a Roman empress with four loin-clothed slaves, a Mediterranean fruit fly, Pac Man, and a 60-ft-long centipede bearing a 250-lb replica of the Golden Gate Bridge.

In midsummer 85-year-old George Adams had reason to remember his first Fourth of July celebration in the U.S. He was 16 at the time, a teenaged emigrant from Albania living in Philadelphia. During the Independence Day festivities someone randomly fired a gun and Adams collapsed when the bullet lodged near his heart. Doctors were afraid to operate. As the Fourth of July approached 69 years later, Adams found himself in a Southfield, Mich., rehabilitation centre where he was recovering from an auto accident. During lunch something caught in his throat. After a fit of coughing he brought up the bullet.

Slice it how you will, Wellston, Ohio, has a problem. Last February town fathers were delighted to welcome a new manufacturing plant that would employ about 1,000 local people and help relieve a 20% unemployment rate. By year's end they had discovered the catch: Wellston's sewage system was clogged by some 400,000 gal of sludgy industrial waste from the plant. The stuff could not be processed by ordinary treatment methods, had a high acid content, was too watery to be buried, and threatened to overflow into a local creek. Exotic new pesticides? Rocket fuel? Secret poison gases for the Army? No; flour, tomato paste, cheese, vegetables, and pepperoni. The plant makes frozen pizzas.

In early August Lon Haldeman of Harvard, Ill., climbed onto his bike in California and headed in an easterly direction. It took him 9 days, 23 hours, and 15 minutes to reach New York City—exactly one day and 12 minutes faster than anyone else had ever pedaled across the U.S. His female counterpart, Susan Notorangelo of St. Louis, Mo., completed a comparable trip in 11 days, 16 hours, and 20 minutes in July. Her astonishing time shortened by nearly three days the record set by Ann Kovich of Texas the previous month.

In mid-February Judge Wallace Anktel of Berlin, N.H., gave Rowland Duchasne the option of spending two 12-hour periods at the city dump in freezing weather or face a $200 fine. Anktel had been found guilty of cruelty to animals for putting four unwanted puppies under a pile of garbage at the dump site.

Drivers in Homewood, Ill., were under unusual police surveillance during the summer. One by one some of the most law-abiding citizens of the community were pulled over by police and given tickets. Subdued anger quickly gave way to a happy surprise when each was told the ticket was redeemable for $5.00 at the police station. The village trustees wanted to promote good driving by rewarding those who observed all the rules of the road.

A municipal court judge in Bowling Green, Ohio, automatically dropped charges of speeding against Michael Groff when a letter arrived from Hillcrest Hospital in Mayfield Heights certifying that Groff had been admitted on March 6 and died on March 11. The local *Sentinel-Tribune* carried the death notice. Later, in a follow-up story, the newspaper reported that Groff was still attending classes at Bowling Green State University. Faced with a life-or-death situation, Groff showed up at court prepared to pay his fine. The judge indicated his amusement by imposing a $250 fine for contempt of court by obstructing justice and avoiding prosecution, 80 days of community service, a letter of apology to the public, and $30 plus court costs for the speeding violation.

Stanton Powers, an artist in Santa Cruz, Calif., needed the help of a Social Security disability check to make ends meet. Then, according to his attorney, he simply prayed for money in front of an automatic teller installed at the County Bank of Santa Cruz, and his prayers were answered. His balance rose from $1.17 to $26, then up through the hundreds, the thousands, and hundreds of thousands. By the next morning Powers was worth, according to the computer, $4.4 million. Powers was able to withdraw about $2,000 before the machine snatched away his card.

Midyear graduation marked an incredible victory for Adeline Becht, a 48-year-old resident of Oregon. As a young woman she became addicted to drugs while being treated for osteomyelitis and alcoholism. The drugs in turn destroyed her sight and hearing. But Becht took hold of herself and straightened out her life. With the help of an interpreter, who sometimes spent 18 hours a day attending lectures and transcribing them into Braille, Becht completed her studies at the University of Oregon. In June, when she graduated with doctoral degrees in both clinical and counseling psychology, she was confident she would be able to treat patients as effectively as any of her peers.

Gertrude Jamison was mighty upset when A. Douglas Thompson notified the Humane Society in Chattanooga, Tenn., that her dog had nipped him while he was delivering mail. She was so angry, in fact, that she phoned Thompson ten times a day to let him know just how she felt. In March a judge threatened to send Jamison to a penal farm if the phone calls persisted. That normally would have satisfied a plaintiff, but Thompson was not convinced his troubles were over. "She'll call again, I guarantee you. As long as she can dial a phone, she'll call." He had good reason to think so. The calls had been going on for 45 years.

WIDE WORLD

"It was something I had to do to achieve inner peace," explained Larry Walters, 33, after the flight. On July 2, Walters tied 45 helium-filled weather balloons to an aluminum lawn chair and soared into the air from a San Pedro, California, backyard. He was spotted by two passenger jetliners as he reached 16,000 feet some 45 minutes later. At length he shot out ten of the balloons with a BB gun brought for the purpose and drifted back to Earth some 20 miles downwind from where he had started. Officials at the Federal Aviation Administration knew immediately that they had to move on Walters, but it took five months for bureaucrats to figure out a charge. In December they cited him for, among other things, operating an aircraft for which there was no airworthiness certificate.

Stephen Thomas complained in January that he had never been paid for the time he served as mayor of Milton, Pa. Some weeks before the election in November 1981 he decided to take another job but at the late date could not legally withdraw his candidacy for mayor. After winning the election, he was dutifully sworn in as mayor but resigned within half an hour. He figured he was owed eight cents for the time he served as chief executive.

HAAR—HARTFORD COURANT/PICTURE GROUP

Lightning may not strike twice in the same place, but how about meteorites? In November a six-pound piece of extraterrestrial masonry crashed through the roof of the Robert Donahue home in Wethersfield, Connecticut. No one was hurt, and scientists were delighted to recover the object for study, but Wethersfield residents were perhaps a little wary. Eleven years before, in April 1971, another meteorite had struck a home just a mile from Donahue's. The odds against such a repeat shelling are incalculable, according to scientists.

State police in Maryland had quite a time bringing William Kayes to a halt on Interstate Highway 70 in early July. As Kayes drove his pickup truck down the wrong side of the highway, he sent some 70 cars screeching and swerving into ditches and onto median strips. And he kept on going after the police had shot out the four tires of his truck and set up roadblocks. Finally the truck's perforated radiator overheated, and the police moved in. All in all it was quite a performance by the 72-year-old resident of Springfield, Va., who was charged with a variety of traffic violations and three counts of assault for allegedly attempting to run down policemen and ram police squad cars.

Circus history was made in Tucson, Ariz., on July 10 when 17-year-old Michael Vazquez of the Vazquez Flying Circus act successfully completed the first aerial quadruple somersault ever performed in public. The feat took place during a Ringling Brothers and Barnum & Bailey show. Only 12 persons have ever succeeded in the triple somersault.

During the summer of 1947 Welby Van Horn was giving tennis lessons at Lookout Mountain, Tenn. On August 8 he sent an air mail letter to his wife in Fountain City, but it never reached its destination. In October, more than 35 years later, the letter reappeared in the Fountain City post office and was routinely returned to Lookout Mountain. The postmaster there was able to locate a friend of Van Horn's who promised to forward it to the sender, now living in Puerto Rico.

Even experienced drivers are sometimes unduly nervous before they take the tests required for renewal of a license. But William Reynolds of Placerville, Calif., was calm and full of confidence when he appeared at the Department of Motor Vehicles in August. According to examiner Jackie Beckham, the confidence Reynolds exhibited was justified because he passed both the written and driving tests with flying colours. He then drove home to celebrate his 100th birthday.

Jim Bonvillain, founder of the Terrebaonne Parish Voters League in Louisiana, can be very persuasive if given enough time. Beatrice Celestain Bolden, for example, finally heeded Bonvillain's advice in April and at the age of 113 registered to vote.

Brazilian police were frustrated in efforts to seize drug smugglers in their jungle hideout until Officer Joao da Silva Bisteme figured out a solution. He evaded the lookouts posted at all the approaches to the camp by sweeping in on a hang glider. His bursts of gunfire permitted police on foot to rush the camp and arrest eight suspects.

A bargain-hunting New Yorker paid $2 in 1981 for a porcelain food stand offered during a tag sale. In January the auction house of Sotheby Parke Bernet found a dealer willing to pay $60,000 for the rare antique. It had been manufactured in the 1770s by Bonin & Morris of Philadelphia, the first porcelain factory in the U.S.

Perfection doesn't count unless you can make it stick. That's what Glenn Allison learned after he bowled a perfect 900 series—three 300 games—in sanctioned league play in La Habra, Calif., on July 1. No one had ever accomplished the feat before; the official record was an 886 rolled in 1939. On July 2 an investigator for the American Bowling Congress flew in to check Allison's claim, and after two months of deliberations the ABC declared that Allison's series was not acceptable because the lanes on which it was bowled did not meet its requirements on oiling.

The fish weren't biting in April, at least not in the waters around Baltimore, so a group of 13 fishermen packed up their gear and called it a day. During a final drink together each accepted a dare and swallowed a couple of live minnows they had bought for bait. The next day two were doubled over with severe abdominal cramps and had to be hospitalized. Surgeons later reported that the seemingly harmless minnows contained live worms that had perforated the men's intestines.

Most wives appreciate a little help around the house, but husbands who do everything, and do it perfectly, are about as rare as flying streetcars. A woman in East Germany, however, had a perfect husband. He did more around the house than any wife could hope for: cooking, baking, shopping, laundry, and taking care of the baby. He did everything so perfectly, in fact, that the woman was granted a divorce in October because she couldn't stand the boredom of having nothing to do.

T. S. Schwaner, curator of reptiles at the South Australian Museum in Adelaide, had to hospitalize one of the world's deadliest snakes for nearly half a year. The 4½-ft-long taipan had a severe infection in the cheek that required intensive care and daily antibiotic injections to control. It seems one of the four mice the taipan had been given for dinner decided not to die without a fight.

U.S. taxpayers often become frustrated trying to figure out the bottom line on their federal returns. But before they reach that point, they sometimes have to make inquiries, only to learn that in some cases the very same query put to different employees of the Internal Revenue Service receives quite different replies. The General Accounting Office added to taxpayers' grief in October when it reported to Congress that the IRS detected about 33 million errors on the 94 million individual tax returns it processed in fiscal 1981. It also noted, on the basis of a sample study of 2,543 returns, that IRS employees made nearly twice as many mistakes in arithmetic as did the taxpayers.

Time and time again, Taiwan's Little League baseball teams have outclassed their U.S. counterparts. The girls at Redwood High in Larkspur, Calif., must have known that and hoped their basketball team would be well prepared when a group of 13 Chinese girls arrived in February. As things turned out they were totally ill-prepared for what took place. The Orientals showed no interest in shooting baskets. But they certainly knew how to sing and dance. Through some misunderstanding, the Chinese had sent a group of entertainers.

In March 6-year-old Scott McKenzie was playing with friends in his backyard in Vinita Park, Mo., when a 100-lb mutt leaped over the fence, attacked the child, and bit off his ear. Scott's father, a policeman, fired six times at the animal, but it escaped. Another policeman later spotted the animal and killed it. When the dog was taken to a veterinarian to be examined for rabies, the boy's ear was found in its stomach. Surgeons succeeded in restoring the ear to the injured child.

Geraldine Gordon's tongue is soft and rubbery even though it is considerably smaller than most. It's a great help, naturally, in eating and talking. And it clamps onto her lower teeth. She lost her own tongue to cancer, but after a five-year interval she received a silicone replacement developed by doctors at the University of California at Davis. It was the first known artificial tongue designed for speech as well as for swallowing.

Jessie Byam graduated from high school in May and publicly pledged to continue her education. Just about everyone in Madison Heights, Michigan, cheered the decision because Jessie was still striving to improve herself at the age of 98. She is believed to be the oldest person ever to graduate from a U.S. high school.

WIDE WORLD

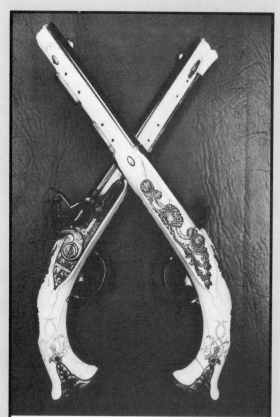

VIC DE LUCIA / THE NEW YORK TIMES

New York City police were preparing to destroy some of the illegal handguns in their collection when they came upon an ornate pair of pistols confiscated in a drug raid nearly ten years earlier. Because the weapons were overlaid with ivory and intricate gold floral patterns, someone decided they should be checked by experts at the Metropolitan Museum of Art. The guns were identified as prized hunting pistols that once belonged to Catherine the Great, empress of Russia, and had an appraised value of $200,000.

On St. Patrick's Day in 1964 Jack Granger dropped 100 sealed bottles into the sea off Miami Beach, Fla. Each contained a note offering an all-expenses-paid vacation to the lucky finders. In October, nearly 18 years after the event, Barbara Karas happened upon one of the bottles at the mouth of Boston Harbor. She managed to get Granger's phone number and called. Though his hotel no longer existed, he assured Karas that the offer of a 12-day free vacation still stood, compliments of the Miami Beach Visitor and Convention Authority.

Michigan State University officials announced in September that the school would continue to supply bed linens for resident students but not pillows. The cost of replacing or repairing the 4,000 pillows that had disappeared or were ripped apart during the previous academic year came to $22,000—considerably more than the budget could bear.

Border Patrol Chief Robert Adams contended that a roadblock set up near Florida City, Fla., was effective: it led to the arrests of 25 illegal aliens in five days in April. Residents of Key West, however, said that it was destroying the area's vital tourist trade. They pointed out that traffic had been backed up 19 mi the previous weekend. When a federal judge refused to grant a temporary injunction against setting up the checkpoint, the citizens of Key West seceded from the Union. They hoisted the flag of the Conch Republic and declared the pelican the state bird and the hibiscus the national flower. Then the mayor declared war on the U.S., but he quickly surrendered in order, he said, to become eligible for foreign aid.

Amelia Salazar was a basketball star at Bledsoe High School in Texas, editor of the yearbook, and top student in her class. Eulogio Guerrero co-captained the varsity basketball team and was president of the student council. He also had the worst academic record among the graduating seniors. None of these things, however, played a role in selecting Amelia as valedictorian of the class of 1982 and Eulogio as salutatorian. Bledsoe's only school, which accepts students from kindergarten through grade 12, had a student body of just 53 and only two high school seniors.

It took five months, but Lynn Rosencrans of Grand Rapids, Mich., finally found what he was looking for. He had had to cruise back alleys, drive through parking lots, and read columns of want ads before his patience and persistence paid off. Finally he located a 1972 red Volkswagen van—the one that had been stolen from him the previous August.

Not all lawyers are willing to fall on their knees before a jury and beg for the acquittal of a client. But the lawyer for Laura E. Clark did just that in August—to no avail. The jury found 82-year-old Clark guilty of possessing nine pounds of marijuana harvested from plants she had cultivated in her vegetable garden. The great-grandmother, who said she got the seeds in Mexico to treat her arthritis, was sentenced to two years of unsupervised probation.

Danny Pocock of Wycheproof, Australia, was on his way to work one July morning when he noticed a 6-ft kangaroo following close behind. The train engineer reckoned it was someone's pet until it knocked him to the ground. He raced for the safety of the station platform but was floored two more times before he made it. "I did somersaults," he later reported, "that I didn't know I could."

Robots are robots, but Robart the Robot is in a class by himself. If you venture into his territory, you had better identify yourself quickly; otherwise he'll order you to leave the room. If you hesitate, he shrieks: "Activate fire control system . . . fire on three." Just seconds later Robart disorients would-be intruders with ultrasound and assails their eardrums with piercing sounds from a wailing siren. Hobart Everett, a 32-year-old navy lieutenant commander, showed off Robart in April. He thought it only proper to give public recognition to the one who helped him fulfill requirements for a degree in engineering.

Impulse buying can wreak havoc with the family budget, but don't try telling that to newlywed Luann Lingle of Bay City, Mich. The night before she got married, her fiancé asked for a cold beer. Happy to oblige, the 23-year-old bride-to-be rushed to the store. When she returned, she handed her future husband the beer—and a lottery ticket she had purchased on impulse. It was worth $100,000.

A. Donald Fass was the chief designer of security devices for the Rollins Protective Service Co. and the firm's top salesman of burglar alarms in the Hartford area of Connecticut. As a salesman, Fass was not easily discouraged. If he failed to make a sale during his first visit to a potential customer's home, he frequently succeeded on his second try about two weeks later. In August Fass pleaded guilty to nine counts of felony and was sentenced to prison for 13 to 26 years. His impressive sales record, he confessed, had been enhanced by burglarizing customers' homes after his initial unsuccessful visit.

Inmates in Nevada State Prison face virtually insurmountable obstacles if they try to escape. The prison is a maximum-security facility, and the officials are well versed in escape techniques. In May, however, they were taken by surprise when guards reported finding a nearly completed one-man helicopter in the maintenance area. The ingenious contraption had been designed and assembled by a plumber, an electrician, and a welder, all of whom were serving long terms. The trio were charged with misuse of state property, a misdemeanor.

Jeremy Cook was only in kindergarten but he thought it would be great if he could win $500 for his school in Elmira, N.Y. So he sent a helium-filled balloon aloft in March hoping it would travel farther than anyone else's and thereby qualify for first prize. In early May Jeremy received a letter from east Africa. His balloon had drifted one-third the distance around the world before landing in Kenya.

Kung Teh-cheng, a university professor in Taiwan, traveled to San Francisco's Chinatown in August to attend the Sacrificial Ceremony to the Sage. His presence was considered so important that officials agreed to hold the ceremony one month early to accommodate Kung's schedule. The honoured guest, after all, represented the 77th generation descended from Confucius, the great Chinese sage born in 551 B.C.

Engineers at the Lockheed Missile and Space Co. in Sunnyvale, Calif., had a problem. They were using sophisticated computer-design techniques in their work and had to get each day's information to the company's test base in Santa Cruz. But the test facility did not have the expensive equipment needed to receive transmissions, and couriers proved to be too slow and too expensive. Finally the perfect solution came to mind: homing pigeons carrying the information on microfilm.

Parks Bonifay of Pensacola, Florida, became the youngest water skier in history when he was still a toothless six-month-old baby. Though he's obviously flying high at a tender age, he still hasn't learned to hot dog it through the air.
WIDE WORLD

429

Deely-Bobbers *added a debonair accent to casual summer wear.*

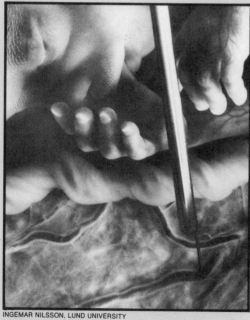

Fetoscopy *provides doctors with startling views of the unborn.*

New Words

Language constantly changes. New words and word meanings are forever coming into the vocabulary; old ones die out. Some new words are only passing fads and are forgotten as soon as the group that originally used them gives them up. Others gain wider acceptance and become part of the living language.

The following list of new words and meanings is a sampling of the continuing change and growth of our language. Some of these entries may be forgotten next year; some may last as long as the English language itself.

biometeorology *n:* the scientific study of how weather affects living things

cosmid *n:* in DNA recombinant technology, a specialized plasmid, or loop of genetic material, that aids the transport of foreign DNA into bacterial cells

Deely Bobbers *n:* plastic headbands ornamented with antenna-like springs ending in pinwheels, stars, or other decorative objects

descope *v:* to reduce the size of, as a project or study

downlink *adj:* pertaining to radio transmissions from a space vehicle to a ground station; *see* uplink

fetology *n:* medical and surgical treatment of fetuses

fetoscopy *n:* a prenatal diagnostic technique in which a periscope-like instrument inserted into the uterus allows the doctor to observe the fetus directly and to obtain tissue samples

gender gap *n:* a difference between male and female perceptions of social and political issues

high five *n:* an over-the-head hand slap exchanged by athletes to convey congratulations

infomercial *n:* a television feature combining a commercial advertisement with an amount of information or instruction, used experimentally on cable television

lipectomy *n:* surgical removal of fat tissue

magnetoid *n:* an extremely massive, rotating, highly magnetic star

out-tro *n:* in television news production, a summary statement on a story by a reporter or anchor;

the opposite of "intro," or introduction

palming *n:* water skiing on the hands

para-skiing *n:* sporting event combining parachuting to a target with slalom skiing

P.L.C. or **PLC** or **plc** *n, abbr:* public liability company; replaces "Ltd." (for limited liability); equivalent to U.S. term "Inc."

pound seizure *n:* use of animals taken from pounds for biomedical research

prion *n:* a life form consisting of tiny protein particles that replicate within the cells of animals, using the host's DNA, and which cause disease states in the host

simulcast *n:* simultaneous broadcast of a program by television and radio stations, usually to achieve better sound quality or stereophonic sound

superstation *n:* a television station whose signal is available nationwide via satellite

telework *n:* work conducted using the computer as the primary communications tool, rather than telephone, typewriter, personal contact, or other traditional means

uplink *adj:* pertaining to radio transmissions from a ground station to a space vehicle; *see* downlink

user friendly *adj:* easy to use, unintimidating; used of computers or other high-technology products designed with simplified controls and instructions

WIDE WORLD

High five *was fast becoming an art form among athletes.*

New word news in 1982 was dominated by a species of slang known sometimes as "Valspeak," purportedly spoken by teenage girls in the San Fernando Valley suburbs of Los Angeles. Valspeak was introduced to less advanced parts of the world via the hit record "Valley Girl," by satirist Frank Zappa and his daughter Moon. Some examples of Valspeak:

airhead *n:* a dumb, boring person

beastie *n:* a repulsive, unacceptable person

space cadet *n:* a weird, out-of-touch person

beige *adj:* boring

bummer *n:* something boring or objectionable

grody *adj:* very bad

gross *adj:* very bad

joanie *adj:* stupid and out-of-date

gag me with a spoon *interj:* how nauseating

barf me out *interj:* how nauseating

to the max *adv:* totally

totally *interj:* totally

awesome *adj:* very good

tubular *adj:* very good

MARK SENNET—GAMMA/LIAISON

BIOGRAPHIES

The following is a selected list of men and women who influenced events significantly in 1982.

Andropov, Yury Vladimirovich

In November 1982, for the first time in the Soviet Union's 60 years of existence, a change at the top of the government was unexpectedly swift and, on the face of it, remarkably harmonious. After Lenin's death Stalin had seized power by ruse and force, doing away with opponents and accomplices alike; when he died, Lavrenty Beria, who had sought to succeed him, was shot, while Georgy Malenkov, who ten days after grasping the rod of power had to pass it to Nikita Khrushchev, was dismissed to oblivion. Khrushchev in turn was pushed aside in a "palace coup" and was succeeded by a group of

three until Leonid Brezhnev eclipsed the other two.

Yury Andropov's accession was an altogether smoother affair. During Brezhnev's illness Politburo members began to consider who among them would be the fittest to succeed him. On April 22, 1982, Andropov was chosen to make the traditional speech commemorating Lenin's birth, and on May 24 he was reelected to the Secretariat of the party Central Committee. (He then automatically relinquished his previous post as head of the State Security Committee [KGB].) Two days after Brezhnev's death on November 10, the 308-member Central Committee unanimously elected Andropov as the sixth leader of the Soviet Union.

Yury Vladimirovich Andropov was born on June 15, 1914, at the village of Nagutskaya in the Stavropol region, the son of a railway worker. Little was known of his schooling, but at the age of 16 he joined the Young Communist League (Komsomol) while working at Mozdok in the North Ossetian Autonomous Republic. For a time he was a boatman on the Volga River, and in 1936 he graduated from the Inland Waterways Transport College at Rybinsk in the Yaroslavl region, where he became a Komsomol organizer. He joined the Communist Party in 1939 and the following year was appointed first secretary of the Komsomol organization in the Karelo-Finnish Autonomous Republic. In 1944 he was appointed second secretary of the party Central Committee at Petrozavodsk, the chief city of Karelia.

The turning point in Andropov's career was his transfer to Moscow, where he was assigned to the central apparat of the Communist Party. In 1953 Khrushchev appointed him ambassador to Hungary, where he was instrumental in the suppression of the 1956 uprising. Recalled to Moscow in 1957, Andropov became head of the Central Committee's department supervising the Communist parties of the "sister" countries. In May 1967 Brezhnev appointed Andropov head of the KGB. A month later he was made a candidate member and in April 1973 a full member of the Politburo.

Aoki, Rocky

He was nearly killed in a fiery crash while racing an offshore powerboat in San Francisco Bay in 1979; his doctors told him he could never race again. Rocky Aoki, nevertheless, returned to the sport on July 14, 1982, and drove a 38-ft (11-m) speedboat to victory in the Benihana Grand Prix off Point Pleasant, N.J. Then, on September 11, Aoki had another brush with death, breaking both his legs in a crash. But the flamboyant Japanese founder of the Benihana of Tokyo steakhouse chain, which had made Japanese cooking an American household word, had always fancied himself a risk taker and a champion.

Considered by many to be a Japanese Horatio Alger, the wiry Aoki's meteoric climb to success in both the business and sports worlds overshadowed his uncertain fate in boat racing. Born Hiroaki Aoki in Tokyo in 1938, Aoki spent many of his early years working around his father's coffee shop. He first traveled to the U.S. in 1959 as a member of the Japanese national team to prepare for the 1960

WILLIAM E. SAURO/THE NEW YORK TIMES

Olympics. He did not make it to Rome, but he later became an excellent flyweight wrestler in the Amateur Athletic Union. Lured by the "American lifestyle," he remained in the U.S., where he attended Springfield College in Massachusetts on a physical education scholarship. But the aspiring wrestling coach quickly realized that big-money opportunities lay elsewhere, so he enrolled in the New York City Community College to study hotel and restaurant management.

While in school Aoki began supporting himself by parking cars and selling ice cream from a truck in Harlem. Working all day and well into the evening, he attracted customers by sticking small red paper parasols into each ice cream. Within months he had saved $10,000. In 1964 he borrowed $20,000 more and opened the first Benihana of Tokyo—a four-table restaurant in New York City. Less than seven years later he ruled a virtual empire of 15 restaurants and 7 franchises around the U.S. By the end of 1982, Benihana of Tokyo was doing $70 million in sales, with 52 restaurants in the U.S. and 24 in Japan.

The highlight—and the selling point—of a meal at one of Aoki's restaurants is the knife-wielding chef who slices up the food with Samurai-like speed and then cooks it on an open steel griddle that is ringed with diners. Aoki, who pioneered the concept, enjoyed being the showman himself and had long counted on his sporting exploits to drum up business for Benihana. He participated in and financially backed the first manned transpacific balloon trip from Japan to California in late 1981. He said he still hoped to undertake a balloon trip from Europe across the Soviet Union to Japan, even though the Soviet government had so far turned down his requests. But there were also times when he doubted whether he should ever take these sorts of risks again. So with his boat racing and ballooning futures in doubt, Aoki was turning his eyes toward business ventures, such as fast food noodle restaurants, to support the expansion of the Benihana empire.

Argüello, Alexis

It might have been a Cinderella story in several respects. Alexis Argüello, born poor in Nicaragua 30 years ago, went to work as a day labourer at the age of 12 to help support his family. While still in his teens he traveled to Canada, where better wages meant more money to send home to his family a continent away. In Canada he also found his way into professional boxing and discovered that prizefighting paid better than construction labour.

In 1974 Argüello won a world boxing title in the 126-lb class. He then moved up twice to win both the World Boxing Council junior lightweight and lightweight championships. Over the years he won 76 professional bouts, 62 by knockouts, and lost only 4. In 1982 he tried to win his fourth title, something that no boxer had ever done. On November 12 he stepped into the ring in the Orange Bowl at Miami, Fla., to face Aaron Pryor, the defending World

Boxing Association junior welterweight champion.

However, the Cinderella story was not to be. Argüello, known as a fighter of superb intelligence and savvy intuition, was the bettors' favourite at 12 to 5 odds despite being outweighed. For 13 rounds the boxers fought almost equally, but when round 14 began the challenger's left hand began to drop, and the defender took advantage with his hard right fist. Argüello took six uncontested blows before the fight was called on a technical knockout. Bleeding from a cut below the eye, Argüello also had a severe concussion and was hospitalized. Pryor thus retained his junior welterweight title, while Argüello kept his lower division crown.

Argüello's brain concussion prompted new concern about the risks of prizefighting. The death of South Korean boxer Duk Koo Kim from injuries that he suffered in a bout the following day brought further demands for the end of bareheaded boxing as a professional sport.

Bechtel, Stephen, Jr.

When U.S. Pres. Ronald Reagan needed a new secretary of state in 1982, he turned to a well-tested source and lured George Shultz away from the presidency of the Bechtel Group, Inc. The San Francisco firm had become the "cradle of the Cabinet," almost a proving ground for his administration's top echelon. Caspar Weinberger, the secretary of defense, had been Bechtel's general counsel; W. Kenneth Davis, the deputy secretary of energy, had been an executive; and diplomatic troubleshooter Philip Habib was a consultant. The remarkable engineering company had employed men who had served other

JAMES D. WILSON/NEWSWEEK

administrations as well; former CIA director Richard Helms had helped the firm avoid potential losses in Iran.

The man who acknowledged the company's debt to Helms was Stephen Bechtel, Jr., the family firm's chief executive officer. Bechtel was used to having close contacts in high places throughout the world. When criticized for his connections in foreign capitals—sometimes unfriendly ones—he said, "I only feel it is appropriate to see leaders when there is business to conduct and it is worth their time."

A giant among privately owned companies, the Bechtel Group stands like a colossus among the world's engineering and construction firms with recent billings of $11 billion a year and 113 "major" simultaneous projects in 21 countries. Bechtel recruited able men of global experience to build such projects as an industrial city in Saudi Arabia, Canada's largest hydroelectric project, the Alaska pipeline, and the subway for Washington, D.C.

The company began modestly enough in 1898 when Bechtel's grandfather hired himself out with a mule team to help build a railroad through Indian territory. It gained national prominence in the 1930s when it headed the consortium that raised the Hoover Dam across the Colorado River. It spanned San Francisco Bay with the Oakland Bay Bridge, concentrated on launching Liberty ships during World War II, and then turned to oil refineries and pipelines under the leadership of Bechtel's father. When nuclear energy came into fashion, the firm took the lead and built nearly half the reactors that would operate in the U.S.

Born May 10, 1925, in Oakland, Calif., Bechtel took a degree in engineering from Purdue University and an M.B.A. from Stanford University. During World War II he served in the U.S. Marine Corps and was awarded the French Legion of Honour.

Betancur Cuartas, Belisario

Belisario Betancur was elected president of Colombia on May 30, 1982. It was the fourth time that he had been a Conservative candidate in a presidential campaign. The first time was in 1962; the second, when he lost to the official Conservative candidate, Misael Pastrana Borrero, was in 1970; and the third was in 1978, when he was beaten by the Liberal Julio César Turbay Ayala. In 1982 a split in the Liberal Party ensured Betancur's victory, the first Conservative win since 1974, when a 16-year agreement to alternate Liberal and Conservative presidencies had ended. Betancur received 47% of the vote, as against 40% for the official Liberal candidate, former president Alfonso López Michelsen, and 11% for the New Liberal, Luis Carlos Galán.

Betancur was born in the Amagá district of Antioquia in 1923. Brought up in severe poverty, he endured considerable hardship in acquiring an education. At the university in Medellín he studied first architecture, then law. At the same time, he worked as a journalist and became increasingly involved in official Conservative politics, moderating his original extreme right-wing opinions. In 1950 Pres. Laureano Gómez appointed him to the constituent assembly, but he was later imprisoned for his opposition to the military rule of Pres. Gustavo Rojas Pinilla. During his career Betancur had been a senator, minister of labour, ambassador to Spain, and professor of law. He was inaugurated in August.

His belief in the Colombian system of power sharing was demonstrated in his first Cabinet, in which six Conservatives and six Liberals were given posts (the Ministry of Defense remained in the hands of the Army). His economic policies pleased the private sector, especially the encouragement of agricultural and industrial exports with increased tax discounts and controls on imports of luxuries and goods that competed unfavourably with domestic products. More important, however, were Betancur's moves to halt guerrilla activity. He restored the Peace Commission (which had resigned under Turbay's administration) and initiated positive steps toward dialogue with the insurgency movements. By the end of September, the two main groups, M-19 and FARC (Colombian Revolutionary Armed Forces), had called cease-fires. One of Betancur's election promises was that guerrilla-dominated areas would receive assistance.

Brown, Charles Lee

You are to reorganize one of the world's largest business enterprises, establishing 22 operating subsidiaries as independent firms and dividing up $100 billion in assets. You are to do this in a manner that maintains public confidence in your company, protects the investment of your three million shareholders, and satisfies the courts of the United States. You have two years to complete the job.

This was the task presented to Charles Lee Brown, board chairman since 1979 of the American Telephone and Telegraph Co. AT&T operates the Bell Telephone System, which provides telephone service in the U.S. It is also the parent firm to Bell Telephone Laboratories, Inc., where research is performed, and Western Electric Co., a communications equipment manufacturer. During the 1970s, 37 smaller firms that manufacture telephones and operate telephone systems had filed suit against AT&T, charging it with monopolistic practices and seeking its breakup. Also, the U.S. government had filed an antitrust suit under federal laws that protect the public against business monopolies. After fighting these actions for some time, AT&T negotiated a settlement. In January 1982 the firm agreed to divest itself of 22 state and regional telephone systems, such as Illinois Bell Telephone Co. and New England Telephone & Telegraph Co. In return, AT&T was allowed to expand into new fields, such as data processing.

If anyone could resolve the immense problems associated with AT&T's divestiture, it appeared to be Charles Brown. In 1977–78, as president and chief operating officer, he directed a reorganization of AT&T—one of the largest such corporate actions in history. Prior to that, as AT&T's chief financial officer, he had helped to reduce the firm's debt. Since joining AT&T during the 1940s as a summer employee and maintenance man, Brown had risen through more than 20 positions. Born on Aug. 23, 1921, in Richmond, Va., he earned a degree in electrical engineering at the University of Virginia in 1943 and served as a radioman in the U.S. Navy before joining AT&T.

Bush, George

In the tradition of his office, Vice-Pres. George Bush had an uneventful year. His major public appearances were at funerals. In June King Khalid, ruler of Saudi Arabia since 1975, died of a heart attack, and Bush headed a large U.S. delegation sent to pay condolences to the ruling Saud family and to new King Fahd, Khalid's half brother and successor. Despite the size of the American party, reportedly intended to show continued U.S. goodwill toward the Saudis during a period of Middle Eastern tension, Bush was kept waiting until the day after his arrival for his audience with King Fahd.

In November, following the death of Soviet leader Leonid Brezhnev, Pres. Ronald Reagan rejected suggestions that he attend the funeral himself and instead sent Bush, who interrupted a state visit to Africa to head the U.S. delegation. Following the funeral Bush met briefly with Brezhnev's successor as head of the Communist Party Central Committee, Yury Andropov.

On February 2, while he was driving to work through an area in downtown Washington about eight blocks from the White House, the roof of Bush's limousine was struck by a chunk of cement. Before it was decided that the object was probably building material that had fallen from one of the several construction projects under way in the neighbourhood and that no assault on the vice-president was involved, police, FBI, and Secret Service agents had sealed off the area, searched buildings, and interrogated bystanders.

. During the last week of April and the first week of May, Bush completed a tour of six Asian nations, visiting Japan, South Korea, Singapore, Australia, New Zealand, and China. In Japan the vice-president attempted to soothe strained relations between that country and the U.S. over trade and defense issues. During Bush's visit to South Korea, scheduled to coincide with the 100th anniversary of the establishment of official relations between Korea and the U.S., he toured the demilitarized zone between North and South Korea and pledged continued American support of the south Korean government.

Bush's visit to China, not originally planned as part of this Asian tour, was included in an attempt to ease recently increased tensions between the People's Republic and the U.S. as a result of the Reagan administration's decision to continue arms sales to

Taiwan. During his five-day visit, Bush met with Foreign Minister Huang Hua, Premier Zhao Ziyang (Chao Tzu-yang), and Deng Xiaoping (Teng Hsiaop'ing), the deputy chairman of the Communist Party, but he conceded in an airport interview at the end of his visit that the Taiwan issue had not been resolved.

It was reported in May that earlier in the year Bush had sought to keep the Reagan administration from tightening a provision of the tax laws beneficial to the drug industry. Bush later abandoned the effort to avoid the appearance of conflict of interest, since he owns a substantial amount of drug company stocks and was a director of Eli Lilly & Co., the pharmaceutical firm, at the time he took office.

Clark, William P.

As U.S. presidential adviser for national security affairs, William P. Clark had the main qualification for success in Ronald Reagan's Washington—Reagan's trust and confidence. He also has earned the respect of a foreign policy establishment that was highly critical when he first came to town to serve as deputy to former secretary of state Alexander Haig.

The U.S. Senate confirmation hearing for the deputy secretary of state's post was an embarrassment to Clark. He was unable to answer even basic questions about foreign affairs, and a number of senators openly expressed doubts about his appointment, which they reluctantly voted to approve. But once on the job, Clark quickly learned what he had to know, and his critics soon were praising him for his intelligence and a calm, judicial manner. Though known as "Reagan's man" in the Department of

State, he also gained Haig's confidence and frequently was responsible for smoothing troubled waters between Haig and the rest of the administration.

Clark was chosen to head the National Security Council after the resignation of Richard Allen. In that sensitive and often controversial position Clark's open-mindedness and quiet, methodical approach to problems proved highly effective. Again, his low-profile style was a sharp contrast to Henry Kissinger and Zbigniew Brzezinski, two flamboyant predecessors.

But Clark could be outspoken and blunt when he believed it was necessary. A devout Roman Catholic, he wrote a strong letter to the chairman of the National Conference of Catholic Bishops, which was drafting a pastoral letter that opposed the Reagan policy on nuclear strategy and disarmament. Clark called for the bishops to support U.S. proposals for nuclear arms reduction and charged that their draft letter reflected "fundamental misreadings of American policies."

Like Reagan, Clark is a former Democrat who became a conservative Republican. Born Oct. 23, 1931, in Oxnard, Calif., he gained his law degree at Loyola University in Los Angeles. He was a county chairman in Reagan's first political campaign and became chief of staff when Reagan was elected governor in 1966. As governor, Reagan appointed Clark to be a county judge and, eventually, a justice of the California Supreme Court.

Cresson, Edith

Since her appointment as French minister of agriculture after Pres. François Mitterrand took office in 1981, Edith Cresson had fully justified the new head of state's confidence in her ability. Mitterrand's desire to promote women to responsible positions had been demonstrated in February 1975 at the Pau congress of the Socialist Party (PS), when Cresson took her place in the PS National Secretariat, in charge of youth and students.

At the end of January 1982 Cresson declared "unacceptable" the prices proposed by the European Commission in Brussels for the agricultural year 1982–83. The Commission had offered an average rise of 9%, while the French farmers were demanding 16%, so the agreement reached by the European Economic Community at the end of April for a rise of 13% in the price of French agricultural products—despite the reservations of the U.K.—might be credited to her. A month later Britain, satisfied with the compensation granted for 1982 by the other European Community countries toward its contribution to the Community budget, stopped blocking the agreement on agricultural prices. European solidarity was maintained—for the time being at least.

Born on Jan. 27, 1934, the daughter of a tax inspector, Edith Cresson was a graduate of the Hautes Études Commerciales—J.F. (the women's section of the business studies school) and joined the Convention des Institutions Républicaines in 1965. She

failed in her attempts to be elected a deputy, first in Vienne, then in the canton of Châtellerault-Nord. As mayor of Thuré from 1977, she stood once more in the March 1978 legislative elections but failed again.

From June 1979 Cresson was a member of the European Parliament, where she showed a special interest in agricultural questions. She gained a doctorate in demography on the subject of "the life of farmers' and workers' wives in the rural canton of Guéméné-Penfao (Loire-Atlantique)." In October 1982 she visited the U.S.S.R. with a confidential mission to improve the French balance of payments deficit through exports of cereal crops. She returned with a draft agreement on deliveries of agricultural and food products for 1982–83.

Cuomo, Mario M.

When voters in New York State went to the polls to elect a governor on Nov. 2, 1982, they were faced with a classic choice of the old versus the new. Republican businessman Lewis Lehrman, a strong supporter of Pres. Ronald Reagan's policies, advocated social welfare cuts, tougher anticrime laws, reinstatement of capital punishment, and a 40% tax cut; while Democratic Lieut. Gov. Mario Cuomo harked back to the Great Society of the 1960s and the necessity of aid to the needy, despite budget deficits. Lehrman waged a powerful campaign using effective television ads and was reported to have spent as much as $8 million. But in the end it was Cuomo's old-fashioned coalition of liberals, labour unions, and minorities that prevailed.

Before he could face Lehrman, however, Cuomo had to wage a fierce rematch against Edward Koch, the popular mayor of New York City, who had defeated him in the Democratic primary for that office in 1977. Koch, who was favoured in the polls, blundered early in the campaign, antagonizing upstate New Yorkers. Cuomo, while advocating liberal policies, capitalized on his simple, conservative family life and upset Koch by more than 80,000 votes.

A lifelong resident of the New York City borough of Queens, Cuomo was born there on June 15, 1932. After high school he briefly played baseball for the farm club of the Pittsburgh Pirates before returning to New York City and receiving a B.A. (1953) and a law degree (1956) from St. John's University. He taught law at St. John's from 1963 to 1974 and also practiced law in Brooklyn. In 1966 he gained public attention by arranging an acceptable compromise between New York City and clients whose neighbourhood was to be destroyed for a new school. New York Mayor John Lindsay asked him to mediate a public housing controversy in 1972, and his success in that endeavour led him to seek public office. He was defeated in his 1974 bid for the nomination for lieutenant governor on a ticket headed by an old friend, Hugh Carey. One of Carey's first appointments as governor was Cuomo as his secretary of state. In 1978, having lost his bid to be mayor, Cuomo joined the ticket in Carey's reelection campaign.

Although he had little administrative experience, Governor Cuomo was expected to be an effective negotiator. It was a skill he would need in order to manage the needs of the poor and the business interests while holding a fragile coalition together in the months ahead.

Decker Tabb, Mary

Winning race after race in 1982, Mary Decker Tabb literally ran off with the record book for women runners in events ranging from 800 to 10,000 m. In October the U.S. runner, who had set nine world and U.S. track records in 1982, was named amateur sportswoman of the year by the Women's Sports Foundation.

In January 1982 Mary Decker Tabb, who had been sidelined for a year and a half by an injured Achilles tendon, began her comeback by winning the women's 1,500-m race at the U.S. Olympic Invitational meet. In this first effort after her injury she set no world records, though she did establish a new meet record of 4 min 8.32 sec in the event. In February at the Los Angeles Times Games she lowered the world indoor record in the 3,000-m race with a time of 8 min 47.3 sec and achieved a new best time of 5 min 53.4 sec at 2,000 m. A few days later she ran the fastest indoor mile ever at the prestigious Wanamaker Millrose Games at Madison Square Garden, where she was timed at 4 min 21.47 sec, winning the race by a comfortable 65 yd. The following week she broke her own record by running the mile in 4 min 20.5 sec at the Jack in the Box Invitational indoor track meet in San Diego, Calif. (A 4-min 17.55-sec

indoor mile that she ran in 1980 was not recognized because it was run on the Houston [Texas] Astrodome's oversized track.)

Decker Tabb also fared well in outdoor events. In June, in her debut in the 5,000-m race, she set a world record at 15 min 8.3 sec. A month later in Paris she ran a 4-min 18.08-sec mile, the first woman to break 4 min 20 sec outdoors. She set a U.S. record of 8 min 29.8 sec in the 3,000-m in Oslo, just missing the world mark of 8 min 27.12 sec in that event. On her return home to Eugene, Ore., she established a time of 31 min 35.3 sec in the 10,000 m at the University of Oregon, the fastest time ever set on a track (though it had been bettered on a road). With this event Decker Tabb became the fastest U.S. woman at all six distances from 800 to 10,000 m.

Mary Decker was born in Flemington, N.J., on Aug 4, 1958. She discovered track and field in 1970, and by 1974 she held world records in the women's 800 m and the 880-yd and 1,000-yd runs indoors. Severe shin splints kept her from competing in the 1976 Olympics. In 1981 she married marathon runner Ron Tabb.

De Lorean, John Zachary

In April 1973 auto executive John Z. De Lorean resigned from his $650,000-per-year job with General Motors Corp. to follow the dream of founding his own auto company. Nine years later the dream became a nightmare as De Lorean was arrested in Los Angeles on charges of drug trafficking on the same day that the British government closed the doors on the bankrupt De Lorean Motor Co. To many people

De Lorean's meteoric rise and fall could serve as a symbol for both the benefits and the potential corruption in American business.

De Lorean was born into the automobile industry on Jan. 6, 1925, in Detroit, Mich., the son of a foundry worker at the Ford Motor Co. After graduating from the Lawrence Institute of Technology in 1948, he became a research engineer, first at Chrysler Corp. and then at the Packard Motor Co. He earned master's degees in engineering and business administration, and in 1956 he joined GM as director of advanced engineering at Pontiac. His work showed a flair for marketing as well as design, and he soon gained recognition for his innovative ideas, particularly the popular Pontiac GTO "muscle car." De Lorean rose through the ranks at GM, becoming vice-president of the North American car and truck group in 1972. It was widely believed that he might one day be president of the corporation, but De Lorean was a maverick with a decidedly uncorporate image. He often disagreed with company policies, and his personal life grew increasingly flamboyant as he divorced his first wife and dated models and actresses before marrying 20-year-old model Kelly Harmon in 1969 and 22-year-old actress-model Cristina Ferrare in 1973.

After his resignation in 1973, De Lorean began to seek financing to develop an "ethical car" that would combine style, fuel efficiency, and a moderate price. In 1978 he announced that the British government would invest at least $110 million in his venture if the new factory were built in Belfast, Northern Ireland. Anticipation was high, but when the first car, the stainless-steel-skinned, gull-winged

DMC-12, finally rolled off the assembly line in 1981, it met mixed reviews and carried a $25,000 price tag in the midst of a worldwide recession. By early 1982 the company was in receivership.

Then on October 19 De Lorean was arrested in Los Angeles and charged with bankrolling a drug deal that would have involved 100 kg (220 lb) of cocaine and netted him as much as $24 million. He denied all charges and at the year's end was free on $5 million bond.

Devine, Grant

In the Saskatchewan provincial election of April 26, 1982, the Progressive Conservative Party won 57 of the 64 seats in the provincial legislature, the largest majority in Saskatchewan history. Party leader Grant Devine, who had never before been elected to public office, thus became the premier of Saskatchewan. His was Saskatchewan's first Conservative government since it became a province in 1905. Once elected, he moved quickly to implement his campaign promises. The legislature abolished the provincial road tax on gasoline and instituted a program giving mortgage relief to homeowners. Saskatchewan was thus provided with the cheapest gasoline and home mortgages in Canada.

Born in Regina, Sask., on July 5, 1944, Devine grew up on his family's farm. He earned three degrees in agricultural economics: a B.S.A. from the University of Saskatchewan (1967), an M.Sc. from the University of Alberta (1969), and a Ph.D. from Ohio State University (1976).

Before making his debut in politics, Devine worked as a marketing specialist and agricultural commodities consultant. From 1970 to 1972 he worked for the Canadian government in Ottawa on agricultural commodities legislation. As an adviser to the Food Prices Review Board, he provided food price comparisons to selected communities across Canada. This endeavour resulted in more competitive retail food prices. In 1970 he obtained an M.B.A. degree from the University of Alberta, and in 1976 he opened an economic consulting firm in Saskatoon.

In the late 1970s Devine decided to enter politics. In November 1979 he became the leader of the Progressive Conservative Party of Saskatchewan, winning on the first ballot at the nominating convention. Winning a seat in the Saskatchewan legislature was not as easy. After losing in elections in 1978 and 1980, he was put in the ignominious position of leading his party from the legislative gallery. In the 1982 election, he finally won a seat as the representative for the riding of Estevan. Thus he could form a government and become premier of the province.

Domingo, Placido

Twenty years after his operatic debut, the critics were saying that Placido Domingo had everything: "the heroic sound, the musical intelligence, the actor's instinct, the good looks, the charm, the stamina, and the adoring crowds." He had more even "than Jon Vickers, Carlo Bergonzi, José Carreras, or even Luciano Pavarotti, he of the golden voice and gilded image." In sum, Domingo had perhaps the most sublime combination of assets in a tenor since Enrico Caruso, whom he surpassed in at least one respect: Domingo was busier. By the end of 1982 he had sung 82 roles in more than 1,600 performances, cut 70 records, and worked on a motion picture.

Born Jan. 21, 1941, in Madrid, Domingo was the scion of the first family of *zarzuela*, the Spanish operetta form that includes spoken dialogue and satire. While he was still a small boy, his parents left Spain for Mexico to found a *zarzuela* company there. Domingo began piano lessons at age eight and won his first competition—a song and dance contest—a year later. After brief studies at Mexico's National Conservatory of Music, he dropped out. He played soccer, tried his hand at amateur bullfighting, and supported himself doing musical odd jobs in clubs and other places.

Returning to serious music, the one-time baritone turned tenor and made his operatic debut in Monterrey, Mexico, in 1961. That same year he sang with Joan Sutherland in Dallas, Texas, and with Lily Pons at her farewell performance in Fort Worth, Texas. Moving to Israel, he spent more than two years there singing in multinational productions. He made his New York City debut in 1965 with the New York City Opera and first sang with the Metropolitan Opera in 1968 on 35 minutes' notice. Seven years later he expanded his musical capabilities by working as a conductor.

Domingo attributes his success in part to his early training. Beyond that, he believes the formula for operatic greatness is "a big chest, a big mouth, 90 percent memory and 10 percent intelligence, lots of hard work and something in the heart."

APESTEGUY—GAMMA/LIAISON

Douglas-Home, Charles Cospatrick

The Times, traditionally the newspaper of the British establishment, acquired a new editor of impeccable establishment qualifications in Charles Douglas-Home, nephew of the former Conservative prime minister, Lord Home of the Hirsel. In March 1982 he replaced Harold Evans, a journalist with a reputation as an innovator and fervent campaigner; only a year earlier Evans had been appointed editor of *The Times* by a new proprietor, the Australian media tycoon Rupert Murdoch. The Evans style, which included a taste for personal publicity, had been an immense success in his 13 years as editor of *The Sunday Times*, but it failed to fit the traditions of *The Times*, and Evans resigned.

The Times's way of doing things was quietly, firmly, and decisively reaffirmed by Douglas-Home. Nobody was better qualified to do this. He was not only an aristocrat by birth but also a professional journalist of remarkably wide experience, having been military correspondent (1961–62) and political and diplomatic correspondent (1962–64) on the *Daily Express* before joining *The Times* in 1965. Born on Sept. 1, 1937, he attended Eton College, served in the Army in the Royal Scots Greys, and after that was for two years the aide-de-camp of the governor of Kenya. During his 17 years on *The Times* he gained a solid grounding in the journal's ways as defense correspondent (1965–70), features editor (1970–73), home editor (1973–78), foreign editor (1978–81), and deputy editor (1981–82).

Douglas-Home did not build himself up as a media personality. On the contrary, he was self-effacing and not well known outside his own circle of colleagues. Though the editorship of *The Times* was a post of great distinction, Douglas-Home determined to keep out of the limelight. He said that he would refuse to be interviewed by anyone about anything. His views were traditionalist, right of centre. His direct impact on *The Times* had not been easy to detect. If it was seen as a paper that was very much what it used to be only more so, that was no doubt his intention.

Dozier, James Lee

During the 1960s a group of left-wing Italian university students organized with the purpose of creating anarchy. Over time their speechmaking and pamphleteering evolved into bombings, kidnappings, and murders. In 1978 this group, by then known as the Red Brigades, gained worldwide notoriety when they abducted, held, and then killed Aldo Moro, a former premier of Italy.

On Dec. 17, 1981, the Red Brigades made their first major mistake. Armed members of the group posing as plumbers kidnapped U.S. Brig. Gen. James Lee Dozier from his apartment in Verona, Italy. Dozier was then the North Atlantic Treaty Organization (NATO) deputy chief of staff of logistics and administration for allied land forces in southern Europe. By abducting Dozier, a representative of NATO, the Red Brigades committed a political act with international implications.

Dozier was hardly a model prisoner. Constantly resistant and watchful, he falsified information on his personal history to confuse his captors. During the 42 days of his captivity he spent most of his time in a pup tent pitched in the middle of a Red Brigades apartment in Padua.

On Jan. 28, 1982, the Leatherheads, an antiterrorist unit of the Italian police, rescued Dozier alive and uninjured. This, only the second such police success against the terrorists, was quickly followed by the capture of several Red Brigades leaders and the recovery of numerous documents linking the group to similar organizations in West Germany and Libya, as well as to the Soviet Union.

Dozier's calm courage under constant threat of death did not surprise anyone who knew him. According to a colleague he was "one of the best army officers" to serve in the Vietnam war. Dozier won the Legion of Merit for his leadership there and four additional medals for bravery under fire.

Dozier was born on April 10, 1931, in Arcadia, Fla. After being graduated from the U.S. Military Academy in 1956, he served with the Army in Kentucky, Vietnam, the Pentagon in Washington, D.C., Kansas, Pennsylvania, Texas, and Europe.

Fahd ibn 'Abd al-'Aziz al-Saud

On the death of King Khalid of Saudi Arabia on June 13, 1982, his half brother Crown Prince Fahd succeeded him. Fahd came to the throne at a time when Middle Eastern affairs were in greater turmoil than at any time since the Arab-Israeli "October war" of 1973 and when Saudi Arabia's strained relations with the West were also a matter for concern. He was, however, well equipped for the task, having had considerable administrative experience before taking the brunt of government decision making at the side of the older but less worldly Khalid.

Fahd was born *c.* 1922 in Riyadh, the son of Ibn Saud. He was the first son of Hassa Sudairi after her remarriage to Ibn Saud, and his full brothers included the minister of defense and aviation, Prince Sultan; the interior minister, Prince Nayif; and the governor of Riyadh, Prince Salman. On being proclaimed crown prince in 1975 after the murder of King Faisal, Fahd made his name as a modernizer, pushing through the ambitious and highly successful second development plan (1975–80). Once thought of as a lazy man, he had from the late 1960s begun an earnest program of self-improvement, making up for his lack of formal schooling. He was minister of education (1953–60) and minister of the interior from 1962 until 1975, when King Khalid, on his accession to the throne, named him crown prince.

The best testaments to Fahd's period as crown prince were the twin industrial cities of Yanbu on the Red Sea and al-Jubayl on the Gulf. Fahd gave them priority and created special agencies to handle projects such as the huge new Jiddah airport, opened in

KEYSTONE

April 1981. His first major political initiative involved his eight principles for a Middle East peace settlement, announced in 1981. These caused considerable interest in Washington because of their implicit recognition of Israel's right to live within secure boundaries. Although the Fahd plan failed to gain Arab endorsement at the Fez, Morocco, summit later in the year, it provided the basis for further progress on a Middle East peace settlement in 1982.

Fedorchuk, Vitaly

The appointment on May 26, 1982, of Col. Gen. Vitaly Fedorchuk as chairman of the Committee for State Security (KGB) of the Soviet Council of Ministers was made by the Presidium of the Supreme Soviet of the U.S.S.R. only two days after Fedorchuk's former chief, Yury Andropov, was elected a secretary of the party Central Committee; Fedorchuk was promoted above two deputy heads of the KGB, and it seemed clear that Andropov had picked him as his successor some time earlier. Then, a month after Andropov succeeded Leonid Brezhnev as general secretary of the Communist Party, came a new promotion for Fedorchuk, when he was appointed minister for internal affairs. He was succeeded as KGB chief by Viktor Chebrikov, one of the deputies he had bypassed.

Fedorchuk was born in 1918 in the Ukraine. After training at a special school for security and intelligence officers, he joined the national security service—then known as NKVD (Narodny Komissariat Vnutrennikh Dyel)—in 1939. A year later he became a member of the Communist Party of the Soviet Union. The secret treaty between Nazi Germany and the Soviet Union that preceded World War II mapped a partition of eastern Europe in general and of Poland in particular. The Polish provinces of Eastern Galicia and Volhynia, with chiefly Ukrainian populations, were incorporated with the Ukrainian Soviet Socialist Republic. The Ukrainians, however, dreamed of independence and religious liberty, especially in Eastern Galicia, where they had been Uniate Catholics in communion with Rome.

The liquidation of the Uniate Church and its forcible merger with the Russian Orthodox Church was the task of the KGB, in which Fedorchuk was involved from the outset of his career with the force. When in 1970 he became head of the Ukrainian branch of the KGB, he had to lead the incessant campaign against the "nationalist bias" in the Ukraine, the homeland of the second largest nationality of the U.S.S.R. Fedorchuk's latest promotion, besides underlining the way in which Andropov was replacing close associates of Brezhnev with his own former KGB colleagues, suggested that the Ministry for Internal Affairs would initiate more vigorous action to combat the growing Soviet crime rate and widespread corruption among the party elites.

Gabler, Mel and Norma

Two of the most influential voices in U.S. education may belong to a Christian fundamentalist couple—high school graduates who operate the nation's largest textbook-reviewing service from their home in Longview, Texas. Mel and Norma Gabler, through their nonprofit organization, Educational Research Analysts, examine textbooks for material that they consider antifamily, anti-American, and anti-Christian. They distribute their reviews to some 13,000 individuals and organizations and work to have textbooks that do not meet their criteria kept out of the nation's elementary and secondary schools.

The Gablers are against not only books that contain errors or omissions but also books that they believe undermine patriotism, the free enterprise system, religion, and parental authority. They oppose sex education in the schools and favour the teaching of the biblical story of creation along with the theory of evolution. They argue that many textbooks have been written by "secular humanists" who do not believe in God or an absolute value system. Their fund-raising pamphlet states: "Until textbooks are changed, there is no possibility that crime, violence, venereal disease and abortion rates will decrease."

The Gablers' successes, especially in their home state of Texas, where a single committee chooses books for the entire state system, have had a national impact. In 1981, of the 15 books against which they testified, 11 were rejected by the Texas textbook committee. Because Texas was expected to spend about $60 million on schoolbooks in 1982, many publishers were believed to consider that state's preferences in planning their books.

The Gablers have been castigated as "self-appointed censors" by such organizations as the National Education Association and the American Library Association. At the 1982 hearings the couple's testimony was opposed by a new group called People for the American Way, which was founded to fight for freedom-of-speech causes.

Mel Gabler, now 67, and Norma Gabler, 59, were married in 1942. He worked as a clerk for the Standard Oil Co. of New Jersey (now Exxon Corp.) for 39 years, though both now devoted full time to their cause, frequently lecturing throughout the U.S. They became concerned with textbooks in 1961, when their 16-year-old son complained about the view of federal-state relations in his history book.

Galtieri, Leopoldo Fortunato

As commander of the Argentine Army in December 1981, Lieut. Gen. Leopoldo Galtieri was a member of the three-man junta ruling Argentina under the presidency of Gen. Roberto Viola. Viola had been in office for just nine months, but his own ill health and the armed forces' dissatisfaction with his administration's policies led to his removal. Galtieri, with the support of newly promoted generals, was sworn in as president on Dec. 22, 1981. For the first time since 1978 the posts of president and army commander were united.

Galtieri's reputation had been that of a moderate, following the policies of the military governments of his predecessors and not associating with civilian political parties. Once installed in the Casa Rosada (the presidential palace), however, he made a number of statements on the need for a gradual return to civilian participation in government. This gained him some popular support, and that support grew

enormously when, on April 2, 1982, Galtieri and his fellow junta members decided on the invasion of the Falkland Islands—the Islas Malvinas. It was a national ambition to make the islands, ownership of which had been disputed with Britain for 149 years, a part of Argentina. The invasion also diverted attention away from widespread anger over the military's handling of the economy and its refusal to provide information on thousands of *desaparecidos*, victims of the 1976–79 suppression of opposition.

Born in 1926 the son of an Italian immigrant, Galtieri rose steadily through the ranks of the Army. After his promotion to army chief, he closed the Argentine-Chilean border in April 1981, thus increasing tension between the two countries. His two visits to Washington in that year were successful in achieving understanding between the U.S. and Argentina on foreign policy and economic planning.

During the war with Britain over the Falklands/Malvinas, Galtieri publicly maintained a rigid attitude toward Argentina's right to the islands, but after the surrender of his forces on June 14, he resigned as army commander on June 17. He was soon replaced as president by retired general Reynaldo Bignone. In his wake he left recrimination and instability within the ruling armed forces.

Garfield

Did two constellations of U.S. culture change their courses in 1982? Traditionally, the dog has been man's best friend, the pet whose picture on a magazine cover assured higher newsstand sales, the very symbol of rectitude and fidelity. Cats of several sorts might be symbols for automobiles and football teams, but they had not worked their way into the nation's heart; even Walt Disney made them villains when he pictured them at all. Horses like Black Beauty and Flicka might enjoy perennial popularity among 13-year-old girls, but it was *Lassie Come Home*—a dog story—that was adapted as a television series. *Pussy Come Home?* Impossible.

Then, nearly a decade ago, a cat named "Heathcliff" was featured in a cartoon strip, followed short-

ly by Bernard Kliban's popular "Cat." Somewhere along the way a live specimen named Morris hawked cat food on television and gained such a personal following that his death was reported deadpan on obituary pages. In time some 250 books appeared, including *101 Uses for a Dead Cat* and *The Official I Hate Cats Book*. Then came Garfield.

Cartoonist Jim Davis conceived him innocently enough in Muncie, Ind., as straight man in a comic strip that he drew for the local newspaper. But the cat started taking over. When the human character introduced himself to readers and then presented the animal, the latter bubbled "Hello. My name is Garfield. I'm a cat and this is my cartoonist . . ." The beast had no manners, no sense of propriety. It soon tyrannized the strip—and then the strip began to sell; first to United Feature Syndicate in 1978 and then in just four years to 1,200 newspapers. By October 1982 a book of Garfield cartoons had knocked *The Joy of Sex* off the paperback best-seller list— and had become the fifth Garfield book on the list. *New York Times* book review editors called it "an unprecedented triumph, to put it mildly." At that point the Garfield paperbacks accounted for 40% of all sales among the top 15. By Thanksgiving there were seven Garfield books on the list, and there had been a Garfield special feature on television.

There were stuffed Garfields, Garfield kittybanks, and a line of Garfield cat food in Canada, to say nothing of china icons of the orange beast with black stripes and bugeyes. (It could have been worse; Davis, 37, had once vainly tried to make another animal star of a strip called "Gnorm the Gnat.")

Garvey, Ed

The executive director of the National Football League Players Association (NFLPA), Ed Garvey was called everything from visionary to wild-eyed radical in 1982 as he led the union through the NFL's first regular-season strike in its 63 years. It lasted eight weeks, from September 21 through November 16, shortened the 1982 regular season from 16 games to 9, and confused onlookers because the union did not follow the traditional sports labour path of fighting for less restricted free-agency, which had allowed baseball and basketball salaries to skyrocket in open-market bidding for players.

Garvey approached negotiations more as a conventional union, reasoning that football players had little more individual bargaining power than pipefitters or electricians. NFL teams had a monopoly in the United States, and they had a bottomless reserve of unemployed potential replacements for a game that rewards team coordination more than individual excellence. Garvey maintained that the teams lacked economic incentive to improve because they shared television and play-off revenues equally and played to near-capacity crowds weekly, leaving few tickets to sell on the basis of a newly acquired star player. Therefore, he proposed that the players be paid according to a wage scale based on experience and

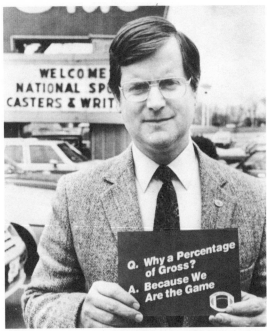

augmented by bonuses for team and individual achievement and that all salaries come from an independently administered league-wide fund.

But Garvey's demands eventually caved in under the burden of player unrest and an important unfavourable court ruling in an unfair-labour-practice suit. Management's only important new concessions in the settlement were immediate bonuses based on experience, severance pay, and union authority to approve players' agents. In return, the NFLPA backed off from its initial demand of a percentage of gross receipts, and the owners preserved the existing system of paying the bulk of players' salaries through individual contract negotiation.

Garvey was born April 18, 1940, in Burlington, Wis. His athletic career ended after he lettered in freshman golf at the University of Wisconsin, where he later was elected president of the student body. After his graduation in 1961 and service in the Army as an intelligence officer, he returned to Wisconsin for law school and was graduated in 1969. Two years later he became executive director of the NFLPA after serving it as an attorney.

Gemayel, Amin

The election of Amin Gemayel as president of Lebanon on Sept. 21, 1982, followed the assassination a week earlier of his younger brother, President-elect Bashir Gemayel. Bashir had been elected on August 23 to succeed the retiring president, Elias Sarkis.

Amin Gemayel came to power as the candidate of the Phalange Party, whose patriarch was his father, Pierre Gemayel. As a politician and businessman Amin was one of the foremost "doves" among Lebanon's Christian leaders. During 12 years as a mem-

CAMERA PRESS, LONDON

González Márquez, Felipe

The Spanish Socialist Workers' Party (PSOE) won a stunning victory in Spain's October 1982 general election under the cool leadership of Felipe González, who at the age of 40 became Europe's youngest head of government. The victory, though widely predicted, was even more sweeping than expected and was all the more surprising in that the PSOE had been legalized only in 1977. The PSOE election campaign was pitched almost exclusively around González's moderation as a leader, and in his victory speech he soberly promised "dialogue and cooperation to help reach solutions to the problems confronting our motherland." He was also determined to see Spain more prominent internationally; in his inaugural address to Parliament on November 30, he said he expected Spain would become a member of the European Communities by 1986, that a referendum would be held on NATO membership, and that negotiations with Britain on the reintegration of Gibraltar into Spanish territory would be a prime foreign policy objective.

Born in Seville on March 5, 1942, González was the only one of five children to attend the university. There he studied first to be a civil engineer before transferring to the law faculty. While still a student, he became involved in the Socialist movement, then in 1964 joined the outlawed PSOE. He started a law practice in Seville, specializing in the defense of workers' rights, and in 1965 moved to Madrid. He and his Andalusian comrades gradually gained ascendancy over the exiled PSOE leadership, and at the party congress at Suresnes, France, in 1974 he was elected secretary-general.

CAMERA PRESS, LONDON

ber of the Lebanese Parliament prior to his election, he earned a reputation as a conciliator, maintaining contact with the Palestinian leftist alliance during the 1975–76 civil war and the troubled years that followed. During the Israeli siege of Beirut in 1982 he crossed the front line for meetings with Palestinian leaders at a time of great tension between the two sides of the divided city. Such an act would have been unthinkable for his brother Bashir, who had a reputation as a man of violence. The two brothers differed widely in character and political views. While Bashir took the military road to power, Amin chose politics. He was first elected to Parliament on the death of his uncle in 1970. When the civil war broke out, he fought and was injured when the jeep he was driving came under attack. The command of the militia, nevertheless, went to his warlike brother.

Aged 40, Amin Gemayel, who was deeply interested in Lebanon's history and culture, was trained as a lawyer. Head of a large business empire that he had built up himself, he was co-founder of the rightist French-language daily newspaper *Le Réveil*. His political philosophy was based on the idea of "dynamic coexistence" both for the diverse creeds and communities of Lebanon and for the warring parties in the Middle East. He showed sympathy for the Palestinians, in sharp contrast to his brother, who said they should leave. His contacts with the Israelis were distant, and he was better known as a friend of Syria. A month after taking office President Gemayel made his international debut when he addressed the UN General Assembly, which accorded him an unusually warm reception. Afterward he was received by U.S. Pres. Ronald Reagan and had talks with Secretary of State George Shultz.

González was conscious of the debt he owed to the Socialist International, which had supported him in his fight to win the leadership of the party from its "old guard" of Civil War veterans under Rodolfo Llopis. A vice-president of the International since 1976, he had traveled extensively, especially in Latin America, to promote its aims. He was a close friend of West Germany's Willy Brandt and other leading Western European Socialists. His election campaign stressed social justice and liberty, and his moral stance accorded well with his youthful good looks and openness of manner.

Guare, John

"Theatre is the last refuge for poetry," said John Guare, who wrote plays in prose but with a lyrical quality similar to the poems of Walt Whitman. In 1982 *Lydie Breeze* and *Gardenia*, two parts of a projected tetralogy set in 19th-century New England, opened separately for short off-Broadway runs. A year earlier his screenplay *Atlantic City* won prizes from the National Society of Film Critics, the Los Angeles Film Critics Society, and the New York Film Critics Circle. Also in 1981 the dramatist won an Award of Merit from the American Academy and Institute of Arts and Letters.

Admired for his rich language and satiric vivacity, Guare first gained fame in the 1960s for arranging "shotgun weddings of lunacy and lyricism," according to the *Saturday Review*. "With a touch of the poet—and the lunatic—Guare conceived contemporary satires that overflowed with lyrical language." Among them were *Marco Polo Sings a Solo* and the autobiographically tinged *House of Blue Leaves*, which won a New York Drama Critics Circle award.

The son of a stock exchange clerk, Guare was born Feb. 5, 1938, in New York City. He received an undergraduate degree from Georgetown University and a master's degree from Yale University's celebrated drama school.

After his New York City debut in the mid-1960s, Guare's plays began appearing almost regularly at the Caffe Cino. *Muzeeka*—about a canned music factory—won him his first Obie (off-Broadway award) in 1968. His adaptation of Shakespeare's *The Two Gentlemen of Verona*—reset in San Juan, P.R., and New York City—won several prizes.

Turning to the screen, Guare teamed up with French director Louis Malle (*Pretty Baby*, *My Dinner with Andre*) and wrote *Atlantic City*, a touchingly sleazy murder-romance about an aging second-rate hoodlum and a casino waitress. (Malle then directed *Lydie Breeze* on stage.) Their next collaboration was to be *Moon over Miami*, a farcical film about drug traffic and police entrapment.

Habib, Philip Charles

For the second time in as many years, Philip Habib was at the eye of the storm in the Middle East in 1982. Once again he performed heroic labours in

CAMERA PRESS, LONDON

bringing a tenuous cease-fire to the strife-torn region. U.S. Pres. Ronald Reagan presented him with the Medal of Freedom, and Charles Percy, chairman of the Senate Foreign Relations Committee, nominated him for the Nobel Peace Prize. But true peace in the Middle East proved as elusive as ever.

Heart trouble had forced Habib's retirement in 1978 after a distinguished 29-year career as a U.S. foreign service officer, most of it as a specialist on the Far East. He suffered a series of heart attacks and underwent coronary bypass surgery. But Pres. Jimmy Carter sent him on a fact-finding mission to the Caribbean, and in 1981 President Reagan made him special envoy to the Middle East with the task of damping down the crisis caused by Syria's installation of surface-to-air missiles in Lebanon. While he was there, fighting broke out between Israeli and Palestine Liberation Organization (PLO) forces in southern Lebanon, but he managed to arrange a cease-fire.

In 1982 the situation was even worse. In June Israel invaded Lebanon in force and drove north to Beirut, where it laid siege to the Muslim part of the city. Working 18 hours a day, shuttling from capital to capital and from meeting to meeting for 11 weeks, Habib hammered out an agreement that ended the hostilities, at least temporarily. He was credited with the idea of bringing in U.S. Marines to help oversee the PLO's evacuation of Beirut—an important point in securing Israeli consent—and with finding other Arab countries where the PLO could go.

With the immediate fire extinguished, it was understood that Habib would leave the working out of a long-range settlement to others, but he was back again in late November, when the Reagan adminis-

445

tration became impatient with the lack of progress. In late December he was again shuttling among capitals, but the year ended with Israeli and Syrian troops still firmly ensconced on Lebanese soil.

Habib was born Feb. 25, 1920, the son of a Lebanese-American grocer, and grew up in a Jewish section of Brooklyn. At the time of his retirement he was undersecretary of state for political affairs, the highest career rank in the State Department.

Haddad, Saad

At the start of 1982 former major Saad Haddad, one of the most ruthless as well as one of the most enigmatic of Lebanon's many militia leaders, was in control of a narrow strip of territory adjacent to the Israeli border, which extended, snakelike, from the Mediterranean Sea to the foothills of Mt. Hermon and the border with Syria. But within a week of the entrance of Israeli troops into Lebanon on June 6, the Israelis had ceded him authority over the entire south of the country, from the Awali River north of Sidon to Lake Qaraaoun in the Bekaa Valley. Haddad expected a major Israeli attack before it came. On June 2 he called for a quick military strike against the Palestinians. "I have no faith in the cease-fire," he said, referring to the agreement negotiated in July 1981 between Israel and the Palestine Liberation Organization (PLO) that had led to ten months of unparalleled calm in southern Lebanon—a calm broken only by a heavy barrage by Israeli and Haddad artillery, and by Israeli aircraft, on April 23, 1982.

Haddad, a 44-year-old Greek Orthodox who had recruited Shi'ah Muslims as well as Maronite Christians for his 2,500-strong pro-Christian force, had long hated the Palestinian guerrillas in Lebanon. In 1979 he used the presence of Palestinian forces in the south as a pretext for his declaration of independence from Lebanon, when he proclaimed the territory under his control to be "Free Lebanon." All Haddad's military supplies came from Israel. Haddad was cashiered from the Lebanese Army after that incident. He had reached the rank of major and had attended a one-year course at the U.S. Advanced Infantry School at Ft. Benning in Georgia.

Haddad was in Beirut in September when the massacre of Palestinians in the Sabra and Shatila camps took place. He initially told reporters that some 10–20 of his men might have been in the city at the time, but he later told an Israeli judicial commission inquiring into the massacre that none of his men were north of the Awali when it occurred. Israel appeared to be hoping that in 1983 Haddad would achieve a reconciliation with the new authorities in Lebanon and become, de facto if not de jure, the Lebanese government's recognized security arm in the south after an Israeli withdrawal.

Henderson, Rickey

Rickey Henderson of the Oakland A's had thought of major league baseball's base stealing record as more of a distraction than a barrier. Lou Brock's record of 118 bases in 162 games was less than three in every four games, and Henderson wondered why nobody had averaged one a game.

He then nearly accomplished that in 1982, when he broke Brock's eight-year-old record with 130. Henderson stole into the record book despite a .399 on-base percentage, which was the lowest of his four-year career. Although his 116 walks were the most in the major leagues, his .267 batting average was 33 points below his career average and 52 points (or 27 hits) below his 1981 average.

Henderson was not the fastest player in the game, but his acceleration to full speed in two strides enabled him to steal second base in 2.9 seconds. A catcher can rarely receive a pitch and deliver the ball to second base in less than 3.2 seconds. Henderson did set another record by being caught stealing 42 times, but 14 were on pickoff attempts and 3 were on attempted steals of home. He also became the unofficial champion of stealing third base, which accounted for more than a quarter of his total.

Born Dec. 25, 1958, in Chicago, Henderson was raised in Oakland, Calif., where he not only was outstanding at baseball but had a football career at Technical High School that attracted major scholarship offers. In his first full major league season, 1980, Henderson's 100 stolen bases broke Ty Cobb's 65-year-old American League record. In 1981 he was a close second in the league's most valuable player voting, won a Gold Glove for his play in left field, and led the league in hits, runs, and stolen bases.

Henderson's prime years as a base stealer appeared to be ahead of him. Brock set his record at the age of 35, and Maury Wills had set the previous record at 29. As 1982 ended, Henderson talked about winning a batting championship and hitting more home runs, but he still said that stealing a base was as exciting as hitting a game-winning grand slam home run in the bottom of the ninth inning.

Hinault, Bernard

During 11 weeks in 1982 French cyclist Bernard Hinault proved beyond all doubt his right to be considered among the sport's all-time greats. Between mid-May and the end of July he won both the Tour of Italy and the Tour de France to join Fausto Coppi, Jacques Anquetil, and Eddy Merckx as the only men to take cycling's two most important stage races during the same season. Although the dominating figure in professional road racing since 1978, Hinault had met with failure when first attempting the double triumph in 1980. As a result he had continued to suffer in comparison with his immediate predecessor Merckx and fellow countryman Anquetil until his victories in 1982 finally ensured the total adulation of an enthusiastic nation.

The Tour of Italy began in Milan on May 13 and finished, after 2,500 mi (4,023 km), in Turin on June 6. Winning and then surrendering the jersey of race

UPI

leader on three occasions, Hinault finally asserted his authority on the mountainous 18th stage between Piamborno and Monte Campione, opening a decisive gap over his nearest challenger when he stretched his advantage to 2 min 35 sec by winning the final time-trial section. In the Tour de France, which began in Basel, Switz., just 26 days later, it was Hinault's ability against the clock on the four individual time-trial stages that gave him the edge; he finished the 2,170-mi (3,492-km) race by leading the field across the line in Paris on July 25. His total victory margin over Joop Zoetemelk of The Netherlands was 6 min 21 sec and, along with his powerful riding in the Pyrenees and Alps, that last stage confirmed his all-round superiority in the face of unjustified criticism.

Born in Yffiniac, Brittany, on Nov. 14, 1954, Hinault began his reign by winning the Tour de France in 1978 and again the following year. After winning the Tour of Italy in 1980, on the first attempt, Hinault was forced to retire from the Tour de France by tendinitis of the knee. He recovered to win the world championship a few weeks later in front of a jubilant home audience at Sallanches, and the following year he won his national tour for the third time. By the end of 1982 Hinault had planned an additional four years of racing and was poised to break the record total of five Tour de France victories held jointly by Anquetil and Merckx.

Imran, Khan

For Khan Imran 1982 was an *annus mirabilis*, a wonder-year. He was appointed captain for the short Pakistan cricket tour of England, and no man could have made a more thrilling attempt to wrest victory than he in a three-match series in which England won two matches and Pakistan one. Imran's leadership was crucial in Pakistan's victory by ten wickets at Lord's. In the two test matches that Pakistan lost, Imran almost played England on his own

and was declared Man of the Match each time. At Edgbaston he took 7 wickets for 52 runs and 2 for 84, and scored 22 runs and 65 (top score). At Headingly he took 5 wickets for 49 runs and 3 for 66, and made 67 runs not out and 46. He was rightly acclaimed Man of the Series, unusual for the captain of the losing side.

Imran first came to England as an 18-year-old all-round cricketer with the Pakistan touring team of 1971. His performances on that tour attracted the attention of the Worcestershire Country Cricket Club, for whom he played for the next few years. During this time he had two years at Oxford University, being captain in 1974, making five centuries, and taking 45 wickets. After transferring from Worcestershire to Sussex in 1977, he became a key member of the latter team. His ability as a menacing fast bowler and number five batsman made Sussex formidable in championship and one-day cricket.

Meanwhile, Imran had become an important player for Pakistan in matches against New Zealand, Australia, and West Indies. He took six wickets in each innings against Australia at Sydney in 1976 and was largely responsible for Pakistan's victory by eight wickets. During the English winter of 1980-81, he played in Pakistan against West Indies and in one memorable match scored his first test century and took ten wickets.

Imran was born on Nov. 25, 1952, the only son of five children of a prosperous civil engineer in Lahore, Pak. On his mother's side two of Pakistan's foremost cricketers, Javed Burki and Majid Khan, were his first cousins and his early heroes. The name Khan signifies that his family are Pathans from the North-West Frontier and that they belong to the Naizi tribe. Imran studied politics and economics at Keble College, Oxford; he stated that he did not know what career he would choose when he gave up cricket but that it would be work in which he was his own master.

447

Jarvik, Robert

Retired dentist Barney Clark was a very special patient when he entered the University of Utah Medical Center in Salt Lake City in November 1982. Possessed of a fierce will to live and a professional interest in advancing science, he suffered a form of heart disease that was amenable to only one form of treatment—a form never before tried. The surgery itself was dangerous and the outcome was unforeseeable. Without the unprecedented operation (which U.S. government authorities approved on an experimental basis) he would have been dead in a matter of days or hours.

When Clark's condition worsened, on December 1 he was wheeled into a specially equipped operating room. Eight hours later he emerged with a new heart—not a transplant from some accident victim's chest but an artificial implant, one made by men out of plastic and aluminum and driven by an electronically controlled air compressor. Because tubes must always connect the new heart to the power source and monitor, Clark would never live a life of normal agility again. But live he did. By Christmas he had taken a few steps around his hospital room, and it appeared that he might soon go home, thanks to the Jarvik-7 beating in his chest.

The device, essentially a pneumatic pump built to exact specifications, was named for its inventor, Robert K. Jarvik, who almost did not make the grade in medicine. Born in Midland, Mich., on May 11, 1946, Jarvik was the son of a surgeon and often observed his father operate. Intrigued with the design of surgical instruments, he invented a surgical stapler to close wounds when he was still a teenager.

Going on to Syracuse University, he studied architecture and mechanical drawing while earning a zoology degree in 1968. When his academic record did not open doors to any U.S. medical schools, he studied at the University of Bologna Medical School in Italy for two years. He then dropped out and transferred to New York University, where he earned a master's degree in occupational biomechanics.

Finally receiving an M.D. degree at the University of Utah College of Medicine in 1976, Jarvik went to work at its medical centre's Artificial Organs Division. His assignment was to design a series of mechanical hearts that could be tested on animals. As these hearts improved, one of them kept a calf alive for 268 days. The heart that extended Barney Clark's life is a two-chambered device that receives blood from the patient's right and left atrias and then pumps it to the pulmonary artery and aorta.

Kadar, Janos

First secretary of the Hungarian Socialist Workers' (Communist) Party, Janos Kadar was one of the most respected leaders within the Soviet bloc. When he assumed power in the sombre November days following the crushing by Soviet tanks of the 1956 Hungarian uprising, most Hungarians believed him to be a puppet of Moscow. Convinced of the Soviet resolve to restore Communism in Hungary, Kadar hoped that if he played a part in this process he would be able to retrieve some of the less contentious goals of the uprising. For a quarter of a century he worked for the welfare of his people and avoided raising hopes impossible to fulfill in the existing world alignment.

Janos Csermanik was born on May 26, 1912, in the then Hungarian Adriatic port of Fiume (now Rijeka, Yugos.). Abandoned by his father, he settled with his mother in Budapest, where he worked as a machinist. In 1930 he joined the Union of Young Communist Workers, was twice jailed, and in 1940 went underground, adopting the nom de guerre of Kadar. After the Hungarian Communist Party was restored by Matyas Rakosi in 1945, Kadar became a member of the Politburo. As part of a Stalinist purge he was arrested in April 1951 on charges of treason and sentenced to four years in prison. However, after Stalin's death and under pressure from Soviet leader Nikita Khrushchev, he was released in July 1954. In February 1956 Khrushchev's denunciation of Stalin precipitated Rakosi's downfall and also set the scene for the uprising of October 23.

After the Soviet intervention Kadar was installed as head of a new government, having become first secretary of the renamed Hungarian Socialist Workers' Party several days earlier. His first efforts in office were to reconstruct the party and the government, and then he started on the long and difficult uphill road to regain the trust of the Hungarian nation and the sympathy of the free world. On June 9, 1977, Pope Paul VI received him in audience at the Vatican—symbolically marking the end of Hungary's moral isolation.

Kemp, Jack

For U.S. Rep. Jack Kemp, 1982 required a strong will and all of his faith in the "supply side" economic theory. That theory had become "Reaganomics" in 1981, but a year later Pres. Ronald Reagan reluc-

tantly asked for and got an increase in certain taxes in an effort to hold down the federal deficit. Kemp not only opposed the tax hike but continued to preach his tax-cutting gospel as he campaigned for Republican candidates throughout the country.

"A recession is *not* the time to raise taxes," Kemp insisted, blaming the Federal Reserve Board for the nation's tight money supply and high interest rates. He also voted against Reagan's balanced budget amendment to the Constitution and found himself bitterly at odds with the White House that had adopted his economic policy only a year earlier.

But the 47-year-old New York congressman was familiar with adversity and accustomed to boos as well as cheers. His previous career as a professional football star was good preparation for the hard knocks of political life. Kemp was cut or traded by a half-dozen teams before becoming the starting quarterback of the Buffalo Bills. He led them to three division titles and two American Football League championships before retiring as an all-pro in 1969.

Always interested in politics, Kemp had been a volunteer in Richard Nixon's presidential campaigns and a special assistant to Reagan when he was governor of California. In 1970 Kemp capitalized on his football fame to be elected to Congress as a conservative Republican in a Buffalo district where he had to win the support of blue-collar Democratic voters. He held it from then on and in 1982 was easily reelected to a seventh term with 75% of the vote.

Kemp was an early and forceful advocate of "supply side" economics—the theory that lower taxes will stimulate the economy and boost productivity, thereby creating jobs and increasing tax revenue by drawing from a broader base. The Kemp-Roth bill became a cornerstone of the Reagan economic policy. But Kemp believed the president's advisers lacked the courage to stick with it through the recession.

Kemp was born July 13, 1935, in Los Angeles. He was graduated from Occidental College in 1957.

Kohl, Helmut

Chairman of the West German Christian Democratic Union (CDU) and a former minister president (prime minister) of the Rhineland-Palatinate, Helmut Kohl became his country's sixth federal chancellor on Oct. 1, 1982, succeeding the Social Democrat Helmut Schmidt. He was elected in the Bundestag with the help of the liberal Free Democratic Party, which had decided to change coalition partners in midterm.

Born on April 3, 1930, in Ludwigshafen, of devout Roman Catholic parents, Kohl was brought up amid the hardships of wartime. He had to interrupt his schooling for a period of premilitary training in Bavaria. He financed his studies at Frankfurt and Heidelberg universities, where he read history, philosophy, law, and economics, by working in a chemical plant.

Kohl joined the CDU at the age of 17 and soon

proved to be a natural politician. He was elected to the Rhineland-Palatinate Parliament in 1959, and four years later he was appointed his party's parliamentary floor leader in the state assembly. He became minister president in 1969 and won a reputation as a sound administrator. Elected chairman of the CDU in 1973, he resigned from the state premiership in 1976 to devote himself to federal politics.

Kohl fought the 1976 federal election as the chancellor candidate of the CDU and its Bavarian sister party, the Christian Social Union (CSU), under the slogan "Freedom Instead of Socialism." The CDU-CSU's poll of 48.6% was its second best result since the formation of the federal republic. But the CSU, led by the conservative Franz-Josef Strauss, had long considered Kohl dull and provincial. In the 1980 election Strauss again contested the chancellorship and lost decisively.

Kohl was a centrist, and in his first government statement he promised that his coalition would pursue centrist policies at home and abroad. He was considered by his detractors to be too much of a generalist for the top job, although he partly compensated for his lack of specialization by a readiness to delegate authority. He was also handicapped by an inability to speak foreign languages.

Koivisto, Mauno Henrik

Elected Finland's chief of state in January 1982, Mauno Koivisto was dubbed the "people's president." The description fitted his background and bearing: born into the family of a ship's carpenter in 1923; a one-time dockworker who wrote a doctorate on conditions in his home port of Turku; a man who did not hide unpalatable truths from his audiences; and an amiable figure with a passion for volleyball and Gary Cooper movies who nevertheless maintained the dignity required by high office.

That Koivisto was the first Finnish president to emerge from the left seemed merely incidental. He was always remote from the grinding apparatus of his party, the Social Democrats, and he was obviously bored with simplistic "isms." Pragmatism was his guideline throughout his terms as prime minister (1968–70 and 1979–82) and central bank governor (1968–82), and he was not afraid to impose draconian measures when other politicians dithered.

Koivisto himself had sometimes appeared vacillating, but he could act decisively when necessary—as when his opponents used the services of his predecessor, the ailing Pres. Urho Kekkonen, in an abortive attempt to dislodge him as prime minister in April 1981. Had Koivisto quit then, he might never have become president in the election forced by Kekkonen's premature resignation, but he invoked the constitutional prerogatives bestowed on Parliament. Koivisto was eager to reactivate Parliament's role in the foreign policy debate. This was a departure, since Juho Paasikivi (president during 1946–56) and Kekkonen, whose personalities remained synonymous with Finland's neutral line, had exercised their responsibilities in this field to the fullest.

The freer atmosphere resulting from this attempt to devolve part of the great power constitutionally bestowed on any Finnish president led to some confusion. However, there was no immediate effect on Finland's international position. Koivisto stressed

continuity at his meeting with Soviet Pres. Leonid Brezhnev in March. Though primarily an economist, Koivisto was quick to grasp the workings of diplomacy, and this, coupled with Finland's innate stability, made the change after the 26 years of Kekkonen's presidency remarkably undramatic.

Lubbers, Rudolphus Franciscus Marie

"Ruud" Lubbers became prime minister of The Netherlands in November 1982, the youngest person ever to hold that office. Like Andreas van Agt, his predecessor, he belonged to the Roman Catholic component of the Christian Democratic Appeal (CDA). His appointment did not surprise anyone. As party leader in the lower house of Parliament since 1978, he had played an important role as mediator between the party and the government. His independence and litheness of mind at times tended to obscure the true nature of his political views and feelings. He had a reputation as a competent negotiator—a person who had at least five solutions for any one problem.

Lubbers was born on May 7, 1939, in Rotterdam. He was educated at Canisius College at Nijmegen and then at Erasmus University, Rotterdam, where he studied economics. After his graduation in 1962 he aspired to a scientific career, but circumstances led him to join the family firm of Lubbers Hollandia Engineering Works, of which he became a director in 1965. During his political career his continuing involvement with this enterprise gave his enemies an opportunity to cast doubts on his integrity. He was reputedly one of the wealthiest of Dutch politicians.

In the 1960s Lubbers belonged to the progressive part of the Catholic People's Party (KVP). He felt emotionally engaged with the Christian Radicals, a movement of progressive politicians within the three great confessional parties, but refused to become a member of the Radical Political Party, founded in 1968, because he felt he owed allegiance to the KVP. During these years he also participated actively in employers' organizations. In 1964 he became chairman of the Christian Young Employers' Organization. Later he was appointed chairman of the Catholic Employers' Organization for the Metal Industry and a member of the board of the influential Dutch Christian Employers' Organization.

From 1973 to 1977 Lubbers served as minister of economic affairs in the government headed by the Socialist Prime Minister Joop den Uyl. During that period he proved his capabilities and succeeded in winning the confidence of the Socialists. In 1977 he became vice-chairman of the CDA in the lower house. After the unexpected and emotional departure of Willem Aantjes in 1978, he was appointed chairman and thereafter was considered to be a key figure in Dutch politics.

Ludlum, Robert

"Robert Ludlum writes spy thrillers the way the rest of us play Scrabble. Ludlum has 25 tiles with words on each, words like World War II, secret documents, Nazi war treasure, CIA. . . . Each year Ludlum chooses half the tiles, face down and turns them over, arranging them this way and that until some reasonably plausible sequence appears. . . ."

His latest opus "is in fact a lousy book. So I stayed up until 3 AM to finish [reading] it. Storytellers like Ludlum sink their hooks into us, and there is only one way to wriggle free. You have to know how it all comes out. . . ."

Thus did some critics pillory this formula writer. Ludlum's tenth novel, *The Parsifal Mosaic*, spent most of 1982 on everybody's best-seller list. Five years earlier his printings had passed the ten million mark, and at last count his works were available in 23 languages.

Each book had a certain sameness that began with the title: *The Bourne Identity*, *The Matarese Circle*, *The Holcroft Covenant*, *The Chancellor Manuscript*, *The Gemini Contenders*, *The Rhinemann Exchange*, *The Matlock Paper*, *The Osterman Weekend*, *The Scarlatti Inheritance*. Never celebrated for their narrative style or literary complexity, Ludlum's novels are fantasies of international intrigue, vengeance, violence, and final victory for the forces of decency as defended by a spectacularly ruthless hero. Each one mixed similar elements into similar plots, and each coined money.

"I write about things that intrigue me," said the author. "I take a theatrical viewpoint . . . sort of melodramatic," he told an interviewer who described the 55-year-old New York City native as a nondescript short man with gray hair and the look of "an off duty professor." In fact, after graduating from Wesleyan University in 1951, he started out as an actor. In 1960 Ludlum founded the Playhouse on the Mall in Paramus, N.J., and found "if you could set your sights low enough in the theatre you could make a killing." After ten years of that he yearned for a change. "I thought I might get published in a small way and then go into teaching at a university or something. In 1971 his first book, *The Scarlatti Inheritance*, was published. It became an instant hit and a Book-of-the-Month Club selection.

Ludwig, Daniel K.

In January 1982 U.S. shipping tycoon Daniel K. Ludwig decided to abandon his most ambitious undertaking—perhaps the largest agricultural-industrial effort ever financed by one person—the $1 billion Jari development project in Brazil. The project, named for the Amazon River tributary along which it is situated, began in 1967 with the purchase of 3.5 million ac (1.6 million ha) for a cost of $3 million, with the aim of producing saw timber and pulp. During the course of the project Ludwig created in the jungle four towns, an airport, a hospital, 3,000 mi (4,850 km) of roads, a 37-mi (60-km) freight railway, a deep-water port, and a $250 million paper and pulp mill that was built in Japan and transported by barge the 17,000 mi (27,400 km) to Jari. In addition to 287,000 ac (114,000 ha) of gmelina, pine, and eucalyptus trees, there were 86,500 ac (34,600 ha) of rice fields, more than 11,000 head of cattle and buffalo, and an enormous mine for kaolin, a clay used in paper production and ceramics.

Although Ludwig's failing health was cited as the reason for abandoning Jari, observers noted many problems in the project, which had recently been losing about $100 million a year. Cost overruns, heavy management turnover (there had been some 30 project directors), disputes with the Brazilian government, and miscalculations about the demand for his products and the adaptability of the fast-growing Southeast Asian gmelina tree to the Amazon soil were all cited. By 1980 financial difficulties had led Ludwig to seek help from the Brazilian government, which was denied. The Jari project was to be taken over by about 20 leading Brazilian firms.

Born on June 24, 1897, in South Haven, Mich., Ludwig left school after the eighth grade. At the age of 19 he went into business for himself, purchasing an excursion boat for $5,000 and converting it into a barge. He later specialized in profitable oil transport. In the 1930s he introduced to the tanker trade the practice of chartering ships before they were built and using the charters as collateral for shipbuilding loans. By the end of World War II Ludwig controlled almost all world oil shipping. He is credited with the development of efficient supertankers, giant ships that can handle cargo more cheaply than several small ships.

Madrid Hurtado, Miguel de la

Elected president of Mexico on July 4, 1982, Miguel de la Madrid assumed power on December 1 for a six-year term. At his inauguration he announced a ten-point plan to combat the country's grave financial crisis. The measures he proposed were in line with the economic policies he had outlined in his election campaign as being essential for Mexico's recovery. They included cuts in public spending, selective investment in labour-intensive industries, and a campaign to drive out corruption. His government was expected to adopt a low profile in foreign affairs and to support reasonable free-market policies when the economic situation improved.

Miguel de la Madrid Hurtado was born in Colima (capital of the state of the same name) on Dec. 12, 1934. He received his primary and secondary education in Mexico City and obtained a law degree with honours at the Universidad Nacional Autónoma (UNAM) in 1957, submitting a dissertation on "Economic Thought in the 1857 Constitution." In 1963 he became a member of the Partido Revolucionario Institucional (PRI). He obtained a master's degree in public administration at Harvard in 1964–65.

During 1953–57 de la Madrid worked in the legal department of the National Foreign Trade Bank. In 1960 he became a consultant to management in the Banco de México, the central bank, which he left in 1965 to spend five years as subdirector of credit in

CAMERA PRESS/PHOTO TRENDS

the Secretariat of Finance and Public Credit. From 1970 until April 1972 he operated as subdirector of finance at Petróleos Mexicanos (PEMEX), the nationalized oil company, but in May he rejoined the Secretariat of Finance as director general of credit. He was appointed undersecretary of finance in October 1975 and from May 1979 occupied the post of secretary for programming and the budget.

On various occasions de la Madrid acted as counselor to bodies concerned with exports and finance, and he was a member of several related technical committees. He attended many economically oriented international meetings on behalf of the government, particularly annual International Monetary Fund, World Bank, and Inter-American Development Bank meetings. He published a book on constitutional law, *Estudios de Derecho Constitucional*, and taught at the UNAM law faculty from 1968.

Marcinkus, Msgr. Paul Casimir

Archbishop Paul Marcinkus first became known to the general public as the tall, balding bodyguard who was always seen shepherding Pope John Paul II on his many international journeys. But in 1982 he became better known in his other role as president of the "Vatican bank" (strictly, the Institute for Religious Works, IOR). The Italian authorities wished to question him about the involvement of the IOR in the Banco Ambrosiano of Milan, which had failed. Its president, Roberto Calvi, was found hanged under Blackfriars Bridge in London on June 18.

Born Jan. 15, 1922, in Cicero, Ill., to immigrant Lithuanian parents, Marcinkus was ordained a priest in 1947. After serving in a Chicago parish, he entered the Pontifical Ecclesiastical Academy in 1952, served as papal diplomat in Bolivia and Cana-

da, and became one of the inner circle of advisers to Pope Paul VI. The chaos of the first papal journey abroad—to the Holy Land in 1964—persuaded the pope to put Marcinkus in charge of future trips. In this he was highly successful. In Manila in 1970 he helped to subdue a deranged Brazilian painter who had approached the pope, knife in hand.

Marcinkus's brusque style offended some, but Paul VI made him bishop and put him in charge of the IOR in 1969. He had no special training in international finance and had to learn on the job. This brought him into contact with various Italian bankers who were not all above suspicion. He worked first with Michele Sindona (currently serving a 25-year sentence for fraud in New York State) and Roberto Calvi. His most imprudent act was to provide Calvi with "letters of comfort" to reassure Ambrosiano's creditors as late as August 1981, when the bank appeared to be doomed. The fact that Calvi gave him in exchange a secret assurance that the IOR would not be liable for any losses incurred by the Banco Ambrosiano looked like conspiracy.

As of the end of 1982 Marcinkus had escaped questioning by staying inside the Vatican. No one suggested that he gained any personal advantage from his financial deals. His misfortune was to be sucked into the Italian banking world. In December it was announced that the Vatican and the Italian government had agreed to set up a joint six-man committee to investigate the IOR-Banco Ambrosiano connection. Meanwhile, Marcinkus no longer acted as the pope's travel organizer and bodyguard, but he remained governor of Vatican City State.

Moi, Daniel Torotich arap

Kenya's reputation as one of Africa's stablest countries was severely shaken by an attempted military coup led by elements in its Air Force in August 1982. Although Pres. Daniel arap Moi was able to put down the challenge with relative ease (but at the cost of several hundred lives), it revealed something of the true extent of economic and political discontent in the country, accentuated since the death of the nation's founding father, Jomo Kenyatta, in 1978. Moi was unfortunate in having come to office at a time when Kenya's rapid economic growth had begun to decline, due mainly to the international financial situation. This meant growing unemployment and fewer opportunities for young Kenyans.

Although President Moi was widely respected, he lacked the charisma of Kenyatta and had no strong independent political base of his own, coming as he did from one of the clans of the minority Kalenjin community. An astute politician, he sought to identify his leadership with Kenyatta's by calling for a policy of *nyayo*, that is, following in the "footsteps" of Kenyatta. But while this slogan was popular among many in the dominant Kikuyu community, it found much less appeal among the second strongest community, the Luo, or among the nation's youth. Although himself a former teacher, Moi found it difficult to win the support of the country's intellectuals. Troubles with university students and staff were a continuing feature of his rule.

Moi was born at Sacho in the Baringo district of Rift Valley Province in 1924 and received a traditional Christian missionary education. He first entered politics as a bitter opponent of Kenyatta and

an outspoken critic of the Kikuyu-led Mau Mau revolt. Fearing domination by the Kikuyu and Luo, he was prominent in establishing the Kenya African Democratic Union (KADU), which favoured a federal type of constitution for the country. During the colonial period he became minister of education in 1961 and later minister of local government. But after independence in 1963, Moi joined Kenyatta's ruling party and became minister for home affairs in 1964 and vice-president in 1967. He was rewarded by being made Kenyatta's designated successor.

Moseley, Mark

Snow was falling, the wind was swirling, and the Washington Redskins were trailing 14–12 with four seconds to play when Mark Moseley lined up for a 42-yd field-goal attempt on Dec. 19, 1982. An opponent tipped the ball, but Moseley kicked it hard enough to put it between the goalposts, winning the game for Washington and breaking the previous National Football League record of 20 consecutive field goals.

Moseley kicked 23 in a row, including 3 in 1981, before missing his final 1982 attempt from 40 yd. His 20-for-21 kicking in one season set an NFL record for field-goal percentage with .952. He led the league in field goals and made the all-star Pro Bowl team for the second time. Most important, Moseley's kicks were the difference in five Redskin victories, two on the last play, prompting the Associated Press to make him the first kicker ever to win the NFL's most valuable player award. In Washington's 27–17 victory over Miami in the Super Bowl, Moseley kicked two field goals.

"We just keep it close and let Mark kick the field

goals," Washington coach Joe Gibbs said. But Moseley was nearly released by Gibbs before the season began. His field-goal percentage the previous two seasons had been .587 on 37-for-63, unacceptable even though he had brought the Redskins from behind to win three games with late kicks and even though he had been 22-for-27 from inside 40 yd. For the 1982 season Moseley did not make the team until his rookie challenger missed two field-goal attempts in the final exhibition game.

Moseley, born March 12, 1948, in Lanesville, Texas, was hardly an instant success in the NFL. Philadelphia cut him in 1971 after one season, and Houston cut him in 1973 after one season, one game, and an injury. From there he returned to Stephen F. Austin State University for his degree. But he continued kicking, and Washington signed him in 1974.

Through 1982, Moseley's career field-goal percentage of .641 was not far behind the NFL record of .688, even though more than half his 273 attempts with Washington had been from 40 yd or farther. His percentage from that distance in nine Redskin seasons was a remarkable .493, despite the apparent disadvantage of kicking with his toe instead of the instep, soccer style, as 26 of 28 NFL kickers did in 1982.

Nakasone, Yasuhiro

With the selection of 64-year-old Yasuhiro Nakasone as Japan's prime minister on Nov. 26, 1982, the nation presumed that Japanese interests would be more forcefully defended than they had been under the former head of government, Zenko Suzuki. Nakasone, who had been the director general of the Administrative Management Agency, had demon-

strated his well-known political talents by first out-polling three other Liberal Democratic Party (LDP) candidates who challenged him for the party presidency. Only the rank and file members of the LDP were allowed to cast ballots. By garnering 57% of the vote, Nakasone was all but assured of the party presidency when the LDP members of the Diet (parliament) made their choice. The presidency of the LDP brought with it the prime ministership.

Though the LDP has held power in Japan since it was founded in 1955, its rule has been severely hampered by bitter factional divisions. Nakasone's victory, therefore, had to be won with the backing of political kingmakers. Chief among those was former prime minister Kakuei Tanaka, who was driven from office when he was accused of involvement in the Lockheed bribery scandal. Though the still incomplete court proceedings began in 1977, Tanaka has remained a powerful force within the LDP, as was evident when six of his closest associates were named to Cabinet posts in the new government.

Nakasone was born in Takasaki City, Gumma Prefecture, on May 27, 1918, the son of a wealthy lumber dealer. He was graduated from Tokyo University School of Law in 1941 and saw action during World War II with the Imperial Japanese Navy. In 1947 he was elected to the first of 14 successive terms in the Diet and in 1959 received a Cabinet post. Since then he has held portfolios in science and technology, defense, and international trade and industry.

Cosmopolitan by choice and capable of carrying on a conversation in English and French, Nakasone has earned a reputation among foreign diplomats as a no-nonsense straight talker. Though said to have admired the stubborn independence of the late French president Charles de Gaulle, Nakasone clearly intends to continue Japan's close relationship with the U.S. He nonetheless has kept his options open on the role Japan will play in the defense of the free world and what economic and trade policies he will pursue.

Nattrass, Susan

For avid competitor Susan Nattrass winning was always a priority. Gaining the women's world trapshooting championship in 1981 gave her the best-ever record in that sport, six consecutive world championships. In recognition of her achievement the Sports Federation of Canada named her the female athlete of the year (1982). She also received the Lou Marsh Trophy as Canadian overall athlete of the year (1981).

Born on Nov. 5, 1950, in Medicine Hat, Alta., Nattrass was introduced to trapshooting at the age of 12 by her father, Floyd Nattrass, himself a champion in the sport and a member of the 1964 Canadian Olympic trapshooting team. Susan Nattrass's first international win came in Reno, Nev., in 1969, when she triumphed over 1,300 other competitors in a trapshooting meet. After that victory she set her sights on world and Olympic Games competition. She won the North American ladies' trapshooting championship every year, beginning in 1972, and she had been the Canadian women's trapshooting champion since 1968. In 1969 she began competing in women's world championships. She finished fourth in 1969 and 1970, second in 1971, and won the gold medal for the first time in 1975. In the 1976 Olympic Games in Montreal, Nattrass was a member of the Canadian team, the first woman to compete in trapshooting in Olympic competition. However, she finished a disappointing 25th.

Competing in both American- and international-style trapshooting, Nattrass won all her major victories in international style. In American style the clay pigeon travels 50 mph, and the shooter has the gun at the shoulder when the target is launched. In international style the pigeon travels at 90 mph, and the shooter has the gun below the waist when the target is launched.

During the winter, when training became difficult because of the weather, Nattrass concentrated on volleyball, squash, and skiing to maintain her reflexes. She also worked toward her degree in physical education. She earned a B.A. at the University of Alberta and an M.A. at the University of Waterloo. While working on her Ph.D. in the sociology of sports at the University of Alberta, she taught physical education and was a sports coach there.

Pawley, Howard

In the Manitoba provincial election of Nov. 17, 1981, the New Democratic Party won a majority of the 57 seats in the Manitoba legislature. Party leader Howard Pawley was sworn in on Nov. 30, 1981, as the 19th premier of the province. Emphasizing economic renewal, Pawley believed that the provincial government should spend money to bring Manitoba out of its economic recession. Once in office, he moved to do just that. A mortgage interest rate relief plan was implemented, as was an income stabilization plan for beef producers. Tenants were not neglected; rent increases were limited to 9% on all older buildings.

Pawley's victory surprised many observers. However, with his easygoing demeanour he had shown himself to be an effective grass-roots politician. First elected to the provincial legislature in 1969, he became the most junior minister in the Cabinet of Premier Edward Schreyer. From 1969 to 1976 he was minister of municipal affairs and was so popular in that position that the municipal secretaries in Manitoba complained when in 1973 Schreyer decided to move him to another Cabinet post. Therefore, Pawley retained the municipal affairs portfolio when he became Manitoba's attorney general and keeper of the great seal in 1973. Known as a civil libertarian, Pawley had a hand in several pioneering pieces of legislation: an automobile insurance bill, a bill outlawing wiretapping, and a bill opening credit files to customers.

Pawley was born on Nov. 21, 1934, in Brampton, Ont. He received an undergraduate degree at the University of Winnipeg and a law degree at the University of Manitoba, and before his entrance into politics he was a practicing lawyer in Selkirk, Man. When he first ran for provincial office in 1958, he was defeated. Two attempts to gain political office in federal elections also ended in failure. However, in 1969 the people of the provincial riding of Selkirk elected him to serve as their representative in the Manitoba legislature.

The government of Edward Schreyer was defeated in the provincial election of 1977, but Pawley retained his seat in the legislature. When Schreyer resigned his post as leader of the Manitoba New Democratic Party to accept the position of governor general of Canada, Pawley succeeded him.

Pérez de Cuéllar, Javier

As his five-year term neared its end late in 1981, Kurt Waldheim, the secretary-general of the United Nations, was seeking reelection. Waldheim, an Austrian, represented an effectively neutral nation in the East-West conflict. He was opposed by Salim A. Salim, foreign minister of Tanzania and a spokesman for the interests of the less developed countries.

In order to win election Waldheim and Salim had to gain the unanimous approval of all five permanent members of the UN Security Council—the United States, the Soviet Union, Great Britain, France, and China. After being chosen by the Security Council, a candidate had to win majority approval from the General Assembly, where every UN member has a vote.

The U.S. opposed Salim's candidacy and vetoed him in the Security Council. China did the same with

Waldheim, and the UN thus appeared to be deadlocked. But on Dec. 11, 1981, in an unexpected move, the Security Council agreed on Javier Pérez de Cuéllar of Peru. Subsequently, he won approval in the General Assembly.

Pérez de Cuéllar's major goal for his term in office was to help achieve independence for Namibia, the territory also known as South West Africa. In 1982 Namibia was controlled by South Africa, a country whose policies of racial separation made it unpopular throughout the world. "I can't forget I come from the third world," Pérez de Cuéllar has said. "I have to give priorities. I've committed myself to solve this problem as soon as possible."

Pérez de Cuéllar was born on Jan. 19, 1920, in Lima, Peru. He joined the foreign ministry in 1940 after graduating from Catholic University in Lima. Since that time he has held numerous diplomatic posts in Europe and Latin America. Before his election as secretary-general, Pérez de Cuéllar had been serving as the UN's special representative to negotiate a Soviet withdrawal from Afghanistan.

Peterson, Roger Tory

More than 30,000 birders hiked through forests and prairies, clambered through thickets, and splashed through swamps in Canada, the U.S., and the Caribbean for the 1982 Audubon Society's Christmas Bird Count. For this important annual wildlife survey, standard equipment included a pair of binoculars and what has become the birdwatcher's bible, Roger Tory Peterson's *A Field Guide to the Birds*. Peterson's *Guide* for the eastern U.S., first published in 1934 and now in its fourth edition (1980), has sold approximately two million copies. The latest edition made the *New York Times* best-seller list, and the first sold out in one week in the midst of the Depression. A companion volume for the western U.S. has sold more than one million copies.

Peterson's stroke of genius in developing the guides was to realize that what the amateur needed was a mentor in the form of a pocket-sized reference work that grouped similar birds and pointed out the distinctive markings of each, the "field marks" that enabled the birder to identify each species at a distance. The 1980 edition, the first in 33 years, was completely redone to incorporate new observations and add new species, including several escapes into the wild by domesticated species. All birds are pictured in colour, with helpful detail drawings of beaks, feet, and heads. Birds are shown in flight as well as at rest. A description of the behaviour, song, and habitat faces the illustration. The phenomenal success of the two guides to the birds has encouraged the issuing of 23 other Peterson *Field Guides*, ranging from mammals and reptiles through minerals and animal tracks.

In 1982, at age 74, Peterson was at work repainting some of the plates for the western *Guide*. He was born on Aug. 28, 1908, in Jamestown, N.Y., and trained at the Art Students League and National Academy of Design in New York City. He has been engaged in painting birds and illustrating and writing bird books since the 1930s, contributing to more than 100 titles as author, illustrator, or editor. In 1981 Peterson reached a milestone in his career: he completed his U.S. life list, the ornithologist's tabulation of sightings of all of the bird species that breed in the U.S. On an April day in the sandhills of northern Texas, Peterson sighted his last bird, the lesser prairie chicken.

Planinc, Milka

Under the system of rotation of offices within the federal government of Yugoslavia, Milka Planinc took office on May 16, 1982, the country's—and Eastern Europe's—first woman head of government. A Croatian, she was appointed by the Federal Assembly to succeed Veselin Djuranovic, a Montenegrin, as president of the Federal Executive Council for a four-year term.

Because of the active role she played in Croatian politics, Premier Planinc had the reputation of being something of an "iron lady." Once in office, she acted to increase the federal government's effectiveness (previously limited by the national governments' decision-making powers) in combating Yugoslavia's mounting economic problems. Among these were an inflation rate of approximately 30%, a per capita foreign indebtedness greater than that of Poland, and an unemployment rate exceeding 13% of the work force. Planinc's measures included the introduction of a greater number of technocrats, particularly economists, into the new government; the raising of the price of gasoline, for the third time in a year, to the highest in Europe; a price freeze

affecting all goods and services apart from privately grown fruit and vegetables for a minimum six-month period beginning in July; and notice to the effect that a wage freeze might also be imposed.

Milka Planinc was born in November 1924 at Drnis, Croatia. She graduated in 1941 from the Senior Administrative School in Zagreb, the Croatian capital. During the same year, she joined the Communist Youth Union of Yugoslavia, and in 1943 she was accepted as a soldier of the Yugoslav Liberation Army. After the war she joined the Yugoslav Communist Party (which in 1952 was renamed the League of Communists). In 1961 Planinc was appointed head of the secretariat for education and culture in Zagreb. Two years later she was named secretary for education and science of the republic of Croatia. She established her political reputation as a loyal supporter of Tito, whom she helped to overcome the outbreak of Croatian nationalism in 1971. A member of the Central Committee of the Croatian branch of the League of Communists since 1959, she became its chairman in 1971 and also a member of the federal Executive Committee.

Podborski, Steve

Seven years of disciplined and concentrated training rewarded Steve Podborski when he became the World Cup downhill ski champion for the 1981–82 season. In the ten-race circuit of the World Cup, scoring is based on five races out of the ten. Podborski garnered three first-place, two second-place, and two fourth-place finishes to end the season with 115 points out of a possible 125. He was the first male North American to capture the World Cup downhill title.

WIDE WORLD

Born on July 25, 1957, Podborski grew up in Don Mills, Ont., a section of Toronto. At the age of two he was introduced to skiing by his parents. His mother, Jackie Podborski, Alpine Ski chairman for southern Ontario and a member of the Canadian Ski Association, was the driving force behind his skiing career. He spent his early years training on a 600-ft (180-m) peak in Ontario, a fact many skiers find hard to believe since the minimum fall in a World Cup downhill course is 3,000 ft (910 m). At the age of 9 Podborski started racing in southern Ontario, and at 13 he competed in the Canadian juvenile championships in British Columbia. In 1974 he went to the fall selection competition of the Canadian national ski team. He won all five downhill races there and made the team.

Podborski's first true win on the World Cup circuit took place in 1981 on the Corviglia downhill course in St. Moritz, Switz. He won the next two races on the circuit, at Garmisch, West Germany, and at Kitzbühl, Austria. He was the first to win three races in a row since world champion Franz Klammer in 1971. At the end of the 1980–81 season Podborski was ranked as the world's premier downhill skier, but he lost the World Cup championship that year by 0.28 sec.

Podborski was a competitor at the 1980 Olympic Games, where he won the bronze medal in downhill skiing. When an accident on the slopes in May 1980 threatened to end his skiing career, he instituted a rigorous training program. Just six months after the surgery on his knee, he was back on the slopes skiing—and winning. In recognition of his achievements the Sports Federation of Canada named him the Canadian male athlete of the year for 1982.

Podhoretz, Norman

Norman Podhoretz, editor in chief since 1960 of *Commentary* magazine, is a neoconservative, a person who relatively recently has been converted to the belief that accommodation with the Soviet Union and other Communist powers is impossible. His views, both past and present, became the subject of controversy in 1982 after he published *Why We Were in Vietnam*, an analysis of U.S. involvement in that war, and "J' Accuse," a defense of Israel and its foreign policy.

In *Why We Were in Vietnam* Podhoretz makes three major points: (1) U.S. entry into the Vietnam war was "an act of imprudent idealism whose moral soundness was overwhelmingly vindicated by the hideous consequences of our defeat"; (2) the effort required to win the war exceeded the "intellectual and moral capabilities" of the U.S. government and its people; and (3) the antiwar movement must accept "a certain measure of responsibility for the horrors that have overtaken the people of Vietnam."

Podhoretz's book provoked a fresh examination of U.S. involvement in Vietnam. Critics accused him of oversimplifying history, confusing the good intentions of American leaders with the evil effects of their deeds, and unreasonably condemning many who opposed the war. (Podhoretz himself had originally opposed the war.)

Podhoretz has become one of the leaders of the neoconservative movement. In the past most Jewish intellectuals in the U.S. were political liberals, and serious Jewish magazines such as *Commentary* reflected a liberal point of view. As U.S. intellectual and political conservatism gained popularity during the 1970s, Podhoretz broke ranks and began to lead *Commentary* rightward.

In "J' Accuse" Podhoretz replied to critics of the Israeli military occupation of Lebanon by arguing that the invasion was a necessity and that Israel was a peace-seeking democracy. He went on to call Israel a tireless enemy of Soviet expansionism, a nation almost uniquely willing among those of the West to make the sacrifices necessary to its survival.

Podhoretz has spent virtually his entire working career at *Commentary*, which is sponsored by the American Jewish Committee. He joined the publication as assistant editor in 1955, left after three years for another publishing job, and then returned to take command in 1960. Born on Jan. 16, 1930, in Brooklyn, N.Y., he obtained bachelor's degrees in 1950 from Columbia University and the Jewish Theological Seminary. He then went to Cambridge University as a Kellett Fellow, where he obtained a B.A. degree in 1952 and an M.A. five years later.

Pritchard, John Michael

A brisk, thoroughgoing musician of wide sympathies, John Pritchard was confirmed in 1982 as principal conductor of the BBC (British Broadcasting Corporation) Symphony Orchestra in succession to Gennadi Rozhdestvensky. It was a safe choice in a time of considerable economic and artistic uncertainty. He had been chief guest conductor of the BBC Symphony since 1979 and chief conductor of the Cologne (West Germany) Opera from 1978.

The son of a distinguished orchestral violinist, Pritchard was born in London on Feb. 5, 1921. He studied piano, viola, and organ under a number of teachers before, in his teens, visiting Italy to study orchestral and operatic rehearsal methods at first hand. Following a spell as conductor of the largely amateur Derby String Orchestra (to which he was appointed in 1943), Pritchard was invited to the Glyndebourne Festival Opera (Sussex, England) in 1947 as a coach. There Fritz Busch, the doyen of Glyndebourne conductors since the house's foundation in 1934, took a keen interest in Pritchard's abilities, infusing him with his own strict concepts of musical excellence. At the same time, Pritchard served as assistant to other major Glyndebourne conductors, among them Rafael Kubelik, Fritz Stiedry, and the veteran Vittorio Gui.

In 1951 the 30-year-old Pritchard found himself in charge of his first full Glyndebourne production, Mozart's *Don Giovanni*. The previous year he had succeeded Reginald Jacques as conductor of the Jacques Orchestra, and in 1952 he substituted, at short notice, for ailing Swiss maestro Ernest Ansermet at the Edinburgh International Festival. Following a spell at Austria's Vienna State Opera, Pritchard in 1955 was appointed principal conductor of the Royal Liverpool Philharmonic Orchestra, a post he held for a number of years. During that time he promoted an especially enterprising "Musica Viva" series of contemporary music programs, in which (under Pritchard's aegis) other young conductors were able to gain wide experience. Also in 1955 he conducted, at London's Royal Opera House, Covent Garden, the premier of Sir Michael Tippett's *The Midsummer Marriage*. Pritchard was made a Commander of the Order of the British Empire in 1962.

Pryor, Richard

In 1980 black comedian Richard Pryor literally caught fire; he accidentally immolated himself while handling a volatile cocaine mixture. In a comic skit concocted after the accident he asks hypothetically what he learned from the experience: "When you're on fire and running down the street, people will get out of your way."

Defusing anxiety with comic common sense is a Pryor trademark: the willingness to look life square in the face and see that it's cross-eyed. As a colleague said, "There is one single reason for his success. Richard tells the truth about the human condition. That's what makes his comedy so wonderful."

Born in Peoria, Ill., on Dec. 1, 1940, Pryor dropped out of school and worked at menial jobs, all the while developing his comic sensibility "on the corner," as he put it. He began working as a comedian in small clubs in Peoria after serving in the Army

and first received national exposure in 1966 with appearances on several television variety shows. He acted in his first film role in 1967 and to date has appeared in more than 25 movies.

Successful on the screen and the nightclub stage, Pryor not only draws grist from his own life but writes all his own material. "Pryor on Fire," his finale at the Hollywood Palladium, was the "reenactment of his incendiary ordeal." The act, according to *Newsweek*'s Jack Kroll, was "a psychodrama at once mirthful and merciless in which he plays everything from himself . . . to the free-base pipe that speaks to Pryor with satanic seductiveness about the ecstacies of getting stoned."

Pryor's movies include vehicles shared with black singer Diana Ross (the Billie Holiday biography *Lady Sings the Blues*) and white comic Gene Wilder (*Silver Streak* and *Stir Crazy*). Other films include *Greased Lightning, The Wiz, Bustin Loose*, and *California Suite*. While a television series was short-lived, in part because of network censorship, he won an Emmy award for a performance with Lily Tomlin. His most famous works are hybridized: concert performances were filmed piecemeal and then edited into one-man movies. Highly unusual in style and content, two have been enormously successful: *Richard Pryor Live in Concert* and *Richard Pryor Live on the Sunset Strip*.

Pym, Francis Leslie

In April 1982, amidst the crisis brought by the Argentine invasion of the Falkland Islands, Francis Pym suddenly found himself appointed British foreign secretary. Lord Carrington, seemingly as firm a fixture as anyone in the U.K. Cabinet, had felt obliged to resign as foreign secretary because of the failure of his department to read Argentine intentions correctly. At a moment when international negotiations would be of crucial importance, Prime Minister Margaret Thatcher turned to Pym. He was not a foreign affairs expert, but for the first two years of the Thatcher government he had been secretary of state for defense. Just as important, perhaps, he understood the Conservative Party better than anyone in the Cabinet, and the party was in angry disarray.

After becoming an MP in 1961, Pym had spent much of his parliamentary career as a "whip" in the administrative office of the party in the House of Commons. As chief whip in the Edward Heath government of 1970–73 and as leader of the Commons since 1981, he was the recognized professional in the business of keeping the party in line. It might be said to run in the family; his father had been a Conservative MP and a whip before him.

Born on Feb. 13, 1922, Pym had the classic Conservative roots in the landed gentry, the traditional education—at Eton College and the University of Cambridge—and a distinguished war record. This was not necessarily the best qualification for the middle-class, aggressive individualism of the

Thatcher wing of the party. In fact, Pym was not in Thatcher's inner ring of confidants and had expressed his doubts about monetarism and the prospects for the economy with some bluntness.

Pym's first mission as foreign secretary, securing a negotiated settlement of the Falklands crisis, failed, but he won the respect and confidence of the diplomatic world by his sharp mind and by a combination of realism and toughness. He had hoped to get the Foreign Office post when the Thatcher government was formed in 1979. After circumstances brought the appointment, he was soon regarded as a great success. Observers of the Westminster scene even began to talk of Pym as the most likely successor to Thatcher as party leader.

Reagan, Nancy

If 1981 was a year of criticism for the wife of U.S. Pres. Ronald Reagan because of her social life and expensive tastes, 1982 was a year of more positive reaction to her work on two social issues—drug abuse among young people, which she believes is related to the breakdown in traditional family life, and the foster grandparents program, which brings together the elderly and handicapped children. In mid-February 1982 Nancy Reagan began her anti-drug campaign by traveling to Florida and Texas, where she visited various facilities to draw attention to the problem. In March she participated in the White House Conference on Drug Use and Families. In support of the foster grandparents program she provided an introduction to a book of case studies entitled *To Love a Child*, published in the fall.

Critics charged that her work on these two issues was intended primarily to draw attention from her public image as a rich man's wife who cared little about the economic problems of ordinary people, an image that arose during her first year in the White House, when she spent some $800,000 to redecorate the living quarters and $200,000 to buy new china. Although these funds came from private contributions, the expenditures were attacked as insensitive in a time of severe recession and federal budget cuts to social welfare programs. The controversy erupted again in 1982 when it was revealed that Mrs. Reagan had accepted free clothes from high-fashion designers, including a $10,000 gown that she wore to the inaugural ball and that was later donated to the Smithsonian Institution.

Nancy Reagan has always said that her first duty is to her family, particularly to her husband, Ronald Reagan. They were married in 1952, when both were actors in Hollywood. Nancy Reagan soon gave up her acting career to become a homemaker. After her husband was elected governor of California in 1966, she became involved in the foster grandparents program and worked to expand it nationwide.

She was born Anne Frances Robbins in New York City. Her official biography gives her birthday as July 6, 1923, though school records state the year as 1921. After her mother's divorce and remarriage she was adopted by her stepfather, a Chicago surgeon, and became Nancy (a nickname from infancy) Davis. She was graduated from Smith College in 1943 and worked as an actress on Broadway and later in motion pictures.

Reagan, Ronald Wilson

The administration of Pres. Ronald Reagan suffered its first significant reversals in 1982. The foreign policy shaped by the president's strenuous anti-Communism led to some badly strained relations with U.S. allies abroad. In June Reagan widened his ban on U.S. sales of pipeline equipment to the Soviet Union to include that produced by foreign subsidiaries and licensees of U.S. companies, arousing strong opposition in Europe. Eventually France, England, and Italy challenged the embargo and told firms in their countries to honour their contracts with the Soviets. The resentment of the European allies was increased when Reagan authorized a one-year extension of the U.S.-Soviet grain accord, prompting charges of American hypocrisy. Opposition to the pipeline sanctions continued to grow until in November Reagan was forced to lift them.

Another consequence of Reagan's anti-Communism was a worsening of relations between the U.S. and the People's Republic of China. Bowing to pressure from American conservatives, the administration announced in April that it would continue limited arms sales to Taiwan, despite sharp protests from the Peking government, which by autumn had decided to resume negotiations with the Soviet Union that had been suspended in 1980, shortly after the Soviet invasion of Afghanistan.

Shuttle diplomacy throughout much of April by Secretary of State Alexander Haig failed to keep Argentina and England from going to war following the Argentine invasion of the Falklands. The Argentines, enthusiastic partners in Reagan's anti-Communist efforts in Central America, felt betrayed by Reagan's eventual support of England in the war, and Argentina's defeat left the country bitterly, if perhaps only temporarily, anti-American.

A casualty of conflict within the administration over foreign policy was Secretary Haig himself, who resigned in June as a result of differences with the president over the pipeline sanctions and U.S. Middle East policy. Reagan named George P. Shultz, a former Cabinet member in the Nixon administration, as Haig's successor.

Administration pressure on Israel—including personal appeals from Reagan to Israeli Prime Minister Menachem Begin—failed to halt Israel's invasion of Lebanon in early June. As the siege of West Beirut continued, relations between the two nations—and the two leaders—suffered. Early in September a Reagan peace plan, urging self-government by the Palestinians of the West Bank in association with Jordan, was rejected by the Israeli Cabinet.

The growing disarmament movement, both abroad and at home, was a continuing problem for Reagan. European fears, already aroused the previous fall by his remarks on the possible use of tactical nuclear weapons there, were not quieted by his statement at a news conference late in March that the Soviet Union had a "definite margin of superiority" over the U.S. in nuclear weapons. The statement was also widely challenged at home, where, despite vigorous criticism by the president, referendums calling for a U.S.-Soviet nuclear-weapons freeze were approved by voters November 2 in eight states and a number of cities.

Even before the November elections, there was evidence of a declining Reagan mandate on domestic issues. Early in September the Senate and House handed the president his first major legislative rebuff by overriding his veto of a major appropriations bill containing what he had charged was "budget-busting" funding for social programs. In December, despite an intense lobbying effort by the administration, the House voted not to begin production of the MX missile, the controversial centrepiece of Reagan's rearmament plan, by a resounding 245–176 margin. In an attempt at compromise, the president agreed that production funds for the missile program would be temporarily frozen to give Congress time to examine various basing plans. But while the final spending bill worked out by a House-Senate conference committee retained $2.5 billion in research and development money for the missile program (to be spent when Congress approved a basing plan), it eliminated the $988 million Reagan had requested for production of the first five MX weapons.

The economy was the predominant issue in the November elections across the country, and widespread dissatisfaction with record high unemployment and Reagan's economic policies resulted in solid gains for the Democrats both in the House and in governorships.

Rossi, Paolo

A major hero of the Italian World Cup soccer triumph in Spain during the summer of 1982, the Juventus (Turin) striker Paolo Rossi was yet another example of the fallen idol returned to his pedestal. Though he strenuously denied any implication, Rossi had been banned for three years by the Italian football authorities in May 1980 for supposed involvement in a football bribery scandal in 1979, a sentence later cut to two years and ending in April 1982. Rossi then so impressed the Italian national team manager, Enzo Bearzot, that he included him in the World Cup team.

Rossi played a crucial part in his country's World Cup triumph by scoring six goals—including three against favoured Brazil and the second of Italy's three goals in the final against West Germany (in which he won his 27th cap). That tally made Rossi top scorer in the finals in Spain and brought him and his family many gifts from a grateful populace, including 1,000 bottles of wine and shoes for his family for life from an Italian shoemaker.

Born in Prato, in the Italian Tyrol, on Sept. 23, 1956, Rossi had a far from easy passage to stardom. He was signed by the Turin club as a teenager, but by the time he reached the age of 18 he had had three cartilages removed from his knees. He went on loan to the lakeside club of Como and made his league debut for them in November 1975, against Perugia. The following season he was sold partly to Vicenza, which later had to sell other star players to buy him outright from Juventus, after an auction. That season, 1976–77, he scored 21 times in 36 games to help Vicenza clinch promotion to the First Division.

Rossi took part in the 1978 World Cup in Argentina, where Italy finished fourth, and played in all games. On his return to Italy he recorded another 15 goals in 28 matches for Vicenza but could not stop their going back to the Second Divison. A year later he was sent on loan to Perugia and scored 13 goals, including both in the 2–2 draw with Avellino, over which result the bribery scandal arose. During his two years in the wilderness Rossi was transferred back to Juventus for a fee of about $5 million. After signing he played in the last three games of 1981–82 to help Turin win its 20th championship.

Schlüter, Poul Holmskov

Poul Schlüter, chairman of Denmark's Conservative Party, took over as his country's prime minister in September 1982 after Anker Jorgensen and his minority Social Democratic government resigned without forcing an election. Schlüter, who had for several months been advocating a broad national coalition as signs of an approaching economic catastrophe became ever more apparent, formed his government with the participation of the Liberal Democrats (Venstre), the Centre Democrats, and the Christian People's Party.

Schlüter replaced Jorgensen after the latter had held office continuously since October 1972 with only one interruption (Poul Hartling's minority Liberal government of December 1973–January 1975). He inherited formidable problems, including soaring balance of payments and budgetary deficits and growing unemployment. Although his appointment was greeted by left-wing demonstrations outside Christiansborg Castle (the Parliament building) and skepticism on the part of the trade unions, Schlüter enjoyed generally good opinion poll ratings; most Danes undoubtedly wished him well.

Schlüter came to office during the half-yearly period for which Denmark assumed the presidency of the Council of Ministers of the European Communities (EC). This in turn coincided with the culmination of intra-Community negotiations over the adoption of a common fisheries policy (CFP). Throughout the negotiations Denmark has been steadfastly opposed to the CFP, and consequently at the Community summit in Copenhagen in December, for which Schlüter served as host, he found himself at odds with the other ministers.

Schlüter was born in 1929 in Tonder, southern Jutland, close to the German border. The son of a wholesaler, he attended the universities of Copenhagen and Århus, graduating with a master's degree in law, and gained his attorney's license. His interest in politics developed early, and at the age of 16 he

chaired the south Jutland Conservative youth organization. He was active in the World Association of Youth and in that connection visited more than 30 countries. In September 1964 he was elected to Parliament, became Conservative Party spokesman in 1971, chaired the party parliamentary group in 1974, and in 1980 became party chairman.

Shultz, George

It came as no surprise to government leaders when U.S. Pres. Ronald Reagan named George Shultz to be secretary of state after the forced resignation of Alexander Haig in the summer of 1982. Shultz had wanted the job when the Reagan administration came to power, but he refused to lobby for it and faced strong opposition from some of Reagan's ultraconservative supporters.

In 1982, however, his nomination to be Haig's replacement sailed through the Senate with no opposition. A former dean of the University of Chicago's Graduate School of Business, Shultz previously had served as secretary of labour, director of the Office of Management and Budget and secretary of the treasury in the administrations of Richard Nixon and Gerald Ford. He had been untouched by the Watergate scandal and was one of the most powerful and popular men in Washington when he left government to become president of Bechtel Corp., an international engineering firm.

Shultz is known as a quiet, soft-spoken team player whose personal style contrasts dramatically with that of the mercurial Haig. Where Haig frequently clashed with the White House and other Cabinet members over questions of policy and jurisdiction, Shultz was willing to compromise for the sake of

UPI

harmony. He also had the advantage of having worked at Bechtel with Secretary of Defense Caspar Weinberger, who had been involved in a running feud with Haig.

In taking over at the State Department, Shultz made the point that policy would not change, since he served the same president. Because of Bechtel's heavy involvement in Middle Eastern development projects and Shultz's personal contacts in Saudi Arabia, he has been careful to appear evenhanded in dealing with Israel and the Arab countries.

Following his visit to Moscow to attend the funeral of Leonid Brezhnev, Shultz warned there would have to be a "change in behaviour" on the part of the Soviet Union before there could be any change in the Reagan administration's tough policies. At the same time, he was instrumental in lifting economic sanctions on the Soviet pipeline in an effort to ease strains with the European allies.

Shultz was born in New York City on Dec. 13, 1920. He received a bachelor's degree from Princeton University and a Ph.D. from MIT.

Singh, Zail

Sworn in as seventh president of the republic of India on July 25, 1982, Zail Singh was the first Sikh to hold that office; he was also a person with a long record of grass-roots politics. His humble origins recalled the phrase "log-cabin to White House." Son of Sardar Kishan Singh, he was born on May 5, 1916, at Sandhwan village in the Faridkot district, in a family of artisans turned small farmers. Originally named Jarnail Singh, when barely 15 he was inspired by the deeds of Bhagat Singh, a revolutionary who was executed by the British in 1931, and became active in the politics of the Akali Dal, a Sikh organization that opposed British rule. Without the benefit of formal education, he pursued traditional studies in Sikh holy books and earned the title of Giani, which means "learned man." In 1938 he established the Praja Mandal (allied to the Indian National Congress) in Faridkot, which was then a princely state. For this act he had to spend four years and ten months in jail. It was about this time that he assumed the name Zail Singh.

In 1946 Zail Singh led a movement to assert the state people's right to hoist the national flag. He even set up a "parallel government" and was arrested again. After India became independent, Faridkot was merged in the Patiala and East Punjab States' Union (PEPSU), which itself was integrated with Punjab in 1956. Zail Singh served as a minister in PEPSU and then in Punjab. He was a member of Rajya Sabha (the upper house of Parliament) from 1956 to 1962. Returning to state politics, he was chief minister of Punjab from 1972 to 1977.

When Indira Gandhi was voted out of power in 1977, Zail Singh stood firmly by her. On her return to office he was named Union home minister, having been elected to Lok Sabha (the lower house of Parliament) from Hoshiarpur. He held the position until

his adoption as Congress candidate for the presidency in 1982. In the election he defeated H. R. Khanna.

Spielberg, Steven

Like the actor who can play Scaramouche and Othello or the musician who can sing plainsong and then conduct Beethoven's Ninth Symphony, Steven Spielberg during the year proved his virtuosity. The filmmaker responsible for *Jaws*, *Close Encounters of the Third Kind*, and *Raiders of the Lost Ark* released two distinctive and impressive box-office smashes back-to-back in 1982. They were *Poltergeist*, a horror film in which malevolent spirits haunt a family by coming and going through a television set, and *E.T. The Extra-Terrestrial*, which spun the space-age fable of a ten-year-old California lad who rescues a creature from a distant planet.

"*E.T.* is my personal resurrection, and *Poltergeist* is my personal nightmare," Spielberg said. *Time* magazine declared that "both succeed beyond anyone's expectations. . . . They re-establish the movie screen as a magic lantern, where science plays tricks on the eye as an artist enters the heart and nervous system with images that bemuse and beguile. . . . Not since the glory days of the Walt Disney Productions—40 years and more ago . . . has a film [*E.T.*] so acutely evoked the twin senses of everyday wonder and otherworldly awe."

Spielberg was born in Cincinnati, Ohio, on Dec. 18, 1947. His father was a computer engineer and his mother a concert pianist, and the family moved frequently from subdivision to subdivision in Ohio, New Jersey, Arizona, and California. "I never mock

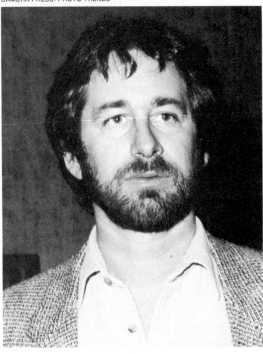

suburbia," Spielberg said. "My life comes from there," as does the context for both of his latest films, which are peopled by suburbanites who encounter the otherworldly right at home.

After two years at California State University in Long Beach, Spielberg wangled an interview with a film studio executive, showed him a short film that he had made, and by the age of 21 had become Hollywood's youngest director with a long-term contract. After directing a number of episodes for television series, he made *The Sugarland Express*, an offbeat tragicomedy with Goldie Hawn. Since then all his features save one (the confused action comedy *1941*) have had remarkable commercial success and received critical acclaim as well.

Stephen, Sir Ninian Martin

Sir Ninian Stephen succeeded Sir Zelman Cowen as governor-general of Australia in July 1982 after a distinguished legal career, climaxed by his appointment as a justice of the High Court of Australia. Australian governors-general had always been in the forefront of political controversy, and Sir Ninian Stephen was no exception. As soon as his appointment was announced, Stephen held a press conference at which he expressed the wish that his term of office be marked, at least as far as the governor-general was concerned, by calm rather than divisiveness. However, most of the reporters wanted to know whether he would follow Sir John Kerr's 1975 example and dismiss an elected government should similar circumstances arise.

Although Stephen could not see this particular piece of history repeating itself, he was prepared to offer a few clues as to his future behaviour. Questioned closely on whether as governor-general he would dissolve both houses of Parliament, he replied that the governor-general "must generally follow the advice of his ministers." He added that he would "seek guidance from my own understanding of the past and the vast resources which now exist, including the great amount of written material on the role of the governor-general."

Stephen's hopes that his appointment be untainted by public controversy were soon dashed. Since Sir John Kerr sacked Gough Whitlam's Australian Labour Party administration, the governor-general had been regarded as fair game for journalists. Stephen was quickly confronted by a press demanding to know why his daughter, then a journalist for the Communist newspaper *Tribune*, had been arrested during Aboriginal land rights demonstrations at the time of the 1982 Commonwealth Games in Brisbane.

Ninian Stephen was born on June 15, 1923, near Oxford in England. After attending schools in Edinburgh, London, and Melbourne, he studied law at the University of Melbourne. During World War II he served in the Australian Army (1941–46). In 1949 he was admitted as barrister and solicitor in the state of Victoria. He was made a queen's counsel in 1966,

was appointed a judge of the Victoria Supreme Court in 1970, and was elevated in 1972 to a justiceship on the Australian High Court bench. He was knighted in 1972.

Suazo Córdova, Roberto

The elections held in Honduras on Nov. 29, 1981, resulted in a clear victory for Roberto Suazo Córdova as president and for his Liberal Party, which gained an absolute majority in the 78-seat National Assembly. The election of a civilian after 17 years of almost continuous military rule (the last civilian president was overthrown in 1972 after only 18 months in office) was greeted with relief both within the country and by other nations, especially the U.S. At his inauguration on Jan. 27, 1982, for a four-year term of office, President Suazo reiterated his campaign promise to carry out "a revolution of work and honesty" and pledged to provide a "government of high public morality."

At the age of 54 Suazo had little experience of government office. His career as a medical doctor was successful (after studying medicine at the University of San Carlos he served in the surgical and maternity wards at Guatemala General Hospital in 1953, followed by 25 years of independent practice in La Paz) and was only on three occasions seriously interrupted by politics. The first was in 1979, when on the death of Modesto Rodas Alvorrado he became general coordinator of the Liberal Party. The second occurred in April 1981, when he was selected as candidate for the Liberal Party at their convention and also became president of the Constituent Assembly. Finally, in the November elections he defeated Ricardo Zúñiga Augustinus, leader of the right-wing National Party.

Suazo was strongly anti-Communist and favoured closer relations with the U.S. But his ambitions, to reactivate the sluggish economy and restore peace, were frustrated on two fronts: in the economic sphere by low foreign credit and commodity prices and politically by increased tension on the country's border with El Salvador and, more recently, Nicaragua. Ultimate power appeared to lie not in the hands of the president but with the hard-line commander in chief of the Army, Gustavo Adolfo Alvarez Martínez. Internal security deteriorated after the president came to power, and it appeared that Suazo would find it difficult to consolidate his position within the country. In December his daughter, also a doctor, was kidnapped by Guatemalan guerrillas and released only after an anti-American statement had been published in Mexican and Central American newspapers.

Sutter, Bruce

In the game that won the 1982 World Series for the St. Louis Cardinals, Bruce Sutter set down the last six batters with dispassionate ease. He did not glare at opposing Milwaukee Brewer hitters from behind his bushy lumberjack beard. He barely acknowl-

edged them. He concerned himself only with the catcher's glove and the split-fingered fastball he throws for virtually every pitch.

He had learned that pitch in 1974 from Freddie Martin, who was his minor-league pitching instructor in the Chicago Cubs organization. Sutter's ordinary fastball and his uninspiring 4.13 earned run average (ERA) had made him consider quitting baseball until Martin taught him to grip the ball between the inside cuticles of his second and third fingers. Only Sutter has been able to master the split-fingered pitch, which does not spin and drops dramatically as it reaches home plate, forcing hitters to beat the ball harmlessly into the ground.

The right-handed relief pitcher, 6 ft 2 in and 190 lb, has been most impressive against the strongest competition. He had two victories and two saves in his only four All-Star game appearances, 1978–81. In his first postseason championship competition Sutter had one victory and one save as the Cardinals defeated Atlanta three games to none in the National League championship series, and he had one win and two saves as they defeated Milwaukee four games to three in the World Series.

Sutter was born Jan. 8, 1953, in Lancaster, Pa. He barged into hitters' nightmares in 1977, his first full major league season, when he had a career-low 1.35 ERA, 31 saves, and a 7–3 won-lost record for a Chicago Cub team that was 81–81. His best season was 1979, when he won the National League's Cy Young award for the pitcher of the year after tying a league record with 37 saves and winning six more games while the Cubs went 80–82. The Cubs traded him to St. Louis after 1980.

Joining a St. Louis team that had recorded just 27 saves altogether in 1980, Sutter supplied 25 in strike-

shortened 1981 and 36 in 1982, when his record was 9–8 for the 92–70 Cardinals. It was the fourth year in a row that Sutter led the National League in saves.

Thatcher, Margaret Hilda

No British prime minister since Winston Churchill in the 1940s enjoyed such massive popular support as Margaret Thatcher did during and after the 1982 Falkland Islands conflict. Her determination to win back the islands by force of arms from the Argentine invaders never faltered. She presented the action as a moral duty and a heroic crusade, and the public for the most part responded to her patriotic appeal. The dominant role she played as war leader was acknowledged by the widely held view that "it was Maggie's war," a judgment that could be taken as critical as well as approving.

Thatcher's leadership improved the reputation of her Conservative government, which was at an exceptionally low ebb at the end of 1981, recording only 25% support in opinion polls. At the time of the Falklands victory the Conservatives' opinion polls rating had risen to 51%, a lead of almost 20 points over the Labour Party. By the end of the year this lead had fallen back somewhat, but it was still enough to suggest that the Thatcher government could win comfortably at the next general election, expected in 1983.

The Falklands dispute was a diversion from Thatcher's primary political objective, to effect a radical shift in the British economy back to private enterprise. She came into office in May 1979 on a program to cut public sector expenditure, to return state-owned enterprise to private ownership wherever possible, to curb the power of the trade unions,

and to squeeze out inflation by monetarist financial policies. She told an exultant party conference in October 1982, "We have done more to roll back the frontiers of Socialism than any other previous government."

Margaret Thatcher, born on Oct. 13, 1925, was the daughter of a successful grocer in the small market town of Grantham. She made her way from the local school to the University of Oxford, where she took a degree in science. Entering Parliament in 1959, she epitomized a new generation of middle-class conservatives who were pushing aside the traditional landed gentry members of the party. She was elected party leader in 1975.

Trottier, Bryan

On a hockey rink Bryan Trottier rarely comes out of the corner without the puck, and he rarely comes out of the play-offs without the Stanley Cup. His durability and dependability have prompted more than one general manager to call him the best player in the National Hockey League, no matter how many records Wayne Gretzky is breaking.

Trottier's New York Islanders won their third consecutive Stanley Cup championship May 16, 1982, by beating Vancouver in four straight games. Trottier was the leading scorer in the play-offs for the second time in three years. He had 29 points on 23 assists and 6 goals to go with his regular-season totals of 79 assists and 50 goals, the most goals in his seven-year NHL career. In an overtime quarterfinal game against the New York Rangers, Trottier won 11 consecutive face-offs in his own zone and scored the winning goal.

"Every facet of the game is important to me," Trottier has said. Beyond being a goal scorer and a passer and a playmaker, he is praised for his defense, his checking, and his face-off skills, ranking in many minds with legendary Gordie Howe as a complete player. Trottier is quiet and businesslike on the rink, appearing to move almost nonchalantly from breakaway spring to body check. Away from the ice his reputation for practical joking makes him the first suspect when a teammate finds his shirt missing or his skate laces tied together.

Trottier was born July 17, 1956, in Val Marie, Sask. A lefthanded shooting centre, he was the NHL's rookie of the year in 1975–76, when he set league rookie records with 63 assists and 95 points. In 1978–79, his second consecutive first-team all-star season, he was the NHL's most valuable player and scoring leader, with 134 points on 47 goals and 87 assists. The next season he was most valuable player in Stanley Cup play as the Islanders won their first championship. His seven-year regular-season averages after 1981–82 were 40 goals, 69 assists, and 109 points.

Trudeau, Pierre Elliott

Pierre Elliott Trudeau, acting on borrowed time during 1982, brought Canada's constitution "home," played world statesman, and recommitted himself energetically to resolving Canada's economic problems. Trudeau teased Canadians throughout the year about his plans to retire. Although in 1979 he had announced his intention to quit, he stayed on to lead the Liberal Party back to power in the election of February 1980 and kindled a national guessing game about how long he would stay. Personal antipathy to the prime minister among Canadians was more evident than at any other time during his 13 years at the job, but Trudeau seemed to relish the environment. He acted with characteristic boldness and confidence, despite opinion polls that showed his party running third behind the Conservatives and New Democrats everywhere in Canada except Quebec.

Queen Elizabeth II proclaimed the Constitution Act at a ceremony in Ottawa on April 17, officially eliminating the last trace of colonial status for Canada. Changes in Canada's constitution had always required ratification by the Parliament of Great Britain until Canada made one last trip to Britain in early 1982 to ask Westminster's approval of a bill permitting constitutional amendments to be made solely by Canada's own Parliament. Trudeau's package, approved by all provinces except Quebec, included both the constitutional amending formula and a hard-won Charter of Rights and Freedoms. As in the United States, the new Canadian constitution proclaims the existence of rights, but it is up to the courts to apply rights in individual civil and criminal cases. This switch from the common law to a constitutional charter had the potential of greatly enhancing the power of the courts in Canada, and

UPI

Trudeau obtained agreement to the charter among the nine provincial premiers only by permitting provincial legislatures to override the charter's provisions in certain circumstances.

A man with unequaled experience among leaders of industrial nations, Trudeau made state visits to Mexico in January and to Yugoslavia in June, cemented Canada's strong traditional and racial ties with France on a trip there in November, and attended the seven-nation economic summit in Versailles during June. Trudeau took along one of his three sons on each state visit and took them all with him for a midsummer holiday tour across Canada in a private railway car. It was a pilgrimage that quickly went sour. For Trudeau's critics the rail trip symbolized Trudeau's private comfort and isolation at a time of high unemployment and economic crisis. At one stop he made an obscene gesture at some peaceful demonstrators. As the trip proceeded, his car was pelted with eggs and tomatoes.

Canada proved in 1982 to be one of the industrial nations hardest hit by recession, and by midyear Trudeau sensed a need to devote himself to solutions. Characteristically, it was an all-out attack. One launching pad was a June 28 budget statement by Finance Minister Allan MacEachen, which reported an alarming escalation of the federal deficit to $19.6 billion from the $10.2 billion predicted only seven months earlier. Strapped on the one hand by the deficit and on the other by 10% inflation and 10% unemployment, the government proposed a so-called six-five solution: an example-setting limit of 6 and 5% in salary increases over the next two years for 500,000 federal public servants. "Six-five" struck a responsive chord across the country, and the government seized on its popularity to pressure provincial governments and the private sector to fall in line.

To signal his rededication to the economy, Trudeau canceled a three-week, six-nation tour of Japan and five other Asian nations in September. He made two extensive shuffles in his Cabinet, changing 18 of 35 portfolios and installing men of action in key economic jobs. He adopted a tone more sympathetic to the business community and to American investors. With a deficit now projected at $23.6 billion, his new minister of finance, Marc Lalonde, reallocated $1 billion for job-creation measures. And Trudeau personally delivered a series of three television statements to Canadians urging them to trust one another and accept sacrifice in the hard times ahead.

Tune, Tommy

His real name is Tommy Tune, he was born to dance, and in 1982 he became one of the hottest names on Broadway. But let him tell it as a *Saturday Review* writer reported in May:

"I was born in Wichita Falls, Texas, 43 years ago. My parents met while dancing, if you can believe it. I started dancing in Houston when I was five years old. It was a class of all boys, 30 minutes tumbling and 30 minutes tap. I was good at tumbling but I

PETER CUNNINGHAM / TIME MAGAZINE

was a speed at tap." The next year all the other boys dropped out, girls enrolled instead, and ballet was offered. "From then on it was all ballet for me. I loved the sensation of flying. I couldn't get over it. Then I started to grow when I was about 12. Before you know it I was six-foot-six. I just looked ridiculous in tights. Right away I knew I'd never make it as the prince in Swan Lake. . . . Anyway, one day the star of our dance studio suggested that I major in drama in high school. 'What's drama?' I asked her. You can't imagine how green I was. 'Well, they put on plays,' she told me. So the first day in high school I signed up to major in drama."

Tune went to *The King and I* and there "for the first time I saw singing and dancing and acting all woven together—color, movement, laughter, tears—laughter and tears at the same time. I couldn't believe it—and that was the place in the road where I turned. From that moment on it had to be musical comedy. And I never turned back."

After graduating from the University of Houston in 1962 Tune headed for New York City. Before nightfall on his first day there he landed a job in the *Irma La Douce* road show chorus. More chorus line jobs followed, and then a major role in 1974 dancing in *Seesaw*. "All my life I'd dreamed of dancing on Broadway, and the first time I did I won a Tony." After that Tune turned to directing. In 1977 *The Club*, his presentation of a satirical Victorian revue with women playing all the male roles, won him an off-Broadway Obie award.

In 1982 *Nine* garnered five major Tony awards,

including one for Tune as best director. Tune was going into rehearsal with Twiggy, the 1960s model, in an adaptation of the film *Funny Face*. "Twiggy and I dance so well together. We have the same bodies, except that I'm a foot taller."

Tutu, the Rt. Rev. Desmond Mpilo

The son of a schoolmaster who taught in South African mission schools later taken over by the state under the "Bantu education" policy, Bishop Desmond Tutu abandoned teaching for preaching early in his career in protest against that system. It was a characteristic gesture. Almost prophetically, he was given the second name Mpilo ("life"), for he was destined to become a vital force in South Africa's racial context—a man loved and hated but always to be reckoned with. When, in August 1982, Columbia University awarded him an honorary degree, he was aptly likened by Columbia's president to Martin Luther King, Jr.

Born on Oct. 7, 1931, at Klerksdorp, Transvaal, of mixed Xhosa and Tswana parentage, Tutu was educated at schools headed by his father. Forced by lack of money to give up the idea of a medical career, he turned to teaching and qualified at the Pretoria Bantu Normal College, gaining a B.A. degree at the same time by private study. He taught for a time but resigned in 1957. In 1961 he was ordained as an Anglican parish priest, and in 1967 he became a theological seminary lecturer in Johannesburg.

His next move was to London, where he obtained an M.A. degree at King's College and ministered for a time in London and Surrey. Back in South Africa,

he worked briefly as student chaplain at Fort Hare and made his first contact with the Black Consciousness movement. Returning to London, he was for three years (1972–75) associate director of theological education funds for the World Council of Churches. His appointment as first black dean of Johannesburg followed, and in 1976 he became Anglican bishop of Lesotho and in 1978 assistant bishop of Johannesburg.

The most stormy chapter of his career lay ahead. Appointed in 1978 as general secretary of the controversial South African Council of Churches, he was brought face to face with the country's basic race and colour problems. As spokesman for an organization radically opposed to apartheid, he was officially cast in the role of "turbulent priest" and agitator. On visits abroad, he did not hesitate to advocate economic pressures on South Africa to hasten change. This led to the withdrawal of his passport in 1981.

Wilson, Bertha

Bertha Wilson once commented that she decided to study law because she lived across the street from the law school. From the time she finished her studies in 1958, she rose steadily until on March 4, 1982, she reached the pinnacle of her profession in Canada, judge of the Supreme Court of Canada. Thus she became the first woman admitted to the select company of nine judges who hold general appellate jurisdiction in civil and criminal cases in Canada and rule on questions of the constitutionality of laws and the powers of Parliament and the provincial legislatures. In making Wilson's appointment Justice Minister Jean Chrétien asserted that she had been appointed not because of her sex but because she was "a very able judge."

Being the first to hold a position was not a new experience for Wilson. In 1975 she became the first woman in Canada named to a provincial supreme court when she was appointed to the Ontario Court of Appeal.

The former Bertha Wenham was born on Sept. 18, 1923, in Kirkcaldy, Fifeshire, Scotland. She earned a master of arts degree from the University of Aberdeen (1944) and a teaching certificate from Aberdeen Training College for Teachers (1945). In 1949 she immigrated to Canada with her husband, an ordained minister. Bertha Wilson entered Dalhousie University law school of Halifax, Nova Scotia, in 1955 and received her degree in 1958. The next year the Wilsons moved to Toronto, and Bertha Wilson became a partner and research director of a large law firm. In 1973 she was appointed a Queen's counsel by the Ontario government.

In 1975 Wilson became a judge. During her seven years on the bench of the Ontario Court of Appeal, she was not afraid to innovate. For her decision in a discrimination case, she was commended by Bora Laskin, chief justice of the Supreme Court of Canada, even though he had to disagree with her decision

UPI

and overturn it. With her expansive view of the law it was thought that she would be a liberal interpreter of the law in her judgments on legal rights and discrimination cases.

Outside the courtroom Wilson was active in the Canadian Bar Association, becoming in 1970 the first woman elected to the national council of that organization. Always interested in religious affairs, she was a member of the board of trustees of the Toronto School of Theology.

Woodward, Sir John

The man chosen to command the British task force that recovered the Falkland Islands was a 49-year-old rear admiral who was then unknown to the public and even to the Cabinet ministers who had set the Falklands operation in motion. Rear Adm. "Sandy" Woodward put to sea on April 5 from Gibraltar, without time to return to London for consultations. Less than three months later Woodward's task force had secured the surrender of the Argentine forces on the Falklands in one of the most daring operations ever undertaken by the British Navy. In Woodward's judgment, adapting a phrase used by Wellington after the Battle of Waterloo, it was a very close run thing. On his return to England he was knighted by Queen Elizabeth.

As it turned out, Woodward was well prepared for the job, with a wide range of experience in different branches of the Navy, though he was too young to have seen action in World War II. Born May 1, 1932, at Marazion, Cornwall, he had fixed his ambitions on the Navy from the time he went, as a small boy, to a preparatory school that had turned out 97 admirals. By the age of 15 he was at Britannia Royal Naval College, Dartmouth, the traditional route to a commission in the Navy. As a young officer he served in submarines, including Britain's first nuclear submarine, and in destroyers. In his 40s he was spotted as a man with a future and was brought into the Ministry of Defence as director of naval plans. He was promoted to rear admiral in July 1981.

Reflecting on the abrupt turn of events that had projected him to the centre of world attention, he said in an interview given as his fleet neared the Falklands, "I am very astonished to find myself in this position. . . . I have been a virtual civil servant for the past three years, commuting into London every day. I do not see myself as a hawk-eyed, sharp-nosed, hard military man leading a battle fleet into the annals of history." In fact he had to make hard decisions, to risk ships and suffer losses in a battle fought almost 8,000 mi (13,000 km) from home bases, without adequate early warning radar systems, with insufficient air cover, and with uncertain supply lines. If the operation was to succeed, it had to succeed quickly. It did.

Worthy, James

Less than eight minutes into the final game of the 1982 Atlantic Coast Conference basketball tournament, James Worthy had 14 points for the University of North Carolina. He was perfect from the field on seven shots. He had a steal and an assist. He had set a pattern not only for the game, which North Carolina won 47–45 against Virginia, but for the entire tournament season, which culminated March 29 with North Carolina's becoming the 1982 national champion of college basketball.

In the championship game Worthy led both teams

with 13-for-17 shooting as North Carolina defeated Georgetown 63–62, but perhaps more significant was his game-saving catch of Georgetown's errant pass in the waning seconds. It was not a spectacular play; he simply was in the right place. Throughout his three college seasons Worthy's value was never so much bellowed by boxcar statistics as it was whispered by the nuances that made him appear to have stepped out of a basketball textbook. Although his close-cropped hair and beard gave Worthy the look of an intimidator, the 6-ft 8-in, 219-lb forward was more consistent than flamboyant, distinguished by grace, fluidity, and economy of motion.

His numbers were impressive enough. He averaged 15.6 points, 6.3 rebounds, and 2.4 assists per game as a junior in the 1981–82 season, and his sophomore averages were 14.2, 8.4, and 2.8 despite playing with a six-inch rod in the ankle he had broken midway through his freshman season. But basketball success at North Carolina is measured by won-lost records, and the Tar Heels were 71–13 with Worthy in the lineup, 32–2 in 1981–82.

The national spotlight did not chase Worthy from the cloak of privacy he had worn since his birth in Gastonia, N.C., on Feb. 27, 1961. He remained reserved, forgoing the traditional press conference of the National Basketball Association's first draft choice when the Los Angeles Lakers selected him for that honour on June 29, 1982. In the fall of 1982 he returned to campus to stay on schedule for his graduation in the summer of 1983.

Wozniak, Stephen

"I've got enough money to sit back in the pool and watch it all go by," a young "Midas" said; then he added in his generation's idiom, "but I want to be in life." Thus, if Stephen Wozniak got a "black eye" staging a three-day rock concert that lost $3 million,

the computer wizard did not blink. What counted in his book, apparently, was the idea of rallying young America around a slogan that echoed John F. Kennedy to older folks' ears. Don't ask "What's in it for me?" Instead Wozniak wanted youth to inquire "What's in it for us?"

Toward that end he founded Unuson (for "Unite Us in Song"), a commercial operation that presented the "Us Festival" and attracted 200,000 people to San Bernardino, Calif. Tickets sold for $37.50 and lemonade for $2, while the pamphlets outlining Wozniakian philosophy were free. When the gate receipts were counted and the books balanced, the event seemed seriously in the red—though sales of records and movie rights were expected to bring additional revenue. If not, Wozniak could still theoretically afford to stage 20 more such shows before feeling any financial pinch. The reason for this is that computers had already made Wozniak, a native Californian born in 1950, very rich.

Six years earlier Wozniak had little more to his public credit than a hand in the "blue box"—a famous or infamous device, the size of a cigarette pack, that enabled telephonic bootleggers to plug into long-distance systems and chat with friends for free around the world, to the Bell system's anger and despair. Wozniak had made the boxes in concert with Steven Jobs, and underground celebrity followed. Then the partners scraped together $1,300, appropriated the garage of Jobs's parents, and built a prototype computer: the Apple. No bigger than a typewriter, it was packed with surprisingly simple electronics and designed for use by nontechnicians. Apple Computers soon found half a million customers, and the company, still run by the two founders, does business amounting to approximately $335 million a year. Wozniak's personal worth amounted to $60 million.

OUR FAMILY RECORD

1983

THIS SPACE FOR FAMILY GROUP PHOTO

WHAT WE DID

AND

HOW WE LOOKED

*Each year important events highlight the life of every
family. Year after year these events may be noted
in the Family Record pages of your Compton Yearbooks.
You will then have a permanent record of your family's
significant achievements, celebrations, and activities.*

OUR FAMILY TREE

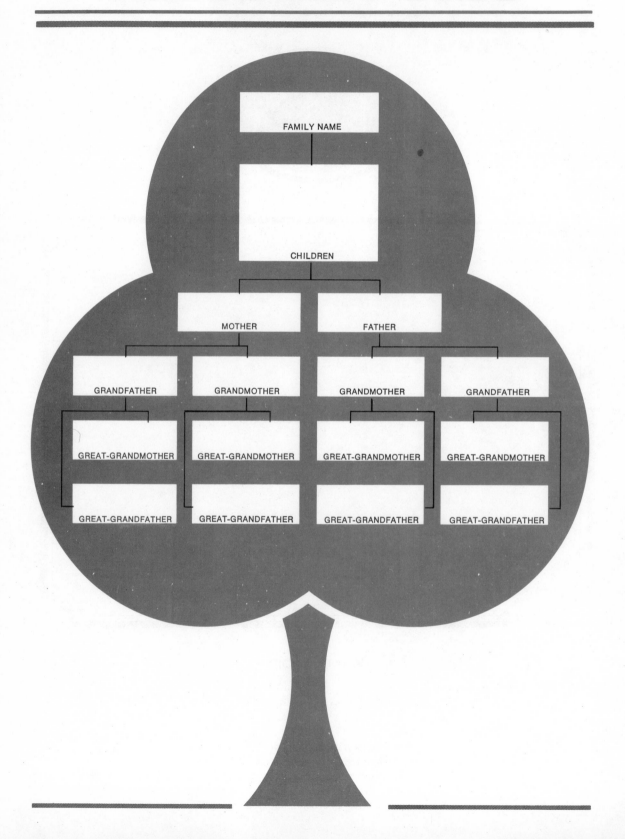

DATES TO REMEMBER

JANUARY

_____
_____
_____
_____
_____
_____

FEBRUARY

_____
_____
_____
_____
_____
_____

MARCH

_____
_____
_____
_____
_____
_____

APRIL

_____
_____
_____
_____
_____
_____

MAY

_____
_____
_____
_____
_____
_____

JUNE

_____
_____
_____
_____
_____
_____

JULY

_____
_____
_____
_____
_____
_____

AUGUST

_____
_____
_____
_____
_____
_____

SEPTEMBER

_____
_____
_____
_____
_____
_____

OCTOBER

_____
_____
_____
_____
_____

NOVEMBER

_____
_____
_____
_____
_____

DECEMBER

_____
_____
_____
_____
_____

Birthdays, weddings, anniversaries, graduations, gifts sent

FAMILY CELEBRATIONS

BIRTHDAYS

NAME

DATE

NAME

DATE

NAME

DATE

NAME

DATE

NAME

DATE

WEDDINGS

NAMES

DATE

NAMES

DATE

NAMES

DATE

NAMES

DATE

NAMES

DATE

ANNIVERSARIES

NAMES

DATE

NAMES

DATE

NAMES

DATE

BIRTHS

NAME

DATE

PARENTS

NAME

DATE

PARENTS

NAME

DATE

PARENTS

PROMOTIONS

NAME

FIRM

TITLE

DATE

NAME

FIRM

TITLE

DATE

HOLIDAYS

OCCASION

OCCASION

OCCASION

SPIRITUAL MILESTONES

NAME _____

MILESTONE _____

_____

_____

NAME _____

MILESTONE _____

_____

NAME _____

MILESTONE _____

_____

NAME _____

MILESTONE _____

_____

NAME _____

MILESTONE _____

_____

_____

OTHER EVENTS

_____

_____

_____

_____

_____

_____

_____

_____

PASTE PHOTO HERE

PASTE PHOTO HERE

PASTE PHOTO HERE

VACATION

WHEN AND WHERE WE WENT

_____
_____
_____
_____
_____
_____
_____
_____
_____
_____
_____
_____
_____
_____
_____
_____
_____
_____
_____
_____
_____
_____
_____
_____
_____
_____
_____
_____

WHAT WE DID

_____
_____
_____
_____
_____
_____
_____
_____
_____
_____
_____
_____
_____
_____
_____
_____
_____
_____
_____
_____
_____

FAVORITE SIGHTS

_____
_____
_____
_____
_____
_____
_____
_____
_____
_____
_____
_____
_____
_____
_____
_____
_____
_____
_____
_____
_____
_____
_____
_____
_____
_____
_____
_____

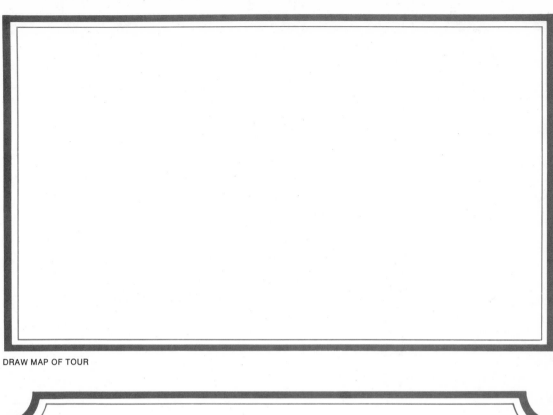

DRAW MAP OF TOUR

PASTE PICTURE HERE

SCHOOL ACTIVITIES

NAME _____

SCHOOL _____

GRADE _____

NAME _____

SCHOOL _____

GRADE _____

NAME _____

SCHOOL _____

GRADE _____

NAME _____

SCHOOL _____

GRADE _____

SCHOOL PARTIES

DATE _____

OCCASION _____

_____

DATE _____

OCCASION _____

_____

DATE _____

OCCASION _____

_____

DATE _____

OCCASION _____

_____

DATE _____

OCCASION _____

_____

DATE _____

OCCASION _____

_____

DATE _____

OCCASION _____

_____

DATE _____

OCCASION _____

_____

SPORTS

NAME _____

SPORT _____

ACHIEVEMENT _____

NAME _____

SPORT _____

ACHIEVEMENT _____

NAME _____

SPORT _____

ACHIEVEMENT _____

NAME _____

SPORT _____

ACHIEVEMENT _____

NAME _____

SPORT _____

ACHIEVEMENT _____

NAME _____

SPORT _____

ACHIEVEMENT _____

NAME _____

SPORT _____

ACHIEVEMENT _____

NAME _____

SPORT _____

ACHIEVEMENT _____

CLUB ACTIVITIES

NAME _____

CLUB _____

ACHIEVEMENT _____

NAME _____

CLUB _____

ACHIEVEMENT _____

NAME _____

CLUB _____

ACHIEVEMENT _____

NAME _____

CLUB _____

ACHIEVEMENT _____

NAME _____

CLUB _____

ACHIEVEMENT _____

NAME _____

CLUB _____

ACHIEVEMENT _____

NAME _____

CLUB _____

ACHIEVEMENT _____

NAME _____

CLUB _____

ACHIEVEMENT _____

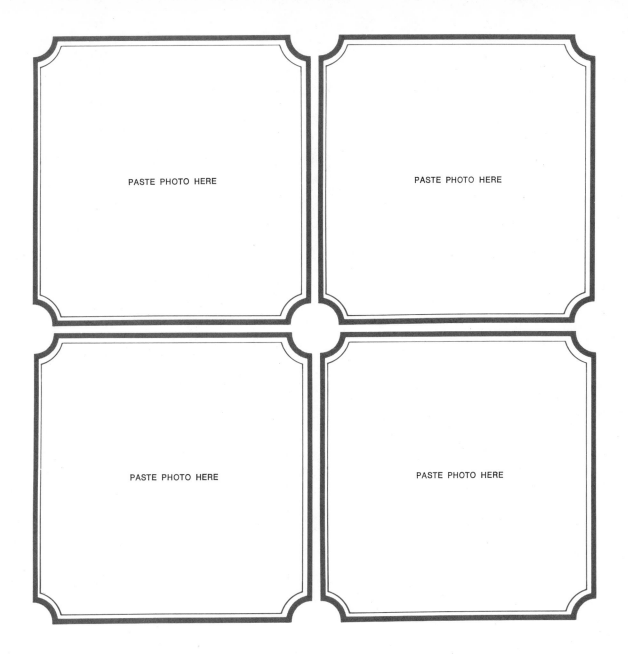

AWARDS, HONORS, AND PRIZES

NAME _____

GRADE _____

HONOR _____

NAME _____

GRADE _____

HONOR _____

NAME _____

GRADE _____

HONOR _____

NAME _____

GRADE _____

HONOR _____

NAME _____

GRADE _____

HONOR _____

NAME _____

GRADE _____

HONOR _____

GRADUATIONS

NAME _____

SCHOOL _____

NAME _____

SCHOOL _____

NAME _____

SCHOOL _____

NAME _____

SCHOOL _____

_____

PETS

NAME AND BREED

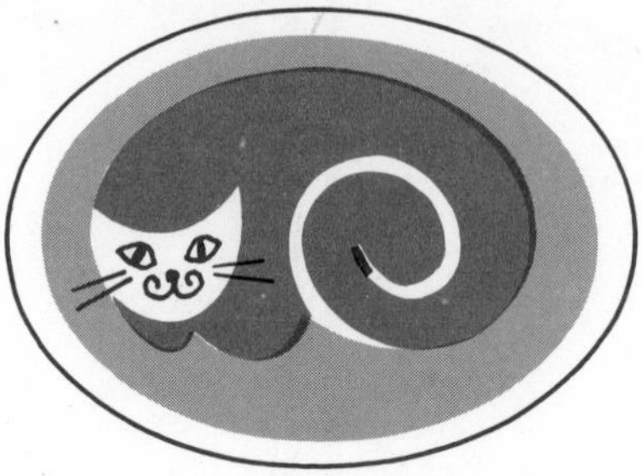

VET'S RECORD

BEHAVIOR AND TRAINING

PASTE PHOTO HERE

LEISURE HOURS

FAVORITE MOVIES

_____
_____
_____
_____
_____
_____
_____
_____
_____
_____
_____
_____

FAVORITE BOOKS

_____
_____
_____
_____
_____
_____
_____
_____
_____
_____

FAVORITE TELEVISION PROGRAMS

_____
_____
_____
_____
_____
_____
_____
_____
_____
_____

FAVORITE RECORDS

_____
_____
_____
_____
_____
_____
_____
_____
_____
_____
_____
_____

_____
_____
_____
_____
_____
_____
_____
_____
_____
_____

HOBBIES

_____
_____
_____
_____
_____
_____
_____
_____
_____
_____

OUR HEALTH RECORD

RECORD OF HEIGHT

FEET   DATE   NAME

6
5
4
3
2
1

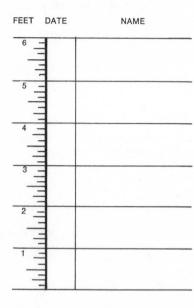

Check Height on
This Scale.
Write Name and
Date Opposite It.

RECORD OF WEIGHT

POUNDS DATE   NAME

225
200
175
150
125
100
75
50
25

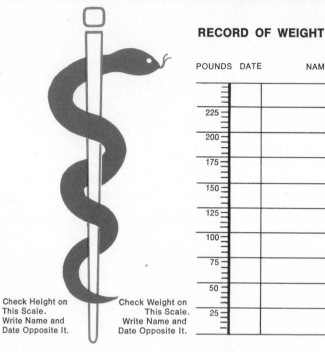

Check Weight on
This Scale.
Write Name and
Date Opposite It.

DOCTORS' NAMES

NAME _____

ADDRESS _____

_____

TELEPHONE NUMBER _____

NAME _____

ADDRESS _____

_____

TELEPHONE NUMBER _____

DENTISTS' NAMES

NAME _____

ADDRESS _____

_____

TELEPHONE NUMBER _____

NAME _____

ADDRESS _____

_____

TELEPHONE NUMBER _____

VISITS

NAME _____

DATE _____

ILLNESS _____

NAME _____

DATE _____

ILLNESS _____

NAME _____

DATE _____

ILLNESS _____

NAME _____

DATE _____

ILLNESS _____

NAME _____

DATE _____

ILLNESS _____

INOCULATIONS

NAME _____

DATE _____

TYPE _____

_____

NAME _____

DATE _____

TYPE _____

_____

OPERATIONS

NAME _____

DATE _____

TYPE _____

_____

NAME _____

DATE _____

TYPE _____

_____

calendar for 1983

JAN

Sat.	1	New Year's Day. Japanese New Year 2643. Circumcision of Christ. St. Basil's Day. Cotton Bowl, Mummers Day, and Tournament of Roses parades, World Communications Year and Year of the Bible begin.
Sun.	2	Earth at perihelion.
Mon.	3	98th Congress assembles.
Tues.	4	Trivia Day.
Thurs.	6	Epiphany, or Twelfth Day. Carl Sandburg's birthday, 1878.
Fri.	7	Munich Fasching Carnival begins, West Germany.
Fri.	14	Julian New Year 6696.
Sat.	15	Martin Luther King, Jr.'s birthday, 1929.
Sun.	16	World Religion Day. Jaycee, Printing, and Worldwide Kiwanis weeks begin.
Thurs.	20	Aquarius begins.
Sun.	23	National Handwriting Day.
Tues.	25	Robert Burns's birthday, 1759.
Wed.	26	Australia Day.
Thurs.	27	Mozart's birthday, 1756.
Sun.	30	Super Bowl XVII.

FEB

Tues.	1	National Freedom Day. American Heart, American History, and International Friendship months begin.
Wed.	2	Candlemas Day. Groundhog Day.
Sun.	6	Mid-Winter's Day. Ronald Reagan's birthday, 1911.
Tues.	8	Anniversary of founding of Boy Scouts of America, 1910.
Fri.	11	Thomas Edison's birthday, 1847. Empire Day, Founding of the Nation, Japan, 660 BC.
Sat.	12	Carnival begins, Brazil. National Inventors Day. Abraham Lincoln's birthday, 1809.
Sun.	13	Chinese New Year 4681, Year of the Pig.
Mon.	14	St. Valentine's Day.
Tues.	15	Mardi Gras.
Wed.	16	Ash Wednesday—Lent begins.
Sat.	19	Pisces begins.
Sun.	20	Brotherhood and International Friendship weeks begin.
Tues.	22	George Washington's birthday, 1732.
Sun.	27	Purim.

MARCH

Tues.	1	National Nutrition, Red Cross, and Youth Art months begin. Water-Drawing Festival begins, Japan.
Fri.	4	World Day of Prayer.
Sun.	6	American Camping, Girl Scout, and Save Your Vision weeks begin.
Tues.	8	International (Working) Women's Day.
Thurs.	10	Harriet Tubman Day.
Fri.	11	Johnny Appleseed Day.
Sat.	12	Rattlesnake Roundup, Claxton, Ga.
Mon.	14	Albert Einstein's birthday, 1879.
Tues.	15	Ides of March. Buzzards return to Hinckley, Ohio.
Wed.	16	Black Press Day.
Thurs.	17	St. Patrick's Day.
Sat.	19	Swallows return to Capistrano, Calif.
Sun.	20	Art and National Wildlife weeks begin. Spring begins.
Mon.	21	National Agriculture Day. Aries begins.
Fri.	25	Feast of Annunciation.
Sun.	27	Palm Sunday.
Tues.	29	Pesach, or first day of Passover.

APRIL

Fri.	1	April Fools' Day. Good Friday.
Sat.	2	Festival '83 begins, Interlochen, Mich. International Children's Book Day.
Sun.	3	Easter. Medic Alert Week begins.
Mon.	4	White House Easter Egg Roll.
Sat.	9	National POW-MIA Recognition Day.
Sun.	10	Lefty Awareness and Pan American weeks begin.
Wed.	13	Thomas Jefferson's birthday, 1743.
Fri.	15	Anniversary of the sinking of the "Titanic," 1912.
Sun.	17	Bike Safety, Jewish Heritage, Keep America Beautiful, National Coin, and National Library weeks begin.
Mon.	18	Boston Marathon. Patriot's Day.
Wed.	20	Taurus begins.
Fri.	22	Arbor Day. Earth Day.
Sat.	23	William Shakespeare's birthday, 1564.
Sun.	24	Daylight Savings Time begins. Grange and National YWCA weeks begin.
Mon.	25	Fast Day, New Hampshire. Save the Children Week begins.
Sat.	30	Walpurgis Night.

MAY

Sun.	1	May Day. Be Kind to Animals, National Goodwill, and National Music weeks begin.
Fri.	6	Nurses' Day. Rudolph Valentino's birthday, 1895.
Sat.	7	Kentucky Derby.
Sun.	8	Mother's Day. VE Day. World Red Cross Day.
Mon.	9	National Salvation Army Week begins.
Tues.	10	National Historic Preservation Week begins.
Thurs.	12	Ascension Day.
Sat.	14	Native American Day. National Windmill Day, The Netherlands.
Wed.	18	Shavuot, or Feast of Weeks.
Sat.	21	Armed Forces Day. Preakness Stakes. Gemini begins.
Sun.	22	Whitsunday, or Pentecost.
Tues.	24	Centennial of building of the Brooklyn Bridge.
Thus.	26	Stratford Festival begins, Canada.
Sun.	29	Trinity Sunday.
Mon.	30	Memorial Day.

JUNE

Wed.	1	June Dairy and National Adopt-a-Cat months begin.
Thurs.	2	Corpus Christi.
Sun.	5	World Environment Day. America the Beautiful Week begins.
Fri.	10	Total eclipse of the Sun.
Sat.	11	Belmont Stakes.
Sun.	12	National Flag Week begins. Ramadan begins.
Mon.	13	National Little League Baseball Week begins.
Tues.	14	Flag Day. Birthday of Univac, 1951. Royal Ascot races begin, England.
Wed.	15	Magna Carta Day.
Fri.	17	World Sauntering Day.
Sat.	18	National Hollerin' Contest, Spivey's Corner, N.C.
Sun.	19	Father's Day.
Tues.	21	Summer begins.
Wed.	22	Cancer begins.
Thurs.	23	Midsummer Eve.
Sun.	26	American Music Festival begins, Philadelphia.

JULY

Fri.	1	Dominion Day, Canada. Anniversary of first U.S. postage stamps, 1847. National Hot Dog and National Peach months begin.
Sun.	3	Dog Days begin.
Mon.	4	Caricom Day. Independence Day. Boy Scouts of America World Scout Jamboree begins.
Wed.	6	Earth at aphelion.
Tues.	12	International Summer Special Olympics Games begin, Baton Rouge, La.
Thus.	14	Bastille Day, France.
Sat.	16	Atomic Bomb Day. Flower Day.
Sun.	17	Captive Nations Week begins.
Wed.	20	Moon Day. Edmonton Klondike Days, Alberta.
Sat.	23	World Frisbee Disc Championships, Pasadena, Calif. Leo begins.
Sun.	24	Pioneer Day.
Mon.	25	World Congress of Esperanto begins, Budapest, Hung.
Fri.	29	Lumberjack World Championships, Hayward, Wis.

AUG

Mon.	1	Francis Scott Key's birthday, 1799.
Thurs.	4	Coast Guard Day.
Sat.	6	Hiroshima Day. Peace Festival, Japan.
Sun.	7	American Family Day.
Mon.	8	All-American Soap Box Derby, Akron, Ohio.
Tues.	9	Ghosts Month begins, Taiwan.
Thurs.	11	Intertribal Indian Ceremonial, Gallup, N.M.
Sun.	14	Atlantic Charter Day. Victory Day. Pan American Games begin, Caracas, Venezuela.
Mon.	15	Anniversary of completion of transcontinental U.S. railway, 1870.
Wed.	17	Anniversary of Klondike Gold Discovery, 1896.
Fri.	19	National Aviation Day.
Sun.	21	Edinburgh International Festival begins, Scotland.
Tues.	23	Virgo begins.
Wed.	24	Saint Bartholomew's Day Massacre, 1572. Vesuvius Day.
Fri.	26	Susan B. Anthony Day. Women's Equality Day.

SEPT

Thurs.	1	Black Reading, National Sight-Saving, and Read a New Book months begin.
Sat.	3	Anniversary of declaration of World War II, 1939. Royal Highland Gathering, Scotland.
Mon.	5	Labor Day. Mackinac Bridge Walk.
Thurs.	8	International Literacy Day. Rosh Hashanah, or Jewish New Year.
Fri.	9	United Tribes International Pow Wow, Bismarck, N.D.
Sun.	11	National Grandparents Day. National Hispanic Heritage Week begins.
Fri.	16	Mayflower Day.
Sat.	17	Citizenship Day. Yom Kippur, or Day of Atonement. Constitution Week begins.
Sun.	18	National Farm Safety and National Rehabilitation weeks begin.
Tues.	20	International Day of Peace.
Thurs.	22	Sukkoth, or Feast of Tabernacles.
Fri.	23	Autumn begins. Checkers Day. Libra begins.
Sat.	24	National Hunting and Fishing Day.
Sun.	25	American Newspaper Week begins.

OCT

Sat.	1	World Vegetarian Day. National Higher Education Week begins.
Sun.	2	National Employ the Handicapped and National 4-H weeks begin.
Mon.	3	Universal Children's Day. National Spinning and Weaving Week begins.
Tues.	4	Anniversary of Sputnik, 1957.
Sat.	8	Muslim New Year 1404.
Sun.	9	Leif Erikson Day. Fire Prevention Week begins.
Mon.	10	Columbus Day. Thanksgiving Day, Canada. International Letter Writing Week begins.
Tues.	11	Baseball's World Series begins.
Sat.	15	Sweetest Day. White Cane Safety Day.
Sun.	16	Dictionary Day. National Shut-In Day.
Sun.	23	Mother-in-Law's Day.
Mon.	24	United Nations Day. Disarmament Week begins. Scorpio begins.
Thus.	27	Anniversary of Cuban Missile Crisis, 1962.
Sun.	30	Return to Standard Time.
Mon.	31	Halloween. National Magic Day. National UNICEF Day.

NOV

Tues.	1	All Saints Day. Aviation History, Good Nutrition, and National Stamp Collecting months begin.
Wed.	2	All-Souls Day.
Fri.	4	World Community Day.
Sat.	5	Guy Fawkes Day. Sadie Hawkins Day.
Sun.	6	French Conversation and National Split Pea Soup weeks begin.
Tues.	8	General Election Day.
Thurs.	10	500th anniversary of Martin Luther's birth. Jewish Book Month begins.
Fri.	11	Veterans, or Armistice, Day.
Mon.	14	National Children's Book Week begins.
Tues.	15	American Enterprise Day.
Fri.	18	Mickey Mouse's birthday, 1928. National Farm-City Week begins.
Sun.	20	Adoption, Latin America, National Bible, and National Family weeks begin.
Tues.	22	Sagittarius begins.
Thurs.	24	Thanksgiving Day.
Sat.	26	Sojourner Truth Day.
Sun.	27	First Sunday in Advent.

DEC

Thurs.	1	Hanukkah begins. Rosa Parks Day.
Mon.	5	Anniversary of Prohibition's repeal, 1933.
Tues.	6	St. Nicholas's Day.
Wed.	7	Pearl Harbor Day.
Sun.	11	Anniversary of UNICEF, 1946.
Tues.	13	Santa Lucia Day, Sweden.
Thurs.	15	Bill of Rights Day. Halcyon Days begin.
Fri.	16	Ludwig van Beethoven's birthday, 1770. Anniversary of Boston Tea Party, 1773.
Sat.	17	Prophet Muhammad's birthday. Pan American Aviation Day. Saturnalia.
Mon.	19	Audubon Christmas Bird Count begins. Penumbral eclipse of the Moon.
Thurs.	22	Capricorn begins.
Sat.	24	Christmas Eve.
Sun.	25	Christmas Day. Isaac Newton's birthday, 1642.
Mon.	26	Boxing Day, Canada. Kwanza.
Wed.	28	Childermas, or Holy Innocents Day.
Sat.	31	New Year's Eve.

Contributors and Consultants

These authorities either wrote the articles listed or supplied information and data that were used in writing them.

Stener Aarsdal, Economic and Political Journalist, *Børsen,* Copenhagen, *Denmark; Biographies* (in part)

Nancy Adams, Reporter, *Chicago Tribune,* and Contributing Editor, *Metropolitan Home* magazine, *Interior Design*

Joseph C. Agrella, Correspondent, *Blood-Horse* magazine; former Turf Editor, *Chicago Sun-Times, Horse Racing* (in part)

Leslie C. Aiello, Lecturer, Department of Anthropology, University College, London, *Anthropology*

J. A. Allan, Senior Lecturer in Geography, School of Oriental and African Studies, University of London, *Libya*

Rex Alston, Broadcaster and Journalist, retired BBC Commentator, *Biographies* (in part)

Peter J. Anderson, Assistant Director, Institute of Polar Studies, Ohio State University, Columbus, *Arctic and Antarctic* (in part)

Johannes Apel, Formerly Curator, Botanic Garden, University of Hamburg, *Zoos and Botanical Gardens* (in part)

John J. Archibald, Feature Writer, *St. Louis Post-Dispatch, Bowling* (in part)

Mavis Arnold, Free-lance Journalist, Dublin, *Ireland*

Ines T. Baptist, Administrative Assistant, Encyclopædia Britannica, Yearbooks, *Belize*

Penelope Barnes, Administrative Assistant, Marketing and Communications, YMCA, Chicago, *Youth Organizations* (in part)

Paul A. Barrett, Managing Editor, *TV World* magazine, *Television and Radio* (in part)

Howard Bass, Journalist and Broadcaster, *Ice Skating; Skiing*

David Bayliss, Chief Transport Planner, Greater London Council, *Transportation* (in part)

John V. Beall, Sales Manager, Davy McKee Corp., *Mines and Mining*

David C. Beckwith, National Economic Correspondent, *Time* magazine, *Elections SPECIAL REPORT: PAC's—The New Force in Politics; State Governments*

John N. Berry III, Editor-in-Chief, *Library Journal, Libraries SPECIAL REPORT: The "New" Censors*

Lucy Blackburn, Economist, Group Economics Department, Lloyds Bank Ltd., London, *Biographies* (in part); *Chile; Costa Rica; El Salvador; Guatemala; Honduras*

Marcia A. Blumenthal, Senior Editor, Computer Industry, *Computerworld* newspaper, *Computers*

William C. Boddy, Editor, *Motor Sport,* Full Member, Guild of Motoring Writers, *Auto Racing* (in part)

Dick Boonstra, Assistant Professor, Department of Political Science, Free University, Amsterdam, *Biographies* (in part); *The Netherlands*

Joan N. Bothell, Free-lance Writer and Editor, *Biographies* (in part)

Russell Bowden, Deputy Secretary-General, The Library Association (U.K.), *Libraries* (in part)

Ben Box, Free-lance Writer and Researcher, *Argentina; Biographies* (in part); *Colombia*

Roger Boye, Coin Columnist, *Chicago Tribune, Stamps and Coins* (in part)

Arnold C. Brackman, Asian Affairs Specialist, *Indonesia*

Henry S. Bradsher, Foreign Affairs Writer, *Philippines*

Robert J. Braidwood, Professor Emeritus of Old World Prehistory, the Oriental Institute, University of Chicago, *Archaeology* (in part)

Rutlage J. Brazee, Geophysical Consultant, *Earth Sciences*

Kenneth Brecher, Professor of Astronomy and Physics, Boston University, *Astronomy*

Hal Bruno, Director of Political Coverage, ABC News, Washington, D.C., *Biographies* (in part)

Joel L. Burdin, Professor of Educational Administration, Ohio University, *Education* (in part)

Ardath W. Burks, Emeritus Professor of Asian Studies, Rutgers University, New Brunswick, N.J., *Japan*

Frank Butler, Former Sports Editor, *News of the World,* London, *Boxing*

Sarah Cameron, Economist, Group Economics Department, Lloyds Bank Ltd., London, *Dominican Republic; Ecuador; Peru; Venezuela*

Roger Caras, Lecturer, Animal Biology, School of Veterinary Medicine, University of Pennsylvania, Special Animal Correspondent, ABC News, *Pets*

Marybeth Carlson, Environmental Writer and Editor, *Animals and Wildlife; Environment*

Elsie J. Carper, Program Analyst, 4-H, *Youth Organizations* (in part)

Victor M. Cassidy, Senior Editor, *Specifying Engineer* magazine, *Biographies* (in part)

Peter B. Cawley, Business Writer, Senior Editor, *The Boston Business Journal, Business and Industry; Financial Institutions; Housing; Insurance; World Trade*

Charles M. Cegielski, Associate Editor, Encyclopædia Britannica, Yearbooks, *Biology* (in part)

Kenneth F. Chapman, Former Editor, *Stamp Collecting* and *Philatelic Magazine,* Philatelic Correspondent, *The Times,* London, *Stamps and Coins* (in part)

Robin Chapman, Senior Economist, Group Economics Department, Lloyds Bank Ltd., London, *Brazil; Caribbean States* (in part); *Latin-American Affairs*

Duncan Chappell, Professor, Department of Criminology, Simon Fraser University, Vancouver, B.C., *Crime and Law Enforcement*

Jeremy Cherfas, Demonstrator in Animal Behaviour, University of Oxford, Life Sciences Consultant, *New Scientist,* London, *Biology SPECIAL REPORT: Reevaluating Darwin*

Hung-Ti Chu, Expert in Far Eastern Affairs, former International Civil Servant and University Professor, *China; Taiwan*

Audrey F. Clough, Communications Editor, Boy Scouts of America, *Youth Organizations* (in part)

Stanley H. Costin, British Correspondent, *Herrenjournal International* and *Men's Wear, Australasia* magazine, *Fashion* (in part)

Rufus W. Crater, Senior Editorial Consultant, *Broadcasting,* New York City, *Television and Radio* (in part)

Norman Crossland, Bonn Correspondent, *The Economist,*

London, *Biographies* (in part); *Germany*

K. F. Cviic, Leader Writer and East European Specialist, *The Economist,* London, *Yugoslavia*

Daphne Daume, Editor, Encyclopædia Britannica, Yearbooks, *Biographies* (in part)

Tudor David, Managing Editor, *Education,* London, *Education* (in part)

Robert R. Davis, Vice-President and Economist, The Harris Bank, Chicago, *International Finance*

Philippe Decraene, Member of Editorial Staff, *Le Monde,* Paris, *Tunisia*

Marta Bekerman de Fainboim, Research Officer, Institute of Development Studies, University of Sussex, England, *Nicaragua*

Kenneth de la Barre, Director, Katimavik, Montreal, *Arctic and Antarctic* (in part)

Robin Denselow, Rock Music Critic, *The Guardian,* London, *Music* (in part)

Elfriede Dirnbacher, Austrian Civil Servant, *Austria*

Chris Drake, Managing Director, Middle East Media Operations, Nicosia, Cyprus, *Cyprus*

Jan R. Engels, Editor, *Vooruitgang* (Bimonthly of the Centre Paul Hymans, liberal study and documentation centre), Brussels, *Belgium*

W. D. Ewart, Editor and Director, *Fairplay International Shipping Weekly,* London, *Shipping*

D. M. L. Farr, Professor of History and Director, Paterson Centre for International Programs, Carleton University, Ottawa, *Canada*

Joan Lee Faust, Garden Editor, *New York Times, Flowers and Gardens* (in part)

Robert Feder, Television Reporter, *Chicago Sun-Times, Television and Radio SPECIAL REPORT: Revolution in the Soaps*

Robert J. Fendell, Auto Editor, *Science & Mechanics,* Auto Contributor, *Gentlemen's Quarterly* magazine, *Auto Racing* (in part)

Peter Fiddick, Specialist Writer, *The Guardian,* London, *Magazines* (in part); *Newspapers* (in part)

Donald Fields, Helsinki Correspondent, BBC, *The Guardian,* and *The Sunday Times,* London, *Biographies* (in part); *Finland*

David Fisher, Civil Engineer, Freeman Fox & Partners, London, formerly Executive Editor, *Engineering,* London, *Engineering Projects* (in part)

Marilyn Francis, Editor, *YWCA Interchange, Youth Organizations* (in part)

Peter W. Gaddum, Chairman, H. T. Gaddum and Company Ltd., Silk Merchants, Macclesfield, Cheshire, England, Honorary President, International Silk Association, Lyons, *Textiles* (in part)

Mary Jo Gallo, Girls Clubs of America, Inc., *Youth Organizations* (in part)

J. Whitfield Gibbons, Research Ecologist, Savannah River Ecology Laboratory, Aiken, S.C., *Biology* (in part)

Frank Gibney, Vice-Chairman, Board of Editors, Encyclopædia Britannica, *Biographies* (in part); *Japan SPECIAL REPORT: Japan's Economic Secret*

Hugh M. Gillespie, Director of Communications, International Road Federation, Washington, D.C., *Engineering Projects* (in part)

Fay Gjester, Oslo Correspondent, *Financial Times,* London, *Norway*

Arthur Goldsmith, Editorial Director, *Popular Photography* and *Camera Arts,* New York City, *Photography*

Harry Golombek, British Chess Champion, 1947, 1949, and 1955, Chess Correspondent, *The Times,* London, *Chess*

Martin Gottfried, Drama Critic, New York City, *Theatre* (in part)

Donald W. Gould, Medical Writer and Broadcaster, U.K., *Medicine* (in part); *Mental Health*

Rowland Gould, Free-lance Writer, Tokyo, *Biographies* (in part)

Benny Green, Record Reviewer, BBC, Contributor to *Encyclopedia of Jazz, Music* (in part)

A. R. G. Griffiths, Senior Lecturer in History, Flinders University of South Australia, *Australia; Biographies* (in part)

Joel W. Grossman, Archaeologist, *Archaeology* (in part)

David A. Harries, Director, Tarmac International Ltd., London, *Engineering Projects* (in part)

H. B. Hawley, Specialist, Human Nutrition and Food Science, Switzerland, *Food*

Peter Hebblethwaite, Vatican Affairs Writer, *National Catholic Reporter,* Kansas City, Mo., *Biographies* (in part)

Myrl C. Hendershott, Professor of Oceanography, Scripps Institution of Oceanography, La Jolla, Calif., *Oceanography*

Robin Cathy Herman, Reporter, *New York Times, Ice Hockey*

G. Fitzgerald Higgins, Editor and Free-lance Writer, *Biographies* (in part); Literature (in part); *Safety*

Harvey J. Hindin, Senior Systems Editor, *Systems and Software* magazine, Rochelle Park, N.J., *Communications*

Louis Hotz, Former Editorial Writer, Johannesburg (S.Af.) *Star, South Africa*

Poli Howard, Public Relations Service, Future Homemakers of America, *Youth Organizations* (in part)

John Howkins, Editor, *InterMedia,* International Institute of Communications, London, *Television and Radio* (in part)

Kenneth Ingham, Professor of History, University of Bristol, England, *Angola; Kenya; Mozambique; Tanzania; Uganda; Zaire; Zambia; Zimbabwe*

Adrian Jardine, Company Director, Member, Guild of Yachting Writers, *Boating*

Peter Jenkins, Policy Editor and Political Columnist, *The Guardian,* London, *Great Britain*

David A. Jessop, Editor, *Caribbean Chronicle* and *Caribbean Insight,* Consultant on Caribbean Affairs, *Caribbean States*

George Joffé, Journalist and Writer on North African Affairs, *Algeria; Morocco*

C. M. Jones, Consultant, *World Bowls* and *Tennis, Bowling* (in part)

D. A. N. Jones, Assistant Editor, *The Listener,* London, *Literature* (in part)

Lou Joseph, Senior Science Writer, Hill and Knowlton, Chicago, *Dentistry*

William A. Katz, Professor, School of Library Science, State University of New York, Albany, *Magazines* (in part)

John A. Kelleher, Group Relations Editor, INL (newspapers), Wellington, N.Z., *New Zealand*

John T. Kenna, Writer on Religious and Cultural Affairs, Chicago, *Minorities, American SPECIAL REPORT: The Latinization of the U.S.*

Richard M. Kennedy, Agricultural Economist, International Economics Division of the Economic Research Service, U.S. Department of Agriculture, *Agriculture*

John V. Killheffer, Associate Editor, Encyclopædia Britan-

Minister, New Delhi, India, *Biographies* (in part); *India*

Margaret H. Quinn, Reporter, *Sun-Gazette*, Williamsport, Pa., *Baseball* (in part)

Robin Ranger, Associate Professor, Defense and Strategic Studies Program, School of International Relations, University of Southern California, *Defense and Arms Control*

Robert Reinhold, Reporter, *New York Times*, Washington, D.C., *Cities and Urban Affairs*

John Roberts, Senior Staff Writer, *Middle East Economic Digest*, London, *Biographies* (in part)

David Robinson, Film Critic, *The Times*, London, *Motion Pictures*

Margaret Rule, Fellow of the Society of Antiquaries, Archaeological Director, The Mary Rose Trust, *Archaeology SPECIAL REPORT: The Raising of the "Mary Rose"*

Yrjö Sarahete, General Secretary, Fédération Internationale des Quilleurs, Helsinki, *Bowling* (in part)

Albert Schoenfield, Former Publisher, *Swimming World*, Vice-Chairman, U.S. Olympic Swimming Committee, *Swimming*

George Schöpflin, Lecturer in East European Political Institutions, London School of Economics and School of Slavonic and East European Studies, University of London, *Czechoslovakia*

Peter Shackleford, Chief of Studies, World Tourism Organization, Madrid, *Tourism*

Mitchell R. Sharpe, Science Writer, Historian, Alabama Space and Rocket Center, Huntsville, *Space Exploration*

Melinda Shepherd, Copy Editor, Encyclopædia Britannica, *Biographies* (in part)

Noel Simpson, Managing Director, Sydney Bloodstock Proprietary Ltd., Sydney, Australia, *Horse Racing* (in part)

K. M. Smogorzewski, Writer on contemporary history, Founder and Editor, *Free Europe*, London, *Albania; Biographies* (in part); *Hungary; Poland; Romania*

Melanie Staerk, Member, Swiss Press Association, former Member, Swiss National Commission for UNESCO, *Switzerland*

Diane M. Stratton, Supervisor, Communications, Big Brothers/Big Sisters of America, *Youth Organizations* (in part)

Zena Sutherland, Associate Professor, Graduate Library School, University of Chicago, *Literature for Children*

Thelma Sweetinburgh, Fashion Writer, Paris, *Fashion* (in part)

Richard N. Swift, Professor of Politics, New York University, New York City, *United Nations*

Lawrence B. Taishoff, President, Broadcasting Publications, Inc., Publisher, *Broadcasting* magazine, *Television and Radio* (in part)

Arthur Tattersall, Textile Trade Statistician, Manchester, England, *Textiles* (in part)

Bruce R. Thomas, Free-lance Writer, Chicago, *Minorities, American*

Harford Thomas, Retired City and Financial Editor, *The Guardian*, London, *Biographies* (in part)

Theodore V. Thomas, Free-lance Journalist and Press Consultant, *Toys and Games*

Lance Tingay, Former Lawn Tennis Correspondent, *The Daily Telegraph*, London, *Tennis*

Edward T. Townsend, National Labor Correspondent, *Christian Science Monitor*, Editor and Consultant, Manpower Education Institute, New York City, *Labour and Employment*

Ossia Trilling, Vice-President, International Association of Theatre Critics (1956–77), Co-editor and Contributor, *International Theatre*, Contributor, BBC, *The Financial Times*, London, *Theatre* (in part)

UNHCR. The Office of the United Nations High Commissioner for Refugees, *Refugees and Migrants* (in part)

Govindan Unny, Agence France-Presse Special Correspondent for India, Nepal, Sri Lanka, and Bangladesh, *Afghanistan; Bangladesh; Burma; Pakistan; Sri Lanka*

Robert William Verdi, Sportswriter, *Chicago Tribune*, *Baseball* (in part)

Peter Ward, Owner and Operator, Ward News Service, Ottawa, Parliamentary Reporter and Commentator, *Canada SPECIAL REPORT: Srains Along the Border*

P. A. Ward-Thomas, Golf Correspondent, *Country Life*, London, *Golf*

Diane Lois Way, Historical Researcher, Ontario Historical Studies Series, *Biographies* (in part)

John Whelan, Deputy Editor and Chief News Editor, *Middle East Economic Digest*, London, Managing Editor, *Arab Banking and Finance*, London, *Biographies* (in part); *Egypt; Iraq; Jordan; Kuwait; Lebanon; Middle Eastern Affairs; Persian Gulf States; Saudi Arabia; Syria*

Richard Whittingham, Free-lance Writer and Editor, *Crime and Law Enforcement SPECIAL REPORT: The New Prohibition*

Barbara Wijngaard, Economist, Group Economics Department, Lloyds Bank Ltd., London, *Biographies* (in part); *Mexico*

Gordon Wilkinson, Information Consultant and Free-lance Science Writer, *Chemistry*

John R. Wilkinson, Sportswriter, East Midland Provincial Newspapers Ltd., U.K., *Biographies* (in part)

David Douglas Willey, Rome Correspondent, BBC, *Italy*

Trevor Williamson, Chief Sports Subeditor, *Daily Telegraph*, London, *Biographies* (in part); *Football* (in part)

Michael Wilson, Consultant Editor, Jane's Publishing Company Ltd., *Aerospace*

Donald E. Witten, Public Affairs Officer, National Oceanographic and Atmospheric Administration, *Weather*

James M. Wolf, Deputy Director, Department of Defense Dependents Schools, Panama Region, *Education SPECIAL REPORT: The Promise of Early Learning*

Anita Wolff, Manager, Copy Department, Encyclopædia Britannica, *Biographies* (in part)

Elizabeth Woods, Writer, *Literature* (in part)

Michael Wooller, Economist, Group Economics Department, Lloyds Bank Ltd., London, *Biographies* (in part); *Bolivia; Paraguay; Portugal; Spain; Uruguay*

David Woolley, Editor, *Airports International*, London, *Transportation* (in part)

Richard L. Worsnop, Associate Editor, Editorial Research Reports, Washington, D.C., *United States*

Almon R. Wright, Retired Senior Historian, U.S. Department of State, *Panama*

Paul Ziemer, Editor, *Detroit Free Press*, Mich., *Congress, U.S.; Elections; Law; Political Parties; Supreme Court, U.S.*

Index

This index is arranged in alphabetical order. Words beginning with "Mc" are alphabetized as "Mac," and "St." is alphabetized as "Saint."

The figures shown in brackets [79, 80] indicate earlier editions of **The Compton Yearbook** in which the topic has appeared since 1979.

Entry headings in boldface type indicate articles in the text.

Cross-references refer to index entries in this volume.

f

h

i

J

u

N ow there's a way to identify all your fine books with flair and style. As part of our continuing service to you, Compton's Encyclopedia (published by Encyclopaedia Britannica, Inc.) is proud to be able to offer you the fine quality item shown on the next page.

B ooklovers will love the heavy-duty personalized **Ex Libris** embosser. Now you can personalize all your fine books with the mark of distinction, just the way all the fine libraries of the world do.

T o order this item , please type or print your name, address and zip code on a plain sheet of paper. (Note special instructions for ordering the embosser). Please send a check or money order only (your money will be refunded in full if you are not delighted) for the full amount of purchase, including postage and handling, to:

Britannica Home Library Service, Inc.
Attn: Yearbook Department
Post Office Box 6137
Chicago, Illinois 60680

17 68

IN THE BRITANNICA TRADITION OF QUALITY...

EX LIBRIS PERSONAL EMBOSSER

A mark of distinction for your fine books. A book embosser just like the ones used in libraries. The 1½" seal imprints "Library of _____" (with the name of your choice) and up to three centered initials. Please type or print clearly BOTH full name (up to 26 letters including spaces between names) and up to three initials.
Please allow six weeks for delivery.

Just **$20.00**

plus $2.00 shipping and handling

This offer available only in the United States.
Illinois residents please add sales tax

Britannica Home Library Service, Inc.